ADVANCED CANCER THERAPEUTICS

ADVANCED CANCER THERAPEUTICS

STRATEGIES AND TECHNOLOGIES FOR TARGETED DRUG DELIVERY

Edited by

MANISH KUMAR
Research and Development, Cadila Pharmaceuticals Limited, Ahmedabad, Gujarat, India

ABHISHEK JHA
Dr. D. Y. Patil Institute of Pharmaceutical Sciences and Research Pimpri, Pune, Maharashtra, India

BRAHMESHWAR MISHRA
Department of Pharmaceutical Engineering and Technology, Indian Institute of Technology (BHU), Varanasi, Uttar Pradesh, India

ELSEVIER

ACADEMIC PRESS
An imprint of Elsevier

Academic Press is an imprint of Elsevier
125 London Wall, London EC2Y 5AS, United Kingdom
50 Hampshire Street, 5th Floor, Cambridge, MA 02139, United States

ISBN: 978-0-443-44185-1

For information on all Academic Press publications visit our website at https://www.elsevier.com/books-and-journals

Publisher: Megan Ball
Acquisitions Editor: Linda Buschman
Editorial Project Manager: Himanshi Yadav
Production Project Manager: Aishwarya R.
Cover Designer: Arumugam Kothandan

Typeset by TNQ Tech

Contents

6. Cancer therapy depending on tumor vasculature and EPR effects

Pralay Maiti and Sudepta Bauri

7. Cancer therapy based on extracellular matrix

Sayali Gaikwad, Ashwani Patil, Abhishek Jha, and Abhishek Sharma

8. Heterogenicity of cancer and drug resistance

Unnati Gupta, Swara Mishra, Mohit Sharma, and Nivedita Bhardwaj

II

Strategies and technologies for cancer therapy

9. Materials and strategies for advanced anticancer drug delivery

Madhu Sharma, Dilip Panwar, Astha Mishra, Yashika Dalal, and Prabhat Ranjan Mishra

10. Drug conjugates for anticancer drug delivery

Disha Marwaha, Priya Gupta, Neha Singh, Ashutosh Gupta, and Abhishek Sharma

11. Self-assembled supramolecular systems for anticancer drug delivery

Radhika Baheti, Vinita Patole, Vinay Chopada, Madhu Kumawat, and Sanjeevani Deshkar

12. Advances in metal-organic frameworks for anticancer drug delivery

Saisritam Kar, Vaibhav Verma, Priya Jha, Divakar Kumar, and Vivek Dave

13. Tumor microenvironment targeted drug delivery systems

Lalit Kumar, Nirmal Morya, Keshav Hirave, Mansi Sharma, and Vikas Anand Saharan

14. Advances in dendrimers for anticancer drug delivery

Abhishek Sharma, Shweta Singh, Himanshu Sharma, Pooja Mittal, and Vishnu Mittal

15. Advances in metallic nanoparticles for anticancer drug delivery

Swati Dubey, Bintu Wadhwani, Mahima Chauhan, Girish Kumar, Tarun Virmani, and Kamla Pathak

16. Advances in polymeric nanoparticles for anticancer drug delivery

Keshav Hirave, Nirmal Morya, Lalit Kumar, Surojit Banerjee, Vikas Anand Saharan, and Anupama Singh

17. Advances in lipid-based nanoparticles for anticancer drug delivery

Sunny Rathee, Sakshi Soni, Adarsh Sharma, Arya Ojha, and Sanjay K. Jain

18. Advances in SNEDDS for anticancer drug delivery

Ashutosh Gupta, Shivani Kunkalienkar, Moumita Saha, Aditya Dev Rajora, Abhishek Sharma, and Sudheer Moorkoth

19. Advances in nanocrystals for anticancer drug delivery

Priya Gupta, Disha Marwaha, Karishma Khan, and Vandana Arora Sethi

20. Theranostic nanoparticles for advanced cancer therapy

Debadatta Mohapatra, Devdutt Sharma, and Rinki Verma

21. DNA based nanomaterials for anticancer therapy

Shweta Singh, Ajay Pandey, Abhishek Sharma, Simran Kanwar, Aman, Ruchi Chawla, and Ravi Bhushan Singh

22. Nanofibrous scaffolds for cancer management

Nirmal Morya, Keshav Hirave, Lalit Kumar, Sujit Erandole, Debadri Banerjee, Anupama Singh, and Vikas Anand Saharan

23. Advances in hydrogel for anticancer drug delivery

Abhishek Sharma, Bhagya Shree, Ruchi Chawla, and Brahmeshwar Mishra

24. Advances in inorganic nanocarriers for anticancer drug delivery

Moumita Saha, Ashutosh Gupta, Shivani Kunkalienkar, Aditya Dev Rajora, Abhishek Sharma, Ruchi Chawla, and Namdev Dhas

25. Microparticles for anticancer drug delivery

Yashika Uniyal, Abhishek Sharma, Bhagya Shree, Arun Kumar Mahato, and Nithya Shanthi

26. Microneedles for anticancer drug delivery

Vikas, Justin Jablonski, Maddelyn Hoehn, Nurhaliza Syukur, and Jason R. McCarthy

27. Implants for anticancer drug delivery

Manish Kumar, Viresh Kumar, Shruti Srivastava, and Abhishek Sharma

28. Phytomedicine for cancer therapy

Hemangini Meher, Alakh N. Sahu, and Debadatta Mohapatra

29. Small molecules as delivery tools for enzymes employed in enzyme-prodrug therapy

Louay Abo Qoura and Vadim S. Pokrovsky

III

Clinical status, challenges, and future prospectives

30. Clinical status of anticancer drug delivery systems

Dilip Panwar, Madhu Sharma, Neha Agarwal, Avijit Kumar Bakshi, Pratiksha Tiwari, Prabhat Kumar Mishra, Sweety Das, and Prabhat Ranjan Mishra

31. Challenges and future prospectives in anticancer drug delivery

Abhishek Sharma, Shreya Singh, Shilpi Arora, and Sundeep Chaurasia

32. Regulatory considerations for anticancer drug delivery systems

Kanchan Bharti, Deepika Deepika, and Vikas Kumar

Contributors

Louay Abo Qoura Research Institute of Molecular and Cellular Medicine, People's Friendship University of Russia (RUDN University), Moscow, Russia; Blokhin National Medical Research Center of Oncology, Ministry of Health of the Russian Federation, Moscow, Russia

Neha Agarwal Division of Pharmaceutics and Pharmacokinetics, CSIR-Central Drug Research Institute, Lucknow, Uttar Pradesh, India; Academy of Scientific and Innovation Research (AcSIR), Ghaziabad, Uttar Pradesh, India

Aman CEPS, Guru Gobind Singh Indraprastha University, Dwarka, New Delhi, India

Shilpi Arora Himachal Institute of Pharmacy, Paonta Sahib, Himachal Pradesh, India

Radhika Baheti School of Pharmacy and Research, Dnyaan Prasad Global University - Dr. D. Y. Patil Unitech Society, Pune, Maharashtra, India; Dr. D. Y. Patil Institute of Pharmaceutical Sciences and Research, Department of Pharmaceutics, Pune, Maharashtra, India

Avijit Kumar Bakshi Division of Pharmaceutics and Pharmacokinetics, CSIR-Central Drug Research Institute, Lucknow, Uttar Pradesh, India; Jawaharlal Nehru University, Delhi, New Delhi, India

Surojit Banerjee School of Pharmaceutical Sciences and Technology, Sardar Bhagwan Singh University, Dehradun, Uttarakhand, India

Debadri Banerjee School of Pharmaceutical Sciences and Technology, Sardar Bhagwan Singh University, Dehradun, Uttarakhand, India

Sudepta Bauri Indian Institute of Technology (BHU), School of Materials Science and Technology, Varanasi, Uttar Pradesh, India

Nivedita Bhardwaj Amity Institute of Pharmacy, Amity University, Noida, Uttar Pradesh, India

Kanchan Bharti Institut de Recerca Biomèdica Catalunya Sud (IRBCatSud), Department of Chemical Engineering, Universitat Rovira I Virgili (URV), Tarragona, Spain

Chahat Chahat Department of Pharmaceutical Science, Hemvati Nandan Bahuguna Garhwal University (HNBGU), Srinagar, Uttarakhand, India

Mahima Chauhan HIMT College of Pharmacy, Greater Noida, Uttar Pradesh, India

Sundeep Chaurasia Department of Pharmaceutics, National Institute of Pharmaceutical Education and Research (NIPER), SAS Nagar, Mohali, Punjab, India

Ruchi Chawla Department of Pharmaceutical Engineering and Technology, Indian Institute of Technology (BHU), Varanasi, Uttar Pradesh, India

Vinay Chopada School of Pharmacy and Research, Dnyaan Prasad Global University - Dr. D. Y. Patil Unitech Society, Pune, Maharashtra, India; Dr. D. Y. Patil Institute of Pharmaceutical Sciences and Research, Department of Pharmaceutics, Pune, Maharashtra, India

Yashika Dalal Division of Pharmaceutics and Pharmacokinetics, CSIR-Central Drug Research Institute, Lucknow, Uttar Pradesh, India

Sweety Das Division of Pharmaceutics and Pharmacokinetics, CSIR-Central Drug Research Institute, Lucknow, Uttar Pradesh, India; Academy of Scientific and Innovation Research (AcSIR), Ghaziabad, Uttar Pradesh, India

Vivek Dave Department of Pharmacy, School of Health Sciences, Central University of South Bihar, Gaya, Bihar, India

Deepika Deepika Institut de Recerca Biomèdica Catalunya Sud (IRBCatSud), Department of Chemical Engineering, Universitat Rovira I Virgili (URV), Tarragona, Spain

Sanjeevani Deshkar School of Pharmacy and Research, Dnyaan Prasad Global University - Dr. D. Y. Patil Unitech Society, Pune, Maharashtra, India; Dr. D. Y. Patil Institute of Pharmaceutical Sciences and Research, Department of Pharmaceutics, Pune, Maharashtra, India

Namdev Dhas Department of Pharmaceutics, Manipal College of Pharmaceutical Sciences, Manipal Academy of Higher Education, Manipal, Karnataka, India

Swati Dubey Maharishi Arvind College of Pharmacy, Jaipur, Rajasthan, India

Sujit Erandole Department of Pharmaceutical Technology (Formulations), National Institute of Pharmaceutical Education and Research, Guwahati (NIPER-G), Sila Katamur (Halugurisuk), Assam, India

Sayali Gaikwad Dr. D. Y. Patil Institute of Pharmaceutical Sciences and Research Pimpri, Pune, Maharashtra, India; DPGU School of Pharmacy and Research Pimpri, Pune, Maharashtra, India

Anurag Kumar Gautam Institute of Pharmacy, Deen Dayal Upadhyaya Gorakhpur University, Gorakhpur, Uttar Pradesh, India

Ashutosh Gupta Department of Pharmaceutical Quality Assurance, Manipal College of Pharmaceutical Sciences, Manipal Academy of Higher Education, Manipal, Karnataka, India; Formulation Research & Development—Non Orals, Sun Pharmaceutical Industries Ltd, Vadodara, Gujarat, India

Priya Gupta Lloyd School of Pharmacy, Greater Noida, Uttar Pradesh, India; Amity Institute of Pharmacy, Amity University, Noida, Uttar Pradesh, India

Shankar Gupta Department of Pharmaceutical Science, Hemvati Nandan Bahuguna Garhwal University (HNBGU), Srinagar, Uttarakhand, India

Unnati Gupta Dr. D. Y. Patil Institute of Pharmaceutical Sciences and Research, Pune, Maharashtra, India

Keshav Hirave Department of Pharmaceutical Technology (Formulations), National Institute of Pharmaceutical Education and Research, Guwahati (NIPER-G), Sila Katamur (Halugurisuk), Assam, India

Maddelyn Hoehn Department of Biomedical Research and Translational Medicine, Masonic Medical Research Institute, Utica, NY, United States

Justin Jablonski Department of Biomedical Research and Translational Medicine, Masonic Medical Research Institute, Utica, NY, United States

Sanjay K. Jain Department of Pharmaceutical Sciences, Dr. Harisingh Gour Vishwavidyalaya, Sagar, Madhya Pradesh, India

Abhishek Jha Dr. D. Y. Patil Institute of Pharmaceutical Sciences and Research Pimpri, Pune, Maharashtra, India; DPGU School of Pharmacy and Research Pimpri, Pune, Maharashtra, India

Priya Jha Department of Pharmacy, School of Health Sciences, Central University of South Bihar, Gaya, Bihar, India

Gaurav Joshi Department of Pharmaceutical Science, Hemvati Nandan Bahuguna Garhwal University (HNBGU), Srinagar, Uttarakhand, India; Institute of Cancer Therapeutics, School of Pharmacy, Optometry and Medical Sciences, University of Bradford, Bradford, United Kingdom

Simran Kanwar CEPS, Guru Gobind Singh Indraprastha University, Dwarka, New Delhi, India

Saisritam Kar Department of Pharmacy, School of Health Sciences, Central University of South Bihar, Gaya, Bihar, India

Abdul Baseer Khan College of Pharmacy, Integral University, Lucknow, Uttar Pradesh, India

Karishma Khan Department of Pharmaceutics, School of Pharmaceutical Education and Research, Jamia Hamdard (Deemed University), New Delhi, India

Bhupinder Kumar Department of Pharmaceutical Science, Hemvati Nandan Bahuguna Garhwal University (HNBGU), Srinagar, Uttarakhand, India

Divakar Kumar Department of Pharmacy, School of Health Sciences, Central University of South Bihar, Gaya, Bihar, India

Girish Kumar Amity University, Greater Noida, Uttar Pradesh, India

Guddu Kumar Department of Pharmaceutics, Manipal College of Pharmaceutical Sciences, Manipal Academy of Higher Education, Manipal, Karnataka, India

Lalit Kumar Department of Pharmaceutical Technology (Formulations), National Institute of Pharmaceutical Education and Research, Guwahati (NIPER-G), Sila Katamur (Halugurisuk), Assam, India

Manvendra Kumar Amity Institue of Pharmacy, Amity University, Noida, Uttar Pradesh, India

Madhu Kumawat School of Pharmacy and Research, Dnyaan Prasad Global University - Dr. D. Y. Patil Unitech Society, Pune, Maharashtra, India; Dr. D. Y. Patil Institute of Pharmaceutical Sciences and Research, Department of Pharmaceutics, Pune, Maharashtra, India

Manish Kumar ISF College of Pharmacy, Moga, Punjab, India; KIET School of Pharmacy, Krishna Institute of Engineering & Technology (KIET), Pharmaceutics, Ghaziabad, Uttar Pradesh, India

Pranesh Kumar Department of Pharmacology, Institute of Pharmaceutical Sciences, University of Lucknow, Lucknow, Uttar Pradesh, India

Vikas Kumar Institut de Recerca Biomèdica Catalunya Sud (IRBCatSud), Department of Chemical Engineering, Universitat Rovira I Virgili (URV), Tarragona, Spain

Viresh Kumar ISF College of Pharmacy, Moga, Punjab, India

Shivani Kunkalienkar Department of Pharmaceutical Quality Assurance, Manipal College of Pharmaceutical Sciences, Manipal Academy of Higher Education, Manipal, Karnataka, India

Arun Kumar Mahato School of Pharmaceutical Sciences & Technology, Sardar Bhagwan Singh University Balawala, Dehradun, Uttarakhand, India

Pralay Maiti IIT BHU, School of Materials Science and Technology, Varanasi, Uttar Pradesh, India

Disha Marwaha Chandigarh University, Unnao, Uttar Pradesh, India; Institute of Pharmaceutical Research, GLA University, Mathura, Uttar Pradesh, India

Jason R. McCarthy Department of Biomedical Research and Translational Medicine, Masonic Medical Research Institute, Utica, NY, United States

Hemangini Meher Department of Pharmacology, Guru Ghasidas Vishwavidyalaya, Bilaspur, Chhattisgarh, India

Astha Mishra Division of Pharmaceutics and Pharmacokinetics, CSIR-Central Drug Research Institute, Lucknow, Uttar Pradesh, India

Brahmeshwar Mishra Department of Pharmaceutical Engineering and Technology, Indian Institute of Technology (BHU), Varanasi, Uttar Pradesh, India

Prabhat Kumar Mishra Division of Pharmaceutics and Pharmacokinetics, CSIR-Central Drug Research Institute, Lucknow, Uttar Pradesh, India; Academy of Scientific and

Innovation Research (AcSIR), Ghaziabad, Uttar Pradesh, India

Prabhat Ranjan Mishra Division of Pharmaceutics and Pharmacokinetics, CSIR-Central Drug Research Institute, Lucknow, Uttar Pradesh, India; Academy of Scientific and Innovation Research (AcSIR), Ghaziabad, Uttar Pradesh, India

Swara Mishra Dr. D. Y. Patil Institute of Pharmaceutical Sciences and Research, Pune, Maharashtra, India

Pooja Mittal GITAM School of Pharmacy, GITAM Deemed to be University, Patancheru, Hyderabad, India

Vishnu Mittal Department of Pharmaceutics, Adesh College of Pharmacy, Shahbad, Haryana, India

Debadatta Mohapatra Leslie Dan Faculty of Pharmacy, University of Toronto, Toronto, ON, Canada; Phytomedicine Research Laboratory, Department of Pharmaceutical Engineering & Technology, Indian Institute of Technology (BHU), Varanasi, Uttar Pradesh, India

Sudheer Moorkoth Department of Pharmaceutical Quality Assurance, Manipal College of Pharmaceutical Sciences, Manipal Academy of Higher Education, Manipal, Karnataka, India

Nirmal Morya Department of Pharmaceutical Technology (Formulations), National Institute of Pharmaceutical Education and Research, Guwahati (NIPER-G), Sila Katamur (Halugurisuk), Assam, India

Arya Ojha Department of Pharmaceutical Sciences, Dr. Harisingh Gour Vishwavidyalaya, Sagar, Madhya Pradesh, India

Ajay Pandey Department of Pharmaceutical Engineering and Technology, Indian Institute of Technology (BHU), Varanasi, Uttar Pradesh, India

Dilip Panwar Division of Pharmaceutics and Pharmacokinetics, CSIR-Central Drug Research Institute, Lucknow, Uttar Pradesh, India; Jawaharlal Nehru University, Delhi, New Delhi, India

Kamla Pathak Faculty of Pharmacy, Uttar Pradesh University of Medical Sciences, Saifai, Uttar Pradesh, India

Ashwani Patil Dr. D. Y. Patil Institute of Pharmaceutical Sciences and Research Pimpri, Pune, Maharashtra, India; DPGU School of Pharmacy and Research Pimpri, Pune, Maharashtra, India

Vinita Patole School of Pharmacy and Research, Dnyaan Prasad Global University - Dr. D. Y. Patil Unitech Society, Pune, Maharashtra, India; Dr. D. Y. Patil Institute of Pharmaceutical Sciences and Research, Department of Pharmaceutics, Pune, Maharashtra, India

Vadim S. Pokrovsky Research Institute of Molecular and Cellular Medicine, People's Friendship University of Russia (RUDN University), Moscow, Russia; Blokhin National Medical Research Center of Oncology, Ministry of Health of the Russian Federation, Moscow, Russia

Sarjana Raikwar Gyan Ganga Institute of Technology and Sciences, Jabalpur, Madhya Pradesh, India

Aditya Dev Rajora Department of Pharmaceutical Quality Assurance, Manipal College of Pharmaceutical Sciences, Manipal Academy of Higher Education, Manipal, Karnataka, India

Sunny Rathee Department of Pharmaceutical Sciences, Dr. Harisingh Gour Vishwavidyalaya, Sagar, Madhya Pradesh, India; National Institute of Pharmaceutical Education and Research-Ahmedabad (NIPER-A), Gandhinagar, Gujarat, India

Moumita Saha Department of Pharmaceutical Quality Assurance, Manipal College of Pharmaceutical Sciences, Manipal Academy of Higher Education, Manipal, Karnataka, India

Vikas Anand Saharan Department of Pharmaceutical Technology (Formulations), National Institute of Pharmaceutical Education and Research, Guwahati (NIPER-G), Sila Katamur (Halugurisuk), Assam, India

Alakh N. Sahu Phytomedicine Research Laboratory, Department of Pharmaceutical Engineering & Technology, Indian Institute of Technology (BHU), Varanasi, Uttar Pradesh, India

Vandana Arora Sethi Lloyd Institute of Management and Technology, Greater Noida, Uttar Pradesh, India

Nithya Shanthi School of Pharmaceutical Sciences & Technology, Sardar Bhagwan Singh University Balawala, Dehradun, Uttarakhand, India

Abhishek Sharma Department of Pharmaceutical Engineering and Technology, Indian Institute of Technology (BHU), Varanasi, Uttar Pradesh, India; School of Pharmaceutical Sciences, SDGI Global University, Ghaziabad, Uttar Pradesh, India

Adarsh Sharma Department of Pharmaceutical Sciences, Dr. Harisingh Gour Vishwavidyalaya, Sagar, Madhya Pradesh, India

Devdutt Sharma Dev Nanotech, Private Limited, Yamunanagar, Haryana, India

Himanshu Sharma Guru Gobind Singh College of Pharmacy, Yamuna Nagar, Haryana, India; Chitkara College of Pharmacy, Chitkara University, Rajpura, Punjab, India

Madhu Sharma Division of Pharmaceutics and Pharmacokinetics, CSIR-Central Drug Research Institute, Lucknow, Uttar Pradesh, India; Academy of Scientific and Innovation Research (AcSIR), Ghaziabad, Uttar Pradesh, India

Mansi Sharma Department of Pharmaceutical Technology (Formulations), National Institute of Pharmaceutical Education and Research, Guwahati (NIPER-G), Sila Katamur (Halugurisuk), Assam, India

Mohit Sharma Dr. D. Y. Patil Institute of Pharmaceutical Sciences and Research, Pune, Maharashtra, India

Devika Shenoy Department of Pharmaceutics, Manipal College of Pharmaceutical Sciences, Manipal Academy of Higher Education, Manipal, Karnataka, India

Bhagya Shree Department of Pharmaceutical Engineering and Technology, Indian Institute of Technology (BHU), Varanasi, Uttar Pradesh, India

Rahul Shukla Department of Pharmaceutics, National Institute of Pharmaceutical Education and Research (NIPER-Raebareli), Lucknow, Uttar Pradesh, India

Anupama Singh School of Pharmaceutical Sciences and Technology, Sardar Bhagwan Singh University, Dehradun, Uttarakhand, India

Neha Singh School of Medical & Allied Sciences, K. R. Mangalam University Sohna, Gurgaon, Haryana, India

Ravi Bhushan Singh CEPS, Guru Gobind Singh Indraprastha University, Dwarka, New Delhi, India

Shreya Singh Pharmacology Department, Bharat Institutions - Pharmacy, Mangalpally, Ibrahimpatnam, Telangana, India

Shweta Singh Department of Pharmaceutical Engineering and Technology, Indian Institute of Technology (BHU), Varanasi, Uttar Pradesh, India

Sakshi Soni Department of Pharmaceutical Sciences, Dr. Harisingh Gour Vishwavidyalaya, Sagar, Madhya Pradesh, India; National Institute of Pharmaceutical Education and Research-Ahmedabad (NIPER-A), Gandhinagar, Gujarat, India

Shruti Srivastava Directorate of Research, Innovation & Consultancy, Chandigarh University, Unnao, Uttar Pradesh, India

Ashish Dilip Sutar Department of Pharmaceutics, National Institute of Pharmaceutical Education and Research (NIPER-Raebareli), Lucknow, Uttar Pradesh, India

Nurhaliza Syukur Department of Biomedical Research and Translational Medicine, Masonic Medical Research Institute, Utica, NY, United States

Pratiksha Tiwari Division of Pharmaceutics and Pharmacokinetics, CSIR-Central Drug Research Institute, Lucknow, Uttar Pradesh, India; Jawaharlal Nehru University, Delhi, New Delhi, India

Yashika Uniyal School of Pharmaceutical Sciences & Technology, Sardar Bhagwan Singh University Balawala, Dehradun, Uttarakhand, India

Mansi Upadhyay Department of Pharmaceutics, Manipal College of Pharmaceutical Sciences, Manipal Academy of Higher Education, Manipal, Karnataka, India

Rinki Verma College of Pharmacy and Health Sciences, St. John's University, Jamaica, NY, United States

Vaibhav Verma Department of Pharmacy, School of Health Sciences, Central University of South Bihar, Gaya, Bihar, India

Vikas Department of Biomedical Research and Translational Medicine, Masonic Medical Research Institute, Utica, NY, United States

Tarun Virmani Amity University, Greater Noida, Uttar Pradesh, India

Nikhar Vishwakarma Gyan Ganga Institute of Technology and Sciences, Jabalpur, Madhya Pradesh, India

Bintu Wadhwani Institute of Chemical Technology (ICT), Mumbai, Maharashtra, India

Muhammad Wahajuddin Institute of Cancer Therapeutics, School of Pharmacy, Optometry and Medical Sciences, University of Bradford, Bradford, United Kingdom

About the editors

Dr. Manish Kumar, PhD

Dr. Kumar holds the position of Formulation Scientist and Deputy Manager in Research and Development, Cadila Pharmaceuticals Limited, Ahmedabad, Gujarat, India. He completed his doctoral degree at the Indian Institute of Technology (Banaras Hindu University), Varanasi—221005, India. He possesses 6 years of academic research experience. His specialization is in pharmaceutics, working on various drug delivery systems, including controlled drug delivery systems, nanoemulsions, polymeric nanoparticles, lipid nanoparticles, nanocrystals, nanofibrous scaffolds, hydrogels, and microneedles for treating cancer, wounds, infections, and inflammatory disorders. To date, he has authored over 50 peer-reviewed articles and about 25 book chapters in well-known international journals. He has four patents in his name and has edited two books. He is working continuously to drive forward cutting-edge research in nanomedicine and drug delivery technologies.

Dr. Abhishek Jha, PhD

Dr. Jha is an Assistant Professor in the Department of Pharmaceutics at Dr. D. Y. Patil Institute of Pharmaceutical Sciences and Research, Pune, Maharashtra, India. He has more than 8 years of professional experience in academic research, specializing in advanced drug delivery systems, cancer nanomedicine, and 3D bioprinting. Holding a PhD from the Indian Institute of Technology (BHU), Varanasi, his work focuses on developing targeted therapeutic interventions for cancer, inflammatory lung disorders, and chronic wounds. His research on modern therapeutics leverages his deep expertise in extracellular vesicles, nanofibers, polymer chemistry, and microneedle technology. So far, he has contributed to three patents, more than 50 peer-reviewed articles and 25 book chapters published in reputed international journals, and edited two books. As an academician, he views education as the art of assisting discovery; empowering students to harness their curiosity, transforming foundational concepts into tangible scientific impact.

Dr. Brahmeshwar Mishra, PhD

Dr. Mishra is a Professor and former Head of the Department of Pharmaceutical Engineering and Technology at the Indian Institute of Technology (Banaras Hindu University), Varanasi, Uttar Pradesh, India. Having earned his BPharm, MPharm as a Gold Medalist, and PhD from the same institution, he has dedicated over 42 years to advancing pharmaceutical sciences. Throughout his career, Prof. Mishra has established a profound commitment to academic guidance, mentoring over a 100 postgraduate, doctoral, and postdoctorate candidates. His research focuses on multiple emulsions, nanomedicine, targeted and rate-controlled drug delivery systems, pharmacokinetics, and bioavailability. His work has yielded over 300 publications, 220 abstracts, 50 book chapters, and 5 patents. With more than 14,000 citations and an h-index exceeding 60, his scholarly impact places him in the top 5% of global researchers as per the SciRank Global database. Beyond his research, Prof. Mishra's institutional leadership, policy contributions, and enduring dedication to his students continue to anchor and advance pharmaceutical education worldwide.

CHAPTER I

Understanding the cancer

The uncontrolled multiplication of cancer cells and their ability to invade other tissues and metastasize to distant sites are the main features of cancer. Cancer results from genetic mutations, which cause the breakdown of the normal control mechanisms for keeping cell growth, differentiation, and death in balance. These genetic defects give rise to cancer cells that grow continuously and can also evade recognition from the immune system. Gaining insights into the tumor microenvironment is essential, as it includes cancer cells, adjacent cells, extracellular matrix, blood vessels, and immune cells. The intricate interaction between cancer and its microenvironment not only drives tumor growth but also significantly impacts therapeutic outcomes. The non-malignant supporting tissue surrounding and interacting with tumor cells can be the primary target of cancer therapy by targeting the tumor stroma. Cancer-associated fibroblasts, immune cells, endothelial cells, and extracellular matrix are numerous cell types present in the tumor's stroma. This tumor microenvironment plays a key role in supporting tumor growth, metastasis, and progression through the provision of structural support, growth factors, and immune responses. However, the tumor stroma is also a source of signals that protect cancer cells and physically block drug entry, which are major drivers of drug resistance. Cancer therapy through the tumor stroma targets cancer-associated fibroblasts, which are responsible for tumor growth, tumor vasculature, and tumor immunity. These therapeutic methods make cancer cells sensitive to conventional cancer therapy by disrupting the tumor niche. The respiration and metabolism of cancer cells are also significant targets for cancer therapy. The Warburg effect, in which cancer cells exhibit a preference to use glycolysis for energy production even in the presence of oxygen, is common in cancer cells. This results in the establishment of an acidic extracellular environment and hypoxia. The hypoxia, which is due to inadequate and disorganized vasculature in the tumor, induces resistance to radiation and chemotherapeutic agents by promoting adaptations in the cells for survival. Hypoxia-activated therapeutics, which activate in hypoxic conditions and spare normal tissues, can be used in cancer therapy to target hypoxic regions in the tumors. The pH-sensitive drug delivery systems can be exploited easily to target the hypoxic regions in the tumors by releasing the drug in the acidic environment.

Tumors are often found to have dense and disordered structures of extracellular matrix, which are also stiffened and often hinder the passage of therapeutic drugs. The constituents of the extracellular matrix, such as collagen, fibronectin, and proteoglycans, not only provide mechanical support but also regulate cell behavior through biochemical signaling. The altered structure of the extracellular matrix prevents the penetration of drugs and provides a microenvironment that is conducive to cancer cell growth and survival. The altered structure of the extracellular matrix is known to be involved in cancer progression and resistance to drugs. The therapeutic strategies to interfere with cancer progression can be implemented that involve reducing the density of the altered structure of the extracellular matrix through enzymatic degradation and inhibiting the remodeling of the extracellular matrix. Additionally, abnormal structure and function, such as irregular vessel structure, increased vessel permeability, and irregular blood flow, are some of the key characteristics of the tumor vasculature. These factors cause the irregular distribution of nutrients, oxygen, and medicinal substances in the tumor mass. The leaky blood vessels and poor lymphatic function in the tumor can be exploited for preferential accumulation of macromolecules and nanoparticles in the tumor tissue, leading to the enhanced permeability and retention (EPR) effect. Most of the nanomedicine-based drug delivery techniques involve exploiting the EPR effect. However, there are some problems in attaining this goal, as the EPR effect is highly variable among different types of tumors and patients. To increase the accumulation and penetration of the drug in the tumor mass, normalizing the vasculature or using the EPR effect in combination with active targeting can be utilized.

Cytotoxic agents, which specifically target rapidly dividing cells, have remained the cornerstone of current cancer chemotherapy. Although these drugs have been found beneficial in reducing the burden of cancer, the non-specific nature of these agents often results in collateral damage to healthy proliferating cells, including those present in the gastrointestinal tract, bone marrow, and hair follicles. Such severe side effects include immunosuppression, mucositis, and alopecia. Additionally, the development of resistance to these agents often limits the effectiveness of chemotherapy. Resistance to these agents has been attributed to changes in the target for the drug, enhanced capacity for DNA repair, increased ability for the efflux of the drug from the cell membrane, and the ability to evade apoptosis. Current trends in anticancer drug delivery systems have focused on increasing the specificity of the anticancer drugs and reducing the side effects. The application of nanotechnology for the delivery of anticancer agents has received considerable interest due to the potential for increasing the pharmacokinetics of the anticancer agents. Nanomedicine has been used as a delivery system for the encapsulation of anticancer agents, protecting them from metabolism and degradation, and for the targeted delivery of the anticancer agents. Nanomedicine has the potential for increasing the accumulation of the anticancer agents at the tumor site by utilizing the tumor-specific characteristics, such as the abnormal vasculature and the enhanced permeability and retention effect. The nanoparticles have the potential for increasing the specificity of the anticancer treatments by conjugating them with the tumor-specific ligands or incorporating tumor microenvironment-responsive moieties.

CHAPTER

1

Introduction to cancer

Ashish Dilip Sutar and Rahul Shukla

Department of Pharmaceutics, National Institute of Pharmaceutical Education and Research (NIPER-Raebareli), Lucknow, Uttar Pradesh, India

Introduction

Cancer is a complex disease that has a significant impact on global health. Uncontrolled proliferation is a hallmark of cancer cells, which invade surrounding tissues and metastasize to distant organs (Montégut et al., 2024). Each body organ is susceptible to cancer, and the likelihood increases markedly with age due to the cumulative effects of genetic mutations, epigenetic alterations, and environmental exposures. Oncology is important for understanding the molecular and physiological mechanisms that explain tumor formation and therapeutic response (Sonkin et al., 2024). Oncology is a whole term that unites cell biology, molecular genetics, immunology, and biochemistry to understand how standard mechanisms, such as cell-cycle control, DNA repair, signal transduction, and metabolic homeostasis, function. These mechanisms get disturbed in cancer (Kiri and Ryba, 2024).

Cancer cells can disrupt the standard mechanisms, such as cell growth and division. In healthy tissues, proliferation is managed by well-organized signaling networks that decide when to divide, differentiate, or undergo programmed cell death. Mutations disrupt this balance and turn off the tumor suppressor genes, eliminating essential growth-inhibitory signals (Shashikant Kamble et al., 2025; Boire et al., 2024; Xiong et al., 2025). Genetic changes activate cancer cells to undergo metabolic and biochemical transformation, which supports their high proliferative demand. Many tumors use glycolysis in oxygen-rich environments to rapidly generate energy, a phenomenon known as the *Warburg effect* (Barba et al., 2024). This transition is mediated by disrupted intracellular signaling, which includes Ras/MAPK and PI3K/Akt/mTOR pathways. These mediate protein synthesis, cellular metabolism, and survival. This flexibility not only maintains tumor persistence under stressful conditions but also presents critical molecular targets for therapeutic intervention (Papaneophytou, 2024).

Advanced Cancer Therapeutics
https://doi.org/10.1016/B978-0-443-44185-1.00011-2

Various extrinsic factors contribute to oncogenesis beyond intrinsic cellular damage. Like, environmental carcinogens (tobacco smoke, ionizing radiation, industrial chemicals, and dietary mutagens) can accelerate genetic damage (Papaneophytou, 2024; Mani et al., 2024). Factors like poor diet, physical inactivity, and alcohol consumption accelerate cancer growth. The combination of these factors forms the base of contemporary cancer research (Marino et al., 2024). A detailed understanding of these complex processes provides a robust scientific foundation for developing therapeutic strategies, identifying diagnostic biomarkers, and exploring innovative treatment paradigms (Mani et al., 2024; Marino et al., 2024; Krupina et al., 2024; Mathure et al., 2023). This chapter explores the various sides of cancer biology, including (a) nature and types of cancer, including differences in benign and malignant growths; (b) causes of cancers (genetic, epigenetic, viral, and environmental); (c) tumor development pathways and progression, focusing on clonal evolution, signaling deregulation, and protein alterations; and (d) hallmarks of malignancy and cancer prevention and early diagnosis.

Cancer and dysregulated proteins

Based on organs and sites, cancers are divided into various types (Fig. 1.1). A few of the cancers and altered proteins responsible for these are discussed in the sections below.

Breast cancer

In breast cancer, there is an overproduction of the HER2 protein due to an amplified HER2 gene. More aggressive tumors and an increased risk of recurrence are mainly due to overexpression of these genes. Standard tests might not show mutations in HER2 but can still boost cancer signaling and lead to metastasis. Finding these mutations has enabled the development of targeted treatments that interfere with HER2 signaling (Cheng, 2024). Another altered gene in breast cancer is p53, in approximately 30% of cases. Mutations primarily affect the DNA-binding domain, impairing its transcriptional regulation. Notably, mutations like R273H and R175H enable mutant p53 to evade programmed cell death by undermining the functions of tumor suppressors like p63 and p73. This interference can lead to genetic instability and is linked to poorer survival outcomes for patients (Marvalim et al., 2023). Pathogenic mutations in the BRCA2 gene disrupt the DNA repair process. The most common are shift and nonsense mutations, which cause a normal amino acid sequence to be interrupted by a premature stop signal. This leads to shorter, malfunctioning proteins that can cause genetic instability, significantly raising the cancer risk for those carrying BRCA2 mutations compared to the general population (Xie et al., 2022).

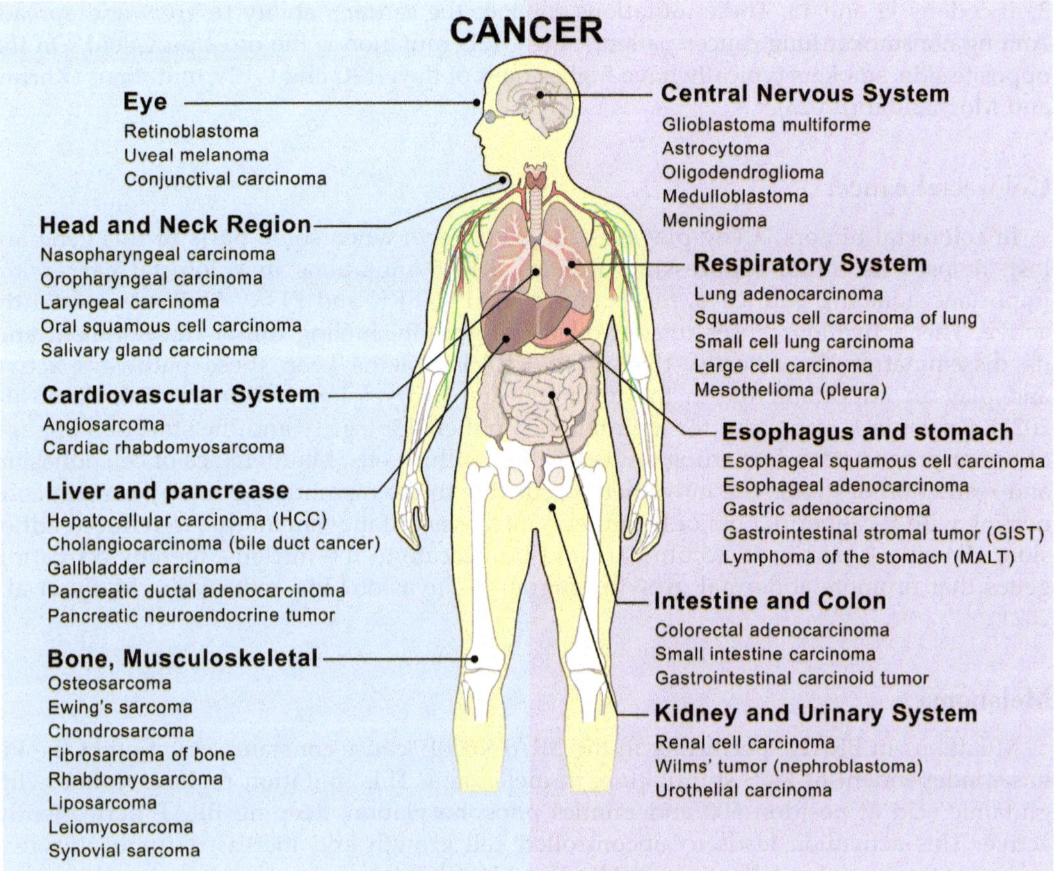

FIGURE 1.1 Types of cancer.

Lung cancer

In lung carcinoma, pathogenic mutations of the BRCA2 gene, such as shifts, nonsense, and deletion mutations, lead to the disruption of the DNA repair process. Shift and nonsense mutations are the most common, causing a disruption of the normal amino acid sequence by introducing a premature stop signal. This mutation leads to shorter, malfunctioning proteins that can cause genetic instability, significantly raising the cancer risk for those carrying BRCA2 mutations compared to the general population (Clusan et al., 2023). Nonsmall cell lung cancer (NSCLC) often features ALK mutations, which can vary based on fusion partners that affect ALK expression and its timing. Currently, 22 known translocation partners have been identified, each creating distinct ALK fusion proteins, with EML4-ALK being a notable example. Some patients have nonfunctioning kinase mutations in ALK, but their role in tumor growth is unclear (Shackelford et al., 2014). In patients with NSCLC, KRAS mutations are frequently found specifically in the KRAS gene, particularly in exons 2 and

3, at codons 12 and 13. These mutations enhance the cancer's ability to grow and spread. Among nonsmoker lung cancer patients, the G12D mutation is the most prevalent. On the opposite side, smokers typically have higher rates of the G12C and G12V mutations (Karimi and Moghaddam, 2023).

Colorectal cancer

In colorectal tumors, a key player is the APC gene; when some parts of this gene are lost, it loses its tumor-suppressing abilities. KRAS mutations in colorectal cancer are important signaling pathways, for example, MAPK/ERK and PI3K/AKT, are constantly active. This activation causes uncontrolled cell growth, fueling tumor development and its dissemination. Specifically, overactive KRAS proteins keep these pathways active and play an important role in the initiation and progression of tumors (Takeda et al., 2025). β-catenin is important for maintaining epithelial integrity and the start or stoppage of tumor progression, depending on its location within cells. Maintenance of cell adhesion and restriction of tumor cell movement occur due to the membrane-bound β-catenin connecting with E-cadherin. Loss of E-cadherin increases cell movement due to reduced adhesion, allowing β-catenin to accumulate and translocate to the nucleus, thereby activating genes that promote abnormal growth, migration, invasion, and metastasis (Matly et al., 2021).

Melanoma

Mutations in BRAF, specifically in the BRAFV600E, cause constant activation of the kinase, independent of RAS stimulation, in melanoma. This mutation replaces valine with glutamic acid at position 600 and mimics phosphorylation, keeping BRAF permanently active. This activation leads to uncontrolled cell growth and increased tumor survival and progression (Mandalà et al., 2014). The p16 (INK4a) protein is an important tumor suppressor that regulates the cell cycle by stopping certain kinases and abnormal cell division. These promote orderly growth of healthy melanocytes, leading to loss of expression of melanoma, which leads to uncontrolled tumor development. The p16 presence in tissues either suppresses or allows cancer progression. Strong staining suggests it's active, while weak or absent staining often signals aggressive melanoma behavior (Smith et al., 2008). The p16 protein has a crucial role in maintaining cell control by regulating cell growth. In melanoma, when p16 is diminished or lost, it opens the way for uncontrollable tumor growth. The p16 through tissue samples help in understanding its functioning in fighting cancer. Strong signals of p16 mean it's in its normal state, but weak or missing signals indicate a more aggressive form of melanoma, which is concerning (Zhu, 2005).

Bone cancer

In osteosarcoma, RUNX2 proteins are normally found at high levels, disrupting normal bone growth. Instead of maturing bone cells, RUNX2 promotes the growth of immature cells, leading to tumor formation. RUNX2 interacts with key cancer pathways like p53 and Wnt, leading to increased tumor growth and spread. RUNX2 also activates enzymes that damage the surrounding tissue, aiding metastasis. Ultimately, high RUNX2 levels are associated with severe tumor characteristics and a worse outlook for patients (Sun et al., 2015).

Cervical cancer progression

Cervical cancer's main cause is human papillomavirus (HPV), driven by three viral proteins: E5, E6, and E7. Specifically, E5 reduces the expression of major histocompatibility complex (MHC) class I, helping infected cells evade the immune system, while enhancing signals that promote further cell growth. And E6 stops the p53 tumor suppressor, causing its degradation and allowing damaged cells to survive and mutate. At the same time, it activates telomerase, giving these cells the ability to live indefinitely. E7 targets the retinoblastoma protein (pRb), which promotes unregulated cell division by activating E2F transcription factors. It also inhibits proteins that normally slow down cell growth. In essence, these proteins help HPV-infected cells proliferate uncontrollably, leading to cancer development (Balasubramaniam Shandra et al., 2019).

Brain tumor

In glioblastoma multiforme (GBM), a critical change involves the EGFR protein. Many tumors have extra copies of the EGFR gene, leading to an overproduction of this protein, which fuels rapid and uncontrolled cell growth. A common mutation, called EGFRvIII, creates a receptor that stays active even without its usual signal. This constant activity makes tumor cells grow faster and more difficult to treat. When EGFRvIII is present alongside regular EGFR amplification, the tumor becomes more aggressive, often resulting in poorer outcomes for patients. Overall, EGFRvIII plays a key role in the challenging nature of GBM (Gan et al., 2013).

Understanding cancer biology

The human body contains trillions of cells, each of which follows a strict timeline of growth, division, and death. Their path is complex and involves a balance of signals that maintain homeostasis within tissues. When this signaling is disturbed, cells begin to multiply beyond physiological control, resulting in a neoplasm. Malignant transformation is a multistep biological process that involves genetic damage, biochemical reprogramming, and cellular adaptation (Steeg, 2021; Errington et al., 2021; Volante et al., 2021). The mechanistic pathway for tumor development is described in Fig. 1.2.

Neoplasia and anaplasia

Neoplasia is an abnormal and uncontrolled cell growth that continues even in the absence of the original stimulus, resulting in a mass that may be benign or malignant. Benign tumors

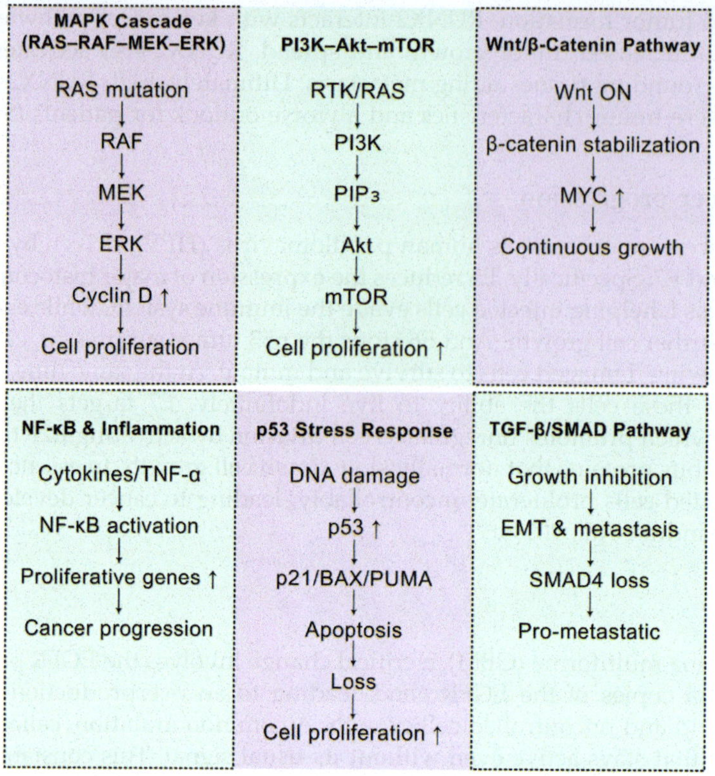

FIGURE 1.2 Mechanistic pathways of tumor development.

are usually well-circumscribed, slow-growing, and noninvasive, remaining confined to their site of origin and resembling the parent tissue in appearance. In contrast, malignant tumors show invasion of surrounding tissues, destroying standard architecture, and have the capacity to metastasize to distant organs (Gu et al., 2023). Anaplasia is a loss of structural and functional differentiation. Cancer cells appear pleomorphic, with irregular nuclei, a high nuclear-to-cytoplasmic ratio, abnormal mitotic figures, and a disorganized arrangement. Functionally, they may produce inappropriate proteins or hormones. These morphological and biochemical changes reflect a profound disruption of the genetic programs that maintain normal identity (Vujanić and Mifsud, 2024).

Cellular basis of malignancy

Growth control loss

In normal tissues, the regulation of the cell cycle is done by external growth factors binding to membrane receptors. These activities involve intracellular signaling in the transcription of genes required for DNA synthesis. When stimulation stops, the cell exits the cycle and enters a resting state in G_0. Cells become self-sufficient due to mutations in growth-regulatory genes. Cancer cells secrete their own growth factors (autocrine stimulation) or present active receptors permanently that signal in the absence of ligand (Ungefroren, 2021). Known examples include mutations in the HER2/neu, EGFR, and RAS families of oncogenes. These activate the *Ras–Raf–MEK–ERK* pathway, continuously driving proliferation (Ungefroren, 2021; Hendrikse et al., 2023).

Failure of inhibitory mechanisms

RB1 and TP53 are the two key tumor suppressor genes that act as molecular brakes in cell division. The retinoblastoma (Rb) protein binds to E2F, preventing cell entry into the S phase. Upon activation of CDK4/6 complexes, Rb is phosphorylated, allowing it to release E2F, which then signals the initiation of DNA replication. Mutations of the RB1 gene eliminate this switch, allowing uncontrolled cell growth to occur. p53 senses DNA damage and either induces cell-cycle arrest to facilitate DNA repair or triggers apoptosis when the damage is irreparable. The mutation of TP53 is most common and found in almost half of human cancers, permitting the survival of genetically unstable cells. Together, Rb and p53 represent the guardians of the genome; their inactivation is central to malignant transformation (Morrison et al., 2024; Goel et al., 2022; Fassl et al., 2022).

Escape from apoptosis

Apoptosis (programmed cell death) is an intrinsic safety mechanism that eliminates damaged cells. Apoptosis is regulated by the Bcl-2 family of proteins and executed by the caspase family of enzymes (Dandoti, 2021). In many cancers, proapoptotic genes, such as Bax and Bak, are suppressed, while antiapoptotic members, including Bcl-2 and Bcl-XL, are overexpressed. Activation of the PI3K–Akt–mTOR pathway also limits apoptosis by phosphorylating and inactivating proteins that induce cell death. Therefore, cells that should be eliminated allow the accumulation of mutations and the development of resistance to therapy (Dandoti, 2021; Castelli et al., 2021).

Limitless replicative potential

Normal cells divide for a finite number of times because their telomeres, protective DNA caps at the ends of chromosomes, shorten with each cycle. Cancer cells upregulate telomerase, an enzyme that rebuilds telomeres, granting them immortality. This feature contributes to tumor persistence and relapse (Liu et al., 2024; Karousou et al., 2023).

Molecular signaling pathways

Dysregulated molecular pathways that result in various cancers (Fig. 1.3).

MAPK cascade

Mutations in RAS genes (H-RAS, K-RAS, N-RAS) make active guanosine triphosphate (GTP)-bound Ras proteins that stimulate the Raf kinase, leading to activation of MEK and ERK. This helps facilitate the transcription of cyclin D and other genes involved in proliferation. These mutations occur commonly in pancreatic, colorectal, and lung cancers (Yan and Jade, 2023; Martin-Vega and Cobb, 2023).

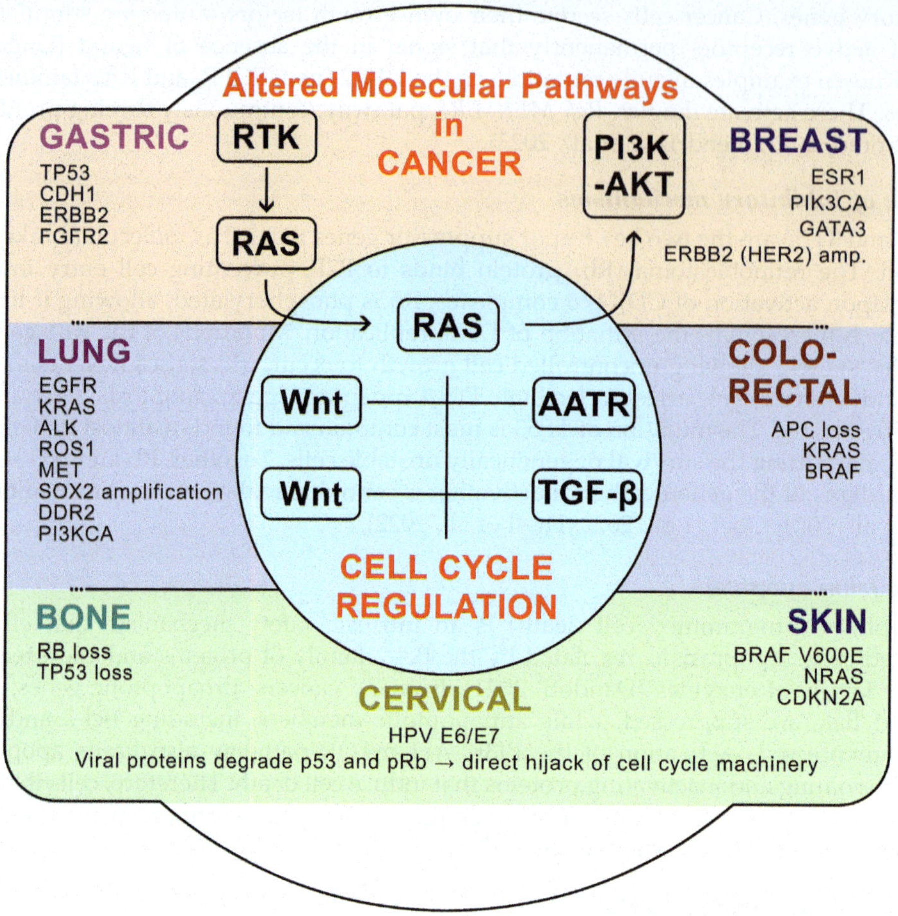

FIGURE 1.3 Altered molecular pathways in various cancers.

PI3K–Akt–mTOR pathway

Tyrosine kinases and Ras activate phosphoinositide 3-kinase (PI3K). PI3K converts PIP_2 to PIP_3, which recruits and activates Akt (protein kinase B). Akt phosphorylates downstream targets controlling metabolism, survival, and growth. Activation of mTOR increases protein synthesis and cell mass. Loss of the inhibitory gene *PTEN* or mutation in PI3K results in the hyperactivation of this pathway (Glaviano et al., 2023; Li et al., 2021).

Wnt/β-catenin pathway

The absence of Wnt signals activates β-catenin degradation through a complex containing APC and GSK-3β. Wnt binding switches off this complex and stabilizes β-catenin, which then enters the nucleus to activate growth genes such as MYC. Changes in β-catenin lead to continuous signaling and are strongly linked to colorectal cancer (Liu et al., 2022; Vallée et al., 2021).

p53 stress response network

Upon DNA damage, hypoxia occurs, p53 accumulates, and transcribes genes for cell-cycle arrest (p21), DNA repair, or apoptosis (*BAX, PUMA*). p53 not only loses its tumor-suppressive ability, but it also gains functions that promote invasion and drug resistance (Hanson and Batchelor, 2022; Vaddavalli and Schumacher, 2022).

NF-κB and inflammatory signaling

Chronic inflammation leads to an environment rich in cytokines and reactive oxygen species. The transcription factor NF-κB, activated by TNF-α and interleukins, triggers expression of antiapoptotic and proliferative genes. Regular or enhanced NF-κB activity is linked to inflammation and cancer progression (Zhang et al., 2021a; Sadati et al., 2025).

TGF-β and SMAD pathway

In the early stages of tumor development, transforming growth factor β acts as a suppressor, inhibiting proliferation. However, later, tumor cells promote invasion and metastasis through epithelial–mesenchymal transition (EMT). Loss of *SMAD4* converts TGF-β signaling from an inhibitory to a prometastatic pathway (Yu et al., 2022; Wang et al., 2023; Aashaq et al., 2022).

Genetic and epigenetic changes

Genetic and epigenetic mutations lead to cancer progression by disrupting standard cellular control mechanisms. Cancer genomes are identified by mutations and chromosomal abnormalities, which include point mutations, deletions, amplifications, and translocations that affect gene function and expression (Parmar and Easwaran, 2022; Zabransky et al., 2022). For example, the Philadelphia chromosome, (9;22), results in the formation of the BCR–ABL fusion gene, which activates a constitutively active tyrosine kinase that drives chronic myeloid leukemia. Similarly, amplification of the *HER2* gene in breast cancer leads to overexpression of its receptor, conferring aggressive tumor behavior and poor prognosis (Hou et al., 2023). In addition to these genetic changes, epigenetic modifications have a profound influence on gene regulation without changing the DNA sequence. Aberrant DNA methylation at CpG islands generally switches off the tumor suppressor genes, while histone deacetylation compacts chromatin and inhibits transcription, both of which contribute to oncogenesis (Gebhard et al., 2021). These modifications are reversible and offer therapeutic opportunities through agents like azacitidine, a DNA methylation inhibitor, and vorinostat, a histone deacetylase inhibitor. Genomic instability, a hallmark of cancer, arises from defects in DNA repair pathways, which include mismatch repair genes (*MLH1, MSH2*), nucleotide-excision repair genes (*XPA*), and double-strand break repair genes (*BRCA1, BRCA2*), leading to the unchecked accumulation of mutations. This genetic damage enhances tumor heterogeneity and adaptability and helps malignant transformation, collectively synergizing the interplay between genetic lesions, epigenetic dysregulation, and impaired genomic maintenance in cancer evolution (Laish et al., 2021; Vietri et al., 2022).

Tumor growth pathophysiology

Tumor growth follows multiple steps, like angiogenesis, metabolic reprogramming, immune evasion, and inflammation.

Angiogenesis

Tumor growth beyond 1–2 mm needs its own blood supply. Hypoxia stabilizes HIF-1α, which induces vascular endothelial growth factor (VEGF) and fibroblast growth factor, thus stimulating new vessel formation. These vessels are leaky and irregular, contributing to metastasis and uneven drug delivery. Antiangiogenic drugs like bevacizumab target this mechanism (Poto et al., 2022; Ozel et al., 2022).

Metabolic reprogramming—the Warburg effect

Cancer cells prefer glycolysis even in the presence of oxygen, producing lactate rather than using oxidative phosphorylation. This "aerobic glycolysis" provides rapid ATP and intermediates for nucleic acid and lipid synthesis. Activation of PI3K/Akt/mTOR and MYC transcription promotes this shift. Lactate acidifies the microenvironment, enhancing invasion (Barba et al., 2024; Papaneophytou, 2024).

Immune evasion

Tumors evade immune destruction by multiple means, such as downregulating MHC class I molecules, expressing immune checkpoint ligands (programmed death-ligand 1 [PD-L1]) that inhibit T cells, and recruiting regulatory T cells and myeloid-derived suppressor cells. Checkpoint-blocker therapies (anti-PD-1, anti-CTLA-4) restore antitumor immunity (Cao et al., 2023).

Inflammation and microenvironment

Inflammatory cells release growth factors (VEGF, epidermal growth factor), proteases, and cytokines that remodel the extracellular matrix. Cancer-associated fibroblasts secrete matrix metalloproteinases (MMPs) that facilitate invasion. Tumor-associated macrophages (TAMs) correlate with poor prognosis (Denk and Greten, 2022; Pereira et al., 2022).

Invasion and metastasis mechanisms

Metastasis is one of the life-threatening features of malignant tumors, leading to the majority of cancer-related deaths. It is a complex and tightly regulated cycle involving local invasion, intravasation, survival in circulation, and extravasation. The cycle begins with local invasion, where cancer cells lose their adhesive properties, primarily due to the downregulation of E-cadherin, a cell–cell adhesion molecule essential for maintaining epithelial integrity. Subsequently, tumor cells release MMPs that degrade the extracellular matrix and basement membrane, which creates a path for invasion into distant tissues (Castaneda et al., 2022; Cambria et al., 2024).

Intravasation occurs when the tumor crosses the local barrier, allowing malignant cells to cross the lymphatic walls. Tumor entry into the bloodstream is facilitated by TAMs, which secrete cytokines and proteolytic enzymes that disrupt endothelial junctions. Cancer cells encounter stressful conditions during circulation, such as immune surveillance. To protect against immune attack and aid in vascular adhesion, they often aggregate with platelets, forming platelet clogs (Wang et al., 2021; Kzhyshkowska et al., 2024).

After extravasation, tumor cells bind to the endothelium lining of other organs via adhesion molecules, integrins, and selectins before migrating through the vessel wall. In the final phase, colonization is most difficult and ineffective. To adapt to a foreign microenvironment, tumor cells activate angiogenic and survival pathways, generally by recruiting local stromal cells and modifying cytokine signaling (Denk and Greten, 2022; Castaneda et al., 2022; Cambria et al., 2024; Wang et al., 2021).

The EMT involves epithelial cells that lose their polarity, acquiring a mesenchymal phenotype, which is characterized by increased motility and invasiveness in the initial stages. Transcription factors regulate EMT by activating genes that promote motility and repressing the expression of E-cadherin (Zhang et al., 2021a). Tumor cells sometimes undergo a reverse process at metastatic sites, called the mesenchymal–epithelial transition (MET), restoring their ability to proliferate and generate new tumors. This dynamic flexibility highlights metastasis as a controlled, reversible biological process, rather than a chance occurrence (Zhang et al., 2021a; Akhmetkaliyev et al., 2023).

Cancer hallmarks

Hanahan and Weinberg discovered that the hallmarks of cancer are complex in the mechanisms of cancer development and progression. These hallmarks show fundamental biological capabilities of tumor, each driven by specialized molecular and signaling pathways as shown in Table 1.1.

TABLE 1.1 Hallmarks and underlying pathways associated with cancer (Pavlova et al., 2022; López-Otín et al., 2023; Hanahan, 2022).

Hallmark	Underlying mechanism/pathway
Sustained proliferative signaling	EGFR–Ras–MAPK, PI3K–Akt–mTOR, Wnt/β-catenin
Insensitivity to antigrowth signals	Loss of TGF-β/SMAD, Rb inactivation
Resistance to apoptosis	Overexpression of Bcl-2, Akt activation
Limitless replication	Telomerase activation
Angiogenesis	HIF-1α → VEGF
Invasion and metastasis	EMT, MMP secretion, integrin switching
Reprogrammed energy metabolism	Warburg effect via MYC and mTOR
Immune evasion	PD-L1/PD-1, CTLA-4, Treg recruitment

Data from N.N. Pavlova, J. Zhu, C.B. Thompson, The hallmarks of cancer metabolism: still emerging. Cell Metab. 34 (3) (2022), 355–377. https://doi.org/10.1016/j.cmet.2022.01.007; C. López-Otín, F. Pietrocola, D. Roiz-Valle, L. Galluzzi, G. Kroemer, Meta-hallmarks of aging and cancer. Cell Metab. 35 (1) (2023), 12–35. https://doi.org/10.1016/j.cmet.2022.11.001; D. Hanahan, Hallmarks of cancer: new dimensions. Cancer Discov. 12 (1) (2022), 31–46. https://doi.org/10.1158/2159-8290.cd-21-1059.

Cancer stem cells and tumor heterogeneity

Cellular heterogeneity can be found within a single tumor, showing differences in responsiveness to cancer treatment. Cancer stem cells (CSCs) are specialized cells that play an important role in this diversification. These cells have a unique capacity to rebuild the tumor after treatment and differentiate into various forms. Critical developmental signaling pathways that control stemness and cellular plasticity, like Notch, Hedgehog, and Wnt, support CSCs (Bayik and Lathia, 2021; Chu et al., 2024).

Importantly, CSCs have strong resistance to chemotherapy and radiation due to their efficient DNA repair mechanisms, activated antiapoptotic pathway, and overexpression of ATP-binding cassette (ABC) transporters, which actively reverse cytotoxic medications. Because of their endurance, CSCs can reform tumors, withstand early treatment, and promote recurrence. Therefore, targeting CSCs is a new area of oncology, with techniques focusing on reducing stemness pathways and blocking niche contacts and making them more susceptible to old treatments. Developing successful cancer treatments and overcoming therapeutic resistance requires an understanding of CSC biology (Bayik and Lathia, 2021; Modi et al., 2022).

Systemic manifestations of cancer

Cancer has significant systemic effects, interfering with normal physiology in addition to local tissue invasion. A syndrome of increasing weight loss, muscle atrophy, and fatigue, called cachexia, is one of the most crippling symptoms. It is primarily caused by chronic inflammation and the release of proinflammatory cytokines. These cytokines change the way energy is metabolized and encourage the breakdown of adipose tissue and skeletal muscle (Aashaq et al., 2022; Poto et al., 2022).

Another group of systemic symptoms produced by tumor cells producing ectopic hormones or peptides is known as paraneoplastic syndromes. A lack of parathyroid hormone-related peptide (PTHrP) causes hypercalcemia, whereas improper secretion of adrenocorticotropic hormone (ACTH) can cause Cushing's syndrome. These endocrine and metabolic abnormalities frequently function as early markers of cancer. Furthermore, metastatic cancer is often accompanied by immunosuppression, which is caused by immune checkpoint activation and tumor-derived cytokines that weaken host immunological responses and make the body more vulnerable to infections. When taken as a whole, these symptoms demonstrate that cancer is a systemic dysfunction of control that affects several organ systems at once rather than just a localized illness (Murakami et al., 2024; Martin, 2022).

Causes of cancer

Environmental exposure and genetic predisposition, in combination, intricately cause cancer. No single cause accounts for all types of cancer; in contrast, the disease starts when multiple risk factors come together over time, disturbing the balance between growth and repair. Genetic and epigenetic alterations provide the biological causes of malignancy, whereas extrinsic agents, including chemical, physical, biological, and lifestyle-related factors, act as initiators or promoters of these changes (Khakoo et al., 2024).

Genetic alterations in oncogenes, tumor suppressor genes, and DNA repair genes basically start the process of carcinogenesis. APC gene mutations cause familial adenomatous polyposis, while BRCA1/2-related breast and ovarian malignancies are examples of hereditary mutations that constitute the basis of familial cancer syndromes. Nonetheless, most mutations are acquired throughout a person's lifetime and are caused by carcinogenic exposures or errors in DNA replication. Many human malignancies have mutational "hotspots" in genes like RAS, TP53, and PIK3CA (Khakoo et al., 2024; Ghojazadeh et al., 2022).

Modifying gene activity, regardless of the underlying DNA sequence, is another essential function of epigenetic change. Tumor suppressor genes can be suppressed by aberrant DNA methylation, and transcription is affected by histone changes that alter chromatin structure. These alterations are desirable therapeutic targets since they are reversible. Certain hematological malignancies are currently treated with medications that block DNA methyltransferases or histone deacetylases, proving that epigenetic dysregulation is a cause of cancer rather than just a side effect (Orsolic et al., 2023; Kopinski et al., 2021).

One of the major extrinsic causes of cancer is chemical carcinogens. Both lifestyle-related and occupational agents are included. Lung and oral cavity cancers are directly linked to polycyclic aromatic hydrocarbons found in tobacco smoking. Aspergillus fungi produce aflatoxins, which are associated with liver cancer. Bladder and stomach tumors have been linked to nitrosamines and aromatic amines. Carcinogens can bind DNA directly or indirectly through metabolic activation by enzymes such as cytochrome P450, which creates reactive intermediates that result in DNA adducts. Permanent mutations arise if such adducts are not fixed before replication (Oliveira and Faustino-Rocha, 2025).

Physical carcinogens are just as potent, especially ultraviolet (UV) light and ionizing radiation. Pyrimidine dimers are formed in DNA by UV radiation, which can cause mutations in essential genes, such as the p53 gene, frequently observed in skin malignancies. Free radicals produced by ionizing radiation can break DNA strands and create chromosomal translocations, as shown in some cases of thyroid and leukemia following nuclear exposure (Oliveira and Faustino-Rocha, 2025; Verma et al., 2024).

The burden of cancer worldwide is primarily caused by biological agents, especially in developing nations. Nearly all cervical cancers and a significant percentage of oropharyngeal cancers are caused by HPV infection. Hepatocellular carcinoma is the result of persistent liver inflammation caused by the hepatitis B and C viruses (HBV and HCV). While *Helicobacter pylori* infection causes atrophic mucosal changes and chronic gastritis, Epstein–Barr virus (EBV) is linked to Burkitt's lymphoma and nasopharyngeal cancer. These infections serve as examples of how chronic inflammation and ongoing immune activation can foster carcinogenesis (Verma et al., 2024; Rumgay et al., 2021; Mustafayev and Torres, 2022).

Systemic and microenvironmental variables significantly influence tumor initiation in addition to these direct causes. An environment that is favorable to aberrant cell proliferation can be created by prolonged oxidative stress, persistent inflammation, and altered hormonal states. TNF-α, IL-6, and prostaglandins are examples of inflammatory mediators that initiate an ongoing cycle of tissue injury and repair, promoting the accumulation of mutations. These molecular changes are synergistically enhanced by lifestyle and behavioral factors, including alcohol and tobacco use, poor diet, obesity, and sedentary behaviors. For example, obesity causes persistent low-grade inflammation and hyperinsulinemia, both of which can trigger protumorigenic signaling pathways, such as NF-κB and PI3K–Akt (Tagliabue, 2021).

Thus, cancer should be seen as a product of prolonged exposure to risk combined with internal vulnerability. The interplay of genes and environment determines not only whether cancer will develop but also its biological behavior, aggressiveness, and response to therapy.

Cancer development mechanism

Cancer develops through multiple steps that include initiation, promotion, and progression. Transformation begins with the initial genetic damage (initiation); this process is irreversible. Growth-stimulating substances promote the proliferation of these modified cells during the promotion phase. Ultimately, as cancer progresses, cells acquire new mutations that confer malignant characteristics, including invasiveness, angiogenesis, and the ability to metastasize (Liu et al., 2022; Cambria et al., 2024).

Oncogenes need to be activated, tumor suppressor genes must be inactivated, and changes must be made to genomic maintenance systems for a normal cell to become malignant. Growth-promoting signals are sent downstream via the Raf–MEK–ERK pathway by Ras proteins that are constantly active due to mutations in RAS genes. Similar to this, loss of PTEN or mutations in PI3K eliminate inhibitory regulation, resulting in the ongoing activation of Akt and mTOR, which support metabolism, protein synthesis, and cell survival. These pathways serve as an example of how regular regulatory circuits can be disrupted to allow unchecked growth (Martin-Vega and Cobb, 2023; Luo et al., 2022).

The ability to disturb cell-cycle checkpoints is another important mechanism. Before replication, DNA integrity is ensured by the G_1/S checkpoint and regulated by the Rb and p53 proteins. This control is lost when Rb is absent, and p53 mutations have the capacity to induce apoptosis or repair ineffectively. Due to this, cells with damaged DNA continue to proliferate, passing on to future generations. Chromosome aberrations and intratumoral heterogeneity, the basis of tumor evolution and medication resistance, are produced over time by such instability (Montégut et al., 2024; Sonkin et al., 2024).

Poor communication between cells and their environment is another factor that contributes to the development of cancer. Signals that typically preserve tissue integrity are released by stromal cells and the extracellular matrix. By releasing enzymes that break down the matrix and altering adhesion molecules, cancer cells change this crosstalk. While integrin flipping enables movement through the extracellular matrix, downregulation of E-cadherin decreases cell-to-cell adhesion, facilitating invasion. Growth factors such as TGF-β and platelet-derived growth factor (PDGF) are secreted by fibroblasts within the tumor microenvironment (TME), which enhances the motility and survival of cancer cells (Huang et al., 2021).

Another characteristic method for cancer progression is angiogenesis. Without a sufficient blood supply, tumors cannot develop larger than a few millimeters. VEGF is expressed when hypoxia causes HIF-1α to stabilize—uneven distribution of nutrients and oxygen results from the convoluted and leaky nature of newly generated tumor arteries. Treatment is made more difficult by this disorganized vasculature, which also leads to metastasis and hinders efficient drug delivery (Elebiyo et al., 2022).

The result of these mechanistic changes is metastasis. Invasion, intravasation, circulation survival, extravasation, and colonization of remote locations are all part of this synchronized process. Epithelial cancer cells undergo the EMT, which transforms them into spindle-shaped, migratory cells. Transcription factors such as Snail and Twist drive this process by upregulating mesenchymal markers, including vimentin, and repressing the expression of E-cadherin. Cancer cells may revert through the MET to form new tumors once they have become embedded in distant tissues (Zhang et al., 2021b; Akhmetkaliyev et al., 2023).

The TME actively contributes to the development of cancer rather than being a passive observer. Tumor survival is supported by a dynamic ecosystem that includes extracellular matrix components, immune cells, endothelial cells, and stromal fibroblasts. Within the TME, macrophages can adopt a tumor-promoting phenotype (M2 type), producing cytokines that promote angiogenesis and suppress immunity. Cancer is a "tissue disease" because of these interactions, which go well beyond single cellular mutations (Tagliabue, 2021; Huang et al., 2021; Elebiyo et al., 2022).

Clinical and biological diversity of cancer

Cancer changes itself based on the cell of origin, molecular structure, and host factors, despite its mechanisms sharing many common characteristics. Thus, tumor classification is important for diagnosis and treatment. Cancers are categorized based on their histological type: sarcomas from mesenchymal tissues, carcinomas from epithelial cells, and hematological malignancies from blood or lymphoid cells. With advances in molecular biology, a second classification approach based on molecular characteristics has emerged (MacDonald et al., 2025; Guo et al., 2019).

For now, there are three kinds of breast cancers: triple-negative, HER2-positive, and hormone receptor-positive. Each has a unique biological behavior and course of treatment. Same as mutations in EGFR, ALK, KRAS, or ROS1 distinguish lung tumors and determine their adequacy for targeted therapies. This approach highlights the shift from morphological to molecular taxonomy by matching classification with underlying mechanisms. Another facet of biological diversity is tumor variability, both intratumoral (differences within the same tumor) and intertumoral (differences between people). As cancer cells multiply, various mutations build up, creating subpopulations with differing degrees of aggression and sensitivity to treatment. Some cells can tolerate radiation or chemotherapy and then relapse as a result of this heterogeneity. The concept of CSCs further complicates the situation. Even after the tumor appears to be in remission, these cells can self-renew (Hu et al., 2023; Asleh et al., 2022).

Tumors exhibit diverse development patterns and modes of spreading from a pathophysiological perspective. While some, like pancreatic adenocarcinoma or small cell lung cancer, spread quickly, others, like basal cell carcinoma, stay locally invasive and seldom metastasize. Organ-specific "soil" conditions, such as prostate cancer favoring bone and colon cancer favoring the liver, are frequently reflected in the pattern of metastatic spread. Adhesion molecules, chemokine receptors, and microenvironmental compatibility all influence these preferences (Caswell and Swanton, 2017; Wandmacher et al., 2021; Sántha et al., 2021).

The host's immunological capacity, hormonal environment, and metabolic condition all have an equal impact on clinical variety. Cancers caused by viruses are more common among immunocompromised people, such as transplant recipients. Gender-specific variations in the incidence of breast, prostate, and endometrial cancers can be explained by hormonal mechanisms that regulate their growth. Insulin resistance and persistent inflammation are two further ways that nutritional and metabolic diseases, such as diabetes and obesity, influence the biological development of the tumor (Caswell and Swanton, 2017; Freedman et al., 2021).

Prevention, early detection, and survivorship

One of the best ways to reduce the burden of cancer worldwide is to prevent it. Primary prevention focuses on environmental management and lifestyle modification because modifiable exposures are a significant cause of many malignancies. Given its association with lung, oral, esophageal, and bladder cancers, quitting tobacco continues to be the most effective intervention. Frequent exercise reduces the risk of obesity by enhancing immunological and metabolic processes. At the same time, a well-balanced diet rich in fruits, vegetables, and antioxidants helps counteract the effects of free radicals. Critical preventive care includes minimizing alcohol consumption, keeping a healthy body weight, and shielding skin from UV rays (Etling et al., 2023; Maresso et al., 2023).

Another effective preventive measure is vaccination, such as hepatitis B vaccination, which avoids chronic infection that results in hepatocellular carcinoma, while the additive effects of the HPV vaccine have decreased the incidence of cervical cancer. Long-term control requires public health strategies that increase access to these vaccines, where infection-related malignancies are still common (Kang et al., 2019).

A component of secondary prevention is the early detection of disease through screening. There are many screening procedures for cancers of various types. Pap smears and HPV tests detect cervical dysplasia before its development, while mammography detects breast abnormalities at preinvasive stages. While low-dose CT scanning increases survival in high-risk smokers by identifying early lung tumors, colonoscopy and fecal occult blood testing enable the early removal of precancerous polyps. Awareness, accessibility, and adherence are essential for screening to be effective; these issues remain significant in underdeveloped nations (Guerra et al., 2024; O'Dowd et al., 2023).

Improving patients' quality of life and preventing recurrence are the main goals of tertiary prevention. Millions of people today live without active treatment thanks to advancements in therapy. Thus, medical, psychological, and social rehabilitation are all part of survivorship care. Common long-term problems that call for coordinated support include neuropathy, emotional distress, infertility, and persistent fatigue. Recovery and reintegration into daily life are improved when follow-up programs incorporate counseling, nutrition, and physical rehabilitation (Cohen and Biesecker, 2010).

Genetic and risk assessment are also part of preventive measures in advanced oncology. Genetic testing for mutations in the BRCA1, BRCA2, or Lynch syndrome genes is an option for patients with a family history of cancer. Understanding risk gives an idea of preventive surgery, which lowers mortality. Such specific prevention will become more sophisticated and popular as precision medicine develops. Finally, the goal of early detection is not merely to reduce incidence but to transform cancer from a life-threatening disease into a manageable condition. By integrating research and compassionate care, we can shift the focus from fear of cancer to empowerment through knowledge and timely action (Maresso et al., 2023; Sloan et al., 2012).

Conclusion

Intrinsic genomic changes and extrinsic environmental factors play an important role in shaping cancer, which is a systemic condition of dysregulated pathways rather than a single entity. Changes in signaling cascades, metabolic adaptability, and immune dysregulation are features that together support tumor survival and transformation of normal cells into malignant phenotypes. Targeted treatments have been made possible by advances in molecular oncology, which have improved our understanding by shifting from descriptive pathology to mechanism-based classification. The problems of tumor heterogeneity, metastasis, and resistance continue to restrict curative outcomes despite significant advancements. Future paths will involve combining immunogenomics, artificial intelligence, and multiomics to create predictive prevention models and adaptive treatment strategies. To turn cancer from a deadly illness into a chronically manageable condition, a comprehensive approach combining molecular understanding, public health policy, and psychological care will be essential.

Acknowledgments

The authors acknowledge the Department of Pharmaceuticals, Ministry of Chemicals and Fertilizers, Govt. of India, for support. The NIPER-R communication number for the book chapter is NIPER-R/Communication/808.

Data availability

Data will be made available on request.

Conflict of interest

The authors declare no competing interests.

References

Aashaq, S., Batool, A., Mir, S.A., Beigh, M.A., Andrabi, K.I., Shah, Z.A., 2022. TGF-β signaling: A recap of SMAD-independent and SMAD-dependent pathways. J. Cell. Physiol. 237 (1), 59–85. https://doi.org/10.1002/jcp.30529.

Akhmetkaliyev, A., Alibrahim, N., Shafiee, D., Tulchinsky, E., 2023. EMT/MET plasticity in cancer and go-or-grow decisions in quiescence: The two sides of the same coin? Mol. Cancer 22 (1). https://doi.org/10.1186/s12943-023-01793-z.

Asleh, K., Riaz, N., Nielsen, T.O., 2022. Heterogeneity of triple negative breast cancer: Current advances in subtyping and treatment implications. J. Exp. Clin. Cancer Res. 41 (1). https://doi.org/10.1186/s13046-022-02476-1.

Bayik, D., Lathia, J.D., 2021. Cancer stem cell–immune cell crosstalk in tumor progression. Nat. Rev. Cancer 21 (8), 526–536. https://doi.org/10.1038/s41568-021-00366-w.

Balasubramaniam Shandra, D., Balakrishnan Venugopal Oon Chern, E., Gurjeet, K., 2019. Key molecular events in cervical cancer development. Medicina 55. https://doi.org/10.3390/medicina55070384.

Barba, I., Carrillo-Bosch, L., Seoane, J., 2024. Targeting the Warburg effect in cancer: Where do we stand? Int. J. Mol. Sci. 25 (6), 3142. https://doi.org/10.3390/ijms25063142.

Boire, A., Burke, K., Cox, T.R., Guise, T., Jamal-Hanjani, M., Janowitz, T., Kaplan, R., Lee, R., Swanton, C., Vander Heiden, M.G., Sahai, E., 2024. Why do patients with cancer die? Nat. Rev. Cancer 24 (8), 578–589. https://doi.org/10.1038/s41568-024-00708-4.

Cambria, E., Coughlin, M.F., Floryan, M.A., Offeddu, G.S., Shelton, S.E., Kamm, R.D., 2024. Linking cell mechanical memory and cancer metastasis. Nat. Rev. Cancer 24 (3), 216–228. https://doi.org/10.1038/s41568-023-00656-5.

Cao, X., Geng, Q., Fan, D., Wang, Q., Wang, X., Zhang, M., Lu, Z., Jiao, Y., Deng, T., Liu, H., Zhou, J., Jia, L., Xiao, C., 2023. m6A methylation: A process reshaping the tumor immune microenvironment and regulating immune evasion. Mol. Cancer 22 (1). https://doi.org/10.1186/s12943-022-01704-8.

Castaneda, M., den Hollander, P., Kuburich, N.A., Rosen, J.M., Mani, S.A., 2022. Mechanisms of cancer metastasis. Semin. Cancer Biol. 87, 17–31. https://doi.org/10.1016/j.semcancer.2022.10.006.

Castelli, V., Giordano, A., Benedetti, E., Giansanti, F., Quintiliani, M., Cimini, A., d'Angelo, M., 2021. The great escape: The power of cancer stem cells to evade programmed cell death. Cancers 13 (2), 328. https://doi.org/10.3390/cancers13020328.

Caswell, D.R., Swanton, C., 2017. The role of tumour heterogeneity and clonal cooperativity in metastasis, immune evasion and clinical outcome. BMC Med. 15 (1). https://doi.org/10.1186/s12916-017-0900-y.

Cheng, X., 2024. A comprehensive review of HER2 in cancer biology and therapeutics. Genes. Available from: 10.3390/genes15070903.

Chu, X., Tian, W., Ning, J., Xiao, G., Zhou, Y., Wang, Z., Zhai, Z., Tanzhu, G., Yang, J., Zhou, R., 2024. Cancer stem cells: Advances in knowledge and implications for cancer therapy. Signal Transduct. Targeted Ther. 9 (1). https://doi.org/10.1038/s41392-024-01851-y.

Clusan, L., Ferrière, F., Flouriot, G., Pakdel, F., 2023. A basic review on estrogen receptor signaling pathways in breast cancer. Int. J. Mol. Sci. Available from: https://doi.org/10.3390/ijms24076834.

Cohen, J.S., Biesecker, B.B., 2010. Quality of life in rare genetic conditions: A systematic review of the literature. Am. J. Med. Genet. 152 (5), 1136–1156. https://doi.org/10.1002/ajmg.a.33380.

Dandoti, S., 2021. Mechanisms adopted by cancer cells to escape apoptosis–a review. Biocell 45 (4), 863–884. https://doi.org/10.32604/biocell.2021.013993.

Denk, D., Greten, F.R., 2022. Inflammation: The incubator of the tumor microenvironment. Trends Cancer 8 (11), 901–914. https://doi.org/10.1016/j.trecan.2022.07.002.

Elebiyo, T.C., Rotimi, D., Evbuomwan, I.O., Maimako, R.F., Iyobhebhe, M., Ojo, O.A., Oluba, O.M., Adeyemi, O.S., 2022. Reassessing vascular endothelial growth factor (VEGF) in anti-angiogenic cancer therapy. Cancer Treat. Res. Commun. 32. https://doi.org/10.1016/j.ctarc.2022.100620.

Errington, T.M., Mathur, M., Soderberg, C.K., Denis, A., Perfito, N., Iorns, E., Nosek, B.A., 2021. Investigating the replicability of preclinical cancer biology. eLife 10. https://doi.org/10.7554/eLife.71601.

Etling, M.A., Vik, T.A., Janota, A.D., Liang, K.L., Kryder-Reid, C.L., Robertson, M., 2023. The continuing evolution of a cancer prevention, screening, and survivorship ECHO: A second year of implementation. Cancer Med. 12, 7398–7405. https://doi.org/10.1002/cam4.5441.

Fassl, A., Geng, Y., Sicinski, P., 2022. CDK4 and CDK6 kinases: From basic science to cancer therapy. Science 375 (6577). https://doi.org/10.1126/science.abc1495.

Freedman, J.A., Al Abo, M., Allen, T.A., Piwarski, S.A., Wegermann, K., Patierno, S.R., 2021. Biological aspects of cancer health disparities. Annu. Rev. Med. 72, 229–241. https://doi.org/10.1146/annurev-med-070119-120305.

Gan, H.K., Cvrljevic, A.N., Johns, T.G., 2013. The epidermal growth factor receptor variant III (EGFRvIII): Where wild things are altered. FEBS J. 280 (21), 5350–5370. https://doi.org/10.1111/febs.12393.

Gebhard, C., Mulet-lazaro, R., Glatz, D., Schwarzfischer-Pfeilschifter, L., Schirmacher, P., Gaedcke, J., Weichert, W., Reuschel, E., Dietmaier, W., Rehli, M., 2021. Aberrant DNA methylation patterns in microsatellite stable human colorectal cancers define a new marker panel for the CpG island methylator phenotype. Cancer Genet. Epigenet. https://doi.org/10.1002/ijc.33831.

Ghojazadeh, M., Hossein Somi, M., Naseri, A., Salehi-Pourmehr, H., Hassannezhad, S., Hajikamanaj Olia, A., Kafshdouz, L., Nikniaz, Z., 2022. Systematic review and meta-analysis of TP53, HER2/ERBB2, KRAS, APC, and PIK3CA genes expression pattern in gastric cancer. Middle East J. Dig. Dis. 14 (3), 335–345. https://doi.org/10.34172/mejdd.2022.292.

Glaviano, A., Foo, A.S.C., Lam, H.Y., Yap, K.C.H., Jacot, W., Jones, R.H., Eng, H., Nair, M.G., Makvandi, P., Geoerger, B., Kulke, M.H., Baird, R.D., Prabhu, J.S., Carbone, D., Pecoraro, C., Teh, D.B.L., Sethi, G., Cavalieri, V., Lin, K.H., Javidi-Sharifi, N.R., Toska, E., Davids, M.S., Brown, J.R., Diana, P., Stebbing, J., Fruman, D.A., Kumar, A.P., 2023. PI3K/AKT/mTOR signaling transduction pathway and targeted therapies in cancer. Mol. Cancer 22 (1). https://doi.org/10.1186/s12943-023-01827-6.

Goel, S., Bergholz, J.S., Zhao, J.J., 2022. Targeting CDK4 and CDK6 in cancer. Nat. Rev. Cancer 22 (6), 356–372. https://doi.org/10.1038/s41568-022-00456-3.

Gu, M., Kovilakam, S.C., Dunn, W.G., Marando, L., Barcena, C., Mohorianu, I., Smith, A., Kar, S.P., Fabre, M.A., Gerstung, M., Cargo, C.A., Malcovati, L., Quiros, P.M., Vassiliou, G.S., 2023. Multiparameter prediction of myeloid neoplasia risk. Nat. Genet. 55 (9), 1523–1530. https://doi.org/10.1038/s41588-023-01472-1.

Guerra, C.E., Sharma, P.V., Castillo, B.S., 2024. Multi-cancer early detection: The new frontier in cancer early detection. Annu. Rev. Med. 75, 67–81. https://doi.org/10.1146/annurev-med-050522-033624.

Guo, M., Peng, Y., Gao, A., Du, C., Herman, J.G., 2019. Epigenetic heterogeneity in cancer. Biomarker Res. 7 (1). https://doi.org/10.1186/s40364-019-0174-y.

Hanahan, D., 2022. Hallmarks of cancer: New dimensions. Cancer Discov. 12 (1), 31–46. https://doi.org/10.1158/2159-8290.cd-21-1059.

Hanson, R.L., Batchelor, E., 2022. Coordination of MAPK and p53 dynamics in the cellular responses to DNA damage and oxidative stress. Mol. Syst. Biol. https://doi.org/10.15252/msb.202211401.

Hendrikse, C.S.E., Theelen, P.M.M., van der Ploeg, P., Westgeest, H.M., Boere, I.A., Thijs, A.M.J., Ottevanger, P.B., van de Stolpe, A., Lambrechts, S., Bekkers, R.L.M., Piek, J.M.J., 2023. The potential of RAS/RAF/MEK/ERK (MAPK) signaling pathway inhibitors in ovarian cancer: A systematic review and meta-analysis. Gynecol. Oncol. 171, 83–94. https://doi.org/10.1016/j.ygyno.2023.01.038.

Hou, Y., Nitta, H., Li, Z., 2023. HER2 intratumoral heterogeneity in breast cancer, an evolving concept. Cancers 15 (10), 2664. https://doi.org/10.3390/cancers15102664.

Hu, X., Yang, P., Chen, S., Wei, G., Yuan, L., Yang, Z., Gong, L., He, L., Yang, L., Peng, S., Dong, Y., He, X., Bao, G., 2023. Clinical and biological heterogeneities in triple-negative breast cancer reveals a non-negligible role of HER2-low. Breast Cancer Res. 25 (1). https://doi.org/10.1186/s13058-023-01639-y.

Huang, J., Zhang, L., Wan, D., Lin, Z., Zheng, S., Lin, S., Qiao, Y., 2021. Extracellular matrix and its therapeutic potential for cancer treatment. Signal Transduct. Targeted Ther. 6 (1). https://doi.org/10.1038/s41392-021-00544-0.

Karimi, N., Moghaddam, S.J., 2023. KRAS-mutant lung cancer: Targeting molecular and immunologic pathways, therapeutic advantages and restrictions. Cells.

Karousou, E., Parnigoni, A., Moretto, P., Passi, A., Viola, M., Vigetti, D., 2023. Hyaluronan in the cancer cells microenvironment. Cancers 15 (3), 798. https://doi.org/10.3390/cancers15030798.

Kang, J., Park, E.J., Lee, J., 2019. Cancer survivorship in primary care. Korean. J. Fam. Med. 40 (6), 353–361. https://doi.org/10.4082/kjfm.19.0108.

Khakoo, N.S., Beecham, A.H., Lyu, J., Quintero, M.A., Gomez, L., Abreu, M.T., Deshpande, A.R., Kerman, D.H., McCauley, J.L., Proksell, S., Damas, O.M., 2024. Early life and childhood environmental exposures, more than genetic predisposition, influence age of diagnosis in a diverse cohort of 2952 patients with IBD. Clin. Gastroenterol. Hepatol. 22 (7), 1462. https://doi.org/10.1016/j.cgh.2024.01.020.

Kiri, S., Ryba, T., 2024. Cancer, metastasis, and the epigenome. Mol. Cancer 23 (1). https://doi.org/10.1186/s12943-024-02069-w.

Kopinski, P.K., Singh, L.N., Zhang, S., Lott, M.T., Wallace, D.C., 2021. Mitochondrial DNA variation and cancer. Nat. Rev. Cancer 21 (7), 431–445. https://doi.org/10.1038/s41568-021-00358-w.

Krupina, K., Goginashvili, A., Cleveland, D.W., 2024. Scrambling the genome in cancer: Causes and consequences of complex chromosome rearrangements. Nat. Rev. Genet. 25 (3), 196–210. https://doi.org/10.1038/s41576-023-00663-0.

Kzhyshkowska, J., Shen, J., Larionova, I., 2024. Targeting of TAMs: Can we be more clever than cancer cells? Cell. Mol. Immunol. 21 (12), 1376–1409. https://doi.org/10.1038/s41423-024-01232-z.

Laish, I., Friedman, E., Levi-Reznick, G., Kedar, I., Katz, L., Levi, Z., Halpern, N., Parnasa, S., Abu-Shatya, A., Half, E., Goldberg, Y., 2021. Double heterozygotes of BRCA1/BRCA2 and mismatch repair gene pathogenic variants: Case series and clinical implications. Breast Cancer Res. Treat. 188 (3), 685–694. https://doi.org/10.1007/s10549-021-06258-9.

Li, H., Prever, L., Hirsch, E., Gulluni, F., 2021. Targeting PI3K/AKT/mTOR signaling pathway in breast cancer. Cancers 13 (14), 3517. https://doi.org/10.3390/cancers13143517.

Liu, J., Xiao, Q., Xiao, J., Niu, C., Li, Y., Zhang, X., Zhou, Z., Shu, G., Yin, G., 2022. Wnt/β-catenin signalling: Function, biological mechanisms, and therapeutic opportunities. Signal Transduct. Targeted Ther. 7 (1). https://doi.org/10.1038/s41392-021-00762-6.

Liu, Y., Xu, Y., Wang, Y., Lv, J., Wang, K., Tang, Z., 2024. Hindering the unlimited proliferation of tumor cells synergizes with destroying tumor blood vessels for effective cancer treatment. Biomater. Sci. 12 (5), 1294–1306. https://doi.org/10.1039/d3bm01858j.

López-Otín, C., Pietrocola, F., Roiz-Valle, D., Galluzzi, L., Kroemer, G., 2023. Meta-hallmarks of aging and cancer. Cell Metab. 35 (1), 12–35. https://doi.org/10.1016/j.cmet.2022.11.001.

Luo, J., Li, Y., Zhai, Y., Liu, Y., Zeng, J., Wang, Di, Li, L., Zhu, Z., Chang, B., Fan, D., Zhang, J., Zhou, J., Sun, L., 2022. D-mannose ameliorates DNCB-induced atopic dermatitis in mice and TNF-α-induced inflammation in human keratinocytes via mTOR/NF-κB pathway. Int. Immunopharmacol. 113 (Pt A), 109378. https://doi.org/10.1016/j.intimp.2022.109378.

MacDonald, W.J., Purcell, C., Pinho-Schwermann, M., Stubbs, N.M., Srinivasan, P.R., El-Deiry, W.S., 2025. Heterogeneity in cancer. Cancers 17 (3). https://doi.org/10.3390/cancers17030441.

Mani, K., Deng, D., Lin, C., Wang, M., Hsu, M.L., Zaorsky, N.G., 2024. Causes of death among people living with metastatic cancer. Nat. Commun. 15 (1). https://doi.org/10.1038/s41467-024-45307-x.

Mandalà, M., Merelli, B., Massi, D., 2014. Nras in melanoma: Targeting the undruggable target. Crit. Rev. Oncol. Hematol. 92 (2), 107–122. https://doi.org/10.1016/j.critrevonc.2014.05.005.

Marino, P., Mininni, M., Deiana, G., Marino, G., Divella, R., Bochicchio, I., Giuliano, A., Lapadula, S., Rocco Lettini, A., Sanseverino, F., 2024. Healthy lifestyle and cancer risk: Modifiable risk factors to prevent cancer. Nutrients 16 (6), 800. https://doi.org/10.3390/nu16060800.

Martin, T.J., 2022. PTH1R actions on bone using the cAMP/protein kinase A pathway. Front. Endocrinol. 12. https://doi.org/10.3389/fendo.2021.833221.

Martin-Vega, A., Cobb, M.H., 2023. Navigating the ERK1/2 MAPK cascade. Biomolecules 13 (10), 1555. https://doi.org/10.3390/biom13101555.

Maresso, K.C., Basen-Engquist, K., Hawk, E., 2023. Cancer Epidemiology, Prevention, and Survivorship Perioperative Care of the Cancer Patient. Elsevier, United States, pp. 3–14. https://doi.org/10.1016/B978-0-323-69584-8.00001-3.

Marvalim, C., Datta, A., Lee, S.C., 2023. Role of p53 in breast cancer progression: An insight into p53 targeted therapy. Theranostics 13 (4).

Mathure, D., Sutar, A.D., Ranpise, H., Pawar, A., Awasthi, R., 2023. Preparation and optimization of liposome containing thermosensitive in situ nasal hydrogel system for brain delivery of sumatriptan succinate. Assay Drug Dev. Technol. 21 (1), 3–16. https://doi.org/10.1089/adt.2022.088.

Matly, A., Quinn, J.A., McMillan, D.C., Park, J.H., Edwards, J., 2021. The relationship between β-catenin and patient survival in colorectal cancer systematic review and meta-analysis. Crit. Rev. Oncol. Hematol. 163, 103337. https://doi.org/10.1016/j.critrevonc.2021.103337.

Modi, A., Roy, D., Sharma, S., Vishnoi, J.R., Pareek, P., Elhence, P., Sharma, P., Purohit, P., 2022. ABC transporters in breast cancer: their roles in multidrug resistance and beyond. J. Drug Target. 30 (9), 927–947. https://doi.org/10.1080/1061186X.2022.2091578.

Montégut, L., López-Otín, C., Kroemer, G., 2024. Aging and cancer. Mol. Cancer 23 (1). https://doi.org/10.1186/s12943-024-02020-z.

Morrison, L., Loibl, S., Turner, N.C., 2024. The CDK4/6 inhibitor revolution — a game-changing era for breast cancer treatment. Nat. Rev. Clin. Oncol. 21 (2), 89–105. https://doi.org/10.1038/s41571-023-00840-4.

Murakami, M., Hirahata, K., Fujimori, N., Yamamoto, T., Oda, Y., Kozono, S., Ueda, K., Ito, T., Nakamura, M., Ogawa, Y., 2024. Two cases of pancreatic neuroendocrine tumors with ectopic ACTH syndrome during their disease course. Clin. J. Gastroenterol. 17 (2), 363–370. https://doi.org/10.1007/s12328-023-01908-5.

Mustafayev, K., Torres, H., 2022. Hepatitis B virus and hepatitis C virus reactivation in cancer patients receiving novel anticancer therapies. Clin. Microbiol. Infection 28 (10), 1321–1327. https://doi.org/10.1016/j.cmi.2022.02.042.

Oliveira, P.A., Faustino-Rocha, A.I., 2025. Chemical Carcinogens. Springer Science and Business Media LLC, pp. 519–541. https://doi.org/10.1007/978-3-032-00761-2_121.

Orsolic, I., Carrier, A., Esteller, M., 2023. Genetic and epigenetic defects of the RNA modification machinery in cancer. Trends Genet. 39 (1), 74–88. https://doi.org/10.1016/j.tig.2022.10.004.

Ozel, I., Duerig, I., Domnich, M., Lang, S., Pylaeva, E., Jablonska, J., 2022. The good, the bad, and the ugly: Neutrophils, angiogenesis, and cancer. Cancers 14 (3), 536. https://doi.org/10.3390/cancers14030536.

O'Dowd, E.L., Merriel, S.W.D., Cheng, V.W.T., Khan, S., Howells, L.M., Gopal, D.P., Roundhill, E.A., Brennan, P.M., Crosbie, P.A.J., Neal, R.D., Brown, K., Crosbie, E.J., Baldwin, D.R., 2023. Clinical trials in cancer screening, prevention and early diagnosis (SPED): A systematic mapping review. BMC Cancer 23 (1). https://doi.org/10.1186/s12885-023-11300-8.

Papaneophytou, C., 2024. The Warburg effect: Is it always an enemy? Front. Biosci. 29 (12). https://doi.org/10.31083/j.fbl2912402.

Parmar, S., Easwaran, H., 2022. Genetic and epigenetic dependencies in colorectal cancer development. Gastroenterol. Rep. 10. https://doi.org/10.1093/gastro/goac035.

Pavlova, N.N., Zhu, J., Thompson, C.B., 2022. The hallmarks of cancer metabolism: Still emerging. Cell Metab. 34 (3), 355–377. https://doi.org/10.1016/j.cmet.2022.01.007.

Pereira, F., Ferreira, A., Reis, C.A., Sousa, M.J., Oliveira, M.J., Preto, A., 2022. KRAS as a modulator of the inflammatory tumor microenvironment: Therapeutic implications. Cells 11 (3). https://doi.org/10.3390/cells11030398.

Poto, R., Cristinziano, L., Modestino, L., de Paulis, A., Marone, G., Loffredo, S., Rosaria Galdiero, M., Varricchi, G., 2022. Neutrophil extracellular traps, angiogenesis and cancer. Biomedicines 10 (2), 431. https://doi.org/10.3390/biomedicines10020431.

Rumgay, H., Murphy, N., Ferrari, P., Soerjomataram, I., 2021. Alcohol and cancer: Epidemiology and biological mechanisms. Nutrients 13 (9), 3173. https://doi.org/10.3390/nu13093173.

Sadati, S., Khalaji, A., Bonyad, A., Khoshdooz, S., Kolbadi, K.S.H., Bahrami, A., Saeid Moeinfar, M., Morshedi, M., Ghamsaraian, A., Eterafi, M., Eshraghi, R., Mahabady, M.K., Mirzaei, H., 2025. NF-κB and apoptosis: Colorectal cancer progression and novel strategies for treatment. Eur. J. Med. Res. 30 (1). https://doi.org/10.1186/s40001-025-02734-w.

Sántha, P., Lenggenhager, D., Finstadsveen, A., Dorg, L., Tøndel, K., Amrutkar, M., Gladhaug, I.P., Verbeke, C., 2021. Morphological heterogeneity in pancreatic cancer reflects structural and functional divergence. Cancers 13 (4), 895. https://doi.org/10.3390/cancers13040895.

Shackelford, R.E., Vora, M., Mayhall, K., Cotelingam, J., 2014. ALK-rearrangements and testing methods in non-small cell lung cancer: A review. Genes.

Shashikant Kamble, A., Sutar, A.D., Shukla, R., 2025. Nanoerythrocytes in Cancer Therapy: Overview of Erythrocytes and Nanoerythrocytes. CRC Press. https://doi.org/10.1016/B978-0-443-28942-2.00014-4.

Sloan, J.A., De Andrade, M., Decker, P., Wampfler, J., Oswold, C., Clark, M., Yang, P., 2012. Genetic variations and patient-reported quality of life among patients with lung cancer. J. Clin. Oncol. 30 (14), 1699–1704. https://doi.org/10.1200/JCO.2010.34.5629.

Smith, E.M., Wang, D., Kim, Y., Rubenstein, L.M., Lee, J.H., Haugen, T.H., Turek, L.P., 2008. p16INK4a Expression, human papillomavirus, and survival in head and neck cancer. Oral Oncology 44 (2), 133–142. https://doi.org/10.1016/j.oraloncology.2007.01.010.

Sonkin, D., Thomas, A., Teicher, B.A., 2024. Cancer treatments: Past, present, and future. Cancer Genet. 286–287, 18–24. https://doi.org/10.1016/j.cancergen.2024.06.002.

Steeg, P.S., 2021. The blood–tumour barrier in cancer biology and therapy. Nat. Rev. Clin. Oncol. 18 (11), 696–714. https://doi.org/10.1038/s41571-021-00529-6.

Sun, S.-S., Zhang, L., Yang, J., Zhou, X., 2015. Role of runt-related transcription factor 2 in signal network of tumors as an inter-mediator. Cancer Lett. 361 (1), 1–7. https://doi.org/10.1016/j.canlet.2015.02.042.

Tagliabue, E., 2021. Special issue: Micro- and macro-environmental factors in solid cancers. Cells 10 (2), 247. https://doi.org/10.3390/cells10020247.

Takeda, M., Shoma, Y., Takuya, I., Yuki, S., Tsuyoshi, H., Atsushi, H., Takayuki, O., Norikatsu, M., Mamoru, U., Hirofumi, Y., Yuichiro, D., Hidetoshi, E., 2025. The role of KRAS mutations in colorectal cancer: Biological insights, clinical implications, and future therapeutic perspectives. Cancers 17. https://doi.org/10.3390/cancers17030428.

Ungefroren, H., 2021. Autocrine TGF-β in cancer: Review of the literature and caveats in experimental analysis. Int. J. Mol. Sci. 22 (2), 977. https://doi.org/10.3390/ijms22020977.

Vaddavalli, P.L., Schumacher, B., 2022. The p53 network: Cellular and systemic DNA damage responses in cancer and aging. Trends Genet. 38 (6), 598–612. https://doi.org/10.1016/j.tig.2022.02.010.

Vallée, A., Lecarpentier, Y., Vallée, J.-N., 2021. The key role of the WNT/β-catenin pathway in metabolic reprogramming in cancers under normoxic conditions. Cancers 13 (21), 5557. https://doi.org/10.3390/cancers13215557.

Verma, A., Zanoletti, A., Kareem, K.Y., Adelodun, B., Kumar, P., Ajibade, F.O., Silva, L.F.O., Phillips, A.J., Kartheeswaran, T., Bontempi, E., Dwivedi, A., 2024. Skin protection from solar ultraviolet radiation using natural compounds: A review. Environ. Chem. Lett. 22 (1), 273–295. https://doi.org/10.1007/s10311-023-01649-4.

Vietri, M.T., D'Elia, G., Caliendo, G., Albanese, L., Signoriello, G., Napoli, C., Molinari, A.M., 2022. Pancreatic cancer with mutation in BRCA1/2, MLH1, and APC genes: Phenotype correlation and detection of a novel germline BRCA2 mutation. Genes 13 (2), 321. https://doi.org/10.3390/genes13020321.

Volante, M., Lam, A.K., Papotti, M., Tallini, G., 2021. Molecular pathology of poorly differentiated and anaplastic thyroid cancer: What do pathologists need to know? Endocr. Pathol. 32 (1), 63–76. https://doi.org/10.1007/s12022-021-09665-2.

Vujanić, G.M., Mifsud, W., 2024. Anaplasia in wilms tumor: A critical review. Pediatr. Blood Cancer 71 (7). https://doi.org/10.1002/pbc.31000.

Wang, Q., Xiong, F., Wu, G., Wang, D., Liu, W., Chen, J., Qi, Y., Wang, B., Chen, Y., 2023. SMAD proteins in TGF-β signalling pathway in cancer: Regulatory mechanisms and clinical applications. Diagnostics 13 (17), 2769. https://doi.org/10.3390/diagnostics13172769.

Wandmacher, A.M., Mehdorn, A.-S., Sebens, S., 2021. The heterogeneity of the tumor microenvironment as essential determinant of development, progression and therapy response of pancreatic cancer. Cancers 13 (19), 4932. https://doi.org/10.3390/cancers13194932.

Wang, H., Tian, T., Zhang, J., 2021. Tumor-associated macrophages (TAMs) in colorectal cancer (CRC): From mechanism to therapy and prognosis. Int. J. Mol. Sci. 22 (16). https://doi.org/10.3390/ijms22168470.

Xie, C., Luo, J., He, Y., Jiang, L., Zhong, L., Shi, Y., 2022. BRCA2 gene mutation in cancer. Medicine.

Xiong, X., Zheng, L.W., Ding, Y., Chen, Y.F., Cai, Y.W., Wang, L.P., Huang, L., Liu, C.C., Shao, Z.M., Yu, K.D., 2025. Breast cancer: Pathogenesis and treatments. Signal Transduct. Targeted Ther. 10 (1). https://doi.org/10.1038/s41392-024-02108-4.

Yan, M.A., Jade, N., 2023. Specificity Models in MAPK Cascade Signaling. FEBSopenBIO. https://doi.org/10.1002/2211-5463.13619.

Yu, X.Y., Sun, Q., Zhang, Y.M., Zou, L., Zhao, Y.Y., 2022. TGF-β/Smad signaling pathway in tubulointerstitial fibrosis. Front. Pharmacol. 13. https://doi.org/10.3389/fphar.2022.860588.

Zabransky, D.J., Jaffee, E.M., Weeraratna, A.T., 2022. Shared genetic and epigenetic changes link aging and cancer. Trends Cell Biol. 32 (4), 338–350. https://doi.org/10.1016/j.tcb.2022.01.004.

Zhang, T., Ma, C., Zhang, Z., Zhang, H., Hu, H., 2021a. NF-κB signaling in inflammation and cancer. MedComm. 2 (4), 618–653. https://doi.org/10.1002/mco2.104.

Zhang, Z., Wuethrich, A., Wang, J., Korbie, D., Lin, L.L., Trau, M., 2021b. Dynamic monitoring of EMT in CTCs as an indicator of cancer metastasis. Anal. Chem. 93 (50), 16787–16795. https://doi.org/10.1021/acs.analchem.1c03167.

Zhu, L., 2005. Tumour suppressor retinoblastoma protein Rb: A transcriptional regulator. Eur. J. Cancer 41 (16), 2415–2427. https://doi.org/10.1016/j.ejca.2005.08.009.

CHAPTER

2

Current practices in cancer chemotherapy

Devika Shenoy[a], *Guddu Kumar*[a] *and Mansi Upadhyay*

Department of Pharmaceutics, Manipal College of Pharmaceutical Sciences, Manipal Academy of Higher Education, Manipal, Karnataka, India

Introduction

The majority of an adult animal's organs and tissues typically maintain a balance between cell death and renewal. The lifespan of each adult cell type in the body has a certain amount of time, and over the period, these cells die, and simultaneously, stem cells multiply and develop to produce new cells. Because new cell creation is regulated, the number of cells remains constant under normal circumstances. However, occasionally, some cells also develop that are insensitive to typical growth-control systems. These cells produce cell clones that have the potential to grow significantly, resulting in a tumor or neoplasm (Iwasa et al., 2020). Cancer is a major cause of death all over the world. It is an uncontrolled proliferation of cells leading to tumors (Upadhyay et al., 2018a; Upadhyay et al., 2019). In recent years, it has been demonstrated that cancer can be treated by surgery, chemotherapy, and radiotherapy (Shewach and Kuchta, 2009). As per the World Health Organization (WHO), an estimated 9.7 million people died from cancer, and 20 million new cases were reported in 2022. By 2050, there will likely be over 35 million new cases of cancer, a 77% increase from the 20 million cases that were anticipated in 2022 (Bray et al., 2024). In healthy tissue, a tightly controlled process of cell division, counterbalanced by cell death, keeps homeostasis intact. A malignant state will arise if there is an imbalance, either during the stage of cell death or during the stage of cellular multiplication. It's been demonstrated that oncogenes and tumor suppressor genes are crucial to this process since they control either cell division or cell death. These distinct functions are reflected in the three groups into which cancer-associated genes can be classified, as summarized in Table 2.1 (Wu et al., 2012).

[a] Equal Contribution.

Advanced Cancer Therapeutics
https://doi.org/10.1016/B978-0-443-44185-1.00028-8

Cancer is caused by mutations in genes (oncogenes). Certain mutations that raise our risk of acquiring cancer can be inherited. The investigation of these mutations has taught us a great deal about how faulty genes might lead to the development of cancer. These genes control cell division, development, proliferation, and survival. Over time, these genetic changes make the cells in sensitive to the body's natural regulatory systems and more skilled at invading normal organs. According to this view, the ability of the cancer-causing cell to divide multiple times is responsible for carcinogenesis. Due to these reasons, the types of cells that are present in a tissue and those that have the capacity to develop into tumors have received a great deal of research. When examined at the molecular level, the tissues that develop into malignant tumors or malignancies can be further classified into dozens of subtypes based on tissue origin and traditional pathology techniques (Cantley and Baselga, 2011). Cancer itself is a sequence of complicated diseases, and to overcome the condition, chemotherapy, surgery, and radiotherapy were among the options (Debela et al., 2021). Among these, chemotherapy is a widely used practice that began in the early 20th century (DeVita and Chu, 2008). The term "chemotherapy" was coined by Paul Ehrlich (Amjad et al., 2025). Although the history of chemotherapy evidence numerous remarkable events in

TABLE 2.1 Functional classification of cancer-associated genes.

Type/name	Nature of gene product
Category I: Genes that promote the growth of cells	
Type/name	**Nature of gene product**
Sis	Regarding platelet-derived growth factor (PDGF)
fms	CSF-1 receptor (colony-stimulating factor1)
erbB	Epidermal growth factor (EGF) receptor
Ha-*ras*	GTPase-active and GTP-binding protein
jun	Part of the AP1 transcription factor
myc	Protein that binds DNA
Category II: Genes that prevent tumor growth and reduce cellular division	
Type/name	**Nature of gene product**
Rb	The retinoblastoma suppressor
P53	A nuclear phosphoprotein that prevents colon and small-cell lung tumors from growing
APC	Inhibitor of adenomatous polyposis
DCC	Inhibitor of colon carcinoma
Category III: Genes controlling programmed cell death	
Type/name	**Nature of gene product**
bcl-2	Inhibitor of apoptosis

Modified from.

the early 1910s, where George Clowes at Rosewell Park Memorial Institute, New York developed a tumor model in rodents, allowing a large number of chemicals to be tested (Zubrod et al., 1977). Later on in 1937, Murray Shear, ran a program involving the screening of drugs for chemotherapy; natural drugs were also included in this therapy. Mainly, the idea of chemotherapy worked in real time during World War II and post period World War II. The report was related to mustard gas and found to be effective against lymphatic tissues and bone marrow (Anand et al., 2023). The first patient who received nitrogen mustard for lymphosarcoma, initially, the cancer, got cleared, but unfortunately, the patient died later, though this was a breakthrough towards the use of chemicals and heading towards the development of cancer chemotherapy for managing various types of cancer (Chen et al., 2018). After mustard gas chemotherapy, another remarkable anticancer chemotherapy that was reported was the application of folate antagonist, Aminopterin, used for leukemia in children (Brianna and Lee, 2023). Indeed, the patients diagnosed with cancer receive chemotherapy, but the approach has overburdened the patients with fatal physical and psychological challenges and causes potential life-threatening adverse effects (Juthani et al., 2024; Upadhyay et al., 2020; Mishra and Upadhyay, 2021). Some of the chemotherapeutic agents and related adverse effects are summarized in Table 2.2.

With the increased cases of cancer and the associated limited conventional therapies, there has been renewed interest in the development of other advanced chemotherapies with improved therapeutic indices. The therapies include cell-based therapy, gene therapy, small-molecule targeted therapy, antibody drug conjugates, etc. These newer modalities not only offer precise tumor targeting but also enhanced therapeutic comfort. The current chapter highlights the basics of conventional chemotherapy and the advancement over traditional therapies.

TABLE 2.2 Chemotherapeutic agent frequently used in chemotherapy and associated adverse effects (Craig et al., 2008).

Category	Therapeutic agent	Mechanism of action	Adverse effect
Platinum analog	Carboplatin, cisplatin,	Selective inhibition of tumor DNA synthesis	Myelosuppression,
Taxane	Docetaxel, paclitaxel	Inhibit DNA replication	Neuropathy, hypersensitivity
Monoclonal antibodies	Rituximab, cetuximab	Inhibits VEGF, inhibit cell growth	Hypersensitivity, cardiotoxicity
Hormone antagonist	Tamoxifen	Estrogen receptor antagonist	Thrombosis
Gonadorelin analogs	Buserelin	Down regulate pituitary symptoms in both males and females	Pituitary gland impairment
Antiandrogen	Cyproterone	Inhibit tumor flare	Hepatotoxicity

Modified from.

Chemotherapeutics

Chemotherapeutics are anticancer agents that slow down the growth of rapidly dividing and multiplying cancer cells. The therapy can reduce the recurrence risk and stop the cancer symptoms by shrinking pain-causing tumors. All anticancer chemotherapeutic agents exhibit their actions by disrupting the cell cycle in various ways. Traditional antineoplastic drugs used in chemotherapy can be classified based on their mechanism of cell cycle arrest or based on their own biological action (Dickens and Ahmed, 2021).

Based on biological action or cell cycle phase, non-specific drugs

Based on the mechanism of action, traditional chemotherapy involves the use of agents such as alkylating agents, antimetabolites, anticancer antibiotics, plant alkaloids, etc. (Table 2.3). These agents show their activity irrespective of the phase of the cell cycle. Generally, the chemicals used in this phase are divided into two categories: cancer chemotherapy and antimicrobial chemotherapy. These medications are cytotoxic in nature and are distinct from one another as they often aim to kill or suppress the target organism while having little or no effect on the host cell (Alam, 2018). Chemotherapy is one sort of treatment that allows for the simultaneous use of multiple therapies, including radiation therapy, surgery, and/or hyperthermia to treat cancer (Adam et al., 2004). Drug combinations are commonly used in cancer chemotherapy treatments, where the dosage of each agent is pushed to the limit of intolerable toxicity. However, new research suggests that this strategy may not be offering

TABLE 2.3 Chemotherapeutics based on mechanism of action.

Chemotherapeutic class	Biological action	Example
Alkylating agent	Impairs the cell function by forming covalent bond with amino, carboxyl, sulfhydryl and phosphate group present in potent biological molecule.	Nitrogen mustard, nitrosourea and platinum complex.
Antimetabolites	Interferes with the DNA synthesis. These agents are most active in S phase. These agents are most active in those tumors that shows fast growth.	Gemcitabine, 5-FU, cytarabine
Antitumor antibiotics	Acts by intercalating DNA at guanine cytosine and guanine thymine sequence resulting in formation of free radicals.	Bleomycin
Anthracyclines	Intercalates between DNA base pair and inhibits DNA topoisomerase I and II	Doxorubicin, epirubicin
Plant alkaloids	They destabilize microtuble dynamics and inhibit its assembly.	Vinca
Camptothecin analog	Inhibit the enzyme topoisomerase and interrupt the elongation phase of DNA replication.	Irinotecan, topotecan

the best efficacy because of the way medications interact. Certain combinations of the medications may provide a synergistic effect, and some may have an antagonistic effect, suggesting that combinations that use specific medications at lower dosages may be the most effective (Mayer and Janoff, 2007).

Traditional chemotherapy includes the following agents.

Alkylating agents

The earliest anticancer compounds identified were alkylating agents, which are still in use. It is further classified based on its chemical structure and mechanism of action. These include triazene compounds, nitrosoureas, epoxides, alkyl sulfonates, nitrogen mustards, and aziridines. These compounds react with DNA, RNA, and proteins either directly or after biological activation to form covalent associations. This leads to DNA damage and causes cell death (Minev, 2011). Alkylating agents constitute a foundational class of chemotherapeutic drugs that target cancer by inflicting irreversible DNA damage, thereby disrupting replication and transcription in malignant cells. These compounds, including classic agents such as Cyclophosphamide and modern ones like Temozolomide, which act by covalently attaching alkyl groups to DNA bases, most commonly at the N-7 or O-6 positions of guanine, or at the N-3 position of adenine, may produce mispairing, strand breaks, or inter- and intra-strand DNA cross-links (Bharti et al., 2017). For example, the activated phosphoramide mustard metabolite of cyclophosphamide cross-links adjacent DNA strands at the guanine N-7 position, preventing DNA unwinding and replication, which triggers apoptosis (Emadi et al., 2009). Temozolomide, a blood–brain–barrier–permeable triazene, methylates guanine bases, especially at the O-6 and N-7 sites, leading to replication arrest and cell death, and forms the mainstay of chemotherapy for high-grade gliomas (Strobel et al., 2019). Because alkylating damage is not cycle-phase specific, these drugs can kill both proliferating and quiescent tumor cells, making them effective against a wide variety of cancers, including lymphomas, leukemias, solid tumors, and brain tumors (Lajous et al., 2019). Despite their potency, their lack of selectivity causes collateral damage to normal, rapidly dividing cells, contributing to common toxicities such as bone marrow suppression, mucositis, and infertility (Nygren, 2001).

Anticancer antibiotics

More than 60% of the anticancer drugs currently approved are derived from natural sources. Microorganisms have played a crucial role in the discovery of drugs with anti-cancer therapeutic benefits. Many important drugs are antibiotics produced by microbes (Demain, 2014). Actinomycin D, anthracyclines, and anthracenones are among the antibiotics that have been approved as anticancer drugs (Saeidnia, 2015; Nagarajan, 2024). Antitumor antibiotics are a class of chemotherapeutic agents derived primarily from microbial sources (e.g., *Streptomyces* species) that combat cancer by disrupting nucleic-acid integrity and function. Among the most important are the anthracyclines, such as Doxorubicin and Daunorubicin, which intercalate between DNA base pairs and inhibit both DNA and RNA synthesis. By stabilizing the drug-DNA complex and inhibiting topoisomerase II-mediated strand passage, they induce DNA strand breaks and prevent DNA replication, ultimately leading to the death of cancer cells (Rasheed and Rubin, 2003). Another key example is Bleomycin, which binds to DNA and, in the presence of iron and oxygen, generates free radicals that produce single- and double-strand DNA breaks. This action is particularly effective in G2-phase cells and is used in the treatment of lymphomas and testicular cancer (Pflug et al., 2016). Additionally, non-anthracycline antibiotics, such as Actinomycin D (also known as Dactinomycin), intercalate preferentially at guanine–cytosine–rich regions, blocking RNA polymerase function and impairing transcription, thereby inhibiting protein synthesis and causing cytotoxicity (Pestell and Rizvanov, 2015). Through these mechanisms, DNA intercalation, free-radical-mediated DNA strand breakage, topoisomerase poisoning, and transcriptional blockade, antitumor antibiotics remain central to chemotherapy regimens for both hematologic malignancies and solid tumors.

Antimetabolites

Cancer cells have higher rates of metabolism as compared to normal cells. These antimetabolites inhibit all forms of metabolism, affecting the rapid division of cells. These also affect normal cells and are produced synthetically. These can be classified into three categories: purine antagonists, pyrimidine antagonists, and folate antagonists (Peters et al., 2000). Antimetabolites are chemotherapeutic agents that mimic natural nucleotides or metabolic cofactors, thus interfering with DNA/RNA synthesis and nucleotide metabolism processes that are often dysregulated in cancer cells. For example, 5-fluorouracil (5-FU) is converted intracellularly to active metabolites such as FdUMP, which irreversibly inhibits the enzyme Thymidylate synthase (TS), leading to depletion of dTMP and subsequent "thymineless death" of cancer cells; additionally, 5-FU metabolites (FUTP, FdUTP) may be incorporated into RNA or DNA to further impair RNA processing or induce DNA damage (Longley et al., 2003). Similarly, antifolate agents such as Methotrexate (MTX) inhibit Dihydrofolate reductase (DHFR), disturbing folate-dependent one-carbon metabolism and thereby impairing both purine and pyrimidine synthesis. More broadly, antimetabolites exploit cancer-specific reliance on high nucleotide turnover and deregulated metabolic pathways, hallmarks of malignant proliferation (Tiwari, 2012). Antimetabolites also target aberrant DNA damage response and replication stress pathways that are frequently activated in malignant cells. Gemcitabine, a deoxycytidine analog, inhibits *ribonucleotide reductase* (RRM1/RRM2) and becomes incorporated into DNA, triggering the stalled replication forks and activation of the ATR-CHK1 signaling pathway, ultimately driving apoptosis in pancreatic and lung tumors (Ciccolini et al., 2016; De Sousa Cavalcante and Monteiro, 2014). Pemetrexed, a multitargeted antifolate, suppresses *thymidylate synthase*, *GARFT*, and *AICARFT*, disrupting purine synthesis and inducing metabolic stress. These drugs are particularly effective in cancers with high replication stress and dysregulated nucleotide biosynthesis (Adjei, 2004).

Plant alkaloids

The anticancer properties of alkaloids are promising because they inhibit the DNA replication-related enzyme topoisomerase, trigger apoptosis, and alter several other intracellular targets and signaling cascades. The chemical structures of these alkaloids contribute to their cytotoxic nature against various cancer cell lines (Mondal et al., 2019). Plant-derived alkaloids remain key anticancer agents that exploit dysregulated mitosis and DNA-processing pathways in tumors. Taxanes (e.g., paclitaxel) bind to β-tubulin and stabilizemicrotubules, leading to mitotic arrest, spindle defects, and subsequent apoptosis; this also elicits immune-dependent tumor clearance in certain contexts (Prota et al., 2023). Vinca alkaloids (vincristine, vinblastine) bind to tubulin at a different site and prevent microtubule-polymerization, resulting in mitotic blockade and neurotoxicity-linked side effects (Taub et al., 2024). Camptothecin derivatives (topotecan, irinotecan) poison topoisomerase I, trapping enzyme-DNA complexes that collapse replication forks and activate DNA damage responses, leading to apoptosis (Pérez-Ortega et al., 2025). Other alkaloid scaffolds (e.g., podophyllotoxin derivatives) target topoisomerase II or microtubule dynamics, demonstrating how plant alkaloids selectively exploit cancer hallmarks, including dysregulated tubulin dynamics, topoisomerase activity, replication stress, and defective DNA damage repair, to produce cytotoxicity (Flavia Serpico et al., 2020). Plant alkaloids remain clinically relevant because they target core vulnerabilities in cancer cells, particularly dysregulated mitosis, replication stress, and impaired DNA-repair signaling. Their diverse structural scaffolds also enable selective action against tubulin, topoisomerases, and other proteins involved in replication. Ongoing research is refining these agents to improve their therapeutic index, reduce resistance, and enhance compatibility with modern combination regimens (Hu et al., 2021).

Antimicrotubular agents

To date, Taxanes and Vinca are considered the most promising antimicrotubular agents. These agents disturb the microtubule dynamics and subsequently cause cell death. Microtubules are dynamic in nature, and during mitosis, through the process of polymerization and depolymerization, they separate the chromosomes and divide the cell into two daughter cells. Agents such as vinca disrupt this microtubule dynamics, thus cell arrest and death occur (Kavallaris, 2006). Microtubule-targeting agents (MTAs) are among the most effective anticancer drugs, because they disrupt microtubule dynamics, a process crucial for mitosis, intracellular transport, and cell structural integrity (Wordeman and Vicente, 2021). Two main classes exist: microtubule-stabilizing agents (e.g., Paclitaxel, Docetaxel), which bind to β-tubulin inside microtubules and enhance tubulin polymerization, thereby preventing the dynamic rearrangements needed for spindle formation (Beretta et al., 2025), and microtubule-destabilizing agents (e.g., Vincristine, Vinblastine), which bind at other sites on tubulin and block polymerization, causing microtubule depolymerization and mitotic arrest (Gigant et al., 2008). At clinically relevant (low) concentrations, both classes mainly suppress microtubule "dynamics" rather than completely depleting microtubules; slowing down microtubule growth and shrinkage is sufficient to prevent proper mitotic spindle assembly, trigger mitotic arrest (often at metaphase), and activate apoptotic signaling (Risinger et al., 2009). Moreover, newer MTAs, such as Eribulin, exhibit additional effects, including the induction of non-functional tubulin aggregates ("tubulin exhaustion"), which leads to irreversible mitotic blockade and cell death (Wang et al., 2023a). Given the essential role of microtubules in rapidly dividing cancer cells, MTAs exploit a core vulnerability of malignancies, the reliance on dynamic cytoskeletal rearrangements for proliferation. However, their long-established clinical success is tempered by limitations, including neurotoxicity (due to effects on neuronal microtubules) and the development of drug resistance (Martino et al., 2018).

Based on cell cycle arrest

Chemotherapeutic drugs used in this phase cause cancer cell death by apoptosis either by directly interfering with DNA or by directly targeting the protein required for cell division. The cell cycle is a process where a cell grows, replicates its DNA, and then divides and forms two daughter cells. The cell cycle has two phases: interphase and mitosis. The longest part of the cell cycle is interphase, which is further divided into G1, S, and G2 phases. When taken during the cell cycle's selective phase, medications that are unique to that phase are more effective (Fig. 2.1). For instance, 5-Fluorouracil is an S-phase specific cell stage (Mishra et al., 2020). Thus, usually, this drug is administered either as an infusion for prolonged

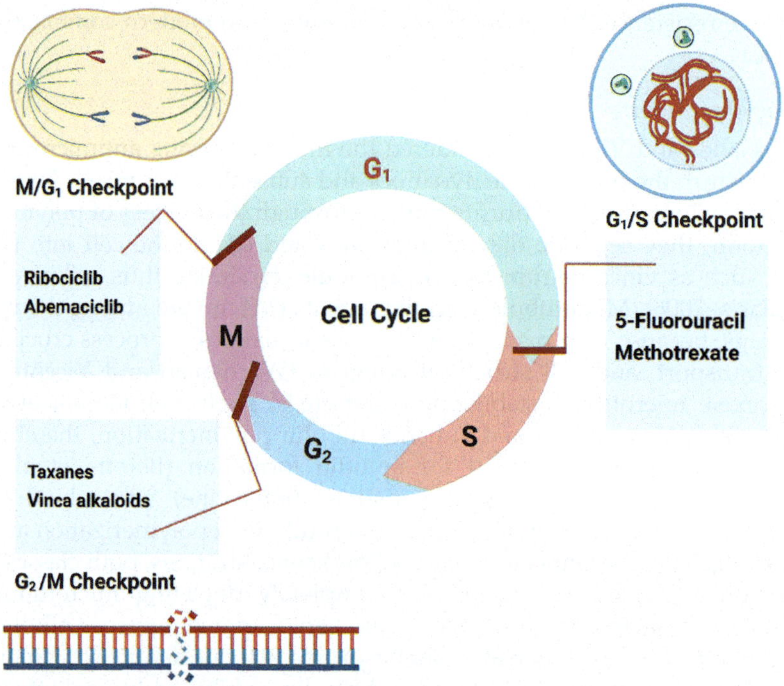

FIGURE 2.1 Cell cycle phase selective active drugs (modified) Dickens and Ahmed (2021). *Modified from: E. Dickens, S. Ahmed, Principles of cancer treatment by chemotherapy. Surgery. 39 (4) (2021), 215–220, https://doi.org/10.1016/j.mpsur.2021.01.009.*

days or in the form of a tablet every day for a week (Dickens and Ahmed, 2021; Almalki, 2023). Methotrexate, another drug, is also an S-phase cell cycle-specific drug. In this stage, the drug competitively inhibits the enzyme dihydrofolate reductase enzyme which eventually results in inhibition of the synthesis of thymidylic acid, ionosinic acid, other purine metabolites, and amino acids such as glycine and methionine. All these are required for DNA and RNA synthesis (Maxwell and Eckhardt, 1990).

Advancements in chemotherapy

Chemotherapy can halt the cell division of cancerous cells completely; however, associated risks exist and can affect healthy cells or organs like bone marrow, hair follicles, liver, kidney, lungs, etc. (Yadav et al., 2022). Over the course of the treatment period, chances of multidrug resistance and relapse of cancer are also reported (Liu, 2009). This could be due to varying and non-selective drug distribution or efflux of the drug, especially Pgp efflux. Chemotoxicity is a major concern that is frequently reported in chemotherapy. Due to the DNA damage, healthy cells also get inflamed, leading to the death of normal cells as well (Juthani et al., 2024). All these drawbacks give a scope for the advancement in chemotherapy. Nanotechnology and chemotherapy, merged with other therapies such as immunotherapy, hormone therapy, gene therapy, etc., are emerging techniques to enhance the therapeutic effect, paving novel ways and new perspectives in clinical practice.

Targeted therapy

This includes drugs acting on a specific target to inhibit the proliferation of cancer cells. Cancer cells can survive and proliferate due to alterations or mutations in selective genes. Such gene mutations can be considered and exploited for targeted therapy with specific drugs. Growth factors, signaling molecules, angiogenesis-promoting chemicals, cell-cycle proteins, apoptosis modulators, and many others are considered key targets for this therapy (Lee et al., 2018). Targeted therapy can be achieved via the use of small molecule inhibitors, antibody drug conjugates, and hormones (Fig. 2.2).

Small molecule inhibitors

These are low molecular weight (<900 Da) compounds and can easily penetrate the cells. They act by inactivating kinases, interfering in the signaling pathways, and ensuring the completeness of the cell cycle, facilitating apoptosis, and regulating DNA repair (Lheureux et al., 2017). They bind to the extracellular and intracellular targets broadly and inhibit protein function by binding to the pocket present on their surface (Liu et al., 2022). Small molecules are generally administered orally and are absorbed better than monoclonal antibodies (Padma, 2015). A few of them have been listed in Table 2.4 with their mechanisms.

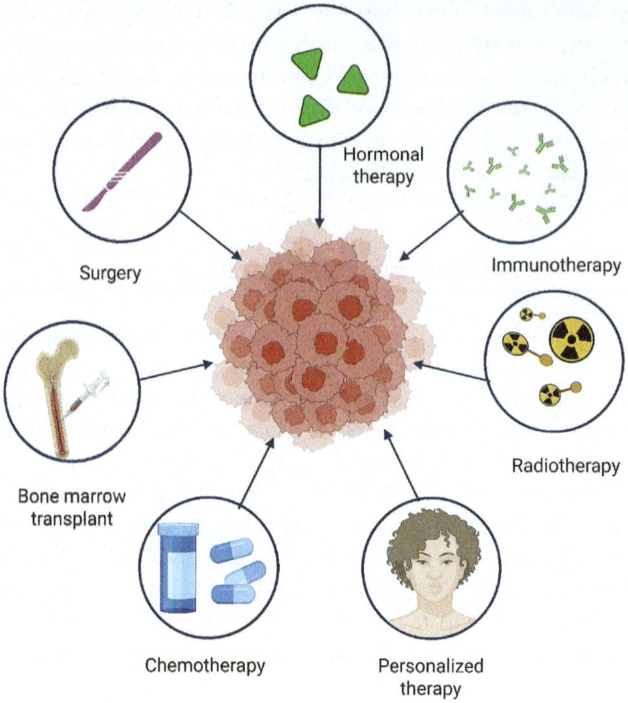

FIGURE 2.2 Types of targeted therapy.

Peptide

Peptides have a wide range of potential uses in the diagnosis and management of diseases, including cancer. Peptide bonds hold short, linear chains of amino acids together, typically including 20–50 amino acids (Derakhshankhah and Jafari, 2018). These have multiple benefits like ease of synthesis and modification, relatively small size, low toxicity due to non-accumulation, high sensitivity and specificity, reduced immunogenicity, and permeability of cell membranes (Tripathi et al., 2018). They can be used as vaccines, hormones, and delivery systems for chemotherapeutic drugs. Cell-penetrating peptides (CPP) are the most widely used peptide form for chemotherapeutic drug delivery. Between 4 and 30 amino acids, CPPs can move across membranes to deliver the medication to the target site. Anti-Cancer Peptides (ACPs) are short bioactive peptides consisting of 10–60 amino acids. ACP exerts anticancer effects through various mechanisms like apoptosis induction, membrane disruption, angiogenesis inhibition, signaling pathway modulation, and

TABLE 2.4 Examples of small-molecule targeted therapies approved by FDA or in pipeline.

Drug (brand name)	Target	Mechanism of action
Imatinib (gleevec), nilotinib (tasigna)	BCR-ABL, KIT, PDGFR	Antagonist of tyrosine kinase
Gefitinib (iressa), erlotinib (tarceva)	EGFR	Antagonist of tyrosine kinase
Sorafenib (nexavar), BRAF, KIT	VEGFR, PDGFR and RAF kinases	Antagonist of kinase
Vorinostat (zolinza), romidepsin (istodax)	HDACs	Prevents histone acetylation
Temsirolimus (torisel), everolimus (afinitor)	mTOR	Suppress the cell-survival pathway.
Bortezomib (velcade), carfilzomib	Proteasome	Prevents protein degradation
BKM120, PX866	PI3K	Blocks cell-survival pathway

immunomodulation. Additionally, ACPs can interfere with key signaling pathways that promote cancer cell survival, proliferation, and metastasis. These peptides may target proteins involved in cell cycle regulation, growth factor signaling, or survival pathways, leading to the inhibition of cancer cell growth and survival (Nhàn et al., 2023). For instance, *p28*, a peptide derived from bacterial protein Azurin, has been shown to stabilize p53 in tumor cells, triggering cell-cycle arrest and apoptosis. Another peptide, *ATX-101*, disrupts PCNA interactions, impairing cancer cell proliferation. Similarly, *PEP-010* can directly induce apoptosis through caspase-9 activation. Among antimicrobial-derived peptides, *Buforin IIb* (and optimized derivative *BR2*) demonstrates strong membrane penetration and cytotoxicity toward cancer cells. Peptides such as *Lactoferricin*, derived from lactoferrin, also show antitumor activity likely via membrane-targeting mechanisms. Beyond direct anticancer activity, peptide-based vaccines and therapeutics, such as Stimuvax, Primovax, and Cilengitide, are under clinical development for various cancers (Bottens and Yamada, 2022; Moreno-Vargas and Prada-Gracia, 2025; Rusiecka et al., 2022; Thundimadathil, 2012; Karami Fath et al., 2022).

Monoclonal antibodies

Monoclonal antibodies can exert anticancer effects by two mechanisms: Direct and Indirect mechanisms. In the direct mechanism, antibodies induce tumor cell death by the blockage of growth factor receptor signaling. For example, epidermal growth factor receptor (EGFR) is overexpressed by many different cancers, and signaling via EGFR leads to tumor cell proliferation, migration, and invasion. Cetuximab, an anti-EGFR mAb, induces apoptosis in tumor cells by blocking ligand binding and receptor dimerization. Human epidermal growth factor receptor 2 (HER2) is a tyrosine kinase receptor that is overexpressed in many cancers, but primarily in breast carcinomas. Antibodies targeting HER2 therefore achieve signaling perturbation by inhibiting heterodimerization and internalization. Trastuzumab was the first FDA-approved anti-HER2 mAb and remains a vital component of treatments for *HER2*-amplified breast cancer (Kumar and Rajnikanth, 2020). Indirect mechanisms of action of mAbs require the engagement of components of the host immune system, and are CDC, antibody-dependent cellular phagocytosis (ADCP), and antibody-dependent cellular cytotoxicity (ADCC). For Example, rituximab, which knocks out the complement cascade component C1q, and the anti-CD20 mAb ofatumumab (Zahavi and Weiner, 2020).

Antibody drug conjugates

ADCs, or antibody–drug conjugates, are a novel type of designed therapies that combine highly effective cytotoxic chemotherapeutics with the monoclonal antibodies that target the proteins on the tumor cell surface. The two substances are joined by chemical linkers. An antibody, a linker, and a payload are the three main parts of an ADC. When ADCs were developed, the cytotoxic efficacy of the payload and the high specificity of an antibody were combined under one roof. An ADC's monoclonal antibody should ideally be extremely selective for the tumor-associated antigen, and its expression is very low or absent in healthy cells (He et al., 2024). A representative example is trastuzumab-emtansine (T-DM1), which links a HER2-specific antibody to the potent microtubule inhibitor DM1; upon binding HER2 on tumor cells, the ADC is internalized and lysosomally processed to release DM1, which disrupts microtubules and triggers apoptosis. Similarly, certain studies highlight a range of payloads (e.g., maytansinoids, auristatins) and diverse linker chemistries, reflecting the evolving ADC design landscape (Najminejad et al., 2023). Indeed, modern ADC development has expanded beyond first-generation drugs, with many compositions improving the therapeutic index and broadening their applicability to various cancer types. The continued refinement of targets, linkers, and payloads underscores the promise of ADCs as a foundational modality in precision oncology (Wang et al., 2023b; Imtiaz et al., 2025).

Hormones

Cancer cells have more hormone-sensitive receptors, leading to rapid cell growth due to hormone activation. Hormone therapies either prevent the body from producing specific hormones or inhibit their action (Feldman and Feldman, 2001). Many tumors, mainly breast, prostate, ovarian, and endometrial cancers, overexpress hormone-responsive receptors, making them highly sensitive to circulating endocrine signals. When hormones such as estrogen, progesterone, or androgens bind to their respective receptors, they activate transcriptional programs that drive rapid cell-cycle progression, angiogenesis, and survival pathways. Hormone therapy, therefore, aims to either reduce systemic hormone production or block receptor activation, thereby limiting the proliferative stimulus that reaches tumor cells (Ulm et al., 2019).

A classic example is estrogen-receptor–positive (ER^+) breast cancer, in which estrogen activates ERα to promote tumor growth. Drugs such as Tamoxifen, a selective estrogen receptor modulator (SERM), competitively bind to ERα and prevent estrogen-induced gene transcription, leading to reduced proliferation and increased apoptosis. Similarly, Aromatase inhibitors (e.g., Letrozole, Anastrozole) suppress estrogen synthesis by inhibiting the aromatase enzyme in peripheral tissues; this is particularly effective in postmenopausal women because it eliminates the primary source of residual estrogen (Chaput and Sumar, 2022; Okwuosa et al., 2021; Clusan et al., 2023). In prostate cancer, androgen signaling through the androgen receptor (AR) plays a key role in disease progression. Androgen deprivation therapies (ADTs) such as Leuprolide or Goserelin act as LHRH (Luteinizing hormone-releasing hormone) agonists, causing long-term downregulation of luteinizing hormone and consequent suppression of testosterone production. Another major example is Enzalutamide, an AR-signaling inhibitor that blocks androgen binding, disrupts nuclear translocation of the AR complex, and prevents AR-driven transcription of survival genes. These mechanisms collectively reduce tumor proliferation and induce apoptosis in AR-dependent cancer cells (Ulm et al., 2019; Ganguly et al., 2021). Hormone-responsive tumors also utilize alternate pathways to maintain growth. For instance, progesterone receptor (PR) signaling promotes proliferation in certain types of endometrial cancers. Agents such as Mifepristone, a PR antagonist, inhibit progesterone-mediated transcription and suppress cell-cycle progression. In addition, Fulvestrant, a selective estrogen receptor degrader (SERD), induces ERα destabilization and proteasomal degradation, effectively eliminating functional receptors from cancer cells and overcoming the resistance seen with earlier hormone therapies (Gucalp et al., 2013). Together, these examples show how hormone-targeted therapies exploit the dependence of certain tumors on endocrine signaling. By interfering with hormone synthesis, receptor binding, or downstream transcriptional activation, these agents substantially slow tumor growth, enhance treatment response, and extend survival in patients with hormone-driven cancers.

Gene therapy

This therapy is recently developed, where a genetic material, either deoxyribonucleic acid (DNA) or ribonucleic acid (RNA), is incorporated into a malignant cell to inhibit its proliferation. Gene therapy can either reverse a cell function by replacing the mutant suppressor gene with a normal gene or incorporate a material like siRNA or antisense oligonucleotide in order to increase the sensitivity of the cancer cells towards cancer treatments (Belete, 2021). Gene therapy has rapidly evolved as a promising therapeutic strategy in oncology by enabling direct modification of the genetic material of malignant cells to suppress tumor progression. In this approach, nucleic acids such as DNA, mRNA, siRNA, or antisense oligonucleotides are delivered into cancer cells to restore tumor-suppressor activity, silence oncogenes, or reprogram signaling pathways that drive malignancy. A prominent example is p53 gene replacement therapy, where adenoviral vectors such as Gendicine introduce a functional TP53 gene into tumor cells, thereby reinstating p53-mediated apoptosis and cell-cycle arrest (Peng, 2005). Another well-studied approach involves the use of oncolytic adenoviruses, such as ONYX-015, which selectively replicate in p53-deficient tumor cells, causing targeted oncolysis without affecting normal tissues (Bischoff et al., 1996). Gene silencing technologies also play a central role; antisense oligonucleotides like oblimersen (G3139) downregulate anti-apoptotic BCL-2, enhancing chemosensitivity in hematologic and solid tumors (Rheingold et al., 2007). Likewise, siRNA-based strategies have been used to inhibit key oncogenic drivers, including VEGF to suppress tumor angiogenesis (Kim et al., 2017), KRAS mutations to block MAPK-dependent proliferation, and HER2 overexpression to reduce growth and drug resistance in HER2-positive breast cancer. Additional gene therapies target survival pathways such as survivin, where antisense or siRNA constructs restore apoptotic signaling (Gu et al., 2016), or immune-evasive molecules such as TGF-β2, where antisense agents like trabedersen reduce tumor invasiveness and enhance immune activity (Oh et al., 2013). Collectively, these gene-based strategies demonstrate the versatility of genetic intervention in cancer therapy, offering opportunities to correct genetic defects, inhibit oncogenic pathways, and sensitize tumors to conventional treatments.

Cancer stem cell therapy

Cancer stem cell therapy needs to survive the main treatment to prevent relapse. This could be caused by a variety of things, such as stem cell quiescence, a protected niche environment, increased xenobiotic efflux pump expression, improved DNA repair and anti-apoptotic pathways, and other survival strategies. The effects of the tyrosine kinase inhibitor imatinib mesylate in chronic myeloid leukemia (CML) provide an example of how important these characteristics are to stem cell survival. A rare group of cells with an HSC-like phenotype may self-renew and differentiate to produce all hematopoietic lineages, which means that they carry the ultimate genetic abnormality. This makes chronic myeloid leukemia a stem cell disease par excellence (Bomken et al., 2010). Cancer stem cells (CSCs), a subpopulation within tumors that is endowed with self-renewal, differentiation potential, and resilience to chemotherapy or radiotherapy, have emerged as critical targets for next-generation cancer therapies (Yang et al., 2020). For example, Salinomycin, originally an antimicrobial agent, was found to preferentially kill CSC-enriched populations (e.g., $CD44^{+}$/$CD133^{+}$ breast cancer cells) by disrupting ion homeostasis and inducing apoptosis, thereby reducing tumor-initiating capacity (Zhu et al., 2020). In a different strategy, immunotherapy using CD133 CAR-T cells selectively targets CSCs that express the surface marker CD133; such CAR-T cells have been shown in preclinical glioma models to efficiently eliminate CSCs and suppress tumor growth (Schmohl and Vallera, 2016). Beyond these, small-molecule inhibitors that interfere with core self-renewal pathways are also promising. For instance, blocking developmental signaling pathways such as Wnt, Notch, Hedgehog, JAK/STAT, or NF-κB, which are often aberrantly activated in CSCs, can suppress CSC self-renewal and sensitize tumors to standard therapies (Yang et al., 2020; Ramos et al., 2017). Additionally, targeting survival mechanisms unique to CSCs, such as the overexpression of anti-apoptotic proteins, is another viable approach. For example, Survivin, which is highly expressed in CSC compartments, has been proposed as a therapeutic target, with efforts underway to develop inhibitors that disrupt its function and thereby trigger CSC apoptosis (Warrier et al., 2020). However, the tumor microenvironment (TME) and niche factors, including extracellular matrix components, stromal cells, and hypoxia, significantly contribute to CSC maintenance, drug resistance, and metastasis (Gaggianesi et al., 2021). Therefore, effective CSC-targeted therapy often requires combinatorial strategies: direct CSC elimination (via agents such as Salinomycin or CAR-T) together with the disruption of supporting niche signals or survival pathways (Mai et al., 2023). In summary, the growing body of evidence supports multiple, complementary approaches to eradicate CSCs, including ionophore-based cytotoxic drugs, surface-marker directed immune therapies, pathway inhibitors targeting self-renewal, and anti-survival protein antagonists, all aimed at removing the root of tumor initiation, relapse, and resistance.

Integration of immunotherapy

In the majority of immunotherapeutic techniques, immune cells are extracted from the patient, altered or activated in vitro, given time to multiply in culture, and then reintroduced into the patient. Recently, two general immune-system-based treatment modalities have been investigated: passive immunotherapy and active immunotherapy. Passive immunotherapy employs antibodies as therapeutic agents to treat cancer patients. These antibodies attach to tumor cells by recognizing particular proteins on their surface. Following binding, the antibody either kills the cells directly or instructs other immune system elements to attack the cells. Scientists have succeeded in producing antibodies with a completely human amino acid composition. Recently, a humanized antibody known as Herceptin was created to target the cell-surface receptor (HER2), which binds a growth factor that encourages the proliferation of breast cancer cells. The idea behind Herceptin is to limit growth factor-induced receptor activation and encourage receptor internalization. Overexpressed cells of the HER2 gene comprise around 25% of breast cancers, making them more susceptible to growth factor stimulation. Before Herceptin was developed, patients whose cancers overexpressed HER2 had an extremely poor prognosis (Carter, 2001). The prognosis has significantly improved.

Active (or adoptive) immunotherapy includes methods to increase the immune system's ability to fight malignant cells. Even though the immune system has evolved to recognize and get rid of foreign substances, cancers start in a person's own cells. Although many tumor cells do include proteins (also known as tumor-associated antigens or neoantigens) that are either changed proteins that are different from those present in normal cells or proteins that are not expressed by their normal counterparts, these proteins are essentially host proteins found in host cells. The immune system usually does not see these proteins as harmful as a result. Although an individual's immune cells may be able to identify certain tumor-associated antigens, malignancies have a variety of defense mechanisms to prevent immune destruction. In recent years, there has been a lot of interest in a novel therapeutic method called chimeric antigen receptor (CAR) T-cell therapy (Fig. 2.3). The process of developing therapeutic cancer vaccines is mostly identical to that of this cell-based therapy. T cells are isolated from the patient and then genetically modified in a lab to generate an antigen receptor that will selectively detect proteins generated by the patient's tumor in the case of CAR T-cell therapy. Two treatments have received FDA approval, and hundreds more clinical trials are actively exploring CAR T-cell therapies despite serious concerns about side effects, toxicity, long-term effectiveness, and expensive treatment costs. Immunotherapies make up a sizable and increasing portion of the experimental anticancer medications presently undergoing clinical testing (Iwasa et al., 2020).

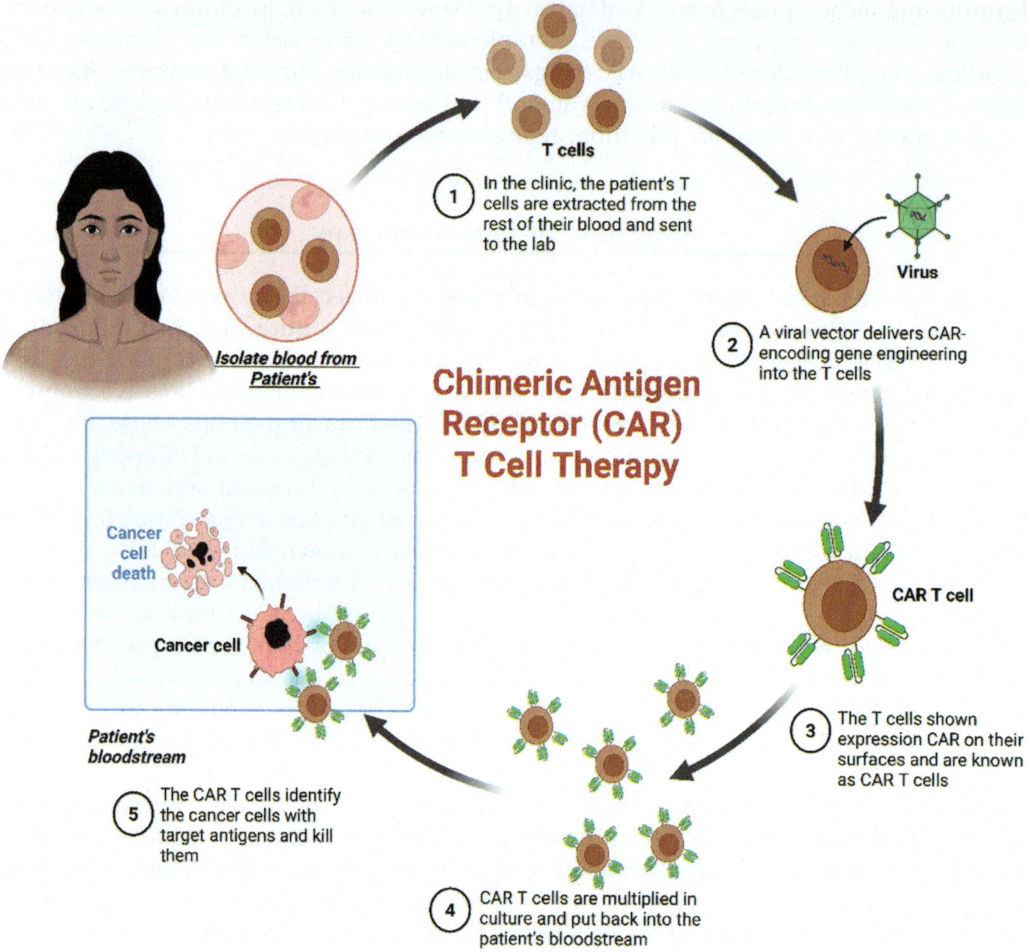

FIGURE 2.3 Chimeric antigen receptor therapy.

Advances in drug delivery

Conventional therapy affects normal cells along with cancer cells. The adverse effects associated with conventional anticancer drugs are very difficult to tackle. This necessitated the advancement in drug delivery systems to improve drug effectiveness as well as minimize toxicity. Advances in drug delivery systems aim to target cancer drugs selectively, thereby avoiding distribution in other organs or normal cells (Li et al., 2025; Upadhyay et al., 2023b; Mishra and Upadhyay, 2020). Nanotechnology in drug delivery systems, also known as nano-oncology, is currently one of the most significant areas of research (Wang et al., 2024). Developing nanotechnology-based chemotherapeutic drug delivery systems claims to enhance the solubility and penetration potential, thereby improving the

TABLE 2.5 Chemotherapeutic delivery agents based on organic nanocarriers that are being clinically studied.

Commercial name	Material composition	Clinical trial phase	Therapeutic usage	References
Docetaxel polymeric NP	Docetaxel encapsulated in polymeric NP made from polylactic acid monovalent salt and mPEG-PLA as copolymer	Phase I	Advanced solid malignancies	Song et al. (2016)
ABI-008	Formulation of albumin bound with docetaxel	Phase I/II	Hormone-refractory prostate cancer	Fu et al. (2009)
CRLX101	Cyclodextrin-based NP conjugated with camptothecin	Phase I phase I/II phase II	Renal cell carcinoma advanced solid tumor ovarian cancer, fallopian tube cancer, primary peritoneal cancer, non-small cell lung cancer, metastatic renal cell carcinoma	Voss et al. (2017)
DHAD-PBCA nanoparticles	Polybutylcyanacrylate NP loaded with mitozantrone	Phase II	Hepatoma	Ruman et al. (2020)

Modified from.

bioavailability of the drug. Nanosystems provide a stealth layer to drugs and augment the biodistribution of chemotherapeutic agents at the cancer site, preventing multidrug resistance and decreasing systemic toxicity (Wang et al., 2020; Upadhyay et al., 2018a, 2018b; Upadhyay et al., 2023a, 2023b). Anticancer drugs can be loaded in various nanosystems like organic nanocarriers, liposomes, micelles, dendrimers, metallic nanoparticles, etc. A few nanoformulations that are under clinical investigation are shown in Table 2.5. Liposomal systems are a novel strategy that can be used for drugs with varying solubility. These are spherical vesicles employed as carriers with a hydrophilic cavity surrounded by one or more lipid bilayers. Liposomes can also encapsulate siRNAs, in addition to hydrophilic and hydrophobic chemotherapeutics (Saraf et al., 2020). Micelles are a core-shell structure with a hydrophilic shell and a hydrophobic core that give loaded drug stability in vivo, a nanoscale architecture, and chemotherapeutic compatibility (Tawfik et al., 2021). The hydrophobic center of the micelle serves as a reservoir for the hydrophobic chemotherapeutics (Senapati et al., 2018). Platelets can also be used as carriers of the drug, which exhibits good biocompatibility and has desirable targeting characteristics (Li et al., 2020). Extracellular vesicles employed for drug delivery are released by normal cells due to external factors or self-stimulation. It contributes to intercellular communication (Qu et al., 2022).

Conclusion

Chemotherapy is a widely used approach to managing cancer; however, due to limitations, the therapy faces several challenges. Encouragingly, with advancements in tumor therapy, a drastic transformation can be observed. Emerging technologies, such as the application of monoclonal antibodies, peptides, immunotherapy, and personalized medicines, have given a new perspective to the oncology field. Furthermore, combining conventional chemotherapy with advanced therapies can provide a broader opportunity with a wider range of treatment choices. Chemotherapy has evolved from traditional cytotoxic drugs into a sophisticated and diverse therapeutic field.

References

Adam, R., Pascal, G., Castaing, D., Azoulay, D., Delvart, V., Paule, B., Levi, F., Bismuth, H., 2004. Tumor progression while on chemotherapy. Ann. Surg. 240 (6), 1052–1064. https://doi.org/10.1097/01.sla.0000145964.08365.01.

Adjei, A.A., 2004. Pharmacology and mechanism of action of pemetrexed. Clin. Lung Cancer 5 (2), S51. https://doi.org/10.3816/CLC.2004.s.003.

Alam, A., 2018. Chemotherapy treatment and strategy schemes: A review. Open Access J. Toxicol. 2 (5). https://doi.org/10.19080/OAJT.2018.02.555600.

Almalki, S.G., 2023. The pathophysiology of the cell cycle in cancer and treatment strategies using various cell cycle checkpoint inhibitors. Pathol. Res. Pract. 251, 154854. https://doi.org/10.1016/j.prp.2023.154854.

Amjad, M.T., Chidharla, A., Kasi, A., 2025. Cancer Chemotherapy.

Anand, U., Dey, A., Chandel, A.K.S., Sanyal, R., Mishra, A., Pandey, D.K., De Falco, V., Upadhyay, A., Kandimalla, R., Chaudhary, A., Dhanjal, J.K., Dewanjee, S., Vallamkondu, J., Pérez de la Lastra, J.M., 2023. Cancer chemotherapy and beyond: Current status, drug candidates, associated risks and progress in targeted therapeutics. Genes. Dis. 10 (4), 1367–1401. https://doi.org/10.1016/j.gendis.2022.02.007.

Belete, T.M., 2021. The current status of gene therapy for the treatment of cancer. Biol. Targets and Ther. 15, 67–77. https://doi.org/10.2147/BTT.S302095.

Beretta, G.L., Cassinelli, G., Rossi, G., Azzariti, A., Corbeau, I., Tosi, D., Perego, P., 2025. Novel insights into taxane pharmacology: An update on drug resistance mechanisms, immunomodulation and drug delivery strategies. Drug. Resist. Updates 81, 101223. https://doi.org/10.1016/j.drup.2025.101223.

Bharti, A.C., Vishnoi, K., Singh, S.M., Aggarwal, B.B., 2017. Pathways linked to cancer chemoresistance and their targeting by nutraceuticals. Role. Nutraceuticals. Cancer Chemosensit. 2, 1–30. https://doi.org/10.1016/B978-0-12-812373-7.00001-2.

Bischoff, J.R., Kirn, D.H., Williams, A., Heise, C., Horn, S., Muna, M., Ng, L., Nye, J.A., Sampson-Johannes, A., Fattaey, A., McCormick, F., 1996. An adenovirus mutant that replicates selectively in p53-deficient human tumor cells. Science 274 (5286), 373–376. https://doi.org/10.1126/science.274.5286.373.

Bomken, S., Fišer, K., Heidenreich, O., Vormoor, J., 2010. Understanding the cancer stem cell. Br. J. Cancer 103 (4), 439–445. https://doi.org/10.1038/sj.bjc.6605821.

Bottens, R.A., Yamada, T., 2022. Cell-penetrating peptides (CPPs) as therapeutic and diagnostic agents for cancer. Cancers 14 (22). https://doi.org/10.3390/cancers14225546.

Bray, F., Laversanne, M., Sung, H., Ferlay, J., Siegel, R.L., Soerjomataram, I., Jemal, A., 2024. Global cancer statistics 2022: Globocan estimates of incidence and mortality worldwide for 36 cancers in 185 countries. CA. Cancer. J. Clin. 74 (3), 229–263. https://doi.org/10.3322/caac.21834.

Brianna, S.H., Lee, 2023. Chemotherapy: How to reduce its adverse effects while maintaining the potency? Med. Oncol. 40 (3). https://doi.org/10.1007/s12032-023-01954-6.

Cantley, L.C., Baselga, J., 2011. The era of cancer discovery. Cancer. Discov. 1 (1), 1. https://doi.org/10.1158/2159-8274.CD-11-0049.

Carter, P., 2001. Improving the efficacy of antibody-based cancer therapies. Nat. Rev. Cancer 1 (2), 118–129. https://doi.org/10.1038/35101072.

Chaput, G., Sumar, N., 2022. Endocrine therapies for breast and prostate cancers essentials for primary care. Can. Fam. Physician 68 (4), 271–276. https://doi.org/10.46747/cfp.6804271.

Chen, Y., Jia, Y., Song, W., Zhang, L., 2018. Therapeutic potential of nitrogen mustard based hybrid molecules. Front. Pharmacol. 9. https://doi.org/10.3389/fphar.2018.01453.

Ciccolini, J., Serdjebi, C., Peters, G.J., Giovannetti, E., 2016. Pharmacokinetics and pharmacogenetics of gemcitabine as a mainstay in adult and pediatric oncology: An EORTC-PAMM perspective. Cancer. Chemother. Pharmacol. 78 (1). https://doi.org/10.1007/s00280-016-3003-0.

Clusan, L., Ferrière, F., Flouriot, G., Farzad, P., 2023. A basic review on estrogen receptor signaling pathways in breast cancer. Int. J. Mol. Sci. 24 (7), 6834. https://doi.org/10.3390/ijms24076834.

Craig, C., Ng, J., Wigmore, T., 2008. The side effects of chemotherapeutic agents. Curr. Anaesth. Crit. Care 19 (2), 70–79. https://doi.org/10.1016/j.cacc.2008.01.004.

De Sousa Cavalcante, L., Monteiro, G., 2014. Gemcitabine: Metabolism and molecular mechanisms of action, sensitivity and chemoresistance in pancreatic cancer. Eur. J. Pharmacol. 741, 8–16. https://doi.org/10.1016/j.ejphar.2014.07.041.

Debela, D.T., Muzazu, S.G.Y., Heraro, K.D., Ndalama, M.T., Mesele, B.W., Haile, D.C., Kitui, S.K., Manyazewal, T., 2021. New approaches and procedures for cancer treatment: Current perspectives. SAGE Open Med. 9. https://doi.org/10.1177/20503121211034366.

Demain, A.L., 2014. Importance of microbial natural products and the need to revitalize their discovery. J. Ind. Microbiol. Biotechnol. 41 (2), 185–201. https://doi.org/10.1007/s10295-013-1325-z.

Derakhshankhah, H., Jafari, S., 2018. Cell penetrating peptides: A concise review with emphasis on biomedical applications. Biomed. Pharmacother. 108, 1090–1096. https://doi.org/10.1016/j.biopha.2018.09.097.

DeVita, V.T., Chu, E., 2008. A history of cancer chemotherapy. Cancer. Res. 68 (21), 8643–8653. https://doi.org/10.1158/0008-5472.CAN-07-6611.

Dickens, E., Ahmed, S., 2021. Principles of cancer treatment by chemotherapy. Surgery 39 (4), 215–220. https://doi.org/10.1016/j.mpsur.2021.01.009.

Emadi, A., Jones, R.J., Brodsky, R.A., 2009. Cyclophosphamide and cancer: Golden anniversary. Nat. Rev. Clin. Oncol. 6 (11), 638–647. https://doi.org/10.1038/nrclinonc.2009.146.

Feldman, B.J., Feldman, D., 2001. The development of androgen-independent prostate cancer. Nat. Rev. Cancer 1 (1), 34–45. https://doi.org/10.1038/35094009.

Fu, Q., Sun, J., Zhang, W., Sui, X., Yan, Z., He, Z., 2009. Nanoparticle albumin-bound (NAB) technology is a promising method for anti-cancer drug delivery. Recent. Pat. Anticancer. Drug. Discov. 4 (3), 262–272. https://doi.org/10.2174/157489209789206869.

Flavia Serpico, A., Visconti, R., Grieco, D., 2020. Exploiting immune-dependent effects of microtubule-targeting agents to improve efficacy and tolerability of cancer treatment. Cell. Death. Dis. 11 (5). https://doi.org/10.1038/s41419-020-2567-0.

Gaggianesi, M., Di Franco, S., Pantina, V.D., Porcelli, G., D'Accardo, C., Verona, F., Veschi, V., Colarossi, L., Faldetta, N., Pistone, G., Bongiorno, M.R., Todaro, M., Stassi, G., 2021. Messing up the cancer stem cell chemoresistance mechanisms supported by tumor microenvironment. Front. Oncol. 11. https://doi.org/10.3389/fonc.2021.702642.

Ganguly, S., Naik, D., Muskara, A., Mian, O.Y., 2021. The nexus of endocrine signaling and cancer: How steroid hormones influence genomic stability. Endocrinology 162 (1). https://doi.org/10.1210/endocr/bqaa177.

Gigant, B., Cormier, A., Dorléans, A., Ravelli, R.B.G., Knossow, M., 2008. Microtubule-destabilizing agents: Structural and mechanistic insights from the interaction of colchicine and vinblastine with tubulin. Top. Curr. Chem 286, 259–278. https://doi.org/10.1007/128_2008_11.

Gu, S., Hu, Z., Ngamcherdtrakul, W., Castro, D.J., Morry, J., Reda, M.M., Gray, J.W., Yantasee, W., 2016. Therapeutic siRNA for drug-resistant HER2-positive breast cancer. Oncotarget 7 (12), 14727–14741. https://doi.org/10.18632/oncotarget.7409.

Gucalp, A., Tolaney, S., Isakoff, S.J., Ingle, J.N., Liu, M.C., Carey, L.A., Blackwell, K., Rugo, H., Nabell, L., Forero, A., Stearns, V., Doane, A.S., Danso, M., Moynahan, M.E., Momen, L.F., Gonzalez, J.M., Akhtar, A., Giri, D.D., Patil, S., Feigin, K.N., Hudis, C.A., Traina, T.A., 2013. Phase II trial of bicalutamide in patients with androgen receptor-positive, estrogen receptor-negative metastatic breast cancer. Clin. Cancer Res. 19 (19), 5505–5512. https://doi.org/10.1158/1078-0432.CCR-12-3327.

He, J., Zeng, X., Wang, C., Wang, E., Li, Y., 2024. Antibody–drug conjugates in cancer therapy: Mechanisms and clinical studies. MedComm. 5 (8). https://doi.org/10.1002/mco2.671.

Hu, D., Yuan, S., Zhong, J., Liu, Z., Wang, Y., Liu, L., Li, J., Wen, F., Liu, J., Zhang, J., 2021. Cellular senescence and hematological malignancies: From pathogenesis to therapeutics. Pharmacol. Ther 223, 107817. https://doi.org/10.1016/j.pharmthera.2021.107817.

Imtiaz, S., Tamanna Ferdous, U., Nizela, A., Hasan, A., Shakoor, A., Zia, A.W., Uddin, S., 2025. Mechanistic study of cancer drug delivery: Current techniques, limitations, and future prospects. Eur. J. Med. Chem. 290, 117535. https://doi.org/10.1016/j.ejmech.2025.117535.

Juthani, R., Punatar, S., Mittra, I., 2024. New light on chemotherapy toxicity and its prevention. BJC. Rep. 2 (1). https://doi.org/10.1038/s44276-024-00064-8.

Iwasa, J., Marshall, W.F., Gerald, K., 2020. Karp's Cell and Molecular Biology: Concepts and Experiments. Wiley, p. 29.

Lee, Y.T., Tan, Y.J., Oon, C.E., 2018. Molecular targeted therapy: treating cancer with specificity. Eur. J. Pharmacol. 834, 188–196. https://doi.org/10.1016/j.ejphar.2018.07.034.

Karami Fath, M., Babakhaniyan, K., Zokaei, M., Yaghoubian, A., Akbari, S., Khorsandi, M., Soofi, A., Nabi-Afjadi, M., Zalpoor, H., Jalalifar, F., Azargoonjahromi, A., Payandeh, Z., Alagheband Bahrami, A., 2022. Anti-cancer peptide-based therapeutic strategies in solid tumors. Cell. Mol. Biol. Lett. 27 (1). https://doi.org/10.1186/s11658-022-00332-w.

Kavallaris, M., 2006. Discovering novel strategies for antimicrotubule cytotoxic therapy. Eur. J. Cancer Suppl. 4 (7), 3–9. https://doi.org/10.1016/j.ejcsup.2006.03.004.

Kim, M.G., Jo, S.D., Yhee, J.Y., Lee, B.S., Lee, S.J., Park, S.G., Kang, S.W., Kim, S.H., Jeong, J.H., 2017. Synergistic anti-tumor effects of bevacizumab and tumor targeted polymerized VEGF siRNA nanoparticles. Biochem. Biophys. Res. Commun. 489 (1), 35–41. https://doi.org/10.1016/j.bbrc.2017.05.103.

Kumar, M., Rajnikanth, P.S., 2020. A mini-review on HER2 positive breast cancer and its metastasis: Resistance and treatment strategies. Curr. Nanomed. 10 (1), 36–47. https://doi.org/10.2174/2468187310666191223141038.

Lajous, H., Lelièvre, B., Vauléon, E., Lecomte, P., Garcion, E., 2019. Rethinking alkylating(-like) agents for solid tumor management. Trends Pharmacol. Sci. 40 (5), 342–357. https://doi.org/10.1016/j.tips.2019.03.003.

Lheureux, S., Denoyelle, C., Ohashi, P.S., De Bono, J.S., Mottaghy, F.M., 2017. Molecularly targeted therapies in cancer: A guide for the nuclear medicine physician. Eur. J. Nucl. Med. Mol. Imag. 44, 41–54. https://doi.org/10.1007/s00259-017-3695-3.

Li, M., Li, J., Chen, J., Liu, Y., Cheng, X., Yang, F., Gu, N., 2020. Platelet membrane biomimetic magnetic nanocarriers for targeted delivery and in situ generation of nitric oxide in early ischemic stroke. ACS. Nano 14 (2), 2024–2035. https://doi.org/10.1021/acsnano.9b08587.

Li, K., Guo, B., Gu, J., Na, T., Gu, J., Yu, H., Sun, M., Han, T., 2025. Emerging advances in drug delivery systems (DDSs) for optimizing cancer complications. Mater. Today Bio 30, 101375. https://doi.org/10.1016/j.mtbio.2024.101375.

Liu, F.S., 2009. Mechanisms of chemotherapeutic drug resistance in cancer therapy-A quick review. Taiwan. J. Obstet. Gynecol. 48 (3), 239–244. https://doi.org/10.1016/S1028-4559(09)60296-5.

Liu, G.H., Chen, T., Zhang, X., Ma, X.L., Shi, H.S., 2022. Small molecule inhibitors targeting the cancers. MedComm. 3 (4). https://doi.org/10.1002/mco2.181.

Longley, D.B., Harkin, D.P., Johnston, P.G., 2003. 5-Fluorouracil: Mechanisms of action and clinical strategies. Nat. Rev. Cancer 3 (5), 330–338. https://doi.org/10.1038/nrc1074.

Mai, Y., Su, J., Yang, C., Xia, C., Fu, L., 2023. The strategies to cure cancer patients by eradicating cancer stem-like cells. Mol. Cancer 22 (1). https://doi.org/10.1186/s12943-023-01867-y.

Martino, E., Casamassima, G., Castiglione, S., Cellupica, E., Pantalone, S., Papagni, F., Rui, M., Siciliano, A.M., Collina, S., 2018. Vinca alkaloids and analogues as anti-cancer agents: Looking back, peering ahead. Bioorg. Med. Chem. Lett. 28 (17), 2816–2826. https://doi.org/10.1016/j.bmcl.2018.06.044.

Mayer, L.D., Janoff, A.S., 2007. Optimizing combination chemotherapy by controlling drug ratios. Mol. Interv. 7 (4), 216–223. https://doi.org/10.1124/mi.7.4.8.

Minev, B.R., 2011. Cancer Management in Man: Chemotherapy, Biological Therapy, Hyperthermia and Supporting Measures. Springer Netherlands. https://doi.org/10.1007/978-90-481-9704-0.

Mishra, B., Upadhyay, M., 2020. Drug Delivery System in Pulmonary Disease: Role of Microparticles Targeting Chronic Inflammatory Lung Diseases Using Advanced Drug Delivery Systems. Elsevier, India, pp. 323–336. https://doi.org/10.1016/B978-0-12-820658-4.00015-7.

Mishra, B., Upadhyay, M., 2021. Advancement on Nanoparticle-Based Drug Delivery Systems for Cancer Therapy Advanced Drug Delivery Systems in the Management of Cancer. Elsevier, India, pp. 319–330. https://doi.org/10.1016/B978-0-323-85503-7.00026-2.

Mishra, B., Upadhyay, M., Bakde, B., 2020. pH Sensed Interpenetrating Polymeric Network: Application in Drug Delivery Interpenetrating Polymer Network: Biomedical Applications. Springer Singapore, India, pp. 119–141. https://doi.org/10.1007/978-981-15-0283-5_5.

Mondal, A., Gandhi, A., Fimognari, C., Atanasov, A.G., Bishayee, A., 2019. Alkaloids for cancer prevention and therapy: current progress and future perspectives. Eur. J. Pharmacol. 858, 172472. https://doi.org/10.1016/j.ejphar.2019.172472.

Moreno-Vargas, L.M., Prada-Gracia, D., 2025. Cancer-targeting applications of cell-penetrating peptides. Int. J. Mol. Sci. 26 (1). https://doi.org/10.3390/ijms26010002.

Maxwell, R.A., Eckhardt, S.B., 1990. Methotrexate. In: Drug Discovery. Humana Press, Totowa, NJ, pp. 249–263.

Nagarajan, D., 2024. Antibiotics and Their Mechanisms of Action. Springer Nature Singapore. https://doi.org/10.1007/978-981-97-6851-6.

Najminejad, Z., Dehghani, F., Mirzaei, Y., Mer, A.H., Saghi, S.A., Abdolvahab, M.H., Bagheri, N., Meyfour, A., Jafari, A., Jahandideh, S., Gharibi, T., Amirkhani, Z., Delam, H., Mashatan, N., Shahsavarani, H., Abdollahpour-Alitappeh, M., 2023. Clinical perspective: Antibody-drug conjugates for the treatment of HER2-positive breast cancer. Mol. Ther. 31 (7), 1874–1903. https://doi.org/10.1016/j.ymthe.2023.03.019.

Nhàn, N.T.T., Yamada, T., Yamada, K.H., 2023. Peptide-based agents for cancer treatment: Current applications and future directions. Int. J. Mol. Sci. 24 (16), 12931. https://doi.org/10.3390/ijms241612931, 1422-0067.

Nygren, P., 2001. What is cancer chemotherapy? Acta. Oncol 40 (2–3), 166–174. https://doi.org/10.1080/02841860117342, 0284-186X.

Oh, S., Kim, E., Kang, D., Kim, M., Kim, J.H., Song, J.J., 2013. Transforming growth factor-β gene silencing using adenovirus expressing TGF-β1 or TGF-β2 shRNA. Cancer Gene Ther. 20 (2), 94–100. https://doi.org/10.1038/cgt.2012.90, 14765500.

Okwuosa, T.M., Morgans, A., Rhee, J.W., Reding, K.W., Maliski, S., Plana, J.C., Volgman, A.S., Moseley, K.F., Porter, C.B., Ismail-Khan, R., 2021. Impact of hormonal therapies for treatment of hormone-dependent cancers (breast and prostate) on the cardiovascular system: Effects and modifications: A scientific statement from the American heart association. Circ. Genom Precis. Med 14 (3), E000082. https://doi.org/10.1161/HCG.0000000000000082.

Padma, V.V., 2015. An overview of targeted cancer therapy. Biomedicine 5 (4). https://doi.org/10.7603/s40681-015-0019-4.

Peng, Z., 2005. Current status of gendicine in China: Recombinant human Ad-p53 agent for treatment of cancers. Hum. Gene Ther. 16 (9), 1016–1027. https://doi.org/10.1089/hum.2005.16.1016.

Pérez-Ortega, H.U., Córdova-Espíritu, R.R., Cano-Serrano, S., García-González, E., Bravo-Sánchez, M.G., Orozco-Mosqueda, M.d.C., Jiménez-Islas, H., Luna-Bárcenas, G., Villaseñor-Ortega, F., 2025. Camptothecin in cancer therapy: Current challenges and emerging strategies with nanoemulsions. Pharmaceutics 17 (11). https://doi.org/10.3390/pharmaceutics17111414.

Pestell, R.G., Rizvanov, A.A., 2015. Antibiotics for cancer therapy. Oncotarget 6 (5), 2587–2588. https://doi.org/10.18632/oncotarget.3388.

Peters, G.J., Van Der Wilt, C.L., Van Moorsel, C.J.A., Kroep, J.R., Bergman, A.M., Ackland, S.P., 2000. Netherlands basis for effective combination cancer chemotherapy with antimetabolites. Pharmacol. Ther. 87. https://doi.org/10.1016/S0163-7258(00)00086-3.

Pflug, N., Kluth, S., Vehreschild, J.J., Bahlo, J., Tacke, D., Biehl, L., Eichhorst, B., Fischer, K., Cramer, P., Fink, A.-M., von Bergwelt-Baildon, M., Stilgenbauer, S., Hallek, M., Cornely, O.A., Vehreschild, M.J.G.T., 2016. Efficacy of antineoplastic treatment is associated with the use of antibiotics that modulate intestinal microbiota. OncoImmunology 5 (6). https://doi.org/10.1080/2162402X.2016.1150399.

Prota, A.E., Lucena-Agell, D., Ma, Y., Estevez-Gallego, J., Li, S., Bargsten, K., Josa-Prado, F., Altmann, K.-H., Gaillard, N., Kamimura, S., Mühlethaler, T., Gago, F., Oliva, M.A., Steinmetz, M.O., Fang, W.-S., Díaz, J.F., 2023. Structural insight into the stabilization of microtubules by taxanes. eLife 12. https://doi.org/10.7554/elife.84791.

Qu, S., Han, Y., Liu, Y., Zhu, J., Acaroz, U., Shen, J., Zhu, K., 2022. Milk exosomes facilitate oral delivery of drugs against intestinal bacterial infections. J. Agric. Food Chem. 70 (51), 16069–16079. https://doi.org/10.1021/acs.jafc.2c04971.

Ramos, E.K., Hoffmann, A.D., Gerson, S.L., Liu, H., 2017. New opportunities and challenges to defeat cancer stem cells. Trends Cancer 3 (11), 780–796. https://doi.org/10.1016/j.trecan.2017.08.007.

Rasheed, Z.A., Rubin, E.H., 2003. Mechanisms of resistance to topoisomerase I-targeting drugs. Oncogene 22 (47), 7296–7304. https://doi.org/10.1038/sj.onc.1206935.

Rheingold, S.R., Hogarty, M.D., Blaney, S.M., Zwiebel, J.A., Sauk-Schubert, C., Chandula, R., Krailo, M.D., Adamson, P.C., 2007. Phase I trial of G3139, a bcl-2 antisense oligonucleotide, combined with doxorubicin and cyclophosphamide in children with relapsed solid tumors: A children's oncology group study. J. Clin. Oncol. 25 (12), 1512–1518. https://doi.org/10.1200/JCO.2006.09.5125.

Risinger, A.L., Giles, F.J., Mooberry, S.L., 2009. Microtubule dynamics as a target in oncology. Cancer. Treat. Rev. 35 (3), 255–261. https://doi.org/10.1016/j.ctrv.2008.11.001.

Ruman, U., Fakurazi, S., Masarudin, M.J., Hussein, M.Z., 2020. Nanocarrier-based therapeutics and theranostics drug delivery systems for next generation of liver cancer nanodrug modalities. Int. J. Nanomed. 15, 1437–1456. https://doi.org/10.2147/ijn.s236927.

Rusiecka, I., Gągało, I., Kocić, I., 2022. Cell-penetrating peptides improve pharmacokinetics and pharmacodynamics of anticancer drugs. Tissue Barriers 10 (1). https://doi.org/10.1080/21688370.2021.1965418.

Saeidnia, S., 2015. New Approaches to Natural Anticancer Drugs SpringerBriefs in Pharmaceutical Science and Drug Development. Springer International Publishing. https://doi.org/10.1007/978-3-319-14027-8.

Saraf, S., Jain, A., Tiwari, A., Verma, A., Panda, P.K., Jain, S.K., 2020. Advances in liposomal drug delivery to cancer: an overview. J. Drug Deliv. Sci. Technol. 56, 101549. https://doi.org/10.1016/j.jddst.2020.101549.

Schmohl, J.U., Vallera, D.A., 2016. CD133, selectively targeting the root of cancer. Toxins 8 (6). https://doi.org/10.3390/toxins8060165.

Senapati, S., Mahanta, A.K., Kumar, S., Maiti, P., 2018. Controlled drug delivery vehicles for cancer treatment and their performance. Signal Transduct. Targeted Ther. 3 (1). https://doi.org/10.1038/s41392-017-0004-3.

Shewach, D.S., Kuchta, R.D., 2009. Introduction to cancer chemotherapeutics. Chem. Rev. 109 (7), 2859–2861. https://doi.org/10.1021/cr900208x.

Song, S.Y., Kim, K.p., Jeong, S.Y., Park, J., Park, J., Jung, J., Chung, H.K., Lee, S.W., Seo, M.H., Lee, J.s., Jung, K.H., Choi, E.K., 2016. Polymeric nanoparticle-docetaxel for the treatment of advanced solid tumors: Phase I clinical trial and preclinical data from an orthotopic pancreatic cancer model. Oncotarget 7 (47), 77348–77357. https://doi.org/10.18632/oncotarget.12668.

Strobel, H., Baisch, T., Fitzel, R., Schilberg, K., Siegelin, M.D., Karpel-Massler, G., Debatin, K.-M., 2019. Mike-andrew westhoff, temozolomide and other alkylating agents in glioblastoma therapy. Biomedicines 7 (3), 69. https://doi.org/10.3390/biomedicines7030069.

Taub, J.W., Buck, S.A., Xavier, A.C., Edwards, H., Matherly, L.H., Ge, Y., 2024. The evolution and history of vinca alkaloids: From the big bang to the treatment of pediatric acute leukemia. Pediatr. Blood Cancer 71 (11). https://doi.org/10.1002/pbc.31247.

Tawfik, S.M., Azizov, S., Elmasry, M.R., Sharipov, M., Lee, Y.I., 2021. Recent advances in nanomicelles delivery systems. Nanomaterials 11 (1), 1–36. https://doi.org/10.3390/nano11010070.

Thundimadathil, J., 2012. Cancer treatment using peptides: Current therapies and future prospects. J. Amino Acids 2012, 1–13. https://doi.org/10.1155/2012/967347.

Tiwari, M., 2012. Antimetabolites: Established cancer therapy. J. Cancer Res. Therapeut. 8 (4), 510–519. https://doi.org/10.4103/0973-1482.106526.

Tripathi, P.P., Arami, H., Banga, I., Gupta, J., Gandhi, S., 2018. Cell penetrating peptides in preclinical and clinical cancer diagnosis and therapy. Oncotarget 9 (98), 37252–37267. https://doi.org/10.18632/oncotarget.26442.

Ulm, M., Ramesh, A.V., McNamara, K.M., Ponnusamy, S., Sasano, H., Narayanan, R., 2019. Therapeutic advances in hormone-dependent cancers: focus on prostate, breast and ovarian cancers. Endocr. Connect 8 (2), R10. https://doi.org/10.1530/EC-18-0425.

Upadhyay, M., Adena, S.K.R., Vardhan, H., Pandey, S., Mishra, B., 2018a. Development and optimization of locust bean gum and sodium alginate interpenetrating polymeric network of capecitabine. Drug Dev. Ind. Pharm. 44 (3), 511–521. https://doi.org/10.1080/03639045.2017.1402921.

Upadhyay, M., Adena, S.K.R., Vardhan, H., Yadav, S.K., Mishra, B., 2018b. Development of biopolymers based interpenetrating polymeric network of capecitabine: A drug delivery vehicle to extend the release of the model drug. Int. J. Biol. Macromol. 115, 907–919. https://doi.org/10.1016/j.ijbiomac.2018.04.123.

Upadhyay, M., Adena, S.K.R., Vardhan, H., Yadav, S.K., Mishra, B., 2019. Locust bean gum and sodium alginate based interpenetrating polymeric network microbeads encapsulating capecitabine: Improved pharmacokinetics, cytotoxicity and in vivo antitumor activity. Mater. Sci. Eng., C 104. https://doi.org/10.1016/j.msec.2019.109958.

Upadhyay, M., Vardhan, H., Mishra, B., 2020. Natural polymers composed mucoadhesive interpenetrating buoyant hydrogel beads of capecitabine: development, characterization and in vivo scintigraphy. J. Drug Deliv. Sci. Technol. 55, 101480. https://doi.org/10.1016/j.jddst.2019.101480.

Upadhyay, M., Hosur, R.V., Jha, A., Bharti, K., Mali, P.S., Jha, A.K., Mishra, B., Kumar, A., 2023a. Myricetin encapsulated chitosan nanoformulation for management of type 2 diabetes: Preparation, optimization, characterization and in vivo activity. Biomater. Adv. 153. https://doi.org/10.1016/j.bioadv.2023.213542.

Upadhyay, M., Kumar, A., Mishra, B., 2023b. Extraction, Structural Properties, and Applications of Locust Bean gum Natural Gums: Extraction, Properties, and Applications. Elsevier, India, pp. 261–275. https://doi.org/10.1016/B978-0-323-99468-2.00008-5.

Voss, M.H., Hussain, A., Vogelzang, N., Lee, J.L., Keam, B., Rha, S.Y., Vaishampayan, U., Harris, W.B., Richey, S., Randall, J.M., Shaffer, D., Cohn, A., Crowell, T., Li, J., Senderowicz, A., Stone, E., Figlin, R., Motzer, R.J., Haas, N. B., Hutson, T., 2017. A randomized phase II trial of CRLX101 in combination with bevacizumab versus standard of care in patients with advanced renal cell carcinoma. Ann. Oncol. 28 (11), 2754–2760. https://doi.org/10.1093/annonc/mdx493.

Wang, S., Guo, X., Xiu, W., Liu, Y., Ren, L., Xiao, H., Yang, F., Gao, Y., Xu, C., Wang, L., 2020. Accelerating thrombolysis using a precision and clot-penetrating drug delivery strategy by nanoparticle-shelled microbubbles. Sci. Adv. 6 (31). https://doi.org/10.1126/sciadv.aaz8204.

Wang, X., Gigant, B., Zheng, X., Chen, Q., 2023a. Microtubule-targeting agents for cancer treatment: Seven binding sites and three strategies. MedComm. Oncol. 2 (3). https://doi.org/10.1002/mog2.46.

Wang, Z., Li, H., Gou, L., Li, W., Wang, Y., 2023b. Antibody–drug conjugates: Recent advances in payloads. Acta Pharm. Sin. B 13 (10), 4025–4059. https://doi.org/10.1016/j.apsb.2023.06.015.

Wang, B., Hu, S., Teng, Y., Chen, J., Wang, H., Xu, Y., Wang, K., Xu, J., Cheng, Y., Xiang, G., 2024. Current advance of nanotechnology in diagnosis and treatment for malignant tumors. Signal. Transduct. Targeted Ther. 9 (1). https://doi.org/10.1038/s41392-024-01889-y.

Warrier, N.M., Agarwal, P., Kumar, P., 2020. Emerging importance of survivin in stem cells and cancer: The development of new cancer therapeutics. Stem Cell Rev. Rep. 16 (5), 828–852. https://doi.org/10.1007/s12015-020-09995-4.

Wordeman, L., Vicente, J.J., 2021. Microtubule targeting agents in disease: Classic drugs, novel roles. Cancers 13 (22). https://doi.org/10.3390/cancers13225650.

Wu, C., Zhu, J., Zhang, X., 2012. Integrating gene expression and protein-protein interaction network to prioritize cancer-associated genes. BMC Bioinf. 13 (1). https://doi.org/10.1186/1471-2105-13-182.

Yadav, A., Singh, S., Sohi, H., Dang, S., 2022. Advances in delivery of chemotherapeutic agents for cancer treatment. AAPS PharmSciTech 23 (1). https://doi.org/10.1208/s12249-021-02174-9.

Yang, L., Shi, P., Zhao, G., Xu, J., Wen, P., Zhang, J., Zhang, G., Wang, X., Dong, Z., Chen, F., Cui, H., 2020. Targeting cancer stem cell pathways for cancer therapy. Signal Transduct. Targeted Ther. 5 (1). https://doi.org/10.1038/s41392-020-0110-5.

Zahavi, D., Weiner, L., 2020. Monoclonal antibodies in cancer therapy. Antibodies 9 (3), 34. https://doi.org/10.3390/antib9030034.

Zhu, Q., Shen, Y., Chen, X., He, J., Liu, J., Zu, X., 2020. Self-renewal signalling pathway inhibitors: perspectives on therapeutic approaches for cancer stem cells. OncoTargets. Ther. 13, 525–540. https://doi.org/10.2147/OTT.S224465.

Zubrod, C.G., Schepartz, S.A., Carter, S.K., 1977. Historical background of the national cancer institute's drug development thrust. Natl. Cancer Inst. Monogr. 45, 7–11.

CHAPTER

3

Emerging trend in anticancer drug delivery

Sarjana Raikwar[1], Nikhar Vishwakarma[1] and Sanjay K. Jain[2]

[1]Gyan Ganga Institute of Technology and Sciences, Jabalpur, Madhya Pradesh, India;
[2]Department of Pharmaceutical Sciences, Dr. Harisingh Gour Vishwavidyalaya, Sagar, Madhya Pradesh, India

Introduction

Cancer is one of the most dangerous diseases, leading to millions of deaths each year. According to 2020 statistics, approximately 19.3 million new cancer cases were reported (Sung et al., 2021). Conventionally, several treatment approaches such as surgery, radiation therapy, chemotherapy, immunotherapy, hormone therapy, and others have been utilized for the management of cancer. However, these conventional approaches have several limitations, including possible side effects on normal tissues in the human body and low therapeutic responses (Anand et al., 2023). Radiation therapy is helpful as a conventional palliative treatment for patients with tumor-related symptoms. This therapy is associated with a direct relationship between radiation dose and the volume of normal tissues exposed, which increases toxicity and leads to damage to healthy tissues. The use of conventional chemotherapy is no longer the preferred choice of cancer treatment, as it also damages normal cells. Moreover, surgery, depending on its extent and location, may result in severe pain, scarring, and long-term functional impairment. Hence, to overcome the drawbacks of traditional treatment methods, it is essential to develop targeted approaches to enhance cancer therapy and reduce adverse effects (Lutz et al., 2014).

Nowadays, new drug delivery systems (NDDSs) are able to efficiently deliver drugs to target sites in a controlled-release manner, thereby maximizing therapeutic efficacy while reducing side effects. These NDDSs include liposomes, nanoparticles, micelles, dendrimers, and others, which have been designed to deliver anticancer drugs. Targeting is achieved by surface modification of these NDDSs using different types of ligands, such as folic acid,

Advanced Cancer Therapeutics
https://doi.org/10.1016/B978-0-443-44185-1.00010-0

transferrin, mannose, hyaluronic acid, and asialoglycoprotein. Overexpressed receptors present on cancer cells are targeted using these ligands through receptor–ligand interactions. Targeted NDDSs have therefore been designed for selective delivery to tumor sites (Khan et al., 2025). Moreover, tumor targeting also involves exploiting the distinct characteristics of the tumor microenvironment (TME) to deliver anticancer drugs to cancer cells. The TME is a dynamic environment consisting of various components, such as abnormal blood vessels, extracellular matrix, and immune cells. These conditions can enhance the specificity and efficacy of drug delivery (Wang et al., 2023). One approach based on the TME involves systems designed to respond to specific stimuli present within the tumor microenvironment. Stimuli-sensitive drug delivery systems—such as pH-, temperature-, hypoxia-, magnetic field-, and light-triggered systems—have been developed for cancer targeting. These systems release drugs upon exposure to particular stimuli or molecules present in the TME. For instance, pH-sensitive nanocarriers are designed to release drugs in response to the acidic pH found in cancer cells (Passive Cancer Targeting).

Another approach targets abnormal blood vessels within the tumor microenvironment. These blood vessels are often leaky and have irregular architecture, allowing enhanced accumulation of drug carriers within tumors. This phenomenon is known as the enhanced permeability and retention (EPR) effect and can be exploited for the selective delivery of anticancer drugs to cancer cells. Additionally, immune cells present in the TME can also be targeted to enhance drug delivery. Thus, tumor targeting through TME-based strategies provides a promising approach to improve the effectiveness of cancer drug delivery (Vagena et al., 2025). Furthermore, theranostic drug delivery systems combine therapeutic and diagnostic agents within a single nanocarrier using nanotechnology. These systems enable simultaneous diagnosis and treatment of diseases such as cancer at the molecular level, facilitating personalized medicine and real-time therapy guidance (Al-Thani et al., 2024). Theranostic drug delivery systems employ smart nanocarriers loaded with imaging agents (e.g., quantum dots and magnetic nanoparticles) along with therapeutic agents such as anticancer drugs or genes, specifically targeting cancer cells. This chapter highlights the challenges associated with conventional cancer treatment approaches and discusses various ligands used for cancer targeting. It also covers multiple targeting strategies, including ligand-mediated drug delivery systems, stimuli-sensitive drug delivery systems and theranostic approaches for cancer targeting, as illustrated in Fig. 3.1. Additionally, it focuses on different clinical trial studies related to cancer treatment.

Limitations and challenges of conventional treatment approaches

Conventional therapies for the treatment of cancer include surgery, chemotherapy, radiotherapy, and hormonal therapy. The different conventional treatment approaches and their associated limitations are discussed below.

Surgery

Surgical intervention is considered an effective approach for the removal and diagnosis of early-stage cancer. For diagnostic purposes, cancer cells are detected using biopsy

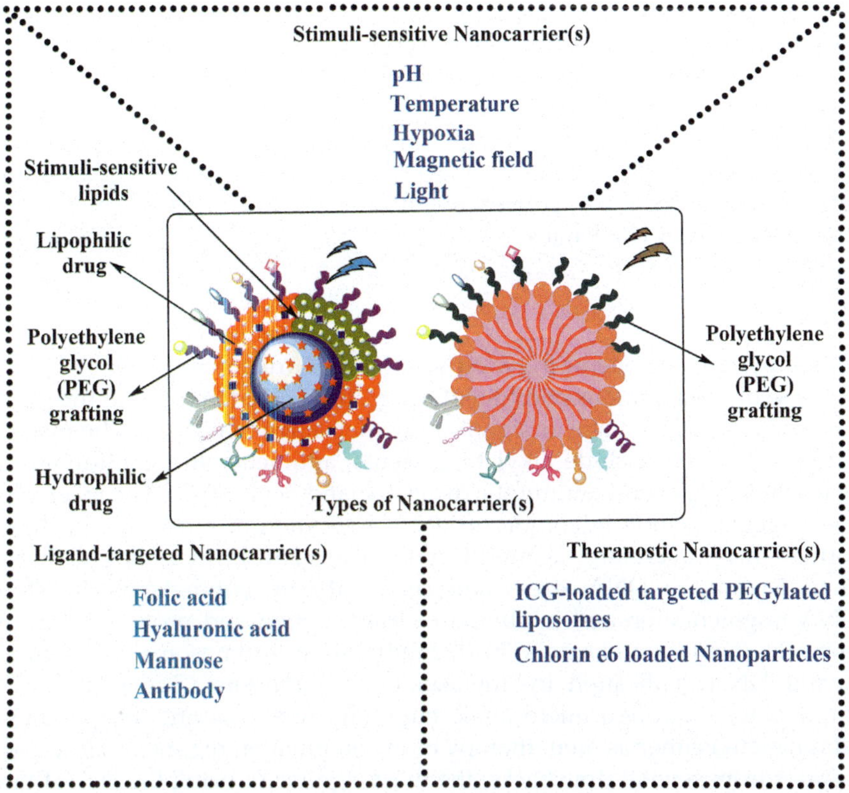

FIGURE 3.1 Different types of nanocarriers used for cancer targeting.

procedures; however, these methods have certain limitations, such as being painful and sometimes providing an insufficient sample size (Zafar et al., 2025). Nowadays, advanced non-invasive techniques such as liquid biopsy using biomarkers, including circulating tumor cells, are employed for early tumor detection. However, detecting these biomarkers in minute quantities poses additional challenges, requiring highly sensitive devices and advanced technologies. Moreover, the success of surgical treatment depends on the size of the tumor and the depth to which cancer cells are embedded within the body. If the tumor size is large, surgical removal may lead to serious damage to adjacent normal tissues or organs (Tohme et al., 2017). One example includes surgical intervention for brain tumors, which can result in impairment of brain functions such as thinking, speaking, and walking (Vijay Gyanani, 2013). Other examples of severe functional impairment include infertility following surgery for prostate, uterine, or ovarian cancers (Schover et al., 2014). Despite successful tumor removal, residual disease may remain in some cases. Several studies have indicated that the presence of minimal residual disease can lead to rapid tumor spread. This rapid progression may result from the surgical procedure itself, a trauma-induced microenvironment, or the use of opioids for pain management (Blatter and Rottenberg,

2015). In some cases, immunosuppressants used to facilitate wound healing after surgery significantly impact macrophage function. Macrophages play a crucial role in immune surveillance following surgery, and their compromised function may contribute to tumor regrowth (Kuo et al., 2025). Recent technological advancements in tumor surgery, such as laparoscopy, laser surgery, cryotechnology, fluorescence-guided surgery, and robotic surgery, have improved surgical outcomes. Nevertheless, several post-surgical complications, including secondary infections, reduced quality of life, and long-term functional impairments, remain significant challenges.

Chemotherapy

Chemotherapy remains one of the most widely used treatment regimens for cancer and involves the use of combinations of different drugs. It is considered one of the primary treatment options for advanced-stage or significantly metastasized cancers. The major classes of chemotherapeutic agents include alkylating agents, antimetabolites, antitumor antibiotics, topoisomerase inhibitors, and antimitotic drugs (Anand et al., 2023). The mechanisms of action of these agents include inhibition of DNA replication or transcription through DNA adduct formation by alkylating agents (Kondo et al., 2010); nucleotide misincorporation or depletion leading to DNA stress and cell death by antimetabolites (Zhang et al., 2016b); DNA fragmentation and inhibition of transcription and protein synthesis by antitumor antibiotics (Santos and Lamers, 2020); inhibition of chromosomal recombination, transcription, and DNA replication by topoisomerase inhibitors (Zuma et al., 2011); and disruption of mitosis through microtubule targeting by antimitotic drugs. Chemotherapy may be administered either as monotherapy or in combination regimens. However, both approaches suffer from several drawbacks, the most significant being the lack of target specificity and selectivity. Cancer cells are rapidly proliferating and share many characteristics with normal cells, making it difficult for chemotherapeutic agents to distinguish between malignant and healthy tissues. This poor selectivity results in severe side effects and toxicity in normal cells and tissues surrounding the tumor (Prieložná et al., 2024). The major adverse effects include dose-dependent hematotoxicity caused by carboplatin, keratitis and skin reactions induced by chlorambucil, renal impairment associated with cisplatin, and cardiotoxicity caused by doxorubicin. Additionally, common side effects such as alopecia, emesis, and neutropenia are frequently observed with chemotherapeutic agents such as 5-fluorouracil, methotrexate, and cyclophosphamides (Abotaleb et al., 2018). Another major challenge associated with chemotherapy is the development of multidrug resistance (MDR). Prolonged use of chemotherapeutic agents, either alone or in combination, often leads to drug resistance or cross-resistance, collectively referred to as MDR (Catalano et al., 2022). As a result, cancer cells continue to proliferate despite ongoing treatment. This phenomenon may be attributed to alterations in drug targets, dysregulation of apoptotic pathways, impaired p53 function, enhanced DNA repair mechanisms, and increased drug efflux (Singhai et al., 2025). These limitations significantly reduce the therapeutic efficacy of chemotherapy and negatively impact patient outcomes, necessitating the development of advanced targeted therapeutic strategies.

Radiotherapy

Radiotherapy is considered one of the most prominent cancer treatment modalities and involves the use of high-energy radiation. These include gamma rays, X-rays, and radioactive isotopes, which are used either to reduce tumor size or to eliminate cancer cells. Compared to chemotherapy, radiotherapy offers improved localization and treatment precision (Shiridokht et al., 2025). Recent advancements in radiation physics have led to the development of advanced techniques such as stereotactic body radiation therapy, image-guided radiation therapy, three-dimensional conformal radiotherapy, and intensity-modulated radiation therapy. These advanced approaches enable effective tumor control while sparing surrounding healthy tissues (Garibaldi et al., 2017). Radiation exposure induces the generation of mitochondrial reactive oxygen species (ROS), resulting in DNA damage and cell death through apoptosis or autophagy. Despite its advantages, radiotherapy is associated with both acute and chronic side effects, including erythema, mucositis, gastrointestinal toxicity, fibrosis, fatigue, and the risk of secondary malignancies (Zheng et al., 2023).

Hormonal therapy

Hormonal therapy is an effective treatment strategy for hormone-dependent cancers such as prostate cancer, hormone receptor–positive breast cancer, and ovarian cancer (Ulm et al., 2019). Hormones, including estrogens, progestogens, and androgens, play critical roles in cell proliferation and differentiation by binding to specific receptors (Mertens et al., 2001). Dysregulation of these hormonal pathways can lead to uncontrolled cell growth and resistance to apoptosis. One therapeutic approach involves targeting the signaling pathways responsible for hormone regulation, while another strategy focuses on reducing hormone production within the body (Mustafa et al., 2024; Victoir et al., 2024). Hormonal therapy primarily acts by inhibiting cell proliferation or inducing tumor regression through receptor antagonism, thereby reducing tumor size before surgical intervention or radiotherapy (Basu and Kopchick, 2019). This therapy is particularly effective in locally advanced and metastatic cancers. However, patients undergoing hormonal therapy often experience challenges such as treatment relapse, development of resistance, and a decline in overall quality of life (Andreu et al., 2022). Currently, the above-mentioned conventional strategies are frequently used either alone or in combination to treat various types of cancer. Nevertheless, these therapies present several. Limitations and challenges that remain to be addressed, highlighting the need for more effective and targeted treatment approaches.

Various types of ligands used in cancer targeting

Conventional strategies for combating cancer suffer from several drawbacks, including low target specificity. This lack of specificity results in systemic toxicity and damage to normal cells located in the vicinity of cancer cells. Therefore, there is a critical need to develop targeted drug delivery strategies that selectively target cancer cells while sparing surrounding healthy tissues (Fan et al., 2023). In this context, researchers have increasingly focused on ligand-based targeting strategies to overcome the shortcomings of conventional therapies. Ligands are molecules that can bind specifically to particular cell types or receptors. By exploiting these interactions, ligands can help in distinguishing cancer cells from normal cells, and their use in targeted drug delivery can lead to significant improvements in therapeutic outcomes (Yan et al., 2024). Various ligands, such as folic acid, hyaluronic acid, mannose, and antibodies, have been widely explored for cancer targeting and are discussed below.

Folic acid

Folic acid is a vitamin that plays a vital role in cell proliferation and nucleotide biosynthesis. It binds to folate receptors and enters cells via receptor-mediated endocytosis. Folate receptors are expressed at low levels on normal tissues but are overexpressed on several cancer cells, particularly in ovarian, kidney, lung, endometrial, and other cancers (Raikwar et al., 2022). Folic acid offers several advantages as a targeting ligand, including small molecular size, lack of immunogenicity, and simple chemical structure, making it an ideal candidate for cancer targeting. Current folate receptor–based targeting strategies primarily involve two approaches: (i) conjugation of anticancer drugs directly with folic acid to form folate–drug conjugates, and (ii) conjugation of folic acid with drug-loaded nanocarriers to form folate–nanocarrier conjugates (Zhang et al., 2025a). Both folate–drug and folate–nanocarrier conjugates readily bind to overexpressed folate receptors on cancer cells due to their inherent affinity. Subsequent receptor-mediated endocytosis facilitates internalization of these conjugates, resulting in enhanced therapeutic efficacy.

Hyaluronic acid

Carbohydrates, also known as saccharides, are natural biomolecules composed of carbon, hydrogen, and oxygen. Based on the number of sugar units, they are classified as monosaccharides, disaccharides, and polysaccharides. Certain carbohydrates with multiple hydroxyl groups, such as glucose and hyaluronic acid, have been extensively investigated for targeting various cellular receptors (Kakade et al., 2022). Hyaluronic acid (HA) is one of the most promising and widely used targeting ligands in cancer therapy. HA is a polysaccharide composed of glycosaminoglycan units and exhibits several favorable properties, including biocompatibility, bioadhesion, long-term stability, biodegradability, and low toxicity (Wang et al., 2025). These properties make HA a suitable ligand for targeted drug delivery. HA can target multiple receptors, including CD44 (cluster of differentiation 44), LAYN, RHAMM (receptor for HA-mediated motility), HARE (hyaluronan receptor for endocytosis), and Toll-like receptors (TLRs) (Pashkina et al., 2025). Among these, CD44 plays a crucial role in cell migration, adhesion, and intercellular interactions and is involved in biological processes such as embryogenesis, regeneration, hematopoiesis, and inflammation. CD44 primarily binds HA but can also interact with other ligands, including chondroitin, serglycin, and osteopontin (Jordan et al., 2015).

CD44 receptors are overexpressed on various cancer cells and are implicated in signaling pathways associated with cancer progression, including cancers of the brain, head and neck, breast, kidney, and other organs (Mattheolabakis et al., 2015). In addition to solid tumors, CD44 is also associated with hematological malignancies, such as acute and chronic lymphoblastic leukemia, acute and chronic myeloid leukemia, and multiple myeloma (Mesrati et al., 2021). Several studies have demonstrated the role of CD44 in tumor metastasis, where binding of HA to CD44 triggers a cascade of intracellular signaling events. HA has been widely exploited for the development of various nanocarriers, including nanoparticles (Choi et al., 2010; Thomas et al., 2015), liposomes (Mukherjee and Raikwar, 2024; Wang et al., 2020), polymer–drug conjugates (Wei et al., 2013) and micelles (Han et al., 2015; Liu et al., 2023). HA-conjugated nanocarriers bind to CD44 receptors and are efficiently internalized by cancer cells. This internalization of nanocarriers loaded with anticancer drugs, imaging agents, or nucleic acids significantly enhances therapeutic efficacy while reducing toxicity to adjacent normal cells (Lee et al., 2020). Furthermore, degradation of HA by hyaluronidase enzymes present in the tumor microenvironment facilitates localized drug release at tumor sites (Pashkina et al., 2025). Targeting CD44 using HA has been shown to reduce side effects, minimize multidrug resistance, and lower the risk of cancer recurrence and metastasis.

Mannose

Mannose receptors are lectin-type transmembrane receptors abundantly expressed on various cells, including endothelial cells, macrophages, and immature dendritic cells. These receptors bind and internalize glycosylated ligands and pathogens, playing a critical role in immune regulation and disease targeting. Structurally, mannose receptors consist of cytosolic and transmembrane domains along with a cytoplasmic tail (van der Zande et al., 2021). Mannose receptors are also found in high abundance on cancer cells, where they facilitate glucose transport—a primary energy source for rapidly proliferating tumor cells. Additionally, these receptors are predominantly expressed on immune cells such as macrophages, tumor-associated macrophages (TAMs), and dendritic cells (Nan et al., 2022). TAMs are commonly present within the tumor microenvironment and play a significant role in cancer progression. While macrophages in the M1-polarized state exhibit anticancer activity, TAMs generally promote tumor growth, angiogenesis, and immune suppression. Mannose-functionalized nanocarriers can be effectively utilized to target cancer by reprogramming TAMs toward the M1 phenotype and enhancing drug delivery to tumor sites (Basak et al., 2023). In some cancers, mannose receptors are also overexpressed on tumor cells, further contributing to enhancing mannose-mediated targeting. The binding of mannose to its receptor triggers receptor-mediated endocytosis and activates intracellular signaling pathways (Dalle Vedove et al., 2018). Moreover, mannose–receptor interactions enhance antitumor immunity by increasing cytokine production (Jin et al., 2025). Thus, mannose receptor–mediated targeting represents a promising strategy for cancer therapy.

Antibodies

Antibodies, particularly monoclonal antibodies, can bind specifically to antigens and are therefore highly effective tools for targeting cancer cells. The use of monoclonal antibodies in chemotherapy began in the 1970s, and to date, approximately 30 antibody-based therapeutics have been approved by the United States Food and Drug Administration (USFDA) for the treatment of various diseases, including cancer, antiviral prophylaxis, and Crohn's disease (Zahavi and Weiner, 2020). Conventional chemotherapy often lacks specificity and causes damage to normal adjacent cells, even when multiple drugs are used in combination (Mokhtari et al., 2017). To enhance therapeutic efficacy, cancer cell–specific antibodies can be combined with chemotherapeutic agents. Due to their high specificity, antibodies selectively target cancer cells, thereby minimizing damage to surrounding healthy tissues (Maiti et al., 2023).

Two major antibody-based targeting strategies—antibody–drug conjugates (ADCs) and antibody–nanocarrier conjugates—have been developed and approved for clinical use. ADCs consist of three main components: a cytotoxic drug, a cleavable or non-cleavable linker, and a cancer-specific antibody (He et al., 2024). ADC conjugation strategies include conventional and site-specific conjugation methods. Conventional conjugation typically utilizes lysine or cysteine residues on antibodies as anchoring points for drug attachment, exploiting abundant thiol groups present in biological systems (Sasso et al., 2023). An FDA-approved ADC, ado-trastuzumab emtansine, has demonstrated effective targeting in HER2-positive breast cancer (Raikwar et al., 2022). While conventional conjugation methods are relatively simple, they often produce heterogeneous products with irregular drug distribution. Other approved ADCs include Tivdak (tisotumab vedotin-tfty) and mirvetuximab soravtansine (ELAHERE) (Approved Antibody-Drug Conjugates for Cancer Therapy). Despite their therapeutic promise, ADCs face challenges such as limited penetration into solid tumors due to their large size, immune-mediated clearance, and premature drug release, which may cause off-target toxicity (Jia et al., 2024). Nevertheless, ADCs continue to show strong potential for treating various cancers. Another antibody-based strategy involves antibody–nanocarrier conjugates, which have been extensively investigated and demonstrated promising results. Antibodies can be conjugated to nanocarriers either through physical adsorption or via covalent chemical bonding (Raikwar et al., 2024). Physical adsorption relies on weak interactions such as hydrogen bonding, van der Waals forces, electrostatic interactions, and hydrophobic interactions. In contrast, covalent conjugation provides more stable and reproducible antibody–nanocarrier constructs (Aparicio-Blanco et al., 2024). Antibody–nanocarrier conjugates generally exhibit superior therapeutic outcomes compared to conventional therapies; however, further studies are required to evaluate their cytotoxicity and long-term in vivo biodistribution.

Targeting approaches

In the field of medicine, improving precision and therapeutic efficacy plays an important role in the treatment of diseases. Traditional drug delivery approaches have several limitations, such as off-target effects, systemic toxicity, and reduced therapeutic outcomes. These challenges have led to the development of targeted drug delivery systems, which have emerged as an innovative frontier capable of revolutionizing medication (Manzari et al., 2021). The conventional approach relies on the circulatory system to distribute drugs throughout the body, whereas targeted drug delivery systems are designed to precisely guide drugs to their desired sites of action. Targeted drug delivery systems aim to treat specific diseased tissues or target particular organs while maximizing therapeutic benefits and minimizing damage to healthy tissues (Singh et al., 2019). Cancer chemotherapy remains a major therapeutic approach for cancer treatment, in which anticancer drugs are administered systemically throughout the body. Although this approach kills tumor cells, it also damages normal cells, leading to systemic side effects such as nausea, vomiting, hair loss, and myelosuppression. This occurs due to the lack of specificity in drug distribution, which has long been a major limitation of cancer chemotherapy. Therefore, there is a pressing need for targeted drug delivery systems that can selectively target malignant cells while sparing healthy tissues (Ahmad et al., 2022). The basic principle of targeted drug delivery is rooted in the concepts of selectivity and localization. Several strategies have been developed to ensure that therapeutic moieties are guided to their intended destinations while minimizing exposure to non-target sites (Pandit et al., 2020). Targeted drug delivery systems require carrier systems or vectors to transport drugs, including liposomes, nanoparticles, micelles, dendrimers, and others. These carriers facilitate the transport of encapsulated drugs through the complex physiological environment of the body (Juillerat-Jeanneret and Schmitt, 2007). In cancer therapy, targeted drug delivery has the potential to enhance the effectiveness of chemotherapy while reducing its adverse effects. Broadly, there are two types of targeting approaches, namely passive targeting and active targeting, which are discussed below.

Passive targeting

Passive targeting is a fundamental strategy used in targeted drug delivery. It exploits the natural and physiological characteristics of the target tissue or site. In contrast, active targeting depends on specific ligands or receptors to guide drug carriers to their desired destinations (Karnwal et al., 2024). Passive targeting is particularly advantageous when the target site exhibits unique characteristics that facilitate drug accumulation. Various passive targeting strategies have been explored for site-specific drug delivery.

Enhanced permeability and retention (EPR) effect

The EPR effect is an important phenomenon in cancer therapy. It takes advantage of the leaky vasculature and poor lymphatic drainage commonly observed in solid tumors. These abnormalities result in the passive accumulation of nanoparticles and macromolecules within tumor tissues. For example, liposomes or nanoparticles carrying anticancer drugs can exploit the EPR effect to accumulate at tumor sites, leading to increased drug concentration in cancer cells while sparing normal tissues (Khan et al., 2026).

Tumor microenvironment

Passive targeting can also depend on the unique microenvironment of cancer cells. Enhanced glycolysis in cancer cells leads to the generation of a localized acidic environment (Raikwar et al., 2025). pH-sensitive drug delivery systems can exploit this acidity to selectively release drugs within the tumor. Moreover, tumor tissues may exhibit elevated levels of specific enzymes, enabling the precise release of bioactive agents within the tumor microenvironment (Jin et al., 2024).

Fenestrated endothelium

Several target tissues, such as the liver and spleen, possess fenestrated endothelial cells in their blood vessels. These fenestrations allow large particles to pass through, making such tissues suitable candidates for passive targeting (Mou et al., 2024). For instance, liposomes can passively accumulate in the liver and spleen due to the presence of fenestrated endothelium and have been employed in the treatment of diseases affecting these organs.

Hypoxic regions

In cancer, hypoxic (low-oxygen) regions arise due to inefficient vasculature. Hypoxia-responsive drug delivery systems can passively target these regions and selectively release bioactive agents in response to low oxygen levels. This strategy overcomes the challenge of treating hypoxic tumor regions, which are often resistant to conventional therapies (Attia et al., 2019). Overall, passive targeting is advantageous because it does not require the design of specific ligands or targeting agents. Instead, it relies on the inherent characteristics of the target tissue. Additionally, passive targeting is often used in combination with active targeting to achieve more precise and efficient drug delivery (Srinivasarao and Low, 2017). Multidrug resistance (MDR) is a major challenge associated with various chemotherapeutic drugs, including paclitaxel (Meng et al., 2016). Developed and characterized paclitaxel (PTX) and baicalein (BA)-loaded nanoemulsions (NEs) for the effective treatment of breast cancer and to overcome MDR by enhancing oxidative stress and inhibiting P-glycoprotein (P-gp). Several studies have reported that BA is a potent MDR-reversal agent with the ability to inhibit P-gp and enhance oxidative stress. The in vitro cytotoxicity of PTX and BA combinations with different weight ratios was evaluated, and the formulation with a 1:1 weight ratio exhibited a strong synergistic effect. The cytotoxicity results suggested that the drug-loaded nanoemulsions demonstrated superior anticancer efficacy in MCF-7/Tax cells compared to other PTX formulations. Cell uptake studies revealed that PTX/BA NEs effectively accumulated in tumor cells. The enhanced cellular uptake was attributed to increased reactive oxygen species (ROS) generation, reduced cellular glutathione (GSH) levels, and enhanced caspase-3 activity in MCF-7/Tax cells. Furthermore, in vivo studies showed that PTX/BA NEs exhibited higher anticancer efficacy than other PTX formulations. Thus, it can be concluded that dual drug-loaded nanoemulsions represent a promising combined therapeutic strategy for overcoming MDR (Meng et al., 2016).

Active targeting

Active targeting is one of the most widely used approaches for directing drugs to cancer cells. This technique utilizes target-specific ligands, molecules, or antibodies and is considered superior to passive targeting, which relies solely on the natural properties of target tissues. Active targeting overcomes the limitations of passive targeting by offering selective and precise drug delivery to the target site. One prominent active targeting strategy is antibody–drug conjugates (ADCs), which employ monoclonal antibodies for target-specific drug delivery. These monoclonal antibody-based drug conjugates bind to specific surface antigens expressed on cancer cells. Upon binding, the antibody–antigen interaction triggers internalization of the drug conjugate, leading to the intracellular release of anticancer drugs. This high specificity minimizes side effects by sparing healthy cells and selectively targeting cancer cells (Bae and Park, 2011; Lammers et al., 2012).

Cancer targeting

Ligand-mediated drug delivery systems

Ligand-mediated drug delivery systems are modified using specific ligands based on ligand– receptor interactions. These systems are designed to selectively target specific cells or tissues within the body. Various new drug delivery systems, such as nanoparticles, liposomes, micelles, and dendrimers, can be functionalized with different ligands to enhance targeting efficiency (Bajracharya et al., 2022).

Folate-targeted drug delivery systems

Folate receptors (FRs) are overexpressed on tumor cells, including those of the ovary, uterus, testis, colon, kidneys and lungs. Folic acid conjugates, linked through the γ-carboxyl group to drug molecules, enter folate-overexpressing cancer cells via receptor-mediated endocytosis (RME). The high affinity of folate conjugates for cancer cell surfaces facilitates efficient internalization. Folic acid conjugation enables targeted delivery of bioactive and diagnostic agents to tumor cells while sparing normal tissues (Marchetti et al., 2014). Therefore, folate-mediated targeting represents an effective strategy for cancer therapy (Gao et al., 2013). Developed tumor microenvironment-sensitive polypeptide (TMSP) and folate-functionalized docetaxel-loaded nanostructured lipid carriers (F/TMSP-DTX-NLCs). TMSPs consisted of polycationic cell-penetrating peptides and polyanionic inhibitory peptides connected via a protease-sensitive linker cleavable by matrix metalloproteinases-2 and -9 (MMP-2/9). Selective cleavage in cancer tissues enhanced cellular uptake. The folate-functionalized nanocarriers selectively bound to FR-positive tumor cells and were internalized via receptor-mediated endocytosis and CPP-mediated penetration. These NLCs exhibited small particle size, high encapsulation efficiency (>95%), sustained drug release, enhanced cellular uptake, and strong cytotoxicity in multiple cancer cell lines. In vivo studies in KB tumor-bearing nude mice demonstrated superior antitumor efficacy and reduced systemic toxicity compared with non-modified formulations (Gao et al., 2013). Zhang et al. (2016a) reported folate-conjugated cisplatin-loaded NLCs (FA–CIS–NLCs) for cervical cancer therapy. Folic acid was conjugated with PEG-DSPE to enhance targeting. The NLCs demonstrated appropriate particle size, high encapsulation efficiency, sustained release, and enhanced cytotoxicity in HeLa cells. The FA–CIS–NLCs showed superior anticancer efficacy both in vitro and in vivo compared with non-targeted formulations (Zhang et al., 2016a; Vinothini et al., 2019) developed folic-acid-conjugated graphene oxide-methyl acrylate nanocarriers loaded with paclitaxel for breast cancer targeting. The nanocarriers demonstrated pH-dependent drug release, significant cytotoxicity, and tumor regression in chemically induced rat tumor models, highlighting their therapeutic potential (Vinothini et al., 2019). Lohade et al. (2016) prepared folic-acid-functionalized liposomes using cholesterol-folate conjugates. These liposomes exhibited enhanced cellular uptake, improved biodistribution, and higher tumor accumulation compared with non-functionalized liposomes, confirming their potential in tumor-targeted drug delivery (Lohade et al., 2016).

Hyaluronic acid-targeted drug delivery systems

Hyaluronic acid (HA) is a glycosaminoglycan widely employed for tumor targeting due to its affinity for CD44 receptors, which are overexpressed on many cancer cells. HA-modified drug delivery systems enhance sustained drug release, tumor accumulation, solubility, and receptor-mediated endocytosis, thereby improving therapeutic efficacy while reducing systemic toxicity. HA-modified paclitaxel-loaded liposomes demonstrated suitable particle size, high drug release, enhanced cellular uptake, and superior cytotoxicity compared with free paclitaxel. In vivo studies confirmed preferential tumor accumulation and improved anticancer efficacy (Ravar et al., 2016). PEGylated HA-coated sorafenib-loaded liposomes exhibited enhanced uptake and cytotoxicity in CD44-overexpressing breast cancer cells, with significant tumor growth inhibition in xenograft models (Mo et al., 2018). HA-conjugated liposomes co-loaded with paclitaxel and ursolic acid showed enhanced cellular uptake, reduced tumor volume, and minimal systemic toxicity in breast cancer models, demonstrating their safety and efficacy (Ma et al., 2023).

Mannose-targeted drug delivery systems

Mannose receptors (CD206) are overexpressed on cancer cells and immune cells such as tumor-associated macrophages. Mannose-functionalized nanocarriers exploit receptor-mediated endocytosis to enhance intracellular drug delivery, improve tumor accumulation, and reduce systemic side effects. Mannose-functionalized liposomes delivering mRNA for immunotherapy significantly enhanced antitumor immune responses and survival in triple-negative breast cancer models (Deng et al., 2025). Mannose-conjugated nanoparticles also improved drug retention and targeting efficiency in liver cancer models (Jain et al., 2021). Mannose-modified iron oxide nanoparticles enabled selective imaging of tumor-associated macrophages in vivo, demonstrating potential for both diagnostic and therapeutic applications (Li et al., 2020).

Antibody-targeted drug delivery systems

Antibody-targeted drug delivery systems employ monoclonal antibodies to selectively deliver chemotherapeutic agents to cancer cells, thereby maximizing efficacy and minimizing off-target toxicity. Antibody-drug conjugates and antibody-functionalized nanocarriers represent advanced targeted therapeutic platforms. Antibody-modified PEGylated liposomes loaded with doxorubicin demonstrated significant tumor reduction in lung cancer models. Dual-targeted liposomes functionalized with anti- GPC3 antibodies and CPP peptides showed enhanced tumor suppression in hepatocellular carcinoma models (Lin et al., 2025). Dextran-based antibody-conjugated prodrug nanoparticles exhibited controlled drug release, enhanced tumor inhibition, and improved safety profiles, highlighting their promise in targeted cancer therapy (Tian et al., 2023).

Stimuli-sensitive drug delivery systems

Stimuli-sensitive drug delivery systems (SSDDS) respond to tumor-specific stimuli such as pH, temperature, hypoxia, magnetic fields, and light. These systems exploit tumor microenvironment characteristics to achieve site-specific drug release, enhanced therapeutic efficacy, and reduced systemic toxicity (Torchilin, 2014).

pH-sensitive drug delivery systems

pH-sensitive systems respond to acidic tumor microenvironments and are widely used for cancer targeting. Curcumin-loaded pH-sensitive nanoparticles demonstrated enhanced anticancer activity and improved bioavailability in colon cancer models (Prajakta et al., 2009; Wang et al., 2020) developed pH-responsive graft copolymer nanoparticles for dual-drug delivery, achieving improved cellular uptake, apoptosis induction, and superior antitumor efficacy in multidrug-resistant cancer models (Li et al., 2020). The synthesis and release mechanism of these nanoparticles is illustrated in Fig. 3.2. Xu et al. (2015) developed and characterized DOX and Bcl-2 siRNA-loaded pH-sensitive nanoparticles (NPs) for the effective treatment of lung cancer. DOX was conjugated onto polyethylenimine (PEI) using cis-aconitic anhydride (CA), a pH-sensitive linker, to form PEI-CA-DOX conjugates. Subsequently, PEI-CA-DOX/siRNA complex NPs were developed through spontaneous electrostatic interactions between cationic PEI-CA-DOX and anionic siRNA. The in vitro drug-release study showed faster DOX release at acidic pH compared to pH 7.4. Moreover, PEI-CA-DOX/siRNA complex NPs exhibited higher cytotoxicity and induced apoptosis in B16F10 cells compared to either DOX or Bcl-2 siRNA alone. The in vivo study was carried out in B16F10 melanoma-bearing mice, where PEI-CA-DOX/Bcl-2 siRNA complex NPs showed improved anticancer efficacy compared to single-drug treatment. Thus, it could be concluded that PEI-CA-DOX/Bcl-2 siRNA complex NPs represent a potential approach for the treatment of metastatic lung cancer via the pulmonary route (Xu et al., 2015). In another study, celastrol (Cel) and ginsenoside Rg3 (RG3)-loaded pH-sensitive prodrug NPs were developed and characterized for pancreatic cancer treatment. Celastrol is a promising antitumor therapeutic agent; however, its clinical applicability is limited due to low solubility, poor cancer selectivity, and high cytotoxicity. In contrast, ginsenoside Rg3 (RG3) is widely used in combination with chemotherapy to enhance anticancer efficacy and reduce side effects. The particle size and zeta potential of the developed NPs were found to be approximately 124.01 nm and −39.89 mV, respectively. These NPs also exhibited good physical stability and controlled drug release. In vivo studies demonstrated high accumulation of NPs in tumor tissues and prolonged blood circulation time. Consequently, the NPs showed

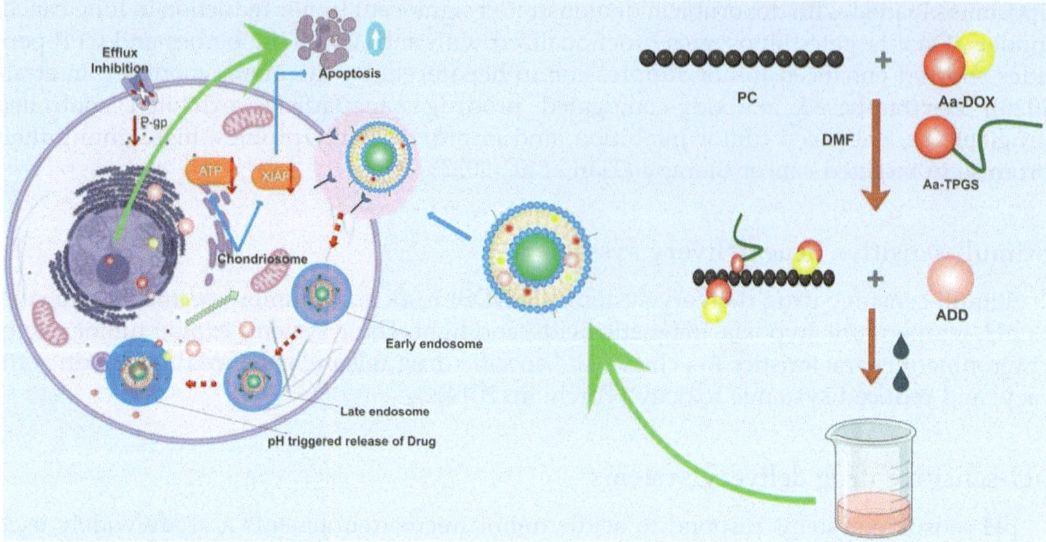

FIGURE 3.2 Synthesis and mechanism of DOX release from pH-sensitive graft copolymer poly (β-amino ester)-g-β-cyclodextrin (PBAE-g-β-CD) NPs.

enhanced tumor growth suppression and reduced systemic toxicity compared to free Cel, free RG3, and the combination of Cel + RG3. These outcomes suggested that the developed NPs could serve as a safe and effective platform for pancreatic cancer treatment (Zhang et al., 2025b).

Temperature-sensitive drug delivery systems

Temperature is an external stimulus employed to trigger drug release from temperature-sensitive drug delivery systems (DDS). Temperature-sensitive DDS are classified into two types: (i) drug delivery systems containing temperature-sensitive components and (ii) temperature-sensitive polymers. These DDS exhibit increased membrane penetration at their gel-to-sol crystalline phase transition temperature. They remain stable at physiological temperature (37°C) but display temperature-triggered drug release above 37°C under hyperthermic conditions (Wang et al., 2017). At elevated temperatures, these DDS show rapid release of the entrapped bioactive compounds. Gold nanoparticle (Au-NP)-coated Pluronic-b-poly(L-lysine) (Pluronic-PLL) nanoparticles loaded with paclitaxel (PTX) were developed and characterized. The deposition of Au-NPs on Pluronic-PLL micelles and the temperature-triggered response of the system were monitored using ultraviolet–visible spectroscopy and dynamic light scattering. The MTT assay was performed to determine the viability of MDA-MB-231 cells treated with PTX-loaded Pluronic- PLL@Au NPs. The results of blood compatibility and in vitro cytotoxicity assays confirmed that PTX-loaded Pluronic-PLL@Au NPs possessed excellent biocompatibility. Confocal laser scanning microscopy (CLSM) analysis revealed higher cellular uptake of PTX-loaded Pluronic-PLL@Au NPs compared to the free drug. Overall, the study concluded that the combination of chemotherapy and photothermal therapy could significantly damage cancer cells compared to chemotherapy or photothermal therapy alone, demonstrating the synergistic effects of chemo-photothermal treatment (Sun et al., 2017).

In another study, tamoxifen- and imatinib-loaded temperature-sensitive liposomes were prepared for the effective treatment of breast cancer. The liposomes were evaluated for average particle size, zeta potential, transition temperature, and drug-release behavior below and above the liposomal transition temperature. Cytotoxicity studies conducted on MCF-7 and MDA- MB-231 breast cancer cells demonstrated synergistic growth inhibition. The liposomes exhibited a transition temperature of 39.4°C and showed more than 70% entrapment efficiency for both tamoxifen and imatinib. Drug-release studies indicated that the temperature-sensitive liposomes released more than 80% of the encapsulated drug within 30 min above the transition temperature. Therefore, dual-drug-loaded temperature-sensitive liposomes could be a promising approach for the treatment of breast cancer (Jose et al., 2019).

Hypoxia-sensitive drug delivery systems

Cancer cells are hypoxic in nature due to insufficient blood supply, which restricts drug penetration into deeper tumor regions. Hypoxic conditions in tumors contribute to drug resistance during chemotherapy, radiotherapy, and phototherapy. Therefore, hypoxia-responsive drug delivery systems are required for the effective delivery of anticancer drugs to tumor sites (Singhai et al., 2025). DOX-loaded, hypoxia-triggered nanoparticles were developed from self-assembled polyethyleneimine-nitroimidazole (PEI-NI) micelles, which were further co-assembled with hyaluronic acid-Ce6 (HC). These drug delivery systems exhibited high cancer selectivity and released bioactive agents in response to dual stimuli, including external (light) and internal (hypoxia) triggers. 3illustrates the DOX-loaded hypoxia-triggered NPs based on self-assembled PEI-NI micelles as a dual-trigger system. Upon reaching the tumor site, light irradiation (600 nm, 10 mW cm^{-2}) generated high levels of reactive oxygen species (ROS), which significantly enhanced hypoxia, leading to nanoparticle dissociation and drug release at the target site. The developed DDS demonstrated synergistic anticancer efficacy through the combination of DOX-mediated chemotherapy and Ce6-mediated photodynamic therapy (PDT), resulting in minimized side effects on normal cells and maximized therapeutic efficacy. Hence, the developed nanocarriers offer a promising strategy for cancer-specific drug delivery through dual-stimuli responsiveness and may serve as a potential platform for programmed combination therapy involving chemotherapy and PDT (He et al., 2018).

In a study, a hypoxia-sensitive diblock copolymer, poly (lactic acid)-azobenzene- poly (ethylene glycol), self-assembled to form polymersomes. These polymersomes released the drug only under hypoxic conditions, as confirmed by dye-loaded polymersomes, which showed that 90% of the entrapped dye was released within 50 min. The polymersomes encapsulated a combination of gemcitabine and erlotinib with encapsulation efficiencies of 40% and 28%, respectively. Cell cytotoxicity studies were conducted using three-dimensional spheroid cultures of pancreatic cancer cells (BxPC-3) to establish hypoxia-mediated release of bioactive compounds from the polymersomes. These polymersomes demonstrated a significant reduction in cell viability in hypoxic spheroidal cultures of BxPC-3 cells. Thus, the polymersomes exhibited promising future applications in the imaging and treatment of hypoxic cancer cells (Kulkarni et al., 2016). Zhang et al. (2016c) developed and characterized triple drug-loaded hypoxia-triggered drug– drug-conjugated nanoparticles (NPs) to synergistically destroy differentiated cancer cells, cancer stem cells (CSCs), and the vascular niche. The hypoxia-sensitive system was developed using an azobenzene (AZO) bond, which imparted hypoxia sensitivity and specificity as a crosslinker conjugating hydrophobic combretastatin A-4 (CA4) with water-soluble irinotecan (IR) to form IR-AZO-CA4 amphiphilic molecules. These molecules self-assembled into NPs capable of entrapping the hydrophobic anti-CSC drug cyclopamine (CP). The drug-release mechanism involved azo-bond cleavage under hypoxic conditions, leading to nanoparticle disassembly and rapid drug release. Cellular uptake studies using confocal laser scanning microscopy (CLSM) showed that IR-AZO-CA4/CP NPs significantly enhanced cellular uptake and penetration of bioactive agents into inner CSC regions. Furthermore, these NPs effectively inhibited migration, invasion, and mammosphere formation. Hence, IR-AZO- CA4/CP NPs represent a potential therapeutic approach for cancer treatment (Zhang et al., 2016c). In another study, digoxin (DIG) and DOX-co-loaded hypoxia-sensitive micelles were prepared for the treatment of triple-negative breast cancer (TNBC). These micelles were designed to improve the therapeutic efficacy and safety of TNBC treatment. DIG, a cardiac steroid with a well-established pharmacological mechanism, was loaded into micelles composed of methoxy-polyethylene glycol (mPEG) and poly (lactic acid) (PLA) copolymers. The incorporation of an azobenzene (AZO) moiety enabled hypoxia-sensitive drug release at the tumor site. In vitro and in vivo studies demonstrated that the micelles efficiently transported the loaded drugs to hypoxic tumor regions, facilitating rapid drug release. Additionally, DIG-mediated inhibition of hypoxia-inducible factor-1α (HIF-1α) enhanced TNBC sensitivity to DOX, resulting in significant suppression of both primary tumor growth and pulmonary metastasis. Therefore, the developed micelles represent a promising strategy for TNBC and other hypoxia-mediated malignancies (Weng et al., 2025).

Magnetic field-sensitive drug delivery systems

The magnetic field (MF) is an important stimulus that plays a crucial role in the sustained release of drugs from magnetic field-sensitive drug delivery systems (Shrivastava et al., 2023). Generally, MF is locally applied to enhance the accumulation of bioactive agents at tumor sites or modulated to induce tumor heating for improved anticancer efficacy. As an external stimulus, MF assists in the transfer of antineoplastic drugs to target sites and helps maintain therapeutic drug concentrations in the bloodstream until complete absorption (Liu et al., 2019). Magnetoliposomes are promising nanocarriers for selective drug delivery in cancer treatment. The magnetic properties of hydrophobic iron oxide nanoparticles combined with a lipid bilayer have been utilized to facilitate the release of entrapped DOX from magnetoliposomes. Cytotoxicity studies of the developed nanocarriers against both normal and cancer cells were conducted, along with evaluations of tumor-killing ability under MF exposure. The results indicated that nanocarriers composed of liposomes and magnetic nanoparticles were non-cytotoxic to normal cells but exhibited significant cytotoxicity toward tumor cells. Thus, DOX-loaded magnetoliposomes show potential applications in tumor treatment, with rapid DOX release observed under the influence of a magnetic field in cancer cells (Szuplewska et al., 2019). In another study, lipid–polymer hybrid nanoparticles containing magnetic beads were developed for stimulus-triggered drug release using a remote radiofrequency (RF) magnetic field. Stability analysis of the hybrid nanoparticles in terms of particle size and polydispersity index (PDI) in phosphate-buffered saline (PBS) showed no significant changes over an extended period, indicating long-term stability. The entrapment efficiencies of camptothecin (CPT) and Fe_3O_4 in the hybrid nanoparticles were determined and RF-controlled drug release was evaluated. In vitro cell-line studies demonstrated a significant reduction in MT2 mouse breast cancer cell growth in the presence of a remote RF field. Hence, the developed nanoparticles represent a promising platform for enhancing drug delivery to cancer cells (Deok Kong et al., 2013).

Light-sensitive drug delivery systems

Light is an extrinsic stimulus employed for the delivery of drugs or bioactive agents to target sites. It plays a significant role in the activation or inactivation of various biochemical processes and is considered an effective strategy for biomedical applications. In biomedical research, parameters such as wavelength, intensity, pulse duration, and irradiation cycles are carefully controlled to enable effective drug delivery (Saraf et al., 2025; Torchilin, 2014). Several photosensitizing agents, including chlorins, porphyrin derivatives, phthalocyanines, and porphycenes, have been utilized for the diagnosis and treatment of cancer. Light-sensitive nanoparticles have been fabricated to achieve efficient cytoplasmic delivery of anticancer drugs for synergistic thermo-chemotherapy. Drug-loaded polymeric nanoparticles based on a selenium-implanted copolymer (I/D-Se-NPs) rapidly disassembled within minutes via reactive oxygen species (ROS)-induced selenium oxidation upon near-infrared (NIR) light exposure. This irreversible dissociation triggered continuous drug release. Moreover, I/D-Se-NPs facilitated cytoplasmic drug delivery through ROS-mediated lysosomal disruption, resulting in preferential nuclear distribution within 5 min post-irradiation. Thus, I/D-Se-NPs represent a promising strategy for achieving synergistic anticancer effects (Wang et al., 2017).

A photoresponsive hollow silica nanoparticle-based nanovesicle was fabricated for the co-delivery of genes and photosensitizers (PSs) for dual-wavelength light-triggered synergistic gene and photodynamic therapy (PDT). The resultant hollow nanoparticles (HNPs) were conjugated with PDMAEMA polycation via a 405 nm light-cleavable coumarin (Cou) linker to form HNP-Cou-PD, which exhibited excellent gene condensation ability, good biocompatibility, and light-triggered gene-release properties. HNP-Cou-PD loaded with chlorin e6 (Ce6) inside the silica cavity and plasmid encoding caspase-8 (CSP8) attached to the PDMAEMA outer layer (Ce6–HNP-Cou-PD/CSP8) demonstrated enhanced anticancer effects under sequential 405 and 670 nm light irradiation both in vitro and in vivo. These effects were attributed to light-stimulated intracellular gene release and ROS generation. Therefore, HNP-Cou-PD nanovesicles represent a promising platform for effective co-delivery of genes and photosensitizers in cancer therapy (Lin et al., 2018).

Theranostic approach

Theranostics is a novel approach in which a nanotherapeutic system is designed to simultaneously diagnose and deliver targeted therapy (Ahmed et al., 2012). It is an emerging strategy in cancer targeting that integrates diagnostic and therapeutic functionalities. Recent advancements in theranostic research have focused on radiotheranostic agents, nanoparticle-based systems, and molecularly targeted drug delivery systems that exploit tumor-specific biomarkers. Theranostic agents enhance cancer targeting by improving drug accumulation at tumor sites while enabling concurrent imaging and therapy (Chen et al., 2016). Due to their ability to be functionalized with ligands, peptides, or antibodies, nanoparticle-based theranostic systems have demonstrated significant potential. Recent research highlights the development of stimuli-responsive theranostic platforms that release drugs in response to tumor-specific conditions such as enzymatic activity or acidic pH, supporting personalized cancer therapy. Various theranostic strategies have been explored, including nanoparticle-based theranostics, radiotheranostic agents, and molecularly targeted theranostics.

Radiotheranostics combine diagnostic imaging and targeted radiotherapy through the use of paired radionuclides, allowing visualization of tumor sites while delivering localized radiation. Clinical studies by Baum and Kulkarni (2012) demonstrated that prostate-specific membrane antigen (PSMA)-targeted radiotheranostics improved outcomes in prostate cancer patients and also showed effectiveness in neuroendocrine tumors. Molecular targeting strategies involve directing theranostic agents toward overexpressed receptors such as HER2, EGFR, or folate receptors on cancer cells, thereby improving targeting accuracy and reducing off-target effects (Baum and Kulkarni, 2012; Kelkar and Reineke, 2011) reported that receptor-targeted theranostics enabled simultaneous imaging and treatment of cancer (Kelkar and Reineke, 2011). Indocyanine green (ICG), an FDA-approved fluorescent probe, has been incorporated into PEGylated liposomes as a contrast agent. Cancer-specific targeting was achieved using the anti-MUC-1 humanized monoclonal antibody (mAb) hCTM01. Following intravenous administration of ICG-loaded targeted and non-targeted PEGylated liposomes in fast-growing (4T1) and slow-growing (HT-29) MUC-1-positive tumor models, targeted liposomes demonstrated significantly higher tumor accumulation compared to non-targeted liposomes. Furthermore, the anticancer drug DOX was successfully incorporated into both targeted and non-targeted PEGylated ICG liposomes. Consequently, DOX-loaded targeted ICG liposomes represent a promising platform for combined tumor-specific therapy and diagnosis (Mura et al., 2013). The application of nanotechnology in anticancer drug delivery has been extensively explored to improve chemotherapy efficacy and reduce associated side effects. Applications include molecular tumor imaging, early detection, molecular diagnosis, targeted therapy, and cancer bioinformatics. Additionally, nanotechnology enables the development of dual-purpose nanomaterials for simultaneous diagnosis and treatment, giving rise to the concept of theranostics, which integrates diagnosis and therapy within a single platform.

Clinical trial studies in cancer treatment

Clinical trials are essential for evaluating the safety and therapeutic effectiveness of drug delivery systems (Selker et al., 2019). Nanocarrier-based drug delivery systems have emerged as promising alternatives to conventional chemotherapy due to their improved tumor-targeting ability and reduced systemic toxicity (Verma et al., 2024). Various nanocarriers, such as liposomes, nanoparticles, dendrimers, and micelles, are currently under clinical investigation. These trials are conducted across different phases to assess safety, clinical efficacy, and dosage optimization (Raikwar et al., 2026). The various clinical trial studies of novel drug delivery systems for cancer treatment are summarized in Table 3.1.

TABLE 3.1 Various clinical trial studies of novel drug delivery systems for cancer treatment.

S.No.	Novel drug delivery systems	Phase	Type of cancer	NCT number
1.	Irinotecan liposome (onivyde)	Phase III	Small cell Lung Cancer	NCT03088813
2.	Liposomal doxorubicin	Phase I	Refractory Solid Tumors	NCT00019630
3.	Lurtotecan liposome (NX 211)	Phase II	Advanced Solid Tumor	NCT00003891
4.	Liposomal cisplatin	Phase I/II	Pancreatic cancer	NCT00080119
5.	Paclitaxel cationic liposomes	Phase II	Advanced Solid Tumor	NCT06632574
6.	Albumin-bound Paclitaxel (Abraxane®)	Phase III	Breast cancer	NCT00629499
7.	2 NBTXR3 crystalline NPs	Phase III	Soft tissue sarcoma	NCT01433068
8.	Ultrasmall silica NPs	Phase I	Prostate cancer	NCT04167969
9.	Immunomodulatory NPs	Phase I	Solid tumors	NCT04751786
10.	Nab-rapamycin NPs	Phase II	Pediatric Solid Tumor	NCT02975882
11.	Gold NPs	Phase I	Brain tumors	NCT00848042
12.	SiRNA loaded dendrimer	Phase I/II	Solid tumor	NCT01591356
13.	Genexol-PM Paclitaxel (Micelles)	Phase I	Breast cancer	NCT02064829
14.	Paclitaxel-loaded micelles	Phase III	Breast cancer	NCT01644890
15.	Cisplatin-loaded micelles	Phase III	Pancreatic cancer	NCT02240238

Conclusion

Cancer continues to represent a formidable global health challenge and remains one of the leading causes of mortality worldwide. Despite the availability of established treatment modalities such as surgery, chemotherapy, radiotherapy, and hormonal therapy, the clinical outcomes of conventional cancer treatments—particularly chemotherapy—are often limited by non-specific targeting, systemic toxicity, suboptimal therapeutic efficacy, and the emergence of multidrug resistance. These inherent limitations have underscored the urgent need for innovative and more precise therapeutic strategies. Advances in nanotechnology have ushered in a transformative era in cancer diagnosis and treatment, offering unprecedented opportunities for improved tumor targeting, real-time imaging, and enhanced therapeutic outcomes. Nanocarrier-based drug delivery systems have emerged as versatile and powerful platforms capable of overcoming the biological and pharmacological barriers associated with conventional chemotherapeutic agents. By enabling controlled drug release, improved bioavailability, and selective accumulation at tumor sites, these systems significantly reduce off-target effects while enhancing anticancer efficacy. The integration of targeting ligands, such as folic acid, hyaluronic acid, mannose, and antibodies, has further strengthened the specificity of nanocarrier systems, facilitating receptor-mediated uptake and improved intracellular delivery of therapeutic agents. In parallel, the development of stimuli-responsive drug delivery systems and theranostic platforms has introduced a new dimension to cancer therapy by enabling site-specific, condition-triggered drug release and simultaneous diagnosis and treatment. These strategies collectively represent a paradigm shift from passive drug administration toward intelligent, personalized cancer

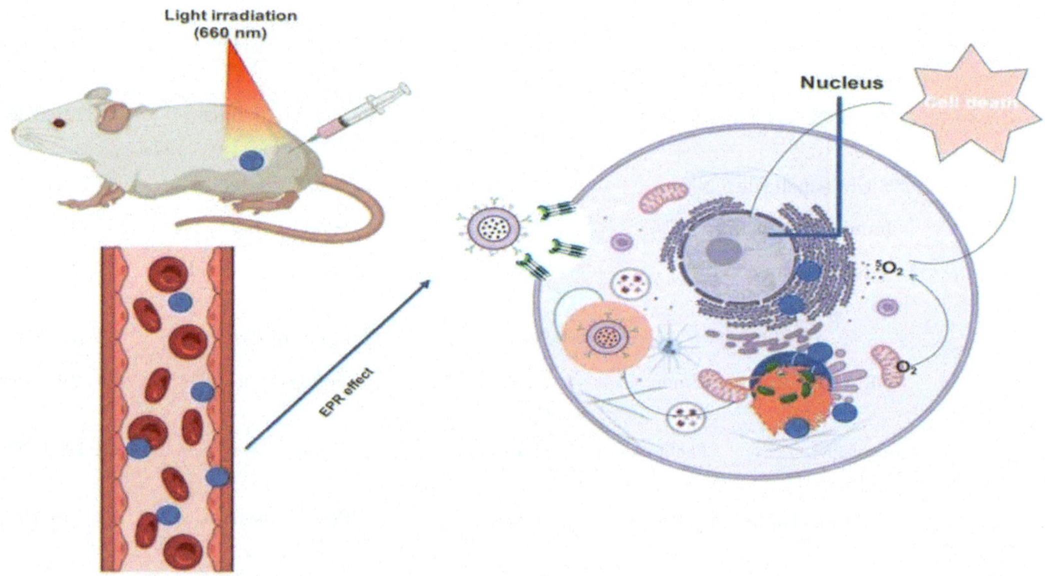

FIGURE 3.3 DOX-loaded, hypoxia-triggered NPs with self-assembled polyethylene polyethylenimine-nitroimidazole (PEI-NI) micelles as a dual trigger system.

therapy. This chapter has comprehensively highlighted the challenges and limitations of conventional chemotherapy, the role of various ligands in cancer targeting, advanced targeting strategies, and the current status of clinical trials involving nanocarrier-based drug delivery systems. Looking ahead, future research efforts will focus on optimizing the safety, scalability, and translational potential of these advanced systems, with particular emphasis on long-term biocompatibility, regulatory approval, and clinical applicability. In summary, the rapid evolution of smart, targeted, and stimuli-responsive drug delivery systems marks a significant advancement in anticancer therapy. These emerging technologies hold immense promise for redefining cancer treatment paradigms, ultimately paving the way toward more effective, safer, and patient-centric therapeutic interventions Fig. 3.3.

Conflict of interest

Authors declare no conflict of interest.

References

Abotaleb, M., Kubatka, P., Caprnda, M., Varghese, E., Zolakova, B., Zubor, P., Opatrilova, R., Kruzliak, P., Stefanicka, P., Büsselberg, D., 2018. Chemotherapeutic agents for the treatment of metastatic breast cancer: An update. Biomed. Pharmacother. 101, 458–477. https://doi.org/10.1016/j.biopha.2018.02.108.

Ahmad, A., Imran, M., Sharma, N., 2022. Precision nanotoxicology in drug development: Current trends and challenges in safety and toxicity implications of customized multifunctional nanocarriers for drug-delivery applications. Pharmaceutics 14, 2463. https://doi.org/10.3390/pharmaceutics14112463.

Ahmed, N., Fessi, H., Elaissari, A., 2012. Theranostic applications of nanoparticles in cancer. Drug Discov. Today 17, 928–934. https://doi.org/10.1016/j.drudis.2012.03.010.

Al-Thani, A.N., Jan, A.G., Abbas, M., Geetha, M., Sadasivuni, K.K., 2024. Nanoparticles in cancer theragnostic and drug delivery: A comprehensive review. Life Sci. 352, 122899. https://doi.org/10.1016/j.lfs.2024.122899.

Anand, U., Dey, A., Chandel, A.K.S., Sanyal, R., Mishra, A., Pandey, D.K., De Falco, V., Upadhyay, A., Kandimalla, R., Chaudhary, A., Dhanjal, J.K., Dewanjee, S., Vallamkondu, J., Pérez de la Lastra, J.M., 2023. Cancer chemotherapy and beyond: Current status, drug candidates, associated risks and progress in targeted therapeutics. Genes Dis. 10 (4), 1367–1401. https://doi.org/10.1016/j.gendis.2022.02.007.

Andreu, Y., Soto-Rubio, A., Ramos-Campos, M., Escriche-Saura, A., Martínez, M., Gavilá, J., 2022. Impact of hormone therapy side effects on health-related quality of life, distress, and well-being of breast cancer survivors. Sci. Rep. 12 (1), 18673. https://doi.org/10.1038/s41598-022-22971-x.

Aparicio-Blanco, J., Vishwakarma, N., Lehr, C.-M., Prestidge, C.A., Thomas, N., Roberts, R.J., Thorn, C.R., Melero, A., 2024. Antibiotic resistance and tolerance: What can drug delivery do against this global threat? Drug Deliv. Transl. Res. 14 (6), 1725–1734. https://doi.org/10.1007/s13346-023-01513-6.

Approved Antibody-Drug Conjugates for Cancer Therapy. Molecules 26, 5847. https://doi.org/10.3390/molecules26195847.

Attia, M.F., Anton, N., Wallyn, J., Omran, Z., Vandamme, T.F., 2019. An overview of active and passive targeting strategies to improve the nanocarriers efficiency to tumor sites. J. Pharm. Pharmacol. 71 (8), 1185–1198. https://doi.org/10.1111/jphp.13098.

Bae, Y.H., Park, K., 2011. Targeted drug delivery to tumors: Myths, reality and possibility. J. Contr. Release 153 (3), 198–205. https://doi.org/10.1016/j.jconrel.2011.06.001.

Bajracharya, R., Song, J.G., Patil, B.R., Lee, S.H., Noh, H.-M., Kim, D.-H., Kim, G.-L., Seo, S.-H., Park, J.-W., Jeong, S.H., Lee, C.H., Han, H.-K., 2022. Functional ligands for improving anticancer drug therapy: Current status and applications to drug delivery systems. Drug Deliv. 29 (1), 1959–1970. https://doi.org/10.1080/10717544.2022.2089296.

Basak, U., Sarkar, T., Mukherjee, S., Chakraborty, S., Dutta, A., Dutta, S., Nayak, D., Kaushik, S., Das, T., Sa, G., 2023. Tumor-associated macrophages: An effective player of the tumor microenvironment. Front. Immunol. 14, 1295257. https://doi.org/10.3389/fimmu.2023.1295257.

Basu, R., Kopchick, J.J., 2019. The effects of growth hormone on therapy resistance in cancer. Cancer. Drug. Resist 2 (3), 827–846. https://doi.org/10.20517/cdr.2019.27.

Baum, R.P., Kulkarni, H.R., 2012. THERANOSTICS: From molecular imaging using Ga-68 labeled tracers and PET/CT to personalized radionuclide therapy - the bad berka experience. Theranostics 2 (5), 437–447. https://doi.org/10.7150/thno.3645.

Blatter, S., Rottenberg, S., 2015. Minimal residual disease in cancer therapy – small things make all the difference. Drug Resist. Updates 21–22, 1–10. https://doi.org/10.1016/j.drup.2015.08.003.

Catalano, A., Iacopetta, D., Ceramella, J., Scumaci, D., Giuzio, F., Saturnino, C., Aquaro, S., Rosano, C., Sinicropi, M. S., 2022. Multidrug resistance (MDR): A widespread phenomenon in pharmacological therapies. Molecules 27 (3), 616. https://doi.org/10.3390/molecules27030616.

Chen, Z., He, N., Chen, M., Zhao, L., Li, X., 2016. Tunable conjugation densities of camptothecin on hyaluronic acid for tumor targeting and reduction-triggered release. Acta Biomater. 43, 195–207. https://doi.org/10.1016/j.actbio.2016.07.020.

Choi, K.Y., Chung, H., Min, K.H., Yoon, H.Y., Kim, K., Park, J.H., Kwon, I.C., Jeong, S.Y., 2010. Self-assembled hyaluronic acid nanoparticles for active tumor targeting. Biomaterials 31 (1), 106–114. https://doi.org/10.1016/j.biomaterials.2009.09.030.

Dalle Vedove, E., Costabile, G., Merkel, O.M., 2018. Mannose and mannose-6-phosphate receptor–targeted drug delivery systems and their application in cancer therapy. Adv. Healthc. Mater. 7. https://doi.org/10.1002/adhm.201701398.

Deng, K., Sun, J., Liu, J., Zhang, Y., Liu, W., Li, X., Wu, H., Li, J., Zhang, J., Jin, C., Zhang, C.Y., 2025. Mannose-modified cationic liposome-based mRNA therapeutics for improved triple-negative breast cancer immunotherapy. Adv. Nanobiomed Res. https://doi.org/10.1002/anbr.202500226.

Deok Kong, S., Sartor, M., Jack Hu, C.-M., Zhang, W., Zhang, L., Jin, S., 2013. Magnetic field activated lipid–polymer hybrid nanoparticles for stimuli-responsive drug release. Acta Biomater. 9 (3), 5447–5452. https://doi.org/10.1016/j.actbio.2012.11.006.

Fan, D., Cao, Y., Cao, M., Wang, Y., Cao, Y., Gong, T., 2023. Nanomedicine in cancer therapy. Signal Transduct. Target Ther. 8 (1), 293. https://doi.org/10.1038/s41392- 023-01536-y.

Gao, W., Xiang, B., Meng, T.-T., Liu, F., Qi, X.-R., 2013. Chemotherapeutic drug delivery to cancer cells using a combination of folate targeting and tumor microenvironment- sensitive polypeptides. Biomaterials 34 (16), 4137–4149. https://doi.org/10.1016/j.biomaterials.2013.02.014.

Garibaldi, C., Jereczek-Fossa, B.A., Marvaso, G., Dicuonzo, S., Rojas, D.P., Cattani, F., Starzyńska, A., Ciardo, D., Surgo, A., Leonardi, M.C., Ricotti, R., 2017. Recent advances in radiation oncology. ecancermedicalscience 11. https://doi.org/10.3332/ecancer.2017.785.

Han, H.S., Choi, K.Y., Ko, H., Jeon, J., Saravanakumar, G., Suh, Y.D., Lee, D.S., Park, J.H., 2015. Bioreducible core-crosslinked hyaluronic acid micelle for targeted cancer therapy. J. Contr. Release 200, 158–166. https://doi.org/10.1016/j.jconrel.2014.12.032.

He, H., Zhu, R., Sun, W., Cai, K., Chen, Y., Yin, L., 2018. Selective cancer treatment *via* photodynamic sensitization of hypoxia-responsive drug delivery. Nanoscale 10 (6), 2856–2865. https://doi.org/10.1039/C7NR07677K.

He, J., Zeng, X., Wang, C., Wang, E., Li, Y., 2024. Antibody–drug conjugates in cancer therapy: Mechanisms and clinical studies. MedComm. 5 (8). https://doi.org/10.1002/mco2.671.

Jain, A.K., Sahu, H., Mishra, K., Thareja, S., 2021. Mannose conjugated starch nanoparticles for preferential targeting of liver cancer. Curr. Drug Deliv. 18, 369–380. https://doi.org/10.2174/1567201817666200903171124.

Jia, G., Jiang, Y., Li, X., 2024. Targeted drug conjugates in cancer therapy: Challenges and opportunities. Pharm. Sci. Adv. 2, 100048. https://doi.org/10.1016/j.pscia.2024.100048.

Jin, Z., Al Amili, M., Guo, S., 2024. Tumor microenvironment-responsive drug delivery based on polymeric micelles for precision cancer therapy: Strategies and prospects. Biomedicines 12, 417. https://doi.org/10.3390/biomedicines12020417.

Jin, H., Wu, P., Lv, C., Zhang, S., Zhang, Y., Li, C., Gao, R., Shan, G., Bi, H., Chang, H., Liu, X., Zeng, Y., 2025. Mannose inhibits PKM2 lactylation to induce pyroptosis in bladder cancer and activate antitumor immune responses. Commun. Biol. 8 (1), 689. https://doi.org/10.1038/s42003-025-08130-8.

Jordan, A.R., Racine, R.R., Hennig, M.J.P., Lokeshwar, V.B., 2015. The role of CD44 in disease pathophysiology and targeted treatment. Front. Immunol. 6. https://doi.org/10.3389/fimmu.2015.00182.

Jose, A., Ninave, K.M., Karnam, S., Venuganti, V.V.K., 2019. Temperature-sensitive liposomes for co-delivery of tamoxifen and imatinib for synergistic breast cancer treatment. J. Liposome Res. 29 (2), 153–162. https://doi.org/10.1080/08982104.2018.1502315.

Juillerat-Jeanneret, L., Schmitt, F., 2007. Chemical modification of therapeutic drugs or drug vector systems to achieve targeted therapy: Looking for the grail. Med. Res. Rev. 27, 574–590. https://doi.org/10.1002/med.20086.

Kakade, P., Chatterjee, A., Pandya, A., Disouza, J., Patravale, V., 2022. Carbohydrate anchored lipid nanoparticles. Int. J. Pharm. 618, 121681. https://doi.org/10.1016/j.ijpharm.2022.121681.

Karnwal, A., Sharma, V., Kumar, G., Jassim, A.Y., Dohroo, A., Sivanesan, I., 2024. Transforming medicine with nanobiotechnology: Nanocarriers and their biomedical applications. Pharmaceutics 16, 1114. https://doi.org/10.3390/pharmaceutics16091114.

Kelkar, S.S., Reineke, T.M., 2011. Theranostics: Combining imaging and therapy. Bioconjug. Chem. 22 (10), 1879–1903. https://doi.org/10.1021/bc200151q.

Khan, H.U., Raza, N., Maheen, S., Abbas, H., Salem, M.E., Khan, I., Naseem, M., Shafqat, S.S., 2025. Advances in targeted drug delivery systems for cancer treatment: Current trends and future prospects. J. Drug Deliv. Sci. Technol. 113, 107402. https://doi.org/10.1016/j.jddst.2025.107402.

Khan, M.S., Alqahtani, T., Al Shmrany, H., Gupta, G., Goh, K.W., Sahebkar, A., Kesharwani, P., 2026. Enhanced permeability and retention (EPR) effect: Advances in nanomedicine for improved tumor targeting. Biomater. Adv. 181, 214636. https://doi.org/10.1016/j.bioadv.2025.214636.

Kondo, N., Takahashi, A., Ono, K., Ohnishi, T., Basu, A., 2010. DNA damage induced by alkylating agents and repair pathways. J. Nucleic Acids 2010 (1). https://doi.org/10.4061/2010/543531.

Kuo, P.-J., Lin, P.-C., Hsieh, C.-H., 2025. Wound healing in cancer patients under immunotherapy. Int. J. Surg. 111, 7087–7098. https://doi.org/10.1097/JS9.0000000000002819.

Kulkarni, P., Haldar, M.K., You, S., Choi, Y., Mallik, S., 2016. Hypoxia-Responsive Polymersomes for Drug Delivery to Hypoxic Pancreatic Cancer Cells.

Lammers, T., Kiessling, F., Hennink, W.E., Storm, G., 2012. Drug targeting to tumors: Principles, pitfalls and (pre-) clinical progress. J. Contr. Release 161 (2), 175–187. https://doi.org/10.1016/j.jconrel.2011.09.063.

Lee, S.Y., Kang, M.S., Jeong, W.Y., Han, D.-W., Kim, K.S., 2020. Hyaluronic acid-based theranostic nanomedicines for targeted cancer therapy. Cancers (Basel) 12 (4), 940. https://doi.org/10.3390/cancers12040940.

Li, Y., Wu, H., Ji, B., Qian, W., Xia, S., Wang, L., Xu, Y., Chen, J., Yang, L., Mao, H., 2020. Targeted imaging of CD206 expressing tumor-associated M2-like macrophages using mannose-conjugated antibiofouling magnetic iron oxide nanoparticles. ACS Appl. Bio Mater. 3, 4335–4347. https://doi.org/10.1021/acsabm.0c00368.

Lin, X., Wu, M., Li, M., Cai, Z., Sun, H., Tan, X., Li, J., Zeng, Y., Liu, X., Liu, J., 2018. Photo-responsive hollow silica nanoparticles for light-triggered genetic and photodynamic synergistic therapy. Acta Biomater. 76, 178–192. https://doi.org/10.1016/j.actbio.2018.07.007.

Lin, C., Sun, J., Yang, Y., Pan, X., Sun, Y., Sun, B., Gan, C., 2025. Anti-GPC3 antibody and cell-penetrating peptide CPP44 dual-ligand modified liposomes for targeted delivery of arsenic trioxide in the treatment of hepatocellular carcinoma. J. Drug Target. 33 (6), 1004–1013. https://doi.org/10.1080/1061186X.2025.2461104.

Liu, J.F., Jang, B., Issadore, D., Tsourkas, A., 2019. Use of magnetic fields and nanoparticles to trigger drug release and improve tumor targeting. WIREs Nanomed. Nanobiotechnol. 11 (6). https://doi.org/10.1002/wnan.1571.

Liu, Z., Chen, X., Jin, Q., Li, M., Zhu, S., Zhang, Y., Zhi, D., Zhao, Y., Li, L., Zhang, S., 2023. Dual functionalized hyaluronic acid micelles loading paclitaxel for the therapy of breast cancer. Front. Bioeng. Biotechnol. 11. https://doi.org/10.3389/fbioe.2023.1230585.

Lohade, A.A., Jain, R.R., Iyer, K., Roy, S.K., Shimpi, H.H., Pawar, Y., Rajan, M.G.R., Menon, M.D., 2016. A novel folate-targeted nanoliposomal system of doxorubicin for cancer targeting. AAPS Pharm. Sci. Tech. 17 (6), 1298–1311. https://doi.org/10.1208/s12249-015-0462-2.

Lutz, S.T., Jones, J., Chow, E., 2014. Role of radiation therapy in palliative care of the patient with cancer. J. Clin. Oncol. 32, 2913–2919. https://doi.org/10.1200/JCO.2014.55.1143.

Ma, T., Zhou, J., Li, J., Chen, Q., 2023. Hyaluronic acid-modified liposomes for ursolic acid-targeted delivery treat lung cancer based on p53/ARTS-mediated mitochondrial apoptosis. Iran. J. Pharm. Res. 22. https://doi.org/10.5812/ijpr- 131758.

Maiti, R., Patel, B., Patel, N., Patel, M., Patel, A., Dhanesha, N., 2023. Antibody drug conjugates as targeted cancer therapy: Past development, present challenges and future opportunities. Arch Pharm. Res. (Seoul) 46 (5), 361–388. https://doi.org/10.1007/s12272-023- 01447-0.

Manzari, M.T., Shamay, Y., Kiguchi, H., Rosen, N., Scaltriti, M., Heller, D.A., 2021. Targeted drug delivery strategies for precision medicines. Nat. Rev. Mater. 6 (4), 351–370. https://doi.org/10.1038/s41578-020-00269-6.

Marchetti, C., Giorgini, M., De Medici, C., Palaia, I., Iadarola, R., Vertechy, L., Muzii, L., Benedetti Panici, P., Domenici, L., Di Donato, V., Tomao, F., 2014. Targeted drug delivery via folate receptors in recurrent ovarian cancer: A review. Onco. Targets. Ther 7, 1223. https://doi.org/10.2147/OTT.S40947.

Mattheolabakis, G., Milane, L., Singh, A., Amiji, M.M., 2015. Hyaluronic acid targeting of CD44 for cancer therapy: From receptor biology to nanomedicine. J. Drug Target. 23 (7–8), 605–618. https://doi.org/10.3109/1061186X.2015.1052072.

Meng, L.uhua, Xia, X.uejun, Yang, Y.anfang, Ye, J.un, Dong, W.ujun, Ma, P.anpan, Jin, Y.iqun, Liu, Y.uling, 2016. Co-encapsulation of paclitaxel and baicalein in nanoemulsions to overcome multidrug resistance via oxidative stress augmentation and P-glycoprotein inhibition. Int. J. Pharm. 513 (1–2), 8–16. https://doi.org/10.1016/j.ijpharm.2016.09.001.

Mertens, H.J.M.M., Heineman, M.J., Theunissen, P.H.M.H., de Jong, F.H., Evers, J.L.H., 2001. Androgen, estrogen and progesterone receptor expression in the human uterus during the menstrual cycle. Eur. J. Obstet. Gynecol. Reprod. Biol. 98 (1), 58–65. https://doi.org/10.1016/S0301-2115(00)00554-6.

Mesrati, M.H., Syafruddin, S.E., Mohtar, M.A., Syahir, A., 2021. CD44: a multifunctional mediator of cancer progression. Biomolecules 11 (12). https://doi.org/10.3390/biom11121850.

Mo, L., Song, J.G., Lee, H., Zhao, M., Kim, H.Y., Lee, Y.J., Ko, H.W., Han, H.-K., 2018. PEGylated hyaluronic acid-coated liposome for enhanced in vivo efficacy of sorafenib via active tumor cell targeting and prolonged systemic exposure. Nanomedicine 14, 557–567. https://doi.org/10.1016/j.nano.2017.12.003.

Mokhtari, R.B., Homayouni, T.S., Baluch, N., Morgatskaya, E., Kumar, S., Das, B., Yeger, H., 2017. Combination therapy in combating cancer. Oncotarget 8 (23), 38022–38043. https://doi.org/10.18632/oncotarget.16723.

Mou, X., Leeman, S.M., Roye, Y., Miller, C., Musah, S., 2024. Fenestrated endothelial cells across organs: Insights into kidney function and disease. Int. J. Mol. Sci. 25 (16), 9107. https://doi.org/10.3390/ijms25169107.

Mukherjee, D., Raikwar, S., 2024. Recent update on nanocarrier(s) as the targeted therapy for breast cancer. AAPS Pharm. Sci. Tech. 25 (6), 153. https://doi.org/10.1208/s12249-024- 02867-x.

Mura, S., Nicolas, J., Couvreur, P., 2013. Stimuli-responsive nanocarriers for drug delivery. Nat. Mater. 12, 991–1003. https://doi.org/10.1038/nmat3776.

Mustafa, M., Ahmad, R., Tantry, I.Q., Ahmad, W., Siddiqui, S., Alam, M., Abbas, K., Moinuddin, H., Habib, S., Islam, S., 2024. Apoptosis: A comprehensive overview of signaling pathways, morphological changes, and physiological significance and therapeutic implications. Cells 13 (22), 1838. https://doi.org/10.3390/cells13221838.

Nan, F., Sun, Y., Liang, H., Zhou, J., Ma, X., Zhang, D., 2022. Mannose: A sweet option in the treatment of cancer and inflammation. Front. Pharmacol. 13. https://doi.org/10.3389/fphar.2022.877543.

Pandit, R., Chen, L., Götz, J., 2020. The blood-brain barrier: Physiology and strategies for drug delivery. Adv. Drug Deliv. Rev. 165–166, 1–14. https://doi.org/10.1016/j.addr.2019.11.009.

Pashkina, E., Bykova, M., Berishvili, M., Lazarev, Y., Kozlov, V., 2025. Hyaluronic aAcid- bBased dDrug dDelivery sSystems for cCancer tTherapy. Cells 14 (2), 61. https://doi.org/10.3390/cells14020061.

Passive Cancer Targeting. Cancers (Basel). 13, 670. https://doi.org/10.3390/cancers13040670.

Prajakta, D., Ratnesh, J., Chandan, K., Suresh, S., Grace, S., Meera, V., Vandana, P., 2009. Curcumin loaded pH-sensitive nanoparticles for the treatment of colon cancer. J. Biomed. Nanotechnol. 5 (5), 445–455. https://doi.org/10.1166/jbn.2009.1038.

Prieložná, J., Mikušová, V., Mikuš, P., 2024. Advances in the delivery of anticancer drugs by nanoparticles and chitosan-based nanoparticles. Int. J. Pharm. X 8, 100281. https://doi.org/10.1016/j.ijpx.2024.100281.

Raikwar, S., Jain, A., Saraf, S., Bidla, P.D., Panda, P.K., Tiwari, A., Verma, A., Jain, S.K., 2022. Opportunities in combinational chemo-immunotherapy for breast cancer using nanotechnology: An emerging landscape. Expert Opin. Drug Deliv. 19 (3), 247–268. https://doi.org/10.1080/17425247.2022.2044785.

Raikwar, S., Vishwakarma, N., Sharma, S., Sharma, R., Jain, S.K., 2024. Polymer/lipid- based nanocomplexes in cancer immunotherapy. In: Nanotechnology Based Strategies for Cancer Immunotherapy. Springer Nature Singapore, Singapore, pp. 279–300. https://doi.org/10.1007/978-981-97-7022-9_10.

Raikwar, S., Vishwakarma, N., Rathee, S., Patil, U.K., Jain, S.K., 2025. Anomalous tumor microenvironment: Exploitable features for drug delivery. In: Tumor-Targeting with Stimuli-Responsive Vesicular Nanocarriers. Elsevier, pp. 1–28. https://doi.org/10.1016/B978-0-443-29125-8.00001-6.

Raikwar, S., Vishwakarma, N., Chourasia, S., Rojekar, S., Jain, S.K., 2026. A clinical and industrial perspective of biodegradable nanofibers in cancer chemotherapy and regenerative medicine. In: Nanofiber Therapeutics. Elsevier, pp. 323–345. https://doi.org/10.1016/B978-0-443-27745-0.00012-0.

Ravar, F., Saadat, E., Gholami, M., Dehghankelishadi, P., Mahdavi, M., Azami, S., Dorkoosh, F.A., 2016. Hyaluronic acid-coated liposomes for targeted delivery of paclitaxel, in-vitro characterization and in-vivo evaluation. J. Contr. Release 229, 10–22. https://doi.org/10.1016/j.jconrel.2016.03.012.

Santos, J.A., Lamers, M.H., 2020. Novel antibiotics targeting bacterial replicative DNA polymerases. Antibiotics 9 (11), 776. https://doi.org/10.3390/antibiotics9110776.

Saraf, S., Rathee, S., Kumari, P., Vishwakarma, N., 2025. Light-triggered vesicular carriers for tumor targeting. In: Tumor-Targeting with Stimuli-Responsive Vesicular Nanocarriers. Elsevier, pp. 259–282.

Sasso, J.M., Tenchov, R., Bird, R., Iyer, K.A., Ralhan, K., Rodriguez, Y., Zhou, Q.A., 2023. The evolving landscape of antibody–drug conjugates: In depth analysis of recent research progress. Bioconjug. Chem. 34 (11), 1951–2000. https://doi.org/10.1021/acs.bioconjchem.3c00374.

Schover, L.R., van der Kaaij, M., van Dorst, E., Creutzberg, C., Huyghe, E., Kiserud, C.E., 2014. Sexual dysfunction and infertility as late effects of cancer treatment. Eur. J. Cancer, Suppl. 12 (1), 41–53. https://doi.org/10.1016/j.ejcsup.2014.03.004.

Selker, H.P., Eichler, H., Stockbridge, N.L., McElwee, N.E., Dere, W.H., Cohen, T., Erban, J.K., Seyfert-Margolis, V. L., Honig, P.K., Kaitin, K.I., Oye, K.A., D'Agostino, R.B., 2019. Efficacy and effectiveness too trials: Clinical trial designs to generate evidence on efficacy and on effectiveness in wide practice. Clin. Pharmacol. Ther. 105 (4), 857–866. https://doi.org/10.1002/cpt.1347.

Shiridokht, F., Kehtari, P., Eskandani, M., Farajollahi, A., Vandghanooni, S., 2025. Advancing cancer radiotherapy: Harnessing radiosensitizers and nanotechnology for enhanced tumor control. Int. J. Pharm. X 10, 100419. https://doi.org/10.1016/j.ijpx.2025.100419.

Shrivastava, P., Vishwakarma, N., Gautam, L., Vyas, S.P., 2023. Magnetically responsive polymeric gels and elastomeric system(s) for drug delivery. In: Smart Polymeric Nano- Constructs in Drug Delivery. Elsevier, pp. 129–150. https://doi.org/10.1016/B978-0- 323-91248-8.00012-X.

Singh, A.P., Biswas, A., Shukla, A., Maiti, P., 2019. Targeted therapy in chronic diseases using nanomaterial-based drug delivery vehicles. Signal Transduct. Target. Ther. 4 (1), 33. https://doi.org/10.1038/s41392-019-0068-3.

Singhai, H., Raikwar, S., Rathee, S., Jain, S.K., 2025. Emerging combinatorial drug delivery strategies for breast cancer: A comprehensive review. Curr. Drug Targets 26 (5), 331–349. https://doi.org/10.2174/011389450135208 1241211090911.

Srinivasarao, M., Low, P.S., 2017. Ligand-targeted drug delivery. Chem. Rev. 117 (19), 12133–12164. https://doi.org/10.1021/acs.chemrev.7b00013.

Sun, Y., Wang, Q., Chen, J., Liu, L., Ding, L., Shen, M., Li, J., Han, B., Duan, Y., 2017. Temperature-sensitive gold nanoparticle-coated pluronic-PLL nanoparticles for drug delivery and chemo-photothermal therapy. Theranostics 7, 4424–4444. https://doi.org/10.7150/thno.18832.

Sung, H., Ferlay, J., Siegel, R.L., Laversanne, M., Soerjomataram, I., Jemal, A., Bray, F., 2021. Global cancer statistics 2020: GLOBOCAN estimates of incidence and mortality worldwide for 36 cancers in 185 countries. CA Cancer J. Clin. 71 (3), 209–249. https://doi.org/10.3322/caac.21660.

Szuplewska, A., Rękorajska (Joniec), A., Pocztańska, E., Krysiński, P., Dybko, A., Chudy, M., 2019. Magnetic field-assisted selective delivery of doxorubicin to cancer cells using magnetoliposomes as drug nanocarriers. Nanotechnology 30 (31), 315101. https://doi.org/10.1088/1361-6528/ab19d3.

Thomas, R.G., Moon, M., Lee, S., Jeong, Y.Y., 2015. Paclitaxel loaded hyaluronic acid nanoparticles for targeted cancer therapy: In vitro and in vivo analysis. Int. J. Biol. Macromol. 72, 510–518. https://doi.org/10.1016/j.ijbiomac.2014.08.054.

Tian, H., Yu, L., Zhang, M., He, J., Sun, X., Ni, P., 2023. Dextran-doxorubicin prodrug nanoparticles conjugated with CD147 monoclonal antibody for targeted drug delivery in hepatoma therapy. Colloids Surf. B Biointerfaces 228, 113400. https://doi.org/10.1016/j.colsurfb.2023.113400.

Tohme, S., Simmons, R.L., Tsung, A., 2017. Surgery for cancer: A trigger for metastases. Cancer Res. 77, 1548–1552. https://doi.org/10.1158/0008-5472.CAN-16-1536.

Torchilin, V.P., 2014. Multifunctional, stimuli-sensitive nanoparticulate systems for drug delivery. Nat. Rev. Drug Discov. 13 (11), 813–827. https://doi.org/10.1038/nrd4333.

Ulm, M., Ramesh, A.V., McNamara, K.M., Ponnusamy, S., Sasano, H., Narayanan, R., 2019. Therapeutic advances in hormone-dependent cancers: Focus on prostate, breast and ovarian cancers. Endocr. Connect. 8, R10–R26. https://doi.org/10.1530/EC-18-0425.

Vagena, I.-A., Malapani, C., Gatou, M.-A., Lagopati, N., Pavlatou, E.A., 2025. Enhancement of EPR effect for passive tumor targeting: Current status and future perspectives. Appl. Sci. 15 (6), 3189. https://doi.org/10.3390/app15063189.

van der Zande, H.J.P., Nitsche, D., Schlautmann, L., Guigas, B., Burgdorf, S., 2021. The mannose receptor: From endocytic receptor and biomarker to regulator of (Meta)Inflammation. Front. Immunol. 12. https://doi.org/10.3389/fimmu.2021.765034.

Verma, M., Jaiswal, A., Vishwakarma, N., Gupta, V., 2024. Design, implementation, and interpretation of clinical trials of cancer immunotherapy. In: Nanotechnology Based Strategies for Cancer Immunotherapy. Springer Nature Singapore, Singapore, pp. 407–417. https://doi.org/10.1007/978-981-97-7022-9_15.

Victoir, B., Croix, C., Gouilleux, F., Prié, G., 2024. Targeted therapeutic strategies for the treatment of cancer. Cancers (Basel) 16 (2), 461. https://doi.org/10.3390/cancers16020461.

Vijay Gyanani, 2013. Turning Stealth Liposomes into Cationic Liposomes for Anticancer Drug Delivery.

Vinothini, K., Rajendran, N.K., Ramu, A., Elumalai, N., Rajan, M., 2019. Folate receptor targeted delivery of paclitaxel to breast cancer cells via folic acid conjugated graphene oxide grafted methyl acrylate nanocarrier. Biomed. Pharmacother. 110, 906–917. https://doi.org/10.1016/j.biopha.2018.12.008.

Wang, Y., Deng, Y., Luo, H., Zhu, A., Ke, H., Yang, H., Chen, H., 2017. Light-rResponsive nNanoparticles for hHighly eEfficient cCytoplasmic dDelivery of aAnticancer aAgents. ACS Nano 11 (12), 12134–12144. https://doi.org/10.1021/acsnano.7b05214.

Wang, J., Liu, D., Guan, S., Zhu, W., Fan, L.i, Qi, Z., Cai, D., 2020. Hyaluronic acid-modified liposomal honokiol nanocarrier: eEnhance anti-metastasis and antitumor efficacy against breast cancer. Carbohydr. Polym.ate Polymers 235, 115981. https://doi.org/10.1016/j.carbpol.2020.115981.

Wang, Q., Shao, X., Zhang, Y., Zhu, M., Wang, F.X.C., Mu, J., Li, J., Yao, H., Chen, K., 2023. Role of tumor microenvironment in cancer progression and therapeutic strategy. Cancer Med. 12 (10), 11149–11165. https://doi.org/10.1002/cam4.5698.

Wang, L., Zhou, F., Xie, W., 2025. Advances in hyaluronic acid-based biomaterials: Applications in cancer therapy, wound healing, and disease management. J. Mater. Sci. Mater. Med. 36, 91. https://doi.org/10.1007/s10856-025-06946-8.

Wei, X., Senanayake, T.H., Warren, G., Vinogradov, S.V., 2013. Hyaluronic acid-based nanogel–drug conjugates with enhanced anticancer activity designed for the targeting of CD44-positive and drug-resistant tumors. Bioconjug. Chem. 24 (4), 658–668. https://doi.org/10.1021/bc300632w.

Weng, L., Zhao, M., Chen, Z., Zhu, L., 2025. Hypoxia-targeted responsive delivery of doxorubicin and digoxin for synergistic treatment of triple-negative breast cancer. Mol. Pharm. 22 (4), 2142–2158. https://doi.org/10.1021/acs.molpharmaceut.4c01325.

Xu, C., Wang, P., Zhang, J., Tian, H., Park, K., Chen, X., 2015. Pulmonary Codelivery of dDoxorubicin and siRNA by pH-sSensitive nNanoparticles for tTherapy of mMetastatic lLung cCancer. Small 11 (34), 4321–4333. https://doi.org/10.1002/smll.201501034.

Yan, S., Na, J., Liu, X., Wu, P., 2024. Different targeting ligands-mediated drug delivery systems for tumor therapy. Pharmaceutics 16, 248. https://doi.org/10.3390/pharmaceutics16020248.

Zafar, A., Khatoon, S., Khan, M.J., Abu, J., Naeem, A., 2025. Advancements and limitations in traditional anti-cancer therapies: A comprehensive review of surgery, chemotherapy, radiation therapy, and hormonal therapy. Discov. Oncol. 16 (1), 607. https://doi.org/10.1007/s12672-025-02198-8.

Zahavi, D., Weiner, L., 2020. Monoclonal antibodies in cancer therapy. Antibodies 9 (3), 34. https://doi.org/10.3390/antib9030034.

Zhang, G., Liu, F., Jia, E., Jia, L., Zhang, Y., 2016a. Folate-modified, cisplatin-loaded lipid carriers for cervical cancer chemotherapy. Drug Deliv. 23, 1393–1397. https://doi.org/10.3109/10717544.2015.1054052.

Zhang, J., Dai, Q., Park, D., Deng, X., 2016b. Targeting DNA replication stress for cancer therapy. Genes 7, 51. https://doi.org/10.3390/genes7080051.

Zhang, R., Li, Y., Zhang, M., Tang, Q., Zhang, X., 2016c. Hypoxia-responsive drug–drug conjugated nanoparticles for breast cancer synergistic therapy. RSC Adv. 6, 30268–30276. https://doi.org/10.1039/C6RA01560C.

Zhang, J., Zhan, B., Du, Y., Liu, N., Liu, S., Li, X., 2025a. Targeted cancer treatment using folic acid-functionalized carbohydrate polymers: A new era in nanomedicine. Ind. Crops Prod. 235, 121704. https://doi.org/10.1016/j.indcrop.2025.121704.

Zhang, Z., Wang, J., Li, X., Zhao, L., Zhao, J., Su, M., Wu, X., Zeng, H., 2025b. Synergistic effect of pH-sensitive PEGylated RG3-chitosan prodrug nanoparticles encapsulated celastrol on pancreatic cancer. Drug Deliv. 32 (1). https://doi.org/10.1080/10717544.2025.2464189.

Zheng, Z., Su, J., Bao, X., Wang, H., Bian, C., Zhao, Q., Jiang, X., 2023. Mechanisms and applications of radiation-induced oxidative stress in regulating cancer immunotherapy. Front. Immunol. 14. https://doi.org/10.3389/fimmu.2023.1247268.

Zuma, A.A., Cavalcanti, D.P., Maia, M.C.P., de Souza, W., Motta, M.C.M., 2011. Effect of topoisomerase inhibitors and DNA-binding drugs on the cell proliferation and ultrastructure of trypanosoma cruzi. Int. J. Antimicrob. Agents 37 (5), 449–456. https://doi.org/10.1016/j.ijantimicag.2010.11.031.

CHAPTER

4

Cancer therapy depending on tumor stroma

Pranesh Kumar[1], *Anurag Kumar Gautam*[2] *and Abdul Baseer Khan*[3]

[1]Department of Pharmacology, Institute of Pharmaceutical Sciences, University of Lucknow, Lucknow, Uttar Pradesh, India; [2]Institute of Pharmacy, Deen Dayal Upadhyaya Gorakhpur University, Gorakhpur, Uttar Pradesh, India; [3]College of Pharmacy, Integral University, Lucknow, Uttar Pradesh, India

Introduction

Despite the continuous improvement of medical technology, diagnosis, and therapeutic strategies, the global cancer burden keeps rising for several malignancies. According to estimates from the American Cancer Society, the incidence of prostate, breast, and uterine corpus cancers is still on the rise. About 19.3 million new cancer cases and 10 million deaths occurred in 2020 alone, which drew attention to cancer as a multifactorial disease with limited therapeutic outcomes and high mortality rates (Siegel et al., 2023). Based on these trends, there is a pressing need to explore the physiology of tumor development and better treatment options that can be utilized. The significance of tumor microenvironment (TME) in cancer biology has been recognized for over a century. As early as the 1880s, Paget proposed the "seed and soil" theory, suggesting that tumor cells ("seed") grow best in favorable microenvironments ("soil") (Paget, 1889; Whiteside, 2008). TME is a complex ecosystem that surrounds tumor cells, consisting of extracellular matrix, stromal cells, immune cells, blood vessels, soluble factors, and various supportive tissue components (Hanahan and Weinberg, 2011). Among these, the tumor stroma plays a crucial role in shaping tumors and their behavior. It impacts cancer initiation and supports cancer cell growth, movement, and invasion, which contributes to resistance to treatments (Kalluri, 2016). The tumor stroma is a dynamic and diverse network made up of cellular components like pericytes, osteoblasts, and chondrocytes, as well as noncellular elements like the extracellular matrix (ECM) (LeBleu and Kalluri, 2018; Dominici et al., 2006). These components create a supportive environment

Advanced Cancer Therapeutics
https://doi.org/10.1016/B978-0-443-44185-1.00030-6

for tumor growth and may serve as important prognostic biomarkers (Hynes, 2009). Several clinical studies show that a low tumor stroma ratio (TSR) is linked to aggressive disease types and poor survival in various cancers (Mesker et al., 2007; Wu et al., 2024a). Surprisingly, stromal elements can also have tumor-suppressive roles in certain situations. For instance, complete removal of the stroma in pancreatic ductal adenocarcinoma led to more invasive tumors and lower overall survival rates (Rhim et al., 2014; Feig et al., 2013). This dual role reveals that the tumor stroma is not a passive structure, but a constantly evolving system with functional flexibility (Danac et al., 2021). Traditional cancer treatments generally focus on cancerous cells and often overlook the significant effects of stromal elements. The TME, which includes ECM remodeling, cancer-associated fibroblast (CAF) activation, cytokines, immune modulation, and the interactions between stromal and cancer cells, shields cancer cells from chemotherapy, radiotherapy, and targeted therapies (van Weverwijk and de Visser, 2023). As a result, stromal behavior is a key factor in treatment resistance and tumor recurrence. Given this context, there has been growing interest in therapies that target the TME and stroma. Various agents, including Edicotinib, Eganelisib, GM-CSF vaccines, and Erdafitinib (JNJ-42,756,493), have received FDA approval for their action on specific TME components; that highlights the importance and clinical potential of stroma-based treatment options (Bejarano et al., 2021). Given the rapidly expanding knowledge of stromal biology, cell communication, and tumor-stroma interactions, stroma-targeted treatment strategies are becoming a promising path for overcoming treatment resistance and improving patient survival (Bejarano et al., 2021). This chapter includes recent advancements in tumor stroma research, highlighting the roles of stromal components in cancer progression, and discussing new developments in stroma-targeted therapies. By combining cancer drugs with strategies aimed at the stroma, future treatment designs may achieve more effective, lasting, and personalized cancer care.

Components of tumor stroma

Extracellular matrix (ECM)

Extracellular matrix (ECM) is the largest non-cellular component of the tumor stroma, and it comprises fibrous proteins, proteoglycans, adhesion molecules, and over 300 different ECM proteins (Beyens and Valkenburg, 2018). In cancer, there is constant remolding of the ECM due to fibroblast-mediated deposition and degradation by matrix metalloproteases (MMPs) (Huang et al., 2022). In cancer, ECM gets abnormally compacted and hardened, thereby increasing tissue rigidity and impairing the entry of immunecells into the tumor mass. A hardened ECM activates the integrin-FAK/Src signaling pathway in cancer cells, thereby facilitating cancer cell migration, invasion, and metabolic alterations (Xiaoxuan Xu et al., 2022). Excessive collagen and hyaluronic acid deposition in the ECM forms a barrier against chemotherapeutic agent penetration, which is a problem in PDAC (Xu et al., 2022b). On the other hand, ECM functions as a storage site for factors like TGF-β, VEGF, and HGF, which are released as a result of ECM degradation and promote immunosuppression, tumor-induced angiogenesis, and cancer cell survival (Xu et al., 2022b).

Fibroblasts

Fibroblasts are key stromal cells that, together with endothelial cells, are crucial in the production of the ECM components collagen and fibronectin, among others. Fibroblasts are equally pivotal in the degradation of the matrix components using their matrix metalloproteinases. Fibroblasts are generally quiescent in normal tissues but play a fundamental role in the homeostasis and repair of tissues, as well as the detoxification of xenobiotics in the body using the cytochrome P450 enzymes. Fibroblasts are equally indispensable in the recruitment of immune cells through the production of cytokines and chemokines. Fibroblasts transform into alpha-smooth muscle actin-producing cells within injured tissues and tumors due to excessive production of collagen (Beyens and Valkenburg, 2018).

Cancer-associated fibroblasts (CAFs)

Cancer-associated fibroblasts (CAFs) are activated fibroblasts in cancer tumors, showing elevated proliferation, migration, and secretory activities. They play decisive roles in promoting tumorigenesis, epithelial–to-mesenchymal transition (EMT), angiogenesis, invasion, and drug resistance. CAFs secreting large amounts of soluble factors such as TGF-β, CXCL12, IL-6, IL-8, HGF, PDGF, and various MMPs have been shown to modulate the ECM to support strong malignancy. Different types of CAFs (CAF-S1, CAF-S2, CAF-S3, CAF-S4) have been proposed to display varied biological properties, in which CAF-S1 promotes immunosuppression, while CAF-S4 promotes matrix remodeling and invasion. CAFs have been demonstrated to support cancer cells in utilizing lactate and pyruvate via the "reverse Warburg effect," promoting cancer cells in performing their unique type of oxidative (Huang et al., 2022; Xu et al., 2022; Luo et al., 2022).

Osteoblasts

Osteoblasts are bone-forming stromal cells responsible for the secretion of type I collagen. They also control the process of bone remodeling through the regulation of osteoclast activity. Osteoblasts secrete RANKL and M-CSF. These factors promote osteoclast differentiation. During the course of bone metastasis, SDF-1/GAS6 is secreted by osteoblasts. These mediators cause the homing of tumor cells. The interaction of tumor cells with osteoblasts gives rise to a "vicious cycle". Osteoblast-induced osteoclast activation results in TGF-β release from the bone matrix. This enhances tumor cell proliferation (Beyens and Valkenburg, 2018).

Chondrocytes

Chondrocytes are unique cells involved in the production of cartilage ECM, such as proteoglycans and type II collagen. Chondrocytes are derived from mesenchymal stem cells (MSCs) and are known to play crucial roles in the development of the skeletal system as well as the upkeep of joints. Though the role of chondrocytes in carcinogenesis has not been investigated as widely as other stromal cells, they may still have a potential ability to affect carcinogenesis in cartilage-related cancers by modulating the stiffness of ECM (Beyens and Valkenburg, 2018).

Stroma–cancer interactions

Tumor-suppressing actions of the stroma

In early tumorigenesis, the normal stroma acts as a barrier against cancer progression by inhibiting epithelial proliferation, migration, and invasion. Fibroblast-derived TGF-β can function as an anti-proliferative factor and contributes to growth suppression in premalignant tissues. Endogenous tissue inhibitors of metalloproteinases (TIMPs) restrict ECM degradation and maintain stromal integrity, and their loss is associated with increased malignancy. In PDAC, the dense stromal matrix has been shown to restrict early tumor expansion; experimental stromal depletion unexpectedly increased tumor aggressiveness and immunosuppression. Some stromal niches also suppress metastatic outgrowth by maintaining disseminated tumor cells in a dormant state (Huang et al., 2022).

Tumor-promoting actions of the stroma

During cancer progression, the stroma becomes "reactive", characterized by desmoplasia, fibroblast activation, and excessive ECM deposition. CAFs alter the ECM by producing collagen, tenascin, and periostin, and by increasing MMP activity that facilitates tumor invasion. CAFs secrete various growth factors, cytokines, chemokines, and exosomes (including TGF-β, IL-6, IL-8, VEGF, PDGF, CXCL12), which promote cancer cell proliferation, EMT, angiogenesis, metastasis, and immune evasion. Senescent stromal cells release a senescence-associated secretory phenotype (SASP) rich in IL-6, IL-8, proteases, and metabolites that accelerate malignancy. Stromal cells in bone also enhance metastatic colonization and drive a sustained cycle of tumor-induced bone destruction. CAF-derived IL-6, NF-κB activation, exosomal miRNAs, and stiff ECM collectively contribute to chemoresistance and poor therapeutic response (Huang et al., 2022).

Interplay and crosstalk between intrastromal components

The tumor stroma is a dynamic and highly interactive network in which fibroblasts, CAFs, ECM, immune cells, endothelial cells, and bone-associated stromal cells continuously communicate to regulate tumor progression. This crosstalk is mediated through cytokines, chemokines, growth factors, ECM remodeling enzymes, and metabolic exchange processes (Liang et al., 2022). ECM not only provides structural support but also regulates signaling between stromal cells by storing growth factors such as TGF-β, VEGF, and HGF, which are released during matrix degradation and subsequently influence fibroblast activation, angiogenesis, and immune responses (Liang et al., 2022; Xu et al., 2022; Sharma et al., 2022). Activated fibroblasts and CAFs react to these cues by secreting a great deal of collagen, hyaluronan, periostin, and MMPs, which contribute to further ECM structural remodeling and an increased stiffness of the tumor microenvironment (Liu et al., 2019). ECM stiffening promotes integrin-FAK/Src pathway activation in both CAFs and cancer cells, and this serves as a positive feedback mechanism enhancing migration, invasion, and metabolic conversion (Zhang et al., 2022).

CAFs engage in incessant bidirectional signaling with immune and endothelial cells. Cytokines, including IL-6, IL-8, and CXCL12, secreted by CAFs regulate the recruitment of immune cells and myeloid suppressor cells, while VEGF stimulation promotes angiogenesis (Kondoh and Mizuno-Kamiya, 2022). The bidirectional signaling is additionally amplified by senescent stromal cells, senescence-associated secretory phenotypes (SASPs) of which accumulate inflammatory cytokines and proteases in the microenvironment, potentiating tumor-stimulating cues in different stromal cell types and compartments. Subpopulations of CAFs, named CAF-S1 and CAF-S4, possess particular roles for other stromal cells, CAF-S1 for the establishment of immunosuppression and CAF-S4 for cancer cell invasion, which stimulate ECM remodeling.

Osteoblasts and osteoclasts are in continuous communication with tumor cells via stromal cytokines such as RANK-L, M-CSF, and TGF-β in bone metastasis, thereby establishing a form of "vicious cycle" that links bone remodeling to the growth of metastasis. Osteoblast-derived SDF-1 and GAS6 attract circulating tumor cells to the bone microenvironment, while ECM degradation during bone resorption releases growth factors that promote tumor outgrowth. Overall, the crosstalk between intrastromal components creates a self-reinforcing system where fibroblasts, ECM, immune cells, endothelial cells, and bone stromal elements cooperate to sustain tumor progression, therapeutic resistance, and metastatic dissemination (Feng et al., 2025).

Effects of tumor stroma on therapy

The tumor stroma strongly influences the outcome of anticancer therapy by creating structural, biochemical, metabolic, and immunological barriers that protect malignant cells. Dense ECM, activated CAFs, abnormal vasculature, inflammatory mediators, stromal hypoxia, and tumor–stromal interactions together limit the effectiveness of chemotherapy, radiotherapy, targeted therapies, hormone antagonists, and immunotherapy. This stromal response supports cancer cell survival, promotes tumor persistence, and contributes to therapeutic failure in many solid tumors (Wu et al., 2024b).

Limiting drug access

The tumor ECM forms a major physical barrier that restricts drug penetration. Excessive deposition of collagen, hyaluronan, and fibronectin increases matrix stiffness and interstitial fluid pressure, which compresses tumor blood vessels and reduces perfusion. This limited vascular access significantly decreases the delivery of therapeutic molecules into the tumor interior. Highly desmoplastic tumors, such as pancreatic cancer, show particularly poor drug uptake because the dense stromal network blocks both diffusion and convection of drugs. CAF-mediated ECM remodeling further thickens the stromal compartment, making drug access progressively more difficult (Olive et al., 2009).

Resistance to cytotoxic chemotherapy

The stromal compartment promotes chemoresistance through cytokine signaling, ECM remodeling, and metabolic support. CAFs secrete IL-6, IL-8, and CXCL12, which activate STAT3, NF-κB, and PI3K/AKT pathways in cancer cells, enhancing survival and drug resistance. CAF-derived exosomes containing regulatory microRNAs suppress tumor-suppressive pathways and promote chemoresistance. Metabolic coupling between CAFs and tumor cells—particularly lactate and pyruvate transfer—further strengthens resistance by increasing cancer cell energy availability and reducing cytotoxic damage. Increased ECM stiffness additionally decreases drug uptake and activates pro-survival mechanotransduction pathways (Xu et al., 2015; Wang et al., 2016).

Resistance to radiation therapy

The stromal microenvironment contributes to radioresistance by generating hypoxia, protecting tumor cells from oxidative stress, and supporting DNA repair. Dense ECM reduces oxygen diffusion, creating hypoxic niches where HIF-1α is stabilized, thereby reducing radiosensitivity. CAFs secrete antioxidants and cytokines that diminish radiation-induced ROS and support cancer cell survival. Senescent stromal cells release SASP factors after radiation, promoting tumor cell regrowth and long-term radioresistance (Cordes, 2006; Hellevik et al., 2012).

Resistance to targeted therapies

Tumor stroma drives resistance to targeted therapies by activating compensatory survival pathways. CAFs release HGF, TGF-β, and PDGF, which trigger bypass signaling through MET, AKT, and Src even when oncogenic drivers are inhibited. ECM components such as fibronectin, tenascin-C, and periostin activate integrin-FAK signaling, enhancing cell survival despite targeted inhibition. CAF-derived cytokines, including IL-6 and CXCL12, increase tumor plasticity, promote EMT, and enable adaptation to targeted agents. Stromal remodeling is strongly associated with reduced effectiveness of kinase inhibitors in desmoplastic tumors (Yoshida et al., 2015; Hirata et al., 2015).

Resistance to hormone antagonists

Stromal signals reduce the response to hormone therapies by activating hormone-independent growth pathways. CAF-derived IL-6 and TGF-β stimulate STAT3 and SMAD signaling, enabling cancer cells to grow without estrogen or androgen stimulation. ECM stiffness activates integrin-FAK signaling, which supports hormone-independent proliferation. Inflammatory mediators within the tumor stroma activate NF-κB and other transcription factors that promote endocrine resistance and tumor persistence (Singh et al., 2014).

Resistance to immunotherapy

The tumor stroma promotes immunotherapy resistance by creating an immunosuppressive and physically restrictive microenvironment. CAFs secrete CXCL12, IL-6, IL-8, and TGF-β, which exclude cytotoxic T cells and recruit immunosuppressive cells such as Tregs and MDSCs. Dense ECM acts as a structural barrier that prevents T-cell infiltration, producing "immune-excluded" tumors unresponsive to checkpoint inhibitors. CAF-S1 subtypes generate highly immunosuppressive niches that reduce T-cell cytotoxicity and impair the immune response. Stromal hypoxia and abnormal vasculature further block immune cell trafficking and reduce immunotherapy efficacy (Pardoll, 2012; Gajewski et al., 2013).

Tumor–stroma targeting strategies

Effective cancer treatment increasingly requires approaches that also target the tumor stroma, because stromal elements can either inhibit or support tumor progression. In many cancers, the activated stroma enhances key malignant features and drives resistance to multiple therapies. In such settings, stroma-directed interventions can significantly improve treatment response and may contribute to more durable or curative outcomes (Özdemir et al., 2014). However, this approach must be used carefully. In certain tumor types, the stroma also performs tumor-restraining functions. Eliminating or suppressing these protective stromal components may unintentionally accelerate tumor growth. Therefore, stromal biomarkers that reflect stromal activity, tumor-promoting behavior, or tumor-suppressive roles are essential to guide appropriate therapeutic choices. Although several classes of stroma-targeting agents are available, using them as standalone treatments is generally insufficient to eradicate the tumor. Cancer cells retain their intrinsic genetic and epigenetic abnormalities, meaning they can eventually reactivate a supportive and reactive stroma even after stromal suppression. For this reason, stromal-targeting therapies are best applied in combination with conventional anticancer strategies such as chemotherapy, radiotherapy, or targeted agents. These combined approaches can weaken the stromal barrier, enhance drug penetration, and simultaneously attack both tumor cells and the supportive microenvironment. Table 4.1 Enlist a few tumor stroma targeting strategies, which are discussed below.

Targeting the ECM

Many therapeutic strategies focus on reducing the density and stiffness of the extracellular matrix (ECM) so that anticancer drugs can penetrate the tumor more effectively. Halofuginone is one such agent that suppresses the production of type I collagen, and this reduction in collagen helps lower desmoplasia (Provenzano et al., 2012). In melanoma xenograft models, halofuginone has been found to reduce the erosion of bone tissue and the extent of metastasis in the bones as well. The strategy in this case involves a functional modification of hyaluronic acid present in tumor stroma. The PEGylated hyaluronidase inhibitor and the 4-umbelliferone inhibitor are known to block the production and secretion of hyaluronic acid in the tumor tissue. By decreasing concentrations of hyaluronic acid, there is a consequent reduction in interstitial fluid pressure, which in turn improves the uptake of pharmacologic therapy in tumor tissue. Lysyl-oxidase is an enzyme improving the cross-linking of collagen fibers in the tumor stroma, which possesses higher levels of LOX activity. An LOX inhibitor will block the aggressive over-cross-linking of collagen, thereby

TABLE 4.1 Tumor–stroma targeting strategies.

Sr. No.	Strategy	Main target	Mechanistic approach	Response	References
1.	Targeting the ECM	Collagen, Hyaluronan, LOX	Halofuginone, PEG-hyaluronidase, HA inhibitors, LOX inhibitors	Reduced ECM stiffness, lower pressure, improved drug penetration	(Kalluri, 2016; Miller et al., 2015)
2.	ECM-based therapeutic delivery	Bone ECM	Bisphosphonates, Radium-223	Blocks bone turnover; targeted killing of bone metastases	(Clézardin, 2013; Weilbaecher et al., 2011)
3.	Targeting stromal cell proteins	FAP, αSMA, TGFβR, CYP3A4, CYP26	Anti-FAP antibodies, FAP-DM1, ATRA, CYP inhibitors	Reduced CAF activity, less ECM secretion, reversed chemoresistance	(Hofheinz et al., 2003; Fischer et al., 2012)
4.	Targeting cancer–stroma signaling	FGFR, TGF-β, CXCR4/SDF-1	RTK inhibitors, ligand traps, anti-TGF-β, AMD3100	Blocks stromal signals; enhanced therapy response	(Bai et al., 2010; Gozgit et al., 2012)
5.	Stromal-antigen immunotherapy	FAP, ECM antigens	FAP-CAR-T, ECM-targeted immune cells	Immune-mediated stromal depletion	Su et al. (2023)
6.	Stromal-component–based drug delivery	Collagen, Fibronectin, HA, FAP	ECM-binding nanoparticles, HA–CD44 targeting, FAP-liposomes	Selective accumulation of drugs in stroma-rich tumors	Kesharwani et al. (2022)
7.	Drug delivery for stromal remodeling	CAF markers, LOX, TGF-β	LOX-inhibitor nanoparticles, CAF-targeted nanocarriers, siRNA	Softer ECM, better perfusion, enhanced intratumoral drug spread	(Huang et al., 2024)

generating a loose or flexible ECM. Other compounds, such as the vitamin D receptor agonist calcipotriol and all-trans retinoic acid (ATRA), also demonstrate antifibrotic effects. Studies using pancreatic ductal adenocarcinoma (PDAC) models show that both agents can reduce stromal fibrosis, which further assists in improving drug penetration and therapeutic outcomes (Miller et al., 2015).

ECM-based approaches to target the TME

A few therapeutic strategies, instead of attacking cancer cells or stromal cells, exploit ECM components to deliver treatment specifically to tumor sites. Bisphosphonates are well-known examples that were originally developed to manage bone metastases. Rather than killing tumor cells directly, bisphosphonates disrupt bone turnover and break the cycle that supports tumor growth in bone (Clézardin, 2013). They are absorbed by osteoclasts and block bone resorption, which also lowers osteoblast activity in the bone microenvironment. Although bisphosphonates reduce skeletal-related events in patients with bone metastases, they rarely improve overall survival (Weilbaecher et al., 2011). Evidence suggests that administering bisphosphonates earlier than tumor cells entery in the pre-metastatic bone niche, may prevent overt metastasis.

Targeting proteins expressed by stromal cells

The tumor stroma can also be targeted by focusing on specific proteins expressed by stromal cells that regulate their growth, secretion, and ECM production. One major target is **fibroblast activation protein (FAP)**. Early trials using the anti-FAP antibody **F19** for colorectal cancer showed no clinical benefit, likely because the antibody could not trigger effective immune-mediated killing of FAP-positive stromal cells. Later, this approach was improved by attaching cytotoxic drugs to anti-FAP antibodies (Hofheinz et al., 2003). One example is **FAP5–DM1,** in which the antibody delivers maytansine (DM1) directly into FAP-positive fibroblasts. After internalization and drug release, strong stromal depletion and tumor regression were observed in several xenograft models. Radio-labeled anti-FAP antibodies, such as those carrying **177Lu,** also produced stromal damage in melanoma models. Another method uses the natural protease activity of FAP to activate the prodrug **promelittin,** releasing melittin, a cytolytic toxin that kills nearby tumor and stromal cells. Although less specific to CAFs, this approach may offer stronger tumor-killing effects but also carries a risk of increased toxicity. **ATRA** is another agent that suppresses CAF activity by reducing FAP, αSMA, and TGFβR expression, lowering ECM and cytokine production, and limiting cancer cell invasion. However, ATRA is metabolized by **CYP26**, reducing its effectiveness; blocking CYP26 restores sensitivity in myeloma models. Similarly, the stromal enzyme **CYP3A4** deactivates docetaxel, and inhibiting CYP3A4 with **clarithromycin** restores docetaxel's cytotoxicity. This approach may help patients with prostate cancer bone metastasis, where docetaxel is widely used but recurrence is common (Fischer et al., 2012; LeBeau et al., 2009).

Targeting cancer cell stroma signaling interactions

Blocking the receptors on cancer cells that respond to stromal-secreted factors is an indirect way to target the tumor stroma. Although these therapies act on cancer cells, they disrupt the growth signals provided by stromal cells. However, many cancer cells carry mutations or overexpress RTKs, allowing them to grow even without stromal support. Still, interfering with these pathways helps reduce stromal-driven tumorprogression. Cancer-associated fibroblasts (CAFs) commonly release FGFs. Several therapies target this pathway, including RTK inhibitors like **dovitinib** (targets FGFR3) and monoclonal antibodies such as **GP369** (targets FGFR2-IIIb) (Bai et al., 2010). Blocking the **FGF2/FGF2R** signaling axis in xenograft models prevents resistance to **bevacizumab**. Another approach uses an FGF ligand trap— a soluble fusion protein combining **FGFR1-IIIc** with an **IgG1 Fc domain**—to block stromal FGFs from binding cancer cell receptors (Gozgit et al., 2012). Combination treatments often show stronger effects than single agents. In breast cancer mouse models, radiation and chemotherapy increased circulating **TGFβ** levels. Adding a TGFβ-neutralizing antibody reduced circulating tumor cells and lung metastasis (Chae et al., 2017). In prostate cancer, osteoblast-secreted **SDF1** attracts tumor cells to the bone marrow niche. The CXCR4 inhibitor **AMD3100** disrupts this interaction, forcing cancer cells out of the niche and into the bloodstream, where they are more vulnerable to therapy. Targeting **CXCR4** in PDAC stroma also increased immune-cell infiltration and improved responses to immunotherapy. These findings suggest that combining AMD3100 with chemotherapy or immunotherapy may produce powerful therapeutic results (Sun et al., 2003).

Targeting stromal antigens with immune cells

CAR-T cells can be engineered to recognize stromal antigens and attack tumor-supporting cells. FAP-targeted CAR-T cells specifically eliminate FAP-positive CAFs and can enter the tumor by moving through the ECM (Stromnes et al., 2014). In mouse models, FAP-CAR-T cells showed strong antitumor effects, and their activity increased further when combined with CAR-T cells directed against tumor antigens such as EphA2. FAP-based cancer vaccines are another stromal-targeting strategy. Eliminating FAP-positive CAFs reduces collagen density in the ECM, improving drug penetration and enhancing immune responses. These vaccines can drive tumor regression alone, but may work even better in combination therapies. Macrophages can also modulate the stroma (Beatty et al., 2011). CD40 agonists activate macrophages and increase MMP activity, leading to ECM breakdown. This enhances the entry of immune cells and stimulates sensitivity to anti-checkpoint drugs, making way for promising future research for CD40-based therapies. Engineered chondrocytes are another novel method. Fibroblasts differentiated into chondrocytes, with targeted overexpression of IL-12, were capable of increasing the number of T and NK cell infiltration into colon cancer models. This impacted the inhibition of tumor growth and angiogenesis, paving the way for immunotherapy combinations (Su et al., 2023).

Targeted drug delivery system based on tumor stromal components

The tumor stromal elements can be employed as target-specific carriers for the drug to be directly administered into the tumor microenvironment. The high ECM density components like collagen, fibronectin, and hyaluronan can be overexpressed in the tumor and can be employed as binding materials for drug-laden nanoparticles. The collagen-targeted peptides, like CREKA and RGD peptides, can guide the nanoparticles to the stromal tumor and can increase the retention of the drug in the tumor. The drug-laden nanoparticles coated with hyaluronan can target the CD44-positive stromal and tumor cells. Fibroblast activation protein (FAP)–targeted liposomes and nanoparticles enable delivery of chemotherapeutic agents specifically to CAF-rich regions, improving drug penetration and therapeutic outcomes. Enzyme-responsive nanocarriers activated by stromal MMPs or LOX release drugs only within the tumor stroma, increasing precision and minimizing off-target effects. These stromal-based delivery systems overcome physical barriers, enhance drug concentration inside tumors, and improve the overall therapeutic response (Kesharwani et al., 2022; Desai et al., 2025).

Targeted drug delivery strategies for tumor stroma remodeling

The goal of targeted drug delivery for stromal remodeling is the reduction and/or modification of the tumor stroma to improve the penetration of drugs. Nanoparticle delivery of matrix-modulating agents like hyaluronidase, LOX inhibitors, and collagenase can resolve the matrix hardness and interstitial pressures while facilitating drug delivery into the tumor. Targeting CAFs using ligands for FAP, PDGFRβ, and/or αSMA can deliver drugs that can suppress the activation of fibroblasts, decrease the production of the extracellular matrix, and modulate the stroma towards a tumor suppressive phenotype. Using TGF-β inhibitors or nanocarried siRNA can modulate the stroma towards suppressing the signaling pathway towards tumor-associated fibrosis. Enzyme-activated nanoplatforms can specifically release drug molecules within the stroma by utilizing stromal matrix metalloproteinases and reactive oxygen species to remodel the stroma, thereby targeting the site of action without distributing drug molecules throughout the entire body. These methods, when combined, can soften the tumor stroma and enhance drug delivery into the tumors (Huang et al., 2024).

Conclusion

Every cellular and non-cellular component of the tumor stroma has the capacity to interact in highly controlled two-way conversations with cancer cells, which are responsible for the growth of cancer, metastasis, and resistance mechanisms to cancer treatments. The potential for stroma-targeted cancer treatments is laid out by these advancements. Understanding the interactions between cancer cells and stroma in stroma-dominant types of malignancy is sufficient to encourage the development of novel therapy modalities. In conclusion, stroma-targeted treatments for cancer are expected to offer a new vista of benefits for cancer patients.

References

Bai, A., Meetze, K., Vo, N.Y., Kollipara, S., Mazsa, E.K., Winston, W.M., Weiler, S., Poling, L.L., Chen, T., Ismail, N. S., Jiang, J., Lerner, L., Gyuris, J., Weng, Z., 2010. GP369, an FGFR2-IIIb-specific antibody, exhibits potent anti-tumor activity against human cancers driven by activated FGFR2 signaling. Cancer Res. 70 (19), 7630–7639. https://doi.org/10.1158/0008-5472.CAN-10-1489.

Beatty, G.L., Chiorean, E.G., Fishman, M.P., Saboury, B., Teitelbaum, U.R., Sun, W., Huhn, R.D., Song, W., Li, D., Sharp, L.L., Torigian, D.A., O'Dwyer, P.J., Vonderheide, R.H., 2011. CD40 agonists alter tumor stroma and show efficacy against pancreatic carcinoma in mice and humans. Science 331 (6024), 1612–1616. https://doi.org/10.1126/science.1198443.

Bejarano, L., Jordão, M.J.C., Joyce, J.A., 2021. Therapeutic targeting of the tumor microenvironment. Cancer Discov. 11 (4), 933–959. https://doi.org/10.1158/2159-8290.CD-20-1808.

Beyens, I., Valkenburg, P.M., 2018. Jessica Taylor Piotrowski, Screen media use and ADHD-related behaviors: Four decades of research. Proc. Natl. Acad. Sci. 115 (40), 9875–9881. https://doi.org/10.1073/pnas.1611611114.

Chae, Y.K., Ranganath, K., Hammerman, P.S., Vaklavas, C., Mohindra, N., Kalyan, A., Matsangou, M., Costa, R., Carneiro, B., Villaflor, V.M., Cristofanilli, M., Giles, F.J., 2017. Inhibition of the fibroblast growth factor receptor (FGFR) pathway: The current landscape and barriers to clinical application. Oncotarget 8 (9), 16052–16074. https://doi.org/10.18632/oncotarget.14109.

Clézardin, P., 2013. Mechanisms of action of bisphosphonates in oncology: A scientific concept evolving from antiresorptive to anticancer activities. Bonekey Rep. 2. https://doi.org/10.1038/bonekey.2013.1.

Cordes, N., 2006. Integrin-mediated cell–matrix interactions for prosurvival and antiapoptotic signaling after genotoxic injury. Cancer Lett. 242 (1), 11–19. https://doi.org/10.1016/j.canlet.2005.12.004.

Danac, J.M.C., Uy, A.G.G., Garcia, R.L., 2021. Exosomal microRNAs in colorectal cancer: Overcoming barriers of the metastatic cascade (Review). Int. J. Mol. Med. 47 (6). https://doi.org/10.3892/ijmm.2021.4945.

Desai, N., Sahel, D., Kubal, B., Postwala, H., Shah, Y., Chavda, V.P., Fernandes, C., Khatri, D.K., Vora, L.K., 2025. Role of the extracellular matrix in cancer: Insights into tumor progression and therapy. Adv. Therapeut. 8 (2). https://doi.org/10.1002/adtp.202400370.

Dominici, M., Le Blanc, K., Mueller, I., Slaper-Cortenbach, I., C Marini, F., Krause, D.S., Deans, R.J., Keating, A., Prockop, D.J., Horwitz, E.M., 2006. Minimal criteria for defining multipotent mesenchymal stromal cells. the international society for cellular therapy position statement. Cytotherapy 8 (4), 315–317. https://doi.org/10.1080/14653240600855905.

Feig, C., Jones, J.O., Kraman, M., Wells, R.J.B., Deonarine, A., Chan, D.S., Connell, C.M., Roberts, E.W., Qi, Z., Caballero, O.L., Teichmann, S.A., Janowitz, T., Jodrell, D.I., Tuveson, D.A., Fearon, D.T., 2013. Targeting CXCL12 from FAP-expressing carcinoma-associated fibroblasts synergizes with anti–PD-L1 immunotherapy in pancreatic cancer. Proc. Natl. Acad. Sci. 110 (50), 20212–20217. https://doi.org/10.1073/pnas.1320318110.

Feng, Q.S., Shan, X.F., Yau, V., Cai, Z.G., Xie, S., 2025. Facilitation of tumor stroma-targeted therapy: Model difficulty and co-culture organoid method. Pharmaceuticals 18 (1). https://doi.org/10.3390/ph18010062.

Fischer, E., Chaitanya, K., Wuëst, T., Wadle, A., Scott, A.M., Van Den Broek, M., Schibli, R., Bauer, S., Renner, C., 2012. Radioimmunotherapy of fibroblast activation protein positive tumors by rapidly internalizing antibodies. Clin. Cancer Res. 18 (22), 6208–6218. https://doi.org/10.1158/1078-0432.CCR-12-0644.

Gajewski, T.F., Schreiber, H., Fu, Y.X., 2013. Innate and adaptive immune cells in the tumor microenvironment. Nat. Immunol. 14 (10), 1014–1022. https://doi.org/10.1038/ni.2703.

Gozgit, J.M., Wong, M.J., Moran, L., Wardwell, S., Mohemmad, Q.K., Narasimhan, N.I., Shakespeare, W.C., Wang, F., Clackson, T., Rivera, V.M., 2012. Ponatinib (AP24534), a multitargeted pan-FGFR inhibitor with activity in multiple FGFR-amplified or mutated cancer models. Mol. Cancer Therapeut. 11 (3), 690–699. https://doi.org/10.1158/1535-7163.MCT-11-0450.

Hanahan, D., Weinberg, R.A., 2011. Hallmarks of cancer: The next generation. Cell 144 (5), 646–674. https://doi.org/10.1016/j.cell.2011.02.013.

Hellevik, T., Pettersen, I., Berg, V., Winberg, J.O., Moe, B.T., Bartnes, K., Paulssen, R.H., Busund, L.T., Bremnes, R., Chalmers, A., Martinez-Zubiaurre, I., 2012. Cancer-associated fibroblasts from human NSCLC survive ablative doses of radiation but their invasive capacity is reduced. Radiat. Oncol. 7 (1). https://doi.org/10.1186/1748-717X-7-59Norway.

Hirata, E., Girotti, M.R., Viros, A., Hooper, S., Spencer-Dene, B., Matsuda, M., Larkin, J., Marais, R., Sahai, E., 2015. Intravital imaging reveals how BRAF inhibition generates drug-tolerant microenvironments with high integrin β1/FAK signaling. Cancer Cell 27 (4), 574–588. https://doi.org/10.1016/j.ccell.2015.03.008.

Hofheinz, R.-D., al-Batran, S.-E., Hartmann, F., Hartung, G., Jäger, D., Renner, C., Tanswell, P., Kunz, U., Amelsberg, A., Kuthan, H., Stehle, G., 2003. Stromal antigen targeting by a humanised monoclonal antibody: An early phase II trial of sibrotuzumab in patients with metastatic colorectal cancer. Oncol. Res. Treat. 26 (1), 44–48. https://doi.org/10.1159/000069863.

Huang, H.Y., Lin, Y.C.D., Cui, S., Huang, Y., Tang, Y., Xu, J., Bao, J., Li, Y., Wen, J., Zuo, H., Wang, W., Li, J., Ni, J., Ruan, Y., Li, L., Chen, Y., Xie, Y., Zhu, Z., Cai, X., Chen, X., Yao, L., Chen, Y., Luo, Y., Luxu, S., Luo, M., Chiu, C. M., Ma, K., Zhu, L., Cheng, G.J., Bai, C., Chiang, Y.C., Wang, L., Wei, F., Lee, T.Y., Huang, H.D., 2022. MiRTarBase update 2022: An informative resource for experimentally validated miRNA-target interactions. Nucleic Acids Res. 50 (1), D222. https://doi.org/10.1093/nar/gkab1079.

Huang, Q., Ge, Y., He, Y., Wu, J., Tong, Y., Shang, H., Liu, X., Ba, X., Xia, D., Peng, E., Chen, Z., Tang, K., 2024. The application of nanoparticles targeting cancer-associated fibroblasts. Int. J. Nanomed. 19, 3333–3365. https://doi.org/10.2147/ijn.s447350.

Hynes, R.O., 2009. The extracellular matrix: Not just pretty fibrils. Science 326 (5957), 1216–1219. https://doi.org/10.1126/science.1176009.

Kalluri, R., 2016. The biology and function of fibroblasts in cancer. Nat. Rev. Cancer 16 (9), 582–598. https://doi.org/10.1038/nrc.2016.73.

Kesharwani, P., Chadar, R., Sheikh, A., Rizg, W.Y., Safhi, A.Y., 2022. CD44-Targeted nanocarrier for cancer therapy. Front Pharmacol 12. https://doi.org/10.3389/fphar.2021.800481.

Kondoh, N., Mizuno-Kamiya, M., 2022. The role of immune modulatory cytokines in the tumor microenvironments of head and neck squamous cell carcinomas. Cancers 14 (12), 2884. https://doi.org/10.3390/cancers14122884.

LeBeau, A.M., Brennen, W.N., Aggarwal, S., Denmeade, S.R., 2009. Targeting the cancer stroma with a fibroblast activation protein-activated promelittin protoxin. Mol. Cancer Therapeut. 8 (5), 1378–1386. https://doi.org/10.1158/1535-7163.MCT-08-1170.

LeBleu, V.S., Kalluri, R., 2018. A peek into cancer-associated fibroblasts: Origins, functions and translational impact. Dis. Model. Mech. 11 (4). https://doi.org/10.1242/dmm.029447.

Liang, L., Li, W., Li, X., Jin, X., Liao, Q., Li, Y., et al., 2022. Reverse Warburg effect' of cancer-associated fibroblasts. Int. J. Oncol. 60, 1–13.

Liu, T., Zhou, L., Li, D., Andl, T., Zhang, Y., 2019. Cancer-associated fibroblasts build and secure the tumor microenvironment. Front. Cell Dev. Biol. 7. https://doi.org/10.3389/fcell.2019.00060.

Luo, H., Xia, X., Huang, L.B., An, H., Cao, M., Kim, G.D., Chen, H.N., Zhang, W.H., Shu, Y., Kong, X., Ren, Z., Li, P. H., Liu, Y., Tang, H., Sun, R., Li, C., Bai, B., Jia, W., Liu, Y., Zhang, W., Yang, L., Peng, Y., Dai, L., Hu, H., Jiang, Y., Hu, Y., Zhu, J., Jiang, H., Li, Z., Caulin, C., Park, J., Xu, H., 2022. Pan-cancer single-cell analysis reveals the heterogeneity and plasticity of cancer-associated fibroblasts in the tumor microenvironment. Nat. Commun. 13 (1). https://doi.org/10.1038/s41467-022-34395-2.

Mesker, W.E., Junggeburt, J.M.C., Szuhai, K., de Heer, P., Morreau, H., Tanke, H.J., Tollenaar, R.A.E.M., 2007. The carcinoma–stromal ratio of colon carcinoma is an independent factor for survival compared to lymph node status and tumor stage. Anal. Cell. Pathol. 29 (5), 387–398. https://doi.org/10.1155/2007/175276.

Miller, B.W., Morton, J.P., Pinese, M., Saturno, G., Jamieson, N.B., Mcghee, E., Timpson, P., Leach, J., Mcgarry, L., Shanks, E., Bailey, P., Chang, D., Oien, K., Karim, S., Au, A., Steele, C., Carter, C.R., Mckay, C., Anderson, K., Evans, T.R.J., Marais, R., Springer, C., Biankin, A., Erler, J.T., Sansom, O.J., 2015. Targeting the LOX/hypoxia axis reverses many of the features that make pancreatic cancer deadly: Inhibition of LOX abrogates metastasis and enhances drug efficacy. EMBO. Mol. Med. 7 (8), 1063–1076. https://doi.org/10.15252/emmm.201404827.

Olive, K.P., Jacobetz, M.A., Davidson, C.J., Gopinathan, A., McIntyre, D., Honess, D., Madhu, B., Goldgraben, M.A., Caldwell, M.E., Allard, D., Frese, K.K., DeNicola, G., Feig, C., Combs, C., Winter, S.P., Ireland-Zecchini, H., Reichelt, S., Howat, W.J., Chang, A., Dhara, M., Wang, L., Rückert, F., Grützmann, R., Pilarsky, C., Izeradjene, K., Hingorani, S.R., Huang, P., Davies, S.E., Plunkett, W., Egorin, M., Hruban, R.H., Whitebread, N., McGovern, K., Adams, J., Iacobuzio-Donahue, C., Griffiths, J., Tuveson, D.A., 2009. Inhibition of Hedgehog signaling enhances delivery of chemotherapy in a mouse model of pancreatic cancer. Science 324 (5933), 1457–1461. https://doi.org/10.1126/science.1171362.

Özdemir, B.C., Pentcheva-Hoang, T., Carstens, J.L., Zheng, X., Wu, C.C., Simpson, T.R., Laklai, H., Sugimoto, H., Kahlert, C., Novitskiy, S.V., DeJesus-Acosta, A., Sharma, P., Heidari, P., Mahmood, U., Chin, L., Moses, H.L., Weaver, V.M., Maitra, A., Allison, J.P., LeBleu, V.S., Kalluri, R., 2014. Depletion of carcinoma-associated fibroblasts and fibrosis induces immunosuppression and accelerates pancreas cancer with reduced survival. Cancer Cell 25 (6), 719–734. https://doi.org/10.1016/j.ccr.2014.04.005.

Paget, S., 1889. The distribution of secondary growths in cancer of the breast. Lancet. 01406736. 133 (3421), 571–573. https://doi.org/10.1016/s0140-6736(00)49915-0.

Pardoll, D.M., 2012. The blockade of immune checkpoints in cancer immunotherapy. Nat. Rev. Cancer 12 (4), 252–264. https://doi.org/10.1038/nrc3239.

Provenzano, P.P., Cuevas, C., Chang, A.E., Goel, V.K., Von Hoff, D.D., Hingorani, S.R., 2012. Enzymatic targeting of the stroma ablates physical barriers to treatment of pancreatic ductal adenocarcinoma. Cancer Cell 21 (3), 418–429. https://doi.org/10.1016/j.ccr.2012.01.007.

Rhim, A.D., Oberstein, P.E., Thomas, D.H., Mirek, E.T., Palermo, C.F., Sastra, S.A., Dekleva, E.N., Saunders, T., Becerra, C.P., Tattersall, I.W., Westphalen, C.B., Kitajewski, J., Fernandez-Barrena, M.G., Fernandez-Zapico, M.E., Iacobuzio-Donahue, C., Olive, K.P., Stanger, B.Z., 2014. Stromal elements act to restrain, rather than support, pancreatic ductal adenocarcinoma. Cancer Cell 25 (6), 735–747. https://doi.org/10.1016/j.ccr.2014.04.021.

Sharma, V., Letson, J., Furuta, S., stroma, F., 2022. Driver and passenger in cancer development. Sci. Signal 15 (724). https://doi.org/10.1126/scisignal.abg3449.

Siegel, R.L., Miller, K.D., Wagle, N.S., Jemal, A., 2023. Cancer statistics, 2023. CA. Cancer J. Clin. 73 (1), 17–48. https://doi.org/10.3322/caac.21763.

Singh, M., Jha, R., Melamed, J., Shapiro, E., Hayward, S.W., Lee, P., 2014. Stromal androgen receptor in prostate development and cancer. Am. J. Pathol. 184 (10), 2598–2607. https://doi.org/10.1016/j.ajpath.2014.06.022.

Stromnes, I.M., Schmitt, T.M., Chapuis, A.G., Hingorani, S.R., Greenberg, P.D., 2014. Re-adapting T cells for cancer therapy: From mouse models to clinical trials. Immunol. Rev. 257 (1), 145–164. https://doi.org/10.1111/imr.12141.

Su, M.C., Nethi, S.K., Dhanyamraju, P.K., Prabha, S., 2023. Nanomedicine strategies for targeting tumor stroma. Cancers 15 (16). https://doi.org/10.3390/cancers15164145.

Sun, Y.X., Wang, J., Shelburne, C.E., Lopatin, D.E., Chinnaiyan, A.M., Rubin, M.A., Pienta, K.J., Taichman, R.S., 2003. Expression of CXCR4 and CXCL12 (SDF-1) in human prostate cancers (PCa) in vivo. J. Cell. Biochem. 89 (3), 462–473. https://doi.org/10.1002/jcb.10522.

van Weverwijk, A., de Visser, K.E., 2023. Mechanisms driving the immunoregulatory function of cancer cells. Nat. Rev. Cancer 23 (4), 193–215. https://doi.org/10.1038/s41568-022-00544-4.

Wang, W., Kryczek, I., Dostál, L., Lin, H., Tan, L., Zhao, L., Lu, F., Wei, S., Maj, T., Peng, D., He, G., Vatan, L., Szeliga, W., Kuick, R., Kotarski, J., Tarkowski, R., Dou, Y., Rattan, R., Munkarah, A., Liu, J.R., Zou, W., 2016. Effector T cells abrogate stroma-mediated chemoresistance in ovarian cancer. Cell 165 (5), 1092–1105. https://doi.org/10.1016/j.cell.2016.04.009.

Weilbaecher, K.N., Guise, T.A., McCauley, L.K., 2011. Cancer to bone: A fatal attraction. Nat. Rev. Cancer 11 (6), 411–425. https://doi.org/10.1038/nrc3055.

Wu, X., Zhang, S., Zhang, Z., He, Z., Xu, Z., Wang, W., Jin, Z., You, J., Guo, Y., Zhang, L., Huang, W., Wang, F., Liu, X., Yan, D., Cheng, J., Yan, J., Zhang, S., Zhang, B., 2024a. Biologically interpretable multi-task deep learning pipeline predicts molecular alterations, grade, and prognosis in glioma patients. NPJ. Precis. Oncol 8 (1). https://doi.org/10.1038/s41698-024-00670-2.

Whiteside, T.L., 2008. The tumor microenvironment and its role in promoting tumor growth. Oncogene 27 (45), 5904–5912. https://doi.org/10.1038/onc.2008.271.

Wu, C., Zhai, Y., Ji, J., Yang, X., Ye, L., Lu, G., Shi, X., Zhai, G., 2024b. Advances in tumor stroma-based targeted delivery. Int. J. Pharm. 664, 124580. https://doi.org/10.1016/j.ijpharm.2024.124580.

Xu, K., Cai, Y.s., Lu, S.M., Li, X.l., Liu, L., Li, Z., Liu, H., Xu, P., 2015. Autophagy induction contributes to the resistance to methotrexate treatment in rheumatoid arthritis fibroblast-like synovial cells through high mobility group box chromosomal protein 1. Arthritis Res. Ther. 17 (1). https://doi.org/10.1186/s13075-015-0892-y.

Xu, M., Zhang, T., Xia, R., Wei, Y., Wei, X., 2022a. Targeting the tumor stroma for cancer therapy. Mol. Cancer 21 (1). https://doi.org/10.1186/s12943-022-01670-1.

Xu, X., Wu, Y., Qian, X., Wang, Y., Wang, J., Li, J., Li, Y., Zhang, Z., 2022b. Nanomedicine strategies to circumvent intratumor extracellular matrix barriers for cancer therapy. Adv. Healthc. Mater. 11 (1). https://doi.org/10.1002/adhm.202101428.

Yoshida, T., Ishii, G., Goto, K., Neri, S., Hashimoto, H., Yoh, K., Niho, S., Umemura, S., Matsumoto, S., Ohmatsu, H., Iida, S., Niimi, A., Nagai, K., Ohe, Y., Ochiai, A., 2015. Podoplanin-positive cancer-associated fibroblasts in the tumor microenvironment induce primary resistance to EGFR-TKIs in lung adenocarcinoma with EGFR mutation. Clin. Cancer Res. 21 (3), 642–651. https://doi.org/10.1158/1078-0432.ccr-14-0846.

Zhang, Z., Li, J., Jiao, S., Han, G., Zhu, J., Liu, T., 2022. Functional and clinical characteristics of focal adhesion kinases in cancer progression. Front. Cell Dev. Biol. 10. https://doi.org/10.3389/fcell.2022.1040311.

CHAPTER

5

Targeting cancer cell respiration in hypoxic and acidic tumor microenvironment: Exploring the therapeutic interventions

Shankar Gupta[1], *Chahat Chahat*[1], *Manvendra Kumar*[2], *Bhupinder Kumar*[1], *Muhammad Wahajuddin*[3] and *Gaurav Joshi*[1, 3]

[1]Department of Pharmaceutical Science, Hemvati Nandan Bahuguna Garhwal University (HNBGU), Srinagar, Uttarakhand, India; [2]Amity Institue of Pharmacy, Amity University, Noida, Uttar Pradesh, India; [3]Institute of Cancer Therapeutics, School of Pharmacy, Optometry and Medical Sciences, University of Bradford, Bradford, United Kingdom

Cancer

Cancer is still considered one of the deadliest diseases worldwide (Zottl et al., 2025). According to the Global Cancer Observatory (Bray et al., 2024) data, approximately 20 million new cancer cases (with lung cancer accounting for the highest incidence, 12.4%) were reported globally in 2022. Additionally, 10 million cancer deaths (with Lung cancer accounting for the highest proportion, 18.7%) were reported worldwide in the same year. Despite advances in cancer diagnosis and therapeutic approaches, the increase in cancer cases underscores the immediate need for better diagnostic methods and the development of new therapeutic agents. Anticancer drug therapies are designed to suppress or kill tumor cells, and their effectiveness does not depend on interactions between tumor cells. Their success also depends on the surrounding non-tumor components, collectively called the tumor microenvironment (TME) (Li and Dalton, 2006). TME functions as a nurturing ecosystem that supplies the cancer cell with essential nutrients, ensures the oxygen supply via angiogenesis, evades the impact of immune attack, remodels the surrounding tissues, and enables

Advanced Cancer Therapeutics
https://doi.org/10.1016/B978-0-443-44185-1.00036-7

the cascade of oncogenic signaling necessary for cancer cell growth and survival. It includes a variety of components, such as stromal cells, immune cells, soluble factors (e.g., cytokines and growth factors), blood vessels, the extracellular matrix (ECM), and physiological conditions, including low oxygen (hypoxia) or acidic pH. These microenvironmental features can reduce drug penetration, provide survival signals, promote repair of drug-induced damage, and suppress programmed cell death, resulting in more drug-resistant characteristics (Fig. 5.1) (Khalaf et al., 2021). Moreover, interactions between tumor cells and non-tumor cells, either through direct contact or via secreted mediators, can trigger various pathways that allow tumor cells to survive at the initial doses of therapy, and later, they develop complete resistance. Therefore, understanding these influences is essential for improving treatment outcomes and circumventing drug resistance in cancer (Li and Dalton, 2006). The present chapter is devoted to elaborating on the interactions between cancer cell respiration, the environment's pH, and hypoxia, and reviews therapeutic approaches that capitalize on these interactions. This chapter also explains the numerous druggable targets and their inhibitors to reduce tumor hypoxia and acidosis.

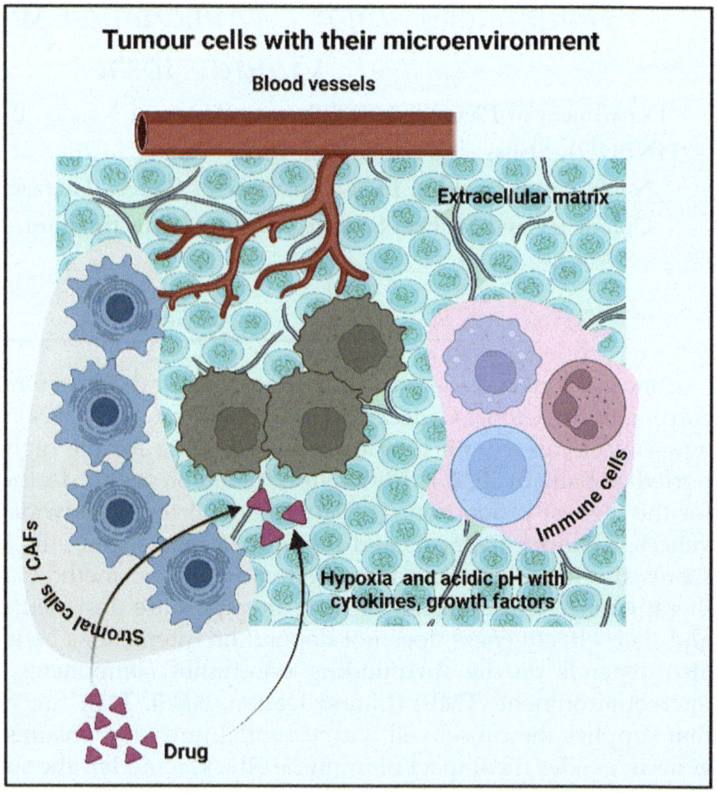

FIGURE 5.1 Tumor microenvironment (TME), including stromal cells (CAFs), immune cells (e.g., TAMs), abnormal vasculature, dense ECM, soluble factors (cytokines, growth factors), and physiological conditions (hypoxia, acidic pH), which reduces anticancer drug penetration.

Correlating pH and hypoxia with cancer cell survival and prognosis

When low oxygen levels (hypoxia) and low pH (acidosis) are observed in the tumor microenvironment (TME), cancer cells exhibit aggressive behavior, and these modifications trigger their survival, development, spread, and resistance to treatment, whereas these conditions are toxic to normal cells. Multiple signaling pathways regulate how cancer cells interact and respond to their surrounding environment. These pathways function both within the cell and within the ECM. The cancer cell microenvironment actively participates in the proliferation, invasion, and metastasis of cancer cells. Basically, in the TME, cancer-associated fibroblasts (CAFs) are capable to recruit stromal cells, immune cells and vascular cells by releasing several stimulatory growth factors, including TGF-β (Transforming Growth Factor-beta), VEGF (Vascular Endothelial Growth Factor), and FGF (Fibroblast Growth Factors), and these factors are responsible for stimulating the angiogenesis process and allow nutrients and oxygen to reach cancer cells. These interactions between tumor cells and such microenvironment ultimately led to a dynamic ecosystem that improves cell proliferation and its metastatic ability and reduces the cancer cell mutation (Zottl et al., 2025; Pawar et al., 2025; Buruiană et al., 2024). Cancer mutations and the activation of several transcription factors result in increased levels of inflammatory mediators, such as cytokines and chemokines, which are released into the TME. This, in turn, recruits and activates numerous inflammatory cells. Further, these recruited cells are responsible for enhanced inflammatory signals and lead to a tumor-related inflammatory environment that helps cancer cells evasion from immune destruction (Vendramini-Costa and Carvalho, 2012; Yoshimura, 2006). The hypoxic-induced conditions in the cancer microenvironment led to stabilization of hypoxia-inducible factors (HIFs), resulting in enhanced angiogenesis and resistance to apoptosis (Chen et al., 2023). Therapeutic approaches, such as targeting the cancer cell microenvironment, hold significant potential. It is already reported that normal cells are probably genetically more stable than cancer cells; thus, therapy targeting the cancer microenvironment has a lower chance of causing mutations and prompt metastasis (Duesberg et al., 1998).

Cellular communication pathways contributing to the TME

Secreted factor (Paracrine) signaling

Small groups of tumor cells can alter the behavior of nearby cells through paracrine signaling. These sub clonal populations release growth factors and cytokines (e.g., WNT16B, VEGFs, and GM-CSF) that act on neighboring cancer cells to stimulate proliferation, trigger epithelial-to-mesenchymal transition (EMT), and activate cancer stem cells (CSC) (Johnson et al., 2013). These secreted molecules also reprogram stromal cells, such as cancer-associated fibroblasts (CAFs), tumor-associated macrophages (TAMs), and endothelial cells, to create a more supportive microenvironment, thereby promoting tumor growth. In this way, a small resistance was developed; for example, therapy-induced WNT16B (regulated by NF-κB) promotes paracrine resistance, and VEGF-C overexpression can accelerate growth and drug-resistant behavior (Fig. 5.2).

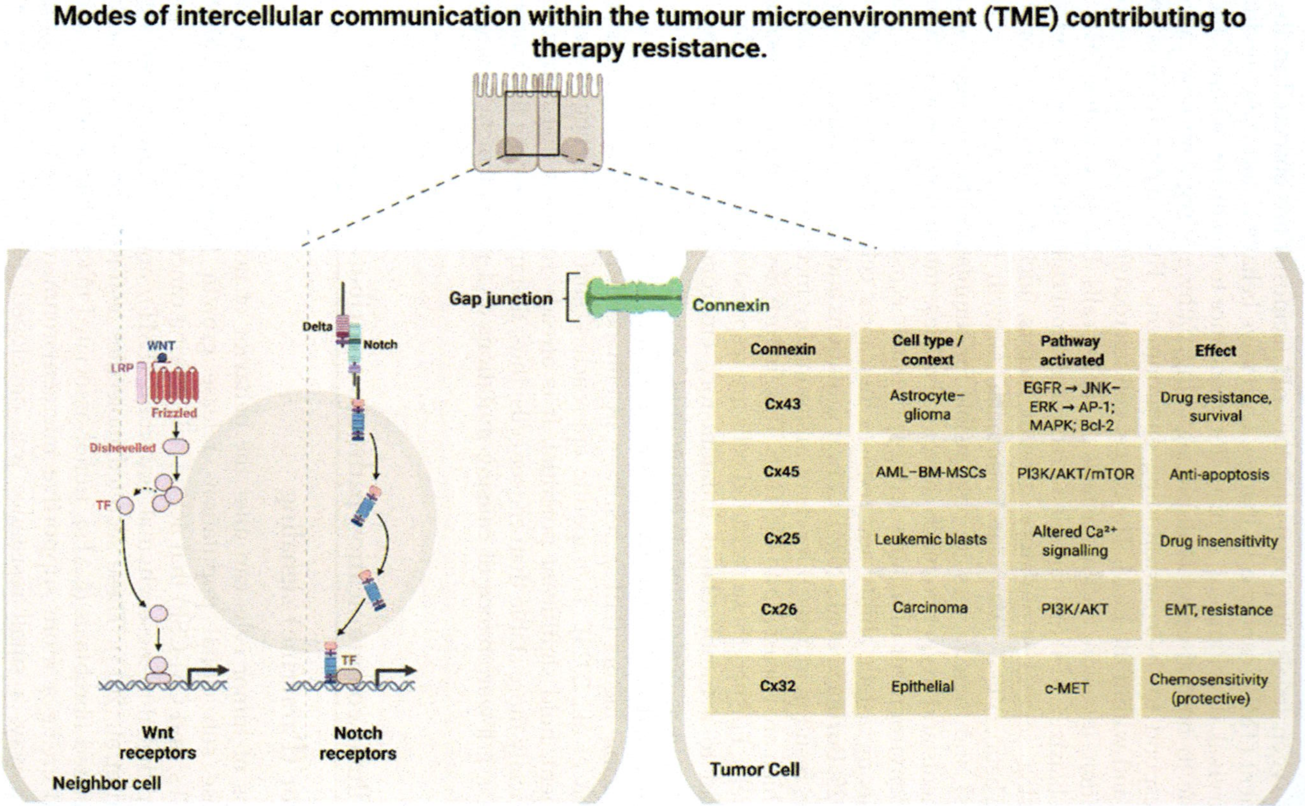

FIGURE 5.2 Different modes of intercellular communication within the tumor microenvironment such as paracrine signaling (WNT16B, VEGFs, IL-6), direct Jagged1–NOTCH contact, and gap junctional exchange via connexins (Cx43, Cx45, Cx26) activate key pathways (NF-κB, Wnt/β-catenin, STAT3, PI3K/AKT/mTOR, MAPK) that promote EMT, cancer stemness, and therapy resistance.

Direct and gap junctional exchange

Direct cell–cell contact and gap junctional communication are also important mechanisms for influencing the tumor microenvironment, which can lead to drug resistance. Direct contact methods or juxtacrine signaling may activate the NOTCH receptor pathway. Gap junctions allow the direct passage of ions, such as Zn^{2+} and Ca^{2+}, small metabolites, mature miRNAs, and even organelles between stromal and cancer cells because of the presence of connexin proteins, which are the basic elements of gap junctions. Astrocytes use Cx43-based GJIC to protect tumor cells from temozolomide and other drugs at the junction between glial cells and glioblastoma. The same Cx43 is often overexpressed in the EGFR → JNK–ERK → AP-1 pathway (Fig. 5.2). Astrocyte–glioma contact alters the expression of hundreds of tumor genes and upregulates pro-survival pathways, such as MAPK and Bcl-2, leading to the formation of Cx43-connected microtube networks that sequester cytotoxic ions, including Ca^{2+}, following radiotherapy. Gap junctions also permit the horizontal transfer of miRNAs (e.g., miR-5096), which can reprogram astrocytes to a more supportive phenotype for tumor development (Cornelison et al., 2022; Hong et al., 2015; Osswald et al., 2015).

In blood cancers and solid tumors, gap junctions create a protective area (niche) to facilitate tumor growth. In the bone marrow niche, functional GJ between leukemic cells and bone marrow mesenchymal stromal cells (BM-MSCs) forms a protected area that supplies survival signals to AML cells. Disruption of GJ increases chemosensitivity. This contract in BM-MSCs activates the PI3K/AKT/mTOR pathway in AML cells and reduces apoptosis. In multiple myeloma, Cx43-mediated GJIC induces BM-MSCs to secrete IL-6, SDF-1, and IL-10 to promote growth and resistance (Han et al., 2023; Yu et al., 2017). The presence of specific connexin proteins (e.g., Cx45 in AML and Cx25 in leukemic blasts) is linked to altered signaling and increased drug insensitivity. In carcinoma, some connexin proteins, such as Cx26, promote epithelial–mesenchymal transition (EMT) and drug resistance through the PI3K/AKT pathway, while other proteins (Cx32) are associated with c-MET (cellular mesenchymal to epithelial transition factor) and chemosensitivity. A novel mechanism for transferring Zn^{2+} to tumor cells involves $ZIP1^{+}$ CAFs created via Cx43, which activate AKT and upregulate ABCB1 (P-gp), causing multidrug resistance. This effect can be reversed by inhibiting AKT (Ni et al., 2022). Similarly, upregulation of the AKT/mTOR pathway, influenced by TME metabolites such as lactate, enhances cell survival and reduces the efficacy of targeted drugs (Allen et al., 2016; Salony et al., 2016). Likewise, cytokines such as IL-6, IL-1β, TAMs, CAFs, or neutrophils rapidly activate the STAT3 pathway. This upregulation promotes resistance by inducing EMT and anti-apoptotic signals and increasing exosome release (Dorayappan et al., 2018; Yin et al., 2017). Another pathway that promotes chemotherapy resistance is triggered by Jagged one or the CAF-derived IL-6 → Notch pathway (Fig. 5.2). Together, these rewired signaling circuits confer phenotypic plasticity to tumor cells, enhancing their ability to survive therapy (Boelens et al., 2014; Lin et al., 2017; Studebaker et al., 2008).

Extracellular vesicle (Exosome) mediated transfer

Exosomes transfer proteins (P-gp) and miRNAs (miR-21 and miR-155) to alter TME components. Tumor and stromal cells release exosomes and larger micro-vesicles that carry proteins, including microRNAs (miRNAs), long non-coding RNAs (lncRNAs), integrins, and drug-efflux proteins. This results in the transmission of resistance traits to sensitive cells, modulation of endothelial and immune cells, and alteration of gene expression in recipient cells, promoting survival. This causes EMT, metastasis, and drug resistance (Pang et al., 2019). For example, exosomal miR-503 alters breast cancer cells after chemotherapy, which is responsible for multidrug resistance (Bovy et al., 2015). Various transporters (MRP2, ATP7A/B, and P-gp) are involved in direct drug efflux (Safaei et al., 2005).

Mechanisms of therapy resistance through cancer-associated fibroblasts (CAF) and macrophages

The TME is also altered by CAFs that actively promote drug resistance. This resistance was obtained through the release of many growth factors (such as HGF, FGF, EGF, TGF-β, and WNT16B) and cytokines (IL-6 and IL-8), which resulted in the up-regulation of pro-survival pathways in cancer cells (Johnson et al., 2013; Aprelikova et al., 2013; Pote and Gacche, 2023). Pathways such as PI3K/AKT, MAPK, and NF-kB-mediated pathways (FAK) are involved in the increase in resistance towards chemotherapy and apoptosis of tumor cells. Cytokines IL-6 and IL-8 assist in maintaining a protective environment in CAF. This environment is favorable to the CSCs. This condition can be determined by using markers like CD10 and GRP77. This habitat further drives chemoresistance (Corso and Giordano, 2013; Kim et al., 2013; Su et al., 2018).

On the same note, TAMs (specifically M2-polarized type) work in conjunction with CAFs to form a resistant environment. The factors released by such macrophages include IL-10, CCL2, as well as cathepsins, which stimulate the activation of the STAT3 and PI3K/Akt/mTOR pathways in cancer cells. To improve the tumor cell survival and enhance stem-like properties and EMT of cancer cells. As an example, IL-10/STAT3 signaling is linked to the resistance of paclitaxel, and the CCL2 factor can help in the development of tamoxifen resistance in cancer cells. The immune response is additionally depressed by these TAMs, which upregulate checkpoint proteins like B7–H4 so that the tumors can avoid immunotherapy, as well as antibody-based therapy (Jinushi and Komohara, 2015; Santoni et al., 2013; Shree et al., 2011). In the case of TAMs (M2 polarized) and TANs (N2 polarized) facilitate a malignant phenotype through the secretion of factors that cause EMT. This shift causes angiogenesis process stimulation and produces a powerful immunosuppressive habitat. As an aside, TAM-generated TGF-β and cathepsins restructure the adjacent tissue, hence expanding the rapid increase in cancerous cells. Angiogenesis is promoted by other factors, including the secretion of growth factor (VEGF) and cytokinin (IL-8). Most importantly, these two types of cells (TAMs and TANs) suppress the immune response; TAMs release IL-10 and CCL chemokines to prevent anti-tumor T-cells, while TANs recruit TAMs to protect the tumor cell against attacks by the immune system (Galdiero et al., 2013; Shamamian et al., 2001).

In addition, the poor vascular organization is also associated with the immune suppression response of the tumor cells. These cells release proangiogenic molecules for the development of blood vessels. Blood vessels that are close to tumor cells exhibit disorganization, leakage, and convoluted forms, and this causes unequal and irregular blood flow. This disorganized structure of vessel combined with increased interstitial fluid pressure, drastically reduces the penetration of therapeutic agents into tumor cells. The tumor cell can also develop resistance to anti-angiogenic drugs, for example, VEGF inhibitors, via increasing other pro-angiogenic signaling pathways, for example, CXCL12-CXCR7 to ensure blood vessel growth in the surroundings of tumor cells is sustained (Flaherty et al., 2015; Queen et al., 2005; Yamada et al., 2015). This abnormal vasculature provides a broader-based therapeutic resistance microenvironment. This poor blood supply causes insufficient oxygen supply (hypoxia), which causes cancerous cells to adapt to glycolytic metabolism. The shift in the metabolism process causes acidosis (an acidic environment). Thus, hypoxia and acidosis are also powerful forces of opposition to numerous treatments (Padera et al., 2004; Arbeit et al., 2006).

Metabolic and physicochemical adaptation

As discussed in the above section, hypoxia, a state of low oxygen within the tumor microenvironment, is a fundamental driver of resistance. This was facilitated by the activation of HIF-1α. This activation initiates a comprehensive pro-survival pathway that inhibits apoptosis by upregulating proteins such as Bcl-xL (Kitange et al., 2009; Zhao et al., 2016). Upregulation of this protein alters cellular metabolism by promoting the switch to glycolysis for energy production. It also regulates drug efflux pumps, such as P-glycoprotein(P-gp), to expel chemotherapeutic agents. Furthermore, HIF-1α enhances cancer stemness by cooperating with signals such as TGF-β2. Ultimately, this results in the creation of aggressive, drug-resistant cell populations that drive tumor recurrence and progression (Kovacic and Osuna, 2000; Meijer et al., 2012; Tang et al., 2018).

Switching to the glycolysis pathway for energy production results in the acidic nature of the TME. These changes directly challenge the efficacy of chemotherapy through multiple mechanisms. The low extracellular pH traps weak-base chemotherapeutic drugs, such as doxorubicin and vincristine, outside cancer cells, preventing their intracellular accumulation and cytotoxic activity. Furthermore, these acidic conditions actively induce resistance in tumor cells by activating the p38 signaling pathway, increasing the activity of drug efflux pumps such as P-glycoprotein. It also promotes a stem-like state by inducing SOX2 expression and driving resistance to targeted agents, creating a formidable barrier to treatment. Alterations in the energy production pathway leading to lactic acidosis can drive resistance to targeted therapies, such as Akt inhibitors (Cowan and Tannock, 2001; Gerweck et al., 1999; Hu et al., 2020; Sauvant et al., 2008).

The metabolites (Lactate, Adenosine, Methylglyoxal) produced by this glycolysis pathway create a powerful resistance and immunosuppressive TME. Tumor cells consume essential nutrients, such as glucose and amino acids (e.g., L-arginine and tryptophan), resulting in a depletion of energy sources and nutrients for effector immune cells. Deprivation of glucose molecules in $CD4^+$ T cells prevents the production of sufficient IFN-γ, thereby weakening the immune system's ability to fight the tumor. Concurrently, the depletion of L-arginine and tryptophan suppresses T-cell function and increases the expression of PD-L1. Exposure of tumor cells to inflammatory cytokines such as IFN-γ activates the kynurenine pathway (via IDO) and leads to the accumulation of kynurenine. This leads to tryptophan depletion and kynurenine accumulation, which have powerful immunosuppressive effects (Aydin et al., 2017; Baumann et al., 2020; Oh et al., 2020; OuYang et al., 2015; Yu et al., 2018). This nutrient deprivation is compounded by the accumulation of metabolic waste products, including lactate and adenosine, which actively inhibit the function of cytotoxic T cells, NK cells, and M1 macrophages while promoting the expansion of immunosuppressive M2 macrophages and MDSCs. Another factor contributing to this immunosuppressive situation is the high level of oxidative stress within the TME. MDSCs utilize ROS to inhibit T-cell proliferation and suppress the T-cell receptor, resulting in T-cell dysfunction. This oxidative stress also paralyzes the tumor-killing capacity of Natural Killer (NK) cells and simultaneously enhances the function and stability of regulatory T cells (Tregs), which further dampens immune responses (Cowan and Tannock, 2001; Oh et al., 2020; Yu et al., 2018; Hugo et al., 2016; Ramapriyan et al., 2019).

Key druggable targets and their inhibitors in cancer that can be targeted to reduce tumor hypoxia and acidosis

Here, we introduce the key possible druggable targets in cancer that can be targeted, and inhibiting these targets helps to reduce hypoxia and acidosis.

Hypoxia-Inducible Factor 1 (HIF-1)

The transcription factor hypoxia-inducible factor 1 (HIF-1) functions to enable cellular adaptation to hypoxic levels by regulating several genes related to energy balance, angiogenesis, and survival. It is found in three forms: HIF-1, 2, and 3. In low oxygen conditions, tumor cells activate adaptive mechanisms that promote survival, angiogenesis, and metabolic reprogramming (Semenza, 1999). The central regulators of these responses are HIF-1, primarily HIF-1α, whose stability is tightly controlled by prolyl hydroxylase domain enzymes (PHD1, PHD2, and PHD3) and von Hippel-Lindau (pVHL) tumor suppressor protein under normoxic conditions (Jaakkola et al., 2001). In a hypoxic condition, the PHD's activity of PHDs decreases, inhibiting the degradation of HIF-1α and stimulating the transcription of several genes, including VEGF, CAIX, GLUT1, LDH-A, CD47, and MCT4, which are involved in regulating pH, metabolism, and angiogenesis. When HIF-1 is active for a prolonged period, it alters the cell's energy needs, making it completely dependent on glycolysis and producing excess lactic acid and hydrogen ions, which creates an acidic environment surrounding the tumor. At the same time, HIF-1α promotes angiogenesis, but in an abnormal way that lacks proper oxygenation and causes tumors to develop in a hypoxic condition. Therefore, by blocking HIF-1α and its related enzymes, the oxygen level of the tumor can be improved, along with this, the growth of abnormal blood vessels can also be reduced, and ultimately, due to this, cancer growth can also be stopped or reduced (Hajizadeh et al., 2020).

To achieve all these points, many inhibitors have been developed that interfere with the production and function of HIF-1. Chetomin and bortezomib inhibit its association with p300, but echinomycin interacts with HIF-1 DNA sites and reduces transcriptional function (Karakashev and Reginato, 2015). Translation blockers such as 2-methoxyestradiol, EZN-2968, and Topotecan block HIF-1 production and nuclear mobility (Shirai et al., 2021). Geldanamycin inhibits Hsp90, which significantly accelerates HIF-1 degradation (D'Oto et al., 2016). These drugs function to reduce the stability and activity of HIF-1, thereby reducing cancer cell viability under low-oxygen conditions. Doxorubicin and daunorubicin inhibit HIF-1 complex to hypoxia-responsive elements, while antisense HIF-1α and PX-478 inhibit its expression and downstream genes like VEGF and Foxp3 (Zaccagna et al., 2021). SCH58261, an A2A receptor antagonist, prevents adenosine-mediated immune suppression, and benzopyranyl-1,2,3-triazole enhances HIF-1 degradation while lowering VEGF expression (Tirpe et al., 2019). The chemical structures of drugs targeting the HIF are compiled in Fig. 5.3.

Hypoxia-activated prodrugs (HAPs)

Another class of drug is hypoxia-activated prodrugs (HAPs), an anti-cancer agent that becomes active only in the hypoxic conditions of tumors. Under normal conditions, they remain inactive; however, in hypoxia, cellular oxidoreductases convert them into toxic forms

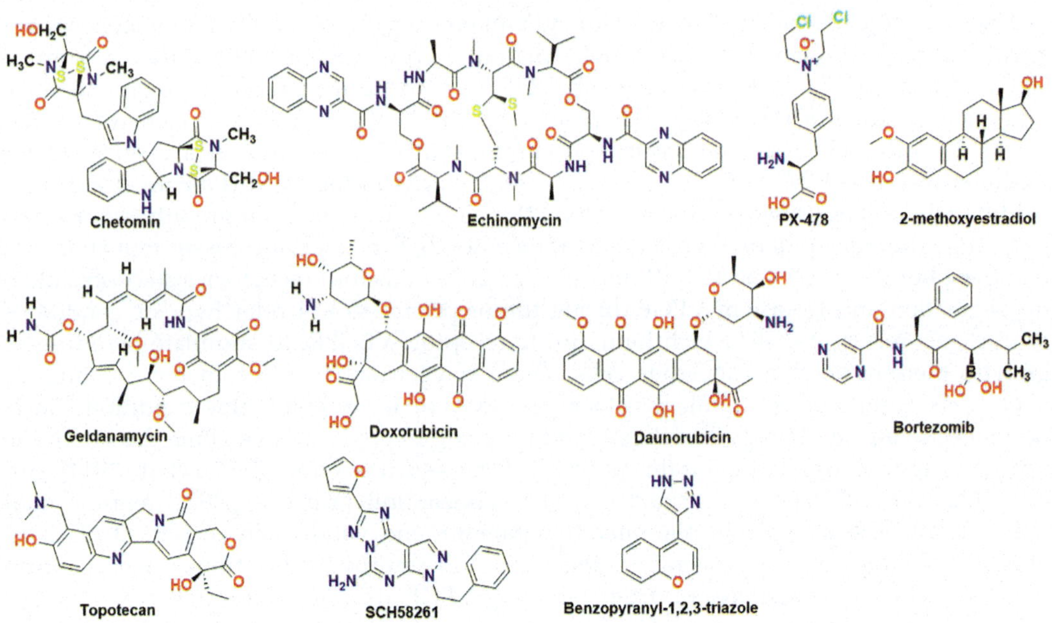

FIGURE 5.3 Chemical structures of key drugs inhibiting HIF-1.

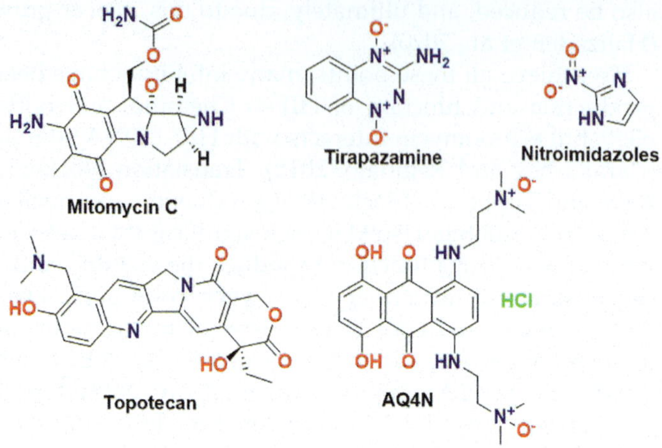

FIGURE 5.4 Chemical structures of the drugs targeting HAPs.

that damage tumor DNA or inhibit key enzymes, such as topoisomerases. Common examples include nitroimidazoles, mitomycin C, topotecan, tirapazamine (TPZ), AQ4N, and metal-based complexes of cobalt or copper (Singleton et al., 2021; Anduran et al., 2022). Thus, HAPs provide a targeted strategy to eradicate hypoxic, treatment-resistant tumor cells. The chemical structures of the drugs targeting HAPs are compiled in Fig. 5.4.

Vascular Endothelial Growth Factor (VEGF)

The vascular endothelial growth factor (VEGF) pathway is essential for angiogenesis, and it includes several members, such a PIGF (placental growth factor), and different forms of VEGF, that is, A, B, C, and D. Amongst all, VEGF-A is the utmost in promoting blood vessel formation in tumors (Hanahan and Weinberg, 2011). VEGF-A is a protein of 45 kDa, encoded by the VEGFA gene located on chromosome 6 (Sherwood et al., 1971). Matrix metalloproteinase-9 (MMP-9) helps release VEGF stored in the ECM (Potente et al., 2011). Additionally, other growth factor receptors, that is, EGFR (epidermal growth factor receptor), HER2 (human epidermal growth factor receptor 2), ErbB2 (erythroblastic leukemia viral oncogene homolog 1,2), and IGF-IR (insulin-like growth factor I receptor), also contribute to the regulation and release of VEGF during tumor progression. Under hypoxic conditions, cancer cells release VEGF, which binds to its receptor, VEGFR, to stimulate blood vessel growth, thereby helping cancerous cells obtain oxygen and survive in these conditions (Gonzalez-Moreno et al., 2010). By blocking VEGF or its receptor, this condition can be normalized, improving oxygen delivery and reducing hypoxia. To overcome this condition, several drugs are used to inhibit this pathway. Drugs such as erlotinib (Yu et al., 2014), gefitinib (Liu et al., 2023), bevacizumab, lenvatinib, cabozantinib (Yan et al., 2024), axitinib, sunitinib, everolimus, pazopanib, regorafenib, sorafenib, and vandetanib (Ansari et al., 2022) inhibit this pathway, suppressing angiogenesis and improving the tumor microenvironment. The chemical structures of drugs targeting VEGF are compiled in Fig. 5.5.

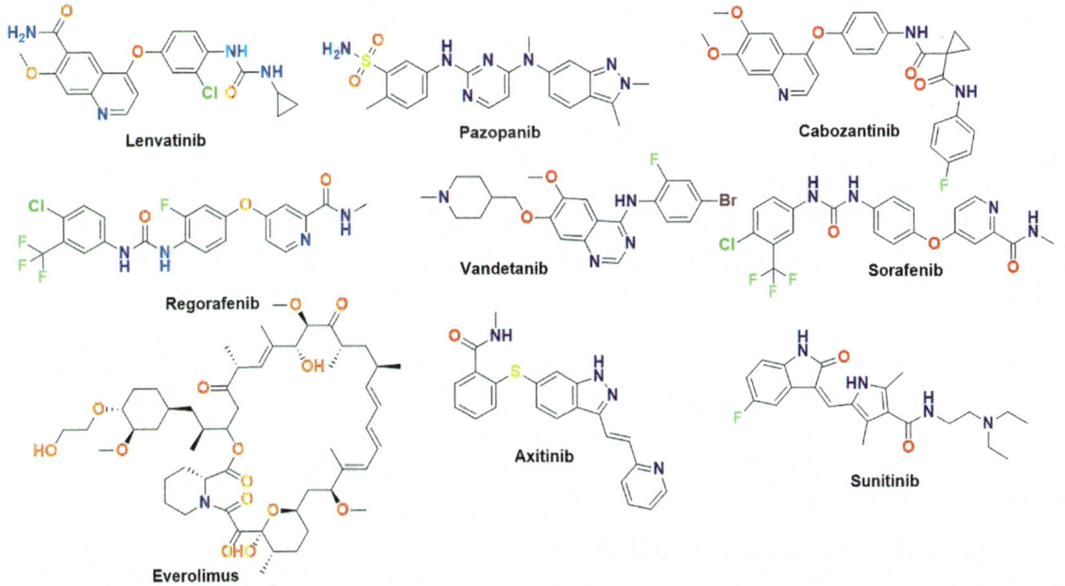

FIGURE 5.5 Chemical structures of key drugs inhibiting VEGF.

Transforming Growth Factor β (TGF-β)

Another growth factor is transforming growth factor β (TGF-β), a signaling molecule that functions in regulating essential cellular processes, including growth, differentiation, movement, aging, and death of cancerous cells. It included TGF-β1, TGF-β2, and TGF-β3 proteins. Among all, TGF-β1 is the most abundant protein, weighing 44 kDa and expressed on chromosome 19. It plays a dualistic role, that is, it can suppress tumors (early stage) as well as promote cancer progression, metastasis, and invasion (advanced stages) (Ali et al., 2023). TGF-β signaling promotes a TME that lowers immune responses by suppressing B cells, T cells, and NK cells. Moreover, it supports regulatory immune cells and increases the expression of programmed cell death protein-1 (PD-1), which decreases immunological activity. TGF-β interacts with its type I and type II receptors to activate Sma- and Mad-related (SMAD) proteins (SMAD2/3 and SMAD4) that control gene expression in the nucleus. It can also trigger MAPK (mitogen-activated protein kinase), AMPK (AMP-activated protein kinase), PI3K (phosphoinositide 3-kinase)/AKT, and Hippo processes using non-SMAD pathways, all of which contribute to tumor development and progression (Park et al., 2016; Shi et al., 2022; Tie et al., 2022). Blocking the PI3K/AKT/mTOR pathway effectively reduces HIF-1α levels, thereby limiting the survival of cancer cells under low oxygen conditions. Drugs like dactolisib (BEZ_{235}) (Peng et al., 2022) block this pathway, while PKI-587 (Xie et al., 2021) functions as a dual inhibitor of PI3K/AKT/mTOR and DNA damage repair pathways, enhancing tumor radiosensitivity. Combining radiotherapy with anti-hypoxic agents offers a promising potential for effective cancer treatment. Another effective combination therapy uses gefitinib, an EGFR inhibitor, together with metformin, an AMPK activator, to target tumor hypoxia and overcome drug resistance (Sulaiman et al., 2020). The chemical structures of drugs targeting TGF-β are compiled in Fig. 5.6.

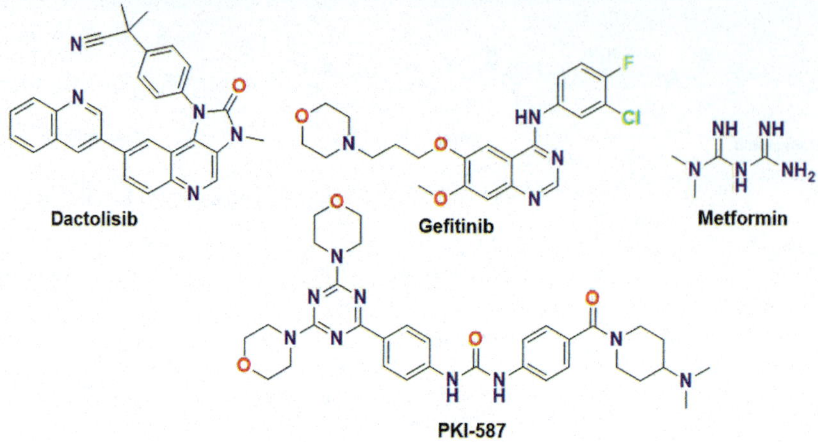

FIGURE 5.6 Chemical structures of drugs targeting TGF-β.

Programmed death-1/L1 (PD-1/PD-L1)

Thiscascade normally controls immune responses, but cancerous cells employ it to avoid recognition and destruction by the immune system. PD-1 (55 kDa) on T-cells interacts with PD-L1 (33 kDa) on tumor or immunological cells, transferring inhibitory signals that restrict T-cell function and cause fatigue (Fanelli et al., 2021). Tumor increases PD-L1 by downregulation of PI3K-Akt kinases, upregulation of STAT3/ALK signaling, and interferon-gamma (IFN-gamma; pro-inflammatory) from the tumor microenvironment, inhibiting T-cells and promoting immunological resistance (Keir et al., 2008; Dosset et al., 2018). Cemiplimab, nivolumab, and pembrolizumab are the PD-1 blockers; however, avelumab, durvalumab, and atezolizumab are the inhibitors of PD-L1 (Vaddepally et al., 2020).

Cytotoxic T-Lymphocyte-Associated Protein 4 (CTLA-4)

It is an immune checkpoint protein located on chromosome 2 (q33-q34). It normally functions by regulating the immune system, preventing the overactivation of T-cells. However, in cancer, its increased activity allows tumor cells to evade detection by the immune system. Its gene contains four exons, which code for three major protein components, that is, a transmembrane area, a ligand binding site, and a cytoplasmic tail (Valk et al., 2008). According to the experiments, increased CTLA-4 expression in breast carcinoma individuals is linked with progressive stages of disease and lymph node metastasis. Furthermore, co-stimulatory molecules such as CD80 (B7-1) and CD86 (B7-2) are situated on the surface of APCs (antigen-presenting cells). In normal conditions, these co-stimulatory fragments join to CD28 on T-cells to activate them. CTLA-4 interacts with CD28 to bind to B7 ligands on APCs, effectively inhibiting activation signals. Additionally, it produces blocking signals, which decrease IL-2 synthesis and halt cell growth. An elevated level of CTLA-4 in regulatory T cells helps to suppress immune responses

(Bour-Jordan et al., 2011; Rowshanravan et al., 2018). A drug that blocks CTLA-4, ipilimumab, is the only single FDA-approved drug. It suppresses the activity of CTLA-4 and improves the tumor microenvironment.

Metabolic Reprogramming and its targets

Underlow oxygen conditions, cancer cells undergo metabolic reprogramming, which alters the way they process nutrients to survive. Hypoxia triggers changes in several key pathways, including glucose transporters (GLUT1, GLUT3), mitochondrial regulators (PDK1), glycolytic enzymes (Aldolase A, HK1, PKM2, LDHA), and lipid metabolism proteins (Lipin-1). These mechanisms allow tumor cells to proliferate and survive under the stress caused by insufficient oxygen. Targeting these hypoxia-induced metabolic processes can be a promising cancer target strategy. Several inhibitors are used in metabolic reprogramming, including WZB117 (GLUT1) (Pliszka and Szablewski, 2021), FX11 (LDHA and PKM2) (Mohammad et al., 2019), dichloroacetate (PDK) (Wang et al., 2021), and fatty acid synthase (FAS) blockers such as cerulenin, C75, orlistat, C93, and GSK837149A (Du et al., 2022). The chemical structures of drugs that impact metabolic reprogramming are compiled in Fig. 5.7.

Carbonic Anhydrase IX (CAIX)

These enzymes, located on the cell membrane, are strongly activated under low-oxygen conditions through HIF-1. They convert carbon dioxide (CO_2) into bicarbonate and protons, allowing cancer cells to release acid outside while maintaining a stable internal pH. It acts on the cell surface, converting CO_2 and H_2O into HCO_3^- and H^+. Bicarbonate is transported back into the cell to maintain intracellular balance, whereas the excess protons increase

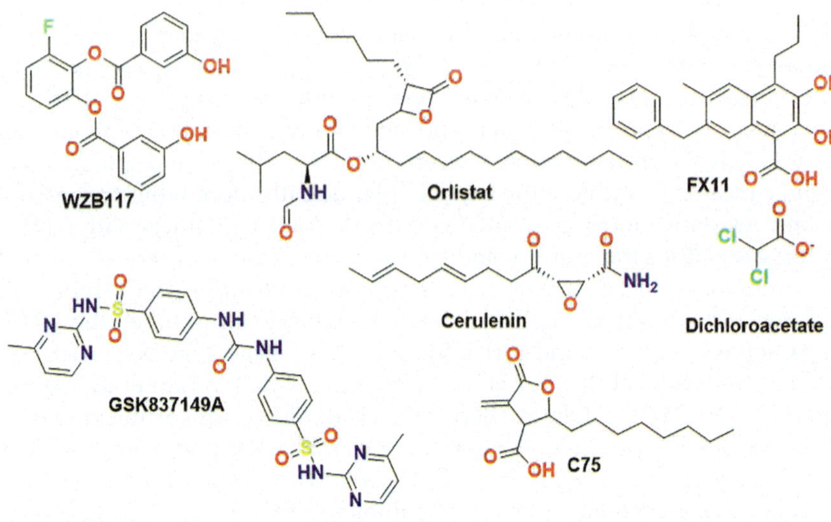

FIGURE 5.7 Chemical structures of drugs that impact metabolic reprogramming.

acidity in the surrounding environment. This maintains intracellular alkalinity (pro-survival) and extracellular acidity (pro-invasion). CAIX level is linked with hypoxic regions and a lethal phenotype by facilitating pH control; it promotes proliferation, invasion, and medication resistance (Pettersen et al., 2015). Indisulam (Ozawa et al., 2004) and VII/20 monoclonal antibody (Zatovicova et al., 2010) are inhibitors of CAIX for cancer treatment. The chemical structures of drugs that inhibit CAIX are compiled in Fig. 5.8**A**.

Monocarboxylate Transporters (MCTs 1 and 4)

MCTs are proton-coupled transporters that transfer lactate and protons across plasma membranes. In tumor cells that rely heavily on glycolysis despite the presence of oxygen, MCT4 facilitates the export of lactate along with protons, whereas MCT1 facilitates the uptake of lactate in cells that have sufficient oxygen for oxidative metabolism. Inhibiting these transporters disrupts the balance of pH and interferes with metabolic symbiosis between the hypoxic and oxygenated regions of the tumor. MCTs carry lactate (or pyruvate) with H^+ down a concentration gradient. By exporting glycolysis byproducts, they avoid intracellular acidification (Halestrap and Wilson, 2012). Inhibition increases intracellular lactate and H+ levels, altering metabolism and reducing the extracellular acidification pathway over time. In hypoxic, highly glycolytic tumor cells, MCT4 expression increases to export excess lactate, whereas MCT1 allows lactate uptake in oxidative cancer cells. This metabolic coupling promotes tumor growth and helps maintain an acidic extracellular environment (Sonveaux et al., 2008). Several inhibitors targeting MCT1 and MCT4 have been developed to interfere with this process, including α-cyano-4-hydroxycinnamate, AZD 3965, and AR-C155858, which can help control hypoxia-associated tumor progression. The chemical structures of drugs that inhibit MCTs 1 and 4 are compiled in Fig. 5.8**B**.

Sodium-proton exchanger 1 (NHE1)

The NHE is a membrane protein, Na^+/H^+ exchanger, and functions in the maintenance of intracellular pH, cell growth, and migration. Among the nine isoforms, NHE1 is most closely associated with cancer development and growth. The activity of NHE1 is increased in conditions such as hypoxia, low pH, and activation pathways involving EGFR, ERK, $p90^{Rsk}$, B-Raf, GPCR (G protein-coupled receptors), PKC, RhoA, and integrin receptors. Its overactivity in cancer cells induces the extracellular acidification, which promotes invasion, metastasis, and resistance to programmed cell death. NHE1 interacts with CD44 and cytoskeletal proteins to reduce the motility and tumor progression (Ward et al., 2020). Inhibiting NHE1 reduces angiogenesis, enhances drug sensitivity, and suppresses tumor development, making it a crucial therapeutic target in cancer. To inhibit or modulate the NHE1 activity, several drugs act as direct and indirect inhibitors, have been reported, such as amiloride (Sailer et al., 1998), paclitaxel (Kumar et al., 2009), etoposide (Akram et al., 2006), daunorubicin (Reshkin et al., 2003), cisplatin (Bernstein et al., 2000), doxorubicin (Miraglia et al., 2005), siRNA-mediated suppression (Mo et al., 2011), PPAR gamma ligands (Kumar et al., 2009), etc., affecting cancer progression. NHE1 activity is directly blocked by amiloride, whereas paclitaxel, an anti-cancer drug, is inhibited directly or via apoptotic cleavage.

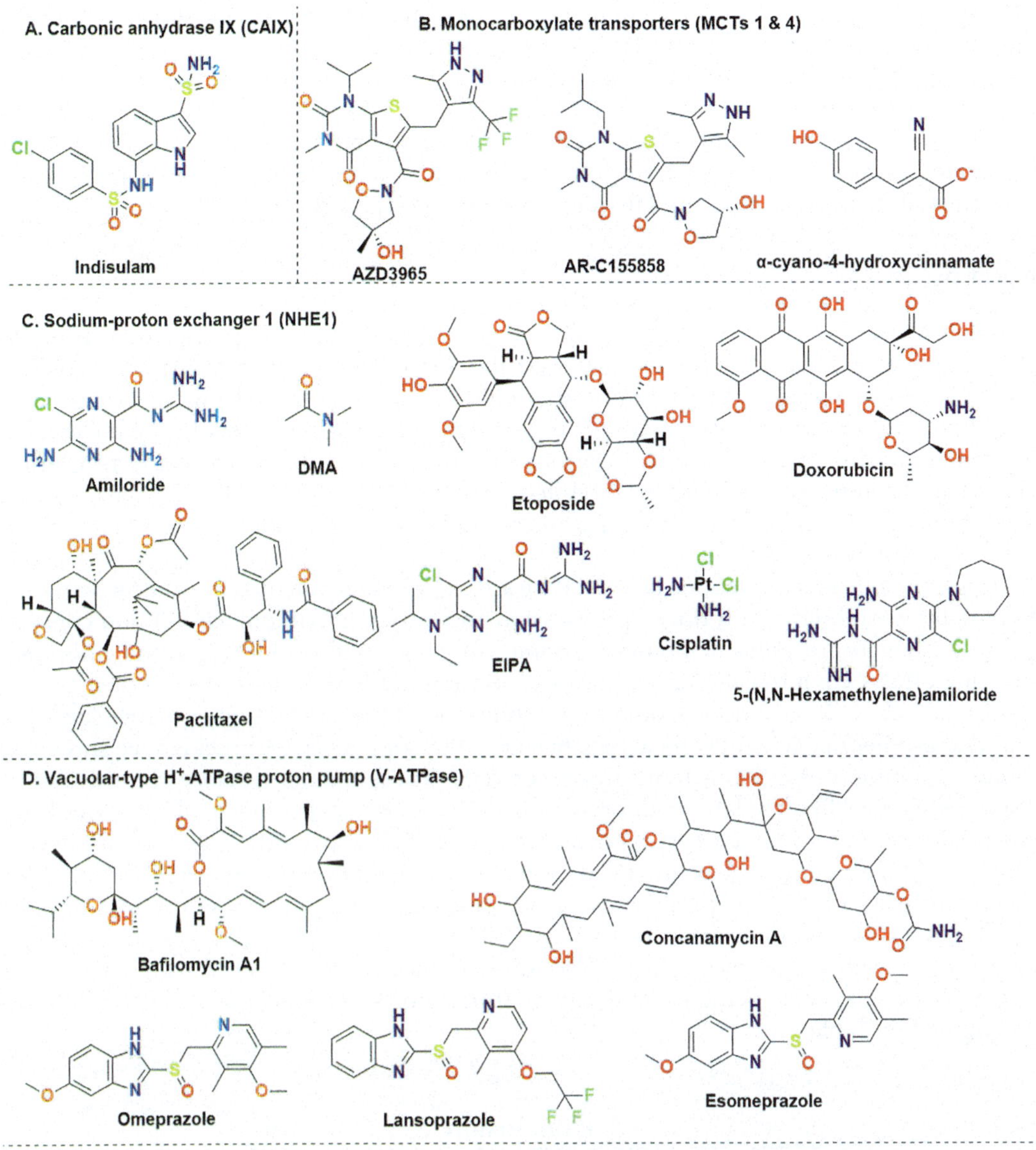

FIGURE 5.8 Chemical structures of the inhibitors targeting A. Carbonic anhydrase IX (CAIX); B. Monocarboxylate transporters (MCTs 1 and 4); C. Sodium-proton exchanger 1 (NHE1); and D. Vacuolar-type H + -ATPase proton pump (V-ATPase).

The amiloride and related compounds are ethylisopropylamiloride (EIPA), dimethylamiloride (DMA), and hexamethyleneamiloride (HMA) (Hosogi et al., 2012; Maidorn et al., 1993; Rich et al., 2000). These compounds block the NHE1 transporter, allowing cancer cells to survive, and also play an important role in drug resistance. When NHE1 is inhibited, cancerous cells become more sensitive to chemotherapy drugs, including cisplatin, etoposide, daunorubicin, and doxorubicin. When NHE1 levels are reduced, angiogenesis is also reduced by decreasing the HIF-1α activity, which is required for tumor growth. A class of drugs may suppress cancer growth by activating PPARγ (a nuclear receptor) to reduce NHE1 production. Knowing all this, it seems that both direct inhibition and generic suppression of NHE1 can make anticancer treatment more effective and also stop tumor growth. The chemical structures of drugs that inhibit NHE1 are compiled in Fig. 5.8**C**.

V-ATPase

The last target is vacuolar-type H^+-ATPase (V-ATPase), a proton pump responsible for maintaining an acidic environment inside specific cellular compartments such as lysosomes and endosomes. In cancer, these pumps are found in excess on the cell surface, from where they expel protons into the surrounding space, thereby increasing the acidity of the external environment. This activity is where cancer cells survive, invade, and become resistant to treatment. Therefore, V-ATPase is inhibited to balance the pH of tumor cells, making them more susceptible to chemotherapy and radiotherapy, and reducing metastatic potential (Nishi and Forgac, 2002).

Drugs that block the functions of V-ATPase are explored as potential anticancer agents for their ability to interfere with tumor progression and survival. Bafilomycin A1 and concanamycin A, which are natural inhibitors, demonstrate growth suppression and apoptosis-inducing effects via intracellular acidification, but are not widely used due to their toxicity (Ohta et al., 1998). In addition, proton pump inhibitors (PPIs) such as omeprazole, lansoprazole, and esomeprazole, which have long been used to suppress gastric acid, have shown the ability to inhibit V-ATPase activity in cancer cells. These agents enhance the therapeutic response to drugs like cisplatin, 5-fluorouracil, and vinblastine (Luciani et al., 2004) and suppress MMP-9 and CXCR4 expression as well as protease immune cell infiltration, and together reduce tumor invasiveness (Jin et al., 2014). Overall, natural V-ATPase inhibitors and repurposed PPIs show promise as supporting agents in cancer therapy by inhibiting tumor growth, overcoming drug resistance, and also preventing metastasis. The chemical structures of drugs that inhibit V-ATPase are compiled in Fig. 5.8**D.** A summary of key druggable targets for reducing tumor hypoxia and acidosis, along with associated inhibitors, is compiled in Table 5.1.

Conclusion

Metabolic vulnerability of cancer cells orchestrated by altered respiration under hypoxia and pH dynamics impacts cancer cell survival and metastasis. Both hypoxia and associated acidosis are not only the byproducts of cancer cell metabolism but, at the same time, considered as "active drivers of malignancy". These reprogram the cancer cell's metabolism, further promoting angiogenesis and allowing immune evasion. This cumulative TME supports tumor survival even under extreme stress and, at the same time, exacerbates the existing cancer chemotherapy resistance. In this chapter, we have covered the signaling

TABLE 5.1 Druggable targets and their inhibitors to reduce tumor hypoxia and acidosis.

S No.	Target	Pathways involved	Effects	Inhibitors
1.	VEGF	VEGF/VEGFR signaling; ECM remodeling; MMP-9 mediated release	Stimulates angiogenesis, improves oxygen supply, and supports tumor survival under hypoxia	Bevacizumab, lenvatinib, cabozantinib, axitinib, sunitinib, everolimus, pazopanib, regorafenib, sorafenib, vandetanib
2.	HIF-1	Hypoxia-induced transcription; regulated by PHD1-3 and pVHL	Promotes glycolysis, angiogenesis, and pH regulation; enhances tumor survival under low oxygen conditions	Chetomin, bortezomib, echinomycin, EZN-2968, topotecan, 2-methoxy estradiol, geldanamycin, doxorubicin, daunorubicin, PX-478, SCH58261, benzopyranyl-1,2,3-triazole
3.	TGF-β	SMAD-dependent and independent (MAPK, PI3K/AKT/mTOR, AMPK)	Facilitates metastasis, immune suppression, invasion, and tumor progression	Dactolisib (BEZ235), PKI-587, gefitinib + metformin (combination therapy)
4.	PD-1/PD-L1	Immune checkpoint: Hinders T-cell properties	Immune evasion; reduced anti-tumor immunity	Cemiplimab, nivolumab, pembrolizumab (PD-1 blockers); however, PD-L1 blockers (avelumab, durvalumab, atezolizumab)
5.	CTLA-4	Participates with CD28 for B7 ligands on APCs; immune checkpoint	Suppresses T-cell activation; facilitates immune escape	Ipilimumab
6.	Metabolic reprogramming	Glycolysis, GLUT1/GLUT3, LDHA, PKM2, PDK1, Lipin-1	Supports survival under hypoxia, maintains pH, and enables proliferation	WZB117 (GLUT1), FX11 (LDHA/PKM2), dichloroacetate (PDK), cerulenin, C75, orlistat, GSK837149A (FAS inhibitors)
7.	CAIX	HIF-1-regulated CO_2 hydration to $HCO_3^- + H^+$	Maintains intracellular alkalinity, extracellular acidity; promotes invasion and chemoresistance	Indisulam, VII/20 monoclonal antibody
8.	MCT1/MCT4	Proton-coupled lactate transport	Maintains intracellular pH, extracellular acidification; metabolic symbiosis	α-cyano-4-hydroxycinnamate, AZD3965, AR-C155858
9.	NHE1	Na^+/H^+ exchanger; EGFR/ERK signaling	Promotes extracellular acidification, invasion, metastasis, and drug resistance	Amiloride, EIPA, DMA, HMA, paclitaxel, cisplatin, doxorubicin, etoposide, PPARγ ligands, siRNA-mediated suppression
10.	V-ATPase	Proton pumps acidify organelles and the extracellular space	Supports extracellular acidification, metastasis; enhances chemo/radioresistance	Bafilomycin A1, concanamycin A, omeprazole, esomeprazole, lansoprazole

pathways and oncogenic drivers that exacerbate tumor hypoxia and acidosis, leading to cancer cell survival and drug resistance. We have considered numerous oncologic targets, including VEGF, HIF-1, TGF-β, PD-1/PD-L1, CTLA-4, CAIX, MCT1/MCT4, NHE1, and V-ATPase, that may be targeted to overcome the TME influenced by hypoxia and acidosis. The key inhibitors targeting these targets, along with their mechanisms, are also presented, along with the chemical structures of the reported inhibitors. Most of the drug candidates have been tested actively in clinical trials; however, the desirable outcomes are still awaited. The ongoing clinical trials may further consider the patient stratification via employing metabolic and hypoxic biomarkers. The adjuvant therapy approach may be tested, whereby approved anticancer agents are combined with drugs that target the TME. In conclusion, the TME influenced by hypoxia and dynamic pH could be an Achilles heel and could bring a paradigm shift in cancer chemotherapeutic treatment. The active clinical trials in this area are expected to yield next-generation anti-cancer therapeutics that will be selective, efficacious, and promising.

Acknowledgments

Authors are thankful to their respective institutes for the necessary infrastructure and support.

References

Akram, S., Teong, H.F.C., Fliegel, L., Pervaiz, S., Clément, M.-V., 2006. Reactive oxygen species-mediated regulation of the Na+–H+ exchanger 1 gene expression connects intracellular redox status with cells' sensitivity to death triggers. Cell Death Differ. 13 (4), 628–641. https://doi.org/10.1038/sj.cdd.4401775.

Ali, S., Rehman, M.U., Yatoo, A.M., Arafah, A., Khan, A., Rashid, S., Majid, S., Ali, A., Ali, M.N., 2023. TGF-β signaling pathway: Therapeutic targeting and potential for anti-cancer immunity. Eur. J. Pharmacol. 947. https://doi.org/10.1016/j.ejphar.2023.175678.

Allen, E., Miéville, P., Warren, C.M., Saghafinia, S., Li, L., Peng, M.W., Hanahan, D., 2016. Metabolic symbiosis enables adaptive resistance to anti-angiogenic therapy that is dependent on mTOR signaling. Cell Rep. 15 (6), 1144–1160. https://doi.org/10.1016/j.celrep.2016.04.029.

Anduran, E., Dubois, L.J., Lambin, P., Winum, J.Y., 2022. Hypoxia-activated prodrug derivatives of anti-cancer drugs: A patent review 2006–2021. Expert Opin. Ther. Pat. 32 (1), 1–12. https://doi.org/10.1080/13543776.2021.1954617.

Ansari, M.J., Bokov, D., Markov, A., Jalil, A.T., Shalaby, M.N., Suksatan, W., Chupradit, S., AL-Ghamdi, H.S., Shomali, N., Zamani, A., Mohammadi, A., Dadashpour, M., 2022. Cancer combination therapies by angiogenesis inhibitors; a comprehensive review. Cell Commun. Signal. 20 (1). https://doi.org/10.1186/s12964-022-00838-y.

Aprelikova, O., Palla, J., Hibler, B., Yu, X., Greer, Y.E., Yi, M., Stephens, R., Maxwell, G.L., Jazaeri, A., Risinger, J.I., Rubin, J.S., Niederhuber, J., 2013. Silencing of miR-148a in cancer-associated fibroblasts results in WNT10B-mediated stimulation of tumor cell motility. Oncogene 32 (27), 3246–3253. https://doi.org/10.1038/onc.2012.351.

Arbeit, J.M., Brown, J.M., Chao, K.S.C., Chapman, J.D., Eckelman, W.C., Fyles, A.W., Giaccia, A.J., Hill, R.P., Koch, C.J., Krishna, M.C., Krohn, K.A., Lewis, J.S., Mason, R.P., Melillo, G., Padhani, A.R., Powis, G., Rajendran, J.G., Reba, R., Robinson, S.P., Semenza, G.L., Swartz, H.M., Vaupel, P., Yang, D., Tatum, J.L., 2006. Hypoxia: Importance in tumor biology, noninvasive measurement by imaing, and value of its measurement in the management of cancer therapy. Int. J. Radiat. Biol. 82 (10), 699–757. https://doi.org/10.1080/09553000601002324.

Aydin, E., Johansson, J., Nazir, F.H., Hellstrand, K., Martner, A., 2017. Role of NOX2-derived reactive oxygen species in NK cell–mediated control of murine melanoma metastasis. Cancer Immunol. Res. 5 (9), 804–811. https://doi.org/10.1158/2326-6066.CIR-16-0382.

Baumann, T., Dunkel, A., Schmid, C., Schmitt, S., Hiltensperger, M., Lohr, K., Laketa, V., Donakonda, S., Ahting, U., Lorenz-Depiereux, B., Heil, J.E., Schredelseker, J., Simeoni, L., Fecher, C., Körber, N., Bauer, T., Hüser, N., Hartmann, D., Laschinger, M., Eyerich, K., Eyerich, S., Anton, M., Streeter, M., Wang, T., Schraven, B., Spiegel, D., Assaad, F., Misgeld, T., Zischka, H., Murray, P.J., Heine, A., Heikenwälder, M., Korn, T., Dawid, C., Hofmann, T., Knolle, P.A., Höchst, B., 2020. Regulatory myeloid cells paralyze T cells through cell–cell transfer of the metabolite methylglyoxal. Nat. Immunol. 21 (5), 555–566. https://doi.org/10.1038/s41590-020-0666-9.

Bernstein, B.W., Painter, W.B., Chen, H., Minamide, L.S., Abe, H., Bamburg, J.R., 2000. Intracellular pH modulation of ADF/cofilin proteins. Cell Motil Cytoskeleton 47 (4), 319–336. https://doi.org/10.1002/1097-0169(200012)47:4<319:aid-cm6>3.0.co;2-i.

Boelens, M.C., Wu, T.J., Nabet, B.Y., Xu, B., Qiu, Y., Yoon, T., Azzam, D.J., Twyman-Saint Victor, C., Wiemann, B.Z., Ishwaran, H., Ter Brugge, P.J., Jonkers, J., Slingerland, J., Minn, A.J., 2014. Exosome transfer from stromal to breast cancer cells regulates therapy resistance pathways. Cell 159 (3), 499–513. https://doi.org/10.1016/j.cell.2014.09.051.

Bour-Jordan, H., Esensten, J.H., Martinez-Llordella, M., Penaranda, C., Stumpf, M., Bluestone, J.A., 2011. Intrinsic and extrinsic control of peripheral T-cell tolerance by costimulatory molecules of the CD28/B7 family. Immunol. Rev. 241 (1), 180–205. https://doi.org/10.1111/j.1600-065X.2011.01011.x.

Bovy, N., Blomme, B., Frères, P., Dederen, S., Nivelles, O., Lion, M., Carnet, O., Martial, J.A., Noël, A., Thiry, M., Jérusalem, G., Josse, C., Bours, V., Tabruyn, S.P., Struman, I., 2015. Endothelial exosomes contribute to the antitumor response during breast cancer neoadjuvant chemotherapy via microRNA transfer. Oncotarget 6 (12), 10253–10266. https://doi.org/10.18632/oncotarget.3520.

Bray, F., Laversanne, M., Sung, H., et al., 2024. Global cancer statistics 2022: GLOBOCAN estimates of incidence and mortality worldwide for 36 cancers in 185 countries. CA Cancer J. Clin. 74 (3), 229–263. https://doi.org/10.3322/caac.21834.

Buruiană, A., Gheban, B.A., Gheban-Roşca, I.A., Georgiu, C., Crişan, D., Crişan, M., 2024. The tumor stroma of squamous cell carcinoma: A complex environment that fuels cancer rogression. Cancers 16 (9). https://doi.org/10.3390/cancers16091727.

Chen, Z., Han, F., Du, Y., Shi, H., Zhou, W., 2023. Hypoxic microenvironment in cancer: Molecular mechanisms and therapeutic interventions. Signal Transduct. Targeted Ther. 8 (1). https://doi.org/10.1038/s41392-023-01332-8.

Cornelison, R.C., Yuan, J.X., Tate, K.M., Petrosky, A., Beeghly, G.F., Bloomfield, M., Schwager, S.C., Berr, A.L., Stine, C.A., Cimini, D., Bafakih, F.F., Mandell, J.W., Purow, B.W., Horton, B.J., Munson, J.M., 2022. A patient-designed tissue-engineered model of the infiltrative glioblastoma microenvironment. NPJ Precis. Oncol. 6 (1). https://doi.org/10.1038/s41698-022-00290-8.

Corso, S., Giordano, S., 2013. Cell-autonomous and non-cell-autonomous mechanisms of HGF/MET-driven resistance to targeted therapies: From basic research to a clinical perspective. Cancer Discov. 3 (9), 978–992. https://doi.org/10.1158/2159-8290.CD-13-0040Italy.

Cowan, D.S.M., Tannock, I.F., 2001. Factors that influence the penetration of methotrexate through solid tissue. Int. J. Cancer 91 (1), 120–125. https://doi.org/10.1002/1097-0215(20010101)91:1<120::AID-IJC1021>3.0.CO;2-Y.

D'Oto, A., Tian, Q.-wu, Davidoff, A.M., Yang, J., 2016. Histone demethylases and their roles in cancer epigenetics. J. Med. Oncol. Ther. 01 (02). https://doi.org/10.35841/medical-oncology.1.2.34-40.

Dorayappan, K.D.P., Wanner, R., Wallbillich, J.J., Saini, U., Zingarelli, R., Suarez, A.A., Cohn, D.E., Selvendiran, K., 2018. Hypoxia-induced exosomes contribute to a more aggressive and chemoresistant ovarian cancer phenotype: A novel mechanism linking STAT3/Rab proteins. Oncogene 37 (28), 3806–3821. https://doi.org/10.1038/s41388-018-0189-0.

Dosset, M., Vargas, T.R., Lagrange, A., Boidot, R., Végran, F., Roussey, A., Chalmin, F., Dondaine, L., Paul, C., Marie-Joseph, E.L., Martin, F., Ryffel, B., Borg, C., Adotévi, O., Ghiringhelli, F., Apetoh, L., 2018. PD-1/PD-L1 pathway: An adaptive immune resistance mechanism to immunogenic chemotherapy in colorectal cancer. Oncoimmunology 7 (6). https://doi.org/10.1080/2162402X.2018.1433981.

Du, D., Liu, C., Qin, M., Zhang, X., Xi, T., Yuan, S., Hao, H., Xiong, J., 2022. Metabolic dysregulation and emerging therapeutical targets for hepatocellular carcinoma. Acta Pharmaceutica Sinica B 12 (2), 558–580. https://doi.org/10.1016/j.apsb.2021.09.019.

Duesberg, P., Rausch, C., Rasnick, D., Hehlmann, R., 1998. Genetic instability of cancer cells is proportional to their degree of aneuploidy. Proc. Natl. Acad. Sci. 95 (23), 13692–13697. https://doi.org/10.1073/pnas.95.23.13692.

Fanelli, G., Romano, M., Nova-Lamperti, E., Sunderland, M.W., Nerviani, A., Scottà, C., Bombardieri, M., Quezada, S.A., Sacks, S.H., Noelle, R.J., Pitzalis, C., Lechler, R.I., Lombardi, G., Becker, P.D., 2021. PD-L1 signaling on human memory CD4+ T cells induces a regulatory phenotype. PLoS Biol. 19 (4). https://doi.org/10.1371/journal.pbio.3001199.

Flaherty, K.T., Manola, J.B., Pins, M., McDermott, D.F., Atkins, M.B., Dutcher, J.J., George, D.J., Margolin, K.A., DiPaola, R.S., 2015. BEST: A randomized phase II study of vascular endothelial growth factor, RAF kinase, and mammalian target of rapamycin combination targeted therapy with bevacizumab, sorafenib, and temsirolimus in advanced renal cell carcinoma - a trial of the ECOG-ACRIN cancer research group (E2804). J. Clin. Oncol. 33 (21), 2384–2391. https://doi.org/10.1200/JCO.2015.60.9727.

Galdiero, M.R., Bonavita, E., Barajon, I., Garlanda, C., Mantovani, A., Jaillon, S., 2013. Tumor associated macrophages and neutrophils in cancer. Immunobiology 218 (11), 1402–1410. https://doi.org/10.1016/j.imbio.2013.06.003.

Gerweck, L., Kozin, S., Stocks, S., 1999. The pH partition theory predicts the accumulation and toxicity of doxorubicin in normal and low-pH-adapted cells. Br J. Cancer 79, 838–842. https://doi.org/10.1038/sj.bjc.6690134.

Gonzalez-Moreno, O., Lecanda, J., Green, J.E., Segura, V., Catena, R., Serrano, D., Calvo, A., 2010. VEGF elicits epithelial-mesenchymal transition (EMT) in prostate intraepithelial neoplasia (PIN)-like cells via an autocrine loop. Exp. Cell Res. 316 (4), 554–567. https://doi.org/10.1016/j.yexcr.2009.11.020.

Hajizadeh, F., Moghadaszadeh Ardebili, S., Baghi Moornani, M., Masjedi, A., Atyabi, F., Kiani, M., Namdar, A., Karpisheh, V., Izadi, S., Baradaran, B., Azizi, G., Ghalamfarsa, G., Sabz, G., Yousefi, M., Jadidi-Niaragh, F., 2020. Silencing of HIF-1α/CD73 axis by siRNA-loaded TAT-chitosan-spion nanoparticles robustly blocks cancer cell progression. Eur. J. Pharmacol. 882. https://doi.org/10.1016/j.ejphar.2020.173235.

Halestrap, A.P., Wilson, M.C., 2012. The monocarboxylate transporter family-role and regulation. IUBMB Life 64 (2), 109–119. https://doi.org/10.1002/iub.572.

Han, Y., Wang, H., Chen, H., Tan, T., Wang, Y., Yang, H., Ding, Y., Wang, S., 2023. CX43 down-regulation promotes cell aggressiveness and 5-fluorouracil-resistance by attenuating cell stiffness in colorectal carcinoma. Cancer Biol. Ther. 24 (1). https://doi.org/10.1080/15384047.2023.2221879.

Hanahan, D., Weinberg, R.A., 2011. Hallmarks of cancer: The next generation. Cell 144 (5), 646–674. https://doi.org/10.1016/j.cell.2011.02.013.

Hong, X., Sin, W.C., Harris, A.L., Naus, C.C., 2015. Gap junctions modulate glioma invasion by direct transfer of microRNA. Oncotarget 6 (17), 15566–15577. https://doi.org/10.18632/oncotarget.3904.

Hosogi, S., Miyazaki, H., Nakajima, K.I., Ashihara, E., Niisato, N., Kusuzaki, K., Marunaka, Y., 2012. An inhibitor of Na +/H + exchanger (NHE), ethyl-isopropyl amiloride (EIPA), diminishes proliferation of MKN28 human gastric cancer cells by decreasing the cytosolic Cl - concentration via DIDS-sensitive pathways. Cell. Physiol. Biochem. 30 (5), 1241–1253. https://doi.org/10.1159/000343315.

Hu, P.S., Li, T., Lin, J.F., Qiu, M.Z., Wang, D.S., Liu, Z.X., Chen, Z.H., Yang, L.P., Zhang, X.L., Zhao, Q., Chen, Y.X., Lu, Y.X., Wu, Q.N., Pu, H.Y., Zeng, Z.L., Xie, D., Ju, H.Q., Luo, H.Y., Xu, R.H., 2020. VDR–SOX2 signaling promotes colorectal cancer stemness and malignancy in an acidic microenvironment. Signal Transduct. Targeted Ther. 5 (1). https://doi.org/10.1038/s41392-020-00230-7.

Hugo, W., Zaretsky, J.M., Sun, L., Song, C., Moreno, B.H., Hu-Lieskovan, S., Berent-Maoz, B., Pang, J., Chmielowski, B., Cherry, G., Seja, E., Lomeli, S., Kong, X., Kelley, M.C., Sosman, J.A., Johnson, D.B., Ribas, A., Lo, R.S., 2016. Genomic and transcriptomic features of response to anti-PD-1 therapy in metastatic melanoma. Cell 165 (1), 35–44. https://doi.org/10.1016/j.cell.2016.02.065.

Jaakkola, P., Mole, D.R., Tian, Y.M., Wilson, M.I., Gielbert, J., Gaskell, S.J., Von Kriegsheim, A., Hebestreit, H.F., Mukherji, M., Schofield, C.J., Maxwell, P.H., Pugh, C.W., Ratcliffe, P.J., 2001. Targeting of HIF-α to the von hippel-lindau ubiquitylation complex by O2-regulated prolyl hydroxylation. Science 292 (5516), 468–472. https://doi.org/10.1126/science.1059796.

Jin, U.H., Lee, S.O., Pfent, C., Safe, S., 2014. The aryl hydrocarbon receptor ligand omeprazole inhibits breast cancer cell invasion and metastasis. BMC Cancer 14 (1). https://doi.org/10.1186/1471-2407-14-498.

Jinushi, M., Komohara, Y., 2015. Tumor-associated macrophages as an emerging target against tumors: Creating a new path from bench to bedside. Biochim. Biophys. Acta. 1855 (2), 123–130. https://doi.org/10.1016/j.bbcan.2015.01.002.

Johnson, L.M., Price, D.K., Figg, W.D., 2013. Treatment-induced secretion of WNT16B promotes tumor growth and acquired resistance to chemotherapy: Implications for potential use of inhibitors in cancer treatment. Cancer Biol. Ther. 14 (2), 90–91. https://doi.org/10.4161/cbt.22636.

Karakashev, S.V., Reginato, M.J., 2015. Progress toward overcoming hypoxia-induced resistance to solid tumor therapy. Cancer Manag. Res. 7, 253–264. https://doi.org/10.2147/CMAR.S58285.

Keir, M.E., Butte, M.J., Freeman, G.J., Sharpe, A.H., 2008. PD-1 and its ligands in tolerance and immunity. Annu. Rev. Immunol. 26, 677–704. https://doi.org/10.1146/annurev.immunol.26.021607.090331.

Khalaf, K., Hana, D., Chou, J.T.T., Singh, C., Mackiewicz, A., Kaczmarek, M., 2021. Aspects of the tumor microenvironment involved in immune resistance and drug resistance. Front. Immunol. 12. https://doi.org/10.3389/fimmu.2021.656364.

Kim, H., Paraiso, T., Smalley, K.S.M., 2013. Fibroblast-mediated drug resistance in cancer. Biochem. Pharmacol. 85 (8), 1033–1041. https://doi.org/10.1016/j.bcp.2013.01.018.

Kitange, G.J., Carlson, B.L., Schroeder, M.A., Grogan, P.T., Lamont, J.D., Decker, P.A., Wu, W., James, C.D., Sarkaria, J.N., 2009. Induction of MGMT expression is associated with temozolomide resistance in glioblastoma xenografts. Neuro Oncol. 11 (3), 281–291. https://doi.org/10.1215/15228517-2008-090.

Kovacic, P., Osuna, J.A., 2000. Mechanisms of anti-cancer agents: Emphasis on oxidative stress and electron transfer. Curr. Pharm. Des. 6 (3), 277–309. https://doi.org/10.2174/1381612003401046.

Kumar, A.P., Quake, A.L., Chang, M.K.X., Zhou, T., Lim, K.S.Y., Singh, R., Hewitt, R.E., Salto-Tellez, M., Pervaiz, S., Clément, M.V., 2009. Repression of NHE1 expression by PPARγ activation is a potential new approach for specific inhibition of the growth of tumor cells in vitro and in vivo. Cancer Res. 69 (22), 8636–8644. https://doi.org/10.1158/0008-5472.CAN-09-0219Singapore.

Li, Z.W., Dalton, W.S., 2006. Tumor microenvironment and drug resistance in hematologic malignancies. Blood Rev. 20 (6), 333–342. https://doi.org/10.1016/j.blre.2005.08.003.

Lin, S., Negulescu, A., Bulusu, S., Gibert, B., Delcros, J.G., Ducarouge, B., Rama, N., Gadot, N., Treilleux, I., Saintigny, P., Meurette, O., Mehlen, P., 2017. Non-canonical NOTCH3 signalling limits tumour angiogenesis. Nat. Commun. 8. https://doi.org/10.1038/ncomms16074.

Liu, Z.L., Chen, H.H., Zheng, L.L., Sun, L.P., Shi, L., 2023. Angiogenic signaling pathways and anti-angiogenic therapy for cancer. Signal Transduct. Targeted Ther. 8 (1). https://doi.org/10.1038/s41392-023-01460-1.

Luciani, F., Spada, M., De Milito, A., Molinari, A., Rivoltini, L., Montinaro, A., Marra, M., Lugini, L., Logozzi, M., Lozupone, F., Federici, C., Iessi, E., Parmiani, G., Arancia, G., Belardelli, F., Fais, S., 2004. Effect of proton pump inhibitor pretreatment on resistance of solid tumors to cytotoxic drugs. J. Natl. Cancer Inst. 96 (22), 1702–1713. https://doi.org/10.1093/jnci/djh305.

Maidorn, R.P., Cragoe, E.J., Tannock, I.F., 1993. Therapeutic potential of analogues of amiloride: Inhibition of the regulation of intracellular pH as a possible mechanism of tumour selective therapy. Br. J. Cancer 67 (2), 297–303. https://doi.org/10.1038/bjc.1993.56.

Meijer, T.W.H., Kaanders, J.H.A.M., Span, P.N., Bussink, J., 2012. Targeting hypoxia, HIF-1, and tumor glucose metabolism to improve radiotherapy efficacy. Clin. Cancer Res. 18 (20), 5585–5594. https://doi.org/10.1158/1078-0432.CCR-12-0858.

Miraglia, E., Viarisio, D., Riganti, C., Costamagna, C., Ghigo, D., Bosia, A., 2005. Na+/H+ exchanger activity is increased in doxorubicin-resistant human colon cancer cells and its modulation modifies the sensitivity of the cells to doxorubicin. Int. J. Cancer 115 (6), 924–929. https://doi.org/10.1002/ijc.20959.

Mo, X.G., Chen, Q.W., Li, X.S., Zheng, M.M., Ke, D.Z., Deng, W., Li, G.Q., Jiang, J., Wu, Z.Q., Wang, L., Wang, P., Yang, Y., Cao, G.Y., 2011. Suppression of NHE1 by small interfering RNA inhibits HIF-1α-induced angiogenesis in vitro via modulation of calpain activity. Microvasc. Res. 81 (2), 160–168. https://doi.org/10.1016/j.mvr.2010.12.004.

Mohammad, G.H., Vassileva, V., Acedo, P., Damink, S.W.M.O., Malago, M., Dhar, D.K., Pereira, S.P., 2019. Targeting pyruvate kinase m2 and lactate dehydrogenase a is an effective combination strategy for the treatment of pancreatic cancer. Cancers 11 (9). https://doi.org/10.3390/cancers11091372.

Ni, C., Lou, X., Yao, X., Wang, L., Wan, J., Duan, X., Liang, J., Zhang, K., Yang, Y., Zhang, L., Sun, C., Li, Z., Wang, M., Zhu, L., Lv, D., Qin, Z., 2022. ZIP1+ fibroblasts protect lung cancer against chemotherapy via connexin-43 mediated intercellular Zn2+ transfer. Nat. Commun. 13 (1). https://doi.org/10.1038/s41467-022-33521-4.

Nishi, T., Forgac, M., 2002. The vacuolar (H+)-ATPases - nature's most versatile proton pumps. Nat. Rev. Mol. Cell Biol. 3 (2), 94–103. https://doi.org/10.1038/nrm729.

Oh, M.H., Sun, I.H., Zhao, L., Leone, R.D., Sun, I.M., Xu, W., Collins, S.L., Tam, A.J., Blosser, R.L., Patel, C.H., Englert, J.M., Arwood, M.L., Wen, J., Chan-Li, Y., Tenora, L., Majer, P., Rais, R., Slusher, B.S., Horton, M.R., Powell, J.D., 2020. Targeting glutamine metabolism enhances tumor-specific immunity by modulating suppressive myeloid cells. J. Clin. Investig. 130 (7), 3865–3884. https://doi.org/10.1172/JCI131859.

Ohta, T., Arakawa, H., Futagami, F., Fushida, S., Kitagawa, H., Kayahara, M., Nagakawa, T., Miwa, K., Kurashima, K., Numata, M., Kitamura, Y., Terada, T., Ohkuma, S., 1998. Bafilomycin A1 induces apoptosis in the human pancreatic cancer cell line Capan-1. J. Pathol. 185 (3), 324–330. https://doi.org/10.1002/(sici)1096-9896(199807)185:3<324:aid-path72>3.0.co;2-9.

Osswald, M., Jung, E., Sahm, F., Solecki, G., Venkataramani, V., Blaes, J., Weil, S., Horstmann, H., Wiestler, B., Syed, M., Huang, L., Ratliff, M., Karimian Jazi, K., Kurz, F.T., Schmenger, T., Lemke, D., Gömmel, M., Pauli, M., Liao, Y., Häring, P., Pusch, S., Herl, V., Steinhäuser, C., Krunic, D., Jarahian, M., Miletic, H., Berghoff, A.S., Griesbeck, O., Kalamakis, G., Garaschuk, O., Preusser, M., Weiss, S., Liu, H., Heiland, S., Platten, M., Huber, P.E., Kuner, T., Von Deimling, A., Wick, W., Winkler, F., 2015. Brain tumour cells interconnect to a functional and resistant network. Nature 528 (7580), 93–98. https://doi.org/10.1038/nature16071.

OuYang, L.Y., Wu, X.J., Ye, S.B., Zhang, R.x., Li, Z.L., Liao, W., Pan, Z.Z., Zheng, L.M., Zhang, X.S., Wang, Z., Li, Q., Ma, G., Li, J., 2015. Tumor-induced myeloid-derived suppressor cells promote tumor progression through oxidative metabolism in human colorectal cancer. J. Transl. Med. 13 (1). https://doi.org/10.1186/s12967-015-0410-7.

Ozawa, Y., Owa, T., Yokoi, A., Yoshimatsu, K., Asada, M., 2004. 420 the combination of Indisulam (E7070) with cisplatin, oxaliplatin and 5-fluorouracil are synergistic in vitro and in vivo. Eur. J. Cancer Suppl. 2 (8), 126. https://doi.org/10.1016/s1359-6349(04)80428-2.

Padera, T.P., Stoll, B.R., Tooredman, J.B., Capen, D., Di Tomaso, E., Jain, R.K., 2004. Cancer cells compress intratumour vessels. Nature 427 (6976), 695. https://doi.org/10.1038/427695a.

Pang, Y., Lin, H., Ou, C., Cao, Y., An, B., Yan, J., Li, X., 2019. Design, synthesis, and biological evaluation of novel benzodiazepine derivatives as anticancer agents through inhibition of tubulin polymerization in vitro and in vivo. Eur. J. Med. Chem. 182, 111670. https://doi.org/10.1016/j.ejmech.2019.111670.

Park, B.V., Freeman, Z.T., Ghasemzadeh, A., Chattergoon, M.A., Rutebemberwa, A., Steigner, J., Winter, M.E., Huynh, T.V., Sebald, S.M., Lee, S.J., Pan, F., Pardoll, D.M., Cox, A.L., 2016. TGFβ1-mediated SMAD3 enhances PD-1 expression on antigen-specific T cells in cancer. Cancer Discov. 6 (12), 1366–1381. https://doi.org/10.1158/2159-8290.CD-15-1347.

Pawar, J.S., Salam, M.A., Dipto, M.S.U., Al-Amin, M.Y., Salam, M.T., Sengupta, S., Kumari, S., Gujjari, L., Yadagiri, G., 2025. Cancer-associated fibroblasts: Immunosuppressive crosstalk with tumor-infiltrating immune cells and implications for therapeutic resistance. Cancers 17 (15). https://doi.org/10.3390/cancers17152484.

Peng, Y., Wang, Y., Zhou, C., Mei, W., Zeng, C., 2022. PI3K/Akt/mTOR pathway and its role in cancer therapeutics: Are we making headway? Front. Oncol. 12. https://doi.org/10.3389/fonc.2022.819128.

Pettersen, E.O., Ebbesen, P., Gieling, R.G., Williams, K.J., Dubois, L., Lambin, P., Ward, C., Meehan, J., Kunkler, I.H., Langdon, S.P., Ree, A.H., Flatmark, K., Lyng, H., Calzada, M.J., Peso, L.D., Landazuri, M.O., Görlach, A., Flamm, H., Kieninger, J., Urban, G., Weltin, A., Singleton, D.C., Haider, S., Buffa, F.M., Harris, A.L., Scozzafava, A., Supuran, C.T., Moser, I., Jobst, G., Busk, M., Toustrup, K., Overgaard, J., Alsner, J., Pouyssegur, J., Chiche, J., Mazure, N., Marchiq, I., Parks, S., Ahmed, A., Ashcroft, M., Pastorekova, S., Cao, Y., Rouschop, K.M., Wouters, B.G., Koritzinsky, M., Mujcic, H., Cojocari, D., 2015. Targeting tumour hypoxia to prevent cancer metastasis. From biology, biosensing and technology to drug development: The METOXIA consortium. J. Enzym. Inhib. Med. Chem. 30 (5), 689–721. https://doi.org/10.3109/14756366.2014.966704.

Pliszka, M., Szablewski, L., 2021. Glucose transporters as a target for anticancer therapy. Cancers 13 (16), 4184. https://doi.org/10.3390/cancers13164184.

Pote, M.S., Gacche, R.N., 2023. ATP-binding cassette efflux transporters and MDR in cancer. Drug Discov. Today 28 (5). https://doi.org/10.1016/j.drudis.2023.103537.

Potente, M., Gerhardt, H., Carmeliet, P., 2011. Basic and therapeutic aspects of angiogenesis. Cell 146 (6), 873–887. https://doi.org/10.1016/j.cell.2011.08.039.

Queen, M.M., Ryan, R.E., Holzer, R.G., Keller-Peck, C.R., Jorcyk, C.L., 2005. Breast cancer cells stimulate neutrophils to produce oncostatin M: Potential implications for tumor progression. Cancer Res. 65 (19), 8896–8904. https://doi.org/10.1158/0008-5472.CAN-05-1734.

Ramapriyan, R., Caetano, M.S., Barsoumian, H.B., Mafra, A.C.P., Zambalde, E.P., Menon, H., Tsouko, E., Welsh, J. W., Cortez, M.A., 2019. Altered cancer metabolism in mechanisms of immunotherapy resistance. Pharmacol Ther. 195, 162–171. https://doi.org/10.1016/j.pharmthera.2018.11.004.

Reshkin, S.J., Bellizzi, A., Cardone, R.A., Tommasino, M., Casavola, V., Paradiso, A., 2003. Paclitaxel induces apoptosis via protein kinase A- and p38 mitogen-activated protein-dependent inhibition of the Na+/H+ exchanger (NHE) NHE isoform 1 in human breast cancer cells. Clin. Cancer Res. 9 (6), 2366–2373.

Rich, I.N., Worthington-White, D., Garden, O.A., Musk, P., 2000. Apoptosis of leukemic cells accompanies reduction in intracellular pH after targeted inhibition of the Na+/H+exchanger. Blood 95 (4), 1427–1434. https://doi.org/10.1182/blood.v95.4.1427.004k48_1427_1434.

Rowshanravan, B., Halliday, N., Sansom, D.M., 2018. CTLA-4: A moving target in immunotherapy. Blood 131 (1), 58–67. https://doi.org/10.1182/blood-2017-06-741033.

Safaei, R., Larson, B.J., Cheng, T.C., Gibson, M.A., Otani, S., Naerdemann, W., Howell, S.B., 2005. Abnormal lysosomal trafficking and enhanced exosomal export of cisplatin in drug-resistant human ovarian carcinoma cells. Mol. Cancer Therapeut. 4 (10), 1595–1604. https://doi.org/10.1158/1535-7163.MCT-05-0102.

Sailer, B.L., Barrasso, A.M., Valdez, J.G., Cobo, J.M., D'Anna, J.A., Crissman, H.A., 1998. Reduction in the radiation-induced late S phase and G2 blocks in HL-60 cell populations by amiloride, an efficient inhibitor of the Na+/H+ transporter. Cancer Res. 58 (3), 413–420.

Salony, X.S., Alves, C.P., Dey-Guha, I., Ritsma, L., Boukhali, M., Lee, J.H., Chowdhury, J., Ross, K.N., Haas, W., Vasudevan, S., Ramaswamy, S., 2016. AKT inhibition promotes nonautonomous cancer cell survival. Mol. Cancer Therapeut. 15 (1), 142–153. https://doi.org/10.1158/1535-7163.MCT-15-0414.

Santoni, M., Massari, F., Amantini, C., Nabissi, M., Maines, F., Burattini, L., Berardi, R., Santoni, G., Montironi, R., Tortora, G., Cascinu, S., 2013. Emerging role of tumor-associated macrophages as therapeutic targets in patients with metastatic renal cell carcinoma. Cancer Immunol. Immunother. 62 (12), 1757–1768. https://doi.org/10.1007/s00262-013-1487-6.

Sauvant, C., Nowak, M., Wirth, C., Schneider, B., Riemann, A., Gekle, M., Thews, O., 2008. Acidosis induces multidrug resistance in rat prostate cancer cells (AT1) in vitro and in vivo by increasing the activity of the p-glycoprotein via activation of p38. Int. J. Cancer 123 (11), 2532–2542. https://doi.org/10.1002/ijc.23818.

Semenza, G.L., 1999. Perspectives on oxygen sensing. Cell 98 (3), 281–284. https://doi.org/10.1016/S0092-8674(00)81957-1.

Singleton, D.C., Macann, A., Wilson, W.R., 2021. Therapeutic targeting of the hypoxic tumour microenvironment. Nat. Rev. Clin. Oncol. 18 (12), 751–772. https://doi.org/10.1038/s41571-021-00539-4.

Shamamian, P., Schwartz, J.D., Pocock, B.J.Z., Monea, S., Whiting, D., Marcus, S.G., Mignatti, P., 2001. Activation of progelatinase A (MMP-2) by neutrophil elastase, cathepsin G, and proteinase-3: A role for inflammatory cells in tumor invasion and angiogenesis. J. Cell. Physiol. 189 (2), 197–206. https://doi.org/10.1002/jcp.10014.

Sherwood, L.M., Parris, E.E., Folkman, J., 1971. Tumor angiogenesis: Therapeutic implications. N. Engl. J. Med. 285 (21), 1182–1186. https://doi.org/10.1056/NEJM197111182852108.

Shi, X., Yang, J., Deng, S., Xu, H., Wu, D., Zeng, Q., Wang, S., Hu, T., Wu, F., Zhou, H., 2022. TGF-β signaling in the tumor metabolic microenvironment and targeted therapies. J. Hematol. Oncol. 15 (1). https://doi.org/10.1186/s13045-022-01349-6.

Shirai, Y., Chow, C.C.T., Kambe, G., Suwa, T., Kobayashi, M., Takahashi, I., Harada, H., Nam, J.M., 2021. An overview of the recent development of anticancer agents targeting the hif-1 transcription factor. Cancers 13 (11). https://doi.org/10.3390/cancers13112813.

Shree, T., Olson, O.C., Elie, B.T., Kester, J.C., Garfall, A.L., Simpson, K., Bell-Mcguinn, K.M., Zabor, E.C., Brogi, E., Joyce, J.A., 2011. Macrophages and cathepsin proteases blunt chemotherapeutic response in breast cancer. Genes Dev. 25 (23), 2465–2479. https://doi.org/10.1101/gad.180331.111.

Sonveaux, P., Végran, F., Schroeder, T., Wergin, M.C., Verrax, J., Rabbani, Z.N., De Saedeleer, C.J., Kennedy, K.M., Diepart, C., Jordan, B.F., Kelley, M.J., Gallez, B., Wahl, M.L., Feron, O., Dewhirst, M.W., 2008. Targeting lactate-fueled respiration selectively kills hypoxic tumor cells in mice. J. Clin. Investig. 118 (12), 3930–3942. https://doi.org/10.1172/JCI36843.

Studebaker, A.W., Storci, G., Werbeck, J.L., Sansone, P., Sasser, A.K., Tavolari, S., Huang, T., Chan, M.W.Y., Marini, F.C., Roso, T.J., Bonafé, M., Hall, B.M., 2008. Fibroblasts isolated from common sites of breast cancer metastasis enhance cancer cell growth rates and invasiveness in an interleukin-6-dependent manner. Cancer Res. 68 (21), 9087–9095. https://doi.org/10.1158/0008-5472.CAN-08-0400.

Su, S., Chen, J., Yao, H., Liu, J., Yu, S., Lao, L., Wang, M., Luo, M., Xing, Y., Chen, F., 2018. CD10+ GPR77+ cancer-associated fibroblasts promote cancer formation and chemoresistance by sustaining cancer stemness. Cell 172 (4), 841–856.

Sulaiman, A., McGarry, S., Chambers, J., Al-Kadi, E., Phan, A., Li, L., Mediratta, K., Dimitroulakos, J., Addison, C., Li, X., Wang, L., 2020. Targeting hypoxia sensitizes TNBC to cisplatin and promotes inhibition of both bulk and cancer stem cells. Int. J. Mol. Sci. 21 (16), 5788. https://doi.org/10.3390/ijms21165788.

Tang, Y.A., Chen, Y.f., Bao, Y., Mahara, S., Yatim, S.M.J.M., Oguz, G., Lee, P.L., Feng, M., Cai, Y., Tan, E.Y., Fong, S. S., Yang, Z.h., Lan, P., Wu, X.j., Yu, Q., 2018. Hypoxic tumor microenvironment activates GLI2 via HIF-1α and TGF-β2 to promote chemoresistance in colorectal cancer. Proc. Natl. Acad. Sci. U S A. 115 (26), E5990. https://doi.org/10.1073/pnas.1801348115.

Tie, Y., Tang, F., Peng, D., Zhang, Y., Shi, H., 2022. TGF-beta signal transduction: Biology, function and therapy for diseases. Mol. Biomed. 3 (1). https://doi.org/10.1186/s43556-022-00109-9.

Tirpe, A.A., Gulei, D., Ciortea, S.M., Crivii, C., Berindan-Neagoe, I., 2019. Hypoxia: Overview on hypoxia-mediated mechanisms with a focus on the role of hif genes. Int. J. Mol. Sci. 20 (24). https://doi.org/10.3390/ijms20246140.

Vaddepally, R.K., Kharel, P., Pandey, R., Garje, R., Chandra, A.B., 2020. Review of indications of FDA-approved immune checkpoint inhibitors per NCCN guidelines with the level of evidence. Cancers 12 (3). https://doi.org/10.3390/cancers12030738.

Valk, E., Rudd, C.E., Schneider, H., 2008. CTLA-4 trafficking and surface expression. Trends Immunol. 29 (6), 272–279. https://doi.org/10.1016/j.it.2008.02.011.

Vendramini-Costa, D.B., Carvalho, J.E., 2012. Molecular link mechanisms between inflammation and cancer. Curr. Pharm. Des. 18 (26), 3831–3852. https://doi.org/10.2174/138161212802083707.

Wang, X., Shen, X., Yan, Y., Li, H., 2021. Pyruvate dehydrogenase kinases (PDKs): An overview toward clinical applications. Biosci. Rep. 41 (4). https://doi.org/10.1042/BSR20204402.

Ward, C., Meehan, J., Gray, M.E., Murray, A.F., Argyle, D.J., Kunkler, I.H., Langdon, S.P., 2020. The impact of tumour pH on cancer progression: Strategies for clinical intervention. Explor Target Antitumor Ther. 1 (2), 71–100. https://doi.org/10.37349/etat.2020.00005.

Xie, Y., Liu, C., Zhang, Y., Amin, L., Sun, C., Li, R., Xing, Y., Shi, M., Qi, W., Hsieh, Y.-H., 2021. PKI-587 enhances radiosensitization of hepatocellular carcinoma by inhibiting the PI3K/AKT/mTOR pathways and DNA damage repair. PLoS One 16 (10), e0258817. https://doi.org/10.1371/journal.pone.0258817.

Yamada, K., Maishi, N., Akiyama, K., Towfik Alam, M., Ohga, N., Kawamoto, T., Shindoh, M., Takahashi, N., Kamiyama, T., Hida, Y., Taketomi, A., Hida, K., 2015. CXCL12-CXCR7 axis is important for tumor endothelial cell angiogenic property. Int. J. Cancer 137 (12), 2825–2836. https://doi.org/10.1002/ijc.29655.

Yan, M., Yang, R., Qi, L., Wang, C., Chen, J., Wu, Z., Han, L., Fan, J., 2024. Anti-angiogenic and antitumor effects of anlotinib combined with bevacizumab for colorectal cancer. Transl. Oncol. 41, 101887. https://doi.org/10.1016/j.tranon.2024.101887.

Yin, Y., Yao, S., Hu, Y., Feng, Y., Li, M., Bian, Z., Zhang, J., Qin, Y., Qi, X., Zhou, L., Fei, B., Zou, J., Dong, H., Huang, Z., 2017. The immune-microenvironment confers chemoresistance of colorectal cancer through macrophage-derived IL6. Clin. Cancer Res. 23 (23), 7375–7387. https://doi.org/10.1158/1078-0432.ccr-17-1283.

Yoshimura, A., 2006. Signal transduction of inflammatory cytokines and tumor development. Cancer Sci. 97 (6), 439–447. https://doi.org/10.1111/j.1349-7006.2006.00197.x.

Yu, H.A., Arcila, M.E., Hellmann, M.D., Kris, M.G., Ladanyi, M., Riely, G.J., 2014. Poor response to erlotinib in patients with tumors containing baseline EGFR T790M mutations found by routine clinical molecular testing. Ann. Oncol. 25 (2), 423–428. https://doi.org/10.1093/annonc/mdt573.

Yu, M., Han, G., Qi, B., Wu, X., 2017. Cx32 reverses epithelial-mesenchymal transition in doxorubicin-resistant hepatocellular carcinoma. Oncol. Rep. 37 (4), 2121–2128. https://doi.org/10.3892/or.2017.5462.

Yu, X., Lao, Y., Teng, X.L., Li, S., Zhou, Y., Wang, F., Guo, X., Deng, S., Chang, Y., Wu, X., Liu, Z., Chen, L., Lu, L.M., Cheng, J., Li, B., Su, B., Jiang, J., Li, H.B., Huang, C., Yi, J., Zou, Q., 2018. SENP3 maintains the stability and function of regulatory T cells via BACH2 deSUMOylation. Nat. Commun. 9 (1). https://doi.org/10.1038/s41467-018-05676-6.

Zaccagna, F., Grist, J.T., Quartuccio, N., Riemer, F., Fraioli, F., Caracò, C., Halsey, R., Aldalilah, Y., Cunningham, C. H., Massoud, T.F., Aloj, L., Gallagher, F.A., 2021. Imaging and treatment of brain tumors through molecular targeting: Recent clinical advances. Eur. J. Radiol. 142. https://doi.org/10.1016/j.ejrad.2021.109842.

Zatovicova, M., Jelenska, L., Hulikova, A., Csaderova, L., Ditte, Z., Ditte, P., Goliasova, T., Pastorek, J., Pastorekova, S., 2010. Carbonic anhydrase IX as an anticancer therapy target: Preclinical evaluation of internalizing monoclonal antibody directed to catalytic domain. Curr. Pharm. Des. 16 (29), 3255–3263. https://doi.org/10.2174/138161210793429832.

Zhao, Q., Tan, B.B., Li, Y., Fan, L.Q., Yang, P.G., Tian, Y., 2016. Enhancement of drug sensitivity by knockdown of HIF-1α in gastric carcinoma cells. Oncol. Res. 23 (3), 129–136. https://doi.org/10.3727/096504015X14500513118029.

Zottl, J., Sebesta, C.G., Tomosel, E., Sebesta, M.C., Sebesta, C., 2025. Unraveling the burden of pancreatic cancer in the 21st century: Trends in incidence, mortality, survival, and key contributing factors. Cancers 17 (10). https://doi.org/10.3390/cancers17101607.

CHAPTER

6

Cancer therapy depending on tumor vasculature and EPR effects

Pralay Maiti[1] *and Sudepta Bauri*[2]
[1]IIT BHU, School of Materials Science and Technology, Varanasi, Uttar Pradesh, India;
[2]Indian Institute of Technology (BHU), School of Materials Science and Technology, Varanasi, Uttar Pradesh, India

Introduction

World Health Organization predicted more than 14 million new cases of cancer annually by 2035 (Pilleron et al., 2019). In the development of cancers, tumor microenvironment (TME) is crucial, which refers to the cellular environment in which (Weber and Kuo, 2012) tumors or cancer stem cells are present[2]. Numerous cellular components make up the TME (Fig. 6.1). The first is endothelial cells that participate in tumor growth and immune system defense. Typically, tumor angiogenic arteries originating from endothelial progenitor cells or branch off the preexisting capillaries provide nutritional support for tumor growth (Arneth, 2019). Immune cells, including macrophages, lymphocytes, and granulocytes, make up the second main component of TME. These participate in a range of immunological activities and responses, including inflammatory responses for adaptation. The macrophages are involved in the onset and spread of cancer as it can inhibit antitumor immune responses and can facilitate the extravasation of circulating cancer cells to distant locations, like the lungs, resulting in development of metastatic colonies (Whiteside, 2008).

The tumor vasculature significantly influences the tumor growth and treatment responses. Normal tissues receiving blood flow from an effective vascular network maintain equilibrium between pro-apoptotic and anti-apoptotic agents. Conversely, lymphatic tubes clear the interstitium of metabolic waste. The vascular network's architecture thus can provide oxygen and nourishment to cells. In cancer, tumor tissue grows quickly that farther away the cells from the supplying blood artery and thus run out of oxygen and nutrients (Forster et al., 2017). When the tumor reaches a certain size

https://doi.org/10.1016/B978-0-443-44185-1.00031-8

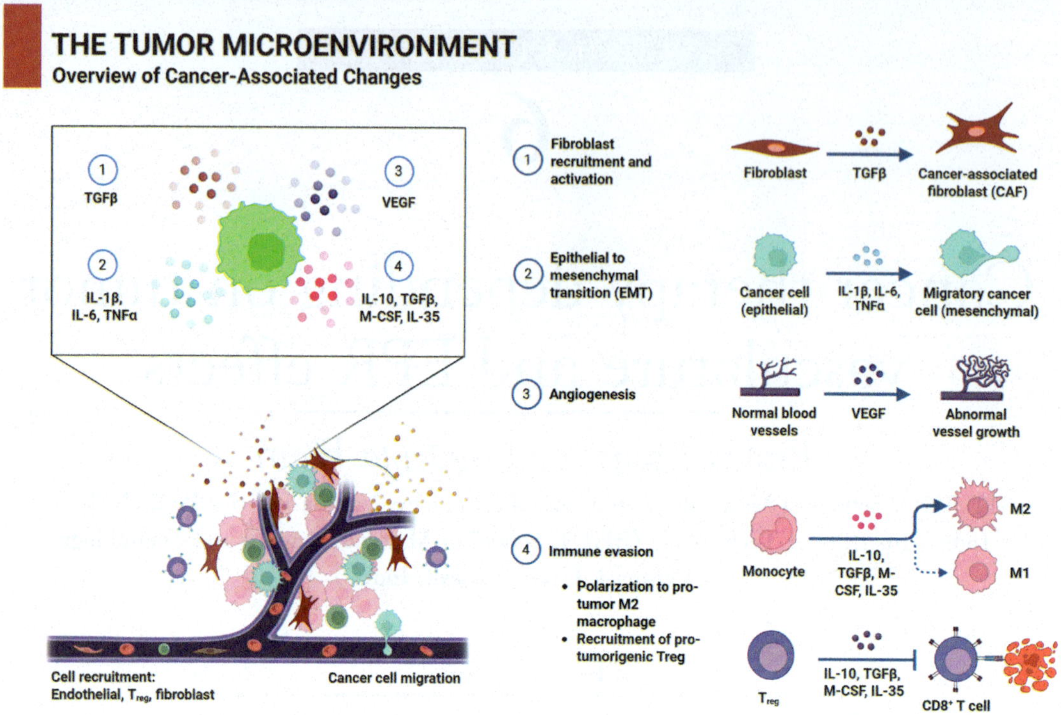

FIGURE 6.1 An overview of tumor microenvironment. Vascular changes associated with tumor microenvironment.

(1–2 mm^3) (Ghosh Dastidar et al., 2020), growth of the tumor and a pathway for metastasis are provided by tumor angiogenesis (Hammersen, 1983). Tumor vasculatures are highly disorganized, irregular, and leaky due to rapid and abnormal angiogenesis. In tumor, a few sites are hyperperfused while few are hypoxic. The tumor vasculature thus plays vital role in cancer progression, metastasis, and treatment resistance.

The enhanced permeability and retention (EPR) effect is another important factor in cancer treatment, first discovered in 1986 by Matsumura and Maeda (Maeda, no date). EPR effect is responsible for preferential accumulation of nanoparticles and macromolecules in tumor tissues. The leaky vasculature results in passive diffusion of drugs, while poor lymphatic drainage results in prolonged retention. However, EPR effect is highly variable within tumors and between tumor types. Additionally, heterogeneous vascular permeability and high interstitial pressure can affect drug retention. The tumor vasculature and EPR effect are double edge strategy that can be exploited for targeted drug delivery, cancer treatment, and minimizing side effects. This chapter discusses the strategies to utilize tumor vasculature and EPR effect in achieving therapeutic outcomes for effective management of cancer.

Tumor vasculature: Structure and function

Tumors have an elevated extracellular matrix (ECM) formation made up of fibrous proteins and polysaccharide meshwork (Campbell et al., 2010). ECM remodeling is necessary for tumor development, where tumor cells acquire immune cells, smooth muscle cells, endothelial cells, and fibroblasts into the extracellular matrix (Radisky et al., 2001). For this, surrounding host tissue's vasculature perfuses small tumors, which have a diameter of less than 2 mm (Gimbrone et al., 1972). Higher metabolic tissue demand and higher cell distance from the preexisting vasculature promote angiogenesis, resulting in the growth and extension of existing blood vessels to establish new vascular networks in the tumors. Below are a few features of vascular architecture in tumors that can be exploited for drug delivery.

Abnormal vascular architecture in tumors

Konerding et al., (1999) used SEM and corrosion casting to investigate the vascular architecture of subcutaneous mouse tumors. Smooth muscle cells, pericytes, lymphatic drainage, and appropriate vessel hierarchy were absent in tumor vasculature. Additionally, the vasculature was complicated, disorderly branched, brought on by random angiogenic signaling, uneven basement membranes, and discontinuous endothelium. Invasion percolation (Baish et al., 1996), which causes such disorderly growth, results in an unequal blood supply, hypoxic condition, and variable nutrient supply. The high supply at its edges results in tumor growth and poor treatment.

Angiogenesis and vascular remodeling

Angiogenesis and vascular remodeling work together as critical processes for tumor progression. High oxygen and nutrient demand result in angiogenesis and restructuring of existing vasculature to meet the demand. The imbalance of interactions between diffusible pro- and anti-angiogenic chemicals secreted by cancer cells and other cells, including stromal cells, endothelial cells, and biological components of the extracellular matrix, also leads to angiogenesis. The angiogenic switch (Bouck et al., 1996) can be due to mechanical or metabolic stress, immunological or inflammatory responses, and genetic abnormalities that trigger the transition. Vascular endothelial cells can respond to such angiogenic stimuli by increasing the rates of migration, differentiation, and proliferation while decreasing the apoptosis rate. Tumor angiogenesis usually results in disorganized, leaky, irregular, and fragile vessels with poor perfusion potential and heterogeneous oxygen supply. For further improving nutrient access, altering immune cell infiltration and facilitating metastasis, vascular remodeling occurs to form torturous and dilated abnormal vascular system via basement membrane degradation and remodeling of matrix metalloproteinases (MMPs). Antiangiogenic therapy and vascular normalization therapy thus can be utilized for improved drug delivery and cancer therapy.

Vascular permeability and tumor heterogeneity

Permeability is a complex process depending on size, shape, and charge of extravasating molecules, affinity towards endothelial membrane and surface of cancer cells, vascular permeability of tumor cells, and tumor heterogenicity (Zhao et al., 2007). The higher permeability in tumors can be due to disorganized endothelial junctions, basement membrane degradation via MMPs, low structural support due to poor pericyte coverage, and high fenestrations in endothelial cells. This can be exploited for EPR effect for nanoparticle-based drug delivery. Targeted treatment using tiny permeable molecules and/or monoclonal antibodies is possible by the identification of particular molecular changes in malignancies. For instance, the estrogen receptor in breast cancer benefited from anti-estrogen therapy (Jordan, 2008). Lapatinib, a HER2 tyrosine kinase inhibitor, and trastuzumab, an antibody targeting breast cancer that expresses HER2. BRAF (Turski et al., 2016) inhibitors like dabrafenib and vemurafenib can be used for melanoma with BRAF aberrations. However, genetic changes like KRAS mutation in colorectal cancer may result in resistance to anti-EGFR (Misale et al., 2014) antibodies cetuximab or panitumumab by dysregulating RAS-MEK-ERK signaling cascade. Therefore, vascular permeability and tumor heterogeneity can contribute to drug selection, target check, drug delivery, and precise therapy.

Implications of tumor vasculature in drug delivery

The drug delivery in tumors is diffusion-limited, where higher concentration is achieved in high vascular sites, while lower concentrations in avascular tumor sections. Convection inside the vasculature further transports drugs to the tumor tissue. Drug distribution to the avascular tumor tissue surrounding the vasculature is regulated by extravasation from the vasculature and diffusion in the avascular space. The linear distance of oxygen's diffusional capacity (~100 μm) is greater than the vessel spacing in a healthy capillary bed (Narang and Varia, 2011). However, tumors have extremely uneven artery spacing, which impedes the diffusional access of medications and oxygen to the tumor's avascular regions. This creates a diffusional barrier to drug transport to target cells. Tumor heterogeneity is emphasized by variance in drug delivery between primary tumors and metastases, showing higher concentrations in smaller tumors (Pervez et al., 1988). Tumor size can also impact drug penetration as a result of solid stress and interstitial fluid pressure (Stylianopoulos et al., 2013). The heightened vascular permeability, inflammation, and disruption of the blood-brain barrier may allow the drug to penetrate areas otherwise shielded.

Tumor vasculature targeting strategies and role in cancer therapy

Targeting tumor vasculature or overexpressed receptors on the tumor vascular endothelial cells via the use of nanoparticles is a novel approach. Targeting tumor angiogenesis and vasculature can be highly applicable to the majority of solid tumors in vivo (Narang and Varia, 2011). Tumor endothelial cells instantly exposed to circulating blood can facilitate drug-loaded nanoparticles delivery without an extravasation barrier. A number of proteins are overexpressed on the surface of tumor vascular endothelial cells that can be used to target tumors with functionalized nanoparticles, creating new avenues for cancer therapy and targeted molecular imaging.

Anti-angiogenic therapy

Anti-angiogenic therapy is a conventional cancer treatment that aims to reduce the vascular network and inhibit the growth of new blood vessels. Folkman (1989) proposed blocking blood vessels to slow the growth of tumors by limiting oxygen and nutrient supply. Treatments such as bevacizumab (Vasudev and Reynolds, 2014), the first VEGF-targeted antibody authorized by the FDA, were made available. However, VEGF pathway inhibitors become ineffective on their own, and resistance usually arises as a result of adaptive and compensating mechanisms (Taylor et al., 2003). Overcoming it is still quite difficult. A few resistance mechanisms that contribute to the limited success of single-targeted therapies are reactivation of alternative angiogenic pathways (Casanovas et al., 2005), upregulation of other pro-angiogenic factors (Li et al., 2014), vascular co-option (Frentzas et al., 2016), where tumors use existing vessels, vascular mimicry (Marchat et al., 2019), where cancer cells form vessel-like structures, recruitment of endothelial progenitor cells (Haider et al., 2017), and mobilization of pro-inflammatory/pro-angiogenic cells (Li et al., 2016). New medications have been developed to target VEGF and other angiogenic pathways to increase anti-tumor efficacy (Kim et al., 1993). For instance, it has been demonstrated that dual inhibition of the VEGF and FGF pathways inhibits the migration and proliferation of endothelial cells (Li et al., 2016). Arylamide-5-anilinoquinazoline-8-nitro is one of the unique VEGF inhibitors that exhibits encouraging anti-tumor and anti-angiogenic qualities in vitro (Zhao et al., 2019).

Normalization versus destruction approaches

Both opposing strategies of normalization and destruction can be utilized in cancer therapy. The destruction strategy destroys cancer cells and associated structures directly with methods such as radiation, chemotherapy, or high-dose anti-angiogenic therapy (Fig. 6.2).

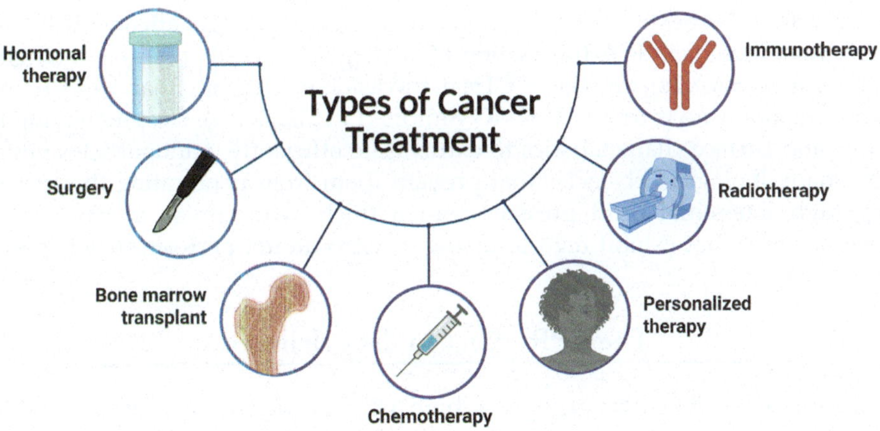

FIGURE 6.2 **Methods of cancer eradication.** Destruction strategies for cancer treatment.

Although it reduces tumor size, but can also cause hypoxia, destroy healthy tissue, and increase tumor resistance. Conversely, normalization seeks to return the tumor microenvironment to normal, particularly in relation to immune and blood vessel function. This enhances oxygen delivery, increases drug absorption, and activates the immune system for promising anticancer effect.

Tumor vasculature modification approaches

By altering the perivascular milieu, medicinal compounds, oncolytic viruses, and nanoparticles uptake and retention can be improved (McKee et al., 2006). Another strategy is to improve transvascular convective flow to raise the perfusing pressure and improve drug delivery (Matsumura et al., 1988). Angiotensin II and other hypertensive drugs can increase the extravasation of colloids. Angiotensin converting enzyme (ACE) inhibitors, such as enalapril, may exacerbate antibody accumulation (Netti et al., 1999). ACE inhibitors increase the permeability to large molecules by preventing the breakdown of bradykinin, a potent physiological vasodilatory peptide. Giving both the ACE inhibitor and angiotensin II is a great method to increase the EPR since angiotensin II will counteract the hypotensive effect of enalapril, an ACE inhibitor (Maeda, 2010a).

Nanoparticles for targeting tumor vasculature and drug delivery

Targeted nanoparticles and tumor microenvironment-responsive nanotherapeutics have recently been developed to alter the tumor vasculature (Fig. 6.3) shows various types of NPs that have been used for decades. The coagulation protein, thrombin, is delivered into tumor tissues using a temperature-sensitive polymeric nanogel or a DNA nanorobot to selectively block tumor vasculature (Ding et al., 2013). The pH-responsive nanotherapeutics are used to correct abnormalities in tumor vasculature and promote medication perfusion, and polymeric nanotherapeutics are also employed to boost tumor vascular permeability by locally lowering tumor-associated platelets (TAPs) (Chen et al., 2018; Zhao et al., 2014). Nanoparticles must first extravasate through blood arteries to target effectively. In xenograft SKOV-3 tumors, there is little extravasation of both quantum dots (QDs) and single-walled carbon nanotubes (SWNTs). However, QDs extravasate more easily than SWNTs in LS174T tumors, but the opposite is true in U87MG tumors (Li et al., 2019). Despite having the right size, shape, and surface characteristics to extravasate efficiently, nanoparticles nevertheless encounter many biological obstacles that prevent them from penetrating the tumor tissue, including high interstitial fluid pressure and a thick extracellular matrix. As a result, many nanoparticles that exhibit high targeting in vitro do not perform better in vivo.

The EPR effect in drug delivery

Early tumors (less than 100 μm) have a high vascular density and a strong EPR effect. Drugs must possess macromolecular properties (or nanomedicines) that allow selective extravasation into tumor tissues via EPR effect but not normal tissues.

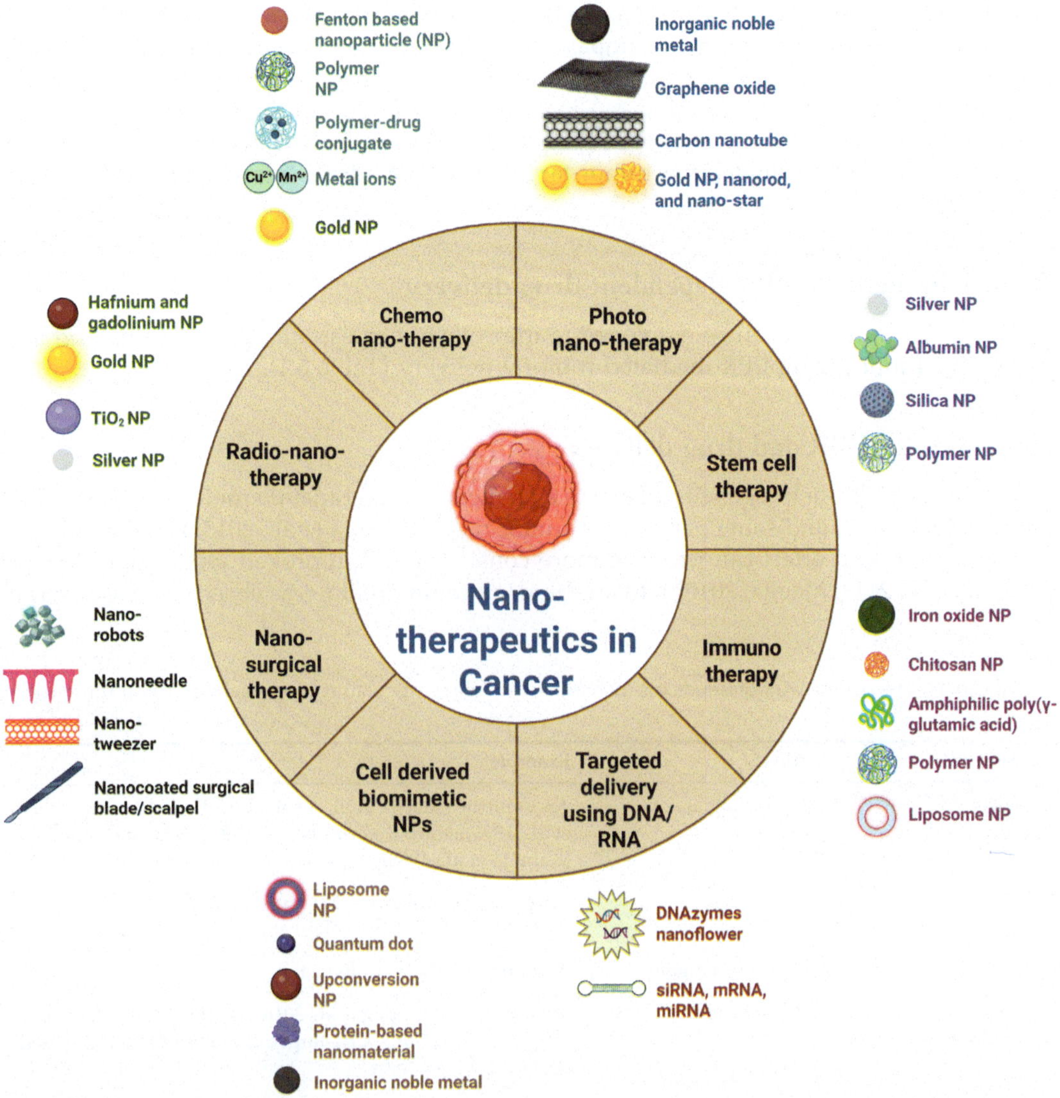

FIGURE 6.3 **Nanomaterials for cancer treatment.** Various nano formulations like polymeric nanoparticles, lipid-based nanoparticles, inorganic nanoparticles, genetic nanoparticles, carbon tube, drug conjugates and proteins or peptides for cancer management.

Mechanism of EPR effect

The Enhanced Permeability and Retention (EPR) effect, initially described by Matsumura and Maeda (1986) in 1986, is the basic mechanism of tumor-targeting of nanomedicines and has been regarded as the "cornerstone" for the creation of nanodrugs for cancer treatment. The study showed that defective vasculature and elevated vascular mediator production caused solid tumors to have large gaps between endothelial cells of approximately 400 nm (Maeda et al., 2016). This allows nanoparticles to leak out and accumulate in tumor cells. Furthermore, impaired lymphatic systems are unable to transport macro- and nanoparticles from tissue to the blood circulation can increase the retention in the tumoral extracellular matrix (Greish, 2010). The difference in lymphatic and vascular architecture between tumor and normal tissues facilitates the tumor-targeting of nanodrugs via the EPR effect (Fang et al., 2011).

Factors influencing EPR-dependent drug delivery

Various technologies can be employed to improve tumor vascular permeability and alter tumor ECM influencing EPR-mediated tumoral delivery (Table 6.1).

Variability of EPR and drug delivery

The EPR effect's heterogeneity presents a challenge to therapeutic molecules in reaching tumor interstitium, and some parts of the tumor tissue (Maeda et al., 2013; Fang et al.,2011). Increasing the EPR effect can produce more consistent and improved medication delivery (Maeda et al., 2013; Maeda, 2010b). Evans blue/albumin uptake was absent in large necrotic

TABLE 6.1 An overview of methods for increasing the tumor vasculature's permeability to optimize the EPR.

Techniques	Methods	Examples
Vascular Permeabilization	NO releasing agents	Amyl-nitrite (Maeda et al., 1996), Sosorbide dinitrate (Maeda et al., 1996), Nitroglycerin (Islam et al., 2018), Bradykinin (Kamata et al., 1985)
	TAP blockage	Anti-platelet antibody R300 (Li et al., 2017), Perfluorotributylamine (Zhou et al., 2018)
	Hypertension agent	Angiotensin II (Nagamitsu et al., 2009)
Vascular Normalization	TAM blockage	nRGD-Lipo-Dox (Song et al., 2016), Histidine-rich glycoprotein (Theek et al., 2018), CCR2-targeting Cu@CuOx (Zhang et al., 2021)
	Proangiogenic signal blockage	Bevacizumab (Seo et al., 2018), DC101 (Chauhan et al., 2020), Sorafenib (Kano et al., 2009), Tie-2-activating antibody (Park et al., 2016)
Oxygen supply	In situ oxygen production	MnO_2 and CaO_2, Catalase (Izci et al., 2021)
	Oxygen delivery	Fluorocarbons (FCs) (Ma et al., 2019), Hemoglobin (Hb) (Yang et al., 2018)
Thrombolysis	Activation of coagulation/fibrinolysis	Streptokinase (SK) (Keramati et al., 2013), Staphylokinase (Sak) (Li et al., 2020)

sections of the tumor, but was more noticeable toward the tumor perimeter, where tumor growth is rapid. According to angiography, prostate and pancreatic tumors are hypovascular, and thus contrast agent is not well absorbed (Tsuchiya et al., 2000). However, angiotensin II-induced hypertension can enhance medication delivery to tumors, even in hypovascular tumors (2012) (Urology, 2000) Bauri et al. (Fig. 6.4) in their work have also shown the EPR superiority in cancer cells compared to 3T3 cells via adhesion and MTT assay data, where drug-loaded PU-CYS system shows enhanced cancer cell killing, where normal cells remain viable up to 95% (Bauri et al., 2024).

Imaging and EPR estimation

Visualizing tumor features non-invasively and measuring important EPR-determining parameters for correlation with tumor accumulation of nanomedicines is a straightforward approach. For instance, MRI, CT, ultrasound, and microscope are examples of multi-model imaging that can be used to determine the relative blood volume (rBV) in a tumor (Golombek et al., 2018). The effect of EPR-mediated tumor targeting can be predicted through direct correlation between the rBV and the accumulation of nanoparticles in tumors. Nanoparticles tagged with an imaging agent can also be used to assess the EPR effect. For example, 89Zr was added to liposomes that facilitate PET imaging. By comparing their tumoral accumulation, it shows a perfect correlation with Doxil. As a result, 89Zr-labeled liposomes can be used to predict the patient's EPR response to Doxil. 89Zr-labeling is a potent nano diagnostics technique that can be used for PET imaging of PEG-PLGA nanoparticles (Pérez-Medina et al., 2016).

Nanomedicine as therapeutic strategy

Nanomedicine (Bauri et al., 2023) has gained widespread popularity for its role in targeted drug delivery. A chronology of significant events in cancer nanomedicine is shown in Fig. 6.5. Various types of nanocarriers been exploited for the delivery of anticancer drugs to enhance therapeutic efficiency while reducing off-target toxicity (Table 6.2). This shows the potential of nanomedicine in effective cancer therapy. Nanomedicine can modulate the pharmacokinetics and pharmacodynamics of multiple therapeutic agents, prolong the systemic circulation, and result in selective accumulation of large bioavailable drugs at the target site, thereby enhancing the therapeutic efficacy.

Nanoparticles can reach tumor tissues mainly by two mechanisms (Fig. 6.6), either by passive or active targeting (Alavi and Hamidi, 2019). Passive targeting involves the accumulation of nanoparticles at the tumor site through EPR via high vascular permeability and low lymphatic outflow. The FDA-approved nanomedicines Doxil and Apealea are well known for their reliance on the EPR effect, and about 15 clinically used nano formulations that employ EPR-mediated passive targeting (He et al., 2019). The heterogeneous nature of tumors can lead to such varying results, and thus, researchers are concentrating on active strategies for nanomedicine delivery as alternatives to passive mechanisms. The strategies include molecular recognition, receptor-mediated transport, or engineered responsiveness for improved intracellular uptake and selectivity, especially in tumors with poor EPR effect

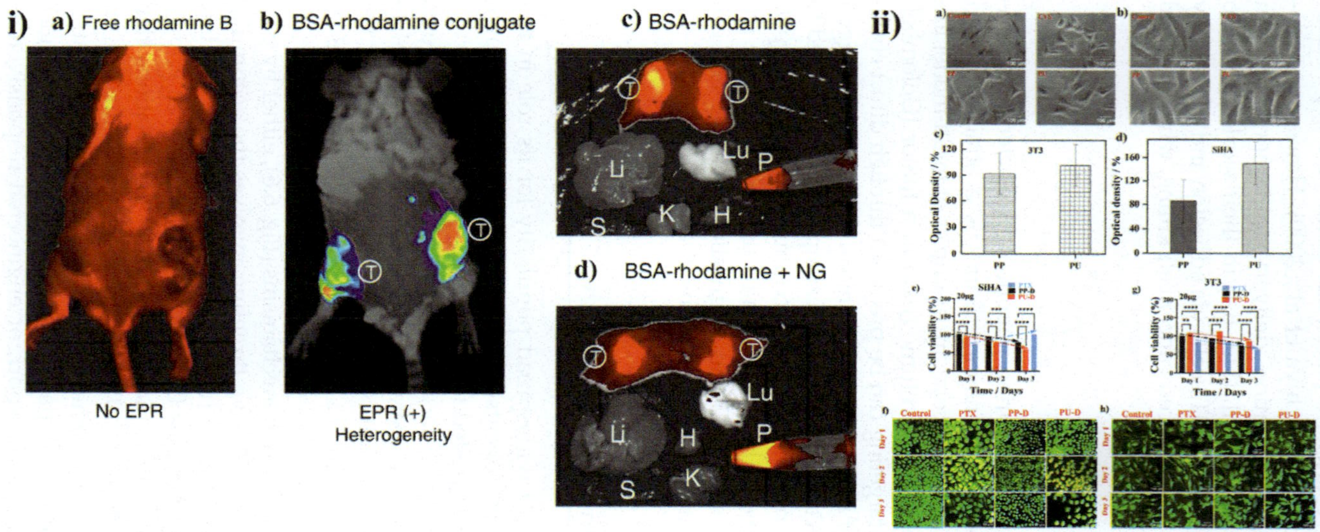

FIGURE 6.4 **EPR-effect-based fluorescence tumor imaging with better tumor killing.** i) The uptake of parental LMW fluorescent probe in-vivo is contrasted with the EPR effect-based uptake of fluorescent nanoprobes in malignancies. a) No clear tumor picture appears 24 hours after the LMW fluorescent probe, rhodamine B, was intravenously injected into S-180 tumor-bearing mice, b) in contrast, under the same experimental conditions, injection of tetraethyl rhodamine isothiocyanate (TRITC)-conjugated BSA (67 k Da) produces highly tumor-selective fluorescence, c) S-180 tumor-bearing mice were dissected after 24 hours, and the IVIS system was used to view each organ. Significant fluorescence was only seen in tumor tissues, d) the same as c), except after applying nitro-glycerine (NG) ointment to the skin, the tumor medication delivery and EPR impact were assessed. The EPR effect would gradually increase over time, as shown in d, where the cut surface of tumor tissues exhibits a more uniform tumor uptake of fluorescent drug (TRITC-BSA) and more fluorescent drug remains in the blood. Not all other normal organs in c and d exhibit fluorescence. T stands for tumor; Li for liver; K for kidney; H for heart; S for spleen; Lu for lung; and P for plasma, reproduced with permission from ref (Maeda et al). ii) all of the polymers' biological responses were evaluated using cellular study. After 1 day of sample proliferation, the morphology of 3T3 cells (cell adhesion magnification: 20×) and SiHA cells (cell adhesion magnification: 40×) grown on PP and PU surfaces was observed using microscopy on a gray filter, respectively, a), b). Using the OD profile information for adhered 3T3 cells and SiHA cells throughout the sample bed, cell adhesion is assessed in c) and d), respectively. Using the MTT assay at a concentration of 20 μg/mL, the in-vitro cytotoxicity of pure drug and drug-loaded PUs on SiHA cells and 3T3 cells at different time intervals was evaluated, respectively, in e) and g). Following AO/EB staining, fluorescence images of SiHA cells and 3T3 cells treated with pure drug and drug-loaded polymers at a concentration of 20 μg/mL were obtained at a magnification of 20× in f) and h), respectively, supporting the EPR effect. *i) Reused with Permission from Hiroshi Maeda, Hideaki Nakamura and Jun Fung Advanced drug delivery reviews (2013). 65(23), 71–79. https://doi.org/10.1016/j.addr.2012.10.002. Copyright from Elsevier. ii) Reused with Permission from Bauri, S., Tripathi, S., Choudhury, A.M., Mandal, S.S., H. Raj, P. Maiti, Nanomaterials as theranostic agents for cancer therapy, ACS Applied Nano Materials, 6(23), 21,462–21,495. https://doi.org/10.1021/acsanm.3c04235.*

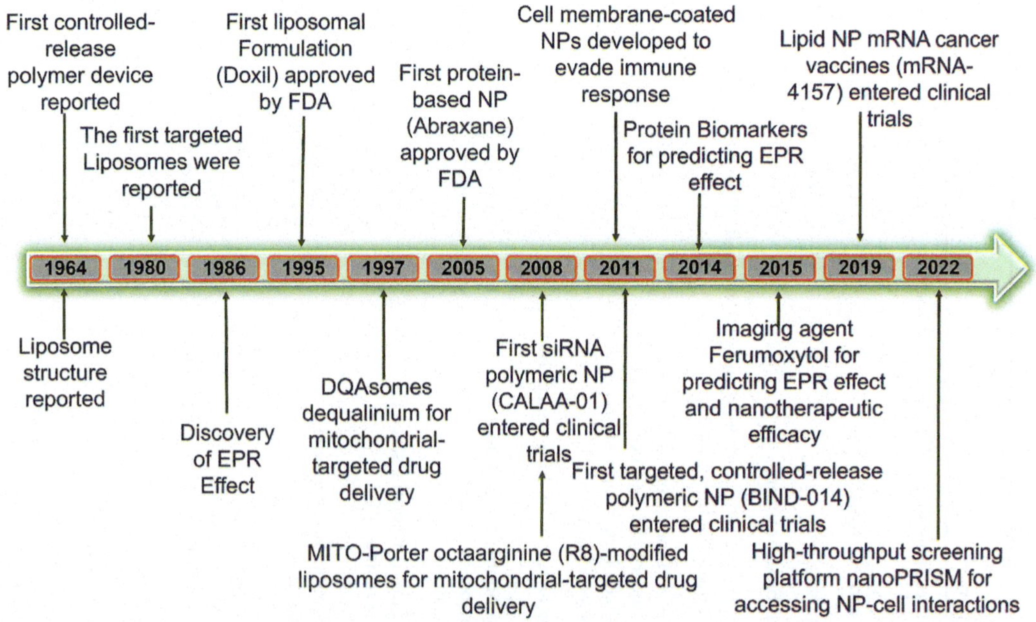

FIGURE 6.5 **Cancer nanomedicine taxonomy.** Schematic representation of cancer nanomedicine progresswith time. [Use of silicone rubber (1964) Folkman and Long (1964); Bangham and Horne (1964) monoclonal antibody and *Staphylococcus aureus* protein with liposome (1980) Heath et al. (1980); Leserman et al. (1980), discovery of EPR Gerlowski and Jain (1986), liposomal-Doxil Patel (1996), DQAsomes Weissig et al. (1998), protein-based NP-Abraxane(Moreno-Aspitia, cancer and –C, 2005), MITO-Porter octaarginine (R8)-modified liposomes made of 1,2-dioleoyl-sn-glycero-3-phosphoethanolamine and sphingomyelinmada Yamada et al. (2008), siRNA/CALAA-01 (*Study Details | Safety Study of CALAA-01 to Treat Solid Tumor Cancers | ClinicalTrials*, no date), Erythrocyte membrane camouflaged polymeric NPs(2011) Hu et al. (2011), BIND-014 (*Study Details | A Study of BIND-014 Given to Patients With Advanced or Metastatic Cancer | ClinicalTrials*, no date), protein biomarkers Yokoi et al. (2014), Ferumoxytol for imaging Aghighi et al. (2015), lipid NP mRNA-4157 Burris et al. (2019), nano-PRISM Boehnke et al. (2022)].

(Byrne et al., 2008). The identification of cell surface receptors via binding of ligand-linked nanoparticles is a widely used approach for active targeting. Nanomedicines can effectively exploit the EPR effect for accumulation in cancer cells or tumors. Table 6.3 includes various drug delivery systems where the EPR effect has been exploited.

Nanomedicine-mediated tumor vasculature and EPR targeting

The two strategies for modulation of tumor vasculature include reducing the oxygen and nutrition supply to starve tumors and enhancing the vascular function to facilitate medication delivery to tumors (Fig. 6.7). Co-delivering anticancer drugs via nanomedicine is more efficient approach to improve anticancer efficacy of a drug and achieve combination or synergistic effect. For example, liposome co-loaded with floxuridine (CPX-1) and irinotecan (CPT-11) to treat advanced colorectal cancer is in Phase II trials, while a liposome co-loaded with cytarabine and daunorubicin (CPX-351 or Vyxeos) to treat acute myeloid leukemia in phase III

TABLE 6.2 Examples of nanomedicine involved in cancer therapy.

Approved formulations	Drug + combintaion	Cancer type	Status
Polymeric micelles	Paclitaxel	Breast cancer non-small cell lung cancer ovarian cancer	Approved
		Stomach cancer breast cancer	Phase III
		Solid tumors	Phase I
		Advanced breast cancer	Phase I
	DACH-platin	Pancreatic cancer head and neck cancer non-small cell lung cancer bladder cancer	Phase III
Polymeric nanoparticles	Docetaxel + prostate-specific membrane antigen (PSMA) AZD2811 (AZD1152 hydroxyquinazoline pyrazol anilide; Aurora-B kinase inhibitor)	Cholangiocarcinoma cervical cancer bladder cancer head and neck cancer non-small cell lung cancer subtypes Advanced solid tumors	Phase II Phase I
Polymeric conjugates	Camptothecin Asparaginase Irinotecan Diaminocyclohexane (DACH) platinum	Renal cancer small cell lung cancer ovarian cancer Acute lymphoblastic leukemia Metastatic breast cancer Ovarian cancer	Phase II Approved Phase III Phase II
Liposomes	• DaunoXome, daunorubicin + liposome • Doxil (caelyx) doxorubicin + PEGylated liposome • Myocet, doxorubicin + liposome • Mepact, muramyl tripeptide phosphatidyl ethanolamide + liposome • Lipusu, paclitaxel + liposome • Marqibo, vincristine + liposome • Onivyde, irinotecan + liposome • Vyxeos, daunorubicin + cytarabine + liposome • Zolsketil, doxorubicin + PEGylated liposome	Ovarian cancer, Kaposi's sarcoma Kaposi's sarcoma Breast cancer Non-metastatic osteosarcoma Breast cancer, NSCLC Leukemia Pancreatic cancer Acute myeloid leukemia Metastatic breast cancer, ovarian cancer	FDA in 1995 FDA in 1996 EMA in 2000 EMA in 2009 EMA in 2013 FDA in 2012 FDA in 2015 FDA in 2017 EMA in 2022

Protein NPs	• Ontak, denileukin diftitox + recombinant DNA-derived cytotoxic protein • Abraxane, paclitaxel + protein carrier • Pazenir, paclitaxel + albumin-bound nanoparticles	Cutaneous T-cell lymphoma Metastatic and pancreatic cancer Metastatic breast cancer, metastatic adenocarcinoma of the pancreas, NSCLC	FDA in 1999 FDA in 2005 EMA in 2019
Magnetic NPS	• NanoTherm, amino silane + nanoparticles of superparamagnetic iron oxide • Magnetic tracers (FerroTrace) + Indocyanine green (ICG) + Magnetic nanoparticles	Glioblastoma, prostate, and pancreatic cancer Colorectal cancer	EMA in 2013 Phase I and phase II
Lipid NPs	• Paclitaxel + liposome and S-1 (NCT04217096) • PLD (PEG + liposome + doxorubicin) + carboplatin VS paclitaxel + carboplatin (NCT03794778) • Ceramide + liposome (NCT04716452) • Irinotecan sucrosofate + liposome (NCT04753216) • CPT -11 + liposome (NCT00734682)	Pancreatic cancer Ovarian cancer Acute myeloid leukemia Platinum-resistant ovarian, fallopian tube, or primary peritoneal ovary Glioma	Phase IV Phase IV Phase I Phase II Phase I
Carbon NPs	• Carbon nanoparticle (NCT02123407) • Indocyanine green + carbon nanoparticles (NCT04759820) • Folic acid analogs + silicon core/Polyethylene glycol + carbon dots nanoparticles	Advanced gastric cancer Colorectal cancer Solid tumors	Phase III Phase II and phase III Phase I and phase II
Metal/Metal Oxide NPs	• AGuIX + Gadolinium-based nanoparticles (NCT04789486) • Hafnium oxide nanoparticle (NCT04615013) • Silica nanoparticle (NCT02106598) • Hafnium oxide nanoparticle (NCT04484909)	Centrally located lung tumors and pancreatic cancer Esophageal cancer Head and neck melanoma Locally advanced or borderline-resectable pancreatic cancer	Phase I and Phase II Phase I Phase I and Phase II Phase I

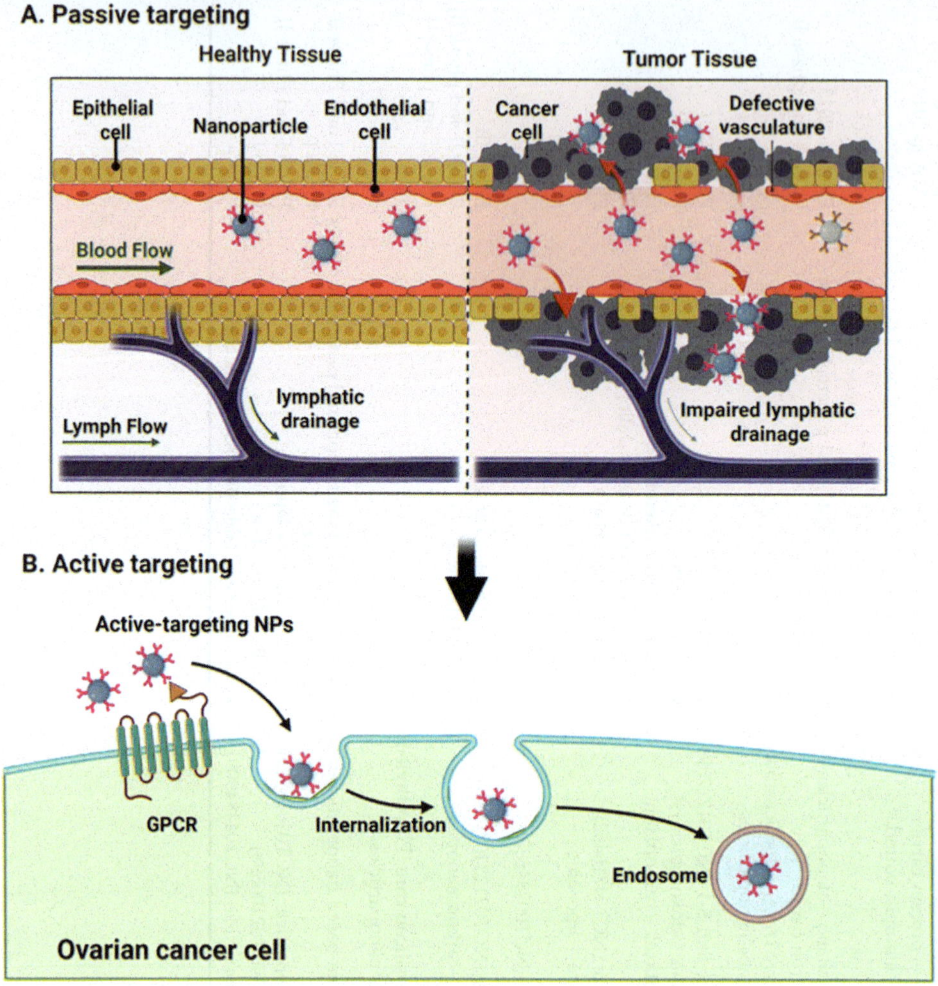

FIGURE 6.6 **Strategies for cancer drug delivery.** Passive versus active targeting in cancer therapy.

(Tabernero et al., 2013). A combinational gene therapy has been exploited that targets kinesin spindle protein and vascular endothelial growth factor (VEGF) with small interfering RNAs (siRNAs) formulated in lipid nanoparticles. It showed improved efficacy in Phase I studies for the treatment of liver metastases and advanced cancers.

Theranostic nanoparticles

Nanoparticles with photothermal (PTT) and photodynamic (PDT) effects can be used in theranostics applications for cancer treatment via receptor-mediated internalization or EPR

TABLE 6.3 Formulations exploiting EPR for drug delivery.

Drug name	Carrier	Scientific name	Clinical trial status
SMANCS	Polymer conjugate	Neocarzinostatin	Approved by Japan (1993)
Doxil	Liposome	Doxorubicin	Approved by USA, 1995
DaunoXome	Liposome	Doxorubicin	Approved by USA, 1996
Ontak	Fusion protein	Diphtheria toxin	Approved by USA, 1999
Myocet	Liposome	Doxorubicin	Approved by Europe (2000)
Zevalin	Anti-CD20 antibody	Yttrium 90	Approved by USA, 2002
Abraxane	Aluminum-bound nanoparticle	Paclitaxel	Approved by USA, 2005
Genexol-PM	Polymeric micelle	Paclitaxel	Approved by Korea (2007)
Marqibo	Liposome	Vincristine	Approved by USA, 2012
Onivyde	Liposome	Irinotecan	Approved by USA, 2015
Vyxeos	Liposome	Daunorubicin and cytarabine	Approved by USA, 2017
Mylotarg	Anti-CD33 antibody	Calicheamicin	Approved by USA, 2017
Hensify	Nanoparticle	Hafnium oxide	Approved by USA, 2019
CPC634	Polymeric micelle	Docetaxel	In clinical phase II trial
NC-4016	Polymeric micelle	Oxaliplatin	In clinical phase I trial
P-THP	Polymer conjugate	Pirarubicin	Preclinical
HPMA-ZnPP	Polymeric micelle	Zn-protoporphyrin	Preclinical
SGB	Polymer conjugate	Boric acid and glucosamine	Preclinical
NK105	Micelle	Paclitaxel	In clinical phase III trial
NC-6004	Micelle	Cisplatin	In clinical phase II trial

effect. Under near-infrared (NIR) light, PTT breaks down cancer cells by rupturing membranes and denaturing proteins with heat produced by nanomaterials such as carbon nanotubes (Wang et al., 2013), graphene oxide (Shi et al., 2014), and gold nanostructures (Fazal et al., 2014). The strong surface plasmon resonance in the near-infrared spectrum of these nanomaterials allows deeper tissue penetration. In PDT, photosensitizers (PSs) are used that accumulate in tumors to release reactive oxygen species (ROS) when exposed to light to kill the cancer cells. However, typical PSs suffer from poor water solubility, limited tumor targeting, and poor tissue penetration. To address this, their nanoparticles are preferred. Besides, gold nanoparticles can also be used as alternative PSs with enhanced optical properties and biocompatibility. Under single-photon NIR (915 nm, <130 mW/cm2) light irradiation, Vankayala et al. found that gold nanorods (Au NRs) (Vankayala et al., 2014) alone can stimulate the creation of singlet oxygen ($^1O_2$) and have remarkable PDT effects

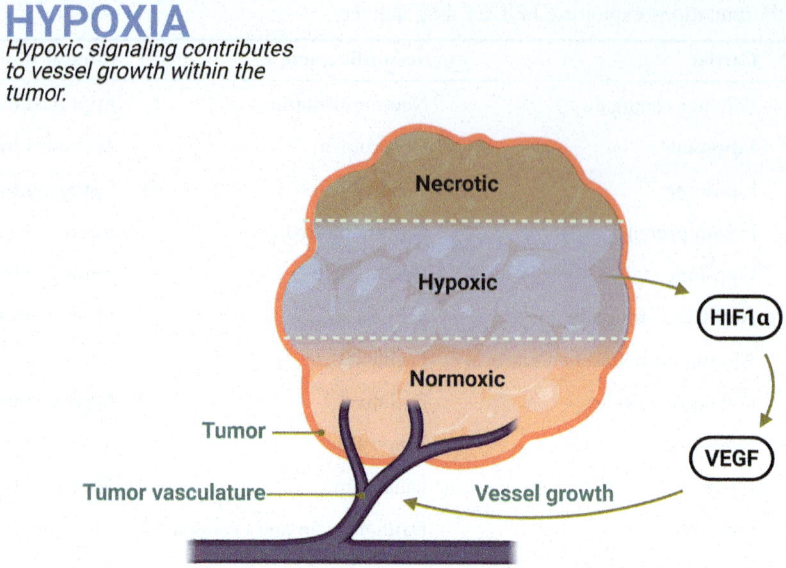

FIGURE 6.7 **Hypoxic signaling contributes to vessel growth within the tumor.** Tumor vasculature is characterized by abnormal vessel growth driven by hypoxia.

on the total eradication of tumors in mice. Gold nanocages, nanorods in shell, and nanoparticles may also stimulate the creation of singlet oxygen and destroy solid tumors for photodynamic therapy. Gold nanostars (GNSTs) (Vankayala et al., 2014) show a long-wavelength plasmon band (nanostar arms) and a short-wavelength plasmon band (nanostar core) in the mid-visible region. GNSTs had the properties of both gold nanoparticles and Au NRs. Iron-oxide nanoparticles can also be employed as a directed hyperthermia agent (Yang et al., 2007). Ultrasonic contrast compounds can preferentially extravasate into tumor tissue in the form of nanobubbles via EPR effect. Therefore, tumor-directed ultrasonography can be used to activate these drugs for controlled distribution and imaging. Using nanobubbles to increase tumor penetration and cell permeability by cavitation can boost the cytotoxic effect. Gao et al., (2008) claim that DOX-containing nano emulsions using perfluorocarbon nanodroplets stabilized by biodegradable block-copolymer micelles showed cavitation effect at the tumor site to enhance permeation at the tumor site and facilitated the release of payload for efficient anticancer effect.

Challenges and limitations

Despite incredibly promising preclinical results, nanomedicines have nearly always failed to increase efficacy in the clinic. Laboratory models used to research EPR are not accurate enough and need to be re-examined. The higher variation could be due to human malignancies with high variations in tumor microenvironment as compared to animal models.

The pharmacokinetics may be considerably changed due to huge tumor-to-body weight ratio in mice as opposed to human patients. Moreover, the patients experience high variability in tumor vasculature and EPR effect. The tumor microenvironment in human cancers differs in the following ways: (i) the tumor endothelium is heterogeneous or lacks fenestrations; (ii) blood flow through tissues is heterogeneous, resulting in areas that are acidic or hypoxic; (iii) pericyte coverage is lower and heterogeneous; (iv) the basement membrane (BM) is heterogeneous; and (v) the extracellular matrix (ECM) has a higher and heterogeneous density, causing an elevated IFP that forces nanomedicines to escape the blood compartment by diffusion rather than the much more effective convective transport (Gillies et al., 1999). Additionally, assessing the EPR effect in human malignancies is time-consuming and expensive. Examining the relationship between vascularization (permeability, perfusion, and IFP) and intra-tumor accumulation can require imaging techniques such as computer tomography, magnetic resonance imaging (MRI), or functional ultrasonography.

Future perspectives

Despite the tremendous advancements in nanomedicine, the complexity of tumor anatomy and heterogeneity make pharmacological and kinetic studies challenging. Developing 3D spheroid models that mimic tumors can be useful but is a complex task. Theranostic techniques offer real-time imaging in addition to therapy. Additionally, phytomedicines combined with nanotechnology could be significant with high stability, efficacy, and safety. Personalized EPR-based therapy can aid in an advanced strategy for targeted cancer treatment. High-throughput screening technique to identify cancer biomarkers could be an important aspect. Shao et al. (2021) used nanoparticles to modify the ROS-responsive tripeptide sequence of Arg-Gly-Asp (RGD) for the simultaneous detection of cancer by near-infrared (NIR) imaging and photothermal treatment (PTT). Compared to non-targeted nanoparticles, targeted nanoparticles of CMCh-BAPE-RGD@ICG precisely depict the position and margin of the SGC7901 tumor by NIR imaging. CMCh-BAPE-RGD@ICG-mediated PTT successfully inhibited the tumor growth (Krishnan, Wang and Vo-Dinh, no date). Phytonanomedicines with immunomodulatory qualities may improve the survival period. The regulatory aspects and innovative clinical trial designs are needed to obtain safe, effective, and readily accessible cancer nanomedicines.

Declaration

The figures in this chapter were created using BioRender (www.biorender.com). The illustrations were produced using a licensed BioRender account with the permission of the account holder (Alok Kumar, alokkumar.rs.mst23@iitbhu.ac.in). All content complies with BioRender's Academic License Terms and Conditions.

References

Aghighi, M., Golovko, D., Ansari, C., Marina, N.M., Pisani, L., Kurlander, L., Klenk, C., Bhaumik, S., Wendland, M., Daldrup-Link, H.E., Karathanasis, E., 2015. Imaging tumor necrosis with ferumoxytol. PLoS One 10 (11), e0142665. https://doi.org/10.1371/journal.pone.0142665.

Alavi, M., Hamidi, M., 2019. Passive and active targeting in cancer therapy by liposomes and lipid nanoparticles. Drug Metab. Pers. Ther. 34 (1). https://doi.org/10.1515/dmpt-2018-0032.

Arneth, B., 2019. Tumor microenvironment. Medicina 56 (1). https://doi.org/10.3390/MEDICINA56010015.

Baish, J.W., Gazit, Y., Berk, D.A., Nozue, M., Baxter, L.T., Jain, R.K., 1996. Role of tumor vascular architecture in nutrient and drug delivery: An invasion percolation-based network model. Microvasc. Res. 51 (3), 327–346. https://doi.org/10.1006/mvre.1996.0031.

Bangham, A.D., Horne, R.W., 1964. Negative staining of phospholipids and their structural modification by surface-active agents as observed in the electron microscope. J. Mol. Biol. 8 (5), 660. https://doi.org/10.1016/s0022-2836(64)80115-7.

Bauri, S., Tripathi, S., Choudhury, A.M., Mandal, S.S., Raj, H., Maiti, P., 2023. Nanomaterials as theranostic agents for cancer therapy. ACS Appl. Nano Mater. 6 (23), 21462–21495. https://doi.org/10.1021/acsanm.3c04235.

Bauri, S., Yadav, P.K., Choudhury, A.M., Maiti, P., 2024. l-Cystine-based polyurethane as a drug-delivery vehicle in targeted cancer therapy and biomedical applications. ACS Appl. Bio Mater. 7 (12), 8671–8684. https://doi.org/10.1021/acsabm.4c01479.

Boehnke, N., Straehla, J.P., Safford, H.C., Kocak, M., Rees, M.G., Ronan, M., Rosenberg, D., Adelmann, C.H., Chivukula, R.R., Nabar, N., Berger, A.G., Lamson, N.G., Cheah, J.H., Li, H., Roth, J.A., Koehler, A.N., Hammond, P.T., 2022. Massively parallel pooled screening reveals genomic determinants of nanoparticle delivery. Science 377 (6604). https://doi.org/10.1126/science.abm5551.

Bouck, N., Stellmach, V., Hsu, S.C., 1996. How tumors become angiogenic. Adv. Cancer Res. 69, 135–174. https://doi.org/10.1016/s0065-230x(08)60862-3.

Burris, H.A., Patel, M.R., Cho, D.C., Clarke, J.M., Gutierrez, M., Zaks, T.Z., Frederick, J., Hopson, K., Mody, K., Binanti-Berube, A., Robert-Tissot, C., Goldstein, B., Ben, B., Sun, J., Zhong, S., Pruitt, S.K., Keating, K., Meehan, R.S., Gainor, J.F., 2019. A phase I multicenter study to assess the safety, tolerability, and immunogenicity of mRNA-4157 alone in patients with resected solid tumors and in combination with pembrolizumab in patients with unresectable solid tumors. J. Clin. Oncol. 37 (Suppl. 15). https://doi.org/10.1200/jco.2019.37.15_suppl.2523.

Byrne, J.D., Betancourt, T., Brannon-Peppas, L., 2008. Active targeting schemes for nanoparticle systems in cancer therapeutics. Adv. Drug Deliv. Rev. 60 (15), 1615–1626. https://doi.org/10.1016/j.addr.2008.08.005.

Campbell, N.E., Kellenberger, L., Greenaway, J., Moorehead, R.A., Linnerth-Petrik, N.M., Petrik, J., 2010. Extracellular matrix proteins and tumor angiogenesis. J. Oncol. 2010, 1–13. https://doi.org/10.1155/2010/586905.

Casanovas, O., Hicklin, D.J., Bergers, G., Hanahan, D., 2005. Drug resistance by evasion of antiangiogenic targeting of VEGF signaling in late-stage pancreatic islet tumors. Cancer Cell 8 (4), 299–309. https://doi.org/10.1016/j.ccr.2005.09.005.

Chauhan, V.P., Stylianopoulos, T., Martin, J.D., Popović, Z., Chen, O., Kamoun, W.S., Bawendi, M.G., Fukumura, D., Jain, R.K., 2020. Normalization of Tumour Blood Vessels Improves the Delivery of Nanomedicines in a Size-Dependent Manner. Informa UK Limited, pp. 279–311. https://doi.org/10.1201/9780429399039-10.

Chen, H., Gu, Z., An, H., Chen, C., Chen, J., Cui, R., Chen, S., Chen, W., Chen, X., Chen, X., Chen, Z., Ding, B., Dong, Q., Fan, Q., Fu, T., Hou, D., Jiang, Q., Ke, H., Jiang, X., Liu, G., Li, S., Li, T., Liu, Z., Nie, G., Ovais, M., Pang, D., Qiu, N., Shen, Y., Tian, H., Wang, C., Wang, H., Wang, Z., Xu, H., Xu, J.F., Yang, X., Zhu, S., Zheng, X., Zhang, X., Zhao, Y., Tan, W., Zhang, X., Zhao, Y., 2018. Precise nanomedicine for intelligent therapy of cancer. Sci. China Chem. 61 (12), 1503–1552. https://doi.org/10.1007/s11426-018-9397-5.

Ding, Y., Li, S., Nie, G., 2013. Nanotechnological strategies for therapeutic targeting of tumor vasculature. Nanomedicine 8 (7), 1209–1222. https://doi.org/10.2217/nnm.13.106.

Fang, J., Nakamura, H., Maeda, H., 2011. The EPR effect: Unique features of tumor blood vessels for drug delivery, factors involved, and limitations and augmentation of the effect. Adv. Drug Deliv. Rev. 63 (3), 136–151. https://doi.org/10.1016/j.addr.2010.04.009.

Fazal, S., Jayasree, A., Sasidharan, S., Koyakutty, M., Nair, S.V., Menon, D., 2014. Green synthesis of anisotropic gold nanoparticles for photothermal therapy of cancer. ACS Appl. Mater. Interfaces 6 (11), 8080–8089. https://doi.org/10.1021/am500302t.

Folkman, J., 1989. Successful treatment of an angiogenic disease. N. Engl. J. Med 320 (18), 1211–1212. https://doi.org/10.1056/NEJM198905043201811.

Folkman, J., Long, D.M., 1964. The use of silicone rubber as a carrier for prolonged drug therapy. J. Surg. Res. 4 (3), 139–142. https://doi.org/10.1016/S0022-4804(64)80040-8.

Forster, J.C., Harriss-Phillips, W.M., Douglass, M.J.J., Bezak, E., 2017. A review of the development of tumor vasculature and its effects on the tumor microenvironment. Hypoxia 5, 21–32. https://doi.org/10.2147/HP.S133231.

Frentzas, S., Simoneau, E., Bridgeman, V.L., Vermeulen, P.B., Foo, S., Kostaras, E., Nathan, M.R., Wotherspoon, A., Gao, Z.H., Shi, Y., Van Den Eynden, G., Daley, F., Peckitt, C., Tan, X., Salman, A., Lazaris, A., Gazinska, P., Berg, T.J., Eltahir, Z., Ritsma, L., Van Rheenen, J., Khashper, A., Brown, G., Nyström, H., Sund, M., Van Laere, S., Loyer, E., Dirix, L., Cunningham, D., Metrakos, P., Reynolds, A.R., 2016. Vessel co-option mediates resistance to anti-angiogenic therapy in liver metastases. Nat. Med. 22 (11), 1294–1302. https://doi.org/10.1038/nm.4197.

Gao, Z., Kennedy, A.M., Christensen, D.A., Rapoport, N.Y., 2008. Drug-loaded nano/microbubbles for combining ultrasonography and targeted chemotherapy. Ultrasonics 48 (4), 260–270. https://doi.org/10.1016/j.ultras.2007.11.002.

Gerlowski, L.E., Jain, R.K., 1986. Microvascular permeability of normal and neoplastic tissues. Microvasc. Res. 31 (3), 288–305. https://doi.org/10.1016/0026-2862(86)90018-X.

Ghosh Dastidar, D., Ghosh, D., Chakrabarti, G., 2020. Tumour vasculature targeted anti-cancer therapy. Vessel Plus 2020. https://doi.org/10.20517/2574-1209.2019.36.

Gillies, R.J., Schornack, P.A., Secomb, T.W., Raghunand, N., 1999. Causes and effects of heterogeneous perfusion in tumors. Neoplasia 1 (3), 197–207. https://doi.org/10.1038/sj.neo.7900037.

Gimbrone, M.A., Leapman, S.B., Cotran, R.S., Folkman, J., 1972. Tumor dormancy in vivo by prevention of neovascularization. J. Exp. Med. 136 (2), 261–276. https://doi.org/10.1084/jem.136.2.261.

Golombek, S.K., May, J.N., Theek, B., Appold, L., Drude, N., Kiessling, F., Lammers, T., 2018. Tumor targeting via EPR: Strategies to enhance patient responses. Adv. Drug Deliv. Rev. 130, 17–38. https://doi.org/10.1016/j.addr.2018.07.007.

Greish, K., 2010. Enhanced permeability and retention (EPR) effect for anticancer nanomedicine drug targeting. Methods mol. Biol. 624, 25–37. https://doi.org/10.1007/978-1-60761-609-2_3.

Hammersen, F., 1983. Angiogenesis: British Microcirculation Society.

Haider, K.H., Aziz, S., Al-Reshidi, M.A., 2017. Endothelial progenitor cells for cellular angiogenesis and repair: Lessons learned from experimental animal models. Regen. Med. 12 (8), 969–982. https://doi.org/10.2217/rme-2017-0074.

He, H., Liu, L., Morin, E.E., Liu, M., Schwendeman, A., 2019. Survey of clinical translation of cancer nanomedicines - lessons learned from successes and failures. Acc. Chem. Res. 52 (9), 2673–2683. https://doi.org/10.1021/acs.accounts.9b00228.

Heath, T.D., Fraley, R.T., Papahdjopoulos, D., 1980. Antibody targeting of liposomes: Cell specificity obtained by conjugation of F(ab′) 2 to vesicle surface. Science 210 (4469), 539–541. https://doi.org/10.1126/science.7423203.

Hu, C.M.J., Zhang, L., Aryal, S., Cheung, C., Fang, R.H., Zhang, L., 2011. Erythrocyte membrane-camouflaged polymeric nanoparticles as a biomimetic delivery platform. Proc. Natl. Acad. Sci. U.S.A 108 (27), 10980–10985. https://doi.org/10.1073/pnas.1106634108.

Islam, W., Fang, J., Imamura, T., Etrych, T., Subr, V., Ulbrich, K., Maeda, H., 2018. Augmentation of the enhanced permeability and retention effect with nitric oxide–generating agents improves the therapeutic effects of nanomedicines. Mol. Cancer Ther. 17 (12), 2643–2653. https://doi.org/10.1158/1535-7163.MCT-18-0696.

Izci, M., Maksoudian, C., Manshian, B.B., Soenen, S.J., 2021. The use of alternative strategies for enhanced nanoparticle delivery to solid tumors. Chem. Rev. 121 (3), 1746–1803. https://doi.org/10.1021/acs.chemrev.0c00779.

Jordan, V.C., 2008. Tamoxifen: catalyst for the change to targeted therapy. Eur. J. Cancer 44 (1), 30–38.

Kamata, R., Yamamoto, T., Matsumoto, K., Maeda, H., 1985. A serratial protease causes vascular permeability reaction by activation of the Hageman factor-dependent pathway in guinea pigs. Infect. Immun. 48 (3), 747–753. https://doi.org/10.1128/iai.48.3.747-753.1985.

Kano, M.R., Komuta, Y., Iwata, C., Oka, M., Shirai, Y.T., Morishita, Y., Ouchi, Y., Kataoka, K., Miyazono, K., 2009. Comparison of the effects of the kinase inhibitors imatinib, sorafenib, and transforming growth factor-β receptor inhibitor on extravasation of nanoparticles from neovasculature. Cancer Sci. 100 (1), 173–180. https://doi.org/10.1111/j.1349-7006.2008.01003.x.

Keramati, M., Mianroodi, R.A., Memarnejadian, A., Mirzaie, A., Sazvari, S., Aslani, M.M., Roohvand, F., 2013. Towards a superior streptokinase for fibrinolytic therapy of vascular thrombosis. Cardiovasc. Hematol. Agents Med. Chem. 11 (3), 218–229. https://doi.org/10.2174/187152571103140120103816.

Kim, K.J., Li, B., Winer, J., Armanini, M., Gillett, N., Phillips, H.S., Ferrara, N., 1993. Inhibition of vascular endothelial growth factor-induced angiogenesis suppresses tumour growth in vivo. Nature 362 (6423), 841–844. https://doi.org/10.1038/362841a0.

Konerding, M.A., Malkusch, W., Klapthor, B., Van Ackern, C., Fait, E., Hill, S.A., Parklns, C., Chaplin, D.J., Presta, M., Denekamp, J., 1999. Evidence for characteristic vascular patterns in solid tumours: Quantitative studies using corrosion casts. Br. J. Cancer 80 (5–6), 724–732. https://doi.org/10.1038/sj.bjc.6690416.

Leserman, L.D., Barbet, J., Kourilsky, F., Weinstein, J.N., 1980. Targeting to cells of fluorescent liposomes covalently coupled with monoclonal antibody or protein A. Nature 288 (5791), 602–604. https://doi.org/10.1038/288602a0.

Li, D., Xie, K., Ding, G., Li, J., Chen, K., Li, H., Qian, J., Jiang, C., Fang, J., 2014. Tumor resistance to anti-VEGF therapy through up-regulation of VEGF-C expression. Cancer Lett. 346 (1), 45–52. https://doi.org/10.1016/j.canlet.2013.12.004.

Li, D., Xie, K., Zhang, L., Yao, X., Li, H., Xu, Q., Wang, X., Jiang, J., Fang, J., 2016. Dual blockade of vascular endothelial growth factor (VEGF) and basic fibroblast growth factor (FGF-2) exhibits potent anti-angiogenic effects. Cancer Lett. 377 (2), 164–173. https://doi.org/10.1016/j.canlet.2016.04.036.

Li, S., Zhang, Y., Wang, J., Zhao, Y., Ji, T., Zhao, X., Ding, Y., Zhao, X., Zhao, R., Li, F., Yang, X., Liu, S., Liu, Z., Lai, J., Whittaker, A.K., Anderson, G.J., Wei, J., Nie, G., 2017. Nanoparticle-mediated local depletion of tumour-associated platelets disrupts vascular barriers and augments drug accumulation in tumours. Nat. Biomed. Eng. 1 (8), 667–679. https://doi.org/10.1038/s41551-017-0115-8.

Li, Z., Di, C., Li, S., Yang, X., Nie, G., 2019. Smart nanotherapeutic targeting of tumor vasculature. Acc. Chem. Res. 52 (9), 2703–2712. https://doi.org/10.1021/acs.accounts.9b00283.

Li, G., Fang, X.L., Ren, Z., Li, K.Q., Zhou, S.H., Hu, D.Q., Wu, G.Q., Wang, T.L., Li, W.P., 2020. Thrombolytic effects of recombinant staphylokinase on coronary thrombosis in miniature pigs. Chin. j. appl. physiol. 36 (4), 369–374. https://doi.org/10.12047/j.cjap.5994.2020.079.

Ma, S., Zhou, J., Zhang, Y., Yang, B., He, Y., Tian, C., Xu, X., Gu, Z., 2019. An oxygen self-sufficient fluorinated nanoplatform for relieved tumor hypoxia and enhanced photodynamic therapy of cancers. ACS Appl. Mater. Interfaces 11 (8), 7731–7742. https://doi.org/10.1021/acsami.8b19840.

Maeda, H., 2010a. Nitroglycerin enhances vascular blood flow and drug delivery in hypoxic tumor tissues: Analogy between angina pectoris and solid tumors and enhancement of the EPR effect. J. Control. Release 142 (3), 296–298. https://doi.org/10.1016/j.jconrel.2010.01.002.

Maeda, H., 2010b. Tumor-selective delivery of macromolecular drugs via the EPR effect: Background and future prospects. Bioconjugate Chem. 21 (5), 797–802. https://doi.org/10.1021/bc100070g.

Maeda, H., Akaike, T., Wu, J., Noguchi, Y., Sakata, Y., 1996. Bradykinin and nitric oxide in infectious disease and cancer. Immunopharmacology. https://doi.org/10.1016/0162-3109(96)00063-X. www.elsevier.com/locate/immpharm33.

Maeda, H., Tsukigawa, K., Fang, J., 2016. A retrospective 30 years after discovery of the enhanced permeability and retention effect of solid tumors: Next-generation chemotherapeutics and photodynamic therapy—problems, solutions, and prospects. Microcirculation 23 (3), 173–182. https://doi.org/10.1111/micc.12228.

Maeda, H., Nakamura, H., Fang, J., 2013. The EPR effect for macromolecular drug delivery to solid tumors: Improvement of tumor uptake, lowering of systemic toxicity, and distinct tumor imaging in vivo. Adv. Drug Deliv. Rev. 65 (1), 71–79. https://doi.org/10.1016/j.addr.2012.10.002.

Marchat, L.A., Multhoff, G., Al-Mulla, F., Fernández-Cortés, M., 2019. Vasculogenic mimicry: Become an endothelial cell "but not so much". Front. Oncol. 9. https://doi.org/10.3389/FONC.2019.00803/FULL.

Matsumura, Y., Maeda, H., 1986. A new concept for macromolecular therapeutics in cancer chemotherapy: Mechanism of tumoritropic accumulation of proteins and the antitumor agent smancs. Cancer Res. 46 (8), 6387–6392.

Matsumura, Y., Kimura, M., Yamamoto, T., Maeda, H., 1988. Involvement of the kinin-generating cascade in enhanced vascular permeability in tumor tissue. Jpn. J. Cancer Res. 79 (12), 1327–1334. https://doi.org/10.1111/j.1349-7006.1988.tb01563.x.

McKee, T.D., Grandi, P., Mok, W., Alexandrakis, G., Insin, N., Zimmer, J.P., Bawendi, M.G., Boucher, Y., Breakefield, X.O., Jain, R.K., 2006. Degradation of fibrillar collagen in a human melanoma xenograft improves the efficacy of an oncolytic herpes simplex virus vector. Cancer Res. 66 (5), 2509–2513. https://doi.org/10.1158/0008-5472.CAN-05-2242.

Misale, S., Di Nicolantonio, F., Sartore-Bianchi, A., Siena, S., Bardelli, A., 2014. Resistance to anti-EGFR therapy in colorectal cancer: From heterogeneity to convergent evolution. Cancer Discov. 4 (11), 1269–1280. https://doi.org/10.1158/2159-8290.CD-14-0462.

Nagamitsu, A., Greish, K., Maeda, H., 2009. Elevating blood pressure as a strategy to increase tumor-targeted delivery of macromolecular drug SMANCS: Cases of advanced solid tumors. Jpn. J. Clin. Oncol. 39 (11), 756–766. https://doi.org/10.1093/jjco/hyp074.

Narang, A.S., Varia, S., 2011. Role of tumor vascular architecture in drug delivery. Adv. Drug Deliv. Rev. 63 (8), 640–658. https://doi.org/10.1016/j.addr.2011.04.002.

Netti, P.A., Hamberg, L.M., Babich, J.W., Kierstead, D., Graham, W., Hunter, G.J., Wolf, G.L., Fischman, A., Boucher, Y., Jain, R.K., 1999. Enhancement of fluid filtration across tumor vessels: Implication for delivery of macromolecules. Proc. Natl. Acad. Sci. U.S.A. 96 (6), 3137–3142. https://doi.org/10.1073/pnas.96.6.3137.

Park, J.S., Kim, I.K., Han, S., Park, I., Kim, C., Bae, J., Oh, S.J., Lee, S., Kim, J.H., Woo, D.C., He, Y., Augustin, H.G., Kim, I., Lee, D., Koh, G.Y., 2016. Normalization of tumor vessels by Tie2 activation and Ang2 inhibition enhances drug delivery and produces a favorable tumor microenvironment. Cancer Cell 30 (6), 953–967. https://doi.org/10.1016/j.ccell.2016.10.018.

Patel, J., 1996. Liposomal doxorubicin: doxil. J. Oncol. Pharm. Pract. 2 (4), 201–210. https://doi.org/10.1177/107815529600200402.

Pérez-Medina, C., Abdel-Atti, D., Tang, J., Zhao, Y., Fayad, Z.A., Lewis, J.S., Mulder, W.J.M., Reiner, T., 2016. Nanoreporter PET predicts the efficacy of anti-cancer nanotherapy. Nat. Commun. 7. https://doi.org/10.1038/ncomms11838.

Pervez, S., Paganelli, G., Epenetos, A.A., Mooi, W.J., Evans, D.J., Krausz, T., 1988. Localization of biotinylated monoclonal antibody in nude mice bearing subcutaneous and intraperitoneal human tumour xenografts. Int. J. Cancer 41 (S3), 30–33. https://doi.org/10.1002/ijc.2910410807.

Pilleron, S., Sarfati, D., Janssen-Heijnen, M., Vignat, J., Ferlay, J., Bray, F., Soerjomataram, I., 2019. Global cancer incidence in older adults, 2012 and 2035: A population-based study. Int. J. Cancer 144 (1), 49–58. https://doi.org/10.1002/IJC.31664.

Radisky, D., Hagios, C., Bissell, M.J., 2001. Tumors are unique organs defined by abnormal signaling and context. Semin. Cancer Biol. 11 (2), 87–95. https://doi.org/10.1006/scbi.2000.0360.

Seo, N., Polozova, A., Zhang, M., Yates, Z., Cao, S., Li, H., Kuhns, S., Maher, G., McBride, H.J., Liu, J., 2018. Analytical and functional similarity of amgen biosimilar ABP 215 to bevacizumab. mAbs 10 (4), 678–691. https://doi.org/10.1080/19420862.2018.1452580.

Shao, J., Liang, R., Ding, D., Zheng, X., Zhu, X., Hu, S., Wei, H., Wei, B., 2021. A smart multifunctional nanoparticle for enhanced near-infrared image-guided photothermal therapy against gastric cancer. Int. J. Nanomedicine 16, 2897–2915. https://doi.org/10.2147/IJN.S289310.

Shi, J., Wang, L., Zhang, J., Ma, R., Gao, J., Liu, Y., Zhang, C., Zhang, Z., 2014. A tumor-targeting near-infrared laser-triggered drug delivery system based on GO@Ag nanoparticles for chemo-photothermal therapy and X-ray imaging. Biomaterials 35 (22), 5847–5861. https://doi.org/10.1016/j.biomaterials.2014.03.042.

Song, X., Wan, Z., Chen, T., Fu, Y., Jiang, K., Yi, X., Ke, H., Dong, J., Yang, L., Li, L., Sun, X., Gong, T., Zhang, Z., 2016. Development of a multi-target peptide for potentiating chemotherapy by modulating tumor microenvironment. Biomaterials 108, 44–56. https://doi.org/10.1016/j.biomaterials.2016.09.001.

Stylianopoulos, T., Martin, J.D., Snuderl, M., Mpekris, F., Jain, S.R., Jain, R.K., 2013. Coevolution of solid stress and interstitial fluid pressure in tumors during progression: Implications for vascular collapse. Cancer Res. 73 (13), 3833–3841. https://doi.org/10.1158/0008-5472.CAN-12-4521.

Tabernero, J., Shapiro, G.I., LoRusso, P.M., Cervantes, A., Schwartz, G.K., Weiss, G.J., Paz-Ares, L., Cho, D.C., Infante, J.R., Alsina, M., Gounder, M.M., Falzone, R., Harrop, J., White, A.C.S., Toudjarska, I., Bumcrot, D., Meyers, R.E., Hinkle, G., Svrzikapa, N., Hutabarat, R.M., Clausen, V.A., Cehelsky, J., Nochur, S.V., Gamba-Vitalo, C., Vaishnaw, A.K., Sah, D.W.Y., Gollob, J.A., Burris, H.A., 2013. First-in-humans trial of an RNA interference therapeutic targeting VEGF and KSP in cancer patients with liver involvement. Cancer Discov. 3 (4), 406–417. https://doi.org/10.1158/2159-8290.CD-12-0429Spain.

Taylor, A.P., Rodriguez, M., Adams, K., Goldenberg, D.M., Blumenthal, R.D., 2003. Altered tumor vessel maturation and proliferation in placenta growth factor-producing tumors: Potential relationship to post-therapy tumor angiogenesis and recurrence. Int. J. Cancer 105 (2), 158–164. https://doi.org/10.1002/ijc.11059.

Theek, B., Baues, M., Gremse, F., Pola, R., Pechar, M., Negwer, I., Koynov, K., Weber, B., Barz, M., Jahnen-Dechent, W., Storm, G., Kiessling, F., Lammers, T., 2018. Histidine-rich glycoprotein-induced vascular normalization improves EPR-mediated drug targeting to and into tumors. J. Control. Release 282, 25–34. https://doi.org/10.1016/j.jconrel.2018.05.002.

Tsuchiya, K., Uchida, T., Kobayashi, M., Maeda, H., Konno, T., Yamanaka, H., 2000. Tumor-targeted chemotherapy with SMANCS in lipiodol for renal cell carcinoma: Longer survival with larger size tumors. Urology 55 (4), 495–500. https://doi.org/10.1016/s0090-4295(99)00537-3.

Turski, M.L., Vidwans, S.J., Janku, F., Garrido-Laguna, I., Munoz, J., Schwab, R., Subbiah, V., Rodon, J., Kurzrock, R., 2016. Genomically driven tumors and actionability across histologies: BRAF-mutant cancers as a paradigm. Mol. Cancer Ther. 15 (4), 533–547. https://doi.org/10.1158/1535-7163.MCT-15-0643.

Urology, K.T., 2000. Long-Term Survival Rate after Tumor-Targeted Chemotherapy with the Macromolecular Anticancer Drug SMANCS in Lipid Contrast Medium for Renal Cell.

Vankayala, R., Huang, Y.K., Kalluru, P., Chiang, C.S., Hwang, K.C., 2014a. First demonstration of gold nanorods-mediated photodynamic therapeutic destruction of tumors via near infra-red light activation. Small 10 (8), 1612–1622. https://doi.org/10.1002/smll.201302719.

Vankayala, R., Lin, C.C., Kalluru, P., Chiang, C.S., Hwang, K.C., 2014b. Gold nanoshells-mediated bimodal photodynamic and photothermal cancer treatment using ultra-low doses of near infra-red light. Biomaterials 35 (21), 5527–5538. https://doi.org/10.1016/j.biomaterials.2014.03.065.

Vasudev, N.S., Reynolds, A.R., 2014. Anti-angiogenic therapy for cancer: Current progress, unresolved questions and future directions. Angiogenesis 17 (3), 471–494. https://doi.org/10.1007/s10456-014-9420-y.

Wang, L., Shi, J., Jia, X., Liu, R., Wang, H., Wang, Z., Li, L., Zhang, J., Zhang, C., Zhang, Z., 2013. NIR-/pH-Responsive drug delivery of functionalized single-walled carbon nanotubes for potential application in cancer chemo-photothermal therapy. Pharm. Res. 30 (11), 2757–2771. https://doi.org/10.1007/s11095-013-1095-3.

Weber, C.E., Kuo, P.C., 2012. The tumor microenvironment. Surg. Oncol. 21 (3), 172–177. https://doi.org/10.1016/j.suronc.2011.09.001.

Weissig, V., Lasch, J., Erdos, G., Meyer, H.W., Rowe, T.C., Hughes, J., 1998. DQAsomes: A novel potential drug and gene delivery system made from dequalinium (TM). Pharm. Res. 15 (2), 334–337. https://doi.org/10.1023/A:1011991307631.

Whiteside, T.L., 2008. The tumor microenvironment and its role in promoting tumor growth. Oncogene 27 (45), 5904–5912. https://doi.org/10.1038/ONC.2008.271;KWRD=MEDICINE.

Yamada, Y., Akita, H., Kamiya, H., Kogure, K., Yamamoto, T., Shinohara, Y., Yamashita, K., Kobayashi, H., Kikuchi, H., Harashima, H., Porter, M.I.T.O.-, 2008. A liposome-based carrier system for delivery of macromolecules into mitochondria via membrane fusion. BBA –Biomembr. 1778 (2), 423–432. https://doi.org/10.1016/j.bbamem.2007.11.002.

Yang, J., Lee, C.H., Ko, H.J., Suh, J.S., Yoon, H.G., Lee, K., Huh, Y.M., Haam, S., 2007. Multifunctional magneto-polymeric nanohybrids for targeted detection and synergistic therapeutic effects on breast cancer. Angew. Chem. Int. Ed. 46 (46), 8836–8839. https://doi.org/10.1002/anie.200703554.

Yang, J., Li, W., Luo, L., Jiang, M., Zhu, C., Qin, B., Yin, H., Yuan, X., Yin, X., Zhang, J., Luo, Z., Du, Y., You, J., 2018. Hypoxic tumor therapy by hemoglobin-mediated drug delivery and reversal of hypoxia-induced chemoresistance. Biomaterials 182, 145–156. https://doi.org/10.1016/j.biomaterials.2018.08.004.

Yokoi, K., Tanei, T., Godin, B., van de Ven, A.L., Hanibuchi, M., Matsunoki, A., Alexander, J., Ferrari, M., 2014. Serum biomarkers for personalization of nanotherapeutics-based therapy in different tumor and organ microenvironments. Cancer Lett. 345 (1), 48–55. https://doi.org/10.1016/j.canlet.2013.11.015.

Zhang, X., Detering, L., Sultan, D., Luehmann, H., Li, L., Heo, G.S., Zhang, X., Lou, L., Grierson, P.M., Greco, S., Ruzinova, M., Laforest, R., Dehdashti, F., Lim, K.H., Liu, Y., 2021. CC chemokine receptor 2-targeting copper nanoparticles for positron emission tomography-guided delivery of gemcitabine for pancreatic ductal adenocarcinoma. ACS Nano. 15 (1), 1186–1198. https://doi.org/10.1021/acsnano.0c08185.

Zhao, J., Salmon, H., Sarntinoranont, M., 2007. Effect of heterogeneous vasculature on interstitial transport within a solid tumor. Microvasc. Res. 73 (3), 224–236. https://doi.org/10.1016/j.mvr.2006.12.003.

Zhao, Y., Ji, T., Wang, H., Li, S., Zhao, Y., Nie, G., 2014. Self-assembled peptide nanoparticles as tumor microenvironment activatable probes for tumor targeting and imaging. J. Control. Release 177 (1), 11–19. https://doi.org/10.1016/j.jconrel.2013.12.037.

Zhao, Y., Liu, F., He, G., Li, K., Zhu, C., Yu, W., Zhang, C., Xie, M., Lin, J., Zhang, J., Jin, Y., 2019. Discovery of arylamide-5-anilinoquinazoline-8-nitro derivatives as VEGFR-2 kinase inhibitors: Synthesis, in vitro biological evaluation and molecular docking. Bioorg. Med. Chem. Lett. 29 (23). https://doi.org/10.1016/j.bmcl.2019.126711.

Zhou, Z., Zhang, B., Wang, S., Zai, W., Yuan, A., Hu, Y., Wu, J., 2018. Perfluorocarbon nanoparticles mediated platelet blocking disrupt vascular barriers to improve the efficacy of oxygen-sensitive antitumor drugs. Small 14 (45). https://doi.org/10.1002/smll.201801694.

Further reading

H.M., Vascular Permeability in Cancer and Infection as Related to Macromolecular Drug Delivery, with Emphasis on the EPR Effect for Tumor-Selective Drug Targeting. (2012).

Krishnan, T., Wang, H.N., Vo-Dinh, T., 2021. Smartphone-based device for colorimetric detection of micro RNA biomarkers using nanoparticle-based assay. Sensors 23. https://doi.org/10.3390/S21238044/S1.

Maeda, H., 2021. The 35th anniversary of the discovery of EPR effect: a new wave of nanomedicines for tumor-targeted drug delivery-personal remarks and future prospects. J Pers Med. 3. https://doi.org/10.3390/JPM11030229.

Moreno-Aspitia, A., Cancer, E.P., -C., 2005. North Central Cancer Treatment Group N0531: Phase II Trial of Weekly Albumin-Bound Paclitaxel (ABI-007; AbraxaneTM) in Combination with Gemcitabine in. Academia.edu a Moreno-Aspitia, EA Perez Clinical Breast Cancer. (2005).

Study Details | A Study of BIND-014 Given to Patients with Advanced or Metastatic Cancer | Clinical.

Study Details | Safety Study of CALAA-01 to Treat Solid Tumor Cancers Clinical.

CHAPTER

7

Cancer therapy based on extracellular matrix

Sayali Gaikwad[1,2], *Ashwani Patil*[1,2], *Abhishek Jha*[1,2] *and Abhishek Sharma*[3]

[1]**Dr. D. Y. Patil Institute of Pharmaceutical Sciences and Research Pimpri, Pune, Maharashtra, India;** [2]**DPGU School of Pharmacy and Research Pimpri, Pune, Maharashtra, India;** [3]**School of Pharmaceutical Sciences, SDGI Global University, Ghaziabad, Uttar Pradesh, India**

Introduction

In cancer, the extracellular matrix (ECM) undergoes extensive structural changes and becomes abnormally dense and stiff. This occurs because stromal matrix components, including collagen, fibronectin, and proteoglycans, are produced and deposited in excess, a process predominantly mediated by cancer-associated fibroblasts (CAFs). This altered matrix promotes tumor growth, invasion, metastasis, angiogenesis, immune evasion, and cancer cell dormancy. Within the tumor microenvironment (TME), cancer cells, CAFs, macrophages, endothelial cells, and soluble mediators constantly interact and reshape the ECM, creating a supportive niche for tumor progression. Because the remodeled ECM drives multiple hallmarks of cancer, targeting ECM components or the cells that produce them offers a promising strategy to disrupt the tumor-supportive environment and improve therapy outcomes (Lee et al., 2025a).

Cancer grows within a complex tumor microenvironment (TME), where the extracellular matrix (ECM) plays a major supportive role. Normally responsible for regulating cell behavior, the ECM becomes highly remodeled in cancer, altering its structure, stiffness, and composition. These changes promote tumor growth, invasion, metastasis, and affect immune and stromal cell behavior. Although enzymes like MMPs and cross-linking proteins are known to drive this remodeling, many mechanisms linking ECM changes to therapy resistance are still not fully understood (Desai et al., 2025).

Advanced Cancer Therapeutics
https://doi.org/10.1016/B978-0-443-44185-1.00013-6

ECM structure

Macromolecules such as glycoproteins (mucins), proteoglycans, collagens, laminins, fibronectin, elastin fibers, and reticulin make up the extracellular matrix (ECM). Proteoglycans, glycoproteins, and collagens are considered the "core-matrisome" of the extracellular matrix. The primary non-collagen component of the extracellular matrix (ECM) is small leucine-rich proteoglycans (SLRPs), which are essential for the development of cancer, metastasis, cardiac remodeling, osteoarthritis (OA), tissue morphogenesis, and immunological response (Lall et al., 2024). Table 7.1 shows the ECM components and their functions. Each component helps in building tissue structure, giving strength, and allowing cells to interact with their surroundings. Together, they form an environment that is important for normal body functions as well as disease processes (Yue, 2014).

ECM as a therapeutic barrier

Through physical and chemical signals, the extracellular matrix sustains the growth, movement, and activity of cells. Examples of mechanical forces that help cells perceive their environment and maintain healthy tissue balance are stiffness and pressure. Proper ECM stiffness is essential for normal cell behavior and tissue stability (Zhang and Zhang, 2025). Cancer-associated fibroblasts reshape the ECM, changing its stiffness and signals in ways that influence tumor immunity and immune-cell movement. A dense, stiff ECM blocks drug penetration and immune infiltration while activating pathways like YAP/TAZ, mTOR, and calcium signaling that support tumor spread. Mechanical forces also affect T-cell activation and exhaustion, partly through mechano-sensors such as Piezo1. Although abnormal ECM remodeling often helps tumors escape immunity, controlled ECM breakdown can improve drug delivery and sometimes limit tumor invasion (Hu et al., 2025).

Direct ECM-targeted therapeutic strategies

Enhanced permeability and retention effect is the basis of several anticancer nanomedicines, but the dense extracellular matrix inhibits their tumor delivery. In spite of the fact that enzymes that degrade ECM can enhance the penetration of nanoparticles, nonspecific delivery may lead to safety issues. By employing hyaluronic acid-collagen IV-binding peptide conjugate to target bromelain to the tumor ECM increases its concentration in tumors, decreases collagen density, and increases the intratumoral distribution of drugs. The strategy makes chemotherapy more effective and without any adverse effects on the system, an encouraging sign of achieving better tumor drug delivery (Ikeda-Imafuku et al., 2022).

Lysyl oxidase (LOX) is a promising biomarker and therapeutic target of interest in hypoxic-ischemic encephalopathy, with its expression being elevated after hypoxic-ischemic brain damage and changing the mechanics of brain tissue by modulating extracellular matrix remodeling. If there is a high level of LOX, the crosslinking of collagen happens,

TABLE 7.1 The components of extracellular matrix and their functions.

ECM Component/ Receptor	Structural overview	Major types/Subunits	Primary biological roles	Key distinguishing features
Collagen	Built from three α-polypeptide chains that intertwine to form a stable triple helix.	Classical fibrillar collagens (types I–III), network-forming collagen (type IV), FACIT family (e.g., types IX, XII), and specialized forms such as type VI.	Provides mechanical strength, maintains tissue shape, and forms the basic architectural scaffold of most organs.	Requires extensive enzymatic modification (proline/lysine hydroxylation); fibrils strengthened by lysyl oxidase cross-linking; forms either thick fibrils or sheet-like networks.
Proteoglycans	Consist of a core protein decorated with long, negatively charged glycosaminoglycan (GAG) chains.	GAG families include hyaluronic acid, keratan sulfate, chondroitin/dermatan sulfate, and heparan sulfate/heparin. Major proteoglycans: Aggrecan, versican, decorin, lumican, perlecan.	Regulate hydration, compressibility, and spacing within tissues; modulate growth factor availability and influence cell signaling.	Highly variable in size and function; cartilage PGs (e.g., aggrecan) generate resistance to load, while decorin/lumican fine-tune collagen fibril formation.
Glycosaminoglycan chains (GAGs)	Linear polysaccharides composed of repeating disaccharides; strongly anionic.	Same four groups as above; only hyaluronic acid is non-sulfated.	Maintain water balance, contribute to gel-like matrix consistency, and regulate molecular diffusion.	Charge density creates a strong water-binding capacity, crucial for lubrication and shock absorption.
Laminins	Large cross-shaped glycoproteins composed of one α, one β, and one γ chain.	Multiple isoforms are formed from 5 α, 3 β, and 3 γ chains (~20 combinations).	Establish and maintain basement membranes; support cell adhesion, polarity, and tissue organization.	Form self-assembled networks tightly interwoven with collagen IV; indispensable during early embryonic development.
Fibronectin	Dimeric glycoprotein built from repeating type I, II, and III modules.	Contains the classic RGD (Arg-Gly-Asp) sequence for integrin binding.	Guides cell adhesion, migration, and wound repair; organizes other ECM molecules.	Secreted as dimers that polymerize into fibrils; progressively matures into an insoluble fibronectin matrix.
Elastin	Synthesized as a soluble tropoelastin monomer that becomes incorporated into elastic fibers.	Interacts with microfibrillar proteins such as fibrillin-1/2 and with fibulin-4/5.	Provides elastic recoil in tissues that undergo repetitive stretching (e.g., arteries, lungs, skin).	Stabilized by unique desmosine and isodesmosine cross-links formed by lysyl oxidase; assembled through staged micro- and macro-aggregation processes.

(*Continued*)

TABLE 7.1 The components of extracellular matrix and their functions.—cont'd

ECM Component/ Receptor	Structural overview	Major types/Subunits	Primary biological roles	Key distinguishing features
Microfibrils (fibrillin family)	Cable-like glycoprotein polymers forming the scaffold for elastic fiber formation.	Fibrillin-1 and fibrillin-2 are the major structural members.	Support elastin deposition and regulate growth factor availability (e.g., TGF-β).	Essential for organizing elastogenesis; mutations lead to connective-tissue disorders (e.g., Marfan syndrome).
Integrins (ECM receptors)	Transmembrane αβ heterodimers linking extracellular ligands to the actin cytoskeleton.	18 α and 8 β chains combine to form 24 distinct integrins; β1 family binds most matrix proteins.	Anchor cells to the ECM, transmit mechanical forces, and regulate signaling pathways controlling proliferation, migration, and survival.	Mediate "outside-in" (ECM to cell) and "inside-out" (cell to ECM) signaling; activate FAK, ILK, talin, vinculin, and Rho/ MAPK pathways.
Syndecans (cell-surface proteoglycans)	Transmembrane proteoglycans carrying heparan sulfate/ occasionally chondroitin sulfate chains.	Four main syndecan isoforms in vertebrates.	Serve as co-receptors for ECM ligands and growth factors; modulate cell adhesion and signaling.	Bridge biochemical cues between ECM and cytoskeleton; regulate cell-matrix interactions in wound healing and cancer.
Other ECM-interacting receptors	Diverse membrane proteins that bind laminins, collagen, or glycoproteins.	Includes laminin receptors, discoidin domain receptors (collagen receptors), and others.	Reinforce adhesion, guide migration, and fine-tune ECM-driven signaling.	Complement integrin function contributes to the specificity of cell-matrix communication.

Data from B.Yue, Biology of the extracellular matrix: an overview. J. Glaucoma. 23 (8) (2014), https://doi.org/10.1097/IJG.0000000000000108.

and due to that, there is induction of mechanosensitive Piezol, Calcium imflammation, and ferroptotic cellular death. LOX or Piezo1 inhibition decreases neuronal injury and enhances cognitive functions. Recently discovered LOX-specific inhibitor, TA, has other advantages of restricting neuronal damage and encouraging synaptic plasticity, and the new approach to hypoxic brain injury treatment can be discussed (Jiang et al., 2024).

Collagens, laminin, fibronectin, periostin, and hyaluronic acid are key extracellular matrix (ECM) components that regulate tumor growth, invasion, immune evasion, and therapy resistance by altering tissue stiffness, signaling pathways, and cell–matrix interactions. Abnormal ECM remodeling, driven by cancer cells, CAFs, immune cells, and enzymes, creates a stiff, heterogeneous microenvironment that promotes metastasis, angiogenesis, stemness, and poor prognosis, while also limiting drug penetration. Targeting ECM components or their associated pathways (e.g., integrins, PI3K/Akt, YAP/TAZ, Notch, Wnt/β-catenin) can reduce tumor aggressiveness, improve immune infiltration, and enhance chemotherapy and immunotherapy efficacy. Advances in peptide-based and intelligent nanoparticle designs, including ECM-targeting, stimuli-responsive, and multifunctional systems, offer promising strategies to overcome ECM barriers and improve targeted drug delivery in solid tumors (Lee et al., 2025b).

Matrix Metalloproteinases (MMPs) are a family of 23 zinc-dependent enzymes that degrade and remodel the extracellular matrix (ECM). They play key roles in normal physiological processes, which include embryogenesis, angiogenesis, and wound recovery, and are regulated via hormones, growth factors, and cytokines. Altered MMP activity is linked to diseases like cancer and fibrosis. Their function is controlled by MMP inhibitors, which prevent excessive ECM breakdown and are important targets for therapeutic research (Cabral-Pacheco et al., 2020). Table 7.2 provides a concise overview of key matrix metalloproteinases involved in cancer, summarizing their primary biological functions, roles in tumor progression, and major therapeutic inhibition strategies relevant to anticancer drug development (Almutairi et al., 2023).

Emerging ECM-based therapies

CAR T cells based on ECM-targeted are a promising approach in cancer immunotherapy in that they provide a two-fold advantage. They not only destabilize the structural support offered by the tumor extracellular matrix (ECM), but also increase the invasion of the tumors by T cells through tumor microenvironment remodeling, exposing tumors to immune attack. CAR T cells targeting individual ECM components have been demonstrated to have a positive response in preclinical research. Major elements of this group are Glypican-1 (GPC1), Glypican-2 (GPC2), and they are both heparan sulfate proteoglycans, which are localized on the cell surface and play a role in growth-related signaling cascades; cerebroglycan, a proteoglycan mainly expressed in the neural tissue, which has the known involvement in tumor progression; Tenascin-C, an extracellular matrix glycoprotein that contribute to invasion of tumor cells, and Chondroitin Sulf Targeting of these extra-

TABLE 7.2 Overview of key matrix metalloproteinases involved in cancer.

MMP type	Primary function	Key role in cancer	Major inhibitor classes/ Strategies	Therapeutic significance
MMP-1 (Collagenase-1)	Degrades fibrillar collagens (I–III); activates other MMPs	Enhances tumor invasion, EMT, and metastasis; associated with poor prognosis	Methyl rosmarinate derivatives, SAR-transfer inhibitors, thiazoles, arylsulfonamides	Selective inhibition aims to reduce invasion while avoiding musculoskeletal toxicity
MMP-2 (Gelatinase-A)	Degrades basement membrane components (collagen IV, gelatin)	Promotes invasion, angiogenesis, and tumor dissemination	Hydroxamate and non-hydroxamate small molecules, sulfonamides, triazoles, hydroxyquinolines	One of the most explored MMP targets; structure-based inhibitors show strong preclinical potential
MMP-3 (Stromelysin-1)	Broad ECM degradation; activates MMP-1 and MMP-9	Drives tumor growth, inflammation, and metastatic spread	Hydroxamate-based inhibitors, carboxylic acid derivatives, thiirene-based covalent inhibitors	Targeting may suppress ECM remodeling and secondary MMP activation
MMP-7 (Matrilysin-1)	Degrades ECM and adhesion molecules (e.g., E-cadherin)	Facilitates epithelial tumor invasion and angiogenesis	Nitro-based zinc-binding inhibitors with modified P3′ side chains	Selective inhibition remains difficult due to structural similarity with MMP-1
MMP-12 (Macrophage elastase)	Elastin and ECM degradation; immune regulation	Exhibits tumor-promoting or tumor-suppressing effects depending on context	Zinc-binding inhibitors with hydrophobic S1′-targeting frameworks	Emerging target; high selectivity required to prevent immune-related side effects
MMP-14 (MT1-MMP)	Cell-surface ECM degradation activates pro-MMP-2	Central mediator of invasion, angiogenesis, and metastasis	Indirect inhibition of MMP-14–MMP-2–TIMP-2 activation complex	Highly attractive target due to membrane localization and key role in tumor progression

Data from S.Almutairi, H.Moh'd Kalloush, N.A.Manoon, S.K.Bardaweel, Matrix metalloproteinases inhibitors in cancer treatment: an updated review (2013–2023). Molecules. 28 (14) (2023), https://doi.org/10.3390/molecules28145567.

cellular matrix constituents in therapy destabilizes tumor structure and at the same time enhances the efficacy of antitumor immune responses (Day et al., 2025).

ECM-responsive nanoparticles represent a sophisticated class of drug delivery platforms that integrate the size-dependent targeting benefits of nanocarriers with the functional properties of extracellular matrix constituents. Formulated using biomolecules such as gelatin, collagen, fibrin, hyaluronic acid, chondroitin sulfate, and heparin, these systems are designed to sense and adapt to local tissue microenvironments, thereby improving cellular internalization and enabling spatially controlled release of therapeutic or bioactive agents. Such design strategies enhance treatment outcomes in oncology, wound repair, and regenerative applications, while supporting the development of multifunctional and stimuli-adaptive delivery systems (Hogan et al., 2023).

Exosomes are endogenous extracellular vesicles with high biocompatibility, low immunogenicity, and tissue-specific cellular targeting that can enable their use as appealing drug delivery, gene-based therapy, and regenerative therapy vectors. Vesicle loading The therapeutic payloads, which are diverse: low-molecular-weight drugs, proteins, various RNA species, CRISPR Cas9 constructs and others, can be loaded either during the process of vesicle formation by genetic modification or after isolation by using physical methods such as electroporation, sonication, incubation, or freeze-thaw cycling, with each loading method having different loading efficiencies, cargo stability, and translational viability. Modifying exosomal membranes helps drugs reach tumors or immune cells more effectively, while surface changes slow their removal from the body. It is worth noting that exosomes can cross restrictive biological interfaces, such as the blood-brain barrier, to make central nervous system delivery, and can actively mediate immune signaling in inflammatory or autoimmune diseases. All these properties contribute to their growing therapeutic utility in oncology, infectious diseases, neurological disorders, gene therapy, tissue repair, and cosmetical applications, protecting cargo, longer circulation time, and wide functional capabilities (Serrano et al., 2025).

Precision in the depiction of the tumor extracellular matrix (ECM) is imperative in understanding the cancer development mechanisms and direct therapeutic interventions. Although the traditional experimental models can recreate the selected features of the ECM, they fail to replicate its dynamic and very complex architecture. Machine learning (ML) and deep learning (DL) in the context of artificial intelligence offer useful computational structures to overcome these problems. Simple machine-learning models can work with structured data like bioink and scaffold properties, while deep-learning models are useful for analyzing complex data such as 3D images and cell activity over time. The AI systems can predict the processes of ECM remodeling, optimize the selection of biomaterials, and replicate the fundamental structural features of orientations of fibers, pore geometry, and mechanical stiffness. Hyaluronic acid, collagen, gelatin, polyethylene glycol, self-assembling peptides or decellularized ECM are all widely used matrices, which are increasingly optimized using AI-assisted design to more closely recap tumor-specific ECM. In addition, the combination of biochemical, biomechanical, and cellular data into AI applications promotes the prediction of therapeutic responses and the creation of individual ECM-based interventions. Together, AI is a crucial interface connecting experimental and computational approaches, allowing for scalable and high-fidelity tumor microenvironment modeling (Jin et al., 2026).

A very dynamic structure made up of matrisome proteins, the extracellular matrix is a structure whose biological functions are highly influenced by glycosylation and other post-modifications. These kinds of modifications affect protein stability, intermolecular interactions, and the formation of tissue-specific microenvironments. The current state-of-the-art techniques, such as tissue decellularization, targeted enrichment, and advanced mass spectrometry, especially glycopeptide-specific analyse can be used to thoroughly characterize matrisome components and their sites of modification. Combining the ideas of glyco-engineering with high-resolution proteomics offers an essential understanding of the remodeling of the ECM, the pathophysiology of diseases, and the discovery of new therapeutic targets (Raghunathan et al., 2019).

Targeting ECM during metastatic dissemination

One of the initial and most important processes in the formation of pre-metastatic niches is the remodeling of the extracellular matrix, allowing tissues at a distance to become open to the incoming tumor cells. This is coordinated by stringently controlled circuits of extracellular proteases. ECM degradation involves the action of matrix metalloproteinases, especially MMP-2 and MMP-9, which release matrix-sequestered signaling molecules, and these molecules allow the immune cell infiltration and vascular restructuring. The plasminogen-plasmin system is a regulatory node capable of directly remodeling ECM architecture, as well as triggering secondary proteolytic cascades. Other serine proteins, such as neutrophil elastase and cathepsin G, are also involved in further remodeling of the matrix by removing endogenous angiogenic inhibitors. All these proteolytic activities shift the ECM towards a pro-metastatic condition. This remodeling process is extended to the remote internal organs by tumor-promoted pathways, including the production of plasmin by S100A10. In such ways, tumors remotely condition the extracellular landscape. The resultant matrix loses homeostatic properties. Rather, it is biochemically and structurally tolerant to metastatic seeding. Therefore, ECM remodeling is an initial and preemptive objective of anti-metastatic therapeutic intervention (Okura et al., 2025). Alterations of the extracellular matrix that are associated with cancer are highly heterogeneous with respect to tumor type and tissue of origin and are actively mediated by context-dependent changes that promote malignant progression, resistance to therapy, and immune escape. Table 7.3 shows cancer type-selective changes of the extracellular matrix, including fibrotic reactions, changes in collagen arrangement, and functional responses of the cancer-associated fibroblasts, alongside therapeutic approaches meant to regulate these changes. It further recapsulates the clinical and preclinical results associated with ECM-targeted interventions, highlighting the significance of tissue-specific matrix features in guiding precision-based cancer therapies (Karsdal et al., 2025). Metastatic dissemination is a very selective process in which only a small portion of tumor cells survives the circulatory system and develop second set of growth formations. Following arrest in remote organs, crosstalk between disseminated tumor cells and resident ECM, regulates the extravasation and determines the ratio of metastatic colonization and cellular dormancy. Recent technological breakthroughs in intravital imaging, quantitative ECM-centric proteomics, and tissue decellularization technologies have made it possible to map out the spatial and temporal roles of ECM-adhesion signaling across these stages of metastasis with precision. A combination of these findings reveals ECM-controlled adhesion pathways as essential factors of circulating tumor cell survival and metastatic success (Kai et al., 2019).

ECM-instructed angiogenesis and vascular normalization

Besides its long-standing role in supporting tumor angiogenesis, vascular endothelial growth factor (VEGF) has a significant impact on extracellular matrix (ECM) remodeling in the tumor microenvironment, and this is what determines tumor growth, invasiveness, and chemosensitivity. In the most aggressive malignancies, like the triple-negative breast

TABLE 7.3 Cancer specific alterations in ECM and targeting approaches.

Organ	ECM-related alterations	ECM-targeted approach reported	Outcome
Pancreatic ductal adenocarcinoma (PDAC)	Excess fibrillar collagen deposition, increased ECM crosslinking, tumor stiffness, chemotherapy-induced desmoplasia	Inhibition of the LOX family using SYN-5505	Reduced collagen crosslinking, decreased tumor stiffness, reduced liver metastasis, improved survival
PDAC (CAF-driven fibrosis)	Elevated CD105^{+} CAF activity, increased collagen deposition, altered ECM remodeling	Repurposing itraconazole to reprogram CAFs	Reduced collagen deposition, altered ECM remodeling, decreased metastatic spread
Hepatocellular carcinoma (liver)	Increased ECM formation and degradation biomarkers, altered TGF-β signaling	Use of circulating ECM biomarkers	Association with poor survival; predictive value for immunotherapy response
Renal cell carcinoma (kidney)	Dysregulated ECM turnover and collagen signaling	ECM biomarker-based patient stratification	Improved prediction of response to nivolumab and ipilimumab
Fibrotic solid tumors (subset of patients)	High CAF activity; collagen III processing; expression of myCAF-specific collagens (VIII, XI, XII)	PRO-C3 and myCAF collagen biomarker assessment	Prognostic enrichment and patient stratification in clinical trials
Metastatic colonization sites (experimental models)	Altered ECM composition in premetastatic and metastatic niches	Use of decellularised organ ECM scaffolds (ISDoT)	Identification of ECM changes regulating metastatic outgrowth

Data from Karsdal, M., Cox, T. R., Parker, A. L., Willumsen, N., Sand, J. M. B., Jenkins, G., Hansen, H. H., Oldenburger, A., Geillinger-Kaestle, K. E., Larsen, A. T., Black, D., Genovese, F., Eckersley, A., Heinz, A., Nyström, A., Holm Nielsen, S., Bennink, L., Johannsson, L., Bay-Jensen, A.-C., ... S., Ricard-Blum. Advances in Extracellular Matrix-Associated Diagnostics and Therapeutics. J. Clin Med, 14(6). (2025), https://doi.org/10.3390/jcm14061856.

cancer, the high levels of VEGF expression cause tumor-specific ECM re-programming that is characterized by reduced collagen I levels, fibronectin, and hyaluronan, as well as disorganized collagen fiber architecture. These changes are a result of VEGF-orchestrated regulation of matrix-modifying enzymes, such as an increase in the expression of MMP1, uPAR, and lysyl oxidase and the decrease in the expression of MMP2 and ADAMTS1 that shift the matrix towards a degradative state. This remodeled state of ECM is contributed to by both autocrine VEGF signaling in cancer cells, possibly by neuropilin-1, and paracrine activities on the cancer-associated fibroblasts (Goggins et al., 2023).

ECM regulation of epigenetics and gene expression

One of the components of the nuclear architecture and the regulation of chromatin dynamics is the extracellular matrix (ECM) that governs transcriptional programs and cellular processes in the varied physiological and pathological conditions. Biomechanical properties of the matrix, including stiffness and surface geometry, are brought into physical contact with the nucleus, resulting in chromatin reorganization and epigenetic modifications, which ultimately affect cell identity, growth, and lineage commitment. Recent evidence indicates that the regulation of ECM-dependence is not limited to histone modifications but also covers patterns of DNA methylation and regulation by microRNAs, as observed with the case of the stiffness-induced elevation of microRNA-21 in mesenchymal stem cells, which favors the fibrogenic response. These mechanically instigated consequences further rely on the tissue context and pathology and lead to modifications in chromatin accessibility of both stem cells, cancer cells, and other specialized groups of cells. Interestingly, there is also the phenomenon of mechanical memory that suggests that cells can be capable of retaining epigenetic remnants of the previous matrix environment, which can be used in therapeutic applications. CM-mediated nuclear mechano-transduction is the exploitation of which is therefore an appealing way of reprogramming pathogenic cellular dysfunctions or regenerative shootouts in many clinical applications (Lee et al., 2025a).

A generalization of these concepts, the concept of jamming-unjamming transition in multicellular systems, is the basis of a mechanistic explanation of how the extracellular matrix mechanics dictate the behavior of cancer cells. It is the ECM that is responsible for controlling the jammed solid-like to unjammed fluid-like changes and conditions, and it is what regulates the rigidity of the tissues and the force transmission of space, enabling collective migration, invasive migration, and tissue reorganization. Such mechanically activated modification of the cytoskeleton and nuclear stress leads to the modification of transcriptional activity and metabolism adjustment, not associated with canonical epithelial-mesenchymal transition pathways. The unjamming state is more partial toward invasion and metastatic migration in cancerous environments, and the jammed state maintains structure and minimizes energy needs. A combination of ECM-initiated mechano-transduction with dynamic jamming behavior defines a significant potential regulatory pathway in mechanical signal and chromatin organization, gene expression, and tumor growth, and as such offers new prospects of mechanically sensitive therapeutic manipulations (Mierke, 2025).

The mechanical signals of the extracellular matrix have an important role in regulating tumor growth, architecture, and metabolic programs by triggering the mechano-epigenetic feedback. Epigenetic modulators such as JMJD1a are increased by increased matrix rigidity and mechanical forces acting on the cell to anti-proliferate YAP-driven cellular proliferation, coordinate cytoskeletal remodeling through mechanoresponsive proteins, including MYH14, and regulate the action of mitochondria through mechanosensitive channels and the action of DNA/ncRNA. One of such tactics is changing the rigidity of the ECM, tuning epigenetic regulators, or changing the mechanoresponsive effectors, which would restrict the development of the tumors, structural remodeling, and the metastatic ability (Zhao and Lv, 2023).

Future perspectives

Individualized regulation of the extracellular matrix (ECM) is a revolutionary approach to cancer treatment, which demonstrates the high inter-individual variability of ECM composition and its debatable role in tumor development, therapeutic response, and immune regulation. The differences in matrix constituents, mechanical properties, and remodeling dynamics produce different tumor microenvironments that regulate drug penetration and cytotoxic efficacy. The systematic characterization of ECM properties on a per-patient level will make it possible to design interventions aimed at remodeling matrix barriers, improving the delivery of therapeutics, and avoiding resistance mechanisms. Integration of ECM-guided approaches with conventional interventions and immunotherapies allows the use of more specific, effective, and less toxic regimens and makes personalized ECM-targeted therapy a promising approach in precision oncology (Desai et al., 2025). Mechanobiology, immunotherapy, and synthetic biology converge to create a revolutionary paradigm of biomedical interventions of the next generation. Cellular microenvironment mechanical signals are not only important determinants of the stem cell differentiation and tissue architecture, but also control the immune cell trafficking, activation, and cytotoxicity with critical importance. Recent microphysiological systems and ECM-mimetic systems allow the reconstruction of tissue-specific mechanical and vascular environments, allowing the immune-tumor and immune-tissue interactions to be accurately studied in physiologically relevant forces. This can also be increased by synthetic biology, which adds the capability of optogenetic control and engineered signaling circuits, which enables active perturbation of mechanotransduction pathways in immune and stromal populations in a highly space and time-faithful manner. Together, these combined strategies are favorable to the creation of personalized immunotherapies that target both biochemical networks and mechanical microenvironment, which is a crucial step in the direction of adaptive, specific, and effective treatment methods (Hwang et al., 2025). The extracellular matrix acts as a patient-specific regulator of tumor advancement, therapeutic reactivity, and immune regulation in its molecular make-up, stiffness, vasculature, and dynamic remodeling. The integration of ECM profiling into the schemes of precision oncology allows tailoring treatment regimens, improving the delivery of the therapy, immune interactions, and personalised cancer therapy (Qiao et al., 2025).

Conclusion

The extracellular matrix (ECM) has become a key mediator of cancer biology, with immense effects on tumor development, invasive capacity, immune responses, and treatment responses. ECM remodeling of cancer changes the tissue composition, mechanical properties, and spatial organization, creating a microenvironment to promote malignancy and restricting drug accessibility and immune cell invasion at the same time. Such dual functions place the ECM as a catalyst of the disease progression and an obstacle to effective treatment, making it a worthwhile target of modern-day oncology. In addition to gene analysis, newer ECM-based methods also look at the physical structure of the tumor environment to help guide personalized treatment.

The unique characteristics of ECM as applied to the patient, such as matrix composition, stiffness, vascular architecture, and dynamic remodeling, determine tumor progression, immune responsivenes and treatment efficacy. The identification of ECM signatures that determine drug delivery and resistance can be optimized through emerging technologies, including ECM replicating platforms, patient-derived organoids, high-resolution imaging, biosensors, and AI-integrated multi-omics. Allowing these to be incorporated into oncology enables the customization of therapies to increase drug penetration, immune interactions, and general patient-based cancer treatments. This part explains new ECM-based treatments and how they help make cancer treatment work better. New methods like ECM-based nanoparticles, exosomes, and CAR-T cells help immune cells reach tumors and improve treatment response. Other tools, such as computer models and matrix analysis, help understand tumor-specific ECMs and support personalized cancer treatment.

These strategies include enzymatic degradation of matrix elements, disarmament of ECM cross-linking enzymes, selective employment of matrix metalloproteinases, and regulation of ECM-linked signaling pathways, which have demonstrated the capability of reducing tumor aggressiveness and enhancing drug penetration levels. The extracellular matrix (ECM) is a hub regulator of essential tumor processes, such as metastasis, angiogenesis, and vascular normalization, and mechano-epigenetic regulation of gene expression, in which physical cues are converted to transcriptional and metabolic alterations in tumor cells. The importance of these multifaceted interactions provides the idea of precision oncology with more than genetic profiling and a structural and biomechanical context of tumors. In the future, ECM-targeted interventions specific to each patient, integrating the knowledge acquired through mechanobiology, immunotherapy, synthetic biology, and computational models, can change the face of cancer therapy. It is possible that, with tailored interventions based on the ECM features of a specific patient, current barriers to therapy may be overcome, the efficacy of these interventions may be enhanced, their toxicity may be reduced, and long-term responsiveness may be achieved. ECM-centered approaches will become the cornerstone of the next-generation precision oncology.

Funding

The authors confirm that they did not receive any financial support, grants, or other forms of assistance for the development of this book chapter.

Credit authorship contribution statement

SG is responsible for conceptualizing and drafting this chapter, bringing together insights from extracellular matrix biology, mechanobiology, immunotherapy, and precision oncology. Her contributions involved synthesizing current evidence on ECM structure, therapeutic strategies, emerging technologies, and future perspectives into a coherent and scholarly narrative, forming the core scientific and mechanistic framework of the chapter.

Dr. AP, a recognized expert in cancer biology, provided scientific guidance and conducted the final critical review, enhancing the chapter's mechanistic clarity, interpretive depth, and overall academic rigor.

AJ contributed as a detailed scientific reviewer, carefully identifying technical inconsistencies and refining mechanistic explanations to ensure that the final manuscript maintained high standards of accuracy and quality.

References

Almutairi, S., Moh'd Kalloush, H., Manoon, N.A., Bardaweel, S.K., 2023. Matrix metalloproteinases inhibitors in cancer treatment: An updated review (2013–2023). Molecules 28 (14). https://doi.org/10.3390/molecules28145567.

Cabral-Pacheco, G.A., Garza-Veloz, I., Castruita-De La Rosa, C., Ramirez-Acuña, J.M., Perez-Romero, B.A., Guerrero-Rodriguez, J.F., Martinez-Avila, N., Martinez-Fierro, M.L., 2020. The roles of matrix metalloproteinases and their inhibitors in human diseases. Int. J. Mol. Sci. 21 (24), 1–53. https://doi.org/10.3390/ijms21249739.

Day, Z.I., Roberts-Thomson, S., Nouri, Y.J., Dalton, N.S., Wang, S.S., Davenport, A., Ludlow, L.E., Hulett, M.D., Cross, R.S., Jenkins, M.R., 2025. Defining the extracellular matrix for targeted immunotherapy in adult and pediatric brain cancer. Npj. Precisi. Oncol. 9 (1). https://doi.org/10.1038/s41698-025-00956-z.

Desai, N., Sahel, D., Kubal, B., Postwala, H., Shah, Y., Chavda, V.P., Fernandes, C., Khatri, D.K., Vora, L.K., 2025. Role of the extracellular matrix in cancer: Insights into tumor progression and therapy. Adv. Therapeut. 8 (2). https://doi.org/10.1002/adtp.202400370.

Goggins, E., Mironchik, Y., Kakkad, S., Jacob, D., Wildes, F., Bhujwalla, Z.M., Krishnamachary, B., 2023. Reprogramming of VEGF-mediated extracellular matrix changes through autocrine signaling. Cancer. Biol. Ther. 24 (1). https://doi.org/10.1080/15384047.2023.2184145.

Hogan, K.J., Perez, M.R., Mikos, A.G., 2023. Extracellular matrix component-derived nanoparticles for drug delivery and tissue engineering. J. Contr. Release 360, 888–912. https://doi.org/10.1016/j.jconrel.2023.07.034.

Hu, Q., Zhu, Y., Mei, J., Liu, Y., Zhou, G., 2025. Extracellular matrix dynamics in tumor immunoregulation: From tumor microenvironment to immunotherapy. J. Hematol. Oncol. 18 (1). https://doi.org/10.1186/s13045-025-01717-y.

Hwang, P.Y., Mistriotis, P., Cai, H., Liu, L., Zhang, B., Smith, Q., Ferruzzi, J., Wang, P.Y., Li, S., 2025. Frontiers in mechanobiology and mechanomedicine. Med-X 3 (1). https://doi.org/10.1007/s44258-025-00071-5.

Ikeda-Imafuku, M., Gao, Y., Shaha, S., Li-Wen Wang, L., Park, K.S., Nakajima, M., Adebowale, O., Mitragotri, S., 2022. Extracellular matrix degrading enzyme with stroma-targeting peptides enhance the penetration of liposomes into tumors. J. Contr. Release 352, 1093–1103. https://doi.org/10.1016/j.jconrel.2022.11.007.

Jiang, D., Zhao, J., Zheng, J., Zhao, Y., Le, M., Qin, D., Huang, Q., Huang, J., Zhao, Q., Wang, L., Dong, X., 2024. LOX-mediated ECM mechanical stress induces piezo1 activation in hypoxic-ischemic brain damage and identification of novel inhibitor of LOX. Redox. Biol. 76. https://doi.org/10.1016/j.redox.2024.103346.

Jin, Y., Hu, M., Zhao, P., Zhang, C., Lin, J., Shen, Y., Chen, H., Zhang, W., Tang, M., Luan, X., 2026. AI-guided biomaterials and biofabrication strategies for enhanced tumor extracellular matrix mimicry. Cell Biomater. 2 (1). https://doi.org/10.1016/j.celbio.2025.100188.

Kai, B., Allison, P.D., Weaver, V.M., 2019. The extracellular matrix modulates the metastatic journey. Dev. Cell 49 (3), 332–346. https://doi.org/10.1016/j.devcel.2019.03.026.

Karsdal, M., Cox, T.R., Parker, A.L., Willumsen, N., Sand, J.M.B., Jenkins, G., Hansen, H.H., Oldenburger, A., Geillinger-Kaestle, K.E., Larsen, A.T., Black, D., Genovese, F., Eckersley, A., Heinz, A., Nyström, A., Nielsen, S.H., Bennink, L., Johannsson, L., Bay-Jensen, A.-C., Orange, D.E., Friedman, S., Røpke, M., Fiore, V., Schuppan, D., Rieder, F., Simona, B., Borthwick, L., Skarsfeldt, M., Wennbo, H., Thakker, P., Stoffel, R., Clarke, G.W., Kalluri, R., Ruane, D., Zannad, F., Mortensen, J.H., Sinkeviciute, D., Sundberg, F., Coseno, M., Thudium, C., Croft, A.P., Khanna, D., Cooreman, M., Broermann, A., Leeming, D.J., Ali, M., Ricard-Blum, S., 2025. Advances in extracellular matrix-associated diagnostics and therapeutics. J. Clin. Med 14 (6). https://doi.org/10.3390/jcm14061856.

Lall, S.P., Alsafwani, Z.W., Batra, S.K., 2024. Parthasarathy seshacharyulu, ASPORIN: A root of the matter in tumors and their host environment. B.B.A.– Rev. Cancer 1879 (1). https://doi.org/10.1016/j.bbcan.2023.189029.

Lee, J.J., Ng, K.Y., Bakhtiar, A., 2025a. Extracellular matrix: Unlocking new avenues in cancer treatment. Biomarker. Res. 13 (1). https://doi.org/10.1186/s40364-025-00757-3.

Lee, J.-H., Yun, Y.G., Kim, H.-W., 2025b. Matrix-induced nuclear remodeling and mechano-therapeutics. Cell. Rep. 44 (9). https://doi.org/10.1016/j.celrep.2025.116176.

Mierke, C.T., 2025. ECM mechanics control jamming-to-unjamming transition of cancer cells. Cells 14 (13). https://doi.org/10.3390/cells14130943.

Okura, G.C., Bharadwaj, A.G., Waisman, D.M., 2025. The role of extracellular proteases and extracellular matrix remodeling in the pre-metastatic niche. Biomolecules 15 (12). https://doi.org/10.3390/biom15121696.

Qiao, D., Wang, R.C., Wang, Z., 2025. Precision oncology: Current landscape, emerging trends, challenges, and future perspectives. Cells 14 (22). https://doi.org/10.3390/cells14221804.

Raghunathan, R., Sethi, M.K., Klein, J.A., Zaia, J., 2019. Proteomics, glycomics, and glycoproteomics of matrisome molecules. Mol. Cell. Proteomics 18 (11), 2138–2148. https://doi.org/10.1074/mcp.R119.001543.

Serrano, D.R., Juste, F., Anaya, B.J., Ramirez, B.I., Sánchez-Guirales, S.A., Quispillo, J.M., Hernandez, E.M., Simon, J. A., Trallero, J.M., Serrano, C., Rawat, S., Lalatsa, A., 2025. Exosome-based drug delivery: Anext-generation platform for cancer, infection, neurological and immunological diseases, gene therapy and regenerative medicine. Pharmaceutics 17 (10). https://doi.org/10.3390/pharmaceutics17101336.

Yue, B., 2014. Biology of the extracellular matrix: An overview. J. Glaucoma 23 (8). https://doi.org/10.1097/IJG.0000000000000108.

Zhang, M., Zhang, B., 2025. Extracellular matrix stiffness: Mechanisms in tumor progression and therapeutic potential in cancer. Exp. Hematol. Oncol. 14 (1). https://doi.org/10.1186/s40164-025-00647-2.

Zhao, B., Lv, Y., 2023. A biomechanical view of epigenetic tumor regulation. J. Biol. Phys. 49 (3), 283–307. https://doi.org/10.1007/s10867-023-09633-3.

CHAPTER

8

Heterogenicity of cancer and drug resistance

Unnati Gupta[1], *Swara Mishra*[1], *Mohit Sharma*[1] *and Nivedita Bhardwaj*[2]

[1]**Dr. D. Y. Patil Institute of Pharmaceutical Sciences and Research, Pune, Maharashtra, India;** [2]**Amity Institute of Pharmacy, Amity University, Noida, Uttar Pradesh, India**

Introduction

Tumor heterogeneity refers to the differences in genotype and phenotype in recognized or unrecognized tumors, which can exhibit variations in behavior and growth. The origins of heterogeneity include genomic instability, epigenetic factors, the tumor microenvironment, and natural selection. These variables will present complex spatial or temporal heterogeneity in tumor environmental systems. Intertumoral heterogeneity is observed in cases when patients have been diagnosed with the same malignancy and additionally identify cancer subtypes, that have variant biological behavior and therapy responses, as with breast cancer. Intratumoral heterogeneity is the genetic variation in molecular and cellular subclones in a single tumor, as genetic adaptation of tumor cells is naturally selected for clonal variation, promoting treatment resistance, or variation from metabolic stress, such as developmentally acquired epigenetic markers (Caiado et al., 2016). A dramatically reshaped open chromatin landscape provides tumor cells with greater epigenetic latitude compared to non-transformed cells, promoting cellular adaptation. Adaptation is observed either when a tumor cell engages developmental programs that had been locked away from developmental signals, or when epigenetic regulators of cell plasticity have epigenetically enabled rerouting. Tumor cells harbor the option for speedier adaptation than non-transformed or healthy cells, which is beneficial and directly contributes to significant phenotypic heterogeneity not only of tumor cells, but also that of stromal and immune cells of the microenvironment, each of which is likely adopting its own unique, non-physiological cell state (Flavahan et al., 2017).

Advanced Cancer Therapeutics
https://doi.org/10.1016/B978-0-443-44185-1.00019-7

The implications of tumor heterogeneity are crucial to patient management. Biopsying a tumor from a single location rarely provides a true representation of tumor heterogeneity and may create a bias that can lead to an underestimation of the genomic complexity of tumors. There are also heterogeneities associated with time and heterogeneities associated with therapy that may lead to the emergence of pre-existing resistant clones, which can predispose the patient to recurrence of disease. Disease recurrence is often related to the activation of signaling cascades, including the PI3K/AKT/mTOR, RAF–MEK–ERK, JNK/p38 MAPK, and JAK/STAT cascades that act in overlapping and compensatory regulatory networks to promote multidrug resistance and disease progression (Nabi et al., 2025; Sahu et al., 2022). The assessment of heterogeneity has gained rapid momentum in developing new approaches in the last few years. Multi-region whole-exome sequencing to assess spatial heterogeneity at metastatic sites. Single-cell sequencing to assess rare resistant clones. Finally, liquid biopsies to assess the real-time circulation of ctDNA and CTCs. Overall, these studies hold significant potential to change our perception of heterogeneity and inform our utilization of this data in precision oncology to develop adaptive therapeutic strategies, such as combinations of targeted agents, immunotherapy, and evolving dose and dosing schedules to overcome resistance, that we often create based on the genetic and phenotypic characteristics of tumors.

Tumor heterogeneity

Tumor heterogeneity refers to the existence of different subpopulations within a tumor that differ in genetic, epigenetic, and phenotypic differences. Moreover, heterogeneity is dynamic, occurring within a single anatomic location and evolving under selective pressures, such as treatment. Heterogeneity is one of the primary contributors to cancer progression, therapy resistance, and cancer recurrence, which is one of the reasons to better understand tumor heterogeneity within the frame and context of personalized or precision oncology. Tumor cells often exhibit significant intratumor heterogeneity, especially when it comes to all sorts of phenotypic differences from morphology to gene expression patterns, especially surface markers and receptors for growth factors and hormones, metabolism and activity, to motility and functional traits such as angiogenesis, proliferation, immunogenicity, and metastatic potential. When it comes to cancer biology, there are various forms of genetic heterogeneity, where interpatient heterogeneity is one of the most utilized and characterized types of heterogeneity (Hayes and Paoletti, 2013; Stanta and Bonin, 2018). Different types of tumor heterogeneity are discussed and depicted in Fig. 8.1.

Intertumor heterogeneity

Intertumor heterogeneity refers to the differences observed between tumors that arise from two different patients, even when they originate from the same tissue. For instance, breast cancers can be classified into diverse molecular subtypes, including luminal A/B, HER2-enriched, basal-like, and claudin-low, which exhibit different biological properties

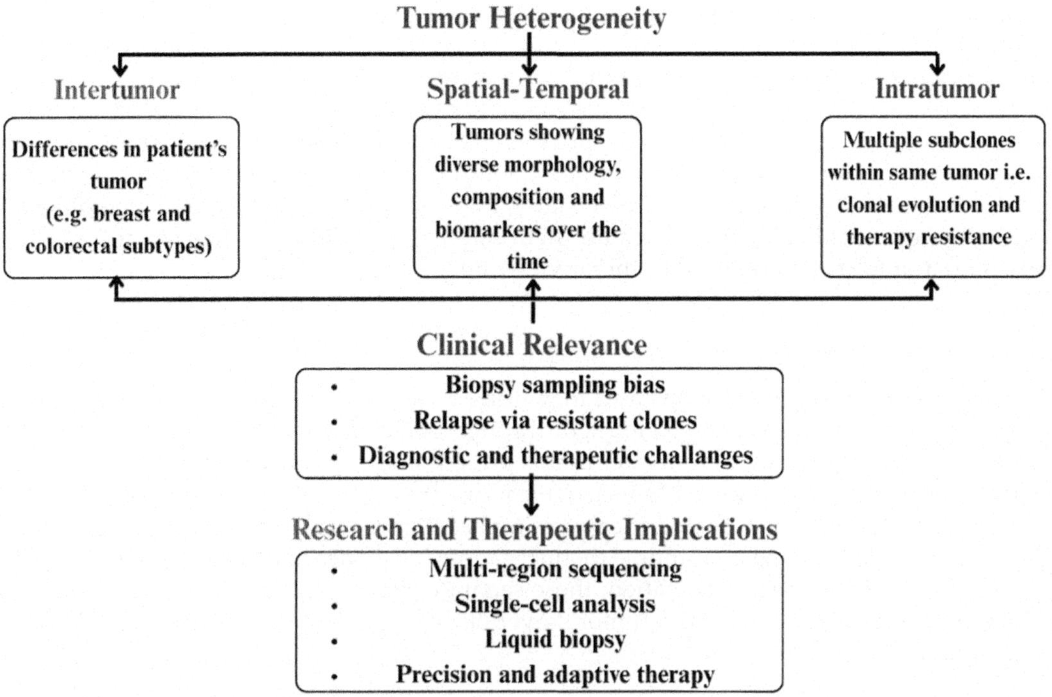

FIGURE 8.1 Types of tumor heterogeneity.

and treatment responses. Similarly, colorectal cancer (CRC) has distinct pathways of development, as identified by microsatellite instability (MSI) with BRAF mutations and chromosomal instability (CIN), which is characterized by TP53 and KRAS mutations. The clinical management question, combined with intertumor heterogeneity, shows a further need for subtype-specific therapy strategies (Hayes and Paoletti, 2013; Stanta and Bonin, 2018; Melo et al., 2013).

Intratumor heterogeneity refers to the presence of two or more distinct genetically subclones in one tumor. This heterogeneity arises from clonal evolution, a reflection of genomic instability. Subclonal variation can occur for multiple reasons. For example, when we refer to heterogeneity on a structural level, we would refer to morphological and histological heterogeneity, wherein different regions of a tumor can be distinct in their physical properties and differentiation states. Much of the heterogeneity can easily be accounted for based on spatial processes that are part of the tumor microenvironment. The distinct histological characteristics of the well-oxygenated tumor periphery versus the hypoxic tumor core, or in the case of lung adenocarcinoma, illustrate this well and reveal different immunohistochemical patterns in tumor samples. Aside from appearance, clonal heterogeneity stems from both accumulating genetic changes, such as mutations in DNA, and epigenetic changes, methylation of promoters. In a Darwinian manner, the selection and fate of subclones are dependent on both the tumor microenvironment and therapeutic interactions. This process of evolution is an important contributing factor to drug resistance (Melo et al., 2013; Wang et al., 2019). Finally, non-clonal heterogeneity suggests that functional variations occur without a change in genotype. In this situation, cells that are genetically identical to each other may act differently simply due to their ability to be phenotypically plastic, including their ability to switch reversibly between states, for example, by going through an epithelial-mesenchymal transition [EMT] or acquire stem cell-like characteristics that can also result in differential outcomes in relation to therapy (Swanton, 2012).

Spatial heterogeneity

Primary tumors and their metastases may differ in biomarker expression. Metastases can originate from minor resistant subclones or through polyclonal seeding, explaining their internal diversity. Therefore, a biomarker that is present in the primary tumor may also be absent in the metastasis, and vice versa, which can be confusing for an oncologist when choosing the appropriate targeted therapies. Metastatic tumors are heterogeneous because they are typically founded by multiple distinct cancer cell clones in a process known as polyclonal seeding. Following colonization, these separate clones continue to evolve in parallel, which progressively increases the tumor's overall diversity (Ramón y Cajal et al., 2020; Li et al., 2014).

Temporal heterogeneity

Tumor cells are heterogeneous, and that heterogeneity may change over time, a phenomenon called temporal heterogeneity. Change in tumor cell properties, like temporal heterogeneity, occurs mainly due to therapy, which acts like a potent selective pressure on the cancer cell population. The therapy destroys the sensitive clone, and in doing so, allows a previously rare resistant clone (which existed before treatment) to prevail and become the dominant tumor clone to relapse clinically. Minimally invasive liquid biopsies can yield unique insights into this dynamic process through longitudinal monitoring. Using ctDNA or CTCs isolated from blood samples and periodically sampled over time, researchers can evaluate tumor evolution, observe the development of mutations conferring resistance, and even update treatment regimens in real time when appropriate (De Bruin et al., 2014; Vieira et al., 2008).

Clinical implications

The challenges of tumor heterogeneity highlight the limitations of single-site biopsies and fixed molecular classifications. Multiregional sampling of tissue combined with liquid biopsies will identify the true complexity of tumors. The understanding of heterogeneity, the differences within and between tumors in the same location, is essential for enhancing adaptive and individualized treatment plans.

The consequences of tumor heterogeneity for good oncology care are mainly evident in diagnostics and management. First, intra-tumor heterogeneity creates substantial clinical complexity for pathology. A biopsy performed on a tumor at a specific site, which is conventionally how biopsies are acquired, may not reflect the tumor's full heterogeneity. The pathologist sometimes is unable to identify the molecular features characterizing the biopsy, which contributes to a 'sampling bias' and limits the pathologist's ability to characterize genomically important subclones, such as those associated with mutations conferring resistance. Also, essential genomic components of characterization are missed out when tumors are assessed without comprehensive clinical sampling associated with traditional biopsy procedures, potentially leading to misconceptions regarding which treatment and/or therapeutic type should be used. Thus, intratumoral heterogeneity is a key factor in both intrinsic drug resistance and acquired drug resistance. It is likely that a small, resistant fraction of cells is present but undetectable in the tumor before the initiation of therapy, which initially allows for the shrinkage of the tumor body but ultimately causes treatment failure when they proliferate and resume tumor growth (Fu et al., 2025; Lim and Ma, 2019).

As a result of the challenges posed by static classifications and single-site biopsies, oncology has shifted towards more comprehensive therapy and treatment approaches. To assess tumor heterogeneity, it will be essential to incorporate multi-regional tissue sampling and liquid biopsy testing with the measurement of circulating tumor cells or circulating tumor DNA (ctDNA) from blood. These strategies provide an in-depth real-time view of the tumor's genomic landscape, enabling clinicians to detect tumor evolution and resistance mutations significantly earlier. Ultimately, understanding more about heterogeneity allows for a better adaptive and personalized treatment approach.

Drug resistance and its mechanism

Drug resistance in cancer is a phenomenon where cancer cells, which were initially responsive to a specific therapeutic agent, either inherently possess or later develop the ability to survive and proliferate despite continued treatment. This can be categorized as either intrinsic or acquired resistance, and is driven by various molecular mechanisms (Fig. 8.2).

Intrinsic drug resistance

Intrinsic resistance refers to the pre-existing and inherent lack of sensitivity of a tumor to a designated anticancer agent before treatment. This is not resistance that has been acquired or induced, but rather a biological property of the cancer cells themselves, related to genetic makeup, cellular diversity, or the microenvironment of the tumor. Some cancers are intrinsically resistant to certain established chemotherapies because they possess inherent mechanisms that neutralize or evade the treatment's effects. For instance, malignant melanoma is intrinsically resistant to many established chemotherapies, partly because of the presence of intrinsic levels of anti-apoptosis proteins (Bcl-2 family) that inhibit programmed cell death, and highly effective mechanisms to repair damage caused by DNA-alkylating agents before lethality. Another clear evidence is colorectal cancers with a KRAS mutation that are

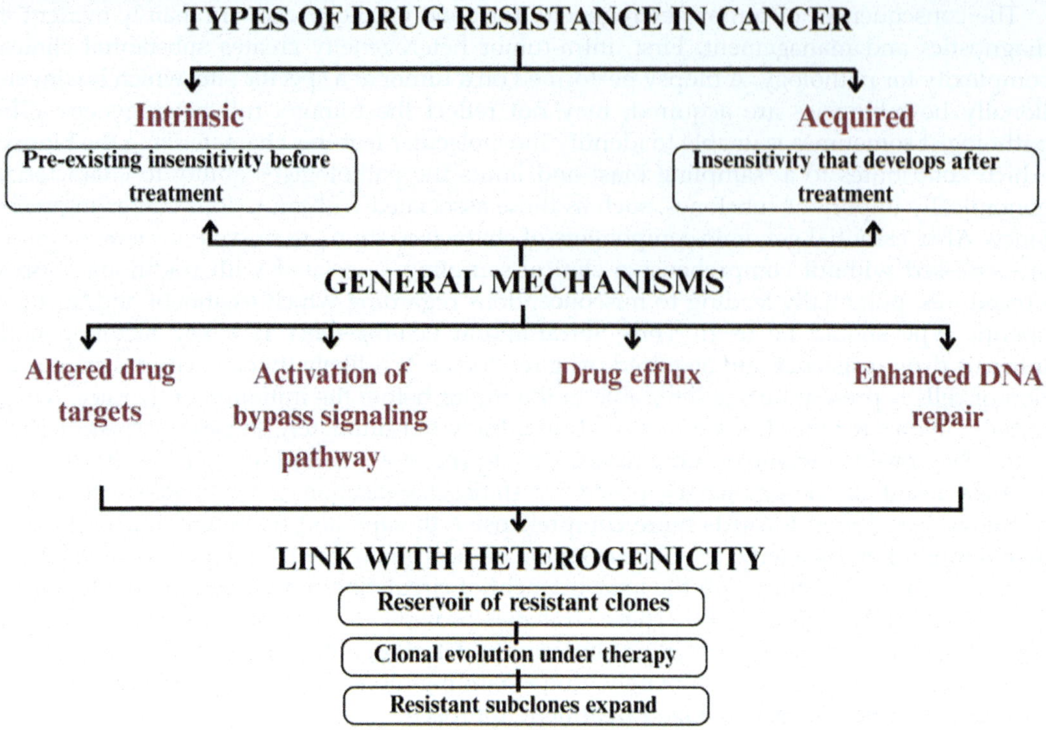

FIGURE 8.2 Molecular and cellular drivers of cancer drug resistance.

inherently resistant to EGFR inhibitors such as cetuximab. KRAS is a critical signaling protein downstream of EGFR. A mutation that locks KRAS "on" removes any potential inhibition by upstream blockade of EGFR from the drug at the initiation of treatment, making the therapy ineffective from the start (Holohan et al., 2013; Kerbel et al., 1994).

Acquired resistance

Acquired resistance is a process in which, after an initial response following exposure to a drug, the cancer cells can potentially gain new properties to withstand the toxicity of the drug. In other words, while a patient may initially be considered to have done well based on a significant decrease in tumor size and even achieving a transient remission, over time, a subclone of cancer cells may evolve new properties that permit their reproduction and proliferation in the presence of the drug. This is an example of Darwinian clonal selection at the cellular level. The drug acts as a strong, selective factor on cancer cells, killing existing, sensitive cancer cells and leaving behind an environment where rare, pre-existing, or even new mutations that lead to resistant cancer cells can proliferate and survive. After the resistant cells continue to proliferate, the tumor is functionally repopulated by resistant progeny cells, and hence the clinical presentation of the relapse condition arises with the tumors that are resistant to the initial drug therapy. An extensively described example of resistance is the development of resistance to the EGFR inhibitor gefitinib in non-small cell lung cancer. Typically, patients with an activating EGFR mutation experience a prominent initial response; however, resistance develops within one to 2 years. In many cases, a secondary "gatekeeper" mutation in the EGFR gene itself (usually T790M) modifies the drug-binding site, preventing the drug from inhibiting the tyrosine kinase (Schmucker et al., 2021).

General mechanisms of drug resistance

Cancer cells employ a wide and often overlapping variety of strategies to become resistant to therapeutic agents. These sophisticated mechanisms can be broadly grouped into several categories.

Altered drug targets

One of the most straightforward mechanisms by which cancer cells develop resistance is by altering the specific molecular target of the drug itself, rendering the therapy ineffective. Resistance can occur when a cancer cell undergoes a genetic change that alters the gene that encodes the target protein. The result of this change to the genetic information is that the three-dimensional structure of the protein is now modified at a key location, which can prevent the effective binding of the drug to its proper binding pocket. This is similar to how changing the tumblers in a lock can prevent the key from functioning. One example of drug resistance occurs when mutations develop in the kinase domain of the BCR-ABL1 fusion protein, commonly found in chronic myeloid leukemia (CML). The mutations physically prevent imatinib from reaching its binding site, allowing cancerous signaling to continue. The resistance can also arise when cancer cells can produce much more target by either gene amplification or protein overexpression. If the target gene is amplified, the cell produces many copies of the target protein, thereby overwhelming the drug target. An example of this is the amplification of the HER2 gene seen in breast cancer, which accounts for resistance to the monoclonal antibody trastuzumab, because the number of surface HER2 receptors overwhelms the antibody and allows for continued receptor signaling (Palmer and Kishony, 2014; Deininger et al., 2005).

Activation of bypass signaling pathways

Cancer cells are often known to rely on specific signaling pathways for growth and survival a concept known as "oncogene addiction." Targeted therapy usually attempts to exploit this addiction by inhibiting a primary molecule in the signaling pathways, or various components, of those pathways. However, cancer cells can escape targeted therapy by signaling through alternative or "bypass" pathways that often provide similar survival signals to those of the original pathway. For example, if the drug involuntarily inhibits a specific growth receptor, such as the epidermal growth factor receptor (EGFR), the cancer cells may downregulate EGFR and/or upregulate a different receptor, like MET, to provide an alternative survival signal. Once a MET receptor is stimulated and upregulated, the MET receptor can signal to downstream events (e.g., PI3K/AKT) that initially relied on the EGFR signal. In this case, the MET receptor provides an alternative route to the survival signal that circumvents the inhibition of the drug (Engelman et al., 2007; Kopetz et al., 2019; Morgillo et al., 2016).

The link between heterogeneity and drug resistance

The specific molecular mechanisms of resistance are not isolated events, but are, at their core, facilitated and amplified by the universal fact of tumor heterogeneity itself, the 'engine' that drives treatment failure to develop adaptive and survival capacities. The extensive genetic and phenotypic diversity observed within a tumor represents a powerful "reservoir" of resistance. Due to the genomic instability seen in cancer cells, a large tumor is not simply a mass of cells that are the same, but a complicated ecosystem with millions (if not billions) of different subclones. In this incredible diversity, it is statistically a certainty that purely by random chance, one or a few cells will have already acquired the particular genetics or epigenetic traits that enable them to survive the specific therapy even before the first dose is given. These traits may be the result of a pre-existing mutation in the target of the drug, the expression of a potent drug efflux pump, or an active DNA repair pathway. When the treatment commences, the only cells that can survive the first assault of the treatment are these rare pre-existing resistant cells. While the treatment will kill most of the tumor, these cells will serve as the "seeds" for the future recurrence of a fully resistant tumor. As such, this is totally consistent with the notion that a treatment that is apparently highly effective will end up appearing to be ineffective (Burrell and Swanton, 2014; Marusyk et al., 2012).

The process of selecting pre-existing resistance occurs through a process of clonal evolution, which is a traditional Darwinian struggle where the therapy is a strong and quick form of selective pressure. The various subclones in a tumor are competing for resources, including oxygen and nutrients, before the therapy. The introduction of a drug disrupts this competition immediately for the tumor, creating a strong bottleneck in the evolutionary landscape where only the "fittest" cells, those utilizing mechanisms of resistance, will survive. The drug-sensitive clones, which make up the majority of the tumor, are killed off. With more resources available for resistant subclones to grow and expand, free from competition, these clones begin to dominate. Due to its ability to grow exponentially, a single surviving resistant cell can establish a large tumor mass. Thus, this tumor that arises at the time of clinical relapse has been selected for in that microenvironment and will often be genetically distinct from the primary tumor, being the progeny of a small number of resistant cells. Tracking this process of evolution will soon be possible for patients who are followed longitudinally, using advanced techniques such as liquid biopsies and analyzing circulating tumor DNA (ctDNA) from blood samples drawn throughout treatment to monitor resistance mutations as they occur over time. The ability to monitor ctDNA will provide almost real-time evidence and tracking of the tumor's evolutionary history, allowing for the possibility of making treatment changes before resistance becomes clinically evident (Fruman and Rommel, 2014; Kandoth et al., 2013).

Interplay of Cancer Heterogeneity and therapeutic failure

The ability of tumors to evolve and withstand therapy is deeply rooted in a complex network of intracellular signaling pathways. Heterogeneity within a tumor means different cells can have varying levels of activation in these pathways, allowing the cancer as a whole to adapt and survive. Understanding these pathways and their interactions is key to overcoming drug resistance, and the interconnection between these pathways (Fig. 8.3).

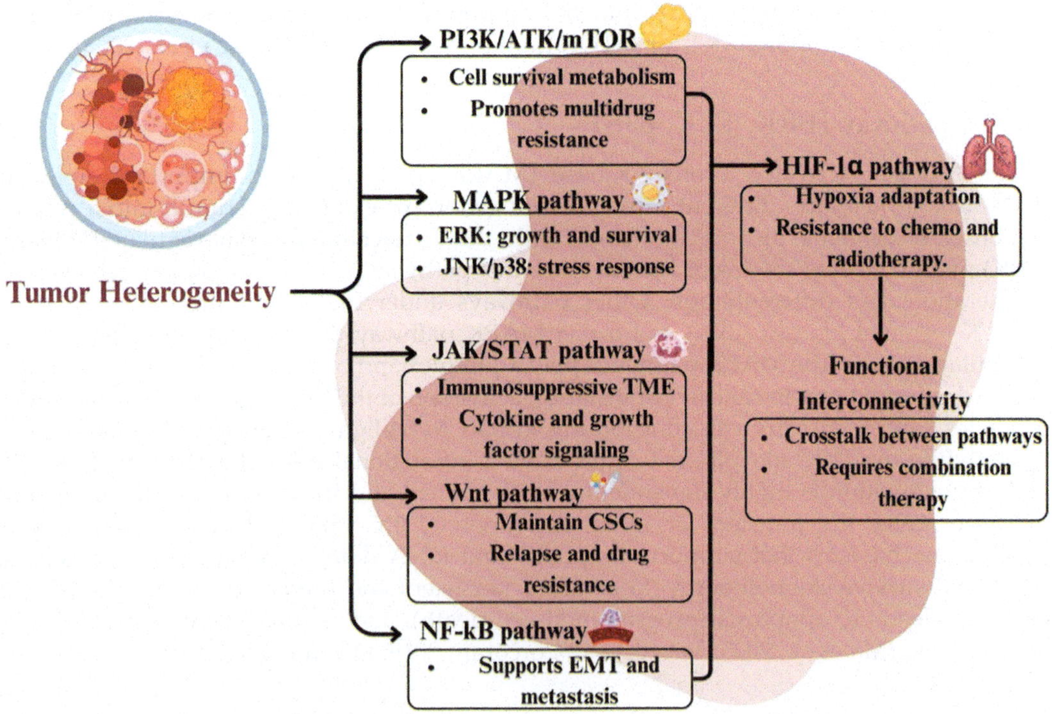

FIGURE 8.3 Signalling pathways involved in cancer heterogeneity.

PI3K/AKT/mTOR (PAM)

The Phosphatidylinositol 3-kinase (PI3K/AKT/mTOR (PAM)) pathway represents a primary and highly conserved signal transduction cascade that regulates cellular homeostasis by responding to extracellular stimuli that modulate essential cellular functions, including cellular growth, metabolism, and cellular survival (Glaviano et al., 2023). Under normal pathophysiological conditions, this signaling cascade is activated by extracellular growth factors that bind to receptors on the cell surface, causing PI3K to phosphorylate cell membrane lipid species either directly or indirectly activating the downstream kinase AKT. This activation is a highly controlled event; however, when considering tumorigenesis, this pathway is the most commonly dysregulated signaling pathway, typically in around 50% or more of human cancers. Dysregulation often occurs through several classic mechanisms: a gain-of-function mutation in the PIK3CA gene that leads to PI3K hyperactivation, loss of the tumor suppressor PTEN, which terminates the signal, or AKT overactivation resulting from a gain-of-function mutation or gene amplification. This constitutive "on" state leads to an enhanced survival capacity for cancer cells and is a key perpetuating pathway that contributes to multidrug resistance (MDR) progression, as a high level of signaling promoting cell survival inhibits programmed cell death in response to anticancer therapies. Due to its significance inside the body, the PAM pathway has become a major target for clinical intervention, resulting in the development of a number of inhibitors that selectively target the central nodes of PI3K, AKT, or mTOR (Janku et al., 2018; Hennessy et al., 2005).

MAPK pathway (ERK, JNK, p38)

The Mitogen-Activated Protein Kinase (MAPK) pathway is an important signaling pathway that mediates different forms of endogenous or exogenous stimuli into a cellular response. It contains distinct branches, with the Extracellular signal-regulated kinases (ERK) pathway being the major branch since this pathway primarily regulates cell growth, proliferation, and differentiation. Other pathways under the MAPK umbrella consist of c-Jun N-terminal kinases (JNK) and a p38 MAPK pathway that are mainly activated due to cellular stresses. The MAPK pathways play a complex and often contradictory role in relation to drug resistance in cancer. For instance, activation of the ERK signaling pathway often promotes cancer cell survival, contributing in part to malignant transformation and resistance, while the JNK and p38 pathways have a bifunctional role. The effect of JNK/p38 pathway activation is highly dependent on cell context and the duration of the signaling. In cancer cells, the transient or initial activation of JNK/p38 pathways leads to pro-survival mechanisms that support autophagy and DNA damage repair, allowing cells to adapt and survive chemotherapy. In contrast, persistent and robust activation of JNK/p38 pathways leads to apoptosis (programmed cell death), and cellular chemoresistance may be overcome (Ma et al., 2025; Yaeger and Corcoran, 2019; Owen et al., 2019).

JAK/STAT pathway

The Janus kinase (JAK)/signal transducer and activator of transcription (STAT) pathway is a primary route for cytokine signaling and is crucial for immune responses and cell proliferation. It mediates the actions of over 50 cytokines, interferons, and growth factors using a series of signaling events that communicate information from the cell surface to the nucleus, directly regulating DNA transcription. The main players in this pathway include transmembrane receptors, receptor-associated cytosolic tyrosine kinases (JAKs: JAK1, JAK2, JAK3, and TYK2), and the transcription factors STATs (STAT1, STAT2, STAT3, STAT4, STAT5A, STAT5B, and STAT6). While important for normal immune responses and cell proliferation, aberrant activation of the JAK/STAT pathway, especially via STAT3, is often detected in the cancer state, where it enhances tumor cell survival, proliferation, and the establishment of an immunosuppressive tumor microenvironment. Additionally, this pathway does not exist in a vacuum but interacts with additional oncogenic signaling networks, thus exacerbating pro-survival signals, which may also promote therapeutic resistance (Tabassum et al., 2019).

NF-κB and Wnt/β-catenin pathways

The Nuclear Factor-kappa B (NF-κB) and Wnt/β-catenin are essential signaling pathways that are frequently hijacked to induce aggressive cancer phenotypes. The NF-κB family of transcription factors typically serves as a master regulator of inflammation and immunity in response to cellular stress or infection. Upon persistent activation in cancer, NF-κB elicits a pro-tumorigenic response by transcribing genes that allow malignant cells to avoid immune detection, resist apoptosis, and establish chronic inflammation that supports tumor growth. In parallel, the Wnt/β-catenin pathway, important for embryonic development, becomes aberrantly activated in cancer cells to sustain cancer stem cell (CSC) populations. This aberrant activity occurs when the central effector of the pathway, β-catenin, accumulates in the nucleus and transcribes genes that confer self-renewal properties to the CSCs, thereby making these cells the source of tumor initiation, treatment resistance, and relapse. The interaction between NF-κB and Wnt/β-catenin signaling is particularly damaging because it drives the epithelial-to-mesenchymal transition (EMT). EMT is a complex program wherein cancer cells acquire migratory and invasive properties associated with mesenchymal cells as they lose their epithelium, stationary cellular characteristics. EMT is the mechanism by which cancer cells can transition and migrate, facilitating metastasis. Additionally, EMT has been strongly linked to the development of multidrug resistance due to the survival gains acquired by cells during this transition, or further, the drug efflux capacity noted in mesenchymal characteristics (Zhang and Yu, 2023; Ghandadi et al., 2019).

HIF-1αpathway

As tumors grow beyond their accessible source of oxygenated blood, they transition into low-oxygen (hypoxic) conditions. In response, the tumor cells adjust their energy expenditure by engaging in an ancillary survival pathway: the hypoxia-inducible factor 1-alpha (HIF−1α) pathway. In normoxic conditions, the HIF−1α protein is subject to degradation. However, under hypoxic conditions, the HIF−1α protein stabilizes and becomes a master transcription factor. The protein undergoes translocation to the cell nucleus and activates hundreds of genes that control the phenotype at its basic level (defining it as a cell). These include forcing the cell to utilize an oxygen-independent pathway to create ATP for fuel (i.e., glycolysis), driving the cells to produce new blood vessels (i.e., angiogenesis) to feed the tumor nutrients, and instigating pro-survival programs. Therefore, HIF−1α is the main regulator of cancer progression and induces an enduring state in tumor cells with sustained resistance to chemotherapeutic drugs and radiation therapies, which is a key driver of treatment failure and malignancy (Schöning et al., 2017; Warfel and El-Deiry, 2014).

Pathway interconnectivity driven resistance

The actual power of cancer lies not in a single pathway, but in the complex dialog in the biological system across multiple signaling pathways. This interplay, which occurs biochemically, allows cells to circumvent therapeutic blockade, making it impossible to address cancer with traditional medications. A specific example is the interaction of the PI3K/AKT signaling pathway and the MAPK signaling pathway. These pathways are co-activated in malignancy. Blocking one of these pathways with a targeted agent, such as a BRAF inhibitor, results in cancer cells using an alternative mechanism through the other pathway to provide an alternative signal that supports survival. This is a common mechanism of acquired resistance. The JAK/STAT pathway frequently coincides and amplifies the signaling inputs stemming from these networks, as STAT3 can be activated from the same upstream signaling, and then enhances the expression of genes that promote cell survival. In agreement, NF-κB frequently serves as a central node, receiving activation signals from PI3K/AKT and MAPK, and connecting them to inflammation and anti-apoptotic signaling to form a powerful survival network. Consequently, the existence of an interlinked web of redundant and compensatory signaling means that targeting a single node will not be sufficient. The implications for cancer treatment are clear: efficacious and durable cancer therapies will likely require a combination therapy approach that targets multiple interlinked nodes to counter the adaptive resistance that arises from tumor heterogeneity (Ignatiadis et al., 2021; Hu et al., 2021; Alexander and Friedl, 2012).

Clinical evidence of pathway-driven resistance

The therapeutic implications of this signaling cross-talk are obvious, since various cancers have been clearly identified that behave as unique molecular escape pathways. Non-small cell lung cancer (NSCLC) with EGFR mutations will often indicate impressive responses to EGFR inhibitors like Osimertinib in patients, but then will develop resistance and disease progression. A common mechanism is the amplification of the MET oncogene, which activates the PI3K/AKT pathway independently of EGFR, thus providing an escape route. This has led to clinical trials combining EGFR and MET inhibitors to prevent or treat this form of resistance. In hormone receptor-positive (HR+) breast cancer, endocrine therapies are a cornerstone of treatment. A major mechanism of acquired resistance is the aberrant activation of growth factor receptor pathways, particularly the PI3K/AKT pathway, often due to mutations in *PIK3CA*. This allows cancer cells to proliferate even in the absence of estrogenic signals. This understanding led directly to the development and approval of the PI3K inhibitor Alpelisib, which is used in combination with endocrine therapy for patients with *PIK3CA*-mutated tumors that have progressed. Patients with BRAF V600E-mutant metastatic colorectal cancer show poor response to BRAF inhibitors alone. This is because inhibiting BRAF leads to a rapid feedback activation of EGFR, which reactivates the MAPK pathway and others. Therefore, the standard of care is now a combination therapy that targets both BRAF and EGFR simultaneously, demonstrating a clinical solution based directly on understanding pathway crosstalk (Massard et al., 2017; McCubrey et al., 2012). Resistance to platinum-based chemotherapy is a major challenge in high-grade serous ovarian cancer. While the mechanisms are complex, hyperactivation of survival pathways, such as the PI3K/AKT pathway, has been shown to play a significant role by inhibiting apoptosis. Furthermore, the loss of functional BRCA proteins, which are crucial for DNA repair, is common in this type of cancer. When tumors develop resistance to PARP inhibitors (a targeted therapy for BRCA-deficient cancers), it is often through mechanisms that restore DNA repair. This highlights a different form of resistance where the cell reactivates a pathway that the drug was designed to exploit (Bhardwaj et al., 2021, 2022).

Advancing methods for mapping cancer heterogeneity and resistance

To examine the complex tumor microenvironment, modern techniques are required to visualize the diversity at different resolutions. Several key techniques have been employed to investigate the mechanisms of heterogeneity and drug resistance (Shao et al., 2021).

Multi-region sampling is the sampling of distinct spatial sites outside of the primary tumor or elsewhere in the body (i.e., in metastases). The genomic sequencing from each biopsy allows for a spatial map of the genetic diversity, to develop inferences regarding the evolutionary path of the tumor and to characterize "private" mutations present in only some of the biopsies. This approach has been crucial to demonstrating how a single biopsy often does not capture the full complexity of the tumor (Chao et al., 2020; Van de Sande et al., 2023). Another technology that marks a major advancement in resolution is Single-Cell Sequencing (SCS), which characterizes single cells from a single tumor sample on a genomic, transcriptomic, or epigenetic level in the thousands. SCS has improved resolution relative to a standard, bulk sequencing that averages genomes of cells within a sample, and does not capture either rare or non-dominant cells. In contrast, SCS can reveal rare cell populations, including pre-existing drug-resistant clones that would not have been detected due to insufficient cell numbers. SCS also permits a very different and detailed interrogation of the tumor microenvironment, providing spatial correlation of the different immune and stromal cells that interact with cancer cells and alter their functioning (Harbst et al., 2016; Hawsawi et al., 2024).

Multi-region and single-cell sequencing generate massive datasets that are not tractable by manual inspection. This data is used in computational modeling with mathematical and statistical algorithms to generate phylogenetic trees of tumor evolution, as well as to predict the response that subclones are likely to have under therapeutic pressures. Such models enable the simulation of different drug regimens and guide the most optimal combination or sequential therapies that may either prevent resistance or at least delay it (Van de Sande et al., 2023).

Therapeutic approaches to overcome heterogeneity and resistance

Historically, the development of novel therapeutics has been driven by the combination of tumor heterogeneity and the co-opting of signal transduction pathways. Unlike traditional therapeutics, these approaches have taken on many forms, but they aim to perturb the majority of cancer's adaptive capabilities. Multi-targeted therapies, managing evolving cancer behaviors, targeting and adaptive immune modulation treatment strategies, and precision medicine, which applies the technique of advanced diagnosis, are all examples of therapies designed to address tumor heterogeneity and adaptive development.

Combination and adaptive therapy

Combination therapy is the bedrock of modern care. The foundational rationale is simply to simultaneously block multiple targets to discourage resistance, which can include treating separate nodes on the same pathway (BRAF and MEK inhibitors) or through independent parallel pathway signaling. By designing synergistic combinations where the combined effect is greater than the sum of their individual effects is possible to achieve a more durable response and overcome the robustness of cancer signaling networks (Lin et al., 2020).

Adaptive therapy is a new and emerging strategy. This approach contrasts with the traditional goal of maximizing tumor cell death; instead, adaptive therapy allows for the continuation of tumor growth, but under the control of a population of cells susceptible to drug therapy. Intermittent or lower-dose drug schedules would allow for the continued survival of drug-sensitive cells while competitively excluding the growth of drug-resistant clones, thereby prolonging treatment (McDonald et al., 2023; Vasan et al., 2019).

Immunotherapy

Immunotherapy is a promising strategy for targeting genetic heterogeneity, particularly through the use of immune checkpoint inhibitors. The immune system is encouraged to recognize a broad spectrum of cancer-associated proteins, in contrast to targeted therapies that specifically target individual mutations. This approach enables T-cells to mediate an immune response against a diverse array of clonal subpopulations. However, tumors can develop resistance. Tumors produce an immunosuppressive tumor microenvironment that excludes or exhausts T-cells. The "non-inflamed", or "immune-desert", phenotype remains a considerable barrier to the immunotherapy field and treating or reversing it, such as using checkpoint inhibitors in combination with a therapy that helps promote T-cell infiltration, remains a major focus of research (Binnewies et al., 2018; Gatenby et al., 2009; Lee et al., 2024; Sharma et al., 2017; Taniguchi and Karin, 2018; Xue et al., 2023).

Precision medicine and its tools

The basic premise of these novel approaches is precision medicine, which boasts new diagnostics that allow therapy to be targeted to the individual tumor. Next-generation sequencing (NGS) is the core technology behind precision oncology. NGS can rapidly sequence either DNA or RNA from a tumor, producing a comprehensive genetic profile of the tumor and identifying driver mutations that may be targets for specific drugs. A breakthrough is the liquid biopsy (Soda et al., 2022). This non-invasive blood test assesses circulating ctDNA, which is released into the bloodstream from cancer cells. Liquid biopsies enable longitudinal assessment of tumor evolution, which informs clinicians about treatment response, as well as early identification of new resistance mutations. The clinical utility of these tools is expanding rapidly, from advanced-stage cancer settings to earlier stages of disease for assessment and detection purposes (Jha et al., 2024a; Jha et al., 2024b; Mokhtari et al., 2017).

Conclusion

Tumor heterogeneity is not only a hallmark of malignancy but also a significant impediment to successful therapeutic targeting of multiple malignancies. Genetic instability, phenotypic plasticity, and impacts of the tumor microenvironment create an ecosystem of selective pressure in which resistant subclones will always emerge with treatment. In addition to providing an ecosystem for tumor heterogeneity, treatment can induce redundant and interconnected dependency on signaling pathways, including but not limited to the cascades involving, PI3K/AKT/mTOR, MAPK, JAK/STAT, NF-κB, and HIF-1α pathways that promote resilience and highlight the inadequacy of monotherapy solutions.

Newer technologies (multi-region sequencing, single-cell technologies, and liquid biopsy) are encouraging renewed interest in how we model the tumor microenvironment and resistance responses. Collectively, these technologies are establishing the framework for precision oncology, where we combine drugs, develop adaptive therapies, and investigate immunotherapy, often incorporating resistance, to deliver clinical value to patients. Integrated, the greatest promise for real-time therapy selection, delaying resistance and altering overall clinical outcomes, may be achieved through the melding of computational modeling of the biophysical properties of tumors and diagnostic molecular technologies in near real-time. In summary, tumor heterogeneity requires addressing not just our static treatment work in single therapy or single targets, but rather through dynamic multi-level treatment strategies that leverage high-resolution genomic complexities and adaptive longitudinal treatment decisions. We must embrace that complexity so that we can begin to transform the field of cancer treatment towards durable scaffold interventions that are temporally more rapid than the evolutionary framework of cancer.

References

Alexander, S., Friedl, P., 2012. Cancer invasion and resistance: Interconnected processes of disease progression and therapy failure. Trends Mol. Med. 18 (1), 13–26. https://doi.org/10.1016/j.molmed.2011.11.003.

Bhardwaj, N., Goel, B., Tripathi, N., Sahu, B., Jain, S.K., 2022. A comprehensive review on chemistry and pharmacology of marine bioactives as antimetastatic agents. Eur. J. Med. Chem. Rep. 4. https://doi.org/10.1016/j.ejmcr.2021.100023.

Bhardwaj, N., Tripathi, N., Goel, B., Jain, S.K., 2021. Anticancer activity of diosgenin and its semi-synthetic derivatives: Role in autophagy mediated cell death and induction of apoptosis. Mini Rev. Med. Chem 21 (13), 1646–1665. https://doi.org/10.2174/1389557521666210105111224.

Binnewies, M., Roberts, E.W., Kersten, K., Chan, V., Fearon, D.F., Merad, M., Coussens, L.M., Gabrilovich, D.I., Ostrand-Rosenberg, S., Hedrick, C.C., Vonderheide, R.H., Pittet, M.J., Jain, R.K., Zou, W., Howcroft, T.K., Woodhouse, E.C., Weinberg, R.A., Krummel, M.F., 2018. Understanding the tumor immune microenvironment (TIME) for effective therapy. Nat. Med. 24 (5), 541–550. https://doi.org/10.1038/s41591-018-0014-x.

Burrell, R.A., Swanton, C., 2014. The evolution of the unstable cancer genome. Curr. Opin. Genet. Dev. 24 (1), 61–67. https://doi.org/10.1016/j.gde.2013.11.011.

Caiado, F., Silva-Santos, B., Norell, H., 2016. Intra-tumour heterogeneity – going beyond genetics. FEBS J. 283 (12), 2245–2258. https://doi.org/10.1111/febs.13705.

Chao, J., Lee, J., Kim, K., Kang, S.Y., Lee, T., Kim, K.M., Kim, S.T., Klempner, S.J., Lee, H., 2020. A pilot study of baseline spatial genomic heterogeneity in primary gastric cancers using multi-region Endoscopic sampling. Front. Oncol. 10. https://doi.org/10.3389/fonc.2020.00225.

De Bruin, E.C., McGranahan, N., Mitter, R., Salm, M., Wedge, D.C., Yates, L., Jamal-Hanjani, M., Shafi, S., Murugaesu, N., Rowan, A.J., Grönroos, E., Muhammad, M.A., Horswell, S., Gerlinger, M., Varela, I., Jones, D., Marshall, J., Voet, T., Van Loo, P., Rassl, D.M., Rintoul, R.C., Janes, S.M., Lee, S.M., Forster, M., Ahmad, T., Lawrence, D., Falzon, M., Capitanio, A., Harkins, T.T., Lee, C.C., Tom, W., Teefe, E., Chen, S.C., Begum, S., Rabinowitz, A., Phillimore, B., Spencer-Dene, B., Stamp, G., Szallasi, Z., Matthews, N., Stewart, A., Campbell, P., Swanton, C., 2014. Spatial and temporal diversity in genomic instability processes defines lung cancer evolution. Science 346 (6206), 251–256. https://doi.org/10.1126/science.1253462.

Deininger, M., Buchdunger, E., Druker, B.J., 2005. The development of imatinib as a therapeutic agent for chronic myeloid leukemia. Blood 105 (7), 2640–2653. https://doi.org/10.1182/blood-2004-08-3097.

Engelman, J.A., Zejnullahu, K., Mitsudomi, T., Song, Y., Hyland, C., Joon, O.P., Lindeman, N., Gale, C.M., Zhao, X., Christensen, J., Kosaka, T., Holmes, A.J., Rogers, A.M., Cappuzzo, F., Mok, T., Lee, C., Johnson, B.E., Cantley, L. C., Jänne, P.A., 2007. MET amplification leads to gefitinib resistance in lung cancer by activating ERBB3 signaling. Science 316 (5827), 1039–1043. https://doi.org/10.1126/science.1141478.

Flavahan, W.A., Gaskell, E., Bernstein, B.E., 2017. Epigenetic plasticity and the hallmarks of cancer. Science 357 (6348). https://doi.org/10.1126/science.aal2380.

Fruman, D.A., Rommel, C., 2014. PI3K and cancer: Lessons, challenges and opportunities. Nat. Rev. Drug Discov. 13 (2), 140–156. https://doi.org/10.1038/nrd4204.

Fu, Y.C., Liang, S.B., Luo, M., Wang, X.P., 2025. Intratumoral heterogeneity and drug resistance in cancer. Cancer Cell Int. 25 (1). https://doi.org/10.1186/s12935-025-03734-w.

Gatenby, R.A., Silva, A.S., Gillies, R.J., Frieden, B.R., 2009. Adaptive therapy. Cancer Res. 69 (11), 4894–4903. https://doi.org/10.1158/0008-5472.CAN-08-3658.

Ghandadi, M., Valadan, R., Mohammadi, H., Akhtari, J., Khodashenas, S., Ashari, S., 2019. Wnt-β-catenin signaling pathway, the achilles' heels of cancer multidrug resistance. Curr. Pharm. Des. 25 (39), 4192–4207. https://doi.org/10.2174/1381612825666191112142943.

Glaviano, A., Foo, A.S.C., Lam, H.Y., Yap, K.C.H., Jacot, W., Jones, R.H., Eng, H., Nair, M.G., Makvandi, P., Geoerger, B., Kulke, M.H., Baird, R.D., Prabhu, J.S., Carbone, D., Pecoraro, C., Teh, D.B.L., Sethi, G., Cavalieri, V., Lin, K.H., Javidi-Sharifi, N.R., Toska, E., Davids, M.S., Brown, J.R., Diana, P., Stebbing, J., Fruman, D.A., Kumar, A.P., 2023. PI3K/AKT/mTOR signaling transduction pathway and targeted therapies in cancer. Mol. Cancer 22 (1). https://doi.org/10.1186/s12943-023-01827-6.

Harbst, K., Lauss, M., Cirenajwis, H., Isaksson, K., Rosengren, F., Törngren, T., Kvist, A., Johansson, M.C., Vallon-Christersson, J., Baldetorp, B., Borg, Å., Olsson, H., Ingvar, C., Carneiro, A., Jönsson, G., 2016. Multiregion whole-exome sequencing uncovers the genetic evolution and mutational heterogeneity of early-stage metastatic melanoma. Cancer Res 76 (16), 4765–4774. https://doi.org/10.1158/0008-5472.CAN-15-3476.

Hawsawi, Y.M., Khoja, B., Aljaylani, A.O., Jaha, R., AlDerbi, R.M., Alnuman, H., Khan, M.I., 2024. Recent progress and applications of single-cell sequencing technology in breast cancer. Front. Genet. 15. https://doi.org/10.3389/fgene.2024.1417415.

Hayes, D.F., Paoletti, C., 2013. Circulating tumour cells: Insights into tumour heterogeneity. J. Intern. Med. 274 (2), 137–143. https://doi.org/10.1111/joim.12047.

Hennessy, B.T., Smith, D.L., Ram, P.T., Lu, Y., Mills, G.B., 2005. Exploiting the PI3K/AKT pathway for cancer drug discovery. Nat. Rev. Drug. Discov. 4 (12), 988–1004. https://doi.org/10.1038/nrd1902.

Holohan, C., Van Schaeybroeck, S., Longley, D.B., Johnston, P.G., 2013. Cancer drug resistance: An evolving paradigm. Nat. Rev. Cancer 13 (10), 714–726. https://doi.org/10.1038/nrc3599.

Hu, X., li, J., Fu, M., Zhao, X., Wang, W., 2021. The JAK/STAT signaling pathway: From bench to clinic. Signal Transduct. Targeted Ther. 6 (1). https://doi.org/10.1038/s41392-021-00791-1.

Ignatiadis, M., Sledge, G.W., Jeffrey, S.S., 2021. Liquid biopsy enters the clinic — implementation issues and future challenges. Nat. Rev. Clin. Oncol. 18 (5), 297–312. https://doi.org/10.1038/s41571-020-00457-x.

Janku, F., Yap, T.A., Meric-Bernstam, F., 2018. Targeting the PI3K pathway in cancer: Are we making headway? Nat. Rev. Clin. Oncol. 15 (5), 273–291. https://doi.org/10.1038/nrclinonc.2018.28.

Jha, A., Kumar, M., Goswami, P., Bharti, K., Manjit, M., Gupta, A., Moorkoth, S., Koch, B., Mishra, B., 2024a. Cabazitaxel-loaded redox-responsive nanocarrier based on d -alpha-tocopheryl-chitosan and hyaluronic acid for improved anti-tumor efficacy in DMBA-induced breast cancer model. Mater. Adv. 5 (19), 7789–7808. https://doi.org/10.1039/d4ma00556b.

Jha, A., Kumar, M., Bharti, K., Manjit, M., Mishra, B., 2024b. Biopolymer-based tumor microenvironment-responsive nanomedicine for targeted cancer therapy. Nanomedicine 19 (7), 633–651. https://doi.org/10.2217/nnm-2023-0302.

Kandoth, C., McLellan, M.D., Vandin, F., Ye, K., Niu, B., Lu, C., Xie, M., Zhang, Q., McMichael, J.F., Wyczalkowski, M.A., Leiserson, M.D.M., Miller, C.A., Welch, J.S., Walter, M.J., Wendl, M.C., Ley, T.J., Wilson, R.K., Raphael, B.J., Ding, L., 2013. Mutational landscape and significance across 12 major cancer types. Nature 502 (7471), 333–339. https://doi.org/10.1038/nature12634.

Kerbel, R.S., Kobayashi, H., Graham, C.H., 1994. Intrinsic or acquired drug resistance and metastasis: are they linked phenotypes? J. Cell. Biochem. 56 (1), 37–47. https://doi.org/10.1002/jcb.240560108.

Kopetz, S., Grothey, A., Yaeger, R., Van Cutsem, E., Desai, J., Yoshino, T., Wasan, H., Ciardiello, F., Loupakis, F., Hong, Y.S., Steeghs, N., Guren, T.K., Arkenau, H.T., Garcia-Alfonso, P., Pfeiffer, P., Orlov, S., Lonardi, S., Elez, E., Kim, T.W., Schellens, J.H.M., Guo, C., Krishnan, A., Dekervel, J., Morris, V., Ferrandiz, A.C., Tarpgaard, L.S., Braun, M., Gollerkeri, A., Keir, C., Maharry, K., Pickard, M., Christy-Bittel, J., Anderson, L., Sandor, V., Tabernero, J., 2019. Encorafenib, binimetinib, and cetuximab in BRAF V600E–mutated colorectal cancer. N. Engl. J. Med. 381 (17), 1632–1643. https://doi.org/10.1056/NEJMoa1908075.

Lee, S., Kim, G., Lee, J.Y., Lee, A.C., Kwon, S., 2024. Mapping cancer biology in space: Applications and perspectives on spatial omics for oncology. Mol. Cancer 23 (1). https://doi.org/10.1186/s12943-024-01941-z.

Li, S.C., Tachiki, L.M.L., Kabeer, M.H., Dethlefs, B.A., Anthony, M.J., Loudon, W.G., 2014. Cancer genomic research at the crossroads: Realizing the changing genetic landscape as intratumoral spatial and temporal heterogeneity becomes a confounding factor. Cancer Cell Int. 14 (1). https://doi.org/10.1186/s12935-014-0115-7.

Lim, Z.F., Ma, P.C., 2019. Emerging insights of tumor heterogeneity and drug resistance mechanisms in lung cancer targeted therapy. J. Hematol. Oncol. 12 (1). https://doi.org/10.1186/s13045-019-0818-2.

Lin, C.C., Fang, Y., Yang, J.C., Lee, J.S., Tiseo, M., Pusztai, L., et al., 2020. A phase 1b/2 study of the MET inhibitor capmatinib in combination with the EGFR inhibitor gefitinib in patients with MET-dysregulated, EGFR-mutant non-small cell lung cancer. J. Thorac. Oncol. 15 (4), 555–565.

Ma, Y.T., Li, C., Shen, Y., You, W.H., Han, M.X., Mu, Y.F., Han, F.J., 2025. Mechanisms of the JNK/p38 MAPK signaling pathway in drug resistance in ovarian cancer. Front. Oncol. 15. https://doi.org/10.3389/fonc.2025.1533352.

Marusyk, A., Almendro, V., Polyak, K., 2012. Intra-tumour heterogeneity: A looking glass for cancer? Nat. Rev. Cancer 12 (5), 323–334. https://doi.org/10.1038/nrc3261.

Massard, C., Michiels, S., Ferte, C., Di Giammarino, D., Le Deley, M.C., Soria, J.C., et al., 2017. High-throughput genomics and drug resistance in cancer: A report of the EORTC-NCI-ASCO-AACR-EAPM-ESMO task force on drug resistance. Clin. Cancer Res 23 (10), 2397–2409.

McCubrey, J.A., Steelman, L.S., Chappell, W.H., 2012. Roles of the Raf/MEK/ERK pathway in cell growth, malignant transformation and drug resistance. Biochim. Biophys. Acta Rev. Cancer 1826 (2), 320–344.

McDonald, T.O., Cheng, Y.C., Graser, C., Nicol, P.B., Temko, D., Michor, F., 2023. Computational approaches to modelling and optimizing cancer treatment. Nat. Rev. Bioeng 1 (10), 695–711. https://doi.org/10.1038/s44222-023-00089-7.

Melo, F.D.S.E., Vermeulen, L., Fessler, E., Medema, J.P., 2013. Cancer heterogeneity - a multifaceted view. EMBO Rep 14 (8), 686–695. https://doi.org/10.1038/embor.2013.92.

Mokhtari, R.B., Homayouni, T.S., Baluch, N., Morgatskaya, E., Kumar, S., Das, B., Yeger, H., 2017. Combination therapy in combating cancer. Oncotarget 8 (23), 38022–38043. https://doi.org/10.18632/oncotarget.16723.

Morgillo, F., Della Corte, C.M., Fasano, M., Ciardiello, F., 2016. Mechanisms of resistance to EGFR-targeted drugs: Lung cancer. ESMO Open 1 (3), e000060. https://doi.org/10.1136/esmoopen-2016-000060.

Nabi, N., Shafat, P.M., Bashir, S., Khan, M.S., 2025. Involvement of Mitogen-Activated Protein (MAP) Kinase Pathway in the Etiopathogenesis of Cancer and its Role in Cancer Therapeutics Cell Signaling Pathways and Their Therapeutic Implication in Cancers, pp. 43–76. https://doi.org/10.1007/978-981-96-2763-9_2.

Owen, K.L., Brockwell, N.K., Parker, B.S., 2019. Jak-stat signaling: A double-edged sword of immune regulation and cancer progression. Cancers 11 (12). https://doi.org/10.3390/cancers11122002.

Palmer, A.C., Kishony, R., 2014. Opposing effects of target overexpression reveal drug mechanisms. Nat. Commun. 5. https://doi.org/10.1038/ncomms5296.

Ramón y Cajal, S., Sesé, M., Capdevila, C., Aasen, T., De Mattos-Arruda, L., Diaz-Cano, S.J., Hernández-Losa, J., Castellví, J., 2020. Clinical implications of intratumor heterogeneity: Challenges and opportunities. J. Mol. Med. 98 (2), 161–177. https://doi.org/10.1007/s00109-020-01874-2.

Sahu, B., Bhardwaj, N., Chatterjee, E., Dey, B., Tripathi, N., Goel, B., Kushwaha, M., Kumar, B., Singh, B., Kumar Guru, S., Jain, S.K., 2022. LCMS-DNP based dereplication of araucaria cunninghamii mudie gum-resin: Identification of new cytotoxic labdane diterpene. Nat. Prod. Res. 36 (24), 6207–6214. https://doi.org/10.1080/14786419.2021.2024530.

Schmucker, R., Farina, G., Faeder, J., Fröhlich, F., Ali, S.S., Sandholm, T., Scott, J.G., 2021. Combination treatment optimization using a pan-cancer pathway model. PLoS Comput. Biol. 17 (12). https://doi.org/10.1371/journal.pcbi.1009689.

Schöning, J.P., Monteiro, M., Gu, W., 2017. Drug resistance and cancer stem cells: The shared but distinct roles of hypoxia-inducible factors HIF1α and HIF2α. Clin. Exp. Pharmacol. Physiol. 44 (2), 153–161. https://doi.org/10.1111/1440-1681.12693.

Shao, F., Duan, Y., Zhao, Y., Li, Y., Liu, J., Zhang, C., He, S., 2021. PARP inhibitors in breast and ovarian cancer with BRCA mutations: A meta-analysis of survival. Aging 13 (6), 8975–8988. https://doi.org/10.18632/aging.202724.

Sharma, P., Hu-Lieskovan, S., Wargo, J.A., Ribas, A., 2017. Primary, adaptive, and acquired resistance to cancer immunotherapy. Cell 168 (4), 707–723. https://doi.org/10.1016/j.cell.2017.01.017.

Soda, N., Clack, K., Shiddiky, M.J.A., 2022. Recent advances in liquid biopsy technologies for cancer biomarker detection. Sens. Diagn. 1 (3), 343–375. https://doi.org/10.1039/d2sd00010e.

Stanta, G., Bonin, S., 2018. Overview on clinical relevance of intra-tumor heterogeneity. Front. Med. 5. https://doi.org/10.3389/fmed.2018.00085/full.

Swanton, C., 2012. Intratumor heterogeneity: Evolution through space and time. Cancer Res. 72 (19), 4875–4882. https://doi.org/10.1158/0008-5472.can-12-2217.

Tabassum, S., Abbasi, R., Ahmad, N., Farooqi, A.A., 2019. Targeting of JAK-STAT signaling in breast cancer: Therapeutic strategies to overcome drug resistance. Adv. Exp. Med. Biol. 1152, 271–281. https://doi.org/10.1007/978-3-030-20301-6_14.

Taniguchi, K., Karin, M., 2018. NF-B, inflammation, immunity and cancer: Coming of age. Nat. Rev. Immunol. 18 (5), 309–324. https://doi.org/10.1038/nri.2017.142.

Van de Sande, B., Lee, J.S., Mutasa-Gottgens, E., Naughton, B., Bacon, W., Manning, J., Wang, Y., Pollard, J., Mendez, M., Hill, J., Kumar, N., Cao, X., Chen, X., Khaladkar, M., Wen, J., Leach, A., Ferran, E., 2023. Applications of single-cell RNA sequencing in drug discovery and development. Nat. Rev. Drug Discov. 22 (6), 496–520. https://doi.org/10.1038/s41573-023-00688-4.

Vasan, N., Baselga, J., Hyman, D.M., 2019. A view on drug resistance in cancer. Nature 575 (7782), 299–309. https://doi.org/10.1038/s41586-019-1730-1.

Vieira, V.M., Webster, T.F., Weinberg, J.M., Aschengrau, A., 2008. Spatial-temporal analysis of breast cancer in upper Cape Cod, Massachusetts. Int. J. Health Geogr. 7. https://doi.org/10.1186/1476-072X-7-46.

Wang, X., Zhang, H., Chen, X., 2019. Drug resistance and combating drug resistance in cancer. Cancer Drug Resist. 2 (2), 141–160. https://doi.org/10.20517/cdr.2019.10.

Warfel, N.A., El-Deiry, W.S., 2014. HIF-1 signaling in drug resistance to chemotherapy. Curr. Med. Chem. 21 (26), 3021–3028. https://doi.org/10.2174/0929867321666140414101056.

Xue, C., Yao, Q., Gu, X., Shi, Q., Yuan, X., Chu, Q., Bao, Z., Lu, J., Li, L., 2023. Evolving cognition of the JAK-STAT signaling pathway: Autoimmune disorders and cancer. Signal Transduct. Targeted Ther. 8 (1). https://doi.org/10.1038/s41392-023-01468-7.

Yaeger, R., Corcoran, R.B., 2019. Targeting alterations in the RAF–MEK pathway. Cancer Discov. 9 (3), 329–341. https://doi.org/10.1158/2159-8290.CD-18-1321.

Zhang, X., Yu, X., 2023. Crosstalk between Wnt/β-catenin signaling pathway and DNA damage response in cancer: A new direction for overcoming therapy resistance. Front. Pharmacol. 14. https://doi.org/10.3389/fphar.2023.1230822.

CHAPTER II

Strategies and technologies for cancer therapy

The segment Strategies and Technologies for Cancer Therapy explores several new drug-delivery approaches and materials that are continually evolving within the paradigm of cancer treatment. Initially the topic focuses on materials and techniques for drug delivery, then moves on to drug conjugates, microparticles, and self-assembled supramolecular structures that enable anticancer drugs to be delivered to the target site. Advanced drug delivery systems incorporating metal-organic frameworks, dendrimers, metallic nanoparticles, polymeric nanoparticles, lipid-based nanoparticles, and self-nanoemulsifying drug delivery systems (SNEDDS) are described. These nanoscale carriers provide advantages in drug solubility, permeability, tumor targeting, cellular uptake, and efficacy of cancer therapy. The scope of the discussion was also enlarged to include the influence of the tumor microenvironment on drug delivery and the strategies used to utilize such specific features for targeted and tumor microenvironment-responsive drug delivery. Besides that, various types of drug delivery formulations such as hydrogels, nanocrystals, theranostic nanoparticles, genetic nanomaterials, and organic nanocarriers are highlighted for anticancer drug delivery and diagnostic purposes. One of the great opportunities offered by the emerging technologies coming to the fore, such as nanofibrous scaffolds, microneedles, and implantable systems, relates to the targeted and continuous release of the drug locally. Besides, the chapter highlights the anticancer therapies based on phytoconstituent-based systems that can be combined with the use of conventional drugs. In the end, enzyme-prodrugs were discussed as a means for accurately delivering the cancer drugs. All these aspects highlight the great progress in the design of new drug delivery systems and point to the future of safer, more effective, and personalized cancer treatments.

CHAPTER

9

Materials and strategies for advanced anticancer drug delivery

Madhu Sharma[1,2], *Dilip Panwar*[1], *Astha Mishra*[1], *Yashika Dalal*[1] *and Prabhat Ranjan Mishra*[1,2]

[1]**Division of Pharmaceutics and Pharmacokinetics, CSIR-Central Drug Research Institute, Lucknow, Uttar Pradesh, India;** [2]**Academy of Scientific and Innovation Research (AcSIR), Ghaziabad, Uttar Pradesh, India**

Introduction

Conventional chemotherapy suffers from intrinsic limitations – many drugs have poor water solubility and bioavailability, non-selective biodistribution, rapid systemic clearance, and dose-limiting toxicities in healthy tissues (Tam et al., 2011). These drawbacks drive the design of advanced delivery platforms that improve the therapeutic index of chemotherapeutics. Encapsulating drugs in carriers can protect labile agents from degradation, enhance aqueous solubility and circulation half-life, and concentrate payloads in tumors (Haque et al., 2023). Nanoscale systems exploit the enhanced permeability and retention (EPR) effect and active targeting to achieve high intratumoral accumulation, reducing off-target exposure (Glasgow and Chougule, 2015). Modern nanomedicines shift cancer therapy toward more precise, patient-centric interventions with controlled spatiotemporal release profiles. A wide array of carrier materials has been explored to optimize pharmacokinetics and tumor targeting. Organic nanocarriers include liposomes and lipid-based vesicles, synthetic and natural polymers (e.g., PLGA, PEGylated polymers), dendritic polymers, and protein or peptide scaffolds. Inorganic carriers (e.g., gold/silica nanoparticles, carbon nanotubes, magnetic or mesoporous oxides) offer high drug loading and tunable release properties. Biomolecule-based and biomimetic platforms are also under active study: for instance, extracellular vesicles or engineered exosome-mimetic vesicles can deliver drugs and nucleic acids to tumors with high efficiency. These naturally derived vesicles inherently improve payload stability and may evade immune clearance, yielding better bioavailability and tumor selectivity. Briefly, biodegradable polymers, lipidic carriers, dendrimers, inorganic nanosystems,

Advanced Cancer Therapeutics
https://doi.org/10.1016/B978-0-443-44185-1.00012-4

and cell-derived vesicles (like exosomes) are being used to modulate circulation time, tissue distribution, and release kinetics. Beyond passive targeting, carriers are frequently endowed with active targeting ligands or biomimetic coatings to home to cancer cells. Nanoparticle surfaces can be decorated with antibodies, peptides, aptamers, or small molecules that bind overexpressed tumor antigens or receptors. For instance, folate or transferrin ligands on nanocarriers facilitate receptor-mediated uptake by cancer cells. Similarly, mannose, RGD peptides, or antibody fragments have been used to recognize specific cancer markers. Active targeting increases cancer-cell uptake and accumulation while sparing healthy cells. A complementary trend is biomimetic cloaking of particles. Nanoparticles can be coated with cell-membrane fragments from red blood cells, platelets, leukocytes, cancer cells, or stem cells to evade immune clearance and exploit natural homing pathways. For example, red-blood-cell-membrane coatings prolong circulation by hiding from phagocytes, and cancer-cell membranes can confer "self" markers for homotypic targeting. These cell-membrane cloaks retain the surface proteins of the source cell (e.g., CD47, integrins), enabling immune evasion and targeted delivery simultaneously. Thus, ligand functionalization and biomimetic coating represent two parallel strategies to enhance tumor specificity and overcome physiological barriers.

Nanocarriers offer rich multifunctionality. Beyond single-drug loading, many platforms co-deliver multiple therapies for a synergistic effect. For example, carriers can encapsulate both a chemotherapeutic and an immunotherapeutic agent (e.g., a checkpoint inhibitor or cytokine) to stimulate an immune response while killing tumor cells. Alternatively, combinations of chemotherapeutics or chemo-photosensitizers in one nanoparticle can attack cancer via complementary mechanisms. Nanocarriers can also transport nucleic acid therapeutics (mRNA, siRNA, plasmids, aptamers) for gene therapy or immunotherapy. In fact, "smart" nanovectors have been engineered for cancer vaccines and gene delivery: they protect fragile oligonucleotides from degradation, enhance targeted uptake, and allow controlled intracellular release. This enables delivery of tumor-specific antigens or RNAi agents directly to immune cells or cancer cells, reinforcing anti-tumor immunity and reprogramming malignant cells. Moreover, nanocarrier physicochemical properties can be precisely tuned. Particle size, shape, and surface charge dictate circulation half-life, tumor penetration, and cell uptake. For example, ~50–150 nm nanoparticles optimally extravasate into tumors via the EPR effect, and spherical or rod-shaped particles display different biodistribution. Surface modifications (PEGylation, zwitterions) reduce non-specific protein adsorption, further prolonging blood residence. By controlling porosity or the polymer matrix, designers regulate drug loading capacity and release rate. In sum, nanocarriers can be fabricated to balance stability in blood versus rapid release in the tumor – a versatility unattainable by free drugs alone. Despite these advances, translating nanosystems into the clinic faces hurdles. Tumor heterogeneity, complex microenvironments, and interpatient variability mean that no single drug delivery system (DDS) fits all cancers. Uncertain long-term biocompatibility and off-target effects of some materials (especially inorganic nanostructures) require careful evaluation (Di Stefano, 2023). Rapid clearance by the mononuclear phagocyte system and limited deep-tumor penetration can still reduce efficacy. Nonetheless, the field is moving toward precision nanomedicine: DDS platforms are increasingly tailored to individual patient tumors and combined with imaging agents for theranostics. Engineered carriers now aim to deliver precise doses to specific cellular targets with minimal collateral damage, aligning with personalized oncology paradigms. In summary, next-generation DDS platforms (from smart polymers and liposomes to biomimetic and multifunctional nanocarriers) are ushering in a paradigm shift. By integrating stimuli-responsive release, active targeting, and combination therapies, a safer and more effective cancer treatment with fewer side effects can be designed. Ongoing research continues to refine these strategies to overcome remaining challenges and fully realize targeted, patient-centric cancer therapy. Building on the above considerations, this chapter will discuss recent advancements in materials and strategies designed to enhance anticancer drug delivery in oncotherapy.

Advanced materials for smart drug delivery

Deviations observed in the tumor microenvironment in comparison to normal tissues are so pronounced, particularly with respect to intracellular parameters of pH, ROS levels, GSH concentrations, hypoxic environments and changes in enzyme expression profiles. These unique physiological properties are crucial sources of targets in designing microenvironment responsive drug delivery systems. With wise exploitation of these differences, formulators can come up with strategies for accurate, localized, and stimuli-driven delivery of therapeutics that will eventually result in improved therapeutic efficacy. Sensitive materials that react to certain stimuli have broadened the scope of drug delivery. They are designed to respond to a variety of internal signals such as changes in pH, reactive oxygen species (ROS), glutathione (GSH) levels, hypoxic microenvironments, and enzyme activity, as well as external signals like changes in temperature, exposure to light, ultrasound, ionizing radiation, and magnetic fields (Webber et al., 2015; Mi, 2020). Through such cues, the stimuli-responsive nanocarrier can release therapeutics in a highly targeted and precise way to improve therapeutic outcomes. The main benefits of these systems are long circulatory persistence, accumulation in targeted tissue (like tumors), and their ability to release the moiety on activation. This unique ability reduces all undesirable off-target side effects and enhances efficacy. Additionally, such materials also demonstrate a promising approach to address not only a therapeutic intervention, but also diagnostic ones, thus supporting the development of even more individualistic treatment paradigms. This section outlines recent studies in the preparation and development of stimuli-responsive materials, especially in a mechanistic way, and their increasing importance in the more complex drug delivery models.

Smart materials for pH responsive drug delivery

The microenvironment of tumor tissues is quite different from normal tissues, not only in terms of structural basis but also in cellular proliferative kinetics and metabolic pathways. The difference in pH between microdomains is an important parameter. Under normal physiological conditions, systemic circulation and normal parenchyma have a near-neutral pH 7.4. Conversely, the extracellular environment of cancerous tumors has a low acidic pH of between 6.5 and 7.2. It is also accompanied by an acidic phenotype, further characterized by endosomal compartments that have a pH range of 5.0–6.5 and lysosomes of even lower pH, between 4.5 and 5.0. The principal cause of pH differences is the elevated glycolytic flux of neoplastic cells, despite sufficient oxygen level, also known as a metabolic reprogramming phenomenon, commonly known as the Warburg effect (Allen and Locasale, 2018). As a result, the glycolytic processes produce large amounts of lactic acid, which is actively produced by tumor cells using proton-coupled transporters. This active extrusion creates a special chemical gradient according to which the pericellular space becomes more acidic, and the intracellular pH is preserved at relatively neutral or slightly alkaline levels. Such pH differences make an attractive strategy for targeted delivery. Selective targeting of the tumor is possible by nanomaterials or polymeric structures that can be subjected to physicochemical changes in response to acidic stimulus. This method increases the localized delivery, high accuracy, and target selectivity of the system. In this connection, pH-responsive systems have been broadly researched in several therapeutic contexts, for example, conventional chemotherapy, nucleic-acid based gene therapy, photothermal treatments, and multimodal combinatoric therapy (Wang et al., 2020; Saw et al., 2019). Several pH-sensitive drug formulation platforms have been outlined in recent academic literature, which can broadly be classified into three main categories as outlined below.

Acidic environment responsive linkages

Formulators designed drug carriers with acid-sensitive linkages to exploit the acidic conditions of the tumor microenvironment for precise drug delivery. Common linkages used include amide, carbonate, imine, oxime, acetal/ketal, hydrazone (HDZ), and certain ortho ester linkages (Liu et al., 2017a; Zheng et al., 2020; Li et al., 2020c). These bonds stay stable under normal physiological conditions (around pH 7.4) and thus nanocarriers circulate for a longer period without releasing the loaded drug. However, once the system reaches an acidic tumor environment or even more acidic compartments like endosomes and lysosomes, these bonds start to break, leading to drug release or structural changes in the carrier. Acid-sensitive chemistry can also be used in polymer-based systems where different polymer blocks are connected through pH-cleavable bonds, allowing the structure to change or break apart under acidic conditions. This can improve biocompatibility and reduce protein interactions in the bloodstream (Ma et al., 2019). Among these, hydrazone bonds are widely used as they are relatively stable in the bloodstream but break quickly in acidic conditions. For example, researchers have attached doxorubicin (DOX) to a dextran-based carrier using hydrazone linkages, allowing the drug to remain intact during systemic circulation and release preferentially inside the tumor cells. Similarly, pH-sensitive lipid-coated nanoparticles have been developed, where acid-labile amide bonds break in the tumor environment, improving cellular uptake and triggering a rapid release of drugs like irinotecan in the intracellular compartment. This strategy not only improves anticancer activity but also reduces side effects. In some advanced systems, the drug itself plays an active role in controlling release. For instance, doxorubicin has been used as a "gatekeeper" in mesoporous silica nanoparticles by forming pH-sensitive bonds at the pore openings. Under acidic conditions, these bonds break, opening the pores and releasing both the drug and other therapeutic agents like siRNA. Targeting groups such as folic acid can also be added to improve delivery to cancer cells, creating multifunctional systems with combined therapeutic effects (Zheng et al., 2020; Fang et al., 2020a). More recently, natural materials have also been explored as carriers. For example, polysaccharides derived from Ganoderma lucidum have been modified with acid-sensitive bonds to deliver drugs like rutin, along with other anticancer agents (Zheng et al., 2020). In acidic tumor conditions, these bonds break, releasing the drugs in a controlled manner. As these carriers are derived from natural sources, they are biocompatible and show minimal side effects.

Proton exchange and ionization behavior

Dynamics of protonation and deprotonation are another popular mechanism of drug delivery systems in modern science. The carrier matrices are usually functionalized by groups, for example, amino, carboxyl, sulfonamide, or nitrogen-containing heterocycles (Fang et al., 2020b). These moieties are capable of accepting and donating protons in the acidic microenvironment of tumor tissue, which results in changing the net surface charge of the vehicle. This not only modifies the physicochemical properties such as hydrophilicity, swelling behavior, and solubility, but also induces the carrier disintegration (Saffioti et al., 2020; Qu et al., 2020; Han et al., 2020; Tian et al., 2020). There is an increase in affinity of the therapeutic cargoes and therapy route, which allows the active drug to pass into the tumorous cell under preciously manner. To avoid premature systemic release, most of these delivery vehicles have been designed to strategically assume a neutral or slightly anionic charge under physiological conditions. This type of electrostatic conformation facilitates long-term circulation in the blood due to decreased opsonization and consequent phagocytic incorporation. Nevertheless, when the acidic tumor microenvironment is met, the subsequent reversal of charges improves the internalization in the cell and the release of the drug, consequently increasing the effectiveness of therapy (Yuan et al., 2019). A recent study, used to exemplify this as a microneedle array, microneedle array used to deliver genetic material to subdermal tumors (Yuan et al., 2019). A microneedle array contained plasmid p53 DNA conjugated with poly (L -lysine -dimethylacrylamide) polymer that experiences charge inversion in acidic conditions. Afterwards, exposed to the tumor microenvironment, the pH changeable charge shift resulted in structural collapse of the assembly, accelerating the release of the DNA (Liu et al., 2017b). Furthermore, the microneedles enabled transdermal penetration, which would result in strong tumor growth inhibition. Many other polymers follow a similar behavior and have been widely utilized in the development of pH-responsive platforms, such as poly (2-diisopropylaminoethyl methacrylate) (PDPAEMA), poly (4-vinylpyridine) (P4VP), poly (2-aminoethyl methacrylate) (PAEMA) and poly (-myristoyl)-ethylenediamine (PBM) (Deirram et al., 2019). Simultaneously, natural polymers are under investigation. Chitosan, a polysaccharide, is especially promising since it has good biocompatibility. Modified chitosan can self-assemble into micellar structures that are able to entrap chemotherapeutics like paclitaxel, while preserving pH sensitivity. At a low PH, the hydrophobicity of these micelles increases, and hence, increases drug release profiling. The distribution of amino and carboxyl functionalities intrinsic to proteins and peptides is also tailored to pH, combined with design strategies. It is through a rational adaptation of these groups that researchers may design biomolecular carriers that change conformation or surface properties with changes in pH and can be used as an appropriate carrier of delicate biological agents in oncologic regimens (Jia et al., 2019).

Polydopamine (PDA): A multifunctional smart material for drug delivery

Along with the pH-sensitive systems considered above, another substance that has gained attention is polydopamine (PDA). Based on the adhesive proteins of mussels, PDA can be characterized by outstanding biocompatibility, strong adhesion levels on surfaces, and efficient photothermal conversion abilities. Another interesting feature of this polymer is the ease with which it can be deposited as a thin conformal layer upon a wide range of surfaces by a simple self-polymerization mechanism. The synthesis of PDA is usually performed in slightly alkaline conditions, and in this case, dopamine is oxidized and reacted further to form a stable polymeric coating (Cheng et al., 2019; Ponzio et al., 2016). The ability of PDA to sense an acidic microenvironment is what makes it especially useful in oncological applications (Cheng et al., 2017a). The exact mechanism of degradation of PDA is not well understood, but it shows significant degradation when the environment is acidic. Therefore, it acts as a convenient compound to use in pH-based drug delivery approaches. PDA-coating of nanoparticles has been demonstrated to increase colloidal stability, reduce premature drug release and increase therapeutic efficacy. An example is the development of PDA, which functionalized black phosphorus nanosystems as multifunctional drug delivery systems with a combinatorial delivery. The amino and hydroxyl groups are abundant in the PDA surface and further chemical conjugation is possible. By using straightforward chemistry, ligand or other therapeutic targeting can be conjugated to enhance specificity and efficacy (Nie et al., 2017). In a research study, scientists produced nanoparticles already loaded with the chemotherapeutic agent docetaxel and then coated with PDA (Zeng et al., 2018). They also conjugated polyethylene glycol folic acid to tumor targets and added a second anticancer effector bortezomib to increase the overall therapeutic efficacy. This dual-delivery mechanism partly due to the acid-responsive of the PDA shell, was found to perform better in chemotherapy (An et al., 2020). The other good example was hollow manganese dioxide nanoparticles, which were loaded with a photosensitizer, followed by the coating with PDA and functionalization with folic acid. This was an integrated system that synergistically combined photodynamic therapy (PDT) and photothermal therapy (PTT) leading to high inhibition levels of tumor growth45. Altogether, PDA is characterized by its versatility, easy modifiability, and the sensitivity to the tumor microenvironment. All these features have set it as one of the most promising platforms on which to develop multifunctional drug delivery systems that are of great potential (Zeng et al., 2020).

Smart materials activated by redox

Examples of reactive oxygen species (ROS) are hydrogen peroxide (H_2O_2), superoxide anions, and hydroxyl radicals (Finkel, 2011). In the physiological system, these species are produced internally and then eliminated in a highly regulated process, playing a key role in the homeostatic regulation of many cellular activities (Tao and He, 2018). Mitochondrial dysfunction, oncogene activation, and increased metabolic demand, however, reach extremely high levels in malignant cellular formations (Pelicano et al., 2004). Although high levels of ROS may lead to genotoxic dysfunction and develop resistance to therapy, the associated redox deficiency is also an opportunity to leverage the rational design of directed interventions (Wu et al., 2020). By taking advantage of such effects, researchers have developed ROS-reactive smart materials that can deliver therapeutics to oxidative microenvironments that are the hallmark of tumors. Most of these systems have been modified to notice either hydrogen peroxide or hydroxyl radicals (Cheng et al., 2017b). Chemically functional groups such as thioethers, thioketals, arylboronic esters, diselenides, and aminoacylates are added strategically to give these platforms selective reactivity (Li et al., 2019a, 2019b). They are typically self-assembled into nanostructured vehicles (micelles) in which the drug cargo is loaded and liberated by redox activation (Yin et al., 2020). A reversible hydrophobic-to-hydrophilic conversion of polymers containing thioether functional groups is an example that can be observed in the presence of ROS, leading to a change in colloidal dispersibility and controlled drug delivery. Quite closely relying on the same strategy, hydrophobic groups entrapped in nanoporous structures are oxidized by ROS, enhancing the degree of hydrophilicity and allowing a progressive, prolonged release of the therapeutic moiety (Yu et al., 2019;Li et al., 2019d). Thioketal linkages can also be exploited for ROS-responsive drug delivery. These cleavable bonds break down selectively in oxidative environments to subsequently release the loaded drugs from the carriers (Wang et al., 2018a; Wang et al., 2019a). Equally, arylboronic ester groups can be oxidized by hydrogen peroxide, which leads to structural rearrangement, allowing the release of the payload. Nanocarriers derived have been effective in mouse models as self-degrading nanoassembly of prodrugs (Li et al., 2019d; Jin et al., 2019). Other directions are the introduction of selenium-containing polymers and the addition of reporter capabilities or functionality, such as a fluorescence reporter, which gives real-time information on redox-induced changes in the cellular environment (Li et al., 2020b; He et al., 2019). Hybrid/natural designs of the systems are also aimed at achieving biocompatibility, reducing off-target effects, and strengthening therapeutic efficacy. Most other treatment strategies combined ROS-responsive platforms with photodynamic therapy (PDT). In PDT, the photosensitizer photoactivation triggers the overproduction of additional ROS in the tumor locus, both enhancing drug delivery and boosting therapeutic efficacy (Sun et al., 2018). ROS sensitivity combined with multimodal treatment modalities provides such smart materials with a powerful ability to provide precise and tumor-selective treatment.

Smart materials responsive to GSH

The difference in intracellular and extracellular GSH levels lies at the basis of using glutathione (GSH)-responsive materials in drug delivery, especially as an oncologic drug. GSH may get up to millimolar in malignant cells and the extracellular environment. This biochemical gradient provides a chance to design a delivery system that is inert at systemic circulation but is activated by translocation into the tumoral space (Wu et al., 2004). The vast majority of GSH-responsive platforms take advantage of reducible linkages between molecules, which are responsible for releasing the drug into the tumor milieu. The use of disulfide bonds, due to their ability to be reduced by GSH easily to form two thiol termini, which, at the same time, releases encapsulated therapeutics (Guo et al., 2020). This could be added to an excess of material geometries, such as linear polymers, cross-linked hydrogels, dendritic systems, and nanoparticle assemblies (Mi et al., 2017; Qiu et al., 2018). Under most conditions, self-assembly of these constructs produces nanostructures with a high loading of therapeutic agents and releases them at high concentrations in intracellular GSH (Liu et al., 2018; Ling et al., 2018). The polymeric nanoparticles connected through a disulfide group have been used to deliver small drugs as well as genetic drugs with an efficient release mechanism within the tumor cells, thus improving the overall therapeutic effect (Yin et al., 2018a; Li et al., 2020a). Multibranched chain polymer drug delivery system assists in amplifying drug loading and targeting selectively in an advanced drug delivery system (Shang et al., 2019; Tang et al., 2019). Other GSH-sensitive moieties that are showing interest beyond the disulfide chemistries, including diselenide linkages, which, though structurally similar, may have different kinetic behaviors and superior response. Nanostructures made of metal and platinum (IV) prodrugs also make use of the reductive tumor microenvironment. As an illustration, reduction of Pt(IV) to the therapeutically active form, Pt(II) is preferentially induced in cancerous cells, thus enhancing antitumor effect and reducing systemic toxicity (Lin et al., 2019; Huang et al., 2019a). Several sophisticated systems have been designed for both diagnostic and therapeutic capabilities. One such case is of manganese-based nanoparticles that deplete when exposed to GSH-releasing chemotherapeutic agents as well as imaging contrast agents (Ling et al., 2019). This is a special feature that enables the delivery dynamics of drugs in real time. Moreover, hybrid nanoplexes that are acidic pH responsive and GSH responsive have been developed, providing a narrow concentration response of drug release and amplified diagnostic responses (Wang et al., 2018b). Altogether, the GSH-responsive materials are an innovative and effective approach to delivering drugs specifically to tumor cells, as it takes advantage of the redox environment peculiarities of malignant tissues to achieve a specific treatment effect.

Smart materials responsive to hypoxia

Essential provision of nutrients and oxygen is required by the exponential increase in the number of tumoral cells. Accordingly, abnormal microvessel tumors with structural malformations will develop in the impaired microcirculation, thus limiting oxygen diffusion gradient in solid tumors (Helmlinger et al., 1997). Damaged vascular networks reduce the distance of oxygen diffusion to about 200 μm in developing tumors. Hypoxia measured in solid tumors is statistically found in 50%–60%, especially in tumors that consist of central tumor cells. The hypoxic tumor areas gain a decreased partial pressure of oxygen ($pO2 \leq 2.5$ mm Hg), which decreases from the tumor surface to its core, and healthy cells are associated with a pO2 of 30–40 mm Hg (Kallinowski and Hoeckel, 1990). Hypoxia not only contributes to the survival of tumor cells (by increasing angiogenesis, invasiveness, and metastasis) but also is the main cause of failure of chemotherapy and radiotherapy, photodynamic therapy, and ultrasound-therapy, ultimately resulting in a poor clinical outcome (Kumari et al., 2020). However, this characteristic physiological cellular activity of tumor tissues has also been stimulated to create hypoxia-responsive materials for targeting poorly oxygenated tumors (Wang et al., 2017). The azobenzene derivatives, a well-developed family of hypoxia-responsive linkers, are widely used with bio-reductive materials to deliver reagents to tumors. The first mode of designing azoreductase-responsive functional metal-organic framework (MOF) to deliver cancer drugs was to coordinate the Fe $3+$ ions with 4, 4-dicarboxylic acid azobenzene linkers (Huang et al., 2019b). Azoreductase is a prototype hypoxia biomarker, which triggers specific degradation and cleavage of azobenzene products. A similar study using carboxymethyl dextran azo bond forms found that azoreductase on hypoxic tumors reduced them to aniline forms, simultaneously releasing doxorubicin (DOX). As hypoxia-responsive moieties in nanocarrier-mediated drug delivery, azo-bond-modified polymers Azo-PEG, PEG-Azo-PLGA, PLGA -g-mPEG/Azo, and Ce_6-PEG-Azo-PCL were derived (Li et al., 2019a, 2019b; Wang et al., 2018c).

Recently, scientists developed new azobenzene-functionalized conjugated polymer (CP)-based nanocarriers bound with chlorin 6 (Ce_6) and camptothein (CPT) to develop a light-enhanced hypoxia-responsive system that combines photodynamic therapy (PDT) and chemotherapy (Zhang et al., 2018). CPs were prepared through a condensation reaction between 4, 4 -azidianiline and terephthalaldehyde. CPs so produced were reprecipitated with both CPT and Ce_6 in a poly (vinylpyrrolidone) solution. When lasers flash, the Ce_6 produces reactive oxygen species, which burn local oxygen, thus making hypoxia worse. This increase in hypoxic conditions leads to a high-intensity cleavage of azo-bonds and liberates CPT. A hypoxia-responsive sulfur dioxide (SO_2) nanocarrier that combines CpG oligodeoxynucleotide and Ce6-loaded SO_2 nanoparticles was developed as a hypoxia-induced immunomodulator to catalyze cancer immunotherapy. These particles were functionalized on their surface by using PEG or chitosan groups of azo bond (Im et al., 2019). The design is intended to synchronize the effect of PDT that causes a decrease of oxygen with the following immune reaction. Another way used to monitor hypoxia-responsive chemotherapy in vivo was by synthesizing an azo near-infrared (NIR) theranostic probe. This probe was made by bonding N,N-bis (2 -chloroethyl) 1, 4 - benzenediamine with an azo bond to an NIR fluorophore (AXPI). It is observed that both processes, the release of the drug and the NIR fluorescence signal, are released concurrently under hypoxic conditions. Other classes of highly hypoxia-responsive materials are nitro scaffold derivatives, such as nitroimidazole, nitroimidazole, 2-nitroimidazole and nitrobenzene (Yin et al., 2018b; Shen et al., 2019). These hydrophobic nitro groups are added onto produce amphiphilic block copolymer hypoxia-sensitizers through degradable polymers, PEG-block-poly(L-glutamic acid), polyethyleneimine, and hyaluronic acid (Tseng et al., 2018).

Exposure to hypoxic environments leads to the reduction of the nitro groups to hydrophilic amine species, resulting in a bulky change in the copolymer solubility, which disrupts nanocarriers, causing drug release to chemotherapy. Moreover, it has utilized macromolecules in hypoxia responsive nanocarriers. As an example, nitro macromolecules made via the conjugation of 2- nitroimidazole to both ends of 1,12-dibromododecane were incorporated inside a phospholipid bilayer with DSPE-PEG 2000 to entrap DOX (Li et al., 2019c). This loss of nitro groups in hypoxia changes the solubility of the macromolecules, which destabilize the phospholipid bi-layer resulting in a burst release of the loaded drug. Additional ones are hypoxic radiosensitizer poly prodrug nanoparticles with angiopep-2 lipid and poly(1,2-metronidazole) assembled as a hypoxia-responsive carrier, which promotes the effective administration of radiotherapy against glioma (Hua et al., 2018). A study by Shen et al. has modified the Toll-like receptor 7 (TLR) agonist, imiquimod, with 4 -nitrobenzyl chloroformate (NBCF) to form a low-molecular-weight prodrug that can modulate the immunologic response caused by combretastatin A4; in this case, nitro reduction is used to suppress anticancer immunity (Shen et al., 2019). To enhance tumor penetration using hypoxic gradients, Zhen et al. designed nanocarriers that have a poly(caprolactone) core and a hybrid shell of NBCF-modified polylysine and PEG. PEG shielding can provide a longer blood circulation time that supplements the effects of hypoxia-driven degradation of NBCF, which returns positively charged amine groups at the nanocarrier surface. The increase of surface charges helps in penetrating into tumor tissue, and as the hypoxia increases in the tumor interiors, more amine groups are lost to the surface, and this further facilitates penetration. Tirapazazine (TPZ) demonstrates the example of a hypoxia-sensitive, activated anticancer agent that is commonly used in modern hypoxia-sensitive systems. In hypoxic conditions, TPZ experiences intracellular reductase metabolism to generate highly reactive radical species, which cause breaks in DNA strands and aberrations in chromosomes, leading to cell death. Conversely, under aerobic conditions, radicals form is effectively scavenged by molecular oxygen, hence releasing the moiety and reducing cytotoxicity (Wang et al., 2017; Wang et al., 2019b). TPZ significantly improves radiation induced tumor regression in hypoxia, dose, and schedule dependence. TPZ is therefore a common treatment of cancer as it is regularly administered as a combination with radiotherapy to create a hypoxia-activated radio-chemotherapeutic regimen.

Smart material triggered by enzymes

Enzymes play critical roles in mediating various biological activities, and the dysregulation of tumor-related enzyme activities has emerged as a paradigm of rational design of responsive DDS in cancer therapy. Intelligent drug release in these nanoplatforms is mainly realized by enzyme-triggered cleavage of the carrier backbone, enzyme-triggered prodrug activation, or enzyme-triggered restructuring of carrier morphology. Amide bonds are regularly used to form hydrolytic proteins because of their calculated stability as part of physiological factors. MMP-2, MMP-7, and MMP-9 are also three of the most overexpressed and active MMPs found in the tumor extracellular space, neoplastic cells, and in the tumor vasculature, thus playing central roles in tumor progression and metastasis (Yang et al., 2019a). The most common stimulus, which is utilized in developing site-specific, enzyme-responsive carriers, is the amplified activity of MMP in the TME. An example of enzyme-sensitive cytotoxic peptide-dendrimer conjugates, polysaccharide matrices cross-linked by an MMP-cleavable peptide linker (Iaccarino et al., 2019), and gold nanoparticles functionalized with an MMP-2 cleavable linker (Yang et al., 2019b) have all been utilized as therapeutically useful constructs based on MMP -2 responsive designs. In the example of the cytotoxic peptide -dendrimer conjugate PKT -GPLGIAGQC -PEG -2000, the three separate peptides - an MMP -2 -sensitive PEGylated peptide, the cytotoxic KLAK sequence, and the tumor-penetrating cell-penetrating TAT motif -were covalently linked to the poly(amidoamine) core, which is the branched dendrimer, leading to increased enzyme -triggered.

A recent study expressed individual living cells in a shell of MMP -7 -reactive polymer, progressing the possibility of clinical cell-therapy applications (Yang et al., 2019a). This study demonstrates the several layers of PEG-modified gelatin attached to surfaces of isolated HeLa or human mesenchymal stem cells through layer-by-layer assembly of cationic gelatin-PEG maleimide (CG-PEG-MAL) and anionic gelatin-PEG maleimide (AG-PEG-MAL). These PEG-gelatin layers were subsequently further cross-linked after clicking an alkyl-terminated peptide (CGGPLGLAGGC) with the cysteine thiols on PEG-gelatin as well as the maleimide groups on the same. This coating enhances the ability to increase the stability to systemic circulation along with the personage into prevention of the autoimmune response and enables the missile delivery to prevent. Battistella et al. synthesized an amphiphilic diblock copolymer consisting of a hydrophobic portion of a Toll-like receptor seven agonist and a hydrophilic MMP9-responsive peptide portion by means of metathesis polymerization into rings by use of ring-opening metathesis. When in contact with the MMP-9, these micellar copolymer systems experience a process of changing to immunostimulatory microscale assemblies, and in the process, this increases the therapeutic effects of copolymer systems. Other MMP nine responsive agents are a DOX prodrug (Fmoc -PLGL -DOX; (Jiang et al., 2019)) that forms MMP nine cleavable nanoparticles when encapsulated into amphiphilic copolymers and a vascular-disruptive agent, combretastatin A4 (CA4) attached to poly(L-glutamic acid) -g-PEG via the Yamaguchi coupling to produce a nanodrug. The CA4 nanodrug selectively disrupts immature tumor vasculature, which amplifies MMP -9 levels in the lesion treated and goes ahead to mediate tumor-selective drug delivery. Moreover, other peptide linkers exhibit dual sensitivity to both MMP-2 and MMP-9, such as PVGLIG, which was first engineered and characterized in 2004 (Sun et al., 2017) and then used in later studies.

The Gly -Phe-Leu-Gly (GFLG) four-peptide is a highly characterized substrate of the lysosomal cysteine protease cathepsin B and has been used as a cleavable linker in many prodrugs and polymer carriers (Duan et al., 2018; Cai et al., 2018). As an example of such an approach, a typical cathepsin B responsive DDS can be considered: a self-assembled amphiphilic triblock copolymer, N two hydroxypropyl methylacryclide (HPMA) grafted with gadolinium and paclitaxel (PTX) and carrying a GFLG linker, which is pHPMA gd ptx(GFLG)-c5.5, in which case the large molecule breaks down into smaller ones upon proteolytic cleavage, releasing the PTX inside the tumor. Also, multidrug-enzaffic nanovectors comprise cathepsin B -cleavable gemcitabine, MMP-9 -cleavable PEG, and ligand-specific CycloRGD motif conjugated with CdSe/ZnS quantum dots (QDs) (Han et al., 2017). These nanovectors can safely survive in the bloodstream, converting into MMP-9-rich TME, where surface exposure of CycloRGD can lead to tumor cell uptake and resultant delivery of gemcitabine, which is triggered by cathepsin-B degradation. Polytyrosine and furin substrate RVRR repeat are responsive to protease K and protease, respectively. Tumor development has been linked to trypsin overexpression, and it can stimulate matrilysin (MMP-7) and hence affect malignancy (Yamamoto et al., 2003). Most recently, poly(casein -g-N -isopropylacrylamide) unimers were found to assemble themselves into biodegradable micelles that could be used to deliver drugs (Cuggino et al., 2020). Poly (N -isopropylacryl amide) consists of monomers that are temperature sensitive and form micelles at temperatures above the lower critical solution temperature (LCST) of poly(N -isopropylacryl amide) of about 32 °C, and below it, the polymers are in the form of an unimer. Doxorubicin loading into these micelles was done through ionic interaction with casein, and its release was achieved after hydrolysis of the casein scaffold by trypsin. Examples of substrates of esterases include carboxylic esters and phospholipids, (Ghavami et al., 2020) and acetylcholine, which have been used to design hydrolytic esterase-sensitive matter. Saxena et al. described self-assembled nanoparticles made of an L-aspartic amphiphilic polyester containing bis -carboxylic acid ester monomers, which effectively entrap curcumin and Nile red (Saxena et al., 2019). These dual-load nanoparticles had a turn-on theranostic FRET response in the extracellular environment, and intracellular exposure to carboxylic-ester hydrolase (CES) inhibited the FRET signal. The need to have donor (curcumin) and acceptor (Nile red) chromophores within a sub-50 A distance in the confinement of the nanoscale is what causes the phenomenon of FRET. Elsewhere, indomethacin-GFFKEH-bicalutamide was engineered as a CES-sensitive prodrug prostate cancer therapy.

Materials for anticancer drug delivery

The development of advanced anticancer DDS relies heavily on the selection of suitable materials that can efficiently encapsulate, protect, and deliver therapeutic agents to tumors with high specificity and minimal toxicity. These materials are designed to improve stability, bioavailability, targeting efficiency, and controlled release of drugs (Tiwari et al., 2024a).

Protein- and peptide-based carriers

Albumin-based systems

The most prevalent plasma protein in human blood is albumin, which has a molecular weight of roughly 67 kDa. Owing to its endogenous origin, it is biocompatible, non-toxic, biodegradable, and non-immunogenic in nature. Various delivery systems have been developed using ovalbumin (OVA), human serum albumin (HSA), and the less expensive bovine serum albumin (BSA). HSA has a large number of ligand-binding regions that can be employed for transfer through both electrostatic and hydrophobic interactions, and the abundance of free cysteine residues on the surface further enhances its binding capacity (Kiarashi and Yasamineh, 2024). It has been demonstrated that certain cancers overexpress certain receptors, such as secreted protein acidic and rich in cysteine (SPARC) and albondin (Gp60), which can mediate albumin transcytosis. Other receptors involved in albumin transport include the megalin/cubilin complex, Gp30 and Gp18 receptors, and the neonatal Fc receptor (FcRn). Therefore, factors other than the EPR effect can cause albumin-based delivery systems to accumulate in tumors (Ji et al., 2024). Several techniques, such as emulsification, thermal gelation, self-assembly, desolvation, and nanospray drying, are used to create albumin-based nanoparticles. The most well-known technique for preparing albumin-based nanoparticles is the patented albumin-bound (NAB) technology, which involves evaporating an emulsion while forming cross-links between albumin units (Qu et al., 2024).

Antibody-drug conjugates (ADCs)

Antibodies play a crucial role as carriers in ADCs, and their selection directly influences the therapeutic efficacy and potency of these systems. Ideal antibodies are expected to possess strong binding affinity for target antigens, extended circulation half-lives, and structural features that support site-specific and uniform attachment of cytotoxic payloads (Hedrich et al., 2018). For effective tumor targeting, the chosen antigens should be predominantly expressed on malignant cells while being minimally present on healthy tissues. Clinically approved ADCs have successfully targeted molecules such as CD22, CD30, CD33, HER2, Nectin-4, and Trop-2. Structurally, antibodies consist of two antigen-binding fragments (Fab), which enable antigen recognition, and a constant fragment (Fc), which mediates immune responses through interactions with effector cell receptors. Human IgGs are classified into four subclasses, each with distinct constant domains and hinge regions that determine their binding affinity to Fcγ receptors on immune cells. Among these, IgG1 antibodies are widely preferred for ADC development due to their strong antibody-dependent cellular cytotoxicity (ADCC), complement-dependent cytotoxicity (CDC), and ease of large-scale production. Consequently, most ADCs are constructed using IgG1 backbones, though some utilize IgG2 or IgG4 (Tiller and Tessier, 2015). With ongoing advances in ADC research, antibody engineering, and drug–antibody conjugation technologies have significantly progressed over the last decade, enabling more precise and efficient therapeutic designs.

Traditional ADC development often uses the native cysteine residues of antibodies to attach cytotoxic drugs. However, this approach typically produces heterogeneous mixtures with variable drug-to-antibody ratios (DARs) and random conjugation sites, resulting in inconsistent pharmacokinetics, efficacy, and safety profiles. Such heterogeneity can limit the therapeutic potential of ADCs (Junutula et al., 2008). To address this, site-specific conjugation technologies have been introduced. For instance, the THIOMAB platform employs site-directed mutagenesis to insert engineered cysteine residues, enabling the creation of homogeneous ADCs with uniform DARs. Compared to nonspecific methods, site-specific conjugation enhances homogeneity, stability, pharmacokinetics, and reduces toxicity (Adhikari et al., 2020). Despite these advances, challenges such as suboptimal conjugation chemistry and potential immunogenicity remain, prompting the development of improved strategies to optimize DAR control. One promising approach involves glycosylation-based modifications of the antibody Fc region (Toftevall et al., 2020). This method uses endoglycosidase-mediated deglycosylation, azide activation, and subsequent attachment of cyclooctyne-functionalized labels, providing a more controlled and precise conjugation process.

The cytotoxic payloads used in ADCs are typically highly potent chemotherapeutic agents, such as microtubule inhibitors (e.g., auristatins, maytansinoids) or DNA-damaging drugs (e.g., calicheamicins, topoisomerase inhibitors). These compounds are far too toxic for systemic administration in their free form, but when conjugated to antibodies, they can be delivered safely and selectively to cancer cells (Yang et al., 2023). This targeted approach allows ADCs to concentrate powerful anticancer agents within tumors while minimizing damage to healthy tissues. Continuous progress in linker chemistry, site-specific conjugation methods, and the development of innovative payloads has significantly expanded their therapeutic window, establishing ADCs as a key and rapidly advancing nanomedicine platform in modern oncology.

Inorganic nanomaterials

Gold nanoparticles (AuNPs)

Gold nanoparticles are commonly employed in biology due to their unique size, decreased frequency of adverse side effects, and controlled drug release compared to other metals. Gold nanoparticle-based supports are most frequently produced via colloidal techniques, wherein gold salts such as hydrogen tetrachloroaurate (III) are reduced, with the help of surface stabilizers that prevent the resultant solution from aggregating. The surfaces of AuNPs can be modified since they can form both covalent and non-covalent bonds. A stabilizing substance, such as citric acid, is in charge of the AuNP surface's total charge. While covalent attachment to AuNPs is typically accomplished by the interaction between gold and amine, thiol, and carboxylate functional groups, the proper selection of a stabilizing agent enables a variety of biomolecules (Antibodies, DNA, and polypeptides) to be conjugated to the surface of AuNPs via electrostatic interactions. Different linkers are used to directly conjugate the drug to the AuNP surface, in contrast to liposomes and micelles (Ajith et al., 2023). Due to their ease of production, low toxicity, and antiangiogenic qualities, AuNPs hold great promise for novel cancer therapy strategies. They are attractive for photothermal therapy, photodynamic therapy, photothermal therapy, biosensors, photoimaging, and targeted medication delivery. Gold nanoparticles (cages, nanorods, and shells) are considered among the most effective optical imaging nanoparticles for cancer therapy due to their inert nature and ability to provide superior spatial and temporal resolution for imaging (Veselov et al., 2022). Gold–polyvinylpyrrolidone nanoparticles (FA–CurAu–PVP NPs) modified with curcumin and folic acid were created by Sneha Mahalunkar et al. for targeted delivery in a breast cancer model system. FA-CurAu-PVP NPs were shown to have a greater potential to suppress the migration and proliferation of breast cancer cells in *in vitro* investigations. FA-CurAu-PVP exhibited higher anticancer activity in triple-negative breast cancer cells that expressed more folate receptors than other breast cancer cells, displaying high selectivity and efficacy (Mahalunkar et al., 2019).

Magnetic nanoparticles (MNPs)

Magnetic targeting has gained significant attention in cancer therapy because it enables both localized drug delivery and real-time tracking of MNPs through magnetic resonance imaging (MRI) (Lim et al., 2011). In this approach, drug-loaded MNPs are directed and concentrated at the tumor site using an external magnetic field, after which the drug is released in a controlled fashion to enhance therapeutic precision (Alromi et al., 2021). MNPs are nanoscale magnetic materials, typically ranging from 10 to 100 nm, characterized by a high surface area, magnetic responsiveness, and superparamagnetic properties. Superparamagnetism allows them to exist in a single-domain state, where the entire particle is uniformly magnetized, and their magnetic orientation can shift with temperature changes (Dan et al., 2015). Commonly, iron oxides such as magnetite (Fe_3O_4) and maghemite (γ-Fe_2O_3) are used for MNP synthesis, often produced through the precipitation of Fe^{2+} and Fe^{3+} salts in aqueous solutions. The particle size can be tailored by adjusting the types and ratios of iron salts, pH, and ionic strength, while reactions are typically performed under inert conditions to avoid oxidation (Hosu et al., 2019). Since freshly formed MNPs have hydrophobic surfaces prone to aggregation, they are usually coated with natural or synthetic polymers, such as PEG, dextran, polyvinylpyrrolidone, chitosan, alginate, fatty acids, or polyaniline, to improve stability and provide functional groups for drug or biomolecule conjugation. These modifications not only reduce agglomeration but also enable targeted drug delivery. Conjugated MNP–drug systems have shown reduced systemic toxicity and improved therapeutic efficiency, with MRI studies further confirming their tumor accumulation (Sharifianjazi et al., 2021).

Porous materials

Zeolites are crystalline, hydrated aluminosilicates composed of interconnected tetrahedral units, $[SiO_4]^{4-}$ and $[AlO_4]^{5-}$, that form a three-dimensional framework. This structure carries a negative charge, balanced by counterions within the lattice. Their highly porous architecture allows zeolites to trap and hold a wide range of molecules, making them attractive candidates for drug delivery applications (Serati-Nouri et al., 2020). To achieve controlled release, zeolites with suitable pore sizes can be selected, or their surfaces can be functionalized with specific ligands. Owing to these properties, zeolites show strong potential as carriers in the development of targeted systems for delivering cytotoxic agents in cancer therapy (Vilaça et al., 2021). Mesoporous silica particles (MSPs) are widely explored porous materials for drug delivery applications. Their pore size, typically ranging from 2 to 50 nm, can be tailored to suit specific therapeutic agents. The abundance of reactive silanol groups on their surface enables easy functionalization with diverse molecules, enhancing versatility in design (Meng et al., 2015). Depending on the synthesis method, both the particle morphology and pore characteristics can be precisely controlled (Shakeran et al., 2021). MSP-based delivery systems are known for their high drug-loading capacity, ability to provide controlled release, and demonstrated potential to enhance antitumor efficacy.

Biomimetic and hybrid systems

Biomimetic and hybrid systems have emerged as innovative materials for advanced anticancer drug delivery, offering unique advantages by combining the strengths of biological and synthetic components. Biomimetic carriers, such as cell membrane-coated nanoparticles, utilize natural membranes derived from red blood cells, leukocytes, platelets, or cancer cells to evade immune clearance, prolong circulation time, and enhance tumor targeting (Wang et al., 2023). These systems can inherit natural functions, including immune evasion and homologous targeting, thereby improving therapeutic selectivity and reducing off-target effects.

Exosomes and cell-membrane coated nanocarriers

Exosomes are nanosized extracellular vesicles secreted by cells, naturally involved in intercellular communication. They possess inherent stability, biocompatibility, and the ability to cross biological barriers such as the blood-brain barrier. Their surfaces are enriched with adhesion molecules and receptors that enable selective uptake by target cells, making them ideal carriers for anticancer drugs, nucleic acids, and therapeutic proteins. Moreover, exosomes derived from patient cells reduce the risk of immunogenicity, supporting personalized therapy. However, challenges remain in the large-scale isolation, purification, and standardization of exosome-based systems (Palakurthi et al., 2024; Tiwari et al., 2025).

Cell-membrane-coated nanocarriers are composed of drug-loaded core particles surrounded by a biomimetic outer membrane with inherent biological activity. The core nanomaterials are generally classified into three categories: organic, inorganic, and organic-inorganic hybrids. Organic nanoparticles such as liposomes, proteins, and polymer-based carriers are widely used due to their favorable safety profile and biocompatibility, with several liposomal and polymeric systems already approved by the FDA and EMA since the 1990s (Farjadian et al., 2019). Inorganic nanoparticles, including metals and their oxides, carbon-based materials, mesoporous silica (MSNs), and hollow manganese dioxide ($HMnO_2$), offer advantages like high drug-loading capacity and unique magnetic, optical, or electrical properties, along with tunable size and shape (Farjadian et al., 2019). Hybrid systems, particularly metal–organic frameworks, combine the benefits of both organic and inorganic components, providing versatile platforms for therapy (Li et al., 2021). The properties of these nanocarriers, such as composition, shape, and structure-determine their drug release behavior, pharmacokinetics, and therapeutic efficiency, making tailored designs essential for different clinical applications. The biomimetic coating, derived from natural cell membranes, engineered membrane derivatives, or synthetic mimics, enhances drug carrier protection, targeting, and overall biocompatibility. However, the performance of cell-membrane coated nanocarriers is influenced by both external and intrinsic factors: tumor microenvironment (TME) abnormalities can hinder drug penetration in solid tumors, while carrier design, preparation methods, and drug loading efficiency impact transport and therapeutic outcomes (Aryal et al., 2013). Together, exosomes and cell-membrane-coated nanocarriers bridge the gap between biological compatibility and engineering flexibility, offering advanced platforms for precise, safe, and effective anticancer therapy.

Hybrid Organic–Inorganic nanoplatforms

Hybrid organic-inorganic nanoplatforms have emerged as promising materials for advanced anticancer drug delivery, combining the structural robustness and multifunctionality of inorganic materials with the biocompatibility and flexibility of organic carriers. These platforms integrate the best features of both systems to enhance stability, drug-loading efficiency, and therapeutic precision (Sierra-Martin and Fernandez-Barbero, 2016). Inorganic components, such as mesoporous silica, gold, iron oxide, or quantum dots, contribute unique optical, magnetic, and catalytic properties that enable controlled drug release, real-time imaging, and external stimuli responsiveness. On the other hand, organic components such as lipids, polymers, or proteins-provide biodegradability, low immunogenicity, and the ability to fine-tune circulation time (Mukherjee et al., 2019). When combined, these hybrids can be engineered for stimuli-responsive drug delivery, where release is triggered by tumor-specific microenvironmental conditions (pH, redox potential, enzymes) or external cues (light, heat, ultrasound, magnetic fields). Additionally, surface functionalization with targeting ligands, including antibodies, peptides, or aptamers, enhances selective accumulation at tumor sites while minimizing systemic toxicity (Yang et al., 2022). Their modular nature also makes them suitable for theranostic applications, integrating diagnostic imaging and therapy into a single platform. Despite these advantages, challenges remain in terms of large-scale production, reproducibility, long-term biosafety, and regulatory approval. However, continued advancements in material design and engineering are expected to establish hybrid organic–inorganic nanoplatforms as a critical component of next-generation personalized cancer therapies.

Strategies for anticancer drug delivery

Strategies for anticancer drug delivery focus on improving drug accumulation at tumors while reducing harm to healthy tissues. Key approaches include passive targeting via the EPR effect, active targeting using ligands like antibodies or peptides, and stimuli-responsive systems that release drugs in response to tumor-specific cues (pH, enzymes, redox) or external triggers (light, heat, magnetic fields). Additionally, nanocarrier-based systems (liposomes, polymers, metal nanoparticles, silica, etc.) enhance drug stability, bioavailability, and controlled release (Hare et al., 2017; Agarwal et al., 2025). Combining these strategies helps overcome tumor heterogeneity, improve penetration, and achieve more effective and safer cancer therapy (Fig. 9.1).

Passive targeting: enhanced permeability and retention (EPR) effect

Passive targeting of nanocarriers refers to their ability to reach specific sites by taking advantage of physiological or pathological features of the body, which promote their accumulation at the target location. This process is largely influenced by a complex interplay of biophysicochemical interactions, governed both by the intrinsic properties of the nanocarriers and by the nature of the surrounding biological environment. After intravenous administration, nano-sized drugs typically circulate through capillaries and preferentially accumulate at tumor sites via passive targeting (Chen et al., 2023). Unlike healthy blood vessels, tumor vasculature often exhibits an incomplete endothelial lining with enlarged pores, leading to enhanced vascular permeability (Gullotti and Yeo, 2009). Manipulating this vascular permeability through chemical or mechanical means can further improve nanocarrier accumulation, thereby strengthening the EPR effect. Moreover, tumors usually lack efficient lymphatic drainage, which results in elevated interstitial fluid pressure and supports the passive buildup and infiltration of nanomedicines into tumor tissue (Natfji et al., 2017). For instance, Goos et al. demonstrated that tumors with pronounced EPR characteristics showed greater uptake of gadolinium-based nanostars (14.8%–21.7% ID), indicating passive accumulation. Nanoparticle size plays a crucial role in the effectiveness of the EPR effect: particles less than 10 nm are rapidly eliminated through the kidneys, while those greater than 100 nm are recognized and taken up by the reticuloendothelial system (RES). As a result, the ideal size range for passive targeting is generally between 10 and 100 nm. In addition to size, other physicochemical properties of nanoparticles are critical in determining cellular uptake and accumulation near tumor sites. The EPR effect remains a central mechanism for delivering nano-sized drugs into the tumor microenvironment. Although multiple parameters influence this process, vascular “permeability” is considered the key factor in nanoparticle uptake, and it can be enhanced by altering local tumor conditions or systemic factors (Shinde et al., 2022).

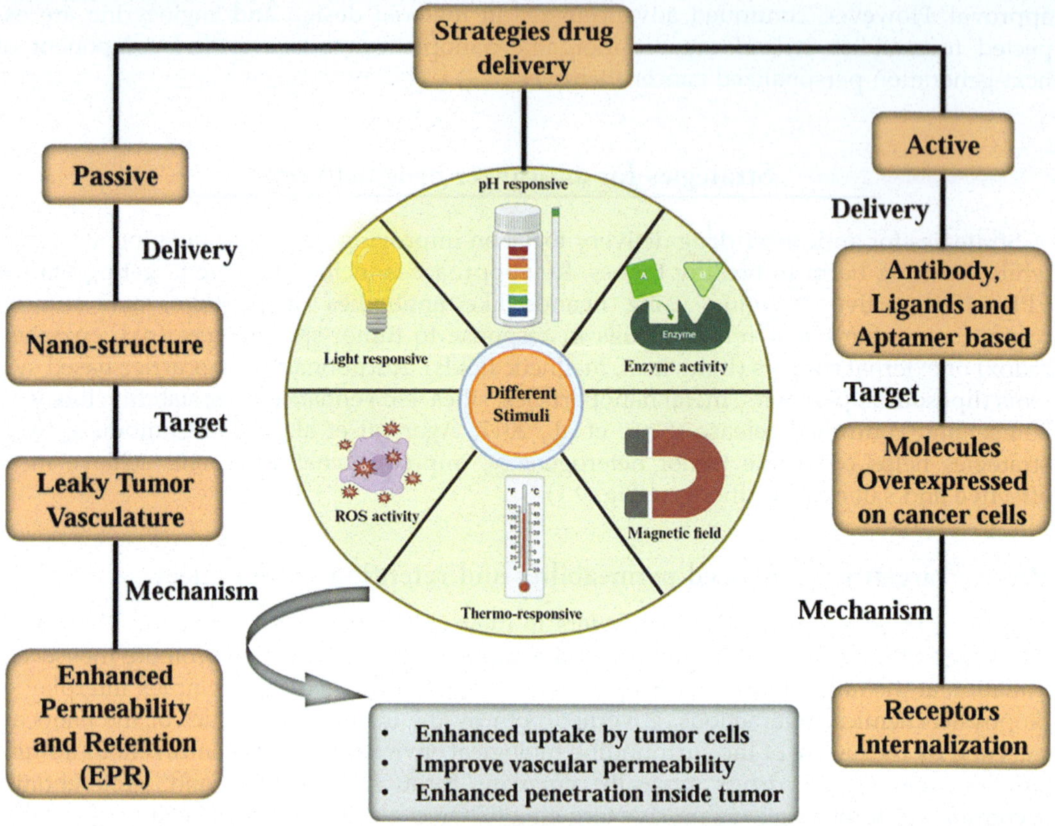

FIGURE 9.1 Graphical representation of anticancer drug delivery strategies.

Active targeting materials

Active targeting is a strategy in which the surface of drug carriers is modified with tumor-specific ligands such as aptamers, antibodies, or receptors that are overexpressed by cancer cells. Also referred to as ligand-mediated targeted drug delivery (TDD), this approach employs ligands that selectively bind to proteins, lipids, or carbohydrates found in high abundance or uniquely expressed under pathological conditions (Srinivasarao and Low, 2017). In anticancer drug delivery, a wide range of ligands is employed to enhance targeting specificity and therapeutic effectiveness. Small molecules such as folate are frequently used, as they bind to folate receptors that are overexpressed in many cancer cells. Monoclonal antibodies, such as trastuzumab, play a crucial role in targeting receptors like HER2 in HER2-positive breast cancer. Additionally, antibody fragments, nanobodies, and aptamers provide versatile options for selective binding, offering advantages like smaller size and better tissue penetration. Other engineered protein or peptide scaffolds are also being developed to improve binding affinity and stability, thereby broadening the scope of precision targeting in cancer therapy. For effective targeting, ligands must have both high binding strength (affinity) and strong selectivity (specificity) for their receptor. Ligands can be linked to drugs in two main ways: a) By chemically attaching them directly to the drug using covalent or electrostatic bonds with specialized linkers (Zhao et al., 2020) and b) By fixing them onto the surface of nanocarriers or microparticles that are loaded with the drug (Chen et al., 2022). After administration, the ligand guides the drug to cells that express the target receptor. Once bound, the ligand–drug complex is taken into the cell, the drug is released, and it produces its therapeutic effect.

Aptamers for directed drug delivery

Aptamers are short, single-stranded RNA or DNA oligonucleotides that can fold into distinct three-dimensional shapes through intramolecular hydrogen bonding and base-pairing interactions. These structural conformations allow aptamers to recognize and bind with high specificity and affinity to a wide range of targets, including proteins, nucleic acids, phospholipids, and even entire cells. When conjugated with therapeutic agents, aptamers can guide drugs directly to target cells, ensuring site-specific delivery of the payload (Zununi Vahed et al., 2019). Their distinctive binding properties, combined with relatively straightforward synthesis and preparation methods, have made aptamers valuable tools in targeted drug delivery systems (TDDS). Along with aptamers, several small molecules such as biotin, folate, and glycyrrhizin are commonly employed as tumor-targeting ligands. For example, folic acid (vitamin B9) binds to folate receptors, which are frequently prominent on the surface of various tumor cells (Sanjanwala and Patravale, 2023).

Carbohydrates and proteins for directed drug delivery

Polysaccharides and proteins can be utilized as a targeting moiety (Bakshi et al., 2025). Examples such as mannose, galactosamine, galactose, and hyaluronic acid are used for research on active targeting strategies and to evaluate their effectiveness in enhancing tumor accumulation (Shchegravina et al., 2021).

Peptides and antibodies for directed drug delivery

More than 40 antibodies have been approved for cancer therapy. Antibodies, such as rituximab and moxetumomab, are capable of specifically binding to receptors expressed on the surface of tumor cells, thereby triggering immune responses or enhancing the effects of chemotherapy. An antibody drug conjugate (ADC) is composed of three key elements: a human-derived monoclonal antibody (mAb), a chemical linker, and a potent cytotoxic agent. In recent years, ADCs have gained significant attention from the pharmaceutical industry as an important class of anticancer therapeutics. Examples of antibodies like Gemtuzumab, Brentuximab, Trastuzumab, Inotuzumab and Polatuzumab based peptides for targeting CD33, CD30, HER2, CD22, and CD79b antigens present on cancerous cells loaded with the Calicheamicin, Monomethyl auristatin E, Mertansine, Calicheamicin, and Monomethyl auristatin E cytotoxic drug Respectively (Dash et al., 2021).

Stimuli-responsive carriers/polymers

Targeted drug delivery strategies are essential for ensuring that therapeutic agents reach the intended site of action. Carrier-based systems are often developed to optimize therapeutic outcomes by improving drug release profiles and directing the drug to the target site with the help of a carrier combined with active therapeutic molecules. Many of these carriers are designed to respond to specific external or internal triggers, and are therefore referred to as "smart biomaterials". Such stimuli-responsive carriers can exist in different forms: they may dissolve in aqueous solutions, adsorb or chemically graft onto aqueous–solid interfaces, form chemical cross-links, bind through hydrogen bonding with drugs or excipients, or interact physically as seen in hydrogels. Their functional groups or components are typically sensitive to stimuli such as changes in temperature, pH, light, magnetic fields, or electric fields (Table 9.1). This allows target-selective delivery in a controlled manner (Rahim et al., 2021; Valamla et al., 2022).

pH-responsive materials

Variations in pH under pathological conditions such as cancer or inflammation have been extensively exploited to achieve site-specific drug release, either within a target organ (e.g., the gastrointestinal tract) or at intracellular sites (e.g., lysosomes or endosomes). Diseased tissues, including tumors and inflamed regions, are typically more acidic (around pH 6.5) compared to normal blood, which maintains a pH of about 7.4. Furthermore, intracellular compartments such as lysosomes and endosomes exhibit even lower pH values, approximately 5.5 and 5.0 respectively (Engin et al., 1995; Panwar et al., 2023). These natural pH gradients provide opportunities to design drug delivery systems that remain stable at physiological pH, thereby preventing premature drug leakage during circulation. Once exposed to the acidic microenvironment of diseased tissues, however, these carriers destabilize and release their therapeutic payload selectively at the site of action, thereby enhancing anticancer efficacy (Ganta et al., 2008; Lee et al., 2008). To exploit this mechanism, two main design strategies for pH-responsive polymeric nanocarriers have been proposed. The first involves incorporating polymers with ionizable functional groups (amine) that can donate or accept protons depending on the surrounding pH. At neutral pH, such polymers generally remain deprotonated and stable, but under acidic conditions, they become protonated, leading to structural changes and altered hydrophobicity. This transition triggers disruption of the carrier and the release of the encapsulated drug. For example, at acidic pH, the protonation of polymeric carboxyl groups can weaken electrostatic interactions between an anionic polymer and a cationic drug like DOX, thereby promoting controlled drug release at the tumor site (Alsehli, 2020).

Enzyme-responsive materials

Enzyme-responsive drug delivery systems have gained significant attention in recent years. Enzymes are essential regulators of biological and metabolic processes in the human body, and many cancers are associated with the abnormal overexpression of various enzymes, such as glycosidases and proteases, which may be membrane-bound or secreted. Harnessing enzymes as natural biological triggers for drug release provides an innovative strategy for cancer therapy. In such systems, specific enzymatic activity breaks chemical

TABLE 9.1 Detailing stimuli-responsive drug delivery systems for advanced therapeutic applications.

Sr. No.	Stimulus	Drug	Stimuli responsive materials/ bonds	Drug delivery system	References
1.	pH	DOX	Acrylic acid-2-methacryloyloxyethyl acrylate, phosphatidyl-ethanolamine, oligo(polyethylene glycol) fumarate-sodium methacrylate, poly(L-histidine)-poly(L-lactic acid), Polydopamine, Chitosan	Nanogels, Liposomes, Microgels, Micelles, Mesoporous silica nanoparticles, Dendrimers	(Chiang et al., 2014; Rehman et al., 2018; Dadsetan et al., 2013; Lee et al., 2005; Sharma et al., 2023; Gou et al., 2023)
		Docetaxel	Phosphatidylethanolamine, carboxymethyl chitosan, hydrazone bond	Liposomes, Mesoporous carbon nanoparticles, Micelles	(Chang et al., 2015; Zhang et al., 2017; Su et al., 2016; Zuluaga and Lange, 2008)
2.	Enzyme	DOX	GPVGLIGK-NH_2 (GK8) linker, Gly-Phe-Leu-Gly (GFLG) linker, Secretory phospholipase A_2, Biotin	Micelles, Dendrimers, liposomes, Mesoporous Silica nanoparticles	(Zhang et al., 2016; Zhang et al., 2014a; Mock et al., 2013; Eskandari et al., 2019)
		Paclitaxel	glycylphenylalanylleucylglycine linker, poly(amdioamine), Hyaluronic acid, Casein	Dendrimers, polymer drug conjugate, Nanogel, Micelles	(Li et al., 2017; Satsangi et al., 2014; Gao et al., 2022; Cuggino et al., 2021)
3.	Temperature	DOX	Pluronic® F127, DPPC:MSPC: DSPE-PEG_{2000},*N*-isopropylacrylamide and *N,N*-dimethylacrylamide,	Hydrogels, Liposomes, Polymeric nanoparticles	(Li et al., 2016; Al-Ahmady et al., 2016; Kang et al., 2003)
		Docetaxel	poly(*N*-isopropylacrylamide-co-acrylamide), (poly(*N*-isopropylacrylamide-*co*-acrylamide)-*b*-poly (DL-lactide)), PLA-L64-PLA, DPPC–DSPE-PEG2000–EPC–MSPC	Nanogel, Micelles, Hydrogel, Liposomes	(Zhang et al., 2009; Yang et al., 2007; Fan et al., 2015; Zhang et al., 2014b)
4.	Magnetic field	Docetaxel	Iron oxide nanoparticles, Fe_3O_4-iSWNTs, superparamagnetic iron oxide nanocrystals,	NLC, Carbon Nanotube, Polymeric micelles,	(Idris et al., 2023; Hossein Panahi et al., 2017; Ling et al., 2011)
		DOX	Iron oxide, $FeCl_3 \cdot 6H_2O$, Polyamidoamine, Fe_3O_4	Micelles, Mesoporous MNPs, dendrimer-coated magnetic nanoparticles, Graphene quantum dots-MNPs	(Varshosaz et al., 2013; Zou et al., 2015; Rouhollah et al., 2013; Javadian et al., 2021)
5.	Electric field	DOX	Platinum	porous Pt NPs	Chen et al. (2020)
6.	Ultrasound	DOX	Succinylated-heparin, Perfluoropentane, Chlorin e6	DOX prodrug-microbubble Complex, eLiposomes, Mesoporous silica NPs	(Luo et al., 2017; Lin et al., 2014; Xu et al., 2020)

(*Continued*)

TABLE 9.1 Detailing stimuli-responsive drug delivery systems for advanced therapeutic applications.—cont'd

Sr. No.	Stimulus	Drug	Stimuli responsive materials/ bonds	Drug delivery system	References
7.	Light	DOX	C_{16}-Nbz-PEG-Nbz-C_{16}, Poly[2-(*N*,*N*-dimethylaminoethyl) methacrylate], Indocyanine green-octadecylamine, Graphene	Lipid-polymer hybrid, Photoresponsive mesoporous silica NPs, Liposomes, Nanogel	(Yao et al., 2017; Wu et al., 2018; Li et al., 2018; Khatun et al., 2015)
		Docetaxel	PEGylated gold nanorod, fullerene-iron oxide-N-succinyl-N′-4-(2-nitrobenzyloxy)-succinyl-chitosan micelles	PEGylated Gold Nanorod Coated Poly(L-lactide) Microneedles, Nanocomposites,	(Hao et al., 2017; Du et al., 2016)

bonds within the carrier, leading to disassembly or degradation of nanostructures such as micelles, thereby releasing the encapsulated drug (Isaacson et al., 2017). Nanocarriers with enzyme-sensitive properties can be engineered by incorporating cleavable moieties either into the polymer backbone or as pendant side groups, allowing the structure to be selectively degraded by the corresponding enzyme. For example, a dual enzyme-responsive nanocarrier based on an N-(2-hydroxypropyl)-methacrylamide (HPMA) copolymer–DOX conjugate (P-DOX-PLGLAG-iRGD) was synthesized. In this system, HPMA copolymer was linked to the DOX via a GFLG tetrapeptide spacer, which is specifically cleaved by cathepsin B, while the tumor-penetrating peptide iRGD was attached via an MMP-2-sensitive PLGLAG linker. Results demonstrated that iRGD conjugation through the MMP-2-cleavable bond improved tumor penetration, enhanced accumulation at the tumor site, and increased cytotoxic activity in prostate cancer cells under both 2D and 3D culture conditions (Peng and Kopeček, 2015).

ROS- and redox-responsive materials

Redox-responsive polymeric nanocarriers represent another class of smart delivery systems that enable controlled and stimuli-triggered drug release. These methods use the redox potential gradient between the oxidizing external and reducing intracellular environments to stimulate drug delivery. This effect is largely attributed to the high intracellular concentration of reduced glutathione (GSH), which averages about 10 mM, in contrast to its much lower extracellular concentration of roughly 2 μM. Moreover, tumor tissues typically exhibit elevated GSH levels compared to healthy tissues, making this difference a useful mechanism for selective intracellular drug release. The design of redox-sensitive nanocarriers generally involves incorporating chemical groups that respond to reducing conditions, with disulfide bonds being the most common example. Disulfide linkages remain stable in oxidizing extracellular environments but undergo cleavage in reductive conditions, producing free thiol groups. This cleavage destabilizes the nanocarrier, leading to its disassembly and subsequent release of the therapeutic payload (Bayat et al., 2024). In such systems, drugs can either be encapsulated within or covalently linked to polymeric nanocarriers containing disulfide units. Various redox-responsive nanomaterials, including block copolymers, dendrimers, and biodegradable polymers such as poly(propylene sulphide), poly (thioketal) urethane, poly[(propylenesulfide)-block-(N,N-dimethylacylamide)-block-(N-isopropylacrylamide)], gelatin-*g*-poly(N-isopropylacrylamide) (Xu et al., 2016), have been investigated for this purpose. Additionally, disulfide bonds may serve as crosslinkers positioned within the core or shell of polymeric micelles, ensuring rapid breakdown of the nanostructure and efficient intracellular drug release in response to elevated glutathione levels (Fathi and Barar, 2017).

Temperature-responsive materials

Temperature-responsive systems are the most widely explored in cancer therapy, designed using thermo-responsive materials (like NIPAM, Pluronic F127). These carriers retain the drug at physiological body temperature (~37 °C) and release it when exposed to the slightly higher temperature of the tumor microenvironment (~40–42°C) (Gulzar et al., 2015). Often, they are paired with hyperthermia therapy, where tumor tissue is exposed to microwave, ultrasound, or radiofrequency heating. While hyperthermia can damage tumor cells or make them more susceptible to chemotherapy and radiotherapy, it also causes collateral harm to normal tissues. Similarly, chemotherapy alone affects both malignant and healthy cells, and when combined with hyperthermia, the toxicity is further amplified (Chen et al., 2014; Sharma, 2023). To address this, thermoresponsive carriers are engineered to take advantage of mild localized hyperthermia (~40 °C), a condition that is harmless to normal cells but enables site-specific drug release. Such systems are usually based on nanoparticles, liposomes, or polymeric micelles that release their cargo only under elevated local temperatures (Gulzar et al., 2015).

Light-responsive materials

Light serves as a particularly attractive external stimulus for drug release because it is non-invasive, controllable, and provides precise spatiotemporal regulation, often functioning in an on/off pulsatile fashion. These systems are primarily applied in photodynamic therapy (PDT), which integrates light irradiation with photosensitizers in the presence of oxygen. Following intravenous administration, the photosensitizer, such as C_{16}-Nbz-PEG-Nbz-C_{16}, Poly[2-(*N,N*-dimethylaminoethyl)methacrylate], Indocyanine green-octadecylamine, and Graphene is activated by light, generating reactive oxygen species (ROS) that selectively damage tumor tissues (Yao et al., 2017; Wu et al., 2018; Li et al., 2018; Khatun et al., 2015). Ultraviolet and visible light are generally limited to superficial treatments such as skin or mucosal lesions, while near-infrared (NIR) light (650–900 nm) is more suitable for clinical use due to its deeper tissue penetration, reaching several millimeters.

Magnetic-field responsive materials

These materials are used for the design of external magnetic field-responsive drug delivery systems. The anticancer drug can be encapsulated in such systems (e.g., iron-oxide nanoparticles), administered either intravenously (i.v.) or intra-arterially (i.a.). An externally applied magnetic field directs and concentrates the carriers at the tumor site. Drug release can be triggered by physiological factors such as changes in pH, temperature, osmolality, or enzymatic activity, thereby reducing systemic exposure and improving local drug accumulation. These systems often follow a core–shell structure, with magnetic materials like

Fe_3O_4 or Fe_2O_3 as the core and polymer, lipid, mesoporous silica, or drug–lipid conjugates (e.g., squalonyl–gemcitabine) forming the shell. Superparamagnetic iron oxide nanoparticles (SPIONs) are the most studied systems as they can be guided under a magnetic field yet lose magnetism once the field is removed- a property associated with quantum effects at the nanoscale (Sahle et al., 2018).

Combination chemotherapy and co-delivery systems

Combination chemotherapy, which uses two or more anticancer agents simultaneously, is well recognized as a means to enhance therapeutic outcomes in clinical oncology (Hu et al., 2010; Sharma et al., 2023). Building on this approach, nanotechnology-enabled co-delivery of anticancer drugs has gained attention as a promising strategy in modern drug delivery research. Nano drug co-delivery systems (NDCDS) integrate at least two therapeutic agents with distinct physicochemical and pharmacological profiles into a single carrier (Teo et al., 2016). Compared with unencapsulated free drugs, NDCDS have demonstrated stronger tumor suppression. Recent advances highlight the development of co-delivery nanoparticles, the use of various nanomaterials, and solutions to current challenges, along with projections for future directions in the field.

Chemo-phototherapy (CPT)

Near-infrared (NIR) light, due to its limited yet safe penetration into tissues, allows nonionizing radiation to be delivered precisely to target sites (Teo et al., 2016). Light-based methods such as PDT and laser-induced thermal therapy are clinically established for both curative and palliative management of solid tumors. However, when applied alone, these approaches often fail to achieve complete tumor elimination and have not replaced traditional ablative methods. To overcome this, combining phototherapy with chemotherapy known as chemophototherapy (CPT) has shown strong efficacy in both laboratory and clinical settings. Chemotherapy enhances PDT by destroying residual tumor cells and preventing regrowth of damaged vasculature. Additionally, PDT can increase vascular permeability, improving tumor uptake of nanoparticle drugs and boosting therapeutic efficiency (Zuluaga and Lange, 2008). Recent work includes multifunctional nanoparticles that incorporate both photosensitizers and chemotherapeutics into one system (Postiglione et al., 2011). Light-activated nanoparticles have also been developed to release drugs upon irradiation, thereby improving bioavailability and treatment outcomes. With its high precision, CPT holds great potential, though further clinical trials are required to validate its effectiveness. While PDT acts locally, chemotherapy works systemically, making CPT a more advanced form of PDT (Olivo et al., 2010). Drugs diffusing beyond the irradiated zone can extend the ablation area, while systemic chemotherapy helps eliminate distant micrometastases, similar to the synergistic effects seen in chemoradiation. Importantly, both preclinical and clinical findings suggest that PDT can trigger antitumor immune responses, which may aid in controlling metastatic disease (Mamon and Tepper, 2014).

Chemo-immunotherapy

Several chemoimmunotherapy combinations have shown promise in cancer treatment, indicating that chemotherapy can enhance immune responses against tumors and improve the activity of immune checkpoint inhibitors (Jenkins et al., 2018). Still, despite numerous clinical trials, relatively few have been successful. Progress is limited by gaps in our understanding of how chemotherapeutics modulate immunity, as well as uncertainties regarding the ideal dosage, timing, and sequencing required to convert immunosuppression into immune activation (Pol et al., 2015). To address this, further studies in preclinical models and well-designed clinical trials are essential. Advanced tools such as spatial transcriptomics and single-cell sequencing offer powerful ways to study the tumor microenvironment (Sistigu et al., 2014). Spatial transcriptomics maps gene expression in intact tissue, revealing diverse cell types and their interactions within the tumor microenvironment (TME). Single cell sequencing provides insight into cellular heterogeneity, enabling detailed profiling of immune cell subsets and functional states. Together, these technologies may clarify the complex interactions among tumor cells, immune cells, and stromal components under chemotherapy, leading to the identification of new therapeutic targets and predictive biomarkers for checkpoint inhibitor therapy. Ultimately, this deeper understanding can refine treatment approaches, enable personalization, and improve patient outcomes (Tiwari et al., 2024b). A major challenge for immunotherapy remains the development of more effective preclinical models to accelerate translation of chemo-immunotherapy strategies into clinical practice. Equally critical is the discovery of biomarkers that can predict which patients will respond best to such treatments. Despite these challenges, the expanding repertoire of checkpoint inhibitors and the wide potential for chemoimmunotherapy combinations across cancer types point to significant progress and innovative therapeutic options in the near future.

Multi-drug nanocarriers

Numerous drug delivery platforms (DDPs) have been documented over the past decade in the literature for the co-delivery of diverse medication combinations, with their performance evaluated in vivo or in vitro for combination therapy. Concurrently, multifunctional nanoparticles capable of executing a variety of therapeutic modalities have been effectively investigated (Gadde, 2015). The opening subsections concentrate on elaborating unique methodologies employed in the development of effective co-delivery platforms for design, delivery, and clinical translatability. Subsequent subsections will focus on RNAi-based co-delivery technologies, encompassing recent advancements. DDPs proficient in co-delivering pharmaceuticals alongside imaging units have been addressed in other sources (Alshawwa et al., 2022). Recent advancements in cellular biology have instigated a paradigm change in cancer therapy, transitioning from "one-drug-one-target" strategies to "combination of drugs-multi-target" methodologies to address various therapeutic obstacles encountered by doctors today (Zeb et al., 2020). Although many drug combinations have been successfully identified via in vitro screening, their clinical efficacy remains elusive due to variations in pharmacokinetics and tissue distribution of each drug in the combination, as well as heightened adverse effects stemming from differing toxicity profiles (Majumder et al., 2019). In recent years, nanoparticles have emerged as a viable category of carriers for the co-delivery of several medications in combination therapy. Encapsulating several drugs/agents within a single carrier (the "two-in-one" strategy) for tumor delivery offers advantages such as synergistic pharmacological profiles, decreased toxicity, and ratiometric drug administration. This evaluation will emphasize the dual techniques employed in various co-delivery platforms and their potential for successful clinical translation (Jabr-Milane et al., 2008).

Challenges and limitations

In recent years, significant progress has been made in developing delivery systems aimed at transporting drugs, including those derived from plants, to specific target sites in the body. Despite these advances, several challenges and limitations remain (Table 9.2). One key obstacle is the scarcity and inconsistency of available literature. Comprehensive and standardized information is essential to guide research in nanomedicine, yet discrepancies in experimental reporting and characterization across studies hinder progress (Youn and Bae, 2018). This lack of uniform data creates difficulties for industrial translation, potentially slowing the shift from laboratory research to clinical application (Pasut, 2019). Moreover, while the therapeutic potential of nanoparticles is well recognized, there is still limited knowledge regarding their safety, unintended protein interactions, and biodistribution in non-target organs. These uncertainties continue to raise concerns about their long-term safety and clinical applicability (Sharma et al., 2021).

Another major hurdle lies in tumor heterogeneity, where variations in the tumor microenvironment, receptor expression, and vascularization reduce the effectiveness of universal targeting approaches (Gullotti and Yeo, 2009). The EPR effect, while widely exploited, is inconsistent across tumor types and patient populations, limiting the predictability of passive targeting. The challenge is ensuring biocompatibility and safety. Many nanomaterials pose risks of immunogenicity, long-term toxicity, or unintended interactions with healthy tissues. Similarly, drug stability and premature release during circulation can compromise therapeutic outcomes (Sharma et al., 2025). While stimuli-responsive systems offer precise control, their performance in complex in vivo conditions often falls short of expectations. On the manufacturing side, scalability and reproducibility remain difficult due to batch-to-batch variations in particle size, charge, and drug loading. High production costs and complex regulatory requirements further restrict large-scale application. Additionally, regulatory frameworks for nanomedicines are still evolving, creating uncertainty in the approval pathways (Hare et al., 2017). Finally, rapid clearance by the mononuclear phagocyte system (MPS), poor tumor penetration, and multidrug resistance in cancer cells often limit therapeutic efficacy. Overcoming these barriers requires interdisciplinary approaches to optimize materials, target strategies, and clinical translation pathways for safe and effective cancer therapy (Lu et al., 2023).

TABLE 9.2 Advantages and disadvantages of various advanced materials for anticancer drug delivery.

Type of carriers	Advantage	Disadvantage	Ref
Polymeric carriers			
Polymeric micelles	• Does not dissociate rapidly due to high molecular weight • Longer shelf life • High stability • Inexpensive and easy to synthesize	• Low drug loading efficiency • Potential toxicity	Yao et al. (2020)
Dendrimers	• Increased surface area • Polyvalency allows multifunctional surface conjugation	• Scattered hyperbranched structure • Unsuitable for incorporation of hydrophilic drugs • Complex synthesis techniques	Bakshi (2025)
Polymer-lipid conjugates	• Prolonged circulation time • Enhanced drug stability • Dual functionality	• Complex design and synthesis • High production costs • Potential immunogenicity	(Giri et al., 2023)
Lipid-based carriers			
Liposomes	• Amphiphilic • Maintains structure at higher temperatures • Highly biocompatible and biodegradable • Excellent cell internalization mechanism	• Low solubility in blood • Shorter half-lives • Low drug loading efficiency	Xiang et al. (2018)
SLNs	• Biocompatibility and biodegradability • Controlled and sustained release • Improved solubility of poorly water-soluble drugs • Scalability	• Limited drug loading capacity • Polymorphic transitions • Stability issues • Potential burst release	Sun et al. (2023)
NLCs	• Higher drug loading capacity • Reduced drug expulsion • Improved stability • Potential for passive and active targeting	• Formulation complexity • Limited large-scale production • Rapid clearance by RES	Liu et al. (2019)
Protein- and peptide-based carriers			
Albumin-based systems	• Non-toxic and non-immunogenic • High drug-binding capacity • Receptor-mediated transport • Avoids harmful solvents	• Stability issues • Shorter shelf-life • Batch-to-batch variability • Production complexity	Zhang et al. (2008)
ADCs	• Targeted delivery of potent drugs • Reduced systemic toxicity • Clinical success	• Antigen heterogeneity • Off-target effects • Complex manufacturing • High cost	Shi et al. (2011)

(Continued)

TABLE 9.2 Advantages and disadvantages of various advanced materials for anticancer drug delivery.—cont'd

Type of carriers	Advantage	Disadvantage	Ref
Inorganic nanomaterials			
AuNPs	• Suitable for photodynamic therapy • Large surface area • High stability	• Expensive for commercial production • Non-biodegradable	(Mohanty et al., 2020)
MNPs	• Easy elimination from the body through metabolic iron pathways • Mechanical and chemical stability • Use as MRI contrast agents • Uniformity in size	• Potential toxicity • Challenge to direct MNPs to desired tissue in the absence of magnetic field	Gao et al. (2014)
Porous materials	• High stability • Excellent loading capacity • Large surface area	• Scattered size distribution • Potential toxicity	Mehta et al. (2023)
Biomimetic and hybrid systems			
Exosomes and cell-membrane coated nanocarriers	• Natural biocompatibility • Intrinsic targeting ability • Biomimetic camouflage • Ability to cross biological barriers	• Complex isolation and purification • Risk of pathogen/immune factors • Scalability and reproducibility	Waheed et al. (2024)
Hybrid organic-inorganic nanoplatforms	• Synergistic properties • Stimuli-responsive release	• Complex synthesis • Scalability issues • Regulatory challenges	Kumar et al. (2023)

Future perspectives and emerging trends

The field of anticancer drug delivery is rapidly evolving, driven by the integration of cutting-edge materials science, nanotechnology, and precision medicine. Future strategies are expected to focus on multifunctional and intelligent nanocarriers capable of simultaneous imaging, therapy, and real-time monitoring of treatment responses (theranostics). Stimuli-responsive systems, triggered by tumor-specific cues such as pH, redox gradients, enzymes, or external fields (light, ultrasound, or magnetic forces), are gaining traction for precise and on-demand drug release. Another major trend is the development of biomimetic and hybrid carriers, including exosomes and cell membrane-coated nanostructures, which leverage natural biological interfaces for enhanced targeting, immune evasion, and improved biocompatibility. Similarly, next-generation ADCs and polymer lipid hybrid nanocarriers are advancing toward more effective, selective, and safer therapies. Personalized medicine is also shaping the future, where patient-specific tumor profiling will guide the design of tailored delivery systems to overcome tumor heterogeneity and drug resistance. Advancements in artificial intelligence (AI) and computational modeling are anticipated to accelerate the design, optimization, and prediction of nanocarrier performance, reducing reliance on trial-and-error experimentation. In parallel, regulatory harmonization and standardized evaluation protocols will be essential to ensure reproducibility, safety, and clinical translation of these complex systems.

Conclusion

The rapid progress in advanced materials and innovative strategies has significantly reshaped the landscape of anticancer drug delivery. From polymer–lipid conjugates, inorganic nanocarriers, and antibody–drug conjugates to biomimetic systems and hybrid organic–inorganic platforms, these technologies are designed to improve therapeutic precision, enhance bioavailability, and minimize systemic toxicity. Targeting approaches whether passive, active, or stimuli-responsive are central to achieving selective drug accumulation in tumors, while smart materials enable controlled and site-specific release. Despite remarkable advancements, challenges such as large-scale production, reproducibility, regulatory complexity, and long-term biosafety remain hurdles to clinical translation. Looking forward, the integration of multifunctional materials, personalized targeting, and theranostic capabilities is expected to drive the next generation of anticancer therapies. Ultimately, the convergence of material science, nanotechnology, and oncology holds great promise in delivering safer, more effective, and patient-centered cancer treatments.

Abbreviations

ADC antibody drug conjugates
ADCC antibody-dependent cellular cytotoxicity
AL artificial learning
AuNPs gold nanoparticles
BCMA B-cell maturation antigen
BSA bovine serum albumin
CD cluster of Differentiation
CMC critical micellar concentration
CPT chemophototherapy
DARs drug-to-antibody ratios
DDPs drug delivery platforms
DDS drug delivery system
DOX Doxorubicin
EBP-1 ErbB3-binding protein 1
EGFR epidermal growth factor receptor
EMA European Medicines Agency
EPR enhanced permeability and retention effect
FDA Food and Drug Administration
GSH tripeptide Glutathione

HAS human serium albumin
HER-2 human epidermal growth factor receptor 2
HPMA N-(2-hydroxypropyl)-methacrylamide
iRGD cell penetration peptide (CRGDKGPDC)
IVIVC in vitro in vivo correlation
IVIVR in vitro in vivo Relationship
ML, machine learning
MMP-2 matrix metalloproteinase-2
MNPs magnetic nanoparticles
MPS mononuclear phagocyte system
MRDD magnetically responsive drug delivery
MRI magnetic resonance image
MSNs mesoporous silica
MSPs mesoporous silica particles
NDCDS nano drug co-delivery system
NIR near infrared
NLC nanostructured lipid carriers
OVA ovalbumin
PAMAM poly(amidoamine)
PBPK physiologically based pharmacokinetic
PDT photodynamic therapy
PEG polyethylene glycol
PEITC poly(ethylene glycol)-block-dendritic polylysine
PLA polylactic acid
PLGA poly(lactide-co-glycolide acid)
PLGLAG prolylleucylglycylleucylalanylglycine
PSMA prostate-specific membrane antigen
PTX Paclitaxel
RGD peptide, arginine-glycine-aspartate
ROS reactive oxygen therapy
SLN solid lipid nanoparticles
SPARC secreted protein acidic and rich in cysteine
SPions superparamagnetic iron oxide nanoparticles
TAT trans-activating transcriptional activator
TDD targeted drug delivery
TME tumor microenvironment

Declaration

Ethical Approval Not applicable. This article does not contain any studies involving human participants or animals performed by the author.
Conflict of Interest The author declares that there is no conflict of interest regarding the publication of this chapter.
Funding No external funding was received for the preparation of this chapter.

Acknowledgments

The authors gratefully acknowledge the support and facilities provided by the Central Drug Research Institute (CSIR-CDRI), Lucknow, for extending resources during the preparation of this manuscript. The authors also thank the University of Connecticut for academic support and Ajay Lale for his valuable assistance in editing this chapter. The CDRI Communication number for the manuscript is 11182.

References

Adhikari, P., Zacharias, N., Ohri, R., Sadowsky, J., 2020. Site-specific conjugation to cys-engineered THIOMAB antibodies. Methods Mol. Biol 2078, 51–69. https://doi.org/10.1007/978-1-4939-9929-3_4.

Agarwal, N., Mishra, P.K., Das, S., Kumar, A., Sharma, M., Panwar, D., Rai, N., Bakshi, A.K., Tiwari, P., Mishra, P. R., 2025. Emerging trends in cervical cancer treatment: Transitioning from traditional to innovative delivery strategies. Int. J. Pharm. 681. https://doi.org/10.1016/j.ijpharm.2025.125878.

Ajith, S., Almomani, F., Elhissi, A., Husseini, G.A., 2023. Nanoparticle-based materials in anticancer drug delivery: Current and future prospects. Heliyon 9 (11). https://doi.org/10.1016/j.heliyon.2023.e21227.

Al-Ahmady, Z., Lozano, N., Mei, K.-C., Al-Jamal, W.'T., Kostarelos, K., 2016. Engineering thermosensitive liposome-nanoparticle hybrids loaded with doxorubicin for heat-triggered drug release. Int. J. Pharm. 514 (1), 133–141. https://doi.org/10.1016/j.ijpharm.2016.09.009.

Allen, A.E., Locasale, J.W., 2018. Glucose metabolism in cancer: The saga of pyruvate kinase continues. Cancer Cell 33 (3), 337–339. https://doi.org/10.1016/j.ccell.2018.02.008.

Alromi, D.A., Madani, S.Y., Seifalian, A., 2021. Emerging application of magnetic nanoparticles for diagnosis and treatment of cancer. Polymers 13 (23). https://doi.org/10.3390/polym13234146.

Alsehli, M., 2020. Polymeric nanocarriers as stimuli-responsive systems for targeted tumor (cancer) therapy: Recent advances in drug delivery. Pharm. J. 28 (3), 255–265. https://doi.org/10.1016/j.jsps.2020.01.004.

Alshawwa, S.Z., Kassem, A.A., Farid, R.M., Mostafa, S.K., Labib, G.S., 2022. Nanocarrier drug delivery systems: Characterization, limitations, future perspectives and implementation of artificial intelligence. Pharmaceutics 14 (4). https://doi.org/10.3390/pharmaceutics14040883.

An, J., Hu, Y.-G., Cheng, K., Cheng, L., Hou, X.-L., Wang, G.-L., Zhang, X.-S., Liu, B., Zhao, Y.-D., Zhang, M.-Z., 2020. ROS-augmented and tumor-microenvironment responsive biodegradable nanoplatform for enhancing chemo-sonodynamic therapy. Biomaterials 234. https://doi.org/10.1016/j.biomaterials.2020.119761.

Aryal, S., Hu, C.M.J., Fang, R.H., Dehaini, D., Carpenter, C., Zhang, D.E., Zhang, L., 2013. Erythrocyte membrane-cloaked polymeric nanoparticles for controlled drug loading and release. Nanomedicine 8 (8), 1271–1280. https://doi.org/10.2217/nnm.12.153.

Bakshi, A.K., Haider, T., Panwar, D., Sharma, M., Tiwari, P., Rai, N., Soni, V., 2025. Ligand density vs mechanistic insight: A ligand conjugated formulation for the treatment of triple-negative breast cancer. J. Nanoparticle Res. 27 (10). https://doi.org/10.1007/s11051-025-06443-7.

Bakshi, A.K., 2025. Smart polymeric nanoconstructs for controlled and novel drug delivery. Concepts in Controlled and Novel Drug Delivery Systems. Available from: https://eduport-global.com/pdfreader/concepts-in-controlled-novel-drug-delivery-systems.

Bayat, M., Mardani, H., Roghani-Mamaqani, H., Hoogenboom, R., 2024. Self-indicating polymers: A pathway to intelligent materials. Chem. Soc. Rev. 53 (8), 4045–4085. https://doi.org/10.1039/d3cs00431g.

Cai, H., Wang, X., Zhang, H., Sun, L., Pan, D., Gong, Q., Gu, Z., Luo, K., 2018. Enzyme-sensitive biodegradable and multifunctional polymeric conjugate as theranostic nanomedicine. Appl. Mater. Today 11, 207–218. https://doi.org/10.1016/j.apmt.2018.02.003.

Chang, M., Lu, S., Zhang, F., Zuo, T., Guan, Y., Ting, W., Shao, W., Lin, G., 2015. RGD-modified pH-sensitive liposomes for docetaxel tumor targeting. Colloids Surf. B Biointerfaces 129, 175–182. https://doi.org/10.1016/j.colsurfb.2015.03.046.

Chen, K., Zhang, Y., Zhu, L., Chu, H., Shao, X., Asakiya, C., Huang, K., Xu, W., 2022. Insights into nucleic acid-based self-assembling nanocarriers for targeted drug delivery and controlled drug release. J. Contr. Release 341, 869–891. https://doi.org/10.1016/j.jconrel.2021.12.020.

Chen, K.J., Chaung, E.Y., Wey, S.P., Lin, K.J., Cheng, F., Lin, C.C., Liu, H.L., Tseng, H.W., Liu, C.P., Wei, M.C., Liu, C.M., Sung, H.W., 2014. Hyperthermia-mediated local drug delivery by a bubble-generating liposomal system for tumor-specific chemotherapy. ACS Nano 8 (5), 5105–5115. https://doi.org/10.1021/nn501162x.

Chen, Z., Kumar Kankala, R., Long, L., Xie, S., Chen, A.Z., Zou, L., 2023. Current understanding of passive and active targeting nanomedicines to enhance tumor accumulation. Coord. Chem. Rev. 481, 215051. https://doi.org/10.1016/j.ccr.2023.215051.

Chen, T., Gu, T., Cheng, L., Xiang, L., Han, G., Liu, Z., 2020. Porous Pt nanoparticles loaded with doxorubicin to enable synergistic chemo-/electrodynamic Therapy. Biomaterials 255. https://doi.org/10.1016/j.biomaterials.2020.120202.

Cheng, W., Liang, C., Xu, L., Liu, G., Gao, N., Tao, W., Luo, L., Zuo, Y., Wang, X., Zhang, X., Zeng, X., Lin, M., 2017a. TPGS-functionalized polydopamine-modified mesoporous silica as drug nanocarriers for enhanced lung cancer chemotherapy against multidrug resistance. Small 13 (29). https://doi.org/10.1002/smll.201700623.

Cheng, W., Zeng, X., Chen, H., Li, Z., Zeng, W., Mei, L., Zhao, Y., 2019. Versatile polydopamine platforms: Synthesis and promising applications for surface modification and advanced nanomedicine. ACS Nano 13 (8), 8537–8565. https://doi.org/10.1021/acsnano.9b04436.

Cheng, Y., Jiao, X., Xu, T., Wang, W., Cao, Y., Wen, Y., Zhang, X., 2017b. Free-blockage mesoporous anticancer nanoparticles based on ROS-responsive wetting behavior of nanopores. Small 13 (40). https://doi.org/10.1002/smll.201701942.

Chiang, W.-H., Huang, W.-C., Chang, Y.-J., Shen, M.-Y., Chen, H.-H., Chern, C.-S., Chiu, H.-C., 2014. Doxorubicin-loaded nanogel assemblies with ph/thermo-triggered payload release for intracellular drug delivery. Macromol. Chem. Phys. 215 (13), 1332–1341. https://doi.org/10.1002/macp.201400145.

Cuggino, J.C., Ambrosioni, F.E., Picchio, M.L., Nicola, M., Jiménez Kairuz, Á.F., Gatti, G., Minari, R.J., Calderón, M., Alvarez Igarzabal, C.I., Gugliotta, L.M., 2020. Thermally self-assembled biodegradable poly(casein-g-N-isopropylacrylamide) unimers and their application in drug delivery for cancer therapy. Int. J. Biol. Macromol. 154, 446–455. https://doi.org/10.1016/j.ijbiomac.2020.03.138.

Cuggino, J.C., Picchio, M.L., Gugliotta, A., Bürgi, M., Ronco, L.I., Calderón, M., Etcheverrigaray, M., Alvarez Igarzabal, C.I., Minari, R.J., Gugliotta, L.M., 2021. Crosslinked casein micelles bound paclitaxel as enzyme activated intracellular drug delivery systems for cancer therapy. Eur. Polym. J. 145. https://doi.org/10.1016/j.eurpolymj.2020.110237.

Dadsetan, M., Efua Taylor, K., Yong, C., Bajzer, Ž., Lu, L., Yaszemski, M.J., 2013. Controlled release of doxorubicin from pH-responsive microgels. Acta Biomater. 9 (3), 5438–5446. https://doi.org/10.1016/j.actbio.2012.09.019.

Dan, M., Bae, Y., Pittman, T.A., Yokel, R.A., 2015. Alternating magnetic field-induced hyperthermia increases iron oxide nanoparticle cell association/uptake and flux in blood-brain barrier models. Pharm. Res. 32 (5), 1615–1625. https://doi.org/10.1007/s11095-014-1561-6.

Dash, A., Blasiak, B., Tomanek, B., Latta, P., van Veggel, F.C.J.M., 2021. Target-specific magnetic resonance imaging of human prostate adenocarcinoma using NaDyF4-NaGdF4 core-shell nanoparticles. ACS Appl. Mater. Interfaces 13 (21), 24345–24355. https://doi.org/10.1021/acsami.0c19273.

Deirram, N., Zhang, C., Kermaniyan, S.S., Johnston, A.P.R., Such, G.K., 2019. pH-responsive polymer nanoparticles for drug delivery. Macromol. Rapid Commun. 40 (10). https://doi.org/10.1002/marc.201800917.

Di Stefano, A., 2023. Nanotechnology in targeted drug delivery. Int. J. Mol. Sci. 24 (9). https://doi.org/10.3390/ijms24098194.

Du, B., Han, S., Zhao, F., Lim, K.H., Xi, H., Su, X., Yao, H., Zhou, J., 2016. A smart upconversion-based light-triggered polymer for synergetic chemo-photodynamic therapy and dual-modal MR/UCL imaging. Nanomed. Nanotechnol. Biol. Med. 12 (7), 2071–2080. https://doi.org/10.1016/j.nano.2016.05.004.

Duan, Z., Cai, H., Zhang, H., Chen, K., Li, N., Xu, Z., Gong, Q., Luo, K., 2018. PEGylated multistimuli-responsive dendritic prodrug-based nanoscale system for enhanced anticancer activity. ACS Appl. Mater. Interfaces 10 (42), 35770–35783. https://doi.org/10.1021/acsami.8b12232.

Engin, K., Leeper, D.B., Cater, J.R., Thistlethwaite, A.J., Tupchong, L., Mcfarlane, J.D., 1995. Extracellular ph distribution in human tumors. Int. J. Hyperther. 11 (2), 211–216. https://doi.org/10.3109/02656739509022457.

Eskandari, P., Bigdeli, B., Porgham Daryasari, M., Baharifar, H., Bazri, B., Shourian, M., Amani, A., Sadighi, A., Goliaei, B., Khoobi, M., Saboury, A.A., 2019. Gold-capped mesoporous silica nanoparticles as an excellent enzyme-responsive nanocarrier for controlled doxorubicin delivery. J. Drug Target. 27 (10), 1084–1093. https://doi.org/10.1080/1061186X.2019.1599379.

Fan, R., Tong, A., Li, X., Gao, X., Mei, L., Zhou, L., Zhang, X., You, C., Guo, G., 2015. Enhanced antitumor effects by docetaxel/LL 37-loaded thermosensitive hydrogel nanoparticles in peritoneal carcinomatosis of colorectal cancer. Int. J. Nanomed. 10, 7291–7305. https://doi.org/10.2147/IJN.S89066.

Fang, L., Lin, H., Wu, Z., Wang, Z., Fan, X., Cheng, Z., Hou, X., Chen, D., 2020a. In vitro/vivo evaluation of novel mitochondrial targeting charge-reversal polysaccharide-based antitumor nanoparticle. Carbohydr. Polym. 234. https://doi.org/10.1016/j.carbpol.2020.115930.

Fang, Z., Pan, S., Gao, P., Sheng, H., Li, L., Shi, L., Zhang, Y., Cai, X., 2020b. Stimuli-responsive charge-reversal nano drug delivery system: The promising targeted carriers for tumor therapy. Int. J. Pharm. 575. https://doi.org/10.1016/j.ijpharm.2019.118841.

Farjadian, F., Ghasemi, A., Gohari, O., Roointan, A., Karimi, M., Hamblin, M.R., 2019. Nanopharmaceuticals and nanomedicines currently on the market: Challenges and opportunities. Nanomedicine 14 (1), 93–126. https://doi.org/10.2217/nnm-2018-0120.

Fathi, M., Barar, J., 2017. Perspective highlights on biodegradable polymeric nanosystems for targeted therapy of solid tumors. Bioimpacts 7 (1), 49–57. https://doi.org/10.15171/bi.2017.07.

Finkel, T., 2011. Signal transduction by reactive oxygen species. JCB (J. Cell Biol.) 194 (1), 7–15. https://doi.org/10.1083/jcb.201102095.

Gadde, S., 2015. Multi-drug delivery nanocarriers for combination therapy. Medchemcomm 6 (11), 1916–1929. https://doi.org/10.1039/C5MD00365B.

Ganta, S., Devalapally, H., Shahiwala, A., Amiji, M., 2008. A review of stimuli-responsive nanocarriers for drug and gene delivery. J. Contr. Release 126 (3), 187–204. https://doi.org/10.1016/j.jconrel.2007.12.017.

Gao, L.Y., Liu, X.Y., Chen, C.J., Wang, J.C., Feng, Q., Yu, M.Z., Ma, X.F., Pei, X.W., Niu, Y.J., Qiu, C., Pang, W.H., Zhang, Q., 2014. Core-Shell type lipid/rPAA-Chol polymer hybrid nanoparticles for invivo siRNA delivery. Biomaterials 35 (6), 2066–2078. https://doi.org/10.1016/j.biomaterials.2013.11.046.

Gao, D., Asghar, S., Ye, J., Zhang, M., Hu, R., Wang, Y., Huang, L., Yuan, C., Chen, Z., Xiao, Y., 2022. Dual-targeted enzyme-sensitive hyaluronic acid nanogels loading paclitaxel for the therapy of breast cancer. Carbohydr. Polym. 294. https://doi.org/10.1016/j.carbpol.2022.119785.

Ghavami, M., Shiraishi, T., Nielsen, P.E., 2020. Enzyme-triggered release of the antisense octaarginine-PNA conjugate from phospholipase A2 sensitive liposomes. ACS Appl. Bio Mater. 3 (2), 1018–1025. https://doi.org/10.1021/acsabm.9b01022.

Giri, P.M., Banerjee, A., Layek, B., 2023. A recent review on cancer nanomedicine. Cancers 15 (8). https://doi.org/10.3390/cancers15082256.

Glasgow, M.D.K., Chougule, M.B., 2015. Recent developments in active tumor targeted multifunctional nanoparticles for combination chemotherapy in cancer treatment and imaging. J. Biomed. Nanotechnol. 11 (11), 1859–1898. https://doi.org/10.1166/jbn.2015.2145.

Gou, K., Xin, W., Lv, J., Ma, Z., Yang, J., Lin, Z., Cheng, Y., Chen, X., Zeng, R., Li, H., 2023. A pH-responsive chiral mesoporous silica nanoparticles for delivery of doxorubicin in tumor-targeted therapy. Colloids Surf. B Biointerfaces 221. https://doi.org/10.1016/j.colsurfb.2022.113027.

Gullotti, E., Yeo, Y., 2009. Extracellularly activated nanocarriers: A new paradigm of tumor targeted drug delivery. Mol. Pharm. 6 (4), 1041–1051. https://doi.org/10.1021/mp900090z.

Gulzar, A., Gai, S., Yang, P., Li, C., Ansari, M.B., Lin, J., 2015. Stimuli responsive drug delivery application of polymer and silica in biomedicine. J. Mater. Chem. B 3 (44), 8599–8622. https://doi.org/10.1039/C5TB00757G.

Guo, W.-W., Zhang, Z.-T., Wei, Q., Zhou, Y., Lin, M.-T., Chen, J.-J., Wang, T.-T., Guo, N.-N., Zhong, X.-C., Lu, Y.-Y., Yang, Q.-Y., Han, M., Gao, J., 2020. Intracellular restructured reduced glutathione-responsive peptide nanofibers for synergetic tumor chemotherapy. Biomacromolecules 21 (2), 444–453. https://doi.org/10.1021/acs.biomac.9b01202.

Han, H., Valdepérez, D., Jin, Q., Yang, B., Li, Z., Wu, Y., Pelaz, B., Parak, W.J., Ji, J., 2017. Dual enzymatic reaction-assisted gemcitabine delivery systems for programmed pancreatic cancer therapy. ACS Nano 11 (2), 1281–1291. https://doi.org/10.1021/acsnano.6b05541.

Han, X., Cheng, K., Xu, Y., Wang, Y., Min, H., Zhang, Y., Zhao, X., Zhao, R., Anderson, G.J., Ren, L., Nie, G., Li, Y., 2020. Modularly designed peptide nanoprodrug augments antitumor immunity of PD-L1 checkpoint blockade by targeting indoleamine 2,3-dioxygenase. J. Am. Chem. Soc. 142 (5), 2490–2496. https://doi.org/10.1021/jacs.9b12232.

Hao, Y., Dong, M.L., Zhang, T.Y., Peng, J.R., Jia, Y.P., Cao, Y.P., Qian, Z.Y., 2017. Novel approach of using near-infrared responsive PEGylated gold nanorod coated poly(l-lactide) microneedles to enhance the antitumor efficiency of docetaxel-loaded MPEG-PDLLA micelles for treating an A431 tumor. ACS Appl. Mater. Interfaces 9 (18), 15317–15327. https://doi.org/10.1021/acsami.7b03604.

Hare, J.I., Lammers, T., Ashford, M.B., Puri, S., Storm, G., Barry, S.T., 2017. Challenges and strategies in anti-cancer nanomedicine development: An industry perspective. Adv. Drug Deliv. Rev. 108, 25–38. https://doi.org/10.1016/j.addr.2016.04.025.

Haque, M., Shakil, M.S., Mahmud, K.M., 2023. The promise of nanoparticles-based radiotherapy in cancer treatment. Cancers 15 (6). https://doi.org/10.3390/cancers15061892.

He, Y., Guo, S., Wu, L., Chen, P., Wang, L., Liu, Y., Ju, H., 2019. Near-infrared boosted ROS responsive siRNA delivery and cancer therapy with sequentially peeled upconversion nano-onions. Biomaterials 225. https://doi.org/10.1016/j.biomaterials.2019.119501.

Hedrich, W.D., Fandy, T.E., Ashour, H.M., Wang, H., Hassan, H.E., 2018. Antibody–drug conjugates: Pharmacokinetic/pharmacodynamic modeling, preclinical characterization, clinical studies, and lessons learned. Clin. Pharmacokinet. 57 (6), 687–703. https://doi.org/10.1007/s40262-017-0619-0.

Helmlinger, G., Yuan, F., Dellian, M., Jain, R.K., 1997. Interstitial pH and pO2 gradients in solid tumors in vivo: High-resolution measurements reveal a lack of correlation. Nat. Med. 3 (2), 177–182. https://doi.org/10.1038/nm0297-177.

Hossein Panahi, F., Jamaleddin Peighambardoust, S., Davaran, S., Salehi, R., 2017. Development and characterization of PLA-mPEG copolymer containing iron nanoparticle-coated carbon nanotubes for controlled delivery of docetaxel. Polymer 117, 117–131. https://doi.org/10.1016/j.polymer.2017.03.084.

Hosu, O., Tertis, M., Cristea, C., 2019. Implication of magnetic nanoparticles in cancer detection, screening and treatment. Magnetochemistry 5 (4). https://doi.org/10.3390/magnetochemistry5040055.

Hu, C.M.J., Aryal, S., Zhang, L., 2010. Nanoparticle-assisted combination therapies for effective cancer treatment. Ther. Deliv. 1 (2), 323–334. https://doi.org/10.4155/tde.10.13.

Hua, L., Wang, Z., Zhao, L., Mao, H., Wang, G., Zhang, K., Liu, X., Wu, D., Zheng, Y., Lu, J., Yu, R., Liu, H., 2018. Hypoxia-responsive lipid-poly-(hypoxic radiosensitized polyprodrug) nanoparticles for glioma chemo- and radiotherapy. Theranostics 8 (18), 5088–5105. https://doi.org/10.7150/thno.26225.

Huang, C., Tan, W., Zheng, J., Zhu, C., Huo, J., Yang, R., 2019a. Azoreductase-responsive metal-organic framework-based nanodrug for enhanced cancer therapy via breaking hypoxia-induced chemoresistance. ACS Appl. Mater. Interfaces 11 (29), 25740–25749. https://doi.org/10.1021/acsami.9b08115.

Huang, H., Dong, Y., Zhang, Y., Ru, D., Wu, Z., Zhang, J., Shen, M., Duan, Y., Sun, Y., 2019b. GSH-sensitive Pt(IV) prodrug-loaded phase-transitional nanoparticles with a hybrid lipid-polymer shell for precise theranostics against ovarian cancer. Theranostics 9 (4), 1047–1065. https://doi.org/10.7150/thno.29820.

Iaccarino, G., Profeta, M., Vecchione, R., Netti, P.A., 2019. Matrix metalloproteinase-cleavable nanocapsules for tumor-activated drug release. Acta Biomater. 89, 265–278. https://doi.org/10.1016/j.actbio.2019.02.043.

Idris, A.H., Abdullah, C.A.C., Yusof, N.A., Asmawi, A.A., Rahman, M.B.A., 2023. Nanostructured lipid carrier Co-loaded with docetaxel and magnetic nanoparticles: Physicochemical characterization and in vitro evaluation. Pharmaceutics 15 (5). https://doi.org/10.3390/pharmaceutics15051319.

Im, S., Lee, J., Park, D., Park, A., Kim, Y.-M., Kim, W.J., 2019. Hypoxia-triggered transforming immunomodulator for cancer immunotherapy via photodynamically enhanced antigen presentation of dendritic cell. ACS Nano 13 (1), 476–488. https://doi.org/10.1021/acsnano.8b07045.

Isaacson, K.J., Martin Jensen, M., Subrahmanyam, N.B., Ghandehari, H., 2017. Matrix-metalloproteinases as targets for controlled delivery in cancer: An analysis of upregulation and expression. J. Contr. Release 259, 62–75. https://doi.org/10.1016/j.jconrel.2017.01.034.

Jabr-Milane, L., van Vlerken, L., Devalapally, H., Shenoy, D., Komareddy, S., Bhavsar, M., Amiji, M., 2008. Multifunctional nanocarriers for targeted delivery of drugs and genes. J. Contr. Release 130 (2), 121–128. https://doi.org/10.1016/j.jconrel.2008.04.016.

Jenkins, R.W., Barbie, D.A., Flaherty, K.T., 2018. Mechanisms of resistance to immune checkpoint inhibitors. Br. J. Cancer 118 (1), 9–16. https://doi.org/10.1038/bjc.2017.434.

Javadian, S., Najafi, K., Morteza Sadrpoor, S., Ektefa, F., Dalir, N., Nikkhah, M., 2021. Graphene quantum dots based magnetic nanoparticles as a promising delivery system for controlled doxorubicin release. J. Mol. Liq. 331. https://doi.org/10.1016/j.molliq.2021.115746.

Ji, Q., Zhu, H., Qin, Y., Zhang, R., Wang, L., Zhang, E., Zhou, X., Meng, R., 2024. GP60 and SPARC as albumin receptors: Key targeted sites for the delivery of antitumor drugs. Front. Pharmacol. 15. https://doi.org/10.3389/fphar.2024.1329636.

Jia, H.-R., Zhu, Y.-X., Liu, X., Pan, G.-Y., Gao, G., Sun, W., Zhang, X., Jiang, Y.-W., Wu, F.-G., 2019. Construction of dually responsive nanotransformers with nanosphere-nanofiber-nanosphere transition for overcoming the size paradox of anticancer nanodrugs. ACS Nano 13 (10), 11781–11792. https://doi.org/10.1021/acsnano.9b05749.

Jiang, J., Shen, N., Ci, T., Tang, Z., Gu, Z., Li, G., Chen, X., 2019. Combretastatin A4 nanodrug-induced MMP9 amplification boosts tumor-selective release of doxorubicin prodrug. Adv. Mater. 31 (44). https://doi.org/10.1002/adma.201904278.

Jin, H., Zhu, T., Huang, X., Sun, Mo., Li, H., Zhu, X., Liu, M., Xie, Y., Huang, W., Yan, D., 2019. ROS-responsive nanoparticles based on amphiphilic hyperbranched polyphosphoester for drug delivery: Light-triggered size-reducing and enhanced tumor penetration. Biomaterials 211, 68–80. https://doi.org/10.1016/j.biomaterials.2019.04.029.

Junutula, J.R., Raab, H., Clark, S., Bhakta, S., Leipold, D.D., Weir, S., Chen, Y., Simpson, M., Tsai, S.P., Dennis, M.S., Lu, Y., Meng, Y.G., Ng, C., Yang, J., Lee, C.C., Duenas, E., Gorrell, J., Katta, V., Kim, A., McDorman, K., Flagella, K., Venook, R., Ross, S., Spencer, S.D., Lee Wong, W., Lowman, H.B., Vandlen, R., Sliwkowski, M. X., Scheller, R.H., Polakis, P., Mallet, W., 2008. Site-specific conjugation of a cytotoxic drug to an antibody improves the therapeutic index. Nat. Biotechnol. 26 (8), 925–932. https://doi.org/10.1038/nbt.1480.

Kallinowski, Z., Hoeckel, V., 1990. Tumor tissue oxygenation as evaluated by computerized-po2-histography. Int. J. Radiat. Oncol. Biol. Phys. 19 (4), 953–961. https://doi.org/10.1016/0360-3016(90)90018-F.

Kang, S.I., Na, K., Bae, Y.H., 2003. Physicochemical characteristics and doxorubicin-release behaviors of pH/temperature-sensitive polymeric nanoparticles. Colloids Surf. A Physicochem. Eng. Asp. 231 (1–3), 103–112. https://doi.org/10.1016/j.colsurfa.2003.09.006.

Khatun, Z., Nurunnabi, Md, Nafiujjaman, Md, Reeck, G.R., Khan, H.A., Cho, K.J., Lee, Y.-K., 2015. A hyaluronic acid nanogel for photo-chemo theranostics of lung cancer with simultaneous light-responsive controlled release of doxorubicin. Nanoscale 7 (24), 10680–10689. https://doi.org/10.1039/C5NR01075F.

Kiarashi, M., Yasamineh, S., 2024. Albumin nanoparticles are a promising drug delivery system in dentistry. Biomed. Eng. Online 23 (1). https://doi.org/10.1186/s12938-024-01318-9.

Kumar, A., Panwar, D., Bhavana, V., Thakor, P., Singh, P.K., Mehra, N.K., 2023. Lipid-based Nanomaterials: A Brief Note on Composition, Development, and Drug Delivery Applications Nanomaterial-Based Drug Delivery Systems: Therapeutic and Theranostic Applications. Springer International Publishing, India, pp. 65–98. https://doi.org/10.1007/978-3-031-30529-0_3.

Kumari, R., Sunil, D., Ningthoujam, R.S., 2020. Hypoxia-responsive nanoparticle based drug delivery systems in cancer therapy: an up-to-date review. J. Contr. Release 319, 135–156. https://doi.org/10.1016/j.jconrel.2019.12.041.

Lee, E.S., Na, K., Bae, Y.H., 2005. Doxorubicin loaded pH-sensitive polymeric micelles for reversal of resistant MCF-7 tumor. J. Contr. Release 103 (2), 405–418. https://doi.org/10.1016/j.jconrel.2004.12.018.

Lee, E.S., Gao, Z., Bae, Y.H., 2008. Recent progress in tumor pH targeting nanotechnology. J. Contr. Release 132 (3), 164–170. https://doi.org/10.1016/j.jconrel.2008.05.003.

Li, N., Cui, W., Cong, P., Tang, J., Guan, Y., Huang, C., Liu, Y., Yu, C., Yang, R., Zhang, X., 2021. Biomimetic inorganic-organic hybrid nanoparticles from magnesium-substituted amorphous calcium phosphate clusters and polyacrylic acid molecules. Bioact. Mater. 6 (8), 2303–2314. https://doi.org/10.1016/j.bioactmat.2021.01.005.

Li, H., Yan, W., Suo, X., Peng, H., Yang, X., Li, Z., Zhang, J., Liu, D., 2019a. Nucleus-targeted nano delivery system eradicates cancer stem cells by combined thermotherapy and hypoxia-activated chemotherapy. Biomaterials 200, 1–14. https://doi.org/10.1016/j.biomaterials.2019.01.048.

Li, M., Zhao, L., Zhang, T., Shu, Y., He, Z., Ma, Y., Liu, D., Wang, Y., 2019b. Redox-sensitive prodrug nanoassemblies based on linoleic acid-modified docetaxel to resist breast cancers. Acta Pharm. Sin. B 9 (2), 421–432. https://doi.org/10.1016/j.apsb.2018.08.008.

Li, N., Cai, H., Jiang, L., Hu, J., Bains, A., Hu, J., Gong, Q., Luo, K., Gu, Z., 2017. Enzyme-sensitive and amphiphilic PEGylated dendrimer-paclitaxel prodrug-based nanoparticles for enhanced stability and anticancer efficacy. ACS Appl. Mater. Interfaces 9 (8), 6865–6877. https://doi.org/10.1021/acsami.6b15505.

Li, Q., Li, W., Di, H., Luo, L., Zhu, C., Yang, J., Yin, X., Yin, H., Gao, J., Du, Y., You, J., 2018. A photosensitive liposome with NIR light triggered doxorubicin release as a combined photodynamic-chemo therapy system. J. Contr. Release 277, 114–125. https://doi.org/10.1016/j.jconrel.2018.02.001.

Li, S., Saw, P.E., Lin, C., Nie, Y., Tao, W., Farokhzad, O.C., Zhang, L., Xu, X., 2020a. Redox-responsive polyprodrug nanoparticles for targeted siRNA delivery and synergistic liver cancer therapy. Biomaterials 234. https://doi.org/10.1016/j.biomaterials.2020.119760.

Li, T., Zhang, M., Wang, J., Wang, T., Yao, Y., Zhang, X., Zhang, C., Zhang, N., 2016. Thermosensitive hydrogel Co-loaded with gold nanoparticles and doxorubicin for effective chemoradiotherapy. AAPS J. 18 (1), 146–155. https://doi.org/10.1208/s12248-015-9828-3.

Li, T., Pan, S., Zhuang, H., Gao, S., Xu, H., 2020b. Selenium-containing carrier-free assemblies with aggregation-induced emission property combine cancer radiotherapy with chemotherapy. ACS Appl. Bio Mater. 3 (2), 1283–1292. https://doi.org/10.1021/acsabm.9b01172.

Li, Y., Lu, A., Long, M., Cui, L., Chen, Z., Zhu, L., 2019c. Nitroimidazole derivative incorporated liposomes for hypoxia-triggered drug delivery and enhanced therapeutic efficacy in patient-derived tumor xenografts. Acta Biomater. 83, 334–348. https://doi.org/10.1016/j.actbio.2018.10.029.

Li, Y., Hu, J., Liu, X., Liu, Y., Lv, S., Dang, J., Ji, Y., He, J., Yin, L., 2019d. Photodynamic therapy-triggered on-demand drug release from ROS-responsive core-cross-linked micelles toward synergistic anti-cancer treatment. Nano Res. 12 (5), 999–1008. https://doi.org/10.1007/s12274-019-2330-y.

Li, Y., Miao, Y., Chen, M., Chen, X., Li, F., Zhang, X., Gan, Y., 2020c. Stepwise targeting and responsive lipid-coated nanoparticles for enhanced tumor cell sensitivity and hepatocellular carcinoma therapy. Theranostics 10 (8), 3722–3736. https://doi.org/10.7150/thno.42008.

Lim, E.K., Huh, Y.M., Yang, J., Lee, K., Suh, J.S., Haam, S., 2011. PH-triggered drug-releasing magnetic nanoparticles for cancer therapy guided by molecular imaging by MRI. Adv. Mater. 23 (21), 2436–2442. https://doi.org/10.1002/adma.201100351.

Lin, C.-Y., Javadi, M., Belnap, D.M., Barrow, J.R., Pitt, W.G., 2014. Ultrasound sensitive eLiposomes containing doxorubicin for drug targeting therapy. Nanomed. Nanotechnol. Biol. Med. 10 (1), 67–76. https://doi.org/10.1016/j.nano.2013.06.011.

Lin, Y.-X., Wang, Y., An, H.-W., Qi, B., Wang, J., Wang, L., Shi, J., Lin, M., Wang, H., 2019. Peptide-based autophagic gene and cisplatin co-delivery systems enable improved chemotherapy resistance. Nano Lett. 19 (5), 2968–2978. https://doi.org/10.1021/acs.nanolett.9b00083.

Ling, X., Chen, X., Riddell, I.A., Tao, W., Wang, J., Hollett, G., Lippard, S.J., Farokhzad, O.C., Shi, J., Wu, J., 2018. Glutathione-scavenging poly(disulfide amide) nanoparticles for the effective delivery of Pt(IV) prodrugs and reversal of cisplatin resistance. Nano Lett. 18 (7), 4618–4625. https://doi.org/10.1021/acs.nanolett.8b01924.

Ling, X., Tu, J., Wang, J., Shajii, A., Kong, N., Feng, C., Zhang, Y., Yu, M., Xie, T., Bharwani, Z., Aljaeid, B.M., Shi, B., Tao, W., Farokhzad, O.C., 2019. Glutathione-responsive prodrug nanoparticles for effective drug delivery and cancer therapy. ACS Nano 13 (1), 357–370. https://doi.org/10.1021/acsnano.8b06400.

Ling, Y., Kun, W., Luo, Y., Gao, X., Zhong, S., 2011. Dual docetaxel/superparamagnetic iron oxide loaded nanoparticles for both targeting magnetic resonance imaging and cancer therapy. Biomaterials 32 (29), 7139–7150. https://doi.org/10.1016/j.biomaterials.2011.05.089.

Liu, C., Gao, H., Zhao, Z., Rostami, I., Wang, C., Zhu, L., Yang, Y., 2019. Improved tumor targeting and penetration by a dual-functional poly(amidoamine) dendrimer for the therapy of triple-negative breast cancer. J. Mater. Chem. B 7 (23), 3724–3736. https://doi.org/10.1039/c9tb00433e.

Liu, G., Tsai, H.-i, Zeng, X., Zuo, Y., Tao, W., Han, J., Mei, L., 2017a. Phosphorylcholine-based stealthy nanocapsules enabling tumor microenvironment-responsive doxorubicin release for tumor suppression. Theranostics 7 (5), 1192–1203. https://doi.org/10.7150/thno.17881.

Liu, L.-H., Qiu, W.-X., Zhang, Y.-H., Li, B., Zhang, C., Gao, F., Zhang, L., Zhang, X.-Z., 2017b. A charge reversible self-delivery chimeric peptide with cell membrane-targeting properties for enhanced photodynamic therapy. Adv. Funct. Mater. 27 (25). https://doi.org/10.1002/adfm.201700220.

Liu, Y., Zhen, W., Jin, L., Zhang, S., Sun, G., Zhang, T., Xu, X., Song, S., Wang, Y., Liu, J., Zhang, H., 2018. All-in-One theranostic nanoagent with enhanced reactive oxygen species generation and modulating tumor microenvironment ability for effective tumor eradication. ACS Nano 12 (5), 4886–4893. https://doi.org/10.1021/acsnano.8b01893.

Lu, J., Gao, X., Wang, S., He, Y., Ma, X., Zhang, T., Liu, X., 2023. Advanced strategies to evade the mononuclear phagocyte system clearance of nanomaterials. Exploration 3 (1). https://doi.org/10.1002/EXP.20220045.

Luo, W., Wen, G., Yang, L., Tang, J., Wang, J., Wang, J., Zhang, S., Zhang, L., Ma, F., Xiao, L., Wang, Y., Li, Y., 2017. Dual-targeted and pH-sensitive doxorubicin prodrug-microbubble complex with ultrasound for tumor treatment. Theranostics 7 (2), 452–465. https://doi.org/10.7150/thno.16677.

Ma, B., Zhuang, W., Xu, H., Li, G., Wang, Y., 2019. Hierarchical responsive nanoplatform with two-photon aggregation-induced emission imaging for efficient cancer theranostics. ACS Appl. Mater. Interfaces 11 (50), 47259–47269. https://doi.org/10.1021/acsami.9b17587.

Majumder, J., Taratula, O., Minko, T., 2019. Nanocarrier-based systems for targeted and site specific therapeutic delivery. Adv. Drug Deliv. Rev. 144, 57–77. https://doi.org/10.1016/j.addr.2019.07.010.

Mahalunkar, S., Singh Yadav, A., Gorain, M., Pawar, V., Braathen, R., Weiss, S., Bogen, B., Gosavi, S.W., Kundu, G. C., 2019. Functional design of pH-responsive folate-targeted polymer-coated gold nanoparticles for drug delivery and in vivo therapy in breast cancer. Int. J. Nanomed. 14, 8285–8302. https://doi.org/10.2147/ijn.s215142.

Mamon, H.J., Tepper, J.E., 2014. Combination chemoradiation therapy: The whole is more than the sum of the parts. J. Clin. Oncol. 32 (5), 367–369. https://doi.org/10.1200/JCO.2013.54.3108.

Mehta, M., Bui, T.A., Yang, X., Aksoy, Y., Goldys, E.M., Deng, W., 2023. Lipid-based nanoparticles for drug/gene delivery: An overview of the production techniques and difficulties encountered in their industrial development. ACS Mater. Au 3 (6), 600–619. https://doi.org/10.1021/acsmaterialsau.3c00032.

Meng, H., Wang, M., Liu, H., Liu, X., Situ, A., Wu, B., Ji, Z., Chang, C.H., Nel, A.E., 2015. Use of a lipid-coated mesoporous silica nanoparticle platform for synergistic gmcitabine and pclitaxel dlivery to hman pncreatic cncer in mice. ACS Nano 9 (4), 3540–3557. https://doi.org/10.1021/acsnano.5b00510.

Mi, P., Yanagie, H., Dewi, N., Yen, H.-C., Liu, X., Suzuki, M., Sakurai, Y., Ono, K., Takahashi, H., Cabral, H., Kataoka, K., Nishiyama, N., 2017. Block copolymer-boron cluster conjugate for effective boron neutron capture therapy of solid tumors. J. Contr. Release 254, 1–9. https://doi.org/10.1016/j.jconrel.2017.03.036.

Mi, P., 2020. Stimuli-responsive nanocarriers for drug delivery, tumor imaging, therapy and theranostics. Theranostics 10 (10), 4557–4588. https://doi.org/10.7150/thno.38069.

Mock, Costyn, Wilding, Arnold, 2013. Cummings, Evidence for distinct mechanisms of uptake and antitumor activity of secretory phospholipase A2 responsive liposome in prostate cancer. Integr. Biol. 5 (1), 172–182. https://doi.org/10.1039/c2ib20108a.

Mohanty, A., Uthaman, S., Park, I.K., 2020. Utilization of polymer-lipid hybrid nanoparticles for targeted anticancer therapy. Molecules 25 (19). https://doi.org/10.3390/molecules25194377.

Mukherjee, A., Waters, A.K., Kalyan, P., Achrol, A.S., Kesari, S., Yenugonda, V.M., 2019. Lipid–polymer hybrid nanoparticles as a next-generation drug delivery platform: State of the art, emerging technologies, and perspectives. Int. J. Nanomed. 14, 1937–1952. https://doi.org/10.2147/ijn.s198353.

Natfji, A.A., Ravishankar, D., Osborn, H.M.I., Greco, F., 2017. Parameters affecting the enhanced permeability and retention effect: The need for patient selection. J. Pharmaceut. Sci. 106 (11), 3179–3187. https://doi.org/10.1016/j.xphs.2017.06.019.

Nie, J., Cheng, W., Peng, Y., Liu, G., Chen, Y., Wang, X., Liang, C., Tao, W., Wei, Y., Zeng, X., Lin, M., 2017. Co-delivery of docetaxel and bortezomib based on a targeting nanoplatform for enhancing cancer chemotherapy effects. Drug Deliv. 24 (1), 1124–1138. https://doi.org/10.1080/10717544.2017.1362677.

Olivo, M., Bhuvaneswari, R., Lucky, S.S., Dendukuri, N., Thong, P.S.P., 2010. Targeted therapy of cancer using photodynamic therapy in combination with multi-faceted anti-tumor modalities. Pharmaceuticals 3 (5), 1507–1529. https://doi.org/10.3390/ph3051507.

Palakurthi, S.S., Shah, B., Kapre, S., Charbe, N., Immanuel, S., Pasham, S., Thalla, M., Jain, A., Palakurthi, S., 2024. A comprehensive review of challenges and advances in exosome-based drug delivery systems. Nanoscale Adv. 6 (23), 5803–5826. https://doi.org/10.1039/d4na00501e.

Panwar, D., Thakor, P., Sharma, M., Bakshi, A.K., Bhavana, V., Srivastava, V., Mishra, P.R., Singh, S.B., Mehra, N.K., 2023. Hyaluronic acid-engineered Bcl-2 inhibitor nanocrystals for site-specific delivery to breast tumor cells. Nanomedicine 18 (15), 1005–1023. https://doi.org/10.2217/nnm-2023-0132.

Pasut, G., 2019. Grand challenges in nano-based drug delivery. Frontiers in Medical Technology 1. https://doi.org/10.3389/fmedt.2019.00001.

Pelicano, H., Carney, D., Huang, P., 2004. ROS stress in cancer cells and therapeutic implications. Drug Resist. Updates 7 (2), 97–110. https://doi.org/10.1016/j.drup.2004.01.004.

Peng, Z.H., Kopeček, J., 2015. Enhancing accumulation and penetration of HPMA copolymer-doxorubicin conjugates in 2d and 3d prostate cancer cells via irgd conjugation with an MMP-2 Cleavable Spacer. J. Am. Chem. Soc. 137 (21), 6726–6729. https://doi.org/10.1021/jacs.5b00922.

Pol, J., Vacchelli, E., Aranda, F., Castoldi, F., Eggermont, A., Cremer, I., Sautès-Fridman, C., Fucikova, J., Galon, J., Spisek, R., Tartour, E., Zitvogel, L., Kroemer, G., Galluzzi, L., 2015. Trial watch: Immunogenic cell death inducers for anticancer chemotherapy. OncoImmunology 4 (4), e1008866. https://doi.org/10.1080/2162402x.2015.1008866.

Ponzio, F., Barthès, J., Bour, J., Michel, M., Bertani, P., Hemmerlé, J., D'Ischia, M., Ball, V., 2016. Oxidant control of polydopamine surface chemistry in acids: A mechanism-based entry to superhydrophilic-superoleophobic coatings. Chem. Mater. 28 (13), 4697–4705. https://doi.org/10.1021/acs.chemmater.6b01587.

Postiglione, I., Chiaviello, A., Palumbo, G., 2011. Enhancing photodynamyc therapy efficacy by combination therapy: Dated, current and oncoming strategies. Cancers 3 (2), 2597–2629. https://doi.org/10.3390/cancers3022597Italy.

Qiu, L., Zhao, L., Xing, C., Zhan, Y., 2018. Redox-responsive polymer prodrug/AgNPs hybrid nanoparticles for drug delivery. Chin. Chem. Lett. 29 (2), 301–304. https://doi.org/10.1016/j.cclet.2017.09.048.

Qu, N., Song, K., Ji, Y., Liu, M., Chen, L., Lee, R.J., Teng, L., 2024. Albumin nanoparticle-based drug delivery systems. Int. J. Nanomed. 19, 6945–6980. https://doi.org/10.2147/IJN.S467876.

Qu, D., Jiao, M., Lin, H., Tian, C., Qu, G., Xue, J., Xue, L., Ju, C., Zhang, C., 2020. Anisamide-functionalized pH-responsive amphiphilic chitosan-based paclitaxel micelles for sigma-1 receptor targeted prostate cancer treatment. Carbohydr. Polym. 229. https://doi.org/10.1016/j.carbpol.2019.115498.

Rahim, M.A., Jan, N., Khan, S., Shah, H., Madni, A., Khan, A., Jabar, A., Khan, S., Elhissi, A., Hussain, Z., Aziz, H.C., Sohail, M., Khan, M., Thu, H.E., 2021. Recent advancements in stimuli responsive drug delivery platforms for active and passive cancer targeting. Cancers 13 (4), 1–52. https://doi.org/10.3390/cancers13040670.

Rehman, A.U., Omran, Z., Anton, H., Mély, Y., Akram, S., Vandamme, T.F., Anton, N., 2018. Development of doxorubicin hydrochloride loaded pH-sensitive liposomes: Investigation on the impact of chemical nature of lipids and liposome composition on pH-sensitivity. Eur. J. Pharm. Biopharm 133, 331–338. https://doi.org/10.1016/j.ejpb.2018.11.001.

Rouhollah, K., Pelin, M., Serap, Y., Gozde, U., Ufuk, G., 2013. Doxorubicin loading, release, and stability of polyamidoamine dendrimer-coated magnetic nanoparticles. J. Pharmaceut. Sci 102 (6), 1825–1835. https://doi.org/10.1002/jps.23524.

Sahle, F.F., Gulfam, M., Lowe, T.L., 2018. Design strategies for physical-stimuli-responsive programmable nanotherapeutics. Drug Discov. Today 23 (5), 992–1006. https://doi.org/10.1016/j.drudis.2018.04.003.

Sanjanwala, D., Patravale, V., 2023. Aptamers and nanobodies as alternatives to antibodies for ligand-targeted drug delivery in cancer. Drug Discov. Today 28 (5), 103550. https://doi.org/10.1016/j.drudis.2023.103550.

Satsangi, A., Roy, S.S., Satsangi, R.K., Vadlamudi, R.K., Ong, J.L., 2014. Design of a paclitaxel prodrug conjugate for active targeting of an enzyme upregulated in breast cancer cells. Mol. Pharm 11 (6), 1906–1918. https://doi.org/10.1021/mp500128k.

Saffioti, N.A., Cavalcanti-Adam, E.A., Pallarola, D., 2020. Biosensors for studies on adhesion-mediated cellular responses to their microenvironment. Front. Bioeng. Biotechnol. 8. https://doi.org/10.3389/fbioe.2020.597950.

Saw, P.E., Yao, H., Lin, C., Tao, W., Farokhzad, O.C., Xu, X., 2019. Stimuli-responsive polymer-prodrug hybrid nanoplatform for multistage siRNA delivery and combination cancer therapy. Nano Lett. 19 (9), 5967–5974. https://doi.org/10.1021/acs.nanolett.9b01660.

Saxena, S., Pradeep, A., Jayakannan, M., 2019. Enzyme-responsive theranostic FRET probe based on l -aspartic amphiphilic polyester nanoassemblies for intracellular bioimaging in cancer cells. ACS Appl. Bio Mater. 2 (12), 5245–5262. https://doi.org/10.1021/acsabm.9b00450.

Serati-Nouri, H., Jafari, A., Roshangar, L., Dadashpour, M., Pilehvar-Soltanahmadi, Y., Zarghami, N., 2020. Biomedical applications of zeolite-based materials: A review. Mater. Sci. Eng. C 116, 111225. https://doi.org/10.1016/j.msec.2020.111225.

Shakeran, Z., Keyhanfar, M., Varshosaz, J., Sutherland, D.S., 2021. Biodegradable nanocarriers based on chitosan-modified mesoporous silica nanoparticles for delivery of methotrexate for application in breast cancer treatment. Mater. Sci. Eng. C 118, 111526. https://doi.org/10.1016/j.msec.2020.111526.

Shang, Y., Zheng, N., Wang, Z., 2019. Tetraphenylsilane-cored star-shaped polymer micelles with pH/redox dual response and active targeting function for drug-controlled release. Biomacromolecules 20 (12), 4602–4610. https://doi.org/10.1021/acs.biomac.9b01472.

Sharifianjazi, F., Irani, M., Esmaeilkhanian, A., Bazli, L., Asl, M.S., Jang, H.W., Kim, S.Y., Ramakrishna, S., Shokouhimehr, M., Varma, R.S., 2021. Polymer incorporated magnetic nanoparticles: Applications for magneto-responsive targeted drug delivery. Mater. Sci. Eng., B 272, 115358. https://doi.org/10.1016/j.mseb.2021.115358.

Sharma, S., Parveen, R., Chatterji, B.P., 2021. Toxicology of nanoparticles in drug delivery. Current Pathobiology Reports 9 (4), 133–144. https://doi.org/10.1007/s40139-021-00227-z.

Sharma, M., Panwar, D., Tiwari, P., Kumar, A., Gautam, S., Marwaha, D., Rai, N., Singh, N., Bakshi, A.K., Agarwal, N., Singh, N.K.C., Mitra, K., Prajapati, V.M., Mishra, P.R., 2023. Immobilized doxorubicin and ribociclib carbamate linkers encaged in surface modified cubosomes spatially target tumor reductive environment to enhance antitumor efficacy. Biomater. Adv. 155. https://doi.org/10.1016/j.bioadv.2023.213672.

Sharma, M., 2023. Nanotheranostic Drug Delivery Controlled and Novel Drug Delivery, pp. 605–650.

Sharma, S., Kumar, C., Kushwaha, H., Sahil, Kumar Jha, S., Chawla, S., Sharma, A., Midha, T., Huddar, V., 2025. Advancing anticancer drug development: Overcoming challenges and exploring new therapeutic strategies. Ayush J. Integr. Oncol. 2 (1), 8–27. https://doi.org/10.4103/ajio.ajio_3_25.

Shchegravina, S., Usova, N., Gracheva, Y.A., Fedorov, A.Y., 2021. Carbohydrate systems in targeted drug delivery: Expectation and reality. Russ. J. Bioorg. Chem. 47 (1), 71–98. https://doi.org/10.1134/S1068162021010222.

Shen, N., Wu, J., Yang, C., Yu, H., Yang, S., Li, T., Chen, J., Tang, Z., Chen, X., 2019. Combretastatin A4 nanoparticles combined with hypoxia-sensitive imiquimod: A new paradigm for the modulation of Host immunological responses during cancer treatment. Nano Lett. 19 (11), 8021–8031. https://doi.org/10.1021/acs.nanolett.9b03214.

Shi, J., Xiao, Z., Votruba, A.R., Vilos, C., Farokhzad, O.C., 2011. Differentially charged hollow core/shell lipid-polymer-lipid hybrid nanoparticles for small interfering rna delivery. Angew. Chem. In. Ed. Engl. 50 (31), 7027–7031. https://doi.org/10.1002/anie.201101554.

Shinde, V.R., Revi, N., Murugappan, S., Singh, S.P., Kumar Rengan, A., 2022. Enhanced permeability and retention effect: A key facilitator for solid tumor targeting by nanoparticles. Photodiagnosis Photodyn. Ther. 39, 102915. https://doi.org/10.1016/j.pdpdt.2022.102915.

Sierra-Martin, B., Fernandez-Barbero, A., 2016. Inorganic/polymer hybrid nanoparticles for sensing applications. Adv. Colloid Interface Sci. 233, 25–37. https://doi.org/10.1016/j.cis.2015.12.001.

Sistigu, A., Yamazaki, T., Vacchelli, E., Chaba, K., Enot, D.P., Adam, J., Vitale, I., Goubar, A., Baracco, E.E., Remédios, C., Fend, L., Hannani, D., Aymeric, L., Ma, Y., Niso-Santano, M., Kepp, O., Schultze, J.L., Tüting, T., Belardelli, F., Bracci, L., La Sorsa, V., Ziccheddu, G., Sestili, P., Urbani, F., Delorenzi, M., Lacroix-Triki, M., Quidville, V., Conforti, R., Spano, J.P., Pusztai, L., Poirier-Colame, V., Delaloge, S., Penault-Llorca, F., Ladoire, S., Arnould, L., Cyrta, J., Dessoliers, M.C., Eggermont, A., Bianchi, M.E., Pittet, M., Engblom, C., Pfirschke, C., Préville, X., Uzè, G., Schreiber, R.D., Chow, M.T., Smyth, M.J., Proietti, E., André, F., Kroemer, G., Zitvogel, L., 2014. Cancer cell–autonomous contribution of type I interferon signaling to the efficacy of chemotherapy. Nat. Med. 20 (11), 1301–1309. https://doi.org/10.1038/nm.3708.

Srinivasarao, M., Low, P.S., 2017. Ligand-targeted drug delivery. Chem. Rev. 117 (19), 12133–12164. https://doi.org/10.1021/acs.chemrev.7b00013.

Su, Z., Liang, Y., Yao, Y., Wang, T., Zhang, N., 2016. Polymeric complex micelles based on the double-hydrazone linkage and dual drug-loading strategy for pH-sensitive docetaxel delivery. J. Mater. Chem. B 4 (6), 1122–1133. https://doi.org/10.1039/C5TB02188J.

Sun, L., Liu, H., Ye, Y., Lei, Y., Islam, R., Tan, S., Tong, R., Miao, Y.B., Cai, L., 2023. Smart nanoparticles for cancer therapy. Signal Transduct. Targeted Ther. 8 (1). https://doi.org/10.1038/s41392-023-01642-x.

Sun, C.-Y., Cao, Z., Zhang, X.-J., Sun, R., Yu, C.-S., Yang, X., 2018. Cascade-amplifying synergistic effects of chemo-photodynamic therapy using ROS-responsive polymeric nanocarriers. Theranostics 8 (11), 2939–2953. https://doi.org/10.7150/thno.24015.

Sun, Z., Li, R., Sun, J., Peng, Y., Xiao, L., Zhang, X., Xu, Y., Wang, M., 2017. Matrix metalloproteinase cleavable nanoparticles for tumor microenvironment and tumor cell dual-targeting drug delivery. ACS Appl. Mater. Interfaces 9 (46), 40614–40627. https://doi.org/10.1021/acsami.7b11614.

Tam, K.Y., Leung, K.C.F., Wang, Y.X.J., 2011 9 18. Chemoembolization agents for cancer treatment. Eur. J. Pharmaceut. Sci. 44. https://doi.org/10.1016/j.ejps.2011.06.013.

Tang, J., Zeng, Z., Yan, J., Chen, C., Liu, J., Feng, X., 2019. Quantitative and high drug loading of self-assembled prodrug with defined molecular structures for effective cancer therapy. J. Contr. Release 307, 90–97. https://doi.org/10.1016/j.jconrel.2019.06.010.

Tao, W., He, Z., 2018. ROS-responsive drug delivery systems for biomedical applications. Asian J. Pharm. Sci. 13 (2), 101–112. https://doi.org/10.1016/j.ajps.2017.11.002.

Teo, P.Y., Cheng, W., Hedrick, J.L., Yang, Y.Y., 2016. Co-delivery of drugs and plasmid DNA for cancer therapy. Adv. Drug Deliv. Rev. 98, 41–63. https://doi.org/10.1016/j.addr.2015.10.014.

Tian, H., Zhang, J., Zhang, H., Jiang, Y., Song, A., Luan, Y., 2020. Low side-effect and heat-shock protein-inhibited chemo-phototherapy nanoplatform via co-assembling strategy of biotin-tailored IR780 and quercetin. Chem. Eng. J. 382. https://doi.org/10.1016/j.cej.2019.123043.

Tiller, K.E., Tessier, P.M., 2015. Advances in antibody design. Annu. Rev. Biomed. Eng. 17, 191–216. https://doi.org/10.1146/annurev-bioeng-071114-040733.

Tiwari, P., Shukla, R.P., Yadav, K., Panwar, D., Agarwal, N., Kumar, A., Singh, N., Bakshi, A.K., Marwaha, D., Gautam, S., Rai, N., Mishra, P.R., 2024a. Exploring nanocarriers as innovative materials for advanced drug delivery strategies in onco-immunotherapies. J. Mol. Graph. Model. 128. https://doi.org/10.1016/j.jmgm.2024.108702.

Tiwari, P., Yadav, K., Shukla, R.P., Bakshi, A.K., Panwar, D., Das, S., Mishra, P.R., 2024b. Extracellular vesicles-powered immunotherapy: Unleashing the potential for safer and more effective cancer treatment. Arch. Biochem. Biophys. 756. https://doi.org/10.1016/j.abb.2024.110022.

Tiwari, P., Shukla, R.P., Yadav, K., Sharma, M., Bakshi, A.K., Panwar, D., Singh, N., Agarwal, N., Mugale, M.N., Mishra, P.R., 2025. YIGSR functionalized hybrid exosomes spatially target dasatinib to laminin receptors for precision therapy in breast cancer. Adv. Healthcare Mater. 14 (9). https://doi.org/10.1002/adhm.202402673.

Toftevall, H., Nyhlén, H., Olsson, F., Sjögren, J., 2020. Antibody conjugations via glycosyl remodeling. Methods Mol. Biol. 2078, 131–145. https://doi.org/10.1007/978-1-4939-9929-3_9.

Tseng, I.M.K., Huang, K.-Y., Li, H.-J., Fa, Y.-C., Ho, Y.-C., Liao, Z.-X., Yang, P.-C., 2018. Targeting tumor microenvironment by Bioreduction-activated nanoparticles for light-triggered virotherapy. ACS Nano 12 (10), 9894–9902. https://doi.org/10.1021/acsnano.8b02813.

Valamla, B., Thakor, P., Phuse, R., Dalvi, M., Kharat, P., Kumar, A., Panwar, D., Singh, S.B., Giorgia, P., Mehra, N.K., 2022. Engineering drug delivery systems to overcome the vaginal mucosal barrier: Current understanding and research agenda of mucoadhesive formulations of vaginal delivery. J. Drug Deliv. Sci. Technol. 70. https://doi.org/10.1016/j.jddst.2022.103162.

Varshosaz, J., Sadeghi-Aliabadi, H., Ghasemi, S., Behdadfar, B., 2013. Use of magnetic folate-dextran-retinoic acid micelles for dual targeting of doxorubicin in breast cancer. BioMed Res. Int. 2013. https://doi.org/10.1155/2013/680712.

Veselov, V.V., Nosyrev, A.E., Jicsinszky, L., Alyautdin, R.N., Cravotto, G., 2022. Targeted delivery methods for anticancer drugs. Cancers 14 (3). https://doi.org/10.3390/cancers14030622.

Vilaça, N., Bertão, A.R., Adi Prasetyanto, E., Granja, S., Costa, M., Fernandes, R., Figueiredo, F., Fonseca, A.M., De Cola, L., Baltazar, F., Neves, I.C., 2021. Surface functionalization of zeolite-based drug delivery systems enhances their antitumoral activity in vivo. Mater. Sci. Eng. C 120, 111721. https://doi.org/10.1016/j.msec.2020.111721.

Waheed, I., Ali, A., Tabassum, H., Khatoon, N., Lai, W.F., Zhou, X., 2024. Lipid-based nanoparticles as drug delivery carriers for cancer therapy. Front. Oncol. 14. https://doi.org/10.3389/fonc.2024.1296091.

Wang, X., Xia, Z., Wang, H., Wang, D., Sun, T., Hossain, E., Pang, X., Liu, Y., 2023. Cell-membrane-coated nanoparticles for the fight against pathogenic bacteria, toxins, and inflammatory cytokines associated with sepsis. Theranostics 13 (10), 3224–3244. https://doi.org/10.7150/thno.81520.

Wang, C., Huang, B., Yang, G., Ouyang, Y., Jia, T., Zhang, W., 2019a. NIR-triggered multifunctional and degradable nanoplatform based on an ROS-sensitive block copolymer for imaging-guided chemo-phototherapy. Biomacromolecules 20 (11), 4218–4229. https://doi.org/10.1021/acs.biomac.9b01123.

Wang, J., He, H., Xu, X., Wang, X., Chen, Y., Yin, L., 2018a. Far-red light-mediated programmable anti-cancer gene delivery in cooperation with photodynamic therapy. Biomaterials 171, 72–82. https://doi.org/10.1016/j.biomaterials.2018.04.020.

Wang, L., Niu, X., Song, Q., Jia, J., Yongwei, H., Zheng, C., Ding, K., Xiao, H., Liu, X., Zhang, Z., Zhang, Y., 2020. A two-step precise targeting nanoplatform for tumor therapy via the alkyl radicals activated by the microenvironment of organelles. J. Contr. Release 318, 197–209. https://doi.org/10.1016/j.jconrel.2019.10.017.

Wang, S., Li, F., Qiao, R., Hu, X., Liao, H., Chen, L., Wu, J., Wu, H., Zhao, M., Liu, J., Chen, R., Ma, X., Kim, D., Sun, J., Davis, T.P., Chen, C., Tian, J., Hyeon, T., Ling, D., 2018b. Arginine-rich manganese silicate nanobubbles as a ferroptosis-inducing agent for tumor-targeted theranostics. ACS Nano 12 (12), 12380–12392. https://doi.org/10.1021/acsnano.8b06399.

Wang, W., Lin, L., Ma, X., Wang, B., Liu, S., Yan, X., Li, S., Tian, H., Yu, X., 2018c. Light-induced hypoxia-triggered living nanocarriers for synergistic cancer therapy. ACS Appl. Mater. Interfaces 10 (23), 19398–19407. https://doi.org/10.1021/acsami.8b03506.

Wang, Y., Xie, Y., Li, J., Peng, Z.-H., Sheinin, Y., Zhou, J., Oupický, D., 2017. Tumor-penetrating nanoparticles for enhanced anticancer activity of combined photodynamic and hypoxia-activated therapy. ACS Nano 11 (2), 2227–2238. https://doi.org/10.1021/acsnano.6b08731.

Wang, Z., Chang, Z.-M., Shao, D., Zhang, F., Chen, F., Li, L., Ge, M.-F., Hu, R., Zheng, X., Wang, Y., Dong, W.-F., 2019b. Janus gold triangle-mesoporous silica nanoplatforms for hypoxia-activated radio-chemo-photothermal therapy of liver cancer. ACS Appl. Mater. Interfaces 11 (38), 34755–34765. https://doi.org/10.1021/acsami.9b12879.

Webber, M.J., Appel, E.A., Meijer, R.L., 2015. Supramolecular biomaterials. Nat. Mater. 15 (1), 13–26. https://doi.org/10.1038/nmat4474.

Wu, G., Fang, Y.-Z., Yang, S., Lupton, J.R., Turner, N.D., 2004. Glutathione metabolism and its implications for health. J. Nutr. 134 (3), 489–492. https://doi.org/10.1093/jn/134.3.489.

Wu, M., Lin, X., Tan, X., Li, J., Wei, Z., Zhang, D., Zheng, Y., Zheng, A.-X., Zhao, B., Zeng, Y., Liu, X., Liu, J., 2018. Photoresponsive Nanovehicle for two independent Wavelength light-triggered sequential release of P-gp shRNA and doxorubicin to optimize and enhance synergistic therapy of multidrug-resistant cancer. ACS Appl. Mater. Interfaces 10 (23), 19416–19427. https://doi.org/10.1021/acsami.8b03823.

Wu, W., Chen, M., Luo, T., Fan, Y., Zhang, J., Zhang, Y., Zhang, Q., Sapin-Minet, A., Gaucher, C., Xia, X., 2020. ROS and GSH-responsive S-nitrosoglutathione functionalized polymeric nanoparticles to overcome multidrug resistance in cancer. Acta Biomater. 103, 259–271. https://doi.org/10.1016/j.actbio.2019.12.016.

Xiang, J., Wu, B., Zhou, Z., Hu, S., Piao, Y., Zhou, Q., Wang, G., Tang, J., Liu, X., Shen, Y., 2018. Synthesis and evaluation of a paclitaxel-binding polymeric micelle for efficient breast cancer therapy. Sci. China Life Sci. 61 (4), 436–447. https://doi.org/10.1007/s11427-017-9274-9.

Xu, P., Jia, Y., Li, Z., Wang, M., Zhou, L., Zhong, G., Yi, Z., Li, N., Zhai, Z., Yang, S., Wu, Y., Zhang, D., Dai, Z., 2020. Therapeutic effect of doxorubicin-chlorin e6-loaded mesoporous silica nanoparticles combined with ultrasound on triple-negative breast cancer. Int. J. Nanomed. 15, 2659–2668. https://doi.org/10.2147/IJN.S243037.

Xu, Q., He, C., Xiao, C., Chen, X., 2016. Reactive oxygen species (ROS) responsive polymers for biomedical applications. Macromol. Biosci. 16 (5), 635–646. https://doi.org/10.1002/mabi.201500440.

Yamamoto, H., Iku, S., Adachi, Y., Imsumran, A., Taniguchi, H., Nosho, K., Min, Y., Horiuchi, S., Yoshida, M., Itoh, F., Imai, K., 2003. Association of trypsin expression with tumor progression and matrilysin expression in human colorectal cancer. J. Pathol. 199 (2), 176–184. https://doi.org/10.1002/path.1277.

Yang, C., Lin, Z.I., Chen, J.A., Xu, Z., Gu, J., Law, W.C., Yang, J.H.C., Chen, C.K., 2022. Organic/inorganic self-assembled hybrid nano-architectures for cancer therapy applications. Macromol. Biosci. 22 (2). https://doi.org/10.1002/mabi.202100349.

Yang, Y., Wang, S., Ma, P., Jiang, Y., Cheng, K., Yu, Y., Jiang, N., Miao, H., Tang, Q., Liu, F., Zha, Y., Li, N., 2023. Drug conjugate-based anticancer therapy - current status and perspectives. Cancer Lett. 552. https://doi.org/10.1016/j.canlet.2022.215969.

Yang, J., Yang, Y., Kawazoe, N., Chen, G., 2019a. Encapsulation of individual living cells with enzyme responsive polymer nanoshell. Biomaterials 197, 317–326. https://doi.org/10.1016/j.biomaterials.2019.01.029.

Yang, K., Liu, Y., Wang, Y., Ren, Q., Guo, H., Matson, J.B., Chen, X., Nie, Z., 2019b. Enzyme-induced in vivo assembly of gold nanoparticles for imaging-guided synergistic chemo-photothermal therapy of tumor. Biomaterials 223. https://doi.org/10.1016/j.biomaterials.2019.119460.

Yang, M., Ding, Y., Zhang, L., Qian, X., Jiang, X., Liu, B., 2007. Novel thermosensitive polymeric micelles for docetaxel delivery. J. Biomed. Mater. Res. A. 81n (4), 847–857. https://doi.org/10.1002/jbm.a.31129.

Yao, Y., Zhou, Y., Liu, L., Xu, Y., Chen, Q., Wang, Y., Wu, S., Deng, Y., Zhang, J., Shao, A., 2020. Nanoparticle-based drug delivery in cancer therapy and its role in overcoming drug resistance. Front. Mol. Biosci. 7. https://doi.org/10.3389/fmolb.2020.00193.

Yao, C., Wu, M., Zhang, C., Lin, X., Wei, Z., Zheng, Y., Zhang, D., Zhang, Z., Liu, X., 2017. Photoresponsive lipid-polymer hybrid nanoparticles for controlled doxorubicin release. Nanotechnology 28 (25). https://doi.org/10.1088/1361-6528/aa702a.

Yin, T., Wang, Y., Chu, X., Fu, Y., Wang, L., Zhou, J., Tang, X., Liu, J., Huo, M., 2018a. Free adriamycin-loaded pH/reduction dual-responsive hyaluronic acid-adriamycin prodrug micelles for efficient cancer therapy. ACS Appl. Mater. Interfaces 10 (42), 35693–35704. https://doi.org/10.1021/acsami.8b09342.

Yin, W., Qiang, M., Ke, W., Han, Y., Mukerabigwi, J.F., Ge, Z., 2018b. Hypoxia-responsive block copolymer radiosensitizers as anticancer drug nanocarriers for enhanced chemoradiotherapy of bulky solid tumors. Biomaterials 181, 360–371. https://doi.org/10.1016/j.biomaterials.2018.08.014.

Yin, W., Ke, W., Lu, N., Wang, Y., Japir, A.A.-W.M.M., Mohammed, F., Wang, Y., Pan, Y., Ge, Z., 2020. Glutathione and reactive oxygen species dual-responsive block copolymer prodrugs for boosting tumor site-specific drug release and enhanced antitumor efficacy. Biomacromolecules 21 (2), 921–929. https://doi.org/10.1021/acs.biomac.9b01578.

Youn, Y.S., Bae, Y.H., 2018. Perspectives on the past, present, and future of cancer nanomedicine. Adv. Drug Deliv. Rev. 130, 3–11. https://doi.org/10.1016/j.addr.2018.05.008.

Yu, L., Ke, H.-L., Du, F.-S., Li, Z.-C., 2019. Redox-responsive fluorescent polycarbonates based on selenide for chemotherapy of triple-negative breast cancer. Biomacromolecules 20 (7), 2809–2820. https://doi.org/10.1021/acs.biomac.9b00583.

Yuan, X., Peng, S., Lin, W., Wang, J., Zhang, L., 2019. Multistage pH-responsive mesoporous silica nanohybrids with charge reversal and intracellular release for efficient anticancer drug delivery. J. Colloid Interface Sci. 555, 82–93. https://doi.org/10.1016/j.jcis.2019.07.061.

Zeb, A., Rana, I., Choi, H.-I., Lee, C.-H., Baek, S.-W., Lim, C.-W., Khan, N., Arif, S.T., Sahar, N.us, Alvi, A.M., Ali Shah, F., ud Din, F., Bae, O.-N., Park, J.-S., Kim, J.-K., 2020. Potential and applications of nanocarriers for efficient delivery of biopharmaceuticals. Pharmaceutics 12 (12), 1184. https://doi.org/10.3390/pharmaceutics12121184.

Zeng, W., Zhang, H., Deng, Y., Jiang, A., Bao, X., Guo, M., Li, Z., Wu, M., Ji, X., Zeng, X., Lin, M., 2020. Dual-response oxygen-generating MnO2 nanoparticles with polydopamine modification for combined photothermal-photodynamic therapy. Chem. Eng. J. 389. https://doi.org/10.1016/j.cej.2020.124494.

Zeng, X., Luo, M., Liu, G., Wang, X., Tao, W., Lin, Y., Ji, X., Lin, N., Lin, M., 2018. Polydopamine-modified black phosphorous nanocapsule with enhanced stability and photothermal performance for tumor multimodal treatments. Adv. Sci. 5 (10). https://doi.org/10.1002/advs.201800510.

Zhang, L., Chan, J.M., Gu, F.X., Rhee, J.W., Wang, A.Z., Radovic-Moreno, A.F., Alexis, F., Langer, R., Farokhzad, O. C., 2008. Self-assembled lipid-polymer hybrid nanoparticles: A robust drug delivery platform. ACS Nano 2 (8), 1696–1702. https://doi.org/10.1021/nn800275r.

Zhang, J., Qian, Z., Gu, Y., 2009. In vivo anti-tumor efficacy of docetaxel-loaded thermally responsive nanohydrogel. Nanotechnology 20 (32). https://doi.org/10.1088/0957-4484/20/32/325102.

Zhang, C., Pan, D., Luo, K., She, W., Guo, C., Yang, Y., Gu, Z., 2014a. Peptide dendrimer-doxorubicin conjugate-based nanoparticles as an enzyme-responsive drug delivery system for cancer therapy. Adv. Healthcare Mater. 3 (8), 1299–1308. https://doi.org/10.1002/adhm.201300601.

Zhang, H., Gong, W., Wang, Z.-Y., Yuan, S.-J., Xie, X.-Y., Yang, Y.-F., Yang, Y., Wang, S.-S., Yang, D.-X., Xuan, Z.-X., Mei, X.-G., 2014b. Preparation, characterization, and pharmacodynamics of thermosensitive liposomes containing docetaxel. J. Pharmaceut. Sci. 103 (7), 2177–2183. https://doi.org/10.1002/jps.24019.

Zhang, X., Wang, X., Zhong, W., Ren, X., Sha, X., Fang, X., 2016. Matrix metalloproteinases-2/9-sensitive peptide-conjugated polymer micelles for site-specific release of drugs and enhancing tumor accumulation: Preparation and in vitro and in vivo evaluation. Int. J. Nanomed. 11, 1643–1661. https://doi.org/10.2147/IJN.S101030.

Zhang, X., Wu, M., Li, J., Lan, S., Zeng, Y., Liu, X., Liu, J., 2018. Light-enhanced hypoxia-response of conjugated polymer nanocarrier for successive synergistic photodynamic and chemo-therapy. ACS Appl. Mater. Interfaces 10 (26), 21909–21919. https://doi.org/10.1021/acsami.8b06491.

Zhang, Y., Zhu, W., Zhang, H., Han, J., Zhang, L., Lin, Q., Ai, F., 2017. Carboxymethyl chitosan/phospholipid bilayer-capped mesoporous carbon nanoparticles with pH-responsive and prolonged release properties for oral delivery of the antitumor drug, docetaxel. Int. J. Pharm. 532 (1), 384–392. https://doi.org/10.1016/j.ijpharm.2017.09.023.

Zhao, P., Zhang, Y., Li, W., Jeanty, C., Xiang, G., Dong, Y., 2020. Recent advances of antibody drug conjugates for clinical applications. Acta Pharm. Sin. B 10 (9), 1589–1600. https://doi.org/10.1016/j.apsb.2020.04.012.

Zheng, D., Zhao, J., Tao, Y., Liu, J., Wang, L., He, J., Lei, J., Liu, K., 2020. pH and glutathione dual responsive nanoparticles based on Ganoderma lucidum polysaccharide for potential programmable release of three drugs. Chem. Eng. J. 389. https://doi.org/10.1016/j.cej.2020.124418.

Zou, Y., Liu, P., Liu, C.-H., Zhi, X.-T., 2015. Doxorubicin-loaded mesoporous magnetic nanoparticles to induce apoptosis in breast cancer cells. Biomed. Pharmacother. 69, 355–360. https://doi.org/10.1016/j.biopha.2014.12.012.

Zuluaga, M.-F., Lange, N., 2008. Combination of photodynamic therapy with anti-cancer agents. Curr. Med. Chem. 15 (17), 1655–1673. https://doi.org/10.2174/092986708784872401.

Zununi Vahed, S., Fathi, N., Samiei, M., Maleki Dizaj, S., Sharifi, S., 2019. Targeted cancer drug delivery with aptamer-functionalized polymeric nanoparticles. J. Drug Target. 27 (3), 292–299. https://doi.org/10.1080/1061186X.2018.1491978.

CHAPTER

10

Drug conjugates for anticancer drug delivery

Disha Marwaha[1], *Priya Gupta*[2], *Neha Singh*[3], *Ashutosh Gupta*[4, 5] and *Abhishek Sharma*[6]

[1]Chandigarh University, Unnao, Uttar Pradesh, India; [2]Amity Institute of Pharmacy, Amity University, Noida, Uttar Pradesh, India; [3]School of Medical & Allied Sciences, K. R. Mangalam University Sohna, Gurgaon, Haryana, India; [4]Department of Pharmaceutical Quality Assurance, Manipal College of Pharmaceutical Sciences, Manipal Academy of Higher Education, Manipal, Karnataka, India; [5]Formulation Research & Development–Non Orals, Sun Pharmaceutical Industries Ltd, Vadodara, Gujarat, India; [6]School of Pharmaceutical Sciences, SDGI Global University, Ghaziabad, Uttar Pradesh, India

Introduction

The primary feature of cancer is the occurrence of uncontrolled cell proliferation. Chemotherapeutics can eradicate cancer; however, most anti-cancer drugs cannot differentiate between malignant cells and rapidly dividing normal cells, eventually leading to side effects and toxicity. Due to the severity of side effects, dose reduction was necessary, leading to an inadequate amount of drug reaching the site of action. The development of drug conjugates has led to a paradigm shift in the drug delivery system. The drug conjugates address the drawbacks of conventional chemotherapy by increasing drug distribution in tumor tissue, decreasing concentration in normal cells, and reducing toxicity and side effects.

Conventional cancer chemotherapy employs small-molecule cytotoxic drugs that confer therapeutic advantages by suppressing the rapid growth of cancer cells or triggering death in tumor cells. The combination of chemotherapeutic drugs is progressively transforming the paradigm of chemotherapy. However, the therapeutic efficacy of chemotherapy may not consistently be seen, especially in metastatic solid tumors. This lack of response may lead to drug resistance, culminating in elevated mortality rates among patients with

Advanced Cancer Therapeutics
https://doi.org/10.1016/B978-0-443-44185-1.00023-9

metastatic solid tumors. The principal drawback of conventional small-molecule chemotherapeutic agents is their lack of target specificity, which invariably leads to off-target adverse effects. Chemotherapeutic agents may concentrate in specific healthy tissues and fail to reach diseased locations to exert their therapeutic effects. Targeted drug conjugates (TDCs) represent a promising strategy in oncological treatment, capable of selectively eliminating cancer cells. TDCs are created by conjugating cytotoxic drugs with highly precise targeting molecules, thereby improving the specificity of cancer treatment and reducing systemic toxicity compared to conventional chemotherapy (Lammers et al., 2016). This improved specificity and less toxicity facilitate a wider therapeutic window, potentially augmenting the safety and efficacy of cancer treatment (de Lázaro and Mooney, 2021).

Antibodies, being innate immune molecules, exhibit remarkable specificity and affinity, enabling the targeting of certain disease indicators. Antibody-based therapeutics have gained prominence in the pharmaceutical sector due to developments in monoclonal antibody (mAb) technology. Antibodies serve as effective delivery vehicles for chemotherapeutics due to their capacity to target tumors, facilitating the accumulation of cytotoxic drugs at tumor sites, minimizing off-target adverse effects, and enhancing the therapeutic index for cancer treatment. Antibody-drug conjugates (ADCs) have developed as a unique approach in cancer therapy, bridging the gap between monoclonal antibody (mAb) and cytotoxic agents, thereby offering patients innovative therapeutic alternatives. In the early 20th century, Paul Ehrlich proposed the concept of "magic bullets," envisioning a targeted drug delivery system capable of selectively eliminating dangerous cells while preserving the integrity of healthy tissues. The clinical efficacy of ADCs is apparent in their improved therapeutic window and notable therapeutic effects; yet, obstacles such as drug resistance, complex pharmacokinetic profiles, and production expenses remain.

Alternative delivery systems could potentially supplant antibodies by employing the design principles of ADCs, thereby overcoming challenges like inadequate permeability and immunogenicity linked to antibodies (Fig. 10.1). Tumor-targeting peptides and small-molecule ligands specific to tumor-associated antigens may function as alternatives to antibodies. This has led to the emergence of peptide-drug conjugates (PDCs) and small molecule-drug conjugates (SMDCs), which have gained popularity due to the swift progress in medical technology. This conjugation trend generally adheres to a ternary framework aimed at ligand-linker-effector compounds. PDCs and SMDCs could represent prospective next-generation therapeutics. Their reduced molecular size may provide improved penetration into tumor tissues, streamline manufacturing processes, and potentially diminish deleterious effects relative to ADCs. Moreover, the diminished dimensions of PDCs and SMDCs often yield more predictable pharmacokinetic profiles compared to the complex processes of ADCs. ADCs continue to demonstrate therapeutic efficacy; however, PDCs and SMDCs may develop into significant adjuncts or alternatives for targeted therapy in the future. Numerous inherent constraints in TDC development require new solutions, including possible immunogenic reactions that could impair therapeutic tolerability and escalate costs due to intricate production methods. Furthermore, the development of drug resistance in tumor cells is a considerable risk to the sustained effectiveness of TDCs, while pharmacokinetic and pharmacodynamic intricacies introduce analytical difficulties. The clinical trial designs must be meticulously developed to precisely evaluate the safety and efficacy profiles

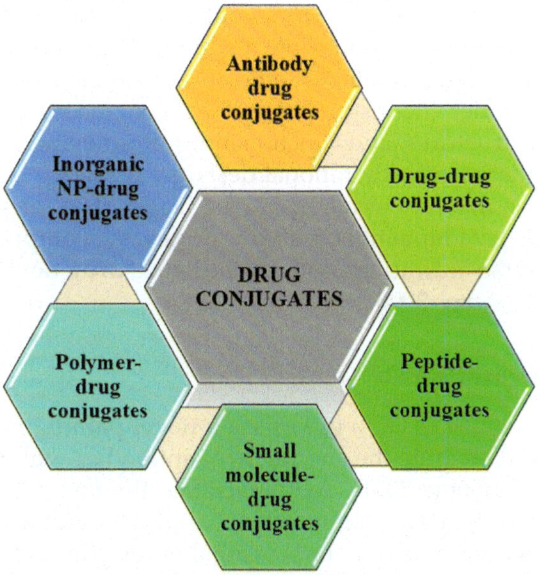

FIGURE 10.1 Types of drug conjugates.

of TDCs. Drug design optimization seeks to augment the infiltration and specificity towards tumor tissues, hence potentially enhancing treatment efficacy. Technological improvements, especially in nanotechnology, have optimized TDC pharmacokinetics, potentially lowering production costs and enhancing therapeutic indices. An extensive examination of TDCs could provide an understanding of their therapeutic effectiveness and constraints, therefore informing subsequent research and clinical applications.

Drug conjugates are at the forefront of the fast-growing field of nanotechnology, offering various applications for drug delivery. They are generally made up of biocompatible polymers or lipids. Drug conjugate nanoparticles can provide high-loading capacities for hydrophilic as well as hydrophobic drugs. A drug conjugate is an exponential field of nanotechnology that has the potential to target administered drugs to a particular organ of interest. By taking advantage of lipid metabolic pathways, they can be designed to overcome drug delivery problems and target specificity. This chapter enumerates different chemical approaches for conjugation to form drug conjugates, the design of drug conjugates, and the advancement in drug conjugates, including stimuli-based drug delivery systems.

Types of drug conjugates

Polymer-drug conjugates

Polymer–drug conjugate treatments are pharmacologically active macromolecular constructions that consist of one or more therapeutic agents—such as small molecules, peptides, proteins, and aptamers—covalently linked to a polymeric carrier (Maeda, 2015). The conjugation of bioactives to polymers has multiple advantages, such as improved drug solubilization, regulated distribution, heightened efficacy, and enhanced pharmacokinetics. The progress in synthetic polymer chemistry and materials engineering is broadening the range of accessible materials, structures, and functionalities. Responsive and multifunctional carriers provide the potential to employ rational design and precise molecular engineering to regulate and enhance the delivery of medicinal medicines. The integration of current polymer–drug conjugate design adaptability with our expanding comprehension of the intricate pathophysiology of diverse indications will revolutionize drug development initiatives and treatment paradigms (Duncan, 2006).

Antibody-drug conjugates (ADCs)

Antibody-Drug Conjugates (ADCs) exemplify a novel paradigm in oncological therapy. These novel therapeutics integrate the specificity of antibodies with the efficacy of cytotoxic agents (de Lázaro and Mooney, 2021). ADCs facilitate the targeted delivery of a cytotoxic agent to cancer cells by conjugating a monoclonal antibody with a chemical linker, thereby reducing damage to healthy tissues and improving therapy efficacy. ADCs are an innovative strategy for targeted cancer treatment and are expected to serve as alternatives to conventional chemotherapeutic drugs in the future (Drago et al., 2021; Hafeez et al., 2020; Mullard, 2023).

ADCs have a monoclonal antibody (mAb), a cytotoxic payload, and a linker for the formation of drug conjugates (Tsuchikama et al., 2024). The antibody part of the ADC binds to the antigen on the tumor cells. After that, receptor-mediated endocytosis delivers the ADC-antigen complex into the cell. The linker is cut inside the cell, or the antibody is broken down, which lets the cytotoxic chemical out. This drug kills cells by disrupting DNA or breaking down microtubules. ADCs have worked well for treating cancer, especially blood malignancies and some solid tumors (Tsuchikama et al., 2024; Fosgerau and Hoffmann, 2015). These conjugates enhance the selectivity, stability, and pharmacokinetic characteristics of monoclonal antibody. Antibody-drug conjugates (ADCs) are an innovative strategy for targeted cancer treatment and are expected to serve as alternatives to conventional chemotherapeutic drugs in the future (Drago et al., 2021; Hafeez et al., 2020; Mullard, 2023).

Peptide-drug conjugates (PDCs)

Peptide-drug conjugates (PDCs) are a new type of targeted therapy that employs small peptides to detect tumors and send powerful medications right to cancer cells. Peptides are smaller and more flexible than antibodies, which usually makes it easier for them to get into solid tumors (Fosgerau and Hoffmann, 2015; Krall et al., 2013). They don't usually cause immunological reactions, which makes them a good choice in some situations. This strategic conjugation presents multiple potential benefits, such as improved tissue infiltration, less immunogenicity, and streamlined production procedures (Leamon and Low, 2001). Notwithstanding the considerable specificity and efficacy of ADCs, obstacles including their substantial size, elevated immunogenicity, intricate manufacturing procedures, and restricted tissue penetration have prompted the investigation of alternate delivery strategies, PDCs (Demeule et al., 2024). They exhibit structural parallels with ADCs, consisting of three fundamental components: the targeting peptide, linker, and cytotoxic payload. PDCs have arisen as a viable therapeutic strategy, especially in oncology, seeking to address the shortcomings of ADCs while preserving the advantages of targeted drug delivery (Zhou et al., 2021).

Small molecule-drug conjugates (SMDCs)

Small molecule-drug conjugates (SMDCs) are garnering heightened interest as a viable alternative to antibodies for drug delivery and tumor-targeting applications due to their superior tumor penetration, in contrast to high-molecular-weight ADCs (Zhuang et al., 2019). This generally comprises a targeted ligand, a spacer, a cleavable linker, and a therapeutic payload. The ratio of payload to small-molecule-targeting ligands in the formulation of SMDCs is more meticulously regulated than that of ADCs (Srinivasarao et al., 2015). Additionally, SMDCs exhibit advantages like facile synthesis and a non-immunogenic characteristic. The molecular weights of SMDCs are generally low, which may augment cell permeability in solid tumors and enhance stability both in vitro and in vivo. The diminutive size of SMDCs is the principal factor contributing to their exceedingly brief half-life in circulation, hence restricting their progressive accumulation in tumors and undermining their therapeutic effectiveness.

Inorganic NP-drug conjugate

Inorganic nanoparticle-drug conjugates are an innovative technique that involve use of nanoparticles consisting of metals or other inorganic materials as pharmaceutical carriers. Such nanoparticles can improve the delivery of anticancer drugs as well as provide additional benefits, such as imaging or photothermal effects (Li et al., 2012; Dreaden et al., 2011). Additionally, these nanoparticles can exert therapeutic action, providing a synergistic or additional therapeutic effect with anticancer drugs (Gupta and Gupta, 2005). Example: inorganic nanoparticles like gold, silver, graphene-based, hydroxyapatite, iron oxide, ZnO, and CeO_2 nanoparticles as drug carrier systems (Unnikrishnan et al., 2023). These function as the core of a carrier, an imaging agent, or even a photothermal or photodynamic instrument, depending on the application. The anticancer drugs are usually conjugated to the surface of inorganic nanoparticles to facilitate the delivery, or can be encapsulated within nanoparticles.

Strategy for designing drug conjugates

Effective drug conjugation necessitates resilient linker strategies to optimize drug delivery to cancer cells. The linker serves as a conduit between the carrier and payload, and its configuration must confer unique characteristics that ensure optimal selectivity and biological efficacy (Kovtun et al., 2006). A linker typically possesses two reactive groups: linker-

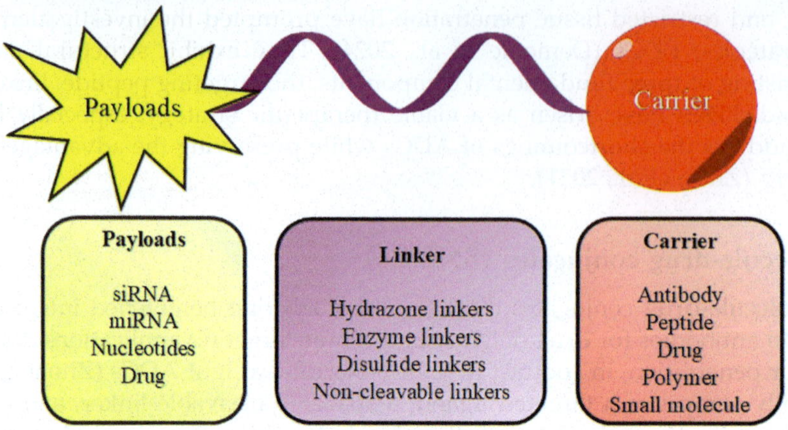

FIGURE 10.2 Design of drug conjugates.

carrier and linker-payload interactions. An ideal linker should be water-soluble to facilitate bioconjugation, not affect the carrier's affinity for its receptor, and prevent the development of inactive aggregates. Also, the attachment of the linker with the payload and carrier must be stable and ensure persistent payload retention in circulation to prevent premature release (Burton et al., 2020; Staudacher and Brown, 2017) Fig. 10.2.

Cleavable linkers

Cleavable linkers are engineered to discharge the payload into target cells in response to specific tumor-associated physiological stimuli, like low pH, elevated glutathione (GSH) levels, or hydrolytic enzymes. They typically enhance the bystander effect and are preferred in the development of drug conjugates, particularly antibody-drug conjugates (ADCs), that target antigens expressed heterogeneously in malignancies. Nonetheless, cleavable linkers demonstrate differing levels of stability in circulation (Staudacher and Brown, 2017).

Acid-cleavable linkers/hydrazone linkages

Tumor tissues typically exhibit inadequate food and oxygen supply, resulting in the accumulation of substantial lactic acid via anaerobic glycolysis. The acidic tumor microenvironment (TME) with a pH of 6.5–6.9 facilitates the cleavage of acid-sensitive linkers, thereby releasing payloads in acidic cellular compartments while ensuring stability in neutral blood circulation (Mollaev et al., 2019). The predominant acid-sensitive or pH-sensitive linker employed in conjugate design is hydrazone. Hydrazones exhibit minimal or no breakdown at neutral pH; however, the bond readily decomposes at a lower pH. Consequently, the breaking of the hydrazone link occurs under acidic conditions, specifically in tumor cells with a pH of 6-8 and in endosomes with a pH of 4-6 (Ziaei et al., 2019).

Disulfide linkers

Disulfide bonds remain stable in extracellular environments, but they undergo cleavage following cellular uptake due to intracellular conditions or being vulnerable to nucleophilic attack from thiols (Bernardes et al., 2012). The levels of antioxidants in the cytoplasm are greater than those found in plasma. Additionally, GSH levels in cancer cells might be higher than in normal cells as a result of hypoxia and oxidative stress within the tumor microenvironment. Therefore, the highly reductive environment of tumor cells can promote the release of the payload connected to a disulfide linker within cancer cells (Forman et al., 2009).

Enzyme cleavable linkers

Enzyme-cleavable ester or amide bonds are favored as linkers in the construction of therapeutic conjugates because of their preferential intracellular cleavage in the tumor microenvironment. Certain intracellular compartments of cancer cells, including endosomes and lysosomes, are abundant in enzymes like esterases and amidases, whose control can be utilized for the targeted release of payloads. Linker structures comprise dipeptide-containing linkers, as well as galactosidase and phosphatase, among others (Dal Corso et al., 2019).

Peptide-based linkers, or lysosomal protease-sensitive linkers, function through intracellular proteases by specifically targeting cathepsin B, which is frequently associated with tumor growth, exhibiting overexpression and extracellular activity in numerous malignancies. Cathepsin B identifies and cleaves a dipeptide link, releasing the payloads. Peptide-based linkers are predominantly utilized in drug conjugate construction owing to their serum stability and fast payload release in tumor cells (Dubowchik et al., 1998).

Glycosidases, including β-glucuronidases, are a category of hydrolytic lysosomal enzymes exclusively located in the lysosomal compartment of cells. They catalyze the degradation of β-glucuronic acid residues into polysaccharides, facilitating the release of payloads from conjugates in hydrophilic environments. This method is utilized in the covalent attachment of many kinds of cytotoxic drugs to carriers through a β-glucuronide linker (Tranoy-Opalinski et al., 2014).

Non-cleavable linkers

Non-cleavable linkers have greater stability in plasma. They have been utilized for the fabrication of drug conjugates. Non-cleavable linkers, upon arriving at tumor sites, depend on lysosomal degradation of the complete carrier-linker structures to liberate the payloads, which can accumulate within tumor cells without permeating the cell membrane, thereby providing an enhanced therapeutic window (Tang et al., 2019). This technique has demonstrated success in two FDA-approved ADCs, trastuzumab emtansine and belantamab mafodotin, due to the previously described advantages (Keam, 2020; Markham and Mafodotin, 2020).

Advancements in drug conjugates

Synergistic delivery of chemotherapeutics

Drug conjugates amplify the synergistic effects of medications, increasing therapeutic efficacy and minimizing systemic toxicity. This method deviates from the conventional approach of drug distribution, which typically entails administering a singular chemical via injection. Synergy occurs when multiple drugs interact on distinct yet interconnected metabolic pathways. Conjugates of pharmaceuticals and polymers can amalgamate chemotherapy with photodynamic or photothermal therapy to create innovative medicines; examples of such conjugates include paclitaxel-doxorubicin and irinotecan-chlorambucil. These designs are particularly beneficial for overcoming multidrug resistance (MDR), minimizing off-target toxicity, and facilitating personalized combination therapy.

Stimuli-responsive delivery of anti-cancer drugs

To address the issues posed by traditional drug delivery systems, such as the delayed release of the charged drugs or the inability to fuse with the endosome post-internalization (Gupta et al., 2023). The stimulus-sensitive nanocarriers preserve their stealth characteristics throughout circulation and undergo rapid alterations upon reaching the designated tumor site and target (Singh et al., 2023). Drug retention in nanocarriers can also be resolved by means of external stimuli that enable targeted and regulated drug release to the targeted tumor cells. A variety of site-specific methodologies were analyzed for drug release, encompassing internal stimuli from the tumor microenvironment (low pH, redox sensitivity, elevated temperature, and enzymes) as well as exterior stimuli such as magnetic fields and light.

pH-responsive

The synthesis of environment-responsive nanoparticles aims to both boost plasma stability and improve drugs retention within tumor cells by potentially releasing the drug in response to stimuli such as pH. pH-sensitive stimuli are frequently employed due to significant variations in pH within biological systems. The tumor's extracellular environment has a much lower pH (5.8–6.5) compared to blood (pH 7.2), whereas the pH of the endosome is even lower (5.0–5.5). Similarly, the pH sensitivity of nanoparticles for endosomal lysis is crucial for effective intracellular delivery of antineoplastic drugs (Marwaha et al., 2025). Zhao et al. developed a pH-sensitive conjugate of oleic acid and doxorubicin hydrochloride. An ionic conjugate was synthesized utilizing oleic acid as an ion-pairing agent. The ion pair demonstrated stability at pH 7.4 instead of $pH < 7$, facilitating increased drug accumulation at the target region while preserving normal tissues. The conjugation improved stability and trapping efficiency, as well as pH-dependent drug release of doxorubicin. The results indicated this as a tumor-specific drug delivery method for doxorubicin as shown in Fig. 10.3 (Zhao et al., 2016).

Redox-sensitive

The insights gained from redox-active polymers, dendrimers, and monolayers utilized for molecular capture and/or release have significantly enhanced these systems. The essence of research on redox-stimulated content delivery from molecular assemblies or aggregates is in the breakdown of the aggregate structure into individual amphiphile monomers, thereby exposing the contents to the surrounding medium (Marwaha et al., 2023; McCarley, 2012). Wang et al. synthesized self-assembled nanoparticles by conjugating cabazitaxel to

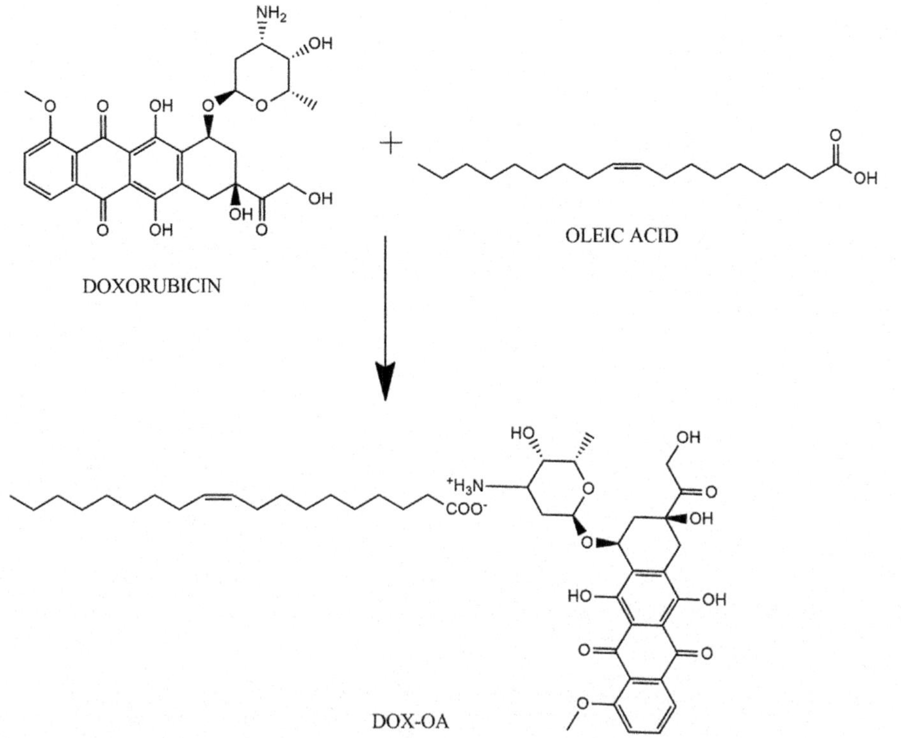

FIGURE 10.3 Doxorubicin (DOX) and oleic acid (OA) conjugation DOX-OA.

citronellol through a disulfide link that is redox-sensitive to elevated glutathione levels in intracellular cancer cells. These nanospherical micelles, featuring disulfide linkers, exhibited stability in systemic circulation and facilitated the release of cabazitaxel within intracellular tumor cells via a thiol-disulfide exchange process. These conjugated nano-assemblies can address toxicity concerns, augment drug loading capacity, and facilitate the release of cabazitaxel into tumor cells more effectively than the drug alone. Du et al. developed redox-sensitive lipid drug-conjugated nanoparticles of camptothecin with palmitic acid. Camptothecin, a chemotherapeutic drug, is restricted for oral administration due to its inadequate bioavailability. This conjugate was synthesized via disulfide linkage and assessed for drug release at varying pH levels. In vitro investigations (cytotoxicity, cellular uptake, confocal laser scanning microscopy) were conducted on Caco-2 cells, whereas in vivo pharmacokinetic assessments were executed to evaluate oral bioavailability. Consequently, redox-sensitive conjugation led to improved bioavailability and is regarded as an efficient oral transport mechanism for camptothecin, as shown in Fig. 10.4 (Du et al., 2018).

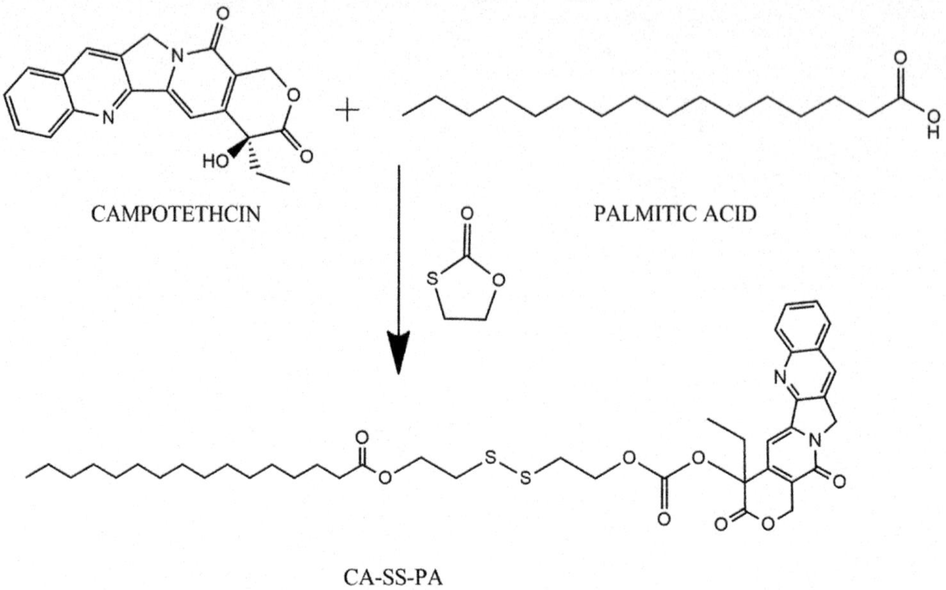

FIGURE 10.4 Camptothecin (CA) and palmitic acid (PA) conjugation CA–SS–PA.

Transport and drug release mechanism of drug-conjugates

Transport of the drug conjugate across the biological membrane or barrier to reach the target site can follow multiple pathways. This depends on the type of drug conjugate and its composition, specific to the polymeric chemistry and materials in drug conjugates (He et al., 2024). For cancer-targeted drug delivery, the drug conjugate should be capable of releasing the drug near tumor tissues in the tumor microenvironment or inside the cancer cells. For this, two kinds of linkers, that is, cleavable and non-cleavable linkers, can be used between the drug and polymer. For example, antibody-drug conjugates have been seen to contain non-cleavable linkers, such as thioether linkers. The polypeptide backbone of the antibody can be hydrolyzed in cell lysosomes to release the drug (Feng and Tong, 2016). For pH-sensitive drug conjugates, the slightly acidic pH of tumor tissue (pH 6.7–7.0) and endosomal intracellular compartments (pH 4.5–6.5) works as a trigger to initiate the drug release. Cis-aconityl amide, hydrazone, imine, oxime, acetal/ketal/orthoester, and other groups like trityl, N-ethoxybenzylimidazoles, thiopropionate, and silyl ether are a few pH-sensitive bonds in drug conjugates that have been developed (Wang et al., 2012; Ge and Liu, 2013). drdug conjugates responsive to differences in redox potential between normal and malignant tissues, as well as between the intracellular and external environments, can also be developed. The concentration of glutathione, a reducing tripeptide with a thiol group, is 100–1000 times higher in cancer cells than in blood, and 100-fold in a tumor mass than in normal tissue. The research revealed that tumor tissues in mice had a glutathione level that was four times higher than that of normal tissues, and that the redox state of the tumor tissue varied significantly and thus can be exploited in drug delivery

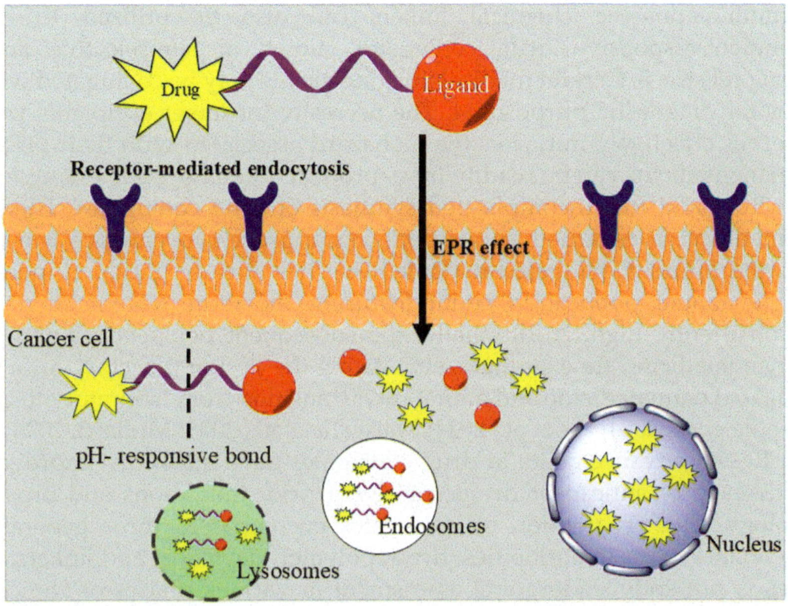

FIGURE 10.5 **Drug release mechanism from drug conjugates.** The major steps involved in drug release from drug conjugates include cellular interaction (binding of drug conjugates at cell surface), cellular internalization (endocytic uptake) and release or free drug for exerting theraputic action.

(Kuppusamy et al., 2002). Additionally, elevated expression of local enzymes in cancer, such as MMP, can also be exploited for enzyme-triggered drug release in tumors from MMP-responsive drug-polymer conjugates. The short peptide GFLG, which is unique to capthepsin B, was discovered in early research on in-depth degradation investigation of oligopeptide sequences connected to polyHPMA-based drug conjugates (Fig. 10.5) (Rejmanová et al., 1983).

Nanotechnology-enhanced drug conjugates

Nanotechnology is considered the forthcoming revolution poised to impact multiple industrial sectors, including biomedicine. Nanomedicine for cancer treatment has made significant advancements in recent decades. Nanomedicine, owing to its distinctive physical and chemical features, might augment the pharmacokinetics of pharmaceuticals by enhancing their stability, solubility, penetration potential, systemic circulation, half-life, and targeting capability, overcoming drug resistance and ultimately improving chemotherapeutic efficiency. Conjugated nanomedicine, composed of drug conjugates linked by chemical connectors, has garnered increased interest for its distinctive potential in cancer therapy in various ways: 1) It enhances the delivery of chemotherapeutic agents to the desired site. Nanomedicine, consisting of hydrophilic as well as hydrophobic materials, can encapsulate and deliver both hydrophilic and lipophilic chemotherapeutics to tumor cells. 2) Conjugated nanomedicines can achieve passive and active targeting through incorporated targeting ligands.

Various stimuli-responsive chemical linkers can also be utilized to create smart microenvironment-responsive drug conjugates, aimed at site-selective and stimulus-regulated drug release. 3. Certain medical imaging agents may be conjugated with therapeutic medicines for diagnostic purposes. 4. The necessity for fewer excipients without therapeutic properties effectively mitigates the biohazard associated with their breakdown. The conjugated nanomedicine can be readily mass-produced in large scale owing to its straightforward structure and the uncomplicated synthesis of drug conjugates. Therefore, conjugated nanomedicine is regarded as a promising approach to enhance cancer treatment outcomes in the future. Conjugated nanomedicine has already garnered increasing attention, with the annual publication count featuring the term "conjugate nanomedicine" remaining consistently high. Additionally, the subsequent perspectives and problems of conjugated nanomedicine are examined, elucidating the design trajectory for a new generation of conjugated nanomedicine and aiding their transition from laboratory to clinical application (Demeule et al., 2024; He et al., 2024; Marwaha et al., 2025; Mullard, 2023; Tsuchikama et al., 2024). Recent advancements in drug conjugates have markedly improved the therapeutic effectiveness of anticancer drugs, resolving prior limitations and broadening their use in oncology. The progression of conjugates encompasses three generations, distinguished by enhancements in antibodies/drug/polymer, payloads, and linkers. A multitude of conjugates is presently undergoing assessment in various phases of clinical trials, and some are FDA approved, indicating the sustained progress of this targeted therapeutic strategy for cancer treatment (Table 10.1).

TABLE 10.1 List of drug conjugates under clinical trials or FDA approved.

Name	Target	Payloads	Cancer/Tumor types	Company	Approval year
Loncastuximab tesirine (zynlonta)	CD19	Loncastuximab	Diffuse large B-cell lympoma	ADC therapeutics	2021
Distamab vedotin (aidixi)	HER2	Disitamab	Urothelial cancer	RemeGen	2021
Tisotumab vedotin (tivdak)	TF	Tisotumab	Cervical cancer	Seagen	2021
Mirvetuximab soravtansine (elahere)	FRα	Mirvetuximab	Ovarian cancer	ImmunoGen	2022
Datopotamab deruxtecan	TROP-2	Datroway	Breast cancer	AstraZeneca/ Daiichi sankyo	2025
Telisotuzumab vedotin	c-Met	EMRELIS	Non- small lung cancer	AbbVie	2025
Melfufen (pepaxto)	Aminopeptidase	Melphalan	Relapsed or refractory multiple myeloma	Oncopeptides AB	2021

TABLE 10.1 List of drug conjugates under clinical trials or FDA approved.—cont'd

Name	Target	Payloads	Cancer/Tumor types	Company	Approval year
ANG-1005	Low-desnsity lipoprotein receptor	Paclitaxel	Different types of cancer		Phase III
NGR-Htnf	Aminopeptidase N	hTNF	Malignant pleural		Phase III
CBX-12	TOP1	Exatecan	Different types of cancer		Phase I/II
BT8009	Nectin-4	Monomethyl auristatin E	Different types of cancer		Phase I/II
BT-1718	Metalloproteinase 14	Maytansine derivative	Solid tumor		Phase I/II
BTP-277	SSTR2	Maytansine derivative	Endocrine cancer and small cell lung cancer		Phase I/II
G-202	PSMA	Thapsigargin	Solid tumors		Phase II
CBP-1008	FRα	Monomethyl auristatin E	Advanced solid tumors		Phase I
TH-1902	Sortilin receptor	Docetaxel	Different types of cancer		Phase I
SOZR-C13	Transient receptor potential cation channel subfamily V member	Monomethyl auristatin E	Solid tumors		Phase I
PEN-866	Heat shock protein	SN-38	Solid tumors		Phase II
177Lu-PSMA-617	PSMA	177Lu	Prostate cancer		Phase II
Epofolate	FR	Epothilone	Solid tumors		Phase II
EC1456	FR	Tubulysin	Solid tumors		Phase I
EC1169	PSMA	Tubulysin	Prostate cancer		Phase I
EC0489	FR	Vinblastine	Solid tumors		Phase I
EC0225	FR	Mitomycin C	Solid tumors		Phase I
PEN-221	Somatostatin receptor 2	Maytansine derivative	Solid tumors		Phase I

Conclusion and future perspectives

The design of drug conjugates is a novel approach for the treatment of cancer, as it can make treatments more precise, site-specific, improving biodistribution, pharmacokinetics, and pharmacodynamics, as well as mitigating the harmful adverse effects of anticancer drugs. It involved affixing chemotherapeutics to specific ligands, such as antibodies, peptides, small molecules, polymers, nanoparticles, or photosensitizers, to specify their transport. In recent decades, there has been an unparalleled growth in the treatment of cancer through drug-conjugate approaches. The tremendous advancements in bioengineering and conjugation technologies have facilitated the development of innovative drug conjugates with enhanced efficacy and a wide spectrum of targetability towards various malignancies. Further research should be done to improve conjugation characteristics, encompassing the precise selection of structural components for synthesis, the optimization and correlation of the physicochemical properties of the conjugates, and the identification of specific biomarkers to forecast conjugate efficacy, thereby facilitating clinical translation. Despite numerous challenges, conjugates possess the potential to improve the efficacy of existing anticancer treatment modalities, thereby providing improved clinical outcomes for patients with diverse cancer types, particularly those with prior treatment failures, a lack of standard therapies, or drug resistance. Drug conjugates with immunotherapy, radiation therapy, or gene therapy can elicit clinical responses that are long-lasting and avoid cancer relapse. Artificial intelligence (AI) and machine learning (ML) assisted computer models can be employed to examine drug and ligand interactions with one another, as well as determine linker chemistry functioning, to expedite the search for novel conjugates. In conclusion, drug conjugates represent a significant advancement in the delivery of anticancer medications. They can provide precision oncology to tailor the treatment as per tumor type and location. Drug conjugates are thus cutting-edge new strategies for targeted therapy of cancer.

References

Bernardes, G.J.L., Casi, G., Trüssel, S., Hartmann, I., Schwager, K., Jörg, S., Neri, D., 2012. A traceless vascular-targeting antibody–drug conjugate for cancer therapy. Angew. Chem. Int. Ed. 51 (4), 941–944. https://doi.org/10.1002/anie.201106527.

Burton, J.K., Bottino, D., Secomb, T.W., 2020. A systems pharmacology model for drug delivery to solid tumors by antibody-drug conjugates: Implications for bystander effects. AAPS J. 22 (1). https://doi.org/10.1208/s12248-019-0390-2. h.springerlink.com/content/1550-7416/.

Dal Corso, A., Pignataro, L., Belvisi, L., Gennari, C., 2019. Innovative linker strategies for tumor-targeted drug conjugates. Chem. Eur J. 25 (65), 14740–14757. https://doi.org/10.1002/chem.201903127.

de Lázaro, I., Mooney, D.J., 2021. Obstacles and opportunities in a forward vision for cancer nanomedicine. nature research. Nat. Mater. 20 (11), 1469–1479. https://doi.org/10.1038/s41563-021-01047-7.

Demeule, M., Currie, J.-C., Charfi, C., Zgheib, A., Cousineau, I., Lullier, V., Béliveau, R., Marsolais, C., Annabi, B., Zendusortide, S., 2024. TH1902) triggers the cGAS/STING pathway and potentiates anti-PD-L1 immune-mediated tumor cell killing. Front. Immunol. 15. https://doi.org/10.3389/fimmu.2024.1355945.

Dreaden, E.C., Mac key, M.A., Huang, X., Kang, B., El-Sayed, M.A., 2011. Beating cancer in multiple ways using nanogold. Chem. Soc. Rev. 40 (7), 3391–3404. https://doi.org/10.1039/c0cs00180e.

Drago, J.Z., Modi, S., Chandarlapaty, S., 2021. Unlocking the potential of antibody–drug conjugates for cancer therapy. Nat. Rev. Clin. Oncol. 18 (6), 327–344. https://doi.org/10.1038/s41571-021-00470-8.

Du, Y., Ling, L., Ismail, M., He, W., Xia, Q., Zhou, W., Yao, C., Li, X., 2018. Redox sensitive lipid-camptothecin conjugate encapsulated solid lipid nanoparticles for oral delivery. Int. J. Pharm. 549 (1–2), 352–362. https://doi.org/10.1016/j.ijpharm.2018.08.010.

Dubowchik, G.M., Mosure, K., Knipe, J.O., Firestone, R.A., 1998. Cathepsin B-sensitive dipeptide prodrugs. 2. models of anticancer drugs paclitaxel (taxol), mitomycin C and doxorubicin. Bioorg. Med. Chem. Lett. 8 (23), 3347–3352. https://doi.org/10.1016/S0960-894X(98)00610-6.

Duncan, R., 2006. Polymer conjugates as anticancer nanomedicines. Nat. Rev. Cancer 6 (9), 688–701. https://doi.org/10.1038/nrc1958.

Feng, Q., Tong, R., 2016. Anticancer nanoparticulate polymer-drug conjugate. Bioeng. Transl. Med. 1 (3), 277–296. https://doi.org/10.1002/btm2.10033.

Forman, H.J., Zhang, H., Rinna, A., 2009. Glutathione: Overview of its protective roles, measurement, and biosynthesis. Mol. Aspect. Med. 30 (1–2), 1–12. https://doi.org/10.1016/j.mam.2008.08.006.

Fosgerau, K., Hoffmann, T., 2015. Peptide therapeutics: Current status and future directions. Drug Discov. Today 20 (1), 122–128. https://doi.org/10.1016/j.drudis.2014.10.003.

Ge, Z., Liu, S., 2013. Functional block copolymer assemblies responsive to tumor and intracellular microenvironments for site-specific drug delivery and enhanced imaging performance. Chem. Soc. Rev. 42 (17), 7289–7325. https://doi.org/10.1039/c3cs60048c.

Gupta, A.K., Gupta, M., 2005. Synthesis and surface engineering of iron oxide nanoparticles for biomedical applications. Biomaterials 26 (18), 3995–4021. https://doi.org/10.1016/j.biomaterials.2004.10.012.

Gupta, P., Sharma, S., Raj Neupane, Y., Khan, Z., Ahmad, S., Emad, N.A., Aqil, M., Kohli, K., Sultana, Y., 2023. Co-delivery of exemestane and thymoquinone via nanostructured lipid carriers for efficient breast cancer therapy. J. Drug Deliv. Sci. Technol. 88, 104892. https://doi.org/10.1016/j.jddst.2023.104892.

Hafeez, U., Parakh, S., Gan, H.K., 2020. Andrew M. scott, antibody–drug conjugates for cancer therapy. Molecules 25 (20), 4764. https://doi.org/10.3390/molecules25204764.

He, J., Zeng, X., Wang, C., Wang, E., Li, Y., 2024. Antibody–drug conjugates in cancer therapy: Mechanisms and clinical studies. MedComm. 5 (8). https://doi.org/10.1002/mco2.671.

Keam, S.J., 2020. Trastuzumab deruxtecan: First approval. Drugs 80 (5), 501–508. https://doi.org/10.1007/s40265-020-01281-4.

Kovtun, Y.V., Audette, C.A., Ye, Y., Xie, H., Ruberti, M.F., Phinney, S.J., Leece, B.A., Chittenden, T., Blättler, W.A., Goldmacher, V.S., 2006. Antibody-drug conjugates designed to eradicate tumors with homogeneous and heterogeneous expression of the target antigen. Cancer Res. 66 (6), 3214–3221. https://doi.org/10.1158/0008-5472.CAN-05-3973.

Krall, N., Scheuermann, J., Neri, D., 2013. Small targeted cytotoxics: Current state and promises from DNA-encoded chemical libraries. Angew. Chem. Int. Ed. Engl. 52 (5), 1384–1402. https://doi.org/10.1002/anie.201204631.

Kuppusamy, P., Li, H., Ilangovan, G., Cardounel, A.J., Zweier, J.L., Yamada, K., Krishna, M.C., Mitchell, J.B., 2002. Noninvasive imaging of tumor redox status and its modification by tissue glutathione levels. Cancer Res. 62 (1), 307–312.

Lammers, T., Kiessling, F., Ashford, M., Hennink, W., Crommelin, D., Storm, G., 2016. Cancer nanomedicine: Is targeting our target? Nat. Rev. Mater. 1 (9). https://doi.org/10.1038/natrevmats.2016.69.

Leamon, C.P., Low, P.S., 2001. Folate-mediated targeting: From diagnostics to drug and gene delivery. Drug Discov. Today 6 (1), 44–51. https://doi.org/10.1016/S1359-6446(00)01594-4.

Li, Z., Barnes, J.C., Bosoy, A., Stoddart, J.F., Zink, J.I., 2012. Mesoporous silica nanoparticles in biomedical applications. Chem. Soc. Rev. 41 (7), 2590–2605. https://doi.org/10.1039/c1cs15246g.

Maeda, H., 2015. Toward a full understanding of the EPR effect in primary and metastatic tumors as well as issues related to its heterogeneity. Adv. Drug Deliv. Rev. 91, 3–6. https://doi.org/10.1016/j.addr.2015.01.002.

Marwaha, D., Gautam, S., Singh, N., Rai, N., Sharma, M., Tiwari, P., Shukla, R.P., Urandur, S., Banala, V.T., Mugale, M.N., Kumar, A., Mishra, P.R., 2023. Synergistic delivery of imatinib through multifunctional nanocrystalline capsules, in response to redox environment for improved breast cancer therapy. Colloids Surf. B Biointerfaces 226, 113316. https://doi.org/10.1016/j.colsurfb.2023.113316.

Marwaha, D., Singh, N., Gautam, S., Rai, N., Tiwari, P., Kumar Bakshi, A., Kumar, A., Agarwal, N., Sharma, M., Shukla, R.P., Mishra, P.R., 2025. Pemetrexed-loaded supramolecular acetal-functionalized pH-responsive nanocarriers selectively induce apoptosis through biotin receptors to enhance antitumor efficacy. Colloids Surf. B Biointerfaces 245, 114247. https://doi.org/10.1016/j.colsurfb.2024.114247.

Markham, A., Mafodotin, B., 2020. First approval. Drugs 80 (15), 1607–1613. https://doi.org/10.1007/s40265-020-01404-x.

McCarley, R.L., 2012. Redox-responsive delivery systems. Annu. Rev. Anal. Chem. 5 (1), 391–411. https://doi.org/10.1146/annurev-anchem-062011-143157.

Mollaev, M., Gorokhovets, N., Nikolskaya, E., Faustova, M., Zabolotsky, A., Zhunina, O., Sokol, M., Zamulaeva, I., Severin, E., Yabbarov, N., 2019. Type of pH sensitive linker reveals different time-dependent intracellular localization, in vitro and in vivo efficiency in alpha-fetoprotein receptor targeted doxorubicin conjugate. Int. J. Pharm. 559, 138–146. https://doi.org/10.1016/j.ijpharm.2018.12.073.

Mullard, A., 2023. FDA approvals. Nat. Rev. Drug Discov. 23 (2), 88–95. https://doi.org/10.1038/d41573-024-00001-x.

Rejmanová, P., Kopeček, J., Pohl, J., Baudyš, M., Kostka, V., 1983. Polymers containing enzymatically degradable bonds, 8. degradation of oligopeptide sequences in N -(2-hydroxypropyl) methacrylamide copolymers by bovine spleen cathepsin B. Makromol. Chem. 184 (10), 2009–2020. https://doi.org/10.1002/macp.1983.021841006.

Singh, N., Marwaha, D., Gautam, S., Rai, N., Tiwari, P., Sharma, M., Shukla, R.P., Mugale, M.N., Kumar, A., Mishra, P.R., 2023. Surface-modified lyotropic crystalline nanoconstructs bearing doxorubicin and buparvaquone target sigma receptors through pH-sensitive charge conversion to improve breast cancer therapy. Biomacromolecules 24 (12), 5780–5796. https://doi.org/10.1021/acs.biomac.3c00795.

Srinivasarao, M., Galliford, C.V., Low, P.S., 2015. Principles in the design of ligand-targeted cancer therapeutics and imaging agents. Nat. Rev. Drug Discov. 14 (3), 203–219. https://doi.org/10.1038/nrd4519.

Staudacher, A.H., Brown, M.P., 2017. Antibody drug conjugates and bystander killing: Is antigen-dependent internalisation required. Br. J. Cancer 117 (12), 1736–1742. https://doi.org/10.1038/bjc.2017.367.

Tang, H., Liu, Y., Yu, Z., Sun, M., Lin, L., Liu, W., Han, Q., Wei, M., Jin, Y., 2019. The analysis of key factors related to ADCs structural design. Front. Pharmacol. 10. https://doi.org/10.3389/fphar.2019.00373.

Tranoy-Opalinski, I., Legigan, T., Barat, R., Clarhaut, J., Thomas, M., Renoux, B., Papot, S., 2014. β-Glucuronidase-responsive prodrugs for selective cancer chemotherapy: An update. Eur. J. Med. Chem. 74, 302–313. https://doi.org/10.1016/j.ejmech.2013.12.045.

Tsuchikama, K., Anami, Y., Ha, S.Y.Y., Yamazaki, C.M., 2024. Exploring the next generation of antibody–drug conjugates. Nat. Rev. Clin. Oncol. 21 (3), 203–223. https://doi.org/10.1038/s41571-023-00850-2.

Unnikrishnan, G., Joy, A., Megha, M., Kolanthai, E., Senthilkumar, M., 2023. Exploration of inorganic nanoparticles for revolutionary drug delivery applications: A critical review. Discov. Nano 18 (1). https://doi.org/10.1186/s11671-023-03943-0. h.springer.com/journal/11671.

Wang, Y., Byrne, J.D., Napier, M.E., DeSimone, J.M., 2012. Engineering nanomedicines using stimuli-responsive biomaterials. Adv. Drug Deliv. Rev. 64 (11), 1021–1030. https://doi.org/10.1016/j.addr.2012.01.003.

Zhao, S., Van Minh, Le, Li, N., Garamus, V.M., Handge, U.A., Liu, J., Zhang, R., Willumeit-Römer, R., Zou, A., 2016. Doxorubicin hydrochloride-oleic acid conjugate loaded nanostructured lipid carriers for tumor specific drug release. Colloids Surf. B Biointerfaces 145, 95–103. https://doi.org/10.1016/j.colsurfb.2016.04.027.

Zhuang, C., Guan, X., Ma, H., Cong, H., Zhang, W., Miao, Z., 2019. Small molecule-drug conjugates: A novel strategy for cancer-targeted treatment. Eur. J. Med. Chem. 163, 883–895. https://doi.org/10.1016/j.ejmech.2018.12.035.

Zhou, X., Smith, Q.R., Liu, X., 2021. Brain penetrating peptides and peptide–drug conjugates to overcome the blood–brain barrier and target CNS diseases. Wiley Interdiscip. Rev. Nanomed. Nanobiotechnol. 13 (4). https://doi.org/10.1002/wnan.1695. http://onlinelibrary.wiley.com/journal/10.1002/(ISSN)1939-0041.

Ziaei, E., Saghaeidehkordi, A., Dill, C., Maslennikov, I., Chen, S., Kaur, K., 2019. Targeting triple negative breast cancer cells with novel cytotoxic peptide–doxorubicin conjugates. Bioconjug. Chem. 30 (12), 3098–3106. https://doi.org/10.1021/acs.bioconjchem.9b00755.

CHAPTER

11

Self-assembled supramolecular systems for anticancer drug delivery

Radhika Baheti[1,2], *Vinita Patole*[1,2], *Vinay Chopada*[1,2], *Madhu Kumawat*[1,2] *and Sanjeevani Deshkar*[1,2]

[1]School of Pharmacy and Research, Dnyaan Prasad Global University - Dr. D. Y. Patil Unitech Society, Pune, Maharashtra, India; [2]Dr. D. Y. Patil Institute of Pharmaceutical Sciences and Research, Department of Pharmaceutics, Pune, Maharashtra, India

Introduction

Cancer remains a leading cause of death worldwide despite significant advances in treatment modalities. While conventional therapies, including surgery, chemotherapy, and radiation, have improved patient outcomes, they suffer from fundamental limitations that compromise therapeutic efficacy and patient quality of life. Traditional chemotherapeutic agents exhibit poor tumor selectivity, causing severe systemic toxicity. Antimitotic drugs often induce severe peripheral neuropathy, while systemic chemotherapy frequently leads to gastrointestinal complications and hematologic disorders that may cause treatment delays or discontinuation (Veselov et al., 2022). Moreover, the inevitable development of drug resistance, driven by genetic mutations and tumor heterogeneity, further limits long-term therapeutic success. These challenges are compounded by inherent pharmacokinetic limitations of conventional formulations, including poor aqueous solubility, rapid systemic degradation, and non-specific biodistribution patterns (Nammas, 2025). The urgent clinical need for more precise and effective therapeutic strategies has driven the development of advanced drug delivery systems that can optimize pharmacokinetic profiles while enabling tumor-specific targeting. Inspired by biological systems such as protein folding and membrane formation, supramolecular self-assembly utilizes weak but cooperative forces, including hydrogen bonding, π-π stacking, electrostatic attractions, and hydrophobic interactions, to spontaneously organize molecular building blocks into complex, functional nanostructures. This approach enables the rational design of “smart” nanocarriers that demonstrate exceptional modularity, environmental responsiveness, and the ability to

Advanced Cancer Therapeutics
https://doi.org/10.1016/B978-0-443-44185-1.00020-3

encapsulate poorly soluble therapeutic agents while protecting them from premature degradation (Wang et al., 2022). Besides their passive targeting and stimuli-responsive release, self-assembled supramolecular drug delivery systems provide several significant advantages over traditional chemotherapy formulations. Their modular and adaptable structures allow customization of size, surface properties, and release profiles to match different drug cargos and tumor types. At the same time, cooperative host–guest interactions enable high drug loading capacities. Encasing drugs within supramolecular cores improves the water solubility and stability of poorly soluble therapeutics, and direct intracellular delivery at high local concentrations helps to overcome multidrug resistance mechanisms (Rahim et al., 2021). Additionally, many supramolecular components—such as Cyclodextrins (CDs), peptide assemblies, and lipid-based amphiphiles are naturally biocompatible and biodegradable, supporting safe metabolism and elimination. Overall, these features lead to better therapeutic effectiveness, less off-target toxicity, and the potential for personalized, precision oncology treatments.

Core molecular interactions underpinning the design of supramolecular self-assembly

Within the field of nanomedicine, supramolecular chemistry has become a transformative discipline. Inspired by the complex biological systems found in nature, such as the spontaneous formation of cell membranes and folded proteins, supramolecular chemistry focuses on the principles of self-assembly. This process involves the spontaneous organization of molecular building blocks into higher-order, functional structures. The design of these structures is driven not by strong covalent bonds, but by a wide range of weak, noncovalent interactions, hydrogen bonding, halogen bonding, chalcogen bonding, π–π stacking interactions, halogen-halogen interactions, electrostatic forces, and van der Waals forces, also known as dispersion forces (Rahim et al., 2021). These weak, but cooperative interactions enable the formation of supramolecular self-assembly, which can direct the individual molecules to organize themselves into a functional, dynamic, stimuli-responsive nanocarrier for cancer therapy.

Among these non-covalent forces, hydrogen bonding is the most prominent interaction and is mostly observed in peptide and polymer assemblies, which respond to enzymatic and pH signals. A hydrogen bond forms when a hydrogen atom, covalently attached to an electronegative donor such as–OH or–NH, interacts with an electronegative acceptor atom (usually oxygen or nitrogen). The strength of hydrogen bonds typically ranges from 4 to 30 kJ/mol, and their strong directionality and reversibility make them essential in molecular recognition, crystal engineering, and biological processes like protein folding and DNA base pairing. Significantly, their reversibility is also utilized in designing dynamic materials, such as self-healing polymers. These directional interactions, with typical energies of 1–5 kcal/mol, enable precise structural control and pH-responsive behavior (Patel, 2023). The synergistic combination of hydrogen bonding with π-π stacking creates highly stable drug-carrier complexes, as demonstrated in hexakis macrocycle systems where both interactions cooperatively stabilize doxorubicin binding with energies exceeding −115 kJ/mol (Pasban and Raissi, 2021).

Electrostatic interactions, such as ion–ion, ion–dipole, and dipole–dipole forces, are equally crucial for enhanced drug loading and stabilizing biomolecular structures, salt bridges, and host–guest complexes. Conversely, van der Waals and London dispersion forces, though individually weak and non-directional, are ubiquitous; their cumulative effect contributes significantly to molecular packing within crystals, surface adhesion, and the stabilization of hydrophobic regions in aqueous environments.

Within the aromatic systems, π–π stacking interactions provide additional stabilization, arising from quadrupole and dispersion contributions. These are fundamental in DNA base stacking, supramolecular frameworks, and in the development of optoelectronic materials. Closely related are cation-π and anion-π interactions, where charged species interact with the electron-rich or electron-deficient π-clouds of aromatic systems; such forces govern enzyme–substrate binding, neurotransmitter recognition, and ion sensing (Dougherty, 2025). In aqueous environments, hydrophobic interactions significantly enhance the self-assembly of amphiphilic molecules into micelles, vesicles, and bilayers, and play a crucial role in protein folding and molecular encapsulation.

Newly identified classes of σ-hole interactions have broadened the range of non-covalent forces that can be used in designing the supramolecular systems. Halogen bonding (involving Cl, Br, and I atoms) and chalcogen bonding (S, Se, and Te) depend on anisotropic electron distributions, which enable the generation of strong and directional non-covalent forces, to guide the formation of ordered supramolecular assemblies that are useful in crystal engineering, drug–protein interactions, and anion recognition. Halogen-halogen interactions also affect packing motifs in crystals, while emerging pnictogen-like bonding (N, P, As) offers new strategies for molecular recognition and material stabilization. More specialized heteroatomic inter-cations (e.g., oxadiazole-π or pyridine-π) present further opportunities for precise binding geometries and contribute to the development of fine-tuned supramolecular structures (Frontera and Bauza, 2021).

Extending beyond organic systems, metal coordination serves as a powerful organizing principle in supramolecular chemistry, enabling the formation of complex and ordered structures. Metal coordination with ions such as Mn^{2+} or Cu^{2+} imparts catalytic and imaging functionalities for chemodynamic and theranostic applications. The binding of multidentate ligands with metal ions creates strong yet flexible structures such as cages, grids, helicates, and metal–organic frameworks (MOFs), whereas weaker metallophilic interactions (e.g., Au–Au or Pt–Pt attractions) facilitate the formation of luminescent materials, catalysts, and nanoscale assemblies (Cué-Sampedro and Sánchez-Fernández, 2024).

Furthermore, encapsulation and host–guest interactions also integrate multiple non-covalent forces such as hydrophobic effects, hydrogen bonding, electrostatic interactions, and dispersion forces—to trap molecules within the confined spaces of macrocyclic hosts, such as cyclodextrins, cucurbiturils, and calixarenes. These systems offer modular, high-affinity encapsulation and on-demand release. Altogether, these non-covalent interactions support the versatility, high drug loading, and precise, multi-modal control that characterize advanced cancer nanomedicines. Thus, Supramolecular assemblies are primarily stabilized not by covalent bonds but by a range of weak yet well-organized non-covalent forces, which collectively provide stability, selectivity, and functionality (Guo and Liu, 2014). Different types of Supramolecular self-assembly systems are diagrammatically represented in Fig. 11.1.

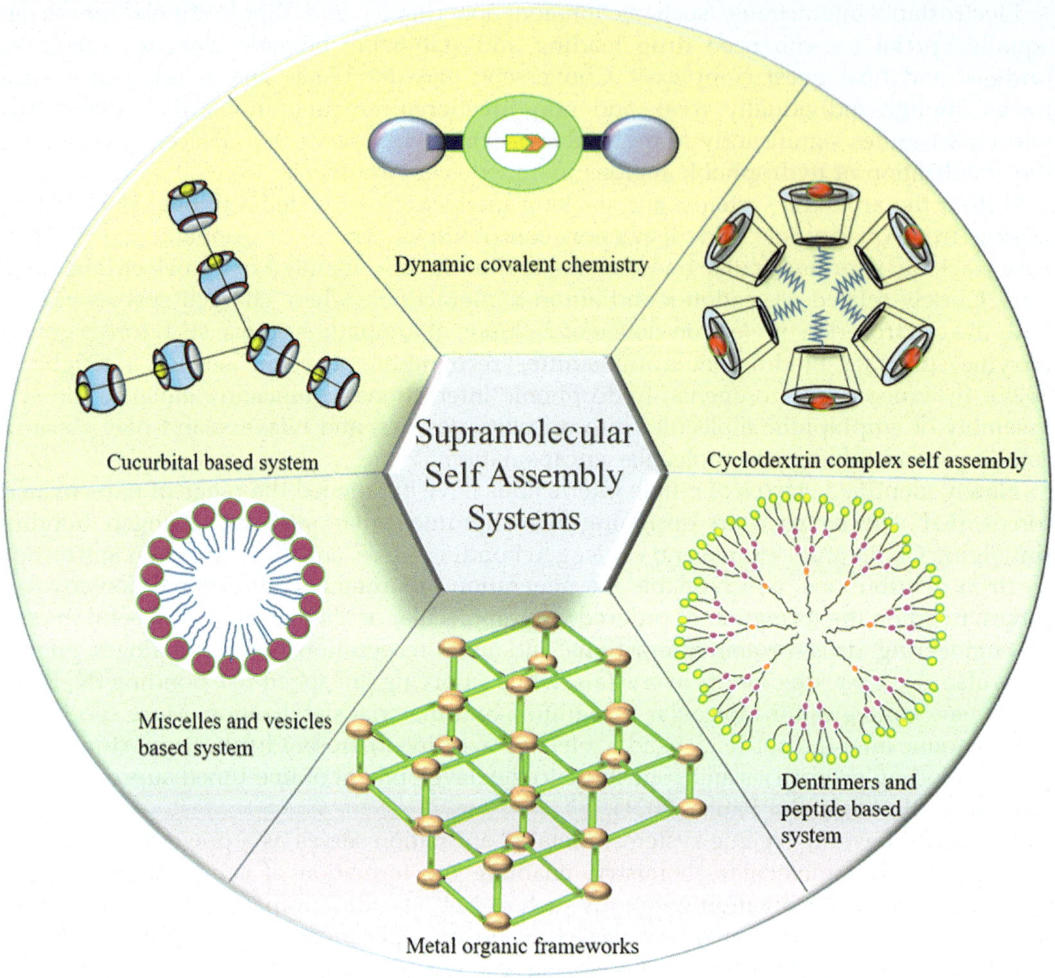

FIGURE 11.1 **Classification of supramolecular self-assembly systems.** The diagram illustrates the primary classes of supramolecular self-assembly systems employed in nanotechnology and pharmaceutical development. The six main categories—dynamic covalent chemistry, cyclodextrin complex self-assembly, dendrimer and peptide-based systems, metal-organic frameworks, micelles and vesicles, and cucurbituril-based systems—represent distinct approaches to creating ordered, hierarchical structures through non-covalent interactions and reversible bonding. These systems are particularly valuable for controlled drug delivery, diagnostic imaging, and therapeutic applications in cancer treatment.

Principles of supramolecular chemistry: Understanding the mechanism of self-assembly

The formation of supramolecular self-assemblies is based on two core concepts: molecular recognition and self-assembly. Molecular recognition refers to the ability of a host molecule to selectively bind a guest molecule, much like a lock and key. This specific binding occurs through a matching fit in size, shape, and charge distribution, facilitated by weak forces such as hydrogen bonds and electrostatic attractions. This principle forms the foundation of host-guest chemistry, where macrocyclic molecules, such as crown ethers, cyclodextrins, and calixarenes, create stable complexes by encapsulating a drug molecule, thereby improving its solubility and stability (Abdelhay and Bani-Yaseen, 2024). The outcome of this precise binding is crucial for applications in sensing, catalysis, and molecular transport. Building on this, self-assembly is a spontaneous process in which these molecular components organize themselves into larger, ordered structures, such as micelles, vesicles, or fibers. This process is driven by the combined action of many non-covalent interactions, resulting in a balance between structural stability and dynamic responsiveness. The resulting structures exhibit hierarchical and long-range order, with small molecular units assembling into larger, functional arrays that span the nanoscale to mesoscale (1–100 nm). The flexible nature of these assemblies, allows them to be reversible, adjustable, and sensitive to external factors such as light or environmental changes. This adaptability offers both flexibility and strength, allowing supramolecular systems to imitate biological processes where organization and order produce unique functions, as seen with enzymes and collagen. The mechanistic basis for the formation of different supramolecular self-assemblies is further discussed.

Cyclodextrin-based self-assembly mechanism

In Cyclodextrin complexation, non-covalent interactions drive the spontaneous organization of the molecules into stable yet dynamic structures. The unique feature of the CDs is their toroidal architecture, possessing a hydrophobic inner cavity and hydrophilic outer surface, which enables the formation of host-guest inclusion complexes wherein a hydrophobic molecule of suitable size can be entrapped. This process of encapsulation is governed by hydrophobic interactions, van der Waals forces, and hydrogen bonding at the rim of the CD cavity. Cyclodextrin-based self-assemblies exhibit a dynamic and reversible nature in which can exhibit controlled and stimuli-responsive behavior, thus making them important drug delivery systems (Lee et al., 2025). The mechanism of cyclodextrin-mediated self-assembly, showing the formation of host–guest inclusion complexes, followed by organization into higher-order supramolecular structures, is shown in the Figure below. The representation of the inclusion complex of Cyclodextrin is represented in Fig. 11.2.

Calixarene and cucurbituril-based self-assembly mechanism

Calixarenes and cucurbiturils belong to two prominent classes of synthetic macrocyclic hosts, resulting in the formation of supramolecular assemblies through non-covalent host-guest interactions. Calixarenes are composed of phenolic units that are linked by methylene bridges and possess a bowl-shaped cavity, which is conformationally flexible, facilitating the inclusion of guest molecules throughhydrophobic, π–π, hydrogen bonding, and electrostatic interactions. This inclusion of the guest molecules allows adaptive binding, resulting in the formation of supramolecular assemblies (Nag and Rao, 2022). On the other hand, cucurbiturilsformed from glycoluril and formaldehyde units exhibit **a** pumpkin-shaped cavity with carbonyl-lined portals thatare rigid and symmetrical. The guest molecules are included

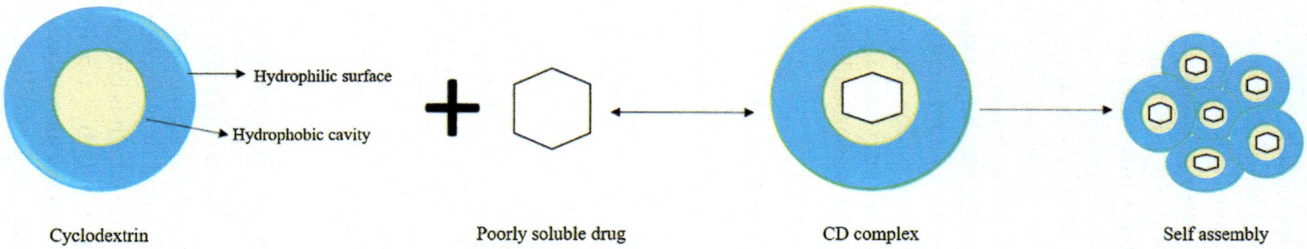

FIGURE 11.2 **Host–guest assembly driven by cyclodextrins.** Mechanism of cyclodextrin-mediated self-assembly showing the formation of host–guest inclusion complexes, followed by organization into higher-order supramolecular structures.

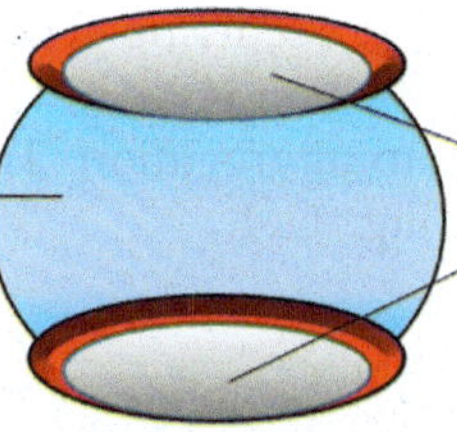

FIGURE 11.3 **Cucurbituril: Hydrophobic cavity and carbonyl portals.** Structure of a cucurbituril host–guest complex showing the hydrophobic cavity and carbonyl-laced portals that facilitate molecular encapsulation through non-covalent interactions.

in this cavity via ion–dipole and hydrogen bonding interactions (Colaco et al., 2025). Both the assemblies' exhibits reversible, responsive, and precise molecular recognition, which employ the core and basic principles of supramolecular chemistry based on the non-covalent interactions. The Structure of a cucurbituril host–guest complex, showing the hydrophobic cavity and carbonyl-laced portals that facilitate molecular encapsulation through non-covalent interactions, is shown below. Figure of structure of a cucurbituril host–guest complex is demonstrated in Fig. 11.3.

Dendrimer- and peptide-based self-assembly mechanism

Dendrimers are highly branched, tree-like architectures having a well-defined internal core, with multiple surface functional groups, self-assembled via hydrogen bonding, electrostatic attraction, π–πstacking. The unique tunable structure of the dendrimers exhibits surface chemistry that enables the encapsulation of the guest molecules or assists in the binding of small molecules, nucleic acids, and drugs. The peptide-based assembly, on the other hand, depends on the sequence-dependent molecular recognition, in which the secondary structures such as α-helices and β-sheets initiate directional hydrogen bonding and π–π stacking between aromatic residues. These interactions, in turn, assist in the formation of supramolecular assemblies (Nag and Rao, 2022).

Micelle- and vesicle-based self-assembly mechanism

Micelle- and Vesicle represent amphiphilic supramolecular assemblies which are formed by the spontaneous organization of molecules containing both hydrophilic and hydrophobic groups. The formation of these assemblies are governed by the hydrophobic effect, in which the amphiphilic molecules reduce the exposure of their non-polar tails to water by aligning the molecules in such a way that their hydrophobic tails are directed inward and the hydrophilic heads are faced outwards towards the aqueous environment leading to the formation of unique spherical or cylindrical structures called as micelles with a single hydrophobic core (Hill et al., 2014). In the case of vesicles, there is a bilayer organization of these hydrophilic and hydrophobic domains, resulting in the formation of an enclosed compartment. These vesicles are additionally stabilized by van der Waals forces, electrostatic interactions, and hydrogen bonding among the amphiphilic molecules. The formation of these vesicles is a thermodynamicallydriven process, occurring when the concentration of the amphiphiles exceeds the critical micelle concentration (CMC), where the decrease in interfacial free energy outweighs entropy loss due to aggregation. These supramolecular assemblies exhibit a reversible and dynamic nature Fig. 11.4.

Dynamic covalent chemistry (DCC) –based self-assembly mechanism

Dynamic covalent chemistry (DCC) showcases a bridge between covalent and noncovalent self-assembly, which enables the formation of reversible structures. Unlike the conventional covalent systems that are static, DCC systems exhibit dynamic bond equilibria, which

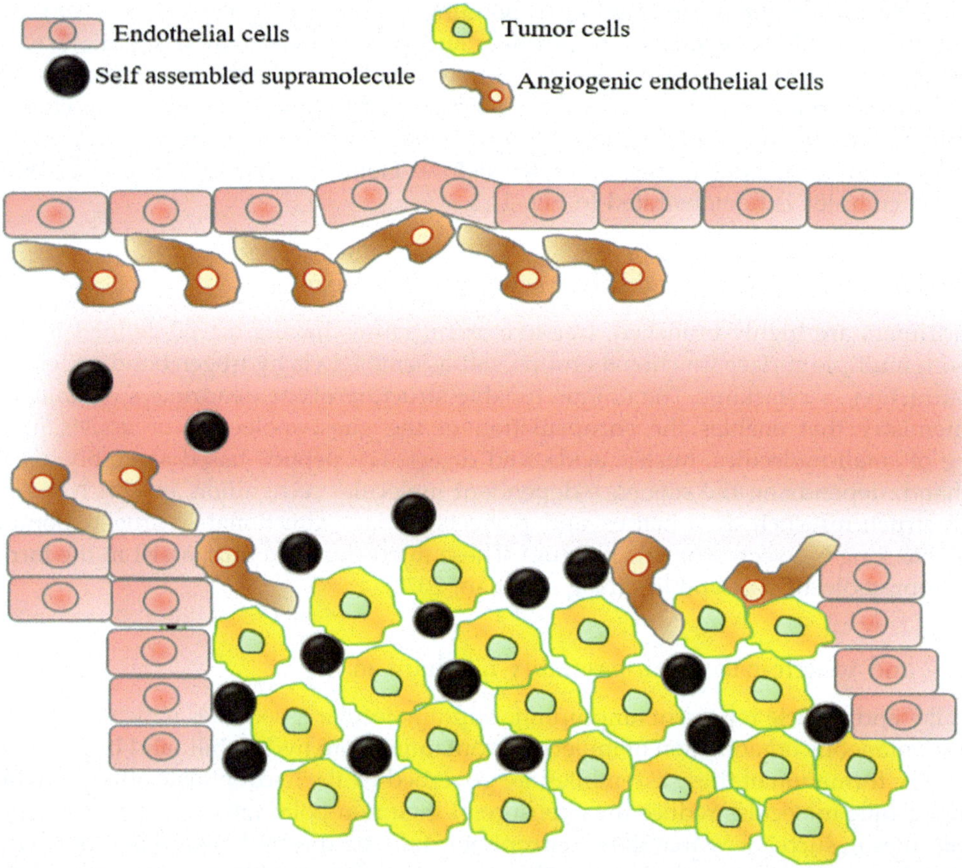

FIGURE 11.4 Targeted delivery of self-assembled supramolecules to tumor vasculature. Schematic representation of the distribution and localization of self-assembled supramolecular nanoparticles within a tumor microenvironment. The figure depicts endothelial cells (pink), tumor cells (yellow), angiogenic endothelial cells (brown), and supramolecular drug carriers (black spheres). Targeted self-assembly enables enhanced delivery and retention of therapeutic agents within tumors by exploiting the abnormal tumor vasculature and angiogenic processes.

allow the structures to rearrange and fix during the assembly process. The common reversible linkages in the DCC include imines, hydrazones, disulfides, boronate esters, and Diels–Alder adducts, which continuously form and break in response to environmental stimuli such as pH, temperature, or redox potential. The DCC supramolecular assemblies, through the interaction of covalent bond reversibility and supramolecular recognition, enable the formation of adaptive networks, molecular cages, covalent organic frameworks (COFs), and dynamic polymers (Mah et al., 2025). They combine the robustness of covalent binding along with the adaptability of supramolecular systems, enabling the systems to rearrange themselves, respond to changes, and evolve in their structures.

Metal–organic framework (MOF) –based self-assembly mechanism

Metal–organic frameworks (MOFs) are crystalline porous materials that are formed via the coordination-driven self-assembly of metal ions or clusters (nodes) with multidentate organic ligands (linkers). The formation of these assemblies depends on the metal–ligand coordination bonds, which combine the strength of the covalent interactions with the reversibility of supramolecular forces, which allows the structure to rearrange itself in an ordered way. The geometry and the metal coordinates together with the arrangement and the chemical nature of the linkers govern the final structure of the framework (Mylonas-Margaritis et al., 2021). Additionally, the framework is stabilized by π–π stacking, hydrogen bonding, and van der Waals forces between the linkers, which assist in the building of the strong three-dimensional structure. The MOF denotes the combined role of metal–ligand bonding and other weak interactions to create well-organized and functional materials through a self-assembly process (Li et al., 2020). Different types of Supramolecular Self-Assembling Systems are summarized in Table 11.1.

Supramolecular strategies in targeted cancer drug delivery

Supramolecular targeted drug delivery systems represent a significant advancement in cancer therapy, offering a sophisticated approach to increase the concentration of anticancer agents specifically within tumor cells while minimizing systemic toxicity. These systems leverage non-covalent interactions, often involving macrocyclic host-guest chemistry, to achieve precise control over drug loading, targeting, and release, providing a robust platform for designing targeted systems. Macrocyclic hosts, such as cyclodextrins and cucurbiturils, can form inclusion complexes with both therapeutic agents and targeting ligands, enabling the creation of complex, multi-ligand carriers without the need for permanent chemical bonds. This method allows for advanced strategies, such as supramolecular pre-targeting, where a host scaffold is first delivered to the tumor, followed by a drug-containing guest molecule that "clicks" to its target with high specificity (Yu and Chen, 2019). Additionally, these systems can release their payload in response to specific tumor microenvironment signals, such as pH or redox gradients, providing an extra level of control to ensure the drug is released exactly where it's needed. The key connecting phenomenon linking self-assembled supramolecular systems and cancer treatment is the enhanced

TABLE 11.1 Types of supramolecular self assembling systems with key structural feature and primary driving force for complexation.

Type	Key structural Feature (Cavity shape/size, portals)	Primary driving force for complexation	Advantages in DDS	Disadvantages/Toxicity	References
Cyclodextrins (CDs)	Toroidal/cone-shaped, hydrophilic exterior, hydrophobic interior cavity; variable cavity sizes (alpha, beta, gamma-CD)	Hydrophobic interactions (key), van der waals forces, hydrogen bonding	Clinically mature (FDA/EMA excipients like Captisol) - enhances solubility, stability, and bioavailability of hydrophobic drugs. Supports passive & active targeting, co-delivery, theranostics.	Native forms (e.g., beta-CD) can cause kidney damage/ hemolysis at high doses - limited stability of some inclusion complexes. Manufacturing complexity for advanced nanostructures	Haider et al. (2025)
Cucurbiturils (CB[n])	Rigid, symmetrical pumpkin-shaped macrocycle; hydrophobic cavity; carbonyl-lined, electronegative portals	Ion-dipole interactions, hydrophobic forces, hydrogen bonding, π–π stacking (depending on guest)	Exceptionally high binding affinities and selectivity for cationic guests. Excellent chemical stability and biocompatibility. Enables stimuli-responsive release (pH, competitive binding). Stabilizes cationic therapeutics	Complex synthesis for larger CB [n] variants. Limited aqueous solubility of some CB[n]s. Strong binding can sometimes hinder drug release.	Li et al. (2021)
Calixarenes	Versatile cup-like conformation; adjustable cavity size; readily modifiable upper and lower rims	Hydrophobic forces, π–π stacking, hydrogen bonding, electrostatic interactions	Highly versatile chemical modification for tailored properties (solubility, targeting). Forms stable complexes with various anticancer agents (doxorubicin, paclitaxel, cisplatin derivatives). Supports multifunctional nanostructures for targeted delivery and theranostics	Potential toxicity (depends heavily on specific derivative and functionalization) less extensively studied clinically compared to CDs synthesis can be challenging for complex modifications	Li et al. (2024)
Dendrimers &peptide-based systems	Uniform spherical capsid-like morphology; spontaneously assembled from peptide dendrimers and complementary peptides	Non-covalent self-assembly of molecular building blocks	Structural precision and nanoscale size. Enhanced drug localization and superior tumor tissue penetration/cellular uptake. pH-responsive release (e.g., DOX release in acidic TME)	Increased complexity compared to simple drug/CD complex. Requires specific building blocks (peptides/dendrimers)	Xie et al. (2022)

Micelles &vesicles (polymersomes)	Micelles: Core-shell structure; hydrophobic core (drug loading) and hydrophilic shell (e.g., PEG for stealth). Vesicles/Polymersomes: Hollow, bilayered structure with an aqueous core.	Hydrophobic segments aggregate in aqueous environments (for core formation)	Passive tumor targeting via the EPR effect. Co-delivery (hydrophilic in core, hydrophobic in membrane for vesicles). Stealth characteristics (prolonged circulation time). Examples have reached clinical trials (e.g., Genexol-PM, Doxil)	Premature drug release in systemic circulation. Poor penetration into the core of solid tumors. Challenges in scalable manufacturing and batch consistency	Bilia et al. (2016)
Dynamic covalent chemistry (DCC)–Based	Not explicitly a macrocycle; involves the use of reversible covalent bonds to create dynamic, adaptable assemblies	Reversible covalent bonds (not detailed in this document) combined with non-covalent forces	Enables assemblies to be reversible, adjustable, and responsive to external factors. Allows for adaptability, responsiveness, and error correction in supramolecular systems	Requires specific synthesis of building blocks with DCC moieties. DCC mechanisms/components were not detailed in the provided text.	Feng and Lei (2024)
Metal–Organic framework (MOF)–Based	Metal coordination complexes forming highly stable yet dynamic assemblies (e.g., cages, grids, helicates, MOFs)	Metal coordination between multidentate ligands and metal ions	Yields highly stable yet dynamic assemblies. Used to form supramolecular containers for encapsulation and host-guest interactions. Provides an alternative to purely organic systems	Metallo-supramolecular systems can be complex to design. Toxicity and long-term stability in biological systems are key challenges.	Cook et al. (2013)

permeability and retention (EPR) effect, along with stimuli-responsive disassembly within the tumor microenvironment. Solid tumors develop abnormal, highly fenestrated vasculature with pore sizes ranging from approximately 100 nm to 2 μm, and they lack adequate lymphatic drainage (Wu, 2021). This "leakiness" allows nanoscale assemblies such as micelles, vesicles, or polymeric nanoparticles formed through supramolecular self-assembly to selectively extravasate from the bloodstream into the tumor interstitium and then be retained there. In contrast, healthy blood vessels exhibit tight endothelial junctions (<10 nm pores) and efficient lymphatic clearance, which prevents the accumulation of similarly sized carriers. Thus, self-assembled nanocarriers such as, PEGylated micelles and liposomes are known to utilize the EPR effect for passive tumor targeting, increasing local drug concentration while reducing systemic exposure and side effects. A well-known example is Doxil, a liposomal doxorubicin formulation that utilizes the EPR effect to concentrate the drug at the tumor site, thereby reducing its cardiotoxicity.

Once localized within the tumor interstitium via EPR, supramolecular carriers utilize the unique biochemical and physicochemical cues of the malignancy—such as acidic extracellular pH (6.5–6.8 compared to 7.4 in normal tissues), elevated glutathione levels, overexpressed enzymes (e.g., matrix metalloproteinases), and hypoxia to induce controlled disassembly and release of drugs at the site (Subhan et al., 2021). The flexible nature of noncovalent interactions enables advanced stimuli-responsive behavior, allowing supramolecular systems to react to tumor-specific environmental signals. pH-responsive strategies are the most clinically developed method, taking advantage of the slightly acidic tumor microenvironment (pH 6.5–7.0) in contrast to normal physiological pH (7.4). Chen and colleagues explained the molecular mechanism of pH-triggered drug release using cucurbituril-oxaliplatin complexes, where protonation of competing molecules at low pH disrupts host-guest interactions, releasing the active drug specifically within tumor tissues. This mechanism maintains a remarkable balance between systemic stability and tumor-specific activation, with binding constants changing by orders of magnitude across physiological pH ranges (Wu et al., 2020).

Although the EPR effect is useful, it is not uniform across all tumors or even within different regions of the same tumor. This heterogeneous nature of the EPR effect limits its reliability, and to overcome the limitations of the EPR effect, many systems use active targeting. This involves enzyme-responsive systems, redox-responsive mechanisms, and functionalizing the nanocarrier's surface with specific ligands that bind to receptors overexpressed on cancer cells, promoting receptor-mediated uptake. Common targeting ligands include folate for folate receptors in ovarian cancer, hyaluronic acid for the CD44 receptor in breast cancer, and RGD peptides for integrin targeting (Belyaev et al., 2025). Enzyme-responsive systems utilize tumor-associated proteases and esterases to trigger the release of drugs by cleaving specific linker molecules. These systems incorporate enzyme-cleavable bonds within supramolecular assemblies, enabling highly targeted activation in response to elevated levels of tumor enzymes, such as matrix metalloproteinases and cathepsins. Redox-responsive mechanisms utilize the high glutathione levels (2–10 mM) found in many tumor cells, compared to the extracellular environment (<20 μM). Disulfide-linked supramolecular systems undergo reductive cleavage after cellular uptake (Yan et al., 2024), resulting in rapid drug release within the cytoplasm while maintaining stability during circulation. Passive targeting via the EPR effect is represented in Fig. 11.4.

Influence of the tumor microenvironment on supramolecular drug delivery systems

When self-assembling supramolecular systems encounter the tumor microenvironment, they undergo significant structural and functional changes driven by the unique physiological conditions found in cancerous tissues. The tumor environment creates a complex interplay of chemical, enzymatic, and physical factors that fundamentally influence the behavior of these complex molecular assemblies.

pH-induced structural modifications

The acidic tumor microenvironment (pH 5.8–6.5) triggers cascading effects on supramolecular system stability through various mechanisms. Protonation of ionizable groups disrupts electrostatic interactions that hold many assemblies together. Histidine-rich systems are especially sensitive to tumor pH because histidine's pKa is around 6.5, making these residues highly responsive to acidification. When protonated, histidine residues carry positive charges that cause electrostatic repulsion, leading to controlled disassembly of supramolecular structures (Saenz et al., 2025). pH-responsive peptide hydrogels show significant morphological changes in acidic conditions, with systems shifting from stable nanofibers to shorter segments or spherical forms when exposed to tumor pH. The swelling behavior of supramolecular assemblies also increases notably under acidic conditions, with some systems experiencing particle size growth from 100 nm to over 400 nm as pH drops from 6.5 to 5.6 (Ye et al., 2024).

Matrix metalloproteinases (MMPs): Primary enzymatic degraders

Matrix metalloproteinases (MMPs) are the most extensively studied group of tumor-associated enzymes that affect the supramolecular structure. These zinc-dependent endopeptidases are highly overexpressed in cancer tissues, with some subtypes showing more than a 10-fold increase in levels. MMP-2 and MMP-9 are particularly significant, as they exhibit increased activity at tumor invasion fronts and metastatic sites. MMP-2 mainly cleaves glycine-proline-arginine-glycine (GPRG) sequences in supramolecular assemblies. When these sequences act as crosslinkers in β-sheet-rich supramolecular filaments, MMP-2-triggered degradation occurs while preserving overall structural integrity until complete disassembly (Mustafa et al., 2022). The secondary structure influences cleavability, as assemblies with stronger β-sheet features tend to reduce MMP-1 cleavage due to the burial of cleavage sites within the supramolecular framework. Patterns of MMP distribution within tumors allow for targeted degradation: MMP-2 is most abundant at invasive fronts, whereas MMP-7 and MMP-14 are concentrated in tumor enters. MMP-9 mostly localizes at the tumor periphery in primary tumors but shifts to the tumor core in metastases (Niland et al., 2022). This spatial distribution supports the design of location-specific responsive systems.

Hyaluronidase-extracellular matrix modifier

Hyaluronidase enzymes are overexpressed in many cancer types and serve as powerful triggers for modifying the supramolecular system. These enzymes cleave hyaluronic acid by breaking β-1,4 glycosidic bonds between N-acetylglucosamine and glucuronic acid through a β-elimination mechanism. Hyaluronidase-responsive supramolecular systems exploit this enzymatic activity for controlled drug release. The enzyme's ability to degrade hyaluronic acid matrices enables the spatially controlled disassembly of HA-based supramolecular carriers, leading to the precise liberation of drugs at sites of elevated enzymatic activity (Lu et al., 2025). Human hyaluronidases (HYAL1-4) show distinct tissue distributions, with HYAL1 being most active in acidic conditions typical of tumor environments.

Cathepsin proteases - lysosomal and extracellular activity

Cathepsin B, a lysosomal cysteine protease, is significantly overexpressed in tumor tissues and is a key target for supramolecular drug delivery systems. This enzyme cleaves specific peptide sequences, especially those containing phenylalanine-lysine (Phe-Lys) and valine-citrulline (Val-Cit) dipeptides. Systems responsive to Cathepsin B demonstrate rapid and complete drug release when exposed to the enzyme, while remaining highly stable in human plasma. The enzyme's presence in lysosomes and extracellular spaces allows for both intracellular and extracellular activation. Cathepsin L, which has similar cysteine protease activity, differs in substrate specificity, enabling orthogonal targeting strategies. Research shows that cathepsin B can trigger nanofiber breakdown, leading to controlled drug release (Egorova et al., 2023). Systems with cathepsin-cleavable linkers exhibit much lower cytotoxicity compared to free drugs until enzymatic activation occurs.

Fibroblast activation protein (FAP) stromal target

Fibroblast Activation Protein is mostly found in disease conditions, making it a perfect target for tumor-specific supramolecular breakdown. This type-II transmembrane serine protease has both dipeptidyl peptidase and endopeptidase functions, cleaving substrates at post-proline bonds. FAP is highly present in reactive stromal fibroblasts in over 90% of human epithelial cancers. The enzyme can break down gelatin and type I collagen, creating pathways for better drug penetration. FAP-responsive peptide systems change from spherical nanoparticles to nanofibers when exposed to cancer-related fibroblasts, which enhances drug retention and penetration. Research shows that FAP cleaves specific GPAX sequences in amphiphilic peptides, causing quick disassembly and drug release at tumor sites (Ma et al., 2023). This targeted action is due to FAP's limited expression, being almost absent in normal adult tissues.

Alkaline phosphatase (ALP): enzyme-instructed assembly

Alkaline phosphatase (ALP), often overexpressed in various cancer types, acts as a trigger for enzyme-instructed self-assembly (EISA) systems. ALP catalyzes the hydrolysis of phosphate monoesters, transforming hydrophilic phosphorylated precursors into hydrophobic molecules that spontaneously self-assemble. This dephosphorylation mechanism causes significant changes in molecular properties, with the removal of phosphate groups by ALP inducing aggregation and gelation at enzymatic sites. Such spatially controlled assembly enables therapeutic agents to be activated precisely where ALP activity is high

(Tyagi and Venkatesh, 2024). Dual-responsive systems, which combine pH sensitivity with ALP activity, show improved selectivity by requiring both acidic conditions and enzymatic activity for optimal drug release. These AND-gate systems ensure activation only occurs within tumor-specific microenvironments.

Carboxylesterases (CES): prodrug activation and disassembly

Carboxylesterase enzymes play essential roles in both prodrug activation and supramolecular disassembly. These enzymes hydrolyze ester bonds in drug delivery systems, with CES1A1 and CES2 being especially important in tumor tissues. Interestingly, some cancer cell lines show CES downregulation, which can be leveraged for selective targeting. Systems designed to disassemble upon CES cleavage will stay stable in CES-deficient cancer cells while disassembling in CES-expressing normal tissues, creating an inverse targeting mechanism (Wang et al., 2022). Esterase-responsive nanoparticles enable controlled drug release through the cleavage of ester linkages in supramolecular structures. Since esterases are widely expressed throughout the body, systemic activation is possible, and combining this with other tumor-specific stimuli can improve selectivity.

β-Galactosidase - reporter and therapeutic target

β-Galactosidase has dual functions as both a reporter enzyme for monitoring tumor burden and a therapeutic target for drug activation. Tumor cells genetically engineered with the lacZ gene produce soluble β-galactosidase, which correlates with tumor size and response to therapy. β-Galactosidase-responsive prodrug systems show excellent therapeutic effectiveness in tumor models. These systems use glucuronide linkages that are cleaved by β-glucuronidase (which has similar substrate specificity to β-galactosidase) to release active drugs specifically within tumor microenvironments (Almammadov et al., 2022). The ability of these systems to bind to albumin improves circulation time and enhances tumor accumulation.

Antioxidant enzymes - altered expression patterns

Superoxide dismutase (SOD) and glutathione peroxidase (GPx) show altered expression patterns in tumor tissues, affecting the stability of the supramolecular system. These antioxidant enzymes influence the redox environment, which can lead to the disassembly of redox-sensitive supramolecular systems (Ranbhise et al., 2025). GPx levels are significantly higher in cancerous tissues compared to normal tissues, while SOD activity varies depending on tumor type and differentiation. In poorly differentiated tumors, both GPx and SOD activities are reduced compared to well-differentiated lesions. These changes in expression create opportunities for redox-responsive supramolecular systems. Manganese superoxide dismutase (SOD2) may promote tumor progression by producing hydrogen peroxide, which can trigger oxidation-sensitive disassembly mechanisms (Abed et al., 2022). The dysregulated antioxidant enzyme expression in tumors offers additional targets for responsive drug delivery systems.

Aminopeptidases and peptidases - sequence-specific cleavage

Various aminopeptidases and peptidases present in tumor microenvironments contribute to supramolecular degradation through sequence-specific cleavage mechanisms. These enzymes can process terminal amino acids or internal peptide bonds in supramolecular assemblies. Leucine aminopeptidase demonstrates step-by-step proteolytic degradation of peptide-based supramolecular systems, enabling controlled and sustained drug release. The sequential nature of aminopeptidase cleavage allows for programmable disassembly kinetics. Peptidase activity creates opportunities for multi-step degradation cascades where initial cleavage events expose secondary cleavage sites, leading to faster disassembly as degradation progresses (Rozans et al., 2024). This mechanism provides built-in amplification of the enzymatic response.

Urease - metabolic enzyme target

Urease activity, which is increased in certain tumor types due to altered metabolism, can act as a trigger for modifying supramolecular systems. This enzyme catalyzes urea hydrolysis, leading to localized pH increases that can initiate pH-sensitive supramolecular disassembly (Panja and Adams, 2021). The metabolic changes in cancer cells often involve shifts in nitrogen metabolism, making urease-responsive systems potentially useful for targeting specific tumor subtypes with altered metabolic profiles.

Applications of supramolecular systems in anticancer therapy

Cyclodextrin-based systems

Cyclodextrins (CDs) are a versatile group of cyclic oligosaccharides with a distinctive molecular structure: a hydrophilic outer surface and a hydrophobic inner cavity. This unique configuration enables them to form host-guest inclusion complexes with poorly water-soluble anticancer drugs, such as paclitaxel and camptothecin. Such supramolecular encapsulation greatly improves the drug's aqueous solubility, chemical stability, and bioavailability by protecting it from premature degradation in the bloodstream. Beyond basic encapsulation, CD-based systems can be engineered into more advanced, multifunctional nanocarriers. By attaching cyclodextrins to polymers or nanoparticles, researchers can develop drug delivery platforms, such as nanosponges and nanogels, that provide better control over drug payloads and release rates. Additionally, modifying the CD's surface with targeting ligands such as folic acid or hyaluronic acid enables receptor-mediated uptake, leading to selective accumulation in tumor cells (Zhang et al., 2025). The flexible nature of these complexes also supports stimuli-responsive drug release triggered by factors like the acidic pH, redox gradients, or enzymatic activity typical of the tumor microenvironment. Despite their significant potential and proven biocompatibility, the clinical translation of CD-based systems faces several obstacles. Important challenges include maintaining consistent and complex stability in physiological fluids, ensuring the long-term safety of chemically modified derivatives, and addressing the high costs and scalability issues associated with large-scale production. However, the clinical approval of specialized CD derivatives, such as Captisol, demonstrates their practical usefulness as pharmaceutical excipients (Beig et al., 2015). The future of this field depends on developing intelligent, theranostic CD platforms that combine drug delivery with imaging, as well as exploring combination therapies that incorporate gene delivery or phototherapy.

Calixarene and cucurbituril-based systems

Beyond cyclodextrins, calixarenes and cucurbiturils are two other major families of macrocyclic hosts that have been widely studied for supramolecular drug delivery. These compounds have distinct, rigid structures that allow them to form highly stable inclusion complexes with various guest molecules. Calixarenes, characterized by their cup-like shape and easily modifiable rims, serve as versatile platforms for encapsulating hydrophobic anticancer drugs, such as doxorubicin and paclitaxel. Calixarene scaffolds are functionalized on both rims to create amphiphilic derivatives that self-assemble into micelles, vesicles, and nanoparticles for highly targeted drug delivery (Pan et al., 2018). Mannose-grafted calixarene micelles selectively bind ovarian and lung cancer cells overexpressing the mannose receptor, increasing cellular DOX uptake by 70%, decreasing the IC_{50} by 50%, and reducing off-target cytotoxicity by 35% compared to free DOX (Sreedevi et al., 2021). Additionally, pseudo-rotaxane nano-valves on mesoporous silica stay sealed at physiological pH and redox potential but open in lysosomal conditions (pH 5.0, 10 mM GSH) to release over 98% of mitoxantrone, doubling median survival from 30 to 60 days in xenograft models while maintaining a good safety profile (Navarro et al., 2025). Their versatility enables the creation of multifunctional nanostructures—including nanoparticles and conjugates—that can be customized for controlled drug release, targeted delivery, and theranostic applications. Mechanistically, they depend on a combination of hydrophobic, electrostatic, and π-π stacking interactions to improve drug solubility and stability, while protecting drugs from enzymatic degradation.

Cucurbiturils (CB[n]) are pumpkin-shaped macrocycles known for their exceptionally high binding affinities and selectivity, especially for cationic guests. This allows for the stabilization and delivery of drugs that might be difficult for other hosts. Drug release from these systems can be precisely triggered by pH shifts, competitive binding, or redox changes, making them ideal for stimuli-responsive applications. Similar to calixarenes, cucurbiturils can be functionalized with targeting moieties and co-loaded with imaging probes to support theranostic strategies. Cucurbituril-based systems leverage rigid, carbonyl-lined portals and hydrophobic cavities to form ultra-tight host–guest complexes with anticancer agents. CB encapsulation of oxaliplatin and carboplatin reduces systemic toxicity by 40%, extends the plasma half-life from 3 to 8 hours, and achieves a 65% tumor volume reduction in colorectal and lung cancer xenografts, compared to 40% with the free drug (Pashkina et al., 2021). Acyclic CB derivatives co-assemble with amphiphilic guest polymers into micelles that co-deliver doxorubicin and camptothecin, thereby increasing tumor drug accumulation from 5% to 10% ID/g and doubling the median survival in breast and pancreatic tumor models (Ahmadian et al., 2020). Injectable CB-enriched hydrogels implanted peritumorally capture guest-modified chemotherapeutics, increasing the local drug concentration threefold (from 5% to 15% ID/g) and enabling five repeat dosing cycles without additional surgery. Furthermore, CB-mediated co-delivery of acridine orange and oxaliplatin in melanoma models results in a 30% greater cell kill (95% vs. 65%) (Wu et al., 2020). At the same time, real-time fluorescence imaging tracks the release kinetics with a temporal resolution of less than 10 minutes.

Calixarenes and cucurbiturils utilize host-guest chemistry to improve drug properties, with their unique structures and binding strengths offering clear advantages. Calixarenes provide a highly adjustable framework suitable for many applications, while cucurbiturils are especially effective at stabilizing certain types of cationic therapeutics and enabling high-affinity, stimuli-responsive release.

Dendrimers and peptide-based systems

Dendrimers are a type of highly branched, monodisperse polymer with a well-defined, tree-like molecular structure. Their unique architecture, which includes a central core, repeating branching units, and a high-density surface, makes them ideal for supramolecular drug delivery. They can encapsulate therapeutic agents inside their internal cavities through non-covalent interactions or carry them on their surface via conjugation. The precise control over their size, shape, and surface chemistry enables highly tunable drug loading and targeted delivery.

One of the most notable platforms is the core–shell tectodendrimer (CSTD), which combines a poly (amidoamine) (PAMAM) dendrimer core with a shell of hydrophilic polymers and targeting ligands (Song et al., 2023). CSTDs co-encapsulate doxorubicin (DOX) within the hydrophobic interior and complex miR-21 inhibitor (miR21i) via electrostatic interactions on the surface (Song et al., 2020). In murine models of triple-negative breast cancer, this system achieved over 95% drug loading, 70% miRNA loading, and pH-triggered release, resulting in an 87% reduction in tumor volume and significant suppression of metastatic lung nodules compared to monotherapies (Scialla et al., 2023). Enhanced apoptosis and downregulation of miR-21 expression resulted in a 60% decrease in cell migration in vitro and a twofold increase in median survival, from 28 to 56 days.

PAMAM dendrimer conjugates have also demonstrated outstanding performance in glioblastoma multiforme (GBM) by simultaneously delivering temozolomide (TMZ) and anti-EGFR small interfering RNA (siRNA). Surface-modified generation-5 PAMAM dendrimers with cRGD peptides for integrin targeting achieved 80% siRNA complexation and 90% TMZ encapsulation (Abedi-Gaballu et al., 2018). Enzyme-responsive linkers enabled the selective release of drugs in the tumor microenvironment overexpressing MMP-2. In orthotopic GBM models, this platform resulted in 75% tumor growth inhibition, increased median survival from 18 to 42 days, and potent gene silencing (>85% EGFR knockdown) in vivo. An anti-angiogenic variant combining dendrimer-mediated delivery of bevacizumab with photodynamic therapy (PDT) agents like chlorin e6 showed two-stage release under near-infrared irradiation, reducing tumor vascular density by 65% and increasing overall survival by 45% in colorectal cancer xenografts (Peng et al., 2018).

Beyond chemotherapy and gene therapy, dendrimer-based photothermal and photodynamic systems demonstrate strong multimodal effectiveness across various cancers.

Gold-dendrimer hybrids self-assemble into 50-nm nanoclusters that deliver indocyanine green (ICG) for photothermal therapy (PTT) and siVEGF for anti-angiogenesis in hepatocellular carcinoma, achieving 90% ablation under 808-nm laser irradiation and an 80% reduction in VEGF, leading to 85% tumor regression and a decrease in metastasis to the lungs (Jiang et al., 2020a). Likewise, dendrimer-enzyme conjugates combining glucose oxidase and catalase within dendrimer shells produce local H_2O_2 and O_2, resulting in enhanced chemodynamic and photodynamic effects, which lead to 70% tumor cell apoptosis and reduced recurrence in melanoma models.

Recent trends highlight multi-stimuli-responsive linkers, including pH-, redox-, and enzyme-sensitive bonds—for the sequential release of therapeutics and targeting ligands (such as folate, RGD, and antibodies) for receptor-mediated uptake. Clinical progress is moving forward, with IND-enabling toxicology studies underway for PAMAM-doxorubicin-miRNA platforms targeting ovarian and pancreatic cancers.

Peptide-based nanocarriers are another vital class of self-assembling systems, inspired by the natural ability of peptides to fold and form organized structures. These systems offer excellent biocompatibility and biodegradability, and can be functionalized with targeting ligands or stimuli-responsive sequences, enabling site-specific drug release. Peptide amphiphiles and self-assembling motifs can form nanostructures, including nanofibers, nanotubes, and hydrogels, which serve as scaffolds for delivering chemotherapeutics, gene modulators, or immune adjuvants. Recent research describes a PA with a matrix metalloproteinase-2(MMP-2) cleavable linker, a tumor-homing RGD motif, and a hydrophobic tail to co-deliver doxorubicin(DOX) and anti-PD-L1 peptides (Zhao and Li, 2025). In orthotopic triple-negative breast cancer (TNBC) models, these PA nanofibers achieved 92% DOX loading, released 85% of the payload within 24 hours under MMP-2 exposure, and increased tumor accumulation by 3.5 times compared to free DOX (Zeng et al., 2023). The co-delivered anti-PD-L1 peptide triggered intense T-cell infiltration, doubling the $CD8^+$/Treg ratio and leading to 78% tumor growth inhibition, as well as a 40% increase in median survival from 32 to 45 days (Wang et al., 2025).

Another emerging approach uses enzyme-responsive peptide–drug conjugates that self-assemble into nanoaggregates directly within the tumor microenvironment. For example, a caspase-3–activatable peptide linked to camptothecin (CPT) remains monomeric in circulation but forms 50-nm nanoworms after caspase-3 cleavage in colon cancer xenografts (Silva et al., 2022). These nanoworms release CPT in stages—about 60% over 12 hours—resulting in 88% tumor apoptosis and significantly reducing hepatic metastases. Similar strategies have been applied to glioblastoma multiforme (GBM), where a cyclic peptide carrying paclitaxel (PTX) and adorned with transferrin-targeting sequences assembles into 100-nm nanospheres (Song et al., 2025). These spheres cross the blood–brain barrier, deliver PTX with 75% encapsulation efficiency, and increase median survival in GBM models from 20 to 38 days.

Co-assembly strategies involving therapeutic peptides and immunomodulatory agents have also shown promise. In melanoma models, α-melanocyte–stimulating hormone analogs co-assembled with Toll-like receptor seven agonists into 200-nm nanovesicles, achieving 95% peptide loading and sustained release over 72 hours (Wu et al., 2023a). The dual payload induced immunogenic cell death and activated dendritic cells, leading to 65% tumor regression and a 50% reduction in lung metastases. Peptide nanozymes, self-assembled from histidine-rich peptides and iron ions, have emerged as catalytic therapeutic platforms for chemodynamic therapy. In hepatocellular carcinoma (HCC) models, these nanozymes generated H_2O_2 in situ to catalyze Fenton reactions, producing hydroxyl radicals that worked synergistically with sorafenib. This combination achieved 80% tumor suppression and minimized off-target toxicity (Yin et al., 2025).

Critically, the repetitive and tunable nature of peptides enables the engineering of assemblies with customized immunogenic profiles, allowing for both direct cytotoxicity against tumor cells and modulation of the tumor immune microenvironment. Emerging evidence emphasizes the increased effectiveness of peptide-based supramolecular vaccines and checkpoint blockade synergists, highlighting their potential to combine chemotherapy with immunotherapy. An excellent example of these principles in action is the development of capsid-like nanocarriers using peptide dendrimers. By mimicking the spontaneous self-assembly of viral capsids, researchers can create uniform, spherical nanostructures with precise control over their size and shape. These structures have shown superior ability to penetrate deep tissue and enhance cellular uptake compared to non-structured carriers. In a notable study, the self-assembly of peptide dendrimers and complementary peptides was used to develop pH-responsive nanocarriers for doxorubicin. The resulting carriers remained stable in circulation but released the drug in response to the acidic tumor microenvironment, leading to effective tumor growth inhibition and reduced systemic toxicity in animal models (Peng et al., 2024).

Micelles and vesicles

Polymeric micelles and supramolecular vesicles are two well-known classes of self-assembling nanocarriers used in cancer therapy. Both are formed by the aggregation of amphiphilic molecules in water, resulting in a core-shell structure that can accommodate therapeutic agents. Polymeric micelles are generally spherical nanostructures formed by the aggregation of amphiphilic block copolymers. Their hydrophobic core provides an ideal environment for encapsulating poorly water-soluble drugs, such as paclitaxel and doxorubicin. The same time, the hydrophilic outer shell, often composed of polyethylene glycol (PEG), confers "stealth" properties. This PEGylated shell reduces clearance by the reticuloendothelial system, extending circulation time and enabling passive tumor targeting through the Enhanced Permeability and Retention (EPR) effect. Several micellar systems have achieved clinical success, such as Genexol-PM, a paclitaxel-loaded micelle that has demonstrated superior efficacy and fewer side effects compared to its conventional formulation (Park et al., 2017).

Supramolecular vesicles, including liposomes and polymersomes, are hollow, bilayered structures that enclose an aqueous core. Polymersomes, particularly those formed from block copolymers such as PEG-PCL, offer enhanced chemical and mechanical stability compared to traditional liposomes. Liposomes have established a clinical standard, with products such as Doxil (PEGylated liposomal doxorubicin) significantly reducing cardiotoxicity and enhancing tumor accumulation (Zhang and Zhang, 2017). The latest research focuses on making these carriers responsive to stimuli. By incorporating elements that respond to natural triggers, such as the tumor microenvironment's low pH or high glutathione (GSH) levels, these systems can be designed to release their payload precisely where needed, thereby improving effectiveness and reducing systemic toxicity (Ashrafizadeh et al., 2022). Despite these advances, the clinical application of these nanocarriers faces significant challenges. Issues such as premature drug release, limited tumor penetration into the core of solid tumors, and manufacturing difficulties in achieving batch-to-batch consistency remain major hurdles that must be addressed for widespread clinical use.

Dynamic covalent chemistry (DCC)

These systems harness reversible covalent bonds—such as imines, hydrazones, boronate esters, and disulfides to assemble single polymer chains into well-defined, protein-like nanostructures known as single-chain nanoparticles (SCNPs). Through mild stimuli, such as pH shifts or redox gradients, these dynamic linkages enable on-demand folding and unfolding, granting SCNPs unparalleled error correction, self-healing, and structural precision. In cancer therapy, DCC-based SCNPs can display targeting ligands with precise spatial control, remain stable during circulation, and then disassemble selectively within acidic endosomes or the reductive intracellular environment (Zeroug-Metz and Lee, 2024). This triggered unfolding promotes efficient endosomal escape and payload release directly into the cytosol, enhancing therapeutic efficacy while minimizing off-target toxicity. The modular nature of DCC also allows customization of bond types and crosslink densities to match specific tumor microenvironment conditions.

Metal–organic frameworks (MOFs)

These frameworks offer a complementary strategy, using crystalline lattices of metal ions (e.g., Zn^{2+}, Zr^{4+}) and organic linkers to create ultraporous, high-surface-area carriers for small-molecule drugs. A prototypical example, DOX@ZIF-8 (a nanocomposite material used in drug delivery), encapsulates doxorubicin within the pores of zeolitic imidazolate framework-8 during synthesis, achieving high loading efficiency (Wu et al., 2023b). Upon exposure to acidic tumor interstitium or endosomal compartments, ZIF-8's coordination bonds weaken and the framework collapses, triggering pH-responsive drug release. This mechanism shields doxorubicin during systemic circulation, reducing systemic toxicity and concentrating the chemotherapeutic at the tumor site. Compared to DCC-SCNPs (Dynamic Covalent Chemistry in the design and formation of Single-Chain Nanoparticles), MOFs excel in payload capacity and well-established synthetic scalability, although their biocompatibility depends on linker selection and metal ion toxicity. Both DCC and MOF platforms are advancing toward hybrid designs that could integrate dynamic covalent linkers within porous frameworks for synergistic control over drug delivery and release (He et al., 2021).

Combination therapy and co-delivery strategies

Monotherapy often fails to provide a lasting cure for cancer because of the complex challenges of tumor heterogeneity and the development of drug resistance. To overcome these limitations, combination therapy has emerged as a more effective strategy. Supramolecular systems, created through non-covalent self-assembly, are particularly suitable for this approach, as they allow for the precise co-delivery of multiple therapeutic agents within a single nanocarrier. This method ensures that drugs reach the tumor site simultaneously and in the correct ratio, leading to strong synergistic effects, lower drug doses, and reduced systemic toxicity.

The field of supramolecular nanomedicine has seen a rapid proliferation of innovative co-delivery platforms, which include, chemo-chemotherapy and chemo-gene therapy. Chemo-Chemotherapy is the most common form of co-delivery, combining two or more traditional chemotherapy drugs. For example, dual-drug-loaded micelle systems containing paclitaxel and doxorubicin have shown increased antitumor activity and synergistic effects in breast cancer models (Jiang et al., 2020). Chemo-Gene Therapy approach combines a chemotherapeutic drug with a genetic payload, such as small interfering RNA (siRNA), miRNA, or plasmid DNA, to overcome drug resistance. A supramolecular carrier can be designed to co-deliver doxorubicin with an siRNA that silences the gene for P-glycoprotein, a drug efflux pump, thereby effectively restoring the therapeutic effectiveness of the drug in resistant cells (Kumar et al., 2022). Song and colleagues developed core-shell tecto-dendrimers (CSTDs) that co-deliver doxorubicin and the therapeutic miR21i gene (Song et al., 2020). The system effectively condenses miR21i through electrostatic interactions while loading doxorubicin into the internal cavity. This dual strategy not only prevents cancer cell migration and triggers apoptosis but also significantly enhances therapeutic outcomes compared to single-drug treatments. Quantitative self-assembled pure drug cocktails combining Cabazitaxel and Dasatinib form stable nano assemblies with nearly 100% drug loading and aggregation-induced emission, enabling real-time delivery tracking (Chen et al., 2021). This approach achieves superior in vivo antitumor effects and minimizes off-target toxicity. Dual-responsive cyclodextrin-based carriers further improve spatiotemporal control by releasing genes in acidic tumor environments and drugs under high glutathione conditions, boosting both gene silencing and chemotherapeutic potency. These innovations represent a new paradigm in precision oncology, offering modular, high-loading, and stimuli-responsive platforms for robust chemo- and gene-combination therapy.

The integration of chemo-immunotherapy using supramolecular carriers has demonstrated remarkable effectiveness. Dual-responsive polymeric nanomedicines co-loading nitric oxide donors and IDO inhibitors induced immunogenic pyroptosis and reversed tumor immunosuppression. In vivo studies showed more than 85% tumor suppression and strong systemic anti immunity, surpassing monotherapies by over three times (Hu et al., 2024). For instance, a survey utilized surfactant-functionalized lipid nanoparticles to co-deliver paclitaxel and an immune checkpoint inhibitor, resulting in a significant increase in immune cell activation and enhanced tumor-targeted delivery (Zhang et al., 2022).

Advanced supramolecular systems are being created that combine multiple treatment methods beyond standard drug combinations. Multimodal therapy is a particularly active research area representing the mix of chemotherapy with photodynamic therapy (PDT) and/or photothermal therapy (PTT). These platforms can be precisely activated by external stimuli, such as near-infrared (NIR). light, providing a highly effective and selective approach. Multi-modal therapeutic combinations utilizing supramolecular self-assembly systems have emerged as revolutionary platforms in cancer treatment, enabling the precise co-delivery and controlled release of multiple agents to maximize synergistic effects and overcome resistance. These systems utilize non-covalent host–guest chemistry, metal coordination, and stimuli-responsive architectures to integrate chemotherapy, immunotherapy, phototherapy, enzyme catalysis, and other modalities into a single nanomedicine (Kwon et al., 2021).

Supramolecular platforms based on cyclodextrins, cucurbiturils, and pillararenes form the foundation of host–guest–mediated multi-modal delivery. Cyclodextrin-based nanocarriers co-encapsulate hydrophobic photosensitizers and hydrophilic immunomodulators, utilizing acid-labile and redox-sensitive linkers to enable the tumor-specific sequential release of photodynamic therapy (PDT) agents and immune checkpoint inhibitors, resulting in a 400% increase in cytotoxic T-cell activity in preclinical studies. Cucurbituril-anchored porphyrin assemblies serve simultaneously as photosensitizers for PDT, carriers for chemotherapeutics, and imaging probes, facilitating combined chemo-photodynamic therapy with a 30% increase in cytotoxicity and real-time tracking capabilities (Özkan et al., 2019). Pillararene-based hosts offer multiple recognition sites for integrating chemotherapeutics, photosensitizers, and targeting ligands, resulting in sophisticated multi-drug nanocomplexes that respond to pH and redox stimuli, facilitating synchronized drug activation.

Metal-coordinated supramolecular assemblies further broaden the multi-modal toolkit. Transition-metal ions like manganese and copper can form coordination networks with organic ligands, creating theranostic nano assemblies that serve as MRI contrast agents, oxygen generators for hypoxia-enhanced PDT, and Fenton-reaction catalysts for chemodynamic therapy. Manganese-based supramolecular systems have shown dual imaging and treatment capabilities, increasing tumor oxygenation by 50% and doubling PDT effectiveness in animal models (Xu et al., 2021).

Phototherapy–immunotherapy combinations represent a significant breakthrough. PDT and photothermal therapy (PTT) induce immunogenic cell death (ICD), releasing tumor-associated antigens and damage signals that turn "cold" tumors into "hot" ones, thereby improving checkpoint blockade therapies. Dual-responsive supramolecular systems that co-deliver photosensitizers and IDO inhibitors achieved an 85% tumor inhibition rate in preclinical glioblastoma models, with 62% of treated animals showing complete regression and extended survival beyond 12 months. Combining PTT with immunotherapy similarly increases tumor vascular permeability and heat shock protein expression, aiding immune cell infiltration and activation (Zhao et al., 2022).

Multi-modal nanozymes are an emerging frontier. Supramolecular nanozymes, assembled from peptides and metal ions, demonstrate catalytic activities such as Fenton-like reactions that produce cytotoxic radicals in situ while delivering chemotherapeutics. Copper-amino acid nanozymes demonstrated a tenfold increase in catalytic efficiency in acidic tumor microenvironments, resulting in a 75% reduction in tumor size compared to free drugs alone (Chen et al., 2024).

Stimuli-responsive architectures enable controlled multi-modal release. Quadruple-stimuli-responsive hydrogels respond to pH, temperature, redox, and light, enabling the temporal programming of sequential therapies. These hydrogels achieved staged release of chemotherapy, PDT agents, and immunomodulators in response to the progressive changes in the tumor environment, leading to sustained tumor remission in preclinical studies (Andrade et al., 2021).

Clinical translation has advanced quickly; several supramolecular multimodal systems received FDA Fast Track designations in 2024–2025, with Phase II trials showing 62% objective response rates in heavily treated patients and abscopal effects in 41% of cases. European approval for a glioblastoma-targeted supramolecular system and India's first domestically developed CAR-T therapy highlight the global momentum (Kong et al., 2025).

Overall, multi-modal supramolecular self-assembly systems provide unmatched synergy by simultaneously targeting various cancer pathways, achieving high drug loading, precise tumor selectivity (>99%), and reduced systemic toxicity. Future directions include AI-guided design for personalized nanomedicines, as well as triple- and quadruple-modal platforms that combine chemotherapy, phototherapy, immunotherapy, and nanozyme catalysis, along with real-time theranostic feedback to optimize treatment strategies. These advances mark a new era of precision, effectiveness, and safety in cancer therapy (Bilgin et al., 2024).

Current clinical landscape, breakthroughs, challenges, and future horizons

Self-assembling supramolecular systems represent a ground-breaking approach in anticancer drug delivery and have shown significant potential in preclinical studies, clinical trials, and approved products, marking a new milestone in precision oncology. The clinical translation of supramolecular anticancer systems has reached significant milestones, with several FDA-approved products showing the viability of this method. The most notable examples include Abraxane (nanoparticle albumin-bound paclitaxel) (Wolfram and Ferrari, 2019) and Doxil (PEGylated liposomal doxorubicin), both of which are supramolecular assemblies that have transformed cancer treatment.

Abraxane, approved by the FDA in 2005 for metastatic breast cancer, exemplifies the clinical success of self-assembling drug delivery systems. This 130-nanometer albumin-bound paclitaxel formulation utilizes supramolecular interactions between albumin and paclitaxel to form stable nanoparticles, eliminating the need for toxic solvents. The system targets the gp 60 receptor-mediated pathway and SPARC (Secreted Protein Acidic and Rich in Cysteine) to enhance tumor accumulation (Tian and Yao, 2022). Clinical trials showed better response rates compared to conventional paclitaxel 1 (33% vs 25%) in non-small cell lung cancer, with significantly improved pharmacokinetic profiles. Doxil is another prime example of approved supramolecular nanomedicine, consisting of intraliposomal doxorubicin-sulfate nano-rod crystals formed through supramolecular assembly. The distinct supramolecular structure within these 85-nanometer PEGylated liposomes enables controlled drug release and enhanced tumor targeting via the enhanced permeability and retention (EPR). Effect (Carretta et al., 2024). This formulation has shown outstanding clinical success in treating various cancers, including ovarian cancer, Kaposi's sarcoma, and multiple myeloma.

The clinical pipeline for supramolecular anticancer systems encompasses several promising candidates at various stages of development. CRLX101(IT-101), a cyclodextrin-based polymer conjugate of camptothecin, has progressed through multiple Phase I and II trials across different cancer types (Sanoff et al., 2019). This system demonstrates the clinical potential of cyclodextrin-based supramolecular drug delivery, showing promising results in small cell lung cancer, ovarian cancer, and advanced solid tumors. Phase I trials of

CALAA-01, a targeted nanocomplex containing siRNA, mark the first clinical assessment of cyclodextrin-based gene delivery systems for cancer treatment. Although preliminary, these studies define the safety profile and dosing parameters for supramolecular nucleic acid delivery platforms (Zuckerman et al., 2014).

The clinical translation challenges for supramolecular systems mainly involve improving stability, scaling up manufacturing, and navigating the regulatory process. Unlike traditional drug formulations, supramolecular systems require detailed characterization of noncovalent interactions and dynamic assembly processes, which makes regulatory approval more complex. Supramolecular self-assembly systems for cancer therapy have demonstrated considerable versatility and efficacy; however, several critical challenges impede their widespread clinical adoption. The intricacy of design and synthesis—often involving multiple functional modules such as macrocyclic hosts, targeting ligands, stimuli-responsive linkers, and imaging agents—can compromise batch consistency and elevate production costs. Developing streamlined, modular chemistries that facilitate the plug-and-play assembly of components without extensive optimization will be essential for scalable manufacturing. Achieving a balance between in vivo stability and on-demand disassembly remains delicate; many systems disassemble prematurely in circulation, leading to off-target release and systemic toxicity, whereas others exhibit excessive stability, hindering therapeutic release within the tumor. Precise adjustment of linker chemistries and the integration of multi-stimuli triggers—such as pH, redox state, enzymatic activity, and temperature—alongside hierarchical activation thresholds, can enhance circulation stability and enable controlled release at the target site (Su et al., 2021). Tumor penetration and heterogeneity present substantial obstacles; dense extracellular matrices and elevated interstitial pressures in deep tumor regions can restrict nanoparticle infiltration. Strategies such as size-switchable assemblies responsive to tumor pH, enzyme-triggered matrix degradation, or the incorporation of cell-penetrating peptides can mitigate these barriers 340 Moreover, intra-tumoural heterogeneity in receptor expression and microenvironmental factors necessitates adaptable systems capable of multi-target engagement or stimulus responsiveness. Currently, limited data are available regarding the immunogenicity and long-term safety of novel supramolecular architectures. Although many components (e.g., cyclodextrins, specific peptides) are biocompatible, comprehensive toxicological evaluations, including assessments of immunotoxicity, complement activation, and long-term biodistribution are required to meet regulatory standards (Geng et al., 2024). Developing standardized evaluation protocols will facilitate the acceleration of safety assessments. Regulatory and commercial challenges also persist; multifunctional nanomedicines often obscure distinctions between drugs, devices, and biologics, resulting in ambiguous approval pathways and unpredictable timelines. Looking forward, AI-driven molecular design holds promise for the rapid identification of optimal macrocycle–guest pairs, linker chemistries, and multi-stimuli architectures customized to individual tumor profiles. The integration of personalized biomarkers, such as genomics, proteomics, and metabolomics, can enable patient-specific triggers and targeted strategies (Mah et al., 2025). Multicompartmental assemblies capable of sequential or cascade release of chemotherapeutics, immunomodulators, and gene therapies may mitigate drug resistance and foster durable immune responses. Ultimately, implementing green chemistry methods in the synthesis of hosts and linkers, combined with continuous-flow manufacturing technologies, will enhance scalability, minimize environmental impact, and lower costs (Caballo, et al., 2017). Addressing these challenges through interdisciplinary collaboration will pave the way for safer, more efficacious, and personalized supramolecular nanomedicines in the realm of cancer treatment.

Conclusion

The exploration of self-assembling supramolecular systems has opened a new doorway, mainly in anticancer therapy, where molecular techniques satisfy clinical purposes. Self-assembling supramolecular systems, whose adaptability, reversibility, and biomimetic principles represent a profound leap forward in therapeutic innovation.

The Chapter explores a variety of carriers, including cyclodextrin inclusion complexes, calixarene and cucurbituril host-guest assemblies, dendrimer conjugates, micelles, vesicles, and peptide-based carriers, to construct functional nanostructures with exceptional precision that can sense, react, and adapt to their biological environment using a multitude of non-covalent bonding mechanisms, including hydrogen bonding, π-π stacking, hydrophobic interactions, and electrostatic attractions. Additionally, the comprehension that, beyond its primary objective, these assemblies also show other benefits through secondary effects, such as enhancing solubility, stability, and bioavailability while lowering systemic toxicity and off-target effects.

Its competence by various mechanisms for targeted and stimuli-responsive delivery using active targeting strategies that employ particular ligands, like folate, hyaluronic acid, or RGD peptides, to identify and target overexpressed receptors on tumor cells has improved the Enhanced Permeability and Retention (EPR) effect, which has long been regarded as a fundamental component of passive targeting. The capacity of these systems to activate on-demand drug release by taking advantage of the distinct biochemical cues of the tumor microenvironment, such as its acidic pH, high glutathione levels, and abundance of enzymes like matrix metalloproteinases (MMPs) and Cathepsin B, which is more appealing, is discussed here. This guarantees precision and safety by ensuring that therapeutic drugs are only active within diseased tissue. By doing this, how supramolecular systems change the idea of "drug delivery" to "drug intelligence," in which the carrier takes part in the therapeutic decision-making process, is addressed herein.

The chapter emphasized the potential of co-delivery and multimodal approaches. Cancer's complexity demands multi-pronged interventions, and supramolecular architectures are ideally suited for this purpose. By co-delivering chemotherapeutic agents with genes, immune modulators, or photosensitizers, these systems enable synergistic therapies—combining chemotherapy with immunotherapy, photodynamic therapy (PDT), or photothermal therapy (PTT). Light-activated, enzyme-triggered, or pH-responsive co-delivery platforms mark a new frontier in personalized and combination oncology, offering improved outcomes even in resistant or metastatic cancers.

Even with the remarkable advancements, there are still difficulties in getting these complex systems from the bench to the bedside. Long-term biocompatibility, batch consistency, and manufacturing scalability necessitate ongoing interdisciplinary cooperation between formulation scientists, pharmacologists, and physicians. However, the clinical success of formulations such as Doxil and Abraxane indicates that this goal is not only feasible but is now in progress.

Future developments in artificial intelligence, machine learning, theranostics, and supramolecular chemistry will speed up the development of customizable nanomedicines based on the tumor profiles of individual patients. The emergence of genuinely personalized oncology is heralded by this combination of biology, chemistry, and data-driven understanding. In the end, supramolecular self-assembly is a paradigm shift that substitutes chemical rigidity with molecular intelligence, turning cancer treatment into an accurate, flexible, and compassionate medical science.

References

Abdelhay, A.H., Bani-Yaseen, A.D., 2024. Recent advances and perspectives of supramolecular host-guest systems for electrochemical energy storage. Mater. Today. Chem. 40. https://doi.org/10.1016/j.mtchem.2024.102259.

Abed, H.F., Abuwatfa, W.H., Husseini, G.A., 2022. Redox-responsive drug delivery systems: Achemical perspective. Nanomaterials 12 (18). https://doi.org/10.3390/nano12183183.

Abedi-Gaballu, F., Dehghan, G., Ghaffari, M., Yekta, R., Abbaspour-Ravasjani, S., Baradaran, B., Ezzati Nazhad Dolatabadi, J., Hamblin, M.R., 2018. PAMAM dendrimers as efficient drug and gene delivery nanosystems for cancer therapy. Appl. Mater. Today 12, 177–190. https://doi.org/10.1016/j.apmt.2018.05.002.

Ahmadian, N., Mehrnejad, F., Amininasab, M., 2020. Molecular insight into the interaction between camptothecin and acyclic cucurbiturils as efficient nanocontainers in comparison with cucurbituril: Molecular docking and molecular dynamics simulation. J. Chem. Inf. Model. 60 (3), 1791–1803. https://doi.org/10.1021/acs.jcim.9b01087.

Almammadov, T., Elmazoglu, Z., Atakan, G., Kepil, D., Aykent, G., Kolemen, S., Gunbas, G., 2022. Locked and loaded: β-galactosidase activated photodynamic therapy agent enables selective imaging and targeted treatment of glioblastoma multiforme cancer cells. ACS. Appl. Bio. Mater 5 (9), 4284–4293. https://doi.org/10.1021/acsabm.2c00484.

Andrade, F., Roca-Melendres, M.M., Durán-Lara, E.F., Rafael, D., Schwartz, S., 2021. Stimuli-responsive hydrogels for cancer treatment: The role of pH, light, ionic strength and magnetic field. Cancers 13 (5), 1164. https://doi.org/10.3390/cancers13051164.

Ashrafizadeh, M., Delfi, M., Zarrabi, A., Bigham, A., Sharifi, E., Rabiee, N., Paiva-Santos, A.C., Kumar, A.P., Tan, S. C., Hushmandi, K., Ren, J., Zare, E.N., Makvandi, P., 2022. Stimuli-responsive liposomal nanoformulations in cancer therapy: Pre-clinical and clinical approaches. J. Contr. Release 351, 50–80. https://doi.org/10.1016/j.jconrel.2022.08.001.

Beig, A., Agbaria, R., Dahan, A., 2015. The use of captisol (SBE7-β-CD) in oral solubility-enabling formulations: Comparison to HPβCD and the solubility–permeability interplay. Eur. J. Pharmaceut. Sci. 77, 73–78. https://doi.org/10.1016/j.ejps.2015.05.024.

Belyaev, I.B., Griaznova, O.Y., Yaremenko, A.V., Deyev, S.M., Zelepukin, I.V., 2025. Beyond the EPR effect: Intravital microscopy analysis of nanoparticle drug delivery to tumors. Adv. Drug. Deliv. Rev. 219. https://doi.org/10.1016/j.addr.2025.115550.

Bilgin, G.B., Bilgin, C., Burkett, B.J., Orme, J.J., Childs, D.S., Thorpe, M.P., Halfdanarson, T.R., Johnson, G.B., Kendi, A.T., Sartor, O., 2024. Theranostics and artificial intelligence: New frontiers in personalized medicine. Theranostics 14 (6), 2367–2378. https://doi.org/10.7150/thno.94788.

Bilia, A.R., Bergonzi, M.C., Guccione, C., Manconi, M., Fadda, A.M., Sinico, C., 2016. Vesicles and micelles: Two versatile vectors for the delivery of natural products. J. Drug. Deliv. Sci. Technol. 32, 241–255. https://doi.org/10.1016/j.jddst.2015.09.007.

Caballo, C., Sicilia, M.D., Rubio, S., 2017. Supramolecular Solvents for Green Chemistry the Application of Green Solvents in Separation Processes. Elsevier Inc., Spain, pp. 111–137. https://doi.org/10.1016/B978-0-12-805297-6.00005-X.

Carretta, A., Moscardini, A., Signore, G., Debellis, D., Catalano, F., Marotta, R., Palmieri, V., Tedeschi, G., Scipioni, L., Pozzi, D., Caracciolo, G., Beltram, F., Cardarelli, F., 2024. The supramolecular processing of liposomal doxorubicin hinders its therapeutic efficacy in cells. Mol. Ther. Oncol. 32 (3), 200836. https://doi.org/10.1016/j.omton.2024.200836.

Chen, X., Xie, B., Huang, L., Wan, J., Wang, Y., Shi, X., Qiao, Y., Song, H., Wang, H., 2021. Quantitative self-assembly of pure drug cocktails as injectable nanomedicines for synergistic drug delivery and cancer therapy. Theranostics 11 (12), 5713–5727. https://doi.org/10.7150/thno.55250.

Chen, C., Chen, N., Qi, Y., Lyu, M., Wu, C., Xie, C., Yu, H., 2024. Copper-based single-atom nanozyme system mimicking platelet cells for enhancing the outcome of radioimmunotherapy. Int. J. Nanomed. 19, 403–414. https://doi.org/10.2147/ijn.s445805.

Colaco, V., Jadhav, S.R., Bandi, S.P., Datta, D., Dhas, N., Thakur, G., Ramesh, B.V., Alizadeh, B., 2025. Multifunctional application of supramolecular cucurbiturils as encapsulating hosts in drug delivery: A review. Int. J. Pharm. 681. https://doi.org/10.1016/j.ijpharm.2025.125801.

Cook, T.R., Zheng, Y.R., Stang, P.J., 2013. Metal-organic frameworks and self-assembled supramolecular coordination complexes: Comparing and contrasting the design, synthesis, and functionality of metal-organic materials. Chem. Rev. 113 (1), 734–777. https://doi.org/10.1021/cr3002824.

Cué-Sampedro, R., Sánchez-Fernández, J.A., 2024. Supramolecular systems and their connection with metal–organic structures. Front. Chem. 12. https://doi.org/10.3389/fchem.2024.1468916.

Dougherty, D.A., 2025. The cation−πinteraction in chemistry and biology. Chem. Rev. 125 (5), 2793–2808. https://doi.org/10.1021/acs.chemrev.4c00707.

Egorova, V.S., Kolesova, E.P., Lopus, M., Yan, N., Parodi, A., Zamyatnin, A.A., 2023. Smart delivery systems responsive to cathepsin B activity for cancer treatment. Pharmaceutics 15 (7). https://doi.org/10.3390/pharmaceutics15071848. http://www.mdpi.com/journal/pharmaceutics.

Feng, G., Lei, S., 2024. Synthesis of covalent nanostructures at the solid-liquid interfaces. In: Encyclopedia of Solid-Liquid Interfaces. Elsevier, pp. 351–359. https://doi.org/10.1016/B978-0-323-85669-0.00065-9.

Frontera, A., Bauza, A., 2021. On the importance of pnictogen and chalcogen bonding interactions in supramolecular catalysis. Int. J. Mol. Sci. 22 (22), 12550. https://doi.org/10.3390/ijms222212550.

Geng, W.C., Jiang, Z.T., Chen, S.L., Guo, D.S., 2024. Supramolecular interaction in the action of drug delivery systems. Chem. Sci. 15 (21), 7811–7823. https://doi.org/10.1039/d3sc04585d.

Guo, D.S., Liu, Y., 2014. Supramolecular chemistry of p -sulfonatocalix[n]arenes and its biological applications. Acc. Chem. Res. 47 (7), 1925–1934. https://doi.org/10.1021/ar500009g.

Haider, S.E.B., Desai, S., Shahiwala, A.F., 2025. Enhanced solubility and rapid delivery of vitamin D3 via Captisol (β-Cyclodextrin sulfobutyl ether) inclusion complex in mouth-dissolving films. Adv. Pharmacol. Pharm. Sci. 2025 (1). https://doi.org/10.1155/adpp/7621311.

He, S., Wu, L., Li, X., Sun, H., Xiong, T., Liu, J., Huang, C., Xu, H., Sun, H., Chen, W., Gref, R., Zhang, J., 2021. Metal-organic frameworks for advanced drug delivery. Acta Pharm. Sin. B. 11 (8), 2362–2395. https://doi.org/10.1016/j.apsb.2021.03.019.

Hill, J., Shrestha, L., Ishihara, S., Ji, Q., Ariga, K., 2014. Self-assembly: From amphiphiles to chromophores and beyond. Molecules 19 (6), 8589–8609. https://doi.org/10.3390/molecules19068589.

Hu, W., Ye, B., Yu, G., Yang, H., Wu, H., Ding, Y., Huang, F., Wang, W., Mao, Z., 2024. Dual-responsive supramolecular polymeric nanomedicine for self-cascade amplified cancer immunotherapy. Adv. Sci. 11 (20). https://doi.org/10.1002/advs.202305382.

Jiang, X., Du, B., Huang, Y., Yu, M., Zheng, J., 2020a. Cancer photothermal therapy with ICG-conjugated gold nanoclusters. Bioconjug. Chem. 31 (5), 1522–1528. https://doi.org/10.1021/acs.bioconjchem.0c00172.

Jiang, Y., Zhou, Y., Zhang, C.Y., Fang, T., 2020b. Co-delivery of paclitaxel and doxorubicin by pH-responsive prodrug micelles for cancer therapy. Int. J. Nanomed. 15, 3319–3331. https://doi.org/10.2147/ijn.s249144.

Kong, Y., Li, J., Zhao, X., Wu, Y., Chen, L., 2025. CAR-T cell therapy: Developments, challenges and expanded applications from cancer to autoimmunity. Front. Immunol. 15. https://doi.org/10.3389/fimmu.2024.1519671.

Kumar, K., Rani, V., Mishra, M., Chawla, R., 2022. New paradigm in combination therapy of siRNA with chemotherapeutic drugs for effective cancer therapy. Curr. Res. Pharmacol. Drug Discov. 3, 100103. https://doi.org/10.1016/j.crphar.2022.100103.

Kwon, N., Kim, H., Li, X., Yoon, J., 2021. Supramolecular agents for combination of photodynamic therapy and other treatments. Chem. Sci. 12 (21), 7248–7268. https://doi.org/10.1039/d1sc01125a.

Lee, Y.B., Kyun, M.L., Lee, Y.J., Shim, H.E., Huh, K.M., Kang, S.W., 2025. Cyclodextrins as multifunctional tools for advanced biomaterials in tissue repair and regeneration. Bioact. Mater. 49, 627–651. https://doi.org/10.1016/j.bioactmat.2025.03.018.

Li, P., Ryder, M.R., Stoddart, J.F., 2020. Hydrogen-bonded organic frameworks: A rising class of porous molecular materials. Acc. Mater. Res. 1 (1), 77–87. https://doi.org/10.1021/accountsmr.0c00019.

Li, S., Gao, Y., Ding, Y., Xu, A., Tan, H., 2021. Supramolecular nano drug delivery systems mediated via host-guest chemistry of cucurbituril (n = 6 and 7). Chin. Chem. Lett. 32 (1), 313–318. https://doi.org/10.1016/j.cclet.2020.04.049.

Li, R., Liu, N., Liu, R., Jin, X., Zheng, L., 2024. Calixarene: Asupramolecular material for treating cancer. Curr. Drug Deliv. 21 (2), 184–192. https://doi.org/10.2174/1567201820666230417084210.

Lu, J., Zhao, Z., Pan, L., Wu, H., Wang, S., Tong, X., Wu, S., 2025. Hyaluronidase: Structure, mechanism of action, diseases and therapeutic targets. Mol. Biomed. 6 (1). https://doi.org/10.1186/s43556-025-00299-y.

Ma, C., Xi, S., Sun, H., Zhang, M., Pei, Y., 2023. Identifying the oncogenic roles of FAP in human cancers based on systematic analysis. Aging 15 (14), 7056–7083. https://doi.org/10.18632/aging.204892.

Mah, J.J.Q., Surat'man, N.E.B., Li, B., Wang, S., Li, Z., 2025. Recent advances of dynamic covalent chemistry polymers aligning with principles of green chemistry. Chem. Sus. Chem. 18 (14). https://doi.org/10.1002/cssc.202500480.

Mustafa, S., Koran, S., AlOmair, L., 2022. Insights into the role of matrix metalloproteinases in cancer and its various therapeutic aspects: Areview. Front. Mol. Biosci. 9. https://doi.org/10.3389/fmolb.2022.896099.

Mylonas-Margaritis, I., Mayans, J., McArdle, P., Papatriantafyllopoulou, C., 2021. ZnII and CuII-based coordination polymers and metal organic frameworks by the of use of 2-pyridyl oximes and 1,3,5-benzenetricarboxylic acid. Molecules 26 (2), 491. https://doi.org/10.3390/molecules26020491.

Nag, R., Rao, C.P., 2022. Calixarene-mediated host-guest interactions leading to supramolecular assemblies: Visualization by microscopy. Chem. Commun. 58 (41), 6044–6063. https://doi.org/10.1039/d2cc01850k.

Nammas, M., 2025. The impact of drug delivery systems on pharmacokinetics and drug-drug interactions in neuropsychiatric treatment. Cureus. 17 (6). https://doi.org/10.7759/cureus.85563.

Navarro, R.P.-, Salmeron, M.C.-, Carrilero-Flores, E., Saura-Sanmartin, A., 2025. Molecular release by the rotaxane and pseudorotaxane approach. Chem. Eur J. 31 (23). https://doi.org/10.1002/chem.202500350.

Niland, S., Riscanevo, A.X., Eble, J.A., 2022. Matrix metalloproteinases shape the tumor microenvironment in cancer progression. Int. J. Mol. Sci. 23 (1). https://doi.org/10.3390/ijms23010146.

Özkan, M., Kumar, Y., Keser, Y., Hadi, S.E., Tuncel, D., 2019. Cucurbituril-Anchored porphyrin-based multifunctional molecular platform for photodynamic antimicrobial and cancer therapy. ACS. Appl. Bio. Mater. 2 (11), 4693–4697. https://doi.org/10.1021/acsabm.9b00763.

Pan, C., Liu, Y., Zhou, M., Wang, W., Shi, M., Xing, M., Liao, W., 2018. Theranostic pH-sensitive nanoparticles for highly efficient targeted delivery of doxorubicin for breast tumor treatment. Int. J. Nanomed. 13, 1119–1137. https://doi.org/10.2147/ijn.s147464.

Panja, S., Adams, D.J., 2021. Urea-urease reaction in controlling properties of supramolecular hydrogels: Pros and cons. Chem. Eur J. 27 (35), 8928–8939. https://doi.org/10.1002/chem.202100490.

Park, I.H., Sohn, J.H., Kim, S.B., Lee, K.S., Chung, J.S., Lee, S.H., Kim, T.Y., Jung, K.H., Cho, E.K., Kim, Y.S., Song, H. S., Seo, J.H., Ryoo, H.M., Lee, S.A., Yoon, S.Y., Kim, C.S., Kim, Y.T., Kim, S.Y., Jin, M.R., Ro, J., 2017. An open-label, randomized, parallel, phase III trial evaluating the efficacy and safety of polymeric micelle-formulated paclitaxel compared to conventional cremophor EL-Based paclitaxel for recurrent or metastatic HER2-negative breast cancer. Cancer. Res. Treat. 49 (3), 569–577. https://doi.org/10.4143/crt.2016.289.

Pasban, S., Raissi, H., 2021. Nanotechnology-based approaches for targeting and delivery of drugs via Hexakis (m-PE) macrocycles. Sci. Rep. 11 (1). https://doi.org/10.1038/s41598-021-87011-6.

Pashkina, E., Aktanova, A., Mirzaeva, I., Kovalenko, E., Andrienko, I., Knauer, N., Pronkina, N., Kozlov, V., 2021. The effect of cucurbit[7]uril on the antitumor and immunomodulating properties of oxaliplatin and carboplatin. Int. J. Mol. Sci. 22 (14), 7337. https://doi.org/10.3390/ijms22147337.

Patel, K., 2023. Structural organization of peptides. In: De Novo Peptide Design. Elsevier, pp. 1–33. https://doi.org/10.1016/B978-0-323-99917-5.00008-1.

Peng, C.L., Lin, H.C., Chiang, W.L., Shih, Y.H., Chiang, P.F., Luo, T.Y., Cheng, C.C., Shieh, M.J., 2018. Anti-angiogenic treatment (bevacizumab) improves the responsiveness of photodynamic therapy in colorectal cancer. Photodiagn. Photodyn. Ther. 23, 111–118. https://doi.org/10.1016/j.pdpdt.2018.06.008.

Peng, S., Yuan, X., Li, H., Huang, H., Li, C., Chen, W., Ren, J., Zhang, Q., Ding, G., Bai, J., 2024. pH-responsive self-assembling peptides potentiate therapeutic efficacy via prolonged drug retention and immunomodulation. Mater. Des. 241, 112893. https://doi.org/10.1016/j.matdes.2024.112893.

Rahim, M.A., Jan, N., Khan, S., Shah, H., Madni, A., Khan, A., Jabar, A., Khan, S., Elhissi, A., Hussain, Z., Aziz, H.C., Sohail, M., Khan, M., Thu, H.E., 2021. Recent advancements in stimuli responsive drug delivery platforms for active and passive cancer targeting. Cancers 13 (4), 1–52. https://doi.org/10.3390/cancers13040670.

Ranbhise, J.S., Singh, M.K., Ju, S., Han, S., Yun, H.R., Kim, S.S., Kang, I., 2025. The redox paradox: Cancer's double-edged sword for malignancy and therapy. Antioxidants 14 (10). https://doi.org/10.3390/antiox14101187.

Rozans, S.J., Moghaddam, A.S., Wu, Y., Atanasoff, K., Nino, L., Dunne, K., Pashuck, E.T., 2024. Quantifying and controlling the proteolytic degradation of cell adhesion peptides. ACS. Biomater. Sci. Eng. 10 (8), 4916–4926. https://doi.org/10.1021/acsbiomaterials.4c00736.

Saenz, G., Pogostin, B.H., Cole, C.C., Agrawal, A., Chew-Martinez, D., Dubackic, M., Pal, A., Olsson, U., McHugh, K.J., Hartgerink, J.D., 2025. Nanofibrous peptide hydrogels leveraging histidine to modulate pH-responsive supramolecular assembly and antibody release. Biomacromolecules 26 (1), 490–502. https://doi.org/10.1021/acs.biomac.4c01296.

Sanoff, H.K., Moon, D.H., Moore, D.T., Boles, J., Bui, C., Blackstock, W., O'Neil, B.H., Subramaniam, S., McRee, A.J., Carlson, C., Lee, M.S., Tepper, J.E., Wang, A.Z., 2019. Phase I/II trial of nano-camptothecin CRLX101 with capecitabine and radiotherapy as neoadjuvant treatment for locally advanced rectal cancer. Nanomedicine 18, 189–195. https://doi.org/10.1016/j.nano.2019.02.021.

Scialla, S., Hanafy, M.S., Wang, J.L., Genicio, N., Costa Da Silva, M., Costa, M., Oliveira-Pinto, S., Baltazar, F., Gallo, J., Cui, Z., Bañobre-López, M., 2023. Targeted treatment of triple-negative-breast cancer through pH-triggered tumour associated macrophages using smart theranostic nanoformulations. Int. J. Pharm. 632. https://doi.org/10.1016/j.ijpharm.2022.122575.

Silva, F., Padín-Iruegas, M., Caponio, V., Lorenzo-Pouso, A., Saavedra-Nieves, P., Chamorro-Petronacci, C., Suaréz-Peñaranda, J., Pérez-Sayáns, M., 2022. Caspase 3 and cleaved caspase 3 expression in tumorogenesis and its correlations with prognosis in head and neck cancer: Asystematic review and meta-analysis. Int. J. Mol. Sci. 23 (19), 11937. https://doi.org/10.3390/ijms231911937.

Song, C., Xiao, Y., Ouyang, Z., Shen, M., Shi, X., 2020. Efficient co-delivery of microRNA 21 inhibitor and doxorubicin to cancer cells using core–shell tecto dendrimers formed via supramolecular host–guest assembly. J. Mater. Chem. B. 8 (14), 2768–2774. https://doi.org/10.1039/d0tb00346h.

Song, C., Zhan, M., Ouyang, Z., Yao, Y., Gao, Y., Shen, M., Shi, X., 2023. Core-shell tecto dendrimer-mediated cooperative chemoimmunotherapy of breast cancer. J. Contr. Release 358, 601–611. https://doi.org/10.1016/j.jconrel.2023.05.021.

Song, N., Xiong, W., Zhu, J., Zhu, C., Gu, X., Yu, Z., 2025. Peptide-based strategies for glioblastoma therapy: From small molecular drugs to delivery vehicles. J. Contr. Release 385, 114023. https://doi.org/10.1016/j.jconrel.2025.114023.

Sreedevi, P., Nair, J.B., Joseph, M.M., Murali, V.P., Suresh, C.H., Varma, R.L., Maiti, K.K., 2021. Dynamic self-assembly of mannosylated-calix[4]arene into micelles for the delivery of hydrophobic drugs. J. Control. Release 339, 284–296. https://doi.org/10.1016/j.jconrel.2021.09.038.

Su, Z., Xiao, D., Xie, F., Liu, L., Wang, Y., Fan, S., Zhou, X., Li, S., 2021. Antibody–drug conjugates: Recent advances in linker chemistry. Acta Pharm. Sin. B. 11 (12), 3889–3907. https://doi.org/10.1016/j.apsb.2021.03.042.

Subhan, M.A., Yalamarty, S.S.K., Filipczak, N., Parveen, F., Torchilin, V.P., 2021. Recent advances in tumor targeting via epr effect for cancer treatment. J. Pers. Med. 11 (6). https://doi.org/10.3390/jpm11060571.

Tian, Z., Yao, W., 2022. Albumin-bound paclitaxel: Worthy of further study in sarcomas. Front. Oncol. 12. https://doi.org/10.3389/fonc.2022.815900.

Tyagi, K., Venkatesh, V., 2024. Emerging potential approaches in alkaline phosphatase (ALP) activatable cancer theranostics. RSC. Med. Chem. 15 (4), 1148–1160. https://doi.org/10.1039/d3md00565h.

Veselov, V.V., Nosyrev, A.E., Jicsinszky, L., Alyautdin, R.N., Cravotto, G., 2022. Targeted delivery methods for anticancer drugs. Cancers 14 (3). https://doi.org/10.3390/cancers14030622.

Wang, X., Li, C., Wang, Y., Chen, H., Zhang, X., Luo, C., Zhou, W., Li, L., Teng, L., Yu, H., Wang, J., 2022. Smart drug delivery systems for precise cancer therapy. Acta Pharm. Sin. B. 12 (11), 4098–4121. https://doi.org/10.1016/j.apsb.2022.08.013.

Wang, Y., Jiang, C., Zhou, H., Han, R., 2025. Transforming cancer immunotherapy: Integration of distinct immune-based approaches as redefined dual immunotherapy with potential third-sensitizer. Exp. Hematol. Oncol. 14 (1). https://doi.org/10.1186/s40164-025-00705-9.

Wolfram, J., Ferrari, M., 2019. Clinical cancer nanomedicine. Nano Today 25, 85–98. https://doi.org/10.1016/j.nantod.2019.02.005.

Wu, J., 2021. The enhanced permeability and retention (EPR) effect: the significance of the concept and methods to enhance its application. J. Personalized. Med. 11 (8), 771. https://doi.org/10.3390/jpm11080771.

Wu, H., Chen, H., Tang, B., Kang, Y., Xu, J.F., Zhang, X., 2020. Host-guest interactions between oxaliplatin and cucurbit[7]uril/cucurbit[7]uril derivatives under pseudo-physiological conditions. Langmuir 36 (5), 1235–1240. https://doi.org/10.1021/acs.langmuir.9b03325.

Wu, C., Wang, M., Sun, J., Jia, Y., Zhu, X., Liu, G., Zhu, Y., Guan, Y., Zhang, Z., Pang, X., 2023a. Peptide-drug co-assembling: a potent armament against cancer. Theranostics 13 (15), 5322–5347. https://doi.org/10.7150/thno.87356.

Wu, W., Yu, X., Sun, J., Han, Y., Ma, Y., Zhang, G., Ma, Q., Li, Q., Xiang, H., 2023b. Zeolitic imidazolate framework (ZIF-8) decorated iron oxide nanoparticles loaded doxorubicin hydrochloride for osteosarcoma treatment - in vitro and in vivo preclinical studies. Int. J. Nanomed. 18, 7985–7999. https://doi.org/10.2147/ijn.s438771.

Xie, F., Li, R., Shu, W., Zhao, L., Wan, J., 2022. Self-assembly of peptide dendrimers and their bio-applications in theranostics. Mater. Today Bio. 14, 100239. https://doi.org/10.1016/j.mtbio.2022.100239.

Xu, J., Wang, J., Ye, J., Jiao, J., Liu, Z., Zhao, C., Li, B., Fu, Y., 2021. Metal-coordinated supramolecular self-assemblies for cancer theranostics. Adv. Sci. 8 (16). https://doi.org/10.1002/advs.202101101.

Yan, S., Na, J., Liu, X., Wu, P., 2024. Different targeting ligands-mediated drug delivery systems for tumor therapy. Pharmaceutics 16 (2), 248. https://doi.org/10.3390/pharmaceutics16020248.

Ye, G., Luo, S., Zafar, H., Ge, H., Liu, B., Wang, N., Jin, Y., Wang, M., Chen, X., Ye, X., 2024. pH-sensitive supramolecular self-assembled peptide hydrogel for the treatment of esophageal cancer. Front. Pharmacol. 15. https://doi.org/10.3389/fphar.2024.1453422.

Yin, Y., Zhao, J., Liu, M., Lu, Y., Cao, J., Zhao, R., Wu, L., Shen, S., 2025. Boosting ferroptosis therapy by sorafenib and ML385 loaded CuFe2O4 nanozymes. Colloids Surf. B Biointerfaces 255, 114968. https://doi.org/10.1016/j.colsurfb.2025.114968.

Yu, G., Chen, X., 2019. Host-guest chemistry in supramolecular theranostics. Theranostics 9 (11), 3041–3074. https://doi.org/10.7150/thno.31653.

Zeng, W., Luo, Y., Gan, D., Zhang, Y., Deng, H., Liu, G., 2023. Advances in doxorubicin-based nano-drug delivery system in triple negative breast cancer. Front. Bioeng. Biotechnol. 11. https://doi.org/10.3389/fbioe.2023.1271420.

Zeroug-Metz, L., Lee, S., 2024. Biodynamers: Applications of dynamic covalent chemistry in single-chain polymer nanoparticles. Drug Deliv. Transl. Res. 14 (12), 3599–3607. https://doi.org/10.1007/s13346-024-01665-z.

Zhang, X.-ying, Zhang, P.-ying, 2017. Polymersomes in nanomedicine - areview. Curr. Nanosci. 13 (2), 124–129. https://doi.org/10.2174/1573413712666161018144519.

Zhang, Z., Yao, S., Hu, Y., Zhao, X., Lee, R.J., 2022. Application of lipid-based nanoparticles in cancer immunotherapy. Front. Immunol. 13. https://doi.org/10.3389/fimmu.2022.967505.

Zhang, J., Zhan, B., Yang, Du, Liu, N., Liu, S., Li, X., 2025. Targeted cancer treatment using folic acid-functionalized carbohydrate polymers: a new era in nanomedicine. Ind. Crop. Prod. 235, 121704. https://doi.org/10.1016/j.indcrop.2025.121704.

Zhao, X., Li, Y., 2025. Matrix metalloproteinase-2-responsive peptide-modified cleavable PEGylated liposomes for paclitaxel delivery. Pharmaceuticals 18 (7), 1042. https://doi.org/10.3390/ph18071042.

Zhao, Y., Liu, X., Liu, X., Yu, J., Bai, X., Wu, X., Guo, X., Liu, Z., Liu, X., 2022. Combination of phototherapy with immune checkpoint blockade: Theory and practice in cancer. Front. Immunol. 13. https://doi.org/10.3389/fimmu.2022.955920.

Zuckerman, J.E., Gritli, I., Tolcher, A., Heidel, J.D., Lim, D., Morgan, R., Chmielowski, B., Ribas, A., Davis, M.E., Yen, Y., 2014. Correlating animal and human phase Ia/Ib clinical data with CALAA-01, a targeted, polymer-based nanoparticle containing siRNA. Proc. Natl. Acad. Sci. U. S. A. 111 (31), 11449–11454. https://doi.org/10.1073/pnas.1411393111.

CHAPTER

12

Advances in metal-organic frameworks for anticancer drug delivery

Saisritam Kar, Vaibhav Verma, Priya Jha, Divakar Kumar and Vivek Dave

Department of Pharmacy, School of Health Sciences, Central University of South Bihar, Gaya, Bihar, India

Introduction

Cancer is a global health concern, accounting for one in every six fatalities worldwide. Traditional treatment approaches, such as surgery, chemotherapy, and radiotherapy, have a low success rate and are associated with cancer relapse or metastasis. Several improvements in cancer therapy have occurred, including stem cell therapy, ablation therapy, natural antioxidants, radionics, chemodynamic therapy, sonodynamic therapy, and ferroptosis-based therapy. However, its inability to target tumor cells rather than healthy cells restricts its capacity to cure cancer. This causes systemic toxicity, the formation of drug-resistant tumor cells, and insufficient drug concentrations in tumors (Debela et al., 2021). Metal-organic Frameworks (MOFs) have received a lot of interest over the last few decades as an advanced nano drug delivery technology for cancer treatment. The extremely flexible architecture has unique qualities such as porous surface area, massive drug payload capacity, structural diversity, and the potential to functionalize with targeted molecules or therapeutics, giving it the pilot position on a novel drug delivery system (Guo et al., 2025).

Metal-organic frameworks (MOFs) are a novel family of highly adjustable hybrid materials comprising organic bridging ligands and metal connecting sites. They are also known as coordination polymers or coordination networks, created in moderate environments through coordination-directed self-assembly processes. Due to high porosity and tunable pore sizes, shapes, and functions, an extensive research is ongoing on MOFs for use in drug delivery and cancer therapy. The huge pore sizes and surface areas can be exploited

Advanced Cancer Therapeutics
https://doi.org/10.1016/B978-0-443-44185-1.00003-3

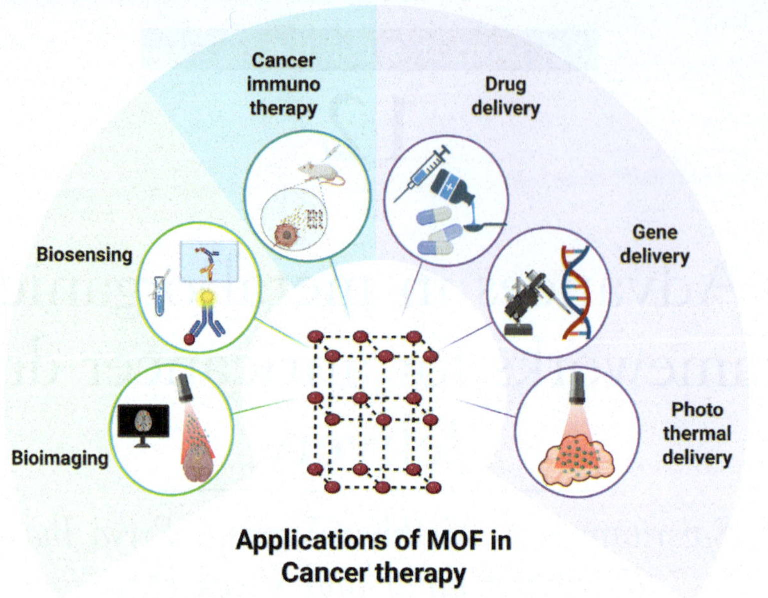

FIGURE 12.1 **Schematic representation of the applications of metal organic framework in cancer therapy.** MOFs can be used as carrier for the delivery of drug, genetic materials, dye, imaging agent, theranostic materials and other therapeutics.

for drug encapsulation and functionalization for post-synthetic grafting of drug particles. These are biodegradable, biocompatible, and non-immunogenic due to their composition and relatively labile metal–ligand bonds. MOFs have been extensively studied for loading and releasing several medicinal compounds. Several methods have been discovered for inorganic and organic polymeric nanoparticles to scale up MOFs down to the nano regime to construct nanoscale metal–organic frameworks (NMOFs). MOFs can be used as nano vectors for delivering therapeutic medicines to specific parts of the human body (Khan et al., 2024). MOF can tackle cancer in various ways, a few of which are shown in Fig. 12.1.

Metal-organic frameworks (MOFs): Structural and functional overview

Metal-organic frameworks (MOF) are porous materials that permit therapeutics to diffuse into the bulk structure. The pores' size and shape determine the guests' size and form selectivity for incorporation. In MOFs, organic linkers or bridging ligands make a coordinative bond with metal ions to form the porous structures. The basic principle of MOFs formation is the attachment of metal-containing units, also known as secondary-building units (SBUs), with organic linkers, as shown in Fig. 12.2. These linkers are typically carboxylate groups, phosphonates, sulfonates, or heterocyclic compounds. The final geometry of the framework largely depends on the coordination number of the metal ions, the geometry of their coordination sphere, and the functional groups present on the organic linkers. This results in an

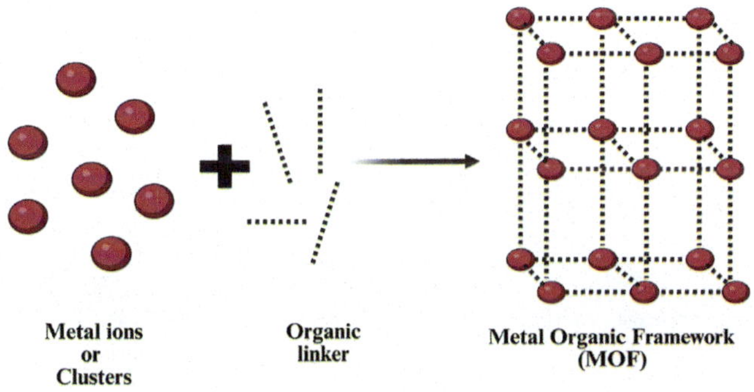

FIGURE 12.2 **Represent formation of metalorganic framework by combination of metal ions and organic linkers.** Metal ions linked with organic linker results in a unit cell structure with void space that can be exploited in drug delivery.

open framework with remarkable characteristics, such as porosity, stability, surface area, and functionality. Long organic linkers provide MOFs with a significant amount of storage space and adsorption sites, resulting in a highly porous nanomaterial. The surface or ligand functionalization can alter the properties of MOFs for targeted drug delivery and effective cancer therapy (Gholami et al., 2022; Parsaei and Akhbari, 2023; Collins, 1987).

Various SBU geometries, such as square paddlewheels, trigonal prisms, triangular arrangements, and octahedra (six points of extension), have been observed in MOF structures. Broad frameworks are formed when inorganic nodes join with ditopic, tritopic, tetratopic, or multitopic linkers. SBUs have an important role in determining the topology of MOFs. This can lead to either closed oligomeric structures or endless polymeric frameworks, depending on the situation. Researchers carefully selected metal-containing units and linkers to generate a range of MOFs with unique properties suitable for certain applications. Pore diameters and spatial arrangement of cavities can be controlled by selecting appropriate metal centers, organic linkers, and reaction conditions. Large pores can cause interpenetration of the frameworks, reducing the available porosity. To avoid this, linkers of appropriate length and capability are chosen. MOFs typically have pore windows of 2 nm in diameter, which is suitable for the adsorption of small molecules. However, accommodating enzymes and proteins becomes more problematic. To overcome this disadvantage, scientists created mesoporous MOFs with pore diameters ranging from 2 to 50 nm, as well as nanosized MOF crystals. These structural advances allow for the encapsulation of higher-molecular-weight biomolecules and surface modification by numerous functional groups, while retaining overall porosity (Collins, 1987). The versatility of MOFs also depends on their synthesis methods (Fig. 12.3). Different processes have a significant impact on crystallinity, particle size, and stability, all of which are important for real-world applications in drug delivery.

Nanostructured MOFs (nano-MOFs) have recently been receiving more interest owing to their role in integrating high surface area, structure versatility, and biocompatibility of traditional nanomedicines with MOFs possessing inherent porosity and functionality. MOFs are also known as "soft porous crystals", which show framework flexibility due to external stimulus-triggered structural modifications (such as changes in pressure, temperature, light). In this regard, the free-cortex flexibility of CSAs makes them attractive for various

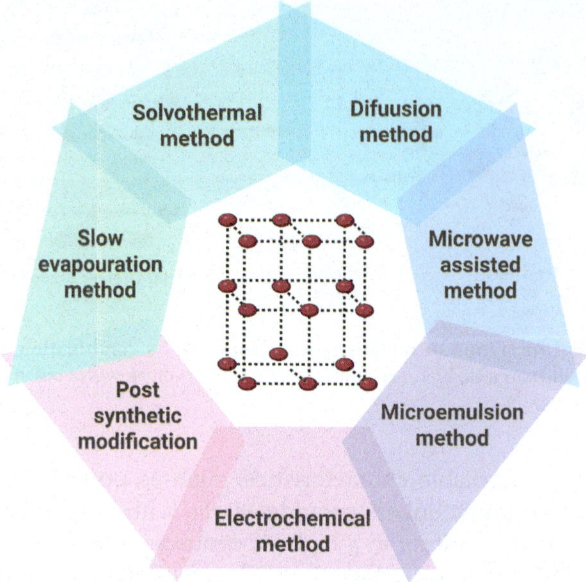

FIGURE 12.3 **Represent the methods of synthesis of metal organic framework.** MOFs can be prepared by solvothermal, electrochemical, microwave, slow evaporation, synthetic and diffusion methods.

applications, such as sensing or catalysis, where binding guest molecules is essential, to drug delivery and innovative material design (Tan et al., 2016). Due to these distinguishing aspects, like structural, porosity, and functionality variability, MOFs have emerged as one of the most promising materials for use in gas storage, separation, catalysis, sensing, microelectronics, bioreactors, and drug delivery. They can be linked with nanoparticles and other functional materials to form hybrid nanocomposites with superior properties. MOF uses a distinct mechanism for drug loading where pore encapsulation, linkage, or in-situ packaging, etc., occur and rely on the stability and adaptability of the formulation. Interestingly, various anticancer drugs can easily encapsulate inside these porous structures and show controlled drug release or release in the tumor microenvironment. Table 12.1 provided a few examples of MOF and their mode of action (Sadiq et al., 2024).

Design strategies for MOFs in anticancer drug delivery

The systematic design of MOFs for therapeutic applications is crucial to their effectiveness as anticancer medicines. The main strategies are to maximize the stability of MOF in biological settings, control payload release kinetics, and maximize loading efficiency. Surface modification of MOF with polymers, lipids, ligands, peptides, proteins, or biomolecules can ensure targeted accumulation in tumor sites (Jha et al., 2024). Additionally, the precise targeting of tumor-specific microenvironments can be achieved by integrating a stimuli-responsive moiety in MOF structures (Jha et al., 2022). Various types of MOFs are designed

TABLE 12.1 MOF and their mode of actions.

MOF	Metal center	Drug	Drug loading method	Drug release mechanism (Stimuli)	Target cell	Types of cancer	References
MIL-53(Fe)	Fe^{3+} (iron)	5-Fu	Pore encapsulation	pH-responsive	MGC-803 and HASMC cells	Stomach, Smooth muscle	Tomar and Singh (2021)
MIL-100(Fe)	Fe^{3+} (iron)	Cyclophosphamide	Surface attachment	pH-responsive	MCF-7 cells	Breast	Cai et al. (2020)
MIl-100(Fe)	Fe^{3+} (iron)	Methotrexate, Collagenase enzyme	Pore encapsulation	pH-responsive	A-375 cell line	Skin	Abuçafy et al. (2022)
MIl-100(Fe)	Fe^{3+} (iron)	DTX	Surface attachment	Redox-responsive	MCF-7 cells	Breast	Rezaei et al. (2018)
MIl-100(Fe)	Fe^{3+} (iron)	Dacarbazine	In situ packaging	pH-responsive	A375 cell lines (melanoma)	Melanoma	Barjasteh et al. (2022)
MIL-101(Fe)	Fe^{3+} (iron)	Curcumin	Pore encapsulation	pH-responsive	HeLa	Cervix	Karimi Alavijeh and Akhbari (2020)
MIL-101(Fe)	Fe^{3+} (iron)	Triptolide	Pore encapsulation	pH-responsive	HepG2 cells	Liver	Cai et al. (2021a)
ZIF-8	Zn^{2+} (Zinc)	DOX	In situ packaging	pH-responsive	MCF-7 cells	Ovary	Liang et al. (2018)
ZIF-8	Zn^{2+} (Zinc)	Rapamycin	In situ packaging	pH-responsive	MCF-7/ADR cells	Ovary	Xu et al. (2020)
ZIF-8	Zn^{2+} (Zinc)	Camptothecin	In situ packaging	Enzyme-triggered	Hela cells	Cervix	Dong et al. (2019)
ZIF-90	Zn^{2+} (Zinc)	DOX, 5-fu	Surface attachment, pore encapsulation	–	–	–	
ZIF-67	Co^{2+} (Cobalt)	DOX, CuSe	Surface attachment, pore encapsulation	Enzyme-triggered	4T1 cells	Breast	Wu et al. (2022)
UiO-66-NH2	Zr^{4+} (zirconium)	Oxaliplatin	Surface attachment	pH-responsive	CT26 cell line	Colon	Gholami et al. (2022)
UiO-66	Zr^{4+} (zirconium)	Quercetin	Surface attachment	pH-responsive	MDA-MB-231 cells	Breast	Parsaei and Akhbari (2023)
UiO-66-PNIPAM	Zr^{4+} (zirconium)	Resorufin, caffeine	Hydrothermal encapsulation	Temperature	–	–	Collins (1987)

for drug delivery applications with unique characteristics (Khan et al., 2024). A few of them are discussed in the sections below.

Stimuli -responsive MOFs

Stimuli-responsive materials are at the forefront of pharmaceutical, biomedical, and food science applications (Guan et al., 2023). This is due to their unique physicochemical properties, self-interaction, and intelligent regulation potential (Karimzadeh et al., 2021). These materials respond to a particular stimulus and readily get activated when exposed to intrinsic (such as pH, redox, enzyme) or external (such as temperature, pressure, light, and magnetic field) triggers (Guan et al., 2023). Several techniques to design stimuli-responsive MOFs include adding switchable molecules, altering the side chain, and altering the topology structure, as shown in Fig. 12.4 (Mondal et al., 2025). Stimuli-responsive MOF can alter their chemical makeup or physical structure according to the surrounding conditions to provide controlled release of payload at the desired site. A MOF have the capacity to prevent premature drug leakage, exhibit high systemic circulation, and release the drug in response to a

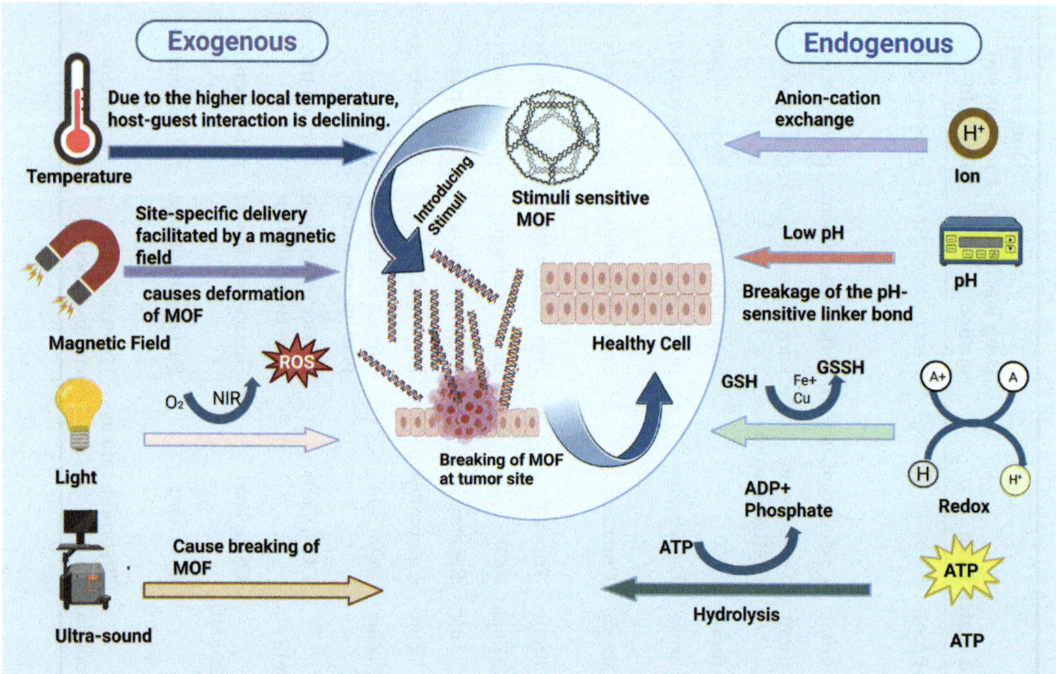

FIGURE 12.4 Representation of various exogenous and endogenous stimuli -ResponsiveMOFs and their mechanism of drug release at tumor site. Exogenous factors include temperature, ultrasound, light, and magnetic field, while endogenous factors are pH, ion, redox, enzyme and ATP.

particular tumor microenvironment. MOF accumulation and payload release at the target site can be influenced by various internal or external environmental conditions (Sadiq et al., 2024).

PH – responsive MOFs

pH is one of the most widely used stimuli in controlled drug delivery, particularly for cancer therapy, due to the distinct pH gradient between healthy and tumor tissues. The extracellular tumor microenvironment (TME) and its intracellular compartments are weakly acidic (pH 5.6–6), a result of elevated glycolysis in cancer cells that produces excess lactic acid. To sustain survival, tumor cells actively expel this acid, creating an acidic milieu. pH-responsive nanocarriers, especially MOF-based drug delivery systems (DDSs) with pH-sensitive groups, can exploit this difference by remaining stable at physiological pH (blood or normal tissues) but degrading in acidic conditions (Abazari et al., 2018a). This enables targeted and efficient drug release at tumor sites as shown in Fig. 12.5.

MOFs can also act as "smart carriers" by using the different surroundings that cancer and normal cells have. When it faces an acidic environment, the coordination bond breaks between organic linkers and metal ions within MOFs, releasing the encapsulated drug within the MOFs into the targeting side and effectively acting there. Also targeting agents like folate attached by surface modification boost the binding efficacy at the targeting site. As a result, MOFs combine active targeting (by ligand-receptor binding) and passive targeting (via superior permeability and retention effect). At the same time, their pH-sensitive breakdown allows for site-specific, regulated drug delivery.

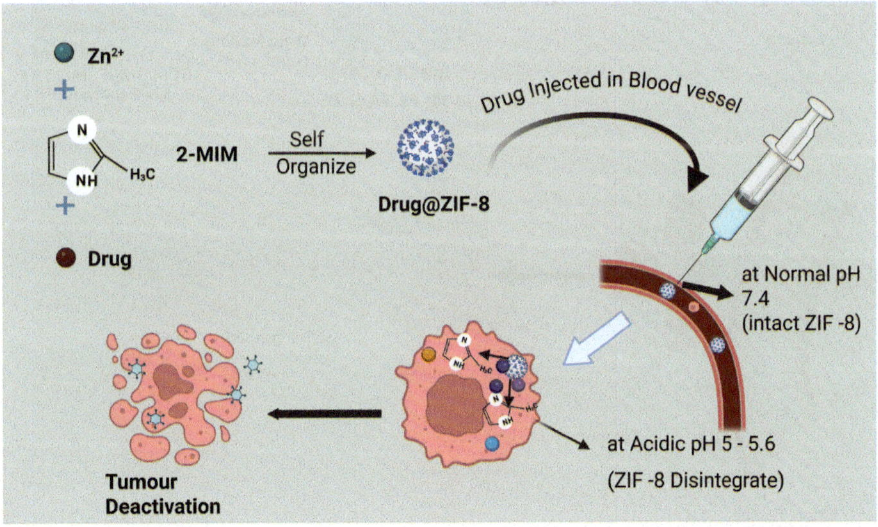

FIGURE 12.5 Schematic representation of redox-responsive MOFs and their mechanism of drug release within the tumor microenvironment. MOF at acidic microenvironment of tumor disintegrate to release the active payload to exert therapeutic action.

Redox responsive system

The drug delivery technique relies on changes in redox potential between healthy and cancerous cells. Tumor cell cytosol contains far more reducing agents, such as glutathione (2–10 mM), than normal cells (2–10 μM) (Liu et al., 2017; Coluccia et al., 2022). Redox-responsive MOFs release the drug in the presence of a large redox potential (Liu et al., 2017; Fu et al., 2022). This strategy has been extensively studied to target tumor cells. Fig. 12.6 provides a detailed overview of the redox-responsive MOFs and their mechanism of drug release within the tumor microenvironment. Stimulus-responsive DDSs exploit the redox potential difference between the intracellular and extracellular regions as a triggering mechanism. Disulfide bonds cause a quick bond cleavage, which can oxidize intracellular GSH as a reducing agent. A redox-responsive DDS could be created by modifying the MOF's surface to incorporate this kind of bond. These disulfide bonds will be broken by the high GSH concentration, which will cause the DDS to disintegrate and release the drug that is encapsulated once more with selectivity and high efficacy at the target site.

Enzyme triggered release

In this system, the encapsulated drug is released at the targeted site in the presence of a specific enzyme overexpressed in tumor tissues. Drugs are encapsulated within MOFs containing linkers like peptides, esters, which are easily broken by enzymes like Matrix metalloproteinases (MMPs), Phospholipases and Esterases, and cathepsins found in cancer cells. The cleavable linker breaks for drug release at the target site (Prakash et al., 2024).

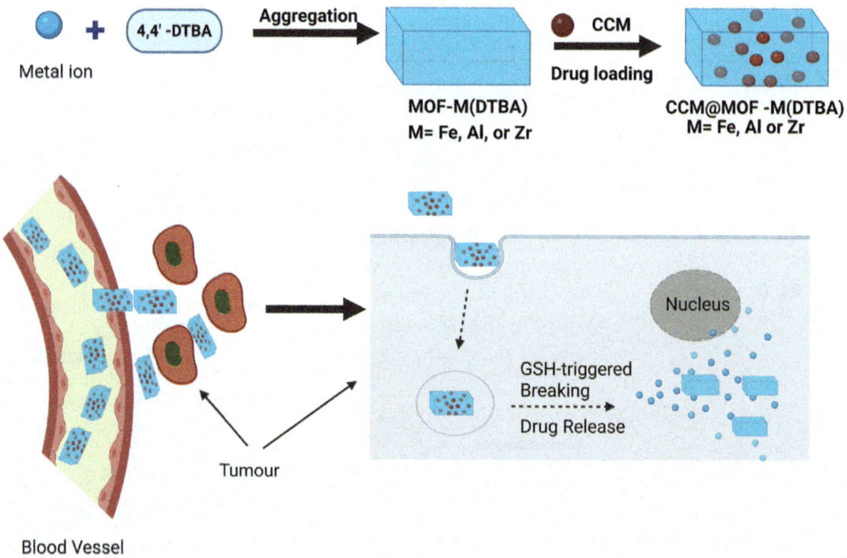

FIGURE 12.6 **Schematic representation of redox-responsive MOFs and their mechanism of drug release within the tumor microenvironment.** MOF with redox-responsive moiety experiences elevated ROS or GSH responsive degradation of MOF structure in cellular environment to release the payload at target site.

Light responsive MOFs

Light-sensitive MOFs are drug delivery systems that kill cancer cells by using ambient light as a stimulus. The MOFs are designed by incorporating photosensitizer molecules sensitive to light into their structure. The MOF system is activated by external light (UV, visible, or NIR), which induces Photosensitizers (such as porphyrins, phthalocyanines, and azobenzenes) present in the MOF structure, resulting in the production of reactive oxygen species (ROS), primarily singlet oxygen (O_2), to damage or kill cancer cells (Tao et al., 2020).

Surface modification for targeted delivery

Surface modification is a novel approach to increase the stability, decrease non-specific interactions, and provide cancer cell-selective delivery of metallic nanoparticles. This can be accomplished using a variety of techniques, such as functional group attachment and polymer coating on MOF (Choi et al., 2020). Nan-MOF stability can be enhanced with polymer coatings, including PEGylation or biopolymers like chitosan (El-Boubbou, 2017). Although functional groups and polymer coatings provide tried-and-true methods for surface modification, newer strategies utilizing nucleic acids have demonstrated encouraging outcomes in improving the stability and functionality of nanoparticles. Interaction between citrate-capped gold nanoparticles and single-stranded DNA increases the durability of nanoparticles, augmenting their use across several applications (Abdelkawi et al., 2023). Functional groups, such as amines and thiols, can be used to bind targeting ligands or drug molecules to the surface of nanoparticles, and the process is known as bioconjugation, greatly improving nanoparticles' targeting capabilities. Drug delivery can be made more precise by bioconjugating the nanoparticles with targeting ligands, which can guide them to particular cells or tissues. This is important in cancer therapy, where targeted delivery improves cancer treatment efficacy, as well as minimizes drug side effects (García-Torra et al., 2021). MOFs have a large internal surface area that can be decorated with various ligands, making them appealing supramolecular matrices for surface functionalization. Proteins, antibodies, peptides, aptamers, small molecules, and polysaccharides are examples of these ligands that can selectively target particular receptors overexpressed on the surface of cancerous cells (Safarkhani et al., 2024). Many receptors, including transferrin, integrin, folate, and epidermal growth factor, have different recognition and binding affinities for a specific ligand. This specific mobility of drugs via membrane receptors improves selectivity and reduces multidrug resistance. The targeting ligands can be implemented to design various ligand-functionalized MOF structures, following a particular mechanism for active targeted drug delivery (Masoudifar et al., 2022). Below sections discuss a few of the surface modification techniques employed in MOF delivery to cancer cells (Table 12.2).

PEGylation for stealth and stability

PEGylation, also known as polyethylene glycol (PEG) functionalization, is a commonly used technique to improve the stability, bioavailability, and circulation time of NPs for cancer treatment. PEGylation efficiently decreases protein adsorption, minimizes opsonization, and stops the mononuclear phagocyte system (MPS) from clearing NPs too soon by creating a hydration shell around them. This prolongs systemic retention and promotes passive

TABLE 12.2 Represent MOF nanocomposites and surface functionalization.

MOF type	Surface modification	Observation	Advantages	Disadvantages	References
Fe_3O_4@Bio-MOF	Core shell hybridization	Magnet basis targeting, high drug loading, pH-responsive release.	Reduce off target effect, image guided cancer therapy	Risk of nanoparticle accumulation, Possibility of toxic chelation form.	Abazari et al. (2018b)
UiO-66 (Zr based)	PEGylation	Avoid lysosomal degradation. Less cytotoxicity due to prolonged blood circulation time.	Better stability with biocompatibility.	Instable in basic media and show missing linker defect.	Abánades Lázaro et al. (2017)
MIL-101(Fe)	Folic acid	FA conjugation enable specify target on HepG-2 cancer cell and enhance cellular uptake.	Targeted delivery and enhanced therapeutic efficacy.	Heterogeneity of folate receptor expression	Majidinia et al. (2025)
PCN-224 (Zr/Ti) NMOFs	Cation exchange	Enhances ROS-mediated cancer cell apoptosis by downregulating of antioxidant enzyme, stability at tumor microenvironment	Act on multidrug resistant on bacteria, control drug release.	Poor recycle and toxicity in long-term use	Matlou and Abrahamse (2022)
ZIF-8(Zn)	Glucose oxidase encapsulation.	Ultra-sensitive cancer biomarker formation	Light-responsive, pH-responsive, active targeting	Complex process	Cai et al. (2020)
UiO-67	Aptamer conjugation	Highly sensitive detection of target (*S. typhimurium*) using UiO-67/graphene sensor; aptamer ensured specificity	fast and accurate analyses, high sensitivity, low-cost, and good reproducibility	Complex modification, not yet strong proof on cancer treatment	Dai et al. (2019)
MOF-808 (Zr)	Galactose based photo click modification	Enhanced endocytosis by hepatic cancer cells (HepG2), targeted carboplatin delivery	Accurate target and controlled release	Required specific photo click knowledge and infrastructure to develop	Wang et al. (2025)
PCN-222 (porphyrinic Zr-MOF)	PEG + Photosensitizer	Effective ROS generation. Also show better binding ability with folic acid and target accumulation.	On light exposure it produces ROS or cytotoxic singlet oxygen that help to kill cancer cell.	Long term use may cause phototoxicity effect.	Matlou and Abrahamse (2022)
NH_2-MIL-125	α-Asarone	Greater cytotoxicity against cancer cells by following ROS mechanism and show synergistic effect.	Improved biocompatibility, controlled and sustained release.	Complex synthesis, Incomplete clinical evidence.	Mukherjee et al. (2024)
Bi-MIL-88B	Folic acid, chitosan	Peroxidase like catalytic activity, FC coating cause target delivery, pH responsive release.	Minimal cytotoxicity, targeted release	Stability, complex synthesis	Akbar et al. (2023)
NU-1000 (Zr)	DNA conjugation	DNA strands fixed on NU-1000 improved selective binding and delivery of oligonucleotides to tumor cells.	Precise gene targeted therapy for change tumor causing gene.	Stearic hinderance cause limited loading	Wang et al. (2019)
MIL-88A (Fe)	Hyaluronic acid coating	Improved dispersibility, biocompatibility, and CD44-targeted doxorubicin delivery.	Active tumor targeting.	Stability concern with Hyaluronic acid.	Zhu et al. (2023)
HKUST-1 (cu)	Bovine Serum Albumin (BSA) capping	BSA capping improved colloidal stability and pH specific release at tumor microenvironments	Slow degradation	Protein coating may block pore	Crawford and Suuberg (2010)
PCN-333(Al)	RNA loaded	siRNA adsorbed into PCN-333 for gene silencing in hepatocellular carcinoma cells	RNA protected from degradation, high loading capacity	Complex control process	Ahmed et al. (2022)

tumor accumulation. PEGylated NPs can fully benefit from the EPR effect, which occurs when NPs extravasate through leaky tumor vasculature and stay in the TME because of inadequate lymphatic drainage, thanks to this extended circulation time. In addition to extending circulation, PEGylation improves NP stability in biological fluids by halting aggregation, enzymatic breakdown, and rapid renal clearance—all of which are typical drawbacks of nonfunctionalized NPs (Hussain et al., 2025). Furthermore, by decreasing non-specific uptake by healthy tissues, PEGylation can alter NP interactions with tumor cells, resulting in increased drug accumulation at the tumor site. PEGylation is a vital tool in nanomedicine because of these benefits, but too much PEG coverage can also cause steric hindrance, which reduces the effectiveness of drug release and cellular internalization. This phenomenon is called the PEG stealthing effect (Ma et al., 2023).

Peptide as a targeting ligand for MOFs

Peptides are brief chains of amino acids that range in length from 2 to 50 units. They are vital for many biological processes and can be synthetic or natural in origin. Depending on their structure, they can function as enzyme substrates and inhibitors, hormones, anti-aging, anti-inflammatory, and antimicrobial agents. Additionally, peptides are good candidates as tumor-targeting ligands to identify overexpressed receptors because of their low cost, moderate size, high specificity/affinity, biocompatibility, and low immunogenicity (Jiang et al., 2019). They have therefore been widely employed in active drug/gene delivery, photodynamic and photothermal therapy, and imaging.

Folic acid: An efficient approach for MOF targeting

As previously stated, proteins and peptides offer special qualities for targeted drug delivery, especially high binding affinity and specificity to their corresponding cell surface receptors. Nevertheless, despite their advantages, they have some practical drawbacks, like high cost and environmental sensitivity. Since small targeting molecules can readily reach the target sites and accumulate in tumor cells, they make good substitutes for peptides and proteins. Several studies have demonstrated that specific small molecules can attach to tumor cell surface receptors and be used for active targeting in cancer treatment (Salahpour Anarjan, 2019). Folic acid (FA) is the most often utilized small molecule targeting agent for active targeting on MOFs. One of the most frequently overexpressed receptors on the surface of cancer cells is the folic acid receptor (FR), which is derived from glycoproteins. Thus, using folate ligands to target tumor cells is a practical method of guaranteeing targeted toxicity to these cells. Numerous human tumor cells, typically of epithelial origin, including those of the breast, ovary, kidney, brain, bladder, and lung, overexpress these receptors (Zhang et al., 2025). Some basic examples of surface modification of MOF and there outcomes discuss below.

Multifunctional MOFs for combination therapy

Chemo dynamic therapy (CDT), photodynamic therapy (PDT), photothermal therapy (PTT), smart chemotherapy, starvation therapy (ST), immunotherapy (IMT), and many other treatment modalities have emerged as a result of the development of medical technology

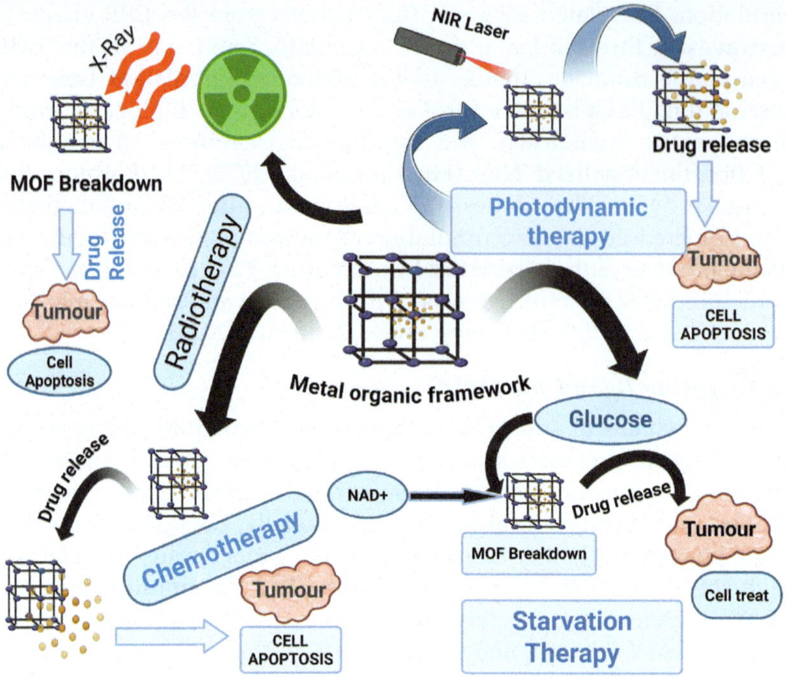

FIGURE 12.7 Schematic representation of the approaches of metal-organic frameworks (MOFs) in cancer therapy. MOF application in chemo, photodynamic (PDT), photothermal (PTT), starvation therapy (ST), and immunotherapy (IMT).

(Fig. 12.7). These new, less invasive or non-invasive techniques have fewer side effects, are easier to use, and are more effective (Ma et al., 2023). Combination therapy offers the several benefits over monotherapy, by using various anticancer pathways to enable lower dosages of individual medications, reducing drug-related toxicities, by changing the drug combination, combination therapy prevents cytotoxic effects on healthy cells while causing toxic effects on cancer cells, changing the "passive" role of cancer treatment, crucially, long-term use of a single compound may cause cancer cells to look for other routes of escape, whereas combination therapy can offer efficient treatment in (Mukhlif et al., 2025) brief cycles, lowering the incidence of drug resistance. Combination therapy works similarly to putting the benefits of separate therapies into a multi-level, multi-functional "container" in order to produce the effect of [1 + 1>2] (Mokhtari et al., 2017; Wang et al., 2016). When compared to monotherapies, combination therapies can greatly increase the effectiveness of cancer treatment (Sun et al., 2021).

Imaging – guided drug delivery with MOFs

Image Guided Drug Delivery (IGDD) offers remarkable control and precision over treatments. This method reduces exposure to healthy tissues while guaranteeing that therapeutic agents are directed precisely to diseased tissues by combining state-of-the-art imaging technologies with targeted drug delivery. Imaging and drug delivery together improve the ability to see, monitor, and adjust treatments in real time in nuclear medicine, where radiopharmaceuticals are used for both diagnostic and therapeutic purposes. This combination reduces adverse effects and increases therapeutic efficacy (Mukhlif et al., 2025). The ability of IGDD to offer real-time feedback on the pharmacokinetics and biodistribution of therapeutic agents is its main benefit. Therefore, image-guided drug delivery offers superior theranostic capabilities and has enormous control. A range of diagnostic imaging techniques carried out in vivo, including positron emission tomography (PET), photoacoustic tomography (PAT), magnetic resonance imaging (MRI), computed tomography (CT), ultrasound (US), etc., have recently been used in studies to detect different types of cancer (Cai et al., 2022).

Advances in MOF-based anticancer drug delivery systems

MOFs can be used for targeted delivery owing to their tunable surface and highly porous structures (Gulati et al., 2023; He et al., 2023). Moreover, the advancement of stimuli-responsive designs and surface modifications has enhanced their translational viability. Recent research has built on these foundations to show four major advances of MOFs in cancer therapy: they can carry traditional chemotherapy drugs, nucleic acids, and gene therapy; serve as platforms for photothermal and photodynamic cancer treatments; and be multifunctional systems that allow the co-delivery of multiple therapeutic agents, as shown in Fig. 12.8 (Gulati et al., 2023; He et al., 2023; Guo et al., 2025).

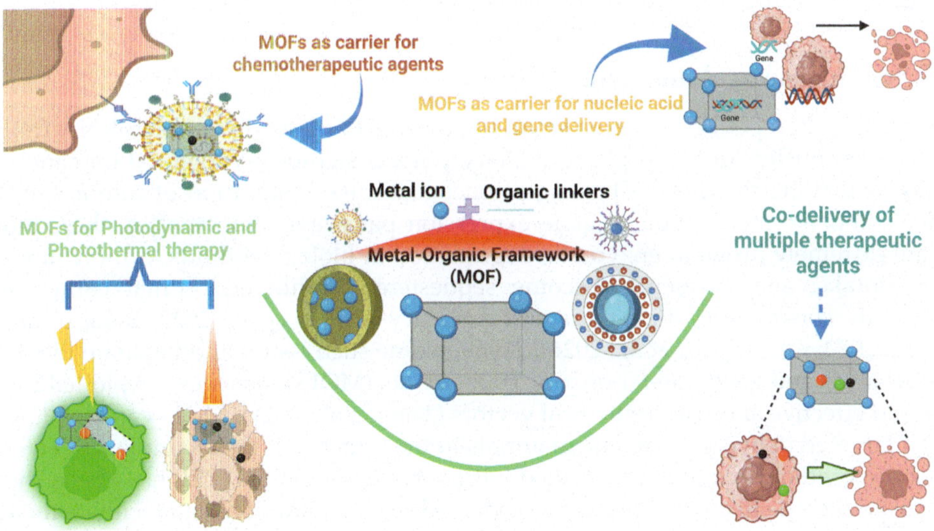

FIGURE 12.8 **Major advances of MOF-based nanoplatforms in cancer therapy.** MOF as carrier for one or more therapeutics for anticancer drug delivery, immunotherapy and theranostic applications.

MOFs as carriers for chemotherapeutic agent

MOFs are Metal-organic frameworks (MOFs) with variable pore dimensions and significant chemical adaptability. These features make it easier to encapsulate large amounts of therapeutic agents (Sun et al., 2013; Dzhardimalieva et al., 2019). Doxorubicin, cisplatin, camptothecin, and paclitaxel are common anticancer drugs that don't dissolve well, are cleared quickly, and are toxic to many different types of cells when given in free form. Because MOFs have porous crystalline networks, these drugs can be stably loaded into the framework and then released in a controlled and long-lasting way (Alavi et al., 2024; Karami et al., 2021; Yan et al., 2020). The zeolitic imidazolate frameworks (ZIF-8) and the MIL-101 series have shown the most promise among the different MOFs that have been studied. For instance, ZIF-8 has shown that it can hold a lot of doxorubicin and release it more easily in acidic conditions that are similar to the tumor microenvironment (Rahman et al., 2025; Yao et al., 2021; He et al., 2014). The localization at the tumor site maintains the release of drugs to be predominantly in response to the pH. This improves site-specific accumulation and reduces the chance of the drug leaking into circulation too soon. In the same way, MIL-101(Cr) has been used to deliver cisplatin, where the framework not only keeps the drug stable during systemic transport but also lets it slowly release in cancerous tissues (Zou et al., 2022; Tran et al., 2023). MOF can exhibit controlled-release properties, providing numerous therapeutic advantages. They increase the systemic circulation and half-life of the drug in the body, making a large fraction of drugs delivered at the target site for internalization by cancer cells, lowering the risk of adverse effects on healthy tissues. Additionally, MOF-based carriers can overcome the multidrug resistance issue by maintaining higher local concentrations of chemotherapeutics at the tumor site. This improves the therapeutic index and overall effectiveness of the free drug. MOFs are being widely studied as new ways to deliver established chemotherapeutic agents to make them work better (Yan et al., 2021; Liu et al., 2024).

MOFs for nucleic acid and gene delivery

Gene-based therapeutics, such as small interfering RNA (siRNA), microRNA (miRNA), antisense oligonucleotides, and plasmid DNA, possess significant potential for cancer treatment by facilitating the direct silencing of oncogenes, the restoration of tumor suppressor functions, and the modulation of gene expression pathways. Nonetheless, these biomolecules are extremely prone to enzymatic degradation in biological fluids, exhibit suboptimal cellular uptake, and frequently become sequestered within endosomal compartments, consequently constraining their therapeutic efficacy (Mokri et al., 2022; Yang et al., 2025; Sun et al., 2020; Khosrojerdi et al., 2024). To overcome such issues and facilitate the delivery of nucleic acids and genes, metal-organic frameworks (MOFs) have been exploited in search of safe and effective alternatives to viral vectors (Tong et al., 2021). MOFs can facilitate effective and targeted delivery of genetic materials to the target site. For example, UiO-66 frameworks composed of zirconium and coated with polyethyleneimine (PEI) have been shown to encapsulate siRNA effectively, protect it from nuclease degradation, and facilitate the knockdown of targeted oncogenes in vitro. The positively charged PEI not only helps the negatively charged phosphate backbone of nucleic acids stick to each other strongly, but it also helps the nucleic acids escape from endosomes by using the "proton sponge effect." This makes sure that the genetic material enters the cytoplasm to exert its anticancer action (Li et al., 2019). MOFs have been designed to co-deliver nucleic acids with chemotherapeutic agents, thereby integrating gene silencing with cytotoxic therapy for enhanced efficacy. MOF-based carriers have a number of advantages over viral vectors, such as higher biosafety, lower immunogenicity, customizable surface chemistry, and the ability to combine different functional modalities. All of these things make MOFs very likely to be the next generation of non-viral gene delivery systems. Their capacity to safeguard nucleic acids, improve intracellular transport, and facilitate targeted gene regulation renders them as adaptable platforms for the progression of nucleic acid therapeutics in cancer therapy (Khosrojerdi et al., 2024).

MOFs for photothermal and photodynamic cancer therapy

Metal-Organic Frameworks (MOFs) can be designed to be multifunctional theranostic platforms for light-triggered cancer therapies, in addition to being nanocarriers for small-molecule drugs. Photodynamic therapy (PDT) and photothermal therapy (PTT) have emerged as two of the most promising non-invasive treatment strategies, and metal-organic frameworks (MOFs) are uniquely suited to enhance their performance (Pattnaik et al., 2024). MOFs based on porphyrins, like PCN-224 and its derivatives, are naturally photosensitive because porphyrins are effective at absorbing light. When these frameworks are exposed to visible or near-infrared (NIR) light, they release a lot of reactive oxygen species (ROS), such as singlet oxygen. This phenomenon causes cancer cells to die by oxidative stress-mediated apoptosis. The porous crystalline structure of MOFs not only stops porphyrins from clumping together and losing their ability to absorb light, which is a common problem with free photosensitizers, but it also makes them more stable and efficient at converting light into chemical energy. This results in increased ROS yields and enhanced tissue penetration, both of which are essential for effective PDT (Wang et al., 2018).

MOFs can be loaded or hybridized with photothermal agents like gold nanoclusters, polydopamine, carbon nanomaterials, or transition-metal oxides, which turn NIR light into heat in a specific area. This heat causes hyperthermia in the tumor microenvironment, which kills cancer cells directly while leaving normal tissues nearby unharmed. The mild photothermal effect also makes the blood vessels in tumors more permeable, which helps drugs get into the tumors and makes combination therapies more effective (Woalder and Tripp, 2017; Wang et al., 2018; Cai et al., 2021b). Recent research has shown that using PDT and PTT together on the same MOF platform can have synergistic effects. For instance, porphyrinic MOFs adorned with gold nanoparticles can concurrently produce reactive oxygen species (ROS) and localized hyperthermia when exposed to dual light, resulting in enhanced tumor regression compared to either treatment individually. Importantly, these systems provide spatiotemporal control, allowing treatment to be precisely activated at the tumor site by external light, thereby minimizing systemic toxicity and reducing collateral damage to healthy tissues (Hu et al., 2022). Overall, MOFs are a very flexible and modular platform for combining PDT and PTT, filling the gap between imaging, diagnosis, and therapy. Their capacity to administer light-activated therapies in a regulated, precise, and minimally invasive fashion underscores their promise as next-generation anticancer nanotheranostics.

Co-delivery of multiple therapeutic agents

Metal-organic frameworks (MOFs) can deliver multiple therapeutic agents on a single nanoplatform. MOFs can combine small-molecule drugs, biomacromolecules, and photosensitizers in a single delivery system. This co-delivery strategy can provide synergistic therapeutic effects by integrating diverse mechanisms of action, surmounting multidrug resistance, and attaining enhanced treatment outcomes relative to monotherapies (Mokri et al., 2022; Pan et al., 2018). For example, ZIF-8 nanoparticles that were loaded with both doxorubicin (a common chemotherapy drug) and siRNA (a genetic silencing agent) showed strong synergistic tumor inhibition by combining chemotherapy and gene silencing into one system. In another instance, porphyrinic MOFs were systematically designed to encapsulate cisplatin with photosensitizers, facilitating a synergistic chemotherapy–photodynamic therapy strategy that enhanced tumor regression and diminished systemic toxicity. Additionally, hybrid MOF systems can combine photothermal agents, immunomodulators, or targeted ligands to widen the therapeutic effect against various cancers. These multifunctional nanoplatforms show the potential of MOFs as a safe and flexible system for personalized multimodal cancer treatments. MOFs have advanced the cancer therapy by allowing for precise control over the release of different therapeutic cargos in space and time and by customizing their combinations to fit the biology of each patient's tumor (Sun et al., 2020; Jiang et al., 2023).

Challenges

Though metal-organic frameworks (MOFs) have immense potential in biological and pharmacological applications, their actual use is hampered by a number of obstacles. One notable disadvantage is their shelf life. MOFs are particularly sensitive to moisture and physiological fluids, which causes structural collapse or medication leaking before reaching their goal. Scalability and reproducibility of synthesis pose further hurdles. Laboratory-scale approaches, such as solvothermal or microwave-assisted synthesis, can produce limited quantities with regulated morphology. However, translating these processes into affordable and environmentally benign large-scale production remains a challenging undertaking. Furthermore, the morphology of drug delivery systems, such as particle size and crystallinity, varies between batches, resulting in changes in porosity within the particles (Khafaga et al., 2024). Biocompatibility and safety are also key issues. Although some studies suggest a favorable safety profile, many elements of their in vivo metabolism, long-term toxicity, and elimination remain unknown. Another limitation is a lack of control over the drug's release kinetics. While MOFs have been proven to react to redox, enzyme, and pH conditions, accurate, predictable, and reproducible release profiles, in vivo are difficult to obtain. Tumor heterogeneity, microenvironmental variety, and dynamic biological barriers can all affect their reactivity. Furthermore, interpenetration and pore clogging concerns can limit the available porosity, lowering the efficiency of drug loading (Saboorizadeh et al., 2024). Finally, the regulatory and translation aspects of MOF-based systems remain unexplored. Comprehensive long-term pharmacokinetics, immunogenicity, and biosafety studies are required for clinical usage, but current data is sparse. These hurdles must be overcome in order to move MOFs from experimental research to real therapeutic usage (Li et al., 2024; Zhang and Chen, 2024).

Future prospects

Metal-organic frameworks (MOFs) are quickly transitioning from the laboratory bench to actual applications in the biomedical field, and the future of MOFs in anticancer therapy appears extremely promising. Among the major areas of focus will be the design of biodegradable and biocompatible MOFs (Horcajada et al., 2012). Scientists are creating frameworks that can resist the rigors of circulation while eventually dissolving into benign constituents using safe metal centers such as iron or zirconium, as well as non-toxic linkers. Furthermore, MOFs offer potential in the field of cancer immunotherapy. MOF-based carriers can stimulate the body's immune system to attack cancer more effectively, either by co-delivering medications and immune stimulants or by modifying the tumor microenvironment. As stable, safe, and multifunctional structures become more extensively created, MOFs are expected to evolve into next-generation nanomedicines that will provide cancer patients with personalized, effective, and less hazardous treatments (Courtenay et al., 2020; Guo et al., 2025).

Conclusion

Metal-organic frameworks (MOFs) have been postulated as a potential anticancer agent in cancer therapy. This chapter demonstrated how various design knowledge (e.g., stimuli-responsive release, surface modification, and the selection of safe metals and biodegradable linkers) could improve the stability, targeting, and therapeutic efficacy of MOFs, making them a reliable and powerful weapon in the fight against cancer. Barriers to clinical translation include physiological stability, large-scale reproducibility, and long-term safety. In the future, the development of biocompatible and multifunctional MOFs for combining drug administration with imaging or immunotherapy has the potential to provide even more accurate and less hazardous treatments. In summary, MOFs represent a potential step toward future guided catalysts in cancer therapy.

References

Abánades Lázaro, I., Haddad, S., Sacca, S., Orellana-Tavra, C., Fairen-Jimenez, D., Forgan, R.S., 2017. Selective surface PEGylation of UiO-66 nanoparticles for enhanced stability, cell uptake, and pH-responsive drug delivery. Chem 2 (4), 561–578. https://doi.org/10.1016/j.chempr.2017.02.005.

Abazari, R., Reza Mahjoub, A., Slawin, A.M.Z., Carpenter-Warren, C.L., 2018a. Morphology- and size-controlled synthesis of a metal-organic framework under ultrasound irradiation: An efficient carrier for pH responsive release of anti-cancer drugs and their applicability for adsorption of amoxicillin from aqueous solution. Ultrason. Sonochem. 42, 594–608. https://doi.org/10.1016/j.ultsonch.2017.12.032.

Abdelkawi, A., Slim, A., Zinoune, Z., Pathak, Y., 2023. Surface modification of metallic nanoparticles for targeting drugs. Coatings 13 (9), 1660. https://doi.org/10.3390/coatings13091660.

Abuçafy, M.P., Frem, R.C.G., Polinario, G., Pavan, F.R., Zhao, H., Mielcarek, A., Boissiere, C., Serre, C., Chiavacci, L. A., 2022. MIL-100(Fe) sub-micrometric capsules as a dual drug delivery system. Int. J. Mol. Sci. 23 (14). https://doi.org/10.3390/ijms23147670.

Ahmed, A., McHugh, D., Papatriantafyllopoulou, C., 2022. Synthesis and biomedical applications of highly porous metal–organic frameworks. Molecules 27 (19). https://doi.org/10.3390/molecules27196585.

Akbar, M.U., Khattak, S., Khan, M.I., Saddozai, U.A.K., Ali, N., AlAsmari, A.F., Zaheer, M., Badar, M., 2023. A pH-responsive bi-MIL-88B MOF coated with folic acid-conjugated chitosan as a promising nanocarrier for targeted drug delivery of 5-Fluorouracil. Front. Pharmacol. 14. https://doi.org/10.3389/fphar.2023.1265440.

Alavi, S.E., Alavi, S.F., Koohi, M., Raza, A., Ebrahimi Shahmabadi, H., 2024. Nanoparticle-integrated metal–organic frameworks: A revolution in next-generation drug delivery systems. J. Pharm. Investig. 54 (6), 751–783. https://doi.org/10.1007/s40005-024-00691-w.

Barjasteh, M., Vossoughi, M., Bagherzadeh, M., Pooshang Bagheri, K., 2022. Green synthesis of PEG-coated MIL-100 (Fe) for controlled release of dacarbazine and its anticancer potential against human melanoma cells. Int. J. Pharm. 618, 121647. https://doi.org/10.1016/j.ijpharm.2022.121647.

Cai, M., Chen, G., Qin, L., Qu, C., Dong, X., Ni, J., Yin, X., 2020. Metal organic frameworks as drug targeting delivery Vehicles in the treatment of cancer. Pharmaceutics 12 (3), 232. https://doi.org/10.3390/pharmaceutics12030232.

Cai, M., Zeng, Y., Liu, M., You, L., Huang, H., Hao, Y., Yin, X., (2021a).

Cai, X., Zhao, Y., Wang, L., Hu, M., Wu, Z., Liu, L., Zhu, W., Pei, R., 2021b. Synthesis of Au@MOF core–shell hybrids for enhanced photodynamic/photothermal therapy. J. Mater. Chem. B 9 (33), 6646–6657. https://doi.org/10.1039/d1tb00800e.

Cai, X., Bao, X., Wu, Y., 2022. Metal–organic frameworks as intelligent drug nanocarriers for cancer therapy. Pharmaceutics 14 (12), 2641. https://doi.org/10.3390/pharmaceutics14122641.

Choi, M., Choi, W.K., Jung, C.H., Kim, S.B., 2020. The surface modification and characterization of SiO2 nanoparticles for higher foam stability. Sci. Rep. 10 (1). https://doi.org/10.1038/s41598-020-76464-w.

Collins, S.J., 1987. The HL-60 promyelocytic leukemia cell line: Proliferation, differentiation, and cellular oncogene expression. Blood 70 (5), 1233–1244. https://doi.org/10.1182/blood.v70.5.1233.1233.

Coluccia, M., Parisse, V., Guglielmi, P., Giannini, G., Secci, D., 2022. Metal-organic frameworks (MOFs) as biomolecules drug delivery systems for anticancer purposes. Eur. J. Med. Chem. 244, 114801. https://doi.org/10.1016/j.ejmech.2022.114801.

Courtenay, A.J., McAlister, E., McCrudden, M.T.C., Vora, L., Steiner, L., Levin, G., Levy-Nissenbaum, E., Shterman, N., Kearney, M.-C., McCarthy, H.O., Donnelly, R.F., 2020. Hydrogel-forming microneedle arrays as a therapeutic option for transdermal esketamine delivery. J. Contr. Release 322, 177–186. https://doi.org/10.1016/j.jconrel.2020.03.026.

Crawford, G., Suuberg, E., 2010. College of science. Area 632.

Dai, G., Li, Z., Luo, F., Ai, S., Chen, B., Wang, Q., 2019. Electrochemical determination of salmonella typhimurium by using aptamer-loaded gold nanoparticles and a composite prepared from a metal-organic framework (type UiO-67) and graphene. Microchim. Acta 186 (9). https://doi.org/10.1007/s00604-019-3724-y.

Debela, D.T., Muzazu, S.G.Y., Heraro, K.D., Ndalama, M.T., Mesele, B.W., Haile, D.C., Kitui, S.K., Manyazewal, T., 2021. New approaches and procedures for cancer treatment: Current perspectives. SAGE Open Med. 9. https://doi.org/10.1177/20503121211034366.

Dong, K., Zhang, Y., Zhang, L., Wang, Z., Ren, J., Qu, X., 2019. Facile preparation of metal−organic frameworks-based hydrophobic anticancer drug delivery nanoplatform for targeted and enhanced cancer treatment. Talanta 194, 703–708. https://doi.org/10.1016/j.talanta.2018.10.101.

Dzhardimalieva, G.I., Rabinskiy, L.N., Kydralieva, K.A., Uflyand, I.E., 2019. Recent advances in metallopolymer-based drug delivery systems. RSC Adv. 9 (63), 37009–37051. https://doi.org/10.1039/c9ra06678k.

El-Boubbou, K., 2017. Multifunctional magnetic iron oxide nanoparticles for intracellular imaging and drug delivery to cancer cells. Int. J. Mater. Mech. Manuf. 5 (4), 231–234. https://doi.org/10.18178/ijmmm.2017.5.4.325.

Fu, S., Rempson, C.M., Puche, V., Zhao, B., Zhang, F., 2022. Construction of disulfide containing redox-responsive polymeric nanomedicine. Methods 199, 67–79. https://doi.org/10.1016/j.ymeth.2021.12.011.

García-Torra, V., Cano, A., Espina, M., Ettcheto, M., Camins, A., Barroso, E., Vazquez-Carrera, M., García, M.L., Sánchez-López, E., Souto, E.B., 2021. State of the art on toxicological mechanisms of metal and metal oxide nanoparticles and strategies to reduce toxicological risks. Toxics 9 (8), 195. https://doi.org/10.3390/toxics9080195.

Gholami, M., Hekmat, A., Khazaei, M., Darroudi, M., 2022. OXA-CuS@UiO-66-NH2 as a drug delivery system for Oxaliplatin to colorectal cancer cells. J. Mater. Sci. Mater. Med. 33 (3). https://doi.org/10.1007/s10856-021-06574-y.

Guan, Q., Fang, Y., Wu, X., Ou, R., Zhang, X., Xie, H., Tang, M., Zeng, G., 2023. Stimuli responsive metal organic framework materials towards advanced smart application. Mater. Today 64, 138–164. https://doi.org/10.1016/j.mattod.2023.02.013.

Gulati, S., Choudhury, A., Mohan, G., Katiyar, R., Mohammed, A.K.M.P., Kumar, S., Varma, R.S., 2023. Metal–organic frameworks (MOFs) as effectual diagnostic and therapeutic tools for cancer. J. Mater. Chem. B 11 (29), 6782–6801. https://doi.org/10.1039/d3tb00706e.

Guo, Z., Xiao, Y., Wu, W., Zhe, M., Yu, P., Shakya, S., Li, Z., Xing, F., 2025. Metal–organic framework-based smart stimuli-responsive drug delivery systems for cancer therapy: Advances, challenges, and future perspectives. J. Nanobiotechnol. 23 (1). https://doi.org/10.1186/s12951-025-03252-x.

He, C., Lu, K., Liu, D., Lin, W., 2014. Nanoscale metal–organic frameworks for the Co-delivery of cisplatin and pooled siRNAs to enhance therapeutic efficacy in drug-resistant ovarian cancer cells. J. Am. Chem. Soc. 136 (14), 5181–5184. https://doi.org/10.1021/ja4098862.

He, Y., Li, D., Wu, L., Yin, X., Zhang, X., Patterson, L.H., Zhang, J., 2023. Metal-organic frameworks for gene therapy and detection. Adv. Funct. Mater. 33 (12). https://doi.org/10.1002/adfm.202212277.

Horcajada, P., Gref, R., Baati, T., Allan, P.K., Maurin, G., Couvreur, P., Férey, G., Morris, R.E., Serre, C., 2012. Metal-organic frameworks in biomedicine. Chem. Rev. 112 (2), 1232–1268. https://doi.org/10.1021/cr200256v.

Hu, L., Xiong, C., Wei, G., Yu, Y., Li, S., Xiong, X., Zou, J.-J., Tian, J., 2022. Stimuli-responsive charge-reversal MOF@polymer hybrid nanocomposites for enhanced co-delivery of chemotherapeutics towards combination therapy of multidrug-resistant cancer. J. Colloid Interface Sci. 608 (Pt 2), 1882–1893. https://doi.org/10.1016/j.jcis.2021.10.070.

Hussain, Z., Hussain Al-Shadidi, J.R.M., Jagal, J., Rawas-Qalaji, M., 2025. Overcoming stealthing effect of PEGylation on chitosan nanoparticles: Optimization, characterization, and assessment of cytotoxicity, apoptosis, cellular internalization, and antimetastatic efficacy. Int. J. Biol. Macromol. 321 (Pt 4), 146514. https://doi.org/10.1016/j.ijbiomac.2025.146514.

Jha, A., Kumar, M., Mishra, B., 2022. Marine Biopolymer-Based Anticancer Drug Delivery Systems Marine Biomaterials: Drug Delivery and Therapeutic Applications. Springer Nature, India, pp. 351–401. https://doi.org/10.1007/978-981-16-4787-1_11.

Jha, A., Kumar, M., Bharti, K., Manjit, M., Mishra, B., 2024. Biopolymer-based tumor microenvironment-responsive nanomedicine for targeted cancer therapy. Nanomedicine (Lond) 19 (7), 633–651. https://doi.org/10.2217/nnm-2023-0302.

Jiang, Z., Guan, J., Qian, J., Zhan, C., 2019. Peptide ligand-mediated targeted drug delivery of nanomedicines. Biomater. Sci. 7 (2), 461–471. https://doi.org/10.1039/c8bm01340c.

Jiang, X., Zhao, Y., Sun, S., Wang, L., Sun, L., Li, W., Wang, Z., Wang, J., Pei, R., 2023. A metal–organic framework complex for enhancing tumor treatments through synergistic effect of chemotherapy and photodynamic therapy. J. Mater. Chem. B 11 (44), 10706–10716. https://doi.org/10.1039/d3tb01592k.

Karami, A., Mohamed, O., Ahmed, A., Husseini, G.A., Sabouni, R., 2021. Recent advances in metal-organic frameworks as anticancer drug delivery systems: A review. Anti. Cancer Agents Med. Chem. 21 (18), 2487–2504. https://doi.org/10.2174/1871520621666210119093844.

Karimi Alavijeh, R., Akhbari, K., 2020. Biocompatible MIL-101(Fe) as a smart carrier with high loading potential and sustained release of curcumin. Inorg. Chem. 59 (6), 3570–3578. https://doi.org/10.1021/acs.inorgchem.9b02756.

Karimzadeh, S., Javanbakht, S., Baradaran, B., Shahbazi, M.A., Hashemzaei, M., Mokhtarzadeh, A., Santos, H.A., 2021. Synthesis and therapeutic potential of stimuli-responsive metal-organic frameworks. Chem. Eng. J. 408. https://doi.org/10.1016/j.cej.2020.127233.

Khafaga, D.S.R., El-Morsy, M.T., Faried, H., Diab, A.H., Shehab, S., Saleh, A.M., Ali, G.A.M., 2024. Metal-organic frameworks in drug delivery: Engineering versatile platforms for therapeutic applications. RSC Adv. 14 (41), 30201–30229. https://doi.org/10.1039/d4ra04441j.

Khan, M.U., Alissa, M., Inam, M., Alsuwat, M.A., Abdulaziz, O., Mostafa, Y.S., Hussain, T., Rehman, K.ur, Zaman, U., Khan, D., 2024. Comprehensive overview of utilizing metal-organic frameworks (MOFs) for precise cancer drug delivery. Microchem. J. 204, 111056. https://doi.org/10.1016/j.microc.2024.111056.

Khosrojerdi, S., Gholami, L., Khazaei, M., Hashemzadeh, A., Darroudi, M., Oskuee, R.K., 2024. Synthesis and evaluation of gene delivery vectors based on PEI-modified metal-organic framework (MOF) nanoparticles. Iran. J. Basic Med. Sci. 27 (2), 203–213. https://doi.org/10.22038/IJBMS.2023.71892.15644.

Li, Y., Zhang, K., Liu, P., Chen, Mo, Zhong, Y., Ye, Q., Wei, M.Q., Zhao, H., Tang, Z., 2019. Encapsulation of plasmid DNA by nanoscale metal–organic frameworks for efficient gene transportation and expression. Adv. Mater. 31 (29). https://doi.org/10.1002/adma.201901570.

Li, D., Yadav, A., Zhou, H., Roy, K., Thanasekaran, P., Lee, C., 2024. Advances and applications of metal-organic frameworks (MOFs) in emerging technologies: A comprehensive review. Glob. Chall. 8 (2). https://doi.org/10.1002/gch2.202300244.

Liang, Z., Yang, Z., Yuan, H., Wang, C., Qi, J., Liu, K., Cao, R., Zheng, H., 2018. A protein@metal–organic framework nanocomposite for pH-triggered anticancer drug delivery. Dalton Trans. 47 (30), 10223–10228. https://doi.org/10.1039/c8dt01789a.

Liu, M., Du, H., Zhang, W., Zhai, G., 2017. Internal stimuli-responsive nanocarriers for drug delivery: Design strategies and applications. Mater. Sci. Eng. C 71, 1267–1280. https://doi.org/10.1016/j.msec.2016.11.030.

Liu, L., Qi, G., Wang, M., He, J., Zheng, Y., Guan, J., Lv, P., Dong, Z., 2024. Construction of intelligent response gene vector based on MOF/Fe3O4/AuNRs for tumor-targeted gene delivery. Int. J. Biol. Macromol. 277 (Pt 3), 134313. https://doi.org/10.1016/j.ijbiomac.2024.134313.

Ma, D., Wang, G., Lu, J., Zeng, X., Cheng, Y., Zhang, Z., Lin, N., Chen, Q., 2023. Multifunctional nano MOF drug delivery platform in combination therapy. Eur. J. Med. Chem. 261, 115884. https://doi.org/10.1016/j.ejmech.2023.115884.

Majidinia, M., Mirhosseyni, M., Abdollahzadeh, N., Ghareghomi, S., Ali, K., 2025. MIL-101(Fe) nanoplatform for pH-triggered quercetin release: Unlocking potent pro-oxidant and anticancer synergy in breast cancer therapy. J. Mol. Struct. 1344, 142966. https://doi.org/10.1016/j.molstruc.2025.142966.

Masoudifar, R., Pouyanfar, N., Liu, D., Ahmadi, M., Landi, B., Akbari, M., Moayeri-Jolandan, S., Ghorbani-Bidkorpeh, F., Asadian, E., Shahbazi, M.-A., 2022. Surface engineered metal-organic frameworks as active targeting nanomedicines for mono- and multi-therapy. Appl. Mater. Today 29, 101646. https://doi.org/10.1016/j.apmt.2022.101646.

Matlou, G.G., Abrahamse, H., 2022. Nanoscale metal–organic frameworks as photosensitizers and nanocarriers in photodynamic therapy. Front. Chem. 10. https://doi.org/10.3389/fchem.2022.971747.

Mokhtari, R.B., Homayouni, T.S., Baluch, N., Morgatskaya, E., Kumar, S., Das, B., Yeger, H., 2017. Combination therapy in combating cancer. Oncotarget 8 (23), 38022–38043. https://doi.org/10.18632/oncotarget.16723.

Mokri, N., Sepehri, Z., Faninam, F., Khaleghi, S., Kazemi, N.M., Hashemi, M., 2022. Chitosan-coated Zn-metal-organic framework nanocomposites for effective targeted delivery of LNA-antisense miR-224 to colon tumor: In vitro studies. Gene Ther. 29 (12), 680–690. https://doi.org/10.1038/s41434-021-00265-7.

Mondal, S., Roy, S., Ksibi, M., Ahmaruzzaman, M., 2025. Harnessing stimuli-responsive moieties for next-gen smart metal-organic frameworks (MOFs): Designing strategies, key advancements and future perspectives. Appl. Mater. Today 44, 102747. https://doi.org/10.1016/j.apmt.2025.102747.

Mukherjee, S., Thakkar, A.B., Agola, A.M., Sargara, P., Mishra, M.K., Subramanian, R.B., Thakor, P., 2024. A mechanistic insight on the biomimetic activity of surface engineered NH2-MIL-125 with α-Asarone for enhanced ROS production in lung cancer cells. Results Surf. Interfaces 17. https://doi.org/10.1016/j.rsurfi.2024.100274.

Mukhlif, B.A.M., Ullah, M.I., Uthirapathy, S., Menon, S.V., Sharma, R.S.K., Kadhim, A.J., Sharma, S., Juneja, B., Abosaoda, M.K., Kadhum, W.R., 2025. Multifunctional nanoparticles for image-guided drug delivery in nuclear medicine: Advancements and applications. J. Radioanal. Nucl. Chem. 334 (2), 1107–1121. https://doi.org/10.1007/s10967-024-09960-2.

Pan, Q.S., Chen, T.T., Nie, C.P., Yi, J.T., Liu, C., Hu, Y.L., Chu, X., 2018. In situ synthesis of ultrathin ZIF-8 film-coated MSNs for codelivering Bcl 2 siRNA and doxorubicin to enhance chemotherapeutic efficacy in drug-resistant cancer cells. ACS Appl. Mater. Interfaces 10 (39), 33070–33077. https://doi.org/10.1021/acsami.8b13393.

Parsaei, M., Akhbari, K., 2023. Magnetic UiO-66-NH 2 core–shell Nanohybrid as a promising carrier for quercetin targeted delivery toward human breast cancer cells. ACS Omega 8 (44), 41321–41338. https://doi.org/10.1021/acsomega.3c04863.

Pattnaik, A.K., Priyadarshini, N., Priyadarshini, P., Behera, G.C., Parida, K., 2024. Recent advancements in metal organic framework-modified multifunctional materials for photodynamic therapy. Mater. Adv. 5 (15), 6030–6051. https://doi.org/10.1039/d4ma00376d.

Prakash, O., Verma, D., Singh, P.C., 2024. Exploring enzyme-immobilized MOFs and their application potential: Biosensing, biocatalysis, targeted drug delivery and cancer therapy. J. Mater. Chem. B 12 (40), 10198–10214. https://doi.org/10.1039/d4tb01556h.

Rahman, M., Kabir, M., Islam, T., Wang, Y., Qi, M., Liu, H., Chen, S., Wu, S., 2025. Curcumin-loaded ZIF-8 nanomaterials: Exploring drug loading efficiency and biomedical performance. ACS Omega 10 (3), 3067–3079. https://doi.org/10.1021/acsomega.4c09945.

Rezaei, M., Abbasi, A., Varshochian, R., Dinarvand, R., Jeddi-Tehrani, M., 2018. NanoMIL-100(Fe) containing docetaxel for breast cancer therapy. Artif. Cell Nanomed. Biotechnol. 46 (7), 1390–1401. https://doi.org/10.1080/21691401.2017.1369425.

Saboorizadeh, B., Zare-Dorabei, R., Safavi, M., Safarifard, V., 2024. Applications of metal–organic frameworks (MOFs) in drug delivery, biosensing, and therapy: A comprehensive review. Langmuir 40 (43), 22477–22503. https://doi.org/10.1021/acs.langmuir.4c02795.

Sadiq, S., Khan, S., Khan, I., Khan, A., Humayun, M., Wu, P., Usman, M., Khan, A., Alanazi, A.F., Bououdina, M., 2024. A critical review on metal-organic frameworks (MOFs) based nanomaterials for biomedical applications: Designing, recent trends, challenges, and prospects. Heliyon 10 (3), e25521. https://doi.org/10.1016/j.heliyon.2024.e25521.

Safarkhani, M., Dana, N., Taghavimandi, F., Najaflu, M., Esmaeili, Y., Zare, E.N., Huh, Y.S., Rahimmanesh, I., Makvandi, P., Xu, Y., Jin, X., 2024. Exploring metal-organic frameworks in gene delivery: From prostate to lung therapeutics. Appl. Mater. Today 41. https://doi.org/10.1016/j.apmt.2024.102449.

Salahpour Anarjan, F., 2019. Active targeting drug delivery nanocarriers: Ligands. Nano-Struct. Nano-Objects 19. https://doi.org/10.1016/j.nanoso.2019.100370.

Sun, C.Y., Qin, C., Wang, X.L., Su, Z.M., 2013. Metal-organic frameworks as potential drug delivery systems. Expert Opin. Drug Deliv. 10 (1), 89–101. https://doi.org/10.1517/17425247.2013.741583.

Sun, Y., Zheng, L., Yang, Y., Qian, X., Fu, T., Li, X., Yang, Z., Yan, H., Cui, C., Tan, W., 2020. Metal–organic framework nanocarriers for drug delivery in biomedical applications. Nano-Micro Lett. 12 (1). https://doi.org/10.1007/s40820-020-00423-3.

Sun, H., Zhang, Q., Li, J., Peng, S., Wang, X., Cai, R., 2021. Near-infrared photoactivated nanomedicines for photothermal synergistic cancer therapy. Nano Today 37, 101073. https://doi.org/10.1016/j.nantod.2020.101073.

Tan, K., Chabal, Y., Keskin, Y., Zhang, X., He, X., Wang, Liu, H., Liu, Y., Mali, G., V. Andre, S., Quaresma, F., 2016. Introduction to Metal–Organic Frameworks Metal–Organic Frameworks, pp. 3–16. https://doi.org/10.5772/61907.

Tao, Y., Chan, H.F., Shi, B., Li, M., Leong, K.W., 2020. Light: A magical tool for controlled drug delivery. Adv. Funct. Mater. 30 (49). https://doi.org/10.1002/adfm.202005029.

Tomar, S., Singh, V.K., 2021. Review on synthesis and application of mil-53. Mater. Today Proc. 43. https://doi.org/10.1016/j.matpr.2021.02.179.

Tong, P.H., Zhu, L., Zang, Y., Li, J., He, X.P., James, T.D., 2021. Metal-organic frameworks (MOFs) as host materials for the enhanced delivery of biomacromolecular therapeutics. Chem. Commun. 57 (91), 12098–12110. https://doi.org/10.1039/d1cc05157a.

Tran, V.A., Thuan Le, V., Doan, V.D., Vo, G.N.L., 2023. Utilization of functionalized metal–organic framework nanoparticle as targeted drug delivery system for cancer therapy. Pharmaceutics 15 (3). https://doi.org/10.3390/pharmaceutics15030931.

Wang, T., Narayanaswamy, R., Ren, H., Torchilin, V.P., 2016. Combination therapy targeting both cancer stem-like cells and bulk tumor cells for improved efficacy of breast cancer treatment. Cancer Biol. Ther. 17 (6), 698–707. https://doi.org/10.1080/15384047.2016.1190488.

Wang, D., Wu, H., Zhou, J., Xu, P., Wang, C., Shi, R., Wang, H., Wang, H., Guo, Z., Chen, Q., 2018. In situ one-pot synthesis of MOF–polydopamine hybrid Nanogels with enhanced photothermal effect for targeted cancer therapy. Adv. Sci. 5 (6). https://doi.org/10.1002/advs.201800287.

Wang, S., Chen, Y., Wang, S., Li, P., Mirkin, C.A., Farha, O.K., 2019. DNA-functionalized metal-organic framework nanoparticles for intracellular delivery of proteins. J. Am. Chem. Soc. 141 (6), 2215–2219. https://doi.org/10.1021/jacs.8b12705.

Wang, Y., Foulkes, R.L., Panagiotou, N., Markopoulou, P., Bistrović Popov, A., Eskandari, A., Fruk, L., Forgan, R.S., 2025. Photoclick surface modification of MOF-808 for galactose-mediated targeted chemotherapy. J. Colloid Interface Sci. 681, 416–424. https://doi.org/10.1016/j.jcis.2024.11.129.

Woalder, M.K., Tripp, P.D.M., 2017. 乳鼠心肌提取 HHS public access. Physiol. Behav. 176 (1), 139–148.

Wu, J., Zhang, Z., Qiao, C., Yi, C., Xu, Z., Chen, T., Dai, X., 2022. Synthesis of monodisperse ZIF-67@CuSe@PVP nanoparticles for pH-responsive drug release and photothermal therapy. ACS Biomater. Sci. Eng. 8 (1), 284–292. https://doi.org/10.1021/acsbiomaterials.1c01124.

Xu, M., Hu, Y., Ding, W., Li, F., Lin, J., Wu, M., Wu, J., Wen, L.P., Qiu, B., Wei, P.F., Li, P., 2020. Rationally designed rapamycin-encapsulated ZIF-8 nanosystem for overcoming chemotherapy resistance. Biomaterials 258. https://doi.org/10.1016/j.biomaterials.2020.120308.

Yan, J., Liu, C., Wu, Q., Zhou, J., Xu, X., Zhang, L., Wang, D., Yang, F., Zhang, H., 2020. Mineralization of pH-sensitive doxorubicin prodrug in ZIF-8 to enable targeted delivery to solid tumors. Anal. Chem. 92 (16), 11453–11461. https://doi.org/10.1021/acs.analchem.0c02599.

Yan, C., Jin, Y., Zhao, C., 2021. Environment responsive metal–organic frameworks as drug delivery system for tumor therapy. Nanoscale Res. Lett. 16 (1). https://doi.org/10.1186/s11671-021-03597-w.

Yang, N., He, Z., Lang, T., 2025. Drug delivery systems based on metal–organic frameworks for tumor immunotherapy. Pharmaceutics 17 (2), 225. https://doi.org/10.3390/pharmaceutics17020225.

Yao, L., Tang, Y., Cao, W., Cui, Y., Qian, G., 2021. Highly efficient encapsulation of doxorubicin hydrochloride in metal–organic frameworks for synergistic chemotherapy and chemodynamic therapy. ACS Biomater. Sci. Eng. 7 (10), 4999–5006. https://doi.org/10.1021/acsbiomaterials.1c00874.

Zhang, Y., Chen, X., 2024. Recent progress and challenges of MOF-based nanocomposites in bioimaging, biosensing and biocarriers for drug delivery. Nanoscale Adv. 6 (2), 290–309. https://doi.org/10.1039/D3NA01075A.

Zhang, J., Zhan, B., Du, Liu, N., Liu, S., 2025. Targeted cancer treatment using folic acid-functionalized carbohydrate polymers: A new era in nanomedicine. Ind. Crops Prod. 235.

Zou, M., Dong, M., Zhao, T., 2022. Advances in metal-organic frameworks MIL-101(Cr). Int. J. Mol. Sci. 23 (16), 9396. https://doi.org/10.3390/ijms23169396.

Zhu, R., Cai, M., Fu, T., Yin, D., Peng, H., Liao, S., Du, Y., Kong, J., Ni, J., Yin, X., 2023. Fe-based metal organic frameworks (Fe-MOFs) for bio-related applications. Pharmaceutics 15 (6), 1599. https://doi.org/10.3390/pharmaceutics15061599.

CHAPTER

13

Tumor microenvironment targeted drug delivery systems

Lalit Kumar, Nirmal Morya, Keshav Hirave, Mansi Sharma and Vikas Anand Saharan

Department of Pharmaceutical Technology (Formulations), National Institute of Pharmaceutical Education and Research, Guwahati (NIPER-G), Sila Katamur (Halugurisuk), Assam, India

Introduction

Cancer is ranked among the top five most critical diseases globally, with its incidence rising every year (Wang et al., 2023). It is characterized by aberrant cellular differentiation, proliferation, as well as by uncontrolled growth, invasion, and metastasis (Yakubu et al., 2021). Some of the cancer therapies are surgical procedures, chemotherapy, radiotherapy, and their combinations. There is still a great challenge in the field of cancer treatment due to drug recurrence, devastating adverse effects, and less effective treatment options available (Yakubu et al., 2021; Yang et al., 2019). The current treatment of cancer requires coordination of clinicians and biological scientists, material scientists, and biomedical engineers. Classical chemotherapeutics do not act selectively, but they spread to both the cancer and normal cells. The application of contemporary pharmacological intervention necessitates tissue selectivity. This restricts the dosage that can be successfully administered in a solid tumor, leading to inferior treatment results because of the high level of toxicity to healthy cells. The main outcome of cancer therapeutics is to enhance both life quality and survival time by minimizing chemoresistance-related systemic toxicity (Byrne et al., 2008). The tumor microenvironment (TME) is one of the areas of priority to explore cancer therapy. More precisely, in-depth knowledge of TME enables the developer to derive therapeutic approaches on the basis of the peculiarities in relation to normal tissue, including vascular alterations, oxygenation, perfusion, pH, and metabolic state (Khawar et al., 2015). This chapter gives a comprehensive view of the tumor microenvironment, its effect on cancer progression, metastatic development, and treatment approaches with TME-based strategies.

Advanced Cancer Therapeutics
https://doi.org/10.1016/B978-0-443-44185-1.00008-2

Tumor microenvironment and its role in cancer progression and metastasis

The tumor microenvironment (TME) refers to the cellular milieu wherein tumors or cancer stem cells reside (Fig. 13.1). Cancer Stem Cells are defined as neoplastic cells possessing self-regenerative capabilities and the potential to initiate tumorigenesis (Khawar et al., 2015). The TME encompasses adjacent immune cells, vasculature, ECM, fibroblasts, lymphocytes, inflammatory cells derived from bone marrow, and various signaling molecules (Del Prete et al., 2017; Spill et al., 2016). TME is the result of the interaction between the malignant and non-malignant cells that affects the development of cancer and its progression (Balkwill et al., 2012; Hanahan and Coussens, 2012).

Tumor development is strongly shaped by an unusual immune response and homeostasis (Tomás-Bort et al., 2020). Central to this process is the TME, a dynamic network in which cancer cells interact with the immune cells, stromal components, and the ECM. These interaction not only enables the tumor survival but also drive the malignant behavior like growth, invasion, and metastasis (Sceneay et al., 2018; Buhrmann et al., 2014). Within the TME, a wide spectrum of innate immune cells, such as macrophages, neutrophils, dendritic cells, innate lymphoid cells and etc., compete with the adaptive immune cells (T cells and B cells), to influence tumor progression (Hinshaw and Shevde, 2019). The contribution of these cellular components is linked to the surrounding anatomical and physiological context, including local metabolism, tissue structure, and specialized function of the host organ. As tumor cell begins to invade adjacent healthy tissues, they actively remodel the microenvironment, providing condition that promotes their own proliferation and dissemination, there establishing the distinct and tumor-promoting landscape characteristics of the TME (Erdogan and Webb, 2017).

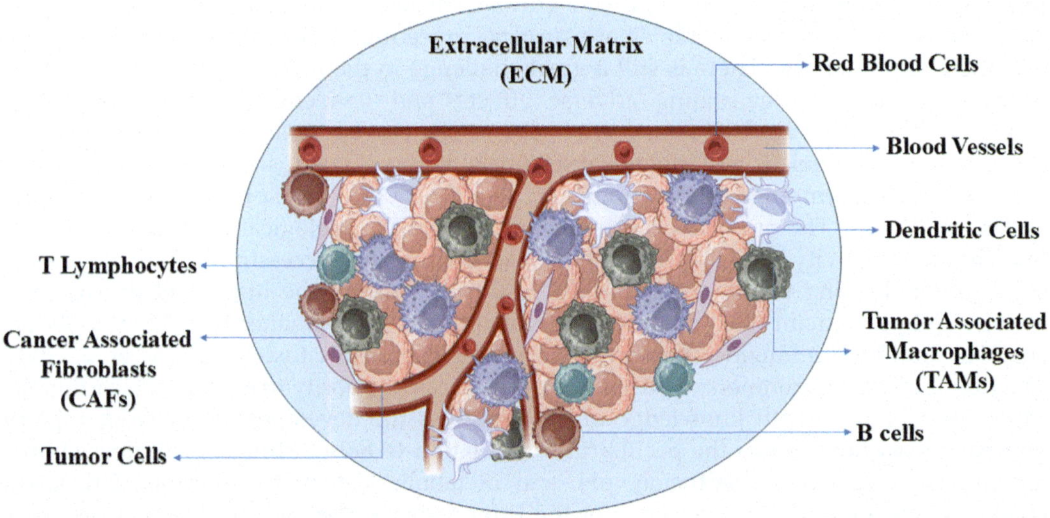

FIGURE 13.1 **Tumor microenvironment.** TME encompasses adjacent immune cells, vasculature, ECM, fibroblasts, lymphocytes, and inflammatory cells.

Tumor microenvironment (TME) consists of multiple non-immune stromal cells, such as endothelial cells, fibroblasts, and organ-specific cells, in addition to immune cells, all of which play significant roles. These components contribute to key tumor activities, including angiogenesis, ECM remodeling, and metastasis. Stromal cells play a pivotal role in assisting the cancer cells in evading the immune surveillance and resisting the immune checkpoint blockade (ICB) therapies (Fukumura et al., 2018; Priego et al., 2018; Fiori et al., 2019). Among these, cancer-associated fibroblasts (CAFs) are the primary stromal cell type in the TME, which influence the ECM remodeling and regulate the interactions between immune cells and cancer cells (Park et al., 2020). Angiogenesis and vascular abnormalities in the TME, together with elevated intratumoral pressure, can further restrict immune cell infiltration and reduce the effectiveness of checkpoint inhibitors (Fukumura et al., 2018). In addition, the stromal cells themselves may contribute to resistance against ICB therapies.

The tumor ECM plays a major role in cancer cell migration, efficiency of treatment, and disease progression (Neophytou et al., 2021). Equally important is the metabolic state of the TME, which strongly affects the tumor's ability to induce an immune response. For example, hypoxic tumors down regulate type 1 major histocompatibility complex (MHC) expression on both tumor cells and dendritic cells (DCs) (Chakravarthy et al., 2018). They also possess reduced T cell and natural killer (NK) cell infiltration, along with impaired mitochondrial biogenesis. It has led to exploring strategies aimed at improving tumor immunogenicity through increased production of mitochondria (Scharping et al., 2016). Furthermore, given the profound impact of hypoxia on tumor immunogenicity, current studies are investigating novel mechanisms of immune escape and resistance to ICBs, particularly those involving other components of TME shaped by metabolic conditions, such as altered nutritional availability (Chakravarthy et al., 2018). Various TME cells and their functions are given in (Table 13.1).

Challenges in drug delivery to the TME

The TME is a complex biological system that impedes effective drug delivery to cancer cells. These barriers can be broadly categorized into physical, cellular, and molecular obstacles, each intricately developed to support tumor growth. By fostering structural, cellular, and microenvironmental defenses, the TME severely limits the effectiveness of available therapeutic strategies (Zhou et al., 2020; Tiwari et al., 2022).

Biological barriers

Abnormal structure of tumor vasculature

The tumor vasculature represents one of the major bottlenecks in effective drug delivery. Unlike normal blood vessels, which are normal in structure and function, tumor vessels are both structurally aberrant and functionally impaired (Stylianopoulos and Jain, 2013; Azzi et al., 2013). The key abnormalities include:

1 **Hyperpermeability and leakage:** Tumor vessels exhibit abnormal inter-endothelial junctions, impoverished pericyte coverage, and an imperfect basement membrane, leading to excessive leakage of fluid from vasculature into the interstitial space.

TABLE 13.1 Cells presents in TME and their functions.

Type of cells	Functions
Cancer associated fibroblasts (CAFs)	Supports proliferative signaling; activation of angiogenesis and metastasis; promoting genome instability and mutation.
Neutrophils	Improvement of angiogenesis and metastasis; linked with poor prognosis
Tumor associated macrophages (TAMs)	ECM degradation; supports the expansion of inflammatory cytokines like TNF-β
Regulatory T cells (Tregs)	Secretion of cytokines such as IL-10, TGF-β; creating an immunosuppressive environment
Myeloid derived suppressor cell (MDSCs)	Suppression of T and NK cells; differentiating into TAMs under hypoxic condition
Mesenchymal stem cells (MSCs)	Advances the cancer initiation and malignancy
Endothelial cells	Comprising of tumor blood vessels; secretion of angiocrine factor like adhesion molecules.
Adipocytes	Controlling the balance of systemic energy and metabolism
Vascular network	Exchange of oxygen and carbon dioxide; gives nutrition support for cancer cells
Lymph vessels	Assist in immune cell avoid immunity and dissemination.
Extracellular matrix (ECM)	Contribution to growth and proliferation signaling, and inhibits cancer apoptosis

2 **Tortuous and compressed architecture:** Their irregular and distorted structures increase resistance to fluid flow while reducing the effective cross-sectional area available for blood flow.
3 **Poor perfusion:** Tumor tissues often receive low blood perfusion compared to the adjacent normal tissue, resulting in hypoxia and impaired drug distribution.

Extracellular matrix density

Dense extracellular matrices in solid tumors act as a prominent barrier to drug penetration (Li et al., 2022; Subrahmanyam and Ghandehari, 2021). About 60% of the solid tumor mass consists of ECM deposits, chiefly collagen, which confer structural stiffness and create the following challenges:

1 **Physical barrier:** Dense collagen fiber networks and other ECM components physically reduce the diffusion of therapeutic agents through tumor tissue.
2 **Increased matrix stiffness:** High stiffness of the matrix, common in an aggressive tumor like triple-negative breast cancer, promotes cancer cell proliferation and is associated with poor prognosis.
3 **Drug binding:** ECM components may bind to the therapeutic agents, thereby reducing their availability to the target cells.

Cellular barriers

Cancer-associated fibroblasts (CAFs)

Cancer-associated fibroblasts, or CAFs, are major obstacles to drug penetration in solid tumors, particularly in high fibrotic cancers like pancreatic ductal adenocarcinoma (Basar et al., 2024; Yuan et al., 2023). CAFs contribute to therapeutic resistance through several mechanisms:

1 **Secretion of ECM:** CAFs continuously produce collagen and other extracellular matrix proteins, generating a dense, fibrotic stroma, often described as "stromal fortress", that blocks drug penetration.
2 **Secretion of growth factors:** CAFs release factors such as TGF-β, VEGF, and PDGF, which not only drive tumor progression but also sustain a distorted and metabolically demanding tumor microenvironment.
3 **Immunosuppressive functions:** CAFs modulate the local immune response by blocking T-cell activity, thereby enabling tumor immune evasion and reducing the efficacy of immunotherapies (Salemme et al., 2023; Zhang et al., 2025).

Tumor associated macrophages (TAMs)

TAMs set up a protective shell around developing tumors and help cancer cells evade treatment through the following mechanisms (Liu et al., 2024; Ji et al., 2024):

1 **Physical barrier:** TAMs pack together at tumor sites, forming a dense shield that blocks both the immune infiltration and incoming drugs.
2 **Immunosuppressive signals:** M2-like TAMs pump out cytokines like IL-10 and TGF-ϐ, which suppress killer T-cell activity.
3 **Therapy-linked resistance:** By releasing growth factors and activating pro-survival pathways, TAMs enhance tumor resistance to chemotherapy, targeted drugs, and even immunotherapy.

Myeloid-derived suppressor cells (MDSCs)

MDSCs represent another important cellular barrier within the TME (Kumar et al., 2024a, 2024b; Li et al., 2021). These immature myeloid cells interfere with therapy in the following ways:

1 **Immunosuppression:** MDSCs suppress T-cell activation and function by multiple mechanisms, including arginase production, nitric oxide synthesis, and cytokine secretion.
2 **Resistance to treatment:** These cells create an immunosuppressive milieu and thus diminish the efficacy of chemotherapy, radiotherapy, and immunotherapy.
3 **Tumor Promotor:** MDSCs may also serve as direct mediators of tumor invasion and metastasis

Microenvironmental barriers

Hypoxia and acidic pH

The acidic and hypoxic nature of the TME poses additional challenges, as given below (Soltani et al., 2021; Dharmaratne et al., 2021):

1 **Restricted drug penetration:** Hypoxic tumor regions, typically characterized by low vascular density, limit the penetration of therapeutic agents.
2 **Impact on drug efficacy:** Acidic pH (6.5–7.0) due to aberrant glucose metabolism and lactate accumulation affects cellular uptake and stability of drugs.
3 **Metabolic adaptation:** Cancer cells reprogram their metabolism to survive hypoxia, leading to resistance against certain therapeutic approaches.

Tregs (regulatory T cells)

Tregs are a key immunosuppressive component in the TME (Chaudhary and Elkord, 2016; Galgani et al., 2021):

1 **Immune suppression:** Type 2 regulatory T cells (Tregs) secrete the inhibitory cytokines TGF-β and IL-10 that inhibit cytotoxic $CD8^+$ T cells, $CD4^+$ T helper cells, and NK cells.
2 **Checkpoint expression:** Tregs express the immune checkpoint molecules CTLA-4, PD-1, LAG-3, and TIM-3, which inhibit immune responses.
3 **Metabolic advantage:** Within the hostile TME, Tregs exhibit better metabolic flexibility than effector T cells, enabling them to survive in nutrient-deprived and acidic conditions.

Strategies for TME-targeted drug delivery

Targeting chemotherapeutic agents to tumors provides several advantages over non-targeted therapies, including reduced adverse effects on healthy tissues and improved drug uptake by cancer cells. Drug delivery to the TME can be achieved through two primary approaches: passive targeting and active targeting.

Passive targeting

Maeda, Matsumura, and co-workers demonstrated that nanoparticles and macromolecular drugs tend to accumulate selectively in solid tumors due to enhanced vascular permeability and retention (EPR effect) of tumor blood vessels and poor lymphatic drainage in tumors (Fig. 13.2) (Matsumura and Maeda, 1986; Maeda et al., 2000). Small drugs entrapped in large macromolecules or water-soluble drugs carried by large molecules don't get drained well and hence accumulate in the tumor (Thanou and Duncan, 2003). The key difference between the normal cells and tumor cells is given in (Table 13.2).

The EPR effect that is often used to assist with the delivery of anticancer drugs is dependent on the characteristics and differences in tumors due to their heterogeneous structures (Maeda, 2012). The structure of the blood vessels and the dimensions of the blood vessels also vary quite a bit, not only from tumor to tumor but from region to region within each tumor (Chauhan et al., 2020). Several factors influence the EPR effect, although the most important factors are: (i) the milieu in which the tumor is growing (extracellular matrix type, blood vessels, and surrounding tissue) plays a critical role in the EPR effect. Tumor ECM is often dense, fibrous, and remolded by proteases, creating physical barriers limiting nanomedicines' penetration. The tumor vasculature is abnormal with poorly aligned

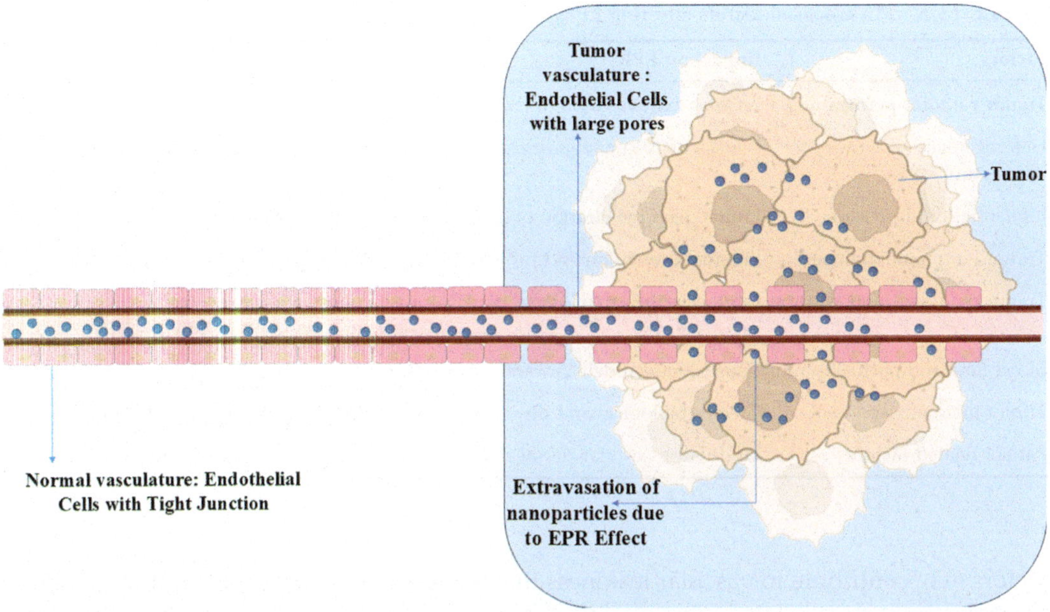

FIGURE 13.2 **Accumulation of nanocarriers in tumor cells due to EPR effect.** Loose vasculature in tumors facilitate EPR effect mediated accumulation of nanoparticles.

TABLE 13.2 Difference between normal cells and cancer cells.

Features	Normal cells	Tumor cells
Endothelial junctions	Tight barrier, no gaps between the endothelial cells	Irregular, leaky (0.1–3 μm)
Basement membrane	Intact, continuous, supports endothelium	Often disrupted or fragmented in tumor vessel
Permeability to macromolecules	Low, regulated, selective	High, leaky, facilitates macromolecule extravasation
Lymphatic drainage	Efficient, prevents edema	Impaired, contributes to high interstitial pressure
Flow pattern	Uniform, controlled perfusion	Heterogeneous, poor perfusion
Pericyte coverage	Dense coverage, maintains vessel stability	Abnormal, destabilizes vasculature

endothelial cells, wide fenestration, deficient basement membrane, and irregular blood flow. These features enable vascular permeability, enabling nanoparticles to extravasate, but also cause heterogeneity in delivery. (ii) Various vascular factors and circulating factors, like VEGF, nitric oxide, prostaglandins, bradykinin, and inflammatory cytokines, promote angiogenesis and vascular permeability, sustaining the EPR effect. However, these same

TABLE 13.3 Physiological factors affecting EPR.

Factors	Impact on EPR
Tumor vascular permeability	Enables extravasation of nanoparticles/macromolecules in the tumor tissue
Heterogenicity of tumor vasculature	Causes uneven nanoparticle accumulation and inconsistent drug delivery
Interstitial fluid pressure	Limits deep penetration of drugs despite vessel leakiness
Tumor lymphatic drainage	Enhances retention and prolonged presence of nanoparticles in tumor tissue
Tumor type, size, and location	Influences the extent of vascularization and penetration; lager/solid tumors are often less accessible
Blood flow and perfusion rate	Causes uneven delivery and distribution of nanoparticles
Tumor microenvironment	Creates biological and physical barriers limiting nanoparticles diffusion
Patient-related factors	Modulates vascular permeability, perfusion, and retention variability

factors may contribute to vascular leakiness that is unevenly distributed, creating regions of poor perfusion and elevated interstitial fluid pressure (IFP), which impedes deep drug penetration. (iii) Other drugs that exert effects on the state of the surrounding tissue and vascular pressure that increases the internal pressure of the tumor and enhance regional blood flow to the tumor. For example, anti-angiogenic drug aiming to normalize tumor vasculature can transiently improve perfusion and reduce vessel leakiness, improving nanoparticle delivery. ECM-modulating agents breaking down fibrous stroma reduce physical barriers. Agents increasing nitric oxide or bradykinin levels temporarily enhance vascular permeability, boosting nanoparticle extravasation (Wang et al., 2012). In addition, physiological factors that affect EPR effect are given in (Table 13.3).

Targeting specific tumor conditions

The second approach of passive targeting uses a specific condition in the tumor environment itself to promote drug release from the delivery system. The condition includes (but is not restricted to) certain pH, specific enzymes, or the microbiome present in the tumor (Hua, 2014; Kadam et al., 2020; Sinha and Kumria, 2002). The main drawback of the approach is that it targets the entire organ rather than just the tumor, which might lead to serious organ cytotoxicity.

pH-responsive systems

Cancer cells use aerobic glycolysis to break down glucose to lactate, even when oxygen is abundant, resulting in increased glucose uptake, which leads to an acidic tumor microenvironment due to lactate accumulation (Warburg effect). The acidic pH in solid tumors, largely a result of the Warburg effect, can be exploited to guide the delivery of the nanocarriers (Dai et al., 2017). There are three common strategies to design pH-responsive NCs. The first strategy involves incorporating molecular components with a pKa close to the pH of the tumor

TABLE 13.4 pH-responsive systems with their responsive moiety.

Responsive moiety	Nanocarrier	Drug	Tumor model	References
Tertiary amine	Micelles (mPEG/HCou-g-MPCL)	Doxorubicin	HeLa	Yang et al. (2020)
Sulfonamides	Polyplexes poly(methacycloylsulfadimethoxine)-b-PEG	DNA	A2780	Sethuraman et al. (2006)
Hydrazone	Polymer-drug conjugate *N*-(2-hydroxypropyl)methacrylamide copolymer	Doxorubicin	EL4	Etrych et al. (2001)
Orthoester	Micelles or micelles like nanoparticles PEG-b-PtNEA27/56/73	Nile red	-	Huang et al. (2009)
Imine	Polymer-drug conjugate dextran	Doxorubicin	B16F10	Feng et al. (2017)
Benzoic imine	Polymeric nanogels Benzoic-imine containing PEI-g-mPEG	Indocyanine green	-	Liao et al. (2020)
Acetals	Mesoporous silica nanoparticles	Resiquimod and OVA	-	Wagner et al. (2021)
pHLIP	Gold nanospheres	Chlorin e6	HeLa	Yu et al. (2016)
PolyHis	Micelles poly (L-lactic acid)-b-PEG-b-polyHis	Doxorubicin	MCF-7	Lee et al. (2007)

TME. In acidic conditions, the functional groups on these molecules become protonated, altering the hydrophilic-lipophilic balance of the nanocarriers and leading to expansion, rearrangement, or disintegration (Zhou et al., 2011). Acid-sensitive moieties such as histidine, sulfonamide, or tertiary amine structures are typically employed. The second strategy uses acid-sensitive bonds that remain stable at neutral pH, but are cleaved in an acidic environment (Du et al., 2014). This enables site-specific drug payloads within the TME. The third strategy involves the use of pH-low insertion peptides (pHLIPs), which enhance cellular uptake of NCs. These peptides weakly associate with cell membranes at neutral pH but undergo stable insertion into the membrane in acidic conditions, thereby improving delivery efficiency (Andreev et al., 2014) (Table 13.4). shows the pH-responsive systems with their responsive moiety.

Enzyme responsive systems

The overexpression of certain enzymes in tumor cells can be exploited as endogenous stimuli for cancer therapy and imaging. Owing to their high substrate specificity, enzymes serve as effective reaction triggers, generating considerable interest in the development of enzyme-responsive nanocarriers. Some key endogenous enzymes investigated for this purpose are glycosidases, phospholipases, MMPs, cathepsin, and others (Table 13.5). For

TABLE 13.5 Enzyme responsive systems.

Enzyme	Responsive moiety	Nanocarriers	Agent	Tumor model	References
α-glucosidase	β- CD	β- CD-MNPs	Prodigiosin	MCF-7/ GFPHepG2	Rastegari et al. (2017)
Galactosidase	Carbohydrate unit	Folate-DOX conjugate	DOX	KG-1 and HL-60	Clarhaut et al. (2013)
Galactosidase	Saccharides	SMPS modified with lactose or starch derivative	$[Ru(bipy)_3]^{2+}$ dye	HeLa	Bernardos et al. (2010)
sPLA2	1-Palmitoyl-2-oleoyl-sn-glycero-3-phosphocholine	Liposome shell and TRAIL-loaded DNA NCs cores	TRAIL	COLO 205 cells	Sun et al. (2016)
MMP-13	PLGLAR	MSNs-PLGLAR-BSA-LA@DOX	DOX	HepG2	Liu et al. (2015)
MMP-9	GFFGLG PhAc-FFAG	MMP-9 responsive peptides in conjuction with Dox	DOX	MDA-MB-231-luc-D3H2LN	Kalafatovic et al. (2016)
MMP-2	GPLGIAGQ	PEG_{2000} – peptide-PTX	PTX	A549	Zhu et al. (2013)
	GPLGLAG	MPV-HOAD	OXApheophorbide a	2 CT26	Zhou et al. (2019)
Cathepsin B	GFLG	DOX@MSN-GFLGR7RGDS/α-CD	DOX	HeLa	Cheng et al. (2015)

example, nanocarriers with MMP cleavable peptide linkers undergo enzymatic cleavage in the TME, releasing the drug payload directly where needed, which improves tumor penetration and therapeutic efficacy (Kapalatiya et al., 2022). Cathepsin B, a protease overexpressed in many cancer types, triggers intracellular drug release by cleaving cathepsin B linkers in the nanocarriers, allowing for selective drug activation inside cancer cell (Li et al., 2020). Additionally, phospholipase A2 responsive systems take advantage of the enzyme's ability to degrade phospholipids in the nanocarrier membranes, releasing drugs specifically in tumors with enzyme levels (Li et al., 2020).

Hypoxia-responsive systems

Nanocarriers designed to deliver drugs specifically to the hypoxic regions via different mechanisms, such as engineered with the hypoxia-responsive linker, prodrugs, or targeting ligands that trigger drug release under low oxygen conditions, are gaining significant attention. Hypoxia, or low oxygen levels, plays a critical role in promoting angiogenesis, metastasis, altered cell motility, increased tumor aggressiveness, and immune suppression (Wilson and Hay, 2011). In one study, micelles capable of releasing anticancer drugs in response to both hypoxic conditions and light were developed. These particles were prepared from the polyethyleneimine-nitroimidazole, and synergistic anticancer efficacy between Dox-mediated chemotherapy and Ce6-mediated photodynamic therapy (PDT) was thus achieved, resulting in reduced side effects to normal tissue (He et al., 2018). The (Table 13.6) shows other hypoxic responsive systems.

Targeting the CAFs

CAFs, activated fibroblasts found abundantly in the TME, secrete growth factors, cytokines, extracellular matrix (ECM) proteins, and enzymes that support tumor growth, angiogenesis, immune suppression, and drug resistance. Targeting CAFs has become an important strategy in cancer therapy and nanomedicine, with various approaches like eliminating CAFs, blocking CAF signaling pathways, and reprogramming CAFs.

Elimination of CAFs

CAF cells comprise the most abundant cell component in TME and have been considered as potential targets in cancer therapy (Sounni and Noel, 2013). One thing that might enable fibroblasts to assume this role is a membrane-bound enzyme known as fibroblast activation protein alpha (FAP). This enzyme exists in cancerous tissue, although not in healthy tissue, indicating it as an ideal target to assault CAFs (Sounni and Noel, 2013). Prodrugs activated by FAP enzymatic activity and immunotoxin-like Anti-FAP-PE39 demonstrated tumor growth inhibition in a preclinical model, underscoring the potential value for CAF depletion strategies (Lan et al., 2025).

Blocking CAFs signaling pathways

Another key strategy for reducing tumor growth and progression. CAFs influence the tumor growth through various pathways, like TGF-β, IL-6, and the CXCL12/CXCR4 axis (Fang et al., 2023). Inhibitors targeting these pathways can reduce CAF activation and immunosuppressive effects, thus restoring immune surveillance and enhancing treatment response. For example, the CXCR4 antagonist plerixafor has been effective in reducing fibrosis and improving immune filtration. Therapeutic targeting of TGF-β, signaling through inhibitors like galunisertinib, helps maintain tumor cells in a dormant state and blocks CAF-mediated tumor promoting signaling (Lan et al., 2025; Chen et al., 2021).

CAFs reprogramming

Reprogramming of CAFs to revert their activated state, tumor supportive state into a quiescent or tumor suppressive phenotype is a highly promising therapeutic strategies (Yamazaki and Ishimoto, 2025). Agents like all-trans retinoic acid (ATRA), minnelide, calcipotrol, and angiotensin receptor blockers like losartan have shown effectiveness in modulating CAFs activation and remodeling the ECM. This reprogramming not only inhibits the tumor-promoting effects of CAFs but also improves the drug delivery by normalizing the tumor stroma and enhancing the efficacy of immunotherapies (Yamazaki and Ishimoto, 2025).

Targeting TAMs

The intricate role of TAMs is closely related to tumor progression and anti-tumor immune responses, as they control the activities of tumor cells and other cells in TME. It is interesting to note that TAM has multiple roles, and its exceptional adaptability has given rise to considerable potential and motivation for TAM-targeted strategies to combat cancer

TABLE 13.6 Hypoxia responsive systems.

Drug delivery system	Agent	Mechanism	References
Hemoglobin microbubbles conjugated with liposomes	Doxorubicin	Oxygen sensitive hemoglobin trigger release	Rastegar et al. (2025)
Azocalixarenes based host-guest drug delivery system	-	Reduction of azo bonds triggers release	Hu et al. (2023)
Poly (N-oxide) – drug conjugates	Interferon alpha	Bior reduction of the polymer triggers release	Zhang et al. (2023)
Polymeric nano prodrug	Photosensitizer 5,10,5,20-tetrakis(4-aminophenyl)-porphine (TAPP) and chlorambucil (CB)	Photodynamic therapy	Zhao et al. (2024)
Polyplexes	SiRNA	The selective nitro-to-amino reduction	Kang et al. (2016)
Magnetosomes	Doxorubicin	Targeting by magnetic field and hypoxia activation	Deng et al. (2025)
Azocalixarene-modified albumin nanoparticles	Hydroxychloroquine and mitochondria-targeting photosensitizer	Host guest dissociation under hypoxia	(Wang et al., 2025)
Hollow gold-platinum bimetallic nanoshells	Doxorubicin	Photothermal effect	Zhang et al. (2025)
Micelles based on angelica polysaccharide	Curcumin	Selective enhancement of ferroptosis in solid tumor, via diminishing glutathione (GSH) under hypoxia	Liu et al. (2022)
Self-assembled polyethyleneimine-nitroimidazole (PEI-NI) micelles	Doxorubicin	NP dissociation in the hypoxic condition	He et al. (2018)

(Bercovici et al., 2019). Targeting TAMs is an approach to overcome the pro-tumor role of tumor-associated macrophages by depleting them, preventing their recruitment (inhibiting signaling pathways), reprogramming them into anti-tumor macrophages, or combining with immunotherapy.

In animal models, these approaches have demonstrated remarkable therapeutic success and synergistic anticancer effects with currently available drugs (Singh et al., 2022; Zhao et al., 2022).

Inhibition of macrophage recruitment to the TME

Many chemokine signals are key to attracting tumor associated macrophages (TAMs) to the tumor microenvironment (TME). Because of this, the main molecules in the chemokine signaling pathway are seen as targets for treatment. Since CCL2/CCR2 signaling is a major factor in attracting TAMs to the TME (Nagarsheth et al., 2017). To achieve this, studies have reported the use of CCL2-neutralizing antibodies or CCR2 inhibitors, such as PF-04,136,309, RS504393, and CCX872, in animal studies. These treatments aim to enhance the efficacy of immune checkpoint inhibitors (ICIs), reduce the number of TAMs in the TME, and stop CCL2/CCR2 signaling (Wang et al., 2021; Wan et al., 2023; Shi et al., 2019; Flores-Toro et al., 2020). However, in clinical trials, these anti-CCR2 antibodies and small-molecule inhibitors have yielded only limited benefits when used alone or in combination with chemotherapy (Brana et al., 2015; Nywening et al., 2016). In a mouse model of breast cancer, blocking CCL2/CCR2 signaling actually accelerated tumor spread by releasing a large number of monocytes (Bonapace et al., 2014), so more compensatory factors need to be considered when developing strategies to target TAMs to get the best and longest results.

Macrophage phagocytosis

Macrophages protect the body by clearing cellular debris, senescent cells, tumor cells, and foreign substances. They play a crucial role in battling infections and suppressing cancer. Normally, healthy cells produce specific molecular signals that prevent macrophages from engulfing them; these are known as phagocytosis checkpoints (Digklia et al., 2022). Tumors exploit these checkpoints by overexpressing inhibitor signals such as CD47 and CD24 or by reprogramming macrophages to promote tumor growth (Chao et al., 2012; Oldenborg et al., 2000; Medzhitov and Janeway, 2002). Researchers are actively investigating strategies to block these signals to enhance the efficacy of cancer therapies (Shi et al., 2021; Wang et al., 2022; Tan, 2022).

One of the extensively explored "don't eat me" signals is CD47, which inhibits phagocytosis by binding to signal regulatory protein alpha (SIRPα) on macrophages and dendritic cells (Xu et al., 2021). Importantly, inhibition of CD47 with specific antibodies has been shown to enhance TAM-mediated phagocytosis, especially when combined with chemotherapeutic agents (Cao et al., 2022). Furthermore, macrophage trogocytosis is a key biological mechanism that affects antibody-opsonized tumor cells. Unlike classical phagocytosis, trogocytosis involves the partial removal (nibbling) of the donor cell's membrane, leading to the transfer of membrane components across cells (Zhang et al., 2022; Singhal et al., 2024), and in some cases killing the donor cells (Finotti et al., 2023). Inhibition of CD47 has been demonstrated to enhance antitumor responses through macrophage trogocytosis in diffuse large B-cell lymphoma and renal cell carcinoma models (Park et al., 2022; Cendrowicz et al., 2022).

Active targeting

Active targeting, also known as ligand-mediated targeting, was accomplished by coupling specific ligands/antibodies to the nanocarriers. This strategy theoretically depends on the paired ligand receptor or antigen antibody expression on the tumor cell surfaces (Mohanraj and Chen, 2006) and can enhance the internalization of the drug delivery system in tumors and improve the therapeutic efficacy of the chemotherapeutic agents. More significantly, it could also reduce the adverse effects, as it binds specifically to a receptor overexpressed on tumors not expressed in normal cells. Various targeting ligands, like asialoglycoprotein receptor (AGPR) are overexpressed on the surface of the tumor cell membrane. Folate receptors are one more common example of the overexpressed receptors (Adams et al., 2001; Gosk et al., 2008). Other examples given in (Table 13.7).

Emerging approaches and technologies

CRISPR/CAS-based systems

CRISPR/Cas system consists of CRISPR-derived RNA (crRNA). The crRNA directs Cas protein to specific genomic sites, where the Cas protein introduces targeted DNA cleavage (Baglaenko et al., 2021; Mohanraju et al., 2016). As one of the emerging gene-editing technologies, the CRISPR/Cas system is also being explored for cancer therapy by modifying target genes within the TME. Gene editing approaches have demonstrated safety and efficacy in several clinical trials (Lu et al., 2020; Stadtmauer et al., 2020).

Engineered cells like CAR T cells

Chimeric antigen receptor (CAR) T cells represent an advancement in cancer therapy, generating considerable interest among medical professionals. These genetically modified T cells express synthetic receptors that specifically recognize tumor-associated antigens with high efficacy under various physiological conditions. A CAR consists of any antibody-derived single-chain variable fragment (scFv) fused to a transmembrane domain and one or more intracellular signaling domains (Newick et al., 2017; Garber, 2018).

To introduce CARs into T cells, plasmids or viral vectors like retroviruses and lentiviruses are frequently employed (Dufait et al., 2012). Lentiviruses have become the most widely used for modifying human T cells, largely due to their efficiency and safety profile. mRNA electroporation enables transient CAR expression, which is useful for assessing the potential side effects during early development. Nonviral gene delivery methods, including DNA or mRNA transposon systems such as Sleeping Beauty system, are also used. This system employs a plasmid housing encoding a transposon enzyme that efficiently integrates the CAR gene into the host genome (Dufait et al., 2012). Sleeping Beauty tends to cause fewer insertional mutations compared to retroviral or lentiviral vectors, which often integrate near transcriptionally active genomic regions (Yant et al., 2005).

Preclinical and clinical advances

Various TME targeted systems are approved by the FDA for the treatment of tumors, and some are still under the clinical trials (Fang and DeClerck, 2013). Clinical status of the TME targeted systems shown in (Table 13.8).

TABLE 13.7 Ligands for various cancers, their respective ligands and examples for active targeting.

Receptor	Location of receptor	Ligand for active targeting	Cancer type(s)	Example of drug delivery system	References
Folate receptor	Cell membrane (glycosylphosphatidylinositol-anchored)	Folic acid, folate-conjugated polymers	Ovarian, breast, lung	Folate-targeted liposomes carrying doxorubicin	Turk et al. (2004)
Transferrin receptor	Cell membrane (iron uptake receptor)	Transferrin protein	Leukemia, breast, liver	Transferrin-modified polymeric nanoparticles	Sawant et al. (2014)
Epidermal growth factor receptor	Cell membrane (tyrosine kinase receptor)	EGF peptide, anti-EGFR antibody (cetuximab)	Lung, breast, colorectal	Cetuximab-conjugated gold nanoparticles	Kao et al. (2014)
HER2/neu (ErbB2)	Cell membrane (tyrosine kinase receptor)	Trastuzumab, anti-HER2 scFv	Breast, gastric	Trastuzumab-decorated liposomes with paclitaxel	Kumar et al. (2024a)
Integrins	Cell membrane (adhesion receptors on tumor and endothelial cells)	RGD peptides (Arg-Gly-Asp)	Melanoma, glioblastoma, angiogenic tumors	RGD-modified micelles delivering paclitaxel	Saraf et al. (2015)
Hyaluronic acid receptor	Cell membrane (stem cell marker, adhesion molecule)	Hyaluronic acid (HA)	Breast, prostate, ovarian, cancer stem cells	HA-decorated chitosan nanoparticles with siRNA	Tirella et al. (2019)
Prostate-specific membrane antigen	Cell membrane (type II transmembrane protein)	PSMA-targeted antibody, aptamer, peptide	Prostate cancer	PSMA-targeted polymeric micelles	Jin et al. (2014)
Vascular endothelial growth factor receptor	Endothelial cell membrane (angiogenesis mediator)	VEGF peptide/antibody, aptamers	Colon, lung, renal (angiogenic tumors)	VEGFR-targeted liposomes for bevacizumab delivery	Hu et al. (2019)
Low-density lipoprotein receptor	Cell membrane (cholesterol uptake receptor)	ApoB, ApoE peptides, LDL-mimicking nanoparticles	Glioblastoma, breast	LDL-mimetic nanoparticles carrying paclitaxel	Kim et al. (2015)

TABLE 13.8 Clinical status of the TME targeted systems.

Targeting strategy	Agents	Brand name	Clinical status	Year of approval
Tumor vasculature	Bevacizumab (Avastin)	Avastin	FDA approved	2004
	IMC-1121B	-	Phase III	-
	Sunitinib (Sutent)	Sutent	FDA approved	2006
	Sorafenib (Nexavat)	Nexavat	FDA approved	2005
	Pazopanib (Votrient)	Votrient	FDA approved	2009
	BMS-582664 (Brivanib)	-	Phase II/III	-
	SU6668	-	Phase I	-
	Cetuximab (Ebitux)	Ebitux	FDA approved	2004
	Panitumumab	Vectibix	FDA approved	2006
	Erlotinib	Tarceva	FDA approved	2004
	Gefitinib	Iressa	FDA approved	2003
Inflammation	CNTO888	-	Preclinical	-
	Binadarit	-	Preclinical	-
	Mouse CSF-1 antisense oligonucleotide, CSF-1 or CSF-1 receptor siRNA	-	Preclinical	-
	Ki20227	-	Preclinical	-
	JNJ-28312141	-	Preclinical	-
	Siltuximab (CNTO-328)	Slyvant	Phase I/II	-
	Tocilizumab	Actemra	Preclinical	-
	AZD 1480	-	Phase I	-
	Ruxolitinib (INCB018424)	Jakavi	Phase II	-
	STAT 3 decoy	-	Phase 0	-
	PS-1145	-	Preclinical	-
	Bortezomib (Velcade)	Velcade	FDA approved	2007
	Curcumin	-	Phase I/II	-
	Arsenic		Phase I/II	-
	Etaneracept (Enbrel)	Enbrel	Phase I/II	-
	Infliximab (cA2, Remicade)	Remicade	Phase II	-
	Celecoxib	Celebrex	Phase II/III	-

TABLE 13.8 Clinical status of the TME targeted systems.—cont'd

Targeting strategy	Agents	Brand name	Clinical status	Year of approval
	Trabedersen (AP12009)	-	Phase II/III	-
	Soluble TGF-βRII/III	-	Preclinical	-
	Soluble TGF-βRII fusion protein	-	Preclinical	-
	LY2109761	-	Preclinical	-
	SB-431542	-	Preclinical	-
	2G7	-	Preclinical	-
	1D11	-	Preclinical	-
Interaction between tumor cells and their microenvironment	Cilengitide	-	Phase II	-
	Etaracizumab (Medi-522)	Abegrin	Phase II/III	-
	Intetumumab (CNTO 95)	Vectibix	Phase II/III	-
	Zoledronic acid	Zometa	FDA approved	2001
	Denosumab	Prolia	FDA approved	2010
	CAL	-	Phase II/III	-
Hypoxia	Tirapzamine (SR4233)	Tirazone	Phase III (closed)	-
	TH-302	-	Phase I/II/III	-
	PR-104	-	Phase I/II	-
	AQ4N	-	Phase I/II	-
	EZN-2968	-	Phase I	-
	PX-478	-	Phase I	-
	Bortezomib	Velcade	FDA approved	2003
	Nelfinavir	Viracept	Phase I/II	-
	Retaspimycin	-	Phase I/II	-
	Tanespimycin	-	Phase II/III	-

Conclusion

Critical research on the understanding of TME is needed to set up new frameworks that would facilitate the evaluation of new treatment strategies. The isolated behavior of the malignant cells is now considered to be highly different compared to their behavior when surrounded by a microenvironment that supports the oncogenic conditions. The expression of cell surface receptors, activation or inhibition of signaling cascades, and the definition of the therapeutic effectiveness and response patterns are some effects that this TME has on them. In order to address the issues of non-responsiveness to treatment or malignant resistance, and to achieve individualized oncological practice, each malignancy must be considered as a complex multifactorial disorder that is different in patients and, by extension, requires customized treatment, especially with a focus on combinatorial therapies. Lastly, the application of nanotechnology can streamline tailored medical applications through the panels of small-scale agents of various interventions.

References

Adams, G.P., Schier, R., McCall, A.M., Simmons, H.H., Horak, E.M., Alpaugh, R.K., Marks, J.D., Weiner, L.M., 2001. High affinity restricts the localization and tumor penetration of single-chain Fv antibody molecules. Cancer Res. 61 (12), 4750–4755.

Andreev, O.A., Engelman, D.M., Reshetnyak, Y.K., 2014. Targeting diseased tissues by pHLIP insertion at low cell surface pH. Front Physiol. 5. https://doi.org/10.3389/fphys.2014.00097.

Azzi, S., Hebda, J.K., Gavard, J., 2013. Vascular permeability and drug delivery in cancers. Front. Oncol. 3. https://doi.org/10.3389/fonc.2013.00211France.

Baglaenko, Y., Macfarlane, D., Marson, A., Nigrovic, P.A., Raychaudhuri, S., 2021. Genome editing to define the function of risk loci and variants in rheumatic disease. Nat. Rev. Rheumatol. 17 (8), 462–474. https://doi.org/10.1038/s41584-021-00637-8.

Basar, E., Mead, H., Shum, B., Rauter, I., Ay, C., Skaletz-Rorowski, A., Brockmeyer, N.H., 2024. Biological barriers for drug delivery and development of innovative therapeutic approaches in HIV, pancreatic cancer, and hemophilia A/B. Pharmaceutics 16 (9), 1207. https://doi.org/10.3390/pharmaceutics16091207.

Balkwill, F.R., Capasso, M., Hagemann, T., 2012. The tumor microenvironment at a glance. J. Cell Sci. 125 (23), 5591–5596. https://doi.org/10.1242/jcs.116392.

Bercovici, N., Guérin, M.V., Trautmann, A., Donnadieu, E., 2019. The remarkable plasticity of macrophages: A chance to fight cancer. Front. Immunol. 10. https://doi.org/10.3389/fimmu.2019.01563.

Bernardos, A., Mondragón, L., Aznar, E., Dolores Marcos, M., Martínez-Máñez, R., Sancenón, F., Soto, J., Barat, J.M., Pérez-Payá, E., Guillem, C., Amorós, P., 2010. Enzyme-responsive intracellular controlled release using nanometric silica mesoporous supports capped with “saccharides”. ACS Nano 4 (11), 6353–6368. https://doi.org/10.1021/nn101499d.

Bonapace, L., Coissieux, M.-M., Wyckoff, J., Mertz, K.D., Varga, Z., Junt, T., Bentires-Alj, M., 2014. Cessation of CCL2 inhibition accelerates breast cancer metastasis by promoting angiogenesis. Nature 515 (7525), 130–133. https://doi.org/10.1038/nature13862.

Brana, I., Calles, A., LoRusso, P.M., Yee, L.K., Puchalski, T.A., Seetharam, S., Zhong, B., de Boer, C.J., Tabernero, J., 2015. Emiliano Calvo, Carlumab, an anti-C-C chemokine ligand 2 monoclonal antibody, in combination with four chemotherapy regimens for the treatment of patients with solid tumors: An open-label, multicenter phase 1b study. Targeted Oncol. 10 (1), 111–123. https://doi.org/10.1007/s11523-014-0320-2.

Buhrmann, C., Kraehe, P., Lueders, C., Shayan, P., Goel, A., Shakibaei, M., Sethi, G., 2014. curcumin suppresses crosstalk between colon cancer stem cells and stromal fibroblasts in the tumor microenvironment: Potential role of EMT. PLoS One 9 (9), e107514. https://doi.org/10.1371/journal.pone.0107514.

Byrne, J.D., Betancourt, T., Brannon-Peppas, L., 2008. Active targeting schemes for nanoparticle systems in cancer therapeutics. Adv. Drug Deliv. Rev. 60 (15), 1615–1626. https://doi.org/10.1016/j.addr.2008.08.005.

Cao, X., Wang, Y., Zhang, W., Zhong, X., Gulsen Gunes, E., Dang, J., Wang, J., Epstein, A.L., Querfeld, C., Sun, Z., Rosen, S.T., Feng, M., 2022. Targeting macrophages for enhancing CD47 blockade–elicited lymphoma clearance and overcoming tumor-induced immunosuppression. Blood 139 (22), 3290–3302. https://doi.org/10.1182/blood.2021013901.

Cendrowicz, E., Jacob, L., Greenwald, S., Tamir, A., Pecker, I., Tabakman, R., Ghantous, L., Tamir, L., Kahn, R., Avichzer, J., Aronin, A., Amsili, S., Zorde-Khvalevsky, E., Gozlan, Y., Vlaming, M., Huls, G., Meerten, T.van,

Dranitzki, M.E., Foley-Comer, A., Pereg, Y., Peled, A., Chajut, A., Bremer, E., 2022. DSP107 combines inhibition of CD47/SIRPα axis with activation of 4-1BB to trigger anticancer immunity. J. Exp. Clin. Cancer Res. 41 (1). https://doi.org/10.1186/s13046-022-02256-x.

Chakravarthy, V., Kaplan, B., Gospodarev, V., Myers, H., De Los Reyes, K., Achiriloaie, A., Tumor, H., 2018. Case report and literature review of pregnancy-associated meningioma. World Neurosurg. 114, e1261. https://doi.org/10.1016/j.wneu.2018.03.187.

Chaudhary, B., Elkord, E., 2016. Regulatory T cells in the tumor microenvironment and cancer progression: Role and therapeutic targeting. Vaccines 4 (3), 28. https://doi.org/10.3390/vaccines4030028.

Chauhan, V.P., Stylianopoulos, T., Martin, J.D., Popović, Z., Chen, O., Kamoun, W.S., Bawendi, M.G., Fukumura, D., Jain, R.K., 2020. Normalization of Tumour Blood Vessels Improves the Delivery of Nanomedicines in a Size-Dependent Manner. Informa UK Limited, pp. 279–311. https://doi.org/10.1201/9780429399039-10.

Chao, M.P., Weissman, I.L., Majeti, R., 2012. The CD47-SIRPα pathway in cancer immune evasion and potential therapeutic implications. Curr. Opin. Immunol. 24 (2), 225–232. https://doi.org/10.1016/j.coi.2012.01.010.

Cheng, Y.J., Luo, G.F., Zhu, J.Y., Xu, X.D., Zeng, X., Cheng, D.B., Li, Y.M., Wu, Y., Zhang, X.Z., Zhuo, R.X., He, F., 2015. Enzyme-induced and tumor-targeted drug delivery system based on multifunctional mesoporous silica nanoparticles. ACS Appl. Mater. Interfaces 7 (17), 9078–9087. https://doi.org/10.1021/acsami.5b00752.

Chen, Y., McAndrews, K.M., Kalluri, R., 2021. Clinical and therapeutic relevance of cancer-associated fibroblasts. Nat. Rev. Clin. 18 (12), 792–804. https://doi.org/10.1038/s41571-021-00546-5.

Clarhaut, J., Fraineau, S., Guilhot, J., Peraudeau, E., Tranoy-Opalinski, I., Thomas, M., Renoux, B., Randriamalala, E., Bois, P., Chatelier, A., Monvoisin, A., Cronier, L., Papot, S., Guilhot, F., 2013. A galactosidase-responsive doxorubicin-folate conjugate for selective targeting of acute myelogenous leukemia blasts. Leuk. Res. 37 (8), 948–955. https://doi.org/10.1016/j.leukres.2013.04.026.

Dai, Y., Xu, C., Sun, X., Chen, X., 2017. Nanoparticle design strategies for enhanced anticancer therapy by exploiting the tumour microenvironment. Chem. Soc. Rev. 46 (12), 3830–3852. https://doi.org/10.1039/C6CS00592F.

Dharmaratne, N.U., Kaplan, A.R., Glazer, P.M., 2021. Targeting the hypoxic and acidic tumor microenvironment with ph-sensitive peptides. Cells 10 (3), 1–14. https://doi.org/10.3390/cells10030541.

Del Prete, A., Schioppa, T., Tiberio, L., Stabile, H., Sozzani, S., 2017. Leukocyte trafficking in tumor microenvironment. Curr. Opin. Pharmacol. 35, 40–47. https://doi.org/10.1016/j.coph.2017.05.004.

Deng, K., Wang, J., Zhou, X., Geng, Y., Liu, W., Zhang, Y., Liu, Y., Jiang, W., 2025. A promising platform of hypoxia sensitive magnetosomes in hepatocellular carcinoma therapy. Sci. Rep. 15 (1). https://doi.org/10.1038/s41598-025-10353-y.

Digklia, A., Coukos, G., Homicsko, K., 2022. Trabectedin and durvalumab combination is feasible and active in relapsing ovarian cancer. Clin. Cancer Res. 28 (9), 1745–1747. https://doi.org/10.1158/1078-0432.CCR-21-4592.

Du, J.Z., Mao, C.Q., Yuan, Y.Y., Yang, X.Z., Wang, J., 2014. Tumor extracellular acidity-activated nanoparticles as drug delivery systems for enhanced cancer therapy. Biotechnol. Adv. 32 (4), 789–803. https://doi.org/10.1016/j.biotechadv.2013.08.002.

Dufait, I., Liechtenstein, T., Lanna, A., Bricogne, C., Laranga, R., Padella, A., Breckpot, K., Escors, D., 2012. Retroviral and lentiviral vectors for the induction of immunological tolerance. Scientifica 2012, 1–14. https://doi.org/10.6064/2012/694137.

Erdogan, B., Webb, D.J., 2017. Cancer-associated fibroblasts modulate growth factor signaling and extracellular matrix remodeling to regulate tumor metastasis. Biochem. Soc. Trans. 45 (1), 229–236. https://doi.org/10.1042/BST20160387.

Etrych, T., Jelinkova, M., Rihova, B., Ulbrich, K., 2001. New HPMA copolymers containing doxorubicin bound via pH-sensitive linkage: Synthesis and preliminary in vitro and in vivo biological properties. J. Contr. Release 73 (1), 89–102. https://doi.org/10.1016/s0168-3659(01)00281-4.

Fang, H., DeClerck, Y.A., 2013. Targeting the tumor microenvironment: From understanding pathways to effective clinical trials. Cancer Res. 73 (16), 4965–4977. https://doi.org/10.1158/0008-5472.CAN-13-0661United States.

Fang, Z., Meng, Q., Xu, J., Wang, W., Zhang, B., Liu, J., Chen, L., Jie, H., Zhao, Y., Yu, X., Shi, S., 2023. Signaling pathways in cancer-associated fibroblasts: Recent advances and future perspectives. Cancer Commun. 43 (1), 3–41. https://doi.org/10.1002/cac2.12392.

Feng, X., Li, Di, Han, J., Zhuang, X., Ding, J., 2017. Schiff base bond-linked polysaccharide–doxorubicin conjugate for upregulated cancer therapy. Mater. Sci. Eng. C 76, 1121–1128. https://doi.org/10.1016/j.msec.2017.03.201.

Finotti, G., Pietronigro, E., Balanzin, C., Lonardi, S., Constantin, G., Chao, M.P., Tecchio, C., Vermi, W., Cassatella, M.A., 2023. slan+ monocytes kill cancer cells coated in therapeutic antibody by trogoptosis. Cancer Immunol. Res. 11 (11), 1538–1552. https://doi.org/10.1158/2326-6066.cir-23-0239.

Fiori, M.E., Di Franco, S., Villanova, L., Bianca, P., Stassi, G., De Maria, R., 2019. Cancer-associated fibroblasts as abettors of tumor progression at the crossroads of EMT and therapy resistance. Mol. Cancer 18 (1). https://doi.org/10.1186/s12943-019-0994-2.

Flores-Toro, J.A., Luo, D., Gopinath, A., Sarkisian, M.R., Campbell, J.J., Charo, I.F., Singh, R., Schall, T.J., Datta, M., Jain, R.K., Mitchell, D.A., Harrison, J.K., 2020. CCR2 inhibition reduces tumor myeloid cells and unmasks a checkpoint inhibitor effect to slow progression of resistant murine gliomas. Proc. Natl. Acad. Sci. 117 (2), 1129–1138. https://doi.org/10.1073/pnas.1910856117.

Fukumura, D., Kloepper, J., Amoozgar, Z., Duda, D.G., Jain, R.K., 2018. Enhancing cancer immunotherapy using antiangiogenics: opportunities and challenges. Nat. Rev. Clin. Oncol. 15 (5), 325–340. https://doi.org/10.1038/nrclinonc.2018.29. PMID: 29508855; PMCID: PMC5921900.

Galgani, M., Bruzzaniti, S., Rocca, C.La, Micillo, T., de Candia, P., Bifulco, M., Matarese, G., 2021. Immunometabolism of regulatory T cells in cancer. Mol. Aspect. Med. 77, 100936. https://doi.org/10.1016/j.mam.2020.100936.

Garber, K., 2018. Driving T-cell immunotherapy to solid tumors. Nat. Biotechnol. 36 (3), 215–219. https://doi.org/10.1038/nbt.4090.

Gosk, S., Moos, T., Gottstein, C., Bendas, G., 2008. VCAM-1 directed immunoliposomes selectively target tumor vasculature in vivo. Biochim. Biophys. Acta Biomembr. 1778 (4), 854–863. https://doi.org/10.1016/j.bbamem.2007.12.021.

Hanahan, D., Coussens, L.M., 2012. Accessories to the crime: Functions of cells recruited to the tumor microenvironment. Cancer Cell 21 (3), 309–322. https://doi.org/10.1016/j.ccr.2012.02.022.

He, H., Zhu, R., Sun, W., Cai, K., Chen, Y., Yin, L., 2018. Selective cancer treatment via photodynamic sensitization of hypoxia-responsive drug delivery. Nanoscale 10 (6), 2856–2865. https://doi.org/10.1039/C7NR07677K.

Hinshaw, D.C., Shevde, L.A., 2019. The tumor microenvironment innately modulates cancer progression. Cancer Res. 79 (18), 4557–4566. https://doi.org/10.1158/0008-5472.can-18-3962.

Hu, Y., Zhou, P., Lin, Y., Yang, D., Wang, B., 2019. Anti-colorectal cancer effect via application of polyethylene glycol modified liposomal apatinib. J. Biomed. Nanotechnol. 15 (6), 1256–1266. https://doi.org/10.1166/jbn.2019.2770.

Hu, X.-Y., Fu, R., Guo, D.-S., 2023. Hypoxia-responsive host–guest drug delivery system. Acc. Mater. Res. 4 (11), 925–938. https://doi.org/10.1021/accountsmr.3c00130.

Hua, S., 2014. Orally administered liposomal formulations for colon targeted drug delivery. Front. Pharmacol. 5. https://doi.org/10.3389/fphar.2014.00138.

Huang, X., Du, F., Cheng, J., Dong, Y., Liang, D., Ji, S., Lin, S.-S., Li, Z., 2009. Acid-sensitive polymeric micelles based on thermoresponsive block copolymers with pendent cyclic orthoester groups. Macromolecules 42 (3), 783–790. https://doi.org/10.1021/ma802138r.

Ji, S., Shi, Y., Yin, B., 2024. Macrophage barrier in the tumor microenvironment and potential clinical applications. Cell Commun. Signal. 22 (1). https://doi.org/10.1186/s12964-023-01424-6.

Jin, J., Sui, B., Gou, J., Liu, J., Tang, X., Xu, H., Zhang, Y., Jin, X., Munirathinam, G., 2014. PSMA ligand conjugated PCL-PEG polymeric micelles targeted to prostate cancer cells. PLoS One 9 (11), e112200. https://doi.org/10.1371/journal.pone.0112200.

Kalafatovic, D., Nobis, M., Son, J., Anderson, K.I., Ulijn, R.V., 2016. MMP-9 triggered self-assembly of doxorubicin nanofiber depots halts tumor growth. Biomaterials 98, 192–202. https://doi.org/10.1016/j.biomaterials.2016.04.039.

Kang, L., Fan, B., Sun, P., Huang, W., Jin, M., Wang, Q., Gao, Z., 2016. An effective tumor-targeting strategy utilizing hypoxia-sensitive siRNA delivery system for improved anti-tumor outcome. Acta Biomater. 44, 341–354. https://doi.org/10.1016/j.actbio.2016.08.029.

Kao, H.-W., Lin, Y.-Y., Chen, C.-C., Chi, K.-H., Tien, D.-C., Hsia, C.-C., Lin, W.-J., Chen, F.-D., Lin, M.-H., Wang, H.-E., 2014. Biological characterization of cetuximab-conjugated gold nanoparticles in a tumor animal model. Nanotechnology 25 (29), 295102. https://doi.org/10.1088/0957-4484/25/29/295102.

Kapalatiya, H., Madav, Y., Sanjay Tambe, V., Wairkar, S., 2022. Enzyme-responsive smart nanocarriers for targeted chemotherapy: An overview. Drug Deliv. Transl. Res. 12 (6), 1293–1305. https://doi.org/10.1007/s13346-021-01020-6.

Kadam, S.D., Dhole, S., Chitlange, S., 2020. Formulation and evaluation of sustained release colon targeted mesalamine tablet. Res. J. Pharm. Technol. 13 (5), 2241–2245. https://doi.org/10.5958/0974-360X.2020.00403.5.

Kim, J.H., Kim, Y., Bae, K.H., Park, T.G., Lee, J.H., Park, K., 2015. Tumor-targeted delivery of paclitaxel using low density lipoprotein-mimetic solid lipid nanoparticles. Mol. Pharm. 12 (4), 1230–1241. https://doi.org/10.1021/mp500737y.

Khawar, I.A., Kim, J.H., Kuh, H.J., 2015. Improving drug delivery to solid tumors: Priming the tumor microenvironment. J. Control Release 201, 78–89. https://doi.org/10.1016/j.jconrel.2014.12.018.

Kumar, D., Silva, V.D., Chaves, N., 2024a. Myeloid-derived suppressor cells as targets of emerging therapies and nanotherapies. Med. Int. 4 (5). https://doi.org/10.3892/mi.2024.170.

Kumar, G., Mullick, P., Andugulapati, S.B., Eedara, A.C., Kumar, N., Mutalik, S., Nandakumar, K., Rao Chamallamudi, M., 2024b. Trastuzumab-conjugated liposomes for co-delivery of paclitaxel and anti-abcb1 siRNA in HER2-positive breast cancer: In vitro and in vivo evaluations. J. Drug Deliv. Sci. Technol. 95, 105614. https://doi.org/10.1016/j.jddst.2024.105614.

Lan, X., Li, W., Zhao, K., Wang, J., Li, S., Zhao, H., 2025. Revisiting the role of cancer-associated fibroblasts in tumor microenvironment. Front. Immunol. 16. https://doi.org/10.3389/fimmu.2025.1582532.

Lee, E.S., Oh, K.T., Kim, D., Youn, Y.S., Bae, Y.H., 2007. Tumor pH-responsive flower-like micelles of poly (l-lactic acid)-b-poly (ethylene glycol)-b-poly(l-histidine). J. Contr. Release 123 (1), 19–26. https://doi.org/10.1016/j.jconrel.2007.08.006.

Li, M., Zhao, G., Su, W.-K., Qi, S., 2020. Enzyme-responsive nanoparticles for anti-tumor drug delivery. Front. Chem. 8. https://doi.org/10.3389/fchem.2020.00647.

Li, K., Shi, H., Zhang, B., Ou, X., Ma, Q., Chen, Y., Pei, S., Li, D., Wang, Y., 2021. Myeloid-derived suppressor cells as immunosuppressive regulators and therapeutic targets. Signal Transduct. Target. Ther. 6 (1). https://doi.org/10.1038/s41392-021-00670-9.

Li, M., Zhang, Y., Zhang, Q., Li, J., 2022. Tumor extracellular matrix modulating strategies for enhanced antitumor therapy of nanomedicines. Mater. Today Bio 16, 100364. https://doi.org/10.1016/j.mtbio.2022.100364.

Liao, S.C., Ting, C.W., Chiang, W.H., 2020. Functionalized polymeric nanogels with pH-sensitive benzoic-imine cross-linkages designed as vehicles for indocyanine green delivery. J. Colloid Interface Sci. 561, 11–22. https://doi.org/10.1016/j.jcis.2019.11.109.

Liu, Y., Ding, X., Li, J., Zhong, L., Hu, Y., Liu, J., Dai, L., Zhou, J., Hou, C., Cai, K., 2015. Enzyme responsive drug delivery system based on mesoporous silica nanoparticles for tumor therapy in vivo. Nanotechnology 26 (14), 145102. https://doi.org/10.1088/0957-4484/26/14/145102.

Liu, X., Wu, Z., Guo, C., Guo, H., Su, Y., Chen, Q., Sun, C., Liu, Q., Chen, D., Mu, H., 2022. Hypoxia responsive nano-drug delivery system based on angelica polysaccharide for liver cancer therapy. Drug Deliv. 29 (1), 138–148. https://doi.org/10.1080/10717544.2021.2021324.

Liu, Y., Liang, J., Zhang, Y., Guo, Q., 2024. Drug resistance and tumor immune microenvironment: An overview of current understandings. Int. J. Oncol. 65 (4). https://doi.org/10.3892/ijo.2024.5684 (Review).

Lu, Y., Xue, J., Deng, T., Zhou, X., Yu, K., Deng, L., Huang, M., Yi, X., Liang, M., Wang, Y., Shen, H., Tong, R., Wang, W., Li, L., Song, J., Li, J., Su, X., Ding, Z., Gong, Y., Zhu, J., Wang, Y., Zou, B., Zhang, Y., Li, Y., Zhou, L., Liu, Y., Yu, M., Wang, Y., Zhang, X., Yin, L., Xia, X., Zeng, Y., Zhou, Q., Ying, B., Chen, C., Wei, Y., Li, W., Mok, T., 2020. Safety and feasibility of CRISPR-edited T cells in patients with refractory non-small-cell lung cancer. Nat. Med. 26 (5), 732–740. https://doi.org/10.1038/s41591-020-0840-5.

Maeda, H., 2012. Macromolecular therapeutics in cancer treatment: The EPR effect and beyond. J. Contr. Release 164 (2), 138–144. https://doi.org/10.1016/j.jconrel.2012.04.038.

Maeda, H., Wu, J., Sawa, T., Matsumura, Y., Hori, K., 2000. Tumor vascular permeability and the EPR effect in macromolecular therapeutics: A review. J. Contr. Release 65 (1–2), 271–284. https://doi.org/10.1016/s0168-3659(99)00248-5.

Matsumura, Y., Maeda, H., 1986. A new concept for macromolecular therapeutics in cancer chemotherapy: Mechanism of tumoritropic accumulation of proteins and the antitumor agent smancs. Cancer Res. 46 (8), 6387–6392.

Medzhitov, R., Janeway, C.A., 2002. Decoding the patterns of self and nonself by the innate immune system. Science 296 (5566), 298–300. https://doi.org/10.1126/science.1068883.

Mohanraj, V., Chen, Y., 2006. Nanoparticles-a review. Trop. J. Pharmaceut. Res. 5 (1), 561–573.

Mohanraju, P., Makarova, K.S., Zetsche, B., Zhang, F., Koonin, E.V., van der Oost, J., 2016. Diverse evolutionary roots and mechanistic variations of the CRISPR-Cas systems. Science 353 (6299). https://doi.org/10.1126/science.aad5147.

Nagarsheth, N., Wicha, M.S., Zou, W., 2017. Chemokines in the cancer microenvironment and their relevance in cancer immunotherapy. Nat Rev Immunol. 17 (9), 559–572. https://doi.org/10.1038/nri.2017.49.

Neophytou, C.M., Panagi, M., Stylianopoulos, T., Papageorgis, P., 2021. The role of tumor microenvironment in cancer metastasis: Molecular mechanisms and therapeutic opportunities. Cancers 13 (9), 2053. https://doi.org/10.3390/cancers13092053.

Newick, K., O'Brien, S., Moon, E., Albelda, S.M., 2017. CAR T Cell therapy for solid tumors. Annu. Rev. Med. 68, 139–152. https://doi.org/10.1146/annurev-med-062315-120245. PMID: 27860544.

Nywening, T.M., Wang-Gillam, A., Sanford, D.E., Belt, B.A., Panni, R.Z., Cusworth, B.M., Toriola, A.T., Nieman, R.K., Worley, L.A., Yano, M., Fowler, K.J., Lockhart, A.C., Suresh, R., Tan, B.R., Lim, K.H., Fields, R.C., Strasberg, S.M., Hawkins, W.G., DeNardo, D.G., Goedegebuure, S.P., Linehan, D.C., 2016. Targeting tumour-associated macrophages with CCR2 inhibition in combination with FOLFIRINOX in patients with borderline resectable and locally advanced pancreatic cancer: A single-centre, open-label, dose-finding, non-randomised, phase 1b trial. Lancet Oncol. 17 (5), 651–662. https://doi.org/10.1016/S1470-2045(16)00078-4.

Oldenborg, P.A., Zheleznyak, A., Fang, Y.F., Lagenaur, C.F., Gresham, H.D., Lindberg, F.P., 2000. Role of CD47 as a marker of self on red blood cells. Science 288 (5473), 2051–2054. https://doi.org/10.1126/science.288.5473.2051.

Park, D., Sahai, E., Rullan, A., 2020. SnapShot: Cancer-associated fibroblasts. Cell 181 (2), 486. https://doi.org/10.1016/j.cell.2020.03.013.

Park, H.R., Kim, S.E., Keam, B., Chung, H., Seok, S.H., Kim, S., Kim, M., Kim, T.M., Doh, J., Kim, D.W., Heo, D.S., 2022. Blockade of CD47 enhances the antitumor effect of macrophages in renal cell carcinoma through trogocytosis. Sci. Rep. 12 (1). https://doi.org/10.1038/s41598-022-16766-3.

Priego, N., Zhu, L., Monteiro, C., Mulders, M., Wasilewski, D., Bindeman, W., Doglio, L., Martínez, L., Martínez-Saez, E., Cajal, S.R.y, Megías, D., Hernández-Encinas, E., Blanco-Aparicio, C., Martínez, L., Zarzuela, E., Muñoz, J., Fustero-Torre, C., Piñeiro-Yáñez, E., Hernández-Laín, A., Bertero, L., Poli, V., Sanchez-Martinez, M., Menendez, J.A., Soffietti, R., Bosch-Barrera, J., Valiente, M., 2018. STAT3 labels a subpopulation of reactive astrocytes required for brain metastasis. Nat. Med. 24 (7), 1024–1035. https://doi.org/10.1038/s41591-018-0044-4.

Rastegari, B., Karbalaei-Heidari, H.R., Zeinali, S., Sheardown, H., 2017. The enzyme-sensitive release of prodigiosin grafted β-cyclodextrin and chitosan magnetic nanoparticles as an anticancer drug delivery system: Synthesis, characterization and cytotoxicity studies. Colloids Surf. B Biointerfaces 158, 589–601. https://doi.org/10.1016/j.colsurfb.2017.07.044.

Rastegar, G., Salman, M.M., Sirsi, S.R., 2025. oxygen sensitive drug release using hemoglobin microbubbles: A new approach to targeting hypoxia in ultrasound-mediated drug delivery. Int J Pharm. 675. https://doi.org/10.1016/j.ijpharm.2025.125521.

Salemme, V., Centonze, G., Avalle, L., Natalini, D., Piccolantonio, A., Arina, P., Morellato, A., Ala, U., Taverna, D., Turco, E., Defilippi, P., 2023. The role of tumor microenvironment in drug resistance: Emerging technologies to unravel breast cancer heterogeneity. Front. Oncol. 13. https://doi.org/10.3389/fonc.2023.1170264.

Saraf, P., Li, X., Wrischnik, L., Jasti, B., 2015. In vitro and in vivo efficacy of self-assembling RGD peptide amphiphiles for targeted delivery of paclitaxel. Pharm. Res. 32 (9), 3087–3101. https://doi.org/10.1007/s11095-015-1689-z.

Sawant, R.R., Jhaveri, A.M., Koshkaryev, A., Zhu, L., Qureshi, F., Torchilin, V.P., 2014. Targeted transferrin-modified polymeric micelles: Enhanced efficacy in vitro and in vivo in ovarian carcinoma. Mol. Pharm. 11 (2), 375–381. https://doi.org/10.1021/mp300633f.

Sethuraman, V.A., Na, K., Bae, Y.H., 2006. pH-Responsive sulfonamide, PEI system for tumor specific gene delivery: An in vitro study. Biomacromolecules 7 (1), 64–70. https://doi.org/10.1021/bm0503571.

Sceneay, J., Griessinger, C.M., Hoffmann, S.H.L., Wen Wen, S., Wong, C.S.F., Krumeich, S., Kneilling, M., Pichler, B.J., Möller, A., Mattei, F., 2018. Tracking the fate of adoptively transferred myeloid-derived suppressor cells in the primary breast tumor microenvironment. PLoS One 13 (4). https://doi.org/10.1371/journal.pone.0196040.

Scharping, N.E., Menk, A.V., Moreci, R.S., Whetstone, R.D., Dadey, R.E., Watkins, S.C., Ferris, R.L., Delgoffe, G.M., 2016. The tumor microenvironment represses T cell mitochondrial biogenesis to drive intratumoral T cell metabolic insufficiency and dysfunction. Immunity 45 (2), 374–388. https://doi.org/10.1016/j.immuni.2016.07.009.

Shi, M., Gu, Y., Jin, K., Fang, H., Chen, Y., Cao, Y., Liu, X., Lv, K., He, X., Lin, C., Liu, H., Li, H., He, H., Qin, J., Li, R., Zhang, H., Zhang, W., 2021. CD47 expression in gastric cancer clinical correlates and association with macrophage infiltration. Cancer Immunol. Immunother. 70 (7), 1831–1840. https://doi.org/10.1007/s00262-020-02806-2.

Shi, L., Wang, J., Ding, N., Zhang, Y., Zhu, Y., Dong, S., Wang, X., Peng, C., Zhou, C., Zhou, L., Li, X., Shi, H., Wu, W., Long, X., Wu, C., Liao, W., 2019. Inflammation induced by incomplete radiofrequency ablation accelerates tumor progression and hinders PD-1 immunotherapy. Nat. Commun. 10 (1). https://doi.org/10.1038/s41467-019-13204-3.

Singh, S., Lee, N., Pedroza, D.A., Bado, I.L., Hamor, C., Zhang, L., Aguirre, S., Hu, J., Shen, Y., Xu, Y., Gao, Y., Zhao, N., Chen, S.-H., Wan, Y.-W., Liu, Z., Chang, J.T., Hollern, D., Perou, C.M., Zhang, X.H.F., Rosen, J.M., 2022. Chemotherapy coupled to macrophage inhibition induces T-cell and B-cell infiltration and durable regression in triple-negative breast cancer. Cancer Res. 82 (12), 2281–2297. https://doi.org/10.1158/0008-5472.can-21-3714.

Sinha, V.R., Kumria, R., 2002. Binders for colon specific drug delivery: An in vitro evaluation. Int. J. Pharm. 249 (1–2), 23–31. https://doi.org/10.1016/S0378-5173(02)00398-8.

Singhal, S., Rao, A.S., Stadanlick, J., Bruns, K., Sullivan, N.T., Bermudez, A., Honig-Frand, A., Krouse, R., Arambepola, S., Guo, E., Moon, E.K., Georgiou, G., Valerius, T., Albelda, S.M., Eruslanov, E.B., 2024. Human tumor–associated macrophages and neutrophils regulate antitumor antibody efficacy through lethal and sublethal trogocytosis. Cancer Res. 84 (7), 1029–1047. https://doi.org/10.1158/0008-5472.can-23-2135.

Sounni, N.E., Noel, A., 2013. Targeting the tumor microenvironment for cancer therapy. Clin. Chem. 59 (1), 85–93. https://doi.org/10.1373/clinchem.2012.185363Belgium.

Soltani, M., Souri, M., Moradi Kashkooli, F., 2021. Effects of hypoxia and nanocarrier size on pH-responsive nanodelivery system to solid tumors. Sci. Rep. 11 (1). https://doi.org/10.1038/s41598-021-98638-w.

Spill, F., Reynolds, D.S., Kamm, R.D., Zaman, M.H., 2016. Impact of the physical microenvironment on tumor progression and metastasis. Curr. Opin. Biotechnol. 40, 41–48. https://doi.org/10.1016/j.copbio.2016.02.007.

Stadtmauer, E.A., Fraietta, J.A., Davis, M.M., Cohen, A.D., Weber, K.L., Lancaster, E., Mangan, P.A., Kulikovskaya, I., Gupta, M., Chen, F., Tian, L., Gonzalez, V.E., Xu, J., Jung, I.y., Joseph Melenhorst, J., Plesa, G., Shea, J., Matlawski, T., Cervini, A., Gaymon, A.L., Desjardins, S., Lamontagne, A., Salas-Mckee, J., Fesnak, A., Siegel, D.L., Levine, B.L., Jadlowsky, J.K., Young, R.M., Chew, A., Hwang, W.T., Hexner, E.O., Carreno, B.M., Nobles, C.L., Bushman, F.D., Parker, K.R., Qi, Y., Satpathy, A.T., Chang, H.Y., Zhao, Y., Lacey, S.F., June, C.H., 2020. CRISPR-engineered T cells in patients with refractory cancer. Science 367 (6481). https://doi.org/10.1126/science.aba7365.

Stylianopoulos, T., Jain, R.K., 2013. Combining two strategies to improve perfusion and drug delivery in solid tumors. Proc. Natl. Acad. Sci. 110 (46), 18632–18637. https://doi.org/10.1073/pnas.1318415110.

Subrahmanyam, N., Ghandehari, H., 2021. Harnessing extracellular matrix biology for tumor drug delivery. J. Personalized Med. 11 (2), 88. https://doi.org/10.3390/jpm11020088.

Sun, W., Ji, W., Hu, Q., Yu, J., Wang, C., Qian, C., Hochu, G., Gu, Z., 2016. Transformable DNA nanocarriers for plasma membrane targeted delivery of cytokine. Biomaterials 96, 1–10. https://doi.org/10.1016/j.biomaterials.2016.04.011.

Tan, Y., 2022. Platinum (IV) complexes as inhibitors of CD47-SIRPα axis for chemoimmunotherapy of cancer. Eur. J. Med. Chem. 229, 114047.

Thanou, M., Duncan, R., 2003. Polymer-protein and polymer-drug conjugates in cancer therapy. Curr. Opin. Invest. Drugs 4 (6), 701–709.

Tirella, A., Kloc-Muniak, K., Good, L., Ridden, J., Ashford, M., Puri, S., Tirelli, N., 2019. CD44 targeted delivery of siRNA by using HA-decorated nanotechnologies for KRAS silencing in cancer treatment. Int. J. Pharm. 561, 114–123. https://doi.org/10.1016/j.ijpharm.2019.02.032.

Tiwari, A., Trivedi, R., Lin, S.Y., 2022. Tumor microenvironment: Barrier or opportunity towards effective cancer therapy. J Biomed Sci. 29 (1). https://doi.org/10.1186/s12929-022-00866-3.

Tomás-Bort, E., Kieler, M., Sharma, S., Candido, J.B., Loessner, D., 2020. 3D approaches to model the tumor microenvironment of pancreatic cancer. Theranostics 10 (11), 5074–5089. https://doi.org/10.7150/thno.42441.

Turk, M.J., Waters, D.J., Low, P.S., 2004. Folate-conjugated liposomes preferentially target macrophages associated with ovarian carcinoma. Cancer Lett. 213 (2), 165–172. https://doi.org/10.1016/j.canlet.2003.12.028.

Wagner, J., Gößl, D., Ustyanovska, N., Xiong, M., Hauser, D., Zhuzhgova, O., Hočevar, S., Taskoparan, B., Poller, L., Datz, S., Hanna, E., Daali, Y., Bein, T., Bourquin, C., 2021. Mesoporous silica nanoparticles as pH-responsive carrier for the immune-activating drug resiquimod enhance the local immune response in mice. ACS Nano 15 (3), 4450–4466. https://doi.org/10.1021/acsnano.0c08384.

Wan, Z., Huang, H., West III, R.E., Zhang, M., Zhang, B., Cai, X., Zhang, Z., Luo, Z., Chen, Y., Zhang, Y., Wen, X., Yang, D., Nolin, T.D., Wang, J., Li, S., Sun, J., 2023. Overcoming pancreatic cancer immune resistance by codelivery of CCR2 antagonist using a STING-activating gemcitabine-based nanocarrier. Mater. Today 62, 33–50. https://doi.org/10.1016/j.mattod.2022.11.008.

Wang, A.Z., Langer, R., Farokhzad, O.C., 2012. Nanoparticle delivery of cancer drugs. Annu. Rev. Med. 63, 185–198. https://doi.org/10.1146/annurev-med-040210-162544.

Wang, Y., Tiruthani, K., Li, S., Hu, M., Zhong, G., Tang, Y., Roy, S., Zhang, L., Tan, J., Liao, C., Liu, R., 2021. mRNA delivery of a bispecific single-domain antibody to polarize tumor-associated macrophages and synergize immunotherapy against liver malignancies. Adv. Mater. 33 (23). https://doi.org/10.1002/adma.202007603.

Wang, Z., Li, B., Li, S., Lin, W., Wang, Z., Wang, S., Chen, W., Shi, W., Chen, T., Zhou, H., Yinwang, E., Zhang, W., Mou, H., Chai, X., Zhang, J., Lu, Z., Ye, Z., 2022. Metabolic control of CD47 expression through LAT2-mediated amino acid uptake promotes tumor immune evasion. Nat. Commun. 13 (1). https://doi.org/10.1038/s41467-022-34064-4.

Wang, Q., Shao, X., Zhang, Y., Zhu, M., Wang, F.X.C., Mu, J., Li, J., Yao, H., Chen, K., 2023. Role of tumor microenvironment in cancer progression and therapeutic strategy. Cancer Med. 12 (10), 11149–11165. https://doi.org/10.1002/cam4.5698.

Wang, W., Yao, S.-Y., Luo, J., Ding, C., Huang, Q., Yang, Y., Shi, Z., Lin, J., Pan, Y.-C., Zeng, X., Guo, D.-S., Chen, H., 2025. Engineered hypoxia-responsive albumin nanoparticles mediating mitophagy regulation for cancer therapy. Nat. Commun. 16 (1). https://doi.org/10.1038/s41467-025-55905-y.

Wilson, W.R., Hay, M.P., 2011. Targeting hypoxia in cancer therapy. Nat. Rev. Cancer 11 (6), 393–410. https://doi.org/10.1038/nrc3064.

Xu, T., Yu, S., Zhang, J., Wu, S., 2021. Dysregulated tumor-associated macrophages in carcinogenesis, progression and targeted therapy of gynecological and breast cancers. J. Hematol. Oncol. (1), 14. https://doi.org/10.1186/s13045-021-01198-9.

Yakubu, M., Meggetto, O., Lai, Y., Peirson, L., Walker, M., Lofters, A., 2021. Impact of postal correspondence letters on participation in cancer screening: A rapid review. Prev. Med. 145, 106404. https://doi.org/10.1016/j.ypmed.2020.106404.

Yamazaki, M., Ishimoto, T., 2025. Targeting cancer-associated fibroblasts: Eliminate or reprogram? Cancer Sci. 116 (3), 613–621. https://doi.org/10.1111/cas.16443.

Yang, L., Li, A., Lei, Q., Zhang, Y., 2019. Tumor-intrinsic signaling pathways: Key roles in the regulation of the immunosuppressive tumor microenvironment. J. Hematol. Oncol. (1), 12. https://doi.org/10.1186/s13045-019-0804-8.

Yang, X.-L., Wu, W.-X., Li, J., Hu, Z.-E., Wang, N., Yu, X.-Q., 2020. A facile strategy to construct fluorescent pH-sensitive drug delivery vehicle. Polymer 197, 122496. https://doi.org/10.1016/j.polymer.2020.122496.

Yant, S.R., Wu, X., Huang, Y., Garrison, B., Burgess, S.M., Kay, M.A., 2005. High-resolution genome-wide mapping of transposon integration in mammals. Mol. Cell Biol. 25 (6), 2085–2094. https://doi.org/10.1128/MCB.25.6.2085-2094.2005.

Yu, M., Guo, F., Wang, J., Tan, F., Li, N., 2016. A pH-Driven and photoresponsive nanocarrier: Remotely-controlled by near-infrared light for stepwise antitumor treatment. Biomaterials 79, 25–35. https://doi.org/10.1016/j.biomaterials.2015.11.049.

Yuan, S., Mu, W., Liu, S., Liu, M., Xia, Z., Liang, S., Gao, T., Fu, S., Liu, J., Huang, X., Liu, Y., Zhang, N., 2023. Transforming cancer-associated fibroblast barrier into drug depots to boost chemo-immunotherapy in "shooting fish in a barrel" pattern. ACS Nano 17 (14), 13611–13626. https://doi.org/10.1021/acsnano.3c02272.

Zhang, H., Feng, L., Mello, P.de A., Mao, C., Near, R., Csizmadia, E., Li-Ying Chan, L., Enjyoji, K., Gao, W., Zhao, H., Robson, S.C., 2022. Glycoengineered anti-CD39 promotes anticancer responses by depleting suppressive cells and inhibiting angiogenesis in tumor models. J. Clin. Investig. (13), 132. https://doi.org/10.1172/jci157431.

Zhang, L., Sun, J., Huang, W., Zhang, S., Deng, X., Gao, W., 2023. Hypoxia-Triggered bioreduction of poly(N -oxide)–drug conjugates enhances tumor penetration and antitumor efficacy. J. Am. Chem. Soc. 145 (3), 1707–1713. https://doi.org/10.1021/jacs.2c10188.

Zhang, L.Y., Chen, X.T., Li, R.T., Meng, W., Huang, G.Q., Chen, Y.J., Ge, F.J., Zhang, Q., Quan, Y.J., Zhang, C.T., Liu, Y.F., Chen, M., Chen, J.X., 2025. Overcoming hypoxia-induced breast cancer drug resistance: a novel strategy using hollow gold-platinum bimetallic nanoshells. J. Nanobiotechnol. 23 (1), 85. https://doi.org/10.1186/s12951-025-03132-4.

Zhang, Z., Wang, R., Chen, L., 2025. Drug delivery system targeting cancer-associated fibroblast for improving immunotherapy. Int J Nanomedicine 20, 483–503. https://doi.org/10.2147/IJN.S500591.

Zhao, Y., Zheng, Y., Zhu, Y., Li, H., Zhu, H., Liu, T., 2022. Docetaxel-loaded M1 macrophage-derived exosomes for a safe and efficient chemoimmunotherapy of breast cancer. J. Nanobiotechnol. 20 (1). https://doi.org/10.1186/s12951-022-01526-2.

Zhao, D., Zhang, Y., Yan, Z., Ding, Y., Liang, F., 2024. Hypoxia-responsive polymeric nanoprodrugs for combo photodynamic and chemotherapy. ACS Omega 9 (1), 1821–1826. https://doi.org/10.1021/acsomega.3c08504.

Zhou, K., Wang, Y., Huang, X., Luby-Phelps, K., Sumer, B.D., Gao, J., 2011. Tunable, ultrasensitive pH-responsive nanoparticles targeting specific endocytic organelles in living cells. Angew. Chem. Int. Ed. 50 (27), 6109–6114. https://doi.org/10.1002/anie.201100884.

Zhou, F., Feng, B., Yu, H., Wang, D., Wang, T., Ma, Y., Wang, S., Li, Y., 2019. Tumor microenvironment-activatable prodrug vesicles for nanoenabled cancer chemoimmunotherapy combining immunogenic cell death induction and CD47 blockade. Adv. Mater. 31 (14). https://doi.org/10.1002/adma.201805888.

Zhou, Y., Chen, X., Cao, J., Gao, H., 2020. Overcoming the biological barriers in the tumor microenvironment for improving drug delivery and efficacy. J. Mater. Chem. B 8 (31), 6765–6781. https://doi.org/10.1039/d0tb00649a.

Zhu, L., Wang, T., Perche, F., Taigind, A., Torchilin, V.P., 2013. Enhanced anticancer activity of nanopreparation containing an MMP2-sensitive PEG-drug conjugate and cell-penetrating moiety. Proc. Natl. Acad. Sci. 110 (42), 17047–17052.

Further reading

Dai, F., Kloepper, J., Amoozgar, Z., Duda, D.G., Jain, R.K., 2018. Enhancing cancer immunotherapy using antiangiogenics: Opportunities and challenges. Nat. Rev. Clin. Oncol. 15 (5), 325–340. https://doi.org/10.1038/nrclinonc.2018.29.

Kheng, N., O'Brien, S., Moon, E., Steven, M., 2017. Albelda, CAR T cell therapy for solid tumors. Annu. Rev. Med. 68 (1), 139–152. https://doi.org/10.1146/annurev-med-062315-120245.

Lin, Z., Wang, T., Perche, F., Taigind, A., Torchilin, V.P., 2013. Enhanced anticancer activity of nanopreparation containing an MMP2-sensitive PEG-drug conjugate and cell-penetrating moiety. Proc. Natl. Acad. Sci. 110 (42), 17047–17052. https://doi.org/10.1073/pnas.1304987110.

Lin, K., Fan, B., Sun, P., Huang, W., Jin, M., Wang, Q., Gao, Z., 2016. An effective tumor-targeting strategy utilizing hypoxia-sensitive siRNA delivery system for improved anti-tumor outcome. Acta Biomater. 44, 341–354. https://doi.org/10.1016/j.actbio.2016.08.029.

CHAPTER

14

Advances in dendrimers for anticancer drug delivery

Abhishek Sharma[1], *Shweta Singh*[1], *Himanshu Sharma*[2,3], *Pooja Mittal*[4] *and Vishnu Mittal*[5]

[1]Department of Pharmaceutical Engineering and Technology, Indian Institute of Technology (BHU), Varanasi, Uttar Pradesh, India; [2]Guru Gobind Singh College of Pharmacy, Yamuna Nagar, Haryana, India; [3]Chitkara College of Pharmacy, Chitkara University, Rajpura, Punjab, India; [4]GITAM School of Pharmacy, GITAM Deemed to be University, Patancheru, Hyderabad, India; [5]Department of Pharmaceutics, Adesh College of Pharmacy, Shahbad, Haryana, India

Introduction

More than 40% of newly developed formulations fail clinical trials due to low aqueous solubility or cell membrane permeation limited absorption, and poor drug bioavailability (Beg et al., 2011). Nanotechnology has gained widespread popularity in overcoming these challenges. These include materials ranging from 1 to 1000 nm. Owing to their definite size and shape, nanomaterials are being thoroughly studied in drug delivery and biological applications. Dendrimers are such a nanomaterial of spherical-shape and are highly branched, monodispersedand three-dimensional structures. Dendrimer chemistry was initially developed by Fritz Vogtle and associates in 1978, and the first dendrimer family was created by Tomalia in 1985 (Vögtle et al., 2009). The term "arborols," which comes from the Latin word "arbour," which means "tree," was chosen by the Newkomes group to describe the synthesis of dendrimers. Dendrimers, as highly branched synthetic polymers made of highly branched monomer units, are referred to as polymers of the 21st century (Thakur and Sharma, 2021). Dendrimer is derived from the Greek word Dendron (tree-like) and meros (parts or units) and has a tree-like appearance and structure. Dendrimers are being studied as promising architectures for serious illnesses, including cancer, TB, and AIDS. The three-dimensional structure, low polydispersity, and high functionality of dendrimers have demonstrated their usefulness as drug carriers (Mhlwatika and

Advanced Cancer Therapeutics
https://doi.org/10.1016/B978-0-443-44185-1.00021-5

Aderibigbe, 2018). Dendrimers may protect a drug from the biological environment, enhancing its bioactivity, prolonging its systemic circulation, and improving accumulation at the target site. Dendrimers' interaction with anticancer drugs has gained a huge research interest. It can involve entrapment of anticancer drugs in the core of dendrimers through electrostatic, hydrophobic, and hydrogen bond interactions. The interaction of an anticancer drug can also be with the surface of a dendrimer, involving electrostatic and covalent interactions. Dendrimers have thus been employed in drug delivery applications for modifying solubility, permeability, release, and targeting to cancer cells. The dendrimer application in the pharmaceutical field depends on various factors, including size, shape, concentration, pH, terminal or surface functionality, and materials used in designing dendrimers. In this chapter, an overview was provided on various generations of dendrimers, their synthesis methods, the mechanism of drug encapsulation and delivery, surface functionalization, and application in anticancer drug delivery.

Molecular structure and properties of dendrimers

The structural control and surface functionality of dendrimers are remarkable (Irfan et al., 2020). The architecture of dendrimers is well known for its well-defined molecular sizes, shapes, and weights (Pérez-Ferreiro et al., 2023). Dendrimers have an inner core for drug entrapment and an o/1uter shell as a surface with functional groups for drug conjugation. The dendrimers' structure is thus divided into three main parts: an initiator core, a shell with expanding arms or branches composed of building blocks, and the outermost surface groups on the branch termini (Gupta et al., 2018). The earliest branches, also known as the first generation, are formed by the monomers that adhere to the core. The end-groups of dendrimers fold back into densely packed interiors or are fully extended with maximum density at the surface. It can be easily tuned for the delivery of drugs, molecular sensors, and enzyme mimics (Darbre and Reymond, 2006). Compared to dendrimers of higher generations, lower generations (0, 1, and 2) have more open structures and a highly asymmetric morphology (Fig. 14.1). The dendrimers, on stretching to a perimeter can become tightly packed, creating a structure that mimics a closed membrane. (Murrar, 2018). Dendrimers of generation three and higher have longer chain length and dense branching to give them a globular shape. Dendrimers can thus be easily tuned for size and shape using polymers of varying length and branching. Dendrimers can show a critical branching condition due to lack of space, and this phenomenon is termed the "starburst effect. (Tomalia et al., 1990)" It is observed with PAMAM dendrimer of higher generation. The diameter of the tenth-generation PAMAM is about 124 Å, and it contains 6141 monomer units. The structure of dendrimers is also thought to be significantly impacted by the growing branch density (Gupta et al., 2018; Maiti et al., 2004). They can be distinguished by their reactive end groups and interior voids. Higher dendrimer generations (5+) offer particle sizes suitable for high drug loading capacity in the inner core, escaping clearance and prolonging systemic circulation for accumulation at the target site, and diversity in surface functionality for modification with ligands or drug conjugations, making them useful carriers for targeted delivery of anticancer drugs. The mean diameters can range from 1 nm for G1 to 14.7 nm for G10, amenable to further modification or conjugation with chemical species such as fluorophores, targeting ligands, drugs, and genes (Table 14.1).

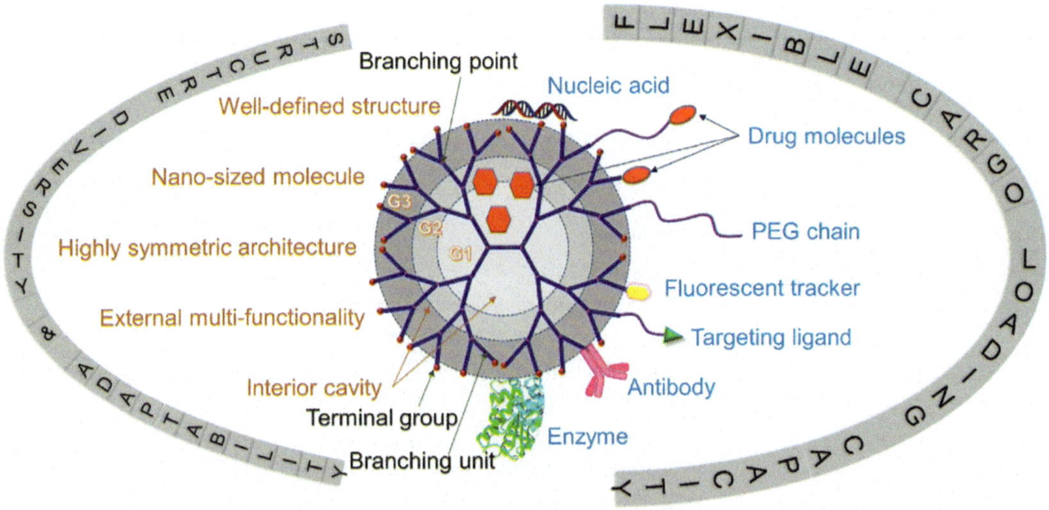

FIGURE 14.1 **Structure diversity, adaptability, and flexible cargo loading capacity of dendrimers.** G1, G2, and G3 represent generation 1, 2, and 3, respectively. *Adapted from Wang J, Li B, Qiu L, Qiao X, Yang H. Dendrimer-based drug delivery systems: History, challenges, and latest developments. J. Biol. Eng. 16 (1) (2022), https://doi.org/10.1186/s13036-022-00298-5*

Synthesis methods of dendrimers

Divergent growth approaches, convergent growth methods, hypercore and branching methods, double exponential, and mixed growth methods are often used in the synthesis of dendrimers (Gawande et al., 2021; Grayson and Fréchet, 2001).

Divergent method (outward growth methodology)

Dendrimers start to develop in the core and spread outward using this method. Tomalia and Newkome coined the word "divergent," which refers to a synthesis method in which dendrimers grow around a core (Patel et al., 2022). Divergent growth is the classical methodology used to synthesize dendrimers, in which construction proceeds outward from a central core bearing multiple reactive sites. In Tomalia's archetypal PAMAM "starburst" dendrimers, synthesis begins from an ethylenediamine core and alternates Michael addition of methyl acrylate with exhaustive amidation, thereby doubling the number of terminal groups with each generation and enabling precise control over size and surface functionality. This stepwise protocol demands near-quantitative conversion at every stage, because incomplete reactions generate "defective" or trailing generations that are extremely difficult to remove chromatographically, leading to slight polydispersity and altered biological performance (Amjad, 2021). Despite these challenges, the divergent route remains attractive for anticancer drug delivery because it readily affords high-generation PAMAM architectures with dense peripheral amines that can be converted into targeting ligands (e.g., folate, PEG–folate) while simultaneously accommodating substantial drug payloads within

TABLE 14.1 Generations of dendrimers in anticancer drug delivery.

Generation	Approx particle size (nm)	Surface functional groups (approx)	Characteristics	Drug delivery use	Example drug
G0	1.0–1.5	04	Very small structure with limited branching	For basic structural studies and research	Rarely used for drug delivery
G1	1.5–2.0	08	Slightly increased branching and cavities	For initial drug loading and improvement of solubility and permeability	Small molecules
G2	2.0–2.9	16	More internal cavities and surface groups	For drug encapsulation in core and drug conjugation on surface	Methotrexate
G3	3.0–3.9	32	Improved drug loading and stability	As drug carrier for anticancer action and imaging applications	Doxorubicin
G4	4.0–4.3	64	High number of terminal groups, good circulation	As carrier for anticancer drug	Paclitaxel
G5	4.3–5.5	128	Large surface area, high drug loading capacity	As targeted drug delivery systems involving ligand attachment	Cisplatin
G6	6.0–6.7	256	Very dense branching and many functional groups	As carrier with antibodies/ligands for advanced targeted therapy	Targeted chemotherapy
G7+	7–10	+512	Extremely large dendrimers with high functionality	As multifunctional systems for targeted drug delivery and imaging applications	Experimental cancer nanomedicine

Data from Tomalia, D.A., Naylor, A.M. and Goddard, W.A. (1990). Starburst Dendrimers: Molecular-Level Control of Size, Shape, Surface Chemistry, Topology, and Flexibility from Atoms to Macroscopic Matter. Angew Chem. Int. Ed. Engl., 29(2), 138–175. https://doi.org/10.1002/anie.199001381. Data from Svenson, S. and Tomalia, D.A. (2012). Dendrimers in biomedical applications-reflections on the field. Advanced Drug Delivery Reviews, 64, 102–115. https://doi.org/10.1016/j.addr.2012.09.030

internal cavities and on the surface (Singh et al., 2008). Such structurally well-defined nanocarriers, obtained through divergent synthesis, have been successfully exploited to improve solubility, tumor-specific accumulation and controlled release of chemotherapeutics in vivo, underscoring the continued relevance of this methodology in modern dendrimer-based oncology formulations (Abedi-Gaballu et al., 2018).

Convergent method

The convergent growth strategy represents one of the most important advances in dendrimer chemistry, providing a highly controlled route for the synthesis of structurally well-defined dendritic macromolecules. This method was first introduced by Hawker and Fréchet in 1990, offering an alternative to the traditional divergent approach. In contrast to divergent synthesis, where dendrimers grow outward from a multifunctional core, the convergent strategy proceeds in the opposite direction, beginning from the molecular periphery and gradually progressing toward the central core (M. Pérez-Ferreiro et al., 2023).

In the convergent approach, small branched fragments known as dendrons are synthesized first through stepwise coupling of branching monomers. Each dendron contains a focal functional group at its apex and multiple terminal groups at the periphery. After constructing dendrons of the desired generation, these fragments are subsequently attached to a multifunctional core molecule in the final step to form the complete dendrimer architecture. This strategy allows the independent synthesis and purification of intermediate dendrons before their coupling with the core, which significantly improves structural precision and reduces defects within the final macromolecule (Grayson and Fréchet, 2001). A pioneering example of convergent dendrimer synthesis was reported by Hawker and Fréchet, who demonstrated the preparation of dendritic polyaryl ether structures using stepwise dendron assembly followed by attachment to a central benzyl core. Their work established the feasibility of producing monodisperse dendrimers with well-defined molecular weights and controlled surface functionalities, which are essential characteristics for applications in nanomedicine and drug delivery systems. Subsequent studies further expanded this methodology to various dendritic architectures, including aryl ester and polyphenylene dendrimers, highlighting the versatility of convergent synthetic design (Miller and Neenan, 1990).

One of the key advantages of the convergent method is the improved control over structural purity and monodispersity. Since dendrons are synthesized separately, incomplete reactions or structural defects can be removed during purification steps before final assembly. This greatly reduces the occurrence of "missing branches" or imperfect growth that often occurs in divergent synthesis. Consequently, dendrimers produced via convergent strategies typically exhibit high structural uniformity and predictable molecular architecture, making them particularly attractive for biomedical applications where reproducibility is critical (Gupta and Nayak, 2015). However, despite its advantages, the convergent approach also presents certain limitations. As dendrons increase in size with higher generations, steric hindrance around the focal point becomes more pronounced during the final coupling with the core. This steric congestion can significantly reduce coupling efficiency and restrict the synthesis of very high-generation dendrimers using this strategy. As a result, the convergent method is generally more suitable for preparing low-to moderate-generation dendrimers, whereas large-scale industrial production often relies on divergent synthesis methods (Sánchez-Navarro and Rojo, 2012).

Hypercore and branched monomer growth method

Hypercore and branched monomer strategies were developed to accelerate dendrimer synthesis by combining advantageous features of both divergent and convergent growth. In this approach, a lower-generation dendritic scaffold is first constructed as a "hypercore" (often a small dendrimer itself), which is then elaborated in a few high-yielding steps using pre-branched oligomeric building blocks or "branched monomers" that already contain multiple branching points. Because much of the branching architecture is pre-assembled before attachment, higher generations can be reached with fewer iterative protection–deprotection and activation cycles, mitigating steric congestion at the periphery and improving overall synthetic efficiency compared with classical stepwise divergent routes. Fréchet and co-workers demonstrated that coupling a G3 aromatic polyester hypercore with G4 dendrons enabled access to a G7 dendrimer that would be synthetically challenging using traditional strategies, illustrating how hypercore concepts can extend to very high generations. For anticancer drug delivery, such methodologies are attractive because they facilitate rapid preparation of large, monodisperse dendritic platforms with dense surface functionality, which can be further decorated with targeting ligands and chemotherapeutic agents to enhance tumor selectivity and loading capacity (Maraval et al., 2005; Ambekar et al., 2020).

The hypercore and branched monomer methods thus represent a powerful evolution in dendrimer synthesis, overcoming limitations of traditional divergent approaches to enable faster production of higher-generation architectures with superior monodispersity and functionality (Kesharwani and Iyer, 2015). These strategies have proven particularly valuable for anticancer applications, as evidenced by studies showing folate-PEG-PAMAM dendrimers synthesized via accelerated hyperbranched routes that achieved 5-fold higher tumor accumulation in mice bearing KB tumors compared to free drug, with minimal off-target toxicity. Such advancements not only streamline scale-up for clinical translation but also enhance drug loading efficiency up to 30–50 wt% in some dendritic carriers, while enabling precise surface engineering for targeted therapies. Overall, they solidify dendrimers as versatile platforms in oncology (Singh et al., 2008).

Double exponential and mixed growth method

The double exponential growth strategy was developed as an accelerated approach to overcome the time-consuming nature of classical divergent and convergent dendrimer synthesis. In this method, dendritic fragments are designed in such a way that they can grow simultaneously in two directions, allowing the number of terminal groups to increase exponentially with each synthetic step. Typically, the approach employs AB_2-type monomers containing orthogonally protected functional groups, enabling selective activation either at the focal point or at the periphery of the dendron. These selectively activated dendritic fragments are then coupled to form higher-generation dendrimers in a significantly reduced number of reaction steps (Boas et al., 2007). One of the earliest demonstrations of this strategy was reported by Moore and co-workers, who showed that a high-generation dendrimer could theoretically be synthesized in far fewer synthetic steps compared with conventional iterative methods. For example, a seventh-generation dendrimer can be obtained in approximately nine steps using the double exponential strategy, whereas traditional stepwise approaches may require more than 14 sequential reactions. This dramatic reduction in the number of synthetic steps highlights the efficiency of the approach for constructing large dendritic macromolecules (Xu et al., 1994).

Double-exponential and mixed-growth methods push dendrimer synthesis to new levels of speed and precision by combining bidirectional branching with orthogonal couplings. In double exponential synthesis, as pioneered by Diederich's group, a dual-purpose monomer splits into two reactive partners, say, an alkyne-bearing branch and an azide-terminated one, that snap together via click chemistry, doubling both the core's multiplicity and surface groups per cycle, so a G4 dendrimer emerges in mere 8–10 steps instead of 20+. Mixed growth builds on this by adding hyperbranched units midway, as in Majoral's phosphorus series, where a G5 core met pre-made G3 wedges to reach G11 with 3000+ phosphorus atoms and 98% purity after simple precipitation. These tricks cut reaction times by 70% and boost yields to 90% per step, perfect for anticancer setups, think doxorubicin-loaded versions showing 4x better cell kill in HeLa models thanks to smarter drug spacing and pH-triggered burst. Researchers love them for scaling up without the usual gunk buildup (Kawaguchi et al., 1995; Abbasi et al., 2014).

Mechanisms of drug loading and release

Owing to the tight, spherical shape and surface functional groups of dendrimers, drug molecules can be confined inside the dendrimers or linked or bound to the surface. Encapsulation in dendrimers can involve entrapment of anticancer drugs through electrostatic, hydrophobic, and hydrogen bond interactions. For the covalent conjugation of an anticancer drug, the functional group present on the polymer's terminal end at the dendrimers' exterior can be exploited (Singh et al., 2016). The loading capacity depends on the density of functional groups on the surface of dendrimers. The release of the drug depends on two mechanisms, mainly passive and active release. Passive release involves hydrolysis or enzymatic degradation of dendrimer conjugates to release the free drug. While active release involves degradation in response to specific stimuli like GSH (disulfide), ROS (thioketal), pH(acetal, hydrozone, cis-aconityl, or di-ester), or temperature (Wang et al., 2016; Wang et al., 2022).

GSH-responsive release

Reductive drug release based on disulfide linkages is one of the most widely explored intracellular triggering mechanisms for dendrimer-based drug delivery. This strategy relies on the large difference in glutathione (GSH) concentrations between extracellular and intracellular environments. The cytoplasm typically contains 1–10 mM GSH, whereas extracellular fluids such as plasma contain only micromolar levels. Because disulfide bonds are stable under normal physiological conditions but undergo cleavage through thiol–disulfide exchange reactions in a reductive environment, they can function as molecular switches for intracellular drug release. When a drug is conjugated to a dendrimer through a disulfide linker, the conjugate remains relatively stable during systemic circulation but undergoes rapid cleavage once internalized into cells where GSH concentrations are significantly higher. This mechanism enables selective intracellular drug liberation and helps minimize premature drug leakage in the bloodstream (Navath et al., 2008).

Experimental studies with PAMAM dendrimer–drug conjugates clearly demonstrate the effectiveness of this mechanism. For example, poly (amidoamine) (PAMAM) dendrimers conjugated with N-acetyl cysteine (NAC) through disulfide linkages were synthesized with approximately 16–18 drug molecules attached per dendrimer, confirmed by NMR and MALDI-TOF analysis. Release studies showed that the conjugates were highly responsive to intracellular glutathione levels: around 60%–70% of the drug payload was released within about 1 h in the presence of intracellular GSH concentrations (~10 mM), whereas negligible drug release occurred at extracellular GSH levels (~2 μM). These findings indicate that the disulfide bond remains stable during circulation but undergoes rapid cleavage inside cells, resulting in efficient intracellular drug release. In addition, the dendrimer–drug conjugates showed significantly enhanced biological activity compared with the free drug, producing up to 16-fold higher inhibition of inflammatory markers in activated microglial cells, which highlights the therapeutic advantage of GSH-responsive dendrimer systems for targeted intracellular drug delivery (Hu et al., 2014; Kurtoglu et al., 2009).

ROS-responsive drug release

Thioketal (TK) linkers are widely used in ROS-responsive drug delivery systems because the thioketal bond is stable under normal physiological conditions but undergoes oxidative cleavage in the presence of elevated reactive oxygen species such as hydrogen peroxide. When ROS levels increase in pathological environments such as tumor tissues or inflamed cells, the TK bond breaks and triggers the release of the conjugated therapeutic agent. This mechanism enables drug carriers to remain stable during systemic circulation while allowing selective activation at disease sites characterized by oxidative stress. Experimental studies have shown that TK-containing nanocarriers maintain minimal drug leakage under normal physiological conditions but undergo rapid degradation and payload release when exposed to ROS. For instance, ROS-cleavable TK-based nanostructures demonstrated significant structural degradation and drug liberation when exposed to oxidative conditions such as H_2O_2, confirming that ROS can efficiently activate TK-containing linkers and initiate controlled drug release (Rinaldi et al., 2022).

Further investigation demonstrates the efficiency of ROS-triggered release from TK-containing drug delivery systems. As an example, a PEG–doxorubicin prodrug containing a thioketal linker exhibited negligible drug release under normal conditions but released approximately 45% of doxorubicin within 24 h in the presence of 100 μM H_2O_2, indicating strong ROS-dependent activation. Similarly, polymeric nanoparticles incorporating TK linkages showed minimal drug leakage in ROS-free environments, whereas exposure to oxidative conditions resulted in drug release approaching ~70%, demonstrating rapid carrier degradation and payload liberation under oxidative stress. Such ROS-responsive behavior highlights the ability of thioketal linkers to act as molecular triggers that convert stable nanocarriers into drug-releasing systems specifically within ROS-rich microenvironments, thereby improving therapeutic selectivity and reducing premature drug leakage during circulation (Chi et al., 2024).

pH-responsive release

Acid-labile linkers are commonly incorporated into dendrimer–drug conjugates to enable selective drug release in response to the acidic conditions typically present in tumor tissues, endosomes, and lysosomes. While the physiological pH of blood and normal tissues is approximately 7.4, the extracellular tumor microenvironment is slightly acidic ($pH \approx 6.5$), and intracellular vesicular compartments may exhibit even lower pH values (pH 5.0–5.5). This pH gradient can be exploited by introducing acid-cleavable linkers such as hydrazone, cis-aconityl, or acetal bonds between the drug molecule and the dendrimer surface. These linkers remain relatively stable at physiological pH but undergo hydrolytic cleavage under acidic conditions, enabling site-specific drug release. For example, PEGylated polylysine dendrimers conjugated with anticancer agents through an acid-labile hydrazone-type linker (HSBA) demonstrated strong pH-dependent behavior. In vitro release studies revealed that less than 10% of the conjugated drug was released at pH 7.4 over 3 days, whereas nearly complete drug liberation occurred at pH 5, confirming efficient acid-triggered cleavage of the linker under conditions that mimic intracellular acidic compartments (Kaminskas et al., 2011).

Dendrimer platforms have also employed acid-sensitive linkages to control the release of different therapeutic agents. For instance, poly (L-glutamic acid) dendrimers incorporating a silsesquioxane core have been developed in which anticancer drugs were attached through hydrazone-type pH-responsive bonds. These dendrimer conjugates formed nanosized particles (~50 nm) and displayed significantly accelerated drug release under acidic conditions compared with neutral environments, demonstrating that proton-mediated cleavage of the linker facilitates drug liberation within tumor cells (Yuan et al., 2010). Similarly, PAMAM dendrimers functionalized with targeting ligands such as folic acid and conjugated with DOX (doxorubicin) through cis-aconityl linkages have shown enhanced drug release at acidic pH values (around pH 5–6) relative to physiological conditions. In these systems, approximately six to seven drug molecules were conjugated per dendrimer, and the acid-sensitive linker enabled efficient intracellular release following receptor-mediated endocytosis into cancer cells (Zhang et al., 2018). Collectively, these studies demonstrate that acid-labile linkers provide an effective mechanism for achieving controlled and tumor-specific drug release from dendrimer nanocarriers, thereby improving therapeutic selectivity and minimizing premature drug leakage during systemic circulation.

Thermo-sensitive release

Thermo-responsive drug delivery systems utilize temperature as an external stimulus to regulate drug release from dendrimer-based nanocarriers. These systems typically incorporate temperature-sensitive polymers such as N-isopropylacrylamide (NIPAM) that exhibit a phase transition near physiological temperature. When the temperature exceeds the polymer's lower critical solution temperature (LCST), the polymer undergoes a conformational change from a hydrated expanded state to a collapsed hydrophobic state. This structural transition can alter the permeability of the nanocarrier and accelerate drug diffusion from the dendrimer system. Thermo-responsive polymers are therefore widely integrated with dendrimer architectures to create smart nanocarriers capable of releasing therapeutic agents in response to localized heating or externally applied stimuli such as near-infrared irradiation (Hassani et al., 2023).

Experimental studies have demonstrated the effectiveness of this approach for controlled drug delivery. In a temperature-responsive nanocarrier composed of polyester dendrimers conjugated with NIPAM-modified nanodiamonds, paclitaxel was loaded into the dendrimer-based system and its release behavior was evaluated at different temperatures. Drug release experiments showed that approximately 64.38% of paclitaxel was released at 37 °C, whereas the release increased to about 92.10% at 45 °C within 48 h, indicating that elevated temperature significantly accelerated drug liberation from the carrier. Furthermore, under near-infrared (NIR) irradiation, photothermal heating generated localized temperature increases that triggered rapid drug release, reaching approximately 97% release within 15 min. These findings demonstrate that thermo-responsive dendrimer nanocarriers can achieve temperature-regulated drug release and enhanced anticancer activity through externally triggered thermal stimulation (Jamshidpour et al., 2024).

Additional thermo-sensitive systems have also been developed using dendrimer-functionalized nanoparticles coated with temperature-responsive polymers. For instance, dendrimer-modified nanocarriers grafted with poly (N-vinylcaprolactam) or related thermo-sensitive polymers exhibit reversible coil-to-globule transitions when exposed to temperature changes, allowing controlled adsorption and release of therapeutic molecules such as letrozole. The release kinetics of such systems have been shown to follow diffusion-controlled mechanisms, and drug liberation increases significantly as the polymer network undergoes temperature-induced structural changes. These studies highlight that thermo-sensitive dendrimer systems provide a promising strategy for achieving controlled and externally regulated drug release in targeted cancer therapy (Hooshyar et al., 2019).

Receptor-mediated endocytosis of surface-modified dendrimer

Surface functionalization of dendrimers with specific ligands allows selective recognition of overexpressed receptors on cancer cells and facilitates receptor-mediated endocytosis, which significantly enhances intracellular drug delivery. In this approach, targeting moieties such as folic acid, transferrin, peptides, or antibodies are conjugated to the dendrimer surface so that the nanocarrier can selectively bind to receptors that are highly expressed on tumor cells but minimally present on normal tissues. Once ligand–receptor interaction occurs, the dendrimer–drug complex is internalized through endocytic pathways such as clathrin-mediated or caveolae-dependent endocytosis, followed by trafficking to endosomal and lysosomal compartments where the drug is subsequently released. Experimental studies using surface-modified PAMAM dendrimers demonstrated that dendrimers can enter cells through multiple uptake routes, including caveolae-dependent endocytosis and macropinocytosis, and intracellular imaging confirmed their localization within endosomes and lysosomes after internalization. These findings highlight that surface chemistry strongly influences cellular uptake mechanisms and governs the intracellular fate of dendrimer-based drug carriers (Saovapakhiran et al., 2009).

Targeting efficiency and therapeutic outcomes can be further improved by engineering dendrimers with receptor-specific ligands and co-delivery strategies. For example, folate-anchored dendrimers loaded with methotrexate (MTX) and all-trans retinoic acid (ATRA) demonstrated enhanced receptor-mediated uptake in cancer cells. In HeLa cell studies, pretreatment with ATRA led to approximately 2.21-fold up-regulation of folate receptors after 48 h, significantly increasing the interaction between folate-modified dendrimers and tumor cells. As a consequence, the targeted dendrimer formulation showed markedly improved cytotoxic activity, with a reduced IC_{50} value of 0.04 μM compared with higher values observed for non-targeted drug combinations. Such receptor-targeted dendrimer systems allow selective accumulation in cancer cells, followed by intracellular drug release triggered by the acidic endosomal environment or enzymatic processes, ultimately resulting in enhanced anticancer efficacy and reduced off-target toxicity (Tekade et al., 2008).

Dendrimers in anticancer drug delivery

Anticancer medications have been delivered by dendrimers in both active and passive methods (Table 14.2). The use of dendrimers as anticancer drug delivery vehicles is discussed below with a few examples. Dendrimers have emerged as versatile nanocarriers for anticancer drug delivery due to their well-defined structure, multivalent surface, and ability to enhance drug solubility, stability, and targeted cellular uptake. Functionalization with ligands such as folic acid, antibodies, and peptides enables receptor-mediated targeting, while advanced modifications allow improved barrier penetration and controlled drug release within the tumor microenvironment. A summarized representation of key dendrimer-based anticancer drug delivery systems along with their experimentally validated outcomes is presented in Table 14.3.

Advantages of dendrimers in anticancer drug delivery

Role in solubility enhancement

One of the most significant advantages of dendrimers is their ability to enhance the solubility of poorly water-soluble anticancer drugs. The unique three-dimensional

TABLE 14.2 Dendrimers-based anticancer drug delivery system.

Anticancer drug	Type of dendrimer used
5-Fluorouracil (5-FU)	PAMAM-mPEG-PDEA dendrimer; PAMAM dendrimer; polyglycerol-based dendrimer
Cisplatin (CDDP)	PAM dendrimer; carboxyl-terminated PAMAM (PAMAM-COOH)
Methotrexate (MTX)	Polyether-co-polyester dendrimer; PAMAM dendrimer
Paclitaxel (PTX)	Polyglycerol dendrimer; PAMAM dendrimer; triazine dendrimer; poly (propylene imine) (PPI) dendrimer; PEGylated PPI and PEGylated PAMAM; FA-DLSP-PLLA modified PAMAM/PPI systems
Doxorubicin (DOX)	PEGylated PAMAM dendrimer; RGD-modified dendrimer formulations

Data from Madaan, K., Kumar, S., Poonia, N., Lather, V. and Pandita, D. (2014). Dendrimers in drug delivery and targeting: Drug-dendrimer interactions and toxicity issues. Journal of Pharmacy and Bioallied Sciences, 6(3), 139–150. https://doi.org/10.4103/0975-7406.130965. Data from Singh, J., Jain, K., Mehra, N.K. and Jain, N.K. Dendrimers in anticancer drug delivery: mechanism of interaction of drug and dendrimers. Artif. Cells Nanomed. Biotechnol., 44(7)(2016). 1626–1634. https://doi.org/10.3109/21691401.2015.1129625

TABLE 14.3 Dendrimer-based anticancer drug delivery systems and their research outcomes.

S. No.	Formulation	Drug	Key mechanistic and experimental outcomes	References
1.	FA/borneol-modified PAMAM G5	**Doxorubicin**	Dual-functional system enabling receptor-mediated uptake and enhanced BBB permeation; demonstrated higher glioma cell internalization, improved brain accumulation, reduced systemic toxicity, and superior anticancer efficacy compared to non-targeted formulations	Xu et al. (2016)
2.	Trastuzumab-grafted PAMAM dendrimer	**Docetaxel**	HER2-targeted nanocarrier promoting selective cellular internalization in HER2-positive breast cancer cells; resulted in enhanced cytotoxicity and improved therapeutic selectivity compared to free drug	Kulhari et al. (2016)
3.	Angiopep-2 grafted PAMAM dendrimer	**Temozolomide**	Ligand-mediated transport across the blood–brain barrier combined with improved systemic stability; exhibited increased brain uptake, prolonged circulation, and enhanced antitumor activity in glioblastoma models	Sahoo et al. (2023)
4.	TPP-functionalized PAMAM dendrimer	**Curcumin**	Mitochondria-targeted delivery exploiting membrane potential differences; resulted in enhanced intracellular localization, induction of mitochondrial dysfunction, and increased apoptosis in hepatocellular carcinoma cells	(S. Kianamiri et al., 2020)
5.	pH-responsive PEG/PDEA/PAMAM nanocarrier	**5-Fluorouracil**	Stimuli-responsive system enabling preferential drug release under acidic tumor microenvironment; improved tumor-specific delivery, sustained release behavior, and enhanced anticancer efficacy compared to free drug	Jin et al. (2011)
6.	G5 PAMAM multivalent conjugate	**Methotrexate**	Drug acts as both therapeutic and targeting ligand; multivalent architecture enhances receptor binding, cellular uptake, and cytotoxic activity relative to free methotrexate	Li et al. (2012)
7.	FA/MTX bifunctional PAMAM conjugate with defined ratio	**Methotrexate**	Precisely controlled ligand–drug ratio improves structural reproducibility and receptor-targeted delivery; demonstrated enhanced selectivity toward folate receptor-positive cancer cells	Zong et al. (2012)
8.	Carboxylate PAMAM 3.5 dendrimer-platinate	**Cisplatin/ platinum conjugate**	Dendrimer conjugation improves aqueous solubility and enables controlled platinum release; significantly enhances tumor accumulation and reduces systemic toxicity compared to free cisplatin	Malik et al., (1999)
9.	PEG-cored Flt-1 antibody-conjugated dendrimer	**Gemcitabine**	Antibody-mediated targeting enhances selective uptake in pancreatic cancer cells; improves intracellular delivery and results in superior tumor inhibition in vivo compared to non-targeted formulations	Öztürk et al. (2017)

hyperbranched architecture of dendrimers provides internal cavities and multiple surface functional groups that facilitate both encapsulation and conjugation of hydrophobic drugs. This dual mechanism allows dendrimers to act as *unimolecular micelles*, thereby improving aqueous solubility and drug dispersion. Additionally, dendrimers can interact with drug molecules through hydrogen bonding, electrostatic interactions, or hydrophobic interactions, leading to improved dissolution and bioavailability. This is particularly important for anticancer drugs such as paclitaxel and camptothecin, which inherently suffer from poor solubility and limited clinical performance (An et al., 2023).

Role in improving permeation

Dendrimers significantly enhance the permeation of anticancer drugs across biological barriers due to their nanoscale size, well-defined architecture, and multivalent surface functionality. Their small and uniform structure enables efficient diffusion through the dense tumor microenvironment, allowing improved distribution of therapeutic agents within tumor tissues. Additionally, dendrimers can exploit the enhanced permeability and retention (EPR) effect, promoting preferential accumulation in tumor sites and facilitating deeper penetration compared to conventional formulations. At the cellular level, dendrimers improve permeation primarily through endocytic uptake mechanisms driven by interactions between their surface groups and the cell membrane. Cationic dendrimers, such as PAMAM, interact strongly with negatively charged cellular membranes, enhancing internalization and intracellular drug delivery. Furthermore, surface modification with targeting ligands enables receptor-mediated uptake, improving selectivity toward cancer cells and reducing off-target effects. These combined properties make dendrimers highly effective carriers for overcoming permeation barriers in anticancer drug delivery (Kukowska-Latallo et al., 2005).

Role in stability enhancement

Dendrimers play a vital role in enhancing the stability of anticancer drugs by protecting them from premature degradation and unfavorable physiological conditions. Their unique branched architecture allows drug molecules to be either encapsulated within internal cavities or conjugated onto surface functional groups, thereby shielding them from hydrolysis, enzymatic degradation, and chemical instability. This protective environment helps maintain drug integrity during systemic circulation and improves overall therapeutic performance. In addition, dendrimers contribute to improved formulation stability and controlled drug release behavior. Their well-defined structure enables precise tuning of drug–carrier interactions, reducing drug leakage and enhancing retention until the drug reaches the target site. Surface modifications, such as PEGylation or ligand conjugation, further improve stability by minimizing aggregation and prolonging circulation time. These properties collectively make dendrimers highly effective nanocarriers for stabilizing anticancer agents and ensuring efficient delivery (Cheng et al., 2008).

Role in cellular internalization and organelle targeting (mitochondria and nucleus)

Dendrimers exhibit excellent capability for cellular internalization owing to their nanoscale size, defined architecture, and multivalent surface. Their surface functional groups, particularly in cationic dendrimers such as PAMAM, enable strong interactions with negatively charged cell membranes, facilitating uptake primarily through endocytic pathways.

This efficient internalization allows dendrimer–drug systems to deliver anticancer agents directly into the intracellular environment, thereby improving therapeutic efficacy compared to conventional formulations (El-Sayed et al., 2002). Beyond cellular uptake, dendrimers can be engineered to target specific organelles, including the mitochondria and nucleus, which are critical sites for anticancer action. Surface modification with targeting moieties such as lipophilic cations or peptide sequences enables dendrimers to localize within mitochondria, inducing apoptosis through mitochondrial dysfunction. Similarly, conjugation with nuclear localization signals allows dendrimers to transport therapeutic agents to the nucleus, enhancing the effectiveness of DNA-targeting drugs. These tunable properties make dendrimers highly promising platforms for site-specific intracellular delivery in cancer therapy (Bae et al., 2021; Kianamiri et al., 2020).

Surface functionalization for targeted delivery

PEGylation

In 1970, Davis and Abuchowsky first used the term "PEGylation." PEGylation is the process of conjugating a surface with polyethylene glycol. To overcome the toxicity issues of dendrimers, PEGylation can be done (Luong et al., 2016). Three methods are usually employed for PEGylation: i) directly conjugating PEG to the dendrimer surface; ii) acting as a bridge between the drug molecule and the dendrimer surface; and iii) binding PEG to the dendrimer surface and reducing steric hindrance with a cross-linking agent. PEGylated drug-loaded dendrimers are reported to minimize toxicity (Kharwade et al., 2022).

Folic acid targeting (FA-dendrimers)

Numerous cancer cell types overexpress the folic acid receptor. Thus, folic acid surface-engineered dendrimers can be used in therapeutic transport, imaging, and diagnosis (Choudhury et al., 2020). Folate-conjugated dendrimers can be a promising platform for safe and targeted delivery of anticancer drugs in cancer cells (Fig. 14.2).

Antibody-functionalized dendrimers

An innovative method for the targeted administration of cytotoxic drug-loaded dendrimer is the use of an antibody for surface functionalization. Antibody-conjugated dendrimers can gain entry into cancer cells via receptor-mediated endocytosis (Jain, 2009). Dendrimers coupled with antibodies target connective tissue and blood vessels that sustain and nourish cancer cells. Additionally, it stops the growth factors needed for tumor development, showing "antiangiogenic impact". Antibody anti-human epidermal growth factor receptor 2 (HER2) PAMAM G 5.0 dimers found to increase the target effectiveness (Fig. 14.3) (Marcinkowska et al., 2019). The result showed high binding and internalization capabilities for HER2-overexpressing mouse fibrosarcoma (MCA-207) cell lines.

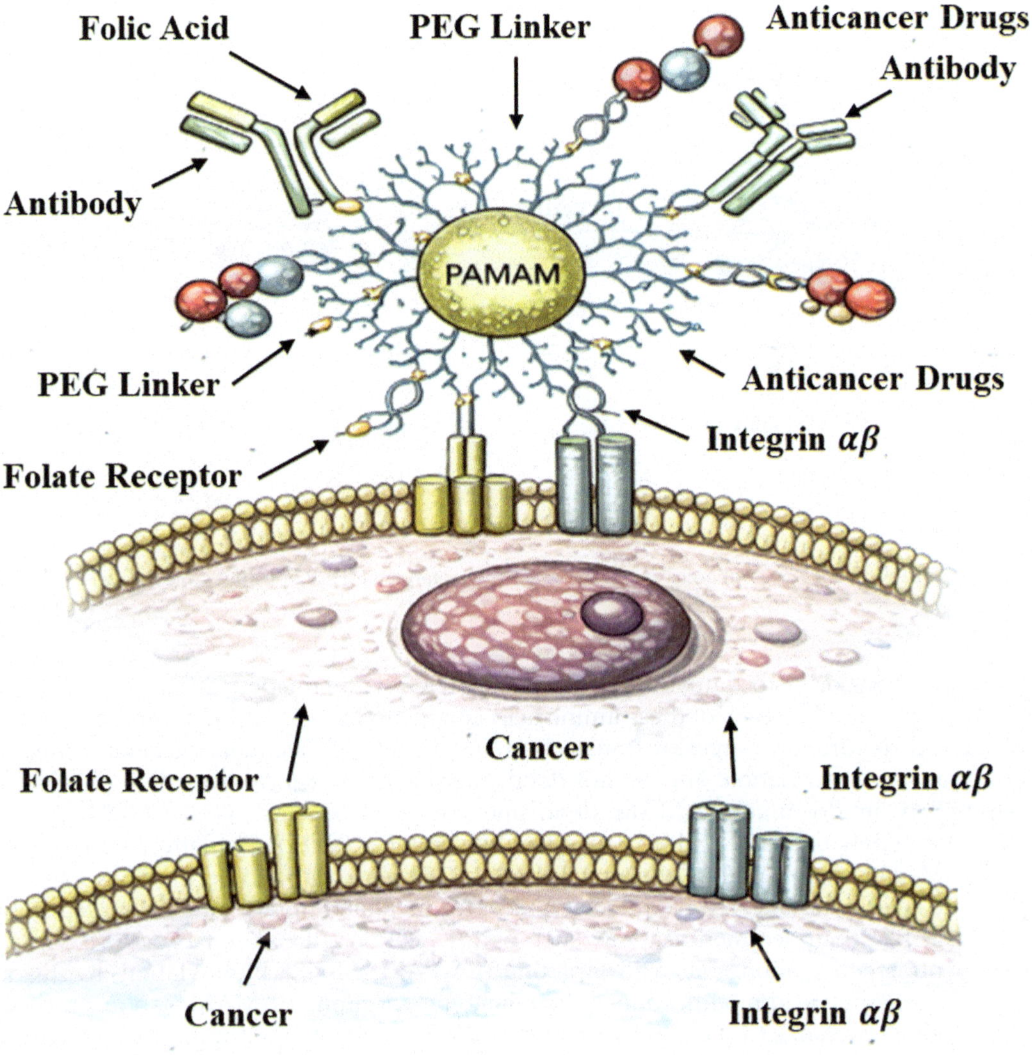

FIGURE 14.2 Advanced dendrimer for targeted cancer therapy.

Amino acid or peptide-conjugated dendrimers

In amino acid conjugation operations, dendrimers are used to conjugate phenylalanine and glycine. They could reduce the hemotoxicity, cytotoxicity, and immunogenicity associated with dendrimers (Janaszewska et al., 2019). The transfection effectiveness of modified PAMAMG 5.0 dimers with surface conjugation of phenylalanine, arginine, and leucine was

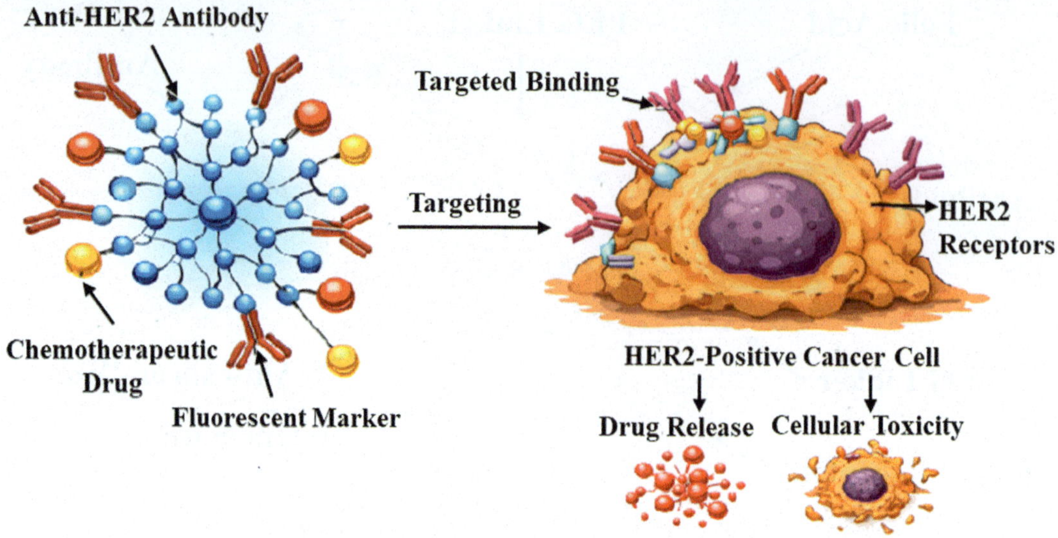

FIGURE 14.3 Antibody-conjugated dendrimers targeting HER2 positive cancer cells.

evaluated. A major histocompatibility complex (MHC) with enhanced immunostimulatory activity is produced by each of these amino acid-conjugated G5.0-PAMAM dimers. PAMAM amino acid dendrimer's superior transfection and targeting effectiveness make it a viable choice for DNA vaccination. The various dendrimer-based anticancer drug delivery systems include Poly(amidoamine) (PAMAM) dendrimers (e.g., G4–NH_2, G3, G3.5–COOH, G4, G5), which are widely used for loading drugs like Doxorubicin (DOX), Cisplatin, 5-Fluorouracil (5-FU), Methotrexate (MTX), Adriamycin, and 10-Hydroxycamptothecin. These showed enhanced cellular uptake, reduced toxicity, receptor-mediated uptake, and improved stability (Table 14.4). Surface modifications such as PEGylation (PEGylated PAMAM G4, G5), RGD peptide conjugation, folic acid targeting (FA-PAMAM G5), biotinylation, hydrazone linkers, and amino acid modifications (phenylalanine-/arginine-PAMAM) can improve targeting, reduce systemic toxicity, enhance bioavailability, and enable stimuli-responsive drug release. Other dendrimer types include Poly(propylene imine) (PPI) dendrimers (e.g., PPI G4, PEGylated PPI) for Paclitaxel (PTX) delivery with increased solubility and tumor selectivity; Polyglycerol dendrimers for PTX and 5-FU with higher solubility and confirmed internal cavity drug encapsulation; Triazine dendrimers for sustained PTX release; Poly-L-lysine dendrimers (PLL G6) for deep tumor penetration; and biodegradable glycerol–succinic acid dendrimers for camptothecin with enhanced uptake and retention. Key observations consistently emphasize improved drug solubility, targeted delivery, reduced toxicity (cardiotoxicity, nephrotoxicity, hemolysis), enhanced cellular uptake, prolonged circulation, and controlled or stimuli-responsive drug release for anticancer dendrimers.

TABLE 14.4 Dendrimer-based anticancer drug delivery systems, materials and drug loading.

Sr. No.	Polymer/Material used	Type of dendrimer	Drug loaded	Key observations	References
1.	Poly (amidoamine) (PAMAM)	PAMAM G4–NH_2	Doxorubicin (DOX)	Enhanced cellular uptake; pH-dependent release; reduced cardiotoxicity	Szota and Jachimska (2023)
2.	PAMAM + PEG	PEGylated PAMAM G5	DOX	Prolonged circulation time; reduced hemolysis; improved tumor accumulation	Luong et al. (2016)
3.	PAMAM + RGD peptide	RGD-modified PAMAM G5	DOX	Active targeting to integrin αvβ3-overexpressing tumor cells	(Ma et al., 2017)
4.	PAMAM (half-generation)	PAMAM G3.5–COOH	Cisplatin	Improved drug loading; reduced nephrotoxicity	Camacho et al. (2021)
5.	PAMAM + Biotin	Biotinylated PAMAM G4	Cisplatin	Enhanced internalization in ovarian cancer cells	Yellepeddi et al. (2013)
6.	Poly(propylene imine) (PPI)	PPI G4	Paclitaxel (PTX)	Increased aqueous solubility; improved cytotoxicity	Jain et al. (2015)
7.	PEG-PPI	PEGylated PPI	PTX	Reduced systemic toxicity; enhanced tumor selectivity	Kesharwani et al. (2011)
8.	Polyglycerol	Polyglycerol dendrimer	PTX	Higher solubility than PEG-400; stable drug encapsulation	Ooya et al. (2004)
9.	Triazine polymer	Triazine dendrimer	PTX	Sustained release; improved intracellular delivery	Lo et al. (2010)
10.	PAMAM	PAMAM G3	5-Fluorouracil (5-FU)	Solubility enhanced linearly with dendrimer concentration	Tokarczyk and Jachimska (2019)
11.	PAMAM-mPEG-PDEA	pH-responsive PAMAM	5-FU	Accelerated drug release at acidic tumor pH	Li et al. (2023)
12.	Polyglycerol	PG dendrimer G2	5-FU	NMR-confirmed internal cavity drug encapsulation	Mariyam et al. (2018)
13.	Polyether-co-polyester	Polyester dendrimer	Methotrexate (MTX)	9–15-fold reduction in IC50; receptor-mediated uptake	Svenson and Chauhan (2008)
14.	PAMAM + folic acid	FA-PAMAM G5	MTX	Selective targeting of folate-receptor-positive tumors	Tunki et al. (2019)
15.	PAMAM + PEG	PEG-PAMAM G4	Adriamycin	Reduced MDR; improved stability and efficacy	Tarach and Janaszewska (2021)
16.	Poly-L-lysine	PLL dendrimer G6	DOX	Deep tumor spheroid penetration; enhanced in vivo efficacy	Al-Jamal et al. (2013)

(Continued)

TABLE 14.4 Dendrimer-based anticancer drug delivery systems, materials and drug loading.—cont'd

Sr. No.	Polymer/Material used	Type of dendrimer	Drug loaded	Key observations	References
17.	Glycerol–succinic acid	Biodegradable dendrimer	Camptothecin	16-Fold increase in cellular uptake; sustained retention	Morgan et al. (2006)
18.	PAMAM	PAMAM G4	10-Hydroxycamptothecin	~600-fold increase in solubility; integrin-targeted activity	Morgan et al. (2006)
19.	PAMAM + hydrazone linker	pH-sensitive PAMAM	DOX	Acid-cleavable release; minimal off-target toxicity	Parshad et al. (2025)
20.	Amino-acid modified PAMAM	Phenylalanine-/ Arginine-PAMAM	Curcumin	Reduced cytotoxicity; enhanced bioavailability	Salem (2014)

Toxicity, biocompatibility, and safety issues

Hematological toxicity

Hematological toxicity is a key limitation that must be addressed before dendrimers can be used safely as anticancer drug carriers. Original experimental work has shown that unmodified cationic PAMAM dendrimers interact strongly with blood cells, especially erythrocytes. In human red blood cells, researchers observed that PAMAM dendrimers altered erythrocyte shape from the normal biconcave form to echinocytic forms, promoted cell aggregation, and induced hemolysis in a concentration- and generation-dependent manner, indicating that higher-generation cationic systems are more damaging to membrane integrity (Domański et al., 2004). A later blood-compatibility study by Han and colleagues confirmed this trend. They showed that cationic PAMAM dendrimers caused clear generation-, concentration-, and time-dependent hemolysis, whereas anionic and neutral PAMAM analogs were far less hemolytic. That study also suggested that blood proteins can partially shield these interactions, which helps explain why surface engineering is essential when designing dendrimer-based anticancer formulations for intravenous use (Han et al., 2010).

Beyond red-cell injury, hematological toxicity can also involve platelet dysfunction and broader systemic blood-related effects. In a primary in vitro study using human platelets, researchers found that only larger cationic PAMAM dendrimers induced platelet aggregation, and that this effect increased with the density of surface amines, suggesting a direct thrombogenic risk linked to membrane disruption rather than classical platelet-activation pathways (Dobrovolskaia et al., 2012). Notably, in vivo studies on dendrimer-mediated anticancer delivery systems suggest that such toxicity can be reduced by rational design. Kaminskas et al. compared free doxorubicin, PEGylated liposomal doxorubicin, and PEGylated dendrimer–doxorubicin in tumor-bearing rats, and reported that systemic toxicity markers, including white blood cell counts and spleen weight changes, were more pronounced with free and liposomal doxorubicin than with the dendrimer conjugate, even though tumor control was similar. Therefore, hematological toxicity is not an inherent barrier for all dendrimer systems, but it is highly dependent on generation, surface charge, and surface modification, with PEGylation or charge neutralization being especially important for safer anticancer delivery (Kaminskas et al., 2012).

In addition to hemolytic effects, the overall biocompatibility and safety profile of dendrimers are strongly influenced by their surface chemistry and functionalization. Studies have shown that modification of dendrimer terminal groups can significantly reduce their interaction with blood components and improve hematological compatibility. For example, acetylation of amine-terminated PAMAM dendrimers has been reported to markedly decrease hemolysis and membrane disruption compared with unmodified cationic dendrimers, demonstrating that surface engineering can enhance blood compatibility while maintaining their drug-delivery potential. These findings emphasize that rational surface modification is essential to improve the safety profile of dendrimer-based anticancer delivery systems and to minimize hematological toxicity during systemic administration (Malik et al., 2000).

Immunogenicity

Immunogenicity is a critical safety concern for dendrimer-based nanocarriers because their interaction with immune components in blood may trigger inflammatory responses. Experimental studies investigating the immune effects of PAMAM dendrimers have shown that cationic dendrimers can stimulate immune cells and induce the production of pro-inflammatory mediators. In vitro research using macrophage cell models demonstrated that higher-generation PAMAM dendrimers (G4–G6) increased reactive oxygen species generation and promoted the secretion of inflammatory cytokines, indicating activation of immune signaling pathways. The study also reported that the intensity of this response increased with dendrimer generation and surface amine density, highlighting the importance of surface chemistry in determining immunological compatibility (Naha et al., 2010).

Besides cytokine-mediated responses, dendrimers can also interact with the complement system, which represents another key mechanism underlying immunogenicity. Research examining the interaction between PAMAM dendrimers and human complement proteins showed that surface functionality strongly influences complement activation. Amine-terminated dendrimers were found to bind natural IgM molecules and subsequently trigger complement activation through the lectin pathway, whereas dendrimers bearing pyrrolidone or carboxyl-terminated groups largely avoided complement recognition. These findings demonstrate that dendrimer-induced immunogenic responses are not intrinsic to the nanocarrier itself but are largely governed by terminal surface groups, emphasizing that appropriate surface modification is essential to improve the immunological safety of dendrimer-based drug delivery systems (Wu et al., 2021).

In Vivo toxicity

In vivo investigations have provided valuable evidence regarding the systemic safety of dendrimers used in biomedical applications. An early animal study evaluated the biological behavior of different generations of PAMAM dendrimers (G3, G5, and G7) in mice. The results showed that most dendrimer generations exhibited relatively low systemic toxicity at moderate doses; however, higher-generation dendrimers with a larger number of surface amine groups displayed increased biological interactions and toxicity at the highest tested concentrations. The same study also reported distinct organ distribution patterns, where G3 dendrimers accumulated predominantly in the kidneys (approximately 15% of the injected dose per gram of tissue over 48 h), while G5 and G7 dendrimers showed higher localization in the pancreas. Additionally, G7 dendrimers demonstrated rapid urinary excretion, with about 46% and 74% of the injected dose recovered in urine at 2 and 4 h, respectively, indicating that dendrimer size and generation significantly influence their biodistribution and in vivo toxicity profile (Roberts et al., 1996).

Further in vivo studies have demonstrated that surface modification can markedly improve the safety profile of dendrimers. For example, research investigating intravenously administered generation-4 poly-L-lysine dendrimers in rats showed that partial PEGylation (≈50% surface PEG coverage) reduced rapid vascular binding and altered biodistribution compared with non-PEGylated dendrimers. PEGylation slowed metabolic degradation and improved plasma circulation stability, while additional acetylation of remaining surface amines further enhanced systemic stability. These findings highlight that surface engineering strategies such as PEGylation and amine capping play a critical role in reducing in vivo toxicity and improving the pharmacokinetic behavior of dendrimer-based nanocarriers for therapeutic applications (Kaminskas et al., 2009).

Conclusion

Dendrimers have gained considerable attention as nanocarriers for anticancer drug delivery owing to their well-defined architecture, nanoscale size, and high density of surface functional groups. Their unique structure, comprising a central core, repetitive branching units, and multiple terminal groups, enables efficient drug loading through encapsulation or chemical conjugation, thereby improving the solubility, stability, and bioavailability of many poorly soluble anticancer drugs. Furthermore, surface functionalization with targeting ligands, antibodies, or peptides allows dendrimers to selectively recognize tumor cells, enhancing targeted drug delivery while reducing damage to healthy tissues. Their ability to provide controlled and sustained drug release also contributes to improved therapeutic efficacy. Despite these advantages, challenges such as potential toxicity, immunogenicity, and the complexity of large-scale synthesis remain important considerations for clinical application. Nevertheless, advances in surface engineering strategies, including PEGylation, charge neutralization, and surface coating, have shown significant potential in improving the biocompatibility and safety of dendrimer systems. With continued research and optimization, dendrimers are expected to play an increasingly important role in the development of safer, more effective, and targeted anticancer drug delivery systems.

References

Abbasi, E., Aval, S.F., Akbarzadeh, A., Milani, M., Nasrabadi, H.T., Joo, S.W., Hanifehpour, Y., Nejati-Koshki, K., Pashaei-Asl, R., 2014. Dendrimers: Synthesis, applications, and properties. Nanoscale Res. Lett. 9 (1), 1–10. https://doi.org/10.1186/1556-276X-9-247.

Abedi-Gaballu, F., Dehghan, G., Ghaffari, M., Yekta, R., Abbaspour-Ravasjani, S., Baradaran, B., Ezzati Nazhad Dolatabadi, J., Hamblin, M.R., 2018. PAMAM dendrimers as efficient drug and gene delivery nanosystems for cancer therapy. Appl. Mater. Today 12, 177–190. https://doi.org/10.1016/j.apmt.2018.05.002.

Al-Jamal, K.T., Al-Jamal, W.T., Wang, J.T.W., Rubio, N., Buddle, J., Gathercole, D., Zloh, M., Kostarelos, K., 2013. Cationic poly- L -lysine dendrimer complexes doxorubicin and delays tumor growth in vitro and in vivo. ACS Nano. 7 (3), 1905–1917. https://doi.org/10.1021/nn305860k.

Ambekar, R.S., Choudhary, M., Kandasubramanian, B., 2020. Recent advances in dendrimer-based nanoplatform for cancer treatment: A review. Eur. Polym. J. 126. https://doi.org/10.1016/j.eurpolymj.2020.109546.

Amjad, A.M., 2021. Dendrimers in anticancer targeted drug delivery: Accomplishments, challenges and directions for future. J. Pharm. Pharmacol. 9 (1), 4–16. https://doi.org/10.19163/2307-9266-2021-9-1-4-16.

An, H., Deng, X., Wang, F., Xu, P., Wang, N., 2023. Dendrimers as nanocarriers for the delivery of drugs obtained from natural products. Polymers 15 (10), 2292. https://doi.org/10.3390/polym15102292.

Bae, Y., Lee, J., Kho, C., Choi, J.S., Han, J., 2021. Apoptin gene delivery by a PAMAM dendrimer modified with a nuclear localization signal peptide as a gene carrier for brain cancer therapy. Korean J. Physiol. Pharmacol. 25 (5), 467–478. https://doi.org/10.4196/kjpp.2021.25.5.467.

Beg, S., Swain, S., Rizwan, M., Irfanuddin, M., Shobha Malini, D., 2011. Bioavailability enhancement strategies: Basics, formulation approaches and regulatory considerations. Curr. Drug Deliv. 8 (6), 691–702. https://doi.org/10.2174/156720111797635504.

Boas, U., Christensen, J.B., Heegaard, P.M.H., 2007. Dendrimers in Medicine and Biotechnology: New Molecular Tools Dendrimers in Medicine and Biotechnology: New Molecular Tools. RSC, Denmark, pp. 1–191. https://doi.org/10.1039/9781847552679.

Camacho, C., Tomás, H., Rodrigues, J., 2021. Use of half-generation PAMAM dendrimers (G0.5–G3.5) with carboxylate end-groups to improve the DACHPtCl2 and 5-FU efficacy as anticancer drugs. Molecules 26 (10), 2924. https://doi.org/10.3390/molecules26102924.

Cheng, Y., Xu, Z., Ma, M., Xu, T., 2008. Dendrimers as drug carriers: Applications in different routes of drug administration. J. Pharmaceut. Sci. 97 (1), 123–143. https://doi.org/10.1002/jps.21079.

Chi, T., Sang, T., Wang, Y., Ye, Z., 2024. Cleavage and noncleavage chemistry in reactive oxygen species (ROS)-Responsive materials for smart drug delivery. Bioconjug. Chem. 35 (1), 1–21. https://doi.org/10.1021/acs.bioconjchem.3c00476.

Choudhury, H., Pandey, M., Wen, L.P., Cien, L.K., Xin, H., Yee, A.N.J., Lee, N.J., Gorain, B., Amin, M.C.I.M., Pichika, M.R., 2020. Folic acid conjugated nanocarriers for efficient targetability and promising anticancer efficacy for treatment of breast cancer: A review of recent up-dates. Curr. Pharm. Des. 26 (42), 5365–5379. https://doi.org/10.2174/1381612826666200721000958.

Darbre, T., Reymond, J.L., 2006. Peptide dendrimers as artificial enzymes, receptors, and drug-delivery agents. Acc. Chem. Res. 39 (12), 925–934. https://doi.org/10.1021/ar050203y.

Dobrovolskaia, M.A., Patri, A.K., Simak, J., Hall, J.B., Semberova, J., De Paoli Lacerda, S.H., McNeil, S.E., 2012. Nanoparticle size and surface charge determine effects of PAMAM dendrimers on human platelets in vitro. Mol. Pharm. 9 (3), 382–393. https://doi.org/10.1021/mp200463e.

Domański, D.M., Klajnert, B., Bryszewska, M., 2004. Poland influence of PAMAM dendrimers on human red blood cells. Bioelectrochemistry 63. https://doi.org/10.1016/j.bioelechem.2003.09.023.

El-Sayed, M., Ginski, M., Rhodes, C., Ghandehari, H., 2002. Transepithelial transport of poly (amidoamine) dendrimers across Caco-2 cell monolayers. J. Contr. Release 81 (3), 355–365. https://doi.org/10.1016/S0168-3659(02)00087-1.

Gawande, V., Choudhury, H., Kesharwani, P., 2021. Dendrimer Nomenclature and Synthesis Methods Dendrimer-Based Nanotherapeutics. Elsevier, India, pp. 75–94. https://doi.org/10.1016/B978-0-12-821250-9.00009-3.

Grayson, S.M., Fréchet, J.M.J., 2001. Convergent dendrons and dendrimers: From synthesis to applications. Chem. Rev. 101 (12), 3819–3868. https://doi.org/10.1021/cr990116h.

Gupta, V., Nayak, S.K., 2015. Dendrimers: A review on synthetic approaches. J. Appl. Pharmaceut. Sci. 5 (3), 117–122. https://doi.org/10.7324/JAPS.2015.50321.

Gupta, A., Dubey, S., Mishra, M., 2018. Unique structures, properties and applications of dendrimers. J. Drug Deliv. Therapeut. 8 (6-s), 328–339. https://doi.org/10.22270/jddt.v8i6-s.2083.

Han, M.H., Chen, J., Wang, J., Chen, S.L., Wang, X.T., 2010. Blood compatibility of polyamidoamine dendrimers and erythrocyte protection. J. Biomed. Nanotechnol. 6 (1), 82–92. https://doi.org/10.1166/jbn.2010.1096.

Hassani, F., Heydarinasab, A., Ahmad Panahi, H., Moniri, E., 2023. Surface modification of tungsten disulfide nanosheets with pH/thermosensitive polymer and polyethylenimine dendrimer for near-infrared triggered drug delivery of letrozole. J. Mol. Liq. 371, 121058. https://doi.org/10.1016/j.molliq.2022.121058.

Hooshyar, S.P., Mehrabian, R.Z., Panahi, H.A., Jouybari, M.H., Jalilian, H., 2019. Synthesis and characterization of magnetized-PEGylated dendrimer anchored to thermosensitive polymer for letrozole drug delivery. Colloids Surf. B Biointerfaces 176, 404–411. https://doi.org/10.1016/j.colsurfb.2019.01.014.

Hu, W., Cheng, L., Cheng, L., Zheng, M., Lei, Q., Hu, Z., Xu, M., Qiu, L., Chen, D., 2014. Redox and pH-responsive poly (amidoamine) dendrimer-poly (ethylene glycol) conjugates with disulfide linkages for efficient intracellular drug release. Colloids Surf. B Biointerfaces 123, 254–263. https://doi.org/10.1016/j.colsurfb.2014.09.024.

Irfan, M., Saeed, A., Akram, S., bin Yameen, S., 2020. Dendrimers chemistry and applications: A short review. Front. Chem. 1 (1), 29–40. https://doi.org/10.52700/fcs.v1i1.6.

Jain, N.K., Tare, M.S., Mishra, V., Tripathi, P.K., 2015. The development, characterization and in vivo anti-ovarian cancer activity of poly (propylene imine) (PPI)-antibody conjugates containing encapsulated paclitaxel. Nanomed. Nanotechnol. Biol. Med. 11 (1), 207–218. https://doi.org/10.1016/j.nano.2014.09.006.

Jain, K.K., 2009. Application of Nanobiotechnology in Cancer Therapeutics Pharmaceutical Perspectives of Cancer Therapeutics. Springer US, Switzerland, pp. 245–268. https://doi.org/10.1007/978-1-4419-0131-6_8.

Jamshidpour, A., Samadi Zadeh, M., Ahmad Panahi, H., Rafiee, A., 2024. Synthesis of stimuli-responsive platform based on polyester dendrimer conjugated to thermo-sensitive polymer coated nanodiamonds as paclitaxel drug delivery system on MCF-7 cell line: An efficient near-infrared photo-thermal therapeutic. J. Polym. Environ. 32 (9), 4268–4281. https://doi.org/10.1007/s10924-024-03213-9.

Janaszewska, A., Lazniewska, J., Trzepiński, P., Marcinkowska, M., Klajnert-Maculewicz, B., 2019. Cytotoxicity of dendrimers. Biomolecules 9 (8), 330. https://doi.org/10.3390/biom9080330.

Jin, Y., Ren, X., Wang, W., Ke, L., Ning, E., Du, L., Bradshaw, J., 2011. A 5-fluorouracil-loaded pH-responsive dendrimer nanocarrier for tumor targeting. Int. J. Pharm. 420 (2), 378–384. https://doi.org/10.1016/j.ijpharm.2011.08.053.

Kaminskas, L.M., Wu, Z., Barlow, N., Krippner, G.Y., Boyd, B.J., Porter, C.J.H., 2009. Partly-PEGylated poly-L-lysine dendrimers have reduced plasma stability and circulation times compared with fully PEGylated dendrimers. J. Pharmaceut. Sci. 98 (10), 3871–3875. https://doi.org/10.1002/jps.21692.

Kaminskas, L.M., Kelly, B.D., McLeod, V.M., Sberna, G., Owen, D.J., Boyd, B.J., Porter, C.J.H., 2011. Characterisation and tumour targeting of PEGylated polylysine dendrimers bearing doxorubicin via a pH labile linker. J. Contr. Release 152 (2), 241–248. https://doi.org/10.1016/j.jconrel.2011.02.005.

Kaminskas, L.M., McLeod, V.M., Kelly, B.D., Sberna, G., Boyd, B.J., Williamson, M., Owen, D.J., Porter, C.J.H., 2012. A comparison of changes to doxorubicin pharmacokinetics, antitumor activity, and toxicity mediated by PEGylated dendrimer and PEGylated liposome drug delivery systems. Nanomed. Nanotechnol. Biol. Med. 8 (1), 103–111. https://doi.org/10.1016/j.nano.2011.05.013.

Kawaguchi, T., Moore, J.S., Walker, K.L., Wilkins, C.L., 1995. Double exponential dendrimer growth. J. Am. Chem. Soc. 117 (8), 2159–2165. https://doi.org/10.1021/ja00113a005.

Kesharwani, P., Iyer, A.K., 2015. Recent advances in dendrimer-based nanovectors for tumor-targeted drug and gene delivery. Drug Discov. Today 20 (5), 536–547. https://doi.org/10.1016/j.drudis.2014.12.012.

Kesharwani, P., Gajbhiye, V., Tekade, R.K., Jain, N.K., 2011. Evaluation of dendrimer safety and efficacy through cell line studies. Curr. Drug Targets 12 (10), 1478–1497. https://doi.org/10.2174/138945011796818135.

Kharwade, R., Badole, P., Mahajan, N., More, S., 2022. Toxicity and surface modification of dendrimers: A critical review. Curr. Drug Deliv. 19 (4), 451–465. https://doi.org/10.2174/1567201818666211021160441.

Kianamiri, S., Dinari, A., Sadeghizadeh, M., Rezaei, M., Daraei, B., Bahsoun, N.E.H., Nomani, A., Sadeghizadeh, M., Nomani, A., 2020. Mitochondria-targeted polyamidoamine dendrimer-curcumin construct for hepatocellular cancer treatment. Mol. Pharm. 17 (12), 4483–4498. https://doi.org/10.1021/acs.molpharmaceut.0c00566.

Kukowska-Latallo, J.F., Candido, K.A., Cao, Z., Nigavekar, S.S., Majoros, I.J., Thomas, T.P., Balogh, L.P., Khan, M. K., Baker, J.R., 2005. Nanoparticle targeting of anticancer drug improves therapeutic response in animal model of human epithelial cancer. Cancer Res. 65 (12), 5317–5324. https://doi.org/10.1158/0008-5472.CAN-04-3921.

Kulhari, H., Pooja, D., Shrivastava, S., Kuncha, M., Naidu, V.G.M., Bansal, V., Sistla, R., Adams, D.J., 2016. Trastuzumab-grafted PAMAM dendrimers for the selective delivery of anticancer drugs to HER2-positive breast cancer. Sci. Rep. 6. https://doi.org/10.1038/srep23179.

Kurtoglu, Y.E., Navath, R.S., Wang, B., Kannan, S., Romero, R., Kannan, R.M., 2009. Poly (amidoamine) dendrimer-drug conjugates with disulfide linkages for intracellular drug delivery. Biomaterials 30 (11), 2112–2121. https://doi.org/10.1016/j.biomaterials.2008.12.054.

Li, M.H., Choi, S.K., Thomas, T.P., Desai, A., Lee, K.H., Kotlyar, A., Banaszak Holl, M.M., Baker, J.R., 2012. Dendrimer-based multivalent methotrexates as dual acting nanoconjugates for cancer cell targeting. Eur. J. Med. Chem. 47 (1), 560–572. https://doi.org/10.1016/j.ejmech.2011.11.027.

Li, L., Deng, Y., Zeng, Y., Yan, B., Deng, Y., Zheng, Z., Li, S., Yang, Y., Jinwei, H., Xiao, X., Wang, X., 2023. The application advances of dendrimers in biomedical field. View 4 (6). https://doi.org/10.1002/viw.20230023.

Lo, S.T., Stern, S., Clogston, J.D., Zheng, J., Adiseshaiah, P.P., Dobrovolskaia, M., Lim, J., Patri, A.K., Sun, X., Simanek, E.E., 2010. Biological assessment of triazine dendrimer: Toxicological profiles, solution behavior, biodistribution, drug release and efficacy in a PEGylated, paclitaxel construct. Mol. Pharm. 7 (4), 993–1006. https://doi.org/10.1021/mp100104x.

Luong, D., Kesharwani, P., Deshmukh, R., Mohd Amin, M.C.I., Gupta, U., Greish, K., Iyer, A.K., 2016. PEGylated PAMAM dendrimers: Enhancing efficacy and mitigating toxicity for effective anticancer drug and gene delivery. Acta Biomater. 43, 14–29. https://doi.org/10.1016/j.actbio.2016.07.015.

Ma, P., Yu, H., Zhang, X., Mu, H., Chu, Y., Ni, L., Xing, P., Wang, Y., Sun, K., 2017. Increased active tumor targeting by an αvβ3-targeting and cell-penetrating bifunctional peptide-mediated dendrimer-based conjugate. Pharm. Res. 34 (1), 121–135. https://doi.org/10.1007/s11095-016-2045-7.

Maiti, P.K., Çağın, T., Wang, G., Goddard, W.A., 2004. Structure of PAMAM dendrimers: Generations 1 through 11. Macromolecules 37 (16), 6236–6254. https://doi.org/10.1021/ma035629b.

Malik, N., Evagorou, E.G., Duncan, R., 1999. Dendrimer-platinate: A novel approach to cancer chemotherapy. Anti Cancer Drugs 10 (8), 767–776. https://doi.org/10.1097/00001813-199909000-00010.

Malik, N., Wiwattanapatapee, R., Klopsch, R., Lorenz, K., Frey, H., Weener, J.W., Meijer, E.W., Paulus, W., Duncan, R., 2000. Dendrimers: Relationship between structure and biocompatibility in vitro, and preliminary studies on the biodistribution of 125I-labelled polyamidoamine dendrimers in vivo. J. Contr. Release 65 (1–2), 133–148. https://doi.org/10.1016/S0168-3659(99)00246-1.

Maraval, V., Laurent, R., Marchand, P., Caminade, A.M., Majoral, J.P., 2005. Accelerated methods of synthesis of phosphorus-containing dendrimers. J. Organomet. Chem. 690. https://doi.org/10.1016/j.jorganchem.2004.10.021.

Marcinkowska, M., Stanczyk, M., Janaszewska, A., Sobierajska, E., Chworos, A., Klajnert-Maculewicz, B., 2019. multicomponent conjugates of anticancer drugs and monoclonal antibody with PAMAM dendrimers to increase efficacy of HER-2 positive breast cancer therapy. Pharm. Res. 36 (11). https://doi.org/10.1007/s11095-019-2683-7.

Mariyam, M., Ghosal, K., Thomas, S., Kalarikkal, N., Latha, M.S., 2018. Dendrimers: General aspects, applications and structural exploitations as prodrug/drug-delivery vehicles in current medicine. Mini Rev. Med. Chem. 18 (5), 439–457. https://doi.org/10.2174/1389557517666170512095151.

Mhlwatika, Z., Aderibigbe, B.A., 2018. Application of dendrimers for the treatment of infectious diseases. Molecules 23 (9), 2205. https://doi.org/10.3390/molecules23092205.

Miller, T.M., Neenan, T.X., 1990. Convergent synthesis of monodisperse dendrimers based upon 1,3,5-trisubstituted benzenes. Chem. Mater. 2 (4), 346–349. https://doi.org/10.1021/cm00010a006.

Morgan, M.T., Nakanishi, Y., Kroll, D.J., Griset, A.P., Carnahan, M.A., Wathier, M., Oberlies, N.H., Manikumar, G., Wani, M.C., Grinstaff, M.W., 2006. Dendrimer-encapsulated camptothecins: Increased solubility, cellular uptake, and cellular retention affords enhanced anticancer activity in vitro. Cancer Res. 66 (24), 11913–11921. https://doi.org/10.1158/0008-5472.CAN-06-2066.

Murrar, A.J.Y., 2018. Brownian Dynamics Simulations for Complexation of DNA with Nano-Cationic Dendrimers. AL-Quds University.

Naha, P.C., Davoren, M., Lyng, F.M., Byrne, H.J., 2010. Reactive oxygen species (ROS) induced cytokine production and cytotoxicity of PAMAM dendrimers in J774A.1 cells. Toxicol. Appl. Pharmacol. 246 (1–2), 91–99. https://doi.org/10.1016/j.taap.2010.04.014.

Navath, R.S., Kurtoglu, Y.E., Wang, B., Kannan, S., Romero, R., Kannan, R.M., 2008. Dendrimer-drug conjugates for tailored intracellular drug release based on glutathione levels. Bioconjug. Chem. 19 (12), 2446–2455. https://doi.org/10.1021/bc800342d.

Ooya, T., Lee, J., Park, K., 2004. Hydrotropic dendrimers of generations 4 and 5: Synthesis, characterization, and hydrotropic solubilization of paclitaxel. Bioconjug. Chem. 15 (6), 1221–1229. https://doi.org/10.1021/bc049814l.

Öztürk, K., Esendağlı, G., Gürbüz, M.U., Tülü, M., Çalış, S., 2017. Effective targeting of gemcitabine to pancreatic cancer through PEG-cored Flt-1 antibody-conjugated dendrimers. Int. J. Pharm. 517 (1–2), 157–167. https://doi.org/10.1016/j.ijpharm.2016.12.009.

Parshad, B., Arora, S., Singh, B., Pan, Y., Tang, J., Hu, Z., Patra, H.K., 2025. Towards precision medicine using biochemically triggered cleavable conjugation. Commun. Chem. 8 (1). https://doi.org/10.1038/s42004-025-01491-5.

Patel, P., Patel, V., Patel, P.M., 2022. Synthetic strategy of dendrimers: A review. J. Indian Chem. Soc. 99 (7), 100514. https://doi.org/10.1016/j.jics.2022.100514.

Pérez-Ferreiro, M., Abelairas, A.M., Criado, A., Gómez, I.J., Mosquera, J., 2023. Dendrimers: Exploring their wide structural variety and applications. Polymers 15 (22). https://doi.org/10.3390/polym15224369.

Rinaldi, A., Caraffi, R., Grazioli, M.V., Oddone, N., Giardino, L., Tosi, G., Vandelli, M.A., Calzà, L., Ruozi, B., Duskey, J.T., 2022. Applications of the ROS-responsive thioketal linker for the production of smart nanomedicines. Polymers 14 (4). https://doi.org/10.3390/polym14040687.

Roberts, J.C., Bhalgat, M.K., Zera, R.T., 1996. Preliminary biological evaluation of polyamidoamine (PAMAM) StarburstTM dendrimers. J. Biomed. Mater. Res. 30 (1), 53–65.

Sahoo, R.K., Kumar, H., Jain, V., Sinha, S., Ajazuddin, N., Gupta, U., 2023. Angiopep-2 grafted PAMAM dendrimers for the targeted delivery of temozolomide: In vitro and in vivo effects of PEGylation in the management of glioblastoma multiforme. ACS Biomater. Sci. Eng. 9 (7), 4288–4301. https://doi.org/10.1021/acsbiomaterials.3c00263.

Salem, M., 2014. Curcumin-Loaded Magnetic Nanoaggregates Conjugated with Folic Acid for Targeted Cancer Treatment. The University of Western Ontario, Canada.

Sánchez-Navarro, M., Rojo, J., 2012. Synthetic strategies to create dendrimers: Advantages and drawbacks. Front. Nanosci. 4, 143–156. https://doi.org/10.1016/B978-0-12-415769-9.00005-4.

Saovapakhiran, A., D'Emanuele, A., Attwood, D., Penny, J., 2009. Surface modification of PAMAM dendrimers modulates the mechanism of cellular internalization. Bioconjug. Chem. 20 (4), 693–701. https://doi.org/10.1021/bc8002343.

Singh, P., Gupta, U., Asthana, A., Jain, N.K., 2008. Folate and folate-PEG-PAMAM dendrimers: Synthesis, characterization, and targeted anticancer drug delivery potential in tumor bearing mice. Bioconjug. Chem. 19 (11), 2239–2252. https://doi.org/10.1021/bc800125u.

Singh, J., Jain, K., Mehra, N.K., Jain, N.K., 2016. Dendrimers in anticancer drug delivery: Mechanism of interaction of drug and dendrimers. Artif. Cells Nanomed. Biotechnol. 44 (7), 1626–1634. https://doi.org/10.3109/21691401.2015.1129625.

Svenson, S., Chauhan, A.S., 2008. Dendrimers for enhanced drug solubilization. Nanomedicine 3 (5), 679–702. https://doi.org/10.2217/17435889.3.5.679.

Szota, M., Jachimska, B., 2023. Effect of alkaline conditions on forming an effective G4.0 PAMAM complex with doxorubicin. Pharmaceutics 15 (3), 875. https://doi.org/10.3390/pharmaceutics15030875.

Tarach, P., Janaszewska, A., 2021. Recent advances in preclinical research using PAMAM dendrimers for cancer gene therapy. Int. J. Mol. Sci. 22 (6), 2912. https://doi.org/10.3390/ijms22062912.

Tekade, R.K., Dutta, T., Tyagi, A., Bharti, A.C., Das, B.C., Jain, N.K., 2008. Surface-engineered dendrimers for dual drug delivery: A receptor up-regulation and enhanced cancer targeting strategy. J. Drug Target. 16 (10), 758–772. https://doi.org/10.1080/10611860802473154.

Thakur, A., Sharma, A., 2021. Synthesis of Dendrimers. Dendrimers in Nanomedicine. CRC Press, pp. 89–122.

Tokarczyk, K., Jachimska, B., 2019. Characterization of G4 PAMAM dendrimer complexes with 5-fluorouracil and their interactions with bovine serum albumin. Colloids Surf. A Physicochem. Eng. Asp. 561, 357–363. https://doi.org/10.1016/j.colsurfa.2018.10.080.

Tomalia, D.A., Naylor, A.M., Goddard, W.A., Dendrimers, S., 1990. Molecular-level control of size, shape, surface chemistry, Topology, and flexibility from atoms to macroscopic matter. Angew Chem. Int. Ed. Engl. 29 (2), 138–175. https://doi.org/10.1002/anie.199001381.

Tunki, L., Kulhari, H., Sistla, R., Pooja, D., 2019. Dendrimer-Based Targeted Drug Delivery Pharmaceutical Applications of Dendrimers. Elsevier, India, pp. 107–129. https://doi.org/10.1016/B978-0-12-814527-2.00005-6.

Vögtle, F., Richardt, G., Werner, N., 2009. Dendrimer Chemistry: Concepts, Syntheses, Properties, Applications. Wiley. https://doi.org/10.1002/9783527626953.

Wang, H., Huang, Q., Chang, H., Xiao, J., Cheng, Y., 2016. Stimuli-responsive dendrimers in drug delivery. Biomater. Sci. 4 (3), 375–390. https://doi.org/10.1039/c5bm00532a.

Wang, J., Li, B., Qiu, L., Qiao, X., Yang, H., 2022. Dendrimer-based drug delivery systems: History, challenges, and latest developments. J. Biol. Eng. 16 (1). https://doi.org/10.1186/s13036-022-00298-5.

Wu, L.P., Ficker, M., Christensen, J.B., Simberg, D., Trohopoulos, P.N., Moghimi, S.M., 2021. Dendrimer end-terminal motif-dependent evasion of human complement and complement activation through IgM hitchhiking. Nat. Commun. 12 (1). https://doi.org/10.1038/s41467-021-24960-6.

Xu, Z., Kahr, M., Walker, K.L., Wilkins, C.L., Moore, J.S., 1994. Phenylacetylene dendrimers by the divergent, convergent, and double-stage convergent methods. J. Am. Chem. Soc. 116 (11), 4537–4550. https://doi.org/10.1021/ja00090a002.

Xu, X.L., Li, J.J., Han, S.P., Tao, C.H., Fang, L., Sun, Y., Zhu, J.Z., Liang, Z.H., Li, F.Z., 2016. A novel doxorubicin loaded folic acid conjugated PAMAM modified with borneol, a nature dual-functional product of reducing PAMAM toxicity and boosting BBB penetration. Eur. J. Pharmaceut. Sci. 88, 178–190. https://doi.org/10.1016/j.ejps.2016.02.015.

Yellepeddi, V.K., Vangara, K.K., Palakurthi, S., 2013. Poly (amido) amine (PAMAM) dendrimer–cisplatin complexes for chemotherapy of cisplatin-resistant ovarian cancer cells. J. Nanoparticle Res. 15 (9), 1897.

Yuan, H., Luo, K., Lai, Y., Pu, Y., He, B., Wang, G., Wu, Y., Gu, Z., 2010. A novel poly (l -glutamic acid) dendrimer based drug delivery system with both pH-sensitive and targeting functions. Mol. Pharm. 7 (4), 953–962. https://doi.org/10.1021/mp1000923.

Zhang, M., Zhu, J., Zheng, Y., Guo, R., Wang, S., Mignani, S., Caminade, A.M., Majoral, J.P., Shi, X., 2018. Doxorubicin-conjugated PAMAM dendrimers for pH-responsive drug release and folic acid-targeted cancer therapy. Pharmaceutics 10 (3). https://doi.org/10.3390/pharmaceutics10030162.

Zong, H., Thomas, T.P., Lee, K.H., Desai, A.M., Li, M.H., Kotlyar, A., Zhang, Y., Leroueil, P.R., Gam, J.J., Holl, M.M. B., Baker, J.R., 2012. Bifunctional PAMAM dendrimer conjugates of folic acid and methotrexate with defined ratio. Biomacromolecules 13 (4), 982–991. https://doi.org/10.1021/bm201639c.

CHAPTER

15

Advances in metallic nanoparticles for anticancer drug delivery

Swati Dubey[1], Bintu Wadhwani[2], Mahima Chauhan[3], Girish Kumar[4], Tarun Virmani[4] and Kamla Pathak[5]

[1]Maharishi Arvind College of Pharmacy, Jaipur, Rajasthan, India; [2]Institute of Chemical Technology (ICT), Mumbai, Maharashtra, India; [3]HIMT College of Pharmacy, Greater Noida, Uttar Pradesh, India; [4]Amity University, Greater Noida, Uttar Pradesh, India; [5]Faculty of Pharmacy, Uttar Pradesh University of Medical Sciences, Saifai, Uttar Pradesh, India

Introduction

Cancer treatments often face challenges from drug resistance, which stems from several interconnected processes. A primary cause is drug deactivation, where cancer cells break down or chemically modify drugs, reducing their effectiveness (Li et al., 2021). Similarly, cancer cells can alter drug targets, decrease drug binding, and make treatments less effective. Resistance is further amplified by evasion of apoptosis, allowing cancer cells to avoid programmed cell death, and by drug efflux mechanisms, where transport proteins pump drugs out of the cell, lowering their internal concentrations (Catalano et al., 2022). Additionally, many cancer cells have an increased ability to repair DNA damage, counteracting the effects of DNA-targeted therapies. Tumor heterogeneity adds more complexity, as genetic and phenotypic diversity exists within a single tumor, complicating uniform treatment delivery. The tumor microenvironment (TME) also plays a crucial role by helping cancer cells evade immune responses (Khalaf et al., 2021). Moreover, genomic instability results in mutation rates that can decrease cancer cell invasiveness. Cancer cells often modify the lipid layer of their membranes, making them more rigid and resistant. This change blocks the entry of chemotherapeutic drugs and reduces their effectiveness (Hheidari et al., 2024). Drug resistance remains a complex, multifaceted issue that can arise from genome changes, interactions with TME, immune responses, and other factors. To address these challenges, multi-targeted therapies are needed to tailor treatment to patients' specific resistance profiles (Nussinov et al., 2021; Luque-Bolivar et al., 2020).

Advanced Cancer Therapeutics
https://doi.org/10.1016/B978-0-443-44185-1.00025-2

In this context, nanotechnology has become a promising option to overcome cancer treatment challenges and drug resistance. Metallic nanoparticles (MNPs) are one of the acceptable and researched platforms for cancer treatment and diagnosis owing to their large surface-to-volume ratio, size, and surface tunability, modified drug release kinetics, coloading potential, and multifunctionality (Tuli et al., 2023). However, the application of MNPs is restricted because of inherent issues, such as nonspecific biodistribution, fast reticuloendothelial clearance, unwanted cytotoxicity to healthy cells, and low stability (Tahir Aminzai et al., 2024). These issues necessitated new advancements in MNPs for drug delivery to cancer cells. This chapter discusses recent advancements in MNPs, including surface functionalization with polymers, lipids, genetic materials, small molecules, targeting ligands, or stimuli-responsive moieties for effective cancer therapy.

Metallic nanoparticles

MNPs have gained widespread popularity in cancer research due to their extraordinary physicochemical characteristics. MNPs of silver, copper, gold, iron, zinc, and platinum exhibit specific surface, electronic, magnetic, and optical characteristics that can be exploited in optical imaging, biosensing, diagnosis, drug delivery, catalysts, and cancer therapy (Dubey et al., 2025). MNPs can generate reactive oxygen species (ROS) by disturbing mitochondrial function, which triggers DNA damage and induces apoptosis in cancer cells (Mustafa et al., 2025). MNPs can be used for safe and effective delivery of linked or entrapped chemotherapeutic drugs, imaging agents, or nucleic acids (Shahalaei et al., 2024). In addition, MNP with a modified surface can improve payload efficacy by improving systemic circulation, minimizing nonselective distribution, and directing delivery to the target site. Researchers are exploring bimetallic nanoparticle design, using two or more metals together or with metal oxides to obtain synergistic catalytic, optical, and therapeutic action for next-generation therapies (Gutiérrez-Cruz et al., 2025). Continuity in green synthesis using biopolymers and a targeted drug delivery approach can result in a safer nanoparticle with minimal toxicities and precise delivery for better cancer management.

Properties

MNPs are nanoscale materials having a size range between 1 and 100 nm. MNPs thus exhibit a large surface area to volume ratio and high quantum effects responsible for higher optical, magnetic, catalytic, and electrical characteristics, compared to bulk metals (Patel et al., 2024). Localized surface plasmon resonance triggered by incident light is one of the remarkable properties, where conduction electrons oscillate collectively. Therefore optical properties are size and shape dependent, requiring a perfect tuning between scattering and absorption through infrared and visible spectra, which can be easily attained with MNPs. Silver and gold nanoparticles have shown different colors at different time intervals due to the surface plasmon effect and have been exploited for photothermal, imaging, and biosensing applications (Ben Amor et al., 2024; Jha et al., 2023). Mechanical, thermal, and chemical properties of MNPs are significantly different from their bulk counterparts (Truong et al., 2024; Chen et al., 2025). A few MNPs (cobalt, iron, and nickel) exhibit superparamagnetic properties that can be used in magnetic field-guided delivery to the target site and magnetic resonance imaging (Ansari et al., 2019). The size, shape, and morphology also determine the bioactivity of MNPs. Small-sized MPPs can have rapid interaction with biological membranes or proteins, while MNPs' composition and surface determine the stability in systemic circulation and specificity toward cancer cells (Saadh et al., 2025).

Anticancer mechanism

MNPs can aid the delivery of anticancer drugs to the tumor site for cellular internalization in cancer cells. Currently, drug-equipped MNPs are being developed to have biological membrane-simulated structures for better monitoring of cellular dynamics and drug kinetics (by facilitating membrane/subcellular trafficking events such as fusion, transplantation, internalization, sequestration, perinuclear localization, and subsequent drug release) (Maji et al., 2018). Surface-modified MNPs can aid drug transport to the tumor site, where they can interact with cancer cells and the nucleus, facilitating the drug's entry. This allows selective damage to cancer cells while protecting normal cells (Mazzaglia et al., 2018). Once the drug enters the cancer cells, it exerts its action by monitoring altered proteins or markers, inhibiting cancer cell growth via regulation of DNA replication, cell cycle arrest, apoptosis, and angiogenesis suppression (Liu et al., 2024). MNPs can gain entry into cancer cells via passive and active targeting. The passive mechanism exploits impaired lymphatic drainage and leaky blood vessels in cancer cells, which allows MNPs to accumulate in cancer cells. This process is known as the enhanced permeability and retention (EPR) effect. However, it does not fit where the EPR effect is limited, and vascularization is poor (Rahim et al., 2021). Active mechanism allows selective delivery to cancer cells by use of targeting ligands such as peptides, antibodies, and small molecules (Nisha et al., 2024). Targeting ligands recognize specific receptors on cancer cells' surface and gain entry via receptor-mediated endocytosis (Argenziano et al., 2021). A dual targeting strategy can also be employed for improving therapeutic action, minimizing organ toxicity, and avoiding drug resistance. The MNPs can also exert anticancer action, providing a synergic effect with linked/entrapped or loaded anticancer drugs.

Advancements in metallic nanoparticles

Biogenic MNPs

Traditional methods of MNPs synthesis involve the use of dangerous or toxic chemical compounds, costly lab equipment, and operation under specific conditions (Todaria et al., 2024). This necessitated a search for alternative techniques for the development of MNPs. To achieve this, biological sources such as plants, bacteria, algae, and fungi have been utilized for MNPs synthesis, known as biogenic MNPs. Compounds found in plants and microbial extracts can transform metal precursors into nanoparticles (Dubey et al., 2024).

Biomolecules function as in situ reducing and capping agents by changing the oxidation state of metal salts from positive to zero and stabilizing the newly formed MNPs to prevent their aggregation by forming a monolayer around them (Patil et al., 2022). For example, biogenic gold nanoparticles were developed by Hellany et al. utilizing *Scabiosa palaestina* for the treatment of cancer. The developed biogenic MNPs were uniformly distributed and spherical, having an absorption at 560 nm and a particle size of 9.9 nm. The developed biogenic MNPs showed potent anticancer activity against MDA-MB-231 and 22Rv1 cell lines, with a reduction in cell viability to $17.48 \pm 8.3\%$ and $16.04 \pm 1.8\%$, respectively, at 100 μg/mL after 3 days (Hellany et al., 2025). Keerthirathna et al. (2025) prepared silver nanoparticles from *Chnoospora minima* using polysaccharides as reducing agents. Silver nanoparticles showed strong potential toward lung cancer (A549 cell line), with an IC_{50} of 13.59 μg/mL, and suggested biocompatible nanotherapeutics (Keerthirathna et al., 2025). Alamelu et al. (2025) developed and characterized the brucine–gold nanoparticles and tested them in vitro against the breast cancer (MCF-7) cell line with an IC_{50} value of 11.47 μg/mL. Results depicted a reduction in cell viability in a dose-dependent manner and promised the successful treatment for targeted breast cancer (Alamelu et al., 2025). A list of biogenic MNPs used for cancer treatment has been given in Table 15.1.

Metal oxide nanoparticles (MONPs) exhibited additional catalytic, semiconductor, and magnetic properties, which make them highly suitable candidates for cancer treatment (targeting and imaging). Among various metal oxides, zinc oxide, titanium dioxide, iron oxide, and silicon dioxide are specifically prominent in cancer research (Joshi et al., 2023). Kimta et al. investigated the crude ethanolic extract of *Adiantum venustum* for the green synthesis of copper oxide nanoparticles (CuO NPs) against cervical cancer. The HeLa cell line depicted an IC50 of 138.07 μg/mL; the findings suggest a promising approach toward biomedical applications (Kimta et al., 2025). Thajuddin et al. (2025) reported that aqueous extract of *Limnospira fusiformis*, utilized for the green synthesis of titanium dioxide nanoparticles (TiO_2 NPs) in biomedicine, showed cytotoxicity against the breast cancer MDA-MB-231 cell line (IC_{50} value - 10 μg/mL) and highlights the broad application of titanium oxide nanoparticles (Thajuddin et al., 2025). Various metal oxide nanoparticles having anticancer activity are given in Table 15.1.

Bimetallic nanoparticles

Bimetallic nanoparticles are a fast-growing category of MNPs for tumor treatment, because they offer synergistic potential that was not attained in monometallic classes. Here, two metals are combined with a metal oxide, which ultimately enhances stability, catalytic properties, optical activity, and therapeutic potential (Goswami et al., 2025). Commonly, experiments with bimetallic nanoparticles are silver–gold, silver–copper oxide, silver–zinc oxide, etc. (Ismail and Dawes, 2022). Chen et al. investigated the biosynthesized bimetallic silver-copper oxide nanoparticles using endophytic *Clonostachys rosea* ZMS36 from the plant *Anemarrhena asphodeloides* and evaluated biomedical applications, displaying cytotoxicity on HeLa, PDSF, and A549 cell lines with IC50 values of 7.53, 35.03, and 14.93 μg/mL, suggesting their potential in cancer treatment (Chen et al., 2025). Bhiradi

TABLE 15.1 Biogenic metallic nanoparticles for cancer treatment.

Type of extract	Type of nanoparticle	Size (nm)	Anticancer profile	References
Ethanolic leaf extract of *Zinnia elegans*	Silver nanoparticles (AgNPs)	95	Glioblastoma (U-87) cell line IC_{50} value: 0.94 μg/mL	Fakhredin et al. (2025)
Shell extract of *Tamarindus indica*	Silver nanoparticles (AgNPs)	20–52	Breast cancer (MCF-7) cell line IC_{50} value: 20 μg/mL	Gomathi et al. (2020)
Leaf extract of *Ardisia gigantifolia*	Silver nanoparticles (AgNPs)	6	Gastric cancer IC_{50} value: 1.37 and 0.65 μg/mL for Adenocarcinoma gastric stomach (AGS) cell line and 1.03 and 0.96 μg/mL for MKN49 cell line	Le et al. (2023)
Leaf extract of *Syzygium malaccense*	Silver nanoparticles (AgNPs)	40.1	Lung cancer LD_{50} value: 7.62 μg/mL for A549 and 73.55 μg/mL for L-132 cell line	Herbin et al. (2022)
Coffea arabica husk extract	Silver nanoparticles (AgNPs)	147	Breast cancer (MCF-7) cell line IC_{50} value: 16.7 μg/mL	Kavin et al. (2025)
Jasminum sambac leaves	Copper nanoparticle (CuNPs)	180.7	Breast cancer (MCF-7) cell line IC_{50} value: 372 μg/mL	Bidan and Al-Ali (2025)
Pistacia khinjuk leaf extract	Copper nanoparticle (CuNPs)	10–70	IC_{50} value: 322, 365, 247, and 273 μg/mL on NCI–H660, DU 145, Lymph node carcinoma of prostate (LNCaP)[a] Clone FGC, and LNCaP clone FGC-Luc2	Wang et al. (2024)
Priestia megaterium cell-free extract	Copper nanoparticles (CuNPs)	57.73	Human colon epithelial colorectal adenocarcinoma Caco–2– HTB–37 cell lines IC_{50} value: 175.36 μg/mL	Mohamed et al. (2024)
Punica granatum plant extract	Iron nanoparticles (FeNPs)	10 to 40	Prostate cancer (NCI–H660 and DU 145) cell line IC_{50} value: 110 and 117 μg/mL	Jia et al. (2024)
Hydroalcoholic extract of *Lavandula stoechas* L	Zinc nanoparticles (ZnNPs)	40 to 50	Human colon cancer and breast cancer (HT29 and MCF-7 cell lines IC_{50} value: 65.42 μg/mL and 54.65 μg/mL	Mehdipour et al. (2024)
Gelatin and curcumin	Platinum nanoparticles (PtNPs)	120–200	Breast and liver cancer (MCF-7 and HepG2 cell line) IC_{50} value: 6.450 and 7.992 μg/mL	Ünal et al. (2025)
Aspergillus fungus extract	Titanium dioxide nanoparticles (TiO_2 NPs)	1.36 to 20	Breast and liver cancer (MCF-7 and HepG-2) cell line IC_{50} value: 11.2 ± 0.57 μg/mL and 31.1 ± 1.44 μg/mL	Alhadrami et al. (2025)
Hydroalcoholic extract of *Polygonum cuspidatum*	Titanium dioxide nanoparticles (TiO_2 NPs)	23.2 to 25.4	Human colorectal cancer (Caco-2 cell line) IC_{50} value: 25.8 ± 6.1 μg/mL	Fletes-Vargas et al. (2025)

(*Continued*)

TABLE 15.1 Biogenic metallic nanoparticles for cancer treatment.—cont'd

Type of extract	Type of nanoparticle	Size (nm)	Anticancer profile	References
Vitex negundo leaf extract	Zinc oxide nanoparticles (ZnO NPs)	452.5	Colorectal cancer (HT-29 cell line) IC_{50} value: 60.56 μg/mL	Kowsalya et al. (2025)
Syzygium aromaticum (clove) bud extract	Zinc oxide nanoparticles (ZnO NPs)	249.8	Oral squamous cell carcinoma (HNO-97 cell line) IC_{50} value: 69.3 μg/mL	Hussien et al. (2025)
Aerva lanata leaf extract	Iron oxide nanoparticles (Fe_2O_3 NPs)	91.8	Breast cancer (MDA-MB-231 cell line) IC_{50} value: 158.29 ± 4.78 μg/mL	Nagaraj et al. (2025)
3-Aminopropyl-triethoxysilane (APTES)	Iron oxide nanoparticles (Fe_3O_4)	20	Cervical and breast cancer (HeLa and MDA-MB-231) IC_{50} value: 228 and 160 μg/mL	(Kumar et al., 2018)
Curcuma longa (turmeric) rhizomes	Cerium oxide nanoparticles (CeO_2 NPs)	70	Lung cancer (H460 cell line) Dose: 10 μg/μL	Krisshna Gunasekaran et al. (2025)
Arabic gum and extract of okra (*Abelmoschus esculentus*) fruit	Cerium oxide nanoparticles (CeO_2 NPs)	27.31	Retinoblastoma (Y79 cell line) IC_{50} value: 500 μg/mL	Foroutan et al. (2025)
Schiff base	Copper oxide nanoparticle (CuO NPs)	100	Hepatocellular carcinoma, colon cancer, lung cancer, human fibroblast HepG-2, Caco-2, A549, BJ-1 cell line IC_{50} value: 18.68 ± 0.83 μg/mL, 17.08 ± 1.30 μg/mL, 13.87 ± 2.25 μg/mL, 24.23 ± 0.76 μg/mL	Almehizia et al. (2025)

[a]*LNCaP clone FGC-Luc2 is a luciferase-expressing epithelial-like prostate cell ideal for in vivo bioluminescence imaging in xenograft models or in cell-based assays.*

and Hiremath (2025) examined in situ silver–gold bimetallic nanoparticles for cytotoxicity using the MTT assay for lung cancer (A549 cell line), which depicted the IC50 value of 4.42 μg/mL, showing a promising approach for cancer (Bhiradi and Hiremath, 2025). Various research on bimetallic nanoparticles developed using green synthesis has been summarized in Table 15.2.

Biosurfactants modified MNPs

The possession of biocompatibility, ionic nature, high emulsification, nontoxicity, biodegradability, and being harmless to the environment has made the biosurfactants an appealing stabilizing agent for the development of MNPs in the treatment of cancer (Sarubbo et al., 2022). These are biologically active, naturally occurring, and renewable surfactants, often made by plants and microorganisms. These are mainly developed from a variety of microorganisms, such as fungi, bacteria, and yeast, having distinct structures and properties (Bjerk et al., 2021). Biosurfactants prevent agglomeration and offer prolonged

TABLE 15.2 Bimetallic nanoparticles (BMNPs) preparation using green synthesis approaches.

Type of extract	Type of nanoparticle	Method/ Size (nm)	Anticancer profile	Ref.
Aspergillus Niger	Silver-gold nanoparticles (Ag–Au NPs)	8–10	Hepatocellular carcinoma, lung cancer (HepG2 and A549 cell line) IC_{50} value: 15.57 and 27.07 μg/mL	Abu-Tahon et al. (2025)
Gymnascella dankaliensis	Silver–iron nanoparticles (Ag–Fe BMNPs)	96.76	Breast cancer (MDA-MB-231) IC_{50} value: 1 μg/mL	Patel et al. (2025)
Croton caudatus Geisel leaf extract	Gold–platinum nanoparticles (Au–Pt NPs)	96.76	Cervical cancer (HeLa cell line) IC_{50} value: 37.17 μg/mL	Kumar et al. (2025)
Pluchea indica leaf extract	Silver titanium dioxide nanoparticles (Ag–TiO_2 BNPs)	50	Breast cancer (MCF-7 cell line) IC_{50} value: 33.5 μg/mL	Selim et al. (2025)
Lagenaria siceraria leaf extract	Bimetallic copper oxide-selenium nanoparticles (CuO–Se BNPs)	30	Breast cancer and hepatocellular carcinoma (MCF-7 and HepG2 cell line) IC_{50} value: 31.1 and 83.4 μg/mL	Elkady et al. (2025)

stability by forming stable coats around the MNPs. Biosurfactants stabilize the MNPs by adhering to the surface of MNPs through hydrophilic head groups and preventing the aggregation through steric and electrostatic repulsion. The functional moieties assist in improving biocompatibility and enable conjugation with chemotherapeutic agents or targeting ligands, guaranteeing stable, targeted, and effective delivery (Gayathiri et al., 2022). AgNPs stabilized using surfactin biosurfactant were prepared for cancer treatment. The prepared NPs were uniformly distributed and stable. These NPs exhibited potent antibacterial activity and improved anticancer potential due to apoptosis induction and reduced proliferation of cancer cells (Chauhan et al., 2025). In another example, AgNPs were developed using a biosurfactant derived from *Candida lipolytica*, which showed antimicrobial activity. AgNPs had a particle size of 20 nm with a zeta size of −60 mV, showing their stability due to the presence of biosurfactant. These NPs prevented the growth of all microbial strains at a 16.50 μg/mL concentration. Moreover, the developed NPs were found to be nontoxic at the tested concentrations (Lima et al., 2024).

MNPs with zwitterionic coating

The surface of MNPs can be engineered using zwitterionic polymers to improve cancer treatment. The coating of zwitterionic polymers on MNPs inhibits their aggregation, increases water dispersibility, and safeguards the MNPs from premature destruction (Li et al., 2019). The antifouling characteristic of these polymers reduces the interaction between immune cells and plasma proteins, resulting in prolonged retention of MNPs in the blood circulation. Moreover, zwitterionic polymers can be further functionalized using various ligands, which leads to active targeting of cancer cells (Wen et al., 2024). Some zwitterionic polymer coatings are designed to be redox or pH-responsive, meaning that they release the therapeutic payload in the acidic or reductive TME while staying stable in the blood (neutral pH). This reduces systemic toxicity by guaranteeing site-specific release of nucleic acids, photosensitizers, or chemotherapeutic agents (Qu et al., 2022). For example, a zwitterionic polymer-coated Au@TiO_2 nanoparticles of doxorubicin were developed for cancer treatment. These nanoparticles showed quick attachment to cancer cells under an acidic environment, higher photothermal conversion efficiency, effective production of ROS, and pH-responsive release of doxorubicin. Furthermore, the small size of the nanoparticles enabled substantial tumor absorption in vivo and partial renal clearance, indicating that the theranostic agent is a promising option for further clinical translation (Zheng et al., 2019).

PEGylated MNPs

The MNPs' surface coating with polyethylene glycol (PEG) is an effective technique for improving systemic circulation, escaping endosomal clearance, and enhancing drug translation to the target site (Mansouri et al., 2024). PEG creates a protective layer on MNPs' surface, providing a stealth layer to protein adsorption and immunological recognition. It also extends blood circulation required for the establishment of efficient tumor accumulation through the increased permeability and retention (EPR) effect (Acharya et al., 2025). PEG-engineered gold nanoparticles of nitroimidazole were developed by Mittal et al. for the treatment of cancer. The nanoparticles had an average diameter of 28.9 ± 1.50 nm and a zeta potential of -20.62 ± 0.05 mV, indicating the development of stable nanoparticles. The results of in vivo studies showed that the coating of gold nanoparticles with PEG reduces the uptake of nanoparticles by the reticuloendothelial system and increases their retention in cancer cells for a prolonged time (Mittal et al., 2024).

Biomolecules linked to MNPs

The MNPs can be functionalized with biomolecules such as peptides, aptamers, antibodies, and polysaccharides. This merges the unique properties of MNPs with the biological specificity of biomolecules to facilitate improved functionality and specificity (Sanità et al., 2020). In addition to increasing colloidal stability under physiological settings, functionalization gives MNPs the capacity for biological recognition, which enables them to engage with cancer cells, receptors, or enzymes in a targeted manner. This design creates tailored, multipurpose theranostic platforms, resulting in encouraged anticancer activity, specific drug targeting, lessening off-target toxicity, and permitting combo treatments (Chen et al., 2024). For instance, gold NPs functionalized with an aptamer were developed for intracellular delivery of $BRAF^{V600E}$ antibody to treat cancer. These NPs showed a 70% reduction in the viability of cancer cells. Moreover, in a melanoma cancer model, the subcutaneous administration of these NPs caused induction of apoptosis and prevention of cancer cell proliferation, resulting in cancer regression in animals (Yeom et al., 2023). In another example, an anti-PD-L1 antibody functionalized gold nanoparticles of doxorubicin were developed to treat colorectal cancer. These NPs exhibited improved uptake of doxorubicin intracellularly, as shown by distinct apoptosis induction of 66% in cancer cells. In addition to it, NIR irradiation was employed for a synergistic effect, which showed more improvement in anticancer activity (Emami et al., 2019). Recent research on biomolecule-functionalized MNPs to treat cancer has been summarized in Table 15.3.

Stimuli-responsive moiety integrated MNPs

Various external stimuli (such as magnetic field, heat, light, and ultrasound) and internal triggers (enzyme activity, pH, redox potential, or hypoxia in the TME) can be used to trigger drug release at the tumor site. Such responses ensure drug accumulation at the target site of cancer, enhancing therapeutic efficiency and minimizing systemic effects, as illustrated in Fig. 15.1. Polymer-coated MNPs have been widely used in cancer therapy due to their biodegradability and biocompatibility (Kumar et al., 2023). For example, in the 4T1 model, the functionalized zinc oxide/chitosan NPs coated with homologous cancer cell membranes demonstrated enhanced siRNA protection, cancer targeting, and synergistic cancer growth inhibition. These NPs also damaged lysosomes, released siRNA, and increased ROS upon dissolving at an acidic pH. The findings showed an average size of 5.6 nm with improved siRNA protection up to 8 h from 2 h, along with enhanced cancer suppression in animals (Zhang et al., 2025). In another example, GSH/pH-responsive copper-based nanocomplexes were developed for the treatment of oral cancer. The developed nanocomplexes released the drug and copper ions, utilizing the acidic and reducing TME, which sets off a series of cell death processes such as ferroptosis, necroptosis, and cuproptosis. Strong tumor inhibition results from this multipurpose system's reduction of glutathione, promotion of lipid peroxidation, disruption of mitochondrial function, and enhancement of oxidative stress (Sun et al., 2025).

TABLE 15.3 Biomolecules-functionalized MNPs to treat cancer.

Biomolecule	Type of metallic nanoparticle	Targeted cancer	Key findings	References
Herceptin	Gold nanocapsules	Breast cancer	Outstanding cytotoxicity resulting in apoptotic cell death	Singh et al. (2025)
Antibody	Gold nanoparticles	Carcinoma cancer	Higher anticancer activity on the covalent binding of the antibody than on the adsorption	Anaki et al. (2024)
AS1411 aptamer	Silver nanoparticles	Breast cancer	Superior activity on breast cancer and higher targeting ability of it	Li et al. (2023)
DNA aptamer	Gold nanoparticles	Not specific	Excellent apoptosis induction and inhibition of cancer cell proliferation	Yeom et al. (2023)
Folic acid	Gold nanoparticles	Breast cancer	Great reduction in the viability of MCF-7 cells up to 10%	Dayekh et al. (2025)
Folate	Magnetic-gold nanoparticles	Liver cancer	Superior reduction in tumor size	Alnasraui et al. (2024)

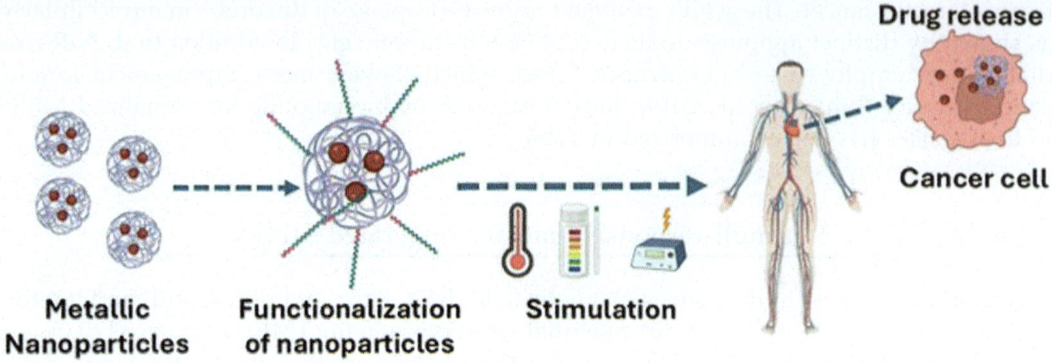

FIGURE 15.1 Drug targeting of metallic nanoparticles employing functionalization and stimuli-responsive release. Schematic representation of metallic nanoparticle-based drug targeting using surface functionalization and stimuli-responsive release mechanisms.

Conclusion

MNPs become highly effective platforms for drug administration along with imaging and theranostic applications due to their distinct physicochemical characteristics. The advancement in MNPs, such as biogenic MNPs, bimetallic nanoparticles, biosurfactants modified MNPs, MNPs with zwitterionic coating, PEGylated MNPs, and stimuli-responsive MNPs, has resulted in more precise and selective delivery for effective cancer therapy. However, there are still significant obstacles that hamper clinical translation, long-term safety, biodegradability, large-scale reproducibility, and regulatory approval. The heterogeneity of tumor biology also calls for the creation of patient-specific nanoparticles for better anticancer response. Future studies are anticipated to concentrate on combining nanotechnology with AI-driven design, tailored medicine, and sustainable green synthesis techniques to produce metallic nanoplatforms that are safer, more intelligent, and clinically applicable.

AI disclosure

During the preparation of this work the author(s) used Quilbot in order to Quilbot were used exclusively for editing and improving the language quality of the chapter. No generative AI tools contributed to the creation of scientific content. After using this tool/service, the author(s) reviewed and edited the content as needed and take(s) full responsibility for the content of the publication.

References

Abu-Tahon, M.A., Alshammari, F.A., Shahhat, I.M., Ghareib, M., Abdallah, W.E., 2025. Eco-Friendly synthesis, characterization, and biomedical applications of biosynthesized bimetallic silver-gold nanoparticles by culture supernatant of Aspergillus Niger. Appl. Biochem. Biotechnol. 197 (1), 137–158. https://doi.org/10.1007/s12010-024-05035-w.

Acharya, B., Behera, A., Moharana, S., 2025. Chapter 5 - functionalization and surface modification techniques of gold nanoparticles and their influence on the physical, chemical, and biological properties. In: Pasha, S.K.K., Deshmukh, K., Mustansar Hussain, C. (Eds.), Gold Nanoparticles, Nanomaterials and Nanocomposites, pp. 149–199.

Alamelu, S., Venkatesan, K.B., Srinivasan, M.K., Pachaiappan, P., 2025. Synthesis and characterization of brucine gold nanoparticles for targeted breast cancer therapy: Mechanistic insights into apoptosis and antioxidant disruption in MCF-7 cells. Biotechnol. Appl. Biochem. 72 (4), 1028–1044. https://doi.org/10.1002/bab.2719.

Alhadrami, H.A., Hassan, H.M., Alhadrami, A.H., Rateb, M.E., Ahmed, A.H., 2025. Green synthesis and anticancer activity of titanium dioxide nanoparticles using the endophytic fungus Aspergillus sp. J. Radiat. Res. Appl. Sci. 18 (1), 101–229. https://doi.org/10.1016/j.jrras.2024.101229.

Almehizia, A.A., Naglah, A.M., Aljafen, S.S., Hassan, A.S., Aboulthana, W.M., 2025. Assessment of the in vitro biological activities of schiff base-synthesized copper oxide nanoparticles as an anti-diabetic, anti-alzheimer, and anti-cancer agent. Pharmaceutics 17 (2). https://doi.org/10.3390/pharmaceutics17020180.

Alnasraui, A.H.F., Joe, I.H., Al-Musawi, S., 2024. Investigation of folate-functionalized magnetic-gold nanoparticles based targeted drug delivery for liver: In vitro, in vivo and docking studies. ACS Biomater. Sci. Eng. 10 (10), 6299–6313. https://doi.org/10.1021/acsbiomaterials.4c01039.

Anaki, A., Tzror-Azankot, C., Motiei, M., Sadan, T., Popovtzer, R., 2024. Impact of synthesis methods on the functionality of antibody-conjugated gold nanoparticles for targeted therapy. Nanoscale Adv. 6 (21), 5420–5429. https://doi.org/10.1039/d4na00134f.

Ansari, S.A.M.K., Ficiarà, E., Ruffinatti, F.A., Stura, I., Argenziano, M., Abollino, O., Cavalli, R., Guiot, C., D'Agata, F., 2019. Magnetic iron oxide nanoparticles: Synthesis, characterization and functionalization for biomedical applications in the Central Nervous System. Materials 12 (3). https://doi.org/10.3390/ma12030465.

Argenziano, M., Arpicco, S., Brusa, P., Cavalli, R., Chirio, D., Dosio, F., Gallarate, M., Peira, E., Stella, B., Ugazio, E., 2021. Developing actively targeted nanoparticles to fight cancer: Focus on Italian research. Pharmaceutics 13 (10), 1538. https://doi.org/10.3390/pharmaceutics13101538.

Ben Amor, I., Hemmami, H., Grara, N., Aidat, O., Ben Amor, A., Zeghoud, S., Bellucci, S., 2024. Chitosan: a green approach to metallic nanoparticle/nanocomposite synthesis and applications. Polymers 16 (18), 2662. https://doi.org/10.3390/polym16182662.

Bhiradi, I., Hiremath, S.S., 2025. Investigations on cytotoxicity of in-situ silver-gold bimetallic nanoparticles. J. Mech. Med. Biol. https://doi.org/10.1142/S0219519425400524.

Bidan, A.K., Al-Ali, Z.S.A., 2025. The role of biomaterial constituents of Jasminum sambac (L.) Aiton leaves in copper nanoparticles synthesis and evaluates their activities as anti-breast cancer and antibacterial agents. Inorg. Nano-Met. Chem. 55 (6), 641–656. https://doi.org/10.1080/24701556.2024.2354480.

Bjerk, T.R., Severino, P., Jain, S., Marques, C., Silva, A.M., Pashirova, T., Eliana, B., 2021. Biosurfactants: properties and applications in drug delivery, biotechnology and ecotoxicology. Bioengineering 8 (8), 115. https://doi.org/10.3390/bioengineering8080115.

Catalano, A., Iacopetta, D., Ceramella, J., Scumaci, D., Giuzio, F., Saturnino, C., Aquaro, S., Rosano, C., Sinicropi, M. S., 2022. Multidrug resistance (MDR): A widespread phenomenon in pharmacological therapies. Molecules 27 (3), 616. https://doi.org/10.3390/molecules27030616.

Chauhan, V., Pandey, A., Mahajan, G., Dhiman, V., Kanwar, S.S., 2025. Synergistic exploration of Surfactin-capped silver nanoparticles: Bioinformatics insights, antibacterial potency, and anticancer activity. 3 Biotech 15 (1). https://doi.org/10.1007/s13205-024-04174-5.

Chen, X., Argandona, S.M., Melle, F., Rampal, N., Fairen-Jimenez, D., 2024. Advances in surface functionalization of next-generation metal-organic frameworks for biomedical applications: Design, strategies, and prospects. Chem 10 (2), 504–543. https://doi.org/10.1016/j.chempr.2023.09.016.

Chen, Y., Zohaib, A., Sun, H., Sun, S., 2025. Multi-metallic nanoparticles: Synthesis and their catalytic applications. Chem. Commun. 61 (65), 12097–12114. https://doi.org/10.1039/d5cc01468a.

Chen, Z., Lv, T., Zhang, Y., Kong, W., Li, X., Xie, S., Li, J., Long, Y., Chen, L., Liu, J., Li, Z., Zeng, X., Deng, Z., 2025. Biosynthesis of bimetallic silver–copper oxide nanoparticles using endophytic Clonostachys rosea ZMS36 and their biomedical applications. Front. Microbiol. 16. https://doi.org/10.3389/fmicb.2025.1581486.

Dayekh, F.R., Sulaiman, G.M., Mohammed, H.A., Khan, R.A., 2025. Chitosan-coated gold nanoparticles' folic acid conjugates for targeted delivery of papain enzyme: An extended nanoplatform approach for cancer therapy. Appl. Organomet. Chem. 39 (4).

Dubey, S., Virmani, T., Yadav, S.K., Sharma, A., Kumar, G., Alhalmi, A., 2024. Breaking Barriers in Eco-Friendly Synthesis of Plant-Mediated Metal/Metal Oxide/Bimetallic Nanoparticles: Antibacterial, Anticancer, Mechanism Elucidation, and Versatile Utilizations. J. Nanomater. https://doi.org/10.1155/2024/9914079.

Dubey, S., Virmani, T., Yadav, S.K., Kumar, G., Sharma, A., Gugulothu, D., 2025. Utilizing plant phytoconstituents in metal oxide nanoparticle synthesis for cancer therapies. Curr. Pharm. Des. 31 (16), 1270–1289. https://doi.org/10.2174/0113816128329342241120105041.

Elkady, F.M., Badr, B.M., Saied, E., Hashem, A.H., Abdel-Maksoud, M.A., Fatima, S., Malik, A., Aufy, M., Hussein, A.M., Abdulrahman, M.S., Hashem, H.R., 2025. Green biosynthesis of bimetallic copper oxide-selenium nanoparticles using leaf extract of lagenaria siceraria: Antibacterial, anti-virulence activities against multidrug-resistant Pseudomonas aeruginosa. Int. J. Nanomed. 20, 4705–4727. https://doi.org/10.2147/IJN.S497494.

Emami, F., Banstola, A., Vatanara, A., Lee, S., Kim, J.O., Jeong, J.H., Yook, S., 2019. Doxorubicin and anti-PD-L1 antibody conjugated gold nanoparticles for colorectal cancer photochemotherapy. Mol. Pharm. 16 (3), 1184–1199. https://doi.org/10.1021/acs.molpharmaceut.8b01157.

Fakhredin, M., Shariatmadar Tehrani, F., Aliannezhadi, M., 2025. The role of reaction temperature in synthesizing clove-derived copper oxide nanoparticles for brain cancer treatment. Results Phys. 68. https://doi.org/10.1016/j.rinp.2024.108101.

Fletes-Vargas, G., Rodríguez-Rodríguez, R., Luna-Bárcenas, G., González-Vargas, O.A., Pérez-Larios, A., Espinosa-Andrews, H., 2025. Titanium dioxide (TiO2) nanoparticles as carriers of Polygonum cuspidatum root hydroalcoholic extract: Physicochemical, structural, and anticancer properties. Discover Mater 5 (1). https://doi.org/10.1007/s43939-025-00326-3.

Foroutan, Z., Afshari, S., Njafi, S., Afshari, A.R., Ahmadi, S.S., Nemati, S., Mirzaei, S.M., Bahrami, A., 2025. Biosynthesis of sulfur quantum dots and cerium oxide nanoparticles for bioimaging and reactive oxygen species modulation. In: Bioimpacts in Y79 Retinoblastoma Cancer Cells, Vol 15, p. 30954. https://doi.org/10.34172/bi.30954.

Gayathiri, E., Prakash, P., Karmegam, N., Varjani, S., Awasthi, M.K., Ravindran, B., 2022. Biosurfactants: Potential and eco-friendly material for sustainable agriculture and environmental safety—a review. Agronomy 12 (3). https://doi.org/10.3390/agronomy12030662.

Gutiérrez-Cruz, S.G., Muñoz-Diosdado, A., Gutiérrez-Calleja, R.A., Rodríguez-Cortés, O., Ortiz-Reyez, A.E., Flores-Mejía, R., 2025. Influence of physicochemical factors on the interaction of metallic nanoparticles with immune system cells. Front. Nanotechnol. 6.

Gomathi, A.C., Xavier Rajarathinam, S.R., Mohammed Sadiq, A., Rajeshkumar, S., 2020. Anticancer activity of silver nanoparticles synthesized using aqueous fruit shell extract of tamarindus indica on MCF-7 human breast cancer cell line. J. Drug Deliv. Sci. Technol. 55. https://doi.org/10.1016/j.jddst.2019.101376.

Goswami, M., Pal, D., Ghosh, M.K., Dwivedi, S., Chandraker, S.K., 2025. Bimetallic nanoparticles: A comprehensive review of synthesis methods and their potential application. ChemistrySelect 10 (29).

Hellany, H., Badran, A., Albahri, G., Kafrouny, N., El Kurdi, R., Maresca, M., Patra, D., Baydoun, E., 2025. Biogenic synthesis of gold nanoparticles using Scabiosa palaestina extract: Characterization, anticancer and antioxidant activities. Nanomaterials 15 (17), 1368. https://doi.org/10.3390/nano15171368.

Herbin, H.B., Aravind, M., Amalanathan, M., Mary, M.S.M., Lenin, M.M., Parvathiraja, C., Siddiqui, M.R., Wabaidur, S.M., Islam, M.A., 2022. Synthesis of silver nanoparticles using syzygium malaccense fruit extract and evaluation of their catalytic activity and antibacterial properties. J. Inorg. Organomet. Polym. Mater. 32 (3), 1103–1115. https://doi.org/10.1007/s10904-021-02210-y.

Hheidari, A., Mohammadi, J., Ghodousi, M., Mahmoodi, M., Ebrahimi, S., Pishbin, E., Rahdar, A., 2024. Metal-based nanoparticle in cancer treatment: lessons learned and challenges. Front. Bioeng. Biotechnol. 12, 2296–4185. https://doi.org/10.3389/fbioe.2024.1436297.

Hussien, N.A., Khalil, M.A.E.F., Schagerl, M., Ali, S.S., 2025. Green synthesis of zinc oxide nanoparticles as a promising nanomedicine approach for anticancer, antibacterial, and anti-inflammatory therapies. J. Nanomed. 20, 4299–4317. https://doi.org/10.2147/IJN.S507214.

Ismail, W.Z.W., Dawes, J.M., 2022. Synthesis and characterization of silver-gold bimetallic nanoparticles for random lasing. Nanomaterials 12 (4). https://doi.org/10.3390/nano12040607.

Jha, A., Kumar, M., Mishra, B., 2023. Gold nanoparticles as theranostic platform. In: In Inorganic Nanosystems, 1, pp. 279–321.

Jia, L., Liu, G., Li, J., Li, X., Zhou, H., Qiu, C., Liu, Y., Tan, S., Almasi, M., 2024. Green formulation of iron nanoparticles by plant extract induces apoptosis via P53 and STAT3 signaling pathways in prostate cancer cells. Inorg. Chem. Commun. 162, 112–164. https://doi.org/10.1016/j.inoche.2024.112164.

Joshi, N., Pandey, D.K., Mistry, B.G., Singh, D.K., 2023. Metal oxide nanoparticles: Synthesis, properties, characterization, and applications. In: Singh, D.K., Singh, S., Singh, P. (Eds.), Nanomaterials: Advances and Applications [Internet], pp. 103–144. https://doi.org/10.1007/978-981-19-7963-7_5.

Kavin, T., Murugaiyah, V., Tan, J.K., Kassim, M.N.I., Ramakrishna, S., Vigneswari, S., 2025. Eco-friendly synthesis of silver nanoparticles using Coffea arabica husk for enhanced antibacterial and anti-cancer applications. Biomass Bioenergy 194. https://doi.org/10.1016/j.biombioe.2025.107625.

Keerthirathna, L., Sigera, S., Rathnayake, M., Senarathne, A., Udeshika, H., Kodikara, C., Sirimuthu, N.M., Samarakoon, K.W., Boudjelal, M., Ali, R., Peiris, D.C., 2025. Chnoospora minima polysaccharide-mediated green synthesis of silver nanoparticles: Potent anticancer and antimicrobial activities. Biology 14 (7), 904. https://doi.org/10.3390/biology14070904.

Khalaf, K., Hana, D., Chou, J.T.T., Singh, C., Mackiewicz, A., Kaczmarek, M., 2021. Aspects of the tumor microenvironment involved in immune resistance and drug resistance. Front. Immunol. 12. https://doi.org/10.3389/fimmu.2021.656364.

Kimta, N., Chauhan, A., Puri, S., Kumari, A., Sharma, R., Kumar, A., Kapoor, D., 2025. Phytomediated copper oxide nanoparticles derived from the fronds of Adiantum venustum D Don: Evaluation of their biomedical potential. Appl. Biochem. Biotechnol. 197 (1), 398–426. https://doi.org/10.1007/s12010-024-05031-0.

Kowsalya, K., Gunasangkaran, G., Halka, J., Dharani, E., Saradhadevi, M., Anand, A.V., Anand, M., Gurusaravanan, P., Bupesh, G., Arun, M., 2025. Green synthesis and characterization of zinc oxide nanoparticles using Vitex negundo methanolic extract and its anticancer efficacy in colorectal cancer. Cytotechnology 77 (3). https://doi.org/10.1007/s10616-025-00775-x.

Krisshna Gunasekaran, N., Nazario Bayon, N., Prabhu Tumkur, P., Prabhakaran, K., Hall, J.C., Ramesh, G.T., 2025. Anticancer activity of cerium oxide nanoparticles towards human lung cancer cells. Nanomanufacturing 5 (2), 6. https://doi.org/10.3390/nanomanufacturing5020006.

Kumar, P.V., Pushpavalli, K.S., Kumar, B.G., Jelastin Kala, S.M., Prakash, K.S., 2025. Green synthesis of Au-Pt bimetallic nanoparticels using Croton caudatus Geisel leaf extract and their biological studies. Results Chem. 13. https://doi.org/10.1016/j.rechem.2024.101945.

Kumar, P., Agnihotri, S., Roy, I., 2018. Preparation and characterization of superparamagnetic iron oxide nanoparticles for magnetically guided drug delivery. Int. J. Nanomed. 13, 43–46. https://doi.org/10.2147/IJN.S125002.

Kumar, M., Jha, A., Mishra, B., 2023. Polymeric nanosystems for cancer theranostics. In: InPolymeric Nanosystems, 1, pp. 657–697.

Le, T.T.H., Ngo, T.H., Nguyen, T.H., Hoang, V.H., Nguyen, V.H., Nguyen, P.H., 2023. Anti-cancer activity of green synthesized silver nanoparticles using Ardisia gigantifolia leaf extract against gastric cancer cells. Biochem. Biophys. Res. Commun. 661, 99–107. https://doi.org/10.1016/j.bbrc.2023.04.037.

Li, S., Huang, P., Ye, Z., Wang, Y., Wang, W., Kong, D., Zhang, J., Deng, L., Dong, A., 2019. Layer-by-layer zwitterionic modification of diverse substrates with durable anti-corrosion and anti-fouling properties. J. Mater. Chem. B 7 (39), 6024–6034. https://doi.org/10.1039/c9tb01337g.

Li, Y., Wang, Z., Ajani, J.A., Song, S., 2021. Drug resistance and Cancer stem cells. Cell Commun. Signal. 19 (1). https://doi.org/10.1186/s12964-020-00627-5.

Li, F., Cao, Y., Kan, X., Li, D., Li, Y., Huang, C., Liu, P., 2023. AS1411-conjugated doxorubicin-loaded silver nanotriangles for targeted chemo-photothermal therapy of breast cancer. Nanomedicine 18 (17), 1077–1094. https://doi.org/10.2217/nnm-2023-0158.

Lima, B.G.A., Silva, R.R., Meira, H.M., Durval, I.J.B., Macedo Bezerra Filho, C., Silva, T.A.L., Sarubbo, L.A., Luna, J.M., 2024. Synthesis and characterization of silver nanoparticles stabilized with biosurfactant and application as an antimicrobial agent. Microorganisms 12 (9). https://doi.org/10.3390/microorganisms12091849.

Liu, Z., Lu, T., Qian, R., Wang, Z., Qi, R., Zhang, Z., 2024. Exploiting nanotechnology for drug delivery: Advancing the anti-cancer effects of Autophagy-Modulating compounds in traditional Chinese medicine. Int. J. Nanomedicine 19, 2507–2528. https://doi.org/10.2147/IJN.S455407.

Luque-Bolivar, A., Pérez-Mora, E., Eugenia Villegas, V., Rondón-Lagos, M., 2020. Resistance and overcoming resistance in breast cancer. Breast Cancer Targ. Ther. 12, 211–229. https://doi.org/10.2147/bctt.s270799.

Maji, D., Lu, J., Sarder, P., Schmieder, A.H., Cui, G., Yang, X., Pan, D., Achilefu, S., Lanza, G.M., 2018. Cellular trafficking of Sn-2 phosphatidylcholine prodrugs studied with fluorescence lifetime imaging and super-resolution microscopy. Precis. Nanomed. 1 (2), 128–145. https://doi.org/10.33218/prnano1(2).180724.1.

Mansouri, E., Rajabpour, S., Mesbahi, A., 2024. In silico estimation of polyethylene glycol coating effect on metallic NPs radio-sensitization in kilovoltage energy beams. BMC Chem. 18 (1). https://doi.org/10.1186/s13065-024-01322-z.

Mazzaglia, A., Scala, A., Sortino, G., Zagami, R., Zhu, Y., Sciortino, M.T., Pennisi, R., Pizzo, M.M., Neri, G., Grassi, G., Piperno, A., 2018. Intracellular trafficking and therapeutic outcome of multiwalled carbon nanotubes modified with cyclodextrins and polyethylenimine. Colloids Surf. B Biointerf. 163, 55–63. https://doi.org/10.1016/j.colsurfb.2017.12.028.

Mehdipour, A., Reza, M.A.S., Rasouli, A., Baravati, M.H.J., Jafari, G.A., Heidari, F., 2024. Green synthesis of zinc nanoparticles by hydroalcoholic extract of lavender (*Lavandula stoechas* L.), characterization, and cytotoxic effects on human breast and colon cancer. Sci. Rep. 14 (1).

Mittal, S., Kumar, C., Mallia, M.B., Sarma, H.D., 2024. Re-engineered theranostic gold nanoparticles for targeting tumor hypoxia. Mater. Adv. 5 (2), 513–520. https://doi.org/10.1039/d3ma00679d.

Mohamed, S.H., Othman, B.A., Abd-Elhalim, B.T., Seada, M.N.A., 2024. Copper nanoparticles biosynthesis by Priestia megaterium and its application as antibacterial and antitumor agents. Sci. Rep. 14 (1). https://doi.org/10.1038/s41598-024-72598-3.

Mustafa, S., Abbas, R.Z., Saeed, Z., Baazaoui, N., Khan, A.M.A., 2025. Use of metallic nanoparticles against eimeria—the coccidiosis-causing agents: A Comprehensive Review. Biol. Trace Elem. Res. 203 (6), 3412–3431. https://doi.org/10.1007/s12011-024-04399-8.

Nagaraj, A., Ghosh, O.S.N., Ghneim, H.K., AlSheikh, Y.A., Mohammed, K., Poda, S., Kalagatur, N.K., 2025. Fe2O3-type iron oxide nanoparticles from Aerva lanata leaf extract exhibit antibiofilm, discriminatory toxicity in cancer cells, and theranostic against oxidative stress in zebrafish. Chem. Phys. Impact 10. https://doi.org/10.1016/j.chphi.2025.100849.

Nisha, Sachan, R.S.K., Singh, A., Karnwal, A., Shidiki, A., Kumar, G., 2024. Plant-mediated gold nanoparticles in cancer therapy: Exploring anti-cancer mechanisms, drug delivery applications, and future prospects. Front. Nanotechnol. 6. https://doi.org/10.3389/fnano.2024.1490980.

Nussinov, R., Tsai, C.J., Jang, H., 2021. Anticancer drug resistance: An update and perspective. Drug Resist. Updat. 59. https://doi.org/10.1016/j.drup.2021.100796.

Patel, J., Kumar, G.S., Roy, H., Maddiboyina, B., Leporatti, S., Bohara, R.A., 2024. From nature to nanomedicine: Bioengineered metallic nanoparticles bridge the gap for medical applications. Discover Nano 19 (1). https://doi.org/10.1186/s11671-024-04021-9.

Patel, B., Choudhary, N., Dudhagara, D., Shahid, M., Syed, R., Yadav, V.K., Sahoo, D.K., Patel, A., 2025. Green synthesis of Ag-Fe bimetallic nanoparticles using fungal filtrates: Unlocking multifunctional medical and environmental applications. RSC Adv. 15 (3), 1565–1575. https://doi.org/10.1039/d4ra07541b.

Patil, S.P., Chaudhari, R.Y., Nemade, M.S., 2022. *Azadirachta indica* leaves mediated green synthesis of metal oxide nanoparticles: A review. Talanta Open 5. https://doi.org/10.1016/j.talo.2022.100083.

Qu, K., Yuan, Z., Wang, Y., Song, Z., Gong, X., Zhao, Y., Mu, Q., Zhan, Q., Xu, W., Wang, L., 2022. Structures, properties, and applications of zwitterionic polymers. ChemPhysMater 1 (4), 294–309. https://doi.org/10.1016/j.chphma.2022.04.003.

Rahim, M.A., Jan, N., Khan, S., Shah, H., Madni, A., Khan, A., Jabar, A., Khan, S., Elhissi, A., Hussain, Z., Aziz, H.C., Sohail, M., Khan, M., Thu, H.E., 2021. Recent advancements in stimuli responsive drug delivery platforms for active and passive cancer targeting. Cancers 13 (4), 1–52. https://doi.org/10.3390/cancers13040670.

Saadh, M.J., Khidr, W.A., Alfarttoosi, K.H., Bishoyi, A.K., Ganesan, S., Shankhyan, A., Gayathri, S., Rizaev, J., Taher, W.M., Alwan, M., Jawad, M.J., Al-Nuaimi, A.M.A., 2025. Metal nanoparticles as a promising therapeutic approach for prostate cancer diagnosis and therapy: A comprehensive review. Med. Oncol. 42 (4). https://doi.org/10.1007/s12032-025-02633-4.

Sanità, G., Carrese, B., Lamberti, A., 2020. Nanoparticle surface functionalization: How to improve biocompatibility and cellular internalization. Front. Mol. Biosci. 7. https://doi.org/10.3389/fmolb.2020.587012.

Sarubbo, L.A., Silva, M.d.G.C., Durval, I.J.B., Bezerra, K.G.O., Ribeiro, B.G., Silva, I.A., Twigg, M.S., Banat, I.M., 2022. Biosurfactants: Production, properties, applications, trends, and general perspectives. Biochem. Eng. J. 181. https://doi.org/10.1016/j.bej.2022.108377.

Selim, S., Badr, B.M., Moustafa, M.H., Saied, E., Elkady, F.M., salama, A., Aloufi, A.S., Algamdi, N.A., Alzahofi, N. N., Abada, E., Alshammari, M.S., Al Jaouni, S.K., Hashem, A.H., 2025. Green biosynthesis of bimetallic silver titanium dioxide nanoparticles using Pluchea indica with their anticancer, antimicrobial, and antioxidant activities. Sci. Rep. 15 (1). https://doi.org/10.1038/s41598-025-10349-8.

Shahalaei, M., Azad, A.K., Sulaiman, W.M.A.W., Derakhshani, A., Mofakham, E.B., Mallandrich, M., Kumarasamy, V., Subramaniyan, V., 2024. A review of metallic nanoparticles: Present issues and prospects focused on the preparation methods, characterization techniques, and their theranostic applications. Front. Chem. 12. https://doi.org/10.3389/fchem.2024.1398979.

Singh, P., Sarkar, A., Mukherjee, N., Jaiswal, A., 2025. Herceptin-conjugated plasmonic gold nanocapsules for targeted NIR-II photothermal therapy. RSC Pharm. 2 (1), 124–134. https://doi.org/10.1039/d4pm00244j.

Sun, Y., Li, E., Zhong, W., Deng, Z., Zhou, Z., Wong, K.H., Li, X., 2025. GSH/pH-responsive copper-based cascade nanocomplexes inducing immunogenic cell death through cuproptosis/ferroptosis/necroptosis in oral squamous cell carcinoma. Mater. Today Bio 30. https://doi.org/10.1016/j.mtbio.2024.101434.

Tahir Aminzai, M., Yildirim, M., Yabalak, E., 2024. Metallic nanoparticles unveiled: Synthesis, characterization, and their environmental, medicinal, and agricultural applications. Talanta 280. https://doi.org/10.1016/j.talanta.2024.126790.

Thajuddin, F., Palanivel, P., Chithirai, A., Thajuddin, S.F., Arivalagan, P., Saravanan, C., Nooruddin, T., Dharumadurai, D., 2025. Green Synthesis of Titanium Oxide Nanoparticles Using Aqueous Extracts of Limnospira Fusiformis and Their Multifunctional Applications in Biomedical and Biodiesel Production. Algal Res. 89. https://doi.org/10.1016/j.algal.2025.104082.

Truong, T.T., Mondal, S., Doan, V.H.M., Tak, S., Choi, J., Oh, H., Nguyen, T.D., Misra, M., Lee, B., Oh, J., 2024. Precision-engineered metal and metal-oxide nanoparticles for biomedical imaging and healthcare applications. Adv. Colloid Interf. Sci. 332. https://doi.org/10.1016/j.cis.2024.103263.

Tuli, H.S., Joshi, R., Kaur, G., Garg, V.K., Sak, K., Varol, M., Kaur, J., Alharbi, S.A., Alahmadi, T.A., Aggarwal, D., Dhama, K., Jaswal, V.S., Mittal, S., Sethi, G., 2023. Metal nanoparticles in cancer: From synthesis and metabolism to cellular interactions. J. Nanostruct. Chem. 13 (3), 321–348. https://doi.org/10.1007/s40097-022-00504-2.

Todaria, M., Maity, D., Awasthi, R., 2024. Biogenic metallic nanoparticles as game-changers in targeted cancer therapy: Recent innovations and prospects. Future J. Pharmaceut. Sci. 10 (1). https://doi.org/10.1186/s43094-024-00601-9.

Ünal, E.D., Duymaz, E., Kavukcu, S.B., Rethinam, S., Türkmen, G., Başaran, B., Türkmen, H., 2025. Novel water-soluble gelatin-based platinum nanoparticles for targeted cancer therapy with enhanced cytotoxicity. J. Nanopart. Res. 27 (1). https://doi.org/10.1007/s11051-024-06212-y.

Wang, Z., Li, M., Zhang, Q., Xu, L., 2024. Green formulation of copper nanoparticles by Pistacia khinjuk leaf aqueous extract: Introducing a novel chemotherapeutic drug for the treatment of prostate cancer. Open Chem. 22 (1). https://doi.org/10.1515/chem-2024-0034.

Wen, J., Huang, S., Hu, Q., He, W., Wei, Z., Wang, L., Lu, J., Yue, X., Men, S., Miao, C., He, Z., Yang, X., Zhai, G., Li, J., Ye, L., 2024. Recent advances in zwitterionic polymers-based non-fouling coating strategies for biomedical applications. Mater. Today Chem. 40. https://doi.org/10.1016/j.mtchem.2024.102232.

Yeom, J.H., Shin, E., Jin, H., Liu, H., Luo, Y., Nam, Y., Ryu, M., Song, W., Chi, H., Kim, J., Lee, K., Bae, J., 2023. Aptamer-conjugated gold nanoparticles platform as the intracellular delivery of antibodies for cancer therapy. J. Ind. Eng. Chem. 126, 480–491. https://doi.org/10.1016/j.jiec.2023.06.036.

Zhang, J., Zhang, Y.P., Qi, S., Wang, Y., Mei, D., Wang, X., Su, Y., Yang, T., Huo, R., Liu, D., Liu, S., Baldan, M., Zhang, S., Cui, C., 2025. Cancer cell membrane-camouflaged pH-responsive nanoparticles for enhancing siRNA effect and synergistic anti-tumor therapy. J. Nanobiotechnol. 23 (1). https://doi.org/10.1186/s12951-025-03508-6.

Zheng, T., Wang, W., Wu, F., Zhang, M., Shen, J., Sun, Y., 2019. Zwitterionic polymer-gated Au@TiO 2 core-shell nanoparticles for imaging-guided combined cancer therapy. Theranostics 9 (17), 5035–5048. https://doi.org/10.7150/thno.35418.

CHAPTER

16

Advances in polymeric nanoparticles for anticancer drug delivery

Keshav Hirave[1], *Nirmal Morya*[1], *Lalit Kumar*[1], *Surojit Banerjee*[2], *Vikas Anand Saharan*[1] and *Anupama Singh*[2]

[1]Department of Pharmaceutical Technology (Formulations), National Institute of Pharmaceutical Education and Research, Guwahati (NIPER-G), Sila Katamur (Halugurisuk), Assam, India; [2]School of Pharmaceutical Sciences and Technology, Sardar Bhagwan Singh University, Dehradun, Uttarakhand, India

Introduction

Polymeric nanoparticles (PNPs) have a wide array of physicochemical features, biocompatibility, and versatility in entrapping therapeutic chemicals, making them an appealing drug delivery strategy for anticancer drugs (Beach et al., 2024). PNPs can range in size from 10 to 600 nm, with a greater surface area-to-volume ratio, controlled drug release, and ligand surface modification for targeted cancer cell therapy. Their capacity to encapsulate both hydrophobic and hydrophilic moieties while protecting them from enzymatic degradation makes them attractive carriers for anticancer drugs (Kumar et al., 2025). Nanoparticles can circumvent the limits of traditional chemotherapy by passive and active targeting (Xiao et al., 2022). Passive targeting accumulates nanoparticles in tumor microenvironments with leaky vasculature and inadequate lymphatic outflow through enhanced permeability and retention effect. Active targeting can improve selectivity and reduce off-target toxicity by conjugating nanoparticles with ligands, antibodies, aptamers, or peptides that have been identified as binding molecules to receptors on the surface of cancer cells. PNPs enable surface modification with proteins, lipids, or other protective coatings toward the immune system, minimizing their recognition, avoiding clearance, and thus

Advanced Cancer Therapeutics
https://doi.org/10.1016/B978-0-443-44185-1.00027-6

making them highly versatile vehicles for drug delivery (Begines et al., 2020). Stimuli-responsive nanoparticles, which respond to pH, enzymes, redox gradients, or temperature, allow active moieties to transport medications to particular sites in the tumor microenvironment on demand. PNPs are versatile in nature and can imitate both diagnostic and therapeutic activities on a single platform, allowing for the development of theragnostic systems (Jia et al., 2025). These multifunctional nanocarriers carry anticancer medicines, track biodistribution, and provide real-time imaging and therapy monitoring. Recent breakthroughs have also focused on codelivering various therapeutic drugs, such as chemotherapeutics with siRNA, immunomodulators, or photosensitizers in a polymeric system to overcome multidrug resistance. In preclinical cancer models, polymer-based hybrid nanocarriers combine chemotherapeutic and gene silencing drugs to reduce tumor growth and overcome resistance. Despite advances, transferring PNPs from bench to bedside remains tough (Prasad et al., 2016). Scaling up, regulatory approval, long-term toxicity, and immunological interaction all require careful consideration. Patient-specific characteristics, such as tumor heterogeneity and genetic diversity, necessitate personalized polymeric nanomedicine. Addressing these difficulties requires interdisciplinary approaches in polymer science, pharmaceutical technology, molecular biology, and clinical research. This chapter examines current advances in PNPs for anticancer drug delivery, emphasizing design techniques, drug targeting, therapeutic uses, and translational issues.

Polymeric nanoparticles: Definition and classification

The International Organization for Standardization (ISO) defines nanoparticles as "nano-object with all external dimensions in the nanoscale where the lengths of the longest and the shortest axes of the nano-object do not differ significantly" (ISO, 2017). If dimensions differ by more than 3 times, the term "nanoplate" or "nanofiber" is preferred over "nanoparticle." Nanoparticles are colloidal carriers composed of natural or synthetic polymers designed to deliver the therapeutic agent, as illustrated in Fig. 16.1. The nanosize provides a high specific surface area, enabling improved solubility, stability, and bioavailability of encapsulated drugs. The term "nanoparticle" encompasses nanocapsules and nanospheres, which differ in their morphological attributes. Nanocapsules typically have an oily core that contains the drug in a dissolved form, surrounded by a polymeric shell that regulates the drug's release kinetics from the core. Nanospheres comprise a continuous polymeric matrix that facilitates the preservation of drug(s) either encapsulated inside their structure or adsorbed onto their surface (Zielińska et al., 2020). PNPs can either encapsulate or adsorb, or conjugate, a drug on their surface for its delivery to the target site. PNPs with porous structure allow delivery of a higher payload to cancer cells (Zielińska et al., 2020). Polymers such as poly(lactide-co-glycolide) (PLGA), polyethylene glycol (PEG), gelatin, hyaluronic acid (HA), alginate, and others are a favored option for biocompatible nanoparticle coatings with diverse constituents. This method effectively inhibits premature clearance by circulating phagocytic cells, ensuring that upon reaching target cells, lysosomal compartments can easily digest PNPs (Eltaib, 2025). PNPs can be of various types, including PNPs, micelles, dendrimers, polymersomes, and polyplexes, as discussed below.

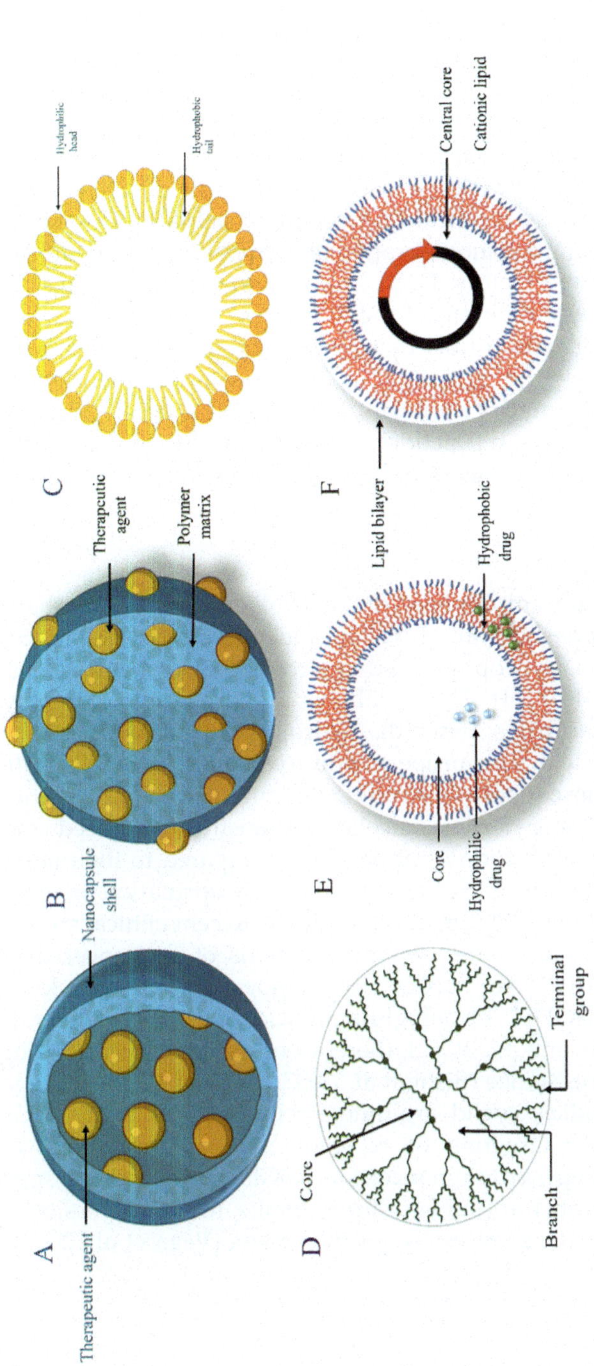

FIGURE 16.1 Structure of polymeric nanoparticles: (A) nanocapsule, (B) nanosphere, (C) micelle, (D) dendrimer, (E) polymerosome, and (F) polyplexes.

Polymeric nanoparticles

PNPs are tiny, solid, and colloidal particles that fall within the size range of 1–1000 nm, in which the therapeutic agent is dissolved on a polymer matrix, entangled, encapsulated, or adsorbed (Zielińska et al., 2020; Letchford and Burt, 2007). PNPs are frequently employed as drug carriers due to their biodegradability, biocompatibility, and high drug loading capacity. It demonstrates low toxicity, enhances therapeutic effectiveness, ensures controlled drug release, and improves physical and chemical stability. This system is widely used for drug delivery, enabling the incorporation of both natural and synthetic agents, including proteins, peptides, growth factors, DNA, mRNA, and various drugs. The PNP formation process profoundly affects their structural attributes, resulting in variations such as nanospheres, where the drug is uniformly distributed, and nanocapsules, which possess a vesicular reservoir containing the drug within an aqueous or oily cavity surrounded by a polymeric membrane. A range of polymers, such as PLGA, polylactide (PLA), polyglycolide, polycaprolactone (PCL), poly(d,L-lactide), chitosan, and PLGA–PEG, have been formulated for both passive and ligand-targeted delivery of therapeutic agents (Prabhu et al., 2015).

Polymeric micelles

Polymeric micelles are amphiphilic di- or triblock copolymers that self-assemble into spherical nanosized core-shell structures in aqueous environments (Sutton et al., 2007). Typically, it consists of hydrophilic and hydrophobic segments such as PEG-b-PLA or PEG-b-PCL (Beach et al., 2024). The copolymer's hydrophobic core plays a crucial role in encapsulating anticancer drugs, while the hydrophilic shell enhances the stealth characteristics of the micellar system. This property effectively hinders its absorption by the reticuloendothelial system, consequently extending its circulation time within the bloodstream (Wang et al., 2018). Polymer-derived micelles demonstrate enhanced stability and a significantly lower critical micellar concentration when compared to their surfactant-based counterparts. It shows a higher drug loading by passive encapsulation or conjugation, supported by noncovalent interactions (Oerlemans et al., 2010). Recent clinical studies have highlighted the potential of specific micellar-based formulations of anticancer drugs, demonstrating their promise as effective drug carriers in oncology therapy. Block copolymer micelles, composed of PEG, PLGA, PCL, or polyglutamic acid, effectively deliver drugs such as doxorubicin (DOX), cisplatin, and paclitaxel, thereby enhancing circulation, tumor accumulation, and overcoming drug resistance (Bisht et al., 2007; Xiang et al., 2014). Ligand-functionalized micelles (folate, antibodies, cyclid arginine-glycine aspartic acid (cRGD), galactose, and aptamers) show precise targeting of receptors like epidermal growth factor receptor (EGFR), integrins, asialoglycoprotein receptor (ASGPR), and prostate specific membrane antigen (PSMA), significantly improving cellular uptake, tumor regression, and therapeutic efficacy compared to free drugs or nontargeted carriers (Vega et al., 2003).

Dendrimers

Dendrimers are branched, monodisperse, synthetic macromolecules characterized by their repeatedly branched structure. A central core and internal repeating units are referred to as generations and surface functional groups. These well-defined nanostructures make them an efficient nanocarrier for cancer drug delivery. It encapsulates hydrophobic and hydrophilic drugs within its internal cavities or forms electrostatic and hydrogen bonds. Poly (amidoamine) (PAMAM), polypropylene imine (PPI), and poly(L-lysine) (PLL) dendrimers are widely utilized in cancer drug delivery due to their biodegradability and surface modification (Vega et al., 2003). Surface modification can enhance the targeting with ligands, showing drug accumulation in the tumor microenvironment, while PEGylation increases circulation time and reduces immunogenicity. Exploring poly(glycerol-succinic acid) dendrimers as potential carriers for camptothecin presents an intriguing avenue for research and application (Morgan et al., 2003). PAMAM dendrimers were studied for the targeted delivery of methotrexate (MTX) by examining two aspects of drug loading into the dendrimer system: encapsulated and covalently bound drug (Qi et al., 2015). The cytotoxicity study revealed that G5 PAMAM dendrimer and MTX conjugates retained anticancer activity similar to the free drug in in vitro conditions of free and blocked folic acid receptors. Folic acid-targeted MTX conjugates demonstrated high specificity and antiproliferative activity against Kaposi's B (KB) cells, which overexpress folic acid receptors. However, when these receptors are blocked, these conjugates lose their antiproliferative effect, indicating that the drug is delivered intracellularly through receptor-mediated endocytosis.

Polymersomes

Polymersomes are self-assembled polymeric nanocarriers composed of amphiphilic block copolymers, which enable them to encapsulate a diverse range of molecules, making them ideal for use in drug delivery systems. The capacity to customize their dimensions and surface properties further amplifies their potential in biomedical applications (Sharma et al., 2020). Polymersomes represent a promising frontier for advancements in nanotechnology and medicinal applications. Polymersomes are vesicles composed of synthetic amphiphilic block copolymers, characterized by unique hydrophilic and hydrophobic portions. Their distinctive structure has intriguing opportunities across several applications. Polymersomes, although architecturally similar to liposomes, viz., vesicles composed of phospholipids, distinguish themselves by their increased stability, higher storage capacity, and prolonged circulation time (Anajafi and Mallik, 2015). The research investigated the efficacy of polymersomes generated from polyphosphazene as delivery vehicles for hydrophilic DOX hydrochloride and hydrophobic DOX base in breast cancer therapy. The strong interaction with polymersomes enhanced the encapsulation of DOX·HCl or DOX. The in vivo delivery of these polymersomes in nude mice bearing MCF-7 xenograft tumors demonstrated similar tumor growth suppression while markedly improving the safety of life (Xu et al., 2014).

Polyplexes

Polyplexes are supramolecular complexes formed by the interaction between cationic polymers and anionic nucleic acids, such as plasmid DNA or small interfering RNA (Ita, 2020). These drug delivery systems have emerged as key tools in drug administration and gene therapy due to their ability to condense genetic material efficiently, protect it from enzymatic degradation, and enable targeted intracellular distribution without compromising bioactivity (Uchida et al., 2023). It can also stabilize nucleic acids within a nanoscale carrier, highlighting their increasing significance in biopolymer research and healthcare applications. Recently, a polyplex system was evaluated for targeted cancer therapy by incorporating targeting ligands and biocompatible modifications to enhance effectiveness. Zhao et al. studied a PLL vector with histidine residues for endosomal escape (Zhao et al., 2014). The cationic peptide moiety allows pDNA polyplex formation and acts as a substrate for protein kinase Cα (PKCα). A biocompatible vector for targeted DNA delivery in cancer therapy is phosphorylcholine-modified polyethyleneimine (PEI). These systems were better absorbed by HepG2 liver cancer cells than PEGylated ones. The therapeutic potential of phosphorylcholine-functionalized PEI was shown by its 6-fold increase in gene expression compared to normal hepatocytes.

Polymers used in anticancer drug delivery

Polymers play a pivotal role in the development of anticancer drug delivery systems enabling the sustained, controlled, and targeted delivery of therapeutic cargo, as illustrated in Fig. 16.2. These systems aim to reduce the systemic toxicity of anticancer drugs to normal cells while increasing penetration in the tumor microenvironment, thereby enhancing therapeutic efficacy.

Natural polymers

Natural polymers like polysaccharides stand out in polymer-based drug delivery systems for their widespread availability, biodegradability, biocompatibility, nonimmunogenicity, and sustainable release nature (Jha et al., 2024a). The nontoxic nature, water solubility, surface versatility, and composition are additional features over those of synthetic polymers. It can exert anticancer action to provide a synergistic effect with anticancer drugs, along with improving drug solubility, penetration, and stability and minimizing systemic toxicity. Some of the polymers used in drug encapsulation and delivery are discussed below.

Chitosan

Chitosan is a biocompatible, biodegradable polysaccharide derived from the N-deacetylation of chitin. It is mainly found in fungi and crustacean exoskeletons (Divya and Jisha, 2018). Chitosan is a flexible cationic polymer comprising repeating units of D-glucosamine and N-acetyl D-glucosamine linked by 1–4 glycosidic linkage. Chitosan, the only natural polycation, has a charge density that depends on acetylation and pH. Due to amine protonation, chitosan dissolves easily in acidic pH but not in alkaline or neutral pH (Bhatta et al., 2012). Chitosan is an effective permeation enhancer, regardless of the degree of deacetylation in low-molecular-weight polymers. Chitosan nanoparticles are emerging as a promising carrier for anticancer agents (Garg et al., 2019). Chitosan is a mucoadhesive and biodegradable polymer for the design of nanoparticles using techniques such as ionic gelation, cross-linking (either ionic or covalent), emulsion solvent diffusion,

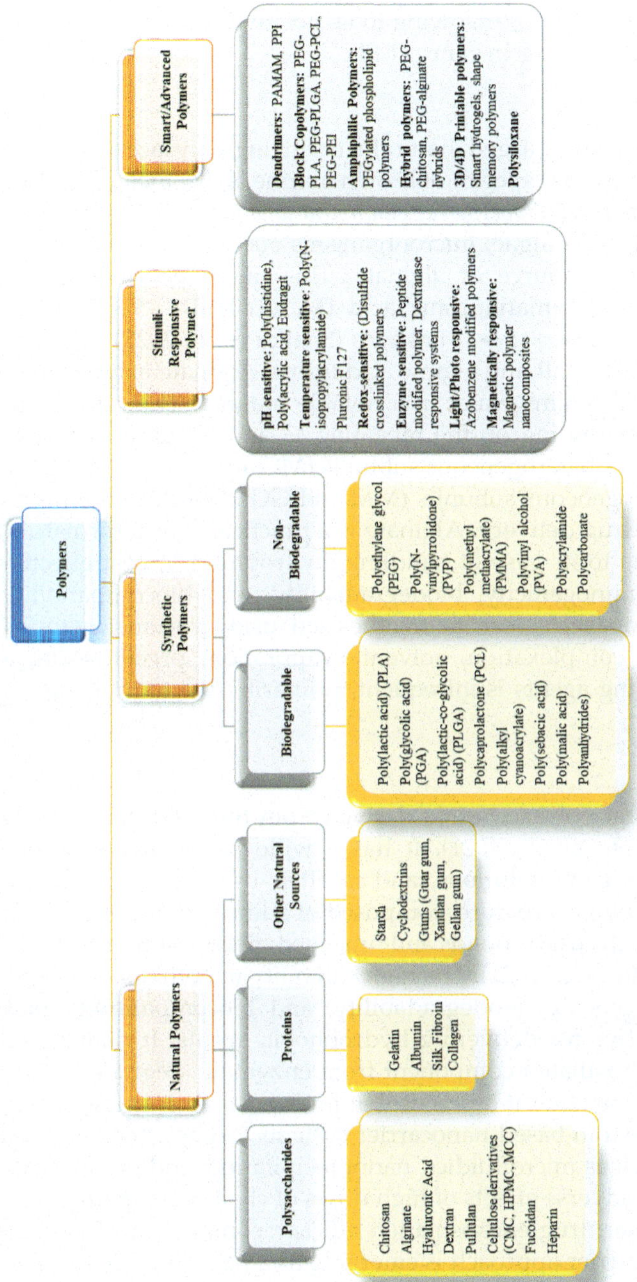

FIGURE 16.2 Polymers utilized in preparing polymeric nanoparticles for anticancer drug delivery.

and precipitation, either alone or in combination. Chitosan nanoparticles efficiently reach tumor sites through passive diffusion, utilizing the solid tumors' enhanced permeation and retention characteristics. Chitosan, owing to its positive charge, can enhance the cellular uptake of the encapsulated drug in cancer cells.

Alginate

Alginate is a negatively charged, naturally occurring polysaccharide found abundantly in nature, sourced from several species of brown marine algae, including *Ascophyllum nodosum*, *Laminaria digitata*, *Laminaria hyperborea*, *Laminaria japonica*, and *Macrocystis pyrifera* (Lee and Mooney, 2012). Alongside algae, microorganisms such as *Azotobacter* sp. and *Pseudomonas* sp. can also provide a source of alginate. This linear polymer consists of irregularly repeating subunits of β-D-mannuronic acid (M, m) and C-5 epimer α-L-guluronic acid (G, n) blocks, connected by β(1→4) linkages (Shaikh et al., 2022). Alginate is commercially available in both sodium salt and alginic acid forms. Alginate exhibits excellent solubility at neutral pH levels and retains water in a notable manner. The physicochemical properties differ significantly depending on the repeating M and G subunits (Lopes et al., 2017). At an acidic pH, repetitive heterogeneous subunits (MG and GM) exhibit a lower solubilization likelihood than homogeneous subunits (MM and GG). Selecting the right polymer grade is crucial for effective drug delivery. Alginate is a practical choice for natural polymeric drug delivery systems due to its ease of handling, hydrophilicity, cost-effectiveness, versatility, nontoxicity, nonimmunogenicity, biodegradability, and biocompatibility (Parmar et al., 2023). Alginate nanoparticles can be synthesized using various methods, including gelation/emulsification, complexation, solvent evaporation, precipitation, and crosslinking. The use of crosslinking agents is infrequent, primarily due to their toxic nature (Tønnesen and Karlsen, 2002).

Dextran

Dextran is a natural polysaccharide derived from the catalytic conversion of sucrose by anaerobic bacteria (Hu et al., 2021). It has a wide range of applications, is known for enhancing the viscosity of solutions, and is often used as a volume expander. It has a branched and hydrophilic structure, composed of a linear chain of repeating glucose monomers linked by α-1,6 glycosidic bonds and branched glucose subunits. It has a broad range of molecular weight (Hu et al., 2021). The high solubility in both aqueous and organic environments, nonimmunogenicity, biodegradability, and biocompatibility make dextran-based carriers highly effective for delivering hydrophobic agents. It demonstrates high stability and protects the encapsulated component from enzymatic degradation. The neutral charge enhances absorption, making it a practical approach for oral drug delivery (He et al., 2023; Huo et al., 2020). Dextran-based nanocarrier systems can be effectively formulated through various methods such as microfluidics, nanoprecipitation, and emulsification. It has the potential to reduce the adverse effects of high doses of chemotherapeutics and drug resistance. It demonstrates higher drug encapsulation efficacy compared to PLGA nanoparticles. The dextran-based nanocarrier approach is emerging as a new strategy for delivering anticancer therapeutics; nonetheless, various challenges must be addressed before entering the translational phase (Roxana Petrovici et al., 2023). Maintaining consistency from source to source and batch to batch is essential for biopolymers. Thorough optimization and biosafety assessments are essential for dextran-based drug delivery systems. Dextran is a versatile nanocarrier that can be adapted into different forms, such as nanogels or prodrugs (Chen et al., 2020; Sameer Khan et al., 2023). It offers a promising strategy to address usual challenges in chemotherapy, including chronic treatment, poor aqueous solubility, and the instability of antitumor agents. It offers effective preventive measures, characterized by their biocompatibility, biodegradability, low toxicity, and low immunogenicity. This strategy promotes cellular uptake, enables controlled and sustained drug release, facilitates targeted delivery, offers customizability, and ensures compatibility in combination therapy. Dextrans, as a carrier, can effectively address numerous issues associated with current chemotherapy practices.

Gelatin

Gelatin, sourced from collagen, is a natural polymer known for its low toxicity, biocompatibility, and biodegradability (Milano et al., 2023). Collagen comprises approximately 30% of the key structural proteins in the human body, occurring in various forms, including fibrous tissues, bones, blood vessels, and the gastrointestinal tract. Bovine is the primary source of commercially available gelatin, derived from the partial acid or alkali hydrolysis of collagen, which produces type A or type B gelatin accordingly (Tan et al., 2018). Gelatin is a unique macromolecule characterized by its amphiphilic nature, featuring a blend of positively charged amino acids like lysine and arginine, lipophilic residues such as valine and leucine, and negatively charged components including aspartic and glutamic acid. These elements make up approximately 35% of its structure. Gelatin's unique helical structure and abundance of active anionic and cationic groups make it a reliable and adaptable carrier for various therapeutic agents. Gelatin serves multiple functions in the biopharmaceutical sector, including as a binder, stabilizer, gelling agent, and hemostatic agent (Jiang et al., 2023). This has led to its recognition as an effective drug carrier for widely used hydrophilic and lipophilic anticancer agents such as paclitaxel, DOX, docetaxel, cisplatin, and gemcitabine. Gelatin nanoparticles are prepared using various techniques, including emulsification, solvent evaporation, desolvation, coacervation-phase separation, and nanoprecipitation. Gelatin nanoparticles exhibit multiple drug release mechanisms that can operate independently or in tandem. These mechanisms include self-diffusion, bioerosion, and degradation of matrix metalloproteinases (MMPs). Gelatin serves as a substrate for MMPs, which are found to be overexpressed at the blood–brain barrier and in the tumor microenvironment. This feature offers a promising approach for the design of nanoparticles and targeted drug delivery (Ding et al., 2024; Manjit et al., 2024).

Hyaluronic acid

HA, also known as hyaluronan, is a naturally occurring substance found in all vertebrates, including humans (Gagneja et al., 2024). It is especially prevalent in synovial fluid and the vitreous humor. HA synthase in plasma membranes is synthesized (Jha et al., 2024b) as part of the extracellular systems. HA is a linear anionic polymer comprising a nonsulfated glycosaminoglycan chain featuring repeating disaccharide units of N-acetyl D-glucosamine and D-glucuronic acid (Huang and Huang, 2018). The polymer's size and concentration differ based on the source. Low molecular weight HA demonstrates good solubility in water, whereas polymers exceeding 200 kDa exhibit exceptional water retention, which is crucial for maintaining hydration. The molecular weight of the HA polymer plays a crucial role in determining its impact on cancer progression. LMW or oligo-HA is predominantly found at the tumor cell periphery and is frequently associated with elevated CD44 expression (Pashkina et al., 2025). CD44 is a transmembrane glycoprotein commonly overexpressed in cancer cells, demonstrating a strong affinity for HA, contributing to cancer progression. The interaction of HA with its receptor enhances the aggressiveness of solid tumors, primarily through the migration and proliferation of tumor cells (Yasin et al., 2022). The uncontrolled growth can be addressed by externally administering high molecular weight (HMW) HA, known for its lower affinity for CD44. The bio-adhesive property of HA enhances cellular uptake by working synergistically with its affinity for overexpressed receptors. HA, being a negatively charged molecule, notably extends the circulation half-life of the encapsulated therapeutics. Reactive oxygen species (ROS) and enzymes such as hyaluronidase-like protein and hyaluronidases effectively degrade HA in extreme pH conditions (below 4 or above 11), promoting the targeted release of antitumor agents (Bhattacharyya et al., 2023). This could improve the overall effectiveness of antitumor treatments. HA nanoparticles have become increasingly favored in polymer-based drug delivery systems, functioning effectively as independent carriers and copolymers to target metal nanoparticle frameworks within the tumor microenvironment.

Cellulose

Cellulose is an organic compound characterized as a linear polysaccharide, consisting of D-glucose monomer subunits interconnected by β (Beach et al., 2024; Kumar et al., 2025; Xiao et al., 2022; Jia et al., 2025) glycosidic linkages (Das et al., 2022). It offers several advantages, including cost-effectiveness and high mechanical strength. The choice of cellulose source, whether from plants, tree bark, marine plants, algae, or bacteria, affects the particle size, morphology, and crystallinity of the resulting nanoparticles. The surface charge of the cellulose carrier depends on the extraction method used. It can include various techniques, such as acid hydrolysis with agents like sulfuric acid, hydrochloric acid, maleic acid, or phosphoric acid (Lugoloobi et al., 2021). Enzyme hydrolysis is another option that utilizes cellulase and endoglucanase. Alternatively, oxidation can be employed using $NaIO_4$, HA, 2,2,6,6-tetramethyl-1-piperidine-N-oxide, or ammonium persulfate. They are noted for their mucoadhesive properties, gel formation ability, and hydrophilic nature. Its unique structure is characterized by inter- and intramolecular hydrogen bonding, which makes it insoluble in water and organic solvents. Despite its solubility challenges, it has proven to be an effective material for preparing highly stable nanoparticles (Aziz et al., 2022; Raghav et al., 2023). Chemically altering the hydroxyl groups via esterification, etherification, carboxylation, and acetylation can increase the solubility of cellulose. Among the cellulose derivatives, methylcellulose, carboxymethyl cellulose, and hydroxypropyl methylcellulose are notable examples. The cellulose nanoparticles are prepared using cross-linking, ionic gelation, and nanoprecipitation. The modified cellulose is a versatile component that can be employed independently or in conjunction with various organic or inorganic ligands, thereby enhancing the precision of the delivery system. The cellulose nanocarrier has been investigated for multiple administration routes, including oral, local, and topical applications. IV dosing is generally avoided because of the crystalline structure associated with it. The sustained release, enhanced cellular interaction, increased absorption, and reduction of dose linked to the cellulose nanoparticles present a promising avenue to mitigate the adverse effects of chemotherapy. Several limitations are associated with it, including the potential for immunogenic responses to the substance, cytotoxicity, and lower degradation of cellulose both in vitro and in vivo (Garg et al., 2025). A standard recommendation is to apply a coating of biocompatible polymers to overcome these challenges.

Synthetic polymers

Synthetic polymers are widely used in current cancer therapies as they improve drug solubility, stability, circulation time, and tumor-targeting potency. They also reduce systemic toxicity by enabling targeted and localized distribution. It can be engineered to produce precise medication release characteristics, avoid degradation while in circulation, and allow active targeting to tumor cells while limiting exposure to healthy tissues and providing systems that respond to pH, temperature, or enzyme levels to release the drug only in the tumor environment. A few synthetic polymers utilized in the formulation of PNPs are given below.

Poly(lactic-co-glycolic acid) (PLGA)

PLGA is a biodegradable polymer for the design of nanoparticles for drug delivery (Tabatabaei Mirakabad et al., 2014). The U.S. Food and Drug Administration (FDA) has approved its application emphasizing its controlled and sustained-release characteristics, low toxicity, and superior biocompatibility with tissues and cells. PLGA nanoparticles undergo degradation in vivo via the hydrolysis of ester bonds, resulting in the formation of their monomeric anions, which include lactate and glycolate (Ochi et al., 2021; Rezvantalab et al., 2018). PLGA is generally synthesized through a catalyzed ring-opening copolymerization process involving LA (lactic acid) and GA (glycolic acid). PLGA, being a copolymer of both components, possesses the inherent characteristics of its constituent monomers (Yang et al., 2024). The degradation rate of this polymer is significantly influenced by the ratio of LA to GA and its molecular weight. An increase in the LA/GA ratio results in heightened hydrophobicity of PLGA, which subsequently causes a reduction in degradation and a slower rate of drug release. Reducing molecular weight increases degradation and drug release rates. The degradation, release kinetics, and molecular weight are also related to the size of the resulting nanoparticles formulated (Rezvantalab et al., 2018). These elements are essential for the effectiveness of PLGA nanoparticles in therapy. While larger formulations have a greater capacity for drug loading, it is crucial to attain a smaller nano-size range. This smaller size is vital for nanoparticles to effectively navigate biological barriers and reach the targeted disease site.

Poly(ε-caprolactone)

PCL is a biodegradable and biocompatible polyester widely used for drug delivery due to its slow degradation rate (Mulinti et al., 2018). Notably, it can incorporate a range of functionalities into its backbone. PCL is a semicrystalline polymer known for its remarkable ability to modify its crystallinity with its molecular weight. It demonstrates impressive elastic behavior at room temperature, allowing for transformation into different structural forms (Bhadran et al., 2023). For the synthesis of a polymer, primarily two strategies are employed, namely polycondensation and ring-opening polymerization. Recently, a green synthesis strategy has emerged as a favored approach to addressing the toxicity concern associated with stannous-based catalysts used in synthesis, as well as safety issues (Bhadran et al., 2023). The copolymerization process can modify the PCL, which plays a crucial role in the advancement of nano-drug delivery systems, including nanoparticles, micelles, and dendrimers (Rainbolt et al., 2015). It has proven to be an effective vehicle for delivering diverse therapeutic agents, including proteins, oligonucleotides, DNA, siRNA, and peptides. In addition, a new strategy has emerged in tissue engineering to design and develop PCL-based materials through surface functionalization with various components, including antibodies, collagen, laminin, fibrin, and peptides.

Poly(2-hydroxyethyl methacrylate) (pHEMA)

pHEMA is a remarkable polymer due to its biocompatibility, cytocompatibility, and minimal immunological response from host tissue. Initially, pHEMA rendered it an ideal biomaterial for developing contact lenses (Zare et al., 2021). Shima Ghaffari et al. formulate ibuprofen-HEMA and diclofenac-HEMA monomers. In this process, poly(ibuprofen-HEMA-co-HEMA) (PIHH), poly(diclofenac-HEMA-co-HEMA) (PDHH), and pHEMA particles are synthesized using distillation precipitation polymerization (Ghaffari et al., 2024). Additionally, this study involved loading DOX into the prepared particles, demonstrating that DOX exhibits a higher release rate in acidic pH, attributed to the enhanced solubility of DOX, as well as the accelerated release of DOX molecules from the nanocarriers. The study delves into the toxicity of particles, revealing that when the drug is loaded into pHEMA particles, the release results in fewer toxic effects compared to its free state (without any nanocarrier). Notably, the inclusion of ibuprofen and diclofenac in the particles, specifically PIHH and PDHH, significantly reduces cytotoxicity.

Poly(N-isopropylacrylamide) (PNIPAAm)

Poly(N-isopropylacrylamide) (PNIPAAm) is a thermoresponsive polymer that can be employed in the design of stimuli-responsive PNPs for precise drug delivery. Such nanoparticles release the drug when exposed to temperature changes.

Recent advances and innovations

PNPs have gained significant attention in the landscape of anticancer drug delivery for controlled release, precise targeting, and minimized systemic toxicity, as summarized in Fig. 16.3. The structural flexibility of PNPs resulted in the discovery of various advanced systems like receptor-targeted nanoparticles, microenvironment-responsive systems, and hybrid and multifunctional systems (Fig. 16.4). Additionally, smart polymers responsive to certain physiological conditions represent a promising strategy in drug delivery. These stimuli-responsive polymers enable site-specific delivery, thus reducing off-target effects and maximizing therapeutic responses. The incorporation of such high-tech materials in drug delivery systems not only maximizes the therapeutic effectiveness but also minimizes side effects. As research and technology advance in this area, the potential for PNPs to transform drug delivery in an unprecedented manner is promising, underscoring the need for

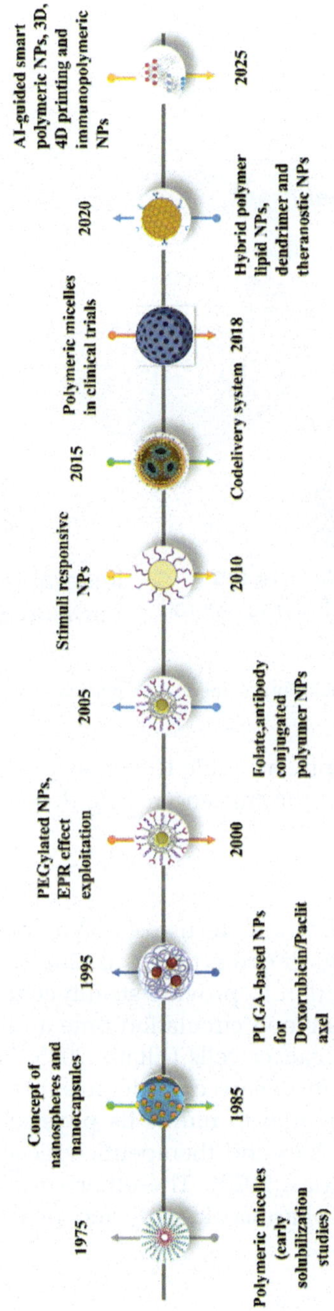

FIGURE 16.3 Historical development in polymeric nanoparticles.

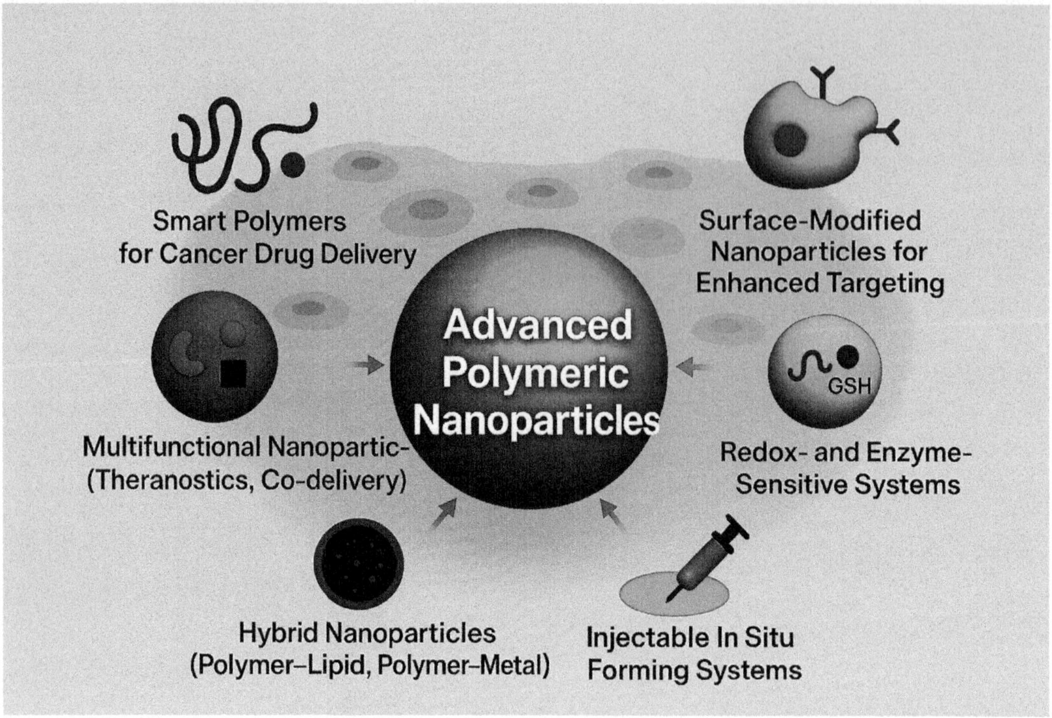

FIGURE 16.4 Advancement in polymeric nanoparticles for anticancer drug delivery.

continued innovation and development. Table 16.1 shows a few examples of advanced polymeric nanoformulations exploited for anticancer drug delivery.

Surface-functionalized PNPs

Recent advancements in PNPs include the use of polymers, lipids, ligands, and antibodies for the targeted delivery of anticancer drugs (Jha et al., 2022). PEGylation is one such widely used method in polymer conjugation to provide stealth coating (Banerjee et al., 2025). The stealth coating of PNPs enhances blood circulation time and diminishes particular interactions between nanoparticles and cancer cells (Eltaib, 2025; Bajracharya et al., 2022; Pearce and O'Reilly, 2019). Over the last few years, considerable interest has focused on developing alternatives to PEG with the potential to mimic its physicochemical benefits and possess favorable pharmacokinetic properties and therapeutic efficacy of nanosystems (Hoang Thi et al., 2020; El-Hammadi and Arias, 2022). The other surface modification strategy used for improving physicochemical, pharmacokinetic, and pharmacodynamic performance of drugs in PNPs is discussed below.

TABLE 16.1 Recent advancements in polymeric nanoparticles for cancer drug delivery.

Polymeric system	Polymer	Drug/active agent	Nanoparticle type/ modification	Target cancer type	Mechanism/delivery strategy	Key finding/outcome	Clinical status	References
Polymersome	Poly(ethylene oxide) (PEO), poly (γ-methyl-ε-caprolactone)	Cisplatin	Bioresorbable polymersomes	Colon cancer	Drug release after binding with the α5β1 integrin	Improved delivery efficacy, increased cisplatin-induced losses to targeted DLD-1 colon cancer cell viability, low toxicity	Ex vivo investigation	Petersen et al. (2013)
Polymersome	Methoxy-poly (ethylene glycol), amino-terminal PEG 2000	Doxorubicin	Poly(methoxy-poly (ethylene glycol)/ ethyl-p-aminobenzoate) phosphazenes (PEPs)	Breast cancer	-	Growth inhibition of MCF-7 xenograft tumors in nude mice demonstrated that PEP polymersomes could enhance safety and encapsulation efficacy	In vivo	Xu et al. (2014)
Nanoparticles	Polyethene glycol and poly(lactide-co-glycolide)	Puerarin and 5-fluorouracil	5-fluorouracil-puerarin nanomaterial coated with dioleoylphosphatidic acids (DOPAs)	Lung cancer	-	5FU-PRN NMs improve biocompatibility and effectiveness in lung cancer cells	In vitro and in vivo	Zhao et al. (2021)
Nanoparticles	Poly(vanillyl alcohol-co-oxalate), PLGA	Curcumin	Oxidation-responsive PNPs	Breast cancer	ROS-responsive PVAX nanoparticles degrade in the oxidative tumor microenvironment and release the drug at the tumor site	Exhibit ROS-triggered degradation and drug release, enhance anticancer efficacy in breast cancer, and show synergistic therapeutic effect	In vitro and in vivo	Huang et al. (2018)
Trastuzumab PAMAM dendrimer	PAMAM dendrimer (G4, amine terminated) + PEG linker (MAL-PEG-NHS)	Docetaxel	Trastuzumab-grafted PAMAM dendrimer	HER2-positive breast cancer	Active targeting via Trastuzumab-HER2 receptor interaction (receptor-mediated endocytosis)	Enhanced uptake and cytotoxicity, 2.5-fold higher apoptosis compared with free DTX, active targeting to the tumor microenvironment	Preclinical	Kulhari et al. (2016)
Micelle-like structure	Poloxamer	Methotrexate	Micelle-like nanoparticles,	Broad range of	Dual-phase drug release, initially releasing entrapped drug followed by sustained	Increase MRT and AUC and improve systemic exposure	Preclinical	Ren et al. (2015)

(*Continued*)

TABLE 16.1 Recent advancements in polymeric nanoparticles for cancer drug delivery.—cont'd

Polymeric system	Polymer	Drug/active agent	Nanoparticle type/ modification	Target cancer type	Mechanism/delivery strategy	Key finding/outcome	Clinical status	References
			self-assembled conjugates	anticancer potential	release from conjugated drug via ester bond hydrolysis	and pharmacokinetics compared with the free drug		
Nanoparticles	PLGA, TPGS	Docetaxel and P-gp inhibitor	Codelivery of docetaxel and poloxamer 235 using PLGA-TPGS nanoparticles	Breast cancer	TPGS and P235 act as P-gp inhibitors, which enhance intracellular accumulation of DTX, passive targeting, and sustained drug release	Overcome MDR, significantly higher cytotoxicity in resistant MCF-7/ADR cells	Preclinical	Tang et al. (2015)
Nanoparticles	Poly(ethylene glycol), poly (lactic-co-glycolic acid)	Docetaxel	APRPG peptide-conjugated PEG-PLGA nanoparticles	Ovarian cancer	APRPG-conjugated PEG-PLGA nanoparticles bind to angiogenic endothelial cells and tumor vasculature, which enhances accumulation at the tumor microenvironment	APRPG-PEG-PLGA nanoparticles showed improved tumor targeting, higher cytotoxicity, increased apoptosis, and superior antitumor efficacy compared to nontargeted nanoparticles and reduced systemic toxicity	Preclinical	Wang et al. (2014)
Micelles	Polycaprolactone, polyethene glycol	Doxorubicin, chlorin	Self-assembled star-shaped micelles	Breast cancer	Micelles enable codelivery—chlorin generates ROS upon light irradiation	Enhance cellular uptake, improve ROS generation, synergistic cytotoxicity, and tumor suppression, and reduce systemic toxicity	Preclinical	Peng et al. (2008)
Micelles	Polycaprolactone, polyethene glycol	Doxorubicin	Self-assembled biodegradable star-shaped micelles	Breast cancer	Enhance solubility and stability, passive targeting, controlled release in an acidic environment	It showed higher drug loading capacity, sustained release, enhanced cytotoxicity, improved tumor suppression, and reduced systemic toxicity compared to the free drug	Preclinical	Dong et al. (2010)

Polymersomes	Poly(ethylene glycol)-b-polycarbonate with pH-sensitive/ROS-sensitive linkages	Gemcitabine and doxorubicin	Polymersomes with dual drug encapsulation	Pancreatic cancer	Enable cytosolic delivery via endosomal escape, dual drug codelivery enhances synergistic anticancer efficacy, pH-responsive drug delivery	Efficient coloading of hydrophilic and hydrophobic drugs and synergistic activity	Preclinical	Nahire et al. (2014)
Polymersomes	Pluronic F127 and polylactic acid	Doxorubicin	Polymersomes modified with transferrin and folate ligand	Breast cancer	Ligand targeting via transferrin receptor and folate receptor	Significantly enhanced tumor-specific uptake and improved cytotoxicity	Preclinical	Wang et al. (2022)
Polymersomes	Amphiphilic block copolymer (PEG-PCL or PEG-PLA)	Doxorubicin, camptothecin	Polymersomes conjugated with FOXM1 aptamer for self-targeting and coencapsulation of dual drugs	Nonsmall cell lung cancer	FOXM1 aptamer facilitates self-targeting to FOXM1-overexpressing NSCLC cells	Enhanced selective uptake, synergistic cytotoxicity from DOX and CPT, and aptamer-mediated tumor targeting significantly improved therapeutic efficacy	Preclinical	Shahriari et al. (2021)

Receptor-targeted nanoparticles

PNPs can be integrated with polymers, antibodies, peptides, or small molecules having binding affinity toward the overexpressed receptors on tumor cells for targeted delivery to cancer cells. Heparin, a glycosaminoglycan with high affinity for growth factors and intrinsic biocompatibility, has been employed as a surface modification (Liang and Kiick, 2014). Heparin-functionalized PLGA nanoparticles had increased cellular uptake and tumor accumulation in mouse models compared to unmodified controls (Chung et al., 2010). The approach of active targeting improves the concentration of the drug at the site, simultaneously minimizing systemic toxicity and unintended exposure to nontarget areas (Ly et al., 2024). Frequently utilized ligands for targeted delivery in cancer cells include transferrin, antibodies, antibody fragments, peptides specifically RGD peptide (Arginylglycylaspartic acid) sequences targeting integrins, and tiny compounds like folic acid. These ligands enhance receptor-mediated endocytosis and optimize intracellular drug delivery. For example, transferrin is overexpressed up to 100-fold in tumor cells relative to normal cells, rendering it an appealing targeting moiety. Antibody-based targeting, especially against HER2 receptors, has shown considerable efficacy in breast cancer treatment (Kumar and Rajnikanth, 2020). Moreover, addressing the tumor microenvironment presents an alternative strategy. Ligands such as vascular endothelial growth factor (VEGF) antibodies or RGD peptides specifically target angiogenic endothelial cells, whereas enzymes and extracellular matrix components are utilized for localized accumulation.

Stimuli-responsive and smart polymers

Stimuli-responsive nanoparticles have emerged as an advanced method in drug delivery, offering precise drug delivery and low dosing frequency while maintaining therapeutic drug concentrations at disease sites for longer durations. These nanoparticles are equipped with stimuli-responsive polymers that respond to physiological triggers, including pH, temperature, and redox systems (Jha et al., 2024a). Through modulating their composition, response to internal or external stimulus can be tuned for drug encapsulation in and release from the nanoparticle for target-specific therapeutic effects (Taghizadeh et al., 2015; Gil and Hudson, 2004; MacEwan et al., 2010). These systems have generally been termed "smart" or "environment-sensitive" polymers due to their dynamic responsiveness to biological conditions. Extensive work has focused on formulating such materials for selective drug delivery, with changes in pH, ROS, and temperature (Gil and Hudson, 2004; Cheng et al., 2014). Polymeric micelles with pH-sensitive substances allow drugs to be released in an acidic tumor microenvironment or in tumor cells only, maximizing efficacy and minimizing systemic side effects (Ulbrich and Šubr, 2004). Another important approach exploits redox variations in diseased and healthy tissues. Tumor tissues exhibit elevated levels of glutathione (GSH) within the cytoplasm. Redox-responsive linkages, including diselenide bonds, play a significant role in various applications. Single bonds, disulfide bonds, platinum conjugation, thioether bonds, and thiol groups are commonly utilized in drug delivery systems to effectively target redox-responsive sites. Reduction-sensitive nanocarriers that cleave in GSH-rich conditions utilize the diselenide bond (-Se-Se-) and the disulfide bond (Ma et al., 2018; Mollazadeh et al., 2021). Se bonds are effective cross-linking agents and are integral to diblock copolymers, strategically positioned between hydrophilic and hydrophobic segments. The responsiveness of selenium bonds to low concentrations in redox environments is effectively harnessed in innovative drug delivery systems, given that selenium atoms also exhibit anti-cancer properties (He et al., 2019). The reduction of Pt(IV) derivatives plays a crucial role in releasing cisplatin from redox-sensitive drug carriers, serving as an effective redox-responsive linkage that can be reduced to a thiol group in the presence of a reducing agent. On the other hand, the thioether bond undergoes oxidation to form a hydrophilic sulfoxide or sulfone when exposed to an oxidizing agent. Thioether moieties exhibit a notable responsiveness to oxidation, whereas disulfide bonds can be cleaved by reducing and oxidizing agents. Integrating a redox-responsive chemical linker within the nanoparticle structure significantly enhances the potential for controlled degradation and drug release. Another example is the use of HA–PCL copolymers, which contain disulfide bonds in the HA shell, allowing for redox-responsive breakdown (Han et al., 2015). Temperature-responsive nanocarriers are another important intelligent drug delivery technique. Tumors have greater baseline temperatures than healthy tissues (Danhier et al., 2010). External stimuli, such as ultrasound or magnetic fields, can locally raise tumor temperature, improving treatment accuracy (Zhao et al., 2011; Shi et al., 2013a; Shi et al., 2013b; Liu et al., 2009; Alvarez-Lorenzo and Concheiro, 2014).

Dual-responsive nanoparticles

Single-function nanoparticles often fail to meet clinical requirements; hence, multifunctional designs that integrate stealth, targeting, and stimulus responsiveness are gaining wide popularity (Bao et al., 2013). These systems incorporate PEGylation to enhance blood circulation time, ligand conjugation for active targeting, and stimuli-sensitive linkages for regulated release. For instance, nanoparticle-based PCL–SS–PEG and PCL-PEI-Fol copolymers demonstrate prolonged circulation, tumor accumulation, selective targeting mediated by folate receptors, and reduction-responsive drug release (Siafaka et al., 2016). Likewise, dual pH and redox-sensitive systems use the unique tumor microenvironment for improved treatment accuracy (Li et al., 2020). Thermally sensitive, ligand-decorated nanoparticles and magnetic field-responsive platforms enhance the potential for image-guided, on-demand medication delivery. Multifunctional surface-modified nanoparticles are the next generation of polymeric drug carriers, designed to surmount biological barriers, augment tumor selectivity, and boost therapeutic efficacy while minimizing systemic toxicity (Siafaka et al., 2016).

Biomimetic nanoparticles

Biomimetic nanoparticles mimic natural cellular components to enhance biocompatibility and therapeutic effectiveness. Typically, it has a core-shell structure, where the core provides mechanical stability and the shell, often formed of phospholipids, enhances biocompatibility (Tikhonov et al., 2024). The electrostatic adsorption of lipid bilayers accomplishes phospholipid coating onto a polymeric core with an opposing charge or via hydrophobic interactions, wherein lipid tails attach to the hydrophobic surface and hydrophilic heads project into the aqueous environment. Phosphorylcholine has been extensively employed to enhance dispersion stability and diminish protein adsorption on nanoparticle surfaces, attributable to the hydrophilic head group in phospholipids (Goto et al., 2008; Carmona-Ribeiro, 2010). Moreover, biomimetic techniques utilize membrane proteins or peptides that enhance cellular trafficking, intercellular recognition, and receptor-specific targeting. Surface modification using particular ligands, such as peptides or antigens, facilitates accurate identification of receptors on cancer cells. Furthermore, carbohydrates integrated into natural cell membranes are crucial for maintaining steric stability and facilitating targeting. N-acetylglucosamine functionalized nanoparticles have exhibited selective targeting of vimentin-expressing cancer cells (Kitagawa et al., 2025). Embedding cyclodextrin or chitosan PEG-based nanoparticles greatly extends blood circulation and enhances retention duration by minimizing nonspecific interactions (Najm et al., 2024).

Prolonged circulation of nanoparticles

Prolonged systemic circulation is crucial for successful drug accumulation in the tumor microenvironment or in cancer cells (Fan et al., 2022). The mononuclear phagocyte system swiftly eliminates the nanoparticles by opsonization, which is more apparent in hydrophobic and positively charged particles. To overcome this issue, surface modification using hydrophilic polymers such as PEG, poloxamer, polyacrylamide, or polyvinyl alcohol creates a protective hydration layer that diminishes protein adsorption and macrophage adhesion. PEGylation, accomplished by adsorption or covalent conjugation, is the most recognized stealth method (Suk et al., 2016). PEG-PLA and PEG-PCL block copolymers are extensively utilized, with the PEG chain on the outer surface providing flexibility and steric hindrance, so nonspecific interactions are efficiently reduced. Recent advancements encompass triblock copolymers, such as PCL-PEO-PCL, which self-assemble into nanoparticles featuring a thick hydrophilic brush structure, effectively inhibiting opsonization. Hyperbranched polyphosphates are a potential polymer family characterized by their biodegradability and biomimetic properties. These prolonged circulation systems enhance pharmacokinetics and diminish elimination, facilitating increased tumor drug accumulation. Zwitterionic coatings (betaine-, sulfobetaine-, and phosphorylcholine-based) are next-generation stealth layers as PEG alternatives emerge (Ouyang et al., 2024).

Hybrid nanoparticles

The integration of polymeric and lipid substances yields a hybrid nanoparticle with distinctive features compared to PNPs (Tahir et al., 2020; Jain et al., 2023). Incorporating polymers into conjugates and assessing hybrid materials for drug delivery can improve stability, enhance drug cargo capabilities, control release, and improve in vivo efficiency. Incorporating synthetic polymers in their lower state, rather than through a conventional mixing approach, represents a notable development in polymer science. This approach facilitates a seamless interaction between lipids and polymers, thereby eliminating the separation phase that typically occurs when natural or inorganic polymers are mixed. This method offers several benefits, primarily focused on conjugate solubility or stability and ultimately decreasing system toxicity (Gajbhiye et al., 2023). Hybrid nanoparticles are the most promising strategy for encapsulating various therapeutic agents within polymer lipid hybrid nanoparticles (PLHNPs), thereby enhancing their synergistic activity. Polymer and metal complexes also come under the hybrid nanoparticle, which integrates metallic components, such as gold or iron oxide nanoparticles, with multifunctional properties for theragnostic applications (Oh and Park, 2011). The gold polymer hybrids enable photothermal therapy, where near-infrared irradiation generates localized heat to ablate tumor cells while simultaneously releasing the encapsulated drugs. Similarly, iron oxide polymer hybrids allow magnetic resonance imaging guidance and magnetically triggered drug release. Beyond PEGylation, emerging functionalization strategies, such as dual ligand modification, have gained attention to improve drug delivery to specific sites (Negi et al., 2024). For example, surface-modified nanoparticles with folic acid and transferrin target overexpressed receptors in tumor cells. Enhanced stability, therapeutic efficacy, and multifunctionality make them promising candidates for next-generation anticancer therapies. However, large-scale manufacturing reproducibility and regulatory approval remain challenges.

Theranostic polymeric nanoparticles

Theranostic PNPs are inorganic nanoparticles designed using a polymer for anticancer drug delivery and theranostic applications (Jha et al., 2022). Unimodal, dual, or multimodal imaging is possible when PNPs are loaded with one or more imaging agents. Photoacoustic imaging, magnetic resonance imaging, ultrasound imaging, positron emission tomography, single-photon emission computed tomography, and other optical imaging are a few of the imaging techniques that can be combined with chemo/photothermal/photodynamic therapy using theranostic PNPs.

Clinical, regulatory, and patent perspectives

Clinical trials, patents, and regulations on PNPs in cancer therapy serve as the bridge between scientific creativity and practical implementation. Due to their role in targeted delivery, modulated release, and multifunctional theranostic applications, PNPs require rigorous clinical testing to confirm safety, pharmacokinetics, and therapeutic impact. Oncology drug and therapeutic intervention development and commercialization are heavily patent-driven, so patents protect intellectual property and indicate innovation and competition. In a more globally harmonized approach, the FDA and European Medicines Agency (EMA) are focusing on nanoscale PNP issues like long-term toxicity, immunogenicity, scalability, and reproducibility. The U.S. Clinical Trials Registry (https://clinicaltrials.gov/), the U.K. ISRCTN (https://www.isrctn.com/), and ReBEC (https://ensaiosclinicos.gov.br/) are just a few of the many international registries searched to find comprehensive clinical trials on the therapeutic usefulness of PNPs in cancer treatment. All of these resources provide relevant and up-to-date information regarding PNP-based formulations and their clinical translational research. PNPs for anticancer drug delivery-related clinical trials and patents are listed in Tables 16.2 and 16.3, respectively.

TABLE 16.2 Patents on polymeric nanoparticles for anticancer drug delivery.

Patent No./ Applicant No.	Drug	Polymer/key excipients	Therapeutic use	Inventor and Applicant	Reference
US20230033582A1	Mefloquine	PLGA, PLA, PGA, polyvinyl alcohol (PVA), PEG	Colorectal, lung, pancreatic cancer	Scott C., Longley D., Humphreys L., McDaid W. (Queen's University Belfast)	Scott et al., (2023)
US20220354787A1	Nucleic acids (e.g., siRNA, miRNA), plasmid DNA (e.g., STAT3 or FoxF1 gene constructs), stabilized RNA (e.g., eGFP RNA	Polyethylenimine (PEI), fatty acids, poly(ethylene glycol) (PEG)	Pulmonary vascular disease	Kalininchenko V., Dunn A., and Shi D. (Cincinnati Children's Hospital Medical Center and University of Cincinnati)	Kalinichenko et al. (2017)
US11344627B2	Methotrexate	Poly(amidoamine) (PAMAM) dendrimers incorporated into exosome shells	Cancer therapeutics: broad spectrum (solid and liquid tumors)	Hong S.-P. and Park S.-J. (Wisconsin Alumni Research Foundation)	Hong and Park (2022)
US2021170040A1	Immunomodulatory agents such as STING agonists, CSF1R inhibitors, PARP inhibitors, VEGFR tyrosine kinase inhibitors, MEK inhibitors, glutaminase inhibitors, TIE II antagonists, CXCR2 inhibitors, and STING antagonists	PAMAM dendrimers (G4-G10, hydroxyl terminated)	Small molecules/ biologics for cancer	Cleland J., Sharma R., Sun M., Appiani S., Slusher B., Rais R., Rangaramanujam K. (Ashvattha Therapeutics Inc.)	Cleland et al. (2021)
US9782342B2	Methotrexate (MTX), 5-fluorouracil (5-FU)	Poly(lactic-co-glycolic acid) (PLGA), PLA, PGA, PCL, or chitosan; human serum albumin as a targeting agent; magnetite or cobalt ferrite as a magnetic core	Osteosarcoma, rheumatoid arthritis (RA)	Asmatulu R., Misak H., Yang S-Y., Wooley P. (Wichita State University)	Asmatulu et al. (2017)
US20160303053A1	Camptothecin	Poly(ε-caprolactone) (PCL)	Solid tumors	Barua S. (University of Missouri-St. Louis)	Barua, 2016
US9023395B2	Curcumin, paclitaxel	PLGA, PVA, and bis-succinimidyl suberate (BS3) were used as surface-active linker/ spacer	Prostate cancer	Braden A. R. C. and Vishwanatha J. K. (University of North Texas Health Science Centre)	Braden and Vishwanatha (2015)

US 8,945,629 B2	Cisplatin	Poly(ethylene glycol) (PEG), PDMA, PDEA	Solid tumor chemotherapy	Radosz M., Xu P., Shen Y. (University of Wyoming)	Radosz et al. (2015)
WO2015023775A1	Nucleic acids (e.g., DNA, RNA, miRNA)	PLGA-modified polyethylenimine (PLGA-PEI) conjugates; optionally APMP-PLGA-PEI	Pancreatic cancer	Lu J-M., Yao Q., Chen C. (Baylor College of Medicine)	Lu et al. (2019)
WO2014210485A1	Docetaxel	PLA-PEG nanoparticles	Prostate and other solid tumors	Wright J. (Bind Therapeutics Inc.)	Wright (2014)
US2010015051A1	Paclitaxel	Biodegradable polymeric nanoparticles (PLGA, transferrin)	Prostate cancer	Labhasetwar V. D. , Sahoo S. K. (University of Nebraska Medical School)	Labhasetwar and Sahoo (2010)
US6585956B2	Cisplatin	Polyamidoamine (PAMAM)	Malignant tumors (ovarian, lung, testicular, breast, stomach cancers, lymphoma, melanoma, leukemia)	Malik N. and Duncan R. (Dow Chemical Company initially, later assigned to Dendritic Nanotechnologies Inc.)	Malik and Duncan (2003)

TABLE 16.3 Some formulations under clinical trial for anticancer drug delivery.

Product/ Platform	Carrier and cargo	Indication(s)	Phase	Key findings	References
BIND-014 (Accurin)	PLGA-based PSMA-targeted docetaxel	Metastatic prostate cancer	Phase II	~12% response rate; manageable toxicity profile	Von Hoff et al. (2016)
CRLX101 (NLG207/ IT-101)	Cyclodextrin-PEG polymer-camptothecin	Advanced solid tumors (lung, ovarian, etc.)	Phase I/IIa and II	MTD = 15 mg/m^2 biweekly; ~64% stable disease, NSCLC subgroup PFS ~4.4 mo	Weiss et al. (2013)
NK012	PEG-PGlu SN-38 polymeric micelle	Metastatic colorectal, TNBC, relapsed SCLC	Phase II	ORR ~3.8% but low diarrhea; acceptable neutropenia	Hamaguchi et al. (2018)
NK105	PEG-P (Asp-4-phenyl-1-butanol) paclitaxel micelle	Gastric, breast cancer	Phase III	Completed phase III in metastatic/recurrent breast cancer	Hamaguchi et al. (2007)
NK911	PEG-P (Asp)–doxorubicin micelle	Pancreatic and colorectal cancer	Phase I/II	MTD ~50 mg/m^2; disease stabilization in multiple pts	Matsumura et al. (2004)
NC-6004 (Nanoplatin)	PEG-P (Glu) cisplatin micelle	Pancreatic, H and N, bladder, lung	Phase III	Improved safety, reduced nephrotoxicity; efficacy comparable	Plummer et al. (2011)
NC-6300	PEG-P (Asp-hydrazone) epirubicin micelle	Solid tumors	Phase I	Acid-labile release system, early safety established	Chawla et al. (2020)
NC-4016	PEG-P (Glu) DACH-platinum micelle	Solid tumors, lymphoma	Phase I	Early-stage proof-of-concept with limited toxicity	Varela-Moreira et al. (2017)
SP1049C	Pluronic-based doxorubicin micelle	Esophageal/GEJ adenocarcinoma	Phase II	Activity seen in advanced gastroesophageal cancer	Valle et al. (2011)
AZD2811 (Accurin)	PLGA-based Aurora B inhibitor nanoparticle	Advanced solid tumors	Phase I	Dose escalation ongoing for safety and PK (NCBI)	AstraZeneca (2017)
ThermoDox	Polymer-encapsulated doxorubicin (thermosensitive)	Chest-wall recurrent breast cancer	Phase I/II	Combined with heat; early safety data reported (NCBI)	Zagar et al. (2014)
ABI-011	Albumin nanoparticle–thiocolchicine	Recurrent tumors	Phase I	Early dose-finding study ongoing (NCBI)	Celgene (2011)
CRLX301	Cyclodextrin-based nanoparticle docetaxel	Solid tumors	Phase I/II	Combination and monotherapy early-stage trials (NCBI)	Piha-Paul et al. (2021)

Marketed products

Several commercialized products that utilize PNPs as anticancer therapeutics have been developed, marking a significant milestone in the process of translating nanotechnology-based research into clinically confirmed and commercially available therapeutics. These formulations demonstrate that PNPs can be utilized to enhance targeted drug delivery, thereby

TABLE 16.4 Commercially available marketed formulation for anticancer drug delivery.

Brand name/ Trade name	API	Route of administration	Polymer used	Dosage form	Indication	Regulatory approval	Manufacturer
Abraxane (021,660)	Paclitaxel	IV	Albumin (natural polymer)	Inj. Suspension	Metastatic breast cancer, NSCLC, pancreatic cancer	US FDA, 2005	Bristol Myers Squibb
Genexol-PM	Paclitaxel	Powder; IV	mPEG-PLA (amphiphilic block copolymer)	Polymeric micelles	Breast, lung, ovarian cancer	MFDS Korea, 2007	Samyang Biopharmaceuticals Corporation
Nanoxel (DR-XY42006)	Docetaxel	Intravenous infusion	mPEG-PLA)	Polymeric nanoparticle	Breast, prostate, and gastric cancer	CDSCO, India, 2010	Fresenius Kabi Oncology Limited
Paclitaxel/ Apealea	Paclitaxel	Intravenous infusion	XR-17 (poly(ethylidene glycol)-octadecyl polymer)	Polymeric micelles	Ovarian cancer	EMA, 2018	Oasmia Pharmaceutical
Genexol	Paclitaxel	Intravenous infusion	Poly(ethylene glycol)-poly(D,L-lactide)	Polymeric micelles	Metastatic breast cancer, pancreatic cancer	MFDS, Korea	Samyang Biopharmaceuticals Corporation
Eligard	Leuprolide acetate	Subcutaneous injection	PLG, PLGH	Inj/Infusion	Prostate cancer	US FDA	ATRIX Laboratories, Inc.
Opaxio	Paclitaxel	IV infusion/ powder for reconstitution	Polyglutamete	Polymeric nanoparticle	Glioblastoma	No	Cell Therapeutics, Inc.
Eligard	Leuprolide acetate	Depot suspension	PLGA copolymer (DL-lactide/glycolide	Subcutaneous depot injection	Prostate cancer	US FDA and EMA	Tolmar Inc.
Transdrug	Doxorubicin	Hepatic intraarterial injection	Polyalkylcynoacrylate nanoparticles	Lyophilized powder to be reconstituted	Hepatocellular carcinoma	Orphan drug/ US FDA and EMA	BioAlliance Pharma SA
Oncaspar	Pegylated L-asparaginase	IM, IV	PEG conjugate protein nanoparticle	Injection, solution	Lymphoblastic leukemia	US FDA	Enzo/Les Laboratoires Servier

overcoming the significant limitations of traditional anticancer drugs. Their availability in the market supports not only their therapeutic efficacy and safety evidence, as demonstrated through rigorous clinical trials, but also their approval in regulatory frameworks across various regions. A brief overview of these products commercialized, including composition, therapeutic application, and clinical significance, is outlined in an organized manner in Table 16.4 that validates the transfer of polymeric nanomedicine from laboratory innovation to real-world cancer management.

Future prospects and opportunities

The future of PNPs holds a revolutionary opportunity for convergence with diagnostics, paving the way for the design of actual theranostic systems (Karam et al., 2022). These platforms will integrate treatment with drug delivery, real-time imaging, disease monitoring, and response to treatment. Imaging agents, fluorescent probes, or contrast molecule-containing PNPs can serve dual purposes, enabling physicians to monitor both biodistribution and tumor accumulation, as well as treatment efficacy over time. This theranostic strategy can accelerate precision oncology through personalizing the treatment regimen depending on each patient's response, reducing undue drug exposure, and enhancing long-term survival rates. Furthermore, coupling polymeric carriers with molecular biomarkers and genotypic profiling will provide the means for making personalized cancer treatments a feasible part of the broader scheme of personalized medicine. Artificial intelligence (AI) and machine learning (ML) represent a new frontier in the design and improvement of PNPs (Logakannan et al., 2025). The intricacy of nanoparticle systems, with many adjustable parameters including polymer composition, molecular weight, surface modification, particle size, and drug loading capacity, renders classical trial-and-error methods time-consuming and resource-wasting. AI-based modeling, big data analysis, and in silico simulations have the potential to significantly accelerate the discovery and optimization process. ML models can predict how nanoparticles interact with tumors, improve formulation strategies, and even use preclinical data to forecast clinical outcomes (Musa et al., 2025). AI-powered molecular docking and virtual screening may also aid in creating polymer–drug conjugates and ligand-modified polymeric systems that are more specific and less toxic (Vora et al., 2023). These advancements are likely to reduce developmental costs and timelines, thereby facilitating the faster clinical translation of novel PNP formulations. In parallel, GSH-sensitive polymeric micelles and nanoparticles exploit the higher GSH concentrations in the tumor to initiate drug release. Notably, cisplatin-loaded polyurethane nanoparticles demonstrated effective tumor targeting and inhibition of growth in lung cancer models (Iyer et al., 2020). Another viable material is the pullulan bioconjugate, a pH-sensitive polysaccharide that exhibits improved drug release and targeting properties when bioconjugated with agents such as DOX or folate (Thomas et al., 2024). These formulations have demonstrated heightened cytotoxicity in cancer cells, enhanced solubility, and lesser toxicity to normal tissues. Sophisticated platforms combining light, imaging, and therapeutic modalities are emerging. Eventually, PNPs have the potential to contribute to adjuvant cancer care by offering smarter, safer, and patient-tailored therapeutic alternatives that will reshape the future of oncology.

Conclusion

PNPs have emerged as a versatile and promising carrier for anticancer drug delivery, which addresses current limitations such as poor solubility, low bioavailability, systemic toxicity, rapid clearance, and a lack of tumor specificity. The physicochemical characteristics, biocompatibility, and tunable surface functionalities enable meticulous regulation of drug encapsulation, release kinetics, and biodistribution. The formulation of various PNPs, including nanospheres, nanocapsules, micelles, dendrimers, polymerosomes, polyplexes, etc., facilitates customized strategies based on therapeutic needs. Natural and synthetic polymers, such as PLGA, PEG, PCL, PLA, chitosan, and HA, offer versatility in achieving biodegradability, stability, and targeted interactions with tumor microenvironments. Recent advancements in intelligent and multifunctional polymers have markedly improved the therapeutic capabilities of nanoparticulate systems. Stimuli-responsive nanoparticles utilize pH, temperature, redox gradients, and enzymatic activity to selectively induce controlled drug release at tumor sites. Surface modifications with ligands or antibodies enhance active targeting, while hybrid systems combining polymers with lipids or metals enable the codelivery of chemotherapeutics, genes, or imaging agents, supporting theragnostic applications and combination therapy. These strategies hold particular promise in overcoming multidrug resistance and heterogeneity in the tumor microenvironment. Despite the advantages, clinical translation faces challenges, including large-scale manufacturing, stability, storage, toxicity, and regulatory hurdles. Nevertheless, ongoing clinical trials and preclinical successes demonstrate the feasibility and therapeutic potential of PNP systems. Further perspectives emphasize personalized nanomedicine, integration with diagnostics and imaging, and application of AI in rational design to optimize efficacy and safety. Collectively, PNPs represent a transformative approach in oncology, with the potential to deliver safer and more effective and patient-tailored cancer therapies. Ultimately, bridging the gap between experimental innovation and clinical application.

References

Alvarez-Lorenzo, C., Concheiro, A., 2014. Smart drug delivery systems: From fundamentals to the clinic. Chem. Commun. 50 (58), 7743–7765. https://doi.org/10.1039/c4cc01429d.

Anajafi, T., Mallik, S., 2015. Polymersome-based drug-delivery strategies for cancer therapeutics. Ther. Deliv. 6 (4), 521–534. https://doi.org/10.4155/tde.14.125.

Asmatulu, R., Misak, H., Yang, S-y., Wooley, P., inventors, Wichita State University, assignee, 2017. Composite magnetic nanoparticle drug delivery system. US Patent 9782342B2.

AstraZeneca (2017). Safety, tolerability, pharmacokinetics, and efficacy of AZD2811 nanoparticles as monotherapy or in combination in acute myeloid leukemia participants. Clinicaltrials.gov, NCT03217838, Available at: https://clinicaltrials.gov/study/NCT03217838 (Accessed 8th July 2026)

Aziz, T., Farid, A., Haq, F., Kiran, M., Ullah, A., Zhang, K., Cheng, L., Ghazanfar, S., Sun, H., Ullah, R., Ali, A., Muzammal, M., Shah, M., Akhtar, N., Selim, S., Hagagy, N., Samy, M., Soad, K., Al, J., 2022. A review on the modification of cellulose and its applications. Polymers 14 (15), 3206. https://doi.org/10.3390/polym14153206.

Bajracharya, R., Song, J.G., Patil, B.R., Lee, S.H., Noh, H.M., Kim, D.H., Kim, G.L., Seo, S.H., Park, J.W., Jeong, S.H., Lee, C.H., Han, H.K., 2022. Functional ligands for improving anticancer drug therapy: Current status and applications to drug delivery systems. Drug Deliv. 29 (1), 1959–1970. https://doi.org/10.1080/10717544.2022.2089296.

Banerjee, S., Hirave, K., Pooja, D., Kulhari, H., Singh, A., Saharan, V.A., 2025. Dendrimers as nanocarriers for phytoceuticals. In: Singh, A., Kulhari, H., Saharan, V.A. (Eds.), Formulating pharma-, nutra-, and cosmeceutical products from herbal substances: Dosage forms and delivery systems. John Wiley & Sons, Inc, New Jersey, pp. 495–532. https://doi.org/10.1002/9781119769484.ch18.

Bao, G., Mitragotri, S., Tong, S., 2013. Multifunctional nanoparticles for drug delivery and molecular imaging. Annu. Rev. Biomed. Eng. 15 (1), 253–282. https://doi.org/10.1146/annurev-bioeng-071812-152409.

Beach, M.A., Nayanathara, U., Gao, Y., Zhang, C., Xiong, Y., Wang, Y., Such, G.K., 2024. Polymeric nanoparticles for drug delivery. Chem. Rev. 124 (9), 5505–5616. https://doi.org/10.1021/acs.chemrev.3c00705.

Begines, B., Ortiz, T., Pérez-Aranda, M., Martínez, G., Merinero, M., Argüelles-Arias, F., Alcudia, A., 2020. Polymeric nanoparticles for drug delivery: Recent developments and future prospects. Nanomaterials 10 (7), 1403. https://doi.org/10.3390/nano10071403.

Bhadran, A., Shah, T., Babanyinah, G.K., Polara, H., Taslimy, S., Biewer, M.C., Stefan, M.C., 2023. Recent advances in polycaprolactones for anticancer drug delivery. Pharmaceutics 15 (7), 1977. https://doi.org/10.3390/pharmaceutics15071977.

Bhatta, R.S., Chandasana, H., Chhonker, Y.S., Rathi, C., Kumar, D., Mitra, K., Shukla, P.K., 2012. Mucoadhesive nanoparticles for prolonged ocular delivery of natamycin: In vitro and pharmacokinetics studies. Int. J. Pharm. 432 (1–2), 105–112. https://doi.org/10.1016/j.ijpharm.2012.04.060.

Bhattacharyya, M., Jariyal, H., Srivastava, A., 2023. Hyaluronic acid: More than a carrier, having an overpowering extracellular and intracellular impact on cancer. Carbohydr. Polym. 317, 121081. https://doi.org/10.1016/j.carbpol.2023.121081.

Bisht, S., Feldmann, G., Soni, S., Ravi, R., Karikar, C., Maitra, A., Maitra, A., 2007. Polymeric nanoparticle-encapsulated curcumin ("nanocurcumin"): A novel strategy for human cancer therapy. J. Nanobiotechnol. 5 (3). https://doi.org/10.1186/1477-3155-5-3.

Braden, A.R.C., Vishwanatha, J.K., 2015. Polymeric Nanoparticles for Enhanced Cancer Treatment. US Patent No. US9023395B2.

Carmona-Ribeiro, A.M., 2010. Biomimetic nanoparticles: Preparation, characterization and biomedical applications. Int. J. Nanomed. 5 (1), 249–259. https://doi.org/10.2147/ijn.s9035.

Celgene, 2011. A Phase 1 Trial of ABI-011 in Patients With Advanced Solid Tumors or Lymphomas [cited 2026 Jul 8] Available from: https://clinicaltrials.gov/study/NCT01163071 [cited 2026 Jul 8] Available from:

Chawla, S.P., Goel, S., Chow, W., Braiteh, F., Singh, A.S., Grilley Olson, J.E., Osada, A., Bobe, I., Riedel, R.F., 2020. A phase 1b dose escalation trial of NC-6300 (nanoparticle epirubicin) in patients with advanced solid tumors or advanced, metastatic, or unresectable soft-tissue sarcoma. Clin. Cancer Res. 26 (16), 4225–4232. https://doi.org/10.1158/1078-0432.CCR-20-0591.

Cheng, W., Gu, L., Ren, W., Liu, Y., 2014. Stimuli-responsive polymers for anti-cancer drug delivery. Mater. Sci. Eng. C 45, 600–608. https://doi.org/10.1016/j.msec.2014.05.050.

Chen, Huang, G., Huang, H., 2020. Preparation and application of dextran and its derivatives as carriers. Int. J. Biol. Macromol. 145, 827–834. https://doi.org/10.1016/j.ijbiomac.2019.11.151.

Chung, Y.I., Kim, J.C., Kim, Y.H., Tae, G., Lee, S.Y., Kim, K., Kwon, I.C., 2010. The effect of surface functionalization of PLGA nanoparticles by heparin- or chitosan-conjugated pluronic on tumor targeting. J. Contr. Release 143 (3), 374–382. https://doi.org/10.1016/j.jconrel.2010.01.017.

Cleland, J., Sharma, R., Sun, M., Appiani, S., Slusher, B., Rais, R., Rangaramanujam, K., inventors, Prgrammable Medicine, LLC, Johns Hopkins University, assignee, 2021. Dendrimer compositions and methods for drug delivery. US Patent Application 2021170040A1.

Danhier, F., Feron, O., Préat, V., 2010. To exploit the tumor microenvironment: Passive and active tumor targeting of nanocarriers for anti-cancer drug delivery. J. Contr. Release 148 (2), 135–146. https://doi.org/10.1016/j.jconrel.2010.08.027.

Das, S., Ghosh, B., Sarkar, K., 2022. Nanocellulose as sustainable biomaterials for drug delivery. Sens. Int. 3, 100135. https://doi.org/10.1016/j.sintl.2021.100135.

Ding, L., Agrawal, P., Singh, S.K., Chhonker, Y.S., Sun, J., Murry, D.J., 2024. Polymer-based drug delivery systems for cancer therapeutics. Polymers 16 (6). https://doi.org/10.3390/polym16060843.

Divya, K., Jisha, M.S., 2018. Chitosan nanoparticles preparation and applications. Environ. Chem. Lett. 16 (1), 101–112. https://doi.org/10.1007/s10311-017-0670-y.

Dong, P.W., Wang, X.H., Gu, Y.C., Wang, Y.J., Wang, Y.J., Gong, C.Y., Luo, F., Guo, G., Zhao, X., Wei, Y.Q., Qian, Z. Y., 2010. Self-assembled biodegradable micelles based on star-shaped PCL-b-PEG copolymers for chemotherapeutic drug delivery. Colloids Surf. A Physicochem. Eng. Asp. 358 (1–3), 128–134. https://doi.org/10.1016/j.colsurfa.2010.01.037.

El-Hammadi, M.M., Arias, J.L., 2022. Recent advances in the surface functionalization of PLGA-based nanomedicines. Nanomaterials 12 (3). https://doi.org/10.3390/nano12030354.

Eltaib, L., 2025. Polymeric nanoparticles in targeted drug delivery: Unveiling the impact of polymer characterization and fabrication. Polymers 17 (7), 833. https://doi.org/10.3390/polym17070833.

Fan, W., Peng, H., Yu, Z., Wang, L., He, H., Ma, Y., Qi, J., Lu, Y., Wu, W., 2022. The long-circulating effect of pegylated nanoparticles revisited via simultaneous monitoring of both the drug payloads and nanocarriers. Acta Pharm. Sin. B 12 (5), 2479–2493. https://doi.org/10.1016/j.apsb.2021.11.016.

Gagneja, S., Capalash, N., Sharma, P., 2024. Hyaluronic acid as a tumor progression agent and a potential chemotherapeutic biomolecule against cancer: A review on its dual role. Int. J. Biol. Macromol. 275 (Pt 2), 133744. https://doi.org/10.1016/j.ijbiomac.2024.133744.

Gajbhiye, K.R., Salve, R., Narwade, M., Sheikh, A., Kesharwani, P., Gajbhiye, V., 2023. Lipid polymer hybrid nanoparticles: A custom-tailored next-generation approach for cancer therapeutics. Mol. Cancer 22 (1). https://doi.org/10.1186/s12943-023-01849-0.

Garg, U., Chauhan, S., Nagaich, U., Jain, N., 2019. Current advances in chitosan nanoparticles based drug delivery and targeting. Adv. Pharmaceut. Bull. 9 (2), 195–204. https://doi.org/10.15171/apb.2019.023.

Garg, T., Arora, S., Pahwa, R., 2025. Cellulose and its derivatives: Structure, modification, and application in controlled drug delivery. Future J. Pharmaceut. Sci. 11 (1). https://doi.org/10.1186/s43094-025-00834-2.

Ghaffari, S., Golshan, M., Jalili, K., Salami-Kalajahi, M., 2024. Anti-inflammatory drugs-modified poly (2-hydroxyethyl methacrylate) particles as anticancer drug carriers. Macromol. Mater. Eng. 309 (11), 2400147.

Gil, E., Hudson, S., 2004. Stimuli-reponsive polymers and their bioconjugates. Prog. Polym. Sci. 29 (12), 1173–1222. https://doi.org/10.1016/j.progpolymsci.2004.08.003.

Goto, Y., Matsuno, R., Konno, T., Takai, M., Ishihara, K., 2008. Polymer nanoparticles covered with phosphorylcholine groups and immobilized with antibody for high-affinity separation of proteins. Biomacromolecules 9 (3), 828–833. https://doi.org/10.1021/bm701161d.

Hamaguchi, T., Kato, K., Yasui, H., Morizane, C., Ikeda, M., Ueno, H., Muro, K., Yamada, Y., Okusaka, T., Shirao, K., Shimada, Y., Nakahama, H., Matsumura, Y., 2007. A phase I and pharmacokinetic study of NK105, a paclitaxel-incorporating micellar nanoparticle formulation. Br. J. Cancer 97 (2), 170–176. https://doi.org/10.1038/sj.bjc.6603855.

Hamaguchi, T., Tsuji, A., Yamaguchi, K., Takeda, K., Uetake, H., Esaki, T., Amagai, K., Sakai, D., Baba, H., Kimura, M., Matsumura, Y., Tsukamoto, T., 2018. A phase II study of NK012, a polymeric micelle formulation of SN-38, in unresectable, metastatic or recurrent colorectal cancer patients. Cancer Chemother. Pharmacol. 82 (6), 1021–1029. https://doi.org/10.1007/s00280-018-3693-6.

Han, H.S., Thambi, T., Choi, K.Y., Son, S., Ko, H., Lee, M.C., Jo, D.G., Chae, Y.S., Kang, Y.M., Lee, J.Y., Park, J.H., 2015. Bioreducible shell-cross-linked hyaluronic acid nanoparticles for tumor-targeted drug delivery. Biomacromolecules 16 (2), 447–456. https://doi.org/10.1021/bm5017755.

He, Le, Sun, M., Cheng, X., Xu, Y., Lv, X., Wang, X., Tang, R., 2019. pH/redox dual-sensitive platinum (IV)-based micelles with greatly enhanced antitumor effect for combination chemotherapy. J. Colloid Interface Sci. 541, 30–41. https://doi.org/10.1016/j.jcis.2019.01.076.

He, Z., Liu, Y., Wang, H., Li, P., Chen, Y., Wang, C., Zhou, C., Song, S., Chen, S., Huang, G., Yang, Z., 2023. Dual-grafted dextran based nanomicelles: Higher antioxidant, anti-inflammatory and cellular uptake efficiency for quercetin. Int. J. Biol. Macromol. 224, 1361–1372. https://doi.org/10.1016/j.ijbiomac.2022.10.222.

Huang, Y., Chen Huang, Y., Chen, Q., Ma, P., Song, H., Ma, X., Ma, Y., Zhou, X., Gou, S., Xu, Z., Chen, J., Xiao, B., 2018. Facile fabrication of oxidationresponsive polymeric nanoparticles for effective anticancer drug delivery. Mol. Pharm. 16 (1), 49–59. https://doi.org/10.1021/acs.molpharmaceut.8b00634.

Huang, G., Huang, H., 2018. Application of hyaluronic acid as carriers in drug delivery. Drug Deliv. 25 (1), 766–772. https://doi.org/10.1080/10717544.2018.1450910.

Huo, M., Wang, H., Zhang, Y., Cai, H., Zhang, P., Li, L., Zhou, J., Yin, T., 2020. Co-delivery of silybin and paclitaxel by dextran-based nanoparticles for effective anti-tumor treatment through chemotherapy sensitization and microenvironment modulation. J. Contr. Release 321, 198–210. https://doi.org/10.1016/j.jconrel.2020.02.017.

Hoang Thi, T.T., Pilkington, E.H., Nguyen, D.H., Lee, J.S., Park, K.D., Truong, N.P., 2020. The importance of poly (ethylene glycol) alternatives for overcoming PEG immunogenicity in drug delivery and bioconjugation. Polymers 12 (2), 298. https://doi.org/10.3390/polym12020298.

Barua, S. inventor, 2016. Polymer-Coated Therapeutic Nanoparticles. US Patent 20160303053A1.

Hong, S., Park, S., inventors, Wisconsin Alumni Research Foundation, asignee, 2022. Dendrimer-exosome hybrid nanoparticles as a delivery platform. US Patent 11344627B2.

Hu, Q., Lu, Y., Luo, Y., 2021. Recent advances in dextran-based drug delivery systems: From fabrication strategies to applications. Carbohydr. Polym. 264, 117999. https://doi.org/10.1016/j.carbpol.2021.117999.

International Organization for Standardization. ISO/TR 18401:2017 - Nanotechnologies — Plain language explanation of selected terms from the ISO/IEC 80004 series. [cited 2026 Jul 8]. Available from: https://www.iso.org/standard/62384.html

Ita, K., 2020. Polyplexes for gene and nucleic acid delivery: Progress and bottlenecks. Eur. J. Pharmaceut. Sci. 150, 105358. https://doi.org/10.1016/j.ejps.2020.105358.

Iyer, R., Nguyen, T., Padanilam, D., Xu, C., Saha, D., Nguyen, K.T., Hong, Y., 2020. Glutathione-responsive biodegradable polyurethane nanoparticles for lung cancer treatment. J. Contr. Release 321, 363–371. https://doi.org/10.1016/j.jconrel.2020.02.021.

Jain, S., Kumar, M., Kumar, P., Verma, J., Rosenholm, J.M., Bansal, K.K., Vaidya, A., 2023. Lipid–polymer hybrid nanosystems: A rational fusion for advanced therapeutic delivery. J. Funct. Biomater. 14 (9). https://doi.org/10.3390/jfb14090437.

Jha, A., Kumar, M., Bharti, K., Manjit, M., Mishra, B., 2024a. Biopolymer-based tumor microenvironment-responsive nanomedicine for targeted cancer therapy. Nanomedicine (Lond). 19 (7), 633–651. https://doi.org/10.2217/nnm-2023-0302.

Jha, A., Kumar, M., Goswami, P., Bharti, K., Manjit, M., Gupta, A., Moorkoth, S., Koch, B., Mishra, B., 2024b. Cabazitaxel-loaded redox-responsive nanocarrier based on d-alpha-tocopheryl-chitosan and hyaluronic acid for improved anti-tumor efficacy in DMBA-induced breast cancer model. Mater. Adv. 5 (19), 7789–7808. https://doi.org/10.1039/d4ma00556b.

Jha, A., Kumar, M., Mishra, B., 2022. Marine biopolymer-based anticancer drug delivery systems. In: Jana, S., Jana, S. (Eds.), Marine biomaterials: drug delivery and therapeutic applications. Springer, Singapore, pp. 351–401. https://doi.org/10.1007/978-981-16-4787-1_11.

Jia, W., Wu, Y., Xie, Y., Yu, M., Chen, Y., 2025. Advanced polymeric nanoparticles for cancer immunotherapy: Materials engineering, immunotherapeutic mechanism and clinical translation. Adv. Mater. 37 (8). https://doi.org/10.1002/adma.202413603.

Jiang, X., Du, Z., Zhang, X., Zaman, F., Song, Z., Guan, Y., Yu, T., Huang, Y., 2023. Gelatin-based anticancer drug delivery nanosystems: A mini review. Front. Bioeng. Biotechnol. 11. https://doi.org/10.3389/fbioe.2023.1158749.

Karam, M., Fahs, D., Maatouk, B., Safi, B., Jaffa, A.A., Mhanna, R., 2022. Polymeric nanoparticles in the diagnosis and treatment of myocardial infarction: Challenges and future prospects. Mater. Today Bio 14, 100249. https://doi.org/10.1016/j.mtbio.2022.100249.

Kalinichenko, V, Dunn, A, Shi, D; inventors, Childrens Hospital Med CT and University Cincinnati, assignee, 2017. Polyethylenimine nanoparticles and methods of using same. US Patent 0220354787A1.

Kitagawa, K., Kobayashi, S., Miura, Y., Tanaka, M., Ise, H., 2025. Targeting and suppression of survivin in cancer cells based on the interaction of cell surface vimentin with N-acetylglucosamine-bearing polymers. ACS Omega 10 (33), 37162–37175. https://doi.org/10.1021/acsomega.5c02098.

Kulhari, H., Pooja, D., Shrivastava, S., Kuncha, M., Naidu, V.G.M., Bansal, V., Sistla, R., Adams, D.J., 2016. Trastuzumab-grafted PAMAM dendrimers for the selective delivery of anticancer drugs to HER2-positive breast cancer. Sci. Rep. 6 (1). https://doi.org/10.1038/srep23179.

Kumar, M., Rajnikanth, P.S., 2020. A mini-review on HER2 positive breast cancer and its metastasis: Resistance and treatment strategies. Curr. Nanomed. 10 (1), 36–47. https://doi.org/10.2174/2468187310666191223141038.

Kumar, V., Jha, S.K., Gupta, G., Sahebkar, A., Kesharwani, P., 2025. Unveiling the power of polymeric nanoparticles: Pioneering advances in breast cancer treatment. Adv. Colloid Interface Sci. 344, 103606. https://doi.org/10.1016/j.cis.2025.103606.

Labhasetwar, V.D., Sahoo, S.K., inventors, University of Nebraska Medical Center UNMC, assignee, 2010. Transferrin-conjugated nanoparticles for increasing efficacy of a therapeutic agent. US Patent Application 2010015051A1.

Lee, K.Y., Mooney, D.J., 2012. Alginate: Properties and biomedical applications. Prog. Polym. Sci. 37 (1), 106–126. https://doi.org/10.1016/j.progpolymsci.2011.06.003.

Letchford, K., Burt, H., 2007. A review of the formation and classification of amphiphilic block copolymer nanoparticulate structures: Micelles, nanospheres, nanocapsules and polymersomes. Eur. J. Pharm. Biopharm. 65 (3), 259–269. https://doi.org/10.1016/j.ejpb.2006.11.009.

Li, R., Peng, F., Cai, J., Yang, D., Zhang, P., 2020. Redox dual-stimuli responsive drug delivery systems for improving tumor-targeting ability and reducing adverse side effects. Asian J. Pharm. Sci. 15 (3), 311–325. https://doi.org/10.1016/j.ajps.2019.06.003.

Liang, Y., Kiick, K.L., 2014. Heparin-functionalized polymeric biomaterials in tissue engineering and drug delivery applications. Acta Biomater. 10 (4), 1588–1600. https://doi.org/10.1016/j.actbio.2013.07.031.

Liu, T.Y., Hu, S.H., Liu, D.M., Chen, S.Y., Chen, I.W., 2009. Biomedical nanoparticle carriers with combined thermal and magnetic responses. Nano Today 4 (1), 52–65. https://doi.org/10.1016/j.nantod.2008.10.011.

Logakannan, K.P., Guven, I., Odegard, G., Wang, K., Zhang, C., Liang, Z., Spear, A., 2025. A review of artificial intelligence (AI)-based applications to nanocomposites. Compos. Appl. Sci. Manuf. 197, 109027. https://doi.org/10.1016/j.compositesa.2025.109027.

Lopes, M., Abrahim, B., Veiga, F., Seiça, R., Cabral, L.M., Arnaud, P., Andrade, J.C., Ribeiro, A.J., 2017. Preparation methods and applications behind alginate-based particles. Expert Opin. Drug Deliv. 14 (6), 769–782. https://doi.org/10.1080/17425247.2016.1214564.

Lugoloobi, I., Maniriho, H., Jia, L., Namulinda, T., Shi, X., Zhao, Y., 2021. Cellulose nanocrystals in cancer diagnostics and treatment. J. Contr. Release 336, 207–232. https://doi.org/10.1016/j.jconrel.2021.06.004.

Lu, J-M., Yao. Q., Chen, C., inventors, Baylor College of Medicine, assignee, 2019. PLGA-modified polyethylenimine self-assembly nanotechnology for nucleic acid and drug delivery. WO Patent Application 2015023775A1.

Ly, P.D., Ly, K.N., Phan, H.L., Nguyen, H.H.T., Duong, V.A., Nguyen, H.V., 2024. Recent advances in surface decoration of nanoparticles in drug delivery. Front. Nanotechnol. 6, 1456939. https://doi.org/10.3389/fnano.2024.1456939.

Ma, G., Liu, J., He, J., Zhang, M., Ni, P., 2018. Dual-responsive polyphosphoester-doxorubicin prodrug containing a diselenide bond: Synthesis, characterization, and drug delivery. ACS Biomater. Sci. Eng. 4 (7), 2443–2452. https://doi.org/10.1021/acsbiomaterials.8b00429.

MacEwan, S.R., Callahan, D.J., Chilkoti, A., 2010. Stimulus-responsive macromolecules and nanoparticles for cancer drug delivery. Nanomedicine 5 (5), 793–806. https://doi.org/10.2217/nnm.10.50.

Malik, N., Duncan, R., inventors, Dendritic Nanotechnologies Inc, assignee, 2003. Dendritic-platinate drug delivery system. US Patent No. US6585956B2.

Manjit, M., Kumar, M., Kumar, K., Dhondale, M.R., Jha, A., Bharti, K., Rain, Z., Prakash, P., Mishra, B., 2024. Fabrication of dual drug-loaded polycaprolactone–gelatin composite nanofibers for full thickness diabetic wound healing. Ther. Deliv. 15 (1), 5–21. https://doi.org/10.4155/tde-2023-0083.

Matsumura, Y., Hamaguchi, T., Ura, T., Muro, K., Yamada, Y., Shimada, Y., Shirao, K., Okusaka, T., Ueno, H., Ikeda, M., Watanabe, N., 2004. Phase I clinical trial and pharmacokinetic evaluation of NK911, a micelle-encapsulated doxorubicin. Br. J. Cancer 91 (10), 1775–1781. https://doi.org/10.1038/sj.bjc.6602204.

Milano, F., Masi, A., Madaghiele, M., Sannino, A., Salvatore, L., Gallo, N., 2023. Current trends in gelatin-based drug delivery systems. Pharmaceutics 15 (5), 1499. https://doi.org/10.3390/pharmaceutics15051499.

Morgan, M.T., Carnahan, M.A., Immoos, C.E., Ribeiro, A.A., Finkelstein, S., Lee, S.J., Grinstaff, M.W., 2003. Dendritic molecular capsules for hydrophobic compounds. J. Am. Chem. Soc. 125 (50), 15485–15489. https://doi.org/10.1021/ja0347383.

Mollazadeh, S., Mackiewicz, M., Yazdimamaghani, M., 2021. Recent advances in the redox-responsive drug delivery nanoplatforms: A chemical structure and physical property perspective. Mater. Sci. Eng. C. Mater. Biol. Appl. 118, 111536. https://doi.org/10.1016/j.msec.2020.111536.

Mulinti, P., Brooks, J.E., Lervick, B., Pullan, J.E., Brooks, A.E., 2018. Strategies to Improve the Hemocompatibility of Biodegradable Biomaterials. Elsevier BV, pp. 253–278. https://doi.org/10.1016/b978-0-08-100497-5.00017-3.

Musa, S.S., Ibrahim, A.M., Alhassan, M.Y., Musa, A.H., Jibo, A.G., Auwal, A.R., Okesanya, O.J., Othman, Z.K., Abubakar, M.S., Ahmed, M.M., Barroso, C.J.V., Sium, A.F., Garcia, M.B., Flores, J.B., Maikifi, A.S.,

Kouwenhoven, M.B.N., Lucero-Prisno, D.E., 2025. Nanotechnology and machine learning: A promising confluence for the advancement of precision medicine. Intell. Based Med. 12, 100267. https://doi.org/10.1016/j.ibmed.2025.100267.

Nahire, R., Haldar, M.K., Paul, S., Ambre, A.H., Meghnani, V., Layek, B., Katti, K.S., Gange, K.N., Singh, J., Sarkar, K., Mallik, S., 2014. Multifunctional polymersomes for cytosolic delivery of gemcitabine and doxorubicin to cancer cells. Biomaterials 35 (24), 6482–6497. https://doi.org/10.1016/j.biomaterials.2014.04.026.

Najm, A., Niculescu, A.G., Bolocan, A., Rădulescu, M., Grumezescu, A.M., Beuran, M., Gaspar, B.S., 2024. Chitosan and cyclodextrins—Versatile materials used to create drug delivery systems for gastrointestinal cancers. Pharmaceutics 16 (1), 43. https://doi.org/10.3390/pharmaceutics16010043.

Negi, S., Tandel, N., Garg, N.K., Sharma, P., Kumar, R., Sharma, P., Kumar, R., Saini, S., Sharma, A., Tyagi, R.K., 2024. Co-delivery of aceclofenac and methotrexate nanoparticles presents an effective treatment for rheumatoid arthritis. Int. J. Nanomed. 19, 2149–2177. https://doi.org/10.2147/IJN.S439359.

Ochi, M., Wan, B., Bao, Q., Burgess, D.J., 2021. Influence of PLGA molecular weight distribution on leuprolide release from microspheres. Int. J. Pharm. 599, 120450. https://doi.org/10.1016/j.ijpharm.2021.120450.

Oerlemans, C., Bult, W., Bos, M., Storm, G., Nijsen, J.F.W., Hennink, W.E., 2010. Polymeric micelles in anticancer therapy: Targeting, imaging and triggered release. Pharm. Res. 27 (12), 2569–2589. https://doi.org/10.1007/s11095-010-0233-4.

Oh, J.K., Park, J.M., 2011. Iron oxide-based superparamagnetic polymeric nanomaterials: Design, preparation, and biomedical application. Prog. Polym. Sci. 36 (1), 168–189. https://doi.org/10.1016/j.progpolymsci.2010.08.005.

Ouyang, X., Liu, Y., Zheng, K., Pang, Z., Peng, S., 2024. Recent advances in zwitterionic nanoscale drug delivery systems to overcome biological barriers. Asian J. Pharm. Sci. 19 (1), 100883. https://doi.org/10.1016/j.ajps.2023.100883.

Parmar, G., Kumar, M., Jha, A., Mishra, B., 2023. Alginate based carriers for topical drug delivery. In: Jana, S., Jana, S. (Eds.), Alginate biomaterial: drug delivery strategies and biomedical engineering. Springer Nature, Singapore, pp. 85–107. https://doi.org/10.1007/978-981-19-6937-9_4.

Pashkina, E., Bykova, M., Berishvili, M., Lazarev, Y., Kozlov, V., 2025. Hyaluronic acid-based drug delivery systems for cancer therapy. Cells 14 (2), 61. https://doi.org/10.3390/cells14020061.

Pearce, A.K., O'Reilly, R.K., 2019. Insights into active targeting of nanoparticles in drug delivery: Advances in clinical studies and design considerations for cancer nanomedicine. Bioconjug. Chem. 30 (9), 2300–2311. https://doi.org/10.1021/acs.bioconjchem.9b00456.

Peng, C.L., Shieh, M.J., Tsai, M.H., Chang, C.C., Lai, P.S., 2008. Self-assembled star-shaped chlorin-core poly(ε-caprolactone)-poly(ethylene glycol) diblock copolymer micelles for dual chemo-photodynamic therapies. Biomaterials 29 (26), 3599–3608. https://doi.org/10.1016/j.biomaterials.2008.05.018.

Petersen, M.A., Hillmyer, M.A., Kokkoli, E., 2013. Bioresorbable polymersomes for targeted delivery of cisplatin. Bioconjug. Chem. 24 (4), 533–543. https://doi.org/10.1021/bc3003259.

Piha-Paul, S.A., Thein, K.Z., De Souza, P., Kefford, R., Gangadhar, T., Smith, C., Schuster, S., Zamboni, W.C., Dees, C.E., Markman, B., 2021. First-in-human, phase I/IIa study of CRLX301, a nanoparticle drug conjugate containing docetaxel, in patients with advanced or metastatic solid malignancies. Invest. N. Drugs 39 (4), 1047–1056. https://doi.org/10.1007/s10637-021-01081-x.

Plummer, R., Wilson, R.H., Calvert, H., Boddy, A.V., Griffin, M., Sludden, J., Tilby, M.J., Eatock, M., Pearson, D.G., Ottley, C.J., Matsumura, Y., Kataoka, K., Nishiya, T., 2011. A Phase I clinical study of cisplatin-incorporated polymeric micelles (NC-6004) in patients with solid tumors. Br. J. Cancer 104 (4), 593–598. https://doi.org/10.1038/bjc.2011.6.

Prabhu, R.H., Patravale, V.B., Joshi, M.D., 2015. Polymeric nanoparticles for targeted treatment in oncology: Current insights. Int. J. Nanomed. 10, 1001–1018. https://doi.org/10.2147/IJN.S56932.

Prasad, R., Pandey, R., Varma, A., Barman, I., 2016. Polymer-based nanoparticles for drug delivery systems and cancer therapeutics. In: Kharkwal, H, Janaswamy, S (Eds.), Natural polymers for drug delivery. CABI, Wallingford UK, pp. 53–70. https://doi.org/10.1079/9781780644479.0053.

Qi, R., Majoros, I., Misra, A.C., Koch, A.E., Campbell, P., Marotte, H., Bergin, I.L., Cao, Z., Goonewardena, S., Morry, J., Zhang, S., Beer, M., Makidon, P., Kotlyar, A., Thomas, T.P., Baker Jr., J.R., 2015. Folate receptor-targeted dendrimer-methotrexate conjugate for inflammatory arthritis. J. Biomed. Nanotechnol. 11 (8), 1431–1441. https://doi.org/10.1166/jbn.2015.2077.

Radosz, M., Xu, P., Shen, Y., inventors, University of Wyoming, assignee, 2015. Nanoparticles for cytoplasmic drug delivery to cancer cells. US Patent 8945629B2.

Raghav, N., Vashisth, C., Mor, N., Arya, P., Sharma, M.R., Kaur, R., Bhatti, S.P., Kennedy, J.F., 2023. Recent advances in cellulose, pectin, carrageenan and alginate-based oral drug delivery systems. Int. J. Biol. Macromol. 244, 125357. https://doi.org/10.1016/j.ijbiomac.2023.125357.

Rainbolt, E.A., Washington, K.E., Biewer, M.C., Stefan, M.C., 2015. Recent developments in micellar drug carriers featuring substituted poly(ε-caprolactone)s. Polym. Chem. 6 (13), 2369–2381. https://doi.org/10.1039/c4py01628a.

Ren, J., Fang, Z., Yao, L., Dahmani, F.Z., Yin, L., Zhou, J., Yao, J., 2015. A micelle-like structure of poloxamer-methotrexate conjugates as nanocarrier for methotrexate delivery. Int. J. Pharm. 487 (1–2), 177–186. https://doi.org/10.1016/j.ijpharm.2015.04.014.

Rezvantalab, S., Drude, N.I., Moraveji, M.K., Güvener, N., Koons, E.K., Shi, Y., Lammers, T., Kiessling, F., 2018. PLGA-based nanoparticles in cancer treatment. Front. Pharmacol. 9, 1260. https://doi.org/10.3389/fphar.2018.01260.

Roxana Petrovici, Pinteala, M., Simionescu, N., 2023. Dextran formulations as effective delivery systems of therapeutic agents. Molecules 28 (3), 1086. https://doi.org/10.3390/molecules28031086.

Sameer Khan, M., Jaswanth Gowda, B.H., Nasir, N., Wahab, S., Rao Pichika, M., Sahebkar, A., Kesharwani, P., 2023. Advancements in dextran-based nanocarriers for treatment and imaging of breast cancer. Int. J. Pharm. 643, 123276. https://doi.org/10.1016/j.ijpharm.2023.123276.

Scott, C., Longley, D., Humphreys, L., Mcdaid, W., inventors, The Queen's University of Belfast, assignee, 2023. Polymeric nanoparticles for enhanced cancer treatment. US Patent 20230033582A1.

Shahriari, M., Taghdisi, S.M., Abnous, K., Ramezani, M., Alibolandi, M., 2021. Self-targeted polymersomal co-formulation of doxorubicin, camptothecin and FOXM1 aptamer for efficient treatment of non-small cell lung cancer. J. Contr. Release 335, 369–388. https://doi.org/10.1016/j.jconrel.2021.05.039.

Shaikh, M.A.J., Alharbi, K.S., Almalki, W.H., Imam, S.S., Albratty, M., Meraya, A.M., Alzarea, S.I., Kazmi, I., Al-Abbasi, F.A., Afzal, O., Altamimi, A.S.A., Singh, Y., Singh, S.K., Dua, K., Gupta, G., 2022. Sodium alginate based drug delivery in management of breast cancer. Carbohydr. Polym. 292. https://doi.org/10.1016/j.carbpol.2022.119689.

Sharma, A.K., Prasher, P., Aljabali, A.A., Mishra, V., Gandhi, H., Kumar, S., Mutalik, S., Chellappan, D.K., Tambuwala, M.M., Dua, K., Kapoor, D.N., 2020. Emerging era of "somes": Polymersomes as versatile drug delivery carrier for cancer diagnostics and therapy. Drug Deliv. Transl. Res. 10 (5), 1171–1190. https://doi.org/10.1007/s13346-020-00789-2.

Shi, Y., Van Den Dungen, E.T.A., Klumperman, B., Van Nostrum, C.F., Hennink, W.E., 2013a. Reversible addition-fragmentation chain transfer synthesis of a micelle-forming, structure reversible thermosensitive diblock copolymer based on the N-(2-hydroxy propyl) methacrylamide backbone. ACS Macro Lett. 2 (5), 403–408. https://doi.org/10.1021/mz300662b.

Shi, Y., Van Steenbergen, M.J., Teunissen, E.A., Novo, L., Gradmann, S., Baldus, M., Van Nostrum, C.F., Hennink, W.E., 2013b. Π-Π Stacking increases the stability and loading capacity of thermosensitive polymeric micelles for chemotherapeutic drugs. Biomacromolecules 14 (6), 1826–1837. https://doi.org/10.1021/bm400234c.

Siafaka, P.I., Üstündağ Okur, N., Karavas, E., Bikiaris, D.N., 2016. Surface modified multifunctional and stimuli responsive nanoparticles for drug targeting: Current status and uses. Int. J. Mol. Sci. 17 (9), 1440. https://doi.org/10.3390/ijms17091440.

Suk, J.S., Xu, Q., Kim, N., Hanes, J., Ensign, L.M., 2016. PEGylation as a strategy for improving nanoparticle-based drug and gene delivery. Adv. Drug Deliv. Rev. 99, 28–51. https://doi.org/10.1016/j.addr.2015.09.012.

Sutton, D., Nasongkla, N., Blanco, E., Gao, J., 2007. Functionalized micellar systems for cancer targeted drug delivery. Pharm. Res. 24 (6), 1029–1046. https://doi.org/10.1007/s11095-006-9223-y.

Tabatabaei Mirakabad, F.S., Nejati-Koshki, K., Akbarzadeh, A., Rahmati Yamchi, M., Milani, M., Zarghami, N., Zeighamian, V., Rahimzadeh, A., Alimohammadi, S., Hanifehpour, Y., Joo, S.W., 2014. PLGA-based nanoparticles as cancer drug delivery systems. Asian Pac. J. Cancer Prev. 15 (2), 517–535. https://doi.org/10.7314/apjcp.2014.15.2.517.

Taghizadeh, B., Taranejoo, S., Monemian, S.A., Moghaddam, Z.S., Daliri, K., Derakhshankhah, H., Derakhshani, Z., 2015. Classification of stimuli-responsive polymers as anticancer drug delivery systems. Drug Deliv. 22 (2), 145–155. https://doi.org/10.3109/10717544.2014.887157.

Tahir, N., Haseeb, M.T., Madni, A., Parveen, F., Khan, M.M., Khan, S., Jan, N., Khan, A., 2020. In: Tyagi, R.K., Garg, N.K., Shukla, R., Bisen, P.S. (Eds.), Lipid polymer hybrid nanoparticles: A novel approach. In: Role of novel drug delivery vehicles in nanobiomedicine. IntechOpen. 2020, London.

Tan, H., Tu, Z., Jia, H., Gou, X., 2018. To ngai, hierarchical porous protein scaffold templated from high internal phase emulsion costabilized by gelatin and gelatin nanoparticles. Langmuir 34 (16), 4820–4829. https://doi.org/10.1021/acs.langmuir.7b04047.

Tang, X., Liang, Y., Feng, X., Zhang, R., Jin, X., Sun, L., 2015. Co-delivery of docetaxel and Poloxamer 235 by PLGA–TPGS nanoparticles for breast cancer treatment. Mater. Sci. Eng. C 49, 348–355. https://doi.org/10.1016/j.msec.2015.01.033.

Thomas, N., Puluhulawa, L.E., Mo'o, F.R.C., Rusdin, A., Gazzali, A.M., Budiman, A., 2024. Potential of pullulan-based polymeric nanoparticles for improving drug physicochemical properties and effectiveness. Polymers 16 (15), 2151. https://doi.org/10.3390/polym16152151.

Tikhonov, A., Kachanov, A., Yudaeva, A., Danilik, O., Ponomareva, N., Karandashov, I., Kostyusheva, A., Zamyatnin, A.A., Parodi, A., Chulanov, V., Brezgin, S., Kostyushev, D., 2024. Biomimetic nanoparticles for basic drug delivery. Pharmaceutics 16 (10), 1306. https://doi.org/10.3390/pharmaceutics16101306.

Tønnesen, H.H., Karlsen, J., 2002. Alginate in drug delivery systems. Drug Dev. Ind. Pharm. 28 (6), 621–630. https://doi.org/10.1081/DDC-120003853.

Uchida, S., Lau, C.Y.J., Oba, M., Miyata, K., 2023. Polyplex designs for improving the stability and safety of RNA therapeutics. Adv. Drug Deliv. Rev. 199, 114972. https://doi.org/10.1016/j.addr.2023.114972.

Ulbrich, K., Šubr, V., 2004. Polymeric anticancer drugs with pH-controlled activation. Adv. Drug Deliv. Rev. 56 (7), 1023–1050. https://doi.org/10.1016/j.addr.2003.10.040.

Valle, J.W., Armstrong, A., Newman, C., Alakhov, V., Pietrzynski, G., Brewer, J., Campbell, S., Corrie, P., Rowinsky, E.K., Ranson, M., 2011. A phase 2 study of SP1049C, doxorubicin in P-glycoprotein-targeting pluronics, in patients with advanced adenocarcinoma of the esophagus and gastroesophageal junction. Invest. N. Drugs 29 (5), 1029–1037. https://doi.org/10.1007/s10637-010-9399-1.

Varela-Moreira, A., Shi, Y., Fens, M.H.A.M., Lammers, T., Hennink, W.E., Schiffelers, R.M., 2017. Clinical application of polymeric micelles for the treatment of cancer. Mater. Chem. Front. 1 (8), 1485–1501. https://doi.org/10.1039/c6qm00289g.

Vega, J., Ke, S., Fan, Z., Wallace, S., Charsangavej, C., Li, C., 2003. Targeting doxorubicin to epidermal growth factor receptors by site-specific conjugation of C225 to poly (L-glutamic acid) through a polyethylene glycol spacer. Pharm. Res. 20 (5), 826–832. https://doi.org/10.1023/a:1023454107190.

Von Hoff, D.D., Mita, M.M., Ramanathan, R.K., Weiss, G.J., Mita, A.C., Lorusso, P.M., Burris, H.A., Hart, L.L., Low, S.C., Parsons, D.M., Zale, S.E., Summa, J.M., Youssoufian, H., Sachdev, J.C., 2016. Phase I study of PSMA-targeted docetaxel-containing nanoparticle BIND-014 in patients with advanced solid tumors. Clin. Cancer Res. 22 (13), 3157–3163. https://doi.org/10.1158/1078-0432.CCR-15-2548.

Vora, L.K., Gholap, A.D., Jetha, K., Thakur, R.R.S., Solanki, H.K., Chavda, V.P., 2023. Artificial intelligence in pharmaceutical technology and drug delivery design. Pharmaceutics 15 (7), 1916. https://doi.org/10.3390/pharmaceutics15071916.

Wang, Y., Liu, P., Duan, Y., Yin, X., Qi, W., Liu, X., Wang, X., Zhou, J., Wang, W., Qiu, L., Wen, Di., 2014. Specific cell targeting with APRPG conjugated PEG–PLGA nanoparticles for treating ovarian cancer. Biomaterials 35 (3), 983–992. https://doi.org/10.1016/j.biomaterials.2013.09.062.

Wang, Z., Deng, X., Ding, J., Zhou, W., Xing, Z., Tang, G., 2018. Mechanisms of drug release in pH-sensitive micelles for tumor targeted drug delivery system: A review. Int. J. Pharm. 535 (1–2), 253–260. https://doi.org/10.1016/j.ijpharm.2017.11.003.

Wang, Q.X., Chen, X., Li, Z.L., Gong, Y.C., Xiong, X.Y., 2022. Transferrin/folate dual-targeting Pluronic F127/poly (lactic acid) polymersomes for effective anticancer drug delivery. J. Biomater. Sci. Polym. Ed. 33 (9), 1140–1156. https://doi.org/10.1080/09205063.2022.2044434.

Weiss, G.J., Chao, J., Neidhart, J.D., Ramanathan, R.K., Bassett, D., Neidhart, J.A., Choi, C.H.J., Chow, W., Chung, V., Forman, S.J., Garmey, E., Hwang, J., Kalinoski, D.L., Koczywas, M., Longmate, J., Melton, R.J., Morgan, R., Oliver, J., Peterkin, J.J., Ryan, J.L., Schluep, T., Synold, T.W., Twardowski, P., Davis, M.E.,

Yen, Y., 2013. First-in-human phase 1/2a trial of CRLX101, a cyclodextrin-containing polymer-camptothecin nanopharmaceutical in patients with advanced solid tumor malignancies. Invest. N. Drugs 31 (4), 986–1000. https://doi.org/10.1007/s10637-012-9921-8.

Wright, J., inventor, 2014. DNIB Unwind Inc, assignee. Docetaxel polymeric nanoparticles for cancer treatment. WO Patent No. WO2014210485A1.

Xiang, J., Mo, R., Ding, Y., Zheng, W., Zhang, C., 2014. Paclitaxel-loaded N-octyl-O-sulfate chitosan micelles for superior cancer therapeutic efficacy and overcoming drug resistance. Mol. Pharm. 11 (1), 145–157. https://doi.org/10.1021/mp400340k.

Xiao, X., Teng, F., Shi, C., Chen, J., Wu, S., Wang, B., Meng, X., Essiet Imeh, A., Li, W., 2022. Polymeric nanoparticles—Promising carriers for cancer therapy. Front. Bioeng. Biotechnol. 10. https://doi.org/10.3389/fbioe.2022.1024143.

Xu, J., Zhao, Q., Jin, Y., Qiu, L., 2014. High loading of hydrophilic/hydrophobic doxorubicin into polyphosphazene polymersome for breast cancer therapy. Nanomed. Nanotechnol. Biol. Med. 10 (2), 349–358. https://doi.org/10.1016/j.nano.2013.08.004.

Yang, J., Zeng, H., Luo, Y., Chen, Y., Wang, M., Wu, C., Hu, P., 2024. Recent applications of PLGA in drug delivery systems. Polymers 16 (18), 2606. https://doi.org/10.3390/polym16182606.

Yasin, A., Ren, Y., Li, J., Sheng, Y., Cao, C., Zhang, K., 2022. Advances in hyaluronic acid for biomedical applications. Front. Bioeng. Biotechnol. 4;10:910290. https://doi.org/10.3389/fbioe.2022.910290.

Zagar, T.M., Vujaskovic, Z., Formenti, S., Rugo, H., Muggia, F., O'Connor, B., Myerson, R., Stauffer, P., Hsu, I.C., Diederich, C., Straube, W., 2014. Two phase I dose-escalation/pharmacokinetics studies of low temperature liposomal doxorubicin (LTLD) and mild local hyperthermia in heavily pretreated patients with local regionally recurrent breast cancer. Int. J. Hyperth. 30 (5), 285–294. https://doi.org/10.3109/02656736.2014.936049.

Zare, M., Bigham, A., Zare, M., Luo, H., Rezvani Ghomi, E., Ramakrishna, S., 2021. pHEMA: An overview for biomedical applications. Int. J. Mol. Sci. 22 (12), 6376. https://doi.org/10.3390/ijms22126376.

Zhao, Y., Fan, X., Liu, D., Wang, Z., 2011. PEGylated thermo-sensitive poly(amidoamine) dendritic drug delivery systems. Int. J. Pharm. 409 (1–2), 229–236. https://doi.org/10.1016/j.ijpharm.2011.02.005.

Zhao, G.X., Tanaka, H., Kim, C.W., Li, K., Funamoto, D., Nobori, T., Nakamura, Y., Niidome, T., Kishimura, A., Mori, T., Katayama, Y., 2014. Histidinylated poly-L-lysine-based vectors for cancer-specific gene expression via enhancing the endosomal escape. J. Biomater. Sci. Polym. Ed. 25 (5), 519–534. https://doi.org/10.1080/09205063.2013.879562.

Zhao, Y., Liu, K., Li, J., Liao, J., Ma, L., 2021. Engineering of hybrid anticancer drug-loaded polymeric nanoparticles delivery system for the treatment and care of lung cancer therapy. Drug Deliv. 28 (1), 1539–1547. https://doi.org/10.1080/10717544.2021.1934187.

Zielińska, A., Carreiró, F., Oliveira, A.M., Neves, A., Pires, B., Nagasamy Venkatesh, D., Durazzo, A., Lucarini, M., Eder, P., Silva, A.M., Santini, A., Souto, E.B., 2020. Polymeric nanoparticles: Production, characterization, toxicology and ecotoxicology. Molecules 25 (16), 3731. https://doi.org/10.3390/molecules25163731.

CHAPTER

17

Advances in lipid-based nanoparticles for anticancer drug delivery

Sunny Rathee[1, 2], *Sakshi Soni*[1, 2], *Adarsh Sharma*[1], *Arya Ojha*[1] *and Sanjay K. Jain*[1]

[1]**Department of Pharmaceutical Sciences, Dr. Harisingh Gour Vishwavidyalaya, Sagar, Madhya Pradesh, India;** [2]**National Institute of Pharmaceutical Education and Research-Ahmedabad (NIPER-A), Gandhinagar, Gujarat, India**

Introduction

Cancer therapy faces substantial obstacles due to tumors' complicated biology, which includes uncontrolled cell proliferation, genetic instability, resistance to apoptosis, and the capacity to elude immune responses. Despite significant progress in the development of chemotherapeutics, targeted inhibitors, and immune-based treatments, their clinical efficacy is frequently hampered by the low solubility of active drugs, nonspecific biodistribution, fast systemic clearance, and dose-related toxicities. These constraints highlight the need for new drug delivery systems that can improve therapeutic accuracy while minimizing side effects (García-Pinel et al., 2019; Khodaverdi et al., 2022; Sheoran et al., 2022). Among several nanoscale delivery systems, lipid-based nanoparticles (LBNPs) have emerged as a versatile and clinically applicable platform for anticancer drug administration. These nanoparticles, made of physiological or synthetic lipids, closely resemble natural cellular membranes, resulting in superior biocompatibility and low immunogenicity. Their amphiphilic characteristic facilitates the production of self-assembled nanostructures in aqueous conditions, allowing hydrophilic and hydrophobic drugs to be encapsulated. Their structural versatility, combined with the capacity to preserve labile compounds like nucleic acids from degradation, propels LBNPs to the forefront of nanomedicine. An intriguing advantage of LBNPs is their ability to improve the pharmacokinetic profile of anticancer drugs. Their nanoscale size

Advanced Cancer Therapeutics
https://doi.org/10.1016/B978-0-443-44185-1.00034-3

enables passive tumor targeting via the enhanced permeability and retention (EPR) effect, resulting in preferential accumulation in tumor tissues. Furthermore, lipid nanoparticles can be designed for regulated or stimuli-responsive release, assuring drug availability at the tumor location while reducing exposure to healthy tissues. Surface modification methods, such as PEGylation for longer circulation or conjugation of ligands comprising peptides, antibodies, or small molecules for active targeting, improve their therapeutic effectiveness (Buse and El-Aneed, 2010; Waheed et al., 2024; Rajpoot, 2020).

LBNPs are a broad group of delivery vehicles that can be used for anticancer drug administration. Liposomes, the earliest and most widely studied members, are bilayer vesicles capable of transporting both hydrophilic and hydrophobic drugs. Solid lipid nanoparticles (SLNs) are also bilayer vesicles that offer improved physical stability and controlled release. However, the lower drug-loading capacity is the main limitation. This prompted the development of nanostructured lipid carriers (NLCs), which combine solid and liquid lipids to form flexible matrices with improved encapsulation efficiency. Further advancement resulted in hybrid systems such as lipid–polymer hybrid nanoparticles (LPHNPs), which combine the structural strength of polymers with the biomimetic properties of lipids, or exosome-like vesicles that use naturally occurring lipid membranes to achieve intrinsic targeting and immune evasion. Self-emulsifying drug delivery systems (SEDDS) have also aided in the oral delivery of poorly water-soluble anticancer drugs by forming fine emulsions in the gastrointestinal tract. Recent advances have broadened the role of LBNPs beyond passive drug transport. Stimuli-responsive nanoparticles that respond to a pH, redox state, enzymes, or temperature within the tumor microenvironment (TME) also offer precise and regulated drug activation. Theranostic lipid nanoparticles integrated with imaging agents enable real-time assessment of drug distribution and treatment response. The remarkable success of lipid nanoparticles in delivering mRNA vaccines has sparked interest in their application for cancer immunotherapy, gene therapy, and personalized cancer therapy (Yao et al., 2025; Grinberg et al., 2014; Layek et al., 2020). Overall, LBNPs represent a rapidly evolving platform that bridges fundamental nanoscience with translational oncology. Their tunable structures, high biocompatibility, and capacity for functionalization make them promising candidates for addressing longstanding limitations in cancer drug delivery. Ongoing advancements in formulation design, scalable manufacturing, and computational optimization are expected to further enhance their clinical integration and shape the future landscape of precision cancer therapy (Wang et al., 2021; Zhao et al., 2022).

Types of lipid-based nanoparticles in anticancer drug delivery

The diversity of LBNPs reflects their adaptability as versatile carriers for anticancer therapeutics. By manipulating lipid composition, structural organization, and formulation methods, researchers have developed a range of nanosystems capable of overcoming the limitations of conventional chemotherapy. These platforms are designed to encapsulate both hydrophilic and hydrophobic molecules, shield drugs from premature degradation, and optimize biodistribution while minimizing systemic toxicity. The capacity of LBNPs to exploit the EPR effect, combined with opportunities for surface functionalization, makes them especially attractive for tumor-targeted delivery. Over time, different types of LBNPs have been created to address specific challenges in oncology, ranging from stability and drug-loading efficiency to controlled release and active targeting (Table 17.1). Traditional systems, such as liposomes, laid the foundation for clinical translation, while subsequent generations, including SLNs and NLCs, introduced improvements in stability and loading capacity. More advanced platforms, such as lipid–polymer hybrids, self-emulsifying systems, and biomimetic exosomes, have further expanded the scope of applications by integrating structural robustness, multifunctionality, and biological mimicry. Collectively, these diverse nanoparticle types provide a broad toolkit that continues to evolve with emerging technologies, forming the basis for innovative strategies in cancer therapy (Feng and Mumper, 2013).

Liposomes

Liposomes are the earliest and most widely investigated LBNPs, first described in the 1960s and later adapted for drug delivery applications. They are spherical vesicles consisting of one or more concentric phospholipid bilayers surrounding an aqueous core. The amphiphilic architecture of liposomes makes them highly versatile: hydrophilic molecules are entrapped in the aqueous interior, whereas hydrophobic molecules are incorporated into the lipid bilayer. This dual-loading ability, combined with their biocompatibility and structural similarity to biological membranes, has made liposomes one of the most successful nanocarriers in oncology (Samimi et al., 2019). Liposomes are primarily composed of natural or synthetic phospholipids, often stabilized with cholesterol to enhance membrane rigidity and reduce permeability. The lipid composition strongly influences the stability, circulation time, and drug release profile. Over the years, various generations of liposomes have been developed to address the limitations of early formulations. Conventional liposomes are composed solely of phospholipids and cholesterol. While they provide efficient drug encapsulation, they are rapidly cleared from circulation by the mononuclear phagocyte system (MPS), limiting their therapeutic potential. Stealth liposomes are designed to overcome rapid clearance from systemic circulation by modifying the surface with hydrophilic polymers such as polyethylene glycol (PEG). PEGylation reduces protein adsorption and immune recognition, prolonging systemic circulation. This innovation led to the development of Doxil (PEGylated liposomal doxorubicin), the first FDA (U.S. Food and Drug Administration)-approved nanomedicine for cancer therapy. Targeted liposomes involve conjugation to ligands such as antibodies, peptides, aptamers, or small molecules (e.g., folic acid [FA]) to the liposomal surface. These ligands selectively bind to overexpressed receptors on cancer cells, improving specificity and cellular uptake. Targeted liposomes represent a key advance toward precision medicine. Stimuli-responsive liposomes include a specific moiety that responds to a particular stimulus to release their cargo for site-specific drug delivery. For example, pH-sensitive liposomes that destabilize and release drugs in the acidic TME. Thermosensitive liposomes that release payloads under localized hyperthermia. Enzyme- and redox-responsive liposomes that exploit tumor-associated enzymatic activity or redox gradients. Immunoliposomes functionalized with monoclonal antibodies or immune-targeting ligands, combining selective targeting with

TABLE 17.1 Different types of lipid-based nanoparticles.

Nanoformulation	Classification	Key features	References
Liposomes	Liposomes range in size from 50 nm to several micrometers and can be classified as follows: **A.** Small unilamellar vesicles (SUVs): Composed of a single bilayer, usually <100 nm in diameter. **B.** Large unilamellar vesicles (LUVs): Larger vesicles with a single bilayer, typically >100 nm. **C.** Multilamellar vesicles (MLVs): Contain multiple concentric lipid bilayers, resembling an "onion-like" structure.	This structural flexibility enables liposomes to be tailored for specific therapeutic requirements, including circulation time, release kinetics, and targeting capacity.	Loh et al. (2021), Saha et al. (2024)
Solid lipid nanoparticles (SLNs)	Different structural models of SLNs have been proposed to describe the distribution of drug molecules within the lipid matrix: **A.** Homogeneous Matrix Model: Drug molecules are uniformly dispersed throughout the solid lipid core. This type provides sustained drug release but may suffer from lower loading efficiency. **B.** Drug-Enriched Shell Model: The drug is concentrated in the outer shell of the nanoparticle, typically formed during cooling of the lipid melt. This configuration results in rapid drug release. **C.** Drug-Enriched Core Model: The drug is concentrated in the central core, surrounded by a lipid shell. This design offers more controlled release compared to the shell model.	These variations highlight how formulation parameters influence the performance of SLNs in drug delivery.	Mura et al. (2013), Shen et al. (2017)
Nanostructured lipid carriers (NLCs)	Based on the structural arrangement of lipids and drugs, NLCs can be classified into three main types: **A.** Imperfect-Type NLCs: Created by mixing solid lipids with spatially different liquid lipids, which prevents the formation of a perfect crystal lattice. This structure provides enhanced drug-loading capacity and prevents drug expulsion. **B.** Amorphous-Type NLCs: Formulated using special lipids that do not crystallize into an ordered lattice upon cooling. The amorphous structure minimizes drug leakage and improves stability during storage. **C.** Multiple-Type NLCs: Also known as "oil-in-solid lipid-in-water" dispersions, these contain small liquid oil nanocompartments embedded within the solid lipid matrix.	They act as reservoirs for high amounts of lipophilic drugs and are particularly useful for poorly soluble anticancer agents.	Liong et al. (2008), Guo et al. (2008)

Lipid–polymer hybrid nanoparticles	Different design strategies have been explored to fabricate LPHNPs, leading to structural variations: **A.** Monolithic Core–Shell LPHNPs: A polymeric core is uniformly coated with a lipid layer, providing both stability and protection of the encapsulated drug. **B.** Polymer–Lipid Matrix Systems: Drugs are dispersed within a blended matrix of polymers and lipids, offering tunable release profiles. **C.** Layer-by-Layer Assembled LPHNPs: Alternate deposition of lipid and polymer layers allows precise control of drug encapsulation and surface functionality.	Each configuration can be tailored for specific therapeutic needs, including controlled release, targeted delivery, or codelivery of multiple agents.	Chen et al. (2009)
Exosomes and cell-derived lipid vesicles	**A.** Microvesicles: Larger vesicles (100–1000 nm) that bud directly from the plasma membrane, capable of carrying significant amounts of drug cargo. **B.** Apoptotic Bodies: Vesicles formed during programmed cell death, which can be engineered to deliver therapeutic molecules but may carry immunogenic risks. **C.** Engineered Exosome-Mimetic Vesicles: Artificially produced vesicles derived from cell membranes through extrusion or sonication, offering scalable alternatives to natural exosomes.	Each type has unique structural and functional properties, and their selection depends on the intended therapeutic application.	Mohan et al. (2014)
Self-emulsifying drug delivery systems (SEDDS)	SEDDS can be categorized based on droplet size and dispersion characteristics: **A.** Self-Microemulsifying Drug Delivery Systems (SMEDDS): Produce transparent or translucent microemulsions with droplet sizes in the range of 20–200 nm, offering enhanced solubilization and stability. **B.** Self-Nanoemulsifying Drug Delivery Systems (SNEDDS): Generate even smaller droplets (<100 nm), improving absorption and lymphatic transport, which can bypass hepatic first-pass metabolism. **C.** Solid SEDDS (S-SEDDS): Liquid SEDDS are adsorbed onto solid carriers (e.g., silica, polymers) and converted into solid dosage forms such as tablets or capsules, improving stability, portability, and patient compliance.	Upon oral administration and upon contact with gastrointestinal tract fluids, the gentle mixing forces disperse the formulation into submicron or nano-sized particles, significantly increasing the surface area available for drug absorption.	Shah et al. (2013), Garbuzenko et al. (2010)

immunomodulatory effects. They are being explored for cancer immunotherapy, where liposomes act both as drug carriers and immune stimulators (Cano et al., 2020; Kim et al., 2023; Jahangir et al., 2020).

Solid lipid nanoparticles

SLNs represent the first generation of colloidal lipid-based nanocarriers introduced as an alternative to liposomes and polymeric nanoparticles in the early 1990s. They are typically composed of lipids that remain solid at both room and body temperatures, stabilized by surfactants or emulsifiers. Common lipids used include triglycerides, fatty acids, and waxes, while stabilizers such as phospholipids, bile salts, or poloxamers are employed to maintain colloidal stability. Their rigid lipid matrix allows for the encapsulation of lipophilic anticancer drugs while providing enhanced stability, controlled drug release, and protection of sensitive molecules from chemical or enzymatic degradation (Nakayama et al., 2014). The size of SLNs generally ranges between 50 and 500 nm, making them suitable for both intravenous and oral delivery. The solid state of the lipid core is a defining feature, as it influences drug incorporation, release kinetics, and storage stability (Hu et al., 2015). The solid lipid matrix protects encapsulated anticancer drugs such as paclitaxel, doxorubicin, and camptothecin from premature degradation. This also enhances the solubility of poorly water-soluble drugs and can be engineered for sustained or controlled release, thereby reducing dosing frequency and systemic toxicity. SLNs can enable surface modifications, such as PEGylation or ligand conjugation, to improve circulation time and achieve active targeting to tumor cells. Use of biodegradable and biocompatible lipids further reduces the risk of long-term toxicity compared to polymeric or inorganic carriers (Singh and Lillard, 2009). Despite their potential, SLNs face several challenges. One of the major drawbacks is the relatively low drug-loading capacity, particularly for hydrophilic molecules, due to the crystalline nature of the lipid matrix. During storage, lipid crystallization can also lead to drug expulsion, resulting in reduced stability of formulations. Furthermore, large-scale production and reproducibility remain technical barriers, as formulation methods such as high-pressure homogenization and solvent evaporation require careful optimization (Nie et al., 2007).

SLNs have been extensively studied for the delivery of various anticancer drugs, including poorly soluble agents like docetaxel and tamoxifen. Preclinical studies demonstrated improved bioavailability, reduced toxicity, and enhanced tumor accumulation compared to free drugs. SLNs have also been explored for oral delivery of chemotherapeutics, addressing the challenge of poor gastrointestinal absorption. Additionally, ligand-decorated SLNs targeting receptors such as folate or transferrin have shown promise in enhancing tumor specificity. While several SLN formulations are in preclinical and early clinical evaluation, none have yet reached the same level of clinical translation as liposomes (Sawant and Torchilin, 2012). Future research on SLNs is focused on overcoming their limitations by integrating novel formulation strategies and hybrid systems. One approach is combining solid lipids with liquid lipids, leading to the development of NLCs, which provide higher drug-loading capacity and improved stability. Advances in microfluidics and scalable manufacturing methods may further accelerate the clinical translation of SLN-based therapies. The integration of targeting ligands, stimuli-responsiveness, and codelivery of drugs with nucleic acids or imaging agents is expected to expand the role of SLNs in precision oncology (Gao et al., 2004).

Nanostructured lipid carriers

NLCs represent the second generation of solid lipid-based nanocarriers, developed to overcome the inherent limitations of SLNs. While SLNs provided stability and controlled release, their crystalline lipid matrix often led to limited drug-loading capacity and drug expulsion during storage. NLCs address these issues by incorporating a mixture of solid lipids and liquid lipids (oils) into the nanoparticle matrix. This blend creates an imperfect crystalline structure that enhances drug incorporation, minimizes leakage, and improves long-term stability. As a result, NLCs are considered a more flexible and efficient platform for anticancer drug delivery (Kim et al., 2008). NLCs are typically composed of biocompatible and biodegradable solid lipids (e.g., glyceryl monostearate, stearic acid, or triglycerides) mixed with liquid lipids such as oleic acid, medium-chain triglycerides, or isopropyl myristate. Surfactants are used to stabilize the colloidal dispersion. The ratio of solid to liquid lipids is a critical parameter, as it determines the degree of structural imperfections in the lipid matrix. These imperfections prevent the tight packing of lipid chains, thereby creating space for accommodating more drug molecules. NLCs are generally in the size range of 50–300 nm, making them suitable for systemic and targeted cancer delivery (Yang et al., 2007).

NLCs offer several advantages over both liposomes and SLNs. The disordered lipid matrix allows higher encapsulation efficiency for hydrophobic drugs such as paclitaxel, curcumin, and docetaxel. They also provide improved physical stability, reduced risk of drug expulsion, and tunable release kinetics ranging from sustained to burst release. The flexibility in formulation allows NLCs to encapsulate multiple therapeutic agents simultaneously, enabling combination therapy approaches. Additionally, their small size facilitates tumor accumulation via the EPR effect, while surface modification with PEG or ligands (e.g., transferrin, folate, peptides) allows for prolonged circulation and active targeting (Li et al., 2008). Despite their promising attributes, NLCs face some challenges. The complexity of their formulation, including the precise selection and ratio of lipids, requires careful optimization to achieve reproducibility and scalability. Large-scale production remains technically demanding, and long-term safety data are still limited compared to liposomes. Another concern is the potential instability of certain liquid lipids, which may lead to oxidative degradation and reduced shelf life if not properly stabilized (Trapani et al., 2012).

NLCs have been extensively investigated for a range of anticancer drugs, including both conventional chemotherapeutics and natural compounds with poor water solubility. For example, paclitaxel-loaded NLCs have demonstrated enhanced cytotoxicity in tumor models with reduced systemic toxicity compared to free drug formulations. Similarly, curcumin- and resveratrol-loaded NLCs have shown promise in overcoming poor solubility and bioavailability, leading to improved antitumor efficacy in preclinical studies. NLCs are also being explored as carriers for gene delivery, where siRNA or plasmid DNA can be coencapsulated with chemotherapeutic agents to achieve synergistic effects. While most NLC formulations remain at the preclinical stage, several candidates have progressed to early-phase clinical evaluations, highlighting their translational potential. Future directions for NLC research focus on multifunctional and stimuli-responsive systems. For instance, pH-sensitive and redox-sensitive NLCs are being developed to selectively release drugs in the TME. Theranostic NLCs, integrating imaging agents with therapeutic drugs, are under investigation for simultaneous diagnosis and treatment. Advances in microfluidic-based manufacturing and high-pressure homogenization may further enable scalable and reproducible production. Furthermore, the integration of NLCs into personalized medicine approaches where formulations are tailored based on tumor genetics and patient-specific needs represents a promising frontier in precision oncology (Bhaskar et al., 2010).

Lipid–polymer hybrid nanoparticles

LPHNPs represent an emerging class of nanocarriers that combine the complementary strengths of polymeric nanoparticles and lipid-based systems. These hybrids were developed to overcome the limitations of individual systems, such as the limited stability of liposomes and the potential toxicity or rapid clearance of pure polymeric nanoparticles (Chandna et al., 2010). By integrating a polymeric core with a lipid shell, LPHNPs achieve high structural integrity, enhanced drug-loading efficiency, controlled release properties, and excellent biocompatibility, making them highly attractive for anticancer applications (Kumar et al., 2025b). A typical LPHNP is composed of three main components (Fig. 17.1): (a) polymeric core often made from biodegradable polymers such as

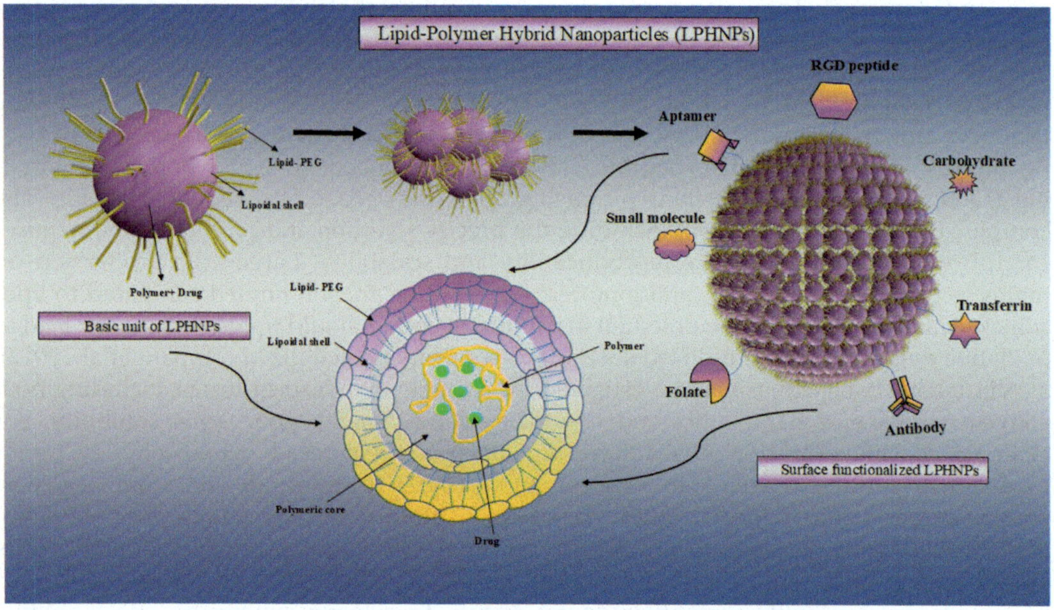

FIGURE 17.1 Lipid–polymer hybrid nanoparticles (LPHNPs).

poly(lactic-co-glycolic acid), polylactic acid, or polycaprolactone. This core provides mechanical strength, high drug-loading capacity, and controlled release of therapeutic agents; (b) lipid shell as a monolayer or bilayer of natural or synthetic lipids that surrounds the polymeric core. The lipid layer improves biocompatibility, enhances interaction with cell membranes, and protects the payload from enzymatic degradation; (c) surface modifications including functionalized groups like PEG for stealth properties or conjugated ligands (antibodies, peptides, aptamers, or small molecules) for active tumor targeting. This hybrid architecture combines the controlled release and robustness of polymers with the biocompatibility and cellular uptake advantages of lipid systems (Zhang et al., 2012). LPHNPs offer several unique benefits for oncology. Their polymeric cores allow encapsulation of a wide range of drugs, including hydrophobic chemotherapeutics and fragile biomolecules such as nucleic acids. The lipid coating enhances systemic stability, reduces premature clearance, and facilitates efficient cellular uptake. Moreover, LPHNPs can be engineered for stimuli-responsive release, enabling precise drug delivery at tumor sites in response to pH, redox gradients, or enzymatic activity. Another major advantage is their suitability for codelivery strategies, where chemotherapeutics can be combined with siRNA, mRNA, or immunomodulators within a single platform, offering synergistic therapeutic effects and overcoming multidrug resistance (Jaimes-Aguirre et al., 2016).

LPHNPs have shown encouraging results in preclinical cancer models. For example, paclitaxel- or docetaxel-loaded LPHNPs demonstrated improved tumor accumulation and reduced systemic toxicity compared to conventional formulations. Gene delivery applications are particularly promising, with siRNA- and mRNA-loaded LPHNPs achieving effective gene silencing and tumor growth inhibition. Immunotherapy is another expanding field, where LPHNPs have been used to deliver tumor-associated antigens or immune adjuvants to enhance antitumor immune responses. While no LPHNP-based anticancer drug has yet been approved for clinical use, several candidates are under investigation in preclinical and early clinical studies (Torchilin, 2007). Future research is focused on designing multifunctional LPHNPs that integrate therapeutic, diagnostic, and immune-modulatory functions. The development of theranostic LPHNPs, which combine drugs with imaging agents, could enable real-time monitoring of treatment response. Advances in scalable production methods such as microfluidics and nanoprecipitation are expected to improve manufacturing consistency. Furthermore, personalized LPHNPs tailored to tumor-specific molecular profiles and patient genetics may represent a major breakthrough in precision oncology (Sutradhar and Amin, 2013). Despite their promise, LPHNPs face several challenges. The complexity of their design requires careful optimization of polymer–lipid interactions to achieve stable formulations. Large-scale production is still difficult due to variability in nanoparticle size, lipid coating uniformity, and batch reproducibility. Additionally, while biodegradable polymers are generally safe, their degradation products may cause local acidity or inflammatory responses in some cases. Long-term toxicity, immunogenicity, and regulatory approval hurdles remain important concerns that need to be addressed for clinical translation (Mendes et al., 2017).

Exosomes and cell-derived lipid vesicles

Exosomes and other cell-derived lipid vesicles have recently emerged as a promising class of naturally occurring nanocarriers for anticancer drug delivery. Unlike synthetic lipid nanoparticles such as liposomes, SLNs, or NLCs, exosomes are nanosized extracellular vesicles (30–150 nm) secreted by various cell types, including immune cells, stem cells, and tumor cells. They play a crucial role in intercellular communication by transferring bioactive molecules such as proteins, lipids, and nucleic acids. Their inherent biocompatibility, stability in circulation, and ability to cross biological barriers such as the blood–brain barrier make them highly attractive for oncology applications (Fig. 17.2; Wang et al., 2017). Exosomes are formed through the endosomal pathway, originating from multivesicular bodies that fuse with the plasma membrane and release vesicles into the extracellular space. Their structure comprises a lipid bilayer enriched with cholesterol, sphingomyelin, and phosphatidylserine, mimicking the composition of cell membranes. They also carry surface proteins such as tetraspanins (CD9, CD63, CD81), integrins, and major histocompatibility complex (MHC) molecules, which contribute to their stability and targeting properties. The interior can encapsulate diverse cargos, ranging from chemotherapeutics to RNA molecules, enabling versatile therapeutic applications (Bozzuto and Molinari, 2015).

Exosomes offer several distinct advantages over synthetic nanoparticles, including natural biocompatibility and biodegradability. As endogenous vesicles, exosomes evade immune clearance more effectively than synthetic carriers, leading to prolonged circulation times. Exosomes have intrinsic targeting capability depending on their cell of origin and can express surface molecules that enable homing to specific tissues, including tumors. Exosomes

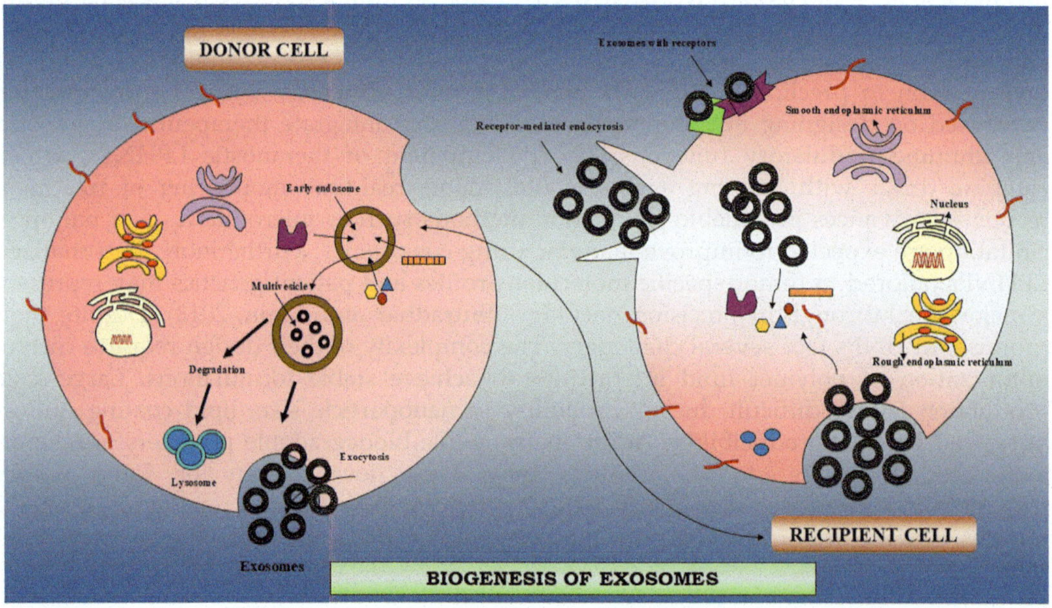

FIGURE 17.2 Biogenesis of exosomes.

have demonstrated the ability to cross the blood–brain barrier, making them particularly useful for brain cancer therapies. They can encapsulate a wide range of therapeutic agents, from small-molecule chemotherapeutics to RNA and protein-based drugs. Compared to synthetic systems, exosomes have reduced risks of triggering unwanted immune responses when properly purified and thus have very low immunogenicity (Kotla et al., 2017). Despite their promise, exosome-based therapies face several challenges. Large-scale production and purification are technically demanding, as exosomes must be isolated from cell culture supernatants or body fluids using ultracentrifugation, size-exclusion chromatography, or microfluidic platforms. Variability in yield, purity, and reproducibility remains a significant bottleneck. Additionally, exosomes derived from tumor cells may carry oncogenic proteins or nucleic acids, raising safety concerns. Standardized protocols for isolation, characterization, and quality control are urgently needed to support regulatory approval and clinical translation (Sercombe et al., 2015).

Exosomes have been employed to deliver a wide variety of anticancer agents. For instance, doxorubicin-loaded exosomes have demonstrated enhanced tumor accumulation and reduced cardiotoxicity compared to free drug. Similarly, exosomes have been engineered to carry siRNA or miRNA for silencing oncogenes, showing promising results in preclinical cancer models. Clinical trials are currently evaluating exosome-based therapies, including dendritic cell-derived exosomes as cancer vaccines. Moreover, stem cell-derived exosomes have gained interest for their regenerative and immunomodulatory properties, which may complement anticancer therapy. The future of exosome research lies in the development of engineered and scalable vesicle systems. Genetic modification of parent cells can produce exosomes with enhanced targeting ability or therapeutic payloads. Hybrid vesicles that combine natural exosome membranes with synthetic lipid or polymeric cores are also being explored to merge the benefits of natural biocompatibility and synthetic versatility. Advances in microfluidic manufacturing may enable large-scale, reproducible production, accelerating clinical translation. Ultimately, exosomes and related cell-derived vesicles are poised to become a powerful platform for precision oncology, particularly in delivering personalized, patient-specific therapies (Lamichhane et al., 2018).

Self-emulsifying drug delivery systems

SEDDS are isotropic mixtures of oils, surfactants, and cosurfactants that spontaneously form fine oil-in-water emulsions or microemulsions upon contact with gastrointestinal fluids under gentle agitation. Unlike conventional lipid nanoparticles such as liposomes, SLNs, or NLCs, SEDDS are liquid or semisolid formulations designed primarily for oral delivery of poorly water-soluble drugs. Their ability to improve solubilization, absorption, and bioavailability of lipophilic anticancer agents has made them an attractive platform for oncology applications, especially for drugs with poor gastrointestinal permeability (Fig. 17.3; Deshpande et al., 2013). A typical SEDDS formulation contains (a) oil phase as long-chain or medium-chain triglycerides, fatty acid esters, or other lipophilic components that act as solvents for poorly soluble drugs; (b) nonionic surfactants such as polysorbates, PEG-based surfactants, or Cremophor EL to stabilize emulsions; and (c) cosurfactants/

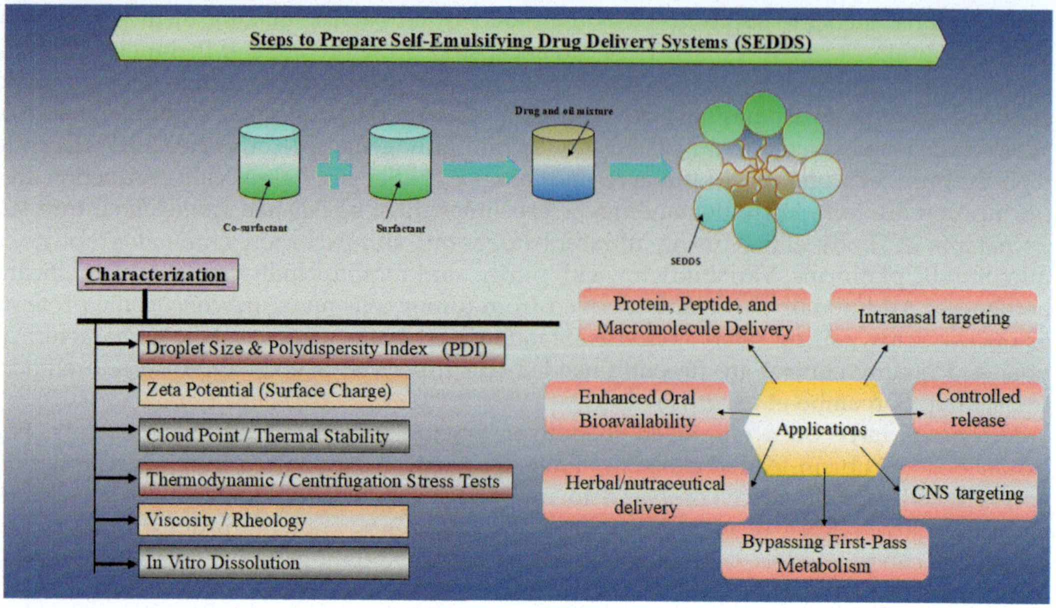

FIGURE 17.3 Method of preparation of self-emulsifying drug delivery systems (SEDDS).

cosolvents like short-chain alcohols (e.g., ethanol, propylene glycol) or glycols that reduce interfacial tension and improve emulsification. Upon oral administration, the gentle mixing forces of the gastrointestinal tract disperse the formulation into submicron droplets (typically 20–200 nm), thereby significantly increasing the surface area available for drug absorption (Garbuzenko et al., 2010). SEDDS can improve the solubilization and gastrointestinal absorption of poorly soluble anticancer drugs. It can bypass first-pass metabolism to avoid lymphatic transport via chylomicron uptake, thereby minimizing hepatic metabolism and enhancing systemic drug exposure. SEDDS can accommodate a broad range of hydrophobic drugs, and solid forms allow for controlled or sustained release (Üner and Yener, 2007). However, they are primarily suitable for lipophilic drugs, making them less effective for hydrophilic or large biomolecule delivery. High concentrations of surfactants may cause gastrointestinal irritation or toxicity. Additionally, physical stability issues such as drug precipitation, phase separation, or lipid oxidation can occur during storage. Scaling up manufacturing and ensuring consistent droplet size upon emulsification remain technical challenges (Khosa et al., 2018).

SEDDS formulations have been widely studied for anticancer drugs with poor solubility and bioavailability. Paclitaxel-loaded self-nanoemulsifying drug delivery systems demonstrated improved oral absorption and antitumor efficacy compared to conventional intravenous formulations. Similarly, tamoxifen and docetaxel have been successfully formulated into SEDDS with enhanced therapeutic outcomes in preclinical studies. Some SEDDS-based formulations are undergoing clinical evaluation, though most remain in the preclinical stage. The ability of SEDDS to provide oral alternatives to traditionally injectable chemotherapeutics is particularly valuable for long-term cancer treatment and palliative care. Future directions for SEDDS research focus on developing targeted and multifunctional systems. Incorporation of ligands or stimuli-responsive components could enable tumor-specific drug release. Hybrid systems combining SEDDS with nanocarriers such as liposomes or polymeric nanoparticles are also being explored to broaden their applicability beyond oral delivery. Advances in solid SEDDS technology may lead to the development of stable, scalable, and patient-friendly formulations that bridge the gap between laboratory innovation and clinical practice (Battaglia et al., 2016).

Formulation strategies and physicochemical properties

The successful design and application of LBNPs in anticancer therapy rely heavily on the choice of formulation strategy and characterization methods. The preparation technique directly influences the physicochemical properties of the nanoparticles, such as size, surface charge, morphology, and drug loading, which in turn determine their biological performance, stability, and therapeutic efficacy. Therefore, understanding the diverse preparation methods is essential for developing reproducible, scalable, and clinically translatable LBNP formulations (Garbuzenko et al., 2019a). Different LBNPs, including liposomes, SLNs, NLCs, lipid–polymer hybrids, exosomes, and self-emulsifying systems, require tailored preparation techniques (Table 17.2). These methods broadly fall into top-down approaches (reducing bulk materials to nanoscale dimensions) and bottom-up approaches (assembling nanoparticles from molecular or atomic building blocks) (Fig. 17.4; Kuzmov and Minko, 2015).

The physicochemical characteristics of LBNPs are critical parameters ensuring the quality, reproducibility, and suitability for anticancer drug delivery. Physicochemical parameters such as particle size, surface charge, polydispersity, morphology, and encapsulation efficiency directly influence biological interactions, stability, pharmacokinetics, and therapeutic performance. A comprehensive understanding of these parameters allows researchers to optimize formulations for clinical translation (Dhar et al., 2008; Hilder and Hill, 2008; Yang et al., 2018; Li et al., 2014).

Particle size and size distribution

Particle size is one of the most important determinants of nanoparticle performance in vivo. LBNPs generally ranging between 20 and 300 nm facilitate prolonged systemic circulation and exhibit high tumor accumulation via the EPR effect. Nanoparticles smaller than 200 nm can efficiently penetrate tumor tissues effectively, while 100 nm particles may even cross biological barriers such as the blood–brain barrier. Size distribution is equally critical and is typically expressed as the polydispersity index (PDI). A low PDI value (<0.3) indicates a homogeneous monodispersed system, essential for predictable drug release and biodistribution. Techniques such as dynamic light scattering and nanoparticle tracking analysis are commonly used to measure particle size and distribution (Hu et al., 2014).

TABLE 17.2 Methods of preparation.

Method	Description	Benefits	Limitations	References
Thin-film hydration method	One of the most widely used methods for liposome preparation. In this technique, lipids are dissolved in an organic solvent and then evaporated to form a thin lipid film on the surface of a round-bottom flask. Upon hydration with an aqueous solution containing the drug, the lipid film self-assembles into multilamellar vesicles (MLVs). These can be further downsized into small unilamellar vesicles (SUVs) using sonication or extrusion	Simple, versatile, and suitable for both hydrophilic and hydrophobic drugs	Batch variability, residual solvent concerns, and limited scalability	Emami et al. (2017)
High-pressure homogenization (HPH)	A common method for producing SLNs and NLCs. In this process, a melted lipid phase (containing the drug) is emulsified in an aqueous surfactant solution, followed by passage through a high-pressure homogenizer. Rapid cooling solidifies the lipid phase into nanoparticles. Hot HPH: Lipid melted above its melting point before homogenization. Cold HPH: Lipid–drug mixture solidified and ground before homogenization to preserve thermolabile drugs	Scalable, reproducible, and solvent-free	High energy input may degrade sensitive biomolecules	Jiang et al. (2013)
Solvent evaporation and solvent injection methods	In the solvent evaporation method, lipids and drugs are dissolved in a volatile organic solvent, emulsified in an aqueous phase, and then evaporated to form nanoparticles. The solvent injection method involves injecting a lipid solution in a water-miscible solvent (e.g., ethanol) into an aqueous phase under stirring, resulting in nanoparticle self-assembly	Good control over particle size, suitable for hydrophobic drugs	Use of organic solvents raises toxicity and regulatory concerns	Marcu et al. (2013)
Microemulsion-based method	This involves preparing an oil-in-water or water-in-oil microemulsion using lipids, surfactants, and cosurfactants, which is then dispersed in cold water to form nanoparticles	Mild conditions, easy scale-up, suitable for heat-sensitive drugs	Requires high surfactant concentrations, which may cause toxicity	Stephen et al. (2016)

Double emulsion (W/O/W) technique	Widely applied for encapsulating hydrophilic drugs in liposomes and lipid–polymer hybrids. The drug is first dissolved in an aqueous phase, emulsified in an oil phase (containing lipids/polymers), and then re-emulsified in an external aqueous phase. Solvent evaporation leads to stable nanoparticles	Effective for hydrophilic drugs, proteins, and peptides	Complexity of process, potential for low encapsulation efficiency	Jin et al. (2019)
Supercritical fluid technology	A greener approach using supercritical carbon dioxide as a solvent or antisolvent to prepare lipid nanoparticles. This avoids toxic organic solvents and allows fine control over particle size	Environmentally friendly, solvent-free, and suitable for sensitive drugs	High operational cost and need for specialized equipment	Wáng and Idée (2017)
Microfluidics-based methods	Emerging microfluidic platforms allow precise mixing of lipid and aqueous phases at microscale levels, leading to highly uniform nanoparticles. This method is particularly suited for lipid–polymer hybrids and gene delivery systems	High reproducibility, scalability, and control over particle properties	Technology still maturing; requires expensive equipment	Cheng et al. (2017), Hom et al. (2010), Yang et al. (2016b)
Biological derivation methods	Exosomes and cell-derived vesicles are isolated from cell culture supernatants or body fluids using ultracentrifugation, size-exclusion chromatography, precipitation, or microfluidic isolation methods. Postisolation, they can be loaded with therapeutic cargo through electroporation, incubation, or membrane permeabilization techniques	Biocompatible and naturally targeted delivery systems	Low yield, high variability, and challenges in large-scale production	Baughman et al. (2002), Wu et al. (2005), Feazell et al. (2007)

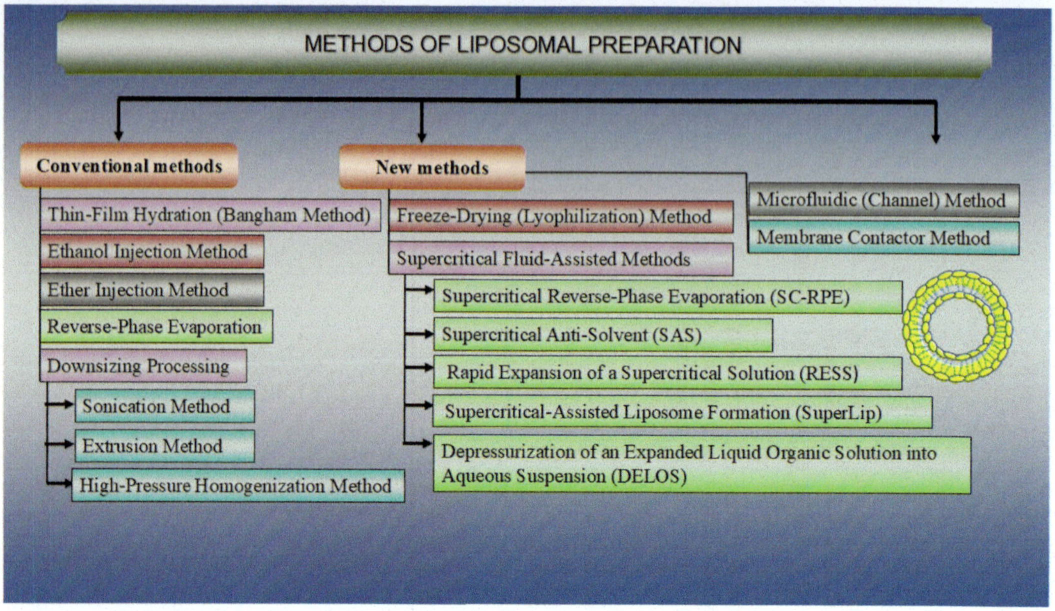

FIGURE 17.4 Method of preparation of liposomes.

Surface charge (zeta potential)

The surface charge, expressed as zeta potential, provides insight into the colloidal stability of nanoparticles. Strongly charged nanoparticles (±30 mV or higher) have good electrostatic repulsion that ensures high dispersion stability. In drug delivery, surface charge also affects cellular uptake and biodistribution. Cationic nanoparticles tend to interact strongly with negatively charged cell membranes, improving uptake, but sometimes may cause cytotoxicity. In contrast, neutral or slightly negative charges are preferred for systemic administration to avoid rapid clearance by the MPS. Zeta potential is typically measured using electrophoretic light scattering techniques (de la Rica et al., 2012).

Morphology and structural characteristics

The morphology of LBNPs influences their stability, release profile, and interaction with biological systems. Spherical nanoparticles are most common due to their thermodynamic stability. However, rod-shaped, cubical, or irregular vesicles have also been reported (Kumar et al., 2024a). Cryo-electron microscopy is increasingly applied to examine liposome lamellarity, exosome ultrastructure, and hybrid nanoparticle assemblies in near-native states. Structural studies also confirm the integrity of surface modifications such as PEGylation or ligand attachment. Transmission electron microscopy, scanning electron microscopy, atomic force microscopy, and X-ray photoelectron spectroscopy are widely used to visualize particle shape and surface architecture (Kanapathipillai et al., 2014; Jha et al., 2024c).

Encapsulation efficiency and drug loading

Encapsulation efficiency (EE%) refers to the percentage of the total drug that is successfully entrapped within nanoparticles, while drug loading (DL%) measures the ratio of encapsulated drug relative to the total weight of the carrier. Both parameters are crucial for determining therapeutic potency, dosing frequency, and the feasibility of large-scale production. High-performance liquid chromatography, UV–Vis spectroscopy, or fluorescence methods are commonly employed to quantify encapsulated drugs after separating free drug using ultracentrifugation, dialysis, or filtration. Optimizing lipid composition and preparation methods is key to achieving high EE% and DL% (Huang et al., 2016).

In vitro drug release profiles

Understanding how drugs are released from LBNPs is essential for predicting therapeutic efficacy. In vitro release studies are typically performed using dialysis membranes, diffusion chambers, or sample-and-separate techniques in simulated physiological conditions. Parameters such as pH, temperature, and enzymatic presence are adjusted to mimic the TME. A controlled or sustained release profile is desirable to maintain therapeutic drug levels while reducing systemic toxicity. Stimuli-responsive nanoparticles are often tested under different conditions (e.g., acidic pH or high glutathione [GSH] levels) to validate their responsiveness (Du et al., 2015; Jha et al., 2024b).

Stability and shelf-life indicators

Stability is a critical parameter, as LBNPs may undergo aggregation, drug leakage, or lipid oxidation during storage. Stability studies involve monitoring particle size, zeta potential, and drug payload over time at different temperature and humidity conditions (Kumar et al., 2025a; Kumar et al., 2019). Lyophilization with cryoprotectants is often used to enhance the long-term stability of liposomes and SLNs. Differential scanning calorimetry and X-ray diffraction are employed to study lipid crystallinity, which influences drug retention and release behavior (Kumar et al., 2024c). For exosomes, stability testing also involves monitoring protein integrity and biological activity (Peng et al., 2019). The long-term stability and proper storage of LBNPs are critical to maintaining their physicochemical properties, therapeutic activity, and safety for clinical applications. Instability during storage can lead to particle aggregation, drug leakage, lipid oxidation, or loss of targeting ligands, which ultimately compromises their efficacy. Therefore, systematic evaluation of stability under different environmental conditions is an essential part of formulation development (Wang et al., 2019).

Physical instability is one of the most common challenges for LBNPs. Aggregation, fusion, and changes in particle size or morphology can occur due to van der Waals forces, electrostatic interactions, or hydration effects. For example, liposomes and SLNs may undergo size growth or gelation during storage. Regular monitoring of particle size, zeta potential, and PDI helps assess physical stability. To improve stability, cryoprotectants such as trehalose, sucrose, or mannitol are often added during lyophilization to prevent vesicle fusion and maintain nanoparticle integrity upon reconstitution (Yang et al., 2019). The chemical stability of lipids must be considered, as they are susceptible to oxidation and hydrolysis, which can alter their chemical structure and compromise nanoparticle function. Unsaturated phospholipids, commonly used in liposome formulations, are particularly prone to peroxidation. Such reactions may cause membrane rigidity, drug leakage, or even the generation of toxic by-products. To minimize chemical instability, antioxidants such as vitamin E or butylated hydroxytoluene are incorporated into formulations. Storage under inert atmospheres (e.g., nitrogen flushing) and protection from light are also effective strategies (Cheng et al., 2013a). Biological stability of LBNPs is also necessary for the successful translation of drugs. For functionalized LBNPs such as those conjugated with targeting ligands, antibodies, or peptides, stability also encompasses the preservation of biological activity. Ligand detachment, conformational changes, or enzymatic degradation during storage can reduce targeting efficiency. Similarly, exosome-based and biomimetic lipid vesicles require stringent storage conditions to maintain their protein and lipid composition. Stabilizers and optimized buffer systems are commonly used to prevent denaturation and preserve bioactivity (Curcio et al., 2012).

Since LBNPs are administered parenterally, maintaining colloidal stability and sterility is also vital. Microbial contamination, aggregation, or precipitation may compromise safety and therapeutic performance. Sterile filtration or aseptic manufacturing conditions are employed to ensure sterility, while pH adjustments and buffer optimization help maintain colloidal stability. For long-term storage, refrigeration (2–8°C) is commonly used, but in some cases, nanoparticles require freezing or lyophilization to retain structural integrity (Hathout et al., 2018). Through long-term and accelerated stability studies under various temperature and humidity conditions, shelf life can be determined following International Council for Harmonisation guidelines. Accelerated testing helps predict potential degradation pathways, while real-time studies confirm actual product stability. These data are essential for regulatory approval and clinical translation of LBNPs (Jia et al., 2018). Regulatory authorities such as the FDA and European Medicines Agency require detailed stability data as part of nanoparticle-based drug submissions. This includes information on recommended storage conditions, validated shelf life, and compatibility with packaging materials. Given the growing clinical interest in LBNPs, standardized guidelines for stability testing are being established to ensure consistent product quality and safety across different formulations (Menon et al., 2017).

Additional biophysical and functional characterizations

Other important parameters include the surface chemistry and functionalization, typically analyzed using Fourier-transform infrared spectroscopy, nuclear magnetic resonance, or X-ray photoelectron spectroscopy. For targeted nanoparticles, binding affinity to receptors can be quantified through ligand–receptor assays. Protein corona studies, conducted by incubating nanoparticles with serum, provide insights into how nanoparticles interact with plasma proteins, which directly impacts their circulation and targeting efficiency. For exosomes and cell-derived vesicles, characterization often includes the detection of surface markers such as CD9, CD63, and CD81 using western blotting or flow cytometry (Fernandes et al., 2018).

Lyophilization and reconstitution strategies

Lyophilization (freeze-drying) is a widely adopted method to extend the shelf life of LBNPs, particularly liposomes, SLNs, and NLCs. By removing water under low temperatures, lyophilization prevents aggregation and lipid degradation. However, improper lyophilization may lead to structural collapse or drug leakage. Therefore, the use of cryoprotectants and optimized freeze–thaw cycles is crucial for the successful preservation of nanoformulation stability and characteristics (Kumar et al., 2024b). After reconstitution, formulations should retain their original physicochemical properties without significant loss of activity (Gan et al., 2011).

Surface engineering and targeting strategies for tumor-specific delivery

The surface properties of LBNPs play a crucial role in determining their circulation time, biodistribution, cellular uptake, and therapeutic efficiency. Unmodified nanoparticles are often rapidly cleared from systemic circulation due to recognition by the MPS. To overcome this challenge and achieve tumor-specific delivery, a variety of surface engineering strategies have been developed. PEG conjugation, commonly referred to as PEGylation, is one of the most widely used surface modifications. By grafting PEG chains onto the nanoparticle surface, a hydrophilic steric barrier is formed, which minimizes protein adsorption (opsonization) and reduces clearance by macrophages. This "stealth" effect increases blood circulation half-life and improves tumor accumulation through the EPR effect. It can reduce immunogenicity and enhance stability. However, repeated administration may trigger anti-PEG antibodies, leading to accelerated blood clearance (ABC phenomenon), and thus, proper care should be taken considering the dose and amount in the formulation. The surface charge of LBNPs may influence the cellular uptake and biodistribution. Positively charged (cationic) modifications, often achieved by incorporating cationic lipids like DOTAP or stearylamine, enhance interaction with negatively charged cell membranes and nucleic acids, making them useful for gene delivery. However, excessive positive charge may cause cytotoxicity and rapid clearance. Neutral or slightly negative charges are generally preferred for systemic delivery. Surface modification not only prolongs systemic stability but also enables targeted delivery, making it a cornerstone in the rational design of LBNPs for anticancer drug delivery.

One of the major advantages of LBNPs in oncology lies in their ability to preferentially accumulate in tumor tissues while sparing healthy organs. Conventional chemotherapy often fails to discriminate between malignant and normal cells, leading to severe systemic toxicity and suboptimal therapeutic outcomes. Nanotechnology-based approaches attempt to address this limitation through both passive and active targeting strategies, as well as more advanced stimuli-responsive and dual-targeted systems. Passive targeting exploits the inherent abnormalities of tumor vasculature and microenvironment to achieve drug accumulation without the need for specific ligands. In contrast, active targeting involves surface modification of nanoparticles with molecules that recognize tumor-specific receptors, leading to enhanced cellular uptake. Stimuli-responsive designs allow nanoparticles to release their therapeutic payload in response to internal (pH, enzymes, redox gradients) or external (heat, light, ultrasound) triggers. Moreover, multimodal and dual-targeting strategies are being increasingly investigated to combine multiple approaches and maximize therapeutic precision. Together, these strategies form a versatile toolkit for designing next-generation LBNPs that can achieve controlled biodistribution, improved efficacy, and reduced toxicity (Lee et al., 2016).

Passive targeting via enhanced permeability and retention effect

Passive targeting is one of the earliest and most widely studied approaches for tumor-specific drug delivery using nanoparticles. It relies on the EPR effect, a unique phenomenon associated with the structure and function of tumor vasculature. Unlike healthy tissues, which have tightly regulated endothelial junctions, tumor blood vessels are often leaky and disorganized due to rapid and uncontrolled angiogenesis. This abnormal architecture allows nanoparticles in the size range of 20–200 nm to extravasate from circulation and accumulate within tumor tissues. Additionally, tumors often lack efficient lymphatic drainage, which leads to prolonged retention of nanoparticles once they have entered the TME. LBNPs, including liposomes, SLNs, and NLCs, are particularly well-suited for exploiting the EPR effect. Their nanoscale size and tunable physicochemical properties enable prolonged circulation in the bloodstream and selective tumor accumulation. For example, PEGylated liposomes exhibit extended half-life and reduced clearance, thereby enhancing their ability to reach tumor tissues through passive targeting. Once accumulated, these nanoparticles release their drug payload either slowly over time or in response to local physiological conditions, leading to higher intratumoral concentrations compared to free drugs. Despite its clinical promise, passive targeting via the EPR effect is not without limitations. The extent of EPR varies significantly across tumor types, stages, and even within different regions of the same tumor, due to heterogeneity in vascular permeability and blood flow. Moreover, the dense extracellular matrix and high interstitial fluid pressure within tumors can hinder deep penetration of nanoparticles, resulting in uneven drug distribution. These limitations have motivated researchers to explore combination strategies such as using EPR for initial accumulation followed by active targeting or stimuli-responsiveness for enhanced uptake and controlled release. In clinical settings, the EPR effect has contributed to the success of several liposomal formulations, such as liposomal doxorubicin (Doxil/Caelyx), which demonstrates reduced systemic toxicity and improved safety compared to free doxorubicin. However, variability in patient responses highlights the need for personalized approaches that can assess the degree of EPR in individual tumors before therapy. Emerging diagnostic techniques, including imaging-based EPR assessment, are being developed to predict treatment outcomes and guide the selection of EPR-dependent nanomedicines. In summary, passive targeting through the EPR effect provides a foundational strategy for tumor-specific delivery of LBNPs. While it offers significant benefits, particularly in reducing off-target toxicity, its effectiveness is influenced by tumor heterogeneity and patient-specific factors. Combining passive targeting with active or stimuli-responsive approaches holds promise for overcoming these limitations and achieving more reliable therapeutic outcomes (Xiong et al., 2018).

Active targeting using ligands for selective drug delivery in cancer cells

While passive targeting via the EPR effect provides a foundation for tumor accumulation, it often lacks precision due to inter- and intratumoral heterogeneity. To achieve more selective and efficient drug delivery, LBNPs have been engineered with active targeting ligands that recognize and bind to specific receptors overexpressed on cancer cells or tumor-associated vasculature. This approach enhances cellular uptake through receptor-mediated endocytosis, thereby improving therapeutic efficacy while minimizing systemic side effects (Yang et al., 2016a). Active targeting using FA, peptides, antibodies, aptamers, and other ligands provides precise tumor recognition, surpassing the limitations of passive EPR-based targeting. Ongoing research focuses on multifunctional systems that combine multiple ligands or integrate active targeting with stimuli-responsive features to maximize therapeutic precision and personalization (Liu et al., 2008). Despite the associated advantages of active targeting, several limitations must be considered. Ligand density on the nanoparticle surface needs to be carefully optimized; excessive density may induce rapid clearance or steric hindrance, while insufficient density reduces binding efficiency. Furthermore, receptor expression varies among patients and tumor types, which may lead to inconsistent therapeutic outcomes. Additionally, the production and regulatory approval of ligand-functionalized nanoparticles can be more complex compared to conventional formulations. In summary, ligand-mediated active targeting represents a critical advancement in LBNP design for cancer therapy.

Small molecules as targeting ligands

Among small-molecule ligands, FA has been extensively used for nanoparticle functionalization that targets the folate receptor, highly overexpressed in various cancers, including ovarian, breast, and lung cancers. FA is small, inexpensive, stable, and easy to conjugate to lipid surfaces, which makes it a practical choice for large-scale development. Similarly, hyaluronic acid (HA) targets the CD44 receptor, another molecule frequently upregulated in cancer cells. HA-based targeting not only facilitates drug delivery but also provides biocompatibility and potential antitumor activity by interfering with tumor cell signaling pathways (Barenholz, 2012).

Researchers introduced a target-agnostic DNA-encoded chemical library (DEL) screening strategy to discover small-molecule ligands that selectively bind cancer cell surfaces without predefined molecular targets. By screening an ultra-large DEL (~10^8 members) directly against live breast cancer cells with distinct metastatic phenotypes (MDA-MB-231 and MCF-7), the approach enabled unbiased identification of cell-specific ligands capable of discriminating between aggressive and less metastatic cancer phenotypes. This expands active targeting beyond conventional receptor-preselected strategies and opens a data-driven route to uncover ligands that reflect functional cell-surface phenotypes. The identified ligands were further validated for cell-targeting applications in photodynamic therapy and targeted drug delivery, demonstrating translational relevance for precision nanomedicine. Importantly, the DNA barcode inherent to DEL compounds enabled rapid receptor deconvolution, leading to the identification of α-enolase (ENO1) as a functional cell-surface receptor for one ligand enriched on aggressive breast cancer cells. This work establishes DEL-based, target-agnostic screening as a powerful platform for discovering novel small-molecule targeting ligands and their cognate receptors, accelerating the development of actively targeted cancer therapeutics when classical biomarkers are unknown or heterogeneous.

Peptide-mediated targeting

Peptides offer high specificity and tunable binding affinity while being relatively easy to synthesize and modify. The arginylglycylaspartic acid (RGD) peptide, which recognizes integrins ($\alpha v\beta 3$ and $\alpha v\beta 5$) commonly expressed in tumor angiogenesis, has been widely utilized for enhancing tumor vasculature targeting. Other examples include trans-activator of transcription (TAT) peptides, which facilitate intracellular delivery by enhancing nanoparticle penetration across cellular membranes, and tumor-homing peptides identified through phage display libraries. Peptide-decorated LBNPs have shown improved penetration into solid tumors and increased cytotoxicity against cancer cells when compared to untargeted systems (Ta and Porter, 2013). Researchers reported a series of peptide–drug conjugates (PDCs) combining the BRAF inhibitor vemurafenib with bioactive cell-penetrating peptides to address acquired drug resistance in melanoma. By covalently linking vemurafenib to peptides possessing either membrane-disruptive anticancer activity or nondisruptive carrier properties, the conjugates enabled efficient transmembrane transport of the drug while introducing complementary cytotoxic mechanisms. This integrated design ensured intracellular delivery of the drug cargo together with the peptide carrier, overcoming limitations associated with poor cellular uptake and reduced drug exposure in resistant melanoma cells. The therapeutic performance of the PDCs was strongly dependent on the choice of peptide carrier, with membrane-active peptides conferring superior potency and selectivity compared with nondisruptive counterparts. An optimized vemurafenib–peptide conjugate exhibited effective activity against both drug-naïve and drug-resistant melanoma cells while maintaining selectivity toward noncancerous cells. These findings underscore the potential of peptide-mediated targeting and delivery strategies to bypass resistance pathways and enhance the clinical utility of small-molecule kinase inhibitors in refractory cancers.

Antibody-based targeting (immunoliposomes)

Antibodies and their fragments provide one of the most powerful tools for active targeting. Immunoliposomes, liposomes conjugated with monoclonal antibodies, can selectively recognize tumor-associated antigens such as HER2, EGFR, or PSMA. By exploiting well-characterized antibody–antigen interactions, these systems achieve precise tumor recognition and internalization. Trastuzumab-modified liposomes targeting HER2-positive breast cancer are a prominent example, demonstrating superior tumor accumulation and enhanced therapeutic response compared to conventional liposomes. However, the complexity and cost of antibody production, as well as potential immunogenicity, remain challenges for widespread clinical use (Pantarotto et al., 2004). Researchers report a dual-ligand immunoliposome system for targeted delivery of arsenic trioxide in hepatocellular carcinoma (HCC), combining an anti-GPC3 monoclonal antibody for tumor-specific recognition with a cell-penetrating peptide (CPP44) to enhance intracellular drug delivery. GPC3 is highly and selectively expressed on HCC cells, enabling active targeting of the liposomes to tumor tissue following initial passive accumulation via the EPR effect. Molecular dynamics simulations confirmed that covalent conjugation of the anti-GPC3 antibody preserved its antigen-binding capability, ensuring effective ligand–receptor recognition at the tumor site. Functionally, the dual-ligand liposomes exhibited significantly enhanced cellular uptake and cytotoxicity compared with nontargeted and single-ligand formulations. In vivo studies in HCC-bearing mice demonstrated efficient tumor accumulation and a marked tumor inhibition rate (~63%), highlighting the synergistic effect of antibody-mediated targeting and CPP-assisted membrane penetration. This work exemplifies how immunoliposomes integrated with peptide-mediated internalization strategies can overcome biological barriers, improve intracellular drug delivery, and enhance therapeutic outcomes, representing a powerful approach for precision nanomedicine in solid tumor therapy.

Aptamers and other emerging ligands

In addition to traditional ligands, aptamers, short single-stranded DNA or RNA sequences, are emerging as attractive targeting moieties. Aptamers can bind to receptors with high specificity and affinity, similar to antibodies, but with advantages such as lower immunogenicity, easier synthesis, and improved stability. Other novel targeting ligands under investigation include carbohydrates, vitamins, and cell-penetrating ligands that can enhance delivery to hard-to-reach tumors (Singh et al., 2005). Recent work by Park et al. (2026) demonstrates how precision glycosylation of albumin nanocarriers can be used as an effective ligand-based strategy for selective targeting within the TME. By engineering clickable albumin nanoparticles with a controlled number of specific sugar moieties (mannose, galactose, or glucose), the authors achieved programmable biodistribution and cell-type selectivity in vivo. Mannosylated albumin preferentially targeted mannose receptor (MRC1)-expressing tumor-associated macrophages (TAMs), while galactosylated and glucosylated albumins showed enhanced accumulation in glycolytic and hypoxic tumor regions enriched in GLUT1-expressing cancer cells. This highlights how ligand–receptor interactions mediated by surface glycans can be rationally exploited to direct nanocarriers toward distinct cellular components of the TME. Importantly, the study integrated positron emission tomography (PET) with spatial transcriptomics to map nanoparticle localization with gene expression-defined tumor niches, providing unbiased mechanistic insight into active targeting at the tissue and cellular levels. Therapeutically, mannosylated albumin loaded with clodronate achieved selective depletion of $CD206^{+}$ TAMs without altering drug release kinetics, demonstrating the immunomodulatory potential of ligand-guided nanomedicine. Overall, this work establishes glycan ligands as tunable targeting moieties and offers a robust framework for designing actively targeted, cell-specific nanotherapeutics for improved precision in cancer drug delivery (Park et al., 2026).

Stimuli-responsive LBNPs for precise drug delivery at the tumor site/in cancer cells

Stimuli-responsive nanomedicine represents an advanced generation of drug delivery systems designed to release their therapeutic cargo selectively in response to specific triggers (Jha et al., 2024a; Jha et al., 2022). These triggers may originate from the TME (endogenous stimuli) or be applied externally (exogenous stimuli). By exploiting these stimuli, LBNPs can achieve site-specific drug release, thereby enhancing therapeutic efficacy while reducing systemic toxicity. This strategy addresses one of the major challenges of conventional chemotherapy: the uncontrolled distribution of drugs throughout the body (Cheng et al., 2013b).

pH-responsive LBNPs

The acidic environment of tumors (pH ~6.5–6.8) and intracellular compartments such as endosomes and lysosomes (pH ~4.5–5.5) provides an ideal trigger for pH-sensitive nanoparticles. pH-responsive LBNPs are engineered with lipids or polymers that destabilize or degrade under acidic conditions, releasing the encapsulated drug at the tumor site. For instance, liposomes containing pH-sensitive lipids such as dioleoylphosphatidylethanolamine (DOPE) undergo conformational changes in acidic environments, enhancing membrane fusion and drug release. This approach has been particularly effective in improving the intracellular delivery of chemotherapeutics and nucleic acids (Mehra and Jain, 2015). Researchers developed pH-responsive LPHNPs for actively targeted delivery of docetaxel to breast cancer cells by integrating FA as a small-molecule targeting ligand with a poly (β-amino ester) (PBAE) polymeric core. The FA-decorated lipid shell enabled receptor-mediated uptake via folate receptors overexpressed on breast cancer cells, while the hybrid core–shell architecture provided excellent colloidal stability and efficient drug encapsulation. This design addressed key delivery barriers, including poor tumor uptake and intracellular sequestration, by combining ligand-mediated targeting with microenvironment-responsive functionality. Functionally, the PBAE core imparted pH-triggered drug release and endosomal/lysosomal escape through the proton sponge effect, enabling rapid intracellular release of docetaxel in the acidic tumor and endosomal compartments. The nanoparticles demonstrated strong cytotoxicity toward 4T1 breast cancer cells in vitro while remaining biocompatible in their blank form and exhibited enhanced tumor accumulation, potent antitumor efficacy, and minimal systemic toxicity in vivo. This work highlights how small-molecule ligands coupled with stimuli-responsive nanocarriers can synergistically improve tumor selectivity, intracellular delivery, and chemotherapeutic efficacy in breast cancer.

Redox-responsive LBNPs

Tumor cells are characterized by a higher concentration of reducing agents, particularly GSH, compared to normal tissues. Redox-responsive nanoparticles leverage this difference by incorporating disulfide bonds or other redox-sensitive linkages within their structure. Upon exposure to the high intracellular GSH levels in cancer cells, these linkages are cleaved, leading to drug release. Redox-sensitive LBNPs are especially valuable for delivering anticancer drugs and genetic materials such as siRNA, as they enable rapid intracellular release while maintaining stability during systemic circulation (Valizadeh et al., 2012). Researchers designed redox-responsive, self-assembled albumin nanoparticles for intracellularly targeted delivery of palbociclib in breast cancer, using a Quality by Design (Box–Behnken DoE) framework to optimize critical formulation attributes. The bovine serum albumin–based nanocarriers exhibited uniform nanoscale size, high drug entrapment efficiency, and excellent physicochemical stability. By exploiting the elevated intracellular GSH levels and acidic microenvironment of tumor cells, the nanoparticles enabled on-demand drug release, achieving near-complete palbociclib release under tumor-relevant redox and pH conditions. Functionally, these redox-responsive nanoparticles showed markedly enhanced anticancer activity compared to free palbociclib across both 2D monolayers and 3D mammosphere models, with higher cellular uptake, increased apoptosis, mitochondrial depolarization, reactive oxygen species (ROS) generation, and suppression of migration and clonogenicity. The formulation also induced G0/G1 cell-cycle arrest via reduced retinoblastoma protein phosphorylation and favorable modulation of BAX/Bcl-2 expression. Although ligand-free, this work exemplifies microenvironment-responsive active targeting at the intracellular level, demonstrating how smart protein nanocarriers can selectively trigger drug release within cancer cells to improve therapeutic efficacy while maintaining hemocompatibility and stability.

Enzyme-responsive LBNPs

Many tumors overexpress specific enzymes, including matrix metalloproteinases (MMPs), phospholipases, and proteases, which can serve as biological triggers for enzyme-sensitive drug release. Enzyme-responsive LBNPs are designed by incorporating peptide sequences or lipid linkages that are cleaved in the presence of these enzymes, leading to site-specific drug release. For example, MMP-sensitive liposomes can release their contents within the tumor extracellular matrix, where MMP activity is particularly high. This strategy enhances local drug concentration and minimizes off-target effects in normal tissues (Ozkan, 2004). Researchers demonstrated an innovative nanoparticle-enabled prodrug activation strategy for head and neck squamous cell carcinoma, aiming to reduce the systemic toxicity associated with conventional chemoradiotherapy. Instead of delivering a cytotoxic drug directly, lipid nanoparticles (LNPs) were engineered to deliver mRNA encoding a bacterial enzyme, purine nucleoside phosphorylase (PNP), which locally converts the clinically used prodrug fludarabine into the highly toxic metabolite 2-fluoroadenine specifically within tumor tissue. By screening 44 chemically distinct LNP formulations using in vivo DNA barcoding, the authors identified a lead formulation (LNPIT) with superior intratumoral delivery and expression efficiency. Tumor cells transfected with LNPIT exhibited enhanced RNA and protein metabolism pathways, indicating efficient mRNA translation and cellular engagement with the nanocarrier system. Therapeutically, sequential administration of LNPIT–PNP followed by fludarabine phosphate induced robust antitumor responses in vivo, validating a tumor-restricted enzyme–prodrug activation paradigm. Although this strategy does not rely on classical ligand–receptor targeting, it represents an advanced form of functional active targeting, where nanoparticle-mediated, localized gene expression confers tumor selectivity at the biochemical level, offering a promising route to improve efficacy while minimizing off-target toxicity in solid tumors.

Temperature-responsive LBNPs

Tumor sites often exhibit slightly elevated temperatures compared to normal tissues, and externally applied hyperthermia can further enhance this difference. Thermosensitive liposomes and lipid carriers are formulated with lipids that undergo phase transitions at specific temperatures, typically between 40 and 45°C. Under localized hyperthermia, the lipid bilayer becomes destabilized, resulting in rapid drug release. ThermoDox, a temperature-sensitive liposomal formulation of doxorubicin, has been investigated in clinical trials in combination with radiofrequency ablation for liver cancer, demonstrating the clinical potential of this strategy (Chen et al., 2015). Researchers developed temperature-responsive, biocompatible nanocarriers based on halloysite clay nanotubes functionalized with poly (N-isopropylacrylamide) (PNIPAM) brushes for controlled anticancer drug release. By integrating mussel-inspired polydopamine coating with surface-initiated atom transfer radical polymerization (ATRP), a thermoresponsive polymer layer was grafted onto the nanotubes, conferring a phase transition temperature (~32°C) suitable for hyperthermia-assisted therapy. This design enabled stable drug loading and temperature-dependent release of doxorubicin, aligning drug liberation with localized heating to exploit the synergistic cytotoxic effects of chemotherapy and hyperthermia. Importantly, PNIPAM grafting improved biocompatibility by suppressing polydopamine-associated cytotoxicity, while maintaining efficient cellular internalization, as confirmed by superresolution imaging in HeLa cells. Although not ligand-directed, this system exemplifies stimuli-responsive active targeting, where spatiotemporal control over drug release is achieved by exploiting externally applied thermal cues at the tumor site. Such temperature-triggered nanocarriers offer a complementary strategy to ligand-mediated targeting by improving on-site drug availability, reducing premature release, and enhancing therapeutic precision during hyperthermia-based cancer treatments.

Externally triggered stimuli (light, ultrasound, magnetic fields)

Beyond endogenous triggers, LBNPs can also be engineered to respond to externally applied stimuli such as light, ultrasound, or magnetic fields. For instance, photosensitive liposomes release drugs upon irradiation with near-infrared (NIR) light, enabling spatiotemporal control over drug delivery. Ultrasound-sensitive nanoparticles can undergo cavitation or membrane disruption when exposed to focused ultrasound waves, enhancing drug penetration and release. Similarly, magnetic nanoparticles incorporated into LBNPs can be directed to tumor sites using external magnetic fields and triggered for on-demand release through magnetic hyperthermia. In summary, stimuli-responsive LBNPs represent a sophisticated and adaptable approach to tumor-targeted drug delivery. By responding to pH, redox gradients, enzymes, or temperature, these systems ensure selective release at the tumor site, overcoming many limitations of conventional drug carriers. The integration of multiple stimuli-responsive mechanisms and their combination with passive and active targeting strategies is paving the way for highly precise and personalized cancer therapies. Table 17.3 summarizes stimuli-responsive LBNPs for cancer therapy (Olerile et al., 2017).

Conjugation schemes for surface functionalization of LBNPs

Effective surface functionalization of LBNPs relies not only on the choice of targeting ligand but also on the conjugation chemistry used to anchor these ligands onto the nanoparticle surface. The conjugation strategy directly influences ligand orientation, density, binding affinity, and overall in vivo behavior. Several well-established chemical coupling methods are employed to functionalize liposomes, SLNs, NLCs, and lipid–polymer hybrids (Table 17.4). Below is an overview of the most widely used schemes in targeted nanocarrier

TABLE 17.3 Stimuli-responsive lipid-based nanoparticles for cancer therapy.

Stimulus type	Nanocarrier type	Stimulus-responsive material	Drug/Gene	Therapeutic application	References
Temperature-responsive	Liposomes; polymeric nanoparticles	Thermosensitive lipids (e.g., DPPC, MSPC), heat-labile polymer matrices	Lucifer yellow iodoacetamide; doxorubicin	Inhibition of CT-26 colon tumors; activity against Lewis lung carcinoma cells	Mahajan et al. (2010)
pH-sensitive	Liposomes; micelles	pH-sensitive lipids (DOPE, CHEMS), acid-cleavable hydrazone linkers	Doxorubicin	Cytotoxic activity in B-lymphoma cells; effective against MCF-7 breast cancer cells	Savla et al. (2011)
Redox-responsive	Gelatin nanoparticles; cationic lipoic acid systems	Disulfide linkages, thiolated lipids, GSH-responsive polymers	Plasmid DNA	Enhanced gene transfection and DNA delivery via glutathione-mediated redox response; increased transgene expression	An et al. (2016)
Enzyme-responsive	Silica-coated magnetic nanoparticles; hyaluronic acid nanocapsules; LIPOSOMAL carriers	MMP-cleavable peptides, HA susceptible to hyaluronidase, phospholipase-sensitive lipids	Doxorubicin; polyhexanide	Colon carcinoma treatment; infection management; breast cancer therapy	Castillo et al. (2012)

design. Conjugation chemistry is a critical determinant of nanoparticle targeting performance. Choosing the appropriate conjugation strategy allows optimization of ligand orientation, binding affinity, stability under physiological conditions, stimuli-responsiveness, and clinical scalability. Incorporating robust and biologically compatible conjugation schemes ensures that targeting ligands remain functional during circulation and effectively engage tumor receptors, thereby improving therapeutic precision.

Recent advances and innovations

The field of LBNPs has witnessed remarkable progress over the past decade, with innovations that extend far beyond conventional drug encapsulation. As the understanding of tumor biology, nanotechnology, and molecular medicine deepens, LBNPs are being engineered to perform multifunctional tasks, including simultaneous drug delivery, gene regulation, immunomodulation, and real-time imaging. These advanced systems not only

TABLE 17.4 Conjugation schemes for surface functionalization of nanoparticles.

Conjugation strategy	Description	Mechanism	Applications	Advantages	Limitations	References
Carbodiimide (EDC/NHS) coupling	Carbodiimide chemistry is one of the most frequently applied methods for linking carboxyl groups (–COOH) on lipid headgroups or polymer coatings with primary amine groups (–NH_2) on ligands	EDC activates carboxyl groups to form an O-acylisourea intermediate, which is stabilized by NHS to yield an NHS ester. This ester reacts with amines to form stable amide bonds	Conjugation of folic acid to DSPE-PEG–COOH on liposomes. HA or RGD peptide surface functionalization	Simple, aqueous-compatible, forms stable bonds	Risk of ligand cross-linking if not optimized	. Civril et al. (2026)
Maleimide–thiol (Michael addition) coupling	The maleimide–thiol reaction is highly selective and efficient under mild conditions, making it ideal for sensitive biomolecules	Maleimide-activated lipids (e.g., DSPE-PEG-maleimide) react with thiolated ligands (–SH) to form stable thioether linkages	Antibody fragments conjugated to liposomal PEG–maleimide. Thiolated aptamers attached to NLCs. Peptides modified with terminal cysteine residues	Fast, biocompatible, highly specific	Thiol oxidation must be carefully controlled	Ansari et al. (2022)
Click chemistry (CuAAC and SPAAC)	Click chemistry has gained popularity because of its rapid kinetics and orthogonality. Types **A.** Cu(I)-catalyzed azide–alkyne cycloaddition (CuAAC) **B.** Strain-promoted azide–alkyne cycloaddition (SPAAC), a copper-free variant suitable for biological systems	Azide-functionalized lipids react with alkyne-containing ligands to form stable triazole rings	Aptamer attachment to liposomes via azide–alkyne click. Click-enabled PEGylated SLNs for controlled ligand density. Copper-free SPAAC for encapsulating sensitive peptides or proteins	High efficiency, tunable ligand density, bioorthogonal	Copper catalysts may be toxic (CuAAC)	Ragab et al. (2022)

Streptavidin–biotin binding	This noncovalent approach relies on the extremely strong streptavidin–biotin affinity (Kd $\approx 10^{-15}$ M)	Biotinylated lipids are incorporated into nanoparticles, and streptavidin serves as a bridge to link biotinylated targeting ligands	Modular assembly of immunoliposomes. Rapid screening of ligand combinations. Hybrid systems require reversible binding	High affinity, flexible modular design	Streptavidin is immunogenic; not ideal for clinical formulations	Obozina et al. (2026)
Hydrazone and Schiff base linkages	These pH-sensitive conjugation strategies allow ligand release or NP disassembly in acidic tumor microenvironments	Hydrazides or amines on ligands react with aldehyde- or ketone-functionalized lipids to form acid-labile hydrazone or imine bonds	pH-responsive targeting ligands. Acid-triggered shedding of shielding layers to expose targeting moieties ("smart targeting")	Stimuli-responsive, reversible	Less stable at physiological pH	Sant et al. (2026)
Electrostatic adsorption	Some targeting moieties, especially nucleic acid-based ligands (aptamers), can be adsorbed via charge interactions	Cationic lipid surfaces electrostatically bind anionic ligands or polynucleotides	Cationic liposomes binding siRNA or aptamers. Surface loading of HA on positively charged SLNs	No chemical modification required	Less stable; desorption possible in vivo	Das et al. (2026)

enhance therapeutic efficacy but also enable precision medicine by tailoring treatments to the unique characteristics of individual patients and their tumors. Recent advances focus on expanding the capabilities of LBNPs through theranostics, gene and mRNA delivery, immunotherapy applications, and codelivery platforms. Innovations in material design, surface functionalization, and manufacturing technologies have further facilitated the clinical translation of these systems. Moreover, the integration of emerging tools such as artificial intelligence (AI) and microfluidic technologies into LBNP development is accelerating optimization and enabling scalable production. Together, these innovations are shaping the next generation of nanomedicine in oncology (Uthaman et al., 2018).

Theranostic lipid nanoparticles

Theranostic nanoparticles are multifunctional systems designed to combine therapeutic and diagnostic capabilities within a single nanoplatform. In the context of LBNPs, theranostic approaches enable drug delivery while simultaneously providing real-time information about biodistribution, accumulation, drug release, and treatment response. This dual functionality allows clinicians to tailor therapies to individual patients and adjust treatment regimens based on feedback, thereby advancing the goals of personalized oncology. Theranostic LBNPs are typically developed by coencapsulating anticancer drugs and imaging agents or by chemically conjugating imaging moieties onto the nanoparticle surface. Imaging modalities such as magnetic resonance imaging (MRI), computed tomography (CT), PET, optical imaging, and photoacoustic imaging can be integrated into these systems. For example, liposomes loaded with doxorubicin and gadolinium complexes provide both therapeutic and MRI contrast capabilities, enabling visualization of drug delivery in real time (Ganguly and Ghosh, 2026). Similarly, LBNPs incorporating fluorescent dyes or NIR probes facilitate intraoperative imaging, helping surgeons delineate tumor margins more accurately (Gahlot, 2026). Beyond imaging, theranostic LBNPs have also been investigated for photothermal and photodynamic therapies. In these systems, nanoparticles are loaded with photosensitizers or plasmonic agents that, upon exposure to light, generate heat or reactive oxygen species to induce localized tumor cell death (Zhu et al., 2026). Such nanoparticles can simultaneously deliver chemotherapy while enhancing treatment efficacy through phototherapy, offering a synergistic multimodal approach. The clinical potential of theranostic nanoparticles lies in their ability to monitor treatment efficacy in real time and personalize therapeutic regimens. However, challenges remain, particularly regarding the complexity of design, potential toxicity of imaging agents, and regulatory requirements for multifunctional products. Nevertheless, theranostic LBNPs are gaining momentum as powerful tools in precision oncology, bridging the gap between therapy and diagnostics (Liu et al., 2017). Researchers developed low-density lipoprotein (LDL)-mimicking lipid nanoparticles as a biomimetic theranostic platform for tumor-targeted codelivery of paclitaxel and superparamagnetic iron oxide nanocrystals. By functionalizing the nanoparticle surface with FA, the system achieved receptor-mediated targeting of folate receptor–overexpressing breast cancer cells (MCF-7), enabling both enhanced intracellular drug delivery and T2-weighted MRI contrast for noninvasive tumor detection. The LDL-like architecture supported efficient coencapsulation of therapeutic and imaging agents while maintaining a favorable nanoscale size and surface charge for in vivo circulation and tumor accumulation. Functionally, folate-decorated LDL-mimetic nanoparticles demonstrated selective uptake by cancer cells, potent antitumor efficacy in vivo, and excellent biocompatibility, as drug-free carriers exhibited minimal cytotoxicity. This work illustrates how small-molecule ligand–mediated targeting combined with biomimicry can be leveraged to create integrated theranostic nanoplatforms, enabling simultaneous tumor imaging and targeted chemotherapy. The strategy highlights the translational potential of folate-functionalized lipid nanoparticles for precision delivery of both drugs and diagnostic agents in cancer therapy.

Codelivery of therapeutics

Cancer is a multifactorial disease that involves complex signaling networks, genetic alterations, and resistance mechanisms. Single-agent chemotherapy often fails to achieve durable responses due to the rapid development of drug resistance and tumor heterogeneity. As a result, combination therapy has become a cornerstone of modern oncology, where two or more agents with complementary mechanisms of action are administered to achieve synergistic effects. LBNPs provide a versatile platform for codelivery of multiple therapeutics, ensuring that drugs reach the tumor site simultaneously, in optimal ratios, and with controlled release kinetics (Cook et al., 1991). The rationale for codelivery lies in the ability to target multiple pathways within cancer cells or the TME. For example, combining a chemotherapeutic drug with a molecularly targeted agent can kill rapidly dividing cells and block survival signaling pathways. Similarly, delivering chemotherapy together with an immunomodulator can simultaneously reduce tumor burden and stimulate antitumor immunity. Traditional combination therapy often suffers from pharmacokinetic mismatches, as different drugs have distinct circulation times and biodistribution profiles, leading to suboptimal outcomes. Encapsulating multiple agents within a single LBNP overcomes these limitations by synchronizing their pharmacokinetics and tumor accumulation (Cho et al., 2012).

Chemotherapy–chemotherapy combinations

One of the earliest applications of codelivery LBNPs has been the encapsulation of two chemotherapeutic agents. For instance, liposomes coloaded with doxorubicin and paclitaxel have demonstrated synergistic cytotoxicity in breast and ovarian cancers. By encapsulating both drugs within a lipid bilayer or lipid matrix, these nanoparticles improve drug solubility, reduce systemic toxicity, and maintain synergistic ratios at the tumor site (Ong et al., 2008). Paulson et al. (2026) reported interim findings from the multicenter phase 1b DeLLphi-303 study evaluating tarlatamab, a DLL3×CD3 bispecific T-cell engager, in combination with PD-L1 inhibitors (atezolizumab or durvalumab) as first-line maintenance therapy after platinum–etoposide chemo-immunotherapy in patients with extensive-stage small cell lung cancer (SCLC). This antibody-based active targeting strategy redirects cytotoxic T cells specifically toward DLL3-expressing tumor cells, while concurrent PD-L1 blockade sustains antitumor immune activation to delay disease progression following induction therapy. The combination demonstrated a manageable safety profile, with cytokine release syndrome and immune effector cell–associated neurotoxicity syndrome as the most notable immune-related adverse events (irAEs) and no treatment-related deaths. At interim analysis, the regimen showed promising clinical activity, with a median overall survival of approximately 25 months, suggesting meaningful benefit over historical outcomes in extensive-stage SCLC. These results underscore the potential of bispecific antibody–mediated targeting integrated with immune checkpoint inhibition as an effective maintenance strategy for aggressive, relapsing cancers (Paulson et al., 2026).

Chemotherapy–gene therapy combinations

Another innovative approach is the codelivery of chemotherapeutics and nucleic acids such as siRNA or mRNA. For example, LBNPs delivering doxorubicin alongside siRNA targeting multidrug resistance genes (e.g., MDR1) can both kill tumor cells and silence the pathways responsible for drug efflux, thereby overcoming resistance. Similarly, codelivery of paclitaxel with mRNA encoding tumor suppressor proteins can induce both direct cytotoxicity and tumor reprogramming, offering a powerful dual mechanism (Ryu et al., 2010). Pirouzmand et al. (2026) developed pH-responsive Janus Ag/mesoporous silica nanoparticles conjugated with a MUC-1 aptamer for receptor-specific targeting of breast cancer cells and codelivery of chemotherapy (doxorubicin), gene therapy (P-glycoprotein antisense oligonucleotides), and photothermal therapy. The dumbbell-shaped Janus nanostructure enabled spatial segregation of functions, with mesoporous silica hosting doxorubicin and chitosan acting as a pH-responsive gatekeeper to protect and release antisense cargo in the acidic TME. The MUC-1 aptamer provided selective binding to MUC-1–overexpressing breast cancer cells, enhancing cellular uptake and tumor selectivity. Functionally, the multifunctional nanoplatform achieved robust cytotoxicity in drug-resistant MCF-7/ADR cells, with marked suppression of P-glycoprotein expression, effectively sensitizing resistant tumors to chemotherapy. Synergistic integration of chemotherapy, antisense-mediated MDR gene silencing, and photothermal therapy under NIR irradiation produced significantly higher tumor cell killing compared to single-modality treatments, while maintaining relatively lower toxicity toward nonresistant cells. This work exemplifies how aptamer-mediated active targeting combined with stimuli-responsive, multimodal nanotherapy can overcome multidrug resistance and enhance therapeutic outcomes in refractory breast cancer (Pirouzmand et al., 2026).

Chemotherapy–immunotherapy combinations

LBNPs are also being explored for combining chemotherapy with immunotherapy. For example, nanoparticles encapsulating oxaliplatin (a chemotherapy drug that induces immunogenic cell death) along with a toll-like receptor agonist can simultaneously destroy tumor cells and activate dendritic cells, leading to robust antitumor immunity. This dual approach not only enhances therapeutic efficacy but also helps establish long-term immune memory against cancer recurrence (Yang et al., 2017). Rached et al. (2025) provided a comprehensive review of the toxicity profile of chemotherapy combined with immune checkpoint inhibitors across multiple tumor indications, including lung, breast, head and neck, gastrointestinal, cervical, and biliary tract cancers. While chemo–immunotherapy has become a standard-of-care approach due to consistent improvements in progression-free survival, overall survival, and pathological complete response, the combination introduces overlapping toxicity spectra from cytotoxic chemotherapy and irAEs. Metalevel analysis across pivotal randomized trials demonstrated a modest increase in all-grade adverse events and serious (grade $\geq$3) toxicities compared with chemotherapy alone, without an associated increase in treatment-related mortality. Clinically, the review highlights common high-grade toxicities such as diarrhea, dyspnea, fatigue, rash, and hepatotoxicity, emphasizing the diagnostic challenge of distinguishing chemotherapy-related side effects from immune-mediated toxicities that require different management strategies. The authors propose practical, multidisciplinary management recommendations involving organ-specific specialists to improve early recognition and tailored treatment of irAEs during combination therapy. This synthesis is particularly relevant for targeted immunotherapies, underscoring that while antibody-based checkpoint blockade enhances antitumor efficacy when combined with chemotherapy, toxicity-aware clinical pathways are essential to safely translate these regimens into routine oncology practice (Rached et al., 2025). While codelivery platforms show great promise, several challenges hinder clinical translation. Ensuring the stability of multiple drugs within the same carrier, preventing premature drug leakage, and achieving scalable manufacturing processes are ongoing concerns. Furthermore, regulatory approval for multicomponent nanomedicines is more complex than for single-agent formulations. Despite these hurdles, advancements in formulation technologies such as microfluidics, modular lipid design, and AI-driven optimization are accelerating progress in this field. Codelivery of multiple therapeutics using LBNPs represents a paradigm shift in cancer nanomedicine, offering the ability to overcome resistance, enhance synergistic effects, and personalize treatment regimens. These multifunctional systems hold great promise for future clinical applications, especially as precision oncology continues to evolve (Terada et al., 2006).

Preclinical and clinical applications

The translation of LBNPs from laboratory research into clinical oncology requires systematic evaluation through preclinical and clinical studies. Preclinical investigations, encompassing both in vitro and in vivo models, serve as the foundation for understanding nanoparticle behavior, therapeutic potential, and safety profiles. These studies provide critical insights into drug loading, release kinetics, cytotoxicity, biodistribution, tumor accumulation, and pharmacokinetics. Following encouraging preclinical outcomes, selected formulations advance to clinical trials, where safety, efficacy, tolerability, and therapeutic superiority over conventional treatments are evaluated in cancer patients. Over the past decades, several LBNP formulations have successfully transitioned from bench to bedside. The clinical landscape now includes FDA-approved formulations, ongoing phase I–III trials, and case studies demonstrating real-world applications. Together, preclinical and clinical research highlight the tremendous potential of LBNPs while also identifying challenges that must be overcome for broader clinical translation (Banerjee et al., 2009).

In vitro and in vivo evaluation in cancer models

In vitro studies are the first step in evaluating the potential of LBNPs for anticancer drug delivery. These experiments typically involve cultured cancer cell lines to assess nanoparticle uptake, intracellular trafficking, drug release, and cytotoxicity. Cellular assays such as 3-[4,5-dimethylthiazol-2-yl]-2,5-diphenyltetrazolium bromide. [1, 2] (MTT), flow cytometry, and confocal microscopy are used to determine nanoparticle-mediated drug internalization and efficacy. Importantly, in vitro models also allow investigation of targeted delivery strategies by comparing uptake in receptor-positive versus receptor-negative cells. For gene and mRNA delivery, in vitro transfection efficiency and protein expression are quantified to validate nanoparticle functionality. Although highly informative, in vitro models lack the complexity of the TME, making them complementary but not definitive predictors of in vivo performance (Singh et al., 2011). Animal models, particularly murine xenografts and genetically engineered mouse models, are critical for assessing LBNP biodistribution, pharmacokinetics, therapeutic efficacy, and toxicity. In vivo studies provide insights into nanoparticle circulation time, tumor accumulation via the EPR effect, and clearance pathways. Tumor-bearing animal models are used to evaluate tumor regression, survival benefits, and immune responses following LBNP treatment. Advanced imaging techniques, such as fluorescence, PET, or MRI, are often integrated with theranostic LBNPs to monitor nanoparticle localization in real time. Moreover, in vivo toxicology studies assess potential adverse effects on major organs, immune activation, and systemic safety (Hatakeyama et al., 2011). To enhance translational relevance, researchers are increasingly using 3D tumor spheroids, organoids, and patient-derived xenograft (PDX) models that better recapitulate the TME and heterogeneity. These models bridge the gap between simplified in vitro assays and complex in vivo studies, improving the predictive accuracy of preclinical evaluations. Incorporating such models into the preclinical pipeline helps identify promising LBNP formulations with a higher likelihood of clinical success (Zhang et al., 2016).

FDA-approved and clinical-stage lipid nanoparticle formulations

The clinical translation of LBNPs has been marked by significant milestones, beginning with the approval of liposomal formulations in the 1990s and more recently with the success of lipid nanoparticles in delivering mRNA vaccines. These approvals validate the safety, efficacy, and scalability of lipid nanocarriers and provide a strong foundation for their application in oncology. Several LBNPs have been approved by the FDA and other regulatory agencies for cancer therapy, while many others are undergoing evaluation in clinical trials across various stages (Bleich et al., 1981). Case studies of LBNPs in oncology highlight the real-world impact of these technologies and provide insight into their clinical performance. They demonstrate how rational formulation design, targeting strategies, and therapeutic payload selection have translated into improved patient outcomes compared to conventional therapies. The following examples represent some of the most significant clinical applications of LBNPs in anticancer therapy (Chen et al., 2013). These approvals highlight the success of liposomal formulations in improving therapeutic index, reducing systemic toxicity, and addressing drug solubility limitations (Lee et al., 2008). Table 17.5 summarizes FDA-approved liposomal formulations and their clinical applications.

TABLE 17.5 FDA-approved liposomal formulations and their clinical applications.

Name	Material Description	Nanoparticle advantages	Indication(s)	Year approved	References
Doxil/Caelyx (Janssen)	Liposomal doxorubicin	Enhanced delivery to disease sites; reduced systemic toxicity	Kaposi's sarcoma	1995	Chandna et al. (2007)
Abelcet (Sigma-Tau)	Lipid-complexed amphotericin B	Lower toxicity compared to conventional formulations	Fungal infections	1995	Dharap et al. (2003)
DaunoXome (Galen)	Liposomal daunorubicin	Targeted tumor delivery; minimized systemic side effects	Kaposi's sarcoma	1996	Dharap et al. (2005)
DepoCyt© (Sigma-Tau)	Liposomal cytarabine	Improved tumor site delivery; decreased systemic toxicity	Lymphomatous meningitis	1996	Garbuzenko et al. (2019b)
AmBisome (Gilead Sciences)	Liposomal amphotericin B	Reduced nephrotoxicity; improved therapeutic index	Fungal/protozoal infections	1997	Saad et al. (2008)
Curosurf/ Poractant alfa (Chiesi Farmaceutici)	Liposome proteins SP-B and SP-C	Efficient delivery with smaller volumes; minimized toxicity	Pulmonary surfactant replacement in respiratory distress syndrome	1999	Savla et al. (2014)
Visudyne (Bausch and Lomb)	Liposomal verteporfin	Targeted delivery to diseased vessels; controlled photosensitive release	Wet age-related macular degeneration, myopia, ocular histoplasmosis	2000	Li et al. (2017)
Marqibo (Onco TCS)	Liposomal vincristine	Enhanced tumor site delivery; reduced systemic toxicity	Acute lymphoblastic leukemia	2012	Onaca et al. (2009)
Onivyde (Merrimack)	Liposomal irinotecan	Targeted tumor delivery; decreased systemic side effects	Pancreatic cancer	2015	Vijayakameswara Rao et al. (2018)

Doxil and DaunoXome in Kaposi's sarcoma

Doxil, the first FDA-approved liposomal formulation, has been extensively used in patients with ovarian cancer, multiple myeloma, and Kaposi's sarcoma. Encapsulating doxorubicin in PEGylated liposomes extends circulation time, reduces cardiotoxicity, and enhances tumor accumulation via the EPR effect, as compared to conventional doxorubicin use. Clinical trials demonstrated prolonged progression-free survival and improved quality of life, with fewer severe adverse effects. This case underscores how LBNPs can repurpose established chemotherapeutics by improving their safety profile and extending therapeutic windows (Rapoport et al., 2009). DaunoXome is liposomal daunorubicin approved for HIV-associated Kaposi's sarcoma. DaunoXome improves the pharmacokinetics of daunorubicin and reduces systemic toxicity compared to the free drug.

Vyxeos and Marqibo in leukemia

Vyxeos is a liposomal formulation coencapsulating cytarabine and daunorubicin at a fixed molar ratio. This ratio was chosen based on preclinical evidence of strong synergistic cytotoxicity. Clinical studies in high-risk acute myeloid leukemia patients showed that Vyxeos significantly improved overall survival compared to the conventional "7 + 3" regimen (cytarabine + daunorubicin given separately). The success of Vyxeos highlights the potential of LBNPs for controlled codelivery of multiple drugs to achieve synergistic therapeutic outcomes (Wang et al., 2012). Marqibo, vincristine sulfate liposome, is approved for acute lymphoblastic leukemia. Marqibo enhances vincristine delivery, minimizes neurotoxicity, and allows higher effective dosing.

Onivyde in pancreatic cancer

Onivyde, a liposomal irinotecan formulation, has shown significant clinical benefit in metastatic pancreatic cancer when combined with fluorouracil and leucovorin. Clinical trials demonstrated increased overall survival compared to standard therapy, establishing Onivyde as a second-line treatment option for this aggressive cancer. By improving the pharmacokinetics and tumor accumulation of irinotecan, Onivyde addressed challenges of drug instability and poor bioavailability seen with the free drug (Schroeder et al., 2009). Liposomal encapsulation enhances the stability and tumor delivery of irinotecan, leading to improved patient outcomes.

mRNA-LNP cancer vaccines in melanoma

The clinical success of LBNPs for mRNA delivery in infectious diseases has rapidly expanded into oncology. Personalized mRNA-LNP vaccines encoding patient-specific neoantigens have entered clinical trials for melanoma. Early-phase studies have reported encouraging outcomes, with robust induction of tumor-specific T-cell responses and preliminary evidence of tumor regression in some patients. These case studies suggest that LBNPs may play a central role in the next generation of cancer vaccines (Kheirolomoom et al., 2010).

Challenges and limitations

While LBNPs have demonstrated considerable promise in anticancer drug delivery, their clinical translation is still hindered by multiple obstacles. These challenges stem from biological interactions in vivo, safety concerns related to long-term use, and practical issues associated with large-scale production and regulatory approval. Addressing these limitations is essential for advancing LBNPs from laboratory innovation to widely adopted therapeutic solutions in oncology.

Biological barriers to effective delivery

Following systemic administration, LBNPs encounter several biological hurdles that compromise delivery efficiency. Circulating nanoparticles are rapidly recognized by plasma proteins (opsonization) and cleared by the MPS, primarily in the liver and spleen. PEGylation and surface modifications extend circulation times but are not absolute solutions, as repeated dosing can trigger accelerated clearance. Even when LBNPs reach the tumor site, intratumoral distribution remains uneven. The dense extracellular matrix, high interstitial fluid pressure, and disorganized vasculature hinder nanoparticle penetration. Endosomal entrapment further restricts intracellular release, particularly for gene and mRNA therapeutics. Tumor heterogeneity compounds the challenge, as differences in receptor expression and microenvironmental conditions limit the effectiveness of receptor-targeted or stimuli-responsive designs. Moreover, the immunosuppressive TME can blunt the efficacy of immunotherapy-loaded LBNPs, reducing overall treatment impact (Gao et al., 2005).

Toxicity and immunogenicity concerns

Although generally regarded as biocompatible, LBNPs are not without safety risks. Certain cationic lipids, frequently used for nucleic acid delivery, can induce dose-dependent cytotoxicity, membrane disruption, and inflammatory responses. Ionizable lipids, while safer, may still accumulate in the liver and trigger metabolic stress with prolonged use. Immunogenicity also poses challenges. PEGylated lipids, widely used to extend circulation time, may elicit anti-PEG antibodies upon repeated administration, leading to hypersensitivity reactions and accelerated blood clearance. Similarly, lipid components or encapsulated payloads may activate complement pathways, resulting in infusion-related reactions. These safety concerns highlight the delicate balance between achieving potent therapeutic effects and maintaining tolerability. Long-term safety data remain limited, and careful optimization of lipid composition and dosing regimens is needed to minimize adverse outcomes (Jung et al., 2012).

Manufacturing, scale-up, and regulatory hurdles

Beyond biological and safety issues, the path to clinical translation is also challenged by manufacturing and regulatory complexities. Laboratory-scale methods such as thin-film hydration or solvent evaporation often lack reproducibility and scalability. While microfluidic platforms offer better control over particle size and reproducibility, translating these techniques into large-scale, GMP-compliant manufacturing remains resource-intensive. Batch-to-batch variability in lipid composition, encapsulation efficiency, and stability further complicates production consistency. Stability during storage and transport is another practical limitation, particularly for nucleic acid–loaded LBNPs, which often require ultra-low temperatures to maintain activity. This dependence on cold-chain logistics increases costs and reduces accessibility, especially in resource-limited settings. From a regulatory standpoint, LBNPs are classified as complex drug products, requiring extensive characterization of their physical, chemical, and biological properties. Regulatory agencies demand detailed data on pharmacokinetics, toxicity, immunogenicity, and long-term safety. Multifunctional formulations, such as theranostic or codelivery systems, face additional scrutiny due to their multicomponent nature, which complicates approval pathways. These regulatory hurdles slow down the clinical adoption of otherwise promising therapies. Overall, the clinical translation of LBNPs is constrained by biological barriers that limit delivery efficiency, toxicity and immunogenicity risks that affect safety, and manufacturing and regulatory challenges that hinder scalability and approval. Overcoming these limitations will require interdisciplinary strategies, including novel lipid chemistries, biomimetic coatings, scalable manufacturing technologies, and adaptive regulatory frameworks tailored for complex nanomedicines (Yang et al., 2023).

Future perspectives and opportunities

The field of LBNPs is evolving rapidly, and their role in cancer therapy is expected to expand significantly in the coming years. Future progress will depend on addressing current limitations while harnessing emerging scientific and technological innovations. Several key directions stand out as transformative opportunities for advancing LBNPs in oncology. One promising avenue is the design of next-generation lipid chemistries tailored for enhanced biocompatibility, biodegradability, and tumor specificity. Novel ionizable and stimuli-responsive lipids are being developed to enable precise drug release in response to pH, redox gradients, or enzymatic activity within the TME. Additionally, biomimetic strategies, such as coating LBNPs with cell membranes derived from cancer cells, red blood cells, or immune cells, hold potential for improving immune evasion and homotypic tumor targeting (Liu et al., 2009). Personalized nanomedicine is another important frontier. With the rise of genomics and AI, LBNPs can be engineered to deliver patient-specific therapies, including mRNA vaccines, siRNA, or CRISPR-based genome editing tools targeting oncogenic mutations. AI-driven formulation design and predictive modeling are expected to accelerate the discovery of optimized nanoparticle compositions and targeting strategies tailored to individual patients.

Combination therapies delivered via LBNPs also present an exciting opportunity. By coencapsulating chemotherapeutics, immunomodulators, and gene regulators within a single nanoparticle, it is possible to achieve synergistic effects, overcome drug resistance, and modulate the tumor immune microenvironment. This is particularly relevant for "cold" tumors, which are typically resistant to immunotherapy. Theranostic formulations that integrate imaging agents alongside therapeutic payloads further open avenues for real-time monitoring of biodistribution, treatment response, and personalized dosing adjustments. On the translational side, advances in manufacturing and scale-up technologies are expected to bridge the gap between laboratory innovation and commercial production. Continuous-flow microfluidic systems and automated production platforms are being optimized for reproducibility and GMP compliance, reducing variability and costs. Improvements in lyophilization and storage technologies may also reduce dependence on extreme cold-chain logistics, expanding global accessibility of LBNP-based therapies. Finally, regulatory science is gradually adapting to the unique challenges of nanomedicine. Collaborative frameworks between researchers, industry, and regulatory agencies will be critical in establishing standardized evaluation protocols for LBNPs. Such frameworks will not only streamline approval processes but also ensure patient safety while fostering innovation. In the future, LBNPs are expected to move beyond conventional drug delivery systems toward becoming multifunctional, patient-tailored platforms capable of integrating therapy, diagnosis, and immune modulation. By leveraging advances in materials science, computational modeling, precision medicine, and scalable manufacturing, lipid-based nanocarriers have the potential to revolutionize cancer treatment and establish themselves as cornerstone technologies in precision oncology (Tong et al., 2012).

Conclusion

LBNPs have emerged as one of the most versatile and clinically impactful nanocarrier systems in modern oncology. Over the past 3 decades, their development has advanced from simple liposomal formulations to sophisticated, multifunctional platforms capable of targeted delivery, controlled release, and integration with genetic and immunotherapeutic strategies. Their inherent advantages, biocompatibility, tunable design, and ability to encapsulate a broad range of therapeutic agents have positioned them at the forefront of cancer nanomedicine. Clinical successes such as Doxil, Vyxeos, and Onivyde have validated the translational potential of LBNPs, while ongoing trials in mRNA vaccines, siRNA therapies, and combination regimens point toward an even broader clinical impact. At the same time, innovations in lipid chemistry, biomimetic coatings, and stimuli-responsive systems are enabling new levels of precision in tumor targeting and therapeutic control. These advances underscore the adaptability of LBNPs in addressing the complex and heterogeneous nature of cancer. Nevertheless, significant challenges remain. Biological barriers, immunogenicity risks, and manufacturing constraints continue to limit their universal application. Regulatory hurdles further complicate translation, particularly for complex multifunctional systems. Overcoming these obstacles will require interdisciplinary collaboration, including expertise in nanotechnology, cancer biology, clinical medicine, regulatory science, and computational modeling. Looking ahead, the integration of AI, precision medicine, and next-generation nanomaterials holds promise to unlock the full potential of LBNPs. By bridging fundamental science with clinical translation, LBNPs are poised not only to improve cancer outcomes but also to reshape the therapeutic landscape toward more personalized, safer, and effective treatment strategies. In conclusion, LBNPs represent a transformative platform in cancer therapeutics. With continued innovation, optimization, and clinical validation, they are likely to become central to the next era of precision oncology, delivering not just drugs but also hope for improved survival and quality of life in patients facing cancer.

References

An, X., Zhu, A., Luo, H., Ke, H., Chen, H., Zhao, Y., 2016. Rational design of multi-stimuli-responsive nanoparticles for precise cancer therapy. ACS Nano 10 (6), 5947–5958. https://doi.org/10.1021/acsnano.6b01296.

Ansari, P., Tabasumma, N., Snigdha, N.N., Siam, N.H., Panduru, R.V., Azam, S., Hannan, J.M., Abdel-Wahab, Y.H., 2022. Diabetic retinopathy: an overview on mechanisms, pathophysiology and pharmacotherapy. Diabetology 3 (1), 159–175.

Banerjee, J., Hanson, A.J., Gadam, B., Elegbede, A.I., Tobwala, S., Ganguly, B., Wagh, A.V., Muhonen, W.W., Law, B., Shabb, J.B., Srivastava, D.K., Mallik, S., 2009. Release of liposomal contents by cell-secreted matrix metalloproteinase-9. Bioconjug. Chem. 20 (7), 1332–1339. https://doi.org/10.1021/bc9000646. http://pubs.acs.org/doi/pdfplus/10.1021/bc9000646.

Barenholz, Y., 2012. Doxil - the first FDA-approved nano-drug: Lessons learned. J. Contr. Release 160 (2), 117–134. https://doi.org/10.1016/j.jconrel.2012.03.020.

Battaglia, L., Serpe, L., Foglietta, F., Muntoni, E., Gallarate, M., Del Pozo Rodriguez, A., Solinis, M.A., 2016. Application of lipid nanoparticles to ocular drug delivery. Expert Opin. Drug Deliv. 13 (12), 1743–1757. https://doi.org/10.1080/17425247.2016.1201059.

Baughman, R.H., Zakhidov, A.A., de Heer, W.A., 2002. Carbon nanotubes–the route toward applications. Science 297 (5582), 787–792. https://doi.org/10.1126/science.1060928.

Bhaskar, S., Tian, F., Stoeger, T., Kreyling, W., de la Fuente, J.M., Grazú, V., Borm, P., Estrada, G., Ntziachristos, V., Razansky, D., 2010. Multifunctional nanocarriers for diagnostics, drug delivery and targeted treatment across blood-brain barrier: Perspectives on tracking and neuroimaging. Part. Fibre Toxicol. 7 (1). https://doi.org/10.1186/1743-8977-7-3.

Bleich, H.L., Moore, M.J., Rodbard, D., Rodbard, D., 1981. The role of regional body temperature in the pathogenesis of disease. N. Engl. J. Med. 305 (14), 808–814. https://doi.org/10.1056/NEJM198110013051406.

Bozzuto, G., Molinari, A., 2015. Liposomes as nanomedical devices. Int. J. Nanomedicine 10, 975–999. https://doi.org/10.2147/IJN.S68861.

Buse, J., El-Aneed, A., 2010. Properties, engineering and applications of lipid-based nanoparticle drug-delivery systems: Current research and advances. Nanomedicine 5 (8), 1237–1260. https://doi.org/10.2217/nnm.10.107.

Cano, A., Espina, M., García, M.L., 2020. Recent advances on antitumor agents-loaded polymeric and lipid-based nanocarriers for the treatment of brain cancer. Curr. Pharm. Des. 26 (12), 1316–1330. https://doi.org/10.2174/1381612826666200116142922.

Castillo, B., Bromberg, L., López, X., Badillo, V., González Feliciano, J.A., González, C.I., Alan Hatton, T., Barletta, G., 2012. Intracellular delivery of siRNA by polycationic superparamagnetic nanoparticles. J. Drug. Deliv. 1–12. https://doi.org/10.1155/2012/218940.

Chandna, P., Saad, M., Wang, Y., Ber, E., Khandare, J., Vetcher, A.A., Soldatenkov, V.A., Minko, T., 2007. Targeted proapoptotic anticancer drug delivery system. Mol. Pharm. 4 (5), 668–678. https://doi.org/10.1021/mp070053o.

Chandna, P., Khandare, J.J., Ber, E., Rodriguez-Rodriguez, L., Minko, T., 2010. Multifunctional tumor-targeted polymer-peptide-drug delivery system for treatment of primary and metastatic cancers. Pharm. Res. 27 (11), 2296–2306. https://doi.org/10.1007/s11095-010-0235-2.

Chen, A.M., Zhang, M., Wei, D., Stueber, D., Taratula, O., Minko, T., He, H., 2009. Co-delivery of doxorubicin and Bcl-2 siRNA by mesoporous silica nanoparticles enhances the efficacy of chemotherapy in multidrug-resistant cancer cells. Small 5 (23), 2673–2677. https://doi.org/10.1002/smll.200900621.

Chen, K.J., Liang, H.F., Chen, H.L., Wang, Y., Cheng, P.Y., Liu, H.L., Xia, Y., Sung, H.W., 2013. A thermoresponsive bubble-generating liposomal system for triggering localized extracellular drug delivery. ACS Nano 7 (1), 438–446. https://doi.org/10.1021/nn304474j.

Chen, H., Wang, Z., Zong, S., Chen, P., Zhu, D., Wu, L., Cui, Y., 2015. A graphene quantum dot-based FRET system for nuclear-targeted and real-time monitoring of drug delivery. Nanoscale 7 (37), 15477–15486. https://doi.org/10.1039/c5nr03454j.

Cheng, Q., Blais, M.O., Harris, G., Jabbarzadeh, E., 2013a. PLGA-carbon nanotube conjugates for intercellular delivery of caspase-3 into osteosarcoma cells. PLoS ONE 8 (12). https://doi.org/10.1371/journal.pone.0081947.

Cheng, R., Meng, F., Deng, C., Klok, H.A., Zhong, Z., 2013b. Dual and multi-stimuli responsive polymeric nanoparticles for programmed site-specific drug delivery. Biomaterials 34 (14), 3647–3657. https://doi.org/10.1016/j.biomaterials.2013.01.084.

Cheng, W., Nie, J., Xu, L., Liang, C., Peng, Y., Liu, G., Wang, T., Mei, L., Huang, L., Zeng, X., 2017. pH-sensitive delivery vehicle based on folic acid-conjugated polydopamine-modified mesoporous silica nanoparticles for targeted cancer therapy. ACS Appl. Mater. Interfaces 9 (22), 18462–18473. https://doi.org/10.1021/acsami.7b02457.

Cho, H., Bae, J., Garripelli, V.K., Anderson, J.M., Jun, H.W., Jo, S., 2012. Redox-sensitive polymeric nanoparticles for drug delivery. Chem. Commun. 48 (48), 6043–6045. https://doi.org/10.1039/c2cc31463k.

Civril, E., Sanyal, R., Sanyal, A., 2026. Engineering polymeric micelles for targeted drug delivery: "click" chemistry enabled bioconjugation strategies and emerging applications. J. Mater. Chem. B 14 (1), 12–44.

Cook, J.A., Pass, H.I., Iype, S.N., Friedman, N., DeGraff, W., Russo, A., Mitchell, J.B., 1991. Cellular glutathione and thiol measurements from surgically resected human lung tumor and normal lung tissue. Cancer Res. 51 (16), 4287–4294.

Curcio, A., Marotta, R., Riedinger, A., Palumberi, D., Falqui, A., Pellegrino, T., 2012. Magnetic pH-responsive nanogels as multifunctional delivery tools for small interfering RNA (siRNA) molecules and iron oxide nanoparticles (IONPs). Chem. Commun. 48 (18), 2400. https://doi.org/10.1039/c2cc17223b.

Das, N.K., Mukhida, S., Kannuri, S., Desai, D., Dudhat, V.L., 2026. Analyzing the WHO's 2024 priority pathogens: successes and omissions. J. Mar. Med. Soc. 28 (1), 105–106.

de la Rica, R., Aili, D., Stevens, M.M., 2012. Enzyme-responsive nanoparticles for drug release and diagnostics. Adv. Drug Deliv. Rev. 64 (11), 967–978. https://doi.org/10.1016/j.addr.2012.01.002.

Deshpande, P.P., Biswas, S., Torchilin, V.P., 2013. Current trends in the use of liposomes for tumor targeting. Nanomedicine 8 (9), 1509–1528. https://doi.org/10.2217/nnm.13.118.

Dhar, S., Liu, Z., Thomale, J., Dai, H., Lippard, S.J., 2008. Targeted single-wall carbon nanotube-mediated Pt (IV) prodrug delivery using folate as a homing device. J. Am. Chem. Soc. 130 (34), 11467–11476. https://doi.org/10.1021/ja803036e.

Dharap, S.S., Qiu, B., Williams, G.C., Sinko, P., Stein, S., Minko, T., 2003. Molecular Targeting of Drug Delivery Systems to Ovarian Cancer by BH3 and LHRH Peptides. J. Controll. Release 91 (1-2), 61–73. https://doi.org/10.1016/S0168-3659(03)00209-8.

Dharap, S.S., Wang, Y., Chandna, P., Khandare, J.J., Qiu, B., Gunaseelan, S., Sinko, P.J., Stein, S., Farmanfarmaian, A., Minko, T., 2005. Tumor-specific targeting of an anticancer drug delivery system by LHRH peptide. Proc. Natl. Acad. Sci. U S A. 102 (36), 12962–12967. https://doi.org/10.1073/pnas.0504274102.

Du, J., Lane, L.A., Nie, S., 2015. Stimuli-responsive nanoparticles for targeting the tumor microenvironment. J. Contr. Release 219, 205–214. https://doi.org/10.1016/j.jconrel.2015.08.050.

Emami, J., Rezazadeh, M., Sadeghi, H., Khadivar, K., 2017. Development and optimization of transferrin-conjugated nanostructured lipid carriers for brain delivery of paclitaxel using box–behnken design. Pharmaceut. Dev. Technol. 22 (3), 370–382. https://doi.org/10.1080/10837450.2016.1189933.

Feazell, R.P., Nakayama-Ratchford, N., Dai, H., Lippard, S.J., 2007. Soluble single-walled carbon nanotubes as longboat delivery systems for platinum (IV) anticancer drug design. J. Am. Chem. Soc. 129 (27), 8438–8439. https://doi.org/10.1021/ja073231f.

Feng, L., Mumper, R.J., 2013. A critical review of lipid-based nanoparticles for taxane delivery. Cancer Lett. 334 (2), 157–175. https://doi.org/10.1016/j.canlet.2012.07.006.

Fernandes, C., Suares, D., Yergeri, M.C., 2018. Tumor microenvironment targeted nanotherapy. Front. Pharmacol 9. https://doi.org/10.3389/fphar.2018.01230.

Gahlot, K.D., 2026. Dietary modulation of the gut resistome: ecological and metabolic pathways driving antimicrobial resistance. Front. Nutr. 13, 1–7.

Gan, Q., Lu, X., Yuan, Y., Qian, J., Zhou, H., Lu, X., Shi, J., Liu, C., 2011. A magnetic, reversible pH-responsive nanogated ensemble based on Fe3O4 nanoparticles-capped mesoporous silica. Biomaterials 32 (7), 1932–1942. https://doi.org/10.1016/j.biomaterials.2010.11.020.

Ganguly, A., Ghosh, S., 2026. A study on the overall trade structure and drivers of intra-industry trade in the pharmaceutical sector of India. J. Econ. Stud. 53 (1), 135–156.

Gao, X., Cui, Y., Levenson, R.M., Chung, L.W.K., Nie, S., 2004. In vivo cancer targeting and imaging with semiconductor quantum dots. Nat. Biotechnol. 22 (8), 969–976. https://doi.org/10.1038/nbt994.

Gao, Z.G., Fain, H.D., Rapoport, N., 2005. Controlled and targeted tumor chemotherapy by micellar-encapsulated drug and ultrasound. J. Contr. Release 102 (1), 203–222. https://doi.org/10.1016/j.jconrel.2004.09.021.

Garbuzenko, O.B., Saad, M., Pozharov, V.P., Reuhl, K.R., Mainelis, G., Minko, T., 2010. Inhibition of lung tumor growth by complex pulmonary delivery of drugs with oligonucleotides as suppressors of cellular resistance. Proc. Natl. Acad. Sci. U S A. 107 (23), 10737–10742. https://doi.org/10.1073/pnas.1004604107.

Garbuzenko, O.B., Kbah, N., Kuzmov, A., Pogrebnyak, N., Pozharov, V., Minko, T., 2019a. Inhalation treatment of cystic fibrosis with lumacaftor and ivacaftor co-delivered by nanostructured lipid carriers. J. Control. Release 296, 225–231. https://doi.org/10.1016/j.jconrel.2019.01.025.

Garbuzenko, O.B., Kuzmov, A., Taratula, O., Pine, S.R., Minko, T., 2019b. Strategy to enhance lung cancer treatment by five essential elements: Inhalation delivery, nanotechnology, tumor-receptor targeting, chemo- and gene therapy. Theranostics 9 (26), 8362–8376. https://doi.org/10.7150/thno.39816.

García-Pinel, B., Porras-Alcalá, C., Ortega-Rodríguez, A., Sarabia, F., Prados, J., Melguizo, C., López-Romero, J.M., 2019. Lipid-based nanoparticles: Application and recent advances in cancer treatment. Nanomaterials 9 (4). https://doi.org/10.3390/nano9040638.

Guo, Y., Shi, D., Cho, H., Dong, Z., Kulkarni, A., Pauletti, G.M., Wang, W., Lian, J., Wen, L., Ren, L., Zhang, Q., Liu, G., Huth, C., Wang, L., Ewing, R.C., 2008. In vivo imaging and drug storage by quantum-dot-conjugated carbon nanotubes. Adv. Funct. Mater. 18 (17), 2489–2497. https://doi.org/10.1002/adfm.200800406.

Grinberg, S., Linder, C., Heldman, E., 2014. Progress in lipid-based nanoparticles for cancer therapy. Crit. Rev. Oncog. 19 (3–4), 247–260. https://doi.org/10.1615/critrevoncog.2014011815.

Hatakeyama, H., Akita, H., Ito, E., Hayashi, Y., Oishi, M., Nagasaki, Y., Danev, R., Nagayama, K., Kaji, N., Kikuchi, H., Baba, Y., Harashima, H., 2011. Systemic delivery of siRNA to tumors using a lipid nanoparticle containing a tumor-specific cleavable PEG-lipid. Biomaterials 32 (18), 4306–4316. https://doi.org/10.1016/j.biomaterials.2011.02.045.

Hathout, R.M., Metwally, A.A., El-Ahmady, S.H., Metwally, E.S., Ghonim, N.A., Bayoumy, S.A., Erfan, T., Ashraf, R., Fadel, M., El-Kholy, A.I., Hardy, J.G., 2018. Dual stimuli-responsive polypyrrole nanoparticles for anticancer therapy. J. Drug Deliv. Sci. Technol. 47, 176–180. https://doi.org/10.1016/j.jddst.2018.07.002.

Hilder, T.A., Hill, J.M., 2008. Probability of encapsulation of paclitaxel and doxorubicin into carbon nanotubes. Micro Nano Lett. 3 (2), 41–49. https://doi.org/10.1049/mnl:20080008.

Hom, C., Lu, J., Liong, M., Luo, H., Li, Z., Zink, J.I., Tamanoi, F., 2010. Mesoporous silica nanoparticles facilitate delivery of siRNA to shutdown signaling pathways in mammalian cells. Small 6 (11), 1185–1190. https://doi.org/10.1002/smll.200901966.

Hu, Q., Katti, P.S., Gu, Z., 2014. Enzyme-responsive nanomaterials for controlled drug delivery. Nanoscale 6 (21), 12273–12286. https://doi.org/10.1039/c4nr04249b.

Hu, Y.W., Du, Y.Z., Liu, N., Liu, X., Meng, T.T., Cheng, B.L., He, J.B., You, J., Yuan, H., Hu, F.Q., 2015. Selective redox-responsive drug release in tumor cells mediated by chitosan based glycolipid-like nanocarrier. J. Contr. Release 206, 91–100. https://doi.org/10.1016/j.jconrel.2015.03.018.

Huang, W.C., Chen, S.H., Chiang, W.H., Huang, C.W., Lo, C.L., Chern, C.S., Chiu, H.C., 2016. Tumor microenvironment-responsive nanoparticle delivery of chemotherapy for enhanced selective cellular uptake and transportation within tumor. Biomacromolecules 17 (12), 3883–3892. https://doi.org/10.1021/acs.biomac.6b00956.

Jahangir, M.A., Taleuzzaman, M., Kala, C., Gilani, S.J., 2020. Advancements in polymer and lipid-based nanotherapeutics for cancer drug targeting. Curr. Pharm. Des. 26 (40), 5119–5127. https://doi.org/10.2174/1381612826999200820173253.

Jaimes-Aguirre, L., Gibbens-Bandala, B.V., Morales-Avila, E., Ocampo-García, B.E., Seyedeh-Fatemeh, M., Amirhosein, A., 2016. Polymer-based drug delivery systems, development and pre-clinical status. Curr. Pharm. Des. 22 (19), 2886–2903. https://doi.org/10.2174/1381612822666160217125028.

Jha, A., Kumar, M., Mishra, B., 2022. Marine Biopolymer-Based Anticancer Drug Delivery Systems Marine Biomaterials: Drug Delivery and Therapeutic Applications. Springer Nature, India, pp. 351–401. https://doi.org/10.1007/978-981-16-4787-1.

Jha, A., Kumar, M., Bharti, K., Manjit, M., Mishra, B., 2024a. Biopolymer-based tumor microenvironment-responsive nanomedicine for targeted cancer therapy. Nanomedicine 19 (7), 633–651. https://doi.org/10.2217/nnm-2023-0302.

Jha, A., Kumar, M., Goswami, P., Bharti, K., Manjit, M., Gupta, A., Moorkoth, S., Koch, B., Mishra, B., 2024b. Cabazitaxel-loaded redox-responsive nanocarrier based on d-alpha-tocopheryl-chitosan and hyaluronic acid for improved anti-tumor efficacy in DMBA-induced breast cancer model. Mate. Adv. 5 (19), 7789–7808. https://doi.org/10.1039/d4ma00556b.

Jha, A., Goswami, P., Kumar, M., Bharti, K., Manjit, M., Satpute, A.P., Gupta, A., Moorkoth, S., Koch, B., Mishra, B., 2024c. Cetuximab functionalized chitosan/hyaluronic acid-based nanoparticles loaded with cabazitaxel enhances anti-tumor efficacy in DMBA-induced breast cancer model in rats through spatial targeting. Chem. Phys. Impact 9. https://doi.org/10.1016/j.chphi.2024.100750.

Jia, X., Zhang, Y., Zou, Y., Wang, Y., Niu, D., He, Q., Huang, Z., Zhu, W., Tian, H., Shi, J., Li, Y., 2018. Dual intratumoral redox/enzyme-responsive no-releasing nanomedicine for the specific, high-efficacy, and low-toxic cancer therapy. Adv. Mater. 30 (30). https://doi.org/10.1002/adma.201704490. http://onlinelibrary.wiley.com/journal/10.1002/(ISSN)1521-4095.

Jiang, S., Eltoukhy, A.A., Love, K.T., Langer, R., Anderson, D.G., 2013. Lipidoid-coated iron oxide nanoparticles for efficient DNA and siRNA delivery. Nano Lett. 13 (3), 1059–1064. https://doi.org/10.1021/nl304287a.

Jin, L., Wang, Q., Chen, J., Wang, Z., Xin, H., Zhang, D., 2019. Efficient delivery of therapeutic siRNA by Fe3O4 magnetic nanoparticles into oral cancer cells. Pharmaceutics 11 (11), 615. https://doi.org/10.3390/pharmaceutics11110615.

Jung, S.H., Na, K., Lee, S.A., Cho, S.H., Seong, H., 2012. Byung Cheol Shin, Gd (III)-DOTA-modified sonosensitive liposomes for ultrasound-triggered release and MR imaging. Nanoscale Res. Lett. 7 (1). https://doi.org/10.1186/1556-276x-7-462.

Kanapathipillai, M., Brock, A., Ingber, D.E., 2014. Nanoparticle targeting of anti-cancer drugs that alter intracellular signaling or influence the tumor microenvironment. Adv. Drug Deliv. Rev. 79, 107–118. https://doi.org/10.1016/j.addr.2014.05.005.

Kheirolomoom, A., Mahakian, L.M., Lai, C.Y., Lindfors, H.A., Seo, J.W., Paoli, E.E., Watson, K.D., Haynam, E.M., Ingham, E.S., Xing, L., Cheng, R.H., Borowsky, A.D., Cardiff, R.D., Ferrara, K.W., 2010. Copper-doxorubicin as a nanoparticle cargo retains efficacy with minimal toxicity. Mol. Pharm. 7 (6), 1948–1958. https://doi.org/10.1021/mp100245u.

Khodaverdi, H., Zeini, M.S., Moghaddam, M.M., Vazifedust, S., Akbariqomi, M., Tebyaniyan, H., 2022. Lipid-based nanoparticles for the targeted delivery of anticancer drugs: a review. Curr. Drug Deliv. 19 (10), 1012–1033. https://doi.org/10.2174/1567201819666220117102658.

Khosa, A., Reddi, S., Saha, R.N., 2018. Nanostructured lipid carriers for site-specific drug delivery. Biomed. Pharmacother. 103, 598–613. https://doi.org/10.1016/j.biopha.2018.04.055.

Kim, J., Lee, J.E., Lee, S.H., Yu, J.H., Lee, J.H., Park, T.G., Hyeon, T., 2008. Designed fabrication of a multifunctional polymer nanomedical platform for simultaneous cancer-targeted imaging and magnetically guided drug delivery. Adv. Mater. 20 (3), 478–483. https://doi.org/10.1002/adma.200701726.

Kim, S.-J., Puranik, N., Yadav, D., Jin, J.-O., Lee, P.C.W., 2023. Lipid nanocarrier-based drug delivery systems: therapeutic advances in the treatment of lung cancer. Int. J. Nanomed. 18, 2659–2676. https://doi.org/10.2147/ijn.s406415.

Kotla, N.G., Chandrasekar, B., Rooney, P., Sivaraman, G., Larrañaga, A., Vijaya Krishna, K., Pandit, A., Rochev, Y., 2017. Biomimetic lipid-based nanosystems for enhanced dermal delivery of drugs and bioactive agents. ACS Biomater. Sci. Eng. 3 (7), 1262–1272. https://doi.org/10.1021/acsbiomaterials.6b00681.

Kumar, M., Shanthi, N., Mahato, A.K., Soni, S., Rajnikanth, P.S., 2019. Preparation of luliconazole nanocrystals loaded hydrogel for improvement of dissolution and antifungal activity. Heliyon 5 (5). https://doi.org/10.1016/j.heliyon.2019.e01688. journals.elsevier.com/heliyon/.

Kumar, M., Goswami, P., Jha, A., Manjit, M., Satpute, A.P., Koch, B., Mishra, B., 2024a. Formulation and evaluation of cetuximab functionalized phospholipid modified nanocrystals of paclitaxel for non-small cell lung cancer therapy. Sci. Rep 14 (1). https://doi.org/10.1038/s41598-024-80283-8.

Kumar, M., Jha, A., Bharti, K., Manjit, M., Kumbhar, P., Dhapte-Pawar, V., Mishra, B., 2024b. Lipid-coated nanocrystals of paclitaxel as dry powder for inhalation: characterization, in-vitro performance, and pharmacokinetic assessment. Colloids Surf. B Biointerfaces 237. https://doi.org/10.1016/j.colsurfb.2024.113865. .sciencedirect.com/science/journal/09277765.

Kumar, M., Jha, A., Bharti, K., Manjit, M., Mishra, B., 2024c. Fucoidan-based bosutinib nanocrystals for pulmonary drug delivery: Solid state characterization and in-vitro assessment. Chem. Phys. Impact (8). https://doi.org/10.1016/j.chphi.2024.100644.

Kumar, M., Jha, A., Goswami, P., Srivastava, R., Manjit, M., Bharti, K., Koch, B., Mishra, B., 2025a. Fabrication of lipid-modified drug nanocrystals loaded injectable hydrogel for breast cancer therapy. Discov. Nano 20 (1). https://doi.org/10.1186/s11671-025-04195-w. .springer.com/journal/11671.

Kumar, M., Goswami, P., Jha, A., Dhapte-Pawar, V., Koch, B., Mishra, B., 2025b. Formulation and evaluation of lipid/soluplus-stabilized nanocrystals of paclitaxel and bosutinib for a synergistic effect in non-small cell lung cancer therapy. Mol. Pharm. 22 (2), 1061–1078. https://doi.org/10.1021/acs.molpharmaceut.4c01334.

Kuzmov, A., Minko, T., 2015. Nanotechnology approaches for inhalation treatment of lung diseases. J. Contr. Release 219, 500–518. https://doi.org/10.1016/j.jconrel.2015.07.024.

Lamichhane, N., Udayakumar, T.S., D'Souza, W.D., Simone, C.B., Raghavan, S.R., Polf, J., Mahmood, J., 2018. Liposomes: Clinical applications and potential for image-guided drug delivery. Molecules 23 (2). https://doi.org/10.3390/molecules23020288.

Layek, B., Gidwani, B., Tiwari, S., Joshi, V., Jain, V., Vyas, A., 2020. Recent advances in lipid-based nanodrug delivery systems in cancer therapy. Curr. Pharm. Des. 26 (27), 3218–3233. https://doi.org/10.2174/1381612826666200622133407.

Lee, S.H., Choi, S.H., Kim, S.H., Park, T.G., 2008. Thermally sensitive cationic polymer nanocapsules for specific cytosolic delivery and efficient gene silencing of siRNA: Swelling induced physical disruption of endosome by cold shock. J. Contr. Release 125 (1), 25–32. https://doi.org/10.1016/j.jconrel.2007.09.011.

Lee, Y., Lee, S., Lee, D.Y., Yu, B., Miao, W., Jon, S., 2016. Multistimuli-responsive bilirubin nanoparticles for anticancer therapy. Angew. Chem. Int. Ed. Engl. 55 (36), 10676–10680. https://doi.org/10.1002/anie.201604858.

Li, J.L., Day, D., Gu, M., 2008. Ultra-low energy threshold for cancer photothermal therapy using transferrin-conjugated gold nanorods. Adv. Mater. 20 (20), 3866–3871. https://doi.org/10.1002/adma.200800941.

Li, J., Liu, F., Shao, Q., Min, Y., Costa, M., Yeow, E.K.L., Xing, B., 2014. Enzyme-responsive cell-penetrating peptide conjugated mesoporous silica quantum dot nanocarriers for controlled release of nucleus-targeted drug molecules and real-time intracellular fluorescence imaging of tumor cells. Adv. Healthc. Mater. 3 (8), 1230–1239. https://doi.org/10.1002/adhm.201300613.

Li, X., Taratula, O., Taratula, O., Schumann, C., Minko, T., 2017. LHRH-targeted drug delivery systems for cancer therapy. Mini Rev. Med. Chem. 17 (3), 258–267. https://doi.org/10.2174/1389557516666161013111155.

Liong, M., Lu, J., Kovochich, M., Xia, T., Ruehm, S.G., Nel, A.E., Tamanoi, F., Zink, J.I., 2008. Multifunctional inorganic nanoparticles for imaging, targeting, and drug delivery. ACS Nano 2 (5), 889–896. https://doi.org/10.1021/nn800072t.

Liu, Z., Chen, K., Davis, C., Sherlock, S., Cao, Q., Chen, X., Dai, H., 2008. Drug delivery with carbon nanotubes for in vivo cancer treatment. Cancer Res. 68 (16), 6652–6660. https://doi.org/10.1158/0008-5472.CAN-08-1468.

Liu, Y.C., Ny, A.L.M.L., Schmidt, J., Talmon, Y., Chmelka, B.F., Lee, C.T., 2009. Photo-assisted gene delivery using light-responsive catanionic vesicles. Langmuir 25 (10), 5713–5724. https://doi.org/10.1021/la803588d.

Liu, M., Du, H., Zhang, W., Zhai, G., 2017. Internal stimuli-responsive nanocarriers for drug delivery: Design strategies and applications. Mater. Sci. Eng. C 71, 1267–1280. https://doi.org/10.1016/j.msec.2016.11.030.

Loh, J.S., Tan, L.K.S., Lee, W.L., Ming, L.C., How, C.W., Foo, J.B., Kifli, N., Goh, B.H., Ong, Y.S., 2021. Do lipid-based nanoparticles hold promise for advancing the clinical translation of anticancer alkaloids? Cancers 13 (21). https://doi.org/10.3390/cancers13215346.

Mahajan, S.D., Roy, I., Xu, G., Yong, K., Ding, H., Aalinkeel, R., Reynolds, J.L., Sykes, D.E., Nair, B.B., Lin, E.Y., Prasad, P.N., Schwartz, S.A., 2010. Enhancing the delivery of anti retroviral drug "Saquinavir" across the blood brain barrier using nanoparticles. Curr. HIV Res. 8 (5), 396–404. https://doi.org/10.2174/157016210791330356.

Marcu, A., Pop, S., Dumitrache, F., Mocanu, M., Niculite, C.M., Gherghiceanu, M., Lungu, C.P., Fleaca, C., Ianchis, R., Barbut, A., Grigoriu, C., Morjan, I., 2013. Magnetic iron oxide nanoparticles as drug delivery system in breast cancer. Appl. Surf. Sci. 281, 60–65. https://doi.org/10.1016/j.apsusc.2013.02.072.

Mehra, N.K., Jain, N.K., 2015. One platform comparison of estrone and folic acid anchored surface engineered MWCNTs for doxorubicin delivery. Mol. Pharm. 12 (2), 630–643. https://doi.org/10.1021/mp500720a.

Mendes, L.P., Pan, J., Torchilin, V.P., 2017. Dendrimers as nanocarriers for nucleic acid and drug delivery in cancer therapy. Molecules 22 (9). https://doi.org/10.3390/molecules22091401.

Menon, J.U., Kuriakose, A., Iyer, R., Hernandez, E., Gandee, L., Zhang, S., Takahashi, M., Zhang, Z., Saha, D., Nguyen, K.T., 2017. Dual-drug containing core-shell nanoparticles for lung cancer therapy. Sci. Rep. 7 (1). https://doi.org/10.1038/s41598-017-13320-4.

Mohan, A., Narayanan, S., Sethuraman, S., Krishnan, U.M., 2014. Novel resveratrol and 5-fluorouracil coencapsulated in PEGylated nanoliposomes improve chemotherapeutic efficacy of combination against head and neck squamous cell carcinoma. BioMed Res. Int. 1–14. https://doi.org/10.1155/2014/424239.

Mura, S., Nicolas, J., Couvreur, P., 2013. Stimuli-responsive nanocarriers for drug delivery. Nat. Mater. 12 (11), 991–1003. https://doi.org/10.1038/nmat3776.

Nakayama, M., Akimoto, J., Okano, T., 2014. Polymeric micelles with stimuli-triggering systems for advanced cancer drug targeting. J. Drug Target. 22 (7), 584–599. https://doi.org/10.3109/1061186X.2014.936872.

Nie, S., Xing, Y., Kim, G.J., Simons, J.W., 2007. Nanotechnology applications in cancer. Annu. Rev. Biomed. Eng. 9 (1), 257–288. https://doi.org/10.1146/annurev.bioeng.9.060906.152025.

Obozina, A.S., Gopanenko, A.V., Zvereva, S.D., Okonechnikov, K.V., Shipunova, V.O., 2026. Genetically encoded in vivo ligation-driven targeted drug delivery system for oncotheranostics. Adv. Healthc. Mater. 15 (9), e04119.

Olerile, L.D., Liu, Y., Zhang, B., Wang, T., Mu, S., Zhang, J., Selotlegeng, L., Zhang, N., 2017. Near-infrared mediated quantum dots and paclitaxel co-loaded nanostructured lipid carriers for cancer theragnostic. Colloids Surf B Biointerfaces 150, 121–130. https://doi.org/10.1016/j.colsurfb.2016.11.032.

Onaca, O., Enea, R., Hughes, D.W., Meier, W., 2009. Stimuli-responsive polymersomes as nanocarriers for drug and gene delivery. Macromol. Biosci. 9 (2), 129–139. https://doi.org/10.1002/mabi.200800248.

Ong, W., Yang, Y., Cruciano, A.C., McCarley, R.L., 2008. Redox-triggered contents release from liposomes. J. Am. Chem. Soc. 130 (44), 14739–14744. https://doi.org/10.1021/ja8050469.

Ozkan, M., 2004. Quantum dots and other nanoparticles: what can they offer to drug discovery? Drug Discov. Today 9 (24), 1065–1071. https://doi.org/10.1016/s1359-6446(04)03291-x.

Pantarotto, D., Singh, R., McCarthy, D., Erhardt, M., Briand, J.P., Prato, M., Kostarelos, K., Bianco, A., 2004. Functionalized carbon nanotubes for plasmid DNA gene delivery. Angew. Chem. Int. Ed. Engl. 43 (39), 5242–5246. https://doi.org/10.1002/anie.200460437.

Park, J.Y., An, J.N., Lee, S.M., Ann, Y.C., Bae, E., Yoo, K.D., Kim, Y.C., Chae, H., Oh, J.Y., Yoo, R.J., Kim, D.K., 2026. Optimization of M1 macrophage targeting using a glucosylated albumin nanoplatform for ROS scavenging and mitochondrial rescue in acute kidney injury. J. Nanobiotechnol. 24, 187.

Paulson, R.S., Gautam, S., Medhekar, R., Mahmud, S., Mirsalehi, A., Ensley, L., Shelley, B., Brisbin, L., Lisi, M., Khare, V., Kaila, S., 2026. Front-line treatment approaches in multiple myeloma: real-world data from a community-based oncology network. Front. Oncol. 16, 1736892.

Peng, J., Yang, Q., Xiao, Y., Shi, K., Liu, Q., Ying, H., Yang, F., Han, R., Qian, Z., 2019. Tumor microenvironment responsive drug-dye-peptide nanoassembly for enhanced tumor-targeting, penetration, and photo-chemo-immunotherapy. Adv. Funct. Mater. 29 (19). https://doi.org/10.1002/adfm.201900004.

Pirouzmand, M., Najibi, N.M., Khadivi-Derakhshan, S., Mahmoudi Gharehbaba, A., Soleymani, J., 2026. Biocompatible manganese-tannic acid-βcyclodextrin compounds as catalytic antioxidants. Res. Chem. Intermed. 52 (2), 1289–1307.

Rached, S., Mzioud, K., Rehioui, M., Khattabi, M., Imtara, H., Kharbouch, O., Er-rajy, M., Habsaoui, A., Touhami, M.E., Al-Rimawi, F., 2025. Natural solutions to environmental degradation: antioxidant and anticorrosive activities of *Mentha pulegium* L. essential oil. Chemistry 8 (4), 53.

Ragab, M., Albukhari, A., Alyami, J., Mansour, R.F., 2022. Ensemble deep-learning-enabled clinical decision support system for breast cancer diagnosis and classification on ultrasound images. Biology 11 (3), 439.

Rajpoot, K., 2020. Lipid-based nanoplatforms in cancer therapy: Recent advances and applications. Curr. Cancer Drug Targets 20 (4), 271–287. https://doi.org/10.2174/1568009620666200115160805.

Rapoport, N.Y., Kennedy, A.M., Shea, J.E., Scaife, C.L., Nam, K.H., 2009. Controlled and targeted tumor chemotherapy by ultrasound-activated nanoemulsions/microbubbles. J. Contr. Release 138 (3), 268–276. https://doi.org/10.1016/j.jconrel.2009.05.026.

Ryu, J.H., Chacko, R.T., Jiwpanich, S., Bickerton, S., Babu, R.P., Thayumanavan, S., 2010. Self-cross-linked polymer nanogels: A versatile nanoscopic drug delivery platform. J. Am. Chem. Soc. 132 (48), 17227–17235. https://doi.org/10.1021/ja1069932.

Saad, M., Garbuzenko, O.B., Ber, E., Chandna, P., Khandare, J.J., Pozharov, V.P., Minko, T., 2008. Receptor targeted polymers, dendrimers, liposomes: Which nanocarrier is the most efficient for tumor-specific treatment and imaging? J. Contr. Release 130 (2), 107–114. https://doi.org/10.1016/j.jconrel.2008.05.024.

Saha, A., Chauhan, S.B., Singh, I., 2024. Targeted drug delivery with lipid-based nanoparticles: Innovations for improved cancer therapy. Nanosci. Nanotechnol. - Asia 14 (5). https://doi.org/10.2174/0122106812316387240822075859.

Samimi, S., Maghsoudnia, N., Eftekhari, R.B., Dorkoosh, F., January 1, 2019. Lipid-Based Nanoparticles for Drug Delivery Systems. Characterization and Biology of Nanomaterials for Drug Delivery, pp. 47–76.

Sant, V.R., ElNakieb, Y., Rousseau, J.F., Liu, Y.L., Rubin, C.D., Maalouf, N.M., 2026. Use and implications of the fracture risk assessment tool in primary hyperparathyroidism. JAMA Netw. Open 9 (3), e261549.

Savla, R., Taratula, O., Garbuzenko, O., Minko, T., 2011. Tumor targeted quantum dot-mucin 1 aptamer-doxorubicin conjugate for imaging and treatment of cancer. J. Control. Release 153, 16–22. https://doi.org/10.1016/j.jconrel.2011.02.015.

Savla, R., Garbuzenko, O.B., Chen, S., Rodriguez-Rodriguez, L., Minko, T., 2014. Tumor-targeted responsive nanoparticle-based systems for magnetic resonance imaging and therapy. Pharm. Res. 31 (12), 3487–3502. https://doi.org/10.1007/s11095-014-1436-x.

Sawant, R.R., Torchilin, V.P., 2012. Multifunctional nanocarriers and intracellular drug delivery. Curr. Opin. Solid State Mater. Sci. 16 (6), 269–275. https://doi.org/10.1016/j.cossms.2012.09.001.

Schroeder, A., Honen, R., Turjeman, K., Gabizon, A., Kost, J., Barenholz, Y., 2009. Ultrasound triggered release of cisplatin from liposomes in murine tumors. J. Contr. Release 137 (1), 63–68. https://doi.org/10.1016/j.jconrel.2009.03.007.

Sercombe, L., Veerati, T., Moheimani, F., Wu, S.Y., Sood, A.K., Hua, S., 2015. Advances and challenges of liposome assisted drug delivery. Front. Pharmacol. 6. https://doi.org/10.3389/fphar.2015.00286.

Shah, V., Taratula, O., Garbuzenko, O.B., Patil, M.L., Savla, R., Zhang, M., Minko, T., 2013. Genotoxicity of different nanocarriers: Possible modifications for the delivery of nucleic acids. Curr. Drug Discov. Technol. 10 (1), 8–15. https://doi.org/10.2174/157016313804998870.

Shen, S., Wu, Y., Liu, Y., Wu, D., 2017. High drug-loading nanomedicines: Progress, current status, and prospects. Int. J. Nanomed. 12, 4085–4109. https://doi.org/10.2147/IJN.S132780.

Sheoran, S., Arora, S., Samsonraj, R., Govindaiah, P., vuree, S., 2022. Lipid-based nanoparticles for treatment of cancer. Heliyon 8 (5). https://doi.org/10.1016/j.heliyon.2022.e09403.

Singh, R., Pantarotto, D., McCarthy, D., Chaloin, O., Hoebeke, J., Partidos, C.D., Briand, J.-P., Prato, M., Bianco, A., Kostarelos, K., 2005. Binding and condensation of plasmid DNA onto functionalized carbon nanotubes: Toward the Construction of nanotube-based gene delivery vectors. J. Am. Chem. Soc. 127 (12), 4388–4396. https://doi.org/10.1021/ja0441561.

Singh, R., Lillard, J.W., 2009. Nanoparticle-based targeted drug delivery. Exp. Mol. Pathol. 86 (3), 215–223. https://doi.org/10.1016/j.yexmp.2008.12.004.

Singh, N., Karambelkar, A., Gu, L., Lin, K., Miller, J.S., Chen, C.S., Sailor, M.J., Bhatia, S.N., 2011. Bioresponsive mesoporous silica nanoparticles for triggered drug release. J. Am. Chem. Soc. 133 (49), 19582–19585. https://doi.org/10.1021/ja206998x.

Stephen, Z.R., Dayringer, C.J., Lim, J.J., Revia, R.A., Halbert, M.V., Jeon, M., Bakthavatsalam, A., Ellenbogen, R.G., Zhang, M., 2016. Approach to rapid synthesis and functionalization of iron oxide nanoparticles for high gene transfection. ACS. Appl. Mater. Interfaces 8 (10), 6320–6328. https://doi.org/10.1021/acsami.5b10883.

Sutradhar, K.B., Amin, L., 2013. Nanoemulsions: Increasing possibilities in drug delivery. Eur. J. Nanomed. 5 (2), 97–110. https://doi.org/10.1515/ejnm-2013-0001.

Ta, T., Porter, T.M., 2013. Thermosensitive liposomes for localized delivery and triggered release of chemotherapy. J. Contr. Release 169 (1–2), 112–125. https://doi.org/10.1016/j.jconrel.2013.03.036.

Terada, T., Iwai, M., Kawakami, S., Yamashita, F., Hashida, M., 2006. Novel PEG-matrix metalloproteinase-2 cleavable peptide-lipid containing galactosylated liposomes for hepatocellular carcinoma-selective targeting. J. Contr. Release 111 (3), 333–342. https://doi.org/10.1016/j.jconrel.2005.12.023.

Tong, R., Hemmati, H.D., Langer, R., Kohane, D.S., 2012. Photoswitchable nanoparticles for triggered tissue penetration and drug delivery. J. Am. Chem. Soc. 134 (21), 8848–8855. https://doi.org/10.1021/ja211888a.

Torchilin, V.P., 2007. Micellar nanocarriers: Pharmaceutical perspectives. Pharm. Res. 24 (1), 1–16. https://doi.org/10.1007/s11095-006-9132-0.

Trapani, G., Denora, N., Trapani, A., Laquintana, V., 2012. Recent advances in ligand targeted therapy. J. Drug Target. 20 (1), 1–22. https://doi.org/10.3109/1061186X.2011.611518.

Üner, M., Yener, G., 2007. Importance of solid lipid nanoparticles (SLN) in various administration routes and future perspective. Int. J. Nanomed. 2 (3), 289–300.

Uthaman, S., Huh, K.M., Park, I.K., 2018. Tumor microenvironment-responsive nanoparticles for cancer theragnostic applications. Biomater. Res. 22 (1). https://doi.org/10.1186/s40824-018-0132-z.

Valizadeh, A., Mikaeili, H., Samiei, M., Mussa Farkhani, S., Zarghami, N., Kouhi, M., Akbarzadeh, A., Davaran, S., 2012. Quantum dots: synthesis, bioapplications, and toxicity. Nanoscale Res. Lett. 7 (1). https://doi.org/10.1186/1556-276x-7-480.

Vijayakameswara Rao, N., Ko, H., Lee, J., Park, J.H., 2018. Recent progress and advances in stimuli-responsive polymers for cancer therapy. Front. Bioeng. Biotechnol. 6. https://doi.org/10.3389/fbioe.2018.00110.

Waheed, I., Ali, A., Tabassum, H., Khatoon, N., Lai, W.F., Zhou, X., 2024. Lipid-based nanoparticles as drug delivery carriers for cancer therapy. Front. Oncol. 14. https://doi.org/10.3389/fonc.2024.1296091.

Wang, C.H., Kang, S.T., Lee, Y.H., Luo, Y.L., Huang, Y.F., Yeh, C.K., 2012. Aptamer-conjugated and drug-loaded acoustic droplets for ultrasound theranosis. Biomaterials 33 (6), 1939–1947. https://doi.org/10.1016/j.biomaterials.2011.11.036.

Wang, Z., Qiao, R., Tang, N., Lu, Z., Wang, H., Zhang, Z., Xue, X., Huang, Z., Zhang, S., Zhang, G., Li, Y., 2017. Active targeting theranostic iron oxide nanoparticles for MRI and magnetic resonance-guided focused ultrasound ablation of lung cancer. Biomaterials 127, 25–35. https://doi.org/10.1016/j.biomaterials.2017.02.037.

Wang, Z., Ju, Y., Ali, Z., Yin, H., Sheng, F., Lin, J., Wang, B., Hou, Y., 2019. Near-infrared light and tumor microenvironment dual responsive size-switchable nanocapsules for multimodal tumor theranostics. Nat. Commun. 10 (1). https://doi.org/10.1038/s41467-019-12142-4.

Wang, T., Suita, Y., Miriyala, S., Dean, J., Tapinos, N., Shen, J., 2021. Advances in lipid-based nanoparticles for cancer chemoimmunotherapy. Pharmaceutics 13 (4), 520. https://doi.org/10.3390/pharmaceutics13040520.

Wu, W., Wieckowski, S., Pastorin, G., Benincasa, M., Klumpp, C., Briand, J.P., Gennaro, R., Prato, M., Bianco, A., 2005. Targeted delivery of amphotericin B to cells by using functionalized carbon nanotubes. Angew. Chem. Int. Ed. Engl. 44 (39), 6358–6362. https://doi.org/10.1002/anie.200501613.

Xiong, D., Zhang, X., Peng, S., Gu, H., Zhang, L., 2018. Smart pH-sensitive micelles based on redox degradable polymers as DOX/GNPs carriers for controlled drug release and CT imaging. Colloids Surf. B Biointerfaces 163, 29–40. https://doi.org/10.1016/j.colsurfb.2017.12.008.

Yang, J., Lee, C.-H., Ko, H.-J., Suh, J.-S., Yoon, H.-G., Lee, K., Huh, Y.-M., Haam, S., 2007. Multifunctional magneto-polymeric nanohybrids for targeted detection and synergistic therapeutic effects on breast cancer. Angew. Chem. Int. Ed. 46 (46), 8836–8839. https://doi.org/10.1002/anie.200703554.

Yang, H.Y., Jang, M.S., Gao, G.H., Lee, J.H., Lee, D.S., 2016a. Construction of redox/pH dual stimuli-responsive PEGylated polymeric micelles for intracellular doxorubicin delivery in liver cancer. Polym. Chem. 7 (9), 1813–1825. https://doi.org/10.1039/c5py01808k.

Yang, Y., Wan, J., Niu, Y., Gu, Z., Zhang, J., Yu, M., Yu, C., 2016b. Structure-dependent and glutathione-responsive biodegradable dendritic mesoporous organosilica nanoparticles for safe protein delivery. Chem. Mater. 28 (24), 9008–9016. https://doi.org/10.1021/acs.chemmater.6b03896.

Yang, H.Y., Jang, M.S., Li, Y., Lee, J.H., Lee, D.S., 2017. Multifunctional and redox-responsive self-assembled magnetic nanovectors for protein delivery and dual-modal imaging. ACS Appl. Mater. Interfaces 9 (22), 19184–19192. https://doi.org/10.1021/acsami.7b03747.

Yang, G., Zhang, R., Liang, C., Zhao, H., Yi, X., Shen, S., Yang, K., Cheng, L., Liu, Z., 2018. Manganese dioxide coated WS_2 @Fe_3O_4/sSiO_2 nanocomposites for pH-responsive MR imaging and oxygen-elevated synergetic therapy. Small 14 (2). https://doi.org/10.1002/smll.201702664.

Yang, H.Y., Jang, M.S., Li, Y., Fu, Y., Wu, T.P., Lee, J.H., Lee, D.S., 2019. Hierarchical tumor acidity-responsive self-assembled magnetic nanotheranostics for bimodal bioimaging and photodynamic therapy. J. Control. Release 301, 157–165. https://doi.org/10.1016/j.jconrel.2019.03.019.

Yang, H., Ji, Z., Zhou, H., Wu, D., Gu, Z., Wang, D., ten Dijke, P., 2023. Lipid-based nanoparticles as drug delivery systems for cancer immunotherapy. MedComm 4 (4). https://doi.org/10.1002/mco2.339.

Yao, W., Lin, Y., Yang, W., Wu, Y., Zheng, L., Zheng, D., Qi, X., Zhao, J., 2025. Lipid-based nanoparticles in cancer therapy: Advances in targeted drug delivery and therapeutic potential for renal cell carcinoma. Adv. Sci. 12 (36). https://doi.org/10.1002/advs.202507666.

Zhang, M., Garbuzenko, O.B., Reuhl, K.R., Rodriguez-Rodriguez, L., Minko, T., 2012. Two-in-one: Combined targeted chemo and gene therapy for tumor suppression and prevention of metastases. Nanomedicine 7 (2), 185–197. https://doi.org/10.2217/nnm.11.131.

Zhang, M., Xu, C., Wen, L., Han, M.K., Xiao, B., Zhou, J., Zhang, Y., Zhang, Z., Viennois, E., Merlin, D., 2016. A hyaluronidase-responsive nanoparticle-based drug delivery system for targeting colon cancer cells. Cancer Res. 76 (24), 7208–7218. https://doi.org/10.1158/0008-5472.CAN-16-1681.

Zhao, Y.Q., Li, L.J., Zhou, E.F., Wang, J.Y., Wang, Y., Guo, L.M., Zhang, X.X., 2022. Lipid-based nanocarrier systems for drug delivery: Advances and applications. Pharm. Fronts 4 (2), e43. https://doi.org/10.1055/s-0042-1751036.

Zhu, J., Jiang, B., Zhu, C., Xia, R., Song, L., Wu, W., Lou, Y., Du, L., 2026. Efficacy and cost-effectiveness of extending risk-stratified colorectal cancer screening: evidence from China's first province-wide program. Int. J. Surg. 10–97.

Wáng, Y.X.J., Idée, J.-M., 2017. A comprehensive literatures update of clinical researches of superparamagnetic resonance iron oxide nanoparticles for magnetic resonance imaging. Quant. Imag. Med. Surg. 7 (1), 88–122. https://doi.org/10.21037/qims.2017.02.09.

CHAPTER

18

Advances in SNEDDS for anticancer drug delivery

Ashutosh Gupta[1, 2], *Shivani Kunkalienkar*[1], *Moumita Saha*[1], *Aditya Dev Rajora*[1], *Abhishek Sharma*[3] *and* *Sudheer Moorkoth*[1]

[1]Department of Pharmaceutical Quality Assurance, Manipal College of Pharmaceutical Sciences, Manipal Academy of Higher Education, Manipal, Karnataka, India; [2]Formulation Research & Development–Non Orals, Sun Pharmaceutical Industries Ltd, Vadodara, Gujarat, India; [3]Department of Pharmaceutical Engineering and Technology, Indian Institute of Technology (BHU), Varanasi, Uttar Pradesh, India

Introduction

Cancer is a noncommunicable disease that, if unchecked, causes aberrant cells to proliferate. For cancer therapy, various drugs have been discovered; however, they suffer from low aqueous solubility or low permeation-limited absorption, a key step to reach systemic circulation and exert therapeutic action. Moreover, anticancer drugs suffer from various challenges like degradation in the gastro-intestinal tract (GIT) microenvironment, low retention at the absorption site, first-pass effect, and efflux by P-glycoprotein (P-gp). To overcome these challenges, novel strategies should be employed to improve the efficacy of anticancer drugs, minimizing their systemic toxicity. Design of self-nanoemulsifying drug delivery systems (SNEDDS) is such an approach for effective delivery of anticancer drugs. SNEDDS is a carrier-based technology that employs the use of functional excipients, such as lipids and polymers, to improve absorption through transport (Thanki et al., 2013). SNEDDS are nanosized formulations with high on-site dissolution, modified release profiles, improved aqueous solubility, and better membrane permeation potential. SNEDDS can avoid first-pass metabolism and improve systemic availability of drugs (Cherniakov et al., 2015). This protects the drug from loss due to stomach deterioration or clearance in the feces. The current chapter gives an overview of various anticancer drugs that have been transformed into SNEDDS, highlighting the research gaps and associated difficulties.

Advanced Cancer Therapeutics
https://doi.org/10.1016/B978-0-443-44185-1.00007-0

Overview of SNEDDS

SNEDDS are advanced formulations designed to improve the oral bioavailability of drugs with poor water solubility. SNEDDS are typically isotropic mixtures of oils, surfactants, and cosurfactants (or cosolvents), which upon contact with gastrointestinal (GI) fluids and gentle agitation spontaneously form a fine oil-in-water nanoemulsion, usually with a droplet size below 200 nm (Khan et al., 2015). This rapid self-emulsification enables efficient solubilization and absorption of lipophilic drug molecules, protects them from degradation in the GI tract, facilitates lymphatic transport, and bypassing first-class metabolism often results in enhanced and more consistent plasma drug concentration profiles. SNEDDS are suitable for drugs classified under biopharmaceutics classification system (BCS) class II (low solubility, high permeability) and are valued for their ease of manufacture, scalability, and adaptability for transformation into solid dosage forms, further streamlining storage and patient compliance (Buya et al., 2020; Salawi, 2022). The technology has shown success from bench to market, offering a versatile approach for oral delivery of both hydrophobic drug compounds and combination therapies.

Mechanism of self-emulsification

Self-emulsification is the process by which an SNEDDS spontaneously forms an emulsion when introduced into the GI tract. Unlike traditional emulsions that require high-energy input, this mechanism occurs with little or no energy. This spontaneity is crucial for improving the absorption and bioavailability of poorly water-soluble drugs. The process is driven by the unique thermodynamic properties of the formulation. The ability of an SNEDDS to self-emulsify is a function of the change in free energy (ΔG) required to create a new surface area between the oil and water phases (Ujhelyi et al., 2018). This relationship is represented by Eq. (18.1):

$$\Delta G = \sum Ni\pi ri2\sigma \tag{18.1}$$

where N_i is the number of droplets, r_i is the radius, and σ is the interfacial tension. For a process to occur on its own, it needs a very low or negative free energy change. The SNEDDS is designed to achieve this by using a specific mix of components: an oil to dissolve the medication, a surfactant for lowering the boundary tension between the oil and water, and sometimes a cosurfactant to minimize tension and improve overall flow.

As the SNEDDS enters the GI tract, its water-soluble part rapidly spreads, causing turbulence and a sudden drop in the interfacial tension. This energy change causes the bulk oil to spontaneously break down into vast numbers of submicron droplets; the enormous surface area of these droplets increases drug absorption. Surfactants immediately stabilize these droplets by forming a monolayer, preventing them from merging. By forming a fine, stable emulsion spontaneously, SNEDDS eliminates the slow dissolution of conventional drugs, thus enhancing bioavailability (Raman Kallakunta et al., 2023). The mechanism of self-emulsification is shown in Fig. 18.1.

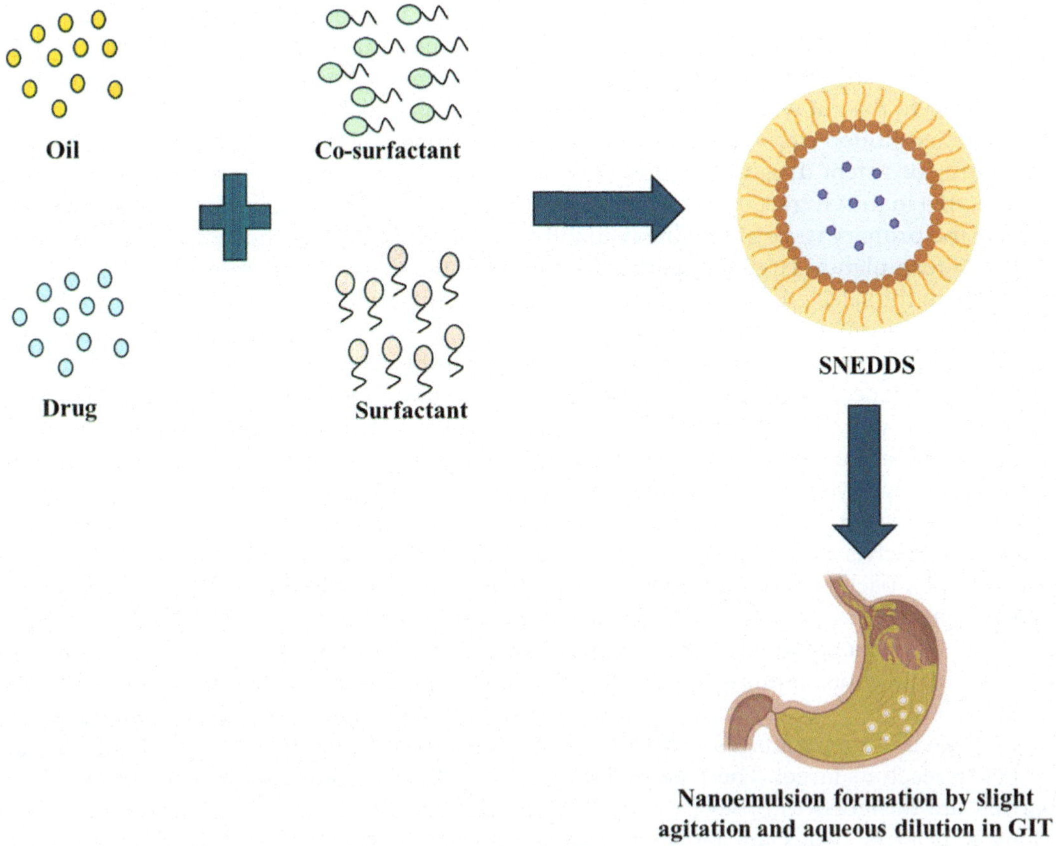

FIGURE 18.1 SNEDDS composition and drug delivery.

Biopharmaceutical challenges in anticancer therapy and the role of SNEDDS

Treating cancer is incredibly complex, and a major reason for this is the significant biopharmaceutical challenges that a drug must overcome to be effective. Overcoming obstacles like poor solubility, low permeability, efflux, and tumor microenvironment (TME) barriers is essential for effective anticancer therapy.

Poor solubility and permeability

SNEDDS is a stable, uniform mixture of oil, water, and surfactant, characterized by small droplets, typically less than 100 nm across (Park et al., 2020). The mild agitation of the stomach initiates the SNEDDS process. The system's surfactants rapidly lower the interfacial tension, causing oil to break into nanosized droplets spontaneously. The rapid formation of ultra-small droplets creates a massive surface area, significantly enhancing the potential for drug uptake. Once in the small intestine, the nanoemulsion benefits from natural digestive processes: lipase breaks down the oil, forming monoglycerides and fatty acids that combine with bile salts and surfactants to create mixed micelles (Algahtani et al., 2022). These micelles efficiently solubilize the drug. In essence, SNEDDS ensures that the drug is delivered to the gut wall in a presolubilized, highly absorbable form, effectively bypassing the slow dissolution step typical of poorly soluble drugs. This ultimately leads to enhanced and more consistent drug absorption (Acevedo-Fani and Singh, 2022). By creating a larger surface area in the GI tract, the nanoemulsion improves the drug's solubility and absorption, solving the primary issue of low bioavailability (Salawi, 2022). The choice of excipients in an SNEDDS formulation largely depends on how well the drug dissolves in them. The drug's solubility in the selected oil, surfactant, and cosurfactant directly dictates how much of it can be effectively loaded into the system. Better solubility within these components allows for higher drug incorporation and a more efficient formulation (Kommana et al., 2020).

Many anticancer agents are lipophilic, or "fat-loving," molecules. While this can help them interact with the cellular membranes of cancer cells, it also makes them poorly soluble in water. Since the human body is primarily an aqueous environment, an oral drug that doesn't dissolve well in the GI tract will have very limited absorption. This can lead to low and unpredictable bioavailability, meaning only a small fraction of the administered drug ever reaches the bloodstream to do its job (Narvekar et al., 2014; Gala et al., 2020). For example, paclitaxel is extremely hydrophobic. It doesn't dissolve well in water, which makes it nearly impossible to administer as a simple injection. To solve this, the drug is formulated with a nonionic surfactant and a dehydrated alcohol. While this formulation allows for intravenous administration, the high concentration of the solubilizing agents can cause severe side effects, including hypersensitivity reactions in patients (Singla et al., 2002). Even if a drug manages to dissolve, it must still pass through various biological membranes to reach its target. These membranes, such as the intestinal lining or the blood–brain barrier, are designed to protect the body from foreign substances (Algahtani et al., 2022). Many anticancer drugs are large or chemically structured in a way that prevents them from passively crossing biological barriers. Such poor bioavailability prevents the drug from attaining therapeutic concentrations at the tumor site and frequently results in its rapid systemic elimination. A chemotherapeutic drug, like etoposide, is a prime example of this challenge. While it works well in in vitro for treating cancers like lung cancer and lymphomas, its large, rigid molecular structure makes oral delivery difficult. The gut's natural function is to absorb nutrients, not large, complex molecules like etoposide. Because the drug cannot efficiently pass through the intestinal wall, a large amount of the oral dose goes unabsorbed and is eliminated, resulting in low and variable bioavailability. Due to this poor permeability, etoposide frequently must be administered intravenously, which is a more invasive and less convenient option for patients (Jang et al., 2025). Droplets smaller than 100 nm allow for faster intestinal diffusion. Further, the system promotes lymphatic absorption, which helps the drug circumvent destructive first-pass metabolism in the liver (Shaker et al., 2019). The SNEDDS formulation significantly enhanced the drug's saturation solubility, achieving a 93.65-fold increase, while the supersaturated S-SNEDDS further boosted solubility to 150 times that of the pure drug. Incorporation of proton pump inhibitor (PPIs) (especially hydroxypropyl methylcellulose [HPMC] K4M) enabled higher drug payload and maintained supersaturation, effectively preventing drug precipitation. Overall, the solid S-SNEDDS markedly improved aqueous solubility, supporting enhanced dissolution and bioavailability (Shanthi et al., 2024).

Efflux and enzymatic degradation

Efflux is a major barrier, particularly for cancer treatments. It's a process where specialized protein pumps on the cell membrane actively eject drug molecules from the cell's interior, essentially spitting them back into the bloodstream. This is a critical mechanism of multidrug resistance, where cancer cells become resistant to a wide variety of chemotherapy drugs. A prime example is the P-gp pump, which is overexpressed in many cancer types. Chemotherapeutic drugs, such as doxorubicin, serve as substrates for this pump. When doxorubicin enters a cancer cell, the P-gp pump immediately recognizes it and ejects it before it can exert its cytotoxic effect, leading to treatment failure (Ughachukwu and Unekwe, 2012; Bao et al., 2012). SNEDDS overcome efflux-mediated resistance in cancer by incorporating surfactants like D-α-Tocopheryl polyethylene glycol succinate (TPGS) or codrugs such as resveratrol, which inhibit P-gp pumps, enhancing intracellular drug retention and uptake in resistant cells like MCF-7. These systems also protect hydrophobic anticancer agents from enzymatic degradation by gastric lipases and tumor proteases through lipid encapsulation and rapid nanoemulsification upon dilution. Recent studies demonstrate 1.6- to 4-fold improved bioavailability and reduced IC50 in breast cancer models via efflux inhibition and stability (Akhtar et al., 2015; Shrivastava et al., 2022).

Enzymatic degradation is another major challenge. Once a drug is absorbed into the bloodstream, it's immediately subject to the body's vast network of enzymes, particularly those in the liver. These enzymes are designed to metabolize and inactivate foreign compounds, including drugs, so they can be eliminated from the body. This process is known as first-pass metabolism. If a drug is extensively metabolized during its first pass through the liver, very little of it will reach its intended target (Wu et al., 2024). A good example of this is the drug 6-mercaptopurine (6-MP), which is used to treat acute leukemia. It undergoes rapid and extensive metabolism by the enzyme thiopurine methyltransferase (TPMT) in the liver. This can lead to low and unpredictable bioavailability, with some patients metabolizing the drug so quickly that it has little therapeutic effect (Urbančič et al., 2025). The drug in the oil phase of SNEDDS can protect it from chemical degradation by enzymes or the harsh and acidic environment of the stomach (Ravi Smitha et al., 2025). The approaches to prevent efflux and enzymatic degradation in SNEDDS include incorporating P-gp inhibitors (e.g., surfactants such as TPGS) to block drug efflux pumps and utilizing lipid-based nanoemulsions to shield drugs from enzymatic breakdown. Additionally, enzyme-responsive coatings or coencapsulation with enzyme inhibitors can enhance drug stability and targeted release within the TME (Li et al., 2020).

Tumor microenvironment barriers

SNEDDS enhance anticancer efficacy by exploiting TME features like hypoxia and acidity, enabling superior drug penetration through enhanced permeability and retention effects. These lipid-based nanoemulsions improve solubility and bioavailability of hydrophobic chemotherapeutics, facilitating targeted accumulation in dense extracellular matrices and overcoming multidrug resistance barriers posed by stromal cells and abnormal vasculature. Recent nano-drug delivery innovations, including SNEDDS-like platforms, demonstrate stimulus-responsive release in TME, boosting therapeutic precision while minimizing systemic toxicity (Shao et al., 2025). Even if an anticancer drug manages to overcome the previous challenges, it still must navigate the complex and hostile TME. This is the area immediately surrounding a tumor, which includes blood vessels, immune cells, and the extracellular matrix. The TME poses severe physical and biological challenges to drug delivery, making it distinct from healthy tissue (Gupta et al., 2025). The combined effect of leaky blood vessels leading to uneven drug distribution and nonfunctional lymphatic drainage causes fluid accumulation and results in high intestinal fluid pressure (Xiao and Yu, 2021). This pressure actively repels drugs, pushing them away from the tumor core. Further, a dense extracellular matrix acts as a physical barrier, blocking drug movement and penetration. These obstacles prevent many potent drugs from reaching therapeutic concentrations. The drug gemcitabine, used for pancreatic cancer, is a prime example. Pancreatic tumors are notoriously difficult to treat, largely because they possess an extremely dense, fibrotic stroma. This physical density, along with the high intestinal fluid pressure, prevents gemcitabine from penetrating effectively, severely limiting its overall efficacy and contributing to the prognosis for pancreatic cancer (Okoro, 2025).

Large-scale production

The manufacturing of pharmaceutical formulations should be economic and reproducible on a large scale. The development of SNEDDS is simple, and large scale-up manufacturing is highly feasible as compared to other complex delivery technologies. Large-scale production of pharmaceutical formulations demands cost-effective, robust, and reproducible processes, which SNEDDS can readily fulfill. Unlike many complex nanocarriers, SNEDDS are prepared by simple mixing of oils, surfactants, and cosolvents using conventional equipment, followed by filling into capsules or conversion into solid SNEDDS, enabling straightforward scale-up under good manufacturing practices (GMP) conditions. Recent work highlights SNEDDS and solid SNEDDS as industrially attractive platforms due to their low manufacturing cost, high batch-to-batch reproducibility, and proven scalability for commercial-scale production (Buya et al., 2020; Kumar et al., 2025). Large-scale production of SNEDDS for anticancer drugs leverages their inherent stability and adaptability, enabling seamless transition from lab to industrial manufacturing via high-throughput techniques like spray drying and adsorption onto solid carriers such as Aerosil 200. Solid SNEDDS (S-SNEDDS) formulations preserve self-emulsifying properties postscaling, achieving nanosized droplets (e.g., 106 nm) and polydispersity index (PDI) <0.3 while boosting drug loading for oncology agents like paclitaxel and enzalutamide. Spray drying offers cost-effective, continuous processing with high yields, mitigating liquid SNEDDS leakage issues during tableting or capsule filling. Pilot-scale batches (e.g., 5 kg) demonstrate reproducibility in droplet size, zeta potential, and release profiles, with excipient optimization ensuring batch-to-batch consistency under GMP conditions. Quality by Design (QbD)-driven design spaces address scale-up challenges like viscosity changes and emulsification efficiency, facilitating FDA-compliant production for enhanced bioavailability in cancer therapies (Buddhadev et al., 2025; Verma et al., 2016).

Pharmacokinetic variability

SNEDDS can provide a highly reproducible absorption profile, offering greater predictability than traditional formulas. The drug absorption can fluctuate based on meals or the individual patient. The SNEDDS can standardize absorption, minimizing interpatient and intrapatient variability, leading to more reliable treatment outcomes (Singh and Thagale, 2025). SNEDDS deliver consistent pharmacokinetic profiles by generating fine nanoemulsions that promote uniform drug solubilization and absorption across the GI tract, independent of fed or fasted states. This minimizes inter- and intrapatient variability compared to conventional formulations, where meal composition or patient factors cause fluctuations in drug exposure. Studies report 1.9- to 2.5-fold bioavailability enhancements with reduced variability coefficients (10%–20% CV) for anticancer agents like dasatinib in solid SNEDDS (Mohd Ateeq et al., 2024). Similarly, a recent study on solid supersaturated self-nanoemulsifying drug delivery systems (ssSNEDDS) for abiraterone acetate, an anticancer agent for prostate cancer, demonstrated significantly reduced pharmacokinetic variability with consistent nanoemulsion formation (106 nm droplet size, PDI 0.234) and enhanced oral absorption in PC-3 cell models. Compared to conventional formulations, ssSNEDDS minimized inter- and intrasubject fluctuations by maintaining supersaturation via HPMC E5 precipitation inhibition, achieving uniform plasma profiles independent of GI conditions. This supports SNEDDS superiority in delivering reproducible bioavailability for oncology drugs (Nair et al., 2025). Overall, SNEDDS ensure reliable dosing, optimized therapeutic indices, and enhanced patient compliance in anticancer regimens by minimizing pharmacokinetic variability through consistent nanoemulsion formation and food-independent absorption.

Formulation strategies of SNEDDS for anticancer drugs

A successful delivery system must enhance bioavailability, ensure transport across barriers, and protect the drug from rapid clearance. One strategy is passive targeting via the enhanced permeation and retention effect, which exploits the leaky tumor vasculature to allow drug accumulation. SNEDDS are a powerful tool in this context (Liu et al., 2024). Their ability to spontaneously form a nanoemulsion significantly boosts a drug's solubility and bioavailability. Importantly, the small, uniform droplets generated by SNEDDS are perfectly sized to leverage the enhanced permeation and retention effect, enabling superior penetration through leaky tumor vessels. Without changing the TME structure, this mechanism ensures a more concentrated and targeted delivery of the anticancer agent, fundamentally improving therapeutic results (Sánchez-López et al., 2019).

Selection of oils

Choice of oils is crucial in the formulation of SNEDDS for anticancer drugs, as the oil phase affects drug solubility, loading, bioavailability, and overall therapeutic efficiency (Buya et al., 2020). The most critical choice parameter is the ability of the oil to solubilize the anticancer drug at sufficiently high levels, which ensures effective encapsulation and contributes to the stability of the nanodispersion (Gupta et al., 2025; Saha et al., 2025). Emulsification is also important to facilitate the spontaneous formation of transparent, stable nanoemulsions with droplet sizes usually less than 200 nm and low polydispersity when mixed with surfactants and water (Priani et al., 2025). Oils favoring lymphatic uptake, long-chain triglycerides (LCTs) in particular, are desirable since they improve oral bioavailability by enabling drugs to avoid hepatic first-pass metabolism, which is beneficial for chemotherapeutics subject to fast hepatic degradation (Aya et al., 2024).

Medium-chain triglycerides (MCTs) like Captex 300, Labrafac CC, and Capryol 90 have been frequently used because they possess outstanding solubilizing ability and greater emulsification performance. Although they do not contribute much to lymphatic transport, these oils allow for quick absorption via the portal vein (Alghananim et al., 2020). LCTs, like Lauroglycol 90, Maisine 35-1, and Peceol, are particularly advantageous for medications that are prone to hepatic metabolism since they facilitate lymphatic transport and circumvent first-pass metabolism while improving bioavailability. Blends of MCTs and LCTs are frequently used to achieve the lymphatic uptake characteristic of LCT and the rapid absorption of MCT (Buya et al., 2020). Nigella sativa oil has been shown to have therapeutic properties beyond emulsification and solubilization, including antioxidant and anticancer activity and the ability to prevent drug-related toxicities, including doxorubicin-induced cardiotoxicity (Usmani et al., 2019).

Choice of surfactants and cosurfactants

Surfactants are essential for enhancing solubilization and spontaneous emulsification in SNEDDS. Through lowering interfacial tension between oil and aqueous phases, they allow the achievement of well-fine and stable nanoemulsions that enhance the dissolution and absorption of poorly soluble chemotherapeutic drugs. Nonionic surfactants like Tween 80, Cremophor EL, and polyethylene glycol (PEG) derivatives are used most frequently due to their lower toxicity, greater biocompatibility, and greater stability with regard to changing pH and ionic strength (Morakul et al., 2024; Nottingham et al., 2020; Senapati et al., 2016). Hydrophilic–lipophilic balance (HLB) is the major factor in the choice of surfactant, for values greater than 10, and preferably greater than 12, are most useful in oil-in-water systems. These surfactants enhance the creation of tiny droplets (<200 nm), which further increase surface area, absorption, and oral bioavailability (Morakul et al., 2024). Surfactant concentration in SNEDDS directly influences droplet size and PDI by modulating interfacial tension and emulsion stability. PDI decreases with rising surfactant concentration up to an optimum, yielding monodisperse nanoemulsions (PDI <0.3), due to uniform interfacial packing that resists Ostwald ripening and flocculation. Excessive concentrations (>60% w/w) may elevate PDI through micellar aggregation or phase inversion, compromising uniformity. Optimization via phase diagrams balances these parameters for anticancer SNEDDS stability (Lin et al., 2023).

Cosurfactants play a pivotal role in SNEDDS for anticancer drugs by lowering interfacial tension, enhancing nanoemulsion flexibility, and boosting drug solubilization for BCS Class II/IV oncology agents like paclitaxel and naringin. Selection criteria prioritize high drug solubility, emulsification efficiency, and biocompatibility, with screening via solubility studies and pseudo-ternary phase diagrams to identify optimal surfactant/cosurfactant ratios (typically 1:1 to 1:3) that yield droplets <200 nm (Shukla et al., 2023). Cosurfactants increase drug solubilization and provide additional interfacial flexibility. PEG 400, Transcutol HP, propylene glycol, and Carbitol are examples of compounds that work in concert to reduce interfacial tension, increase the nanoemulsification zone in phase diagrams, and speed up the generation of nanoemulsions upon dilution with water. Additionally, they stabilize the system under physiological conditions and prevent the drug from precipitating. Another important factor is the ratio of surfactant to cosurfactant, which determines stability, droplet size, and phase separation (Aziz et al., 2024; Khan et al., 2015).

Selection of precipitation inhibitor

The selection of a precipitation inhibitor in SNEDDS formulation strategies is crucial for maintaining supersaturation and preventing premature drug precipitation, thereby enhancing the oral bioavailability of anticancer drugs. Polymers such as HPMC, polyvinylpyrrolidone (PVP), and Soluplus are widely used due to their ability to inhibit nucleation and crystal growth, thereby prolonging the metastable supersaturated state, which is essential for effective drug absorption. The choice of inhibitor must be tailored to the specific drug and lipid system, considering factors such as solubility, compatibility, and supersaturation holding capacity, to maximize therapeutic efficacy and minimize precipitation risks (Mageshvaran et al., 2025). Supersaturable SNEDDS can be designed using a precipitation inhibitor like HPMC to attain a supersaturated state of a drug during dilution by GI fluids (Subramanian et al., 2020). This increases drug levels above equilibrium solubility for a sufficient duration to allow maximum absorption before precipitation occurs. This approach is based on the addition of precipitation inhibitors, such as HPMC or PVP, which retard crystallization and extend the supersaturated state (Alothaid et al., 2021; Thomas et al., 2013).

Other excipients

Recently, the design of solid SNEDDS has gained attention due to its high storage stability. The solution-state SNEDDS can be converted to solid SNEDDS by its adsorption onto the porous carrier, that is, Aerosil200 (Shanthi et al., 2024), Sylysia (350, 550, and 730), and Neusilin US2 (Beg et al., 2012).

Recent advances and modifications

Targeted SNEDDS

Targeted SNEDDS are advanced formulations that distribute drugs to targeted sites, extending their anticancer potency while lowering off-target damage. The systems combine molecular targeting processes with the advantage of classical SNEDDS solubilization and adsorption. SNEDDS also have PEG coatings for stealth to reduce nontarget cell absorption and improve systemic circulation or mucoadhesive polymers, such as acyl chitosan, to prolong GI residency (Sabale et al., 2025). A recent study developed a cell membrane-camouflaged double emulsion-based SNEDDS loaded with *Inula viscosa* extract, demonstrating enhanced biocompatibility and targeted anticancer efficacy by evading immune clearance and improving tumor accumulation. This biomimetic surface modification allowed improved cellular uptake and cytotoxicity in human cancer cell lines, highlighting an innovative strategy for SNEDDS surface engineering to overcome biological barriers in cancer therapy. The study supports the potential of membrane-camouflaged or biomimetic SNEDDS as a promising direction in targeted drug delivery systems for oncology applications (Vizzoni et al., 2025).

These systems offer several benefits for treating cancer, including reduced toxicity to healthy organs, enhanced selectivity for tumor cells, and a reduction in the dosage of drugs needed. Drug accumulation and activity at the target are improved by receptor-mediated endocytosis, which also enhances cellular drug absorption. Designing targeted SNEDDS requires careful consideration of tumor molecular biology to select appropriate ligands based on receptor profiles and microenvironmental characteristics. To enable ligand attachment with a stable nanoemulsion, balancing the composition of oil and surfactant is crucial (Sabale et al., 2025). Ligand-targeted SNEDDS employ polymers like chitosan or pectin for solidification, enabling pulmonary delivery of anticancer agents with aerodynamic diameters of <3 μm for deep lung deposition and systemic circulation. Additionally, chitosan-coated solidified SNEDDS improves atorvastatin-like hydrophobic drug bioavailability by 1.5 times via reduced first-pass metabolism, adaptable for tyrosine kinase inhibitors in lung cancer therapy. These modifications enhance permeability and retention effects, resulting in superior tumor inhibition (up to 5-fold) through the active targeting of folate/transferrin receptors on cancer cells (Mohite et al., 2024; Saeed et al., 2025).

Solid SNEDDS are formulated by transforming liquid SNEDDS into free-flowing solid powders or granules using methods like adsorption on porous carriers (e.g., Neusilin, Syloid, Florite), spray drying, or freeze drying (Shrivastava et al., 2022; Nazlı et al., 2021). This process overcomes various drawbacks of liquid systems, such as capsule leakage, drug precipitation, and incompatibility with shell material, thus improving physical and chemical stability. Solid SNEDDS further enhance patient compliance by allowing for the presentation of the powders, tablets, or capsules as easy-to-handle and easy-to-administer versions, yet maintaining the rapid dispersion, high solubilization, and enhanced dissolution properties of liquid SNEDDS upon their interaction with GI fluids (Shrivastava et al., 2022).

Stimuli-responsive SNEDDS

Stimuli-responsive SNEDDS have emerged as a promising strategy for anticancer drug delivery by enabling site-specific and controlled drug release in response to TME triggers. For instance, pH-responsive SNEDDS have been developed to exploit the acidic TME, releasing anticancer drugs selectively at tumor sites to enhance therapeutic efficacy while minimizing systemic toxicity (Rahim et al., 2021). One study demonstrated that pH-sensitive SNEDDS improved the stability and bioavailability of acid-labile lipophilic drugs, such as silibinin, showing significant enhancement in in vitro drug release profiles compared to conventional formulations. Another example includes thermoresponsive SNEDDS that respond to temperature variations within tumors, allowing triggered drug release and improved cytotoxicity in cancer cells. These smart SNEDDS platforms not only protect the drug during systemic circulation but also provide on-demand release, thereby optimizing drug concentration at the tumor site and minimizing adverse effects (Zhao et al., 2016). Additionally, redox- or enzyme-sensitive SNEDDS utilize elevated glutathione levels or tumor-specific enzymes to further safeguard the selective release of drugs within cancer cells, thereby improving target specificity. These pH-sensitive drug delivery systems enhance tumor targeting by releasing drugs effectively in acidic tumor environments, thereby increasing uptake and cytotoxicity while minimizing effects on normal tissues. The integration of pH sensitivity with ligands for targeting, for example, antibodies or peptides, enhances accumulation and controlled release within tumors. This combination minimizes the dose of required drugs and drug-related systemic side effects, important for cytotoxic chemotherapy, thus enhancing efficacy and patient safety (Alsawaftah et al., 2022).

Hybrid system

Hybrid SNEDDS integrate SNEDDS with functional constituents such as siRNAs, chemotherapeutics, photosensitizers, or polymers to promote solubility, bioavailability, and anticancer activity. Reyna-Lázaro et al. designed oral SNEDDS (~50 nm) codelivering siRNAs, hydrophobic drugs (e.g., doxorubicin), and photosensitizers based on a chitosan–RNA core and lipid shells (Labrafil, Cremophor, phosphatidylcholine). The nanosystems presented high drug loading, pH-triggered release, protection against physiological fluids, increased cancer cell internalization, and strong anticancer activity (Reyna-Lázaro et al., 2024).

Hybrid SNEDDS enhance the oral bioavailability of weakly soluble anticancer drugs through the formation of nanoemulsions, which aid in lymphatic transport and the prevention of drug degradation (Reyna-Lázaro et al., 2024). They allow for multifunctional codelivery of chemotherapeutic, gene silencing, and photodynamic agents for synergistic cancer therapies. ssSNEDDS, like abiraterone acetate ones, deliver better drug loading, nanoscale size, amorphous drug state, increased dissolution, and better anticancer activity in cell models (Nair et al., 2025). Similarly, SNEDDS combined with chitosan is used for the codelivery of doxorubicin and siRNA-RAD51 in breast cancer therapy, leveraging the hybrid lipid-polymer structure to achieve synergistic chemo-gene effects and low cytotoxicity. This hybrid system demonstrated superior cell viability reduction compared to individual components, attributed to enhanced cellular uptake and targeted gene silencing without significant off-target effects in preclinical models. These findings validate hybrid SNEDDS as versatile platforms integrating lipid solubilization with polymeric stability for advanced anticancer applications (Reyna-Lázaro et al., 2024).

Codelivery system

The codelivery system of SNEDDS is a multifunctional approach to deliver multiple therapeutic agents simultaneously. SNEDDS coloaded with chemotherapeutic drugs and siRNA have been designed to synergistically enhance intracellular delivery, counteract drug resistance, and enhance apoptotic action in cancer cells. It is utilized effectively in pancreatic cancer treatment with better pharmacokinetics and drug release behavior than traditional formulations. Nanoemulsions in SNEDDS form droplets less than 100 nm that stabilize drugs and enable lymphatic transport, avoiding first-pass metabolism to enhance systemic delivery of hydrophobic anticancer drugs (Galatage et al., 2023). Codelivery of anticancer drugs using SNEDDS has been extensively validated for its enhanced therapeutic efficacy and improved pharmacokinetics. For example, coloading tamoxifen and resveratrol in a solid SNEDDS significantly enhanced cytotoxicity against breast cancer cells, with a 1.63-fold increase in oral bioavailability compared to conventional formulations, suggesting synergistic effects and improved cellular internalization (Shrivastava et al., 2022). Another study highlighted coloading of antiviral agents remdesivir and baricitinib in bioactive SNEDDS, showing superior anticancer activity against breast and lung cancer cell lines, indicating promising combined therapeutic potential. These studies confirm that SNEDDS-based codelivery systems effectively improve solubility, bioavailability, and tumor-targeted action through enhanced drug release and cellular uptake mechanisms (Kazi et al., 2023). Nanoemulsion formulations of SNEDDS were also documented for the delivery of imatinib with enhanced in vitro anticancer activity by enhancing drug solubilization and uptake in cells. A recent study demonstrated the development of a codelivery SNEDDS system for Ibrutinib (a Bruton's tyrosine kinase inhibitor) combined with Naringenin, aimed at enhancing solubility, oral bioavailability, and synergistic anticancer activity in breast cancer treatment. The optimized SNEDDS showed a 4.89-fold increase in cytotoxic potency against MCF-7 cells compared to free drugs and improved pharmacokinetic profiles with 1.41-fold higher oral bioavailability in vivo, highlighting the significant therapeutic potential of these hybrid SNEDDS for precision cancer therapy. This study underscores the promise of hybrid SNEDDS platforms in addressing drug delivery challenges in oncology through synergistic coloading and nanoplatform engineering (Shetty et al., 2025).

Regulatory guidelines

QbD enhances robustness in SNEDDS development for anticancer drugs by defining Quality Target Product Profiles (QTPPs) and Critical Quality Attributes (CQAs), such as achieving globule size below 200 nm and rapid emulsification time, while identifying Critical Material Attributes (CMAs) through risk assessment tools like FMEA. This tailored approach follows ICH Q8 guidelines, linking formulation variables to drug bioavailability improvements and consistent nanoemulsion performance. SNEDDS formulations employ generally recognized as safe (GRAS) excipients such as medium-chain glycerides, Polysorbate 80, and Transcutol P, which are FDA-approved, balancing efficient drug solubilization with minimal GI toxicity (Priani et al., 2025; Khot et al., 2025). Regulatory challenges for anticancer SNEDDS include excipient variability, scale-up difficulties, and demonstrating bioequivalence under FDA/EMA frameworks. QbD strategies overcome these challenges by establishing design spaces and utilizing Design of Experiments for optimization, coupled with predictive in silico models. Furthermore, transforming liquid SNEDDS into solid forms enhances stability and manufacturability, facilitating regulatory acceptance and reproducible clinical outcomes in oncology drug delivery (Buya et al., 2020).

Conclusion

The use of SNEDDS for oral administration is gaining traction. The use of SNEDDS in cancer treatment has demonstrated improvements in drug stability throughout the GI tract, solubility in aqueous media, and rate of dissolution of BCS class II and IV medications. Additionally, SNEDDS can be made into tablets or soft/hard capsules, which are compact solid unit dosage forms. This provides greater patient compliance, and through the lymphatic circulation, it has improved bioavailability and safeguards first-pass metabolism. The limitations of SNEDDS include the inability to incorporate drugs at high doses, the dependence of drug loading on solubility within the oil phase, the increased risk of precipitation during solubilization, and the sensitivity of formulation stability to pH and temperature variations. Although large-scale production presents challenges in maintaining consistency and stability, advances in solidification techniques and scalable manufacturing under regulatory-compliant frameworks facilitate commercial viability. Use of GRAS excipients and careful selection of surfactants and cosurfactants balances safety with efficient drug release. Therefore, it can be said that while SNEDDS offer a breakthrough for the oral administration of pharmaceutical ingredients that are not sufficiently soluble, further research is necessary to overcome the current limitations. Overall, SNEDDS represent an innovative and scalable platform poised to improve the therapeutic index and patient outcomes in oncology treatment.

Acknowledgment

The authors are thankful to Manipal College of Pharmaceutical Sciences, Manipal Academy of Higher Education, Manipal, for the facilities. BioRender license for creating illustrations for the graphical abstract was provided by the Directorate of Research, MAHE, Manipal.

References

Acevedo-Fani, A., Singh, H., 2022. Biophysical insights into modulating lipid digestion in food emulsions. Prog. Lipid Res. 85, 101129. https://doi.org/10.1016/j.plipres.2021.101129.

Akhtar, N., Talegaonkar, S., Ahad, A., Khar, R.K., Jaggi, M., 2015. Potential of a novel self nanoemulsifying carrier system to overcome P-glycoprotein mediated efflux of etoposide: In vitro and ex vivo investigations. J. Drug Deliv. Sci. Technol. 28, 18–27. https://doi.org/10.1016/j.jddst.2015.05.003.

Algahtani, M.S., Ahmad, M.Z., Ahmad, J., 2022. Investigation of factors influencing formation of nanoemulsion by spontaneous emulsification: Impact on droplet size, polydispersity index, and stability. Bioengineering 9 (8). https://doi.org/10.3390/bioengineering9080384.

Alghananim, A., Özalp, Y., Mesut, B., Serakinci, N., Özsoy, Y., Güngör, S., 2020. A solid ultra fine self-nanoemulsifying drug delivery system (S-SNEDDS) of deferasirox for improved solubility: Optimization, characterization, and in vitro cytotoxicity studies. Pharmaceuticals 13 (8), 162. https://doi.org/10.3390/ph13080162.

Alothaid, H., Aldughaim, M.S., Yusuf, A.O., Yezdani, U., Alhazmi, A., Habibullah, M.M., Khan, M.G., 2021. A comprehensive study of the basic formulation of supersaturated self-nanoemulsifying drug delivery systems (SNEDDS) of albendazolum. Drug Deliv. 28 (1), 2119–2126. https://doi.org/10.1080/10717544.2021.1986601.

Alsawaftah, N.M., Awad, N.S., Pitt, W.G., Husseini, G.A., 2022. pH-responsive nanocarriers in cancer therapy. Polymers 14 (5). https://doi.org/10.3390/polym14050936.

Aya, H., El-Badry, M., Fathy, M., El-Sayed, A.M., 2024. Impact of oil type on the development and oral bioavailability of self-nanoemulsifying drug delivery systems containing simvastatin. Sci. Rep. 14 (1). https://doi.org/10.1038/s41598-024-71980-5.

Aziz, A., Zaman, M., Khan, M.A., Jamshaid, T., Butt, M.H., Hameed, H., Rahman, M.S.U., Shoaib, Q.U.A., 2024. Preparation and evaluation of a self-emulsifying drug delivery system for improving the solubility and permeability of ticagrelor. ACS Omega 9 (9), 10522–10538. https://doi.org/10.1021/acsomega.3c08700.

Bao, L., Hazari, S., Mehra, S., Kaushal, D., Moroz, K., Dash, S., 2012. Increased expression of P-glycoprotein and doxorubicin chemoresistance of metastatic breast cancer is regulated by miR-298. Am. J. Pathol. 180 (6), 2490–2503. https://doi.org/10.1016/j.ajpath.2012.02.024.

Beg, S., Swain, S., Singh, H.P., Patra, C.N., Rao, M.B., 2012. Development, optimization, and characterization of solid self-nanoemulsifying drug delivery systems of valsartan using porous carriers. AAPS PharmSciTech 13 (4), 1416–1427. https://doi.org/10.1208/s12249-012-9865-5.

Buddhadev, S.S., Garala, K.C., Rahamathulla, M., Alamri, A.H., Hani, U., Begum, M.Y., Baghel, S.S., Ahmed, M.M., Pasha, I., 2025. Design, characterization, and evaluation of solid-self-nano-emulsifying drug delivery of benidipine with telmisartan: Quality by design approach. ACS Omega 10 (16), 16440–16456. https://doi.org/10.1021/acsomega.4c10838.

Buya, A.B., Beloqui, A., Memvanga, P.B., Préat, V., 2020. Self-nano-emulsifying drug-delivery systems: From the development to the current applications and challenges in oral drug delivery. Pharmaceutics 12 (12), 1–52. https://doi.org/10.3390/pharmaceutics12121194.

Cherniakov, I., Domb, A.J., Hoffman, A., 2015. Self-nano-emulsifying drug delivery systems: An update of the biopharmaceutical aspects. Expert Opin. Drug Deliv. 12 (7), 1121–1133. https://doi.org/10.1517/17425247.2015.999038.

Gala, U.H., Miller, D.A., Williams, R.O., 2020. Harnessing the therapeutic potential of anticancer drugs through amorphous solid dispersions. Biochim. Biophys. Acta Rev. Cancer 1873 (1). https://doi.org/10.1016/j.bbcan.2019.188319.

Galatage, S.T., Manjappa, A.S., Bhagwat, D.A., Trivedi, R., Salawi, A., Sabei, F.Y., Alsalhi, A., 2023. Oral self-nanoemulsifying drug delivery systems for enhancing bioavailability and anticancer potential of fosfestrol: In vitro and in vivo characterization. Eur. J. Pharm. Biopharm. 193, 28–43. https://doi.org/10.1016/j.ejpb.2023.10.013.

Gupta, A., Jadhav, S.R., Colaco, V., Saha, M., Ghosh, A., Sreedevi, A., Datta, D., Hebbar, S., Moorkoth, S., Ligade, V. S., Dhas, N., 2025. Harnessing unique architecture and emerging strategies of solid lipid nanoparticles to combat colon cancer: A state-of-the-art review. Int. J. Pharm. 675, 125562. https://doi.org/10.1016/j.ijpharm.2025.125562.

Jang, J.Y., Kim, D., Im, E., Kim, N.D., 2025. Etoposide as a key therapeutic agent in lung cancer: Mechanisms, efficacy, and emerging strategies. Int. J. Mol. Sci. 26 (2). https://doi.org/10.3390/ijms26020796.

Kazi, M., Alanazi, Y., Kumar, A., Shahba, A.A.-W., Ahamad, S.R., Alghamdi, K.M., 2023. Oral bioactive self-nanoemulsifying drug delivery systems of remdesivir and baricitinib: A paradigmatic case of drug repositioning for cancer management. Molecules 28 (5), 2237. https://doi.org/10.3390/molecules28052237.

Khan, A.W., Kotta, S., Ansari, S.H., Sharma, R.K., Ali, J., 2015. Self-nanoemulsifying drug delivery system (SNEDDS) of the poorly water-soluble grapefruit flavonoid Naringenin: Design, characterization, in vitro and in vivo evaluation. Drug Deliv. 22 (4), 552–561. https://doi.org/10.3109/10717544.2013.878003.

Khot, S., Sable, P., Kokare, C., 2025. QbD-enabled formulation development of imatinib using self-nanoemulsifying drug delivery system in nose-to-brain treatment of glioblastoma. Int. J. Pharm. 686, 126348. https://doi.org/10.1016/j.ijpharm.2025.126348.

Kommana, N., Bharti, K., Surekha, D.B., Thokala, S., Mishra, B., 2020. Development, optimization and evaluation of losartan potassium loaded self emulsifying drug delivery system. J. Drug Deliv. Sci. Technol. 60. https://doi.org/10.1016/j.jddst.2020.102026.

Kumar, M., Chawla, P.A., Faruk, A., Chawla, V., 2025. Design and evaluation of solid self-nanoemulsifying drug delivery systems of cyclosporine developed with a superior adsorbent base. RSC Pharm. 2 (2), 318–332. https://doi.org/10.1039/d4pm00198b.

Li, M., Zhao, G., Su, W.K., Shuai, Q., 2020. Enzyme-responsive nanoparticles for anti-tumor drug delivery. Front. Chem. 8. https://doi.org/10.3389/fchem.2020.00647.

Lin, L., Chen, Q., Dai, Y., Xia, Y., 2023. Self-nanoemulsifying drug delivery system for enhanced bioavailability of madecassic acid: In vitro and in vivo evaluation. Int. J. Nanumea. 18, 2345–2358. https://doi.org/10.2147/ijn.s408115.

Liu, Y., Liang, Y., Yuhong, J., Xin, P., Han, J.L., Zhu, R., Zhang, M., Chen, W., Ma, Y., Du, Y., Yu, X., 2024. Advances in nanotechnology for enhancing the solubility and bioavailability of poorly soluble drugs. Drug Des. Dev. Ther. 18, 1469–1495. https://doi.org/10.2147/DDDT.S447496.

Mageshvaran, D., Yadav, S., Yadav, V., Kuche, K., Katari, O., Jain, S., 2025. Enhancing oral bioavailability of dasatinib via supersaturable SNEDDS: Investigation of precipitation inhibition and IVIVC through in-vitro lipolysis-permeation model. Int. J. Pharm. 668, 125007. https://doi.org/10.1016/j.ijpharm.2024.125007.

Mohd Ateeq, M.A., Mahajan, S., Saren, B.N., Aalhate, M., Singh, H., Chatterjee, E., Maji, I., Gupta, U., Sriram, A., Guru, S.K., Singh, P.K., 2024. Solid self nano-emulsifying drug delivery system of dasatinib: Optimization, in-vitro, ex-vivo and in-vivo assessment. Ther. Deliv. 15 (10), 749–768. https://doi.org/10.1080/20415990.2024.2397330.

Mohite, P., Sule, S., Pawar, A., Alharbi, H.M., Maitra, S., Subramaniyan, V., Kumarasamy, V., Uti, D.E., Ogbu, C.O., Oodo, S.I., Kumer, A., Idowu, A.O., Okoye, O.N.N., 2024. Development and characterization of a self-nano emulsifying drug delivery system (SNEDDS) for ornidazole to improve solubility and oral bioavailability of BCS class II drugs. Sci. Rep. 14 (1). https://doi.org/10.1038/s41598-024-73760-7.

Morakul, B., Teeranachaideekul, V., Limwikrant, W., Junyaprasert, V.B., 2024. Dissolution and antioxidant potential of apigenin self nanoemulsifying drug delivery system (SNEDDS) for oral delivery. Sci. Rep. 14 (1). https://doi.org/10.1038/s41598-024-59617-z.

Nair, A., Aalhate, M., Mahajan, S., Gupta, U., Maji, I., Singh, P.K., 2025. Solid supersaturated self-nanoemulsifying drug delivery system for abiraterone acetate: Improved drug loading, dissolution, cellular uptake, and anticancer activity. Pharmaceut. Dev. Technol. 30 (5), 604–620. https://doi.org/10.1080/10837450.2025.2505003.

Narvekar, M., Xue, H.Y., Eoh, J.Y., Wong, H.L., 2014. Nanocarrier for poorly water-soluble anticancer drugs - barriers of translation and solutions. AAPS PharmSciTech 15 (4), 822–833. https://doi.org/10.1208/s12249-014-0107-x.

Nazlı, H., Mesut, B., Özsoy, Y., 2021. In vitro evaluation of a solid supersaturated self nanoemulsifying drug delivery system (Super-SNEDDS) of aprepitant for enhanced solubility. Pharmaceuticals 14 (11), 1089. https://doi.org/10.3390/ph14111089.

Nottingham, E., Sekar, V., Mondal, A., Safe, S., Rishi, A.K., Singh, M., 2020. The role of self-nanoemulsifying drug delivery systems of CDODA-Me in sensitizing erlotinib-resistant non–small cell lung cancer. J. Pharmaceut. Sci. 109 (6), 1867–1882. https://doi.org/10.1016/j.xphs.2020.01.010.

Okoro, J., 2025. A novel gemcitabine analog as a potential anticancer agent: Synthesis and in-vitro evaluation against pancreatic cancer. Am. J. Cancer Res. 15 (2), 684–704. https://doi.org/10.62347/kxsr8930.

Park, H., Ha, E.S., Kim, M.S., 2020. Current status of supersaturable self-emulsifying drug delivery systems. Pharmaceutics 12 (4). https://doi.org/10.3390/pharmaceutics12040365.

Priani, S.E., Fakih, T.M., Wilar, G., Chaerunisaa, A.Y., Sopyan, I., 2025. Quality by design and in silico approach in SNEDDS development: A comprehensive formulation framework. Pharmaceutics 17 (6). https://doi.org/10.3390/pharmaceutics17060701.

Rahim, M.A., Jan, N., Khan, S., Shah, H., Madni, A., Khan, A., Jabar, A., Khan, S., Elhissi, A., Hussain, Z., Aziz, H.C., Sohail, M., Khan, M., Thu, H.E., 2021. Recent advancements in stimuli responsive drug delivery platforms for active and passive cancer targeting. Cancers 13 (4), 1–52. https://doi.org/10.3390/cancers13040670.

Raman Kallakunta, V., Dudhipala, N., Nyavanandi, D., Sarabu, S., Yadav Janga, K., Ajjarapu, S., Bandari, S., Repka, M.A., 2023. Formulation and processing of solid self-emulsifying drug delivery systems (HME S-SEDDS): A single-step manufacturing process via hot-melt extrusion technology through response surface methodology. Int. J. Pharm. 641, 123055. https://doi.org/10.1016/j.ijpharm.2023.123055.

Ravi Smitha, A., Mohanan, J., Kuzhiyil Chalil, A., Nourin Karakkunnummal, F., 2025. Advances in self-nanoemulsifying drug delivery systems: Mechanistic insights and formulation strategies. J. Drug Deliv. Therapeut. 15 (8), 217–236. https://doi.org/10.22270/jddt.v15i8.7303.

Reyna-Lázaro, L., Morales-Becerril, A., Aranda-Lara, L., Isaac-Olivé, K., Ocampo-García, B., Gibbens-Bandala, B., Olea-Mejía, O., Morales-Avila, E., 2024. Pharmaceutical nanoplatforms based on self-nanoemulsifying drug delivery systems for optimal transport and co-delivery of siRNAs and anticancer drugs. J. Pharmaceut. Sci. 113 (7), 1907–1918. https://doi.org/10.1016/j.xphs.2024.02.017.

Sabale, V., Girhepunje, M., Ingole, A., Warokar, A., Sawarkar, K., Sabale, P., 2025. Acyl chitosan based self-nanoemulsifying drug delivery system of lipophilic drug with enhanced oral bioavailability and mucoadhesion:

Formulation development, optimization and in vitro/in vivo characterization. Int. J. Biol. Macromol. 306 (Pt 1), 141257. https://doi.org/10.1016/j.ijbiomac.2025.141257.

Saeed, M.D., Shah, K.U., Nawaz, A., Naz, F.F., Metouekel, A., Shazly, G.A., Dauelbait, M., 2025. Fabrication and evaluation of solidified nanoemulsion designs for systemic delivery of atorvastatin through the lung. Sci. Rep. 15 (1). https://doi.org/10.1038/s41598-025-05646-1.

Saha, M., Gupta, A., Kunkalienkar, S., Dhas, N., Shetty, S., Gupta, A., Mutalik, S., Krishnadas, N., Chandrashekar, R., Narasimhaswamy, N., Moorkoth, S., 2025. Nanoemulsion as a promising drug delivery strategy for effective eradication of Helicobacter pylori: Current insights. Drug Deliv. Transl. Res. https://doi.org/10.1007/s13346-025-01986-7.

Salawi, A., 2022. Self-emulsifying drug delivery systems: A novel approach to deliver drugs. Drug Deliv. 29 (1), 1811–1823. https://doi.org/10.1080/10717544.2022.2083724.

Sánchez-López, E., Guerra, M., Dias-Ferreira, J., Lopez-Machado, A., Ettcheto, M., Cano, A., Espina, M., Camins, A., Garcia, M.L., Souto, E.B., 2019. Current applications of nanoemulsions in cancer therapeutics. Nanomaterials 9 (6), 821. https://doi.org/10.3390/nano9060821.

Senapati, P.C., Sahoo, S.K., Sahu, A.N., 2016. Mixed surfactant based (SNEDDS) self-nanoemulsifying drug delivery system presenting efavirenz for enhancement of oral bioavailability. Biomed. Pharmacother. 80, 42–51. https://doi.org/10.1016/j.biopha.2016.02.039.

Shaker, D.S., Ishak, R.A.H., Ghoneim, A., Elhuoni, M.A., 2019. Nanoemulsion: A review on mechanisms for the transdermal delivery of hydrophobic and hydrophilic drugs. Sci. Pharm. 87 (3). https://doi.org/10.3390/scipharm87030017.

Shanthi, N., Mittal, H., Kumar, M., Mahato, A.K., Mishra, B., 2024. Formulation, optimization and evaluation of dabigatran etexilate encapsulated solid supersaturated self-nanoemulsifying drug delivery system. Curr. Nanomed. 14 (2), 143–154. https://doi.org/10.2174/0124681873276409231213115328.

Shao, X., Zhao, X., Wang, B., Fan, J., Wang, J., An, H., 2025. Tumor microenvironment targeted nano-drug delivery systems for multidrug resistant tumor therapy. Theranostics 15 (5), 1689–1714. https://doi.org/10.7150/thno.103636.

Shetty, A., Keerikkadu, M., Bangera, P.D., Tippavajhala, V.K., Rathnanand, M., 2025. An overview of advanced nanocarrier systems for ibrutinib delivery: Overcoming pharmacokinetic barriers and enabling targeted cancer therapy. Int. J. Pharm. X 10. https://doi.org/10.1016/j.ijpx.2025.100417.

Shrivastava, N., Parikh, A., Dewangan, R.P., Biswas, L., Verma, A.K., Mittal, S., Ali, J., Garg, S., Baboota, S., 2022. Solid self-nano emulsifying nanoplatform loaded with tamoxifen and resveratrol for treatment of breast cancer. Pharmaceutics 14 (7). https://doi.org/10.3390/pharmaceutics14071486.

Shukla, E., Kara, D.D., Katikala, T., Rathnanand, M., 2023. Self-nanoemulsifying drug delivery systems (SNEDDS) of anti-cancer drugs: A multifaceted nanoplatform for the enhancement of oral bioavailability. Drug Dev. Ind. Pharm. 49 (1), 1–16. https://doi.org/10.1080/03639045.2023.2182124.

Singh, R., Thagale, R., 2025. Comparative study of SNEDDS and SEDDS for enhancing oral delivery of vildagliptin. Orient. J. Chem. 41 (4), 1414–1433. https://doi.org/10.13005/ojc/410440.

Singla, A.K., Garg, A., Aggarwal, D., 2002. Paclitaxel and its formulations. Int. J. Pharm. 235 (1–2), 179–192. https://doi.org/10.1016/S0378-5173(01)00986-3.

Subramanian, P., Rajnikanth, P.S., Kumar, M., Chidambram, K., 2020. In-vitro and in-vivo evaluation of supersaturable self-nanoemulsifying drug delivery system (SNEDDS) of dutasteride. Curr. Drug Deliv. 17 (1), 74–86. https://doi.org/10.2174/1567201816666191112111610.

Thanki, K., Gangwal, R.P., Sangamwar, A.T., Jain, S., 2013. Oral delivery of anticancer drugs: Challenges and opportunities. J. Contr. Release 170 (1), 15–40. https://doi.org/10.1016/j.jconrel.2013.04.020.

Thomas, N., Holm, R., Garmer, M., Karlsson, J.J., Müllertz, A., Rades, T., 2013. Supersaturated self-nanoemulsifying drug delivery systems (Super-SNEDDS) enhance the bioavailability of the poorly water-soluble drug simvastatin in dogs. AAPS J. 15 (1), 219–227. https://doi.org/10.1208/s12248-012-9433-7.

Ughachukwu, P.O., Unekwe, P.C., 2012. Efflux pump-mediated resistance in chemotherapy. Ann. Med. Health Sci. Res. 2 (2), 191. https://doi.org/10.4103/2141-9248.105671.

Ujhelyi, Z., Vecsernyés, M., Fehér, P., Kósa, D., Arany, P., Nemes, D., Sinka, D., Vasvári, G., Fenyvesi, F., Váradi, J., Bácskay, I., 2018. Physico-chemical characterization of self-emulsifying drug delivery systems. Drug Discov. Today Technol. 27, 81–86. https://doi.org/10.1016/j.ddtec.2018.06.005.

Urbančič, D., Jukič, M., Šmid, A., Gobec, S., Jazbec, J., Mlinarič-Raščan, I., 2025. Thiopurine S-methyltransferase – an important intersection of drug-drug interactions in thiopurine treatment. Biomed. Pharmacother. 184, 117893. https://doi.org/10.1016/j.biopha.2025.117893.

Usmani, A., Mishra, A., Arshad, M., Jafri, A., 2019. Development and evaluation of doxorubicin self nanoemulsifying drug delivery system with Nigella sativa oil against human hepatocellular carcinoma. Artif. Cells Nanomed. Biotechnol. 47 (1), 933–944. https://doi.org/10.1080/21691401.2019.1581791.

Verma, S., Singh, S.K., Verma, P.R.P., 2016. Solidified SNEDDS of loratadine: Formulation using hydrophilic and hydrophobic grades of aerosil, pharmacokinetic evaluations and in vivo-in silico predictions using GastroPlus. RSC Adv. 6 (4), 3099–3116. https://doi.org/10.1039/c5ra21796b.

Vizzoni, L., Caricchio, F., Cerri, L., Migone, C., Piras, A.M., Zambito, Y., Lai, M., Garzella, F., Bizzarri, R., Fabiano, A., 2025. Cell membrane-camouflaged double emulsion-based SNEDDS for targeted melanoma therapy using Inula viscosa. Int. J. Pharm. 686, 126270. https://doi.org/10.1016/j.ijpharm.2025.126270.

Wu, K., Kwon, S.H., Zhou, X., Fuller, C., Wang, X., Vadgama, J., Wu, Y., 2024. Overcoming challenges in small-molecule drug bioavailability: A review of key factors and approaches. Int. J. Mol. Sci. 25 (23), 13121. https://doi.org/10.3390/ijms252313121.

Xiao, Y., Yu, D., 2021. Tumor microenvironment as a therapeutic target in cancer. Pharmocol. Ther. 221, 107753. https://doi.org/10.1016/j.pharmthera.2020.107753.

Zhao, T., Maniglio, D., Chen, J., Chen, B., Migliaresi, C., 2016. Development of pH-sensitive self-nanoemulsifying drug delivery systems for acid-labile lipophilic drugs. Chem. Phys. Lipids 196, 81–88. https://doi.org/10.1016/j.chemphyslip.2016.02.008.

CHAPTER

19

Advances in nanocrystals for anticancer drug delivery

Priya Gupta[1,5], *Disha Marwaha*[2,6], *Karishma Khan*[3] *and Vandana Arora Sethi*[4]

[1]Lloyd School of Pharmacy, Greater Noida, Uttar Pradesh, India; [2]Institute of Pharmaceutical Research, GLA University, Mathura, Uttar Pradesh, India; [3]Department of Pharmaceutics, School of Pharmaceutical Education and Research, Jamia Hamdard (Deemed University), New Delhi, India; [4]Lloyd Institute of Management and Technology, Greater Noida, Uttar Pradesh, India; [5]Amity Institute of Pharmacy, Amity University, Noida, Uttar Pradesh, India; [6]Chandigarh University, Unnao, Uttar Pradesh, India

Introduction

Nanocrystals are nano-sized particles ranging between 10 and 1000 nm. These are formed during the crystallization process and are stabilized with a surfactant, polymer, or both. The nanocrystals, owing to their large specific surface area, possess high saturation solubility, increased dissolution, and improved permeation, thereby increasing the drug bioavailability. Nanocrystals exhibit high structural stability, working as an excellent drug delivery system for anticancer therapy. Nanocrystals involve minimal usage of polymers, surfactants, solubilizing chemicals, or organic solvents and exhibit a high drug loading of approximately 100%. Various lipophilic or hydrophobic drugs, namely thymectacin, cyclosporine, camptothecin, busulfan, and paclitaxel, have been formulated as nanocrystals to showcase their efficacy against cancer. Nanocrystals can exploit the size and surface properties to bypass the biological barriers and gain accumulation at the tumor site or tissues. The surface of nanocrystals can be modified with various materials to endow it with superior properties like prolonged systemic circulation, controlled release, site-specific delivery, high stability, and cell internalization potential. Nanocrystals can acquire passive targeting via size-dependent enhanced permeability and retention (EPR) effect or ligand-guided active targeting. The size, shape, and surface of nanocrystals play a vital role in deciding the pharmacokinetics and pharmacodynamics properties of the drug. Nanocrystals can be designed

Advanced Cancer Therapeutics
https://doi.org/10.1016/B978-0-443-44185-1.00005-7

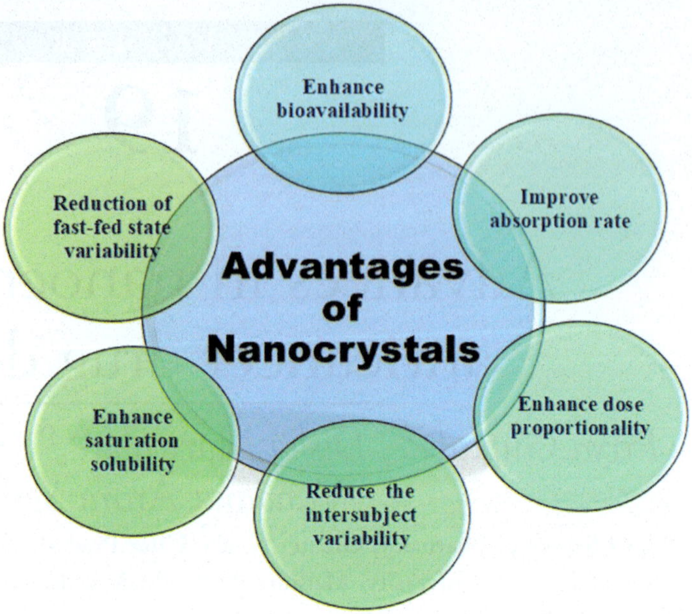

FIGURE 19.1 Advantages of nanocrystals in drug delivery.

for administration via various routes, including intravenous, oral, ocular, and topical. Fig. 19.1 depicts the various advantages offered by the nanocrystals. Nanocrystals can further be incorporated into other carriers like microparticles, hydrogel, microneedles, nanofibrous scaffolds, implants, etc., to give an advanced drug delivery system for site-specific delivery and better therapeutic results.

Nanocrystal stabilization and theory

Nanocrystals are pure drug crystals with 100% drug-loading potential. However, nanocrystals in aqueous media are unstable owing to their large specific surface area and high interfacial energy, which is responsible for thermodynamic instability and aggregation of such nanocrystals (Fan et al., 2018; Peltonen, 2018). The nanocrystals can experience the Ostwald ripening phenomenon, where smaller crystals gradually dissolve and accumulate on larger ones, resulting in a further increase in size. This shows physical instability of nanocrystals and the possibility of aggregation, embolism, vascular blockage, and macrophagic clearance, as well as low blood circulation (Pawar et al., 2014; Zhang et al., 2015b; Skrdla and Yang, 2019). Therefore, to attain good stability for maintaining both safety and efficacy, reduction of interfacial tension and prevention of nanocrystal aggregation are essential by the use of an ideal stabilizer (Fontana et al., 2018). To stabilize nanocrystals and maintain their nano-size, stabilizers like polymers or surfactants, or their combinations, are employed. The stabilizer type and its concentration can effectively determine the nanocrystals' size and stability (Joshi et al., 2019). The stabilizers can be ionic or nonionic, or polymeric surfactants to give nanocrystals an ionic or steric barrier (Joshi et al., 2019; Tuomela et al., 2016). Sodium dodecyl sulfate represents a common ionic surfactant (Rachmawati et al., 2013; Kojima et al., 2018; Rahman et al., 2019; Ueda et al., 2019), while Tween (Sarnes et al., 2013; Sharma et al., 2015; Park et al., 2016), decyl glycoside (Pelikh et al., 2018), and D-α-tocopherol polyethylene glycol 1000 succinate (TPGS) (Rachmawati et al., 2013; Wang et al., 2020) represent nonionic surfactants. The polymeric stabilizers are sodium carboxymethyl cellulose (Rachmawati et al., 2013), polyvinylpyrrolidone (Rachmawati et al., 2013; Kumar and Siril, 2018; Zhang et al., 2015a), hydroxypropyl methylcellulose (Kojima et al., 2018; Ueda et al., 2019; Kumar and Siril, 2018; Tuomela et al., 2014), poloxamer (Sarnes et al., 2013; Park et al., 2016; Gol et al., 2018; Kuroiwa et al., 2018), polyvinyl alcohol (Rachmawati et al., 2013; Kumar and Siril, 2018), and polyethylene glycol (PEG) (Park et al., 2016; Zhang et al., 2015a). The natural stabilizers, such as saponins, can also be used, which are nontoxic and nonirritant (Xie et al., 2016a; Chen et al., 2017; Jin et al., 2019). The ionic surfactants augment the repulsive Coulomb forces between the particles and thus work by providing electrostatic stabilization. While nonionic surfactants and polymeric stabilizers offer steric hindrance by adsorbing on the particle's surface (Tuomela et al., 2016; Soisuwan et al., 2019). The molecular weight of the stabilizer is another crucial factor for deciding nanocrystal size, stability, and performance. The low molecular weight polymeric stabilizers can result in faster mucin diffusion and high oral absorption (Ueda et al., 2019).

Routes of administration

The drug nanocrystals can be administered via multiple routes, including oral, dermal, parenteral, nasal, vaginal, pulmonary, and ophthalmic. Nanocrystals for the oral route are designed to enhance the dissolution of poorly soluble drugs, thereby increasing dissolution-limited absorption and bioavailability (Patel et al., 2014; Fu et al., 2013). However, the nanocrystals when administered by the oral route often face hurdles attributed to the gastrointestinal tract environment, such as the biological membrane as a barrier to permeation, and pH, microbe, and enzyme as factors affecting nanocrystal integrity and stability (Rowlands et al., 1999). In order to improve the stability and avoid abrupt drug release from the nanocrystals, the surface modification technique has been employed. Besides, nanocrystals of anticancer drug can be administered via the intravenous route. Nanocrystals for dermal application create supersaturated conditions, maintaining gradient concentration and absorption for therapeutic effect (Pireddu et al., 2016; Vidlářová et al., 2016). Ophthalmic nanocrystals provide prolonged retention and maintain a concentration gradient due to high solubility at the site, thereby improving the therapeutic action of drug (Tuomela et al., 2014; Romero et al., 2016). The following sections discuss nanocrystals for administration via various routes.

Intravenous route of administration

Recently, nanocrystals for intravenous administration have gained enormous interest due to their capability to mitigate toxicity and accumulate at target sites. The nanocrystals' stability in vivo is dependent mainly on surface charge, morphology, surface hydrophobicity/hydrophilicity, specific surface area, particle size, and polydispersity. Drug nanocrystals in systemic circulation can dissolve gradually to release free drug and can be recognized by phagocytic cells or macrophages present in the spleen, lung, and liver (Müller et al., 2011; Singh et al., 2023). The nanocrystals can be surface modified with PEG for their stabilization, known as PEGylation, which imparts them a stealth layer against reticuloendothelial system uptake, enhancing the systemic circulation time and decreasing enzymatic degradation (Shegokar and Singh, 2011; Tang et al., 2021). Drug nanocrystals formulated using TPGS follow sustained release kinetics and higher tumor efficacy in chemotherapy-resistant cancers (Liu et al., 2010). TPGS can suppress the efflux action of P-glycoprotein (P-gp) pump linked with the development of multidrug resistance in cancer patients (Choudhury et al., 2017).

Various anticancer drugs are formulated as nanocrystals for administration via the intravenous route (Miao et al., 2018). For instance, in a study by Zhang et al., paclitaxel nanocrystals and PEGylated paclitaxel nanocrystals were formulated, wherein the former and the latter depicted particle sizes of 240 and 330 nm, respectively. Furthermore, the augmented inhibition of tumors in the breast cancer xenografted model was achieved by PEGylated paclitaxel nanocrystals compared to the saline solution and the paclitaxel nanocrystals via intravenous administration. Additionally, the PEGylated paclitaxel nanocrystals depicted enhanced anticancer activity in the lung tumor metastasis model, quantified by luciferase activity. It depicted higher anticancer activity compared to the saline, paclitaxel nanocrystals, and Taxol, wherein a remarkable reduction of around 82% was achieved (Zhang et al., 2015a). In another study, paclitaxel nanocrystals resulted in a 4-fold increase in the anticancer activity and a 2-fold reduction in tumor size compared to the pure drug (Tao et al., 2013). The paclitaxel nanocrystals exhibited higher anticancer activity compared to micron-sized formulation due to improved pharmacokinetics of drug (Atia et al., 2022). Similarly, camptothecin nanocrystals demonstrated augmented treatment efficacy on lung metastasis of MDA-MB-231 tumor (Zhang et al., 2014) and MCF-7 tumor (Zhang et al., 2011).

Topical route of administration

The topically administered nanocrystals can successfully permeate through the skin, mainly the stratum corneum, followed by the dermal layer, as well as hair follicles, sebaceous glands, and sweat glands (Kumar et al., 2019). The dexamethasone nanocrystals gained higher absorption via the stratum corneum in contrast to the pure drug (Lohan et al., 2020). The nanocrystals sized >100 nm are absorbed by endocytosis or energy-independent mechanisms, while smaller nanocrystals translocate through pores or channels within the cells. Soni et al. developed silver nanocrystals of noscapinoids showing enhanced apoptosis, better cellular uptake, and improved cytotoxicity in B16-F1 cells (Soni et al., 2017).

Ocular route of administration

The nanocrystals can exhibit dual release behavior in the eye, showing immediate and prolonged release on ocular administration. The nanocrystals, due to their large surface area, lead to increased saturation solubility as well as drug dissolution, which in turn results in absorption and a triggering effect by providing sufficient concentration of drug (Gao et al., 2008). In addition, the large surface area of nanocrystals facilitates enhancing the interaction time with the biological membranes that further aids in imparting them with the mucoadhesive properties, subsequently augmenting the residence time in the cul-de-sac. The increased time of residence ultimately results in sustained or prolonged drug release (Ali et al., 2011; Ravichandran, 2009). Several research groups have demonstrated the remarkable potential of nanocrystals in ocular drug delivery. In a study, Kim et al. fabricated cyclosporine A nanosuspension and performed the Draize test and Schirmer tear test to study the irritation in rabbit eyes. Restasis, a commercially available ophthalmic emulsion, decreased tear flow rate, while no change was reported for nanocrystals (Kim et al., 2011).

Pulmonary route of administration

Compared to micro-sized drug formulations, nanocrystals have low macrophage clearance and high mucus penetration. The enhanced mucus penetration and improved contact with alveoli have been observed with rod-shaped nanocrystals, followed by spherical nanocrystals (Yue et al., 2022). In another study, the PEG-coated C109 nanocrystals resulted in superior mucus penetration, further aiding in diffusion and improving therapeutic efficacy in the model of artificial cystic fibrosis (Costabile et al., 2020). Kumar et al. recently reported the fabrication of marine polysaccharide fucoidan nanocrystals incorporating bosutinib as a dry inhalation powder. Results revealed highly homogenous amorphous nanocrystals exhibiting a size of around 150 nm with about 10-fold increase in saturation solubility and surface area. Additionally, remarkable improvement in drug dissolution (5-fold) as well as mucus penetration (5-fold) was observed compared to the coarse drugs. Lastly, their enhanced ability to deliver the drug to deeper tissues was revealed by the exceptional flowability as well as good aerosolization performance obtained by the flow property analysis and aerosolization investigation (Kumar et al., 2024a).

Fate of nanocrystals

Drug nanocrystals have attracted great attention owing to their immense potential of augmenting dissolution rate and improving water solubility. This renders them effective in combating various hurdles associated with drug lipophilicity, thereby enhancing the bioavailability of the drug and treatment efficacy (Lhaglham et al., 2024). The drug nanocrystals were initially developed for enhancing oral drug administration but are now widely utilized for drug delivery by various routes such as transdermal, pulmonary, parenteral, ocular, and intranasal (McGuckin et al., 2022). The drug nanocrystals administered orally for increasing absorption by the intestine undertake various pathways. Following oral administration, the drug nanocrystals can dissolve quickly to release the drug for prompt

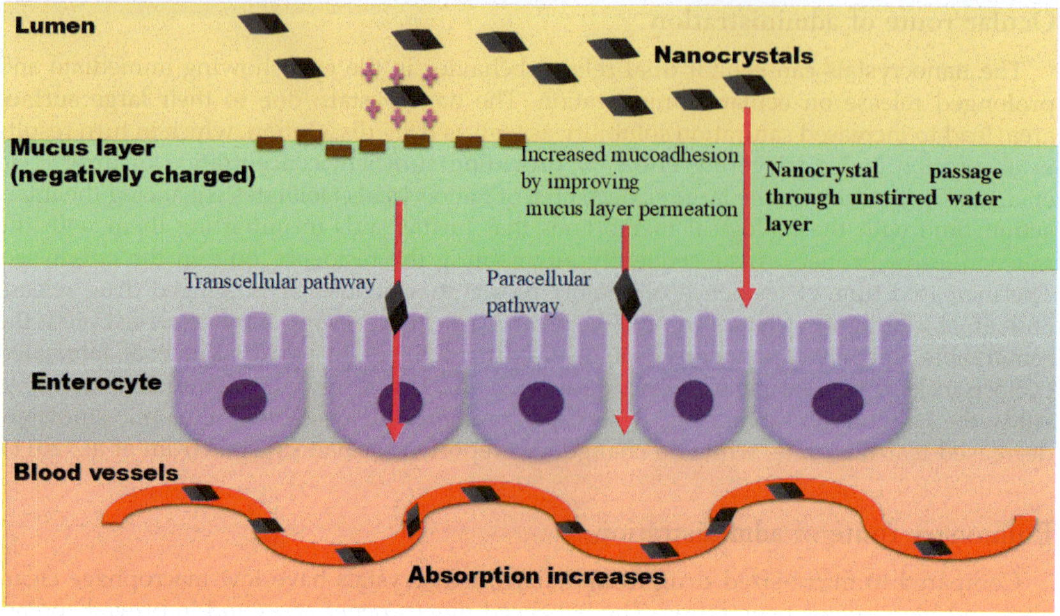

FIGURE 19.2 Schematic representation of various pathways of nanocrystals following oral administration.

absorption. Besides, it can enhance the mucoadhesion due to a large number of contact points, augmenting mucus permeation, and manifest the particle drift effect by passing through the unstirred water layer. Furthermore, these nanocrystals can stimulate paracellular delivery due to their size and incorporated stabilizers (Fig. 19.2). The stabilizers used can facilitate permeation and can inhibit efflux by P-gp to enhance the cellular accumulation (Macedo et al., 2024). The EPR can play a key role in higher retention and accumulation of nanocrystals in tumor tissues on both oral and intravenous administration. The EPR effect takes place due to the anomalous tumor vasculature combined with the disordered endothelium, as well as poor lymphatic drainage at the site of tumor (Miao et al., 2018). The nanocrystals exhibiting a size of less than 500 nm in systemic circulation can accumulate in leaky cancerous tissues via the EPR effect. The nanocrystals can be administered via the pulmonary route for drug delivery in cancerous cells due to advantages like reduced mucociliary clearance, minimal uptake by the macrophages, and avoiding systemic toxicity. Nanocrystals are highly stable to aerosolization pressure and have uniform distribution potential and longer retention in deep lungs, alleviating drug inhomogeneity concerns and facilitating higher drug delivery to cancer cells in the lungs (Kumar et al., 2024b). The pulmonary-administered nanocrystals can reach cancer cells in intact form or may dissolve to release the free drug, maintaining a higher concentration gradient for uptake by cancer cells. Compared to the larger nanocrystals, the smaller nanocrystals facilitate higher drug diffusion and permeation across the membrane, enhancing cellular permeation and uptake. However, lungs have a small fluid volume where nanocrystals can undergo diverse dissolution behavior upon pulmonary delivery. The size of nanocrystals effectively guides their accumulation in tumor tissues by the EPR effect and thus needs to be considered carefully.

Improved mucus penetration as well as cellular internalization can be achieved due to better interaction between mucus/biological membranes possessing mesh-like structures, and the nanocrystals can further favor drug delivery (He et al., 2020).

Advances in nanocrystals

Biopolymer-stabilized nanocrystals

Nanocrystals can be stabilized with biopolymers, including heparin, chitosan, alginate, hyaluronic acid, dextran, cellulose, fucoidan, albumin, and pullulan. Agrawal et al. fabricated lapatinib nanocrystals further coated with hyaluronic acid for efficient action against breast cancer. The results of extensive in vitro and in vivo analysis demonstrated the enhanced anticancer potential of hyaluronic acid-coated nanocrystals, attributing it to the active targeting of the CD44 receptors compared to the native lapatinib and lapatinib nanocrystals. Herein, the external coating of hyaluronic acid caused the preferential accumulation of lapatinib around the cancerous cells owing to its capability of actively targeting CD44 receptors. Furthermore, in the female BALB/C mice bearing a tumor induced by the 4T1 triple-negative cancer cells, remarkable hindrance in the growth of the tumor and overall augmentation in survival probability were observed due to their enhanced residence time and superior tumor localization. Thus, the nanocrystals coated by hyaluronic acid enhance the potential of lapatinib in managing triple-negative breast cancer (Agrawal et al., 2018). In another study, Lee et al. investigated the potential of hyaluronic acid in targeted molecular imaging in the diagnosis and treatment of CD44-overexpressing cancers. The team formulated $MnFe_2O_4$ nanocrystals (MNCs) and conjugated them with varied amounts of hyaluronic acid to serve as explicit magnetic resonance contrast agents (HA-MRCAs) and further compared their biocompatibility, CD44 targeting, and physicochemical properties. Aminated polysorbate 80 was utilized for fabricating hydrophobic MNCs, and different kinds of HA-MRCAs were formulated. The ideal ratio of conjugation of hyaluronic acid was determined not only for showcasing enhanced CD44 ability but also for identifying enhanced cell viability by in vitro studies (Lee et al., 2013).

Park et al. formulated albumin-coated paclitaxel nanocrystals possessing superior serum stability and 90% drug loading. Albumin was chosen due to its manifold advantages, including its ability to bind to SPARC (secreted protein acidic and rich in cysteine), which is abundantly present in the tumor and cancer interstitium once it enters the tumor. Different crystallization conditions were employed for formulating three types of paclitaxel nanocrystals, wherein the smallest size was exhibited by the nanocrystal crystallized in the Pluronic F-127 media, followed by albumin coating ("Cim-F-alb"). It possessed the highest amount of native albumin and also manifested enhanced uptake by SPARC + B16F10 melanoma cells and reduced uptake by the J774A.1 macrophages, thereby demonstrating the most appropriate cell interaction profiles. Moreover, in undiluted serum, Cim-F-alb displayed more stability compared to Abraxane, whereas the comparable cytotoxicity was maintained by Cim-F-alb as that of solvent-dissolved paclitaxel and Abraxane. Furthermore, superior antitumor efficacy at the same dose was exhibited by Cim-F-alb in the B16F10 melanoma mouse model in comparison to Abraxane (Park et al., 2017).

Lipid-stabilized nanocrystals

Lipid-coated nanocrystals amalgamate drug nanocrystals into the liposomes' hydrophilic core, forming a hybrid system. The advantages include nanocrystals' improved dissolution, augmented drug loading, and enhanced aerosolization stability with lipid membranes' fluidity, surface modification potential, colloidal stability, and controlled release characteristic (Lu et al., 2017; Chvatal et al., 2017). Moreover, the nanocrystals are capable of withstanding higher aqueous solubility and enhanced tumor penetration. These lipid-coated nanocrystals aid in the successful fusion of lipid particles with the cell membrane of cancerous cells via phospholipid bilayer diffusion, consequently stimulating intracellular drug delivery (Dyett et al., 2019). Additionally, these exhibit the potential of controlling drug release, thereby facilitating maximum drug retention at the target site, and can be decorated with specific molecules exhibiting selectivity toward malignant cells (Kumar et al., 2025a). In a recently conducted study, Kumar et al. fabricated paclitaxel nanocrystals using fucoidan, a marine biopolymer that was employed as a stabilizer, wherein the resultant nanocrystals were then surface modified with phospholipid for obtaining lipid-coated nanocrystals for lung cancer. The lipid nanocrystals resulted in slower drug release, astounding flow properties, improved aerosolization performance, enhanced drug distribution, and extended retention in the lungs compared to the pure paclitaxel and fucoidan paclitaxel nanocrystals (Kumar et al., 2024). In another study, paclitaxel nanocrystals were created with a surface modification using a fucoidan–oleylamine conjugate, stabilized by Soluplus, and coated with lipids. In comparison to pure paclitaxel, the lipid nanocrystals were stable, homogenous, and displayed enhanced drug release. The obtained nanocrystals were further loaded into an in situ gel-forming injectable hydrogel to demonstrate therapeutic activity against breast cancer. The in vivo studies demonstrated superior inhibition of tumors and systemic toxicity avoidance by nanocrystals compared to pure paclitaxel (Kumar et al., 2025b). It can thus be inferred that although the lipid-coated nanocrystals have demonstrated promising results in the management of cancer, substantial research addressing challenges related to scalability and regulatory concerns must be accomplished for harnessing their potential as a potent drug delivery system.

Surface-functionalized nanocrystals

Nanocrystals can be surface functionalized with various materials like ligands (polymers, proteins, peptides, or antibodies) to achieve targeted delivery (Kumar et al., 2020). Wang et al. formulated hyaluronic acid-coated camptothecin nanocrystals that exhibited sustained release, enhanced aqueous dispersion, high stability, and efficient anticancer potential against CD44-overexpressing cells. Herein, the hyaluronic acid coating functioned as a promising targeting ligand, stabilizer, protective coating, and hydrophilic layer as well. Thus, attributing to their CD44-mediated endocytosis, which further aided in improved absorption and targeted drug delivery, the fabricated nanocrystals demonstrate elevated anticancer activity for managing cancer in overexpressed CD44 cells (Wang et al., 2020b).

In yet another study, the role of cellulose and chitosan-based nanosystems was investigated on folate receptor-positive breast cancer cells by Pinto et al. In the study, chitosan labeled with fluorescein isothiocyanate and modified with folic acid was physically adsorbed on the surface of cellulose nanocrystals. The fabricated nanosystem exhibited enhanced stability in both simulated nonphysiological and physiological conditions. Apart from this, it also demonstrated noncytotoxicity against MDA-MB-231 cells. Furthermore, concentration-dependent cellular internalization was observed, wherein an increase in the concentration of folic acid resulted in about a 5-fold increase in the cellular internalization. Additionally, the formulation had a moderate impact on the metabolic activity of the cell, downregulated the choline uptake, and augmented the release of choline, indicating the potential antiproliferative action of the nanosystem as confirmed by the exometabolic profile of MDA-MB-21 cells (Pinto et al., 2021).

Nanocrystal-equipped nanocarriers as advanced drug delivery systems

Nanocrystal-loaded microparticles

Nanocrystals can be incorporated into microparticles as carriers to form a nano-in-microparticle system. Wang et al. fabricated breviscapine nanocrystals loaded into poly (lactic-co-glycolic acid (PLGA) microparticles. An increase in drug loading from 2.4% to 15.3% and an increase in encapsulation efficiency from 48.5% to 91.9% were observed. Furthermore, a comparatively stable level of serum for approximately 30 days was observed after the intramuscular injection of the formulation in rats (Wang et al., 2017a). Casula et al. developed nanocrystals intended for the delivery of curcumin, which were subsequently incorporated into mannitol microparticles to create a dry powder suitable for inhalation. The resultant nanocrystal-loaded microparticles depicted ideal mass median aerodynamic diameter (MMAD) values less than 5 μm, responsible for effective aerodynamic properties with controlled release, acting as a promising inhalable treatment for respiratory disease management (Casula et al., 2024). Budesonide nanocrystal-loaded hyaluronic acid microparticles for inhalation exhibited significant mucoadhesive properties with a remarkable pharmacological effect (Liu et al., 2018). An enlightening study by Nandi et al. demonstrated the potential of nanocrystal-loaded nano-embedded microparticles for efficient combination delivery of simvastatin and ezetimibe utilizing the NanoCrySP technology. Both drug nanocrystals exhibited a size of approximately 600 nm, which increased the dissolution by 1.65 times and 1.45 times for ezetimibe and simvastatin, respectively. Developed nanocrystals embedded in microparticles were highly stable (Nandi et al., 2020).

Nanocrystal-loaded hydrogels

Hydrogel-based nanocrystal formulations have been garnering immense interest in recent years. Nanocrystal gel was prepared as an extended release formulation for dermal application, aiding tissue adhesion and enhanced residence at site (Pelikh et al., 2021). Kumar et al. formulated niclosamide nanocrystal-loaded hydrogel for antipsoriatic effect. Polyvinylpyrrolidone/vinyl acetate copolymer was utilized for obtaining stable nanocrystals, followed by their modification by hyaluronic acid for achieving CD-44 targeting. The nanosuspension exhibited a 173.3 ± 10.2 nm particle size and a polydispersity index of 0.221 ± 0.09. The niclosamide-loaded hydrogel depicted drug content in the range of 95.5% ± 0.12–96.5% ± 0.4 along with delayed drug release of 8.25 ± 1.6% in 12 h. It was further observed that the drug release pattern followed the Higuchi model and was stable at 25 ± 2 °C. Additionally, compared to the coarse niclosamide, the formulation depicted enhanced inhibitory action on the HaCaT cells, as confirmed by the cytotoxicity assay (Kumar et al., 2022).

Nanocrystal-loaded microneedles

Nanocrystals can be loaded in microneedles as a carrier for aiding application at the site and facilitating accumulation in the dermal layer of skin. Liu and colleagues fabricated biodegradable and dissolvable resveratrol nanocrystal-loaded microneedles. Nanocrystal technology was utilized for enhancing the solubility of resveratrol, while the microneedle was used as a carrier. The amorphous resveratrol nanocrystals had a particle size of 161 ± 9 nm, higher dissolution of about 84.14 ± 2.53% in 120 min, and astounding mechanical strength. On application to the skin of mice, it rapidly dissolves to release the drug while microneedles create a channel, paving the way for an efficient transdermal drug delivery (Liu et al., 2023). In another study, resveratrol nanocrystals were loaded into dissolvable microneedles. The nanocrystals depicted a particle size of approximately 110 nm and showed good release characteristics as well as stability. Moreover, microneedles showed good solubilization properties and high skin-piercing capabilities and improved the drug bioavailability (Diao et al., 2024).

Nanocrystal-loaded scaffolds

The scaffolds possess poor mechanical strength, thereby restricting their application. Incorporating high aspect ratio nanoparticles can increase stress moduli and strength. The polymer scaffolds can be strengthened by utilizing chitin nanocrystals (CNCs) that represent novel emerging nanoparticles and are derived from a biological source (Liu et al., 2016). Liu et al. prepared chitosan–chitin nanocrystal composite scaffolds wherein the CNCs exhibiting 300 nm length and 20 nm width were dispersed in the chitosan solution (CS). Resultant composite scaffolds demonstrated remarkable improvement in modulus and compressive strength in comparison to the pure scaffold of only CS. A composite scaffold comprised of a well-interconnected structure with approximately 80% porosity, exhibiting a 100–200 μm size range. Furthermore, the incorporation of nanocrystals in the scaffold resulted in the elevation of scaffold density while reducing the water swelling ratio. Additionally, their outstanding biocompatibility and low toxicity were observed when applied as scaffolds for the osteoblast cells MC3T3-E1 (Liu et al., 2016). Dang et al. fabricated bioactive glass (BG) scaffolds incorporating $CuFeSe_2$ nanocrystals (BG-CFS) that exhibited outstanding photothermal performance. Furthermore, the prepared scaffolds demonstrated remarkable attrition of Saos-2 bone tumor cells in vitro as well as significant inhibition of the growth of bone tumors in vivo. Additionally, the BG-CFS scaffolds resulted in inducing the production of osteogenic gene expressions in the rabbit bone marrow stromal cells (rBMSCs), rabbit bone marrow stromal cells, thereby facilitating the formation of new bones in the bone defects (Dang et al., 2018). The researchers have developed a cellulose nanocrystal-based, in situ, 3D-printed, injectable hydrogel using poly(ε-caprolactone-co-lactide)-b-poly(ethylene glycol)-b-poly(ε-caprolactone-co-lactide) (PCLA) as copolymers. The release of biologics was controlled by hydrophobic and hydrogen interactions that arose from the effective coordination of cellulose nanocrystal-embedded PCLA copolymer solutions with doxorubicin, a hydrophobic compound, and lysozyme, a water-soluble compound. Moreover, cellulose nanocrystals incorporated into PCLA copolymer sols were subcutaneously injected into BALB/c mice, showing instant formation of hydrogel along with controlled biodegradation without any skin toxicity. The doxorubicin-loaded hydrogel formulation depicted remarkable inhibitory action on in vivo MDA-MB-231 tumor xenograft model (Phan et al., 2022).

Application of anticancer drug nanocrystals

Nanocrystals of anticancer drugs can be designed for effective management of various types of cancer, including breast, lung, colorectal, and skin (Table 19.1). The nanocrystals can be designed considering the cancer type for the selective delivery of therapeutics. For example, nanocrystals can be modified with ligands having specific affinity toward receptors overexpressed on cancer cells, like EGFR, CD4, HER2, folate, etc. Nanocrystals can be formulated for the delivery of dual or codelivery of two therapeutics to obtain an additive or synergistic effect. For example, Zu et al. developed paclitaxel-disulfiram cocrystal-like nanorods and further anchored them with cytochrome C, a basic protein drug. The formulation was also modified with hyaluronic acid. This resulted in synchronous delivery of cytochrome C to malignant cells for inducing apoptosis by utilizing nanorods as a carrier. Additionally, enhanced tumor targeting and extended in vivo circulation reversed the tumor drug resistance and augmented therapeutic efficacy in A549/Taxol drug-resistant tumor-bearing mice (Zou et al., 2024). Table 19.2 summarizes a few of the recently conducted studies of codelivered nanocrystals for the management of various types of cancer.

Nanocrystals for imaging and theranostic applications

Nanocrystals have been reported to play a crucial role in cancer imaging techniques. The field of cancer imaging has been revolutionized owing to the exclusive magnetic and optical properties of the nanocrystals that have rendered cancer imaging with enhanced resolution and sensitive modalities. When decorated with targeting ligands, nanocrystals can be employed as contrast agents for targeted imaging, facilitating the accurate diagnosis, staging, and monitoring of treatment outcomes on a real-time basis (Joseph and Singhvi, 2019; Desai et al., 2021). The successful amalgamation of nanocrystals with imaging techniques offers a multitude of approaches aiding in rigorous cancer diagnosis and personalized treatment regimens (Patel et al., 2024).

TABLE 19.1 Application of drug nanocrystals in various types of cancer.

Anticancer agent	Nanocrystal formulation	Model	Findings	References
Nanocrystals for breast cancer				
Paclitaxel	Folic acid and poly(ethylene glycol)-decorated nanocrystals	In vivo (4T1 orthotopic breast cancer-bearing nude mice)	Superior cellular uptake and cellular growth inhibition action of PTX NC@lipid–PEG–FA over PTX NC or PEGylated paclitaxel nanocrystals without FA modification (PTX NC@lipid–PEG), prolonged circulation of PTX NC@lipid–PEG–FA in blood compared with PTX NC or Taxol, enhanced accumulation of PTX intratumor, significant tumor reduction compared to PTX NC@ lipid–PEG, PTX NC, and Taxol	Zhao et al. (2021)
Paclitaxel	Herceptin (HCT)-functionalized nanocrystals	In vitro (HER2-positive breast cancer cells)	Superior binding affinity, augmented cell internalization in HER2-positive cells in comparison to paclitaxel nanocrystals, higher cell inhibition	Noh et al. (2016)
Paclitaxel	Cellulose nanocrystals labeled with fluorescein-5′-isothiocyanate and conjugated with folic acid	In vitro (KB and MDA-MB-468)	Remarkable and folate receptor binding uptake in KB and MDA-MB-468 cells, uptake by Clathrin-mediated endocytosis in both cell types, caveolae in MDA-MB-468, significant specific internalization of folic acid conjugated cellulose nanocrystals to folic receptor-positive cancer cells and tumors	Bittleman et al. (2018)
Paclitaxel	PEGylated paclitaxel nanocrystals	In vivo (breast cancer xenografted mice with MDA-MB-231/Luc cells, lung tumor metastasis)	Enhanced tumor inhibition in breast cancer model compared to saline and paclitaxel nanocrystals, augmented anticancer activity in lung tumor metastasis model compared to saline, paclitaxel nanocrystals, and Taxol, nearly 82% intensity reduction	Zhang et al. (2015a)
Carfilzomib	Albumin-coated nanocrystals	In vitro (breast cancer cell line) In vivo (4T1 orthotopic breast cancer model)	Better metabolic stability, augmented cellular interactions, elevated uptake and cytotoxic effects, superior anticancer activity compared to cyclodextrin formulation	Park et al. (2019)
Docetaxel	Herceptin nanocrystals	In vitro (MCF-7)	Rapid drug release, enhanced uptake, augmented cytotoxicity by Herceptin-modified docetaxel nanocrystals compared to docetaxel nanocrystals and pure docetaxel	Choi and Park (2017)

Nanocrystals for lung cancer				
Osemertinib	Drug nanocrystals (OS–NCs)	In vitro (A549)	7-fold enhanced solubility, higher in vitro drug release, augmented potency to A549 cells by osimertinib nanocrystals compared to pure osimertinib	Anwer et al. (2025)
Paclitaxel	Porous quaternized chitosan nanoparticles with nanocrystals (HTCC-NP:PTX)	In vitro (CaCo-2 and LLC cells) In vivo (lung cancer model)	Enhanced cellular uptake compared to neat PTX, likely accumulation in subcutaneous tumor tissue, remarkable tumor inhibition, apoptosis induction, reduced toxicity associated with Cremophor-EL compared to Taxol	Lv et al. (2011)
Bexarotene	Drug nanocrystals	In vitro (A549) In vivo (lung cancer xenografted mice with A549 cells)	More steady and durable efficacy, less cardiac accumulation compared to the control group, significantly enhanced cytotoxicity, apoptosis, and G1 cell cycle arrest induction, enhanced antitumor activity	Wang et al. (2017b)
Flubendazole	Drug nanocrystals	In vivo (lung cancer xenografted mouse model with A549R)	Retardation of tumor progression, around 40% reduction in tumor size in the A549R xenograft mouse model compared to the control group	de Souza Gonçalves et al. (2023)
Nanocrystals for colorectal cancer				
Curcumin	Fe_3O_4@cellulose nanocrystal (MCNC)-stabilized Pickering emulsions	In vitro (HCT116)	Efficient inhibition of about 18% of human colon cancer cells in the presence of external magnetic field, 2-fold reduction in 3D multicellular spheroid volume of HCT116 in comparison to the control sample, nontoxic to brine shrimp up to 100 μg/mL concentration	Low et al. (2019)
Salinomycin	Drug nanocrystals	In vitro (HT-29 and HCT116 colorectal cancer cells) In vivo ($APC^{min/+}$ transgenic mice)	Enhanced uptake in cells in comparison with free salinomycin, remarkably augmented cytotoxicity, 1.5–3 times improved Wnt inhibitory effect, 10 times enhanced cancer stem cell inhibitory action compared to the free drug, 2 times better antitumor effect compared to free salinomycin	Wang et al. (2020b)
5-Fluorouracil	Cellulose nanocrystals (CNC/5FU)	In vitro (HCT116 and HT-29 colorectal cancer cells; CCD112 colon normal cells)	Enhanced thermal stability of 5-FU when loaded in CNC, no effect on the viability of CCD112 by CNC, anticancer action on HCT116 and HT-29, apoptosis induction, damage of mitochondrial membrane	Yusefi et al. (2022)
Cisplatin	Mucoadhesive hydrogels based on polyacrylic acid grafted cellulose nanocrystals (CNC-g-PAA9)	In vitro (HCT-116)	Enhanced rheological properties compared to CNC, about 3-fold increased IC_{50} value against HCT116, cisplatin, and CNC-g-PAA9 complex, no intrinsic cytotoxicity	Vakili et al. (2021)

TABLE 19.2 Nanocrystal-based codelivery of chemotherapeutics.

Chemotherapeutic agents	Type of nanocrystal	Type of cancer	Model	Inference	References
Paclitaxel and lapatinib	Polydopamine PEGylated composite nanocrystal coated with (cNC@PDA-PEG)	Breast cancer	In vitro (MCF-7/ADR)	Negligible hemolysis, complete cell uptake via endocytosis, augmented cellular uptake, enhanced drug-resistant cell inhibition	Wang et al. (2020a)
Ropivacaine and doxorubicin	Homogenous nanocrystals based on self-assembled peptides	Melanoma	In vitro (cultured human melanoma cells) In vivo (rat sciatic nerve block model, incisional pain model, nude mouse tumor resection model)	Enhanced antitumor efficacy by synergism, improved cellular uptake, long-acting analgesia, inhibition of tumor recurrence, relieved postoperative pain	Peng et al. (2023)
Paclitaxel and disulfiram	Nanococrystals stabilized by β-lactoglobulin	Lung cancer	In vitro (Taxol-resistant A549 cells; A549/TAX)	Stable, high drug-loading capacity, enhanced uptake in cells, 5-fold elevation in apoptosis, 7-fold IC_{50} reduction, 8.9-fold dose reduction compared to free paclitaxel	Mohammad et al. (2018)
Paclitaxel and LF3	TMTP1-modified biomimetic nanocrystals (TRNC@P + L)	Gastric cancer	In vitro (human gastric cancer cells BGC-823 and HGC-27)	Enhanced tumor targeting, prolonged circulation, improved bioavailability, decreased toxicities of free paclitaxel and LF3, ferroptosis induction, increased ROS accumulation, augmented lipid peroxidation, enhanced anticancer activity by synergism	Zhao et al. (2025)
Paclitaxel and bosutinib	Soluplus/lipid-stabilized nanocrystals	Nonsmall cell lung cancer	In vitro (A549)	Superior anticancer action of nanocrystal combination compared to drug combination, enhanced cellular internalization, ROS generation, apoptosis induction, higher translocation compared to Soluplus nanocrystals, enhanced drug retention in lungs	Kumar et al. (2025)

Guo et al. developed paclitaxel (PTX) nanocrystals labeled with 4-chloro-7-nitro-1,2,3-benzoxadiazole (NBD-Cl), which is a drug fluorophore conjugate; similar work was previously performed by Ma et al. and Wang et al. (PTX-NBD). The resultant PTX-NBD were then employed for the formulation of cube-shaped nanocrystals that were further surface modified by soybean phosphatidylcholine (SPC) and 1,2-diacyl-SN-glycero-3-phosphoethanolamine-N-[methoxy (poly (ethyleneglycol))-2000] (MPEG-DSPE). It was observed that the cube-shaped surface-functionalized nanocrystal (PTX-NBD@PC-PEG NCs) resulted in a significant reduction in the burst release, augmented cellular uptake, and improved cytotoxicity, indicating its potential application in chemotherapy as well as imaging (Guo et al., 2017). In a study conducted by Bujnakova et al., zinc sulfide nanocrystals in CS were prepared. It was reported that the suspension was stable, demonstrated a zeta potential of +57 mV, and had a surface coating by chitosan, confirmed by the altered FTIR spectrum. Moreover, fascinating optical properties as analyzed in vitro were shown to be exhibited by zinc nanocrystals. The results of fluorescence microscopy, as performed on CaCo-2, HCT116, HeLa, and MCF-7, revealed the accumulation of the particles in the cytosol, indicating that they passed the cell membrane and were seen clearly. However, it was also noted that the nanoparticles did not influence the biological activity of the cell and did not initiate cell death, and the cells' granularity alone was increased owing to cellular uptake. All these observations proved the potential of these nanocrystals as bioimaging agents (Bujňáková et al., 2017). In yet another study, Kajani et al. fabricated a series of carbon dots utilizing a one-pot hydrothermal technique for cancer imaging. The taxane diterpenoids were used as the source of carbon, while different diamines and folic acid were used as carbon and nitrogen sources, respectively. The blue and green multicolor carbon nanocrystals demonstrated astounding anticancer activity against MCF-7 and HeLa cells with IC_{50} of 31.3 ± 2.7 and $34.1 \pm 1.1\ \mu g\ mL^{-1}$. Whereas an IC_{50} of $120.5 \pm 3.8\ \mu g\ mL^{-1}$ was displayed by the nanocrystals on the normal human fibroblast cells. Furthermore, the flow cytometry studies revealed cell death due to apoptosis as the primary anticancer mechanism of carbon dots, wherein the induction of both intrinsic and extrinsic pathways was proved to be involved, as per the data obtained from the molecular studies (Abbasi Kajani et al., 2018).

Gold nanocrystals of different shapes and sizes have immense potential for extending resonance from visible light to the near-infrared spectrum, where light can easily penetrate tissues. The gold nanocrystals are recognized as great candidates for biomedical diagnostics due to their ability to absorb and scatter the light at the resonance wavelength, rendering it an exclusive color capable of detection by the naked human eye. These are massively used for carrying out the immunogenic strip test. Additionally, these are considered promising imaging agents for the diagnosis and identification of cancer due to their characteristic, by which the surface electrons present on the gold nanocrystals magnify the signals of Raman scattering, thereby enabling sensitivity and contrast of detection and exhibiting stability on repetitive analysis when combined with antibodies or immune probes (Atapour et al., 2022). In light of this, successful cell labeling and in vivo imaging were achieved by hydroxyapatite nanocrystals possessing luminescence properties, which were fabricated by codoping Eu/Gd (Xie et al., 2016b). Thus, in a nutshell, it can be inferred that although extensive progress has been made in this specific area, still better understanding and approaches are needed for harnessing the full potential of nanocrystals as imaging and theranostic agents for gaining maximum therapeutic efficacy.

Conclusion and future prospect

The drug nanocrystals represent one of the promising drug delivery systems for the administration of poorly soluble drugs, wherein their fascinating properties, such as enhanced structural stability, high drug loading, improved time of circulation, and steady dissolution, render them an outstanding formulation for efficient cancer therapy. Compared with conventional formulations, these also result in improved pharmacokinetics and biodistribution. Furthermore, with the advent of hybrid nanocrystals, bioimaging and concurrent anticancer treatment have been made possible. Moreover, the development of surface-functionalized, lipid-modified, and biopolymer nanocrystals has further aided in the enhanced anticancer therapy. Even though a plethora of research about the role of nanocrystals in managing cancer is still on the preclinical animal level, their potential as novel drug delivery systems in treating various types of cancer cannot be overlooked. However, the major obstacle exists in the successful commercialization of the nanocrystals, which could be resolved by enabling the production of high-quality and uniform nanocrystals on an industrial scale. In this context, extensive knowledge regarding the crystallization process and its control is needed for achieving nanocrystals of ideal shape and size. The researchers must shift their focus to the integration of advanced targeting approaches and the long-term safety of these drug delivery systems. Apart from this, the researchers should focus on addressing the regulatory challenge, the amelioration of which will lead to the expansion of clinical translation of the drug nanocrystals in cancer therapy.

References

Abbasi Kajani, A., Bordbar, A.-K., Ayatollahi Mehrgardi, M., Hamid Zarkesh-Esfahani, S., Motaghi, H., Kardi, M., Khosropour, A.R., Ozdemir, J., Benamara, M., Beyzavi, H., 2018. Green and facile synthesis of highly photoluminescent multicolor carbon nanocrystals for cancer therapy and imaging. ACS Appl. Bio Mater. 1 (5), 1458–1467. https://doi.org/10.1021/acsabm.8b00407.

Agrawal, S., Dwivedi, M., Ahmad, H., Chadchan, S.B., Arya, A., Sikandar, R., Kaushik, S., Mitra, K., Jha, R.K., Dwivedi, A.K., 2018. CD44 targeting hyaluronic acid coated lapatinib nanocrystals foster the efficacy against triple-negative breast cancer. Nanomed. Nanotechnol. Biol. Med. 14 (2), 327–337. https://doi.org/10.1016/j.nano.2017.10.010.

Ali, H.S.M., York, P., Ali, A.M.A., Blagden, N., 2011. Hydrocortisone nanosuspensions for ophthalmic delivery: A comparative study between microfluidic nanoprecipitation and wet milling. J. Contr. Release 149 (2), 175–181. https://doi.org/10.1016/j.jconrel.2010.10.007.

Anwer, Md K., Mirza, M.A., Aleemuddin, M., Alshdefat, R., 2025. Enhanced cytotoxicity of osimertinib nanocrystals against lung cancer: Preparation, characterization and cytotoxicity studies against A549 cell lines. J. Drug Deliv. Sci. Technol. 107, 106805. https://doi.org/10.1016/j.jddst.2025.106805.

Atapour, A., Khajehzadeh, H., Shafie, M., Abbasi, M., Mosleh-Shirazi, S., Kasaee, S.R., Amani, A.M., 2022. Gold nanoparticle-based aptasensors: A promising perspective for early-stage detection of cancer biomarkers. Mater. Today Commun. 30, 103181. https://doi.org/10.1016/j.mtcomm.2022.103181.

Atia, M.M., Abdel-Tawab, H.S., Mostafa, A.M., Mobarak, S.A., 2022. Nanocurcumin and curcumin prevent N, N′-methylenebisacrylamide-induced liver damage and promotion of hepatic cancer cell growth. Sci. Rep. 12 (1). https://doi.org/10.1038/s41598-022-12406-y.

Bittleman, K.R., Dong, S., Roman, M., Lee, Y.W., 2018. Folic acid-conjugated cellulose nanocrystals show high folate-receptor binding affinity and uptake by KB and breast cancer cells. ACS Omega 3 (10), 13952–13959. https://doi.org/10.1021/acsomega.8b01619.

Bujňáková, Z., Dutková, E., Kello, M., Mojžiš, J., Baláž, M., Baláž, P., Shpotyuk, O., 2017. Mechanochemistry of chitosan-coated zinc sulfide (ZnS) nanocrystals for bio-imaging applications. Nanoscale Res. Lett. 12 (1). https://doi.org/10.1186/s11671-017-2103-z.

Casula, L., Craparo, E.F., Lai, E., Scialabba, C., Valenti, D., Schlich, M., Sinico, C., Cavallaro, G., Lai, F., 2024. Encapsulation of nanocrystals in mannitol-based inhalable microparticles via spray-drying: A promising strategy for lung delivery of curcumin. Pharmaceuticals 17 (12), 1708. https://doi.org/10.3390/ph17121708.

Chen, Y., Liu, Y., Xu, J., Xie, Y., Zheng, Q., Yue, P., Yang, M., 2017. A natural triterpenoid saponin as multifunctional stabilizer for drug nanosuspension powder. AAPS PharmSciTech 18 (7), 2744–2753. https://doi.org/10.1208/s12249-017-0756-7.

Choi, J.S., Park, J.S., 2017. Surface modification of docetaxel nanocrystals with HER2 antibody to enhance cell growth inhibition in breast cancer cells. Colloids Surf. B Biointerfaces 159, 139–150. https://doi.org/10.1016/j.colsurfb.2017.07.064.

Choudhury, H., Gorain, B., Pandey, M., Kumbhar, S.A., Tekade, R.K., Iyer, A.K., Kesharwani, P., 2017. Recent advances in TPGS-based nanoparticles of docetaxel for improved chemotherapy. Int. J. Pharm. 529 (1–2), 506–522. https://doi.org/10.1016/j.ijpharm.2017.07.018.

Chvatal, A., Farkas, Á., Balásházy, I., Szabó-Révész, P., Ambrus, R., 2017. Aerodynamic properties and in silico deposition of meloxicam potassium incorporated in a carrier-free DPI pulmonary system. Int. J. Pharm. 520 (1–2), 70–78. https://doi.org/10.1016/j.ijpharm.2017.01.070.

Costabile, G., Provenzano, R., Azzalin, A., Camilla Scoffone, V., Chiarelli, L.R., Rondelli, V., Grillo, I., Zinn, T., Lepioshkin, A., Savina, S., Miro, A., Quaglia, F., Makarov, V., Coenye, T., Brocca, P., Riccardi, G., Buroni, S., Ungaro, F., 2020. PEGylated mucus-penetrating nanocrystals for lung delivery of a new FtsZ inhibitor against Burkholderia cenocepacia infection. Nanomed. Nanotechnol. Biol. Med. 23, 102113. https://doi.org/10.1016/j.nano.2019.102113.

Dang, W., Li, T., Li, B., Ma, H., Dong, Z., Wang, X., Chang, J., Xiao, Y., Wang, J., Wu, C., 2018. A bifunctional scaffold with $CuFeSe_2$ nanocrystals for tumor therapy and bone reconstruction. Biomaterials 160, 92–106. https://doi.org/10.1016/j.biomaterials.2017.11.020.

Desai, N., Momin, M., Khan, T., Gharat, S., Singh Ningthoujam, R., Omri, A., 2021. Metallic nanoparticles as drug delivery system for the treatment of cancer. Expert Opin. Drug Deliv. 18 (9), 1261–1290. https://doi.org/10.1080/17425247.2021.1912008.

Diao, N., Qu, H., Wang, W., Cao, M., Liu, X., Yang, W., Cao, Y., Sun, T., Pei, H., Guo, C., Chen, D., 2024. Preparation and evaluation of a soluble microneedle loaded with resveratrol nanocrystals. J. Drug Deliv. Sci. Technol. 94, 105463. https://doi.org/10.1016/j.jddst.2024.105463.

Dyett, B.P., Yu, H., Strachan, J., Drummond, C.J., Conn, C.E., 2019. Fusion dynamics of cubosome nanocarriers with model cell membranes. Nat. Commun. 10 (1). https://doi.org/10.1038/s41467-019-12508-8.

Fan, M., Geng, S., Liu, Y., Wang, J., Wang, Y., Zhong, J., Yan, Z., Yu, L., 2018. Nanocrystal technology as a strategy to improve drug bioavailability and antitumor efficacy for the cancer treatment. Curr. Pharm. Des. 24 (21), 2416–2424. https://doi.org/10.2174/1381612824666180515154109.

Fontana, F., Figueiredo, P., Zhang, P., Hirvonen, J.T., Liu, D., Santos, H.A., 2018. Production of pure drug nanocrystals and nano co-crystals by confinement methods. Adv. Drug Deliv. Rev. 131, 3–21. https://doi.org/10.1016/j.addr.2018.05.002.

Fu, Q., Sun, J., Ai, X., Zhang, P., Li, M., Wang, Y., Liu, X., Sun, Y., Sui, X., Sun, Le, Han, X., Zhu, M., Zhang, Y., Wang, S., He, Z., 2013. Nimodipine nanocrystals for oral bioavailability improvement: Role of mesenteric lymph transport in the oral absorption. Int. J. Pharm. 448 (1), 290–297. https://doi.org/10.1016/j.ijpharm.2013.01.065.

Gao, L., Zhang, D., Chen, M., 2008. Drug nanocrystals for the formulation of poorly soluble drugs and its application as a potential drug delivery system. J. Nanoparticle Res. 10 (5), 845–862. https://doi.org/10.1007/s11051-008-9357-4.

Guo, F., Shang, J., Zhao, H., Lai, K., Li, Y., Fan, Z., Hou, Z., Su, G., 2017. Cube-shaped theranostic paclitaxel prodrug nanocrystals with surface functionalization of SPC and MPEG-DSPE for imaging and chemotherapy. Colloids Surf. B Biointerfaces 160, 649–660. https://doi.org/10.1016/j.colsurfb.2017.10.013.

Gol, D., Thakkar, S., Misra, M., 2018. Nanocrystal-based drug delivery system of risperidone: Lyophilization and characterization. Drug Dev. Ind. Pharm. 44 (9), 1458–1466. https://doi.org/10.1080/03639045.2018.1460377.

He, Y., Liang, Y., Mak, J.C.W., Liao, Y., Li, T., Yan, R., Li, H.-F., Zheng, Y., 2020. Size effect of curcumin nanocrystals on dissolution, airway mucosa penetration, lung tissue distribution and absorption by pulmonary delivery size effect of curcumin nanocrystals on dissolution, airway mucosa penetration, lung tissue distribution and absorption by pulmonary delivery. Colloids Surf. B Biointerfaces 186, 110703. https://doi.org/10.1016/j.colsurfb.2019.110703.

Jin, X., Luo, Y., Chen, Y., Ma, Y., Yue, P., Yang, M., 2019. Novel breviscapine nanocrystals modified by Panax notoginseng saponins for enhancing bioavailability and synergistic anti-platelet aggregation effect. Colloids Surf. B Biointerfaces 175, 333–342. https://doi.org/10.1016/j.colsurfb.2018.11.067.

Joseph, E., Singhvi, G., 2019. Multifunctional Nanocrystals for Cancer Therapy: A Potential Nanocarrier Nanomaterials for Drug Delivery and Therapy. Elsevier, India, pp. 91–116. https://doi.org/10.1016/B978-0-12-816505-8.00007-2.

Joshi, K., Chandra, A., Jain, K., Talegaonkar, S., 2019. Nanocrystalization: An emerging technology to enhance the bioavailability of poorly soluble drugs. Pharm. Nanotechnol. 7 (4), 259–278. https://doi.org/10.2174/2211738507666190405182524.

Kim, J.H., Jang, S.W., Han, S.D., Hwang, H.D., Choi, H.G., 2011. Development of a novel ophthalmic ciclosporin A-loaded nanosuspension using top-down media milling methods. Pharmazie 66 (7), 491–495. https://doi.org/10.1691/ph.2011.0358.

Kojima, T., Karashima, M., Yamamoto, K., Ikeda, Y., 2018. Combination of NMR methods to reveal the interfacial structure of a pharmaceutical nanocrystal and nanococrystal in the suspended state. Mol. Pharm. 15 (9), 3901–3908. https://doi.org/10.1021/acs.molpharmaceut.8b00360.

Kumar, M., Shanthi, N., Mahato, A.K., 2019. Pharmaceutical drug nanocrystals: Role in dermal delivery. Nanosci. Nanotechnol. - Asia 9 (3), 300–310. https://doi.org/10.2174/2210681208666180516093855.

Kumar, A., Valamla, B., Thakor, P., Sandeep Chary, P., Rajana, N., Kumar Mehra, N., 2022. Development and evaluation of nanocrystals loaded hydrogel for topical application. J. Drug Deliv. Sci. Technol. 74, 103503. https://doi.org/10.1016/j.jddst.2022.103503.

Kumar, M., Shanthi, N., Rajnikanth, P.S., Mahato, A.K., 2020. Authors review on drug nanocrystals: A progress to targeted delivery. Current Nanomedicine 10 (3), 248–270. https://doi.org/10.2174/2468187310666200221103827.

Kumar, M., Jha, A., Goswami, P., Srivastava, R., Manjit, M., Bharti, K., Koch, B., Mishra, B., 2025a. Fabrication of lipid-modified drug nanocrystals loaded injectable hydrogel for breast cancer therapy. Discover Nano 20 (1). https://doi.org/10.1186/s11671-025-04195-w.

Kumar, M., Goswami, P., Jha, A., Dhapte-Pawar, V., Koch, B., Mishra, B., 2025b. Formulation and evaluation of lipid/Soluplus-stabilized nanocrystals of paclitaxel and bosutinib for a synergistic effect in non-small cell lung cancer therapy. Mol. Pharm. 22 (2), 1061–1078. https://doi.org/10.1021/acs.molpharmaceut.4c01334.

Kumar, M., Jha, A., Bharti, K., Manjit, Mishra, B., 2024a. Fucoidan-based bosutinib nanocrystals for pulmonary drug delivery: Solid state characterization and in-vitro assessment. Chem. Phys. Impact 8, 100644. https://doi.org/10.1016/j.chphi.2024.100644.

Kumar, M., Jha, A., Bharti, K., Manjit, M., Kumbhar, P., Dhapte-Pawar, V., Mishra, B., 2024b. Lipid-coated nanocrystals of paclitaxel as dry powder for inhalation: Characterization, in-vitro performance, and pharmacokinetic assessment. Colloids Surf. B Biointerfaces 237, 113865. https://doi.org/10.1016/j.colsurfb.2024.113865.

Kumar, R., Siril, P.F., 2018. Enhancing the solubility of fenofibrate by nanocrystal formation and encapsulation. AAPS PharmSciTech 19 (1), 284–292. https://doi.org/10.1208/s12249-017-0840-z.

Kuroiwa, Y., Higashi, K., Ueda, K., Yamamoto, K., Moribe, K., 2018. Nano-scale and molecular-level understanding of wet-milled indomethacin/poloxamer 407 nanosuspension with TEM, suspended-state NMR, and Raman measurements. Int. J. Pharm. 537 (1–2), 30–39. https://doi.org/10.1016/j.ijpharm.2017.12.028.

Lee, T., Lim, E.-K., Lee, J., Kang, B., Choi, J., Park, H.S., Suh, J.-S., Huh, Y.-M., Haam, S., 2013. Efficient CD44-targeted magnetic resonance imaging (MRI) of breast cancer cells using hyaluronic acid (HA)-modified $MnFe_2O_4$ nanocrystals. Nanoscale Res. Lett. 8 (1). https://doi.org/10.1186/1556-276x-8-149.

Lhaglham, P., Jiramonai, L., Jia, Y., Huang, B., Huang, Y., Gao, X., Zhang, J., Liang, X.-J., Zhu, M., 2024. Drug nanocrystals: Surface engineering and its applications in targeted delivery. iScience 27 (11). https://doi.org/10.1016/j.isci.2024.111185.

Liu, Y., Huang, L., Liu, F., 2010. Paclitaxel nanocrystals for overcoming multidrug resistance in cancer. Mol. Pharm. 7 (3), 863–869. https://doi.org/10.1021/mp100012s.

Liu, M., Zheng, H., Chen, J., Li, S., Huang, J., Zhou, C., 2016. Chitosan-chitin nanocrystal composite scaffolds for tissue engineering. Carbohydr. Polym. 152, 832–840. https://doi.org/10.1016/j.carbpol.2016.07.042.

Liu, T., Han, M., Tian, F., Cun, D., Rantanen, J., Yang, M., 2018. Budesonide nanocrystal-loaded hyaluronic acid microparticles for inhalation: In vitro and in vivo evaluation. Carbohydr. Polym. 181, 1143–1152. https://doi.org/10.1016/j.carbpol.2017.11.018.

Liu, Y., Zhang, Z., Wang, C., Xie, X., Ma, Y., Wang, Y., 2023. Biodegradable and dissolvable resveratrol nanocrystals non-silicon microneedles for transdermal drug delivery. J. Drug Deliv. Sci. Technol. 86, 104653. https://doi.org/10.1016/j.jddst.2023.104653.

Lohan, S.B., Saeidpour, S., Colombo, M., Staufenbiel, S., Unbehauen, M., Wolde-Kidan, A., Netz, R.R., Bodmeier, R., Haag, R., Teutloff, C., Bittl, R., Meinke, M.C., 2020. Nanocrystals for improved drug delivery of dexamethasone in skin investigated by EPR spectroscopy. Pharmaceutics 12 (5), 400. https://doi.org/10.3390/pharmaceutics12050400.

Low, L.E., Tan, L.T.H., Goh, B.H., Tey, B.T., Ong, B.H., Tang, S.Y., 2019. Magnetic cellulose nanocrystal stabilized Pickering emulsions for enhanced bioactive release and human colon cancer therapy. Int. J. Biol. Macromol. 127, 76–84. https://doi.org/10.1016/j.ijbiomac.2019.01.037.

Lu, Y., Qi, J., Dong, X., Zhao, W., Wu, W., 2017. The in vivo fate of nanocrystals. Drug Discov. Today 22 (4), 744–750. https://doi.org/10.1016/j.drudis.2017.01.003.

Lv, P.P., Wei, W., Yue, H., Yang, T.Y., Wang, L.Y., Ma, G.H., 2011. Porous quaternized chitosan nanoparticles containing paclitaxel nanocrystals improved therapeutic efficacy in non-small-cell lung cancer after oral administration. Biomacromolecules 12 (12), 4230–4239. https://doi.org/10.1021/bm2010774.

Macedo, L.D., Masiero, J.F., Bou-Chacra, N.A., 2024. Drug nanocrystals in oral absorption: Factors that influence pharmacokinetics. Pharmaceutics 16 (9), 1141. https://doi.org/10.3390/pharmaceutics16091141.

McGuckin, M.B., Wang, J., Ghanma, R., Qin, N., Palma, S.D., Donnelly, R.F., Paredes, A.J., 2022. Nanocrystals as a master key to deliver hydrophobic drugs via multiple administration routes. J. Contr. Release 345, 334–353. https://doi.org/10.1016/j.jconrel.2022.03.012.

Mohammad, I.S., He, W., Yin, L., 2018. A smart paclitaxel-disulfiram nanococrystals for efficient MDR reversal and enhanced apoptosis. Pharm. Res. 35 (4). https://doi.org/10.1007/s11095-018-2370-0.

Miao, X., Yang, W., Feng, T., Lin, J., Huang, P., 2018. Drug nanocrystals for cancer therapy. Wiley Interdiscip. Rev. Nanomed. Nanobiotechnol. 10 (3). https://doi.org/10.1002/wnan.1499.

Müller, R.H., Gohla, S., Keck, C.M., 2011. State of the art of nanocrystals - special features, production, nanotoxicology aspects and intracellular delivery. Eur. J. Pharm. Biopharm. 78 (1), 1–9. https://doi.org/10.1016/j.ejpb.2011.01.007.

Nandi, S., Kaur, A., Bansal, A.K., 2020. Dual drug nanocrystals loaded microparticles for fixed dose combination of simvastatin and ezetimibe. Pharmaceut. Dev. Technol. 25 (1), 40–53. https://doi.org/10.1080/10837450.2019.1669181.

Noh, J.K., Naeem, M., Cao, J., Lee, E.H., Kim, M.S., Jung, Y., Yoo, J.W., 2016. Herceptin-functionalized pure paclitaxel nanocrystals for enhanced delivery to HER2-positive breast cancer cells. Int. J. Pharm. 513 (1–2), 543–553. https://doi.org/10.1016/j.ijpharm.2016.09.067.

Park, J.E., Park, J., Jun, Y., Oh, Y., Ryoo, G., Jeong, Y.S., Gadalla, H.H., Min, J.S., Jo, J.H., Song, M.G., Kang, K.W., Bae, S.K., Yeo, Y., Lee, W., 2019. Expanding therapeutic utility of carfilzomib for breast cancer therapy by novel albumin-coated nanocrystal formulation. J. Contr. Release 302, 148–159. https://doi.org/10.1016/j.jconrel.2019.04.006.

Park, J.J., Meghani, N., Choi, J.S., Lee, B.J., 2016. Development and evaluation of decorated aceclofenac nanocrystals. Colloids Surf. B Biointerfaces 143, 206–212. https://doi.org/10.1016/j.colsurfb.2016.03.022.

Park, J., Sun, B., Yeo, Y., 2017. Albumin-coated nanocrystals for carrier-free delivery of paclitaxel. J. Contr. Release 263, 90–101. https://doi.org/10.1016/j.jconrel.2016.12.040.

Patel, A., Patel, K., Patel, V., Singh Rajput, M., Patel, R., Rajput, A., 2024. Nanocrystals: An emerging paradigm for cancer therapeutics. Future J. Pharmaceut. Sci. 10 (1). https://doi.org/10.1186/s43094-024-00579-4.

Patel, K., Patil, A., Mehta, M., Gota, V., Vavia, P., 2014. Oral delivery of paclitaxel nanocrystal (PNC) with a dual Pgp-CYP3A4 inhibitor: Preparation, characterization and antitumor activity. Int. J. Pharm. 472 (1–2), 214–223. https://doi.org/10.1016/j.ijpharm.2014.06.031.

Pawar, V.K., Singh, Y., Meher, J.G., Gupta, S., Chourasia, M.K., 2014. Engineered nanocrystal technology: In-vivo fate, targeting and applications in drug delivery. J. Contr. Release 183 (1), 51–66. https://doi.org/10.1016/j.jconrel.2014.03.030.

Pelikh, O., Eckert, R.W., Reddy Pinnapireddy, S., Keck, C.M., 2021. Hair follicle targeting with curcumin nanocrystals: Influence of the formulation properties on the penetration efficacy. J. Contr. Release 329, 598–613. https://doi.org/10.1016/j.jconrel.2020.09.053.

Pelikh, O., Stahr, P.-L., Huang, J., Gerst, M., Scholz, P., Dietrich, H., Geisel, N., Keck, C.M., 2018. Nanocrystals for improved dermal drug delivery. Eur. J. Pharm. Biopharm. 128, 170–178. https://doi.org/10.1016/j.ejpb.2018.04.020.

Peltonen, L., 2018. Practical guidelines for the characterization and quality control of pure drug nanoparticles and nano-cocrystals in the pharmaceutical industry. Adv. Drug Deliv. Rev. 131, 101–115. https://doi.org/10.1016/j.addr.2018.06.009.

Peng, F., Liu, J., Chen, J., Wu, W., Zhang, Y., Zhao, G., Kang, Y., Gong, D., He, L., Wang, J., Zhang, W., Qiu, F., 2023. Nanocrystals slow-releasing ropivacaine and doxorubicin to synergistically suppress tumor recurrence and relieve postoperative pain. ACS Nano 17 (20), 20135–20152. https://doi.org/10.1021/acsnano.3c05831.

Phan, V.H.G., Murugesan, M., Huong, H., Le, T.T., Phan, T.H., Manivasagan, P., Mathiyalagan, R., Jang, E.S., Yang, D.C., Li, Y., Thambi, T., 2022. Cellulose nanocrystals-incorporated thermosensitive hydrogel for controlled release, 3D printing, and breast cancer treatment applications. ACS Appl. Mater. Interfaces 14 (38), 42812–42826. https://doi.org/10.1021/acsami.2c05864.

Pinto, R.J.B., Lameirinhas, N.S., Guedes, G., da Silva, G.H.R., Oskoei, P., Spirk, S., Oliveira, H., Duarte, I.F., Vilela, C., Freire, C.S.R., 2021. Cellulose nanocrystals/chitosan-based nanosystems: Synthesis, characterization, and cellular uptake on breast cancer cells. Nanomaterials 11 (8). https://doi.org/10.3390/nano11082057.

Pireddu, R., Caddeo, C., Valenti, D., Marongiu, F., Scano, A., Ennas, G., Lai, F., Fadda, A.M., Sinico, C., 2016. Diclofenac acid nanocrystals as an effective strategy to reduce in vivo skin inflammation by improving dermal drug bioavailability. Colloids Surf. B Biointerfaces 143, 64–70. https://doi.org/10.1016/j.colsurfb.2016.03.026.

Rachmawati, H., Al Shaal, L., Müller, R.H., Keck, C.M., 2013. Development of curcumin nanocrystal: Physical aspects. J. Pharmaceut. Sci. 102 (1), 204–214. https://doi.org/10.1002/jps.23335.

Rahman, M., Arevalo, F., Coelho, A., Bilgili, E., 2019. Hybrid nanocrystal–amorphous solid dispersions (HyNASDs) as alternative to ASDs for enhanced release of BCS Class II drugs. Eur. J. Pharm. Biopharm. 145, 12–26. https://doi.org/10.1016/j.ejpb.2019.10.002.

Ravichandran, R., 2009. Nanoparticles in drug delivery: Potential green nanobiomedicine applications. Int. J. Green Nanotechnol. Biomed. 1 (2), B108. https://doi.org/10.1080/19430850903430427.

Romero, G.B., Keck, C.M., Müller, R.H., Bou-Chacra, N.A., 2016. Development of cationic nanocrystals for ocular delivery. Eur. J. Pharm. Biopharm. 107, 215–222. https://doi.org/10.1016/j.ejpb.2016.07.005.

Rowlands, B.J., Soong, C.V., Gardiner, K.R., 1999. The gastrointestinal tract as a barrier in sepsis. Br. Med. Bull. 55 (1), 196–211. https://doi.org/10.1258/0007142991902213.

Sarnes, A., Østergaard, J., Jensen, S.S., Aaltonen, J., Rantanen, J., Hirvonen, J., Peltonen, L., 2013. Dissolution study of nanocrystal powders of a poorly soluble drug by UV imaging and channel flow methods. Eur. J. Pharmaceut. Sci. 50 (3–4), 511–519. https://doi.org/10.1016/j.ejps.2013.08.030.

Sharma, S., Verma, A., Venkatesh Teja, B., Shukla, P., Mishra, P.R., 2015. Development of stabilized paclitaxel nanocrystals: In-vitro and in-vivo efficacy studies. Eur. J. Pharmaceut. Sci. 69, 51–60. https://doi.org/10.1016/j.ejps.2014.11.012.

Shegokar, R., Singh, K.K., 2011. Surface modified nevirapine nanosuspensions for viral reservoir targeting: In vitro and in vivo evaluation. Int. J. Pharm. 421 (2), 341–352. https://doi.org/10.1016/j.ijpharm.2011.09.041.

Singh, N., Marwaha, D., Gautam, S., Rai, N., Tiwari, P., Sharma, M., Shukla, R.P., Mugale, M.N., Kumar, A., Mishra, P.R., 2023. Surface-modified lyotropic crystalline nanoconstructs bearing doxorubicin and buparvaquone target sigma receptors through pH-sensitive charge conversion to improve breast cancer therapy. Biomacromolecules 24 (12), 5780–5796. https://doi.org/10.1021/acs.biomac.3c00795.

Skrdla, P.J., Yang, H., 2019. On the stability of nano-formulations prepared by direct synthesis: Simulated Ostwald ripening of a typical nanocrystal distribution post-nucleation. AAPS PharmSciTech 20 (1). https://doi.org/10.1208/s12249-018-1257-z.

Soisuwan, S., Teeranachaideekul, V., Wongrakpanich, A., Langguth, P., Buraphacheep Junyaprasert, V., 2019. Impact of uncharged and charged stabilizers on in vitro drug performances of clarithromycin nanocrystals. Eur. J. Pharm. Biopharm. 137, 68–76. https://doi.org/10.1016/j.ejpb.2019.02.004.

Soni, N., Jyoti, K., Jain, U.K., Katyal, A., Chandra, R., Madan, J., 2017. Noscapinoids bearing silver nanocrystals augmented drug delivery, cytotoxicity, apoptosis and cellular uptake in B16F1, mouse melanoma skin cancer cells. Biomed. Pharmacother. 90, 906–913. https://doi.org/10.1016/j.biopha.2017.04.042.

de Souza Gonçalves, D., Yukuyama, M.N., Miyagi, M.Y.S., Vieira Silva, T.J., Lameu, C., Bou-Chacra, N.A., Barros de Araujo, G.L., 2023. Revisiting flubendazole through nanocrystal technology: Statistical design, characterization and its potential inhibitory effect on xenografted lung tumor progression in mice. J. Cluster Sci. 34 (1), 261–272. https://doi.org/10.1007/s10876-022-02220-x.

Tang, W., Zhang, Z., Li, C., Chu, Y., Qian, J., Ying, T., Lu, W., Zhan, C., 2021. Facile separation of PEGylated liposomes enabled by anti-PEG scFv. Nano Lett. 21 (23), 10107–10113. https://doi.org/10.1021/acs.nanolett.1c03946.

Tao, W., Zeng, X., Liu, T., Wang, Z., Xiong, Q., Ouyang, C., Huang, L., Mei, L., 2013. Docetaxel-loaded nanoparticles based on star-shaped mannitol-core PLGA-TPGS diblock copolymer for breast cancer therapy. Acta Biomater. 9 (11), 8910–8920. https://doi.org/10.1016/j.actbio.2013.06.034.

Tuomela, A., Liu, P., Puranen, J., Rönkkö, S., Laaksonen, T., Kalesnykas, G., Oksala, O., Ilkka, J., Laru, J., Järvinen, K., Hirvonen, J., Peltonen, L., 2014. Brinzolamide nanocrystal formulations for ophthalmic delivery: Reduction of elevated intraocular pressure in vivo. Int. J. Pharm. 467 (1–2), 34–41. https://doi.org/10.1016/j.ijpharm.2014.03.048.

Tuomela, A., Hirvonen, J., Peltonen, L., 2016. Stabilizing agents for drug nanocrystals: Effect on bioavailability. Pharmaceutics 8 (2). https://doi.org/10.3390/pharmaceutics8020016.

Ueda, K., Iwai, T., Sunazuka, Y., Chen, Z., Kato, N., Higashi, K., Moribe, K., 2019. Effect of molecular weight of hypromellose on mucin diffusion and oral absorption behavior of fenofibrate nanocrystal. Int. J. Pharm. 564, 39–47. https://doi.org/10.1016/j.ijpharm.2019.04.033.

Vakili, M.R., Mohammed-Saeid, W., Aljasser, A., Hopwood-Raja, J., Ahvazi, B., Hrynets, Y., Betti, M., Lavasanifar, A., 2021. Development of mucoadhesive hydrogels based on polyacrylic acid grafted cellulose nanocrystals for local cisplatin delivery. Carbohydr. Polym. 255, 117332. https://doi.org/10.1016/j.carbpol.2020.117332.

Vidlářová, L., Romero, G.B., Hanuš, J., Štěpánek, F., Müller, R.H., 2016. Nanocrystals for dermal penetration enhancement – effect of concentration and underlying mechanisms using curcumin as model. Eur. J. Pharm. Biopharm. 104, 216–225. https://doi.org/10.1016/j.ejpb.2016.05.004.

Wang, H., Zhang, G., Ma, X., Liu, Y., Feng, J., Park, K., Wang, W., 2017a. Enhanced encapsulation and bioavailability of breviscapine in PLGA microparticles by nanocrystal and water-soluble polymer template techniques. Eur. J. Pharm. Biopharm. 115, 177–185. https://doi.org/10.1016/j.ejpb.2017.02.021.

Wang, Y., Rong, J., Zhang, J., Liu, Y., Meng, X., Guo, H., Liu, H., Chen, L., 2017b. Morphology, in vivo distribution and antitumor activity of bexarotene nanocrystals in lung cancer. Drug Dev. Ind. Pharm. 43 (1), 132–141. https://doi.org/10.1080/03639045.2016.1225752.

Wang, J., Muhammad, N., Li, T., Wang, H., Liu, Y., Liu, B., Zhan, H., 2020. Hyaluronic acid-coated camptothecin nanocrystals for targeted drug delivery to enhance anticancer efficacy. Mol. Pharm. 17 (7), 2411–2425. https://doi.org/10.1021/acs.molpharmaceut.0c00161.

Wang, J., Lv, F.-M., Wang, D.-L., Du, J.-L., Guo, H.-Y., Chen, H.-N., Zhao, S.-J., Liu, Z.-P., Liu, Y., 2020a. Synergistic antitumor effects on drug-resistant breast cancer of paclitaxel/lapatinib composite nanocrystals. Molecules 25 (3), 604. https://doi.org/10.3390/molecules25030604.

Wang, Z.hongyuan, Feng, T.ao, Zhou, L.iang, Jiang, D.awei, Zhang, Y.ifan, He, G.ang, Lin, J.ing, Huang, P.eng, Lu, D.esheng, 2020b. Salinomycin nanocrystals for colorectal cancer treatment through inhibition of Wnt/β-catenin signaling. Nanoscale 12 (38), 19931–19938. https://doi.org/10.1039/d0nr04552g.

Xie, Y., Ma, Y., Xu, J., Liu, Y., Yue, P., Zheng, Q., Hu, P., Yang, M., 2016a. Panax notoginseng saponins as a novel nature stabilizer for poorly soluble drug nanocrystals: a case study with baicalein. Molecules 21 (9), 1149. https://doi.org/10.3390/molecules21091149.

Xie, Y., He, W., Fang, L., Perera, T.S.H., Gan, L., Han, Y., Wang, X., Li, S., Dai, H., 2016b. Luminescence enhanced Eu^{3+}/Gd^{3+} Co-doped hydroxyapatite nanocrystals as imaging agents in vitro and in vivo. ACS Appl. Mater. Interfaces 8 (16), 10212–10219. https://doi.org/10.1021/acsami.6b01814.

Yue, P., Zhou, W., Huang, G., Lei, F., Chen, Y., Ma, Z., Chen, L., Yang, M., 2022. Nanocrystals based pulmonary inhalation delivery system: advance and challenge. Drug Deliv. 29 (1), 637–651. https://doi.org/10.1080/10717544.2022.2039809.

Yusefi, M., Lee-Kiun Soon, M., Teow, S.-Y., Irene Monchouguy, E., Haleema Mooneerah Neerooa, B.N., Izadiyan, Z., Jahangirian, H., Rafiee-Moghaddam, R., Webster, T.J., Shameli, K., 2022. Fabrication of cellulose nanocrystals as potential anticancer drug delivery systems for colorectal cancer treatment. Int. J. Biol. Macromol. 199, 372–385. https://doi.org/10.1016/j.ijbiomac.2021.12.189.

Zhang, H., Wang, X., Dai, W., Gemeinhart, R.A., Zhang, Q., Li, T., 2014. Pharmacokinetics and treatment efficacy of camptothecin nanocrystals on lung metastasis. Mol. Pharm. 11 (1), 226–233. https://doi.org/10.1021/mp4004018.

Zhang, H., Hu, H., Zhang, H., Dai, W., Wang, X., Wang, X., Zhang, Q., 2015a. Effects of PEGylated paclitaxel nanocrystals on breast cancer and its lung metastasis. Nanoscale 7 (24), 10790–10800. https://doi.org/10.1039/C4NR07450E.

Zhang, Z., Wang, Z., He, S., Wang, C., Jin, M., Yin, Y., 2015b. Redox reaction induced Ostwald ripening for size- and shape-focusing of palladium nanocrystals. Chem. Sci. 6 (9), 5197–5203. https://doi.org/10.1039/C5SC01787D.

Zhang, H., Hollis, C.P., Zhang, Q., Li, T., 2011. Preparation and antitumor study of camptothecin nanocrystals. Int. J. Pharm. 415 (1–2), 293–300. https://doi.org/10.1016/j.ijpharm.2011.05.075.

Zhao, J., Du, J., Wang, J., An, N., Zhou, K., Hu, X., Dong, Z., Liu, Y., 2021. Folic acid and poly (ethylene glycol) decorated paclitaxel nanocrystals exhibit enhanced stability and breast cancer-targeting capability. ACS Appl. Mater. Interfaces 13 (12), 14577–14586. https://doi.org/10.1021/acsami.1c00184.

Zhao, Q., Wu, T., Tang, C., Li, J., Wu, M., Wu, J., Wang, Z., Zhu, Y., Xu, H., Li, X., 2025. Biomimetic nanocrystals co-deliver paclitaxel and small-molecule LF3 for ferroptosis-combined chemotherapy for gastric cancer. Colloids Surf. B Biointerfaces 251, 114586. https://doi.org/10.1016/j.colsurfb.2025.114586.

Zou, J., Xing, X., Teng, C., Zhao, Q., He, W., Wu, X., Xia, Y., 2024. Cocrystal@protein-anchoring nanococktail for combinatorially treating multidrug-resistant cancer. Acta Pharm. Sin. B 14 (10), 4509–4525. https://doi.org/10.1016/j.apsb.2024.08.014.

CHAPTER

20

Theranostic nanoparticles for advanced cancer therapy

Debadatta Mohapatra[1], *Devdutt Sharma*[2] *and Rinki Verma*[3]

[1]Leslie Dan Faculty of Pharmacy, University of Toronto, Toronto, ON, Canada; [2]Dev Nanotech, Private Limited, Yamunanagar, Haryana, India; [3]College of Pharmacy and Health Sciences, St. John's University, Jamaica, NY, United States

Introduction

Cancer is one of the world's most devastating ailments, characterized by uncontrolled cell proliferation, invasion, and metastasis. According to the International Agency for Research on Cancer (IARC) global cancer observatory database, 206,36,441 cases of cancer incidence and 97,62,507 mortality among both males and females in 2024 were reported WHO. GLOBOCAN (2024). Asia has the largest cancer incidence rate, accounting for around 50.7% of all cases worldwide, followed by Europe (21.0%), North America (13.4%), Latin America and the Caribbean (7.7%), Africa (5.9%), and Oceania (1.3%). Similarly, Asia has the highest cancer-related mortality rate (56.1%), followed by Europe (20.4%), Africa (7.8%), Latin America and the Caribbean (7.7%), North America (7.2%), and Oceania (0.76%) (WHO. GLOBOCAN, 2024). Among all cases, breast cancer had the highest age-standardized cancer incidence and death, followed by prostate, lung, colorectal, cervix uteri, thyroid, stomach, corpus uteri, liver, ovary, bladder, nonHodgkin lymphoma, leukemia, pancreas, and esophagus. Cancer incidence and death are steadily growing, highlighting the critical need for novel ways for early detection and treatment with low toxicity and side effects. The poor prognosis of cancer by standard laboratory and imaging approaches causes obstacles in early diagnosis. Many tumors have no identifiable indicators and develop asymptomatically, making early detection challenging. Additionally, conventional therapies such as chemotherapy and radiotherapy frequently lack selectivity, resulting in toxicity to noncancerous tissues and serious adverse effects. Drug resistance, tumor heterogeneity, and metastasis also hinder therapy outcomes. All these can be addressed by the implications of innovative theranostic nanoformulations (Hosseini et al., 2023).

Advanced Cancer Therapeutics
https://doi.org/10.1016/B978-0-443-44185-1.00035-5

Theranostics nanoformulations integrate therapeutics and diagnostics, offering simultaneous diagnosis and therapy (Hosseini et al., 2023). Theranostic nanoformulations ranging from 1 to 100 nm have been extensively applied for both cancer diagnosis, therapy, and real-time monitoring of therapeutic responses (Al-Thani et al., 2024; Hosseini et al., 2023; Kashyap et al., 2023). Incorporating diagnostic agents (fluorescent dyes, radionuclides, or contrast materials) for magnetic resonance imaging (MRI), computed tomography (CT), positron emission tomography (PET), photoacoustic tomography (PAT), and single photon emission computed tomography (SPECT) with therapeutic compounds like drugs, proteins, peptides, or biologicals into the nanoparticles allows effective tracking of biodistribution, precise tumor targeting, and monitoring of treatment outcomes (Hosseini et al., 2023; Akmal Raheem et al., 2023; Gupta et al., 2024). Theranostic nanoparticles circumvent the limitations of conventional cancer treatments, including drug resistance, low targeting accuracy, and adverse effects on healthy tissues (Sharmiladevi et al., 2021). Theranostic nanoparticles such as gold nanoparticles and iron oxide nanoparticles, or silica nanoparticles, polymeric nanoparticles, dendrimers, quantum dots, carbon nanotubes, carbon dots, and liposomes equipped with metals or inorganic materials have been extensively used for diagnosing and treating advanced-stage cancer (Gupta et al., 2024; Xue et al., 2021; Azimizonuzi et al., 2025). Theranostic nanoparticles can be surface-functionalized for site-specific delivery, avoiding off-target distribution and undesirable organ toxicities. The targeting can be achieved by conjugation or surface modifications with targeting ligands (antibodies, proteins, peptides, polysaccharides) specific to receptors on cancer cells' surface or via the Enhanced Permeability and Retention (EPR) effect (Gupta et al., 2024). Additionally, stimuli-responsive nanotheranostics (pH, temperature, enzyme, photon, or magnet) can be designed to release the payload at the tumor microenvironment for cancer cell-selective drug delivery. However, despite promising preclinical success by theranostic nanoparticles, they face several challenges regarding scale-up, stability, safety, biocompatibility, regulatory approval, and clinical translation (Gupta et al., 2024). This chapter comprehensively discusses theranostics nanoparticles, types, associated advantages, targeting strategies, imaging modalities, preclinical and clinical status, challenges, limitations, and future prospects for advanced cancer therapy.

Nanotechnology in cancer theranostics

Nanomedicine is a multidisciplinary field that leverages nanotechnology for the diagnosis, treatment, and prevention of diseases. It employs nanoscale materials, including nanoparticles (NPs), liposomes, niosomes, exosomes, nanoemulsions, dendrimers, nanofibers, and nanogels for effective and targeted drug delivery. These nanoformulations can effectively penetrate biological barriers to reach the target site and allow controlled release of therapeutics. These can be exploited for the design of advanced imaging nanomaterials for selective and early detection of cancer. Nanoparticles loaded or conjugated with imaging agents (MRI, PET, CT, optical) can help to effectively visualize tumors all over the body and track biodistribution in real time. Nanoparticles can bypass drug efflux pumps or co-deliver gene therapy agents (e.g., siRNA or miRNA) to silence resistance-related genes, avoiding or overcoming multidrug resistance (MDR). Incorporating photothermal (e.g., gold nanoparticles) or photodynamic agents (e.g., porphyrins) into nanoparticles results in a theranostic nanoplatform to obtain an additive or synergistic anticancer effect. Such a nanoplatform can avoid the requirement of repeated biopsies for tracking cancer, offering a noninvasive method for tumor monitoring.

Nanoparticles for the design of cancer nanotheranostics

Common nanocarriers used in the formulation of theranostic nanosystems include liposomes, noisome, nanoparticle, nanoemulsion, microemulsion, nanostructured lipid carrier, solid lipid nanoparticle, nanocomposite, quantum dots, carbon dots, carbon nanotube, dendrimers, and metallic nanoparticles (gold and silver nanoparticles), and magnetic nanoparticles (Fig. 20.1). Each nanoparticles exhibit unique characteristics to provide multiple benefits like biodegradability, biocompatibility, nonimmunogenicity, targeting, real-time monitoring, and therapeutic effect.

Polymeric nanoparticles

Polymeric nanoparticles (PNPs) are solid colloidal particles made of both natural and synthetic polymers. Natural polymers include heparin, chitosan, dextran, albumin, gelatin, alginate, and collagen (Kumar et al., 2023). Polyethylene glycol, polyglutamic acid, polyglycolic acid, polylactic acid, polycaprolactone, poly(D, L-lactide-co-glycolic acid), polyaspartate, and N-(2-hydroxypropyl)-methacrylamide copolymers are all synthetic polymers that are widely used in drug delivery research due to their biocompatibility and therapeutic efficacy. These nanoparticles are frequently used as nanocarriers in cancer theranostics because of their superior biocompatibility, customized drug release ability, loading flexibility, and surface modification ability. They can load therapeutics (anticancer drugs, genetic materials, PTT, PDT, and immunomodulating agents) and diagnostic materials (fluorescent, MRI, and PET/SPECT contrast agents) (Wang et al., 2014; Sarcan et al., 2018; Huang et al., 2023; Li et al., 2023b). In a recent study, heavy-atom-free azadipyrromethene boron difluoride (aza-BODIPY) theranostic NPs were developed for PDT to avoid the toxicity of heavy-atom-based conventional photosensitizers. The aza-BODIPY derivative (AB-OH), having a donor-acceptor-donor structure, was conjugated to poly(ethyleneglycol)-succinic acid (mPEG-SA) to produce amphiphilic mPEG-SA-AB. The conjugate was reported to form nanoparticles by self-assembling and generate reactive oxygen species (ROS) with mild heat upon irradiation with 660 nm red light. The nanoparticles showed excellent hemocompatibility and cellular biocompatibility against breast cancer cells (4T1) under dark conditions and developed photocytotoxicity by intracellular ROS generation, followed by apoptosis induction upon irradiation. Confocal laser scanning microscopy revealed improved cellular uptake and accumulation of nanoparticles in endocytic compartments in both 2D and 3D culture models, compared to the free dye. The in vivo study in 4T1 tumor-bearing BALB/c mice demonstrated tumor-targeted accumulation and significantly improved (2.5-fold) antitumor activity of the nanoparticle compared to the parent AB-OH molecule. The developed nanoparticle represented a safe and efficacious nanotheranostic platform, offering synergistic photodynamic and mild photothermal effects for improved

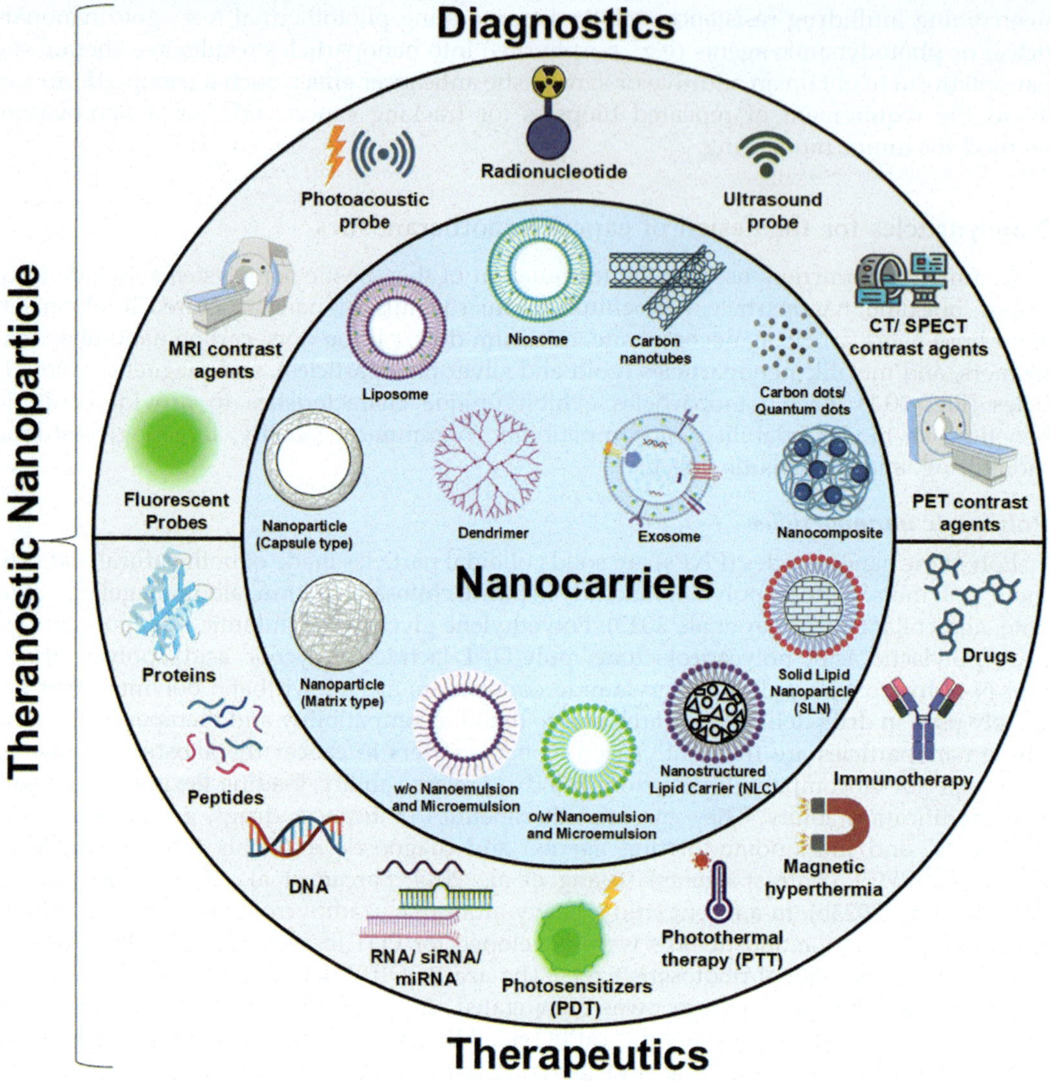

FIGURE 20.1 Schematic representation of theranostic nanoparticles for advanced cancer therapy. Theranostic materials integrated nanocarriers for imaging, diagnosis, and therapeutic effects.

diagnosis and therapy of breast cancer (Muangsopa et al., 2025). In another study, ^{177}Lu-labeled polymeric theranostic nanoparticles (^{177}Lu-PNPs) were designed as a multifunctional platform to treat head and neck cancer with near-infrared II (NIR-II) and SPECT imaging. The PNPs were modified with ethylenediamine and chelated with diethylenetriamine pentaacetic acid (DTPA). The PNPs showed a 15.4% $\pm$ 3.2% radiochemical yield, >95% purity, preserving size distribution and optical properties. The formulation showed effective tumor delivery with peak uptake at 24 h postinjection. The ^{177}Lu-PNPs with PTT significantly improved tumor uptake, suppression of tumor growth, and extended survival of MTCQ-1 tumor-bearing nude mice. The retention of histopathology (kidney, liver, spleen) and body weight maintenance revealed the safety of the ^{177}Lu-PNPs-PTT combination therapy for theranostic use (Hsieh et al., 2025).

Dendrimers

Dendrimers are polymeric branched monomers to which bioactives can be covalently linked for their delivery. Their monodispersity, multifunctionality, controlled release potential, and surface tunability make them suitable for cancer theranostics development. They can simultaneously deliver diagnostics (MRI, PET/SPECT contrast agents, fluorescence moieties) and therapeutics (drugs, gene, proteins, and immunotherapy) for effective cancer therapy (Ray et al., 2018; Kesharwani et al., 2022; Cruz et al., 2023). Fluorinated redox-responsive cross-linked poly(amidoamine) G2 (PAMAM G2) theranostic dendrimers were developed for improving gene delivery. A cross-linker having disulfide bonds and trifluoromethyl groups enables “click” Michael addition with PAMAM G2. The developed cross-linked polymers showed strong ^{19}F nuclear magnetic resonance signals and promising relaxation behavior, allowing their application as ^{19}F MRI molecular tracers. The developed fluorinated polymer (PAMAM G2) showed extremely low cytotoxicity against human umbilical vein endothelial cells (HUVEC), excellent plasmid DNA complexation, glutathione-triggered degradation, and improved transfection efficiency in human cervical carcinoma cells (HeLa) associated with a reducing environment. The selective cleavage of the disulfide bond of the cross-linker in a glutathione-rich environment was found to be effective in promoting plasmid DNA release. The study revealed the potential of the fluorinated dendrimer as a low-toxicity, multifunctional, trackable platform for effective gene delivery and theranostic uses (Romani et al., 2025). In another study, an angiopep-2targeted multifunctional dendrimer-based nanotheranostic was reported to improve the targeted delivery of temozolomide (TMZ) for effective glioblastoma multiforme treatment. The dendrimer was developed using fourth-generation polypropylene imine and functionalized with polyethylene glycol to improve biocompatibility. It was further conjugated with Angiopep-2 (ANG-2) for targeted delivery to glioblastoma multiforme cells. The incorporation of silver sulfide (Ag_2S) quantum dots allowed near-infrared (NIR) imaging and noninvasive real-time monitoring. The dendrimers showed excellent biocompatibility, $56.32 \pm 2.8\%$ TMZ loading, and sustained release properties. Further, it showed significantly improved cellular uptake in brain capillary endothelial cells (BCECs) and C6 glioma cells compared to free TMZ. Sulforhodamine B assay revealed improved cytotoxicity against C6 glioma cells compared to the free drug. In vivo antitumor activity in the C6 glioma xenograft mouse model revealed significant tumor growth inhibition compared to control and free TMZ. The in vivo biodistribution studies by NIR imaging revealed targeted delivery to tumor tissues and their potential for glioblastoma multiforme treatment (Kumar Parashar et al., 2025).

Liposomes

Liposomes are spherical vesicles of phospholipid bilayer. The core of liposome is hydrophilic whereas the bilayers are hydrophobic allowing the loading of both hydrophilic and hydrophobic drugs. It protects the payload in the core and bilayers from degradation, improves stability, and provides controlled release (Azimizonuzi et al., 2025). They can be surface functionalized or equipped with inorganic materials or imaging modalities to give a hybrid structure for theranostic applications and cancer therapy (Azimizonuzi et al., 2025). Radionuclides or gold/iron oxide nanoparticles in liposomes enable imaging techniques like MRI, PET, and optical imaging, while fluorescent dyes allow precise tracking of cancer cells. Liposomes with paramagnetic agents offer high-resolution MRI imaging without damaging healthy tissues (Fernandes, 2023b). Multifaceted theranostic liposome containing doxorubicin (DOX) and indocyanine green (ICG) was reported for improved anticancer activity and imaging in lung adenocarcinoma models. The smart liposome showed excellent cellular uptake in lung adenocarcinoma cells (A549), with ICG and DOX localization in lysosomes and nuclei, respectively, with significant cytotoxicity. In vivo imaging showed accumulation of liposomes in tumor sites in xenograft models, with ICG signals observed in the liver and intestines, indicating metabolic routes. When exposed to 780 nm light, the ICG/DOX-loaded liposomes inhibited tumor growth significantly compared to ICG/DOX liposomes without light irradiation in nude mice through combined ferroptosis and apoptosis induction, reflecting their theranostic potential for lung adenocarcinoma. By offering controlled drug release, apoptosis induction, imaging capabilities, and photothermal effects, the multifunctional liposome offered a comprehensive approach for diagnosing and treating lung cancer (Liao et al., 2025). In a recent study, doxorubicin-loaded integrin-targeting cyclic RGD peptide (cRGD) theranostic liposomes were prepared by microfluidic-assisted synthesis for the treatment of triple-negative breast cancer (TNBC). The cRGD was used as a targeting ligand on liposomes by click chemistry reaction to target overexpressed integrin receptor $\alpha v\beta 3$ in TNBC cells (MDA-MB-231). The liposome was loaded with a fluorescent dye (rhodamine) and a gadolinium complex for dual imaging by fluorescence and magnetic resonance techniques. Compared to the untargeted liposome, the targeted theranostic smart liposome showed improved cellular uptake via integrin-mediated endocytosis, enhanced cytotoxicity against MDA-MB-231 cells, and imaging capabilities. Further, the targeted cRGD liposome significantly inhibited the migration of MDA-MB-231 cells compared to the untargeted liposome and free DOX at 8, 24, and 48 h, thus preventing cancer metastasis (Ovejero-Paredes et al., 2025).

Niosome

Niosomes are vesicular carriers having structures similar to liposomes; however, nonionic surfactants are used as membrane formers instead of phospholipid (Demir et al., 2018). These have greater stability and are easier to process. They are safe, nonimmunogenic, and nontoxic drug delivery systems. Niosomes can be loaded with drugs, imaging agents, and other therapeutic compounds (Demir et al., 2018). Nanoparticles, such as quantum dots (Saharkhiz et al., 2023) and gold nanoparticles (Demir et al., 2018), are integrated with niosomal formulations for theranostic applications. They have been widely explored for theranostic nanovesicles for advanced cancer therapy (Saharkhiz et al., 2023). A novel pH-responsive theranostic niosome loaded with doxorubicin was reported for the treatment of breast cancer. The pH-responsive stealth niosome was formulated via a thin-film hydration method using Span 60, Tween 60, cholesterol, distearoylphosphatidylcholine (DSPC), and pH-sensitive polymer (DSPE-CA-PEG2000). Then, CdSe/ZnS quantum dots were loaded between the surfactant bilayer to provide a tracing feature. The fabricated smart neosome demonstrated excellent cytotoxicity against MCF-7 cells at low concentrations without affecting normal mouse fibroblast cells (L929). The theranostic ability was evaluated against MCF-7 breast cancer cell line by cytotoxicity study, apoptosis assay, and fluorescence microscopy. The neosomes were spherical-shaped, with an average size of 100 ± 10 nm, a zeta potential of -2 mV, and 87% entrapment efficiency. The formulation showed a pH-responsive release behavior of 40%, 60%, and 80% drug release in pH 7.4, 6.5, and 4, respectively. Further, it showed excellent cellular uptake and cytotoxicity via apoptosis induction. The quantum dots enabled an on/off fluorescent property. The prepared neosome was reported as an excellent formulation for cancer theranostic applications (Saharkhiz et al., 2023). In another study, a theranostic pH-responsive noisome was prepared by thin-film hydration and used for direct delivery of docetaxel via antiprostate-specific membrane antigen (PSMA) aptamer. An aptamer A10 conjugation to the neosome was carried out via a disulfide bond. Then, quantum dots (CdSe/ZnS QDs) were functionalized with mercapto propanoic acid ligands and attached to the $3'$ terminal of the aptamer via an amide bond. The neosomes were found to be spherical-shaped vesicles with an average size of 200 nm, and a negative surface charge (-1.8 ± 0.2 mV). The drug release was found to be pH dependent, with a sustained drug release at pH 5. The targeted neosomes demonstrated excellent cellular uptake and cytotoxicity against prostate cancer cells (LNCap) with overexpression of PSMA. The quantum dots allowed the tracing and uptake of particles at the targeted tissue (Nasri et al., 2024).

Silica nanoparticles

Silica nanoparticles can be designed to deliver drugs, imaging agents such as fluorescent dyes, or metals. Mesoporous silica nanoparticles (MSNs), known for their large surface area and adjustable pore size, are popular for efficient cargo loading and controlled release potential (Zhu et al., 2023; Dutta Gupta et al., 2024). Folic acid-targeted fibrous theranostic silica nanoparticles were reported to improve the delivery of chemotherapeutic agents (chlorambucil and organotin metallodrug: organotin (IV) complex) and molecular imaging agent (Alexa Fluor 647) for effective treatment of triple-negative breast cancer. The in vitro results demonstrated a synergistic activity of the two chemotherapeutic agents with improved cytotoxicity and inhibition of cell migration of triple-negative breast cancer cells (MDA-MB-231). The in vivo imaging showed tumor-specific accumulation of nanoparticles and significant inhibition of tumor growth in an orthotopic breast cancer model after 13 days. The nanotheranostics represented negligible systemic toxicity with their promising theranostic applicability for effective treatment of triple-negative breast cancer (Ovejero-Paredes et al., 2022). In another study, programmed death-ligand 1 (PD-L1)-aptamer-functionalized fluorescent silica nanoparticles (FSNPs) were reported for TNBC. The PD-L1 aptamers were conjugated to FSNPs to fabricate AptPD-L1-FSNPs. In vitro cellular targeting was investigated using PD-L1-positive TNBC cells and negative controls. Then, the in vivo biodistribution and tumor targeting were investigated via fluorescence imaging in TNBC-bearing mice. The AptPD-L1-FSNPs demonstrated high specificity to PD-L1-expressing TNBC cells (MDA-MB-231). The in vivo outcomes in the tumor-bearing mice model showed prolonged tumor retention, reduced tumor growth, increased apoptosis, and survival prolongation with negligible toxicity. The theranostic silica nanoparticles offered real-time targeted TNBC imaging and therapy (Tan et al., 2025).

Gold nanoparticles

Gold nanoparticles are a versatile and promising platform in cancer theranostics due to their exceptional optical properties (Jha et al., 2023). It can be surface functionalized with polymers, lipids, peptides, genes, or anticancer agents, allowing targeted delivery for precise imaging, real-time monitoring, and anticancer effects. The tunable size, biocompatibility, and capability to carry contrast agents allow multimodal imaging with minimal immune interference (López-Valverde et al., 2022). Gold nanoparticles can target and penetrate cancer cells with high precision (Kumar and Lim, 1999). It enables stimulus-responsive action at the tumor microenvironment with negligible toxicity to normal cells (Pawar et al., 2023). In gene therapy, gold nanoparticles can be used for carrying nucleic acids in cancer cells, thus enhancing therapeutic outcomes. In PTT, it serves as an efficient heat-generating agent, enabling the selective destruction of tumor cells, further supporting targeted and minimally invasive cancer treatment. Their use in drug delivery systems enables stimulus-responsive targeted release at the tumor microenvironment with negligible toxicity to normal cells (Pawar et al., 2023). In a recent study, resveratrol (RESV)-functionalized gold and theranostic ^{198}gold nanoparticles were reported for the diagnosis and treatment of prostate cancer. The RESV^{-198}AuNP nanoformulation integrated RESV as the anticancer and high antioxidant agent with radioactive gold nanoparticles (^{198}AuNPs). The stability study in rat serum and saline showed the durability of the formulation for up to 15 days. The in vivo biodistribution studies in normal female CF-1 mice and PC-3 tumor-bearing severe combined immunodeficiency mice (SCID) represented optimum tumor retention. The intratumoral administration of theranostic nanoparticles in SCID mice reflected strong retention within prostate cancer xenografts, representing tumor-specific uptake and accumulation. This study revealed the potential of the theranostic gold nanoparticle for prostate cancer theranostics (Sakr et al., 2025). In another study, bovine serum albumin (BSA)-coated bimetallic theranostic manganese dioxide (MnO_2)-gold (MnO_2–Au@curcumin) nanoparticle was reported for synergistic radiochemotherapy of breast cancer. MnO_2 was used for oxygen generation, gold for radiosensitization, BSA for biocompatibility, and curcumin (CUR) was used as an anticancer agent to achieve chemotherapeutic and radioprotective effects. The nanoparticles were found to be spherical in shape with an average size of 190 nm, polydispersity index of 0.391, and zeta potential of −24.7 mV. The in vitro results on breast cancer cells (4T1) showed excellent haemocompatibility, dose-dependent cytotoxicity without affecting normal cells (human foreskin fibroblast 2: HFF-2), and improved radiosensitization under 4 Gy X-ray irradiation. Further, the formulation showed a pH-dependent release behavior under an acidic tumor microenvironment. The computational studies, including molecular docking, molecular dynamics, and density functional theory, represented the stability and interactions of nanoparticles (Naderlou et al., 2025).

Iron oxide nanoparticles

Iron oxide nanoparticles are extensively used as contrast agents for tumor imaging and as targeted therapeutic carriers, owing to their strong magnetic properties. These nanoparticles can be functionalized with drugs, proteins, enzymes, antibodies, or nucleic acids for effective anticancer action (Shakil et al., 2019). Iron oxide nanoparticles have been utilized for magnetic hyperthermia, where nanoparticles raise the temperature of tumor cells to induce cell death. It can be exploited for magnetic labeling and tracking of cells. Magnetic iron oxide nanoparticles (Fe_3O_4NPs) and superparamagnetic iron oxide have shown great theranostic potential because of their inherent biocatalytic activity (nanozyme), magnetic resonance imaging ability, photo-responsive therapy, gene and drug delivery ability (Li et al., 2017; Zhao et al., 2020). In a study, a theranostic nano-vector based on superparamagnetic iron oxide nanoparticles (SPION) containing tumor suppressor miRNA (miR-497-5p) was developed for targeting colorectal cancer (CRC). Bioinformatics tools were used to identify miR-497-5p. *Fusarium oxysporum* fungus was used for the green synthesis of SPION@Ag@Cs nanocomposite targeting programmed cell death protein-1 (PD1)/programmed cell death-ligand 1 (PDL1) and cytotoxic T-lymphocyte-associated protein 4 (CTLA4) pathways for colorectal cancer therapy. In vitro cytotoxicity revealed significant cytotoxicity due to pmiR497-@Nano composite compared to the pNull@Nano control vector ($P < .05$). The immunofluorescence confirmed transfection of cells with miR497@NPs and the downregulation of CTLA4 in Caco2 and HT29 cell lines. The PDL1 showed a significant increase in response to nanoparticle treatment. The miR-497 decreased cell proliferation by inducing cell cycle arrest in S-phase. The outcomes revealed the efficacy of the nanoformulation for suppressing CTLA4 in human CRC cell lines. The SPION/miR-497 nanovector integrated MRI-guided diagnosis with targeted gene therapy, representing a promising theranostic strategy for colorectal cancer (Elfiky et al., 2025). In a recent study, citric acid-coated SPIONs of nintedanib were developed for lung cancer theranostic application. Citric acid was used to improve the stability of magnetic nanoparticles by offering repulsive forces between two particles. The drug-loaded and blank SPIONs showed higher saturation magnetization. The nintedanib esylate-loaded nanoparticles (NE-CA-SPIONs) were found to be spherical-shaped, with 30.65 ± 3.2 nm size, -32.3 ± 2.4 mV zeta potential, 22.09 emu/g magnetic property, and of a semicrystalline nature. The formulation showed a drug release of $98.85 \pm 3.7\%$ in 29 h. The NE-CA-SPIONs were found to be hemocompatible and demonstrated significantly higher cytotoxicity towards human lung cancer cells (A549) compared to nintedanib esylate. The X-ray imaging reflected their use as a contrast agent in diagnosis. Overall, the study demonstrated the use of iron oxide nanoparticles to diagnose and treat lung cancer (Patel and Patel, 2024).

Quantum dots, carbon dots, and carbon nanotubes

Carbon dots (CDs) or carbon quantum dots (CQDs) are zero-dimensional fluorescent nanomaterials, typically measuring between 1 and 10 nm. They are widely utilized in cancer theranostics, biosensing, and drug delivery due to their unique optical properties and biocompatibility (Radnia et al., 2020; Wang et al., 2018). CDs possess inherent fluorescence and exhibit selective anticancer effects while sparing healthy cells. Recently, green carbon dots have gained considerable interest, synthesized from natural sources such as plant extracts, natural polymers, agricultural by-products, and amino acids. These provide cost-effective production, high biocompatibility, strong luminescent properties, and easy surface modification, making them highly suitable for diverse biomedical applications (Mohapatra et al., 2021, 2022; Radnia et al., 2020). Dual fluorescent CDs were synthesized from *Piper longum* leaves using the solvothermal carbonization method for multifaceted theranostic and environmental applications. The developed CDs (PLECDs) showed pink fluorescence in ethanol and green fluorescence in water. The UV spectroscopy, high-performance thin-layer chromatography, fluorescence properties, and transmission electron microscopy revealed effective synthesis of CDs with an average particle size of 2.83 nm. The energy dispersive X-ray and X-ray photoelectron spectroscopy revealed the abundance of C, N, and O. The developed CDs showed excellent cytotoxicity towards human cervical carcinoma (SiHa), human triple-negative breast cancer cells (MDA-MB-231), and murine melanoma (B16F10) cell lines with excellent in vitro bioimaging properties. Further, the PLECDs showed pH-dependent fluorescence properties, photostability, and thermal stability (Mohapatra et al., 2023). Quantum dots (QDs) are tiny semiconductor nanomaterials, similar to CDs, typically below 10 nm, attracting considerable interest in theranostic nanomedicine owing to distinct optical and electronic characteristics (Nowroozi et al., 2018; Tripathi et al., 2015). Their properties can be tailored by adaptable surface chemistry to obtain distinctive optical properties for multiplex detection and higher sensitivity. Their ultralow nano dimension imparts them with effective specific optical and electronic properties (Ahmad et al., 2023). These thus possess size-tunable emission spectra, higher contrast, and exceptional photostability, making them superior imaging agents compared to traditional dyes. In cancer theranostics, QDs serve as multifunctional platforms that can simultaneously enable tumor imaging, targeted drug delivery, and therapy monitoring. The integration of QDs with other nanomaterials of organic and inorganic origin forms hybrid QDs for theranostic applications (Ahmad et al., 2023). In a recent study, CdZnSeS QDs were prepared using a single-step hot injection method and were reported as nanotheranostics for prostate and leukemia cancer. The nanoparticles demonstrated a quasi-core/shell structure with a high quantum yield (85%). Then the QDs were encapsulated into gallic acid/alginate (GA-Alg) matrices to fabricate imaging QDs@mod-polyacrylic acid (PAA)/GA-Alg particles with enhanced stability in aqueous media. The QDs demonstrated excellent cytotoxicity against leukemia (HL-60) and human prostate cancer (PC-3). Further, the QDs@mod-PAA/GA-Alg nanoparticles were loaded with betulinic acid (BA) and ceranib-2 (C2). The QDs represented pH-dependent drug release with sustained release at pH 5.5. The BA-loaded QDs demonstrated a three-fold increase in cytotoxicity against HL-60 and PC-3 compared to BA. Similar cytotoxicity improvements were observed with nanocarriers loaded with C2 and simultaneously with both BA and C2. Due to their excellent luminescent properties and cytotoxicity, they are reported as novel cancer theranostics for prostate and leukemia cancer (Tan et al., 2024). Carbon nanotubes (CNTs) are other promising carbon-based tubular theranostic nanomaterials with excellent optical and thermal properties, along with drug loading and functionalization capability (Mostafavi et al., 2022; Tang et al., 2021). Carbon nanotubes, as single-walled (SWCNTs) or multi-walled (MWCNTs) nanosystems, have been widely explored for drug delivery and superior mechanical, thermal, and electrical properties. The strong near-infrared absorption of CNTs makes them suitable for photothermal therapy (PTT). CNTs can deliver payload to the nucleus, mitochondria, or cytoplasm, or can target components of the tumor microenvironment, for enhanced antitumor effect (Tang et al., 2021). Additionally, carbon-nanomaterials conjugated with photosensitizers or chemotherapeutic drugs enable photodynamic therapy or chemotherapy responsive to specific stimuli such as light or pH. Such integration of diagnostic and therapeutic functions into a single nanoparticle offers multifunctional therapeutics for precise cancer treatment. In a recent study, aptamer-assisted MWCNTs were developed as an MRI contrast and photothermal agent for breast cancer therapy. The developed MWCNTs were ligand exchanged with butyric acid (BA) to achieve a hydrophilic property. Then, a breast cancer aptamer specific to Mucin-1 (MUC-1) was conjugated with the functionalized MWCNTs. The MWCNTs successfully targeted triple-negative breast cancer cells (MDA-MB-231) with excellent cellular uptake. The quantitative polymerase chain reaction and immunoblotting revealed a reduction in cancer-induced inflammation and protein expression. The Immunoblot and confocal-based immunofluorescence assay demonstrated the ability of MWCNTs to induce photothermal cell death of MDA-MB-231 cells. The MCNTs acted as MRI contrast agents, allowing visualization of cancer cells. In addition to that, the MWCNTs showed photothermal capabilities. The outcomes revealed the theranostic potential of the CNTs for breast cancer treatment (Khajuria et al., 2024).

Functionalization of theranostic nanoparticles

Theranostic nanoparticles can be functionalized with targeting moieties such as proteins, peptides, antibodies, or aptamers to achieve passive and active targeting (Fig. 20.2). Both

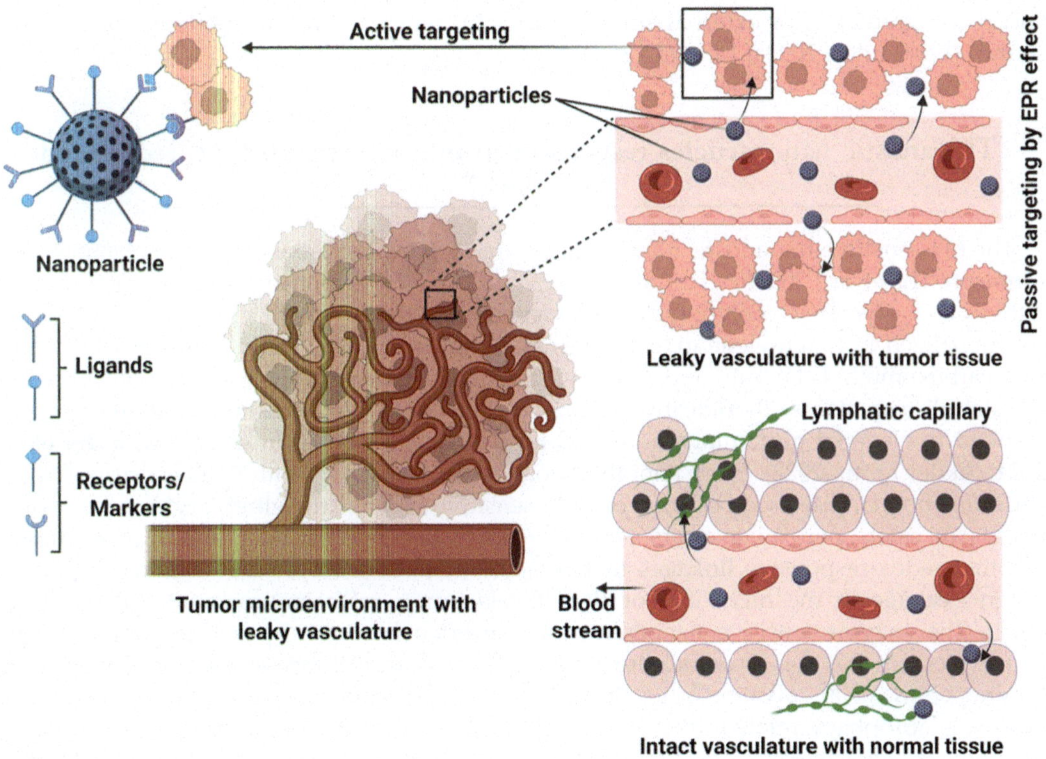

FIGURE 20.2 Targeting pathways for theranostic nanoparticles. Enhanced Permeation and Retention effect assisted passive targeting and cancer cell surface receptor-mediated endocytosis-based active targeting.

strategies enable the selective accumulation of the payload in tumor cells, improving theranostic properties while minimizing off-target toxicities (Gupta et al., 2024). Passive targeting allows theranostics accumulation at the tumor site via the enhanced permeability and retention (EPR) effect (Carrese et al., 2021; Karthikeyan et al., 2023; Akmal Raheem et al., 2023; Al-Thani et al., 2024). The leaky abnormal blood vessels (pore size: 100–1200 nm) at the tumor microenvironment cause the accumulation of theranostics materials, whereas the low lymphatic drainage prevents their rapid clearance, leading to prolonged retention for longer imaging and anticancer action. The active targeting of theranostics with targeting ligands allows recognition of specific receptors (folate receptor, integrin αvβ3) or markers (prostate-specific membrane antigen) overexpressed at the cancer site, thus providing precise theranostic application (Chen et al., 2014b; Carrese et al., 2022; Gupta et al., 2024). Ligands, such as monoclonal antibodies (rituximab, trastuzumab, cetuximab, bevacizumab), aptamers (VEGF-aptamer, antiMUC1 aptamer, antiEGFR aptamer), peptides (RGD4C, MiRGD), or small molecules (folic acid, transferrin) can be anchored to the surface of theranostic nanoparticles for active targeting (Karthikeyan et al., 2023). PEGylation is another surface modification technique widely employed to enhance the biocompatibility and systemic circulation of theranostic nanoparticles. Stimuli-responsive molecules can also be integrated into theranostic nanoparticles to achieve controlled/sustained drug release and real-time imaging in response to a specific tumor microenvironment or external stimuli. Stimuli-responsive theranostics respond to a particular stimulus (internal stimuli like pH, enzymes, and redox gradients, or external stimuli like light, temperature, magnetic fields, or ultrasound) (Fernandes, 2023a; Li et al., 2023a).

Theranostic nanoparticles responsive to internal stimuli (pH, redox, and enzyme)

The pH-sensitive theranostic nanoparticles are responsive to the acidic tumor microenvironments (Li et al., 2023b; Li et al., 2023c). Various pH-responsive agents, such as poly (ethylene glycol)- poly(2-(hexamethyleneimino)ethyl methacrylate), hydrazine-functionalized poly (ethylene glycol), hydrazide-tailored poly(methyl methacrylate), chitosan, carboxymethyl dextran, and pH low insertion peptide are used for the development of stimuli-responsive theranostic nanoformulations. Redox-sensitive nanotheranostics respond to elevated glutathione and ROS levels in cancer cells (Li et al., 2023a; Jia et al., 2024; Sikder et al., 2022). Such nanotheranostics are fabricated with GSH-sensitive linkers (disulfide bonds, diselenide bonds), or ROS sensitive linkers (thioether, aryl boronic esters, peroxalate esters, peroxalate esters, peroxalate ester, aryl boronic ester, and thioketal bond), or other redox-responsive linkages that remain stable in the systemic circulation but undergo cleavage in the high-GSH or ROS levels tumor microenvironment (Sikder et al., 2022). The enzyme-sensitive nanotheranostics exert action as response to tumor specific overexpressed enzymes at extracellular region (matrix metalloproteinases), cell membrane (aminopeptidase N, alkaline phosphatase, and γ-glutamyltranspeptidase), cytosol (caspase-3/7, autophagy-related 4B cysteine peptidase, transglutaminase, and nitroreductase), lysosome (β-galactosidase, β-glucuronidase, and cathepsin B), endoplasmic reticulum (protein tyrosine phosphatase 1B, carboxylesterase), mitochondrion (enterokinase), golgi body (furin), and nucleus (endonuclease histone deacetylases) (Li et al., 2023a). Such theranostic nanoparticles contain enzyme-cleavable linkers that remain stable in normal tissues but are selectively cleaved at the tumor site by the enzymes.

External stimuli (temperature, light, magnetic field, and ultrasound)

Temperature-sensitive theranostic nanomaterials release the contained materials upon local hyperthermia (Michael et al., 2025). Temperature-sensitive theranostic nanomaterials contain thermoresponsive materials or linkers such as poly(N-isopropylacrylamide), poly [(N–N-diethyl) acrylamide], dipalmitoyl phosphatidylcholine, polyethylene glycol, poly (propylene glycol), poly(N-vinylcaprolactam), elastin like polypeptides, collagen, and silk. On exposure to external heat, their activation provides thermal imaging or therapeutic action (Amin et al., 2020; Li et al., 2023a; Michael et al., 2025). Localized heating in response to external stimulus provides theranostic action like magnetic hyperthermia, focused ultrasound, and microwave therapy (Li et al., 2023a; Michael et al., 2025). Light-sensitive nanotheranostics work in response to NIR to provide PDT/PTT (Li et al., 2023a). Apart from PDT and PTT, photosensitive linkers (O-nitrobenzyl ester, coumarin ester) incorporated in theranostic nanostems trigger the release of payload through photo-degradation, photo-decrosslinking, photo-isomerization, and photo-crosslinking mechanisms (Li et al., 2023a; Yao et al., 2016). Such nanotheranostics remain dormant and inefficacious in the absence of light and get activated upon exposure to light or a photon (Yao et al., 2016). Magnetic nanoparticles (magnetite: Fe_3O_4 and maghemite: γ-Fe_2O_3) are responsive to an external magnetic field to accumulate and generate magnetic hyperthermia at the intended site (Yao et al., 2016). The intrinsic magnetic properties also assist transport to the target site and provide selective magnetic resonance imaging and magnetothermal effect (Li et al., 2023a; Yao et al., 2016). Ultrasound-responsive theranostics can trigger the killing of tumor cells by ultrasonic cavitation, mechanical, and thermal effects. It can generate sonoluminescence for cancer diagnosis and offer noninvasive, deeper tumor tissue penetration for effective cancer therapy (Li et al., 2023a; Yao et al., 2016).

Applications of theranostic nanoparticles

Photothermal therapy

Photothermal therapy (PTT) utilizes gold, copper, silver, carbon nanoparticles/carbon nanotubes, quantum dots, or nanoparticles with optical absorbers (e.g., cyanine, IR dyes) that convert near-infrared light (NIR) into heat, selectively killing cancer cells with minimal injury to noncancerous tissues (Xue et al., 2021; Michael et al., 2025; Al-Thani et al., 2024; Gupta et al., 2024). The site-specific hyperthermia acts as an effective tool for the precise destruction of abnormal cancerous cells (Li et al., 2023a). The anticancer effect primarily results from direct thermal ablation, causing irreversible damage to tumor tissue and apoptosis in cancer cells. When the temperature exceeds 49°C, it leads to protein denaturation, cell membrane disruption, inflammation, damage to the cytoskeleton, and inhibition of DNA synthesis (Fernandes, 2023a).

Photodynamic therapy

Theranostic nanoparticles for photodynamic therapy (PDT) utilize photosensitizers (e.g., IR780 NIR dye, chlorin e6, ZnF16Pc, tetraphenylporphyrin) that produce reactive oxygen species (ROS) (e.g., reactive superoxide anion radicals, hydrogen peroxide, and hydroxyl radicals) upon activation by light (Xue et al., 2021; Karthikeyan et al., 2023). The oxidative stress destroys cancer cells and abnormal vasculature without affecting normal tissues (Gupta et al., 2024; Karthikeyan et al., 2023). The cancer cells' destruction occurs through the processes of necrosis, apoptosis, and mitotic cell death (Fernandes, 2023a). PDT elevates hypoxia within the tumor microenvironment due to the consumption of oxygen and the resulting shutdown of blood vessels (Karthikeyan et al., 2023). In addition, the optical characteristics of the photosensitizer or its carrier enable real-time imaging alongside photodynamic therapy (Xia et al., 2021). PDT also enhances the efficacy of chemotherapy, radiation, and gene therapy (Al-Thani et al., 2024).

Magnetic hyperthermia

Magnetic theranostic nanoparticles (e.g., iron oxide) produce localized heat when exposed to an alternating magnetic field. The generated heat causes the death of surrounding cancer cells without affecting noncancerous tissue. Magnetic nanoparticles can be remotely sensed and controlled by applying external magnetic fields (Coene and Leliaert, 2022; Kandasamy and Maity, 2021). When such particles are coated with thermo-sensitive coatings, spatial and controlled drug release is achieved (Coene and Leliaert, 2022). Additionally, combining targeted heating with drug release can create a synergistic therapeutic effect. However, magnetic nanoparticles may occasionally accumulate in unintended areas of the body, potentially causing unwanted heat damage to healthy tissues (Coene and Leliaert, 2022).

Combination therapies

Combination therapies are mostly preferred due to the insufficiency and limitations of single oncotherapy. The administration of multimodal diagnostic and therapeutic strategies, called "cocktail" theranostics, is used to achieve the desired anticancer property (Xue et al., 2021). Coloading of multiple therapeutic agents (e.g., chemo with PTT or PDT) in therapeutic nanoparticles provides synergistic therapeutic effects, overcoming drug resistance, and enhancing therapeutic outcomes with diagnostic capabilities (Xue et al., 2021; Karthikeyan et al., 2023; Gupta et al., 2024; Kumar Rajora et al., 2024).

Imaging modalities integrated with nanoparticles

Magnetic resonance imaging

Combining nanoparticles with MRI materials has significantly improved diagnostic accuracy by enhancing image contrast. Magnetic nanoparticles, such as those made from iron oxide, gadolinium, or manganese, alter relaxation times to boost signal intensity and clarity (Abbasi et al., 2016; Sharma et al., 2024). Surface modifications further enable selective interaction with specific cells or disease markers, reducing background noise and enhancing diagnostic accuracy. Theranostic nanoparticles expand this capability by combining imaging with therapeutic delivery, allowing real-time monitoring of treatment responses. Additionally, advanced MRI techniques like magnetic resonance spectroscopy (MRS) benefit from nanoparticle-enhanced contrast, enabling detailed visualization of biochemical tissue profiles for more accurate cancer diagnosis and treatment monitoring (Gujar et al., 2005).

Computed tomography

CT has significantly improved the reliability of medical imaging, particularly with the incorporation of nanoparticles (Gupta et al., 2024). CT imaging offers the ability to differentiate tumors from healthy tissues based on variations in X-ray attenuation. This is enhanced by radiopaque nanoparticles, which improve image contrast due to their high atomic number and electron density. Commonly used contrast-enhancing elements in nanoparticles include iodine, bismuth, and gold, as they provide strong X-ray absorption and are highly electron-dense (Tang et al., 2024). In CT images, tumor regions that absorb more X-rays appear white, while areas with lower absorption appear darker. The major advantages of CT imaging are its high spatial resolution (ranging from 0.05 to 0.2 mm in preclinical imaging to 0.5–1.0 mm in clinical settings), rapid image acquisition, and deep tissue penetration enabled by high-energy ionizing radiation. However, repeated exposure to ionizing radiation poses health risks, limiting the frequency of scans. Additionally, the contrast agents typically required in high doses may lead to toxicity and adverse effects, particularly in vital organs.

Positron emission tomography

Positron emission tomography (PET) plays a pivotal role in theranostic nanomedicine for advanced cancer therapy by enabling precise, noninvasive visualization of biological processes at the molecular level (Goel et al., 2017). As a highly sensitive imaging modality, PET allows real-time tracking of radiolabeled nanocarriers, providing crucial information on biodistribution, tumor targeting, and therapeutic response. In theranostic applications, nanoparticles are engineered to carry both therapeutic agents and PET-compatible radioisotopes such as 18F, 64Cu, or 68Ga, allowing simultaneous diagnosis and treatment monitoring. PET imaging also aids in identifying tumor heterogeneity, evaluating receptor expression, and predicting therapeutic outcomes, which are essential for optimizing targeted therapies. PET-integrated theranostic nanomedicine represents a transformative approach in cancer management, offering high sensitivity, early detection, and real-time therapy assessment that significantly improve the precision and efficacy of advanced cancer treatments (Gupta et al., 2024).

Optical imaging (Fluorescence, bioluminescence)

Photoluminescent nanoparticles (PLNPs), such as lanthanide-doped upconversion nanoparticles (UCNPs) and quantum dots (QDs), have garnered significant interest in cancer theranostics. Their appeal lies in their ultra-small size, customizable surface chemistry, high quantum yield, and unique optical and photophysical characteristics such as strong near-infrared (NIR) absorption and multi-color luminescence. These properties enable real-time monitoring of both drug delivery and release, supporting simultaneous imaging and therapeutic applications. Additionally, PLNPs, including UCNPs and QDs, exhibit reduced background autofluorescence due to their longer emission wavelengths. This characteristic is particularly beneficial for deep-tissue imaging, as it allows for better tissue penetration with minimal damage to surrounding tissues (Chen et al., 2014a; Wang et al., 2017a). Furthermore, cadmium-free quantum dots are considered more biocompatible, leading to reduced cytotoxicity compared to their cadmium-containing counterparts (Xu et al., 2016).

Photoacoustic Imaging

Photoacoustic Imaging (PAI) combines laser-induced ultrasound with the light-absorbing properties of nanoparticles to produce high-resolution, deep-tissue images (Liu et al., 2019). When pulsed laser light strikes nanoparticles, particularly gold nanoparticles, they absorb the energy and emit ultrasonic waves, enabling detailed visualization of vascular structures and tumors. PAI is especially valuable in cancer diagnosis and monitoring due to its ability to provide real-time, high-quality molecular imaging (Yang et al., 2019). Its integration with nanoparticles allows targeted imaging and tracking of therapeutic agents, such as gene delivery vectors, in breast cancer treatment, ensuring gene expression at tumor sites. However, challenges remain, including achieving uniform nanoparticle distribution in tissues and the complexity of nanoparticle synthesis and regulatory approval. Addressing these issues is crucial to advancing PAI for broader clinical use in diagnostics and theranostics (Gupta et al., 2024).

Preclinical and clinical studies

Preclinical studies

In vitro and in vivo studies play a pivotal role in the preclinical evaluation of theranostic nanomedicine for advanced cancer therapy, enabling a comprehensive assessment of their dual diagnostic and therapeutic functions. In vitro studies involve testing on cancer cell lines to evaluate cytotoxicity, cellular uptake, apoptosis, cell cycle analysis, and imaging capabilities. While, in vivo studies in tumor-bearing animal models assess pharmacokinetics, biodistribution, tumor accumulation via passive or active targeting, therapeutic efficacy, and real-time imaging using modalities like PET, MRI, or optical imaging. These models enable assessment of toxicity and safety, as well as anticancer effects. The integration of therapy and imaging in these studies enables dynamic monitoring of treatment progress. Some recent preclinical studies on theranostic nanoparticles are summarized in Table 20.1.

Clinical studies

Few reports have been made to highlight promising preclinical results and ongoing clinical trials that showcase their translational potential. Table 20.2 shows the summaries of

TABLE 20.1 Preclinical studies on various theranostic nanoparticles for advanced cancer therapy.

Nanocarrier	Diagnosis	Therapeutic agent	Cell line use and animal model	References
Iron oxide NPs	MRI	Magnetic resonance-guided focused ultrasound surgery	H460 cell line and H460 xenograft mice	Wang et al. (2017a)
Iridium oxide NPs size	Fluorescence imaging	Doxorubicin PTT	HepG2 cell line and HepG2 xenograft mice	Zhang et al. (2022)
NaGdF4:Yb/Er@ MIL-53(Fe)	MRI	Doxorubicin	B16–F10 and HEK293 cell line	Mukherjee et al. (2020)
Gold NPs	Fluorescence imaging	PDT	PC-3 cells line and PC-3 xenograft mice	Mangadlao et al. (2018)
	Photoacoustic imaging	PTT	U-87MG xenograft mice	Yoon et al. (2018)
Lanthanide-doped NPs NaYF4:Yb, Tm@NaYF4:Eu	Upconversion luminescence imaging	PDT	AGS xenograft mice	Zhou et al. (2022)
Lanthanide-doped NPs NaLuF4	NIR-II imaging	Doxorubicin PTT	HCT 116 xenograft mice and LLC	Li et al. (2019)
Silicon-based	PET imaging	Radiotherapy	4T1 tumor-bearing mice	Ferreira et al. (2021)
	Photoacoustic imaging	Doxorubicin PTT	MCF10a and HS578T cell line	Silvestri et al. (2019)
PLGA-based NPs	MRI	Radio frequency hyperthermia, Docetaxel	S180 xenograft mice	Wang et al. (2017b)
	Photoacoustic imaging	Photothermal therapy	MDA-MB-231 xenograft mice	Li et al. (2021)
PLGA-based NPs	MRI Dual-modal ultrasound	PTT	SKBR3 and MDA-MB-231 cells line	Dong et al. (2019)
Chitosan-based NPs	Fluorescence imaging	Nucleic acid	HeLa cell line	Gholami et al. (2019)
Liposomes-based NPs	PET Fluorescence photoacoustic imaging	PDT AQ4N	4T1 Balb/c mice	Feng et al. (2017)
	Fluorescence imaging	Doxorubicin PTT	4T1 Balb/c mice	Prasad et al. (2019)

(Continued)

TABLE 20.1 Preclinical studies on various theranostic nanoparticles for advanced cancer therapy.—cont'd

Nanocarrier	Diagnosis	Therapeutic agent	Cell line use and animal model	References
pH-sensitive niosome	Fluorescence imaging.	Doxorubicin	MCF-7 breast cancer cells	Saharkhiz et al. (2023)
Folate targeted niosome	Fluorescence imaging	Gold nanoparticles and Protoporphyrin IX-based PDT and radiotherapy	Human cervical cancer (HeLa) and A549 human lung adenocarcinoma cell line	Demir et al. (2018)
Hyaluronic acid-modified niosome	Fluorescence imaging	Fingolimod	MDA-MB-231 triple-negative breast cancer cell line	Hashemi et al. (2025)
Carbon quantum dots	NIR fluorescence imaging	Carbon quantum dots, functionalized with multiple paired α-carboxyl and amino groups	HeLa cells and A549 cells and tumor-bearing BALB/c mice	Li et al. (2020)
Carbon dots	NIR fluorescence imaging	Sulfur and nitrogen codoped NIR CDs PTT	HeLa cells H22 tumor models of the ICR mice	Bao et al. (2018)
Carbon nanotubes	Fluorescence imaging Raman spectroscopy	Single-walled carbon nanotubes	C6 rat glioma cells	Golubewa et al. (2020)
Radiolabeled SLN	Fluorescence imaging	Trastuzumab	Human breast cancer cells (MCF-7 and MDA-MB-231)	Ozgenc et al. (2022)
Albumin NPs	Fluorescence imaging	Paclitaxel PTT	4T1 Balb/c mice	Xia et al. (2021)
Nanoemulsion	MRI	Myrisplatin	Nu/nu mice bearing subcutaneous flank ovarian SKOV-3 tumors	Ganta et al. (2015)
Nanoemulsion	Fluorescence imaging	Paclitaxel	Human oral epidermoid carcinoma cell line (KB-3–1) and nude mice inoculated with KB-8–5 cells	Yang et al. (2014)
Dendrimers	MRI	Doxorubicin hydrochloride and PTT	Human hepatoma HepG2 cell line	Jędrzak et al. (2019)
Exosomes	Fluorescence imaging	Olaparib	MDA-MB-231 breast cancer cells and0 BALB/c nu/nu mice containing MDA-MB-231	Jung et al. (2018)

TABLE 20.2 Nanocarrier-based strategies in cancer therapy: Overview of active clinical trials. ClinicalTrials.gov.

ClinicalTrials.gov ID	Title	Type of cancer	Status	Last update
NCT06111417	Use of an ultra-rapid BRCA1/2 status screening test in diagnostic and theranostic indications: Performance and interest for patients and practitioners (TURBO)	Breast cancer		22-04-2025
NCT04674722	HER2 expression detection and radionuclide therapy in breast cancer using 99mTc/188Re labeled single domain antibody	Breast cancer	Early phase 1	09-12-2024
NCT06337084	Diagnostic efficacy and dosimetry of MNPR-101-DFO*-89Zr in patients with solid tumors	Solid tumors	Phase 1	22-05-2025
NCT06228482	Molecularly targeted radionuclide therapy via the integrin Alphavbeta6	Lung cancer	Phase 1	28-05-2025
NCT05501665	Split course adaptive radiation therapy with pembrolizumab With/Without chemotherapy for treating stage IV lung cancer	Lung cancer	Phase 1	17-10-2024
NCT04789486	Nano-SMART: Nanoparticles with MR-guided SBRT in centrally located lung tumors and pancreatic cancer	Lung cancer and pancreatic cancer	Phase 2	23-05-2025
NCT06693375	To evaluate dose and safety of NanoEcho Particle-1 using NanoEcho imaging device examinations of rectal lymph nodes in healthy volunteers and rectal cancer patients	Rectal cancer	Phase 2	18-11-2024
NCT06589401	Oral paclitaxel for patients with advanced solid tumors	Solid tumor	Phase 1	19-09-2024
NCT06423326	Gemcitabine, cisplatin and nab-paclitaxel as neoadjuvant treatment for patients with resectable or borderline resectable pancreatic cancer	Pancreatic cancer	Phase 2	19-09-2024
NCT06173349	PLZ4-coated paclitaxel-loaded micelles for the treatment of patients with recurrent or refractory nonmuscle invasive bladder cancer	Bladder cancer	Phase 1	18-12-2024
NCT06169072	Sentinel lymph node localisation with an ultra-low dose of magtrace in breast cancer patients (MagSnow2)	Breast cancer and sentinel lymph node	Phase 2	26-01-2024
NCT06048367	Carbon nanoparticle-loaded iron [CNSI–Fe (II)] in the treatment of advanced solid tumor (CNSI–Fe (II))	Solid tumor	Phase 1	27-06-2025
NCT05685602	CA-4948 added to standard chemotherapy to treat metastatic or unresectable pancreatic cancer	Pancreatic cancer	Phase 2	03-07-2025
NCT05666700	CAR-T cell therapy in RelApsed/Refractory myeloma with ExtrameduLlary disease - an in vivo imaging and molecular monitoring study (CARAMEL)	Extramedullary myeloma	Phase 1	11-04-2024
NCT05285358	Pressurized intraperitoneal aerosolized nab-paclitaxel in combination with gemcitabine and cisplatin for the treatment of biliary tract cancer patients with peritoneal metastases	Bile duct adenocarcinoma	Phase 1	07-03-2025
NCT05267899	A phase I first-in-human study to evaluate the safety, tolerability, and pharmacokinetics of WGI-0301 in patients with advanced solid tumors	Advanced solid tumors	Phase 1	26-09-2023

(*Continued*)

TABLE 20.2 Nanocarrier-based strategies in cancer therapy: Overview of active clinical trials. ClinicalTrials.gov.—cont'd

ClinicalTrials.gov ID	Title	Type of cancer	Status	Last update
NCT05048082	A study to evaluate pegsitacianine, an intraoperative fluorescence imaging agent for the detection of lung malignancies	Lung cancer	Phase 2	08-11-2024
NCT05039632	Phase I/II randomized study of NBTXR3 activated by abscopal or RadScopal radiation in combination with immunotherapy (anti-PD-1/L-1) for patients with advanced solid malignancies	Advanced solid malignancies	Phase 1 Phase 2	18-05-2025
NCT04899908	Stereotactic brain-directed radiation with or without aguix gadolinium-based nanoparticles in brain metastases	Brain cancer	Phase 2	24-10-2024
NCT05969041	Study of MT-302 in adults with advanced or metastatic epithelial tumors (MYE symphony)	Epithelial tumors	Phase 1	18-01-2024
NCT04486833	Quaratusugene ozeplasmid (Reqorsa) and osimertinib in patients with advanced lung cancer who progressed on osimertinib (Acclaim-1)	Lung cancer	Phase 1 Phase 2	25-03-2025
NCT07047560	Liposomal irinotecan (II) fractionated dosing combined with 5-FU/LV (FOLFIRInali-3) and bevacizumab in second-line treatment of advanced colorectal cancer: A single-arm, phase II clinical study	Colorectal cancer	Phase 2	02-07-2025
NCT07044921	Clinical study of irinotecan liposome (II)-based combination treatment for irinotecan-resistant colorectal cancer.	Colorectal cancer	Phase 2	01-07-2025
NCT06801730	Irinotecan liposomes combined with bevacizumab in the treatment of recurrent glioma (NALIRIBVRG)	Glioma	Phase 2	30-01-2025
NCT06791460	Pegylated liposomal doxorubicin plus adebrelimab with or without mirabegron in relapsed ovarian cancer	Ovarian cancer	Phase 2 Phase 3	18-03-2025

some recent clinical trials on theranostic nanoparticles for the diagnosis and treatment of cancer. For instance, Clinical Trial NCT04674722 is evaluating the safety, dosimetry, and efficacy of 99mTc/188Re-labeled antiHER2 single-domain antibodies (99mTc-NM-02 and 188Re-NM-02) for SPECT/CT imaging and radionuclide therapy in patients with HER2-positive breast cancer. This study compares the novel approach with standard HER2 detection methods such as IHC/FISH and 18F-FDG PET/CT, aiming to establish a noninvasive alternative for both diagnostic imaging and targeted treatment. Similarly, NCT06337084 is a pilot study investigating MNPR-101-DFO-^{89}Zr*, a radiolabeled monoclonal antibody targeting uPAR-expressing solid tumors, using PET/CT. The trial focuses on evaluating biodistribution, tumor uptake, safety, and pharmacokinetics, supporting its use as a dual-functional diagnostic and therapeutic tool. NCT06228482 explores the theranostic pairing of [^{68}Ga] Ga DOTA-5G for PET-based patient selection and [^{177}Lu] Lu DOTA-ABM-5G for radionuclide therapy in metastatic nonsmall cell lung cancer (NSCLC). This Phase I trial aims to determine safety, tolerability, and therapeutic response in patients with progressive disease, reinforcing the potential of theranostic combinations in personalized oncology. NCT04789486 focuses on AGuIX, a gadolinium-based nanoparticle, combined with MRI-guided stereotactic body radiation therapy for pancreatic and lung tumors. This study investigates the nanoparticle's radiosensitizing properties and its potential to enhance both targeting precision and therapeutic outcomes under image guidance. The NCT06169072 trial examines superparamagnetic iron oxide nanoparticles in an ultra-low dose (0.1 mL) for sentinel lymph node detection in breast cancer, comparing it to the standard Tc99m $\pm$ blue dye dual technique. It also assesses MRI artifacts and skin staining over time, addressing key safety and imaging considerations in clinical practice. Finally, NCT06048367 is a Phase I study evaluating the intratumoral injection of carbon nanoparticle-loaded iron in patients with advanced solid tumors, particularly those harboring KRAS mutations, such as pancreatic cancer. The study investigates dose-limiting toxicities, the maximum tolerated dose, and the therapeutic potential of CNSI–Fe (II) as a ferroptosis-inducing agent. Collectively, these ongoing clinical trials highlight the versatility and promise of theranostic nanoparticles in oncology. By integrating targeted therapy with noninvasive imaging, these systems represent a transformative step toward personalized, adaptive, and precision-based cancer treatment with real-time monitoring and improved therapeutic control. NCT04899908 is a clinical trial evaluating whether AGuIX gadolinium-based nanoparticles can enhance the effectiveness of stereotactic radiation therapy in treating brain metastases that are difficult to control with radiation alone. NCT07047560 is a Phase II, single-arm trial assessing the efficacy and safety of fractionated liposomal irinotecan (FOLFIRInali-3) plus bevacizumab as a second-line treatment for advanced colorectal cancer, with objective response rate as the primary endpoint.

Challenges and limitations

Although theranostic nanoparticles show great promise for advanced cancer treatment, their clinical application faces several obstacles. Major challenges include ensuring biocompatibility, managing long-term toxicity, and preventing unpredictable immune reactions caused by differences in NPs' size, shape, surface charge, and composition. Additionally, balancing both therapeutic and diagnostic capabilities within a single nanoparticle is difficult, often leading to compromises in one function to enhance the other. Limited tumor penetration, fast clearance, and off-target accumulation further reduce therapeutic and imaging potential. Additionally, interpatient variability in tumor biology complicates the design of universally effective theranostic platforms. Standardization in manufacturing, quality control, and scalability is lacking, and regulatory classification, whether as drugs, biologics, or devices, remains ambiguous, delaying approval pathways. Finally, high production costs and insufficient long-term preclinical and clinical data present significant barriers to commercialization and widespread clinical adoption.

Future perspectives

Theranostic nanoparticles represent a cutting-edge approach in cancer treatment by combining targeted therapy with real-time diagnostic capabilities in a single, precisely engineered platform. New developments in nanotechnology aim to deliver treatments like chemotherapy drugs, genetic material, or immune modulators directly to tumors while simultaneously enabling imaging to track how well the therapy is working. Improvements in nanoparticle surface design and responsive materials help these particles overcome biological barriers and adjust to the tumor environment, boosting effectiveness and reducing side effects. Integrating multiple treatment methods, such as photodynamic therapy, heat-based therapy, and radiation enhancement, into one nanoparticle offers a way to tackle drug resistance and achieve enhanced therapeutic results. With the rise of personalized medicine, these multifunctional nanoparticles are set to become key tools for customizing cancer treatments based on individual molecular characteristics, enabling earlier detection, precise therapy, and ongoing monitoring throughout the course of treatment.

Summary and conclusion

Nanoparticles provide unique advantages in delivering drugs directly to target sites, improving imaging techniques, and enabling advanced therapies like photothermal treatment and controlled drug release. Their ability to specifically attack cancer cells while minimizing adverse effects represents a major advancement in cancer care. However, issues concerning their safety, potential toxicity, and integration with existing therapies require additional investigation. Nanotechnology is set to play a crucial role in predictive oncology by improving early diagnosis, enabling precise therapies, and boosting patient outcomes. Nanotheranostics, which integrates diagnostic and therapeutic functions, holds the potential to transform cancer care through more effective, minimally invasive, and personalized treatment strategies.

References

Abbasi, A.Z., Gordijo, C.R., Amini, M.A., Maeda, A., Rauth, A.M., DaCosta, R.S., Wu, X.Y., 2016. Hybrid manganese dioxide nanoparticles potentiate radiation therapy by modulating tumor hypoxia. Cancer Res. 76 (22), 6643–6656. https://doi.org/10.1158/0008-5472.CAN-15-3475.

Ahmad, J., Garg, A., Mustafa, G., Ahmad, M.Z., Aslam, M., Mishra, A., 2023. Hybrid quantum dot as promising tools for theranostic application in cancer. Electronics 12 (4), 972. https://doi.org/10.3390/electronics 12040972.

Akmal Raheem, M., Rahim, M.A., Gul, I., Zhong, X., Xiao, C., Zhang, H., Wei, J., He, Q., Hassan, M., Zhang, C.Y., Yu, D., Pandey, V., Du, K., Wang, R., Han, S., Han, Y., Qin, P., 2023. Advances in nanoparticles-based approaches in cancer theranostics. OpenNano 12. https://doi.org/10.1016/j.onano.2023.100152.

Al-Thani, A.N., Ghafoor Jan, A., Abbas, M., Geetha, M., Kumar Sadasivuni, K., 2024. Nanoparticles in cancer theragnostic and drug delivery: A comprehensive review. Life Sci. 352. https://doi.org/10.1016/j.lfs. 2024.122899.

Amin, M., Huang, W., Seynhaeve, A.L.B., ten Hagen, T.L.M., 2020. Hyperthermia and temperature-sensitive nanomaterials for spatiotemporal drug delivery to solid tumors. Pharmaceutics 12 (11), 1007. https://doi.org/ 10.3390/pharmaceutics12111007.

Azimizonuzi, H., Ghayourvahdat, A., Mareb, H.A., Abdul Kareem, R., Zrzor, A.J., Salah Mansoor, A., Athab, Z.H., Kalavi, S., 2025. A state-of-the-art review of the recent advances of theranostic liposome hybrid nanoparticles in cancer treatment and diagnosis. Cancer Cell Int. 25 (1). https://doi.org/10.1186/s12935-024-03610-z.

Bao, X., Yuan, Y., Chen, J., Zhang, B., Li, Di, Zhou, D., Jing, P., Xu, G., Wang, Y., Holá, K., Shen, D., Wu, C., Song, L., Liu, C., Zbořil, R., Qu, S., 2018. In vivo theranostics with near-infrared-emitting carbon dots—Highly efficient photothermal therapy based on passive targeting after intravenous administration. Light Sci. Appl. 7 (1). https://doi.org/10.1038/s41377-018-0090-1.

Carrese, B., Cavallini, C., Sanità, G., Armanetti, P., Silvestri, B., Calì, G., Pota, G., Luciani, G., Menichetti, L., Lamberti, A., 2021. Controlled release of doxorubicin for targeted chemo-photothermal therapy in breast cancer HS578T cells using albumin modified hybrid nanocarriers. Int. J. Mol. Sci. 22 (20). https://doi.org/10.3390/ ijms222011228.

Carrese, B., Sanità, G., Lamberti, A., 2022. Nanoparticle's design for theranostic approach in cancer disease. Cancers 14 (19), 4654. https://doi.org/10.3390/cancers14194654.

Chen, F., Ehlerding, E.B., Cai, W., 2014a. Theranostic nanoparticles. J. Nucl. Med. 55 (12), 1919–1922. https://doi.org/10.2967/jnumed.114.146019.

Chen, G., Qiu, H., Prasad, P.N., Chen, X., 2014b. Upconversion nanoparticles: Design, nanochemistry, and applications in theranostics. Chem. Rev. 114 (10), 5161–5214. https://doi.org/10.1021/cr400425h.

Coene, A., Leliaert, J., 2022. Magnetic nanoparticles in theranostic applications. J. Appl. Phys. 131 (16). https://doi.org/10.1063/5.0085202.

Cruz, A., Barbosa, J., Antunes, P., Bonifácio, V.D., Pinto, S.N., 2023. A Glimpse into dendrimers integration in cancer imaging and theranostics. Int. J. Mol. Sci. 24 (6), 5430.

Demir, B., Baris Barlas, F., Pinar Gumus, Z., Unak, P., Timur, S., 2018. Theranostic niosomes as a promising tool for combined therapy and diagnosis: "All-in-one" approach. ACS Appl. Nano Mater. 1 (6), 2827–2835. https://doi.org/10.1021/acsanm.8b00468.

Dong, Q., Yang, H., Wan, C., Zheng, D., Zhou, Z., Xie, S., Xu, L., Du, J., Li, F., 2019. Her2-Functionalized gold-nanoshelled magnetic hybrid nanoparticles: A theranostic agent for dual-modal imaging and photothermal therapy of breast cancer. Nanoscale Res. Lett. 14 (1). https://doi.org/10.1186/s11671-019-3053-4.

Dutta Gupta, Y., Mackeyev, Y., Krishnan, S., Bhandary, S., 2024. Mesoporous silica nanotechnology: promising advances in augmenting cancer theranostics. Cancer Nanotechnol. 15 (1), 9.

Elfiky, A.M., Eid, M.M., El-Manawaty, M., Elshahid, Z.A., Mohamed Youssef, E., Mahmoud, K., 2025. Production of novel theranostic nano-vector based on superparamagnetic iron oxide nanoparticles/miR-497 targeting colorectal cancer. Sci. Rep. 15 (1). https://doi.org/10.1038/s41598-025-88165-3.

Feng, L., Cheng, L., Dong, Z., Tao, D., Barnhart, T.E., Cai, W., Chen, M., Liu, Z., 2017. Theranostic liposomes with hypoxia-activated prodrug to effectively destruct hypoxic tumors post-photodynamic therapy. ACS Nano 11 (1), 927–937. https://doi.org/10.1021/acsnano.6b07525.

Fernandes, D.A., 2023a. Review on metal-based theranostic nanoparticles for cancer therapy and imaging. Technol. Cancer Res. Treat. 22. https://doi.org/10.1177/15330338231191493.

Fernandes, D.A., 2023b. Liposomes for cancer theranostics. Pharmaceutics 15 (10), 2448. https://doi.org/10.3390/pharmaceutics15102448.

Ferreira, C.A., Goel, S., Ehlerding, E.B., Rosenkrans, Z.T., Jiang, D., Sun, T., Aluicio-Sarduy, E., Engle, J.W., Ni, D., Cai, W., 2021. Ultrasmall porous silica nanoparticles with enhanced pharmacokinetics for cancer theranostics. Nano Lett. 21 (11), 4692–4699. https://doi.org/10.1021/acs.nanolett.1c00895.

Ganta, S., Singh, A., Kulkarni, P., Keeler, A.W., Piroyan, A., Sawant, R.R., Patel, N.R., Davis, B., Ferris, C., O'Neal, S., Zamboni, W., Amiji, M.M., Coleman, T.P., 2015. EGFR targeted theranostic Nanoemulsion for image-guided ovarian cancer therapy. Pharm. Res. 32 (8), 2753–2763. https://doi.org/10.1007/s11095-015-1660-z.

Gholami, L., Tafaghodi, M., Abbasi, B., Daroudi, M., Kazemi Oskuee, R., 2019. Preparation of superparamagnetic iron oxide/doxorubicin loaded chitosan nanoparticles as a promising glioblastoma theranostic tool. J. Cell. Physiol. 234 (2), 1547–1559. https://doi.org/10.1002/jcp.27019.

Goel, S., England, C.G., Chen, F., Cai, W., 2017. Positron emission tomography and nanotechnology: A dynamic duo for cancer theranostics. Adv. Drug Deliv. Rev. 157–176. https://doi.org/10.1016/j.addr.2016.08.001.

Golubewa, L., Timoshchenko, I., Romanov, O., Karpicz, R., Kulahava, T., Rutkauskas, D., Shuba, M., Dementjev, A., Svirko, Y., Kuzhir, P., 2020. Single-walled carbon nanotubes as a photo-thermo-acoustic cancer theranostic agent: Theory and proof of the concept experiment. Sci. Rep. 10 (1). https://doi.org/10.1038/s41598-020-79238-6.

Gujar, S.K., Maheshwari, S., Björkman-Burtscher, I., Sundgren, P.C., 2005. Magnetic resonance spectroscopy. J. Neuroophthalmol. 25 (3), 217–226. https://doi.org/10.1097/01.wno.0000177307.21081.81.

Gupta, D., Roy, P., Sharma, R., Kasana, R., Rathore, P., Gupta, T.K., 2024. Recent nanotheranostic approaches in cancer research. Clin. Exp. Med. 24 (1). https://doi.org/10.1007/s10238-023-01262-3.

Hashemi, Z., Kaveh Zenjanab, M., Pourbakhsh, M., Doustmihan, A., Fathi, M., Rana, J.E., 2025. Hyaluronic acid-modified theranostic niosomes for targeted fingolimod delivery and inhibition of triple-negative breast cancer metastasis. Med. Oncol. 42 (7). https://doi.org/10.1007/s12032-025-02796-0.

Hosseini, S.M., Mohammadnejad, J., Salamat, S., Beiram Zadeh, Z., Tanhaei, M., Ramakrishna, S., 2023. Theranostic polymeric nanoparticles as a new approach in cancer therapy and diagnosis: A review. Mater. Today Chem. 29. https://doi.org/10.1016/j.mtchem.2023.101400.

Hsieh, H.H., Su, S.P., Chan, Y.H., Chiang, H.K., Lee, Y.J., Wu, C.Y., 2025. Development of theranostic 177Lu-labeled polymeric nanoparticles (177Lu-PNPs) for the treatment of head and neck cancer. ACS Appl. Bio Mater. 8 (6), 5266–5275. https://doi.org/10.1021/acsabm.5c00579.

Huang, P., Wang, C., Deng, H., Zhou, Y., Chen, X., 2023. Surface engineering of nanoparticles toward cancer theranostics. Acc. of Chem. Res. 56 (13), 1766–1779. https://doi.org/10.1021/acs.accounts.3c00122.

Jha, A., Kumar, M., Mishra, B., 2023. Gold Nanoparticles as Theranostic Platform Inorganic Nanosystems: Theranostic Nanosystems, vol2. Elsevier, India, pp. 279–321. https://doi.org/10.1016/B978-0-323-85784-0.00007-8.

Jędrzak, A., Grześkowiak, B.F., Coy, E., Wojnarowicz, J., Szutkowski, K., Jurga, S., Jesionowski, T., Mrówczyński, R., 2019. Dendrimer based theranostic nanostructures for combined chemo- and photothermal therapy of liver cancer cells in vitro. Colloids Surf. B Biointerfaces 173, 698–708. https://doi.org/10.1016/j.colsurfb.2018.10.045.

Jia, X., Wang, Y., Qiao, Y., Jiang, X., Li, J., 2024. Nanomaterial-based regulation of redox metabolism for enhancing cancer therapy. Chem. Soc. Rev. 53 (23), 11590–11656. https://doi.org/10.1039/d4cs00404c.

Jung, K.O., Jo, H., Yu, J.H., Gambhir, S.S., Pratx, G., 2018. Development and MPI tracking of novel hypoxia-targeted theranostic exosomes. Biomaterials 177, 139–148. https://doi.org/10.1016/j.biomaterials.2018.05.048.

Kandasamy, G., Maity, D., 2021. Multifunctional theranostic nanoparticles for biomedical cancer treatments - a comprehensive review. Mater. Sci. Eng. C Mater. Biol. Appl. 127. https://doi.org/10.1016/j.msec.2021.112199.

Karthikeyan, L., Sobhana, S., Yasothamani, V., Gowsalya, K., Vivek, R., 2023. Multifunctional theranostic nanomedicines for cancer treatment: Recent progress and challenges. Biomed. Eng. Adv. 5. https://doi.org/10.1016/j.bea.2023.100082.

Kashyap, B.K., Singh, V.V., Solanki, M.K., Kumar, A., Ruokolainen, J., Kesari, K.K., 2023. Smart nanomaterials in cancer theranostics: Challenges and opportunities. ACS Omega 8 (16), 14290–14320. https://doi.org/10.1021/acsomega.2c07840.

Kesharwani, P., Chadar, R., Shukla, R., Jain, G.K., Aggarwal, G., Abourehab, M.A., Sahebkar, A., 2022. Recent advances in multifunctional dendrimer-based nanoprobes for breast cancer theranostics. J. Biomater. Sci. Polymer Ed. 33 (18), 2433–2471.

Khajuria, A., Alajangi, H.K., Sharma, A., Kaur, H., Sharma, P., Negi, S., Kumari, L., Trivedi, M., Yadav, A.K., Kumar, R., Raghuvanshi, R.S., Kaur, I.P., Tyagi, R.K., Jaiswal, P.K., Lim, Y.-beom, Barnwal, R.P., Singh, G., 2024. Theranostics: Aptamer-assisted carbon nanotubes as MRI contrast and photothermal agent for breast cancer therapy. Discov. Nano 19 (1). https://doi.org/10.1186/s11671-024-04095-5.

Kumar, P.P.P., Lim, D.-K., 2023. Photothermal effect of gold nanoparticles as a nanomedicine for diagnosis and therapeutics. Pharmaceutics 15 (9), 2349. https://doi.org/10.3390/pharmaceutics15092349.

Kumar Parashar, A., Saraogi, G.K., Shrivastava, V., Bagri, R., Tyagi, L.K., Arora Sethi, V., Jain, P.K., 2025. Development of angiopep-2 targeted dendrimer-based nanotheranostic system for enhanced temozolomide delivery to glioblastoma multiforme. Bull. Natl. Res. Cent. 49 (1). https://doi.org/10.1186/s42269-025-01309-3.

Kumar Rajora, A., Ahire, E.D., Rajora, M., Singh, S., Bhattacharya, J., Zhang, H., 2024. Emergence and impact of theranostic-nanoformulation of triple therapeutics for combination cancer therapy. Smart Med. 3 (1). https://doi.org/10.1002/smmd.20230035.

Kumar, M., Jha, A., Mishra, B., 2023. Polymeric Nanosystems for Cancer Theranostics Polymeric Nanosystems: Theranostic Nanosystems, vol. 1. Elsevier, India Elsevier, India, pp. 657–697. https://doi.org/10.1016/B978-0-323-85656-0.00004-8.

Li, K., Nejadnik, H., Daldrup-Link, H.E., 2017. Next-generation superparamagnetic iron oxide nanoparticles for cancer theranostics. Drug Discov. Today 22 (9), 1421–1429. https://doi.org/10.1016/j.drudis.2017.04.008.

Li, X., Jiang, M., Zeng, S., Liu, H., 2019. Polydopamine coated multifunctional lanthanide theranostic agent for vascular malformation and tumor vessel imaging beyond 1500 nm and imaging-guided photothermal therapy. Theranostics 9 (13), 3866–3878. https://doi.org/10.7150/thno.31864.

Li, S., Su, W., Wu, H., Yuan, T., Yuan, C., Liu, J., Deng, G., Gao, X., Chen, Z., Bao, Y., Yuan, F., Zhou, S., Tan, H., Li, Y., Li, X., Fan, L., Zhu, J., Chen, A.T., Liu, F., Zhou, Y., Miao, L., Zhai, X., Zhou, J., 2020. Targeted tumour theranostics in mice via carbon quantum dots structurally mimicking large amino acids. Nat. Biomed. Eng. 4 (7), 704–716. https://doi.org/10.1038/s41551-020-0540-y.

Li, S., Kwok-Ho, L., Li, X., Fang, X., Wai-Sum, L., Gu, Y.-J., Wong, W.-T., 2021. pH-triggered poly (ethylene glycol)–Poly (lactic acid/glycolic acid)/croconaine nanoparticles-assisted multiplexed photoacoustic imaging and enhanced photothermal cancer therapy. ACS Appl. Bio Mater. 4 (5), 4152–4164. https://doi.org/10.1021/acsabm.0c01578.

Li, H., Yue, F., Luo, Q., Li, Z., Li, X., Gan, H., Gu, Z., Gong, Q., Luo, K., 2023a. Stimuli-activatable nanomedicine meets cancer theranostics. Theranostics 13 (15), 5386–5417. https://doi.org/10.7150/thno.87854.

Li, T., Wu, M., Wei, Q., Xu, D., He, X., Wang, J., Wu, J., Chen, L., 2023b. Conjugated polymer nanoparticles for tumor theranostics. Biomacromolecules 24 (5), 1943–1979. https://doi.org/10.1021/acs.biomac.2c01446.

Li, X., Yue, R., Guan, G., Zhang, C., Zhou, Y., Song, G., 2023c. Recent development of pH-responsive theranostic nanoplatforms for magnetic resonance imaging-guided cancer therapy. Exploration 3 (3). https://doi.org/10.1002/exp.20220002.

Liao, W.-T., Chang, D.-M., Lin, M.-X., Chou, T.-S., Tung, Y.-C., Hsiao, J.-K., 2025. Multifaceted functional liposomes: theranostic potential of liposomal indocyanine green and doxorubicin for enhanced anticancer efficacy and imaging. Pharmaceutics 17 (3), 344. https://doi.org/10.3390/pharmaceutics17030344.

Liu, Y., Bhattarai, P., Dai, Z., Chen, X., 2019. Photothermal therapy and photoacoustic imaging via nanotheranostics in fighting cancer. Chem. Soc. Rev. 48 (7), 2053–2108. https://doi.org/10.1039/c8cs00618k.

López-Valverde, J.A., Jiménez-Ortega, E., Leal, A., 2022. Clinical feasibility study of gold nanoparticles as theragnostic agents for precision radiotherapy. Biomedicines 10 (5). https://doi.org/10.3390/biomedicines10051214.

Mangadlao, J.D., Wang, X., McCleese, C., Escamilla, M., Ramamurthy, G., Wang, Z., Govande, M., Basilion, J.P., Burda, C., 2018. Prostate-specific membrane antigen targeted gold nanoparticles for theranostics of prostate cancer. ACS Nano 12 (4), 3714–3725. https://doi.org/10.1021/acsnano.8b00940.

Michael, B., Srinivasan, M., Elumalai, K., Ravikumar, L., Kathiresan, S., Jayaprakash, N., 2025. Thermoresponsive nanomaterials: Revolutionizing cancer theranostics. Biomed. Mater. Devices 2731–4812. https://doi.org/10.1007/s44174-025-00400-7.

Mohapatra, D., Bayazeed Alam, Md, Pandey, V., Pratap, R., Dubey, P.K., Parmar, A.S., Sahu, A.N., 2021. Carbon dots from an immunomodulatory plant for cancer cell imaging, free radical scavenging and metal sensing applications. Nanomedicine 16 (23), 2039–2059. https://doi.org/10.2217/nnm-2021-0190.

Mohapatra, D., Pratap, R., Pandey, V., Dubey, P.K., Agrawal, A.K., Parmar, A.S., Sahu, A.N., 2022. Tinospora cordifolia leaves derived carbon dots for cancer cell bioimaging, free radical scavenging, and Fe3+ sensing applications. J. Fluoresc. 32 (1), 275–292. https://doi.org/10.1007/s10895-021-02846-6.

Mohapatra, D., Pratap, R., Pandey, V., Singh, S., Naik, G.G., Mandal, S.C., Otimenyin, S.O., Dubey, P.K., Parmar, A. S., Sahu, A.N., 2023. Bioengineered dual fluorescent carbon nano dots from Indian long pepper leaves for multifaceted environmental and health utilities. Environ. Sci. Pollut. Control Ser. 30 (18), 52182–52208. https://doi.org/10.1007/s11356-023-25887-9.

Mostafavi, E., Iravani, S., Varma, R.S., Khatami, M., Rahbarizadeh, F., 2022. Eco-friendly synthesis of carbon nanotubes and their cancer theranostic applications. Mater. Adv. 3 (12), 4765–4782. https://doi.org/10.1039/d2ma00341d.

Muangsopa, P., Yong, G.Y., Thathong, Y., Kampaengsri, S., Chansaenpak, K., Saetiew, J., Khrootkaew, T., Jantasin, A., Meemon, P., Sukwattanasinitt, M., Kue, C.S., Kamkaew, A., 2025. Heavy-atom-free aza-BODIPY polymeric nanoparticles for theranostic-guided photodynamic cancer therapy. ACS Appl. Bio Mater. 2576–6422. https://doi.org/10.1021/acsabm.5c00878.

Mukherjee, P., Kumar, A., Bhamidipati, K., Puvvada, N., Sahu, S.K., 2020. Facile strategy to synthesize magnetic upconversion nanoscale metal–organic framework composites for theranostics application. ACS Appl. Bio Mater. 3 (2), 869–880. https://doi.org/10.1021/acsabm.9b00949.

Naderlou, S., Mohammadi, A., Zareian, D.A., Torkzaban, M., Danafar, H., 2025. Computational modeling and experimental synthesis of BSA-coated bimetallic theranostic MnO_2-Au@curcumin nanoplatform for synergistic radiochemotherapy of breast cancer. Int. J. Biol. Macromol. 318 (Pt 4). https://doi.org/10.1016/j.ijbiomac.2025.145184.

Nasri, N., Saharkhiz, S., Dini, G., Ghasemvand, F., 2024. In vitro study of a new theranostic smart niosomal nanostructure for direct delivery of docetaxel via anti-PSMA aptamer. Heliyon 10 (17). https://doi.org/10.1016/j.heliyon.2024.e37341.

Nowroozi, F., Dadashzadeh, S., Soleimanjahi, H., Haeri, A., Shahhosseini, S., Javidi, J., Karimi, H., 2018. Theranostic niosomes for direct intratumoral injection: Marked enhancement in tumor retention and anticancer efficacy. Nanomedicine 13 (17), 2201–2219. https://doi.org/10.2217/nnm-2018-0091.

Ovejero-Paredes, K., Díaz-García, D., Mena-Palomo, I., Marciello, M., Lozano-Chamizo, L., Morato, Y.L., Prashar, S., Gómez-Ruiz, S., Filice, M., 2022. Synthesis of a theranostic platform based on fibrous silica nanoparticles for the enhanced treatment of triple-negative breast cancer promoted by a combination of chemotherapeutic agents. Biomater. Adv 137. https://doi.org/10.1016/j.bioadv.2022.212823.

Ovejero-Paredes, K., Bisbano, G., Flier, I., González-Simón, A., Marciello, M., Oliveira, S., Zupi, M., Rubes, D., Ayash, F., Doria, F., Pirota, V., Terreni, M., Serra, M., Filice, M., 2025. Microfluidic-assisted synthesis of integrin-targeting cRGD liposomes as a scalable strategy for theranostic applications in triple-negative breast cancer. Eur. J. Pharmaceut. Sci. 213. https://doi.org/10.1016/j.ejps.2025.107216.

Ozgenc, E., Karpuz, M., Arzuk, E., Gonzalez-Alvarez, M., Sanz, M.B., Gundogdu, E., Gonzalez-Alvarez, I., 2022. Radiolabeled trastuzumab solid lipid nanoparticles for breast cancer cell: in vitro and in vivo studies. ACS Omega 7 (34), 30015–30027.

Patel, M., Patel, M., 2024. Design and characterization of superparamagnetic iron oxide nanoparticles of nintedanib for theranostic application. Colloids Surf. A Physicochem. Eng. Asp. 697. https://doi.org/10.1016/j.colsurfa.2024.134446.

Pawar, V., Maske, P., Khan, A., Ghosh, A., Keshari, R., Bhatt, M., Srivastava, R., 2023. Responsive nanostructure for targeted drug delivery. J. Nanotheranostics 4 (1), 55–85. https://doi.org/10.3390/jnt4010004.

Prasad, R., Yadav, A.S., Gorain, M., Chauhan, D.S., Kundu, G.C., Srivastava, R., Selvaraj, K., 2019. Graphene oxide supported liposomes as red emissive theranostics for phototriggered tissue visualization and tumor regression. ACS App. Bio Mater. 2 (8), 3312–3320. https://doi.org/10.1021/acsabm.9b00335.

Radnia, F., Mohajeri, N., Zarghami, N., 2020. New insight into the engineering of green carbon dots: Possible applications in emerging cancer theranostics. Talanta 209. https://doi.org/10.1016/j.talanta.2019.120547.

Ray, S., Li, Z., Hsu, C.-H., Hwang, L.-P., Lin, Y.-C., Chou, P.-T., Lin, Y.-Y., 2018. Dendrimer-and copolymer-based nanoparticles for magnetic resonance cancer theranostics. Theranostics 8 (22), 6322.

Romani, C., Bellucci, M.C., Di Pietro, M.E., Gagni, P., Sponchioni, M., Volonterio, A., 2025. Fluorinated redox-responsive cross-linked poly (amidoamine) G2 as smart theranostic dendrimers. Biomacromolecules 1525–7797. https://doi.org/10.1021/acs.biomac.5c00914.

Saharkhiz, S., Zarepour, A., Ali, Z., 2023. A new theranostic pH-responsive niosome formulation for doxorubicin delivery and bio-imaging against breast cancer. Int. J. Pharm. 637. https://doi.org/10.1016/j.ijpharm.2023.122845.

Sakr, T.M., Thipe, V.C., Katti, K.K., Watkinson, L., Carmack, T., Smith, C.J., Cutler, C., Hegde, P., Hegde, A., Lugão, A.B., Katti, K.V., 2025. Immunomodulatory green nanomedicine production, tumor cellular targeting, in vivo biodistributions and preclinical therapeutic efficacy investigations of resveratrol-functionalized gold and theranostic 198 gold nanoparticles. J. Mater. Chem. B 13 (27), 8038–8050. https://doi.org/10.1039/d5tb00815h.

Sarcan, E.T., Silindir-Gunay, M., Ozer, A.Y., 2018. Theranostic polymeric nanoparticles for NIR imaging and photodynamic therapy. Int. J. Pharm. 551 (1–2), 329–338. https://doi.org/10.1016/j.ijpharm.2018.09.019.

Sharma, A., Modgil, M., Joshi, G., Bisht, P., 2024. Recent update on nanoparticles based approaches for management of cancer: Wave from traditional to advanced technology. Curr. Cancer Drug Targets 25. https://doi.org/10.2174/0115680096323618240911140624.

Sharmiladevi, P., Girigoswami, K., Haribabu, V., Girigoswami, A., 2021. Nano-enabled theranostics for cancer. Mater. Adv. 2 (9), 2876–2891. https://doi.org/10.1039/d1ma00069a.

Shakil, M.S., Hasan, M.A., Sarker, S.R., 2019. Iron oxide nanoparticles for breast cancer theranostics. Curr. Drug Metab. 20 (6), 446–456. https://doi.org/10.2174/1389200220666181122105043.

Sikder, A., Vambhurkar, G., Amulya, E., Bagasariya, D., Famta, P., Shah, S., Khatri, D.K., Singh, S.B., Sinha, V.R., Srivastava, S., 2022. Advancements in redox-sensitive micelles as nanotheranostics: A new horizon in cancer management. J. Contr. Release 349, 1009–1030. https://doi.org/10.1016/j.jconrel.2022.08.008.

Silvestri, B., Armanetti, P., Sanità, G., Vitiello, G., Lamberti, A., Calì, G., Pezzella, A., Luciani, G., Menichetti, L., Luin, S., d'Ischia, M., 2019. Silver-nanoparticles as plasmon-resonant enhancers for eumelanin's photoacoustic signal in a self-structured hybrid nanoprobe. Mater. Sci. Eng. C Mater Biol Appl. 102, 788–797. https://doi.org/10.1016/j.msec.2019.04.066.

Tan, E., Snee, P.T., Danışman-Kalındemirtaş, F., 2024. An investigation of quantum dot theranostic probes for prostate and leukemia cancer cells using a CdZnSeS QD-based nanoformulation. J. Colloid Interface Sci. 675, 1032–1039. https://doi.org/10.1016/j.jcis.2024.07.075.

Tan, J., Zhu, D., Li, G., Hu, H., Lai, Z., Li, Z., 2025. A novel theranostic system of PD-L1-Aptamer-functionalized fluorescent silica nanoparticles for triple-negative breast cancer. Nanomed. Nanotechnol. Biol. Med. 68. https://doi.org/10.1016/j.nano.2025.102834.

Tang, L., Xiao, Q., Mei, Y., He, S., Zhang, Z., Wang, R., Wang, W., 2021. Insights on functionalized carbon nanotubes for cancer theranostics. J. Nanobiotechnol. 19 (1). https://doi.org/10.1186/s12951-021-01174-y.

Tang, C., Zhou, K., Wu, Di, Zhu, H., 2024. Nanoparticles as a novel platform for cardiovascular disease diagnosis and therapy. Int. J. Nanomed. 19, 8831–8846. https://doi.org/10.2147/ijn.s474888.

Tripathi, S.K., Kaur, G., Kaur Khurana, R., Kapoor, S., Singh, B., 2015. Quantum dots and their potential role in cancer theranostics. Crit. Rev. Ther. Drug Carrier Syst. 32 (6), 461–502. https://doi.org/10.1615/critrevtherdrugcarriersyst.2015012360.

Wang, C., Sun, X., Cheng, L., Yin, S., Yang, G., Li, Y., Liu, Z., 2014. Multifunctional theranostic red blood cells for magnetic-field-enhanced in vivo combination therapy of cancer. Adv. Mater. 26 (28), 4794–4802. https://doi.org/10.1002/adma.201400158.

Wang, Z., Qiao, R., Tang, N., Lu, Z., Wang, H., Zhang, Z., Xue, X., Huang, Z., Zhang, S., Zhang, G., Li, Y., 2017a. Active targeting theranostic iron oxide nanoparticles for MRI and magnetic resonance-guided focused ultrasound ablation of lung cancer. Biomaterials 127, 25–35. https://doi.org/10.1016/j.biomaterials.2017.02.037.

Wang, H., Bi, J., Zhu, B.-W., Tan, M., 2018. Multicolorful carbon dots for tumor theranostics. Curr. Med. Chem. 25 (25), 2894–2909. https://doi.org/10.2174/0929867324666170316110810.

Wang, L., Li, D., Hao, Y., Niu, M., Hu, Y., Zhao, H., Chang, J., Zhang, Z., Zhang, Y., 2017b. Gold nanorod–based poly (lactic-co-glycolic acid) with manganese dioxide core–shell structured multifunctional nanoplatform for cancer theranostic applications. Int. J. Nanomed. 12, 3059–3075. https://doi.org/10.2147/ijn.s128844.

WHO, 2024. GLOBOCAN. International Agency for Research on Cancer. Available from: https://gco.iarc.fr/en. Available from: (Accessed 25 July 2025).

Xia, W., Tao, Z., Zhu, B., Zhang, W., Liu, C., Chen, S., Song, M., 2021. Targeted delivery of drugs and genes using polymer nanocarriers for cancer therapy. Int. J. Mol. Sci. 22 (17), 9118. https://doi.org/10.3390/ijms22179118.

Xu, G., Lin, G., Lin, S., Wu, N., Deng, Y., Feng, G., Chen, Q., Qu, J., Chen, D., Chen, S., Niu, H., Mei, S., Yong, K.-T., Wang, X., 2016. The reproductive toxicity of CdSe/ZnS quantum dots on the in vivo ovarian function and in vitro fertilization. Sci. Rep. 6 (1). https://doi.org/10.1038/srep37677.

Xue, Y., Gao, Y., Meng, F., Luo, L., 2021. Recent progress of nanotechnology-based theranostic systems in cancer treatments. Cancer Biol. Med. 18 (2), 336–351. https://doi.org/10.20892/j.issn.2095-3941.2020.0510.

Yang, X., Wang, D., Ma, Y., Zhao, Q., Fallon, J.K., Liu, D., Xu, X.E., Wang, Y., He, Z., Liu, F., Nanoemulsions, T., 2014. Codelivery of hydrophobic drug and hydrophilic imaging probe for cancer therapy and imaging. Nanomedicine 9 (18), 2773–2785. https://doi.org/10.2217/nnm.14.50.

Yang, Z., Song, J., Tang, W., Fan, W., Dai, Y., Shen, Z., Lin, L., Cheng, S., Liu, Y., Niu, G., Rong, P., Wang, W., Chen, X., 2019. Stimuli-responsive nanotheranostics for real-time monitoring drug release by photoacoustic imaging. Theranostics 9 (2), 526–536. https://doi.org/10.7150/thno.30779.

Yao, J., Feng, J., Chen, J., 2016. External-stimuli responsive systems for cancer theranostic. Asian J. Pharm. Sci 11 (5), 585–595. https://doi.org/10.1016/j.ajps.2016.06.001.

Yoon, Y.I., Pang, X., Jung, S., Zhang, G., Kong, M., Liu, G., Chen, X., 2018. Smart gold nanoparticle-stabilized ultrasound microbubbles as cancer theranostics. J. Mater. Chem. B 6 (20), 3235–3239. https://doi.org/10.1039/c8tb00368h.

Zhang, H., Zhang, L.X., Zhong, H., Niu, S., Ding, C., Lv, S., 2022. Iridium oxide nanoparticles-based theranostic probe for in vivo tumor imaging and synergistic chem/photothermal treatments of cancer cells. Chem. Eng. J. 430. https://doi.org/10.1016/j.cej.2021.132675.

Zhao, S., Yu, X., Qian, Y., Chen, W., Shen, J., 2020. Multifunctional magnetic iron oxide nanoparticles: An advanced platform for cancer theranostics. Theranostics 10 (14), 6278–6309. https://doi.org/10.7150/thno.42564.

Zhou, T., Cheng, Q., Zhang, L., Zhang, D., Lin, L., Jiang, T., Huang, L., Xu, H., Hu, M., Jing, S., 2022. Ferrocene-functionalized core–shell lanthanide-doped upconversion nanoparticles: NIR light promoted chemodynamic therapy and luminescence imaging of solid tumors. Chem. Eng. J. 438. https://doi.org/10.1016/j.cej.2022.135637.

Zhu, Y., Bai, Y., He, J., Qiu, X., 2023. Advances in the stimuli-responsive mesoporous silica nanoparticles as drug delivery system nanotechnology for controlled release and cancer therapy. 3 Biotech 13 (8), 274.

CHAPTER

21

DNA based nanomaterials for anticancer therapy

Shweta Singh[1], *Ajay Pandey*[1], *Abhishek Sharma*[1], *Simran Kanwar*[2], *Aman*[2], *Ruchi Chawla*[1] and *Ravi Bhushan Singh*[2]

[1]Department of Pharmaceutical Engineering and Technology, Indian Institute of Technology (BHU), Varanasi, Uttar Pradesh, India; [2]CEPS, Guru Gobind Singh Indraprastha University, Dwarka, New Delhi, India

Introduction

Cancer remains a dominant global health burden characterized by rising incidence, high mortality, and substantial socioeconomic impact. Despite advancements in targeted biologics, chemotherapy, radiation, immunotherapy, and surgical oncology, long-term clinical results are still constrained by tumor heterogeneity, systemic toxicity, and treatment resistance. Traditional chemotherapeutics often have limited therapeutic indices and poor tumor selectivity, leading to off-target cytotoxicity and mechanisms of multidrug resistance fueled by genomic instability and efflux pumps. The biological complexity of the tumor microenvironment, which includes immune evasion, stromal barriers, and hypoxia, further impairs the effectiveness of treatment. These restrictions have led to extensive research on nanoscale delivery technologies that can increase tumor accumulation, reduce systemic exposure, and facilitate multipurpose treatment approaches (Shi et al., 2017).

DNA-based nanomaterials have emerged as a revolutionary class of programmable therapeutic platforms in this evolving environment. DNA nanostructures, in contrast to traditional polymeric or lipid nanoparticles, are assembled via predictable Watson–Crick base pairing, enabling stoichiometric cargo organization and nanoscale architectural accuracy. DNA's molecular recognition, enzymatic biodegradability, and intrinsic biocompatibility make it an exceptionally adaptable platform for anticancer treatment. Developments in structural DNA nanotechnology, such as dynamic strand displacement circuits and DNA origami, have increased the number of useful nanodevices available for theranostic

Advanced Cancer Therapeutics
https://doi.org/10.1016/B978-0-443-44185-1.00016-1

integration, logic-gated release, and targeted distribution (Seeman, 2003). DNA nanoparticles offer a significant conceptual advantage in cancer beyond their structural programmability: they enable therapeutic integration at the molecular information level. Mutations, epigenetic dysregulation, and abnormal signaling networks are the main causes of cancer, which is essentially a genomic illness. DNA-based nanostructures can directly interact with nucleic acid pathways using antisense oligonucleotides, siRNA, miRNA mimics, or CRISPR-associated components, in contrast to conventional carriers that just deliver medications. DNA nanotechnology is positioned at the intersection of gene therapy and nanomedicine due to its inherent compatibility with genetic therapies. Additionally, the precise spatial organization of several therapeutic modules enabled by DNA scaffolds allows for the synergistic codelivery of gene-silencing drugs and chemotherapeutics within a single nanoscale construct. In preclinical models, this kind of multimodal integration has been shown to increase intracellular uptake and enhance tumor inhibition (Ammar et al., 2025).

Crucially, the tumor microenvironment (TME) presents intricate biological barriers that limit efficient drug penetration, including high interstitial fluid pressure, thick extracellular matrix deposition, and aberrant vasculature. To limit tumor penetration and cellular internalization, DNA nanostructures with regulated size, shape, and surface topology can be created. According to new data, the structural geometry of DNA has a major impact on biodistribution profiles and cellular uptake pathways; wireframe or tubular DNA designs exhibit better tissue distribution than compact spherical designs. This design flexibility enables rational optimization tailored to specific tumor types and anatomical constraints. In translational research, the structure-dependent biological performance of DNA nanoparticles has been thoroughly examined (Zhao et al., 2025). The ability of DNA nanotechnology to precisely deliver ligands is another characteristic that sets it apart in cancer treatment. To increase binding avidity to overexpressed tumor receptors, multivalent display of targeting moieties, such as folate, RGD peptides, HER2 aptamers, or antibody fragments, may be strategically arranged with nanoscale precision. DNA-based assembly offers precise control over ligand quantity and orientation, in contrast to polymeric nanoparticles that employ stochastic conjugation techniques. This degree of architectural control might greatly enhance receptor internalization and clustering, thereby increasing the therapeutic index (Chehelgerdi et al., 2023). Various hallmarks of cancer are mentioned in Fig. 21.1. Collectively, these characteristics demonstrate how DNA nanoparticles in anticancer treatment constitute a paradigm change. DNA nanostructures are programmable molecular platforms that can sense, compute, and respond within biological systems, rather than merely serving as passive carriers. This intersection of molecular oncology and structural nanotechnology serves as the foundation for the current chapter, which methodically examines the design principles, therapeutic potential, translational challenges, and potential applications of DNA-based nanomaterials in precision cancer treatment.

Cancer burden and limitations of conventional anticancer therapies

Cancer is still one of the leading causes of illness and death globally, and its prevalence is growing gradually due to environmental factors, changing lifestyles, and population aging. Over the next 20 years, it is anticipated that there will be more than 28 million new instances

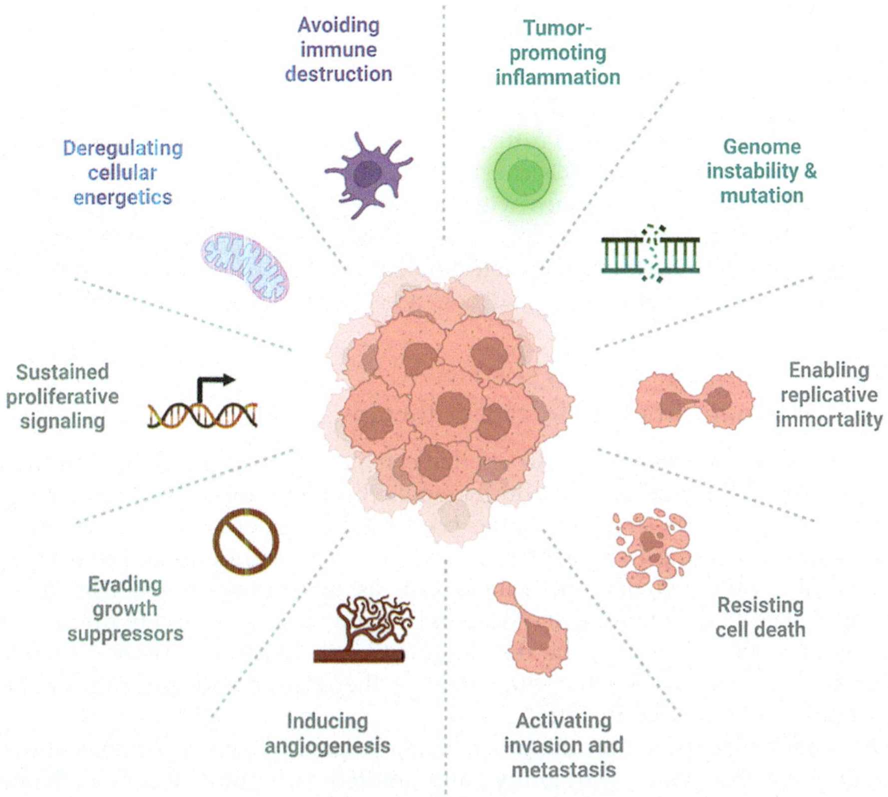

FIGURE 21.1 Hallmarks of cancer.

of cancer annually, putting an unprecedented strain on healthcare systems and drug development pipelines, according to current epidemiological assessments. For many solid tumors, especially those that are lung, pancreatic, or glioblastoma malignancies, survival results are still below ideal levels despite improvements in early identification and multimodal therapy. Adaptive resistance mechanisms, tumor heterogeneity, and metastatic progression significantly reduce the long-term therapeutic effectiveness, underscoring the need for novel therapeutic paradigms that go beyond traditional cytotoxic approaches. The ongoing increase in cancer-related fatalities, together with the serious side effects and inherent hazards of current therapies, emphasizes the pressing need for more individualized and efficient solutions. Because of their affordability and wide applicability, conventional treatments remain the most widely used, even as cutting-edge medicines such as gene therapy and immunotherapy are developed. Thus, as shown in Fig. 21.1, continuous efforts to enhance traditional cancer treatments, such as surgery, radiation, chemotherapy, and hormone therapy, remain crucial. The goal of this study is to provide a thorough analysis of the strengths and limitations of these conventional treatments. By examining their current situation, development, and persistent difficulties, we aim to pinpoint unmet needs and identify possible directions for further study and creativity (Zafar et al., 2025).

Systemic toxicity, poor tumor selectivity, and dose-limiting side effects are common limitations of conventional anticancer modalities, such as chemotherapy, radiation, and surgical resection. Due to their limited therapeutic indices, small-molecule chemotherapeutics often cause off-target cytotoxicity in rapidly proliferating healthy tissues, such as the gastrointestinal epithelium and bone marrow. Furthermore, treatment effectiveness is compromised by multidrug resistance (MDR), which is caused by genomic instability and efflux transporters. Biological treatments still face issues with immunogenicity, pharmacokinetics, and challenges in the tumor microenvironment, while being more targeted. Together, these difficulties support the investigation of nanotechnology-enabled delivery methods to increase accuracy, reduce systemic exposure, and enhance therapeutic results (Minh Haong et al., 2025).

Emergence of nanotechnology in cancer therapy

The rational design of nanoscale carriers that can alter pharmacokinetics and tumor accumulation has revolutionized oncological therapies through nanotechnology. The increased permeability and retention (EPR) effect has been used to target tumors passively by developing nanocarriers ranging from liposomes and polymeric nanoparticles to inorganic platforms. Clinically validated nanomedicines, such as liposomal doxorubicin, demonstrate the translational potential of nanoscale systems by exhibiting better safety profiles than their free-drug equivalents. Crucially, the development of theranostic systems is facilitated by nanotechnology, which enables the integration of therapeutic and imaging capabilities on a single platform (Ammar et al., 2025).

Conventional nanocarriers, on the other hand, frequently have poor control over cargo stoichiometry, batch-to-batch variability, and limited structural accuracy. Biomolecule-based nanomaterials, especially those derived from nucleic acids, have emerged as highly programmable and structurally specified alternatives in this setting. DNA nanotechnology enables the construction of structures with predictable self-assembly, adjustable shape, and nanometer-scale precision. Because of these characteristics, DNA-based nanomaterials are positioned as potential next-generation materials that can get beyond the drawbacks of synthetic polymeric or lipid systems (Gressler et al., 2025).

Why DNA as a nanomaterial?

DNA's intrinsic biocompatibility and molecular recognition make it a particularly adaptable building element. DNA is a naturally occurring biopolymer that degrades predictably by enzymes into physiologically acceptable nucleotides and has little inherent toxicity. In biological systems, DNA nanostructures are often well tolerated when properly constructed, whereas synthetic polymers can accumulate or trigger inflammatory responses. Moreover, PEGylation and phosphorothioate linkages are examples of chemical changes that might improve stability without sacrificing biocompatibility (Mathur and Medintz, 2019). Through Watson–Crick base pairing, DNA offers unmatched programmability beyond biocompatibility, enabling precise control over the size, shape, and spatial arrangement of functional moieties. Chemotherapeutic drugs, targeting ligands, and imaging probes can be stoichiometrically loaded with nanoscale precision through sequence-defined assembly. It is challenging to get this molecular accuracy with traditional nanoparticle technologies. As a result, DNA nanostructures offer a modular framework for building multipurpose anticancer systems with logic-responsive behavior, controlled release, and targeted delivery (Ding et al., 2025).

Scope and objectives of the chapter

To provide a thorough and critical assessment of DNA-based nanomaterials in anticancer therapy, this chapter will focus on their therapeutic mechanisms, structural underpinnings, translational challenges, and future prospects. The rational engineering of DNA nanostructures to overcome tumor-specific obstacles, such as immunological evasion, drug resistance, and heterogeneity, is given special consideration. By incorporating new research from prestigious publications, the chapter situates DNA nanotechnology within the context of precision oncology (Kumar et al., 2016). To determine the viability of clinical translation, the chapter also assesses practical factors, including stability, pharmacokinetics, scalability, and regulatory considerations. The discussion of cutting-edge ideas such as AI-assisted design and logic-gated nanodevices aims to highlight revolutionary trends shaping the next 10 years of research. Together, these analyses aim to connect basic nanotechnology concepts with pharmaceutical development strategies, offering a path forward for bringing DNA nanoparticles from the lab to clinical use (Panda and Mohapatra, 2025).

Fundamentals of DNA-based nanomaterials

The physicochemical and structural characteristics of nucleic acids provide DNA-based nanomaterials with their functional capabilities. While the negatively charged phosphate backbone permits electrostatic interactions with cationic drugs and biomolecules, the double-helical structure, supported by hydrogen bonding and base stacking, provides a predictable geometry and mechanical stability. Two- and three-dimensional nanostructures with precisely specified dimensions, surface patterns, and cargo placement may be formed using scaffolded DNA origami and tile-based assembly techniques. The structural control achievable with the majority of synthetic nanocarriers is surpassed by the atomic-level programmability (Rothemund, 2006; Wang et al., 2025). DNA nanoparticles provide functional versatility, biodegradability, and adjustable stability in addition to structural accuracy. While maintaining regulated enzymatic degradation, protective coatings, crosslinking techniques, and chemical backbone changes can improve serum stability. Additionally, dynamic strand displacement methods enable the development of sensitive systems that can release drugs in response to environmental stimuli or tumor-associated nucleic acids. These characteristics enhance multifunctional anticancer applications by enabling the integration of therapeutic payloads, imaging agents, and targeting ligands within a single scaffold (Wilhelm et al., 2016) Fig. 21.2.

Beyond structural precision, DNA nanomaterials offer tunable stability, biodegradability, and functional modularity. Chemical backbone modifications, crosslinking strategies, and

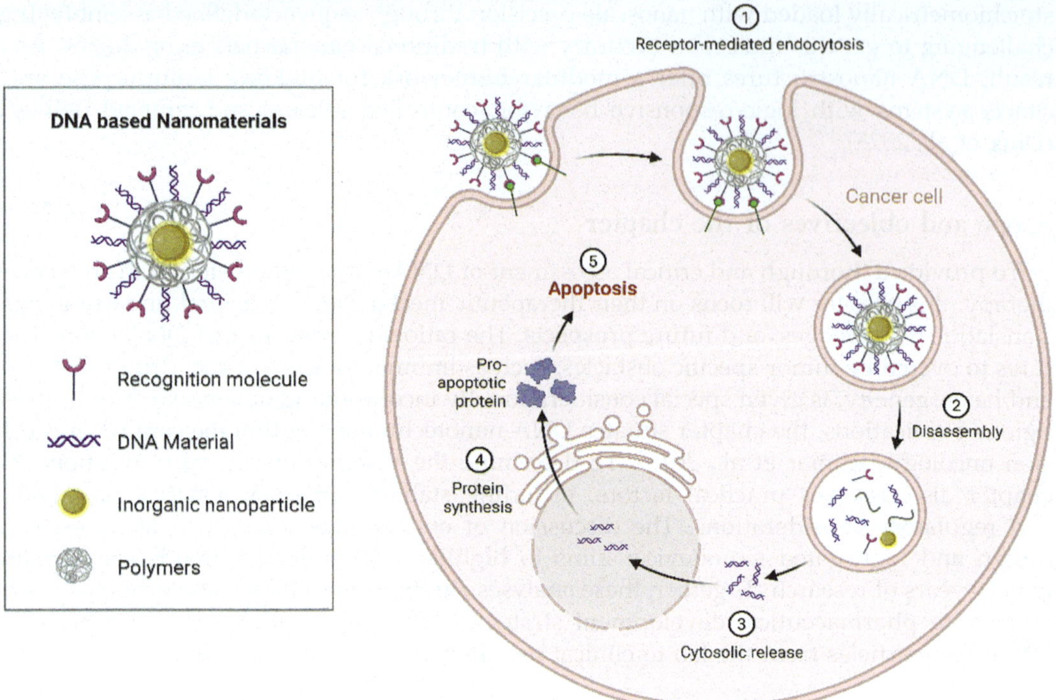

FIGURE 21.2 DNA-based nanomaterials for cancer therapy.

protective coatings can enhance serum stability while preserving controlled enzymatic degradation. Moreover, dynamic strand displacement mechanisms enable the construction of responsive systems that trigger drug release upon exposure to tumor-associated nucleic acids or environmental stimuli. These features enable the integration of targeting ligands, imaging agents, and therapeutic payloads within a single scaffold, supporting multifunctional anticancer applications (Nasiri et al., 2024).

Structural and physicochemical properties of DNA relevant to nanomedicine

DNA is a polyanionic biopolymer composed of repeating nucleotide units linked by phosphodiester bonds, forming a double-helical structure stabilized by Watson–Crick base pairing and π–π stacking interactions. The predictable hydrogen-bonding rules (A–T and G–C) confer molecular recognition fidelity, while the 2 nm diameter and 0.34 nm base-pair spacing enable nanoscale architectural precision. DNA's persistence length (~50 nm for double-stranded DNA) imparts semiflexibility, enabling controlled curvature and mechanical stability during the construction of nanostructures. Importantly, the negative phosphate backbone facilitates electrostatic interactions with cationic drugs and proteins, making DNA an attractive scaffold for loading chemotherapeutics and for nucleic acid therapeutics (Zhan et al., 2023).

From a physicochemical standpoint, DNA nanostructures have a specified stoichiometry, programmable surface activity, and a controllable size (10–200 nm). While chemical modifications such as methylation, phosphorothioate substitution, and PEG conjugation can alter nuclease resistance and circulation half-life, their hydrophilic nature enhances water solubility. Furthermore, targeted ligands (such as aptamers and antibodies) can be spatially conjugated without random dispersion using DNA scaffolds. These characteristics set DNA nanomaterials apart from polymeric nanoparticles, which frequently have uncontrollable surface chemistry and polydispersity (Hong et al., 2025).

Principles of DNA self-assembly

Based on base-pairing specificity and carefully regulated annealing temperatures, DNA self-assembly depends on thermodynamically driven hybridization between complementary sequences. By creating distinct sequence domains, scientists can engineer hierarchical assembly, strand-displacement reactions, and error-corrected complex nanostructure development. While scaffolded DNA origami significantly increased geometric complexity, periodic lattices were made possible by the advent of "DNA tiles" and crossover motifs. Because GC content, ionic strength, and melting temperature factors determine the thermodynamic stability of these structures, assembly kinetics can be precisely modulated (Han et al., 2026). Strand displacement circuits and responsive nanodevices are examples of dynamic DNA nanotechnology that go beyond static structures. Tumor-associated nucleic acid biomarkers can cause conditional cargo release by toehold-mediated strand exchange. Logic-gated therapy methods that can selectively activate cancer cells are based on these principles. Crucially, delicate medicinal payloads are preserved, as self-assembly occurs under gentle aqueous conditions without the need for harsh solvents (Han et al., 2026).

For self-assembly to be successful, thermodynamic control is essential. Base composition, strand length, ionic strength, and annealing kinetics all affect hybridization efficiency. The negatively charged phosphate backbone is often protected by magnesium ions, which reduce electrostatic repulsion and promote stable duplex formation. By enabling mispaired strands to properly dissociate and rehybridize, controlled thermal annealing—typically involving progressive cooling from denaturing temperatures—facilitates mistake repair. These days, computational methods aid secondary structure prediction, minimize cross-hybridization events, and optimize melting temperatures for robust assembly. Rational sequence engineering for biological constructions is now possible thanks to the integration of computational design platforms, which have significantly reduced the need for trial-and-error testing (Han et al., 2026). Dynamic self-assembly techniques have enabled DNA nanotechnology to achieve functional responsiveness beyond static designs. One of the strongest instruments in this field is toehold-mediated strand displacement. A prehybridized strand is gradually displaced by an invading strand by branch migration when it attaches to an exposed single-stranded "toehold" area. Under particular molecular circumstances, this process enables signal amplification, cargo release, and programmable molecular switching (Wu et al., 2025).

The structural palette of DNA nanoparticles is further extended by hierarchical assembly. Higher-order assemblies can be constructed from individual nanostructures by shape-complementary interactions or sticky-end cohesion. Wireframe cages, tubular nanorods, polyhedral containers, and hybrid nanocomposites containing proteins or inorganic nanoparticles can all be created from this multiscale structure. Such structures enable multivalent ligand presentation, spatially regulated drug loading, and adjustable mechanical qualities that affect cellular absorption in anticancer applications (Saji et al., 2025). The concepts of DNA self-assembly combine dynamic molecular programming, computational design, structural geometry, and thermodynamics into a single production approach. This convergence sets DNA nanotechnology apart from traditional nanoparticle engineering techniques, in which bulk physicochemical processes rather than stored molecular instructions are often responsible for the shapes that result. Such programmable precision enables the design of nanostructures that are not only carriers but also functioning molecular systems that can sense, calculate, and react in intricate biological settings, which is useful for anticancer treatment (Zhan et al., 2023).

Stability, biodegradability, and biocompatibility of DNA nanostructures

The intrinsic biodegradability of DNA nanoparticles is one of their main benefits. Long-term accumulation concerns are decreased by endogenous nucleases, which progressively break down DNA into nucleotides that enter physiological metabolic processes. Unaltered DNA nanostructures, however, are prone to rapid enzymatic breakdown in serum. Cross-linking, backbone modification, and encapsulation within lipid or polymeric shells are methods to improve stability (Perrault and Shih, 2014).

Assessments of biocompatibility often show that structurally designed DNA nanostructures at therapeutic doses have little cytotoxicity. It is important to note that sequence design that eliminates CpG motifs that are known to activate Toll like receptors can reduce immunogenicity. Comparing in vivo studies to other synthesized nanomaterials, good tolerance profiles are found. However, dose-dependent inflammatory reactions are still possible and need to be carefully considered (Jiang et al., 2021). The endurance of DNA nanostructures in vivo is largely determined by their structural design, which goes beyond chemical stabilizing techniques. In comparison to loosely formed frameworks, it has been demonstrated that multilayer origami constructions with densely packed helices exhibit improved resistance against nuclease-mediated cleavage. Similarly, because of their greater solvent accessibility, wireframe geometries with lower steric hindrance could show different degradation rates. Crucially, regulated enzymatic breakdown can decrease long-term tissue buildup and enable progressive drug release; thus, degradation is not always harmful. DNA nanomaterials are distinguished from inorganic nanoparticles, which may remain in biological systems indefinitely, by their inherent biodegradability (Nasiri et al., 2024).

Advantages of DNA nanomaterials over conventional nanocarriers

DNA nanostructures have unmatched structural precision, enabling the precise arrangement of ligands and the determination of atomic geometry features that are seldom achievable with liposomes or polymeric nanoparticles. With multivalent targeting and spatially ordered drug loading enabled by this precision, systemic exposure is decreased, and therapeutic efficacy is increased. In contrast to stochastic polymer assembly, batch repeatability is intrinsically tied to sequence fidelity, which enhances manufacturing consistency. Furthermore, sensing, targeting, and therapeutic modules can be integrated into a single programmable scaffold using DNA nanoparticles. DNA devices, unlike traditional carriers, can respond to intracellular stimuli, enabling regulated drug release and reduced off-target toxicity. DNA's modularity enables rapid redesign to account for various tumor markers, enabling tailored treatment approaches.

The digital addressability of DNA nanomaterials, in which each nucleotide position within a structure can be individually programmed and functionally altered, is another unique feature. The ability to precisely manage inter-ligand spacing and cooperative contacts is made possible by the deterministic positioning of therapeutic molecules at predetermined coordinates. In cancer cells, this kind of nanoscale spatial arrangement can have a major impact on downstream signaling cascades, intracellular trafficking, and receptor clustering. Conventional liposomal or polymeric systems, on the other hand, typically rely on the statistical distribution of surface ligands, which limits molecular reproducibility (Ding et al., 2025; Wilhelm et al., 2016).

Types of DNA nanostructures

DNA nanostructures are a versatile and rapidly evolving field in nanotechnology, leveraging the predictable base-pairing properties of DNA to create a variety of structures with applications in medicine, computation, and materials science. These structures can be categorized into several types, each with unique characteristics and applications. The following sections provide an overview of the main types of DNA nanostructures, highlighting their design principles and potential uses Fig. 21.3.

Linear and branched DNA nanostructures

Linear DNA nanostructures are the simplest form, consisting of straight chains of DNA. They serve as basic building blocks for more complex structures and are often used in applications requiring straightforward assembly and disassembly processes. Branched DNA nanostructures involve multiple DNA strands forming junctions, creating more complex geometries. These structures are used in the synthesis of functional materials and have applications in diagnostics, drug delivery, and protein engineering (Dong et al., 2020).

DNA tiles and lattices

DNA tiles are formed by the self-assembly of short DNA strands into specific shapes, such as TX tiles and 4×4 cross-tiles. These tiles can further assemble into one - and two-dimensional lattices, which are used in molecular computation and templated assembly of materials. The ability to form micrometer-scale arrays makes DNA tiles suitable for applications in biosensing and the patterning of nanoscale materials (Rangnekar and Labean, 2014).

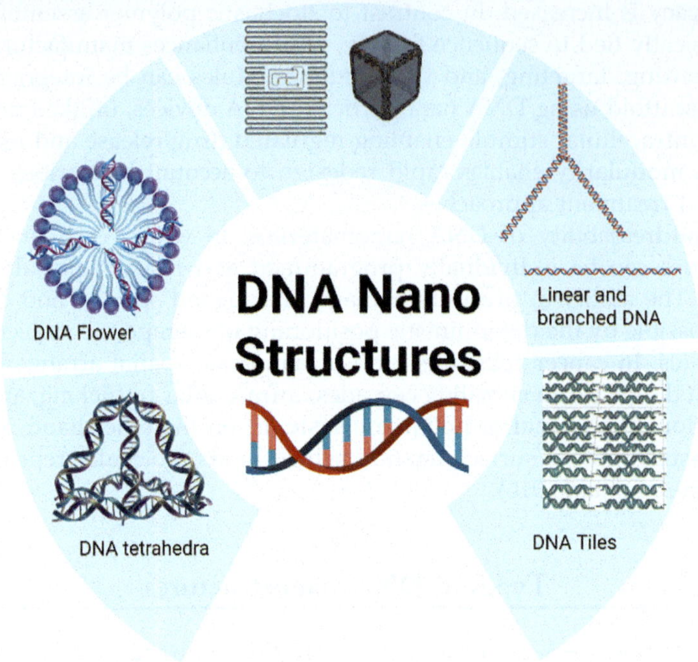

FIGURE 21.3 DNA nanostructures.

DNA origami nanostructures

DNA origami involves folding a long single-stranded DNA scaffold into desired shapes using multiple short staple strands. This technique allows for the creation of intricate two- and three-dimensional structures. It is used in a wide range of applications, including drug delivery systems, biosensors, and the construction of dynamic devices that can change shape in response to environmental stimuli (Yoon et al., 2021).

DNA tetrahedra and polyhedral nanostructures

DNA tetrahedra are simple polyhedral structures formed by the self-assembly of DNA strands into a three-dimensional shape. These structures are highly stable and can be used for drug delivery and as scaffolds for biomolecular interactions (Chen et al., 2024b). More complex polyhedral structures can be designed for specific applications, such as encapsulating molecules or creating nanoscale containers for chemical reactions (Yoon et al., 2021).

Dynamic and stimuli-responsive DNA nanostructures

Dynamic DNA nanostructures can change their conformation in response to environmental stimuli, such as pH, temperature, or the presence of specific molecules. This adaptability makes them ideal for applications in biosensing and targeted drug delivery. These structures often incorporate reconfigurable elements like strand displacement reactions and aptamers, allowing them to perform complex tasks and respond to specific cues with high precision (Zhang et al., 2019). While DNA nanostructures offer significant potential across various fields, challenges remain in their practical application. Issues such as scalability, immunocompatibility, and long-term stability need to be addressed to fully realize their potential in clinical and industrial settings. Additionally, integrating DNA nanostructures with other technologies, such as artificial intelligence, could further enhance their capabilities and applications (Hong et al., 2025).

DNA nanostructures in drug delivery

DNA nanostructures have emerged as a promising platform for drug delivery, particularly in the field of cancer therapy. These structures offer several advantages over traditional drug delivery systems, including precise control over size, shape, and function, as well as the ability to integrate with various functional moieties. DNA nanostructures can enhance the delivery of anticancer agents by improving cellular uptake, protecting drugs from degradation, and facilitating targeted delivery to tumor cells. This response will explore the rationale for using DNA nanostructures in drug delivery, their encapsulation and protection capabilities, cellular uptake and intracellular trafficking, and a comparison with polymeric and inorganic nanocarriers.

Rationale for use

DNA nanostructures are biocompatible, biodegradable, and nontoxic, making them ideal for drug delivery applications. They can be precisely engineered to have specific shapes and sizes, which allows for the customization of drug delivery systems to meet specific therapeutic needs. DNA nanostructures can be functionalized with targeting ligands, proteins, and other molecules to enhance their stability and specificity for drug delivery (Kumar et al., 2024).

Encapsulation and protection of anticancer agents

DNA nanostructures can encapsulate a variety of anticancer drugs, such as doxorubicin, and protect them from premature degradation (Shishparenok et al., 2023). Covalent attachment of drugs to DNA nanostructures can prevent premature release and ensure precise delivery to target sites (Navarro et al., 2024). DNA origami, a specific type of DNA nanostructure, offers increased stability and reduced biotoxicity, making it suitable for transporting anticancer agents (Zhang et al., 2023).

Cellular uptake and intracellular trafficking

DNA nanostructures can traverse cell membranes and deliver drugs directly to the nucleus, enhancing the efficacy of anticancer therapies (Safarkhani et al., 2024). Strategies such as the incorporation of folate units or the use of transfection agents like Lipofectamine can improve the cellular uptake of DNA nanostructures (Navarro et al., 2024). Tetrahedral DNA nanostructures (TDNs) are particularly effective in promoting intracellular uptake due to their compact structure and natural biocompatibility (Huang et al., 2023; Zhang et al., 2020b).

Comparison with polymeric and inorganic nanocarriers

Unlike polymeric and inorganic nanocarriers, DNA nanostructures offer unsurpassed programmability and ease of functional modification. DNA nanostructures exhibit lower cytotoxicity and higher specificity compared to traditional nanocarriers, reducing the risk of adverse effects (Zhang et al., 2020b). While polymeric and inorganic nanocarriers have inherent flexibility, DNA nanostructures provide a more precise and customizable platform for drug delivery. Despite the promising potential of DNA nanostructures in drug delivery, there are challenges that need to be addressed for their clinical application. These include overcoming biological barriers, ensuring efficient cellular uptake, and achieving precise control over drug release (Jiang et al., 2021). Additionally, while DNA nanostructures offer advantages over traditional nanocarriers, further research is needed to fully understand their long-term safety and efficacy in clinical settings.

Mechanisms of drug loading and release

DNA-based nanostructures, such as DNA origami, offer versatile mechanisms for loading and releasing therapeutic agents, primarily leveraging the unique physicochemical properties of DNA. These methods are crucial for developing effective drug delivery systems that can target cancer cells while minimizing systemic toxicity. The primary loading strategies include intercalation, covalent bonding, and physical entrapment, while release is often triggered by specific environmental stimuli within the tumor microenvironment or the cell itself (Wang et al., 2022a).

Drug loading onto DNA nanostructures can be achieved through several distinct mechanisms. One common method is intercalation, where drug molecules like doxorubicin (DOX) insert themselves between the base pairs of the DNA double helix. This noncovalent interaction is driven by forces like fluorescence resonance energy transfer (FRET) (Wang et al., 2022a). Another approach involves covalently connecting drugs to the DNA chains that form the nanostructure, effectively making the drug part of the carrier itself. Physical entrapment is also used, where drugs are encapsulated within the cavities of DNA cages or nanoboxes. For larger molecules or nucleic acid drugs like siRNA, a complementary single-strand extension can be added to the DNA nanostructure to facilitate loading via hybridization. The choice of loading method depends on the specific characteristics of the drug being delivered (Shishparenok et al., 2023; Zhang et al., 2023).

Once the drug-loaded nanocarrier reaches its target, the release of the therapeutic payload is often triggered by specific conditions. For DNA origami nanostructures, release can be initiated by changes in the cellular environment. For instance, after being internalized by cells through endocytosis, the nanostructure is often trafficked to lysosomes. The acidic pH within the lysosome can cause the DNA nanostructure to degrade, thereby releasing the drug cargo. Some systems are designed to be responsive to other stimuli like temperature, enzymes, or the presence of specific molecules such as ATP (Yang et al., 2023). For example, DNA nanostructures can be designed to disassemble and release their cargo when they encounter the acidic environment of a tumor or the enzymatic activity within a lysosome. This controlled release ensures that the drug is delivered precisely where it is needed, enhancing its therapeutic effect while reducing off-target toxicity (Wang et al., 2022a).

Intercalation-based drug loading

Intercalation is a common, noncovalent method for loading therapeutic agents, particularly small-molecule drugs, into various types of nanostructures for drug delivery applications. This process involves the insertion of drug molecules between the base pairs or into the grooves of DNA-based nanocarriers, or within the porous structures of other nanomaterials. The stability and efficiency of this loading method depend on the specific interactions between the drug and the carrier, such as electrostatic forces, hydrogen bonding, and π-π interactions (Yang et al., 2023).

Several types of DNA nanostructures utilize intercalation for drug loading. For instance, DNA tetrahedrons (TDNs) can be loaded with anticancer drugs like doxorubicin (DOX), paclitaxel, and methylene blue through intercalation. Similarly, DNA origami structures can easily accommodate a variety of therapeutic compounds, including DOX and daunorubicin, via intercalation. DNA nanotubes are also capable of absorbing hydrophobic anticancer drugs like doxorubicin and daunorubicin at their ends due to electrostatic and van der Waals forces. The loading of DOX into a ZIF-8 metal-organic framework (MOF) is another example, achieved through a combination of coordination bonds and π-π interactions with the ligand (Shishparenok et al., 2023; Yadav et al., 2023; Zhuang et al., 2016).

This loading strategy is often straightforward, sometimes requiring only direct mixing of the nanostructure and the drug. However, a notable challenge with simple intercalation is the lack of precise quantitative control over the amount of drug loaded. The kinetics of drug release and the degradation rate of the carrier in vivo are not always strongly correlated, which can affect therapeutic outcomes. Despite this, intercalation remains a widely used and effective method for creating drug-loaded nanocarriers for targeted cancer therapy and other biomedical applications (Shishparenok et al., 2023; Huang et al., 2023).

Groove binding and electrostatic interactions

Electrostatic interactions and groove binding are key mechanisms for loading therapeutic agents into nanocarriers, particularly those based on DNA and proteins. In DNA-based drug delivery systems (DDS), the molecular structure of DNA itself facilitates these interactions. For instance, the anticancer drug doxorubicin (Dox) can be embedded into the base pairs of a DNA origami structure, a process that involves groove binding. Similarly, the electrostatic gradient within protein nanocages like ferritin, which has a positive outer surface and a negative inner surface, enables drug loading. Cationic dendrimers also utilize electrostatic interactions with their surface amino groups to solubilize and carry negatively charged hydrophobic drugs (Liu and Fan, 2013; Berlin Heidelberg, 2013; Yang et al., 2019).

These noncovalent interactions are fundamental to the design of smart, stimulus-responsive DDS. For example, in a DNA nanohydrogel designed for gene therapy, therapeutic oligonucleotides are incorporated via electrostatic interactions, and their release can be triggered by intracellular conditions. The strength of these interactions can also be modulated to control drug release. In a study comparing iron-based and zinc-based metal-organic frameworks (MOFs) for Dox delivery, the stronger binding affinity between Dox and the iron-based framework, which includes electrostatic interactions, resulted in a slower, more controlled release compared to the zinc-based framework. Therefore, both groove binding and electrostatic forces are crucial for the encapsulation, stability, and controlled release of therapeutics from advanced nanocarrier systems (Shishparenok et al., 2023; Li et al., 2024b).

Covalent conjugation strategies

Covalent conjugation is a key strategy for enhancing the functionality of DNA-based nanomaterials, particularly for applications in cancer therapy. This method involves chemically linking various functional molecules, such as therapeutic agents, targeting ligands, or other nanoparticles, to the DNA structure, thereby creating hybrid systems with tailored properties for drug delivery and diagnostics. These covalent modifications improve the stability, targeting specificity, and therapeutic efficacy of the nanocarriers.

Several methods are employed to achieve covalent conjugation. One common approach is to modify the DNA backbone or its ends with reactive groups like azides, amino groups, or sulfhydryl groups, which can then participate in reactions such as "click chemistry" to attach other molecules. For instance, the MUC1 aptamer has been coupled with polymers or nanoparticles for targeted drug delivery. Similarly, therapeutic drugs like docetaxel have been encapsulated in nanoparticles functionalized with the A10 RNA aptamer to improve drug delivery and uptake. Another strategy involves directly linking drug molecules to the DNA strands that will form the nanostructure. For example, researchers have covalently connected drugs to component DNA chains, which are then assembled as part of the final structure (Zhang et al., 2023; Shishparenok et al., 2023).

Covalent linkages are also crucial for integrating peptides and proteins. Therapeutic DNA has been covalently linked to a mitochondrion targeting signal peptide (MTS) to transport it into mitochondria (Sun et al., 2022b). In another application, the antiCD28 antibody was conjugated with an antiEGFR aptamer to combine their inhibitory properties and enhance cancer cell-killing activity. Furthermore, covalent crosslinking between DNA strands is a technique used to stabilize the entire nanostructure, making it more resistant to degradation by nucleases and improving its overall stability for in vivo applications (Shishparenok et al., 2023).

In summary, covalent conjugation strategies are fundamental to the design of advanced DNA nanomaterials. By permanently linking therapeutic agents, targeting moieties, and stabilizing components, researchers can create sophisticated and robust nanocarriers. These covalent modifications are essential for overcoming challenges in drug delivery, such as poor stability and nonspecific targeting, thereby enhancing the potential of DNA nanotechnology in cancer treatment (Yadav et al., 2023; Shishparenok et al., 2023).

Stimuli-responsive drug release mechanisms

Smart drug delivery systems (DDSs) that respond to specific physical or chemical stimuli in the tumor microenvironment (TME) have become a prominent area of research for antitumor therapies. DNA-based nanostructures can be engineered to release their therapeutic payloads in response to various endogenous triggers, including pH, enzymes, and specific small molecules like adenosine triphosphate (ATP) and glutathione (GSH). This targeted release enhances treatment efficacy while minimizing systemic side effects (Hong et al., 2025; Shishparenok et al., 2023; Li et al., 2024a).

pH-responsive release

The TME is characterized by a weakly acidic environment (pH 6.5–7.2) compared to normal tissues (pH 7.4), a phenomenon known as the Warburg effect. This pH difference can be exploited to trigger drug release. DNA nanostructures can incorporate pH-sensitive elements like the i-motif, a cytosine-rich quadruplex structure that forms under acidic conditions. This structural change can lead to the disassembly of the nanocarrier and subsequent release of the drug. For instance, a pH-responsive DNA nanomicelles was developed using rolling circle amplification (RCA) to generate long single-stranded DNA with sequences complementary to pH-responsive DNA triplex structures. In the acidic microenvironment of tumor cells, the formation of these triplex structures triggered the release of coloaded doxorubicin (DOX) and siRNA. Another approach involves using DNA origami to create a nanocapsule with pH-responsive latches. These latches open at high pH for cargo loading and close at a lower pH to seal the capsule, which can then be triggered to open and release its payload in the acidic TME (Hong et al., 2025; Yadav et al., 2023; Li et al., 2024b).

Enzyme-triggered release

The TME often exhibits abnormally high expression of enzymes like matrix metalloproteinases (MMPs) and telomerase, which can serve as triggers for drug release. MMPs, a family of zinc-containing proteolytic enzymes, are overexpressed in the TME and can cleave specific substrates. Researchers have designed spherical nucleic acids (SNAs) encapsulated by an amphipathic peptide containing MMP recognition sequences. In the TME, MMPs cleave the peptide shell, promoting the SNA's accumulation and cellular uptake. Telomerase, another enzyme highly active in most tumors, can also be used as a trigger. A telomerase-responsive DNA icosahedron was constructed from two conical DNA cages linked by telomerase primers and telomeric repeats. In the presence of telomerase, the primers are elongated, causing the disassembly of the icosahedron and the release of its encapsulated platinum drug payload (Hong et al., 2025; Yadav et al., 2023; Li et al., 2024a).

Redox- and ATP-triggered release

Tumor cells have higher concentrations of reducing agents like glutathione (GSH) and energy molecules like ATP compared to normal cells (Li et al., 2023; Hong et al., 2021; Cancer Letters, 2021). This disparity can be exploited for targeted drug release. DNA nanostructures can be modified with disulfide bonds, which are stable in the extracellular environment but are cleaved by the high intracellular GSH concentrations, triggering drug release. For example, a GSH-responsive triangular DNA origami nanostructure was designed to codeliver a therapeutic gene (p53) and a chemotherapy drug (DOX), with both payloads attached via disulfide linkers for precise release upon redox reaction with GSH. Similarly, the significantly higher ATP levels in the TME (1–10 mM) versus normal tissue can be used as a trigger. ATP-responsive systems often use an ATP aptamer. In the absence of ATP, the drug is loaded onto the aptamer-based nanostructure. When exposed to high ATP concentrations in tumor cells, a structural transformation of the aptamer occurs, leading to drug release (Li et al., 2024a).

DNA-based nanostructures can be intricately designed to respond to a variety of stimuli present in the tumor microenvironment, such as pH, enzymes, GSH, and ATP. These smart systems enable the controlled and targeted release of therapeutic agents, which enhances the efficacy of cancer treatments and reduces off-target toxicity. The programmability and versatility of DNA make it an ideal material for creating sophisticated, multi-responsive drug delivery platforms for precision medicine (Li et al., 2025).

Targeted DNA nanostructures for cancer therapy

Targeted DNA nanostructures represent a significant advancement in cancer therapy, offering a precise method for delivering therapeutic agents directly to tumor cells while minimizing damage to healthy tissue. These nanostructures can be engineered with specific ligands such as aptamers, peptides, antibodies, or folic acid that selectively bind to receptors overexpressed on the surface of cancer cells. This targeted approach enhances the accumulation of drugs in tumor tissues, improves therapeutic efficacy, and reduces systemic side effects associated with conventional chemotherapy. The inherent biocompatibility, biodegradability, and programmability of DNA make it an ideal material for creating these sophisticated delivery vehicles (Chen et al., 2024b).

Various types of DNA nanostructures, including tetrahedrons, origami, hydrogels, and spherical nucleic acids (SNAs), have been developed for targeted cancer therapy. For instance, a DNA tetrahedron modified with a cell-penetrating peptide was shown to effectively deliver doxorubicin (DOX) to glioblastoma cells. Similarly, an aptamer-modified DNA nanostructure (Apt-NS) was created to specifically recognize nonsmall cell lung cancer (NSCLC) A549 cells, leading to the internalization of the nanostructure and subsequent release of its drug payload inside the tumor cells. This targeted delivery resulted in enhanced antitumor effects, including suppression of cell proliferation, invasion, and migration, as well as increased apoptosis (Wang et al., 2022a). Beyond targeting the cell surface, DNA nanostructures can also be designed to target specific subcellular organelles like the nucleus or mitochondria, further refining the precision of the therapy. For example, a tetrahedral DNA nanostructure modified with a nuclear localization signal (NLS) peptide was shown to successfully deliver antisense oligonucleotides to the nucleus of A549 cells (Sun et al., 2022a).

In vivo studies have confirmed the potential of these targeted systems. Aptamer-modified DNA nanostructures have demonstrated significant accumulation in tumor tissue in mouse models, leading to superior antitumor efficacy compared to free drugs. Moreover, these systems exhibit good biosafety with no significant organ toxicity. The ability to precisely control the design, size, and surface chemistry of DNA nanostructures allows for the creation of versatile platforms that can carry various therapeutic cargoes, including small molecule drugs, nucleic acids, and proteins, making them a promising strategy for personalized cancer treatment.

In summary, targeted DNA nanostructures offer a highly programmable and effective platform for cancer therapy. By utilizing specific recognition molecules, these systems can deliver anticancer agents directly to tumor cells and even specific subcellular locations, thereby enhancing treatment efficacy and reducing toxicity. Continued research in this area holds the potential to overcome many of the limitations of traditional cancer treatments and usher in a new era of precision medicine (Yadav et al., 2023; Sun et al., 2022b; Chen et al., 2024a).

Passive targeting via enhanced permeability and retention effect

Passive targeting is a strategy that leverages the enhanced permeability and retention (EPR) effect to increase the concentration of therapeutic agents, such as nanoparticles, in tumor tissues compared to normal tissues. This phenomenon occurs because blood vessels in malignant lesions are more permeable to macromolecules, typically those larger than 10 nm, than blood vessels in healthy tissues. Following extravasation into the tumor, these macromolecules are retained for longer periods due to impaired lymphatic clearance (Nicolson et al., 2020). This increased accumulation and retention within the tumor microenvironment is a key principle in designing nanomedicines for cancer therapy.

DNA nanostructures and nanoparticles are particularly well-suited to exploit the EPR effect for passive targeting. Their size can be engineered to fall within the optimal range for permeating tumor vasculature while avoiding rapid elimination by the kidneys, which typically clear particles smaller than 10 nm. For instance, DNA nanostructures can be designed with specific hydrodynamic diameters (10–200 nm) to facilitate accumulation at tumor. By taking advantage of the EPR effect, these nanocarriers can improve drug penetration and accumulation, thereby enhancing therapeutic efficacy and minimizing systemic toxicity and side effects (Li et al., 2024b; Zhang et al., 2019).

Active targeting using ligands and aptamers

Active targeting is a crucial strategy in drug delivery, particularly for cancer therapy, that utilizes specific molecules to direct nanocarriers to their intended sites, such as tumor cells. This approach enhances therapeutic efficacy while minimizing off-target effects. Common targeting molecules include ligands like peptides, proteins, antibodies, and folic acid, as well as nucleic acid aptamers, which are conjugated to the surface of DNA nanostructures. These molecules bind to specific receptors that are overexpressed on the surface of target cells, facilitating precise recognition and delivery of therapeutic agents (Sun et al., 2022a).

Ligands function by binding to specific receptors on the cell surface. For example, folic acid can be used to target the folate receptor, which is often overexpressed on cancer cells. Similarly, peptides can be designed to bind to various receptors, enabling the targeted delivery of nanocarriers. An important consideration for ligand-based targeting is that the interaction is often sensitive to environmental factors like pH, which can be exploited to trigger drug release in the acidic tumor microenvironment. Viral capsid proteins have also been shown to interact electrostatically with DNA origami nanostructures (DONs), improving their internalization into cells (Sun et al., 2022a; Shishparenok et al., 2023; Zhang et al., 2023).

Aptamers are short, single-stranded DNA or RNA molecules that fold into unique three-dimensional structures, allowing them to bind to cellular targets with high selectivity and affinity. They are often used to target cell surface receptors and can be easily integrated into DNA nanostructures through hybridization or conjugation. For instance, the AS1411 aptamer targets the nucleolin protein, which is commonly found on the surface of cancer cells, providing a vector for directed drug delivery. Similarly, the MUC1 aptamer has been used to target the MUC1 receptor, which is overexpressed in many cancers, including breast and pancreatic cancer. Both ligands and aptamers are essential tools for achieving active targeting in DNA-based drug delivery systems. By modifying nanostructures with these molecules, researchers can guide therapeutic payloads to specific cancer cells, overcoming limitations of traditional chemotherapy and improving treatment precision (Sun et al., 2022b; Shishparenok et al., 2023).

Cell-specific and receptor-mediated targeting strategies

DNA nanostructures can be engineered for cell-specific and receptor-mediated targeting, primarily for applications in cancer therapy and diagnosis. This is achieved by modifying the nanostructures with various targeting molecules or ligands that recognize and bind to specific receptors overexpressed on the surface of target cells, particularly cancer cells. This approach enhances the selective delivery of therapeutic agents, improves drug efficacy, and reduces toxicity to healthy tissues (Sun et al., 2022b).

Several types of targeting ligands are commonly used to functionalize DNA nanostructures. These include aptamers, which are short synthetic single-stranded DNA or RNA oligonucleotides with high affinity and specificity for their targets. Other frequently used molecules are peptides, proteins, antibodies, and small molecules like folic acid. For instance, DNA origami nanostructures can be modified with folate to target folate receptors, which are often overexpressed in various cancers, including triple-negative breast cancer (Zhang et al., 2023). Similarly, tetrahedral DNA nanostructures (TDNs) have been modified with MUC1 aptamers to specifically bind to Mucin one proteins, which are highly expressed on many cancer cells. This strategy allows for the selective delivery of drugs like doxorubicin to cancer cells while minimizing uptake by normal cells. The internalization of these targeted nanostructures often occurs through receptor-mediated endocytosis, a process where the cell membrane engulfs the nanostructure after it binds to its specific surface receptor.

In summary, the functionalization of DNA nanostructures with specific ligands is a key strategy for achieving receptor-mediated and cell-specific targeting. By leveraging the overexpression of certain receptors on cancer cells, these modified nanostructures can selectively deliver therapeutic payloads, thereby increasing treatment precision and efficacy. Common targeting agents include aptamers, folic acid, and various peptides and antibodies, which guide the nanostructures to their intended cellular destinations (Duangrat et al., 2020; Sun et al., 2022a).

Tumor microenvironment-responsive DNA nanostructures

DNA nanostructures can be engineered to be "smart" carriers that respond to specific cues within the tumor microenvironment (TME), enabling precise, on-demand drug release. The TME is characterized by unique physiological conditions such as low pH (acidity), altered redox potential, hyperthermia, and the overexpression of certain enzymes, which can be exploited as triggers for these stimuli-responsive nanomaterials.

One of the most significant features of the TME is its mild acidity (pH 6.5–6.9), a result of the Warburg effect where cancer cells favor anaerobic glycolysis. This acidic environment is utilized by pH-responsive DNA nanostructures, which often incorporate i-motif structures. An i-motif is a cytosine-rich quadruplex that forms under acidic conditions, triggering a conformational change in the nanostructure to release its therapeutic cargo. For instance, researchers have developed a DNA hydrogel based on an i-motif that releases doxorubicin in the acidic TME. Another strategy involves using the enzyme-rich environment of tumors. Matrix metalloproteinases (MMPs) are often overexpressed in the TME and can cleave specific peptide sequences integrated into DNA assemblies, leading to drug release. Similarly, telomerase, an enzyme highly active in most tumors, can trigger the disassembly of DNA icosahedrons to release platinum-based drugs. The TME also has a distinct redox environment, with high intracellular concentrations of antioxidants like glutathione (GSH). This has been exploited by creating DNA tetrahedrons that release drugs like camptothecin in response to high GSH levels. Furthermore, the elevated temperature (hyperthermia) found in some tumors can also be used as a trigger for thermo-responsive DNA nanocarriers (Hong et al., 2025; Yadav et al., 2023).

Applications of DNA-based nanomaterials in cancer therapy

DNA-based nanomaterials are increasingly utilized in cancer therapy due to their unique properties, including sequence programmability, biocompatibility, and structural controllability. These materials serve as versatile platforms for delivering therapeutic agents, overcoming limitations of traditional treatments such as poor water solubility, low targeting, and drug resistance. Their applications span chemotherapy, gene therapy, and immunotherapy, often in combination to achieve synergistic effects and improve treatment outcomes (Liu et al., 2018a; Lv et al., 2021). Table 21.1 show examples of engineered nanostructures in the delivery of various therapeutics.

TABLE 21.1 Engineered DNA nanostructures serve as innovative carriers for therapeutic agents.

Nanomaterial	Method/Strategy	Target	Model	Payload	References.
DNA tetrahedron	HER2 aptamer covalently anchored to tetrahedral framework nucleic acid	HER2	SKBR-3; MCF-7; MCF-10A	HApt–tetrahedral DNA	Li et al. (2025)
FUdR–DNA-affibody chimera	5′-terminal attachment of 10 FUdR residues per strand	HER2	BT474; MCF-7	5-Fluorodeoxyuridine	(Zhang et al., 2020a)
HER2 aptamer–drug conjugate	Aptamer chemically conjugated to mertansine (small-molecule payload)	HER2	BT-474; MDA-MB-231	Mertansine	Jeong et al. (2020)
HER2–EGFR bivalent aptamer	Bivalent HER2 aptamer combined with EGFR siRNA (chimera)	HER2, EGFR	BT474; SKBR3; MDA-MB-231; MCF7; Hs578T	siRNA	Xue et al. (2018)
HER2-targeted MSNs	β-cyclodextrin pH-sensitive capping of DOX-loaded mesoporous silica nanoparticles functionalized with HER2 aptamer	HER2	SKBR3; MCF7; HEK-293T	Doxorubicin	(Shen et al., 2019)
HER2 oligobody (cotinine-aptamer)	MMAE-conjugated cotinine-based oligobody incorporating HER2 aptamer	HER2	SKBR3; NCI–N87	MMAE	Kim et al. (2020)
HER2 aptamer on gold nanostars	Dense grafting of HER2 aptamer onto Au nanostars	HER2	SKBR-3; MCF-10A	HApt–AuNS	Lee et al. (2015)
Aptamer A6 (HER2)	Liposomal display of A6 aptamer (varied lipid compositions)	HER2	SKBR3; MCF7; MDA-MB-231	Doxorubicin	Powell et al. (2017)
HER2 + AS1411 dual hydrogel	DNA hydrogel decorated with HER2 and AS1411 aptamers	HER2, nucleolin	SKBR-3; MCF7; MDA-MB-23	Doxorubicin	Jin et al. (2022)
Carboxylated chitosan MSNs	pH-responsive chitosan coating with HER2 aptamer on DOX-loaded MSNs	HER2, EGFR	SKBR-3; MCF7	Doxorubicin	Lohiya and Katti (2022)
HER2 aptamer-bearing micelle	pH-responsive micelle carrying fluorescently labelled HER2 aptamer	HER2	SKBR3; MCF7; HeLa	HER2 aptamer (payload/label)	Shen et al. (2018)
HER2 aptamer carrier-free NPs	Carrier-free nanoparticles combining ursolic acid and DOX with HER2 aptamer	HER2	BT474	Ursolic acid + Doxorubicin	(Jiang et al., 2017)

AS1411-modified DNA tetrahedron/MOF	miR-21/miR-155/AS1411 sequences integrated into TDN–MOF hybrids	Nucleolin	MDA-MB-231; HepG2	Doxorubicin; camptothecin; rhodamine 6G; fluorescein	(Zhang et al., 2021b)
AS1411-TDN (intercalation)	DOX and TMPyP4 intercalated into AS1411-functionalized tetrahedra	Nucleolin	HeLa	Doxorubicin; TMPyP4	(Wang et al., 2022b)
AS1411-conjugated nanoparticles (broad set)	Multiple platforms: PEG-PLA micelles, PLGA-lecithin-PEG, PAMAM, albumin NPs, PLGA-PVP, etc. (AS1411 surface decoration or covalent attachment)	Nucleolin	diverse (MCF-7, A549, HepG2, HT29, CT26, etc.)	Doxorubicin; Paclitaxel; Camptothecin; 5-FU; multiple siRNAs/miRNAs	(Li et al., 2015; Alibolandi et al., 2017; Barzegar Behrooz et al., 2017; Xu et al., 2018; Qi et al., 2016; Yu et al., 2020; Saravanakumar et al., 2019)
AS1411-functionalized inorganic NPs/MOFs	AS1411 attached to AuNPs, ZIF-8, ZnO-gated porphyrinic MOF, γ-CD-MOF with GQDs, Mn-doped MSNs, Zn-doped magnetic iron oxide NPs	Nucleolin	HeLa; MCF-7; HEK293T; others	Doxorubicin; phototherapeutic agents; imaging agents	(Lopes-Nunes et al., 2021; Dong et al., 2018; Zhao et al., 2018; Jia et al., 2019)
AS1411-liposome/EV platforms	AS1411 displayed on DC-Chol/DOPE liposomes, DOPE/sphingomyelin/DSPE-PEG liposomes, or carried by extracellular vesicles	Nucleolin	A375; MDA-MB-231; MCF-7; MDA-MB-231 (EV)	anti-BRAF siRNA; paclitaxel + siRNA; miRNA let-7; VEGF siRNA	(Li et al., 2014; Yu et al., 2019; Wang et al., 2017)
AS1411-nanotrains and DNA nanostructures	AS1411-tethered DNA nanotrains, three-way junction pocket DNA nanostructures, aptamer-tethered nanotrains	Nucleolin	HeLa; L02; PC-3; 4T1; CHO	Anthracyclines; Doxorubicin	(Pei et al., 2020; Taghdisi et al., 2018)
AS1411 + phototherapeutics/multimodal probes	AS1411-AuNP conjugates carrying TMPyP4 + DOX; AS1411-decorated AuNPs with DNAzyme + ZnO QDs; AS1411-upconversion NPs with PPIX	Nucleolin	HeLa; MCF-7; others	TMPyP4 + Doxorubicin; Doxorubicin + miRNA-21; Protoporphyrin IX (PDT)	(Shiao et al., 2014; He et al., 2016; Lin et al., 2020)
AS1411-smart platforms	AS1411 photo-sensitive OliP conjugates, AS1411-ATP fusion bivalent aptamer polyplexes, Click-nucleic-acid codelivery platforms	Nucleolin; ATP; PFKFB4	4T1; MCF-7/DOX; HEK293	siRNAs, DOX, rapamycin, anti-PFKFB4 siRNA	(Zhao et al., 2020; Guo et al., 2020: Gao et al., 2020)

(*Continued*)

TABLE 21.1 Engineered DNA nanostructures serve as innovative carriers for therapeutic agents.—cont'd

Nanomaterial	Method/Strategy	Target	Model	Payload	References.
AS1411-enzyme/ peptide co-delivery	AS1411 conjugated silica supra-assemblies, PAMAM grafted persistent luminescence NPs, MoS_2 nanosheet hybrids, and cyt *c* co-delivery	Nucleolin	HCT116; HeLa; MCF-7; HepG2	Doxorubicin; Docetaxel; Cytochrome *c*	(Thorat et al., 2020; Zhang et al., 2020c; Cai et al., 2020; Zhang et al., 2014)
Cy5.5-AS1411	Covalent assembly of Cy5.5-AS1411 on GO-wrapped DOX-loaded MSNs (imaging + delivery)	Nucleolin	MCF-7	Doxorubicin	(Zhang et al., 2014)
AS1411-PAMAM with nucleic acid cargo	PAMAM-10C–10C-PEG NPs bearing bcl-xl shRNA; AS1411-PAMAM-PEG systems	Nucleolin	A549; L929; MKN45	bcl-xl shRNA; 5-Fluorouracil	(Barzegar Behrooz et al., 2017; Ayatollahi et al., 2017)
AS1411-anchored liposomal SDT	AS1411 anchored on MnO_2-coated liposomes loaded with acriflavine and HMME for sonodynamic therapy	Nucleolin	SKOV3; HL-7702	Acriflavine; HMME (SDT)	Wang et al. (2018)
AS1411 variants and combinatorial systems	AS1411-PGG-PTX, AS1411 + cRGD gold nanoclusters, AS1411 + siRNA/ MSN hybrids, AS1411-DNCA lipid NPs, AS1411-PDA	Nucleolin	diverse	Paclitaxel; Doxorubicin; NIR agents; siRNAs	(Luo et al., 2017; Chen et al., 2016a; Zhuang et al., 2021; Ma et al., 2018a; Xu et al., 2016)
ATP-AS1411 bivalent aptamer	ATP-responsive AS1411 conjugated to DOX-loaded silica nanoparticles	ATP, Nucleolin	CHO	Doxorubicin	Charbgoo et al. (2021)
Apta-12 (APTA12) DOX conjugate	DOX-APTA12 conjugate for nucleolin targeting	Nucleolin	MCF-10A; MDA-MB-231	Doxorubicin + Gemcitabine	Joshi et al. (2019)
DNA tetrahedron (MUC1 + AS1411)	TDN modified with MUC1 and AS1411 aptamers; DOX intercalation	MUC1, Nucleolin	MCF-7; HL-7702	Doxorubicin	(Liu et al., 2018b)
MUC1 aptamer–siRNA chimera	Aptamer–siR-29b chimera synthesis (PTEN modulation)	MUC-1, PTEN	OVCAR-3	miRNA-29b	Dai et al. (2012)
MUC1 aptamer-MSNs (smart sensor)	MUC1-responsive hairpin DNA motif conjugated to DOX-loaded MSNs	MUC-1	MCF-7; Hs578bst	Doxorubicin	Si et al. (2020)

MUC1 aptamer-$CaCO_3$ complexes	Dimer aptamer–calcium carbonate complexes loaded with epirubicin and melittin	MUC-1	MCF7; C26; HepG2	Epirubicin; melittin	Yazdian-Robati et al. (2019)
MUC1 aptamer–ferritin NPs	Ferritin conjugation for epirubicin delivery	MUC-1	Colon cancer cells	Epirubicin	Yazdian-Robati et al. (2022)
MUC1 aptamer-KLA conjugate	KLA peptide–MUC1 aptamer conjugated to DNA nanoparticles surface	MUC-1	MCF-7	Doxorubicin; KLA peptide	Charbgoo et al. (2018)
MUC1 aptamer-SPIONs	PEGylated SPIONs armed with DOX-conjugated MUC1 aptamer	MUC-1	MDA-MB-231	Doxorubicin	Aghanejad et al. (2018)
MUC1 aptamer-QDs/PDT	ZnSe/ZnS QD–PPIX conjugates; Protoporphyrin IX loading on MUC1 aptamer NPs	MUC-1	HeLa; RAW; MCF-7	PPIX (PDT); Paclitaxel + sodium oxamate	(Singh et al., 2016; Ranjbar-Navazi et al., 2021)
MUC1 aptamer-chitosan NPs	Chitosan nanoparticles bearing siRNA and docetaxel; chitosan-SN38 NPs	MUC-1	SKBR3; HT-29	siRNA + Docetaxel; SN38	(Jafari et al., 2019; Sayari et al., 2014)
MUC1 aptamer-liposomes/hydrogels	Aptamer-conjugated liposomes for docetaxel; CpG–MUC1 hydrogel with intercalated DOX	MUC-1; Tubulin	multiple (MCF-7, MCF10A, MDA-MB-231, HeLa)	Docetaxel; Doxorubicin	(Mohapatra et al., 2017; Wei et al., 2019)
5TR1 aptamer systems	5TR1-conjugated PEGylated liposomes, PLGA NPs, SPION conjugates	MUC-1	C26; MDA-MB-231; MCF7	Doxorubicin; Epirubicin	(Moosavian et al., 2018; Luo et al., 2018; Taghavi et al., 2017; Jalalian et al., 2013)
Nucleoside-modified aptamers	Replacement of natural nucleosides (clofarabine, etc.) within MUC1 aptamer sequence for therapeutic action	MUC-1	—	Therapeutic nucleoside analogues	(Zhu et al., 2022)
DNA tetrahedron (drug loading)	Intercalation or physical loading of small molecules/photosensitisers	apoptosis/MDR cell apoptosis	B6F10; SCC7; MDA-MB-231; A549; A549/T	Methylene blue (PDT); Paclitaxel	(Kim et al., 2016; Xue et al., 2018)
DNA tetrahedron (ASO/NLS)	ASOs loaded into TDNs with nuclear localization sequence	c-raf	A549	ASO	Yang et al. (2018)

(*Continued*)

TABLE 21.1 Engineered DNA nanostructures serve as innovative carriers for therapeutic agents.—cont'd

Nanomaterial	Method/Strategy	Target	Model	Payload	References.
Streptavidin-decorated mirror TDN	Biotinylated mirror strand conjugated to streptavidin for enzyme loading	apoptosis; gene modification; carbohydrate hydrolysis	HeLa; nanofibroblasts	Caspase-3; Cre recombinase; β-galactosidase	Kim et al. (2018)
Double-bundle DNA tetrahedron	Intercalation of platinum-based DNA intercalator 56MESS	EGFR	A431; A549; A549/DDP; MCF-7; A2780	56MESS (platinum intercalator)	Wu et al. (2019)
DNA origami (intercalation)	Intercalative drug loading for cytotoxicity and PDT	apoptosis, MDR apoptosis	MDA-MB-231; MDA-MB-468; MCF-7; HL-60/ADR	Doxorubicin; Daunorubicin; BMEPC (PDT agent)	(Zhao et al., 2012; Halley et al., 2016; Zhuang et al., 2016)
DNA nanorobot (tubular origami)	Fastener strands unzip upon aptamer binding to expose payload (molecular trigger)	Tumor endothelial cell marker (nucleolin)	HUVEC; MDA-MB-231	Thrombin (coagulation protease)	(Li et al., 2019)
DNA nanotubes	Cholesterol modification and conjugation to cytochrome *c*	apoptosis	HeLa	Cytochrome *c*	Kocabey et al. (2021)
Self-assembled DNA nanotubes	Cy3 labeling and folate conjugation for FR targeting	Folate receptor	KB (nasopharyngeal)	Cy3 (label)	Ko et al. (2008)
MUC1-modified DNA nanotube–peptide	Capsulation and dual DOX/PTX loading	MUC-1; integrin αvβ3	MCF-7	Doxorubicin; Paclitaxel	Ji et al. (2018)
PSMA aptamer-anchored PLGA-b-PEG NPs	Surface-anchored aptamer for targeted DTX delivery	PSMA	LNCaP	Docetaxel	(Chen et al., 2016b)
PSMA RNA aptamer-liposome	Aptamer-conjugated PEGylated liposome	PSMA	LNCaP	Doxorubicin	Baek et al. (2014)
A10 aptamer-CRISPR chimera	DSPE-PEG2000 liposome carrying CRISPR/Cas9 chimeras	PSMA; PLK-1	LNCaP; PC-3	CRISPR gRNA targeting PLK1	Zhen et al. (2017)

A10–3.2 aptamer nanobubbles	Cationic nanobubbles for FoxM1 siRNA delivery	PSMA	LNCaP	FoxM1 siRNA	Wu et al. (2018)
PSMA-targeted micelles	H40-PLA-PEG micelles bearing DOX and PSMA aptamer	PSMA	CWR22Rν1	Doxorubicin	Xu et al. (2013)
A10 aptamer–polylactide	A10-functionalized DOX–polylactide conjugate	PSMA	LNCaP; PC-3	Doxorubicin	Tang et al. (2015)
A10–3.2 ultrasound droplets	Ultrasound-responsive droplets delivering siRNA	PSMA; CAT-1	22RV1; PC-3; 16HBE	siRNA (siCAT-1)	Guo et al. (2022)
B19 aptamer-PAMAM dendrimer	PAMAM G4C12 dendrimer conjugated with B19 aptamer	CD133	U-87; C6	Paclitaxel + Temozolomide	Behrooz et al. (2022)
CD133 aptamer-PLGA-PEG micelle	Aptamer-functionalized micelle for paclitaxel delivery	CD133	A549	Paclitaxel	Pang et al. (2022)
PEGylated CD133-DOX conjugate	PEGylated aptamer–doxorubicin conjugate	CD133	Hep3B; Huh7; HEK293T	Doxorubicin	Zhou et al. (2021)
CD133-SN38 NPs	Self-assembled PEGylated carboxymethylcellulose–SN38 nanoparticles	CD133	HT29; CHO	SN38	Alibolandi et al. (2018)
CD133 aptamer-exosomes	Exosomes decorated with CD133 and angiopep-2 for TMZ + O6-BG delivery	CD133; An2	U87MG; GSC	Temozolomide + O6-benzylguanine	(Liang et al., 2022)
CD133 aptamer-drug nanomicelles	Gefitinib-loaded nanomicelles conjugated with CD133 aptamers	CD133	A549; A431	Gefitinib	Huang et al. (2017)
CD133 aptamer-liposome DTX	DTX liposomes surface-conjugated with CD133 aptamers	CD133	A549	Docetaxel	(Ma et al., 2017)
CD44 aptamer-PEGylated liposomes	Surface-conjugated CD44 aptamer on PEGylated liposomes	CD44	A549; MDA-MB-231; NIH/3T3	—	Alshaer et al. (2015)
CD44 aptamer-DOX conjugate	Direct aptamer–drug conjugation	CD44	Breast cancer cells	Doxorubicin	Natesh et al. (2021)
CD44-anti-PD-L1 dual aptamer liposome	Liposomes co-functionalized with CD44 and anti-PD-L1 aptamers carrying DOX + IDO1 siRNA	CD44; PD-L1	MDA-MB-231; 4T1 (mouse)	DOX; IDO1 siRNA	Kim et al. (2022)

(Continued)

TABLE 21.1 Engineered DNA nanostructures serve as innovative carriers for therapeutic agents.—cont'd

Nanomaterial	Method/Strategy	Target	Model	Payload	References.
CD28 aptamer X-polymers	CAR-like multivalent aptamer nanoparticles combining CD28 aptamer, CTLA-4 tetramer, RNA aptamer (Del60), and folate-labeled ssDNA	CD28; CTLA-4	Mouse melanoma B16	CAR-T-like immunotherapy construct	Bai et al. (2020)
MRP1-CD28 aptamer conjugate	MRP1-CD28 aptamer conjugate developed into translational whole-cell vaccine (Aptvax)	MRP1; CD28	B16F10; resistant tumors	Whole-cell vaccine (Aptvax)	Soldevilla et al. (2016)
CD38 aptamer-DOX conjugate	CD38 aptamer chemically conjugated to DOX	CD38	Multiple myeloma cell lines (HDLM2, Jeko1, L428, K299, CD38-neg cells)	Doxorubicin	Wen et al. (2016)
CD71 aptamer-MMAE	CD71 aptamer conjugated with XQ-2d-MMAE	CD71	OCM-1	Monomethyl auristatin E (MMAE)	(Zhang et al., 2022)
CD117 aptamer-MTX	CD117 aptamer–methotrexate conjugates	CD117	HEL cells (CD117 +)	Methotrexate	Zhao et al. (2015)
VEGF aptamer	VEGF aptamer assembled with DNA fragments and photosensitiser TMPyP	VEGF	MCF-7	Daunomycin + TMPyP (PDT)	Zhao et al. (2021)
EpCAM RNA aptamer liposome	RNA aptamer–conjugated PEGylated liposome for DOX delivery	EpCAM	CHO–K1; C26	Doxorubicin	Mashreghi et al. (2021)
EpCAM aptamer–survivin siRNA fusion	Aptamer–siRNA fusion combined with DOX in resistant MCF-7 subline	EpCAM	MCF-7 (DOX-resistant)	Doxorubicin + survivin siRNA	Wang et al. (2015)
FOXM1 aptamer	FOXM1 aptamer conjugated to HA-b-PCL nanopolymersomes carrying DOX and CPT	FOXM1	A549; SK-MES-1	Doxorubicin; camptothecin	Shahriari et al. (2021)
Sgc8c aptamer–DOX conjugate	PTK7-targeting aptamer–DOX conjugate	PTK7	NB-4; Ramos	Doxorubicin	Huang et al. (2009)

BAFF-R aptamer–siRNA	BAFF-R aptamer conjugated with siRNA	BAFF-R	Jeko-1; Z138	siRNA	Zhou et al. (2013)
DNA nanoflower (RCA)	Rolling circle amplification product dual-functionalized with AS1411 and ASO for co-delivery	Nucleolin; PLK1	MCF-7 (breast cancer)	Doxorubicin + anti-PLK1 ASO	(Shen et al., 2025)
DNA nanorobot	Tubular DNA origami “fastener” strands unzip upon aptamer binding to expose payload	Nucleolin (tumor endothelium)	HUVEC; MDA-MB-231	Thrombin (coagulation protease)	(Hua et al., 2019)
Aptamer–protein (HSA) conjugate	AS1411 conjugated to human serum albumin carrying lidamycin (LDP-AE)	Nucleolin	KYSE520 (esophageal)	Lidamycin	Zheng et al. (2025)
DNA hydrogel + AuNPs	Nanoscale DNA hydrogel functionalized with NGR peptide and AuNPs for peptide release	CD13 (APN)	Broad cancer models	Buforin IIb (anticancer peptide)	Quazi and Park (2023)
Tetrahedral DNA (tFNA)	AntiHER2 aptamer anchored on tFNA to promote lysosomal degradation of HER2	HER2	SK-BR-3; MCF-7	HApt (aptamer as effector)	(Ma et al., 2019)

Chemotherapy delivery

DNA nanomaterials are used as carriers for conventional chemotherapy drugs to enhance their efficacy and reduce side effects.

Doxorubicin (DOX) Delivery: Various DNA nanostructures, including origami (triangles, tubes), tetrahedrons, and nanogels, have been used to deliver DOX. These carriers improve drug loading, facilitate targeted delivery to tumors like breast cancer, and can overcome multidrug resistance by altering intracellular drug distribution. For example, triangular DNA origami has shown optimal tumor accumulation and significant therapeutic effects in multidrug-resistant breast cancer cells (Liu et al., 2018a).

Platinum-Based Drug Delivery: DNA icosahedrons have been designed to encapsulate platinum nanoparticles. These structures can respond to intracellular triggers like telomerase, which is overexpressed in many cancer cells, to precisely release the drug, thereby enhancing treatment efficacy against cisplatin-resistant tumors (Ma et al., 2018b).

Paclitaxel (PTX) Delivery: DNA tetrahedrons (TDNs) have been used to deliver PTX to treat nonsmall cell lung cancer. This system significantly inhibited the proliferation of both wild-type and multidrug-resistant cancer cells, demonstrating its potential to overcome drug resistance (Huang et al., 2023).

Gene therapy and combination therapy

DNA nanostructures can deliver nucleic acid-based drugs, such as siRNA, antisense oligonucleotides (ASO), and components for gene editing, often in combination with chemotherapy.

siRNA Delivery: DNA tetrahedrons have been used for targeted in vivo delivery of small interfering RNA (siRNA), demonstrating effective gene silencing in tumor models without significant immune response. Cross-linked nucleic acid nanogels have also been developed for effective siRNA delivery, showing prolonged blood circulation compared to naked siRNA (Lv et al., 2021).

Combined Gene and Chemotherapy: DNA origami platforms have been engineered for the synergistic delivery of both chemotherapy drugs (like DOX) and gene-based therapies (like p53 or RNAi) to combat multidrug-resistant tumors. Another approach uses a carrier-free system where drug-chemogene conjugates self-assemble into nanoparticles, combining chemotherapy with gene silencing to reverse multi-drug resistance (Liu et al., 2018b).

Gene Editing Delivery: A platform based on branched DNA has been constructed to codeliver sgRNA/Cas9 for gene editing and antisense oligonucleotides for gene silencing. This system targets the tumor-related gene PLK1, showing effective tumor treatment with good biocompatibility (Liu et al., 2019).

Immunotherapy applications

DNA nanomaterials are also explored as vehicles for immunostimulatory agents to enhance antitumor immune responses.

CpG Oligonucleotide Delivery: DNA structures like tetrahedrons, dendrimers, and nanoribbons are used to deliver CpG oligonucleotides, which act as vaccine adjuvants. These nanostructures protect the CpG motifs from degradation, enhance their uptake by immune cells, and lead to a stronger immunostimulatory effect compared to free CpG ODNs (Huang et al., 2023).

Combined Immunotherapy: A DNA nanococoon has been developed for the inflammation-triggered, programmed delivery of CpG and antiPD1 antibody for postoperative cancer immunotherapy. This system enhances T cell activity at tumor inflammation sites and induces a persistent immune response, significantly inhibiting tumor recurrence (Wang et al., 2016).

DNA nanostructures and clinical perspectives

DNA-based nanomaterials are emerging as a versatile and promising platform in cancer therapy due to their unique properties, including sequence programmability, biocompatibility, and structural controllability. These materials can be engineered into various shapes and sizes, such as DNA origami, tetrahedrons (TDNs), and nanogels, to function as sophisticated drug delivery systems. Their applications span chemotherapy, gene therapy, and immunotherapy, aiming to enhance therapeutic efficacy while minimizing side effects (Abdollahzadeh et al., 2025).

In chemotherapy, DNA nanomaterials serve as effective carriers for conventional drugs like doxorubicin (DOX) and paclitaxel (PTX). For instance, DNA origami structures have been used to deliver DOX to breast cancer cells, improving drug accumulation and overcoming resistance. Similarly, tetrahedral DNA nanostructures (TDNs) have been shown to inhibit the proliferation of multidrug-resistant nonsmall cell lung cancer cells by efficiently delivering PTX. These nanocarriers can be designed to respond to the tumor microenvironment, such as acidic pH, to trigger drug release precisely at the tumor site, thereby improving treatment efficiency and reducing systemic toxicity. By combining chemotherapy with gene therapy, such as codelivering DOX with p53 using a DNA nano-kite, these systems can treat multidrug-resistant tumors more effectively (Huang et al., 2023; Abdollahzadeh et al., 2025).

For gene therapy, DNA nanomaterials are used as nonviral vectors to deliver therapeutic nucleic acids like small interfering RNA (siRNA), antisense oligonucleotides (ASO), and CRISPR/Cas9 components. Their structural stability protects the genetic cargo from degradation in the bloodstream. For example, DNA tetrahedrons have been successfully used for targeted in vivo siRNA delivery. Other platforms, like those based on branched DNA, can co-deliver gene-editing tools (sgRNA/Cas9) and gene-silencing agents (antisense) to synergistically target cancer-related genes like PLK1 (Abdollahzadeh et al., 2025).

In the realm of immunotherapy, DNA nanostructures are utilized to deliver immunostimulatory agents like CpG oligonucleotides (CpG ODN). These structures protect CpG ODN from nuclease degradation and enhance their uptake by immune cells, leading to a stronger antitumor immune response. DNA tetrahedrons and nanoribbons loaded with CpG have been shown to induce a significantly higher secretion of proinflammatory cytokines compared to free CpG ODN. Furthermore, these nanomaterials can be designed for the codelivery of agents like antiPD-1 antibodies, offering a combined immunotherapeutic strategy that can inhibit tumor recurrence postsurgery (Kerkmann et al., 2006; Huang et al., 2023).

Nanomaterials are increasingly utilized as carriers for chemotherapeutic agents to enhance targeted delivery and overcome the limitations of conventional chemotherapy, such as systemic toxicity and drug resistance. These nanocarriers are designed to load and protect therapeutic agents, enabling targeted delivery to tumor sites and facilitating stimuli-responsive release. Various materials, including DNA-based nanostructures and graphene derivatives, have been developed for this purpose, often in combination with other functional molecules like polymers, peptides, and aptamers to improve biocompatibility and targeting specificity (Ouyang et al., 2020).

DNA nanotechnology, particularly DNA origami, offers a method to create precisely shaped nanostructures for drug delivery. These structures can be designed in various forms, such as triangles, squares, and tubes, and can be loaded with chemotherapeutic drugs like doxorubicin (DOX) (Zhang et al., 2021a). For example, a DNA nanoscale precision-guided missile (D-PGM) has been developed, consisting of a "warhead" (WH) and a "guidance/control" (GC) system. The WH is a rod like DNA nanostructure that serves as the drug carrier, while the GC is an aptamer-based logic gate that guides the nanostructure to specific cancer cells. The drug-loading capacity of these DNA structures is a key feature; for instance, the WH component of the D-PGM is reported to have a high payload capacity. Studies have shown that the DOX-to-WH system ratio can reach 120:1, indicating a very high drug payload capacity. Once delivered to the target cells, the drugs can be released in response to the intracellular environment, such as low pH or nuclease degradation (Ouyang et al., 2020).

Graphene and its derivatives, such as graphene oxide (GO), are also used as platforms for delivering chemotherapeutic agents. These materials can be functionalized to improve their properties for biomedical applications. For example, GO can be used in drug delivery systems to carry agents like doxorubicin (DOX) and paclitaxel (PTX). The high surface area of graphene derivatives allows for high drug loading capacity. Functionalization with polymers like polyethylene glycol (PEG) can improve solubility and biocompatibility, while targeting ligands such as folic acid (FA) can direct the nanocarrier to specific cancer cells (Angelopoulou et al., 2024).

Challenges and limitations

In vivo stability and nuclease degradation

The vulnerability of DNA-based nanomaterials to enzymatic breakdown in physiological settings is a major drawback for anticancer treatment. Intracellular nucleases in endosomal and lysosomal compartments, as well as circulating DNases in plasma, can rapidly degrade unmodified DNA constructs, reducing their structural integrity and therapeutic half-life. The architecture has a significant impact on the rate of deterioration; multilayer origami structures that are tightly packed tend to be more nuclease-resistant than open wireframe designs. A balance between protection and regulated biodegradability is necessary since overstabilization may impede intracellular cargo release. Many chemical modifications have been investigated to improve serum stability, such as PEGylation, 2′-O-methylation, and phosphorothioate linkages. Resistance to enzymatic assault is further improved by encapsulation within lipid bilayers or polymer coatings (Perrault and Shih, 2014). Importantly, stabilization strategies must consider tumor-specific microenvironments characterized by acidic pH, oxidative stress, and heterogeneous enzymatic activity. Controlled degradation can be advantageous, enabling site-specific drug release while minimizing long-term accumulation. Structural design approaches integrating crosslinking or hybrid DNA–polymer composites are emerging as promising solutions (Jin et al., 2024).

Large-scale production and cost issues

One significant translational constraint is still the scalability of DNA nanoparticles. Solid-phase phosphoramidite chemistry, which is necessary for high-fidelity oligonucleotide synthesis, becomes expensive when lengthy scaffold strands are needed for intricate origami structures. Furthermore, strict purification and quality control are necessary to produce large quantities of high-purity DNA free of endotoxins and truncated sequences. Compared to polymeric or lipid-based nanocarriers, these requirements result in a considerable increase in production costs (Paiva et al., 2025). Although rolling-circle amplification and new enzymatic DNA synthesis techniques are viable and affordable substitutes, industrial standardization is still being developed. To ensure repeatability, automated folding systems and scalable annealing procedures need to be tuned in accordance with GMP guidelines. Additionally, in order to comply with regulations, analytical characterisation instruments such as gel electrophoresis, dynamic light scattering, and atomic force microscopy must be standardized (Hadi et al., 2020).

Pharmacokinetics and biodistribution concerns

The pharmacokinetic behavior of DNA nanostructures is highly dependent on size, geometry, and surface chemistry. Structures smaller than approximately 10 nm are prone to rapid renal clearance, whereas larger constructs may accumulate in the liver and spleen due to uptake by the mononuclear phagocyte system. Shape-dependent biodistribution has also been observed, with elongated or tubular geometries exhibiting altered circulation profiles compared with compact spherical designs. Opsonization and tumor accumulation can be controlled through surface modification techniques, such as PEGylation and targeted ligand attachment. Predictability is limited, though, since the impact of increased permeability and retention (EPR) differs greatly between tumor types and individuals. Furthermore, in the long term, off-target accumulation can pose safety concerns (L.Wu et al.).

Beyond size and geometry, the pharmacokinetic profile of DNA nanostructures is strongly influenced by their structural rigidity, surface charge density, and molecular flexibility. Highly compact multilayer origami structures may exhibit prolonged circulation compared with flexible wireframe assemblies due to reduced deformation and filtration through glomerular membranes. Conversely, excessive negative surface charge can promote rapid opsonization by serum proteins, facilitating clearance by macrophages within the mononuclear phagocyte system. Surface engineering strategies such as PEGylation reduce protein corona formation and extend systemic half-life; however, repeated administration may induce antiPEG antibody responses, complicating long-term therapeutic regimens. The relationship between DNA nanostructures and the tumor microenvironment is another important factor that determines biodistribution. Although the increased permeability and retention (EPR) effect has long been used to promote passive tumor growth, its magnitude varies widely with interstitial pressure, stromal density, and tumor vascularization. According to recent data, the form and mechanical characteristics of nanostructures affect the depth of tumor penetration and the routes of cellular internalization; for example, in dense tumor matrices, wireframe and rod-like designs show better diffusion (Bujold et al., 2018).

Safety, toxicity, and regulatory challenges

The relationship between DNA nanostructures and the tumor microenvironment is another important factor that determines biodistribution. Although the increased permeability and retention (EPR) effect has long been used to promote passive tumor growth, its magnitude varies widely with interstitial pressure, stromal density, and tumor vascularization. According to recent data, the form and mechanical characteristics of nanostructures affect the depth of tumor penetration and the routes for cellular internalization; in dense tumor matrices, for example, wireframe and rod like designs show better diffusion. Since DNA nanoparticles fall between biologics and nanomedicines, regulatory categorization poses an additional challenge. The development of standardized protocols for stability testing, characterization, and long-term biodistribution research is ongoing. Clinical approval will depend on the establishment of standardized preclinical evaluation procedures and analytical frameworks (Kim et al., 2023).

Future perspectives and emerging trends

Smart and logic-gated DNA nanodevices

Growing functional complexity and integration with precision medicine paradigms will determine DNA nanotechnology's future course in cancer. From static drug carriers to dynamic molecular systems that can sense, calculate, and trigger therapeutic responses, next-generation DNA nanodevices are changing rapidly. Tumor-specific nucleic acid signatures can trigger conditional drug release via logic-gated structures based on toehold-mediated strand displacement, enabling multi-input Boolean processing in biological settings. These programmable nanorobots have the potential to minimize systemic toxicity and greatly improve tumor selectivity (Chen et al., 2018).

Rational nanostructure engineering is being accelerated by concurrent developments in computational design and artificial intelligence. By predicting folding efficiency, thermodynamic stability, and hybridization kinetics, machine learning methods can minimize the number of experimental iterations. DNA nanoparticles provide an adaptable framework for patient-specific therapeutic payloads, such as mutation-targeted siRNA, antisense oligonucleotides, or CRISPR components, when paired with tumor genomic analysis. In the direction of genuinely individualized oncology, this intersection of nanotechnology, molecular diagnostics, and AI-driven optimization is revolutionary. The development of synthesis methods and the clarification of regulatory mechanisms will enable DNA nanoparticles to move from experimental constructs to precision medicines for clinical use (Esmaeilpour et al., 2026).

Personalized cancer therapy using DNA nanotechnology

The sequence-defined programmability of DNA nanoparticles makes them a very flexible platform for customized cancer. Rational design of DNA nanostructures, including mutation-targeted siRNA, antisense oligonucleotides, or CRISPR-associated components, can be informed by patient-specific genomic changes when next-generation sequencing is incorporated into regular cancer diagnosis. This modular flexibility enables therapeutic payloads to be quickly reconfigured to address changing tumor genotypes and acquired resistance mechanisms. Sequence redesign is all that is needed to reprogramme DNA-based systems, whereas traditional nanoparticles require reformulation for every therapeutic modification. DNA nanostructures enable the precise spatial arrangement of targeted ligands that are tailored to tumor-specific receptor expression patterns, in addition to genetic tailoring. Quantitative receptor profiling can be used to enhance the multivalent presentation of aptamers or peptide ligands, increasing internalization efficiency and binding avidity. This precision supports the development of adaptive therapy approaches that are sensitive to interpatient variability (Nicolson et al., 2020).

Integration with artificial intelligence and precision medicine

The combination of DNA nanotechnology and artificial intelligence (AI) has the potential to speed up the development of logical nanostructures and therapeutic optimization. Before experimental confirmation, secondary structure formation, hybridization thermodynamics, and possible misfolding events may be predicted using computational modeling platforms. Prediction accuracy for intricate multi-strand assemblies may be improved by machine learning algorithms trained on sizable datasets of nucleic acid folding and interaction characteristics. One of the main translational hurdles in nanomedicine is addressed by such computational support, which decreases experimental iteration cycles and enhances reproducibility. AI-driven pharmacokinetic modeling and systemic biology techniques may improve predictions of biodistribution, tumor penetration, and clearance kinetics, in addition to structural optimization. Selecting targeted ligands and therapeutic payloads for DNA nanocarriers can be guided by integrating patient-derived omics data, including genomic, transcriptomic, and proteomic profiles. The combination of clinical informatics, computational biology, and nanotechnology is a revolutionary step toward data-driven precision oncology (Esmaeilpour et al., 2026).

Translational potential and clinical outlook

Despite DNA nanotechnology's strong preclinical performance, coordinated advancements in manufacturing scalability, regulatory standards, and long-term safety assessment are necessary for effective clinical translation. A crucial milestone is yet to be achieved: the establishment of GMP-compliant manufacturing methods that can produce endotoxin-free, structurally homogeneous DNA nanostructures on an industrial scale. The development of robust analytical frameworks for structural characterization, including high-resolution imaging, purity evaluation, and stability testing in physiological settings, is equally crucial. Clinically, early-stage studies must carefully evaluate immunogenicity, biodistribution, and therapeutic index across a range of tumor types. The significance of stratified clinical design is demonstrated by interpatient variability and the heterogeneity of the improved permeability and retention effect. However, the combination of computational optimization, molecular oncology, and programmable nanotechnology offers a solid scientific basis for potential therapeutic integration (Wages et al., 2018; Seeman and Sleiman, 2017).

Conclusion

Instead of only acting as passive carriers, DNA nanostructures are programmable molecular platforms with the ability to sense, calculate, and react within biological systems. Building on this idea, new research has transformed static DNA scaffolds into useful tools: DNA origami and compact polyhedra now allow ligands and cargo to be placed at the atomic level, enabling real stoichiometric codelivery of chemotherapeutics and gene-silencing agents. While multivalent aptamer displays and regulated geometry enhance receptor engagement and cellular uptake, concurrent advancements in stimuli-responsive design—pH, enzyme, redox, and ATP triggers—have developed designs that release payloads only under tumor-relevant conditions. These characteristics alter the delivery strategy: DNA platforms offer digital addressability and deterministic architecture that are unmatched by polymeric or lipid carriers. This enables the development of modular, synergistic therapies tailored to the tumor's biology. In practical terms, this means the potential to combat heterogeneity and resistance through coordinated molecular actions, more accurate combination therapies, and the capacity to program activation within the tumor microenvironment. However, there are still reasonable boundaries. For instance, rapid clinical expectations are less likely due to shape-dependent biodistribution, nuclease sensitivity, and dose-related immune responses. Real-world issues such as scalable GMP procedures, robust hybrid stability (chemical modification, coatings, or lipid encapsulation), and regulatory routes consistent with the hybrid drug-device character of DNA devices should be taken into account for successful translation. The development process can be accelerated, and the top candidates can be selected by combining normal pharmacokinetic analytics with AI-based sequence and structure design. Measured optimism is justified: programmable DNA nanotechnology has the potential to become a fundamental tool in precision oncology with focused investment in production, safety profiling, and stratified clinical testing.

References

Abdollahzadeh, H., Peeples, T.L., Shahcheraghi, M., 2025. DNA nanotechnology in oligonucleotide drug delivery systems: Prospects for Bio-nanorobots in cancer treatment. Adv. Drug Deliv. Rev. 225. https://doi.org/10.1016/j.addr.2025.115673.

Aghanejad, A., Babamiri, H., Adibkia, K., Barar, J., Omidi, Y., 2018. Mucin-1 aptamer-armed superparamagnetic iron oxide nanoparticles for targeted delivery of doxorubicin to breast cancer cells. Bioimpacts 8 (2), 117–127. https://doi.org/10.15171/bi.2018.14.

Alibolandi, M., Taghdisi, S.M., Ramezani, P., Hosseini Shamili, F., Farzad, S.A., Abnous, K., Ramezani, M., 2017. Smart AS1411-aptamer conjugated pegylated PAMAM dendrimer for the superior delivery of camptothecin to colon adenocarcinoma in vitro and in vivo. Int.J. Pharm. 519 (1–2), 352–364. https://doi.org/10.1016/j.ijpharm.2017.01.044.

Alibolandi, M., Abnous, K., Anvari, S., Mohammadi, M., Ramezani, M., Taghdisi, S.M., 2018. CD133-targeted delivery of self-assembled PEGylated carboxymethylcellulose-SN38 nanoparticles to colorectal cancer. Artif. Cells, Nanomed. Biotechnol. 46 (1), 1159–1169. https://doi.org/10.1080/21691401.2018.1446969.

Alshaer, W., Hillaireau, H., Vergnaud, J., Ismail, S., Elias, F., 2015. Functionalizing liposomes with anti-CD44 aptamer for selective targeting of cancer cells. Bioconjug. Chem. 26 (7), 1307–1313. https://doi.org/10.1021/bc5004313.

Ammar, M.M., Ali, R., Abd Elaziz, N.A., Habib, H., Abbas, F.M., Yassin, M.T., Maniah, K., Abdelaziz, R., 2025. Nanotechnology in oncology: Advances in biosynthesis, drug delivery, and theranostics. Discov. Oncol. 16 (1). https://doi.org/10.1007/s12672-025-02664-3.

Angelopoulou, A., Papachristodoulou, M., Voulgari, E., Mouikis, A., Zygouri, P., Gournis, D.P., Avgoustakis, K., 2024. Paclitaxel-loaded, pegylated carboxylic graphene oxide with high colloidal stability, sustained, pH-responsive release and strong anticancer effects on lung cancer A549 cell line. Pharmaceutics 16 (11), 1452. https://doi.org/10.3390/pharmaceutics16111452.

Ayatollahi, S., Salmasi, Z., Hashemi, M., Askarian, S., Oskuee, R.K., Abnous, K., Ramezani, M., 2017. Aptamer-targeted delivery of Bcl-xL shRNA using alkyl modified PAMAM dendrimers into lung cancer cells. Int. J. Biochem. Cell Biol. 92, 210–217. https://doi.org/10.1016/j.biocel.2017.10.005.

Baek, S.E., Lee, K.H., Park, Y.S., Oh, D.K., Oh, S., Kim, K.S., Kim, D.E., 2014. RNA aptamer-conjugated liposome as an efficient anticancer drug delivery vehicle targeting cancer cells in vivo. J. Contr. Release 196, 234–242. https://doi.org/10.1016/j.jconrel.2014.10.018.

Bai, C., Gao, S., Hu, S., Liu, X., Li, H., Dong, J., Huang, A., Zhu, L., Zhou, P., Li, S., Shao, N., 2020. Self-assembled multivalent aptamer nanoparticles with potential CAR-like characteristics could activate T cells and inhibit melanoma growth. Mol. Ther. Oncolytics 17, 9–20. https://doi.org/10.1016/j.omto.2020.03.002.

Barzegar Behrooz, A., Nabavizadeh, F., Adiban, J., Shafiee Ardestani, M., Vahabpour, R., Aghasadeghi, M.R., Sohanaki, H., 2017. Smart bomb AS1411 aptamer-functionalized/PAMAM dendrimer nanocarriers for targeted drug delivery in the treatment of gastric cancer. Clin. Exp. Pharmacol. Physiol. 44 (1), 41–51. https://doi.org/10.1111/1440-1681.12670.

Behrooz, A.B., Vazifehmand, R., Tajudin, A.A., Masarudin, M.J., Sekawi, Z., Masomian, M., Syahir, A., 2022. Tailoring drug co-delivery nanosystem for mitigating U-87 stem cells drug resistance. Drug Deliv. Trans. Res. 12 (5), 1253–1269. https://doi.org/10.1007/s13346-021-01017-1.

Bujold, K.E., Lacroix, A., Sleiman, H.F., 2018. DNA Nanostructures at the interface with biology. Chem. 4 (3), 495–521. https://doi.org/10.1016/j.chempr.2018.02.005.

Cai, S., Yan, J., Xiong, H., Wu, Q., Xing, H., Liu, Y., Liu, S., Liu, Z., 2020. Aptamer-functionalized molybdenum disulfide nanosheets for tumor cell targeting and lysosomal acidic environment/NIR laser responsive drug delivery to realize synergetic chemo-photothermal therapeutic effects. Int. J. Pharm. 590, 119948. https://doi.org/10.1016/j.ijpharm.2020.119948.

Charbgoo, F., Alibolandi, M., Taghdisi, S.M., Abnous, K., Soltani, F., Ramezani, M., 2018. MUC1 aptamer-targeted DNA micelles for dual tumor therapy using doxorubicin and KLA peptide. Nanomed. Nanotechnol. Biol. Med. 14 (3), 685–697. https://doi.org/10.1016/j.nano.2017.12.010.

Charbgoo, F., Soltani, F., Alibolandi, M., Taghdisi, S.M., Abnous, K., Ramezani, P., Ramezani, M., 2021. Ladder-like targeted and gated doxorubicin delivery using bivalent aptamer in vitro and in vivo. Mater. Sci. Eng. C 119, 111618. https://doi.org/10.1016/j.msec.2020.111618.

Chehelgerdi, M., Chehelgerdi, M., Allela, O.Q.B., Pecho, R.D.C., Jayasankar, N., Rao, D.P., Thamaraikani, T., Vasanthan, M., Viktor, P., Lakshmaiya, N., Saadh, M.J., Amajd, A., Abo-Zaid, M.A., Castillo-Acobo, R.Y., Ismail, A.H., Amin, A.H., Akhavan-Sigari, R., 2023. Progressing nanotechnology to improve targeted cancer treatment: Overcoming hurdles in its clinical implementation. Mol. Cancer 22 (1). https://doi.org/10.1186/s12943-023-01865-0.

Chen, D., Li, B., Cai, S., Wang, P., Peng, S., Sheng, Y., He, Y., Gu, Y., Chen, H., 2016a. Dual targeting luminescent gold nanoclusters for tumor imaging and deep tissue therapy. Biomaterials 100, 1–16. https://doi.org/10.1016/j.biomaterials.2016.05.017.

Chen, Z., Tai, Z., Gu, F., Hu, C., Zhu, Q., Gao, S., 2016b. Aptamer-mediated delivery of docetaxel to prostate cancer through polymeric nanoparticles for enhancement of antitumor efficacy. Eur. J. Pharm. Biopharm. 107, 130–141. https://doi.org/10.1016/j.ejpb.2016.07.007.

Chen, T., Ren, L., Liu, X., Zhou, M., Li, L., Xu, J., Zhu, X., 2018. DNA nanotechnology for cancer diagnosis and therapy. Int. J. Mol. Sci. 19 (6), 1671. https://doi.org/10.3390/ijms19061671.

Chen, M., Hei, J., Huang, Y., Liu, X., Huang, Y., 2024a. In vivo safety evaluation method for nanomaterials for cancer therapy. Clin. Transl. Oncol. 26 (9), 2126–2141. https://doi.org/10.1007/s12094-024-03466-9.

Chen, Q., Liu, Y., Chen, Q., Li, M., Xu, L., Lin, B., Tan, Y., Liu, Z., 2024b. DNA nanostructures: Advancing cancer immunotherapy. Small 20 (49). https://doi.org/10.1002/smll.202405231.

Dai, F., Zhang, Y., Zhu, X., Shan, N., Chen, Y., 2012. Anticancer role of MUC1 aptamer–miR-29b chimera in epithelial ovarian carcinoma cells through regulation of PTEN methylation. Targeted Oncol. 7 (4), 217–225. https://doi.org/10.1007/s11523-012-0236-7.

Duangrat, R., Udomprasert, A., Kangsamaksin, T., 2020. Tetrahedral DNA nanostructures as drug delivery and bioimaging platforms in cancer therapy. Cancer Sci. 111 (9), 3164–3173. https://doi.org/10.1111/cas.14548.

Ding, L., Liu, B., Peil, A., Fan, S., Chao, J., Liu, N., 2025. DNA-directed assembly of photonic nanomaterials for diagnostic and therapeutic applications. Adv. Mater. 37 (49). https://doi.org/10.1002/adma.202500086.

Dong, K., Wang, Z., Zhang, Y., Ren, J., Qu, X., 2018. Metal–organic framework-based nanoplatform for intracellular environment-responsive endo/lysosomal escape and enhanced cancer therapy. ACS Appl. Mater. Interfaces 10 (38), 31998–32005. https://doi.org/10.1021/acsami.8b11972.

Dong, Y., Yao, C., Zhu, Y., Lu, Y., Luo, D., Yang, D., 2020. DNA functional materials assembled from branched DNA: Design, synthesis, and applications. Chem. Rev. 120 (17), 9420–9481. https://doi.org/10.1021/acs.chemrev.0c00294.

Esmaeilpour, D., Hamblin, M.R., Cheng, J., Khosravi, A., Liu, J., Zarepour, A., Zarrabi, A., Sillanpää, M., Nazarzadeh Zare, E., Shen, J., Karimi-Maleh, H., 2026. Artificial intelligence driven protein design and sustainable nanomedicine for advanced theranostics. Bioact. Mater. 60, 425–455. https://doi.org/10.1016/j.bioactmat.2026.01.036.

Gao, D., Zhu, Q., Ruan, J., Sun, T., Han, L., 2020. Polyplexes by polymerized dequalinium and bifunctional aptamer for mitochondrial targeting drug release to overcome drug resistance. ACS Appl. Bio Mater. 3 (8), 5182–5192. https://doi.org/10.1021/acsabm.0c00610.

Gressler, S., Hipfinger, C., Part, F., Pavlicek, A., Zafiu, C., Giese, B., 2025. A systematic review of nanocarriers used in medicine and beyond — Definition and categorization framework. J. Nanobiotechnol. 23 (1). https://doi.org/10.1186/s12951-025-03113-7.

Guo, Q., Chen, Q., Zhang, Y., Zhou, W., Li, X., Li, C., Zhang, Y., Chen, H., Liu, P., chu, Y., Sun, T., Jiang, C., 2020. Click-nucleic-acid-containing codelivery system inducing collapse of cellular homeostasis for tumor therapy through bidirectional regulation of autophagy and glycolysis. ACS Appl. Mater. Interfaces 12 (52), 57757–57767. https://doi.org/10.1021/acsami.0c18361.

Guo, L., Shi, D., Shang, M., Sun, X., Meng, D., Liu, X., Zhou, X., Li, J., 2022. Utilizing RNA nanotechnology to construct negatively charged and ultrasound-responsive nanodroplets for targeted delivery of siRNA. Drug Deliv. 29 (1), 316–327. https://doi.org/10.1080/10717544.2022.2026532.

Hadi, T., Nozzi, N., Melby, J.O., Gao, W., Fuerst, D.E., Kvam, E., 2020. Rolling circle amplification of synthetic DNA accelerates biocatalytic determination of enzyme activity relative to conventional methods. Sci. Rep. 10 (1). https://doi.org/10.1038/s41598-020-67307-9.

Halley, P.D., Lucas, C.R., McWilliams, E.M., Webber, M.J., Patton, R.A., Kural, C., Lucas, D.M., Byrd, J.C., Castro, C. E., 2016. Daunorubicin-loaded DNA origami nanostructures circumvent drug-resistance mechanisms in a leukemia model. Small 12 (3), 308–320. https://doi.org/10.1002/smll.201502118.

Han, L., Yu, Y., Li, P., Tian, Y., 2026. From nanoparticle synthesis to assembly: DNA as a key structural material. RSC Appl. Interfaces 3 (1), 26–44. https://doi.org/10.1039/d5lf00313j.

He, Z.M., Zhang, P.H., Li, X., Zhang, J.R., Zhu, J.J., 2016. A targeted DNAzyme-nanocomposite probe equipped with built-in Zn2+ arsenal for combined treatment of gene regulation and drug delivery. Sci. Rep. 6. https://doi.org/10.1038/srep22737.

Hong, H., Fang, Z., He, W., others, 2021. Single-cell RNA-seq reveals the heterogeneity of tumor microenvironment in triple-negative breast cancer. Cancer Lett. 506, 179–190.

Hong, Y., Ma, W., Wang, M., Wang, H.H., 2025. Advances in programmable DNA nanostructures enabling stimuli-responsive drug delivery and multimodal biosensing. RSC Chem. Biol. 6 (9), 1366–1385. https://doi.org/10.1039/d5cb00057b.

Hua, L., Liu, J., Gu, H., 2019. Targeting nucleolin to obstruct vasculature feeding with an intelligent DNA nanorobot. J. Cell Mol. Med. 23 (3), 2248–2250. https://doi.org/10.1111/jcmm.14127.

Huang, Y.F., Shangguan, D., Liu, H., Phillips, J.A., Zhang, X., Chen, Y., Tan, W., 2009. Molecular assembly of an aptamer-drug conjugate for targeted drug delivery to tumor cells. Chem. Bio. Chem. 10 (5), 862–868. https://doi.org/10.1002/cbic.200800805.

Huang, X., Huang, J., Leng, D., Yang, S., Qi, Y., Sun, J., Hu, J., 2017. Gefitinib-loaded DSPE-PEG2000 nanomicelles with CD133 aptamers target lung cancer stem cells. World J. Surg. Oncol. 15 (1). https://doi.org/10.1186/s12957-017-1230-4.

Huang, H., Gao, S., Cai, X., 2023. DNA-Based nanomaterials in the immunotherapy. Curr. Drug Metabol. 24 (5), 367–384. https://doi.org/10.2174/1389200224666230413082047.

Jafari, R., Majidi Zolbanin, N., Majidi, J., Atyabi, F., Yousefi, M., Jadidi-Niaragh, F., Aghebati-Maleki, L., Shanehbandi, D., Zangbar, M.-S.S., Rafatpanah, H., 2019. Anti-Mucin1 aptamer-conjugated chitosan nanoparticles for targeted co-delivery of docetaxel and IGF-1R siRNA to SKBR3 metastatic breast cancer cells. Iran. Biomed. J. 23 (1), 21–33. https://doi.org/10.29252/ibj.23.1.21.

Jalalian, S.H., Taghdisi, S.M., Hamedani, N.S., Kalat, S.A.M., Lavaee, P., ZandKarimi, M., Ghows, N., Jaafari, M.R., Naghibi, S., Danesh, N.M., Ramezani, M., Abnous, K., 2013. Epirubicin loaded super paramagnetic iron oxide nanoparticle-aptamer bioconjugate for combined colon cancer therapy and imaging in vivo. Eur. J. Pharmaceut. Sci. 50 (2), 191–197. https://doi.org/10.1016/j.ejps.2013.06.015.

Jeong, H.Y., Kim, H., Lee, M., Hong, J., Lee, J.H., Kim, J., Choi, M.J., Park, Y.S., Kim, S.C., 2020. Development of HER2-specific aptamer-drug conjugate for breast cancer therapy. Int. J. Mol. Sci. 21 (24), 1–13. https://doi.org/10.3390/ijms21249764.

Ji, X., Haoyuan, Lv, Guo, J., Ding, C., Luo, X., 2018. A DNA nanotube–peptide biocomplex for mRNA detection and its application in cancer diagnosis and targeted therapy. Chem. Eur J. 24 (40), 10171–10177. https://doi.org/10.1002/chem.201801347.

Jia, Q., Li, Z., Guo, C., Huang, X., Song, Y., Zhou, N., Wang, M., Zhang, Z., He, L., Du, M., 2019. A γ-cyclodextrin-based metal–organic framework embedded with graphene quantum dots and modified with PEGMA via SI-ATRP for anticancer drug delivery and therapy. Nanoscale 11 (43), 20956–20967. https://doi.org/10.1039/c9nr06195a.

Jiang, K., Han, L., Guo, Y., Zheng, G., Fan, L., Shen, Z., Zhao, R., Shao, J., 2017. A carrier-free dual-drug nanodelivery system functionalized with aptamer specific targeting HER2-overexpressing cancer cells. J. Mater. Chem. B 5 (46), 9121–9129. https://doi.org/10.1039/c7tb02562a.

Jiang, S., Ge, Z., Mou, S., Yan, H., Fan, C., 2021. Designer DNA nanostructures for therapeutics. Chem. 7 (5), 1156–1179. https://doi.org/10.1016/j.chempr.2020.10.025.

Jin, F., Zeng, Q., Qian, H., Zhang, D., Wei, Y., Wang, Y., Chai, C., Cheng, W., Ding, S., Chen, T., 2022. Dual-targeted self-assembled DNA hydrogels decorated with multivalent aptamers loaded with DOX for anticancer therapy. Front. Pharmacol. 13. https://doi.org/10.3389/fphar.2022.807498.

Jin, Z., Amili, M.Al, Guo, S., 2024. Tumor microenvironment-responsive drug delivery based on polymeric micelles for precision cancer therapy: strategies and prospects. Biomedicines 12 (2), 417. https://doi.org/10.3390/biomedicines12020417.

Joshi, M., Choi, J.S., Park, J.W., Doh, K.O., 2019. Combination of doxorubicin with gemcitabine-incorporated G-quadruplex aptamer showed synergistic and selective anticancer effect in breast cancer cells. J. Microbiol. Biotechnol. 29 (11), 1799–1805. https://doi.org/10.4014/jmb.1907.07029.

Kerkmann, M., Lochmann, D., Weyermann, J., Marschner, A., Poeck, H., Wagner, M., Battiany, J., Zimmer, A., Endres, S., Hartmann, G., 2006. Immunostimulatory properties of CpG-oligonucleotides are enhanced by the use of protamine nanoparticles. Oligonucleotides 16 (4), 313–322. https://doi.org/10.1089/oli.2006.16.313.

Kim, K.R., Bang, D., Ahn, D.R., 2016. Nano-formulation of a photosensitizer using a DNA tetrahedron and its potential for in vivo photodynamic therapy. Biomater. Sci. 4 (4), 605–609. https://doi.org/10.1039/c5bm00467e.

Kim, K.R., Hwang, D., Kim, J., Lee, C.Y., Lee, W., Yoon, D.S., Shin, D., Min, S.J., Kwon, I.C., Chung, H.S., Ahn, D.R., 2018. Streptavidin-mirror DNA tetrahedron hybrid as a platform for intracellular and tumor delivery of enzymes. J. Contr. Release 280, 1–10. https://doi.org/10.1016/j.jconrel.2018.04.051.

Kim, H.J., Sung, H.J., Lee, Y.M., Choi, S.I., Kim, Y.H., Heo, K., Kim, I.H., 2020. Therapeutic application of drug-conjugated HER2 oligobody (HER2-doligobody). Int. J. Mol. Sci. 21 (9). https://doi.org/10.3390/ijms21093286.

Kim, M., Lee, J.S., Kim, W., Lee, J.H., Jun, B.H., Kim, K.S., Kim, D.E., 2022. Aptamer-conjugated nano-liposome for immunogenic chemotherapy with reversal of immunosuppression. J. Contr. Release 348, 893–910. https://doi.org/10.1016/j.jconrel.2022.06.039.

Kim, J., Cho, H., Lim, D.-K., Joo, M.K., Kim, K., 2023. Perspectives for improving the tumor targeting of nanomedicine via the EPR effect in clinical tumors. Int. J. Mol. Sci. 24 (12), 10082. https://doi.org/10.3390/ijms241210082.

Ko, S.H., Liu, H., Chen, Y., Mao, C., 2008. DNA nanotubes as combinatorial vehicles for cellular delivery. Biomacromolecules 9 (11), 3039–3043. https://doi.org/10.1021/bm800479e.

Kocabey, S., Ekim Kocabey, A., Schneiter, R., Rüegg, C., 2021. Membrane-interacting DNA nanotubes induce cancer cell death. Nanomaterials 11 (8), 2003. https://doi.org/10.3390/nano11082003.

Kumar, V., Palazzolo, S., Bayda, S., Corona, G., Toffoli, G., Rizzolio, F., 2016. DNA nanotechnology for cancer therapeutics. Theranostics 6 (5), 710–725. https://doi.org/10.7150/thno.14203.

Kumar, M., Jha, A., Mishra, B., 2024. DNA-based nanostructured platforms as drug delivery systems. Chem. Bio. Eng. 1 (3), 179–198. https://doi.org/10.1021/cbe.3c00023.

Lee, H., Dam, D.H.M., Ha, J.W., Yue, J., Odom, T.W., 2015. Enhanced human epidermal growth factor receptor 2 degradation in breast cancer cells by lysosome-targeting gold nanoconstructs. ACS Nano 9 (10), 9859–9867. https://doi.org/10.1021/acsnano.5b05138.

Li, L., Hou, J., Liu, X., Guo, Y., Wu, Y., Zhang, L., Yang, Z., 2014. Nucleolin-targeting liposomes guided by aptamer AS1411 for the delivery of siRNA for the treatment of malignant melanomas. Biomaterials 35 (12), 3840–3850. https://doi.org/10.1016/j.biomaterials.2014.01.019.

Li, X., Yang, Y., Ji, Q., Qiu, L., 2015. Targeted delivery of anticancer drugs by aptamer AS1411 mediated Pluronic F127/cyclodextrin-linked polymer composite micelles. Nanomed. Nanotechnol. Biol. Med. 11 (1), 175–184. https://doi.org/10.1016/j.nano.2014.08.013.

Li, M., Yang, G., Zheng, Y., Lv, J., Zhou, W., Zhang, H., You, F., Wu, C., Yang, H., Liu, Y., 2023. NIR/pH-triggered aptamer-functionalized DNA origami nanovehicle for imaging-guided chemo-phototherapy. J. Nanobiotechnol. 21 (1). https://doi.org/10.1186/s12951-023-01953-9.

Li, C., Wang, M., Li, P.F., Sheng, J., Fu, Q., 2024a. Construction of smart DNA-based drug delivery systems for cancer therapy. Small 20 (30). https://doi.org/10.1002/smll.202306257.

Li, M., Zhang, Y., Shi, X., Zhang, Y., Song, X., Shi, P., Zhang, S., 2024b. Controlled assembly strategy and stimuli-responsive sensing mechanism based on nanomaterials for targeted and precise treatment of malignant tumors. Sci. Sin. Chim. 54 (10), 1744–1756. https://doi.org/10.1360/ssc-2024-0115.

Li, S., Xu, M., Yao, C., Yang, D., 2025. DNA-Based nanostructures for tumor microenvironment-responsive drug delivery. Adv. Drug Deliv. Rev. 223, 115610. https://doi.org/10.1016/j.addr.2025.115610.

Liang, S., Xu, H., Ye, B.C., 2022. Membrane-decorated exosomes for combination drug delivery and improved glioma therapy. Langmuir 38 (1), 299–308. Available from: http://pubs.acs.org/journal/langd5. doi: 10.1021/acs.langmuir.1c02500.

Lin, H.C., Li, W.T., Madanayake, T.W., Tao, C., Niu, Q., Yan, S.Q., Gao, B.A., Ping, Z., 2020. Aptamer-guided upconversion nanoplatform for targeted drug delivery and near-infrared light-triggered photodynamic therapy. J. Biomater. Appl. 34 (6), 875–888. https://doi.org/10.1177/0885328219882152.

Liu, H., Fan, C., 2013. DNA origami nanostructures. In: Fan, C. (Ed.), DNA Nanotechnology. Springer, Berlin Heidelberg, pp. 207–224. https://doi.org/10.1007/978-3-642-36077-0_10.

Liu, J., Song, L., Liu, S., Jiang, Q., Liu, Q., Li, N., Wang, Z.G., Ding, B., 2018a. A DNA-based nanocarrier for efficient gene delivery and combined cancer therapy. Nano Lett. 18 (6), 3328–3334. https://doi.org/10.1021/acs.nanolett.7b04812.

Liu, X., Wu, L., Wang, L., Jiang, W., 2018b. A dual-targeting DNA tetrahedron nanocarrier for breast cancer cell imaging and drug delivery. Talanta 179, 356–363. https://doi.org/10.1016/j.talanta.2017.11.034.

Liu, J., Wu, T., Lu, X., Wu, X., Liu, S., Zhao, S., Xu, X., Ding, B., 2019. A self-assembled platform based on branched DNA for sgRNA/Cas9/antisense delivery. J. Am. Chem. Soc. 141 (48), 19032–19037. https://doi.org/10.1021/jacs.9b09043.

Lohiya, G., Katti, D.S., 2022. Carboxylated chitosan-mediated improved efficacy of mesoporous silica nanoparticle-based targeted drug delivery system for breast cancer therapy. Carbohydr. Polym. 277, 118822. https://doi.org/10.1016/j.carbpol.2021.118822.

Lopes-Nunes, J., Agonia, A.S., Rosado, T., Gallardo, E., Palmeira-De-oliveira, R., Palmeira-De-oliveira, A., Martinez-De-oliveira, J., Fonseca-Moutinho, J., Campello, M.P.C., Paiva, A., Paulo, A., Vulgamott, A., Ellignton, A.D., Oliveira, P.A., Cruz, C., 2021. Aptamer-functionalized gold nanoparticles for drug delivery to gynecological carcinoma cells. Cancers 13 (16). https://doi.org/10.3390/cancers13164038.

Luo, Z., Yan, Z., Jin, K., Pang, Q., Jiang, T., Lu, H., Liu, X., Pang, Z., Yu, L., Jiang, X., 2017. Precise glioblastoma targeting by AS1411 aptamer-functionalized poly (l-γ-glutamylglutamine)–paclitaxel nanoconjugates. J. Colloid Interface Sci. 490, 783–796. https://doi.org/10.1016/j.jcis.2016.12.004.

Luo, S., Wang, S., Luo, N., Chen, F., Hu, C., Zhang, K., 2018. The application of aptamer 5TR1 in triple negative breast cancer target therapy. J. Cell. Biochem. 119 (1), 896–908. https://doi.org/10.1002/jcb.26254.

Lv, Z., Zhu, Y., Li, F., 2021. DNA functional nanomaterials for controlled delivery of nucleic acid-based drugs. Front. Bioeng. Biotechnol. 9. https://doi.org/10.3389/fbioe.2021.720291.

Ma, J., Zhuang, H., Zhuang, Z., Lu, Y., Xia, R., Gan, L., Wu, Y., 2017. Development of docetaxel liposome surface modified with CD133 aptamers for lung cancer targeting. Artif. Cell Nanomed. Biotechnol. 46 (8), 1–8. https://doi.org/10.1080/21691401.2017.1394874.

Ma, Y., Zhu, Y., Wang, C., Pan, D., Liu, S., Yang, M., Xiao, Z., Yang, X., Zhao, W., Zhou, X., Li, Y., Pan, Y., Sun, J., Wang, S., Guan, Z., Zhang, L., Yang, Z., 2018a. Annealing novel nucleobase-lipids with oligonucleotides or plasmid DNA based on H-bonding or π-π interaction: assemblies and transfections. Biomaterials 178, 147–157. https://doi.org/10.1016/j.biomaterials.2018.06.012.

Ma, Y., Wang, Z., Ma, Y., Han, Z., Zhang, M., Chen, H., Gu, Y., 2018b. A telomerase-responsive DNA icosahedron for precise delivery of platinum nanodrugs to cisplatin-resistant cancer. Angew. Chem. Int. Ed. 57 (19), 5389–5393. https://doi.org/10.1002/anie.201801195.

Ma, W., Zhan, Y., Zhang, Y., Shao, X., Xie, X., Mao, C., Cui, W., Li, Q., Shi, J., Li, J., Fan, C., Lin, Y., 2019. An intelligent DNA nanorobot with in vitro enhanced protein lysosomal degradation of HER2. Nano Lett. 19 (7), 4505–4517. https://doi.org/10.1021/acs.nanolett.9b01320.

Mashreghi, M., Zamani, P., Karimi, M., Mehrabian, A., Arabsalmani, M., Zarqi, J., Moosavian, S.A., Jaafari, M.R., 2021. Anti-epithelial cell adhesion molecule RNA aptamer-conjugated liposomal doxorubicin as an efficient targeted therapy in mice bearing colon carcinoma tumor model. Biotechnol. Prog. 37 (3). https://doi.org/10.1002/btpr.3116.

Mathur, D., Medintz, I.L., 2019. The growing development of DNA nanostructures for potential healthcare-related applications. Adv. Healthcare Mater. 8 (9). https://doi.org/10.1002/adhm.201801546.

Minh Hoang, C.N., Nguyen, S.H., Tran, M.T., 2025. Nanoparticles in cancer therapy: strategies to penetrate and modulate the tumor microenvironment – A review. KeAi Communications Co. Smart Mater. Med. 6 (2), 270–284. https://doi.org/10.1016/j.smaim.2025.07.004.

Mohapatra, S., Saha, A., Mondal, P., Jana, B., Ghosh, S., Biswas, A., Ghosh, S., 2017. Synergistic anticancer effect of peptide-docetaxel nanoassembly targeted to tubulin: Toward development of dual warhead containing nanomedicine. Adv. Healthcare Mater. 6 (2). https://doi.org/10.1002/adhm.201600718.

Moosavian, S.A., Abnous, K., Akhtari, J., Arabi, L., Gholamzade Dewin, A., Jafari, M., 2018. 5TR1 aptamer-PEGylated liposomal doxorubicin enhances cellular uptake and suppresses tumor growth by targeting MUC1 on the surface of cancer cells. Artif.Cells, Nanomed. Biotechnol. 46 (8), 2054–2065. https://doi.org/10.1080/21691401.2017.1408120.

Nasiri, M., Bahadorani, M., Dellinger, K., Aravamudhan, S., Vivero-Escoto, J.L., Zadegan, R., 2024. Improving DNA nanostructure stability: A review of the biomedical applications and approaches. Int. J. Biol. Macromol. 260 (Pt 1), 129495. https://doi.org/10.1016/j.ijbiomac.2024.129495.

Natesh, J., Chandola, C., Meeran, S.M., Neerathilingam, M., 2021. Targeted delivery of doxorubicin through CD44 aptamer to cancer cells. Ther. Deliv. 12 (10), 693–703. https://doi.org/10.4155/tde-2021-0038.

Navarro, N., Aviñó, A., Domènech, Ò., Borrell, J.H., Eritja, R., Fàbrega, C., 2024. Defined covalent attachment of three cancer drugs to DNA origami increases cytotoxicity at nanomolar concentration. Nanomed. Nanotechnol. Biol. Med. 55, 102722. https://doi.org/10.1016/j.nano.2023.102722.

Nicolson, F., Ali, A., Kircher, M.F., Pal, S., 2020. DNA nanostructures and DNA-functionalized nanoparticles for cancer theranostics. Adv. Sci. 7 (23). https://doi.org/10.1002/advs.202001669.

Ouyang, C., Zhang, S., Xue, C., Yu, X., Xu, H., Wang, Z., Lu, Y., Wu, Z.S., 2020. Precision-guided missile-like DNA nanostructure containing warhead and guidance control for aptamer-based targeted drug delivery into cancer cells in vitro and in vivo. J. Am. Chem. Soc. 142 (3), 1265–1277. https://doi.org/10.1021/jacs.9b09782.

Paiva, W.A., Currier, M.E., Ashooh, S.E., Honan, N.M., Oldenhuis, N.J., 2025. Transforming bio-derived DNA into biotechnology. Trends Chem. 7 (12), 884–899. https://doi.org/10.1016/j.trechm.2025.09.017.

Panda, P., Mohapatra, R., 2025. Advancements in DNA nanotechnology for targeted drug delivery: Design strategies and applications. Hybrid Adv. 10, 100480. https://doi.org/10.1016/j.hybadv.2025.100480.

Pang, L., Huang, X., Zhu, L., Xiao, H., Li, M., Guan, H., Gao, J., Jin, H., 2022. Targeted killing of CD133+ lung cancer stem cells using paclitaxel-loaded PLGA-PEG nanoparticles with CD133 aptamers. J. South. Med. Univ. 42 (1), 26–35. https://doi.org/10.12122/j.issn.1673-4254.2022.01.03.

Pei, W., Liu, M., Wu, Y., Zhao, Y., Liu, T., Sun, B., Liu, Y., Wang, Q., Han, J., 2020. High payload and targeted release of anthracyclines by aptamer-tethered DNA nanotrains — Thermodynamic and release kinetic study. Eur. J. Pharmaceut. Sci. 148, 105319. https://doi.org/10.1016/j.ejps.2020.105319.

Perrault, S.D., Shih, W.M., 2014. Virus-inspired membrane encapsulation of DNA nanostructures to achieve in vivo stability. ACS Nano 8 (5), 5132–5140. https://doi.org/10.1021/nn5011914.

Powell, D., Chandra, S., Dodson, K., Shaheen, F., Wiltz, K., Ireland, S., Syed, M., Dash, S., Wiese, T., Mandal, T., Kundu, A., 2017. Aptamer-functionalized hybrid nanoparticle for the treatment of breast cancer. Eur. J. Pharm. Biopharm. 114, 108–118. https://doi.org/10.1016/j.ejpb.2017.01.011.

Qi, J., Zhang, Y., Gou, Y., Lee, P., Wang, J., Chen, S., Zhou, Z., Wu, X., Yang, F., Liang, H., 2016. Multidrug delivery systems based on human serum albumin for combination therapy with three anticancer agents. Mol. Pharm. 13 (9), 3098–3105. https://doi.org/10.1021/acs.molpharmaceut.6b00277.

Quazi, M.Z., Park, N., 2023. DNA hydrogel-based nanocomplexes with cancer-targeted delivery and light-triggered peptide drug release for cancer-specific therapeutics. Biomacromolecules 24 (5), 2127–2137. https://doi.org/10.1021/acs.biomac.3c00021.

Rangnekar, A., Labean, T.H., 2014. Building DNA nanostructures for molecular computation, templated assembly, and biological applications. Acc. Chem. Res. 47 (6), 1778–1788. https://doi.org/10.1021/ar500023b.

Ranjbar-Navazi, Z., Fathi, M., Dalir Abdolahinia, E., Omidi, Y., Davaran, S., 2021. MUC-1 aptamer conjugated InP/ZnS quantum dots/nanohydrogel fluorescent composite for mitochondria-mediated apoptosis in MCF-7 cells. Mater. Sci. Eng. C 118, 111469. https://doi.org/10.1016/j.msec.2020.111469.

Rothemund, P.W.K., 2006. Folding DNA to create nanoscale shapes and patterns. Nature 440 (7082), 297–302. https://doi.org/10.1038/nature04586.

Safarkhani, M., Ahmadi, S., Ipakchi, H., Saeb, M.R., Makvandi, P., Ebrahimi Warkiani, M., Rabiee, N., Huh, Y.S., 2024. Advancements in aptamer-driven DNA nanostructures for precision drug delivery. Adv. Sci. 11 (26). https://doi.org/10.1002/advs.202401617.

Saji, M., Perumal, D., Yang, Q., Jaekle, F., Zhang, F., 2025. Controlling assembly of hybrid DNA nanostructures into higher-order structures via hydrophobicity. Angew. Chem. Int. Ed. 64 (34). https://doi.org/10.1002/anie.202507844.

Saravanakumar, K., Hu, X., Shanmugam, S., Chelliah, R., Sekar, P., Oh, D.H., Vijayakumar, S., Kathiresan, K., Wang, M.H., 2019. Enhanced cancer therapy with pH-dependent and aptamer functionalized doxorubicin loaded polymeric (poly D, L-lactic-co-glycolic acid) nanoparticles. Arch. Biochem. Biophys. 671, 143–151. https://doi.org/10.1016/j.abb.2019.07.004.

Sayari, E., Dinarvand, M., Amini, M., Azhdarzadeh, M., Mollarazi, E., Ghasemi, Z., Atyabi, F., 2014. MUC1 aptamer conjugated to chitosan nanoparticles, an efficient targeted carrier designed for anticancer SN38 delivery. Int. J. Pharm. 473 (1–2), 304–315. https://doi.org/10.1016/j.ijpharm.2014.05.041.

Seeman, N.C., 2003. DNA in a material world. Nature 421 (6921), 427–431. https://doi.org/10.1038/nature01406.

Seeman, N.C., Sleiman, H.F., 2017. DNA nanotechnology. Nat. Rev. Mater. 3. https://doi.org/10.1038/natrevmats.2017.68.

Shahriari, M., Taghdisi, S.M., Abnous, K., Ramezani, M., Alibolandi, M., 2021. Self-targeted polymersomal co-formulation of doxorubicin, camptothecin and FOXM1 aptamer for efficient treatment of non-small cell lung cancer. J. Contr. Release 335, 369–388. https://doi.org/10.1016/j.jconrel.2021.05.039.

Shen, Y., Zhang, J., Hao, W., Wang, T., Liu, J., Xie, Y., Xu, S., Liu, H., 2018. Copolymer micelles function as pH-responsive nanocarriers to enhance the cytotoxicity of a HER2 aptamer in HER2-positive breast cancer cells. Int. J. Nanomed. 13, 537–553. https://doi.org/10.2147/ijn.s149942.

Shen, X., Zhu, A., Xu, Y., 2025. DNA nanoflower enables controlled Co-delivery of antisense oligodeoxynucleotide and doxorubicin for anti-breast cancer treatment. Micro & Nano Lett. 20 (1). https://doi.org/10.1049/mna2.70008.

Shi, J., Kantoff, P.W., Wooster, R., Farokhzad, O.C., 2017. Cancer nanomedicine: Progress, challenges and opportunities. Nat. Rev. Cancer 17 (1), 20–37. https://doi.org/10.1038/nrc.2016.108.

Shiao, Y.S., Chiu, H.H., Wu, P.H., Huang, Y.F., 2014. Aptamer-functionalized gold nanoparticles as photoresponsive nanoplatform for Co-drug delivery. Am. Chem. Soc. 6 (24), 21832–21841. https://doi.org/10.1021/am5026243.

Shishparenok, A.N., Furman, V.V., Zhdanov, D.D., 2023. DNA-based nanomaterials as drug delivery platforms for increasing the effect of drugs in tumors. Cancers 15 (7). https://doi.org/10.3390/cancers15072151.

Si, P., Shi, J., Zhang, P., Wang, C., Chen, H., Mi, X., Chu, W., Zhai, B., Li, W., 2020. MUC-1 recognition-based activated drug nanoplatform improves doxorubicin chemotherapy in breast cancer. Cancer Lett. 472, 165–174. https://doi.org/10.1016/j.canlet.2019.12.019.

Singh, S., Jha, P., Singh, V., Sinha, K., Hussain, S., Singh, M.K., Das, P., 2016. A quantum dot-MUC1 aptamer conjugate for targeted delivery of protoporphyrin IX and specific photokilling of cancer cells through ROS generation. Integr. Biol. 8 (10), 1040–1048. https://doi.org/10.1039/c6ib00092d.

Soldevilla, M.M., Villanueva, H., Casares, N., Lasarte, J.J., Bendandi, M., Inoges, S., de Cerio, A.L.D., Pastor, F., 2016. MRP1-CD28 bi-specific oligonucleotide aptamers: Target costimulation to drug-resistant melanoma cancer stem cells. Oncotarget 7 (17), 23182–23196. https://doi.org/10.18632/oncotarget.8095.

Sun, S., Yang, Y., Niu, H., Luo, M., Wu, Z.S., 2022a. Design and application of DNA nanostructures for organelle-targeted delivery of anticancer drugs. Expert Opin. Drug Deliv. 19 (6), 707–723. https://doi.org/10.1080/17425247.2022.2083603.

Sun, S., Yang, Y., Gao, Z., Jiang, H., Ye, L., Lai, Y., Shen, Z., Wu, Z.S., 2022b. Endogenous stimuli-responsive autonomous separation of dual-targeting DNA guided missile from nanospacecraft for intelligent targeted cancer therapy. ACS Appl. Mater. Interf. 14 (40), 45201–45216. https://doi.org/10.1021/acsami.2c13624.

Taghavi, S., Ramezani, M., Alibolandi, M., Abnous, K., Taghdisi, S.M., 2017. Chitosan-modified PLGA nanoparticles tagged with 5TR1 aptamer for in vivo tumor-targeted drug delivery. Cancer Lett. 400, 1–8. https://doi.org/10.1016/j.canlet.2017.04.008.

Taghdisi, S.M., Danesh, N.M., Ramezani, M., Yazdian-Robati, R., Abnous, K., 2018. A novel AS1411 aptamer-based three-way junction pocket DNA nanostructure loaded with doxorubicin for targeting cancer cells in vitro and in vivo. Mol. Pharm. 15 (5), 1972–1978. https://doi.org/10.1021/acs.molpharmaceut.8b00124.

Tang, L., Tong, R., Coyle, V.J., Yin, Q., Pondenis, H., Borst, L.B., Cheng, J., Fan, T.M., 2015. Targeting tumor vasculature with aptamer-functionalized doxorubicin-polylactide nanoconjugates for enhanced cancer therapy. ACS Nano 9 (5), 5072–5081. https://doi.org/10.1021/acsnano.5b00166.

Thorat, N.D., Bauer, J., Tofail, S.A.M., Gascón Pérez, V., Bohara, R.A., Yadav, H.M., 2020. Silica nano supra-assembly for the targeted delivery of therapeutic cargo to overcome chemoresistance in cancer. Colloids. Surf. B: Biointerfaces 185. https://doi.org/10.1016/j.colsurfb.2019.110571.

Wang, T., Gantier, M.P., Xiang, D., Bean, A.G., Bruce, M., Zhou, S.F., Khasraw, M., Ward, A., Wang, L., Wei, M.Q., AlShamaileh, H., Chen, L., She, X., Lin, J., Kong, L., Shigdar, S., Duan, W., 2015. EpCAM aptamer-mediated survivin silencing sensitized cancer stem cells to doxorubicin in a breast cancer model. Theranostics 5 (12), 1456–1472. https://doi.org/10.7150/thno.11692.

Wang, C., Sun, W., Wright, G., Wang, A.Z., Gu, Z., 2016. Inflammation-Triggered cancer immunotherapy by programmed delivery of CpG and anti-PD1 antibody. Adv. Mater. 28 (40), 8912–8920. https://doi.org/10.1002/adma.201506312.

Wang, Y., Chen, X., Tian, B., Liu, J., Yang, L., Zeng, L., Chen, T., Hong, A., Wang, X., 2017. Nucleolin-targeted extracellular vesicles as a versatile platform for biologics delivery to breast cancer. Theranostics 7 (5), 1360–1372. https://doi.org/10.7150/thno.16532.

Wang, N., Zheng, Z., Niu, H., Zhang, S., Zhang, A., 2018. Core-shell nanoplatform for synergistic enhanced sonodynamic therapy of hypoxic tumor via cascaded strategy. Adv. Healthcare Mater. 7.

Wang, Q., He, Z., Zhu, H., Gao, W., Zhang, N., Li, J., Yan, J., He, B., Ye, X., 2022a. Targeting drug delivery and efficient lysosomal escape for chemo-photodynamic cancer therapy by a peptide/DNA nanocomplex. J. Mater. Chem. B 10 (3), 438–449. https://doi.org/10.1039/d1tb02441h.

Wang, N., Yu, C., Xu, T., Yao, D., Zhu, L., Shen, Z., Huang, X., 2022b. Self-assembly of DNA nanostructure containing cell-specific aptamer as a precise drug delivery system for cancer therapy in non-small cell lung cancer. J. Nanobiotechnol. 20 (1). https://doi.org/10.1186/s12951-022-01701-5.

Wang, J., Li, K., Li, F., Li, X., Zhou, J., Yang, M., Zhang, X., Wang, M., Li, L., 2025. Interaction of nanomaterials with nucleic acids and their applications in nucleic acid analysis. Int. J. Biol. Sci. 21 (9), 4051–4068. https://doi.org/10.7150/ijbs.113309.

Wages, N.A., Chiuzan, C., Panageas, K.S., 2018. Design considerations for early-phase clinical trials of immune-oncology agents. J. ImmunoTher. Cancer 6 (1). https://doi.org/10.1186/s40425-018-0389-8.

Wei, H., Zhao, Z., Wang, Y., Zou, J., Lin, Q., Duan, Y., 2019. One-step self-assembly of multifunctional DNA nanohydrogels: an enhanced and harmless strategy for guiding combined antitumor therapy. ACS Appl. Mater. Inter. 11 (50), 46479–46489. https://doi.org/10.1021/acsami.9b15874.

Wen, J., Tao, W., Hao, S., Iyer, S.P., Zu, Y., 2016. A unique aptamer-drug conjugate for targeted therapy of multiple myeloma. Leukemia 30 (4), 987–991. https://doi.org/10.1038/leu.2015.216.

Wilhelm, S., Tavares, A.J., Chan, W.C.W., 2016. Reply to "evaluation of nanomedicines: Stick to the basics". Nat. Rev. Mater. 1 (10). https://doi.org/10.1038/natrevmats.2016.74.

Wu, M., Zhao, H., Guo, L., Wang, Y., Song, J., Zhao, X., Li, C., Hao, L., Wang, D., Tang, J., 2018. Ultrasound-mediated nanobubble destruction (UMND) facilitates the delivery of A10-3.2 aptamer targeted and siRNA-loaded cationic nanobubbles for therapy of prostate cancer. Drug Deliv. 25 (1), 226–240. https://doi.org/10.1080/10717544.2017.1422300.

Wu, T., Liu, J., Liu, M., Liu, S., Zhao, S., Tian, R., Wei, D., Liu, Y., Zhao, Y., Xiao, H., Ding, B., 2019. A nanobody-conjugated DNA nanoplatform for targeted platinum-drug delivery. Angew. Chem. – Int. Ed. 58 (40), 14224–14228. https://doi.org/10.1002/anie.201909345.

Wu, Y., Jin, M., Peng, C., Wang, G.A., Li, F., 2025. Kinetics and activation strategies in toehold-mediated and toehold-free DNA strand displacement. Biosensors 15 (10), 683. https://doi.org/10.3390/bios15100683.

Xu, W., Siddiqui, I.A., Nihal, M., Pilla, S., Rosenthal, K., Mukhtar, H., Gong, S., 2013. Aptamer-conjugated and doxorubicin-loaded unimolecular micelles for targeted therapy of prostate cancer. Biomaterials 34 (21), 5244–5253. https://doi.org/10.1016/j.biomaterials.2013.03.006.

Xu, G., Yu, X., Zhang, J., Sheng, Y., Liu, G., Tao, W., Mei, L., 2016. Robust aptamer–polydopamine-functionalized M-PLGA–TPGS nanoparticles for targeted delivery of docetaxel and enhanced cervical cancer therapy. Int. J. Nanomed. 11, 2953–2965. https://doi.org/10.2147/IJN.S103513.

Xu, L., He, X.Y., Liu, B.Y., Xu, C., Ai, S.L., Zhuo, R.X., Cheng, S.X., 2018. Aptamer-functionalized albumin-based nanoparticles for targeted drug delivery. Colloids Surf. B Biointerfaces 171, 24–30. https://doi.org/10.1016/j.colsurfb.2018.07.008.

Xue, L., Maihle, N.J., Yu, X., Tang, S.C., Liu, H.Y., 2018. Synergistic targeting HER2 and EGFR with bivalent aptamer-siRNA chimera efficiently inhibits HER2-positive tumor growth. Mol. Pharm. 15 (11), 4801–4813. https://doi.org/10.1021/acs.molpharmaceut.8b00388.

Yadav, K., Sahu, K.K., Sucheta, Gnanakani, S.P.E., Sure, P., Vijayalakshmi, R., Sundar, V.D., Sharma, V., Antil, R., Jha, M., Minz, S., Bagchi, A., Pradhan, M., 2023. Biomedical applications of nanomaterials in the advancement of nucleic acid therapy: Mechanistic challenges, delivery strategies, and therapeutic applications. Int. J. Biol. Macromol. 241. https://doi.org/10.1016/j.ijbiomac.2023.124582.

Yang, J., Jiang, Q., He, L., Zhan, P., Liu, Q., Liu, S., Fu, M., Liu, J., Li, C., Ding, B., 2018. Self-assembled double-bundle DNA tetrahedron for efficient antisense delivery. ACS Appl. Mater. Interfaces 10 (28), 23693–23699. https://doi.org/10.1021/acsami.8b07889.

Yang, R., Li, Y., Wang, X., Yan, J., Pan, D., Xu, Y., Wang, L., Yang, M., 2019. Doxorubicin loaded ferritin nanoparticles for ferroptosis enhanced targeted killing of cancer cells. RSC Adv. 9 (49), 28548–28553. https://doi.org/10.1039/c9ra04478g.

Yang, Y., Cai, X., Shi, M., Zhang, X., Yang, P., Zhang, Y., Ju, H., Cao, P., 2023. Biomimetic retractable DNA nanocarrier with sensitive responsivity for efficient drug delivery and enhanced photothermal therapy. J. Nanobiotechnol. 21 (1). https://doi.org/10.1186/s12951-023-01806-5.

Yazdian-Robati, R., Arab, A., Ramezani, M., Rafatpanah, H., Bahreyni, A., Nabavinia, M.S., Abnous, K., Taghdisi, S.M., 2019. Smart aptamer-modified calcium carbonate nanoparticles for controlled release and targeted delivery of epirubicin and melittin into cancer cells in vitro and in vivo. Drug Dev. Ind. Pharm. 45 (4), 603–610. https://doi.org/10.1080/03639045.2019.1569029.

Yazdian-Robati, R., Bayat, P., Dehestani, S., Hashemi, M., Taghdisi, S.M., Abnous, K., 2022. Smart delivery of epirubicin to cancer cells using aptamer-modified ferritin nanoparticles. J. Drug Targe. 30 (5), 567–576. https://doi.org/10.1080/1061186X.2022.2025600.

Yu, S., Bi, X., Yang, L., Wu, S., Yu, Y., Jiang, B., Zhang, A., Lan, K., Duan, S., 2019. Co-delivery of paclitaxel and PLK1-targeted siRNA using aptamer-functionalized cationic liposome for synergistic anti-breast cancer effects in vivo. J. Biomed. Nanotechnol. 15 (6), 1135–1148. https://doi.org/10.1166/jbn.2019.2751.

Yoon, Y., Lee, C., Kim, S.J., 2021. Structural DNA nanotechnology towards therapeutic applications. J. Korean Phys. Soc. 78 (5), 343–350. https://doi.org/10.1007/s40042-020-00049-z.

Zafar, A., Khatoon, S., Khan, M.J., Abu, J., Naeem, A., 2025. Advancements and limitations in traditional anti-cancer therapies: a comprehensive review of surgery, chemotherapy, radiation therapy, and hormonal therapy. Discov. Oncol. 16 (1). https://doi.org/10.1007/s12672-025-02198-8.

Zhan, P., Peil, A., Jiang, Q., Wang, D., Mousavi, S., Xiong, Q., Qi, S., Shang, Y., Ding, B., Lin, C., Ke, Y., Liu, N., 2023. Recent advances in DNA origami-engineered nanomaterials and applications. Chem. Rev. 123 (7), 3976–4050. https://doi.org/10.1021/acs.chemrev.3c00028.

Zhang, B., Zhong, L., Liu, J., Ding, X., Li, J., Cai, K., 2014. Cytochrome c end-capped mesoporous silica nanoparticles as redox-responsive drug delivery vehicles for liver tumor-targeted triplex therapy in vitro and in vivo. J. Contr. Release 192, 192–201. https://doi.org/10.1016/j.jconrel.2014.06.037.

Zhang, Y., Pan, V., Li, X., Yang, X., Li, H., Wang, P., Ke, Y., 2019. Dynamic DNA structures. Small 15 (26). https://doi.org/10.1002/smll.201900228.

Zhang, C., Han, M., Zhang, F., Yang, X., Du, J., Honglei, Z., Li, W., Chen, S., 2020a. Enhancing antitumor efficacy of nucleoside analog 5-fluorodeoxyuridine on HER2-overexpressing breast cancer by affibody-engineered DNA nanoparticle. Int. J. Nanomed. 15, 885–900. https://doi.org/10.2147/ijn.s231144.

Zhang, T., Tian, T., Zhou, R., Li, S., Ma, W., Zhang, Y., Liu, N., Shi, S., Li, Q., Xie, X., Ge, Y., Liu, M., Qi, Z., Lin, S., Cai, X., Lin, Y., 2020b. Design, fabrication and applications of tetrahedral DNA nanostructure-based multifunctional complexes in drug delivery and biomedical treatment. Nat. Protoc. 15 (8), 2728–2757. https://doi.org/10.1038/s41596-020-0355-z.

Zhang, H.J., Zhao, X., Chen, L.J., Yang, C.X., Yan, X.P., 2020c. Dendrimer grafted persistent luminescent nanoplatform for aptamer guided tumor imaging and acid-responsive drug delivery. Talanta 219. Available from: www.journals.elsevier.com/talanta.

Zhang, J., Li, C., Xue, Q., Yin, X., Li, Y., He, W., Chen, X., Zhang, J., Reis, R.L., Wang, Y., 2021a. An efficient carbon-based drug delivery system for cancer therapy through the nucleus targeting and mitochondria mediated apoptotic pathway. Small Methods 5 (12). https://doi.org/10.1002/smtd.202100539.

Zhang, P., Ouyang, Y., Sohn, Y.S., Nechushtai, R., Pikarsky, E., Fan, C., Willner, I., 2021b. PH- and miRNA-responsive DNA-tetrahedra/metal-organic framework conjugates: Functional sense-and-treat carriers. ACS Nano 15 (4), 6645–6657. https://doi.org/10.1021/acsnano.0c09996.

Zhang, H., Jin, C., Zhang, L., Peng, B., Zhang, Y., Liu, Y., Li, L., Ye, M., Xiong, W., Tan, W., 2022. CD71-Specific aptamer conjugated with monomethyl auristatin E for the treatment of uveal melanoma. ACS Appl. Mater. Interfaces 14 (1), 32–40. https://doi.org/10.1021/acsami.1c13980.

Zhang, S., Lou, X.Y., Liu, L., Yang, Y.W., 2023. The creation of DNA origami-based supramolecular nanostructures for cancer therapy. Adv. Healthcare Mater. 12 (27). https://doi.org/10.1002/adhm.202301066.

Zhao, Y.X., Shaw, A., Zeng, X., Benson, E., Nyström, A.M., Högberg, B., 2012. DNA origami delivery system for cancer therapy with tunable release properties. ACS Nano 6 (10), 8684–8691. https://doi.org/10.1021/nn3022662.

Zhao, N., Pei, S.N., Qi, J., Zeng, Z., Iyer, S.P., Lin, P., Tung, C.H., Zu, Y., 2015. Oligonucleotide aptamer-drug conjugates for targeted therapy of acute myeloid leukemia. Biomaterials 67, 42–51. https://doi.org/10.1016/j.biomaterials.2015.07.025.

Zhao, Q.-ge, Wang, J., Zhang, Y.-peng, Zhang, J., Tang, A.-na, 2018. De-ming Kong, A ZnO-gated porphyrinic metal–organic framework-based drug delivery system for targeted bimodal cancer therapy. J. Mater. Chem. B 6 (47), 7898–7907. https://doi.org/10.1039/c8tb02663g.

Zhao, D., Yang, G., Liu, Q., Liu, W., Weng, Y., Yi, Z., Qu, F., Li, L., Huang, Y., 2020. A photo-triggerable aptamer nanoswitch for spatiotemporal controllable siRNA delivery. Nanoscale 12 (20), 10939–10943. https://doi.org/10.1039/d0nr00301h.

Zhao, P., Tang, Z.W., Lin, H.C., Djuanda, D., Zhu, Z., Niu, Q., Zhao, L.M., Qian, Y.N., Cao, G., Shen, J.L., Fu, B., 2021. VEGF aptamer/i-motif-based drug co-delivery system for combined chemotherapy and photodynamic therapy. Photodiagn. Photody. Ther. 36. https://doi.org/10.1016/j.pdpdt.2021.102547.

Zhen, S., Takahashi, Y., Narita, S., Yang, Y.C., Li, X., 2017. Targeted delivery of CRISPR/Cas9 to prostate cancer by modified gRNA using a flexible aptamer-cationic liposome. Oncotarget 8 (6), 9375–9387. https://doi.org/10.18632/oncotarget.14072.

Zheng, C., Song, L., Yu, C., Zhu, L., Zhang, J., Wang, N., Liu, M., Li, S., Wang, L., Shen, Z., Huang, X., 2025. Palindrome-mediated DNA nanotubes with cell-specific aptamers to improve targeted antitumor effects and reduce toxicity on non-small cell lung cancer. Sci. China Life Sci. 68 (2), 454–466. https://doi.org/10.1007/s11427-023-2556-4.

Zhou, J., Tiemann, K., Chomchan, P., Alluin, J., Swiderski, P., Burnett, J., Zhang, X., Forman, S., Chen, R., Rossi, J., 2013. Dual functional BAFF receptor aptamers inhibit ligand-induced proliferation and deliver siRNAs to NHL cells. Nucleic Acids Res. 41 (7), 4266–4283. https://doi.org/10.1093/nar/gkt125.

Zhou, G., Da Won Bae, S., Nguyen, R., Huo, X., Han, S., Zhang, Z., Hebbard, L., Duan, W., Eslam, M., Liddle, C., Yuen, L., Lam, V., Qiao, L., George, J., 2021. An aptamer-based drug delivery agent (CD133-apt-Dox) selectively and effectively kills liver cancer stem-like cells. Cancer Lett. 501, 124–132. https://doi.org/10.1016/j.canlet.2020.12.022.

Zhu, L., Yang, J., Ma, Y., Zhu, X., Zhang, C., 2022. Aptamers entirely built from therapeutic nucleoside analogues for targeted cancer therapy. J. Am. Chem. Soc. 144 (4), 1493–1497. https://doi.org/10.1021/jacs.1c09574.

Zhuang, X., Ma, X., Xue, X., Jiang, Q., Song, L., Dai, L., Zhang, C., Jin, S., Yang, K., Ding, B., Wang, P.C., Liang, X.J., 2016. A photosensitizer-loaded DNA origami nanosystem for photodynamic therapy. ACS Nano 10 (3), 3486–3495. https://doi.org/10.1021/acsnano.5b07671.

Zhuang, J., Chen, S., Hu, Y., Yang, F., Huo, Q., Xie, N., 2021. Tumor-targeted and redox-responsive mesoporous silica nanoparticles for controlled release of doxorubicin and an siRNA against metastatic breast cancer. Int. J. Nanomed. 16, 1961–1976. https://doi.org/10.2147/IJN.S278724.

CHAPTER

22

Nanofibrous scaffolds for cancer management

Nirmal Morya[1], *Keshav Hirave*[1], *Lalit Kumar*[1], *Sujit Erandole*[1], *Debadri Banerjee*[2], *Anupama Singh*[2] and *Vikas Anand Saharan*[1]

[1]Department of Pharmaceutical Technology (Formulations), National Institute of Pharmaceutical Education and Research, Guwahati (NIPER-G), Sila Katamur (Halugurisuk), Assam, India; [2]School of Pharmaceutical Sciences and Technology, Sardar Bhagwan Singh University, Dehradun, Uttarakhand, India

Introduction

Nanomaterials offer a wide range of drug delivery options, with exceptional physicochemical, biological, and pharmacological properties. Nanofibers have recently gained interest in the healthcare system. Nanofibrous scaffolds are widely used in a variety of fields, including sensor devices, wound dressings, bone and tissue engineering, controlled drug release, ocular drug delivery, antimicrobial delivery, cancer therapy, cardiovascular regeneration, cosmetics, filter media, medical prosthesis, and haemostatic devices (Gupta et al., 2014). A nanofiber scaffold is a porous, three-dimensional matrix of diameters ranging from 50 to 1000 nm. They are composed of natural, synthetic, and composite polymers and can be produced using various methods, including electrospinning, phase separation, biocomponent extrusion, melt blowing, centrifugal spinning, molecular self-assembly, and drawing. Nanofibers may have lengths ranging from a few micrometers to millimeters, and aspect ratios ranging from 100:1 to more than 1000:1. A high aspect ratio in nanofibers can have an impact on handling, injectability, and dispersibility in specific formulations (for example, injectable fiber suspensions) (Chen et al., 2013). Nanofiber scaffolds have key characteristics such as high surface area and volume ratio compared with conventional fibers. It has high porosity, which provides cell respiration, prevents wound dehydration, and avoids microbial infiltration. Its mechanical strength is comparable with that of natural skin, making it an ideal drug delivery method for achieving regulated and sustained drug release

Advanced Cancer Therapeutics
https://doi.org/10.1016/B978-0-443-44185-1.00022-7

using various biodegradable and nonbiodegradable polymers. It mimics the extracellular matrix (ECM), providing mechanical support and a surface for cell adhesion, proliferation, tissue regeneration, and sustained delivery of drugs (Vojoudi and Babaloo, 2023). In cancer therapy, it can be used as a carrier for drug delivery to the target site. The anticancer drugs can be either loaded in the core of nanofibers or conjugated or adsorbed to the surface of nanofibers. Thus nanofibers can be used as a suitable platform for anticancer drug delivery.

Method of preparation of nanofibrous scaffolds

Various methods that can be employed for the preparation of nanofiber scaffolds are listed in Table 22.1, with associated advantages.

Electrospinning

In the year 1964, Geoffrey Ingram Taylor reported the formation of the Taylor cone, which made the popularity of electrospinning in the 1990s, followed by aligned electrospinning, coaxial electrospinning, and dual electrospinning in the early 2000s (Keirouz et al., 2023). The setup of electrospinning is represented in Fig. 22.1a, the principle of Taylor cone formation is shown in Fig. 22.1b. Electrospinning processes can be further classified into monoaxial electrospinning, coaxial electrospinning, triaxial or multiaxial, centrifugal spinning, portable electrospinning, free-surface roller, wire-based electrospinning, bubble electrospinning, corona electrospinning, high-speed electrospinning, alternating current electrospinning, T-Coil (two-level coil) needleless electrospinning, corona electrospinning, rotary cone needleless electrospinning, quilled nozzle-less electrospinning, annular/multichannel needleless electrospinning, side-by-Side (Janus) electrospinning, and hybrid configurations. The electrospinning process can also be classified into two broader categories: needle and nonneedle systems. The needle system consists of mono-axial, coaxial, triaxial, centrifugal, portable electrospinning (handheld, in-situ), while the nonneedle system consists of roller and wire, bubble, corona, and high-speed electrospinning. Different types of electrospinning processes are discussed briefly below (Keirouz et al., 2023).

Monoaxial electrospinning: This system was introduced in 1902 by Colley and Morton. The principle of monoaxial electrospinning is the formation of a Taylor cone. The distance between the spinneret and the metal collector directly affects the diameter of nanofibers; the greater the distance, the thinner the fibers, and the shorter the distance, the thicker the fibers. Monoaxial electrospinning has some limitations, such as the ability to spin only one polymeric solution at a time (Luraghi et al., 2021).

Coaxial electrospinning: It was invented by Sun Z. in 2003. Coaxial electrospinning is a modification of monoaxial electrospinning in which a coaxial needle is used to spin out two polymeric solutions simultaneously to form a single composite fiber. The core and shell systems use different feeding pumps and have separate flow rates that can affect the formation of nanofibers and their morphology. During the formation of the Taylor cone at the tip of the needle system, the core material is usually covered by shell material (Khan et al., 2024b).

TABLE 22.1 Key advantages and mechanisms of the methods of preparation of nanofiber scaffolds.

Methods of preparation		Advantage	Mechanism	References
Electrospinning	Monoaxial electrospinning	It is a simple, cost-effective electrospinning method compared with others, in which the spinneret is at a fixed distance from the metal collector.	Application of the electrostatic force stretches out the droplet into a wire-like structure and forms nanofibers. The principle of monoaxial electrospinning is the formation of a taylor cone.	Luraghi et al. (2021)
	Coaxial electrospinning	Two different solutions can be spun simultaneously using an inner-core and outer-shell system.	A coaxial needle is used to spin out two polymeric solutions simultaneously to form a single composite fiber. Coaxial needles have two systems: An inner core and an outer shell.	Khan et al. (2024b)
	Triaxial or multiaxial electrospinning	Three or more solutions can be spun simultaneously to produce nanofiber scaffolds.	It has more than two (triaxial has three and multiaxial has more than three) concurrent polymeric solution supplies through the spinneret at a time.	Ghosal et al. (2021)
	Centrifugal electrospinning	Fast process compared with conventional electrospinning.	It is a combined form of conventional electrospinning with centrifugal force.	Zhang et al. (2024)
	Portable electrospinning	Easy-to-carry device for personalized applications, such as wound dressings.	It generates nanofiber scaffolds by a high-voltage, direct current (HV DC) supply to the spinneret.	Xu et al. (2022)
	Free-surface roller and wire-based electrospinning	It is a needle-less system that uses a roller spinneret.	A rotating drum or wire, partially submerged in a polymer bath, carries a thin liquid film upward, and high voltage triggers fiber formation	Jirsak et al. (2009)
	Bubble electrospinning	It is also a needle-less system that requires one-way spinning.	Generation of gas bubbles in the polymeric solution and contact with the airstream, making it fine, and an electrostatic charge converts into nanofiber scaffolds.	Liu et al. (2010)
	Corona electrospinning	It is a high-throughput, needle-less, closed electrospinning system.	The corona electrospinning assembly consists of a circular electrode with a sharp edge, a high-voltage power supply, a feed supply unit, a metal collector, and a corona spinneret.	Molnar and Nagy (2016)
	High-speed electrospinning	Time savings process compared with conventional electrospinning.	A combination of conventional electrospinning with the high-speed rotating jet (up to 50,000 rpm)	Nagy et al. (2015)

(*Continued*)

TABLE 22.1 Key advantages and mechanisms of the methods of preparation of nanofiber scaffolds.—cont'd

Methods of preparation	Advantage	Mechanism	References
Melt blowing	It is a single-step, simple, and versatile method of preparation that yields nanofibrous scaffolds in the micrometer or submicrometer range.	A molten mass of polymer is extruded through a die, and a fiber is formed due to air-drag (elongation of the polymer extruded) that is collected on a collector in the structure of a web.	McCulloch (1999)
Template melt-extrusion	A solvent-free, precise dimension control, and high alignment with polymer versatility.	Combination methodology of template synthesis and extrusion process (anodic aluminium oxide membrane- AAOM) for the production of nanofibers of thermoplastic materials.	Li et al. (2006)
Template synthesis	A desired size of nanofiber can be obtained by selecting the same size of membrane.	A mould or template is typically used to obtain the desired nanofiber size by passing a polymeric solution through a membrane under positive pressure.	Li et al. (2005)
Flash spinning	Suitable for polymers such as polyolefins and high-molecular-weight polymers.	Polymeric material is formed into a nanofiber with a spin agent (liquid) spun out into an area having a lower temperature and pressure to form plexifilaments	Weinberg et al. (2014)
Fibrillated bicomponent fibers extrusion	It offers a large surface area, high production, and good mechanical strength.	Coextrusion of two immiscible polymers through a spinneret with a cross-sectional configuration	Dasdemir et al. (2012)
Phase separation	It is a fast, easy-to-operate procedure with a limitation on fiber diameter and a batch process.	The solvent phase is separated out from the solution, and the polymeric material remains, persisting to form nanofibers	Zhang and Lu (2014)
Drawing	It does not require complex assembly or machinery.	A droplet of polymeric solution material with a size in millimeters is dropped on the surface of silicon dioxide (SiO_2) and allowed to evaporate, followed by pipetting at a speed of 100 μm/s to get fibers.	Tong and Mazur (2008)
Centrifugal spinning	It can be used with various materials, such as ceramics, carbon fibers, and metals.	High-speed centrifugation of polymeric material is performed without worrying about the dielectric constant.	Ren et al. (2014)

TABLE 22.1 Key advantages and mechanisms of the methods of preparation of nanofiber scaffolds.—cont'd

Methods of preparation	Advantage	Mechanism	References
Plasma-induced synthesis	Low temperature procedure with vertical alignment. Enhance surface energy and precise diameter control.	Synthesis of nanofibers takes place by fast bombardment of high-energy radicals on the outer side of electrodes, followed by the generation of a plasma region due to the vaporization of atoms and cloud atoms	Saleem et al. (2020)
Solution blow spinning	It is a hybrid technology that combines the additive advantages of electrospinning and melt blowing.	It is a hybrid technology that uses components of the electrospinning and melt-blown processes to overcome the limitations of individual methods.	Behrens et al. (2014)
Self-assembly	It provides a smaller diameter compared with the conventional method.	Mechanism of self-assembly method of fiber preparation is the reduction of Gibbs free energy. Molecules move from a state of high energy (disorganized) to a state of lower energy (an organized fiber).	Hassanzadeh et al. (2013)

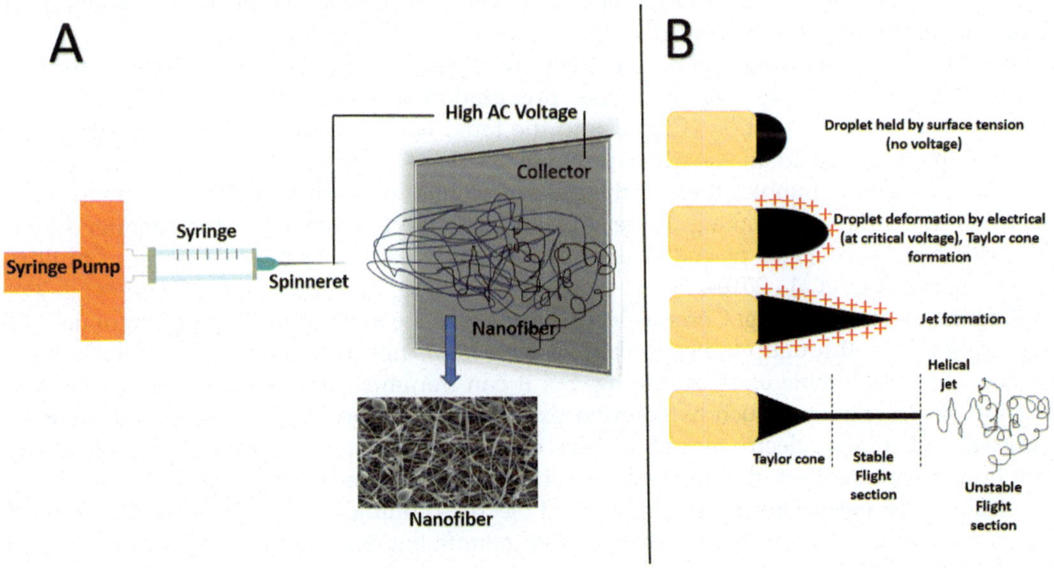

FIGURE 22.1 Electrospinning setup (A) and process of Taylor cone formation (B).

Triaxial or multiaxial electrospinning: It is the process of nanofibers preparation similar to coaxial electrospinning; the basic difference is that it has more than two (triaxial has three and multiaxial has more than three) concurrent polymeric solution supplies through the spinneret at a time. Triaxial electrospinning forms nanofibers with three layers: an outer layer, a middle layer, and an inner layer. Three or more feeding pumps are used to adjust the feeding rate of each solution to get the desired nanofibers (Ghosal et al., 2021).

Centrifugal electrospinning: Centrifugal electrospinning, also called rotary jet electrospinning. It is a combined form of conventional electrospinning with centrifugal force. It was invented first time by Andrey in 2005. Conventional centrifugal spinning uses only centrifugal force to spin the polymeric solution through a tiny orifice toward the collector and form fibers. In addition to the conventional electrospinning assembly, centrifugal electrospinning uses a high-speed rotating spinneret driven by a motor or, in some instances, a rotating metallic collector (Zhang et al., 2024).

Portable electrospinning: Portable electrospinning is the process of nanofiber preparation using a lightweight device; it is easy to carry from one place to another. This type of process comes into light to provide personalized dressing to treat wounds at a mobile location. The major drawback of portable electrospinning is the requirement for a high-voltage power supply at the on-site location (Xu et al., 2022).

Free-surface roller and wire-based electrospinning: It is the first needle-less system invented by Jirsak in 2004 (Patent No. US7585437B2). Its assembly consists of a roller spinneret electrode, an oppositely charged metallic collector, and a high-voltage power supply. During nanofiber preparation, the rotating electrode spinneret is submerged in the polymeric solution and rotated at high speed by a motor. Two motors separately rotate the spinneret and the metal collector individually. In this method, a high-power electric current (over 50 kV) is required to form nanofibers. When a sufficient electric field is applied, the liquid layer electrifies, and multiple Taylor cones form (Waqas et al., 2021).

Bubble electrospinning: Bubble electrospinning was invented by Liu in 2009. In the bubble electrospinning method for nanofiber preparation, a nonneedle system is used. In this process, a polymeric solution is filled into the tank, which is supplied with gas through a gas pump connected to an electric supply (16–35 kV). Due to gas bubbles generated in the polymeric solution, bubbles form at the surface. Polymeric solution bubbles come into contact with the airstream, making it fine. After that, an electrostatic charge is generated by an electrified metal collector placed at the opposite end, leading to the formation of multiple Taylor cones (Liu et al., 2010).

Corona electrospinning: Corona electrospinning is the method of preparation of nanofibers using a high-throughput, needle-less system. It has not developed a polymeric solution system, such as bubble electrospinning. So, it can minimize the problems associated with bubble electrospinning, such as solution exposure. The Corona electrospinning assembly consists of a circular electrode with a sharp edge, a high-voltage power supply, a feed supply unit, a metal collector, and a corona spinneret (Molnar and Nagy, 2016).

High-speed electrospinning: High-speed electrospinning was used for the first time by Nagy et al. (2015) to form Itraconazole-loaded nanofibers. This method contains a combination of conventional electrospinning with the high-speed rotating jet (up to 50,000 rpm) to increase production output (Nagy et al., 2015).

Melt blowing

Melt blowing is the nonelectrostatic method of preparation of nanofibrous scaffolds. It is a single-step, simple, and versatile method of preparation that gives micrometer or below range of nanofibrous scaffolds. A schematic presentation of the melt blowing process for the preparation of nanofibers is shown in Fig. 22.2. Melt blowing technology was first developed by a United States-based laboratory called the Naval Research Laboratory in the 1950s (McCulloch, 1999). In this process, a molten mass of polymer is extruded through a die, and a fiber is formed due to air-drag (elongation of the polymer extruded) that is collected on a collector in the structure of a web. In this process, the diameter of nanofibers depends upon the temperature of the extrusion process, the viscosity of the extrudate, the air-drag process temperature and its velocity (Shambaugh, 1988).

Template synthesis

In this technique, a mould or template is generally used to get the desired size of nanofibers. The polymeric solution passes through a membrane having a pore size in nanometers under positive water pressure. So, after interacting with a salifying solution, a desired range of nanofibers will be obtained (Li et al., 2005). A schematic representation of the template synthesis is shown in Fig. 22.3.

Template melt-extrusion

It is a combination methodology of template synthesis and extrusion process for the production of nanofibers of thermoplastic materials. In the process, a molten mass of polymeric material passes through the membrane (anodic aluminium oxide membrane-AAOM) pores forcefully, followed by cooling at room temperature (Li et al., 2006). Generally, the AAOM thin membrane is placed on a stainless-steel base to bear pressure and make the flow of polymeric solution unidirectional. The polymer solution-containing vessel should be placed on a temperature-controlled heating system to maintain the material molten.

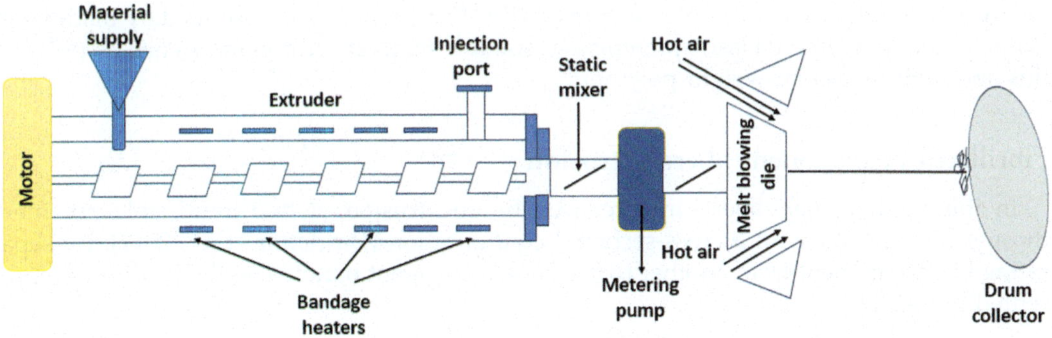

FIGURE 22.2 A schematic presentation of the melt blowing process for the preparation of nanofibers.

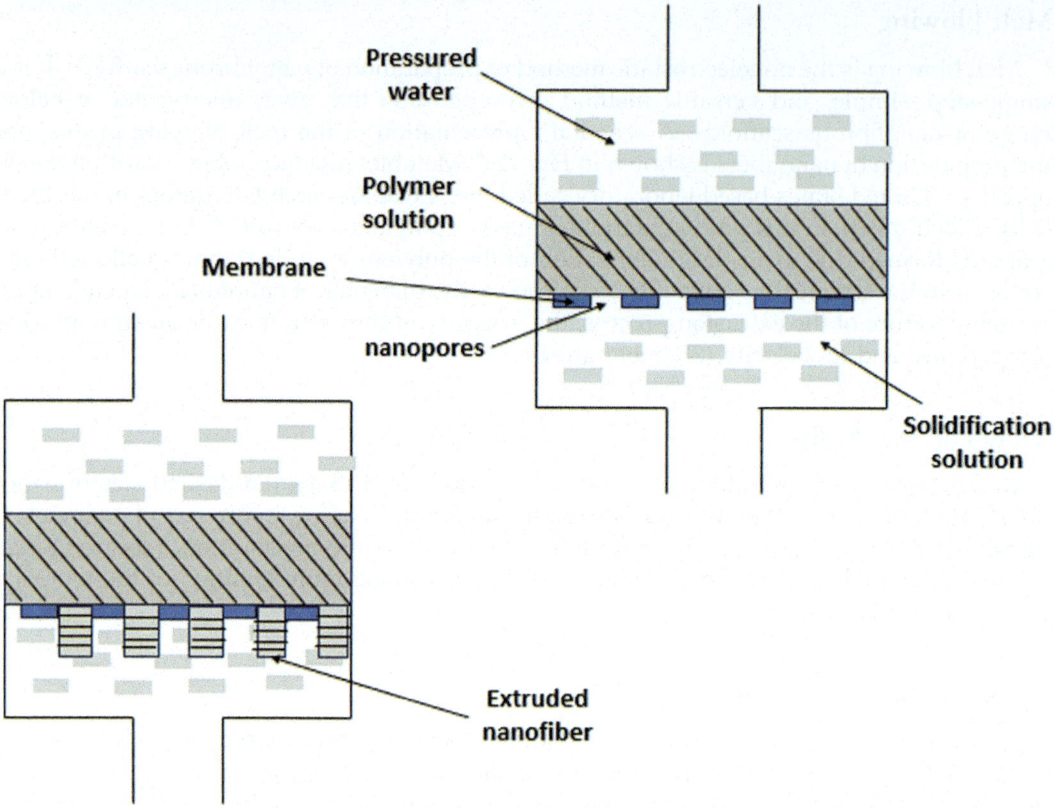

FIGURE 22.3 A schematic representation of the template synthesis.

Flash spinning

Flash spinning is the process of nanofiber preparation in which a polymeric material is formed into a nanofiber with a spin agent (liquid) spun out into an area having a lower temperature and pressure to form plexifilaments (15). This process was described by Blades and White of DuPont (1963). Flash spinning is a suitable method for polymers such as polyolefins and high-molecular-weight polymers.

Fibrillated bicomponent fibers extrusion

In this method, nanofibers are prepared by coextrusion of two immiscible polymers through a spinneret with a cross-sectional configuration (Dasdemir et al., 2012). By separating one component from another to produce subsequent nanofibers, the process is represented in Fig. 22.4.

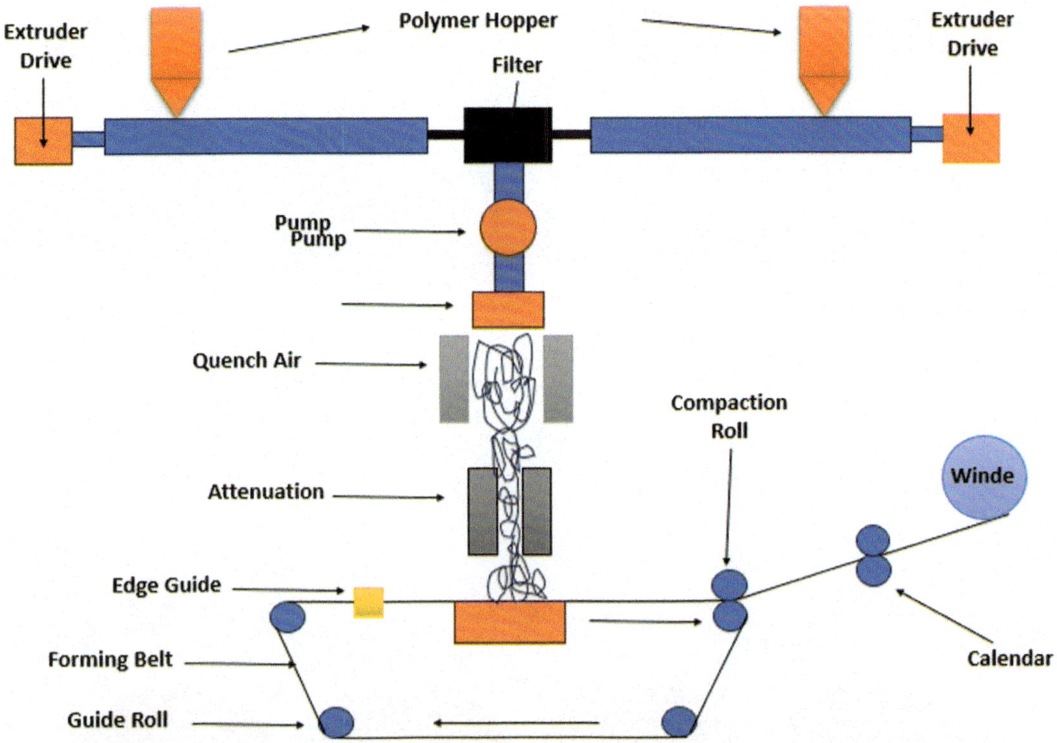

FIGURE 22.4 Fibrillated bicomponent fibers extrusion process.

Phase separation

In the phase separation process of preparing nanofibers, the solvent phase is separated out from the solution, and the polymeric material remains, persisting to form nanofibers (Hae-won et al., 2012). In the phase separation process, a solution was prepared by dissolving the desired polymer at a specific temperature to form a homogeneous solution. Further solution was kept at gelation temperature to form a gel-like structure. Now, the extraction of solvent makes drying of the polymer to form a framework of nanofibers (Jiang et al., 2023). A Schematic representation of the phase separation process is shown in Fig. 22.5.

Drawing

In the drawing process of nanofibers preparation, a droplet of polymeric solution material with a size in millimeters is dropped on the surface of silicon dioxide (SiO_2) and allowed to evaporate. The drawing process is the laboratory-scale preparation of nanofibers (Tong and Mazur, 2008). A schematic representation of the drawing process of nanofiber preparation is shown in Fig. 22.6.

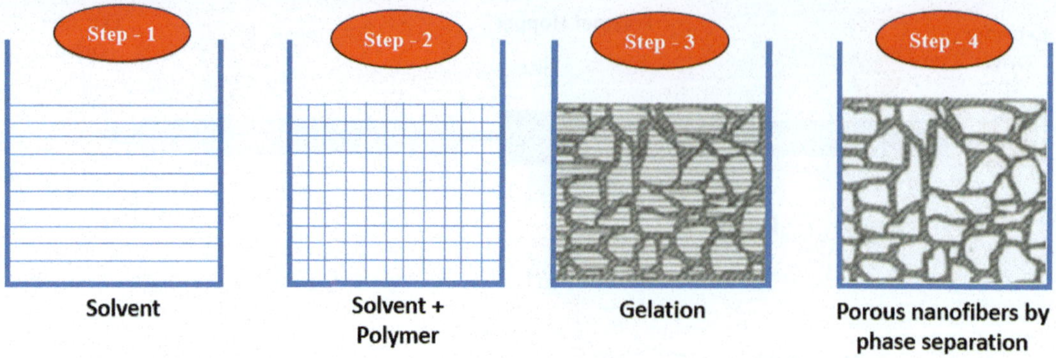

FIGURE 22.5 A schematic representation of the phase separation process.

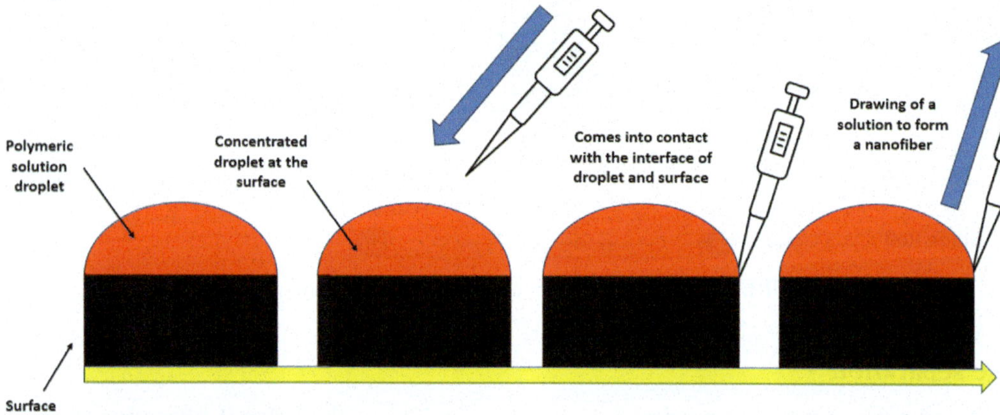

FIGURE 22.6 A schematic representation of the drawing process of nanofiber preparation.

Centrifugal spinning

The centrifugal spinning process has almost 50 times higher production rate compared with conventional spinning methods (Ren et al., 2014). In centrifugal spinning, centrifugal force is used, while an electric field is used in the electrospinning method. Centrifugal spinning can be applied to polymeric solutions without worrying about their dielectric constant and without exposure to high-voltage electric fields. Centrifugal spinning was first used by Hooper (1924) for the preparation of artificial silk fibers (Hooper, 1924). A schematic representation of the centrifugal spinning is shown in Fig. 22.7. Forcespinning is the technology to form a nanofiber using a solution or a solid material that is melted into a spun nanofiber. This technology was invented and commercialized by Dr Karen Lozano and FibeRio Technology Corporation, United States, respectively (Sarkar et al., 2010).

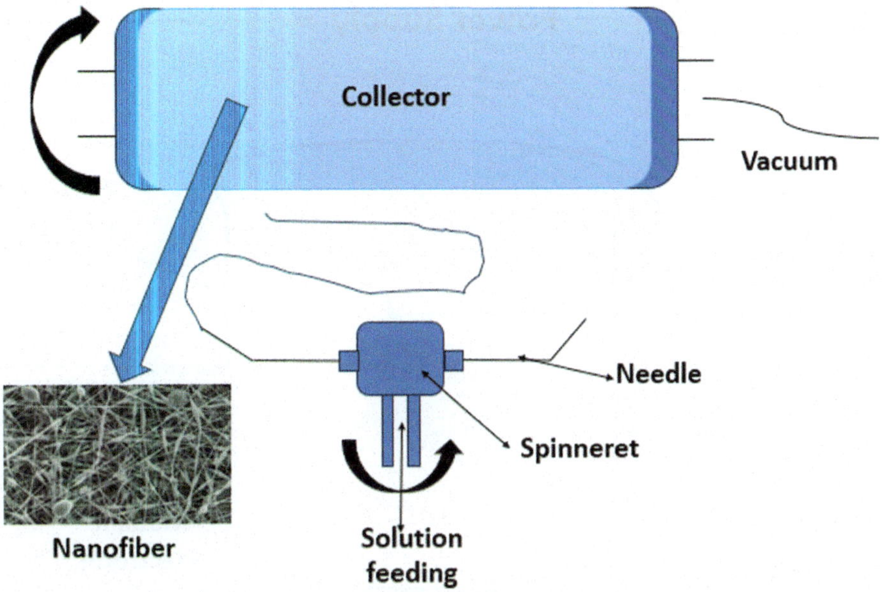

FIGURE 22.7 A schematic representation of the centrifugal spinning.

Plasma-induced synthesis

Plasma is considered the fourth state of matter; it is a gas-like substance where some amount of material remains in ionized form, or simply, they carry a charge on the surface. In the plasma-induced synthesis of nanofibers, a direct current is used to form plasma between both electrodes in the solution. Synthesis of nanofibers takes place by fast bombardment of high-energy radicals on the outer side of electrodes, followed by the generation of a plasma region due to the vaporization of atoms and cloud atoms (Saleem et al., 2020). The Plasma-induced synthesis of nanofibers is diagrammatically represented in Fig. 22.8.

Solution blow spinning

It is the hybrid technology in which component of the electrospinning and melt blowing processes was used. In the solution blow spinning process, a compressed gas source is used to blow the polymeric solution through a nozzle (Dias et al., 2019). The solution of the spinning process is diagrammatically represented in Fig. 22.9.

Formulation of nanofibrous scaffolds

Choice of materials for the fabrication of nanofibrous scaffolds depends on the application site and intended action, such as dissolving nanofibers for instant drug release, slow degrading nanofibers for prolonged drug release, nanofibers for localized administration, etc.

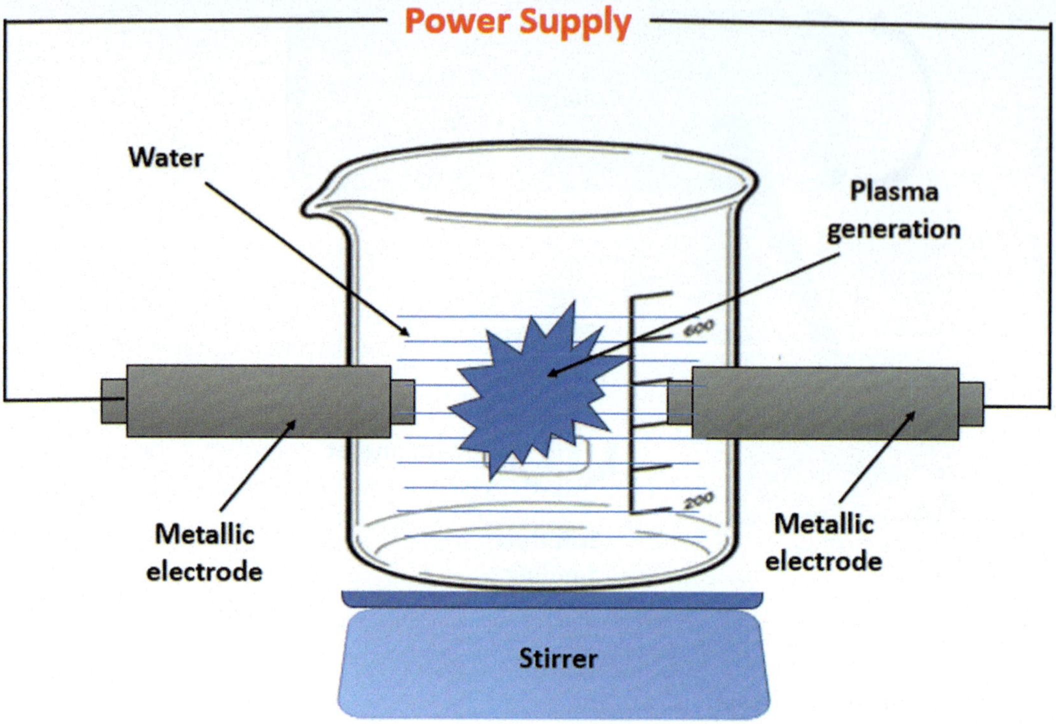

FIGURE 22.8 Plasma-induced synthesis of nanofibers.

(Hayati et al., 1987). For the fabrication of nanofibers, various materials, natural, synthetic, or a combination of two or more, can be used (Brenner et al., 2012) (Table 22.2). Hybrid and composite nanofibrous scaffolds usually consist of two or more polymers (or polymers with functional additives, e.g., nanoparticles) to exploit the best properties of each material (Table 22.3). This cooperative approach has the potential to improve mechanical performance, biological behavior, and therapeutic effects beyond those provided by individual polymer scaffolds (Abadi et al., 2022). A typical approach is to combine natural polymers (such as collagen, chitosan, silk fibroin, or alginate) with synthetic polymers (such as polycaprolactone [PCL], poly lactic acid [PLA], or poly (lactic co-glycolic acid) [PLGA]). The natural component adds bioactive sites and ECM-like properties to the scaffold, which help promote cell adhesion and proliferation, while the synthetic component adds tunable mechanical strength, longer scaffold persistence, and controlled degradation rate (Haaparanta et al., 2014). For example, coupling collagen with PCL in nanofibers led to a hybrid material that was stiffer and maintained its architecture for a longer time, while supporting earlier, higher rates of attachment of cancer cells than pure collagen scaffolds or PCL scaffolds alone. Modifying chitosan with PEO and blending alginate with PCL have been shown to improve electrospinnability and produce consistent nanofibers with quasi-uniform pore structures, allowing enhanced diffusion of nutrients and oxygen in three-dimensional tumor models (Sen et al., 2025). These hybrid systems have value when looking to perform in vitro tumor modelling for breast cancer, cervical cancer, and glioblastoma.

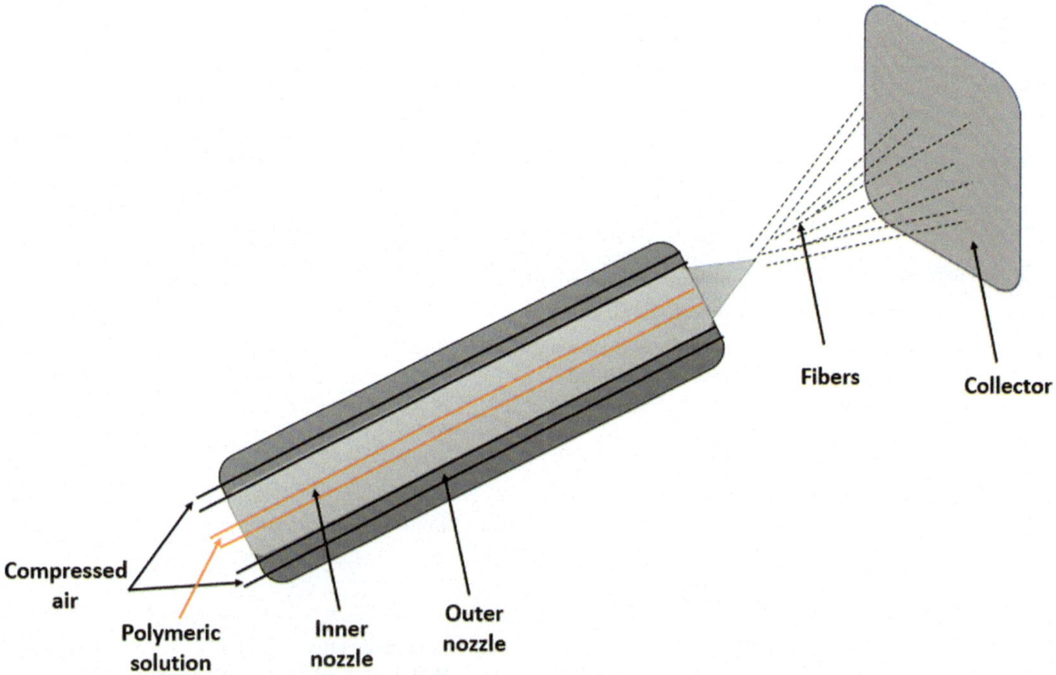

FIGURE 22.9 Solution blow spinning process.

Advanced strategies and functionalization of nanofibrous scaffolds

The power of nanofibrous scaffolds lies in their ability to be tailored such that they interact with the biological system positively and uniquely. These sophisticated functional techniques include surface modification and nanomaterial integration. Surface modification techniques are methods of functionalizing nanofibrous scaffolds in order to improve pharmacological activity and targeted therapy. It can be accomplished using physical and chemical modification approaches.

Physical modification

Physical surface modification involves altering the surface characteristics of biomaterials, such as surface or roughness (Yang et al., 2021), wettability (Misaka et al., 2024), morphology (Rahman et al., 2025), and compatibility with biological systems to enhance their performance, biocompatibility, and targetability (Aminu et al., 2023). Several techniques employed for physical surface modification include plasma treatment (Zarei et al., 2023), ultraviolet (Kolská et al., 2018), or laser treatment (Daskalova et al., 2018). In plasma treatment, polar groups are introduced to the surface, making it hydrophilic and good for cell attachment. This helps in increasing surface wettability and biological attachment property of the nanofiber scaffold (Zarei et al., 2023). In the UV treatment,

TABLE 22.2 Different types natural and synthetic polymers used in the preparation of nanofiber scaffolds for cancer management.

Polymer type	Polymer	Formulation	Advantage	Observation	Pharmacological use	References
Natural	Collagen	3D porous hybrid scaffolds	Mimicking the natural cartilage tissue	Improved porosity and mechanical strength	Cartilage tissue engineering	Haaparanta et al. (2014)
Natural	Silk fibroin	Nanofibrous aerogel	Porous structure	Sustained drug release	Ovarian cancer	Deng et al. (2024)
Natural	Chitosan	Nanofiber scaffolds	Surface roughness, scaffolds' wettability	High proliferation rate of cells compared with 2D structures	3D breast cancer tissue	Rabie et al. (2022)
Natural	Alginate	3D printed alginate scaffolds with nanoparticle	Enhance the generation of ROS and suppression of	Reduction in tumor volume	Local breast cancer	Colak and Ertas (2024)
Synthetic	Polycaprolactone	Gold nanocage-incorporated fiber	Smart stimulation of the system	Synergistic effect of PCL and cold nanocage	Chemo photothermal therapy	Park et al. (2019)
Synthetic	Polycaprolactone, PVA	Nanofiber patch	Sustained drug delivery by PCL, PVA improve water adsorption	Localized nanotherapeutics delivery	Breast cancer	Rehman et al. (2025)
Synthetic	PLA	Nanofibers	High porosity, complex geometry, biodegradability, and biocompatibility	Prolonged release and improved stability of the system	Colorectal cancer	Chi et al. (2020)
Synthetic	PLGA	Nanofiber	Sustained release of paclitaxel	Biodegradable system	Glioma	Xie and Wang (2006)
Synthetic	PVA	Nonwoven nanofibers	Controlled release of drug	Initial burst followed by sustains release of drug	Colorectal cancer	Bhusnure et al. (2021)

the impact of UV-A (longwave ultraviolet) radiation on the surface and bulk properties of nonwoven polyamide nanofibers was investigated by exposing them to varying durations of UV treatment (Kolská et al., 2018). The findings revealed notable modifications in surface chemistry, polarity, surface charge, wettability, roughness, and morphology,

TABLE 22.3 Composite polymeric materials used in nanofiber scaffolds preparation for cancer management.

Polymers	Formulation	Advantage	Pharmacological use	References
Poly (L-lactic acid)-co-poly(3-caprolactone) (PLLACL), silk fibroin (SF) and hydroxyapatite	Electrospun-electrosprayed hydroxyapatite nanostructured composites	Mimic the native extracellular matrix and have good biocompatibility	Bone tissue regeneration	Gandhimathi et al. (2018)
N-carboxymethyl chitosan/polyvinyl alcohol/poly (ε-caprolactone)	Core–shell nanofiber	Controlled drug release, high adsorption	Breast cancer	Abasalta et al. (2022)
PEG-PLGA copolymer	Nanoparticle incorporated in nanofiber	Smart nanofiber system, on-demand system	–	Fazio et al. (2019)
Alginate	3D-printed alginate scaffolds with bismuth sulfide nanoparticles	Enhance formation of RO, enhance the inhibition of breast cancer cells, and suppress their colony formation capacity.	Breast cancer	Colak and Ertas (2024)

particularly evident after short exposure up to 10 min. Laser treatment works without causing much thermal stress, making it ideal for producing precise and controlled surface modifications. The highly employed laser technique uses a femtosecond laser, which helps in creating different textures on nanomaterial scaffolds such as lines, triangles, squares, wells, and pentagonal shapes. The potential of femtosecond (fs) laser surface modification to enhance the biological performance of 3D-printed poly-e-caprolactone (PCL) scaffolds was investigated for bone tissue engineering (Daskalova et al., 2018). Some of the other physical modification techniques are the physical vapor deposition (Bank-Srour et al., 2013) and ion beam implantation (Xiao et al., 2020).

Chemical modification

Chemical modification of NFs has been explored to improve biocompatibility, biodegradability, and targeting potential towards the target site (Miraftab et al., 2015). Various chemical reactions have been employed to chemically modify the NFs by introducing functional groups on the surface of polymers. This includes cross-linking that enables the attachment of functional molecules such as proteins, enzymes, monomers, or polymers onto material surfaces. This enhances the stability of polymeric fibers or modifies the release kinetics through inter- or intramolecular linkages. In a study, curcumin and 5-fluorouracil were loaded into core–shell polyethene oxide and polyethyleneimine nanofibers (Yang et al., 2014). Two distinct formulations were prepared by varying the extent of cross-linking. Each formulation was loaded with an equivalent drug quantity. The study showed that the formulation with higher cross-link density exhibited a delayed release of 5-fluorouracil. This resulted in decreased cytotoxicity at early time points (48 h) compared with the faster-releasing fibers. Chemical grafting involves the covalent attachment reaction and the process can be classified into two main approaches: "grafting to" and "grafting from". The first approach, grafting, involves a coupling reaction in which the end functional group of a polymer reacts with a complementary group on the surface. This results in a chemical change in the polymer backbone (Niemczyk-Soczynska et al., 2020). This approach uses various kinds of polymerization, such as controlled free-radical polymerization, atom-transfer radical polymerization, and anionic polymerization. Grafting from approach, on the other hand involve the alteration of the macromolecular backbone to introduce reactive functional groups onto the surface. This process typically requires an initiator, which can be incorporated onto the surface through postpolymerization, copolymerization, or polycondensation techniques. "Click" chemistry has also been observed to be a highly effective method for modifying the surfaces of polymer fibers by attaching biologically active molecules through selective heteroatom-based bonds (Lancuški et al., 2012).

Incorporation of nanoparticles and other nanomaterials within nanofibers

Nanomaterials have gained immense popularity in drug delivery as they offer a number of advantages due to their unique physicochemical properties, including high surface area, tunable size, and functional versatility. These materials, such as vesicles, micelles, silica nanoparticles, and other nanomaterials such as carbon nanotubes and metal-based nanocarriers, have been engineered and loaded with anticancer drugs for better drug delivery. These nanomaterial-based drug delivery systems enhanced the therapeutic index of chemotherapeutic agents while minimizing systemic toxicity. Nanofiber scaffolds have been widely employed against several cancers, including brain cancer, breast cancer, and many more. To make drug delivery more precise and accurate, attempts have been made where nanomaterials in different forms have been introduced into the nanofiber scaffold, as depicted in Table 22.4. The nano fiber provides a physical structure that can stay in place at the site of a tumor, working as a carrier, whereas the nanomaterial loaded with an anticancer drug facilitates controlled drug delivery at the target site. Some scaffolds have also been designed to respond to certain conditions, such as changes in pH or temperature, thereby releasing the drug in response to a particular stimulus.

Applications of nanofibrous scaffolds in cancer management

Nanofibrous scaffolds have several applications in cancer treatment.

Nanofibrous scaffolds for anticancer drug delivery

Nanofibrous scaffolds can be utilized to treat a variety of cancers, including brain cancer, liver cancer, cervical cancer, oral cancer, colorectal cancer, and pediatric solid tumors (Table 22.5). Carmustine-loaded biodegradable nanofiber membranes were prepared by the

TABLE 22.4 An overview of nanoparticles and other nanomaterials within nanofibers.

Type of nanomaterial incorporated in NF	Drug	Polymer used	Key outcomes	Outcomes related to cancer	References
Vesicle	5-Fluorouracil and paeonolum	Vesicle: Cetyltrimethylammonium bromide (CTAB) and sodium dodecylbenzenesulfonate (SDBS): Poly (ethylene oxide)	Increasing the CTAB/SDBS molar ratio enhanced the release of 5-FU and reduced the release of paeonolum.	Dual anticancer drug delivery was achieved in a controlled and desirable amount.	Li et al. (2015)
Macrovesicles	Rhodamine-B	Polycaprolactone (PCL) and PCL-Pluronic (F127)	Electrospun mesh showed slower drug release due to PCL coating over vesicles and improved hydrophilicity	Promoted higher L929 cell viability due to enhanced hydrophilicity	Nair et al. (2014)
Micelle	5-Fluorouracil and cefradine	PCL doped with PGC-C18 (poly (glycerol monostearate-co-ε-caprolactone))	Increased hydrophobicity slowed drug diffusion and extended release over 90+ days.	Significant cytotoxicity against HT-29 colorectal cancer cells was achieved	Hu et al. (2013)
Folate-targeted micelle	Doxorubicin	Folate-conjugated PCL-PEGC, PVA and micelles shell comprising cross-linked gelatin	The nanofiber system significantly reduced drug dose and administration frequency.	Maintained strong antitumor efficacy and minimized side effects compared with intravenous injection	Yang et al. (2015)
Mesoporous silica and hydroxyapatite nanocarriers	Doxorubicin hydrochloride and hydroxycamptothecin	Mesoporous silica, hydroxyapatite, poly (lactic-co-glycolic acid) (PLGA)	Both drug-loaded nanocarriers were successfully embedded in PLGA nanofibers, enabling sustained release	Higher in vitro inhibition of HeLa cells compared with single-drug systems.	Chen et al. (2014)

electrospinning method using PLGA and poly [(D, L)-lactide-co-glycolide] polymer to treat brain cancer (Tseng et al., 2013). Reduction-responsive Pt(IV) prodrug-backboned micelle and sodium dichloroacetate were coelectrospun into poly(vinyl alcohol) (PVA) nanofibers to prepare an implant for localized delivery of active ingredients (Zhang et al., 2017). A

TABLE 22.5 Application of nanofibrous scaffolds in different types of cancer management.

Drug	Polymer	Method of preparation	Formulation	Pharmacological use	Investigation status	References
Carmustine	PLGA, poly [(D, L)-lactide-co-glycolide]	Electrospinning	Nanofiber membrane	Glioblastoma multiforme (brain cancer)	In vivo	Tseng et al. (2013)
Pt (IV)	Poly-vinyl alcohol	Coelectrospun	Implantable nanofiber micelle	Cervical cancer	In vivo	Zhang et al. (2017)
Cisplatin	Poly-L -lactic acid	electrospinning	Multilayered fiber mat	Liver cancer	In vivo	Zhang et al. (2014)
Docetaxel	Poly-D, L-lactic acid	Electrospinning	Fiber mats	Breast cancer	In vivo	Ding et al. (2016)
Cisplatin	PGC-C18, PCL	Electrospinning	Nanofiber meshes	Lung cancer	In vivo	Kaplan et al. (2016)
7-Ethyl-10-hydroxycamptothecin (SN-38)	PLA	Electrospinning	Microcrystal-loaded nanofibers	Pediatric solid tumor	In vivo	Monterrubio et al. (2016)
5-Flurouracil, oxaliplatin	Poly (l-lactide)	Electrospinning	Nanofiber mats implant	Colorectal cancer	In vivo	Zhang et al. (2016)
Diclofenac sodium	Poly (d, L-lactide-co-glycolide)	Electrospinning	Electrospun nanofiber	Oral cancer	In vivo	Will et al. (2016)

synergistic effect on cancer cells was achieved with Pt. In a study, a cisplatin-loaded polylactide nanofiber multilayer mat was prepared by using the electrospinning process for subcutaneous drug delivery and treatment of liver cancer (Zhang et al., 2014). Biodistribution results confirmed that the drug concentration ratio of armpit SC local tissue and blood was 6.32 (1 h) and 5.47 (24 h). While the cancer survival rate was found to be 23 days (control), 30 days (i.v. route), and 49 days (SC route of nanofiber formulation). Docetaxel-loaded Poly-d, L-lactide electrospun nanofiber mat was prepared by using the electrospinning method to treat breast cancer recurrence in a mouse model (Ding et al., 2016). Biodistribution in the mouse model was found to be 3238 ng/g in thoracic tissue after local administration, while 122 ng/g was observed during i.v. administration. Survival rate in the mouse model was found to be higher in the fiber mat group (83%) compared with nonfiber mat formulations. Cisplatin-loaded nanofiber meshes were prepared by using the electrospinning process with the hydrophobic polycaprolactone and poly (glycerol monostearate-*co*-caprolactone) copolymer (Kaplan et al., 2016). Due to the high hydrophobic nature of meshes, they exhibit the linear cisplatin release over 90 days. In onother study, pediatric solid tumors were treated by radiotherapy and chemotherapy, having serious short-term and long-term side effects. SN-38 (an approved anticancer drug) has low aqueous solubility, so to overcome the problem of low solubility, SN-38 microcrystal-loaded electrospun fiber was prepared to treat paediatric solid tumors (Monterrubio et al., 2016). 5-Fluorouracil (F) and oxaliplatin (O)-loaded poly (l-lactide) electrospun nanofiber mats were prepared to treat colorectal cancer (Zhang et al., 2016). After 10 h of treatment relative tumor volume was found in order of: Oxaliplatin and 5-fluorouracil nanofiber < Oxaliplatin and 5-fluorouracil i.v. < control < poly (l-lactide) fiber (Blank) and survival rate was found in order of: Oxaliplatin and 5-fluorouracilnanofiber > Oxaliplatin and 5-fluorouracil i.v. > control > blank poly l-lactide fiber. Diclofenac sodium is an FDA-approved NSAID drug. In its repurposing attempt, diclofenac sodium-loaded electrospun nanofibers were prepared using electrospinning technology to treat oral cancer by local delivery (Will et al., 2016). Formulation was tested for various tongue cell lines such as SCC-4, SCC-25, SCC-9, and SCC-15. An oral cancer model was developed using SCC-9 cell injection in the oral cavity. Results were examined for tumor recurrence and found that the formulation of nanofiber scaffolds had less tumor recurrence (33%) compared with other groups (90%–100%).

Tissue engineering and regenerative nanofibrous scaffolds in postcancer surgery

Nanofibrous scaffolds have versatile applications in tissue engineering. Diclofenac sodium-loaded Poly (D, L lactide-co-glycolide, 80/20) nanofiber scaffolds were prepared using the electrospinning technique (Nikkola et al., 2015). Nanofibrous scaffolds have also been used in regenerative medicine in postcancer surgery. Much research has been done, including Carmustine, irinotecan, cisplatin, paclitaxel, and temozolomide drug-loaded nanofiber formulations for postcancer surgery of glioblastoma multiforme GBM (Ranganath and Wang, 2008).

Nanofiber-based system for cancer diagnostics and theranostics

Nanofiber scaffold-based drug delivery systems were used for diagnostic and theranostic purposes in cancer management, as presented Table 22.6. For early cancer detection, various biomarkers were investigated, including miRNA-223-3p, which is a promising biomarker for laryngeal cancer diagnosis. Surface-enhanced Raman scattering (SERS) with a nanofiber-based system was used to amplify signals through expedited entrapment and signal redistribution. Prepared diagnostic devices showed a linear detection range of 10–250 fM with the LOD of 19.5 fM (Martino et al., 2025). Nanofiber-based systems for cancer diagnosis were developed using the principles of electrochemical sensing, electrochemical immunosensing, electrochemical genosensing, and fluorescent chemosensing or gas sensing (Hernández and Chauhan, 2020). Therapeutic and diagnostic applications in the same devices or systems are considered as their theranostic application. In a study, coaxial electrospinning was used to form a core–shell nanofiber formulation using indomethacin as a model drug for theranostic application in colon cancer. The core contained the Eudragit S100 polymeric material, while the shell consisted of PEO and a magnet-sensitive contrast agent (GD-DTPA). Drug release was followed by a combination of erosion and diffusion mechanisms. This formulation successfully delivered therapeutic drugs and contrast agents to the colonic area (Jin et al., 2016).

TABLE 22.6 Nanofiber scaffolds-based formulations used for diagnostic and theranostics cancer.

Drug	Method of preparation	Polymer	Formulation	Investigation status	Type of smart formulation	Pharmacological use	References
miRNAs	Nanospider NS 1S500U [Elmarco s.r.o.]	ε-caprolactam and ε-caprolactone	Nanofiber combined with gold nanoparticle	In vitro	Diagnosis	Laryngeal cancer diagnosis	Martino et al. (2025)
Laccase enzyme and reduce graphene oxide	Electrospinning	PVP, chitosan	Nanofibers	In vitro	Electrochemical detection	17α-ethinylestradiol detection	Hernández and Chauhan (2020)
Indomethacin, Gd (diethylenetriaminepentaacetate hydrate)	Coaxial electrospinning	Eudragit S100, poly (ethylene oxide)	Nanofibers	In vitro	Theranostics	Colon imaging	Jin et al. (2016)
Doxorubicin		1-Ethyl-3-(3-dimethyl aminopropyl) carbodiimide, *N*-hydroxysuccinimide	Nanoparticle-conjugated electrospun nanostructure	In vivo	Theranostic	Breast cancer	Khan et al. (2024a)

Doxorubicin-loaded nanofibers are also used for the theranostic application of breast cancer (Khan et al., 2024a).

Smart nanofibrous scaffolds

Smart nanofiber formulations are formulations that turn on by some stimuli, such as photoresponsivity (radiation such as near infrared), thermo-responsive, pH-responsive, acid-responsive or magnet-responsive. pH-responsive doxorubicin-loaded core–shell nanofibrous from polyvinyl alcohol and polycaprolactone were prepared by using coaxial electrospinning (Yan et al., 2020). The pH-sensitive degradation of these polymers at pH 4 resulted in a high drug release, highlighting their potential use in cervical cancers and other solid tumors. The pH-sensitive degradation of the polymers enabled the DOX-loaded fibers to exhibit efficacy against cervical cancer HeLa cells. A few examples of stimuli-responsive nanofibers designed using a variety of polymers and materials are given in Table 22.7, suggesting the applicability of nanofibers in microenvironment-responsive anticancer drug delivery.

Translational challenges and considerations

Nanofiber scaffolds formulation provides a unique drug delivery strategy for cancer therapy. Several translational problems, including as low throughput efficacy, batch-to-batch variability, biocompatibility, regulatory and economic constraints, cause obstacles in the lab-to-market journey.

Manufacturing considerations

Scalability and reproducibility are significant challenges in the clinical translation of nanofibrous formulations. Many preparation techniques, including phase separation and melt blowing, do not yield a consistent diameter (Zhu et al., 2024). Electrospinning may not be repeatable at the industrial scale, despite being acceptable for repeatability at the laboratory scale. The quality control of nanofibrous formulations is an essential component that regulatory authorities monitor in order to achieve the intended results (Maduna and Patnaik, 2024).

Biological consideration

One of the challenges in lab-to-market translation is the cytotoxic effect of nanofibrous scaffolds beyond the intended area. Local therapy for cancer care involves many variables, yet certain shortcomings, such as drug leakage at off-target areas, may increase drug toxicity (Logan et al., 2023). Numerous research methods, including biodistribution, immunogenicity, and long-term degradation investigations, are required to overcome these obstacles. Replicating human cancer behavior in in vitro models is also a challenging task while conducting preclinical research (Yadav et al., 2025). In vivo studies are usually conducted to

TABLE 22.7 Smart and responsive nanofibrous scaffolds for cancer management.

Drug	Method of preparation	Polymer	Formulation	Investigation status	Type of smart formulation	Pharmacological use	References
Doxorubicin	Coaxial electrospinning	PVA, PCL	Nanofibrous scaffolds	In vitro	pH-responsive, achieved by polyvinyl alcohol (PVA)/polycaprolactone (PCL), in which PVA and PCL were present in the core and shell, respectively, for cervical cancer chemotherapy.	Cervical cancer	Yan et al. (2020)
Doxorubicin	-	FFYEE	Nanofiber conjugate	In vivo	Acid responsive, achieved by hydrazone bond (acid hydrolysis) of modified peptide at C-terminal α-D-galactosamine for dual strategy as acid response by hydrazone bond and targeting of doxorubicin using α-D-galactosamine for hepatic cancer treatment.	Hepatic cancer	Liang et al. (2022)
Doxorubicin	Electrospinning	PVA, poly (*N*-isopropyl acrylamide)	Microgel	In vitro	Thermoresponsiveness, achieved by incorporating poly (*N*-isopropyl acrylamide) into the fabrication of microgels and superparamagnetic iron oxide nanoparticles, was utilized to provide magnet responsiveness in poly (vinyl alcohol) nanofibrous membranes.	Anticancer	Gonçalves et al. (2024)
Gold nanorod	Electrospinning	PEG, PLGA, PLA-b-PEG	Electrospun membrane	In vitro	Photo-responsive, achieved using a gold nanorod (GNB) that selectively kills cancerous cells, and the nanofiber membrane was used as a biodegradable carrier and surgical removal material.	Lung, breast, and cervical cancer	Cheng et al. (2014)

Bortezomib, polydopamine	Electrospinning	PCL	Nanofibrous scaffolds	In vitro	Photo-responsive using NIR, achieved by lethal polydopamine nanospheres (PD-NS) loaded nanofiber containing bortezomib (BMT) drug. BMT-PD-NS exhibit an absorption band in the near-infrared (NIR), enabling rapid heating that can induce cancer cell death.	Colorectal cancer	Obiweluozor et al. (2018)
MoS_2, doxorubicin	Blend electrospinning	Chitosan, PVA	Electrospun nanofiber mat	In vivo	Photothermal (808 nm laser) responsive drug delivery of doxorubicin (anticancer drug) was achieved by MoS_2 (photothermal transforming agent) and polymers such as chitosan and PVA with the conversion efficiency of 23.2%.	Colorectal cancer	Zhao et al. (2019)
Doxorubicin	Electrospinning	Polycaprolactone	Nanofiber	In vitro	A photo-responsive nanofiber scaffold for the treatment of breast cancer was formulated by gold nanocage-loaded PCL fibers, with chemotherapeutic agents encapsulated in the core and a phase-transforming fatty acid in the sheath. When the photo-response system was heated, the fatty layer melted, resulting in rapid drug release.	Breast cancer	Park et al. (2019)
Carmofur, rose bengal	Coaxial electrospinning	Eudragit L100-55, HPMC	Electrospun oral formulation	In vitro	Targeting of carmofur for colon cancer was achieved using photosensitive pH-responsive drug delivery. Rose Bengal was used as a photosensitizer because it has sensitivity for the colon site, and pH-sensitive Eudragit L100-55 was used as a pH-responsive material in the shell with HPMC in the core.	Colon cancer	Li et al. (2019)

(*Continued*)

TABLE 22.7 Smart and responsive nanofibrous scaffolds for cancer management.—cont'd

Drug	Method of preparation	Polymer	Formulation	Investigation status	Type of smart formulation	Pharmacological use	References
Camptothecin, doxorubicin	Electrospinning	Poly(N-isopropylacrylamide)	Layer-by-layer nanofiber	In vitro	Dual drug delivery of camptothecin (CPT) and doxorubicin (DOX) was achieved using a light-responsive, layer-by-layer-assembled nanofiber for sequential drug release in which CPT was encapsulated in fiber, while DOX was layered. Polyethyleneimine and sodium 4-styrenesulfonate were used in layering while gold nanorod was used as photo-responsive material.	Skin cancer	Singh et al. (2023)
Doxorubicin hydrochloride	Electrospinning	Polydopamine, polycaprolactone	Nanofiber-loaded implant	In vitro	Dual-responsive (pH and near-IR) smart delivery of doxorubicin (DOX) was achieved using a multifunctional polydopamine (pH and near-IR) and PCL polymer, enabling improved DOX release at acidic pH and near-IR at 808 nm.	Lung, breast cancer	Tiwari et al. (2019)

address these issues, but their translational efforts are constrained by a number of factors, including cancer heterogeneity, metastasis, and the EPR effect (Seruga et al., 2014).

Regulatory consideration

Nanomedicine's clinical translation is still difficult and needs a lot of data to be approved by regulators (Đorđević et al., 2022; Uhljar and Ambrus, 2023). Preclinical data, including physicochemical, stability, repeatability, scalability, and PK-PD data, are necessary for regulatory agencies to perform clinical trials. Choosing participants, establishing an outcome (such as tumor regression or survival rate), and monitoring adverse drug reactions are all challenges in the process of obtaining approval for clinical trials (Agrahari and Hiremath, 2017).

Patents and clinical trials

Nanofiber scaffolds are employed for different applications in biomedical science and cancer management. A few patented inventions are summarized in Table 22.8. Most of the patented nanofibrous scaffold's formulations were developed by the electrospinning technology due to its capability to reproduce and control parameters. Table 22.9 provides a comprehensive summary of clinical research on nanofibrous scaffolds in cancer management. These suggest the wide applicability of nanofibrous scaffolds in drug delivery and cancer therapy.

Future perspectives

Nanotechnology in the delivery of drugs, theranostics, gene therapy, and immunotherapy is continuously developing with rising attempts to overcome current laboratory challenges. Recent developments in drug delivery using nanofibrous scaffolds are creating a potential use for personalized and customized medications. Personalized cancer therapy is a fast-increasing strategy for cancer management. By adopting a nanofibrous scaffold-based technology, patient-centric cancer treatment can be accomplished by formulating scaffolds as per the needs of individual patients and tumor behavior (Kajdič et al., 2019). With the use of clinical evaluation data of cancer patients, such as biopsy data, tailored scaffolds (various alignments, porosity, mechanical strength) can be constructed for drug delivery (O'Meara et al., 2024). The future of nanofibrous scaffolds lies in theranostics, where therapeutic application for cancer can be achieved with diagnostic application. Through this approach, the clinician can keep an eye on the patient's health and modify future treatment plans. The future of systems based on nanofibrous scaffolds includes immunomodulation and combination treatment. Scaffolds functionalized with growth factors, antigens, immune cells, and immunotherapeutic, can be employed for immunomodulation in cancer eradication and recurrence prevention (Zhu et al., 2025). To get personalized therapy for cancer management, modified scaffolds are needed. Major obstacles in the lab to market conversion are

TABLE 22.8 A list of patents of nanofiber-scaffolds for cancer management.

Patent no.	Drug	Method of preparation	Formulation	Polymer used	Pharmacological use	References
US20240122918A1	Acriflavine, PT-2385, temozolomide	Coaxial electrospinning	NanoMesh	Hydrophobic polymer	Glioblastoma multiforme	Steckl et al. (2022)
US11737990B2	–	Dual syringe electrospinning	Implantable fiber scaffolds	Polycaprolactone	Tissue regeneration	Johnson (2024)
US20140030315A1	Naproxen	Electrospinning	Nanofiber scaffolds	Polycaprolactone	Drug delivery	Johnson (2018)
WO2013124867A1	TPGnRH, paclitaxel	Electrostatic complexation	Nanofiber	–	Brain tumor	Manzoor et al. (2013)
US11964000B2	Bone morphogenetic protein 4	Electrospinning	Nanofiber implant	Polyamide	Brain tumors	Stupp et al. (2024)
WO2022101687A1	Fucoidan	Electrospinning	Nanofiber mesh (skin patch)	Polycaprolactone	Melanoma (skin cancer)	Oliveira et al. (2024)
US20180000744A1	5-Flurouracil	Coaxial electrospinning and electrospraying	Nonencapsulated composition	Polycaprolactone, polyethene glycol	Breast cancer	Khan et al. (2018)
EP2813212A1	Ticagrelor	Electrospinning (Nanospider technology)	Nanofiber-loaded tablet	PVP K-90 or Soluplus (BASF)	Tissue engineering	StranskaIvana et al. (2014)
US20060204539A1	–	Electrospinning	Electrospun cell matrices	Collagen, elastin, PLGA	Tissue engineering	Atala et al. (2005)
WO2023083866A	Methotrexate, 5-fluorouracil, irinotecan	Coaxial electrospinning	Nanofiber mat	Polycaprolactone	Pancreatic cancer	Iribarren et al. (2023)
CN111375060B	Doxorubicin	Electrospinning	Smart polymer (pH and NIR responsive)	Polydopamine, polycaprolactone, gelatin	Anticancer	Xiujun et al. (2021)
CN101358383A	Comfrey	Electrospinning	Nanofiber	–	Wounds, anticancer, antioxidant	Limin et al. (2009)
US10799620B2	Gemcitabine	Roller electrospinning	Nanofiber rings implant	Polycaprolactone	Postsurgical pancreatic tumor	Xie et al. (2020)

TABLE 22.9 Nanofibrous scaffolds formulations investigated for clinical trials.

Clinical trial no.	Present recruitment status	Company/ sponsor	Pharmacological action/use	Product	Drug	Design of study	References
NCT06986811	Phase 2	Cebiotex	Locally resectable abdominal tumors	Membrane implant	SN-38 (Active metabolite of irinotecan)	Nonrandomized	Cebiotex (2025)
NCT06538857	Phase 2	Cebiotex	Locally resectable pancreatic tumors	Membrane implant	SN-38 (Active metabolite of irinotecan)	Randomized	Cebiotex (2025)
NCT06578650	Recruiting	Acera Surgical, Inc.	Malignant cutaneous neoplasms	Electrospun fiber matrix	–	Observational study	Cebiotex (2025)
NCT02409628	Complete	Neotherix Limited	Surgical excision wound caused by the surgical removal of nonmelanoma skin cancers	EktoTherix	–	Interventional study	Neotherix Limited (2017)
NCT02967146	Phase 3	Samsung Medical Center	Breast cancer	Mediclore	–	Interventional study	Samsung Medical Centre (2016)

the scalability issue, which is expected to be addressed with industry-scalable approaches such as multineedle and needle-less electrospinning, hybrid manufacturing, and 3D bioprinting. AI-based optimization, prediction, automation, and robotics will be helpful in faster manufacturing and reducing the development timelines (Cho et al., 2025).

Conclusion

This chapter provides a comprehensive overview of the contemporary landscape of nanofibrous scaffolds in cancer therapy and cancer recurrence prevention. To improve drug transport, release profile, biocompatibility, targetability, and therapeutic efficiency of anticancer medicines, advanced scaffold functionalization methodologies can be employed concentrated on surface modification and nanomaterial integration. Nanofibrous scaffolds have been utilized in enhanced cancer therapy through targeted drug delivery and codelivery for gene therapy, immunotherapy, and theranostic applications. However, there are still challenges with scalability, reproducibility, and regulatory approvals in the lab-to-market process. With the integration of robotics-based design, optimization, and personalized therapy, nanofibrous scaffolds have a bright future. Nanofibrous scaffolds are promising carriers for anticancer drug delivery, paving the way for a new era of cancer management.

Author contribution

Nirmal Morya: Writing, review and editing, **Keshav Hirave**: Writing and review, **Lalit Kumar**: Writing and review, **Sujit Erandole**: Writing and review, **Debadri Banerjee**: Writing, **Anupama Singh:** Overall supervision, review and editing, **Vikas Anand Saharan:** Overall supervision, review and editing.

References

Abadi, B., Goshtasbi, N., Bolourian, S., Tahsili, J., Adeli-Sardou, M., Forootanfar, H., 2022. Electrospun hybrid nanofibers: Fabrication, characterization, and biomedical applications. Front. Bioeng. Biotechnol. 10, 986975. https://doi.org/10.3389/fbioe.2022.986975.

Abasalta, M., Asefnejad, A., Khorasani, M.T., Saadatabadi, A.R., Irani, M., 2022. Adsorption and sustained release of doxorubicin from N-carboxymethyl chitosan/polyvinyl alcohol/poly(ε-caprolactone) composite and core-shell nanofibers. Iran J. Drug Deliv. Sci. Technol. 67, 102937. https://doi.org/10.1016/j.jddst.2021.102937.

Agrahari, V., Hiremath, P., 2017. Challenges associated and approaches for successful translation of nanomedicines into commercial products. Nanomedicine 12 (8), 819–823. https://doi.org/10.2217/nnm-2017-0039.

Aminu, N., Ilyasu, S., Al-Kassim Hassan, M., Kurfi, F.S., Jatau, A.I., Chan, S.Y., Alfred-Ugbenbo, D., 2023. Applications of nanofibers drug delivery system in cancer therapy. J. Drug Deliv. Sci. Technol. 90, 105128. https://doi.org/10.1016/j.jddst.2023.105128.

Atala, A., Yoo, J., Lim, G., Czerw, R., Soker, S., Stitzel, inventors, 2005. Wake Forest University, Wake Forest University Health Sciences, assignee. Electrospun Cell Matrices, US Patent US20060204539A1.

Bank-Srour, B., Becker, P., Krasovitsky, L., Gladkikh, A., Rosenberg, Y., Barkay, Z., Rosenman, G., 2013. Physical vapor deposition of peptide nanostructures. Polym. J. 45 (5), 494–503. https://doi.org/10.1038/pj.2013.19.

Behrens, A.M., Casey, B.J., Sikorski, M.J., Wu, K.L., Tutak, W., Sandler, A.D., Kofinas, P., 2014. In situ deposition of PLGA nanofibers via solution blow spinning. ACS Macro Lett. 3 (3), 249–254. https://doi.org/10.1021/mz500049x.

Bhusnure, O.G., Gholve, S.B., Giram, P.S., Gaikwad, A.V., Udumansha, U., Mani, G., Tae, J.H., 2021. Novel 5-flurouracil-Embedded non-woven PVA - PVP electrospun nanofibers with enhanced anti-cancer efficacy: Formulation, evaluation and in vitro anti-cancer activity. J. Drug Deliv. Sci. Technol. 64, 102654. https://doi.org/10.1016/j.jddst.2021.102654.

Brenner, E.K., Schiffman, J.D., Thompson, E.A., Toth, L.J., Schauer, C.L., 2012. Electrospinning of hyaluronic acid nanofibers from aqueous ammonium solutions. Carbohydr. Polym. 87 (1), 926–929. https://doi.org/10.1016/j.carbpol.2011.07.033.

Cebiotex, 2025. CEB-01 in Paediatrics with Locally Resectable Abdominal Tumors (CEB-01-RLP01-C). Clinicaltrials.gov. NCT06986811. Available at https://clinicaltrials.gov/study/NCT06986811. Accessed 10 July 2026.

Cebiotex, 2025. Locally Resectable Pancreatic Cancer. Clinicaltrials.gov. NCT06538857. Available at https://www.trialx.com/clinical-trials/listings/323014/ceb-01-in-locally-resectable. Accessed 10 July 2026.

Chen, H., Truckenmüller, R., Van Blitterswijk, C., Moroni, L., 2013. Fabrication of Nanofibrous Scaffolds for Tissue Engineering Applications. Elsevier BV, pp. 158–183. https://doi.org/10.1533/9780857097231.1.158.

Chen, M., Feng, W., Lin, S., He, C., Gao, Y., Wang, H., 2014. Antitumor efficacy of a PLGA composite nanofiber embedded with doxorubicin@MSNs and hydroxycamptothecin@HANPs. RSC Adv. 4 (95), 53344–53351. https://doi.org/10.1039/c4ra09122a.

Cheng, M., Wang, H., Zhang, Z., Li, N., Fang, X., Xu, S., 2014. Gold nanorod-embedded electrospun fibrous membrane as a photothermal therapy platform. ACS Appl. Mater. Interfaces 6 (3), 1569–1575. https://doi.org/10.1021/am405839b.

Chi, H.Y., Chan, V., Li, C., Hsieh, J.H., Lin, P.H., Tsai, Y.-H., Chen, Y., 2020. Fabrication of polylactic acid/paclitaxel nano fibers by electrospinning for cancer therapeutics. BMC Chem. 14, 63. https://doi.org/10.1186/s13065-020-00711-4.

Cho, Y., Beak, J.W., Sagong, M., Ahn, S., Nam, J.S., Kim, I.D., 2025. Electrospinning and nanofiber technology: Fundamentals, innovations, and applications. Adv. Mater. 37 (28), 2500162. https://doi.org/10.1002/adma.202500162.

Colak, B., Ertas, Y.N., 2024. Implantable, 3D-printed alginate scaffolds with bismuth sulfide nanoparticles for the treatment of local breast cancer via enhanced radiotherapy. ACS Appl. Mater. Interfaces 16 (13), 15718–15729.

Dasdemir, M., Maze, B., Anantharamaiah, N., Pourdeyhimi, B., 2012. Influence of polymer type, composition, and interface on the structural and mechanical properties of core/sheath type bicomponent nonwoven fibers. J. Mater. Sci. 47 (16), 5955–5969. https://doi.org/10.1007/s10853-012-6499-7.

Daskalova, A., Ostrowska, B., Zhelyazkova, A., Święszkowski, W., Trifonov, A., Declercq, H., Nathala, C., Szlazak, K., Lojkowski, M., Husinsky, W., Buchvarov, I., 2018. Improving osteoblasts cells proliferation via femtosecond laser surface modification of 3D-printed poly-ε-caprolactone scaffolds for bone tissue engineering applications. Appl. Phys. A 124 (6), 413. https://doi.org/10.1007/s00339-018-1831-y.

Deng, Z., Liu, H., Chen, G., Deng, H., Dong, X., Wang, L., Tao, F., Dai, F., Cheng, Y., 2024. Coaxial nanofibrous aerogel featuring porous network-structured channels for ovarian cancer treatment by sustained release of chitosan oligosaccharide. Int. J. Biol. Macromol. 276 (Pt 1), 133824. https://doi.org/10.1016/j.ijbiomac.2024.133824.

Dias, G.C., Cellet, T.S.P., Santos, M.C., Sanches, A.O., Malmonge, L.F., 2019. PVDF nanofibers obtained by solution blow spinning with use of a commercial airbrush. J. Polym. Res. 26 (4), 1. https://doi.org/10.1007/s10965-019-1731-7.

Ding, Q., Li, Z., Yang, Y., Guo, G., Luo, F., Chen, Z., Yang, Y., Qian, Z.Y., Shi, S., 2016. Preparation and therapeutic application of docetaxel-loaded poly(d,l-lactide) nanofibers in preventing breast cancer recurrence. Drug Deliv. 23 (8), 2677–2685. https://doi.org/10.3109/10717544.2015.1048490.

Đorđević, S., Gonzalez, M.M., Conejos-Sánchez, I., Carreira, B., Pozzi, S., Acúrcio, R.C., Satchi-Fainaro, R., Florindo, H.F., Vicent, M.J., 2022. Current hurdles to the translation of nanomedicines from bench to the clinic. Drug Deliv. Transl. Res. 12 (3), 500–525. https://doi.org/10.1007/s13346-021-01024-2.

Fazio, E., Ridolfo, A., Neri, G., 2019. Thermally activated noble metal nanoparticles incorporated in electrospun fiber-based drug delivery systems. Curr. Nanomater. 4 (1), 21–31. https://doi.org/10.2174/1573407214666180914121929.

Ghosal, K., Augustine, R., Zaszczynska, A., Barman, M., Jain, A., Hasan, A., Kalarikkal, N., Sajkiewicz, P., Thomas, S., 2021. Novel drug delivery systems based on triaxial electrospinning based nanofibers. React. Funct. Polym. 163, 104895. https://doi.org/10.1016/j.reactfunctpolym.2021.104895.

Gonçalves, A., Cabrita, R., Matos, J., Rodrigues, I., Vieira, T., Borges, J.P., Soares, P.I.P., 2024. Dual-stimuli-responsive poly (vinyl alcohol) nanofibers for localized cancer treatment: Magnetic hyperthermia and drug release studies. J. Drug Deliv. Sci. Technol. 94, 105492. https://doi.org/10.1016/j.jddst.2024.105492.

Gupta, K.C., Haider, A., Choi, Y.R., Kang, I.K., 2014. Nanofibrous scaffolds in biomedical applications. Biomater. Res. 18 (1), 5. https://doi.org/10.1186/2055-7124-18-5.

Haaparanta, A.M., Järvinen, E., Cengiz, I.F., Ellä, V., Kokkonen, H.T., Kiviranta, I., Kellomäki, M., 2014. Preparation and characterization of collagen/PLA, chitosan/PLA, and collagen/chitosan/PLA hybrid scaffolds for cartilage tissue engineering. J. Mater. Sci. Mater. Med. 25 (4), 1129–1136. https://doi.org/10.1007/s10856-013-5129-5.

Hae-won, K., So-hee, B., Hae-won, K., inventors, 2012. Industry Academic Cooperation Foundation of Dankook University, Switzerland, assignee. Preparation Method of Biopolymer Having Nanofiber Structure Using Phase Separation. WIPO Patent Application WO2012046957A2.

Gandhimathi, C., Venugopal, J.R., Ramakrishna, S., Srinivasan, D.K., 2018. Electrospun-electrosprayed hydroxyapatite nanostructured composites for bone tissue regeneration. J. Appl. Polym. Sci. 135 (42), 2301293. https://doi.org/10.1002/app.46756.

Hassanzadeh, P., Kharaziha, M., Nikkhah, M., Shin, S.R., Jin, J., He, S., Sun, W., Zhong, C., Dokmeci, M.R., Khademhosseini, A., Rolandi, M., 2013. Chitin nanofiber micropatterned flexible substrates for tissue engineering. J. Mater. Chem. B 1 (34), 4217–4224. https://doi.org/10.1039/c3tb20782j.

Hayati, I., Bailey, A.I., Tadros, Th.F, 1987. Investigations into the mechanisms of electrohydrodynamic spraying of liquids. J. Colloid Interface Sci. 117 (1), 205–221. https://doi.org/10.1016/0021-9797(87)90185-8.

Hernández, S.N.H., Chauhan, G., 2020. Nanofibers for cancer sensing and diagnostics. Mater. Today Proc. 66–70. https://doi.org/10.1016/j.matpr.2020.10.164.

Hooper, J.P., inventor, 1924. Hooper Manufacturing Co, assignee. Centrifugal spinneret. US Patent US1500931A.

Hu, J., Zeng, F., Wei, J., Chen, Y., Chen, Y., 2013. Novel controlled drug delivery system for multiple drugs based on electrospun nanofibers containing nanomicelles. J. Biomater. Sci. 25 (3), 257–268. https://doi.org/10.1080/09205063.2013.852367.

Iribarren, O.M., Garmendia, M.M., Pons, M.R., Alonso, S.A., Ruiz, J.P., Tuñón, J.M.C., Castero, F.J.C., Arenas, S.P., inventors, 2023. Asociacion Centro tecnologico Ceit, Serviicio Andaluz De Salud 43, Universidad De Sevilla 6, assignee. Drug delivery system using electrospinning of polymers. Patent WO2023083866A.

Jiang, L., Huang, X., Tian, C., Zhong, Y., Yan, M., Miao, C., Wu, T., Zhou, X., 2023. Preparation and characterization of porous cellulose acetate nanofiber hydrogels. Gels 9 (6), 484. https://doi.org/10.3390/gels9060484.

Jin, M., Yu, D.G., Geraldes, C.F.G.C., Williams, G.R., Bligh, S.W.A., 2016. Theranostic fibers for simultaneous imaging and drug delivery. Mole. Pharm. 13 (7), 2457–2465.

Jirsak, O., Sanetrnik, F., Lukas, D., Kotek, V., Martinova, L., Chaloupek, J., Liberci, T.U.V., inventors, 2009. Technicka Univerzita v Liberci., assognee. Method of Nanofibres Production From a Polymer Solution Using Electrostatic Spinning and a Device for Carrying out the Method. US Patent US7585437B2.

Johnson, J.K., inventor, 2018. NEF IP Holdings LLC, assignee. Nanofiber Scaffolds for Biological Structures. US Patent US20140030315A1.

Johnson, J.K., inventor, 2024. NFS IP Holdings LLC, assignee. Nanofiber Scaffolds for Biological Structures. US Patent US11737990B2.

Kajdič, S., Planinšek, O., Gašperlin, M., Kocbek, P., 2019. Electrospun nanofibers for customized drug-delivery systems. J. Drug Deliv. Sci. Technol. 51, 672–681. https://doi.org/10.1016/j.jddst.2019.03.038.

Kaplan, J.A., Liu, R., Freedman, J.D., Padera, R., Schwartz, J., Colson, Y.L., Grinstaff, M.W., 2016. Prevention of lung cancer recurrence using cisplatin-loaded superhydrophobic nanofiber meshes. Biomaterials 76, 273–281. https://doi.org/10.1016/j.biomaterials.2015.10.060.

Keirouz, A., Wang, Z., Reddy, V.S., Nagy, Z.K., Vass, P., Buzgo, M., Ramakrishna, S., Radacsi, N., 2023. The history of electrospinning: Past, present, and future developments. Adv. Mater. Technol. 8 (11), 2201723. https://doi.org/10.1002/admt.202201723.

Khan, A., Tripathi, A., Gandhi, M., Bellare, J., Srivastava, R., 2024a. Development of injectable upconversion nanoparticle-conjugated doxorubicin theranostics electrospun nanostructure for targeted photochemotherapy in breast cancer. J. Biomed. Mater. Res. 112 (9), 1612–1626. https://doi.org/10.1002/jbm.a.37713.

Khan, J., Khan, A., Khan, M.Q., Khan, H., 2024b. Applications of co-axial electrospinning in the biomedical field. Next Mater. 3, 100138. https://doi.org/10.1016/j.nxmate.2024.100138.

Khan, M.R., Iqbal, S., inventors, 2018. Georgia Southern University Research and Service Foundation Inc, assignee. Nanoencapsulated Compositions. US Patent US20180000744A1.

Kolská, Z., Polanský, R., Prosr, P., Zemanová, M., Ryšánek, P., Slepička, P., Švorčík, V., 2018. Properties of polyamide nanofibers treated by UV-A radiation. Mater. Lett. 214, 264–267. https://doi.org/10.1016/j.matlet.2017.12.029.

Lancuški, A., Fort, S., Bossard, F., 2012. Electrospun Azido-PCL nanofibers for enhanced surface functionalization by click chemistry. ACS Appl. Mater. Interfaces 4 (12), 6499–6504. https://doi.org/10.1021/am301458y.

Li, H., Sanchez-Vazquez, B., Trindade, R.P., Zou, Q., Mai, Y., Dou, L., Zhu, L.M., Williams, G.R., 2019. Electrospun oral formulations for combined photo-chemotherapy of colon cancer. Colloids Surf. B Biointerfaces 183, 110411. https://doi.org/10.1016/j.colsurfb.2019.110411.

Li, X., Tian, S., Ping, Y., Kim, D.H., Knoll, W., 2005. One-step route to the fabrication of highly porous polyaniline nanofiber films by using PS-b-PVP diblock copolymers as templates. Langmuir 21 (21), 9393–9397. https://doi.org/10.1021/la0514009.

Li, H., Ke, Y., Hu, Y., 2006. Polymer nanofibers prepared by template melt extrusion. J. Appl. Polym. Sci. 99 (3), 1018–1023. https://doi.org/10.1002/app.22597.

Li, W., Luo, T., Yang, Y., Tan, X., Liu, L., 2015. Formation of controllable hydrophilic/hydrophobic drug delivery systems by electrospinning of vesicles. Langmuir 31 (18), 5141–5146. https://doi.org/10.1021/la504796v.

Liang, J., Guo, R., Xuan, M., Sun, Q., Wu, W., 2022. An acid-sensitive nanofiber conjugate based on a short aromatic peptide for targeted delivery of doxorubicin in liver cancer. Int. J. Nanomed. 17, 2961–2973. https://doi.org/10.2147/ijn.s359642.

Limin, Z., Joe, H., inventors, 2009. Donghua University, assignee. Comfrey Drug-Loaded Nanofibers and its Preparation and Application. China Patent CN101358383A.

Liu, Y., Ren, Z.-F., He, J.-H., 2010. Bubble electrospinning method for preparation of aligned nanofibre mat. Mater. Sci. Technol. 26 (11), 1309–1312. https://doi.org/10.1179/026708310x12798718274359.

Logan, M.K., Irvin, S.D., Enfrin, M., Arafat, H., Dumée, L.F., Gibert, Y., 2023. Toxicity of nanofibers on zebrafish embryogenesis – impact of materials properties on inflammatory responses. J. Environ. Chem. Eng. 11 (5), 110727. https://doi.org/10.1016/j.jece.2023.110727.

Luraghi, A., Peri, F., Moroni, L., 2021. Electrospinning for drug delivery applications: A review. J. Contr. Release 334, 463–484. https://doi.org/10.1016/j.jconrel.2021.03.033.

Maduna, L., Patnaik, A., 2024. Challenges associated with the production of nanofibers. Processes 12 (10), 2100. https://doi.org/10.3390/pr12102100.

Manzoor, K., Parwathy, C., Archana, P.R., Shantikumar, V.N., inventors, 2013. Amrita Vishwa Vidyapeetham University, assignee. Polymer - Polymer or Polymer - Protein Core - Shell Nano Medicine Loaded With Multiple Drug Molecules. WIPO Patent Application WO2013124867A1.

Martino, S., Yilmaz, D., Tammaro, C., Misso, G., Esposito, A., Falco, M., Cossu, A.M., Lombardi, A., Amler, E., Divin, R., Giannetti, A., Scrima, M., Dardano, P., De Stefano, L., Rea, I., De Luca, A.C., Caraglia, M., 2025. Flexible 3D nanofiber-based SERS biosensor for detection of miRNA-223-3p in early laryngeal cancer diagnosis. Talanta 285 (1), 127293. https://doi.org/10.1016/j.talanta.2024.127293.

McCulloch, J.G., 1999. The history of the development of melt blowing technology. Int. Nonwovens J. os-8 (1). https://doi.org/10.1177/1558925099os-800123.

Miraftab, M., Saifullah, A.N., Çay, A., 2015. Physical stabilisation of electrospun poly (vinyl alcohol) nanofibres: Comparative study on methanol and heat-based crosslinking. J. Mater. Sci. 50 (4), 1943–1957. https://doi.org/10.1007/s10853-014-8759-1.

Misaka, M., Teshima, H., Hirokawa, S., Li, Q.-Y., Takahashi, K., 2024. Nano-captured water affects the wettability of cellulose nanofiber films. Surf. Interfaces 46, 103923. https://doi.org/10.1016/j.surfin.2024.103923.

Molnar, K., Nagy, Z.K., 2016. Corona-electrospinning: Needleless method for high-throughput continuous nanofiber production. Eur. Polym. J. 74, 279–286. https://doi.org/10.1016/j.eurpolymj.2015.11.028.

Monterrubio, C., Pascual-Pasto, G., Cano, F., Vila-Ubach, M., Manzanares, A., Schaiquevich, P., Tornero, J.A., Sosnik, A., Mora, J., Carcaboso, A.M., 2016. SN-38-loaded nanofiber matrices for local control of pediatric solid tumors after subtotal resection surgery. Biomaterials 79, 69–78. https://doi.org/10.1016/j.biomaterials.2015.11.055.

Nair, B.P., Vaikkath, D., Mohan, D.S., Nair, P.D., 2014. Fabrication of a microvesicles-incorporated fibrous membrane for controlled delivery applications in tissue engineering. Biofabrication 6 (4), 045008. https://doi.org/10.1088/1758-5082/6/4/045008.

Nagy, Z.K., Balogh, A., Démuth, B., Pataki, H., Vigh, T., Szabó, B., Molnár, K., Schmidt, B.T., Horák, P., Marosi, G., Verreck, G., Van Assche, I., Brewster, M.E., 2015. High speed electrospinning for scaled-up production of amorphous solid dispersion of itraconazole. Int. J. Pharm. 480 (1–2), 137–142. https://doi.org/10.1016/j.ijpharm.2015.01.025.

Neotherix Limited, 2017. Ekto TherixTM Regenerative Tissue Scaffold for Repair of Surgical Excision Wounds. Clinicaltrials.gov. NCT02409628. Available at https://clinicaltrials.gov/study/NCT02409628. Accessed 10 July 2026.

Niemczyk-Soczynska, B., Gradys, A., Sajkiewicz, P., 2020. Hydrophilic surface functionalization of electrospun nanofibrous scaffolds in tissue engineering. Polymers 12 (11), 2636. https://doi.org/10.3390/polym12112636.

Nikkola, L., Morton, T., Balmayor, E.R., Hanna, J., Ali, H., Redl, H., van Griensven, M., Ashammakhi, N., 2015. Fabrication of electrospun poly (d,l lactide-co-glycolide) 80/20 scaffolds loaded with diclofenac sodium for tissue engineering. Eur. J. Med. Res. 20 (1), 54. https://doi.org/10.1186/s40001-015-0145-1.

O'Meara, C.H., Nguyen, T.V., Jafri, Z., Boyer, M., Shonka, D.C., Khachigian, L.M., 2024. Personalised medicine and the potential role of electrospinning for targeted immunotherapeutics in head and neck cancer. Nanomater 14 (1), 6. https://doi.org/10.3390/nano14010006.

Obiweluozor, F.O., Emechebe, G.A., Tiwari, A.P., Kim, J.Y., Park, C.H., Kim, C.S., 2018. Short duration cancer treatment: Inspired by a fast bio-resorbable smart nano-fiber device containing NIR lethal polydopamine nanospheres for effective chemo–photothermal cancer therapy. Int. J. Nanomed. 13, 6375–6390. https://doi.org/10.2147/IJN.S180970.

Oliveira, F.S.D., Catarina, A., Soares, C., Isabel, A., Neves, M.A.D., João, N., Reis, G.D., Luís, R., Marques, P., Margarida, A., Silva, Q., José, T., Martins, P., Manuel, A., inventors. 2024. Association for the Advancement of Tissue Engineering and Cell Based Technologies and Therapies (A4TEC), assignee. Nanofiber Mesh Comprising Fucoidan, Method and Uses Thereof. WIPO Patent Application WO2022101687A1.

Park, J.H., Seo, H., Kim, D.I., Choi, J.H., Son, J.H., Kim, J., Moon, G.D., Hyun, D.C., 2019. Gold nanocage-incorporated poly(ε-caprolactone) (pcl) fibers for chemophotothermal synergistic cancer therapy. Pharmaceutics 11 (2), 60. https://doi.org/10.3390/pharmaceutics11020060.

Rabie, A.M.I., Ali, A.S.M., Al-Zeer, M.A., Barhoum, A., El-Hallouty, S., Shousha, W.G., Berg, J., Kurreck, J., Khalil, A.S.G., 2022. Spontaneous Formation of 3D breast cancer tissues on electrospun chitosan/poly (ethylene oxide) nanofibrous scaffolds. ACS Omega 7 (2), 2114–2126. https://doi.org/10.1021/acsomega.1c05646.

Rahman, S.U., Farooq, S., Kitchamsetti, N., Sajid, M., Gul, S., Farooq, F., Rafiq, M., Fatima, I., Razzaq, H., 2025. Morphology-controlled polyaniline nanofibers via rapid polymerization for enhanced supercapacitor performance. Nano energy Adv. 5 (3), 11. https://doi.org/10.3390/nanoenergyadv5030011.

Ranganath, S.H., Wang, C.H., 2008. Biodegradable microfiber implants delivering paclitaxel for post-surgical chemotherapy against malignant glioma. Biomaterials 29 (20), 2996–3003. https://doi.org/10.1016/j.biomaterials.2008.04.002.

Rehman, R., Rafiq, M., Shafi, H., Rather, A.H., Khan, R.S., Raza, S.N., Rather, S.u., Majeed, S., Khan, N.A., Sheikh, F. A., 2025. Designing sustained release from nanofiber patch for paclitaxel as prospective localized nanotherapeutic delivery in breast cancer. Int. J. Pharm. 671, 125158. https://doi.org/10.1016/j.ijpharm.2024.125158.

Ren, L., Ozisik, R., Kotha, S.P., 2014. Rapid and efficient fabrication of multilevel structured silica micro-/nanofibers by centrifugal jet spinning. J. Colloid Interface Sci. 425, 136–142. https://doi.org/10.1016/j.jcis.2014.03.039.

Saleem, H., Trabzon, L., Ali, K., Javaid Zaidi, S., 2020. Recent advances in nanofibrous membranes: production and applications in water treatment and desalination. Desalination 478, 114. https://doi.org/10.1016/j.desal.2019.114178.

Samsung Medical Centre, 2016. Anti-adhesive Effect and Safety of a Mixed Solid of Poloxamer, Gelatin and Chitosan (Mediclore®) After Axillary Dissection for Breast Cancer. Clinicaltrials.gov. NCT02967146. Available at https://clinicaltrials.gov/study/NCT02967146. Accessed 10 July 2026.

Sarkar, K., Gomez, C., Zambrano, S., Ramirez, M., de Hoyos, E., Vasquez, H., Lozano, K., 2010. Electrospinning to force spinning. Mater. Today 13 (11), 12–14. https://doi.org/10.1016/s1369-7021(10)70199-1.

Sen, O., Jana, S., Nandi, G., Manna, S., 2025. Recent progress in chitosan-based nanofibers as potential drug carriers in cancer therapy. Int. J. Polym. Mater. Polym. Biomater. 74 (6), 555–573. https://doi.org/10.1080/00914037.2024.2344618.

Seruga, B., Sadikov, A., Cazap, E.L., Delgado, L.B., Digumarti, R., Leighl, N.B., Meshref, M.M., Minami, H., Robinson, E., Yamaguchi, N.H., Pyle, D., Cufer, T., 2014. Barriers and challenges to global clinical cancer research. Oncologist 19 (1), 61–67. https://doi.org/10.1634/theoncologist.2013-0290Slovenia.

Shambaugh, R.L., 1988. A macroscopic view of the melt-blowing process for producing microfibers. Ind. Eng. Chem. Res. 27 (12), 2363–2372. https://doi.org/10.1021/ie00084a021.

Singh, B., Yun, S., Park, M.-H., 2023. Light-responsive layer-by-layer assembled nanofibers for sequential drug release. J. Drug Deliv. Sci. Technol. 88, 104910. https://doi.org/10.1016/j.jddst.2023.104910.

Steckl, A., Han, D., Tyler, B.M., Brem, H., Alomari, S., inventors, 2022. University of Cincinnati, Johns Hopkins University, assignee. NanoMesh Drug Delivery for Treatment of Brain Tumours. US Patent US20240122918A1.

StranskaIvana, D., Vladimir, E., Kral, V., Sebek, P., Beranek, J., Dumicic, A., Sedmak, F., Chvojka, T., inventors. 2014. Zentiva KS., assignee. Drug formulation using API in nanofibers. European Patent EP2813212A1.

Stupp, S.I., McClendon, M.T., Xi, G., Fyrner, B.T.B., Smith, C.S., Sather, N.A., inventors, 2024. Northwestern University., assignee. Cancer treatment methods using nanofiber-stabilised growth factors US Patent US11964000B2.

Tiwari, A.P., Bhattarai, D.P., Maharjan, B., Ko, S.W., Kim, H.Y., Park, C.H., Kim, C.S., 2019. Polydopamine-based implantable multifunctional nanocarpet for highly efficient photothermal-chemo therapy. Sci. Rep. 9 (1), 2943. https://doi.org/10.1038/s41598-019-39457-y.

Tong, L., Mazur, E., 2008. Glass nanofibers for micro- and nano-scale photonic devices. J. Non-Cryst. Solids 354 (12–13), 1240–1244. https://doi.org/10.1016/j.jnoncrysol.2006.10.090.

Tseng, Y.-Y., Liao, J.-Y., Chen, W.-A., Kao, Y.-C., Liu, S.-J., 2013. Sustainable release of carmustine from biodegradable poly [(d, l)-lactide- co -glycolide] nanofibrous membranes in the cerebral cavity: In vitro and in vivo studies. Expert Opin. Drug Deliv. 10 (7), 879–888. https://doi.org/10.1517/17425247.2013.758102.

Uhljar, L.É., Ambrus, R., 2023. Electrospinning of potential medical devices (wound dressings, tissue engineering scaffolds, face masks) and their regulatory approach. Pharmaceutics 15 (2), 417. https://doi.org/10.3390/pharmaceutics15020417.

Vojoudi, E., Babaloo, H., 2023. Application of electrospun nanofiber as drug delivery systems: A review. Pharm. Nanotechnol. 11 (1), 10–24. https://doi.org/10.2174/2211738510666220928161957.

Waqas, M., Keirouz, A., Sanira Putri, M.K., Fazal, F., Diaz Sanchez, F.J., Ray, D., Koutsos, V., Radacsi, N., 2021. Design and development of a nozzle-free electrospinning device for the high-throughput production of biomaterial nanofibers. Med. Eng. Phys. 92, 80–87. https://doi.org/10.1016/j.medengphy.2021.04.007.

Weinberg, M.G., Digg, T., Harding, W., Co, A., Du, D.N.A., inventors, 2014. Flash Spun Web Containing Submicron Filaments and Process for Forming Same. Republic of Korea Patent KR101340264B1.

Will, O.M., Purcz, N., Chalaris, A., Heneweer, C., Boretius, S., Purcz, L., Nikkola, L., Ashammakhi, N., Kalthoff, H., Glüer, C.-C., Wiltfang, J., Açil, Y., Tiwari, S., 2016. Increased survival rate by local release of diclofenac in a murine model of recurrent oral carcinoma. Int. J. Nanomed. 11, 5311–5321. https://doi.org/10.2147/ijn.s109199.

Xiao, S., Peng, Q., Yang, Y., Tao, Y., Zhou, Y., Xu, W., Shi, X., 2020. Preparation of [amine-terminated generation 5 poly(amidoamine)]- graft-Poly (lactic- co-glycolic acid) electrospun nanofibrous mats for scaffold-mediated gene transfection. ACS Appl. Bio Mater. 3 (1), 346–357. https://doi.org/10.1021/acsabm.9b00848.

Xie, J., Chen, S., Baxter, T.B., inventors, 2020. University of Nebraska System, assignee. Ring and Tubular Structures and Methods of Synthesis and Use Thereof. US Patent US10799620B2.

Xie, J., Wang, C.-H., 2006. Electrospun micro- and nanofibers for sustained delivery of paclitaxel to treat C6 glioma in vitro. Pharm. Res. 23 (8), 1817–1826. https://doi.org/10.1007/s11095-006-9036-z.

Xiujun, C., Dong, C., Xiang, L., Junjie, X., inventors, 2021. Zhejiang University ZJU, assignee. Composite fiber with pH and near-infrared light-responsive drug release, and preparation method and application thereof. China Patent CN111375060B.

Xu, S., Lu, T., Yang, L., Luo, S., Wang, Z., Ye, C., 2022. In situ cell electrospun using a portable handheld electrospinning apparatus for the repair of wound healing in rats. Int. Wound J. 19 (7), 1693–1704. https://doi.org/10.1111/iwj.13769.

Yadav, S., Sharma, A., Kurmi, B.D., Kaur, K., Sandhu, N.K., Thakur, S., Rai, V.K., 2025. Nanofiber drug delivery systems: Recent advances in nanofabrication and their role in targeted therapy in cancer, neurodegenerative, and cardiovascular diseases. Polym. Adv. Technol. 36 (5), e70198. https://doi.org/10.1002/pat.70198.

Yan, E., Jiang, J., Yang, X., Fan, L., Wang, Y., An, Q., Zhang, Z., Lu, B., Wang, D., Zhang, D., 2020. pH-sensitive core-shell electrospun nanofibers based on polyvinyl alcohol/polycaprolactone as a potential drug delivery system for the chemotherapy against cervical cancer. J. Drug Deliv. Sci. Technol. 55, 101455. https://doi.org/10.1016/j.jddst.2019.101455.

Yang, G., Wang, J., Wang, Y., Li, L., Guo, X., Zhou, S., 2015. An implantable active-targeting micelle-in-nanofiber device for efficient and safe cancer therapy. ACS Nano 9 (2), 1161–1174. https://doi.org/10.1021/nn504573u.

Yang, Y., Li, Y., Cao, L., Wang, Y., Li, L., Li, W., 2021. Electrospun PVDF-SiO2 nanofibrous membranes with enhanced surface roughness for oil-water coalescence separation. Sep. Purif. Technol. 269 (118), 118726. https://doi.org/10.1016/j.seppur.2021.118726.

Yang, Z., Xu, M., Liu, Y., He, F., Gao, F., Su, Y., Wei, H., Zhang, Y., 2014. Nitrogen-doped, carbon-rich, highly photoluminescent carbon dots from ammonium citrate. Nanoscale 6 (3), 1890–1895. https://doi.org/10.1039/c3nr05380f.

Zarei, M., Sayedain, S.S., Askarinya, A., Sabbaghi, M., Alizadeh, R., 2023. Improving physio-mechanical and biological properties of 3D-printed PLA scaffolds via in-situ argon cold plasma treatment. Sci. Rep. 13 (1), 14120. https://doi.org/10.1038/s41598-023-41226-x.

Zhang, X., Lu, Y., 2014. Centrifugal spinning: An alternative approach to fabricate nanofibers at high speed and low cost. Polym. Rev. 54 (4), 677–701. https://doi.org/10.1080/15583724.2014.935858.

Zhang, Y., Liu, S., Wang, X., Zhang, Z.-yun, Jing, X.-bin, Zhang, P., Zhi-gang, Xie., 2014. Prevention of local liver cancer recurrence after surgery using multilayered cisplatin-loaded polylactide electrospun nanofibers. Chin. J. Polym. Sci. 32 (8), 1111–1118. https://doi.org/10.1007/s10118-014-1491-0.

Zhang, J., Wang, X., Liu, T., Liu, S., Jing, X., 2016. Antitumor activity of electrospun polylactide nanofibers loaded with 5-fluorouracil and oxaliplatin against colorectal cancer. Drug Deliv. 23 (3), 784–790. https://doi.org/10.3109/10717544.2014.916768.

Zhang, Y., Wang, P., Shi, Q., Ning, X., Zheng, J., Long, Y.-Z., 2024. Research progress and prospect of centrifugal electrospinning and its application. J. Alloys Compd. 990, 174433. https://doi.org/10.1016/j.jallcom.2024.174433.

Zhang, Z., Wu, Y., Kuang, G., Liu, S., Zhou, D., Chen, X., Jing, X., Huang, Y., 2017. Pt(iv) prodrug-backboned micelle and DCA loaded nanofibers for enhanced local cancer treatment. J. Mater. Chem. B 5 (11), 2115–2125. https://doi.org/10.1039/c7tb00178a.

Zhao, J., Zhu, Y., Ye, C., Chen, Y., Wang, S., Zou, D., Li, Z., 2019. Photothermal transforming agent and chemotherapeutic co-loaded electrospun nanofibers for tumor treatment. Int. J. Nanomed. 14, 3893–3909. https://doi.org/10.2147/ijn.s202876.

Zhu, Q., Song, X., Chen, X., Li, D., Tang, X., Chen, J., Yuan, Q., 2024. A high performance nanocellulose-PVDF based piezoelectric nanogenerator based on the highly active CNF@ZnO via electrospinning technology. Nano Energy 127, 109741. https://doi.org/10.1016/j.nanoen.2024.109741.

Zhu, Y., Yao, Z.C., Li, S., Ma, J., Wei, C., Yu, D., Stelzel, J.L., Ni, B.Y.X., Miao, Y., Van Batavia, K., Lu, X., Lin, J., Dai, Y., Kong, J., Shen, R., Goodier, K.D., Liu, X., Cheng, L., Vuong, I., Howard, G.P., Livingston, N.K., Choy, J., Schneck, J.P., Doloff, J.C., Reddy, S.K., Hickey, J.W., Mao, H.Q., 2025. An mRNA lipid nanoparticle-incorporated nanofiber-hydrogel composite for cancer immunotherapy. Nat. Commun. 16 (1), 5707. https://doi.org/10.1038/s41467-025-61299-8.

CHAPTER

23

Advances in hydrogel for anticancer drug delivery

Abhishek Sharma, Bhagya Shree, Ruchi Chawla and Brahmeshwar Mishra

Department of Pharmaceutical Engineering and Technology, Indian Institute of Technology (BHU), Varanasi, Uttar Pradesh, India

Introduction

Hydrogels are hydrophilic, three-dimensional, crosslinked polymeric networks capable of absorbing large amounts of water and retaining a swollen state without losing their structural integrity. Due to these characteristics, hydrogels have emerged as promising carriers for delivering a wide range of therapeutic agents, including chemotherapeutics, immunotherapeutics, nucleic acids, RNA-based therapeutics, and proteins, in cancer treatment. Their widespread application in anticancer drug delivery is primarily attributed to their excellent biocompatibility, injectability, tunable physicochemical properties, and high drug encapsulation capacity (Xu et al., 2025). Another key advantage of hydrogels is their versatility in terms of size, as they can be fabricated in various forms ranging from macrogels to microgels and nanogels, depending on the intended route of administration and therapeutic application. This size tunability enables hydrogels to be widely explored for diverse delivery strategies, including local and targeted drug delivery at the tumor site, as well as topical, pulmonary, and oral delivery of anticancer agents (Sun et al., 2020). Conventional cancer therapies often suffer from poor tumor specificity, off-target toxicity, and the development of multidrug resistance. These limitations can be effectively addressed using hydrogel-based drug delivery systems, which enable the sustained and controlled release of single or multiple therapeutic agents, thereby enhancing therapeutic efficacy while minimizing systemic exposure and reducing toxicity to healthy tissues (Mohammadzadeh et al., 2025). The potential of hydrogel-based biomaterials to deliver anticancer drugs through both active and passive targeting strategies, while simultaneously enhancing the physical and chemical stability of chemotherapeutic agents, is evidenced by previously FDA-approved hydrogel-based

Advanced Cancer Therapeutics
https://doi.org/10.1016/B978-0-443-44185-1.00024-0

products such as Genexol-PM, which delivers paclitaxel for the treatment of ovarian and breast cancer, and Oncogel, designed for the localized delivery of paclitaxel in esophageal cancer (Wang et al., 2023).

Factors affecting drug encapsulation

Drugs can be incorporated into hydrogels through two primary approaches. The first is the postloading method, in which preformed hydrogels are incubated with a drug solution, allowing the therapeutic molecules to diffuse and become entrapped within the polymeric network. The second approach is in situ loading, where the drug is encapsulated simultaneously during hydrogel formation by coupling with the polymer chains. In both cases, drugs may be either chemically crosslinked with the polymeric biomaterials or physically associated through noncovalent interactions (Hu et al., 2024). The various factors that can influence drug encapsulation within hydrogels are discussed in the following section.

Porosity

The morphology of hydrogels, particularly their microporous structure as characterized by scanning electron microscopy (SEM), plays a crucial role in determining drug loading capacity and encapsulation efficiency. When drug loading occurs simultaneously with the crosslinking process, the physical space provided by the porous network facilitates enhanced entrapment of therapeutic agents such as doxorubicin. Moreover, efficient drug loading is achieved through physical interactions between the drug molecules and the functional groups of the polymeric matrix, provided that an optimal pore size and pore density are maintained (Parvaresh et al., 2023). Porosity is, in turn, influenced by several key factors, including: (i) polymer concentration, where an increase in polymer content generally enhances the water-holding capacity and contributes to higher porosity of the hydrogel matrix; (ii) crosslinking density, as higher crosslinker concentrations typically result in smaller pore sizes due to the formation of a more compact and rigid network; and (iii) nanoparticle incorporation, which may reduce overall porosity by interacting with and occupying spaces within the polymeric network (Hu et al., 2018). Thus, careful consideration of these factors allows precise control over the porosity of hydrogels, enabling the rational design of drug delivery systems that not only achieve efficient loading of anticancer agents but also modulate their release kinetics in a controlled manner (Qi et al., 2015).

Mesh size

The mesh size of the hydrogel network is a critical parameter that can affect drug loading capacity, particularly when loading is achieved using the swelling equilibrium method. In this method, hydrogels are immersed in a drug solution and allowed to swell until equilibrium is attained, and the amount of drug loaded is largely governed by the mesh size of the swollen network. Mesh size is typically estimated from the average molecular weight between adjacent crosslinks, which reflects the degree of crosslinking within the hydrogel structure. The mesh size can be influenced by several polymer characteristics, including molecular weight, polymer concentration, backbone length, and swelling ratio. Generally, higher polymer concentrations result in denser networks with smaller mesh sizes (Bertz et al., 2013). Uniformity in mesh size ensures a homogeneous distribution of drug within the hydrogel matrix, while a small and uniform mesh size provides a high surface area, thereby facilitating enhanced encapsulation of anticancer agents (Xue et al., 2017).

Crosslinking

Crosslinking occurs through interactions between polymeric chains, either via covalent or noncovalent bonds, depending on the nature of the polymer, the drug, and the surrounding environmental conditions. Crosslinking significantly influences the swelling behavior of hydrogels, where high crosslinking densities generally lead to low swelling ratios, modulating drug–polymer interactions and providing structural integrity to the hydrogel network. The type of crosslinker also plays a crucial role in determining drug loading efficiency (Uddin et al., 2024). In the study by Uddin et al. (2024), disulfide-based crosslinkers were found to be unfavorable for loading anticancer drugs, genipin crosslinkers exhibited superior compatibility across different drug molecules. The findings highlighted the importance of selecting appropriate crosslinkers based on drug compatibility. Furthermore, crosslinked hydrogels showed higher loading efficiencies compared to linear, noncrosslinked systems, as the three-dimensional network provides sufficient free volume and interaction sites for effective drug entrapment (Uddin et al., 2024). However, excessively high crosslinking densities may result in the formation of more rigid hydrogel networks, which consequently limit drug loading capacity by reducing the conformational freedom of the polymeric chains. As a result, drug–polymer interactions necessary for efficient encapsulation are hindered (Hu et al., 2018). The molecular weight and size of the crosslinker also significantly influence drug loading efficiency, with larger crosslinkers generally promoting higher loading capacities due to the formation of more flexible networks and increased free volume within the hydrogel matrix (Vu et al., 2023). A recent study investigating the role of free catecholamine groups in the drug loading efficiency of photo-crosslinkable polymeric hydrogels revealed that the presence of dopamine significantly enhances anticancer drug loading. This improvement is primarily attributed to π–π stacking interactions and hydrophobic interactions between dopamine moieties and hydrophobic drug molecules (Kim and Shin, 2022).

Polymer type

The choice of polymer in hydrogel fabrication for anticancer drug delivery is of paramount importance, as the polymer's composition, origin, and structural arrangement directly influence drug loading and encapsulation efficiency. The polymer serves as the core component of the hydrogel system, providing a three-dimensional framework that retains therapeutic agents through various mechanisms, including physical entrapment, covalent bonding, and electrostatic interactions (Wang et al., 2023). Polymers used in hydrogel fabrication are broadly classified into natural, synthetic, and hybrid categories, each offering distinct advantages for drug delivery applications. Natural polymers such as chitosan, cellulose, gelatin, and dextran exhibit excellent bioactivity, biocompatibility, and low toxicity. Owing to their cationic nature, these polymers readily interact with negatively charged anticancer drugs, thereby facilitating efficient drug encapsulation. In particular, the presence of functional groups such as carboxyl and amine moieties in gelatin enables strong electrostatic interactions with drug molecules, further enhancing loading efficiency (Das et al., 2023). Synthetic polymers such as polyethylene glycol (PEG) are widely employed in hydrogel systems due to their ability to encapsulate hydrophobic drugs, enhance their aqueous solubility, and maintain formulation stability during systemic circulation (Wang et al., 2023). Polymers such as poly (methacrylic acid) (PMMA), poly (acrylic acid), poly (N-isopropylacrylamide), and poly (vinyl alcohol) offer precise control over the physical and chemical properties of hydrogels, which in turn significantly influence drug encapsulation behavior. Furthermore, the surfaces of these polymers can be chemically modified to enable specific interactions or covalent bonding with selected drug molecules, thereby enhancing their loading capacity and overall delivery efficiency (Thang et al., 2023). Hybrid or semiinterpenetrating polymer networks that combine natural and synthetic polymers, such as salecan and PMMA, significantly reinforce the mechanical properties of hydrogels while also promoting electrostatic interactions that enable efficient drug loading (up to 84%) and controlled drug release (Qi et al., 2015). The compatibility between the interaction sites of the polymer and the drug is a critical determinant of efficient drug loading. For example, in chitosan-based hydrogel systems, erlotinib exhibits higher loading efficiency than thymoquinone, which can be attributed to its larger polar surface area that provides more interaction sites for binding with the polymer matrix (Uddin et al., 2024).

Molecular weight of the drug

The molecular weight of drug molecules plays a significant role in determining their loading rate, loading capacity, diffusivity, and permeability within the hydrogel matrices. These parameters are generally interrelated, where smaller drug molecules diffuse more rapidly into the hydrogel network, while larger molecules experience greater steric hindrance, leading to slower loading kinetics. However, although lower molecular weight often facilitates faster loading, it does not necessarily translate into higher loading capacity. This is evidenced by the comparatively higher loading of erlotinib and gefitinib relative to thymoquinone (164.2 g/mol), indicating that additional factors such as drug–polymer interactions and molecular structure also govern encapsulation efficiency (Uddin et al., 2024). In addition, drugs with low molecular weight are often challenging to encapsulate within hydrogel systems due to their small size, high aqueous solubility, and limited availability of intermolecular forces such as electrostatic interactions, π–π stacking, and hydrophobic interaction (Hu et al., 2024).

Types of hydrogel

Various types of hydrogels can be fabricated using a wide range of polymers to serve as carriers for anticancer drug delivery. The specific type of hydrogel employed largely dictates the method and efficiency of drug encapsulation, as well as the mechanism by which the therapeutic agent is protected, released, and delivered to the target site. Consequently, a combination of the hydrogel's physical structure, chemical interactions, and dimensional scale governs how effectively the drug is entrapped within the matrix. For instance, macrogels offer a high reservoir capacity for drug loading, whereas nanogels possess a high surface-to-volume ratio, which enhances loading efficiency. Furthermore, in stimuli-responsive hydrogels, environmental triggers such as temperature and pH play a critical role in drug encapsulation and release, and therefore, these systems must be designed in accordance with the intended physiological conditions (Sun et al., 2020).

Advancement in hydrogel

Conjugated hydrogel: Peptide, protein, or antibody conjugation

As the name suggests, in conjugated hydrogels, therapeutic agents are chemically or physically linked to polymer chains, forming a hydrogel-based delivery system with tunable physicochemical properties for controlled and sustained drug release. In addition to small-molecule drugs, biomacromolecules such as DNA, RNA, nucleic acids, peptides, and proteins can also be conjugated with hydrogels to generate stable and functional complexes. Conjugation refers to the process of attaching small chemical molecules or biologics, including monomers, peptides, polysaccharides, proteins, nucleic acids, and even cells, to polymeric carriers to protect them from degradation and enhance their stability. This process can be achieved either through physical interactions or via chemical crosslinking.

Peptide-conjugated hydrogels represent an important subclass, where conjugation typically occurs through coupling reactions between functional groups such as amine or thiol moieties of peptides and reactive groups on hydrophilic polymers. These conjugates subsequently undergo self-assembly or polymerization to form a three-dimensional hydrogel network. In the case of protein conjugation, stable amide bonds are commonly formed between protein functional groups and polymer backbones. Among various polymers, polyethylene glycol (PEG) is one of the most widely used materials for bioconjugation due to its excellent biocompatibility and the ease with which its terminal hydroxyl groups can be modified into reactive functionalities for targeting amine and thiol groups of peptides and proteins. Furthermore, positively charged polymers such as chitosan can electrostatically interact with negatively charged biomolecules, including proteins, RGD peptides, and antibodies, while hydrophobic proteins can be efficiently associated with hydrophobic polymer matrices (Dinh et al., 2025). Thus, in summary, physical crosslinking involves noncovalent interactions such as physical entanglement, hydrogen bonding, hydrophobic interactions, electrostatic interactions, and self-assembly-based conjugation. In contrast, chemical crosslinking is characterized by the formation of covalent bonds, including C–C, C–O, C–N, C–S, S–S, B–O, and Si–O linkages (Dong et al., 2025). A prominent example of peptide-conjugated hydrogels is the P–Y/G@NH system, which has been developed for the treatment of nonsmall cell lung carcinoma. In this system, the YSA peptide is conjugated to a paclitaxel–succinic acid complex, forming a drug–peptide conjugate that enhances targeting efficiency. This conjugate is subsequently incorporated into a hydrogel matrix composed of dextran and gold nanoparticles, enabling improved drug stability, controlled release, and enhanced therapeutic efficacy (Hajareh Haghighi et al., 2023). Antibody-conjugated hydrogels are emerging as a powerful platform in cancer immunotherapy, designed to overcome key limitations associated with conventional antibody-based treatments, such as short circulation time and severe immune-related adverse events, including hepatitis and pneumonitis. In these systems, hydrogels function as localized depots that enable sustained and controlled release of therapeutic antibodies, thereby increasing drug concentration at the target site while minimizing systemic exposure and toxicity. Antibody-conjugated hydrogels primarily act within the tumor microenvironment to modulate and stimulate immune responses. One advanced strategy involves loading hydrogels with platelets conjugated to antiPD-L1 antibodies. These engineered platelets can trigger the formation of antibody-releasing microparticles, facilitating localized immune checkpoint inhibition and effectively reducing postsurgical tumor recurrence (Zhang et al., 2024).

Stimuli response hydrogel

Stimuli-responsive hydrogel-based drug delivery systems represent a smart and transformative platform for the treatment of various cancers. These smart hydrogels are polymeric networks capable of undergoing significant physical or chemical changes, such as volume phase transitions, solubility alterations, or network degradation, in response to specific environmental stimuli. Such responsive behaviour enables the controlled and site-specific release of therapeutic agents (Andrade et al., 2021; Kasiński et al., 2020). In cancer treatment, these systems provide localized, sustained, and on-demand drug delivery, which enhances the therapeutic efficacy while minimizing systemic toxicity to healthy tissues (Sun et al., 2020). Stimulus employed in anticancer drug delivery are generally classified into endogenous triggers (pH, Redox, enzymes, GSH, and glucose), which originate from the tumor microenvironment, and exogenous triggers (heat, light, magnetic field, ultrasound, and X-ray), which are externally applied or controlled by the clinician (Parvaresh et al., 2023).

pH-responsive hydrogels

Tumor tissues typically exhibit a slightly acidic extracellular environment (pH 5.5–7.2) compared to normal physiological tissues (pH ~7.4), primarily due to elevated glycolytic activity and lactic acid production. pH-responsive hydrogels are designed with ionizable functional groups, such as amines, carboxylic acids, and imines, which undergo protonation or deprotonation in response to pH changes. These alterations induce swelling or collapse of the polymeric network, thereby enabling controlled drug release. Generally, cationic hydrogels preferentially release drugs under acidic conditions, whereas anionic hydrogels exhibit drug release at higher pH levels. Alternatively, acid-labile chemical linkages, including Schiff bases, hydrazone, ketal, acetal, and hydrazide bonds, can be incorporated into hydrogel structures, which selectively degrade in the acidic tumor microenvironment to trigger site-specific payload release (Sun et al., 2020; Andrade et al., 2021). In a recent study, a doxorubicin-loaded hydrogel fabricated from 4-formylbenzoic acid–modified poly(vinyl alcohol) and crosslinked with polyethyleneimine demonstrated high pH sensitivity, exhibiting negligible drug release at physiological pH (7.4) but significantly enhanced release at mildly acidic pH (6.8). These findings highlight the strong potential of pH-responsive hydrogels as effective delivery systems for cancer chemotherapy (Yu et al., 2025).

Redox-responsive hydrogels

Redox-responsive systems exploit the significantly higher intracellular concentration of glutathione (GSH) in cancer cells, which is approximately four times greater than that in normal healthy tissues. These hydrogels typically incorporate disulfide bonds within their polymeric network, which remain stable under physiological conditions in the bloodstream but are cleaved in the reductive intracellular tumor environment. Upon exposure to elevated GSH levels, the disulfide bonds are reduced to sulfhydryl groups, leading to network degradation and subsequent drug release. Polyethylene glycol (PEG)-based polymers are widely recognized as effective redox-responsive carriers, as they can be readily functionalized with disulfide linkages and have been extensively utilized in the fabrication of anticancer drug delivery systems over the past decade. Redox-sensitive hydrogels are particularly advantageous for protein delivery and for overcoming drug resistance in tumor cells. In addition to disulfide bonds, diselenide linkers have also gained attention, as they can be cleaved in the presence of reducing agents such as glutathione or dithiothreitol (DTT) within the tumor microenvironment (Kilic Boz et al., 2022). An advanced dual pH- and redox-responsive hydrogel system has been developed for the precise and targeted delivery of doxorubicin. In this system, 2-hydroxyethyl methacrylate and 2-dimethylaminoethyl methacrylate were polymerized using redox-sensitive and pH-sensitive crosslinkers, namely 2,2′-dithiodiethanol diacrylate (DSDA) and N,N′-methylene-bisacrylamide (MBA). The resulting hydrogel exhibited significantly enhanced drug release under acidic conditions (pH 3.5) and in the presence of DTT, demonstrating its potential for controlled and stimuli-specific drug delivery in cancer therapy (Zarrin-Nahand et al., 2025).

Enzyme-responsive hydrogels

Enzyme-responsive systems exploit the overexpression of specific enzymes in the tumor microenvironment, such as matrix metalloproteinases (MMPs), heparinase, and O^6-methylguanine-DNA methyltransferase. These hydrogels are engineered to incorporate enzyme-cleavable peptide or polymeric sequences within their network structure. In the presence of the target enzymes, these sequences get selectively cleaved, leading to degradation of the hydrogel matrix and subsequent localized release of the encapsulated therapeutic agents (Solanki and Bhatia, 2024). Hyaluronic acid–based hydrogels exhibit hyaluronidase-responsive drug release and have been widely explored for the targeted treatment of breast cancer (Asadi et al., 2024).

Glucose-responsive hydrogels

In glucose-responsive systems, hydrogels loaded with glucose oxidase can generate reactive oxygen species or induce tumor starvation by consuming local glucose, thereby exerting cytotoxic effects on cancer cells. Alternatively, changes in glucose concentration can trigger physical responses in boronic acid–containing hydrogels, such as network swelling or contraction, which can be used as a signal for the quantitative detection of glucose levels.

Despite their potential, the development of glucose-responsive hydrogels remains challenging. In particular, the hydrogen peroxide produced during glucose oxidation may induce inflammation and oxidative stress, posing significant safety concerns for glucose oxidase–based drug delivery systems (Asadi et al., 2024).

Thermo-responsive hydrogels

Thermo-responsive systems represent one of the most widely studied categories of stimuli-responsive hydrogels. These hydrogels undergo a sol–gel phase transition at their lower critical solution temperature (LCST). Polymers such as poly(N-isopropylacrylamide) (pNIPAM) and PLGA–PEG–PLGA triblock copolymers are commonly employed in these systems. They remain in a liquid state at room temperature, facilitating easy administration, and subsequently transform into a solid or semisolid gel at physiological body temperature through a process known as reverse thermal gelation, thereby forming an in situ drug depot for sustained release (Sun et al., 2020; Solanki and Bhatia, 2024). An on-demand thermo-responsive hydrogel composed of N-isopropylacrylamide crosslinked with poly (ethylene glycol) diacrylate and loaded with doxorubicin has been developed to achieve sustained and controlled drug release for the treatment of colorectal cancer (Carreño et al., 2021).

Photo/light-responsive hydrogels

Photo-responsive hydrogels utilize external light sources, including ultraviolet (UV), visible light, and near-infrared (NIR) radiation, as stimuli to trigger drug release. Upon light irradiation, specific photo-cleavable bonds within the hydrogel network are broken, leading to the controlled release of the encapsulated anticancer agents. In addition to drug delivery, these systems can also be employed in photothermal and photodynamic therapy by incorporating photosensitizers into the hydrogel matrix. Upon irradiation, the activated photosensitizers generate localized heat or reactive oxygen species, thereby enhancing therapeutic efficacy at the tumor site (Wang et al., 2023). Photo-responsive hydrogels enable precise on–off control over drug release, as changes in hydrogel properties—such as heat transfer, charge transfer, or photoisomerization, occur only upon exposure to external light stimuli. This level of spatiotemporal control is achieved by incorporating photoactive moieties, including nitrobenzyl ester linkers, spiropyrans, and azo groups, into the polymeric backbone, where they act as light-sensitive crosslinkers that regulate network stability and drug release behavior (Asadi et al., 2024).

Magnetic field-responsive hydrogels

Magnetic-responsive hydrogels incorporate magnetic materials such as iron oxide nanoparticles, magnetite, iron–platinum, and cobalt–iron alloys within their polymeric matrix. When exposed to an alternating magnetic field, these materials generate localized heat through magnetic relaxation and hysteresis losses, which can trigger drug release from a thermosensitive hydrogel matrix or induce hyperthermia to selectively destroy tumor cells. In contrast, the application of a static magnetic field enables directional movement and accumulation of magnetic hydrogels at a specific target site, thereby enhancing the precision of targeted drug delivery (Sun et al., 2020; Parvaresh et al., 2023).

Ultrasound-responsive hydrogels

Ultrasound-sensitive hydrogels can trigger site-specific drug release through multiple physical mechanisms. The responsiveness of these systems largely depends on factors such as polymer composition, crosslinking strategy, and fabrication method. High-intensity focused ultrasound (HIFU) applied to tumor tissues generates localized heat through the conversion of acoustic energy and simultaneously induces the formation of microbubbles due to acoustic cavitation. This synergistic combination of thermal effects and mechanical vibrations effectively disrupts the hydrogel network, thereby facilitating efficient and controlled release of the encapsulated therapeutic payload (Sun et al., 2020; Asadi et al., 2024).

Electric field-responsive hydrogels

Electric-responsive systems employ conductive polymers that undergo reversible oxidation–reduction reactions upon the application of an external electric field, leading to structural or conformational changes in the hydrogel network and subsequent controlled release of the encapsulated drugs (Thang et al., 2023; Asadi et al., 2024).

X-ray-responsive hydrogels

X-ray-responsive systems represent an emerging strategy in hydrogel-based drug delivery, where X-ray irradiation is employed to trigger the release of chemotherapeutic agents. This approach enables synergistic chemoradiotherapy, allowing simultaneous radiation and drug treatment at the tumor site while minimizing systemic toxicity (Sun et al., 2025).

Injectable (sol-gel-sol) hydrogel

Injectable in situ hydrogels are local drug delivery systems that undergo phase transition from solution state to gel state at the tumor site and work as a depot formulation to release the drug in a sustained manner when external stimuli (heat) are applied, which causes transition from gel to solution state again (Shi et al., 2026). Injectable hydrogel demonstrates sol–gel–sol behavior for easy administration of anticancer drug to form a depot at the target site for localized drug delivery in a controlled manner (Fig. 23.1). Polymers such as chitosan, poly(N-isopropylacrylamide), and triblock copolymers of polyethylene glycol with polypropylene, polycarbonate, poly (ε-caprolactone), poly (lactic acid), and poly (lactide-co-glycolide) undergo conformational transitions from extended chains to globular or micellar states at physiological body temperature (37°C), owing to their lower critical solution temperature (LCST) lying within this range (Xin and Naficy, 2022). In a recent study, a thermosensitive hydrogel matrix composed of PCL–PEG–PCL was coloaded with rhenium-188 colloid and paclitaxel micelles. Upon injection, the system formed an in situ gel and remained localized at the injection site for up to 2 weeks, enabling sustained drug release. The antitumor efficacy of this formulation was evaluated in tumor-bearing mice, where it demonstrated significantly improved control over tumor volume and enhanced tumor growth inhibition in a hepatocellular carcinoma model (Shih et al., 2026). In another study, an in situ injectable hydrogel system was developed for the treatment of melanoma. In this approach, porous paclitaxel-loaded poly (lactic acid) (PLA) microspheres and cisplatin were

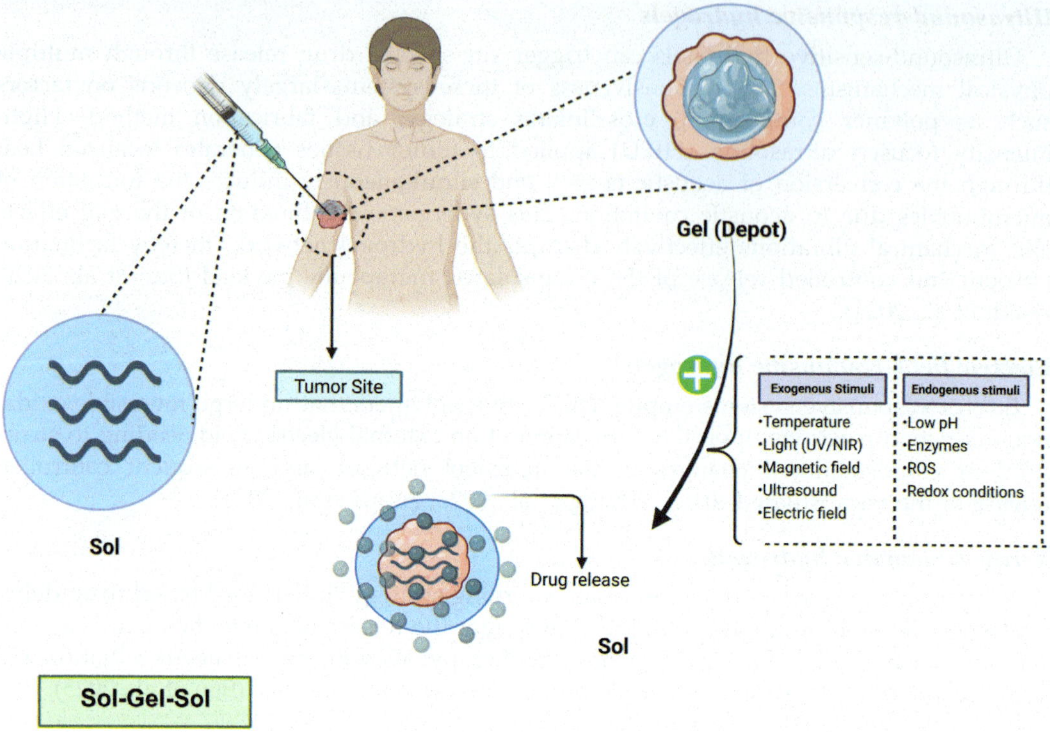

FIGURE 23.1 Sol–gel–sol behavior of injectable hydrogels for site-specific anticancer drug delivery, showing in situ gel depot formation and stimuli-responsive drug release.

coencapsulated within a thermosensitive poly (ethylene glycol)–poly (D,L-lactic acid)–poly (ethylene glycol) (PEG–PDLLA–PEG) hydrogel and administered via intratumoral injection. In vitro release studies demonstrated sustained drug release, with only 58% of paclitaxel released over 1 week and approximately 50% of cisplatin released within 48 h. In vivo antitumor evaluation revealed that the dual drug-loaded thermosensitive hydrogel achieved the smallest tumor volume and the slowest tumor growth rate compared to control groups. Furthermore, histological analysis of major vital organs showed no significant structural abnormalities, and complete degradation of the hydrogel was observed by day 15. These findings highlight that injectable hydrogels offer precise control over drug release kinetics and localization, along with excellent biodegradability, making them highly suitable for localized cancer therapy with enhanced therapeutic efficacy (Liu et al., 2023). A novel pentablock thermoresponsive hydrogel has been developed for the codelivery of oxaliplatin and gemcitabine in the treatment of pancreatic cancer. In this system, poly (D,L-lactide) was incorporated into a methoxy poly (ethylene glycol)–poly (ε-caprolactone)–methoxy poly (ethylene glycol) backbone to enhance the hydrolytic degradation of the hydrogel following the sol–gel transition mediated by micelle formation (Elsherbeny et al., 2025). Another research group prepared active in situ hydrogels that can be controlled externally, instead of relying on passive endogenous stimuli in the tumor environment, which is variable and heterogeneous. A precise drug delivery and release is achieved independent of the fluctuations in the tumor microenvironment. Sol–gel-sol hydrogels based on Pluronic F127 and chitosan have emerged as advanced thermo- and pH-responsive platforms for localized anticancer drug delivery. These systems remain injectable in the sol state and undergo in situ gelation at physiological temperature, forming a drug depot that enhances tumor retention. Studies have shown that the incorporation of paclitaxel nanocrystals or gemcitabine within such hydrogels enables homogeneous drug distribution and sustained release. Furthermore, the sol–gel–sol transition can be externally regulated through photothermal stimulation, where near-infrared irradiation induces localized heating, leading to hydrogel melting and on-demand drug release, thereby improving cellular drug uptake and therapeutic efficacy (Kumar et al., 2025; Shi et al., 2026). An innovative thermosensitive hydrogel system based on poloxamer 407 has been developed for the treatment of bone cancer, incorporating zoledronic acid to induce bone cancer cell death and holmium-doped bioactive glass nanoparticles to promote bone regeneration. This dual-functional system enables a synergistic therapeutic effect, simultaneously supporting tumor eradication and tissue regeneration, while preventing undesirable interactions between bisphosphonates and the bioactive glass components (Borges et al., 2023).

Hydrogel for the design of microneedles

Microneedles represent an emerging, minimally invasive transdermal drug delivery platform, as they create microscopic channels upon penetrating the epidermis while avoiding direct contact with capillaries and nerve endings. Hydrogel-based materials are particularly well-suited for microneedle fabrication due to their excellent biocompatibility and their ability to mimic the extracellular matrix. The inherent water-absorbing capacity of hydrogels allows them to swell after insertion, forming hydrophilic pathways that facilitate sustained drug release through diffusion from the crosslinked polymeric network. Both natural and synthetic hydrophilic polymer blends can be molded into microneedle arrays, depending on the desired mechanical and release characteristics. To date, numerous hydrogel-based microneedle systems have been developed for the delivery of anticancer agents such as doxorubicin, paclitaxel, and cisplatin, as well as photothermal and immunotherapeutic agents for melanoma treatment, using polymers including poly (vinyl alcohol), hyaluronic acid, gelatin, dextran, and poly (vinyl pyrrolidone) (Zhu et al., 2025). Beyond transdermal skin applications, hydrogel-based microneedles have also been explored for deeper and site-specific treatments of various cancers, including breast cancer, cervical cancer, basal cell carcinoma, glioma, and pancreatic cancer. Owing to their biodegradability, ease of dissolution, ability to penetrate deeper epidermal layers, and responsiveness to external or internal stimuli, these systems enable sustained and controlled drug release. As a result, hydrogel-based microneedles can achieve enhanced antitumor efficacy while requiring lower drug doses, thereby reducing systemic toxicity and improving therapeutic outcomes (Filho et al., 2023). The simplicity of fabrication and ease of operation make hydrogel-based microneedles highly suitable for tumor treatment. Moreover, stimuli-responsive microneedle systems can be developed using strategies similar to those employed for stimuli-responsive hydrogels. These include pH-responsive, glutathione-responsive, enzyme-responsive, reactive oxygen species (ROS)-responsive, and glucose-responsive microneedles, which enable precise and efficient drug delivery for cancer therapy (Tang et al., 2024a). Despite their advantages as sustained-release and long-acting drug delivery systems, microneedles exhibit certain limitations, including relatively low drug loading capacity and limited accessibility to deep tissues and vital organs. Consequently, for localized tumor treatment in deeper anatomical sites, injectable hydrogel systems are often more suitable and effective than microneedle-based platforms (Pacheco et al., 2023). In addition to serving as a noninvasive platform for the sustained delivery of chemotherapeutic agents, microneedle-based hydrogel systems are also being explored for the early diagnosis of cancer. These systems enable the extraction of interstitial fluid from tissues, which contains tumor-derived exosomes that can be isolated and analyzed for cancer-specific biomarkers, thereby facilitating rapid and minimally invasive diagnosis. Furthermore, hydrogels can be functionalized with glypican-1 (GPC1) antibodies, as GPC1 proteins are overexpressed in tumor-derived exosomes compared to normal cells. Since these exosomes carry tumor-specific genetic material, such platforms offer significant potential for sensitive and early cancer detection (Park et al., 2023). Recently, an advanced rocket-like microneedle patch was developed as a dual-layer drug delivery system for the treatment of prostate cancer. In this design, the first layer comprised a zeolitic imidazole framework-8 (ZIF-8) loaded with bicalutamide, an androgen receptor antagonist, which served as a rapid-release and short-acting component. The second layer consisted of alginate–tyramine monomers encapsulating goserelin, a gonadotropin-releasing hormone (GnRH) analogue that suppresses male hormone synthesis, forming a long-acting sustained-release depot. Following administration, the hydrogel-based second layer penetrates the stratum corneum and remains stable within the tissue, enabling prolonged and controlled drug release. This innovative microneedle system offers a promising and practical therapeutic strategy for patients with prostate cancer requiring long-term hormonal therapy (Chen et al., 2025). For the treatment of cutaneous melanoma, a novel hydrogel-based microneedle system has been developed as a chemoimmunotherapeutic delivery platform. In this system, a programmed death-ligand 1 (PD-L1) inhibitor and doxorubicin were cocrosslinked within methacryloyl gelatin (GelMA) hydrogel microneedles, resulting in enhanced local drug concentration at the tumor site. This painless and minimally invasive delivery approach enables synergistic drug retention and sustained release, which effectively reduces skin damage while significantly enhancing the cytotoxic and immunotherapeutic killing of melanoma cells (Teng et al., 2025).

Hydrogel for the design of implants

Implantable hydrogels have emerged as a promising strategy in cancer therapy, particularly for preventing postoperative tumor recurrence. These systems can be engineered to incorporate tumor antigens, antibodies, and vaccines, thereby enabling localized immunomodulation at the surgical site. Residual cancer cells often exhibit poor responsiveness to systemic therapies and are frequently inaccessible to repeated injections, making implantable hydrogels an effective alternative for sustained local treatment. In addition, implantable hydrogel platforms are widely utilized for the delivery of chemoimmunotherapeutic agents, offering prolonged drug retention and enhanced therapeutic efficacy at the target site

(Pechnikova et al., 2025). Implantable hydrogels are typically fabricated in the size range of millimeters to centimeters and can be introduced into the body either through surgical implantation in intramuscular or subcutaneous tissues, or via minimally invasive injection owing to their shear-thinning properties and shape-memory behavior, which allows them to recover their original structure after administration. As discussed earlier, both physical and chemical crosslinking strategies can be employed to engineer these hydrogels with tailored mechanical properties, and external stimuli such as light, temperature, ultrasound, electric fields, and magnetic fields can be applied postimplantation to activate their therapeutic function. The functional lifetime of implantable hydrogels generally does not exceed 6 months, and reimplantation may be required for prolonged treatment regimens. Upon exposure to external stimuli, these systems enable controlled and on-demand release of the encapsulated therapeutic cargo, after which the hydrogel network can return to its original state once the stimulus is withdrawn (Sun et al., 2022). Several recently developed implantable hydrogel systems have been reported, particularly for postoperative cancer therapy. To begin with, a three-dimensional (3D)-printed implantable hydrogel scaffold composed of Pluronic F124 and sodium alginate has been engineered for the localized delivery of the anticancer drug doxorubicin complexed with copper (II) ions. This multifunctional system integrates conventional chemotherapy with chemodynamic therapy, thereby inducing apoptosis and ferroptosis in residual tumor cells. The hydrogel paste is fabricated into a cuboidal scaffold using 3D printing and enables sustained and localized release of both copper ions and doxorubicin, enhancing therapeutic efficacy while minimizing systemic toxicity (Dang et al., 2023). In another study, a brain-implantable hydrogel system was developed to prevent the recurrence of glioblastoma arising from residual glial cells by enabling localized delivery of temozolomide. The photo-crosslinked and freeze-dried hydrogel flakes were fabricated using a combination of methacrylated gelatin, chitosan, and hyaluronic acid, resulting in a biocompatible matrix capable of providing controlled and sustained drug release. This localized delivery strategy effectively minimizes systemic toxicity while maintaining therapeutic drug concentrations at the tumor site. Furthermore, the implant demonstrated excellent biocompatibility, biodegradability, and biosafety, highlighting its potential as a promising platform for postoperative brain cancer therapy (Krajcer et al., 2025). In parallel, a group of researchers developed a compact, wireless, and flexible implantable device for brain tumor treatment that operates without the need for an external battery. This system is composed of MXene, which provides excellent electrical conductivity and a high surface area, and poly (vinyl alcohol), sandwiched between polydimethylsiloxane (PDMS) layers on both sides. The device enables precise ultrasonic-driven tribological energy harvesting and transfer, allowing efficient and self-powered operation. This hydrogel-based matrix represents an innovative therapeutic platform and signifies a major advancement in neuro-oncology, offering promising potential for personalized and patient-specific brain cancer treatment (He et al., 2025). Another promising application of hydrogel implants is their use as surface-filling materials for complex anatomical tumor sites during surgical procedures, where complete resection of malignant tissue is often challenging or impossible. These shape-adaptive hydrogels can be loaded with therapeutic agents, proteins, and microRNAs (miRNAs) and applied directly to the surgical cavity. Surface-associated cancers such as mesothelioma, thymoma, colorectal cancer, and ovarian cancer can be locally treated by spraying or applying these hydrogels intraoperatively, leading to effective coverage of the tumor bed and sustained localized therapy. By conforming to the unique and irregular anatomy of tumor sites, these hydrogels can penetrate small gaps and crevices and undergo shape transformation after application, thereby enhancing drug retention and reducing the likelihood of tumor recurrence. This approach offers significant clinical potential for improving postoperative cancer outcomes (Majumder et al., 2021). A major concern in postoperative tumor recurrence is the presence of cancer-associated cells, adipocytes, and angiogenic cells within the tumor microenvironment, which can promote tumor regrowth and metastasis. This challenge can be addressed by incorporating chemotherapeutic agents into hydrogel matrices and engineering them as bioadhesive implants for localized and sustained drug release. For instance, a bioadhesive hydrogel system has been developed by grafting hyaluronic acid with dopamine and 3-aminobenzeneboronic acid, and subsequently loading it with doxorubicin and metformin. This implant can be applied directly to the surgical tumor site, where doxorubicin is released in a controlled manner through the cleavage of borate bonds under acidic conditions characteristic of the tumor microenvironment. Simultaneously, metformin inhibits adipocyte activity at the cancer site, thereby suppressing tumor recurrence and metastasis. Such multifunctional hydrogel implants offer a promising strategy for effective postoperative breast cancer therapy (Li et al., 2023).

Hydrogel in dual drug delivery

Cancer is a highly complex disease involving multiple dysregulated biological pathways, and treatment with a single therapeutic agent often leads to the development of drug resistance, increased systemic toxicity, and reduced cellular uptake. Therefore, combination therapy using multiple drugs that target different molecular pathways simultaneously is considered a more effective and clinically relevant strategy. Hydrogel-based drug delivery systems are particularly well-suited for such combinatorial approaches, as they enable the coencapsulation and controlled release of multiple therapeutic agents. For instance, a dual-drug delivery system was developed using a thiol–ene conjugated hydrogel formed by crosslinking thiol-modified hyaluronic acid with vinyl sulfone–modified β-cyclodextrin, enabling the localized codelivery of doxorubicin and carvacrol for the treatment of triple-negative breast cancer (Sathi Devi et al., 2025). Researchers have also developed a double-crosslinked hydrogel system for combination cancer therapy by integrating a peptide-based hydrogel with alginate nanoparticles. In this system, the peptide chains form covalent bonds with cisplatin, which reinforces the self-assembled hydrogel network and enables rapid initial drug release. Simultaneously, irinotecan is encapsulated within alginate nanoparticles dispersed throughout the matrix, allowing its sustained and controlled release. This hierarchical architecture facilitates a sequential release profile, in which cisplatin is released first to sensitize tumor cells, followed by prolonged release of irinotecan, ultimately resulting in superior antitumor efficacy against A549 lung cancer tumors (Hajareh Haghighi et al., 2023). For the treatment of cervical cancer, disulfide cross-linked biodegradable polymeric nanogels have been developed to codeliver vorinostat, a histone deacetylase inhibitor, and irinotecan, a topoisomerase II inhibitor. These nanogels were fabricated using poly (ethylene glycol) monomethacrylate and enabled sustained and redox-responsive release of both drugs, thereby enhancing therapeutic efficacy while minimizing systemic toxicity (Kumar et al., 2018). For tumors characterized by a dense extracellular matrix, such as oral squamous cell carcinoma and pancreatic cancer, supramolecular hydrogels can be engineered to overcome the major barrier of poor drug penetration into tumor tissues. In such cases, a sequential drug delivery strategy is particularly effective, where one agent is first used to modulate the tumor microenvironment, followed by the delivery of a cytotoxic drug. For example, in one study, pirfenidone was initially released to inhibit collagen production and reduce matrix density, thereby facilitating the subsequent penetration of paclitaxel into the tumor tissue. The hydrogel matrix was fabricated using equimolar concentrations of guanosine, boric acid, and phosphatidylglycerol, which formed borate bonds and self-assembled guanosine quartets, enabling the encapsulation of poorly water-soluble drugs. Both in vitro and in vivo evaluations demonstrated controlled and sequential drug release, prolonged retention of the anticancer agent at the tumor site, and enhanced local drug concentration. Consequently, this coloaded supramolecular hydrogel system exhibited improved tumor suppression and reduced tumor volume, highlighting its strong potential for the treatment of collagen-dense cancers (Cao et al., 2025). Another innovative strategy for utilizing hydrogels as dual drug-delivery systems in anticancer therapy involves the codelivery of a chemotherapeutic agent along with a pain-relieving drug. For instance, Sheng et al. developed a pH-responsive hydrogel system for the treatment of colorectal cancer, composed of alginate and sodium carboxymethyl cellulose crosslinked with calcium ions. This hydrogel was designed to encapsulate aspirin as an analgesic agent and calcium carbonate-loaded methotrexate microspheres as the anticancer component. The formulation remains stable in the acidic environment of the stomach and the neutral conditions of the small intestine, while enabling pH-triggered drug release specifically in the colorectum. This targeted release strategy not only enhances the therapeutic efficacy of methotrexate but also provides localized pain relief, thereby improving patient comfort and treatment outcomes (Sheng et al., 2021). Similarly, an in situ injectable hydrogel system has been developed for the treatment of colorectal cancer using a multi-component combination delivery strategy. This formulation consists of poly(N-isopropylacrylamide) microgels loaded with 5-fluorouracil, aldehyde-functionalized Pluronic F127 micelles encapsulating curcumin, with both components coentrapped within a hydrazide-functionalized gelatin hydrogel matrix. The resulting microgel-embedded, micelle-crosslinked injectable hydrogel enabled sustained and controlled release of both drugs for over 1 month, thereby providing a synergistic therapeutic effect. This combination system significantly enhanced cancer cell apoptosis in HT-29 cell models and effectively overcame the reduced sensitivity associated with 5-fluorouracil-resistant tumor cells. Overall, these findings demonstrate that combination therapy delivered through hydrogel-based platforms not only retains the inherent advantages of hydrogel systems but also substantially improves therapeutic efficacy and treatment outcomes in resistant cancers (Pakian et al., 2022). A research group investigated the application of a drug-eluting, shear-thinning hydrogel system for the treatment of hepatocellular carcinoma using conventional catheter-based arterial chemoembolization. In this approach, a laponite–gelatin hydrogel was engineered for pH-dependent codelivery of doxorubicin, a chemotherapeutic agent released under acidic conditions, and antiPD-1 (aPD-1), an immune checkpoint inhibitor released preferentially at neutral pH. Doxorubicin not only induces direct cytotoxic effects but also enhances interferon production, thereby promoting immune-mediated antitumor activity. Moreover, it has been shown to upregulate PD-L1 expression on tumor cells, which further sensitizes the tumor microenvironment to immune checkpoint blockade. Consequently, the combined delivery of a chemotherapeutic and an immunotherapeutic agent via this hydrogel system resulted in the highest survival rates and the smallest tumor volumes, demonstrating the strong potential of chemoimmunotherapy-based hydrogel platforms for advanced cancer treatment (Falcone et al., 2024). Hydrogels also offer a versatile platform for the simultaneous codelivery of hydrophilic and hydrophobic drugs within a single delivery system. For instance, hydrophilic doxorubicin and hydrophobic camptothecin have been successfully coencapsulated in a third-generation dendrimer-crosslinked γ-polyglutamic acid hydrogel. In this system, the hydrophobic drug is preferentially loaded within the dendrimer core, while the hydrophilic drug is retained within the polyglutamic acid network, enabling differential loading and controlled release. This dual-compartment architecture facilitates sustained and synchronized drug release, resulting in synergistic therapeutic efficacy against cancer cells (Jia et al., 2025). Hydrogel-based delivery systems can also be employed for the dual oral delivery of anticancer drugs, offering a strategy to reduce the individual drug doses and minimize the risk of systemic side effects. For example, a novel polymer matrix composed of pectin grafted with poly (4-acryloylmorpholine-co-2-acrylamido-2-methyl-1-propanesulfonic acid) has been developed using a green chemistry approach and coloaded with doxorubicin and 5-fluorouracil as model anticancer agents. In vitro cytotoxicity studies demonstrated approximately 70% cell viability in normal MCF-10A cells, indicating reduced toxicity toward healthy cells while maintaining anticancer efficacy (Luanda et al., 2025).

Theranostic hydrogel

Theranostics integrate cancer diagnosis and therapy within a single platform, enabling real-time monitoring of disease progression and treatment efficacy, thereby facilitating personalized and patient-specific therapeutic interventions. Injectable polymeric hydrogels have emerged as promising theranostic platforms, as their in vivo behavior can be tracked to provide continuous feedback for optimizing drug delivery and treatment regimens. These systems can simultaneously incorporate multiple therapeutic modalities, including chemotherapy, photothermal therapy, photodynamic therapy, and radiotherapy, along with diagnostic functions based on optical, magnetic, and nuclear imaging techniques, all within a single crosslinked hydrogel matrix. Such noninvasive and multifunctional delivery systems offer significant clinical advantages by improving treatment precision, enhancing patient outcomes, and reducing overall healthcare costs through the use of a single integrated platform (Wang et al., 2021). Hydrogel-based nanotheranostic systems enable the coordinated integration of early cancer detection, targeted therapy, and real-time monitoring of disease progression. These systems function as drug depots that encapsulate and deliver diverse nanoscale platforms, including metallic, polymeric, lipid-based, and carbon-based nanoparticles, which are often integrated with imaging agents. Such agents include magnetic resonance imaging (MRI) contrast materials, radioactive isotopes for positron emission tomography (PET), and fluorescent probes such as quantum dots, allowing precise visualization of tumor sites and continuous tracking of cancer progression. Through this multifunctional approach, hydrogel nanotheranostics offer a powerful strategy for personalized and image-guided cancer therapy (Misra and Acharya, 2021). Several representative examples of theranostic hydrogels demonstrate how diagnosis and therapy can be seamlessly integrated using advanced materials and stimuli-responsive mechanisms. One such system was specifically designed for the treatment of multidrug-resistant hepatocellular carcinoma. This platform consists of a thermosensitive Pluronic F127 hydrogel coloaded with doxorubicin and gold–manganese oxide nanoparticles. Upon injection, the formulation undergoes a sol–gel transition at physiological temperature, forming a stable in situ depot that minimizes premature drug leakage. When exposed to near-infrared (NIR) laser irradiation, the gold nanoparticles generate localized heat, enabling photothermal therapy while simultaneously triggering the controlled release of doxorubicin. In parallel, manganese ions released from the nanoparticles act as efficient MRI contrast agents, allowing real-time visualization of the tumor microenvironment and continuous assessment of therapeutic efficacy (Huang et al., 2022). For locoregional tumor management, a cluster missile–inspired dynamic nanocomposite hydrogel has been developed using a Schiff base reaction between carboxymethyl chitosan and platinum-containing, size-changeable synergistic nanoprodrugs coloaded with cisplatin and demethylcantharidin. These nanoparticles exhibit an isoelectric point at pH 5.0, allowing them to maintain a small particle size (~25 nm) at physiological pH (7.4) and the slightly acidic extracellular tumor pH (6.8), thereby facilitating deep tumor penetration, efficient cellular internalization, and enhanced accumulation within tumor tissues. Upon entering the intracellular tumor environment (pH ~5.0), the nanoparticles undergo aggregation into larger clusters, which triggers selective and localized drug release. Furthermore, the presence of platinum heavy metals within the nanoparticles enables spatiotemporal monitoring through computed tomography (CT) imaging, allowing real-time tracking of dynamic changes in both the hydrogel matrix and tumor tissue without the need for additional contrast agents (Ma et al., 2025). For theranostic applications, hydrogel polymers can interact with therapeutic and diagnostic payloads through diverse crosslinking and interaction mechanisms. For example, fluorescent carbon dots can be noncovalently incorporated within chitosan hydrogels, while 5-fluorouracil can be encapsulated in the same matrix via hydrophobic interactions, enabling simultaneous imaging and drug delivery (Sachdev et al., 2016). Theranostic hydrogels represent a significant advancement in the management of gastrointestinal tumors, including liver, gastric, colorectal, and pancreatic cancers, by addressing major clinical challenges such as late-stage diagnosis, drug resistance, and the presence of a dense tumor microenvironment. Early diagnosis of these tumors can be achieved through the detection of circulating tumor cells (CTCs). For instance, L-histidine–containing hydrogels have been developed to selectively capture sialylated glycans expressed on the surface of CTCs, achieving detection accuracies as high as 94%. Following surgical intervention, theranostic hydrogel formulations such as sodium alginate–calcium lactate systems can provide localized protection and sustained therapeutic delivery, proving beneficial in the management of gastroenterological tumors and polyps.

In pancreatic cancer, diagnosis is commonly based on the detection of the carbohydrate antigen CA19-9, a protein biomarker abundantly released by pancreatic tumor cells. In this context, cellulose-based hydrogels embedded with cadmium quantum dots have been designed to enable real-time monitoring of disease recurrence while simultaneously delivering therapeutic agents. Similarly, for gastric cancer, CD44-targeting supramolecular hydrogels have been developed to facilitate high-resolution fluorescence imaging of CD44 receptors overexpressed on gastric cancer stem cells. Overall, theranostic hydrogel platforms that combine sustained drug release with integrated imaging modalities such as computed tomography (CT), MRI, and PET represent an emerging and clinically promising strategy for personalized diagnosis and treatment of gastrointestinal cancers (Tang et al., 2024b; Zhou et al., 2024).

Conclusion

Hydrogels have emerged as highly effective carriers of anticancer, immunotherapeutic, and photothermal agents in cancer treatment. Their main advantage is their capacity to deliver therapeutic payloads in a sustained and localized manner, which improves therapeutic efficacy while decreasing systemic toxicity and off-target side effects. Hydrogels can be administered by a variety of methods, including oral, transdermal, injectable, and implanted systems. Hydrogels can be classed into natural, synthetic, and hybrid hydrogels according to polymer origin, and their physical, chemical, and mechanical properties can be modified using internal and external stimuli for controlled drug release. Smart hydrogels have received special interest due to their capacity to produce tailored drug release at tumor locations, minimizing the requirement for large systemic dosages. Their water-absorbing and swelling capabilities allow for efficient drug encapsulation and prolonged release while being biocompatible and biodegradable. The efficacy of hydrogel-based delivery systems can be tuned by polymer type, concentration, crosslinking density, and drug molecular weight, all of which influence porosity, mesh size, and release kinetics. In conclusion, hydrogels provide a unique and less invasive smart platform for precise drug delivery and robust therapeutic outcomes.

References

Andrade, F., Roca-Melendres, M.M., Durán-Lara, E.F., Rafael, D., Schwartz, S., 2021. Stimuli-responsive hydrogels for cancer treatment: The role of pH, light, ionic strength and magnetic field. Cancers 13 (5), 1164. https://doi.org/10.3390/cancers13051164.

Asadi, K., Samiraninezhad, N., Akbarizadeh, A.R., Amini, A., Gholami, A., 2024. Stimuli-responsive hydrogel based on natural polymers for breast cancer. Front. Chem. 12. https://doi.org/10.3389/fchem.2024.1325204.

Bertz, A., Wöhl-Bruhn, S., Miethe, S., Tiersch, B., Koetz, J., Hust, M., Bunjes, H., Menzel, H., 2013. Encapsulation of proteins in hydrogel carrier systems for controlled drug delivery: Influence of network structure and drug size on release rate. J. Biotechnol. 163 (2), 243–249. https://doi.org/10.1016/j.jbiotec.2012.06.036.

Borges, R., Zambanini, T., Pelosine, A.M., Justo, G.Z., Souza, A.C.S., Machado, J., Schneider, J.F., de Araujo, D.R., Marchi, J., 2023. A colloidal hydrogel-based drug delivery system overcomes the limitation of combining bisphosphonates with bioactive glasses: In vitro evidence of a potential selective bone cancer treatment allied with bone regeneration. Biomater. Adv. 151. https://doi.org/10.1016/j.bioadv.2023.213441.

Cao, L., Li, Z., Song, J., Xia, X., Zhang, G., Wang, H., Zhao, H., 2025. Sequential drug release system: Targeting the tumor ECM for enhanced chemotherapy efficacy. Proc. Natl. Acad. Sci. 122 (23). https://doi.org/10.1073/pnas.2421061122.

Carreño, G., Pereira, A., Ávila-Salas, F., Marican, A., Andrade, F., Roca-Melendres, M.M., Valdés, O., Vijayakumar, S., Schwartz, S., Abasolo, I., Rafael, D., Durán-Lara, E.F., 2021. Development of "on-demand" thermo-responsive hydrogels for anti-cancer drugs sustained release: Rational design, in silico prediction and in vitro validation in colon cancer models. Mater. Sci. Eng. C 131, 112483. https://doi.org/10.1016/j.msec.2021.112483.

Chen, Y.T., Chen, K.T., Yu, K.J., Pang, S.T., Yang, H.W., 2025. Rocket-like microneedle patch for sustained hormone therapy in prostate cancer. ACS Biomater. Sci. Eng. 11 (8), 4830–4843. https://doi.org/10.1021/acsbiomaterials.5c00127.

Dang, W., Wang, Y., Chen, W.C., Ju, E., Mintz, R.L., Teng, Y., Zhu, L., Wang, K., Lv, S., Chan, H.F., Tao, Y., Li, M., 2023. Implantable 3D printed hydrogel scaffolds loading copper-doxorubicin complexes for postoperative chemo/chemodynamic therapy. ACS Appl. Mater. Interfaces 15 (4), 4911–4923. https://doi.org/10.1021/acsami.2c18494.

Das, S.S., Sharma, D., Rao, B.V.K., Arora, M.K., Ruokolainen, J., Dhanka, M., Singh, H., Kesari, K.K., 2023. Natural cationic polymer-derived injectable hydrogels for targeted chemotherapy. Mater. Adv. 4 (23), 6064–6091. https://doi.org/10.1039/d3ma00484h.

Dinh, L., Hwang, S.-J., Yan, B., 2025. Hydrogel conjugation: Engineering of hydrogels for drug delivery. Pharmaceutics 17 (7), 897. https://doi.org/10.3390/pharmaceutics17070897.

Dong, S., An, S., Saiding, Q., Chen, Q., Liu, B., Kong, N., Chen, W., Tao, W., 2025. Therapeutic hydrogels: Properties and biomedical applications. Chem. Rev. 125 (18), 8835–8920. https://doi.org/10.1021/acs.chemrev.5c00182.

Elsherbeny, A., Bayraktutan, H., Gumus, N., McCrorie, P., Garcia-Sampedro, A., Parmar, S., Ritchie, A.A., Meakin, M., Oz, U.C., Rahman, R., Ashworth, J.C., Grabowska, A.M., Moloney, C., Alexander, C., 2025. Pentablock thermoresponsive hydrogels for chemotherapeutic delivery in a pancreatic cancer model. Biomater. Sci. 13 (7), 1831–1848. https://doi.org/10.1039/d4bm01629g.

Falcone, N., Ermis, M., Gangrade, A., Choroomi, A., Young, P., Mathes, T.G., Monirizad, M., Zehtabi, F., Mecwan, M., Rodriguez, M., Zhu, Y., Byun, Y., Khademhosseini, A., de Barros, N.R., Kim, H.J., 2024. Drug-eluting shear-thinning hydrogel for the delivery of chemo- and immunotherapeutic agents for the treatment of hepatocellular carcinoma. Adv. Funct. Mater. 34 (8). https://doi.org/10.1002/adfm.202309069.

Filho, D., Guerrero, M., Pariguana, M., Marican, A., Durán-Lara, E.F., 2023. Hydrogel-based microneedle as a drug delivery system. Pharmaceutics 15 (10), 2444. https://doi.org/10.3390/pharmaceutics15102444.

Hajareh Haghighi, F., Binaymotlagh, R., Fratoddi, I., Chronopoulou, L., Palocci, C., 2023. Peptide-hydrogel nanocomposites for anti-cancer drug delivery. Gels 9 (12), 953. https://doi.org/10.3390/gels9120953.

He, J., Li, J., Ren, J., Cao, X., Xu, T., Liang, C., Zhuang, B., Lin, X., Li, N., Xu, B., 2025. A wireless millimeter-scale device for in vivo electromagnetic brain tumor therapy by ultrasound-responsive Ti 3 C 2 T x hydrogel. Adv. Healthcare Mater. 14 (15). https://doi.org/10.1002/adhm.202404918.

Hu, X., Zhang, C., Xiong, Y., Ma, S., Sun, C., Xu, W., 2024. A review of recent advances in drug loading, mathematical modeling and applications of hydrogel drug delivery systems. J. Mater. Sci. 59 (32), 15077–15116. https://doi.org/10.1007/s10853-024-10103-x.

Hu, X., Wang, Y., Zhang, L., Xu, M., Zhang, J., Dong, W., 2018. Design of a pH-sensitive magnetic composite hydrogel based on salecan graft copolymer and Fe3O4@SiO2 nanoparticles as drug carrier. Int. J. Biol. Macromol. 107 (Pt B), 1811–1820. https://doi.org/10.1016/j.ijbiomac.2017.10.043.

Huang, S., Ma, Z., Sun, C., Qi, Z., Li, Z., Wang, S., Yan, Q., Liu, C., Hou, B., Zhang, C., 2022. An injectable thermosensitive hydrogel loaded with a theranostic nanoprobe for synergistic chemo–photothermal therapy for multidrug-resistant hepatocellular carcinoma. J. Mater. Chem. B 10 (15), 2828–2843. https://doi.org/10.1039/d2tb00044j.

Jia, X., Wei, Y., Zhang, X., Gu, Q., Liu, Y., Wang, S., Zhu, C., 2025. Dual-drug loaded γ-polyglutamic acid hydrogel with hydrophilic doxorubicin and hydrophobic camptothecin for enhanced tumor therapy. Chem. Asian J. 20 (18). https://doi.org/10.1002/asia.202500058.

Kasiński, A., Zielińska-Pisklak, M., Oledzka, E., Sobczak, M., 2020. Smart hydrogels – synthetic stimuli-responsive antitumor drug release systems. Int. J. Nanomed. 15, 4541–4572. https://doi.org/10.2147/ijn.s248987.

Kilic Boz, R., Aydin, D., Kocak, S., Golba, B., Rana, S., Sanyal, A., 2022. Redox-responsive hydrogels for tunable and "on-demand" release of biomacromolecules. Bioconjug. Chem. 33 (5), 839–847. https://doi.org/10.1021/acs.bioconjchem.2c00094.

Kim, S., Shin, M., 2022. Role of free catecholamine in thiol-ene crosslinking for hyaluronic acid hydrogels with high loading efficiency of anticancer drugs. Tissue Eng. Regen. Med. 19 (2), 281–287. https://doi.org/10.1007/s13770-021-00388-3.

Krajcer, A., Hinz, A., Bzowska, M., Stankiewicz, S., Słomka, J., Horak, W., Grzywna, E., Lewandowska-Łańcucka, J., 2025. Hydrogel-based implantable system for local delivery of temozolomide in postsurgical brain cancer therapy. Chem. Eng. J. 516, 164175. https://doi.org/10.1016/j.cej.2025.164175.

Kumar, M., Jha, A., Goswami, P., Srivastava, R., Manjit, M., Bharti, K., Koch, B., Mishra, B., 2025. Fabrication of lipid-modified drug nanocrystals loaded injectable hydrogel for breast cancer therapy. Discov. Nano 20 (1). https://doi.org/10.1186/s11671-025-04195-w.

Kumar, P., Wasim, L., Chopra, M., Chhikara, A., 2018. Co-Delivery of vorinostat and etoposide via disulfide cross-linked biodegradable polymeric nanogels: Synthesis, characterization, biodegradation, and anticancer activity. AAPS PharmSciTech 19 (2), 634–647. https://doi.org/10.1208/s12249-017-0863-5.

Li, J., Chen, Q., Li, S., Zeng, X., Qin, J., Li, X., Chen, Z., Zheng, W., Zhao, Y., Huang, Z., Yang, X., Gan, L., 2023. An adhesive hydrogel implant combining chemotherapy and tumor microenvironment remodeling for preventing postoperative recurrence and metastasis of breast cancer. Chem. Eng. J. 473, 145212. https://doi.org/10.1016/j.cej.2023.145212.

Liu, Y., Ma, W., Zhou, P., Wen, Q., Wen, Q., Lu, Y., Zhao, L., Shi, H., Dai, J., Li, J., Fu, S., 2023. In situ administration of temperature-sensitive hydrogel composite loading paclitaxel microspheres and cisplatin for the treatment of melanoma. Biomed. Pharmacother. 160, 114380. https://doi.org/10.1016/j.biopha.2023.114380.

Luanda, A., Mahadev, M., Charyulu, R.N., Badalamoole, V., 2025. Evaluation of dual drug delivery efficiency of nanocomposite hydrogel containing pectin for combating cancer. Polym. Adv. Technol. 36 (3). https://doi.org/10.1002/pat.70118.

Ma, J., Gong, B., Hu, W., Liu, J., Wang, Y., Wang, Z., Yang, X., Wang, X., Yang, H., Yan, G., 2025. Cluster missile-inspired dynamic nanocomposite hydrogel precisely mediates robust locoregional tumor theranostics. Adv. Funct. Mater. 35 (15). https://doi.org/10.1002/adfm.202418295.

Majumder, P., Singh, A., Wang, Z., Dutta, K., Pahwa, R., Liang, C., Andrews, C., Patel, N.L., Shi, J., de Val, N., Walsh, S.T.R., Jeon, A.B., Karim, B., Hoang, C.D., Schneider, J.P., 2021. Surface-fill hydrogel attenuates the oncogenic signature of complex anatomical surface cancer in a single application. Nat. Nanotechnol. 16 (11), 1251–1259. https://doi.org/10.1038/s41565-021-00961-w.

Misra, R., Acharya, S., 2021. Smart nanotheranostic hydrogels for on-demand cancer management. Drug Discov. Today 26 (2), 344–359. https://doi.org/10.1016/j.drudis.2020.11.010.

Mohammadzadeh, V., Atapour-Mashhad, H., Shahvali, S., Salehi, B., Shaban, M., Shirzad, M., Salahvarzi, A., Mohammadi, M., 2025. Hydrogels as advanced drug delivery platforms for cancer immunotherapy: Promising innovations and future outlook. J. Nanobiotechnol. 23 (1). https://doi.org/10.1186/s12951-025-03613-6.

Pacheco, C., Baião, A., Ding, T., Cui, W., Sarmento, B., 2023. Recent advances in long-acting drug delivery systems for anticancer drug. Adv. Drug Deliv. Rev. 194, 114724. https://doi.org/10.1016/j.addr.2023.114724.

Pakian, S., Radmanesh, F., Sadeghi-Abandansari, H., Nabid, M.-reza, 2022. Gelatin-based injectable hydrogel/microgel composite as a combinational dual drug delivery system for local co-delivery of curcumin and 5-fluorouracil in synergistic therapy of colorectal cancer. ACS Appl. Polym. Mater. 4 (11), 8238–8252. https://doi.org/10.1021/acsapm.2c01188.

Park, W., Maeng, S.W., Mok, J.W., Choi, M., Cha, H.J., Joo, C.K., Hahn, S.K., 2023. Hydrogel microneedles extracting exosomes for early detection of colorectal cancer. Biomacromolecules 24 (3), 1445–1452. https://doi.org/10.1021/acs.biomac.2c01449.

Parvaresh, A., Izadi, Z., Nemati, H., Derakhshankhah, H., Jaymand, M., 2023. Redox- and pH-responsive alginate-based magnetic hydrogel: "Smart" drug delivery and protein corona studies. J. Mol. Liq. 382, 121990. https://doi.org/10.1016/j.molliq.2023.121990.

Pechnikova, N.A., Aggeli, A., Latypova, A.A., Iaremenko, A.V., Domvri, K., Zubarev, I.V., Liu, C., Yaremenko, A.V., 2025. Implantable biomaterials for cancer immunotherapies. Adv. Funct. Mater. 35 (10). https://doi.org/10.1002/adfm.202416813.

Qi, X., Wei, W., Li, J., Liu, Y., Hu, X., Zhang, J., Bi, L., Dong, W., 2015. Fabrication and characterization of a novel anticancer drug delivery system: Salecan/poly (methacrylic acid) semi-interpenetrating polymer network hydrogel. ACS Biomater. Sci. Eng. 1 (12), 1287–1299. https://doi.org/10.1021/acsbiomaterials.5b00346.

Sachdev, A., Matai, I., Gopinath, P., 2016. Carbon dots incorporated polymeric hydrogels as multifunctional platform for imaging and induction of apoptosis in lung cancer cells. Colloids Surf. B Biointerfaces 141, 242–252. https://doi.org/10.1016/j.colsurfb.2016.01.043.

Sathi Devi, L., Gigliobianco, M.R., Gabrielli, S., Agas, D., Sabbieti, M.G., Morelli, M.B., Amantini, C., Casadidio, C., Di Martino, P., Censi, R., 2025. Localized cancer treatment using thiol-ene hydrogels for dual drug delivery. Biomacromolecules 26 (5), 3234–3254. https://doi.org/10.1021/acs.biomac.5c00387.

Sheng, Y., Gao, J., Yin, Z.-Z., Kang, J., Kong, Y., 2021. Dual-drug delivery system based on the hydrogels of alginate and sodium carboxymethyl cellulose for colorectal cancer treatment. Carbohydr. Polym. 269, 118325. https://doi.org/10.1016/j.carbpol.2021.118325.

Shi, Y., Wu, Q., Yang, T., Lin, J., Yu, Q., Yao, C., Yang, H., Xu, S., Liang, J., Zhang, C., Liu, J., Zhu, W.-H., Wang, Q., 2026. Temperature-activated in situ hydrogel augments tumor treatment. Biomaterials 326, 123633. https://doi.org/10.1016/j.biomaterials.2025.123633.

Shih, Y.-H., Peng, C.-L., Chiang, P.-F., Chen, C.-T., 2026. Antitumor evaluation of rhenium-188 and paclitaxel codelivered via thermosensitive hydrogel in a hepatocellular carcinoma animal model. Int. J. Mol. Sci. 27 (2), 775. https://doi.org/10.3390/ijms27020775.

Solanki, R., Bhatia, D., 2024. Stimulus-responsive hydrogels for targeted cancer therapy. Gels 10 (7), 440. https://doi.org/10.3390/gels10070440.

Sun, K., Qiu, J., Wang, Y., Han, F., Song, H., Wu, T., Wang, Y., Jiao, W., 2025. Recent advances in hydrogel-based therapeutics for lung cancer. RSC Adv. 15 (55), 47676–47699. https://doi.org/10.1039/d5ra06157a.

Sun, Y., Chen, L.G., Fan, X.M., Pang, J.L., 2022. Ultrasound responsive smart implantable hydrogels for targeted delivery of drugs: Reviewing current practices. Int. J. Nanomed. 17, 5001–5026. https://doi.org/10.2147/IJN.S374247.

Sun, Z., Song, C., Wang, C., Hu, Y., Wu, J., 2020. Hydrogel-based controlled drug delivery for cancer treatment: A review. Mol. Pharm. 17 (2). https://doi.org/10.1021/acs.molpharmaceut.9b01020.

Tang, H., Cheng, X., Liang, L., Chen, B.Z., Liu, C., Wang, Y., 2024a. A stimulus responsive microneedle-based drug delivery system for cancer therapy. Biomater. Sci. 12 (24), 6274–6283. https://doi.org/10.1039/d4bm00741g.

Tang, M., Song, J., Zhang, S., Shu, X., Liu, S., Ashrafizadeh, M., Ertas, Y.N., Zhou, Y., Lei, M., 2024b. Innovative theranostic hydrogels for targeted gastrointestinal cancer treatment. J. Transl. Med. 22 (1). https://doi.org/10.1186/s12967-024-05749-9.

Teng, M., Zhang, L., Fan, Y., Fu, M., Li, Z., 2025. Microneedles loaded with PD-L1 inhibitor and doxorubicin GelMA hydrogel for melanoma immunochemotherapy. Mater. Des. 255, 114238. https://doi.org/10.1016/j.matdes.2025.114238.

Thang, N.H., Chien, T.B., Cuong, D.X., 2023. Polymer-based hydrogels applied in drug delivery: An overview. Gels 9 (7). https://doi.org/10.3390/gels9070523.

Md Uddin, S., Khand, S., Dong, C., 2024. Effect of crosslinking agents on chitosan hydrogel carriers for drug loading and release for targeted drug delivery. Gels 10 (7), 421. https://doi.org/10.3390/gels10070421.

Vu, T.T., Gulfam, M., Jo, S.H., Rizwan, A., Joo, S.B., Lee, B., Park, S.H., Lim, K.T., 2023. The effect of molecular weight and chemical structure of cross-linkers on the properties of redox-responsive hyaluronic acid hydrogels. Int. J. Biol. Macromol. 238. https://doi.org/10.1016/j.ijbiomac.2023.124285.

Wang, F., Chen, J., Liu, J., Zeng, H., 2021. Cancer theranostic platforms based on injectable polymer hydrogels. Biomater. Sci. 9 (10), 3543–3575. https://doi.org/10.1039/d0bm02149k.

Wang, Z., Ye, Q., Yu, S., Akhavan, B., 2023. Poly ethylene glycol (PEG)-Based hydrogels for drug delivery in cancer therapy: A comprehensive review. Adv. Healthcare Mater. 12 (18). https://doi.org/10.1002/adhm.202300105.

Xin, H., Naficy, S., 2022. Drug delivery based on stimuli-responsive injectable hydrogels for breast cancer therapy: A review. Gels 8 (1), 45. https://doi.org/10.3390/gels8010045.

Xu, H., Yang, F., Wang, X., Jiao, W., Jin, Y., 2025. Advances in hydrogel-based delivery of RNA drugs for antitumor therapy. Gels 11 (8), 633. https://doi.org/10.3390/gels11080633.

Xue, B., Wang, W., Qin, J.J., Nijampatnam, B., Murugesan, S., Kozlovskaya, V., Zhang, R., Velu, S.E., Kharlampieva, E., 2017. Highly efficient delivery of potent anticancer iminoquinone derivative by multilayer hydrogel cubes. Acta Biomater. 58, 386–398. https://doi.org/10.1016/j.actbio.2017.06.004.

Yu, Y., Zhao, Y., Zou, Y., Lu, C., Li, N., Shi, Z., Li, X., Lai, X., 2025. Ultra-sensitive pH responsive hydrogels with injectable and self-healing performance for controlled drug delivery. Int. J. Pharm. X 9, 100334. https://doi.org/10.1016/j.ijpx.2025.100334.

Zarrin-Nahand, N., Mardani, H., Roghani-Mamaqani, H., Shahi, S., Abdollahi, M., Salami-Kalajahi, M., 2025. Dual pH- and redox-responsive hydrogel particles as smart carriers for controlled release of doxorubicin. Colloids Surf. A Physicochem. Eng. Asp. 725, 137625. https://doi.org/10.1016/j.colsurfa.2025.137625.

Zhang, Z., He, C., Chen, X., 2024. Designing hydrogels for immunomodulation in cancer therapy and regenerative medicine. Adv. Mater. 36 (4). https://doi.org/10.1002/adma.202308894.

Zhou, Y., Pan, M., Lin, R., Huang, H., 2024. Advances in hydrogel materials applied to pancreatic-related diseases. J. Pancreatol. 7 (3), 222–232. https://doi.org/10.1097/jp9.0000000000000158.

Zhu, L., Qiao, G., Gao, H., Jiang, A., Zhang, L., Wang, X., 2025. Enhancing melanoma therapy with hydrogel microneedles. Front. Oncol. 15. https://doi.org/10.3389/fonc.2025.1590534.

CHAPTER

24

Advances in inorganic nanocarriers for anticancer drug delivery

Moumita Saha[1], Ashutosh Gupta[1, 2], Shivani Kunkalienkar[1], Aditya Dev Rajora[1], Abhishek Sharma[3], Ruchi Chawla[3] and Namdev Dhas[4]

[1]Department of Pharmaceutical Quality Assurance, Manipal College of Pharmaceutical Sciences, Manipal Academy of Higher Education, Manipal, Karnataka, India; [2]Formulation Research & Development–Non Orals, Sun Pharmaceutical Industries Ltd, Vadodara, Gujarat, India; [3]Department of Pharmaceutical Engineering and Technology, Indian Institute of Technology (BHU), Varanasi, Uttar Pradesh, India; [4]Department of Pharmaceutics, Manipal College of Pharmaceutical Sciences, Manipal Academy of Higher Education, Manipal, Karnataka, India

Introduction

In anticancer drug delivery, inorganic nanocarriers offer a flexible and highly advanced approach (Xu et al., 2006). The structural skeleton and physicochemical properties of inorganic nanocarriers allow efficient loading of drugs, systemic circulation behavior, and ideal pharmacological activity. They play a major role in the development of next-generation cancer nanomedicine due to their capacity to integrate targeted therapy, controlled release, and diagnostic imaging. Owing to their distinct physicochemical characteristics, structural adaptability, and multipurpose potential, inorganic nanocarriers have become potent platforms in the delivery of anticancer drugs. Inorganic nanocarriers allow for the targeted, controlled, and stimuli-responsive delivery of anticancer agents, improving therapeutic efficacy while reducing side effects, in contrast to conventional chemotherapy, which has poor selectivity and systemic toxicity. High stability, multifunctionality, accurate size control, and theranostic potential are just a few benefits of inorganic nanocarriers. Surface engineering and thorough safety evaluation are necessary to carefully address issues like long-term toxicity, nonbiodegradability, accumulation in off-target organs, and regulatory obstacles. Their

https://doi.org/10.1016/B978-0-443-44185-1.00033-1

successful use in oncology will depend on ongoing research on biocompatibility, scalable synthesis, and clinical translation. For precise drug delivery, tumor microenvironment-responsive systems can be constructed that can distinguish between normal and tumor sites (Shi et al., 2020a). Tumor tissues vary in growth, proliferation, and metabolism from normal tissues, creating distinct features called the tumor microenvironment (TME), which consists of pathological (such as aberrant vascular structure and receptor overexpression) and biochemical (such as pH, redox potential, enzyme activity, and hypoxia) differences (Wang et al., 2025; Pavlova and Thompson, 2016; Shi et al., 2020a; Wang et al., 2018). These differences can be exploited to target the tumor and achieve precise drug delivery. For example, a pH-sensitive system with ionizable groups or acid-labile bonds that change their character as per H^+ concentration at the tumor site or in cancer cells (Long et al., 2022). The drug delivery systems responsive to reactive oxygen species (ROS), or glutathione, can also be designed using a material responsive to these stimuli (Cheng et al., 2011; de la Rica et al., 2012). Gold nanoparticles (AuNPs), graphene oxide (GO), black phosphorus (BP), and MSNs are a few inorganic nanocarriers that are most frequently studied (Huang et al., 2023). The present chapter primarily introduces various inorganic nanoparticles (INPs), drug loading and release mechanisms, as well as various advances and strategies employed in anticancer drug delivery.

Types of inorganic NPs

INPs are nanoscale materials made of inorganic elements like metals, metal oxides, semiconductors, or carbon-based inorganic structures. They usually range in size from 1 to 100 nm. INPs have garnered a lot of attention in the field of biomedicine, especially in imaging, diagnostics, and drug delivery, due to their small size, large surface-area-to-volume ratio, and distinctive physicochemical properties. The characteristics of INPs are very different from those of their bulk counterparts. These include improved mechanical strength, electrical conductivity, chemical reactivity, magnetic characteristics (superparamagnetism), and optical behavior (surface plasmon resonance). Their functional applications can be further expanded by easily modifying their surfaces with polymers, biomolecules, or targeting ligands. A broad and adaptable class of nanomaterials with distinct size-dependent characteristics is represented by INPs. Their composition-based classification—metal, metal oxide, semiconductor, magnetic, and nonmetal INPs—offers a helpful framework for comprehending their behavior and uses. It is anticipated that further developments in synthesis, surface modification, and toxicity assessment will increase their safe and efficient use, especially in complex biomedical and pharmaceutical applications. Various INPs employed in biomedical applications are shown in Fig. 24.1.

Gold NPs

Gold nanoparticles (AuNPs) are suitable for drug conjugation via thiol or amine linkages. Oxaliplatin-conjugated AuNPs with higher cytotoxicity and uptake demonstrate the way AuNPs improve both delivery and efficacy as drug carriers (Brown et al., 2010). In addition, they are in favor of photothermal therapy (PTT), which uses near-infrared (NIR) radiation to

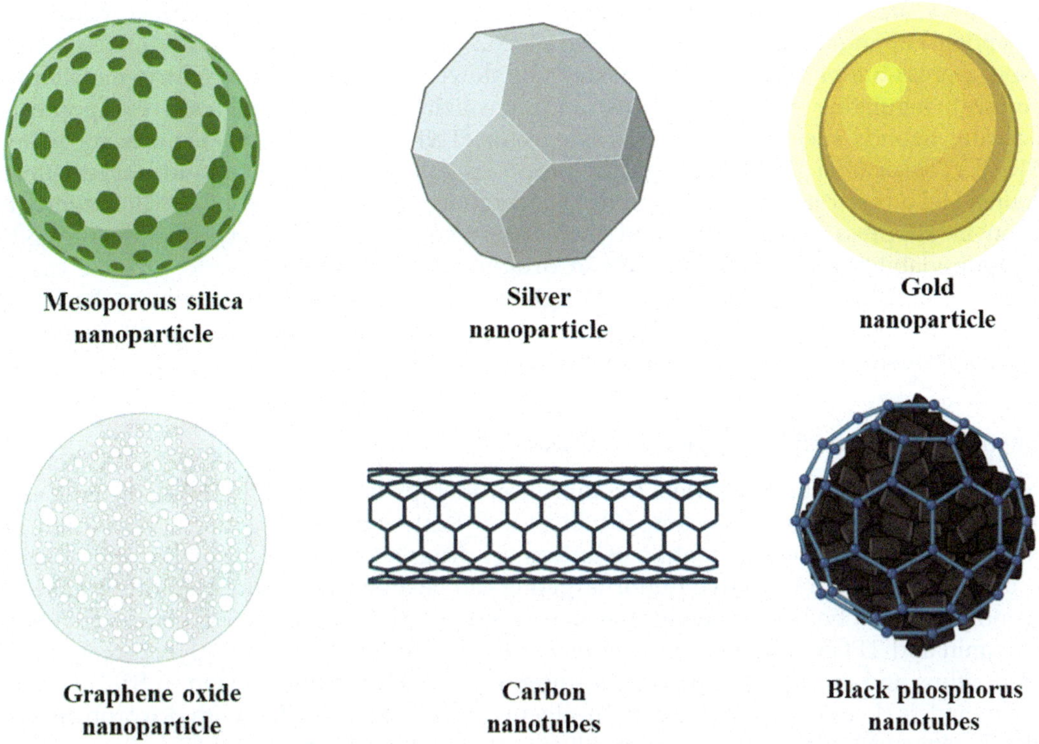

FIGURE 24.1 Pictorial representation of the different types of inorganic nanoparticles.

cause localized tumor ablation. AuNPs are biocompatible and simple to functionalize. AuNPs are used in PTT to selectively ablate tumor cells by absorbing NIR light and producing heat. Experiments have shown that PTT is extremely effective at killing colorectal, fibroblast, and MCF-7 breast cancer cells (Nisha et al., 2024). Through local dose amplification, AuNPs can enhance radiotherapy in vivo, improving tumor control and survival without causing significant damage (Jain et al., 2012). Green synthesis of AuNPs using plant extracts yields biocompatible nanoparticles that can target several tumors. For example, AuNPs derived from Rhus chinensis cause apoptosis in a number of cancer cell lines, while AuNPs derived from *Mangifera indica* seed extract have antiangiogenic qualities (Nisha et al., 2024). Plant-derived AuNPs can exhibit significant anticancer activity by promoting apoptosis through ROS induction and adjustment in apoptotic proteins (Nisha et al., 2024).

Silver NPs

Silver nanoparticles (AgNPs) hold the potential to be used as effective anticancer agents, which possess the intrinsic cytotoxicity and physicochemical structure that enable targeted release, apoptosis induction, and cell signaling modulation. AgNPs induce ROS generation, resulting in oxidative stress, DNA damage, and impairment in the mitochondria, resulting in cell cycle arrest and activation of intrinsic (caspase-9 dependent) and extrinsic (caspase-8 dependent) apoptotic pathways (Takáč et al., 2023; Kanipandian and Ramesh, 2024). They also suppress tumor growth and metastasis by downregulating MMPs (matrix metalloproteinases), regulating p53 and cyclins, and sensitizing drug-resistant cells to apoptosis-inducing ligands such as tumor necrosis factor (TNF)-related apoptosis-inducing ligand (TRAIL) (Takáč et al., 2023). Biologically produced AgNPs exhibit potent anticancer effects against HeLa cervical cancer through ROS generation, DNA damage, and MMP downregulation to suppress proliferation and metastasis (Xu et al., 2020). Hybrid silver–AgNPs decrease viability and affect cell cycle in drug-resistant glioblastoma and prostate cancer (Takáč et al., 2023). Drug conjugation of AgNPs with methotrexate, doxorubicin, Paclitaxel (PTX), and imatinib improves targeted delivery, cytotoxicity, and safety by functional groups like carboxyl, hydroxyl, and amine (Gomes et al., 2021).

Mesoporous silica nanoparticles (MSNs)

MSNs are excellent nanocarriers for anticancer therapy because of their tunable pore size, large surface area, high biocompatibility, and facile functionalization. MSNs can be exploited for effective encapsulation of anticancer drugs such as PTX, cisplatin, and doxorubicin within their pores. Active tumor targeting can be attained by surface modification using polymers, antibodies, or ligands (such as folic acid). PTX-loaded MSNs codelivered with curcumin and TPGS promoted intracellular drug deposition, blocked P-glycoprotein-facilitated efflux, and promoted apoptosis, leading to better tumor suppression in B16F10 melanoma models (Lee et al., 2025). Hierarchically organized MSNs loaded with doxorubicin and siRNA against P-glycoprotein successfully reversed drug resistance, and 87% tumor inhibition was observed in vivo with respect to 50.7% by free drug, through suppression of multidrug resistance proteins and minimized systemic toxicity (Esa et al., 2025). PEGylated and tannic acid–functionalized MSNs (MSN-PEG/TA 25) exhibited strong antimetastatic activities in 4T1 breast cancer models by suppressing lung metastasis, blocking endothelial tube formation, and regulating cancer cell migration, with combined treatment with liposomal doxorubicin enhancing survival (Lee et al., 2024b). Polydopamine-functionalized MSNs with intracellularly loaded umbelliprenin triggered programmed cell death in vitro, validating the efficacy of surface functionalization in targeted therapy (Edalatian Tavakoli et al., 2024). For regulated medication release in the tumor microenvironment, MSNs can also be designed with pH-, redox-, or enzyme-responsive gatekeepers.

Iron oxide NPs

Iron oxide nanoparticles (IONPs) have come into focus in anticancer treatment because of their multifaceted features, such as magnetic responsiveness, compatibility with living organisms, and simplicity of surface modification. IONPs are used in magnetic fluid hyperthermia (MFH), wherein alternating magnetic fields heat nanoparticles localized inside tumors to kill cancer cells. Improved survival has been observed with MFH, although problems persist with optimizing delivery and dose. IONPs can also be used to activate antitumor immunity, such as starch-coated IONPs (ferumoxytol), which polarize macrophages to the proinflammatory M1 phenotype, increase T cell invasion, and inhibit the growth of tumors, evidencing their ability to control innate and adaptive immune responses (Soetaert et al., 2020). Iron oxide nanoparticles (IONs) are also very useful in magnetically guided delivery of drugs due to their versatility in surface functionalization. In breast cancer, drug, antibody, or nucleotide-conjugated IONPs are theranostic agents, offering targeted delivery of drugs, improved MRI contrast, and magnetic targeting for HER2-positive tumors (Kumar et al., 2022). IONPs further utilize ferroptosis, an iron-dependent regulated cell death with lipid peroxidation and ROS production, to make drug-resistant cancer cells extremely vulnerable. This action, in concert with magnetic drug targeting, increases tumor specificity and therapeutic effect (Shubhra, 2023). Silver-doped iron oxide (Ag–Fe_3O_4) nanoparticles also exhibit synergistic anticancer activity and can promote apoptosis and ROS-mediated cytotoxicity in lung cancer cells. These works highlight the versatility of IONPs as multifunctional nanoplatforms for imaging, targeted treatment, immune modulation, and new cell death mechanisms, placing them as very promising candidates for future cancer treatment platforms (Abdelghany et al., 2025).

Quantum dots

Quantum dots (QDs) are tunable nanomaterials with special optical and physicochemical properties, allowing applications in imaging, drug delivery, photodynamic therapy (PDT), and cancer stem cell (CSC) targeting. Ligand-conjugated QDs targeting CSC markers such as CD44 or CD24 deliver PDT selectively and induce ROS upon laser stimulation to overcome chemoresistance and suppress tumor relapse in breast cancer models. CdTe QDs conjugated with anti-CD22 antibodies and encapsulated with doxorubicin and gambogic acid selectively localize in cancer cells, inducing apoptosis through BAX/caspase-3 in lymphoma. Multimodal platforms, such as graphene QDs coupled with magnetic nanospheres and silica shells, integrate PDT, PTT, chemotherapy, and mechanical disturbance to enhance ROS-mediated apoptosis in different cancer cells (Mofokeng et al., 2025). In vivo, biomimetic cancer cell membrane-coated BP QDs support tumor-targeted PTT and anti-PD-L1 immunotherapy, enhancing immune response and fluorescence imaging and inhibiting tumor growth and metastasis (Hamidu et al., 2023). Peptide- and folic acid–functionalized nucleus-targeted graphene QDs selectively accumulate in cancer cell nuclei, cause DNA damage, and induce upregulation of apoptosis-related proteins, effectively inhibiting tumor growth (Qi et al., 2021). Furthermore, nitrogen-phosphorus doped carbon QDs show effective cellular uptake, apoptosis induction, and fluorescent imaging in melanoma cells, and this potential of theirs is pointed out as promising for combined diagnostic and therapeutic ("theranostic") applications (Devi et al., 2022).

Carbon nanotubes

Carbon nanotubes (CNTs), both single-walled CNTs (SWCNTs) and multiwalled CNTs (MWCNTs), have shown immense promise as anticancer drugs and drug delivery vehicles because of their high surface area, biocompatibility, and effective cellular uptake. SWCNTs have been used to deliver chemotherapy drugs such as PTX, doxorubicin, curcumin, survivin siRNA, and gemcitabine to lung cancer cells, with surface engineering such as chitosan and hyaluronic acid (HA) improving targeting and biocompatibility. For example, SWCNTs loaded with survivin siRNA caused apoptosis by suppressing the antiapoptotic protein survivin, whereas MWCNTs coupled with GO and antibodies transported cisplatin and methotrexate to drug-resistant lung cancer cells and reversed resistance via EMT modulation as well as enhancing tumor inhibition in vivo (Boraei et al., 2025). CNTs also make possible new therapeutic approaches beyond classical drug delivery. Photoactivated SWCNTs treated with picosecond laser pulses cause nonthermal mechanical disruption of cancer cells with precise theranostic tumor ablation (Golubewa et al., 2020). Magnetically controlled CNTs tagged with anti-CD44 antibodies mechanically disrupt drug-resistant glioblastoma cells under rotational magnetic fields, representing a nonchemical therapy with low toxicity (Sabir et al., 2025). Further, CNTs are multifunctional platforms for synergistic PTT, PDT, gene therapy, immunotherapy, and chemotherapy by leveraging their high surface area for synergistic effects (Alfei et al., 2025). Molecular dynamics simulation validates strong doxorubicin binding to CNTs, validating their efficacy as good nanocarriers that enhance pharmacokinetics and minimize side effects, underscoring their extensive potential in new cancer therapies (Zheoat et al., 2025).

Metal-organic frameworks (MOFs)

Metal-organic frameworks (MOFs) have appeared as promising anticancer platforms because of their porosity, structural tunability, biodegradability, and large drug loadability. Copper-based MOFs (Cu-MOFs) prepared using glutarate and 1,2-bis (4-pyridyl)ethane linkers exhibited robust cytotoxicity against cell lines of ovarian cancer (SKOV3, U87, LN229) through ROS-mediated apoptosis by Cu (II) interaction with cancer cell membranes, with an IC50 of 12.5 μg/mL in SKOV3 cells within 24 h (Han et al., 2022). Aqueous-medium-synthesized aluminum-based MOFs (Al-MOFs) exhibited increased antiproliferative activities toward breast cancer cells with good biocompatibility, which favors their application as drugs or drug carriers (Zeraati et al., 2021). Bimetallic Ti/Fe MOFs embedded in pH-responsive injectable hydrogels and Au NP-decorated were used to provide multifunctional anticancer therapy for models of breast cancer by combining chemotherapy with sonodynamic (SDT), chemodynamic therapy (CDT), and starvation therapy (ST), inducing ROS and oxygen radicals under ultrasound irradiation for increased killing of tumor cells in vitro and in vivo (Kush et al., 2025). MOFs have also been combined with photosensitizers for PDT to enhance ROS utilization, hydrophilicity, tumor targeting, and deep tissue penetration by upconversion nanoparticles (UCNPs) (Abodunrin et al., 2025). Moreover, MOFs of high pore size and biocompatible surface functionalization have been prepared for the treatment of oral cancer, maximizing drug encapsulation, cellular uptake, and release to enhance therapeutic efficiency (Shaji and Saravanan, 2024).

Drug loading mechanism and targeting strategies

Inorganic nanocarriers, such as MSNs and MOFs, employ multiple mechanisms to load drugs. Physical adsorption and encapsulation take advantage of the high surface area and pore volume of these carriers to immobilize hydrophilic or hydrophobic drugs without disrupting their chemical structure (Yao et al., 2020). Chemical conjugation or coordination enables drugs to become covalently linked or form a metal–drug coordination bond with the functional groups on the nanoparticle surface, facilitating stimuli-responsive release in tumor-specific conditions, such as acidic pH, high glutathione, enzymes, temperature, or outside stimuli such as light, ultrasound, or magnetic fields, enabling preferential drug delivery to tumor tissues (Edis et al., 2021; Shi et al., 2020b). Drug release is usually in a controlled manner that permits a slow release of the drug from the pores or surfaces (Ghosn et al., 2019). Carrier degradation by enzymatic or hydrolytic action also allows the release of the encapsulated or conjugated drugs from INPs (Kush et al., 2025). Other external triggers, such as alternating magnetic fields or photothermal/photodynamic stimulation, also enhance drug release, enabling targeted delivery and local cytotoxicity for anticancer action at the site (Rahimkhoei et al., 2024).

Targeted inorganic nanocarriers can facilitate maximum accumulation of anticancer drugs selectively in tumors, thereby avoiding systemic toxicity. Passive targeted inorganic nanocarriers exploit enhanced permeability and retention (EPR) effect to accumulate preferentially within a tumor due to leaky vasculature and poor lymphatic drainage (Bhattacharyya et al., 2011). Active targeted inorganic nanocarriers surface-functionalized with ligands such as antibodies, peptides, aptamers, folic acid, or transferrin gain entry into cells through receptor-mediated endocytosis (Sun et al., 2021). Microenvironment-responsive inorganic nanosystems release drugs in response to acidic pH, elevated glutathione, enzymes, or hypoxia, ensuring localized action (Sun et al., 2023). Biomimetic coatings such as cancer cell membranes or stealth polymers like PEG extend circulation, avoid immune clearance, and enhance homotypic targeting (Zhang et al., 2022). Magnetic nanoparticles can enable external field-guided delivery to the target site and hyperthermia, resulting in a multimodal system with targeting capability, real-time imaging, and anticancer action (Sun et al., 2021).

Recent advances in inorganic nanocarriers

Inorganic nanocarriers represent a rapidly evolving frontier in drug delivery, offering distinct advantages over traditional organic systems due to their inherent stability, tunable surface chemistry, and robust structural properties. Recent studies have been utilizing the unique characteristics of new materials, including gold nanoparticles, MSNs, magnetic nanoparticles, and QDs for the design of highly tailored and multifunctional delivery systems (Unnikrishnan et al., 2023). Such innovations can drive the design of the next-generation biocompatible nanosystems with high drug payload potential, site-selective and stimuli-responsive release, imaging, diagnostics, and anticancer action.

Ultrasmall-sized inorganic nanocarriers

The development of ultrasmall nanoparticles (particularly under 6 nm in size) is an important strategy to tackle long-term toxicity, as this size enables renal clearance. Such particles can cross the kidney glomerular filtration barrier, thereby preventing long-term accumulation in the liver and spleen. For instance, ultrasmall zwitterionic ligand-coated iron oxide nanoparticles (Fe_3O_4@DMSA), with hydrodynamic sizes below 6 nm, have been designed (Lee et al., 2024a). Similarly, glutathione-coated gold nanoparticles (2–3 nm) used in imaging have demonstrated excellent safety profiles in early human clinical trials, showing less than 50% retention in organs and over 50% excretion through urine within 24 h (Li et al., 2023). Peng et al. systematically framed this concept in the context of "renal-clearable nanocarriers", highlighting that ultrasmall inorganic platforms such as QDs, silica "C-dots", carbon dots, and noble metal nanoclusters can achieve high tumor-–to–background ratios together with >50%–80% injected dose cleared via urine within 24–48 h (Peng et al., 2020). A key advance has been the engineering of ultrasmall gold nanocarriers and coordination polymer nanodots that couple deep tumor penetration with therapeutic functionality. Long-circulating ultrasmall Au nanocarriers (≈5 nm core, ~20 nm hydrodynamic size) functionalized for pH-sensitive doxorubicin release showed up to 8% injected dose accumulating in tumors and homogeneous intratumoral distribution, markedly improving efficacy without obvious off-target toxicity (Lee et al., 2017). More recently, an intratumoral self-assembly strategy using renal-clearable AuNPs (<3 nm) achieved precise photothermal–chemotherapy of liver tumors: two complementary AuNP populations, bearing cyclodextrin/RGD and adamantane/doxorubicin, self-assembled only in the tumor microenvironment, boosting NIR absorption, enhancing tumor uptake (>10% ID/g) and enabling potent ablation while maintaining extremely low nonspecific liver accumulation and rapid renal excretion (Yuan et al., 2025). Ultrasmall lanthanide-based nanodots further illustrate how size control below ~4 nm can be leveraged for tumor-targeted theranostics. HA–functionalized $NaGdF_4$ nanodots (~3.8 nm) combined active CD44 targeting with renal clearance; in a breast cancer model, they reached ~5.3% ID/g tumor accumulation at 2 h postinjection while ~75% of the injected dose was eliminated in urine within 24 h, with negligible histological toxicity (Yan et al., 2020). Collectively, these studies indicate that ultrasmall inorganic nanocarriers can overcome the classical trade-off between deep penetration and safe clearance. By operating in the "small-size EPR" regime and integrating tumor-specific ligands or stimuli-responsive assembly, they enable efficient intratumoral delivery, reduced off-target burden, and a more favorable safety profile, positioning them as promising candidates for next-generation anticancer nanomedicines (Mosleh-Shirazi et al., 2021).

Biocompatible and biodegradable inorganic nanocarriers

The biocompatibility and safety of inorganic nanocarriers are critical for clinical translation and can be achieved through various engineered materials. The surface modification of INPs with materials such as polyethylene glycol (PEG) and other biodegradable polymers helps to minimize recognition by the immune system, reduce the nonspecific adsorption of proteins (opsonization), and considerably extend the systemic circulation. A noteworthy example is IONPs, ferumoxytol, which have a carbohydrate shell that lessens immune recognition, thereby improving blood residence time and, as a result, usefulness in drug delivery, and contrasts with MRI associatively (Suk et al., 2016). PEGylated gold nanoparticles (AuNPs) have enhanced cancer treatment by improving particle stability, enabling targeted therapeutic delivery, and reducing opsonization. Overall, such surface engineering techniques substantially reduce the immune system's ability to clear the nanoparticles, thereby improving the pharmacokinetic behavior of the nanoparticles and advancing the clinical translation of safe, biocompatible inorganic nanocarrier systems (Singh et al., 2025). The assumption that gold nanoparticles (AuNPs) remain biochemically inert in tissues has been fundamentally challenged by recent transcriptomics and ultrastructural studies demonstrating authentic intracellular biodegradation over months. Primary human fibroblasts exposed to citrate-coated AuNPs (4–22 nm diameter) undergo a two-stage biotransformation: initial NADPH oxidase (NOX)-mediated ROS attack in lysosomes dissolves the nanoparticle core into Au^{+} ionic species, followed by unexpected recrystallization into well-defined 2.5-nm nanoleaves self-assembled via metallothionein (MT) chelation. Transcriptomics reveals sustained upregulation (through 2 months) of genes encoding NADPH production, heme oxidase-1, glutathione metabolism, and MT synthesis, a coordinated response to gold degradation products unobservable in short-term studies (Balfourier et al., 2020).

The FDA has designated biodegradable silica as "Generally Recognized as Safe". Cornell dots based on silica started clinical trials for drug delivery and imaging in humans. To achieve controlled nontoxic degradability into the biologically safe and easily cleared (by the body) silicic acid, recent studies concentrated on tuning the chemical composition of the MSNs (Huq et al., 2025). Due to their biocompatibility, high drug loading capacity, and low risk of accumulation, MSNs are rapidly being advanced as multifunctional platforms in Phases I and II clinical trials (Liu et al., 2025). Calcium phosphate (CaP) nanoparticles represent the most extensively validated biodegradable inorganic platform for anticancer applications, leveraging their similarity to natural bone mineral (hydroxyapatite) as both an advantage and a degradation control mechanism. The fundamental innovation is engineering distinct crystallographic phases, each with quantitatively different pH-dependent solubility, to enable triggered release within the acidic tumor microenvironment (pH 4.5–6.0) while maintaining stability in circulation (pH 7.4) (Khalifehzadeh and Arami, 2020). IONPs, predominantly magnetite (Fe_3O_4) and maghemite (γ-Fe_2O_3), represent a distinct biodegradable paradigm leveraging iron's essential but strictly regulated biological metabolism. Rather than being cleared intact, IONPs are degraded intracellularly via an iron-dependent ferroptosis mechanism that is amplified in the acidic, redox-active tumor microenvironment. Within lysosomes, intralysosomal pH (~4.5) and the Warburg effect-associated metabolic state of tumor cells create conditions favoring Fenton chemistry: released ferrous/ferric ions (Fe^{2+}/Fe^{3+}) catalyze cyclic Haber–Weiss reactions that generate hydroxyl radicals from endogenous hydrogen peroxide, overwhelming cellular antioxidant defenses and triggering lipid peroxidation-mediated ferroptotic cell death (Shestovskaya et al., 2023). The biodegradability of inorganic nanocarriers is crucial for their clinical translation and long-term safety. CaP systems undergo complete degradation and metabolic clearance within 2–4 weeks, making them suitable for repeated or chronic dosing without concerns of metal accumulation. IONPs exhibit intermediate clearance kinetics, with hepatic iron levels reaching a transient plateau and returning to baseline within 8–12 weeks through normal iron metabolism. In contrast, MSNs and gold nanoparticles (AuNPs) show much slower, RES-mediated clearance over months to years, with limited renal elimination of very small fragments. This biodegradation hierarchy directly influences dosing strategies: degradable systems such as CaP and IONPs allow frequent dosing schedules, whereas more persistent platforms like MSNs and AuNPs are generally restricted to single or infrequent administrations (Zhou et al., 2020).

Receptor-targeted inorganic nanocarriers

Cancer involves complex molecular interactions that drive abnormal cellular activity. The receptors involved in the mechanism of cancer are epidermal growth factor receptor (EGFR), folate receptor, transferrin receptor, integrins, mucin-1 (MUC1), CD44, hormone receptors, and programmed death-1 receptor (PD-1). Dysregulation of these receptors can lead to cell proliferation, survival, and immune evasion. The development of targeted therapies that show promise for more efficient and individualized tumor treatment is based on this concept (Cheng et al., 2025). Receptor-mediated targeting of inorganic nanocarriers has emerged as a key strategy for improving the selectivity of anticancer drug delivery by integrating the physicochemical advantages of inorganic cores with molecular recognition of overexpressed tumor receptors. In recent years, mesoporous silica, gold, iron oxide, and other metal-based nanoparticles have been extensively functionalized with targeting ligands such as folic acid, RGD/iRGD peptides, and antibodies against HER2 or EGFR to promote active tumor homing, enhanced cellular uptake, and deeper tissue penetration beyond the passive EPR effect. Mechanistically, these systems exploit high-affinity ligand–receptor interactions that trigger receptor clustering and receptor-mediated endocytosis (clathrin- or caveolae-dependent), followed by controlled drug release in response to acidic pH or enzymatically active tumor microenvironments (Fan et al., 2023). Slavkova et al. developed MSNs with pore volume (1.38 cm^3/g) for MCF-7 breast cancer cells. The observation showed that the doxorubicin-loaded MSNs and the folic acid-conjugated doxorubicin-loaded MSNs caused moderate cytotoxicity. Doxorubicin accumulation has been detected by fluorescence-based analysis. These results all showed the potential of MSNs for the treatment of breast cancer (Slavkova et al., 2026). Machado et al. developed gemcitabine (GEM)-loaded and folate (FA)-conjugated calcium phosphate nanoparticles (CaP NPs) for the treatment of FRα-overexpressing cancer cell lines (MCF-7, MDA-MB-231, HeLa). The developed CaP NPs exhibited pH-responsive degradation and controlled release. The GEM-loaded CaP NPs demonstrated cytotoxicity in the FRα-overexpressing cancer cell lines. The FA conjugated NPs showed less toxicity in the hMSCs without compromising the anticancer activity. These observations demonstrated the potential of FA-conjugated and GEM-loaded CaP NPs for the treatment of breast cancer (Machado et al., 2026). Integrin-targeted gold nanocarriers represent a well-established example of receptor-driven inorganic nanomedicine for combined chemo-photothermal therapy. Gold nanorods (AuNRs) and nanospheres have been functionalized with the cyclic RGDfK (cRGDfK) peptide to selectively recognize αvβ3/β5 integrins, which are highly expressed on angiogenic tumor endothelium and invasive cancer cells, and concurrently loaded with a peptidylarginine deiminase 4 (PAD4) inhibitor to suppress neutrophil extracellular trap formation and tumor metastasis. Both in vitro and in vivo studies demonstrated that cRGDfK-modified AuNRs achieved significantly higher cellular uptake than nontargeted systems, while chemophotothermal combination therapy (PAD4 inhibition coupled with NIR irradiation) resulted in pronounced suppression of primary tumor growth, reduced lung metastasis, and decreased inflammatory infiltration compared to monotherapies, without notable systemic toxicity. Mechanistically, RGD-mediated integrin binding promoted efficient nanoparticle internalization and endosomal trafficking, whereas photothermal heating enhanced vascular permeability and intratumoral drug penetration, highlighting the synergistic roles of receptor targeting and photothermal effects in therapeutic efficacy (Lu et al., 2021). Receptor-targeted inorganic nanocarriers enhance the specificity and efficacy of anticancer therapy by enabling active tumor targeting and improved cellular uptake. These systems represent a promising strategy to overcome the limitations of passive nanomedicine and advance precision cancer treatment.

Stimuli-responsive inorganic nanocarriers

Numerous biological applications have been enabled by nanocarriers, which can alter their properties in response to endogenous or external stimuli. One such use is the controlled release of drugs at the intended spot, eliminating adverse effects in healthy tissue that surrounds it. These stimuli-responsive nanocarriers have garnered significant attention from research teams worldwide in recent years for their potential in targeted drug delivery. A hydrophobic inner core and a hydrophilic or amphilic outer shell, typically an amphilic stimulus-responsive polymer sensitive to a number of endogenous or external stimuli, are the typical elements of stimuli-responsive nanocarriers. The inorganic nanocarrier demonstrated stimulus-responsive cancer treatment, including H, redox, temperature, light, enzyme, and magnetic responsiveness. A common approach for controlled drug delivery involves functionalizing MSNs with pH-sensitive coatings or linkers, enabling minimal drug release at physiological pH (7.4) while promoting rapid release in the mildly acidic tumor microenvironment (pH 6.5–6.8) and highly acidic endo/lysosomal compartments (pH 4.5–5.5). Chang et al. developed a targeted pH-responsive system (DOX@MSN-PEI-AA) by loading doxorubicin into carboxylated MSNs and sequentially modifying the surface with polyethyleneimine (PEI) and anisamide (AA) to target sigma receptor–overexpressing breast cancer cells. This system exhibited high drug loading, negligible leakage at pH 7.4, and significantly enhanced DOX release at pH 5.0 because of PEI protonation and weakened electrostatic interactions, resulting in improved cytotoxicity in MCF-7 cells and effective in vivo tumor suppression with minimal systemic toxicity (Chang et al., 2022; Racles et al., 2022). Manganese dioxide (MnO_2) nanostructures represent redox-responsive inorganic platforms that exploit the elevated glutathione (GSH) and ROS levels in tumors for degradable theranostic applications. Chen et al. developed HA–functionalized MnO_2 nanosheets that were both pH- and redox-responsive, enabling targeted cancer therapy and imaging. Under reductive and mildly acidic tumor-like conditions, the MnO_2 nanosheets decomposed into Mn^{2+}, leading to H_2O_2 consumption, hypoxia modulation, and triggered drug release, while the HA coating facilitated CD44-mediated cellular uptake and enhanced tumor accumulation in vivo (Brito et al., 2023). Calcium carbonate ($CaCO_3$) nanoparticles have been widely explored as highly sensitive tumor pH sensors due to their rapid dissolution in mildly acidic tumor environments compared with neutral physiological conditions. Although initially developed for imaging and sensing applications, this pH-responsive behavior can also be effectively exploited for triggered drug release in $CaCO_3$-based inorganic nanocarriers (Dong et al., 2016). A recent study reported dual pH-responsive CaP nanoparticles stabilized with carboxymethyl cellulose (CMC), in which gemcitabine was covalently conjugated to CMC and the system was further coated with a silica shell and functionalized with folic acid (CaP–CMC–GEM/SiO_2–FA). The formulation exhibited minimal gemcitabine release at physiological pH (7.4) but nearly complete (100%) release under endolysosomal pH (4.5), attributed to CaP core dissolution and acid-triggered CMC–GEM bond cleavage. In folate receptor–overexpressing cancer cells, these nanoparticles showed enhanced receptor-mediated uptake and selective cytotoxicity, while folate modification significantly reduced toxicity toward normal mesenchymal stem cells, highlighting the synergistic advantages of pH responsiveness and receptor targeting in inorganic CaP-based nanocarriers (Machado et al., 2026). A core–shell Au@carbon/calcium phosphate (Au@C/CaP) nanostructure was developed to integrate pH- and NIR–triggered drug release with X-ray CT imaging and combined chemophotothermal therapy. The gold core and carbon interlayer enabled efficient photothermal conversion and strong X-ray attenuation, while the CaP shell acted as a pH-sensitive drug reservoir. These nanoparticles remained stable and retained drugs at physiological pH but exhibited rapid drug release and significant heat generation under acidic conditions and NIR irradiation, resulting in synergistic cancer cell killing through combined chemotherapy and photothermal effects, demonstrating the potential of multistimuli-responsive inorganic hybrids for precise cancer therapy (Wang et al., 2017).

Combination strategies

This strategy involves the use of inorganic nanocarriers with other anticancer agents, such as drugs, genes, proteins, peptides, and antibodies, to receive additional or synergistic anticancer effects. It can address the limitations of single-drug treatments, overcome drug resistance, and avoid cancer relapse. Inorganic nanocarriers, owing to their large surface areas and high surface functionality, can be structurally modified to accommodate and deliver multiple therapeutic agents within a single system.

Dual–drug delivery

The inorganic carriers can be designed to encapsulate two different drugs that act on distinct biochemical pathways within cancer cells. By delivering two drugs together at a precisely controlled ratio directly to the tumor site, inorganic nanocarriers can achieve synergistic effects, resulting in markedly higher tumor cell death than single-drug treatments. Vivero-Escoto et al. developed MSNs coloaded with cisplatin and phthalocyanine for combination-based anticancer therapy. The cytotoxicity study of the optimized formulation demonstrated that, after light exposure, it showed a toxic effect on HeLa cells compared with the other free groups. These observations demonstrate the potential of MSNs as an inorganic nanocarrier for the treatment of cancer (Vivero-Escoto and Elnagheeb, 2015). Mehnath et al. developed chrysin- and cisplatin-coloaded nanoparticles for the treatment of oral cancer. The cytotoxic potential of the nanoparticle was at a 25 $\mu g\ mL^{-1}$ concentration. The chrysin caused mitochondrial dysfunction and generated ROS. The nanoformulation has demonstrated 92% tumor volume regression compared with cisplatin alone (Mehnath et al., 2018). Inorganic–polymer hybrid systems have been explored for the codelivery of cytotoxic drugs and chemosensitizers to overcome multidrug resistance. For instance, poly (lactide-co-glycolic acid) (PLGA) nanoparticles coencapsulating vincristine and the P-glycoprotein inhibitor verapamil demonstrated reduced systemic toxicity and enhanced tumor inhibition compared with free drugs or nonnanoparticulate combinations, by ensuring simultaneous cellular delivery at a fixed synergistic ratio (Yang et al., 2022). Similar dual–drug PLGA formulations coloading cisplatin with irinotecan or PTX with thymoquinone achieved sustained co-release and significantly improved cytotoxicity against prostate and breast cancer cells, highlighting the therapeutic advantage of synchronized delivery of mechanistically complementary agents (Gong et al., 2023). Similarly, a PEGylated poly (α-lipoic acid) (mPEG-PαLA) nanocarrier, which can chelate metal ions and form an inorganic–organic hybrid structure, was used to coload PTX and doxorubicin for osteosarcoma treatment. The dual–drug nanoparticles (NP-PTX-DOX) showed efficient cellular uptake, reduction/pH-triggered intracellular release, and synergistic apoptosis in K7 osteosarcoma cells, with significantly higher tumor accumulation (about 1.4-fold higher fluorescence vs. free DOX) and stronger tumor growth inhibition in mice than single-drug or free-drug controls. These results indicate that a dual-responsive nanocarrier can markedly enhance combination chemotherapy efficacy in solid tumors (Li et al., 2020).

Codelivery of drugs and genes

Inorganic nanocarriers such as MSNs can be engineered to enable dual-therapeutic delivery. This can be achieved by loading the anticancer drug within the pores of MSN while simultaneously conjugating nucleic acid, such as siRNA or plasmids, on the particle's surface. This novel system combines chemotherapy with gene silencing to counteract drug resistance in various cancer models. It has shown promising results in early clinical studies and in translational research aimed at cancer treatment (Ul Khaliq et al., 2023; Eljack et al., 2022). MSNs have been designed for the codelivery of chemotherapy agent doxorubicin within the mesopores and siRNA for targeting drug resistance genes such as Bcl-2, on the nanoparticles' surface (Chen et al., 2009). MSN has also integrated gene silencing agents with other anticancer drugs such as epirubicin and p53-containing plasmids, which resulted in greater tumor inhibition than when single agents were used, confirming the potential of MSNs for integrated gene and drug therapies in oncological care (Park et al., 2025; Paris and Vallet-Regí, 2020; Hanafi-Bojd et al., 2016). A CaP–polymeric nanoparticle platform was engineered to codeliver a microRNA-21 inhibitor (anti-miR-21) together with doxorubicin for breast and nonsmall cell lung cancer therapy. The CaP shell electrostatically complexed the negatively charged miR-21 inhibitor, while DOX was encapsulated in the polymeric core; acidic tumor/endosomal pH-triggered CaP dissolution and promoted release of both cargos into the cytosol. Codelivery significantly downregulated miR-21, restored expression of tumor-suppressor targets, and produced markedly higher cytotoxicity and apoptosis than DOX alone or miR-21 inhibitor alone, indicating synergistic chemo–gene effects and partial reversal of chemoresistance (Sriram and Lee, 2021). Similarly, a gold-based nanocarrier was designed for the simultaneous delivery of Bcl-2 siRNA and doxorubicin to overcome antiapoptotic signaling in solid tumors. In this construct, Dox was intercalated or conjugated to the gold surface, while Bcl-2 siRNA was complexed via cationic linkers, yielding stable nanoconjugates with efficient cellular uptake and endosomal escape. In Bcl-2-overexpressing cancer cells, the nanocarrier effectively knocked down Bcl-2 expression and enhanced Dox-induced apoptosis, leading to significantly greater growth inhibition and caspase activation than either free DOX, free siRNA, or single-cargo nanoparticles, highlighting gold-mediated chemo–gene codelivery as a potent strategy to sensitize resistant tumors (Tunç and Aydin, 2022).

Theragnostic and multimodal inorganic nanosystems

Preclinical investigations are increasingly centered on combining therapeutic functions—such as drug delivery, PTT, and PDT—with advanced diagnostic imaging techniques, including MRI, PET, and fluorescence imaging, within a single platform (Alsaab et al., 2020). As examples, gold nanoparticles (AuNPs) are a multifunctional system for codelivery of chemotherapeutic and gene-silencing agents for synergistic effects, while acting as UCNPs to improve treatment by enhancing PDT (Zhuang et al., 2025). Inorganic nanocarriers, including nanoparticles of gold, iron oxide, QDs, and MSNs, allow real-time tracking of drug biodistribution and therapeutic effect using imaging methods such as MRI, CT, fluorescence, or photoacoustic imaging, thus enhancing treatment accuracy and efficacy (Lin et al., 2016).

Chemophotothermal/photodynamic therapy (PTT/PDT)

Building on the chemophotothermal/photodynamic therapy (PTT/PDT) approach, INPs, such as gold nanoparticles (AuNPs), represent a prime clinical example. AuNPs can be loaded with chemotherapeutic drugs and activated by NIR light to generate localized heat that effectively ablates tumor tissue while accelerating drug release, thereby achieving synergistic anticancer effects. Zeho et al. discussed the effect of PDT and PTT on cancer treatment. PDT works by photosensitizers generating ROS to kill cancer cells. PTT works by photothermal heating and kills cancer cells. The combination of PDT and PTT, along with the anticancer drug, can lead to a better cancer treatment strategy. This mechanism demonstrates the potential of combination therapy for cancer treatment (Zhao et al., 2025). A recent study reported a gold nanocage–based nanosystem in which the Au cage itself acted as the photothermal/photodynamic transducer while carrying PTX as the chemotherapeutic cargo. Because of the broad NIR absorbance of the Au cage, a single 808 nm laser irradiation generated both heat and ROS, enabling combined PTT and PDT; at the same time, the temperature rise accelerated PTX release in tumor tissue. In-vivo, this triple-mode system (chemo + PTT + PDT) produced significantly greater tumor regression than free PTX or PTT/PDT alone, without obvious systemic toxicity, showing that a single inorganic framework can coordinate all three modalities (Duan et al., 2023). A further example is a photoresponsive inorganic-containing nanocomposite in which doxorubicin was loaded together with a catalytic component capable of Fenton-like reactions. Upon NIR irradiation, the nanocomposite exhibited a photothermal effect that accelerated DOX release and simultaneously promoted catalytic decomposition of endogenous H_2O_2 into highly toxic hydroxyl radicals (CDT), producing a synergistic PTT + CDT + chemotherapy effect in tumor models. In vivo data showed significantly enhanced tumor suppression versus any single or dual modality, underlining how inorganic photothermal scaffolds can be integrated with both chemotherapy and ROS-generating mechanisms in a single platform (Patnaik et al., 2025).

Translation to the clinic

Iron oxide nanoparticles (IONPs): IONPs are the most clinically advanced inorganic nanocarriers. Advanced formulations, such as Feraheme (Ferumoxytol), are already approved by the FDA and used to treat iron deficiency anemia. In addition, IONPs are actively studied in clinical trials for MRI of numerous cancers and inflammatory diseases due to their magnetic properties (Toth et al., 2017; Bashir et al., 2015). Coupling IONPs with targeting peptides or antibodies to improve tumor selectivity in preclinical studies to aid in the treatment of more difficult cancers like glioblastoma and prostate cancer continues to build on the advancements. In addition to the above, IONPs are also being used for next-generation biomedical sensing to magnetically segregate and accurately identify rare biological targets such as circulating tumor cells (CTCs) (Raucher, 2019; Li et al., 2021).

Silica nanoparticles (Cornell dots): The FDA authorized small silica nanoparticles for human clinical studies as imaging agents and for drug delivery and immunotherapy. Silica nanoparticles show versatility and biocompatibility as diagnostic and therapeutic platforms because a fluorophore and targeting peptide are often incorporated (Corma et al., 2022). The creation of MSNs represents a significant advancement in this area. With internal pore structures, MSNs can hold an unprecedented amount of drugs. Currently, research is being conducted on designing systems where drugs are released upon a stimulus that could potentially be used to treat certain tumors in a more effective way. For example, doxorubicin could be encapsulated and released in an acidic or reducing environment. Moving to the next stage and long-term safe biocompatibility is more controlled renal circumvention of mesoporous nanoparticles to meet regulatory hurdles for clinical translation (Castillo et al., 2019; Vallet-Regí et al., 2018).

Silica–gold nanoshells (AuroLase): These hybrid nanoparticles are tailored for use in PTT. They integrate silica's remarkable safety and biocompatibility with a thin gold shell's remarkable photothermal efficacy. This innovative design enables them to capture NIR laser light and transform it into heat for precise thermal ablation of solid tumors. Clinical trials investigated their use in head and neck and lung cancer photothermal therapies. This technique is noninvasive and offers considerable precision by exploiting tumor accumulation through EPR effect. This means targeted therapy with a little damage to adjacent healthy tissue (Yu et al., 2025; Bort et al., 2020).

Hafnium oxide nanoparticles (NBTXR3): NBTXR3 nanoparticles are unique in their category. These engineered hybrid silica–gold nanoparticles are designed to enhance the efficacy of radiotherapy. Using high Z of hafnium, these nanocrystals can absorb X-rays during traditional radiation therapy. Once inside tumor cells, hafnium oxide nanoparticles increase the radiation dose within the tumor while decreasing the dose to the surrounding healthy tissue (Wang et al., 2023; Stergioula et al., 2023). This X-ray responsive mechanism has been validated in advanced clinical trials for soft tissue sarcoma and is being investigated for a variety of other solid tumors. This mechanism will improve the therapeutic ratio of radiotherapy (Zachou et al., 2024; Kim and Bui, 2023).

Challenges in clinical translation

The overall clinical success of inorganic nanocarriers is still complex because of issues related to safety, manufacturing, biological performance, and regulatory approvals. The most important is long-term safety and toxicity, which calls for proof that these NPs can be biodegraded into innocuous components and that the body can get rid of them—ideally through the hepatic or renal systems—without affecting internal organs or triggering an immune response. Ensuring scalability and reproducibility in good manufacturing practices (GMP) is a challenging task. This is particularly true for complex inorganic systems, where it is frequently challenging to maintain a high degree of uniformity in physicochemical features, including size, shape, surface chemistry, and drug loading. As a result, these systems are expensive to create, which limits their commercial viability (Chehelgerdi et al., 2023). Clinical success is also hampered by biological factors. Poor therapy outcomes result from the well-discussed EPR phenomenon, which allows nanoparticles to collect in tumors but varies greatly between tumor types and even between people. In addition, as soon as nanoparticles enter the bloodstream, they rapidly form a covering of adsorbed biomolecules known as a "protein corona," which alters their surface properties, targeting behavior, and clearance kinetics and ultimately affects in vivo behavior (Carrese et al., 2022; Golombek et al., 2018; Xuan et al., 2023; Đorđević et al., 2022; Ye et al., 2022). One major obstacle is the regulatory setting. Agencies need comprehensive information on long-term metabolism, biodistribution, and potential toxicity in addition to short-term safety and efficacy. Preclinical and clinical trials must be carried out extensively to determine the safety, dependability, and compliance of nanomedicines due to the ongoing changes in their regulatory frameworks (Bai et al., 2025). All of these intricate problems of biodegradation, immunological compatibility, scalable manufacture, and regulatory licensing must be resolved to fully realize the clinical promise of inorganic nanocarriers in precision medicine.

Conclusion

Many novel inorganic materials have drawn interest as materials science expands. The remarkable properties of inorganic materials, such as their ease of synthesis and functionalization, high compliance and stability, and superior safety and biocompatibility, have attracted attention. Inorganic nanocarriers have undergone a clear conceptual transformation from passive drug vehicles into highly engineered, intelligent therapeutic systems. Through precise control over particle size, composition, and surface functionalization, modern inorganic platforms are now capable of remaining stable during systemic circulation, selectively accumulating within tumor tissues, and responding dynamically to tumor-specific stimuli such as acidic pH, elevated redox potential, enzymatic activity, or external triggers such as light and magnetic fields. The incorporation of targeting ligands further enhances cellular specificity, enabling receptor-mediated uptake and minimizing off-target interactions with healthy tissues. Importantly, the field has progressed beyond conventional single-drug delivery toward integrated combination nanomedicine, where a single inorganic carrier can codeliver multiple therapeutic agents or simultaneously combine chemotherapy with gene therapy, photothermal, photodynamic, or chemodynamic modalities. These multifunctional systems consistently demonstrate superior therapeutic outcomes in preclinical models, including enhanced tumor regression, improved modulation of drug resistance mechanisms, and, in some cases, stimulation of antitumor immune responses. Collectively, these advances position inorganic nanocarriers as a powerful and versatile class of smart nanotherapeutics, with future challenges centered on achieving scalable synthesis, long-term biosafety, regulatory standardization, and successful clinical translation.

References

Abdelghany, S., Elsayed, A., Kabary, H., Salaheldin, H., 2025. Iron oxide/silver-doped iron oxide nanoparticles: Facile synthesis, characterization, antibacterial activity, genotoxicity and anticancer evaluation. Sci. Rep. 15 (1). https://doi.org/10.1038/s41598-025-14098-6.

Abodunrin, T.O., Egharevba, G.O., Owoeye, F.D., Omojola, J.A., Adeyemi, O.S., 2025. Metal organic frameworks in photodynamic therapy of cancer: Functional roles of active metal centres and integrated and loaded photosensitizers in the framework. Materials Advances 6 (5), 1554–1577. https://doi.org/10.1039/d4ma00425f.

Alfei, S., Reggio, C., Zuccari, G., 2025. Carbon nanotubes as excellent adjuvants for anticancer therapeutics and cancer diagnosis: A plethora of laboratory studies versus few clinical trials. Cells 14 (14), 1052. https://doi.org/10.3390/cells14141052.

Alsaab, H.O., Alghamdi, M.S., Alotaibi, A.S., Alzhrani, R., Alwuthaynani, F., Althobaiti, Y.S., Almalki, A.H., Sau, S., Iyer, A.K., 2020. Progress in clinical trials of photodynamic therapy for solid tumors and the role of nanomedicine. Cancers (Basel) 12 (10), 1–26. https://doi.org/10.3390/cancers12102793.

Bai, J.W., Zhang, G.J., Gao, Y.Y., 2025. Challenges in the Clinical Application of NIRF Imaging Application of Near-Infrared Fluorescence Imaging in Cancer Surgery. Springer Science+Business Media, China, pp. 369–381. https://doi.org/10.1007/978-981-96-6875-5_19.

Balfourier, A., Luciani, N., Wang, G., Lelong, G., Ersen, O., Khelfa, A., Alloyeau, D., Gazeau, F., Carn, F., 2020. Unexpected intracellular biodegradation and recrystallization of gold nanoparticles. Proc. Natl. Acad. Sci. 117 (1), 103–113. https://doi.org/10.1073/pnas.1911734116.

Bashir, M.R., Bhatti, L., Marin, D., Nelson, R.C., 2015. Emerging applications for ferumoxytol as a contrast agent in MRI. J. Magn. Reson. Imaging 41 (4), 884–898. https://doi.org/10.1002/jmri.24691.

Bhattacharyya, S., Kudgus, R.A., Bhattacharya, R., Mukherjee, P., 2011. Inorganic nanoparticles in cancer therapy. Pharm. Res. 28 (2), 237–259. https://doi.org/10.1007/s11095-010-0318-0.

Bort, G., Lux, F., Dufort, S., Crémillieux, Y., Verry, C., Tillement, O., 2020. EPR-mediated tumor targeting using ultrasmall-hybrid nanoparticles: From animal to human with theranostic AGuIX nanoparticles. Theranostics 10 (3), 1319–1331. https://doi.org/10.7150/thno.37543.

Boraei, S.B.A., Kamalinejad, F., Kiaei, N., 2025. The cutting-edge applications and properties of carbon nanotubes in diagnosis and treatment of lung cancer: A review. Front. Biomater. Sci. 4. https://doi.org/10.3389/fbiom.2025.1500758.

Brito, B., Ruggiero, M.R., Price, T.W., da Costa Silva, M., Genicio, N., Wilson, A.J., Tyurina, O., Rosecker, V., Eykyn, T.R., Bañobre-López, M., Stasiuk, G.J., Gallo, J., 2023. Redox double-switch cancer theranostics through Pt(iv) functionalised manganese dioxide nanostructures. Nanoscale 15 (25), 10763–10775. https://doi.org/10.1039/d3nr00076a.

Brown, S.D., Nativo, P., Smith, J.A., Stirling, D., Edwards, P.R., Venugopal, B., Flint, D.J., Plumb, J.A., Graham, D., Wheate, N.J., 2010. Gold nanoparticles for the improved anticancer drug delivery of the active component of oxaliplatin. J. Am. Chem. Soc. 132 (13), 4678–4684. https://doi.org/10.1021/ja908117a.

Carrese, B., Sanità, G., Lamberti, A., 2022. Nanoparticles design for theranostic approach in cancer disease. Cancers 14 (19), 4654. https://doi.org/10.3390/cancers14194654.

Castillo, R.R., Lozano, D., González, B., Manzano, M., Izquierdo-Barba, I., Vallet-Regí, M., 2019. Advances in mesoporous silica nanoparticles for targeted stimuli-responsive drug delivery: An update. Expert Opin. Drug Deliv. 16 (4), 415–439. https://doi.org/10.1080/17425247.2019.1598375.

Chang, J., Mo, L., Song, J., Wang, X., Liu, H., Meng, C., Wu, Y., 2022. A pH-responsive mesoporous silica nanoparticle-based drug delivery system for targeted breast cancer therapy. J. Mater. Chem. B 10 (17), 3375–3385. https://doi.org/10.1039/d1tb02828f.

Chehelgerdi, M., Chehelgerdi, M., Allela, O.Q.B., Pecho, R.D.C., Jayasankar, N., Rao, D.P., Thamaraikani, T., Vasanthan, M., Viktor, P., Lakshmaiya, N., Saadh, M.J., Amajd, A., Abo-Zaid, M.A., Castillo-Acobo, R.Y., Ismail, A.H., Amin, A.H., Akhavan-Sigari, R., 2023. Progressing nanotechnology to improve targeted cancer treatment: Overcoming hurdles in its clinical implementation. Mol. Cancer 22 (1). https://doi.org/10.1186/s12943-023-01865-0.

Chen, A.M., Zhang, M., Wei, D., Stueber, D., Taratula, O., Minko, T., He, H., 2009. Co-delivery of Doxorubicin and Bcl-2 siRNA by mesoporous silica nanoparticles enhances the efficacy of chemotherapy in multidrug-resistant cancer cells. Small 5 (23), 2673–2677. https://doi.org/10.1002/smll.200900621.

Cheng, R., Feng, F., Meng, F., Deng, C., Feijen, J., Zhong, Z., 2011. Glutathione-responsive nano-vehicles as a promising platform for targeted intracellular drug and gene delivery. J. Contr. Release 152 (1), 2–12. https://doi.org/10.1016/j.jconrel.2011.01.030.

Cheng, H., Liao, J., Ma, Y., Sarwar, M.T., Yang, H., 2025. Advances in targeted therapy for tumor with nanocarriers: A review. Mater. Today Bio 31. https://doi.org/10.1016/j.mtbio.2025.101583.

Corma, A., Botella, P., Rivero-Buceta, E., 2022. Silica-based stimuli-responsive systems for antitumor drug delivery and controlled release. Pharmaceutics 14 (1), 110. https://doi.org/10.3390/pharmaceutics14010110.

de la Rica, R., Aili, D., Stevens, M.M., 2012. Enzyme-responsive nanoparticles for drug release and diagnostics. Adv. Drug Deliv. Rev. 64 (11), 967–978. https://doi.org/10.1016/j.addr.2012.01.002.

Devi, S., Kumar, M., Tiwari, A., Tiwari, V., Kaushik, D., Verma, R., Bhatt, S., Sahoo, B.M., Bhattacharya, T., Alshehri, S., Ghoneim, M.M., Babalghith, A.O., Batiha, G.E.S., 2022. Quantum dots: An emerging approach for cancer therapy. Front. Mater. 8. https://doi.org/10.3389/fmats.2021.798440.

Dong, Z., Feng, L., Zhu, W., Sun, X., Gao, M., Zhao, H., Chao, Y., Liu, Z., 2016. CaCO3 nanoparticles as an ultra-sensitive tumor-pH-responsive nanoplatform enabling real-time drug release monitoring and cancer combination therapy. Biomaterials 110, 60–70. https://doi.org/10.1016/j.biomaterials.2016.09.025.

Đorđević, S., Gonzalez, M.M., Conejos-Sánchez, I., Carreira, B., Pozzi, S., Acúrcio, R.C., Satchi-Fainaro, R., Florindo, H.F., Vicent, M.J., 2022. Current hurdles to the translation of nanomedicines from bench to the clinic. Drug. Deliv. Transl. Res. 12 (3), 500–525. https://doi.org/10.1007/s13346-021-01024-2.

Duan, S., Hu, Y., Zhao, Y., Tang, K., Zhang, Z., Liu, Z., Wang, Y., Guo, H., Miao, Y., Du, H., Yang, D., Li, S., Zhang, J., 2023. Nanomaterials for photothermal cancer therapy. RSC Adv. 13 (21), 14443–14460. https://doi.org/10.1039/d3ra02620e.

Edalatian Tavakoli, S., Motavalizadehkakhky, A., Homayouni Tabrizi, M., Mehrzad, J., Zhiani, R., 2024. Study of the anti-cancer activity of a mesoporous silica nanoparticle surface coated with polydopamine loaded with umbelliprenin. Sci. Rep. 14 (1). https://doi.org/10.1038/s41598-024-62409-0.

Edis, Z., Wang, J., Waqas, M.K., Ijaz, M., Ijaz, M., 2021. Nanocarriers-mediated drug delivery systems for anticancer agents: An overview and perspectives. Int. J. Nanomed. 16, 1313–1330. https://doi.org/10.2147/ijn.s289443.

Eljack, S., David, S., Faggad, A., Chourpa, I., Allard-Vannier, E., 2022. Nanoparticles design considerations to co-deliver nucleic acids and anti-cancer drugs for chemoresistance reversal. Int. J. Pharm.X (4). https://doi.org/10.1016/j.ijpx.2022.100126.

Esa, M., Kaewpaiboon, S., Srichana, T., 2025. Fabrication, biodistribution, and toxicological evaluation of mesoporous silica nanoparticles based on preclinical studies intended for cancer therapy: A review. J.Appl. Pharm. Sci. 15 (7), 1–26. https://doi.org/10.7324/JAPS.2025.220858.

Fan, D., Cao, Y., Cao, M., Wang, Y., Cao, Y., Gong, T., 2023. Nanomedicine in cancer therapy. Signal Transduct. Targeted Ther. 8 (1). https://doi.org/10.1038/s41392-023-01536-y.

Ghosn, Y., Kamareddine, M.H., Tawk, A., Elia, C., El Mahmoud, A., Terro, K., El Harake, N., El-Baba, B., Makdessi, J., Farhat, S., 2019. Inorganic nanoparticles as drug delivery systems and their potential role in the treatment of chronic myelogenous leukaemia. Technol. Cancer Res. Treat. 18. https://doi.org/10.1177/1533033819853241.

Golombek, S.K., May, J.N., Theek, B., Appold, L., Drude, N., Kiessling, F., Lammers, T., 2018. Tumor targeting via EPR: Strategies to enhance patient responses. Adv. Drug Deliv. Rev. 130, 17–38. https://doi.org/10.1016/j.addr.2018.07.007.

Golubewa, L., Timoshchenko, I., Romanov, O., Karpicz, R., Kulahava, T., Rutkauskas, D., Shuba, M., Dementjev, A., Svirko, Y., Kuzhir, P., 2020. Single-walled carbon nanotubes as a photo-thermo-acoustic cancer theranostic agent: Theory and proof of the concept experiment. Sci. Rep. 10 (1). https://doi.org/10.1038/s41598-020-79238-6.

Gomes, H.I.O., Martins, C.S.M., Prior, J.A.V., 2021. Silver nanoparticles as carriers of anticancer drugs for efficient target treatment of cancer cells. Nanomaterials (Basel) 11 (4). https://doi.org/10.3390/nano11040964.

Gong, J., Shi, T., Liu, J., Pei, Z., Liu, J., Ren, X., Li, F., Qiu, F., 2023. Dual-drug codelivery nanosystems: An emerging approach for overcoming cancer multidrug resistance. Biomed. Pharmacother. 161. https://doi.org/10.1016/j.biopha.2023.114505.

Hamidu, A., Pitt, W.G., Husseini, G.A., 2023. Recent breakthroughs in using quantum dots for cancer imaging and drug delivery purposes. Nanomaterials (Basel) 13 (18). https://doi.org/10.3390/nano13182566.

Hanafi-Bojd, M.Y., Jaafari, M.R., Ramezanian, N., Abnous, K., Malaekeh-Nikouei, B., 2016. Co-delivery of epirubicin and siRNA using functionalized mesoporous silica nanoparticles enhances in vitro and in vivo drug efficacy. Curr. Drug Deliv. 13 (7), 1176–1182. https://doi.org/10.2174/1567201813666151231094056.

Han, I., Choi, S.A., Lee, D.N., 2022. Therapeutic application of metal–organic frameworks composed of copper, cobalt, and zinc: Their anticancer activity and mechanism. Pharmaceutics 14 (2). https://doi.org/10.3390/pharmaceutics14020378.

Huang, H., Liu, R., Yang, J., Dai, J., Fan, S., Pi, J., Wei, Y., Guo, X., 2023. Gold nanoparticles: Construction for drug delivery and application in cancer immunotherapy. Pharmaceutics 15 (7), 1868. https://doi.org/10.3390/pharmaceutics15071868.

Huq, T.B., Anil Kumar Jeeja, P., Dam, S.K., Das, S.S., Vivero-Escoto, J.L., 2025. Recent applications of mesoporous silica nanoparticles in gene therapy. Adv. Healthc. Mater. 14 (26). https://doi.org/10.1002/adhm.202404781.

Jain, S., Hirst, D.G., O'Sullivan, J.M., 2012. Gold nanoparticles as novel agents for cancer therapy. Br. J. Radiol. 85 (1010), 101–113. https://doi.org/10.1259/bjr/59448833.

Kanipandian, N., Ramesh, R., 2024. Biosynthesis and characterization of silver nanoparticles using cleistanthus collinus; investigation on molecular mechanism of apoptosis cell death against lung cancer cells. Asian Pac. J. Cancer Biol. 9 (4), 527–535. https://doi.org/10.31557/apjcb.2024.9.4.527-535.

Khalifehzadeh, R., Arami, H., 2020. Biodegradable calcium phosphate nanoparticles for cancer therapy. Adv. Colloid Interface Sci. 279. https://doi.org/10.1016/j.cis.2020.102157.

Kim, T., Bui, N.Q., 2023. The next frontier in sarcoma: Molecular pathways and associated targeted therapies. Cancers 15 (6). https://doi.org/10.3390/cancers15061692.

Kumar, M., Kumar, P., Sagar, S., Chaudhary, A., 2022. Iron oxide nanoparticles approaching to eradicate her2-positive breast cancer. Int. J. Health Sci. 12680–12707. https://doi.org/10.53730/ijhs.v6ns2.8308.

Kush, P., Singh, R., Kumar, P., 2025. Recent advances in metal–organic framework-based anticancer hydrogels. Gels 11 (1). https://doi.org/10.3390/gels11010076.

Lee, K.Y.J., Lee, G.Y., Lane, L.A., Li, B., Wang, J., Lu, Q., Wang, Y., Nie, S., 2017. Functionalized, long-circulating, and ultrasmall gold nanocarriers for overcoming the barriers of low nanoparticle delivery efficiency and poor tumor penetration. Bioconjugate Chem. 28 (1), 244–252. https://doi.org/10.1021/acs.bioconjchem.6b00224.

Lee, S., Byun, A., Jo, J., Suh, J.M., Yoo, J., Lim, M.H., Kim, J.W., Shin, T.H., Choi, J.S., 2024a. Ultrasmall Mn-doped iron oxide nanoparticles with dual hepatobiliary and renal clearances for T1 MR liver imaging. Nanoscale Adv. 6 (8), 2177–2184. https://doi.org/10.1039/d3na00933e.

Lee, Y.T., Wu, S.H., Wu, C.H., Lin, Y.H., Lin, C.K., Chen, Z.A., Sun, T.C., Chen, Y.J., Chen, P., Mou, C.Y., Chen, Y.P., 2024b. Drug-free mesoporous silica nanoparticles enable suppression of cancer metastasis and confer survival advantages to mice with tumor xenografts. ACS Appl. Mater. Interfaces 16 (45), 61787–61804. https://doi.org/10.1021/acsami.4c16609.

Lee, J., Kim, J.M., Baek, Y.J., Kang, H., Choi, M.K., Song, I.S., 2025. Anticancer activity of paclitaxel-loaded mesoporous silica nanoparticles in B16F10 melanoma-bearing mice. Pharmaceutics 17 (8). https://doi.org/10.3390/pharmaceutics17081042.

Li, Y., Hou, H., Zhang, P., Zhang, Z., 2020. Co-delivery of doxorubicin and paclitaxel by reduction/pH dual responsive nanocarriers for osteosarcoma therapy. Drug Deliv. 27 (1), 1044–1053. https://doi.org/10.1080/10717544.2020.1785049.

Li, F., Xu, H., Zhao, Y., 2021. Magnetic particles as promising circulating tumor cell catchers assisting liquid biopsy in cancer diagnosis: A review. TrAC, Trends Anal. Chem. 145. https://doi.org/10.1016/j.trac.2021.116453.

Li, L., Shen, Y., Tang, Z., Yang, Y., Fu, Z., Ni, D., Cai, X., 2023. Engineered nanodrug targeting oxidative stress for treatment of acute kidney injury. Exploration 3 (6). https://doi.org/10.1002/EXP.20220148.

Lin, G., Mi, P., Chu, C., Zhang, J., Liu, G., 2016. Inorganic nanocarriers overcoming multidrug resistance for cancer theranostics. Adv. Sci. 3 (11). https://doi.org/10.1002/advs.201600134.

Liu, Y., Zhao, M., Zhang, M., Yang, B., Qi, Y.-K., Fu, Q., 2025. Mesoporous silica nanoparticle-based nanomedicine: Preparation, functional modification, and theranostic applications. Mater. Today Bio 34. https://doi.org/10.1016/j.mtbio.2025.102223.

Long, H., Tian, W., Jiang, S., Zhao, J., Zhou, J., He, Q., Tang, Z., Shen, W., Wang, J., 2022. A dual drug delivery platform based on thermo-responsive polymeric micelle capped mesoporous silica nanoparticles for cancer therapy. Microporous Mesoporous Mater. 338. https://doi.org/10.1016/j.micromeso.2022.111943.

Lu, Y., Peng, Z., Zhu, D., Jia, Y., Taledaohan, A., Li, Y., Liu, J., Wang, Y., Wang, Y., 2021. RGD peptide and pad4 inhibitor-loaded gold nanorods for chemo-photothermal combined therapy to inhibit tumor growth, prevent lung metastasis and improve biosafety. Int. J. Nanomedicine 16, 5565–5580. https://doi.org/10.2147/IJN.S319210.

Machado, T.R., Winter, A., Loza, K., Kostka, K., Zucolotto, V., Epple, M., 2026. Dual pH-responsive calcium phosphate nanoparticles conjugated with folate by CuAAC click chemistry for targeted gemcitabine delivery to cancer cells. ACS Appl. Bio Mater. 9 (1), 137–152. https://doi.org/10.1021/acsabm.5c01683.

Mehnath, S., Arjama, M., Rajan, M., Annamalai, G., Jeyaraj, M., 2018. Co-encapsulation of dual drug loaded in MLNPs: Implication on sustained drug release and effectively inducing apoptosis in oral carcinoma cells. Biomed. Pharmacother. 104, 661–671. https://doi.org/10.1016/j.biopha.2018.05.096.

Mofokeng, M.T., Didamson, O.C., Abrahamse, H., 2025. The role of quantum dots in enhancing the therapeutic targeting of cancer stem cells. Chem. Commun. 61 (77), 14870–14887. https://doi.org/10.1039/d5cc02925b.

Mosleh-Shirazi, S., Abbasi, M., Shafiee, M., Kasaee, S.R., Amani, A.M., 2021. Renal clearable nanoparticles: An expanding horizon for improving biomedical imaging and cancer therapy. Mater. Today Commun. 26. https://doi.org/10.1016/j.mtcomm.2021.102064.

Nisha, Sachan, R.S.K., Singh, A., Karnwal, A., Shidiki, A., Kumar, G., 2024. Plant-mediated gold nanoparticles in cancer therapy: Exploring anti-cancer mechanisms, drug delivery applications, and future prospects. Front. Nanotechnol. 6. https://doi.org/10.3389/fnano.2024.1490980.

Paris, J.L., Vallet-Regí, M., 2020. Mesoporous silica nanoparticles for Co-delivery of drugs and nucleic acids in oncology: A review. Pharmaceutics 12 (6), 526. https://doi.org/10.3390/pharmaceutics12060526.

Park, S., Lu, G.L., Zheng, Y.C., Davison, E.K., Li, Y., 2025. Nanoparticle-based delivery strategies for combating drug resistance in cancer therapeutics. Cancers 17 (16). https://doi.org/10.3390/cancers17162628.

Pavlova, N.N., Thompson, C.B., 2016. The emerging hallmarks of cancer metabolism. Cell Metab. 23 (1), 27–47. https://doi.org/10.1016/j.cmet.2015.12.006.

Patnaik, C., Rath, S., De, A., 2025. Avenues for integrating photothermal therapy in cancer clinic. Commun. Chem. 8 (1). https://doi.org/10.1038/s42004-025-01705-w.

Peng, C., Huang, Y., Zheng, J., 2020. Renal clearable nanocarriers: Overcoming the physiological barriers for precise drug delivery and clearance. J. Contr. Release 322, 64–80. https://doi.org/10.1016/j.jconrel.2020.03.020.

Qi, L., Pan, T., Ou, L., Ye, Z., Yu, C., Bao, B., Wu, Z., Cao, D., Dai, L., 2021. Biocompatible nucleus-targeted graphene quantum dots for selective killing of cancer cells via DNA damage. Commun Biol. 4 (1). https://doi.org/10.1038/s42003-021-017131.

Racles, C., Zaltariov, M.-F., Peptanariu, D., Vasiliu, T., Cazacu, M., 2022. Functionalized mesoporous silica as doxorubicin carriers and cytotoxicity boosters. Nanomaterials 12 (11), 1823. https://doi.org/10.3390/nano12111823.

Rahimkhoei, V., Alzaidy, A.H., Abed, M.J., Rashki, S., Salavati-Niasari, M., 2024. Advances in inorganic nanoparticles-based drug delivery in targeted breast cancer theranostics. Adv. Colloid Interface Sci. 329. https://doi.org/10.1016/j.cis.2024.103204.

Raucher, D., 2019. Tumor targeting peptides: Novel therapeutic strategies in glioblastoma. Curr. Opin. Pharmacol. 47, 14–19. https://doi.org/10.1016/j.coph.2019.01.006.

Sabir, S., Thani, A.S.B., Abbas, Q., 2025. Nanotechnology in cancer treatment: Revolutionizing strategies against drug resistance. Front Bioeng Biotechnol 13. https://doi.org/10.3389/fbioe.2025.1548588.

Shaji, A., Saravanan, A., 2024. Targeted oral therapy: Utilization of metal-organic frameworks. Asian Pac. J. Cancer Biol. 9 (3), 441–443. https://doi.org/10.31557/apjcb.2024.9.3.441-443.

Shestovskaya, M.V., Luss, A.L., Bezborodova, O.A., Makarov, V.V., Keskinov, A.A., 2023. Iron oxide nanoparticles in cancer treatment: Cell responses and the potency to improve radiosensitivity. Pharmaceutics 15 (10). https://doi.org/10.3390/pharmaceutics15102406.

Shi, Z., Zhou, Y., Fan, T., Lin, Y., Zhang, H., Mei, L., 2020a. Inorganic nano-carriers based smart drug delivery systems for tumor therapy. Smart Mater. Med. 1, 32–47. https://doi.org/10.1016/j.smaim.2020.05.002.

Shi, Z., Li, Q., Mei, L., 2020b. pH-Sensitive nanoscale materials as robust drug delivery systems for cancer therapy. Chin. Chem. Lett. 31 (6), 1345–1356. https://doi.org/10.1016/j.cclet.2020.03.001.

Shubhra, Q.T.H., 2023. Iron oxide nanoparticles in magnetic drug targeting and ferroptosis-based cancer therapy. Med. Rev. 3 (5), 444–447. https://doi.org/10.1515/mr-2023-0029.

Singh, P., Joshi, A.S., Singh, H., Mijakovic, I., 2025. Medical importance and pharmacokinetics of gold nanoparticles in the human body. Mol. Cancer 24 (1). https://doi.org/10.1186/s12943-025-02418-3.

Slavkova, M., ordanov, Y.Y., Voycheva, C., Popova, T., Spassova, I., Kovacheva, D., Tzankova, V., Tzankov, B., 2026. Synthesis of folic acid-functionalized hybrid mesoporous silica nanoparticles and in vitro evaluation on MCF-7 breast cancer cells. Int. J. Mol. Sci. 27 (2). https://doi.org/10.3390/ijms27021092.

Soetaert, F., Korangath, P., Serantes, D., Fiering, S., Ivkov, R., 2020. Cancer therapy with iron oxide nanoparticles: Agents of thermal and immune therapies. Adv. Drug Deliv. Rev. 65–83. https://doi.org/10.1016/j.addr.2020.06.025.

Sriram, V., Lee, J.Y., 2021. Calcium phosphate-polymeric nanoparticle system for co-delivery of microRNA-21 inhibitor and doxorubicin. Colloids Surf. B Biointerfaces 208. https://doi.org/10.1016/j.colsurfb.2021.112061.

Stergioula, A., Pantelis, E., Kontogeorgakos, V., Lazaris, A.C., Agrogiannis, G., 2023. Understanding the role of radio-sensitizing nanoparticles in enhancing pathologic response in soft tissue sarcomas. Cancers 15 (23). https://doi.org/10.3390/cancers15235572.

Suk, J.S., Xu, Q., Kim, N., Hanes, J., Ensign, L.M., 2016. PEGylation as a strategy for improving nanoparticle-based drug and gene delivery. Adv. Drug Deliv. Rev. 99, 28–51. https://doi.org/10.1016/j.addr.2015.09.012.

Sun, M., Wang, T., Li, L., Li, X., Zhai, Y., Zhang, J., Li, W., 2021. The application of inorganic nanoparticles in molecular targeted cancer therapy: EGFR targeting. Front. Pharmacol. 12. https://doi.org/10.3389/fphar.2021.702445.

Sun, L., Liu, H., Ye, Y., Lei, Y., Islam, R., Tan, S., Tong, R., Miao, Y.B., Cai, L., 2023. Smart nanoparticles for cancer therapy. Signal Transduct. Target. Ther. 8 (1). https://doi.org/10.1038/s41392-023-01642-x.

Takáč, P., Michalková, R., Čižmáriková, M., Bedlovičová, Z., Balážová, Ľ., Takáčová, G., 2023. The role of silver nanoparticles in the diagnosis and treatment of cancer: Are there any perspectives for the future? Life 13 (2), 466. https://doi.org/10.3390/life13020466.

Toth, G.B., Varallyay, C.G., Horvath, A., Bashir, M.R., Choyke, P.L., Daldrup-Link, H.E., Dosa, E., Finn, J.P., Gahramanov, S., Harisinghani, M., Macdougall, I., Neuwelt, A., Vasanawala, S.S., Ambady, P., Barajas, R., Cetas, J.S., Ciporen, J., DeLoughery, T.J., Doolittle, N.D., Fu, R., Grinstead, J., Guimaraes, A.R., Hamilton, B. E., Li, X., McConnell, H.L., Muldoon, L.L., Nesbit, G., Netto, J.P., Petterson, D., Rooney, W.D., Schwartz, D., Szidonya, L., Neuwelt, E.A., 2017. Current and potential imaging applications of ferumoxytol for magnetic resonance imaging. Kidney Int. 92 (1), 47–66. https://doi.org/10.1016/j.kint.2016.12.037.

Tunç, C.Ü., Aydin, O., 2022. Co-delivery of Bcl-2 siRNA and doxorubicin through gold nanoparticle-based delivery system for a combined cancer therapy approach. J. Drug Deliv. Sci. Technol. 74. https://doi.org/10.1016/j.jddst.2022.103603.

Ul Khaliq, N., Lee, J., Kim, J., Kim, Y., Yu, S., Kim, J., Kim, S., Sung, D., Kim, H., 2023. Mesoporous silica nanoparticles as a gene delivery platform for cancer therapy. Pharmaceutics 15 (5), 1432. https://doi.org/10.3390/pharmaceutics15051432.

Unnikrishnan, G., Joy, A., Megha, M., Kolanthai, E., Senthilkumar, M., 2023. Exploration of inorganic nanoparticles for revolutionary drug delivery applications: A critical review. Discov Nano 18 (1). https://doi.org/10.1186/s11671-023-039430.

Vallet-Regí, M., Colilla, M., Izquierdo-Barba, I., Manzano, M., 2018. Mesoporous silica nanoparticles for drug delivery: Current insights. Molecules 23 (1), 47. https://doi.org/10.3390/molecules23010047.

Vivero-Escoto, J.L., Elnagheeb, M., 2015. Mesoporous silica nanoparticles loaded with cisplatin and phthalocyanine for combination chemotherapy and photodynamic therapy in vitro. Nanomaterials 5 (4), 2302–2316. https://doi.org/10.3390/nano5042302.

Wang, H., Zhang, M., Zhang, L., Li, S., Li, L., Li, X., Yu, M., Mou, Z., Wang, T., Wang, C., Su, Z., 2017. Near-infrared light and pH-responsive Au@carbon/calcium phosphate nanoparticles for imaging and chemo-photothermal cancer therapy of cancer cells. Dalton Trans. 46 (43), 14746–14751. https://doi.org/10.1039/C7DT02274C.

Wang, J., Zhang, L., Peng, F., Shi, X., Leong, D.T., 2018. Targeting endothelial cell junctions with negatively charged gold nanoparticles. Chem Mater. 30 (11), 3759–3767. https://doi.org/10.1021/acs.chemmater.8b00840.

Wang, J., Pan, J., Tang, Y., Chen, J., Fei, X., Xue, W., Liu, X., 2023. Advances of hafnium based nanomaterials for cancer theranostics. Front. Chem. 11. https://doi.org/10.3389/fchem.2023.1283924.

Wang, M., Yu, F., Zhang, Y., 2025. Present and future of cancer nano-immunotherapy: Opportunities, obstacles and challenges. Mol. Cancer 24 (1). https://doi.org/10.1186/s12943-024-02214-5.

Xu, Z.P., Zeng, Q.H., Lu, G.Q., Yu, A.B., 2006. Inorganic nanoparticles as carriers for efficient cellular delivery. Chem. Eng. Sci. 61 (3), 1027–1040. https://doi.org/10.1016/j.ces.2005.06.019.

Xu, L., Wang, Y.Y., Huang, J., Chen, C.Y., Wang, Z.X., Xie, H., 2020. Silver nanoparticles: Synthesis, medical applications and biosafety. Theranostics 10 (20), 8996–9031. https://doi.org/10.7150/thno.45413.

Xuan, L., Ju, Z., Skonieczna, M., Zhou, P.K., Huang, R., 2023. Nanoparticles-induced potential toxicity on human health: Applications, toxicity mechanisms, and evaluation models. MedComm 4 (4). https://doi.org/10.1002/mco2.327.

Yan, Y., Ding, L., Liu, L., Abualrejal, M.M.A., Chen, H., Wang, Z., 2020. Renal-clearable hyaluronic acid functionalized NaGdF 4 nanodots with enhanced tumor accumulation. RSC Adv. 10 (23), 13872–13878. https://doi.org/10.1039/c9ra08974h.

Yang, C., Lin, Z.I., Chen, J.A., Xu, Z., Gu, J., Cheung Law, W., Yang, J.H.C., Chen, C.-K., 2022. Organic/inorganic self-assembled hybrid nano-architectures for cancer therapy applications. Macromol. Biosci. (2), 22. https://doi.org/10.1002/mabi.202100349.

Yao, Y., Zhou, Y., Liu, L., Xu, Y., Chen, Q., Wang, Y., Wu, S., Deng, Y., Zhang, J., Shao, A., 2020. Nanoparticle-based drug delivery in cancer therapy and its role in overcoming drug resistance. Front. Mol. Biosci. 7. https://doi.org/10.3389/fmolb.2020.00193.

Ye, Q., Lin, Y., Li, R., Wang, H., Dong, C., 2022. Recent advances of nanodrug delivery system in the treatment of hematologic malignancies. Semin. Cancer Biol. 86, 607–623. https://doi.org/10.1016/j.semcancer.2022.03.016.

Yu, X., Fan, S., Zhu, B., El-Hout, S.I., Zhang, J., Chen, C., 2025. Recent progress on photothermal nanomaterials: Design, mechanism, and applications. Green Energy Environ. 10 (7), 1377–1436. https://doi.org/10.1016/j.gee.2024.09.002.

Yuan, G., Luo, X., He, K., Tan, Y., Luo, C., Liu, B., Sun, Y., Liu, J., 2025. Intratumoral self-assembly of renal-clearable gold nanoparticles as precise photothermal nanomedicine for liver tumor therapy. Sci. Adv. 11 (17). https://doi.org/10.1126/sciadv.adw7032.

Zachou, M.E., Kouloulias, V., Chalkia, M., Efstathopoulos, E., Platoni, K., 2024. The impact of nanomedicine on soft tissue sarcoma treated by radiotherapy and/or hyperthermia: A review. Cancers 16 (2). https://doi.org/10.3390/cancers16020393.

Zeraati, M., Rahdar, A., Medina, D.I., Sargazi, G., 2021. Synthesis of Al-based metal-organic framework in water with caffeic acid ligand and NaOH as linker sources with highly efficient anticancer treatment. Front. Chem. 9. https://doi.org/10.3389/fchem.2021.784461.

Zhang, Y., Chen, Q., Zhu, Y., Pei, M., Wang, K., Qu, X., Zhang, Y., Gao, J., Qin, H., 2022. Targeting inorganic nanoparticles to tumors using biological membrane-coated technology. MedComm 3 (4). https://doi.org/10.1002/mco2.192.

Zhao, R., Li, S., Zhao, J., Yao, C., 2025. Advancements in nano-delivery systems for photodynamic and photothermal therapy to induce immunogenic cell death in tumor immunotherapy. Int. J. Nanomed. 20, 8221–8248. https://doi.org/10.2147/IJN.S514659.

Zheoat, A.M.A., Al Luaibi, A.I.M., Darraji, R.K.A.A., Singh, N.S.S., Salahshour, S., Sajadi, S.M., Hekmatifar, M., 2025. Interaction of doxorubicin with carbon nanotubes in the capillaries surrounding cancer tumors using molecular dynamics simulation: The impact of pH on the thermal properties. Results Chem. 16. https://doi.org/10.1016/j.rechem.2025.102418.

Zhou, H., Ge, J., Miao, Q., Zhu, R., Wen, L., Zeng, J., Gao, M., 2020. Biodegradable inorganic nanoparticles for cancer theranostics: Insights into the degradation behavior. Bioconjugate Chem. 31 (2), 315–331. https://doi.org/10.1021/acs.bioconjchem.9b00699.

Zhuang, L., Lian, Y., Zhu, T., 2025. Multifunctional gold nanoparticles: Bridging detection, diagnosis, and targeted therapy in cancer. Mol. Cancer 24 (1). https://doi.org/10.1186/s12943-025-02431-6.

CHAPTER

25

Microparticles for anticancer drug delivery

Yashika Uniyal[1], *Abhishek Sharma*[2], *Bhagya Shree*[2], *Arun Kumar Mahato*[1] *and Nithya Shanthi*[1]

[1]School of Pharmaceutical Sciences & Technology, Sardar Bhagwan Singh University Balawala, Dehradun, Uttarakhand, India; [2]Department of Pharmaceutical Engineering and Technology, Indian Institute of Technology (BHU), Varanasi, Uttar Pradesh, India

Introduction

Traditional anticancer drug delivery systems struggle with various drawbacks, including poor drug release kinetics, low selectivity, rapid degradation, and harmful effects on healthy tissues. These limitations necessitate delivery systems that can direct anticancer agents precisely to tumor sites while maintaining steady and effective concentrations for longer durations. Microparticles (MPs) have recently gained widespread popularity for anticancer drug delivery. It belongs to a broad category of extracellular vesicles called microvesicles (MVs), which include a population of membrane vesicles with a variety of shapes and sizes, ranging from 0.1 to 1 μm (Verma et al., 2021). Microparticle based drug delivery systems can be effectively employed for anticancer drug encapsulation with controlled release capabilities. Additionally, the degradation rate of the polymer matrix can be modified to control drug release, ensuring consistent therapeutic levels within the tumor microenvironment (Verma et al., 2021). Microparticles are essential to contemporary drug delivery systems as they can improve anticancer drug stability, bioavailability, and distribution at the target site. It can shield the encapsulated drug before its delivery to the intended site of action and can reduce the dosing frequency, thereby increasing patient compliance. Their versatility in carrying a wide range of drug types including proteins, peptides, and small molecules positions microparticles as a key component in the development of advanced, targeted, and personalized medical therapies (Kumar et al., 2021). The size and surface can be tailored to achieve preferential accumulation in cancerous tissues through passive targeting or receptor recognition, reducing unwanted side effects and enhancing therapeutic performance. They can be

Advanced Cancer Therapeutics
https://doi.org/10.1016/B978-0-443-44185-1.00001-X

designed to release their payload at a particular physiological variable, including pH, ROS, enzymes, or in response to external stimuli like ultrasound, light, and magnetic field. Microparticles can thus be tuned with various materials for modified release and targeted delivery of an anticancer drug.

Materials for the design of microparticles

Microparticles can be designed using various materials, including biopolymers, synthetic polymers, lipids, or inorganic materials. Natural polymers like chitosan, alginate, gelatin, carrageenan, pullulan, dextran, cellulose, starch, etc., are preferred for the design of microparticles owing to their biocompatibility, biodegradability, nonimmunogenicity, easy processing, and low cost. However, synthetic polymers such as polyethylene glycol (PEG), polylactic acid (PLA), and polylactic-co-glycolic acid (PLGA) can also be incorporated to modulate mechanical properties or modify drug release patterns (Table 25.1).

TABLE 25.1 Polymer-based microparticle formulation for targeted cancer therapy.

S. No.	Polymer/Formulation	Type of cancer targeted	Key observations/Outcomes	References
1.	Polycaprolactone (PCL) microspheres–sorafenib tosylate	Lung cancer	Lower IC_{50} compared to free drug in A549 cells; promising for inhaled targeting with reduced systemic exposure.	(Yadav et al., 2023)
2.	Poloxamer 407-based solid lipid microparticles –erlotinib	Nonsmall cell lung cancer	Enhanced cytotoxicity versus free drug in A549 cells; potential for local inhaled delivery with reduced systemic toxicity.	Bakhtiary et al. (2017)
3.	Nano-structured microparticles for extracellular modulation	Lung cancer	Enabled delivery of therapeutic nanoparticles (NPs) and enhanced intratumoral penetration.	Abdel-Hafez et al. (2024)
4.	Chitosan, dextran sulfate, and mannose-g-PEI-based inhalable nano-in-microparticles for codelivery of small molecules and miRNAs	Lung cancer	Coloaded system showed higher cytotoxicity versus DOX alone; better aerosolization; potential to overcome drug resistance via miR delivery.	Motiei et al. (2023)
5.	PLGA microparticles for pulsatile release of STING agonists	Various solid tumors/pancreatic cancer (cancer immunotherapy)	Comparable antitumor immune responses and survival benefits as multiple soluble injections; reduced metastasis.	Lu et al. (2020)

TABLE 25.1 Polymer-based microparticle formulation for targeted cancer therapy.—cont'd

S. No.	Polymer/Formulation	Type of cancer targeted	Key observations/Outcomes	References
6.	Carboxymethyl cellulose (CMC)–curcumin-loaded microspheres	Oral cancer	Improved mucosal adhesion and curcumin bioavailability.	Esthar et al. (2023)
7.	Curcumin-loaded magnetic microspheres	Breast cancer	Delayed tumor appearance, reduced tumor burden, decreased abnormal mammary tissue, and lower vascularization marker (CD-31).	Esthar et al. (2023)
8.	Polyethylene glycol (PEG)–PLGA copolymer – gemcitabine-loaded microspheres	Pancreatic cancer	Enhanced circulation time; improved antitumor efficacy.	Li et al. (2019)
9.	Quercetin microparticles via electrospraying	Lung cancer (A549 model)	Showed stronger inhibition of A549 cell growth, reduced migration, induced G0/G1 arrest versus free quercetin.	Li et al. (2019)
10.	PLGA–CS–PEG microspheres for hyperthermia-modulated release	Triple-negative breast cancer	Exhibited cytotoxicity toward TNBC cells; temperature modulation improved release; potential for combined hyperthermia therapy.	Jusu et al. (2021)
11.	Poly (lactic-co-glycolic acid) (PLGA) microspheres	Breast cancer	Sustained release and targeted activity in tumor models.	Jusu et al. (2021)
12.	Chitosan microspheres	Multiple cancer models	Effective in both local and systemic delivery studies.	Zhao et al, (2022)
13.	PLGA porous microparticles for pulmonary delivery	Pulmonary metastatic lung cancer models	Controlled release profile and efficient lung deposition.	Luna Lazo et al. (2023)
14.	Alginate microspheres – curcumin-loaded	Liver cancer	Improved bioavailability and localized delivery.	Sood et al. (2023)
15.	Dextran sulfate microspheres – cisplatin-loaded	Melanoma	Controlled cytotoxicity and prolonged release.	(An et al., 2023)
16.	Carrageenan microspheres	Colon cancer	Exhibited selective cytotoxicity and good stability.	Campos et al. (2022)
17.	Poly(ethyleneimine) (PEI) gene-loaded microspheres	Breast cancer	Promoted tumor suppression via gene delivery.	Fahira et al. (2022)

Drug encapsulation in microparticles

Drug Loading refers to the amount of active compound successfully incorporated within the microparticles relative to the total weight of the carrier. The efficiency of drug loading depends on several parameters, such as the physicochemical properties of the drug, the type of polymer or material used for formulation, the preparation technique, and the interaction between the drug and matrix. High loading capacity is generally desirable to minimize the amount of carrier material administered and to ensure an effective therapeutic dose. The effectiveness of drug delivery systems that use microparticles depends a lot on how well the drug is wrapped and shielded during the manufacturing process. Drug Encapsulation Techniques mainly include three methods. Physical Entrapment involves the spreading or mixing of the drug into the polymer material. In surface adsorption, the drug sticks or is adsorbed onto the surface of the particle through weak forces, which can cause a quick release of the drug at first. Covalent Conjugation is the method of attaching the drug chemically to the polymer structure, which helps control and slow down the release over time (Kállai-Szabó et al., 2024). How the drug is encapsulated depends on the technique employed; primarily, it is due to hydrophobic interactions, hydrogen bonding, precipitation of solvent onto the drugs, evaporation of the solvent, phase separation, and also electrostatic interactions or weak van der Waals forces. Drug release from the microparticles that is., microspheres and microcapsules, is via various mechanisms including diffusion, where drug moves from a high concentration to a low concentration through polymeric matrix/shell, dissolution which depends on the thickness and solubility of the polymeric coating in the medium, osmosis due to difference in osmotic pressure, disintegration, swelling and erosion due to physical, chemical and enzymatic mediated hydrolysis. The capacity of microparticles to encapsulate and retain therapeutic agents depends on multiple physicochemical and formulation-related parameters. Drug loading efficiency is a critical determinant of the performance, stability, and therapeutic potential of the delivery system (Vlachopoulos et al., 2022). The following factors play a major role.

Physicochemical properties of the drug

The solubility, molecular weight, charge, and polarity of the drug strongly influence encapsulation. Hydrophilic drugs often show lower entrapment in hydrophobic polymeric carriers, while hydrophobic compounds are generally loaded more efficiently (Vlachopoulos et al., 2022). Increasing the drug concentration beyond a certain point results in a decline in the encapsulation and drug loading efficiency. If the pH of the aqueous phase is kept below the pKa of the drug, the encapsulation efficiency would increase due to the lower solubility of the drug in the external phase (Arabia et al., 2025).

Polymer characteristics

Type of polymer, its molecular weight, composition, and degradation profile dictate drug–polymer interactions. Polymers with higher hydrophobicity or functional groups that can interact with the drug tend to enhance encapsulation. Increasing the molecular weight of the polymer increases the encapsulation. The same goes for polymer concentration, an increase in which increases the encapsulation efficiency due to an increase in viscosity. Polymer crystallinity also plays a role in drug release (Miles et al., 2021). The type of polymer material being used for a particular drug and route of administration is critical.

Natural polymers like cellulose and starch derivatives are biodegradable, biocompatible, have low cost, and thus show good encapsulating and controlled drug delivery properties to the microparticles developed using them. The presence of free hydroxyl groups in the polymeric chains causes molecular interactions, which in turn lead to increased viscosity, ideal for uniform drug-loaded microparticle formation (Lukova et al., 2023). The source of polymer also plays a role in drug loading, size, porosity, and drug release characteristics of the microparticles, as changing the source of polymer changes the viscosity, molecular weight, and blockiness of the polymer (Wan et al., 2021).

Method of preparation

Techniques such as solvent evaporation, spray drying, coacervation, or nanoprecipitation, microfluidization, spray congealing, emulsification, freeze drying, emulsion extraction, etc, differ in their encapsulation outcomes. Factors like emulsification energy, solvent selection, and phase ratios during preparation significantly affect loading efficiency. In 3D printed smart microparticles, the nozzle size, printing pressure, and printing speed affect the drug loading efficiency. Smaller nozzle size, higher printing speed, and pressure showed an increase in the drug loading efficiency (Wang et al., 2022). In the spray drying technique, the concentration of the starting material that includes both polymer and drug is crucial to prepare microparticles with optimum properties, in addition to other variables like the amount of compressed gas, pump speed, and air flow rate. In the coacervation technique, if opposing charges have been established between two polymers, an ideal pH is maintained depending on the polymers used, and optimal stirring speed and duration have been used, then microparticles with good morphology, size, and high drug-loading efficiency can be formed (Lukova et al., 2023).

Drug-to-polymer ratio

The proportion of drug relative to the carrier matrix determines the encapsulation yield, size, loading efficiency, release kinetics, and production yield. While higher drug content can increase loading, it may also lead to drug crystallization or leakage if the polymer cannot accommodate excess molecules. The optimal drug-to-polymer ratio depends on the individual drug and polymer characteristics being used. It is found that high molar concentration of the right polymeric blends, when compared to the drug, increases the loading efficiency of the drug, entrapment efficiency of the drug, but also increases the size of the microparticles in case of a few polymers and vice versa in others (Jelvehgari et al., 2011; Medipelli and Chinthala, 2025). Also, high drug to polymer ratio in hollow microparticles shows better encapsulation and release profiles when compared to solid microparticles with lower drug-to-polymer concentration (Baek et al., 2017).

The choice of organic and aqueous solvents, their miscibility, and volatility influence both drug entrapment and particle formation. A poorly optimized solvent system can cause premature drug diffusion, reducing efficiency. The organic solvent must ideally be able to dissolve the polymers, be water-insoluble for emulsion formation, and be volatile for its easy removal during processing. Recently, green solvents like ethyl lactate are being studied for chemotherapeutic drug-loaded microparticles to overcome the toxic properties of organic solvents like dichloromethane, chloroform, acetone, etc in addition to their ability to provide the smallest size range, spherical morphology and high drug loading efficiency while providing a safe, sustainable and environment friendly alternative to common toxic organic solvents (Alvarez et al., 2025).

Stabilizers and additives

Surfactants, emulsifiers, and stabilizers regulate droplet size during microparticle formation. Their concentration and type can control drug partitioning and minimize drug loss to the external phase. The addition of various additives apart from the polymer influences the properties of microparticles. Surface modification, like pegylation, decreases the encapsulation efficiency and increases the release rate of the drugs from the microparticles. The addition of sufficient concentration of surfactant, like PVA, in the external water phase enhances the encapsulation and drug loading efficiency, and the same goes for the addition of osmotic agents like sodium chloride of sufficient osmolarity, which is due to an increase in the osmotic pressure in the external phase. The initial release of the drug when osmogens are added is dependent on their concentration; low concentrations of osmogen increased the release, whereas high concentrations decreased it due to the formation of denser microparticles when high concentration is used (Bhatt and Shah, 2012).

Processing parameters

Parameters such as stirring speed, homogenization pressure, temperature, and pH of the medium directly impact particle size, morphology, and drug encapsulation levels. Stirring speed affects particle size; higher speed reduces the size of the particle. Control over the processing and storage temperature changes, especially in polymers with variable glass transition temperature, is essential for efficient formation of a solid matrix. In the emulsion extraction manufacturing method, multiple processing variables affect the final microparticles formed. These include interfacial tension between the two phases, mixing point of the two phases, stirring rate and time, viscosity of oil phase, etc during the initial emulsion formation, and water volume, water-solvent miscibility, temperature, and stirring rate, solvent removal rate, etc. during the subsequent solvent evaporation. The solubility of the solvent in the water must not be more than 15%(w/w) for the formation of spherical microparticles. The drug release from the microparticles depends on their internal network structure, which is formed during the mixing stage itself when both the phases exchange at the interface (Park et al., 2021).

Drug excipient interactions and compatibility

Hydrogen bonding, ionic interactions, electrostatic attraction, donor-acceptor coordination, or hydrophobic effects between drug molecules and excipients enhance retention within the microparticles, thereby improving loading efficiency (Vlachopoulos et al., 2022). The interaction between the drug and the polymeric materials, limits the loading efficiency of the drug due to compatibility issues which further makes the microparticulate system incapable of unlocking its full potential as delivery system in giving controlled release, increased duration of action of drug and reduced frequency of administration, thus such methods which employ high mass fraction of the drug when compared to the polymer used must be employed in microsphere formation, for example, using sequential solidification approach in which the drug nanoparticles are oversaturated and precipitated in the polymer droplet before solidification (Li et al., 2022).

Particle size and shape

The size and shape of the microparticles are affected by production method, polymer concentration, processing parameters, etc., which in turn affects the release of the drug, as lower particle size has a high surface area to volume ratio, thus faster release, spherical shape gives sustained release, and the presence of porous channels increases the drug released.

Mechanism of drug release

Drug release from a matrix-type microparticulate system

A matrix-type microparticulate system consists of drug molecules uniformly dispersed within a polymeric matrix (lipid, polymer, or hybrid) as shown in Fig. 25.1. The drug is

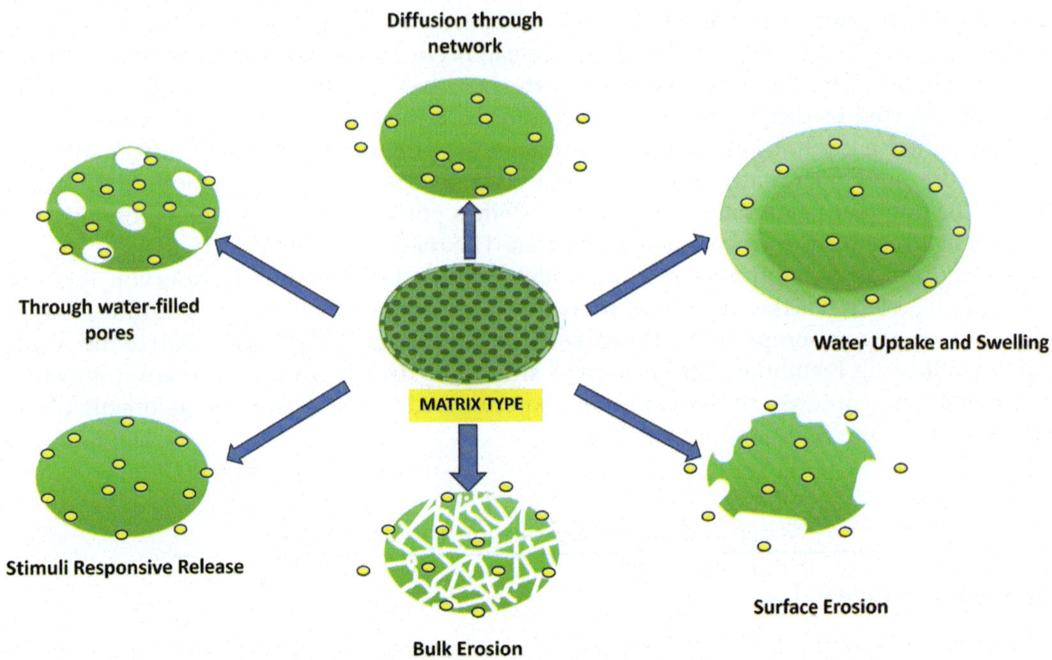

FIGURE 25.1 Drug release from a matrix-type microparticulate system.

not coated or encapsulated in a separate shell but is embedded throughout the particles. Drug release typically occurs through diffusion-controlled, polymer degradation, or erosion-controlled, swelling-controlled, or a combination of two or more mechanisms. Diffusion-controlled release occurs when the drug diffuses out through the polymer matrix into the surrounding biological fluid. Initially, the surface drug is rapidly released (burst effect). Later, the drug's release slows as it travels longer distances via the polymer network, following Fick's law of diffusion. Polymer crosslinking, drug solubility, matrix porosity, and particle size all have an impact on diffusion-controlled release. Polymer degradation-controlled release is determined by the type of polymer utilized in microparticle design. In this case, the polymer degrades gradually (by hydrolysis or enzymatic activity), forming channels for drug release. Bulk erosion (e.g., PLGA microparticles). Swellable controlled systems make use of swellable hydrophilic polymers (such as HPMC and alginate). The polymer absorbs water, swelling and increasing pore size to release the drug. The drug diffuses out of the enlarged matrix and is commonly employed with hydrophilic drugs. Many microparticles may follow a combination pathway of initial diffusion, polymer swelling, and eventual erosion. Such a technology enables sustained and regulated release, reduces dose frequency, increases patient compliance, protects sensitive medications, and allows for target site-responsive release. Examples include alginate and gelatin microparticles.

Drug release from a reservoir-type microparticulate system

A reservoir-type microparticle consists of a drug-containing core surrounded by a rate-controlling polymer membrane (Fig. 25.2). The drug is concentrated in the center (core) and released via the outer shell. Drug release can occur by diffusion through the polymeric membrane, whereby the drug dissolves in the core before diffusing across the membrane into the external medium. The polymer coating is critical in limiting drug release, which is determined entirely by the membrane thickness, polymer permeability, drug solubility in the core, and microparticle surface area. Pore-mediated release is another process in which the polymer membrane is porous or becomes porous when hydrated, allowing drugs to diffuse through aqueous channels in the coat. The release rate increases with pore number and size. Erosion or rupture of polymer membranes is less common in reservoir-type, but can lead to release of the drug over time. The membrane serves as a rate-limiting barrier for reservoir-type microparticles. It can keep plasma drug levels stable, control the release rate by adjusting membrane thickness, and shield the drug from the microenvironment. If the membrane ruptures, the system may experience dose dumping and is unsuitable for drugs that require high loading efficiency.

Recent advances and emerging technologies

Hybrid microparticles

Hybrid microparticles are an advanced class of carriers designed by combining two or more materials to achieve complementary advantages. Among these, lipid–polymer and

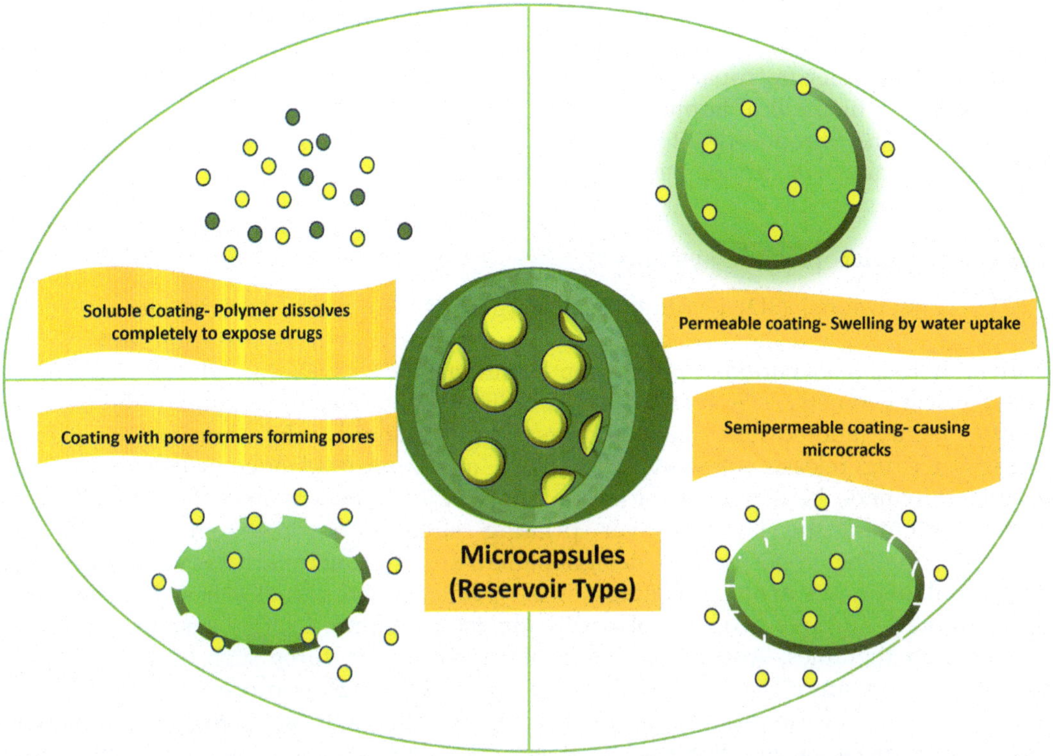

FIGURE 25.2 Drug release from a reservoir-type microparticulate system.

metal–polymer composites are widely explored due to their unique structural and functional properties. for example., 1. Poly (methyl methacrylate) (PMMA) and lanthanum (III) oxide PMMA_La $_2O_3$ hybrid microspheres through suspension polymerization using the Radioactive Particle Tracking (RPT) technique (Vieira et al., 2020).

2. pH-sensitive ternary Iron (II, III) oxide nanoparticles and graphene quantum dots Fe3O4/GQDs hybrid microspheres as an anticancer drug carrier (Pooresmaeil and Namazi, 2020).

Lipid Microparticles: These systems integrate the biocompatibility and biodegradability of lipids with the mechanical strength and stability of polymers. The lipid layer often enhances drug solubility and provides a biomimetic surface, while the polymeric matrix ensures controlled release and structural integrity. Such combinations improve encapsulation efficiency, extend circulation time, and enhance the targeted delivery of therapeutic agents, for example., Solid lipid microparticles were formed using the PGSS technique (López-Iglesias et al., 2020). Solid Lipid Microparticles were formed containing Asiatic acid for topical delivery (Chutoprapat et al., 2024).

Metal–Polymer Microparticles: In these composites, metals such as gold, silver, or iron oxide are incorporated into a polymeric framework. The polymer component ensures biocompatibility and sustained release, while the metallic phase imparts unique features like magnetic responsiveness, photothermal activity, or antimicrobial action. These properties make metal–polymer microparticles particularly valuable in cancer therapy, imaging, and multifunctional biomedical applications. 30 different metal elements, most of them transition metals, are introduced into polymeric frameworks for interactions with biology-relevant substrates via various means (Yan et al., 2016).

3D-printed microparticle systems

Three-dimensional (3D) printing has emerged as a powerful tool for designing and fabricating microparticle-based drug delivery systems with high precision and customization. Unlike conventional fabrication techniques, 3D printing allows fine control over particle geometry, size distribution, and internal architecture, enabling the development of highly tailored therapeutic carriers. These systems can be engineered to provide controlled drug release, site-specific delivery, and multifunctional properties by integrating polymers, biomaterials, or even inorganic components into the printed structures. Moreover, the layer-by-layer printing strategy ensures reproducibility and flexibility, making it possible to design patient-specific microparticles with optimized pharmacokinetics. A major advantage of 3D printed microparticles lies in their ability to incorporate multiple drugs or bioactive molecules within a single system, facilitating combination therapies. Additionally, stimuli-responsive features such as pH, temperature, or light sensitivity can be programmed during the printing process to achieve smart and on-demand release profiles. In biomedical applications, these systems hold immense promise for personalized medicine, regenerative therapies, and next-generation anticancer treatments, where precise control over drug delivery is crucial (Xu et al., 2024).

Microspheres-in-gel systems

Injectable hydrogel systems containing microspheres have emerged as a promising strategy for localized and sustained cancer treatment. In these hybrid delivery systems, drug-loaded microspheres are dispersed within a biocompatible hydrogel matrix, forming a semisolid depot after administration. This unique configuration allows precise and prolonged drug exposure directly at the tumor site, minimizing systemic toxicity and maximizing therapeutic efficacy.

The injectable nature of these hydrogels offers significant advantages for minimally invasive cancer therapy. They can be administered directly into the tumor bed or postsurgical cavity, where they undergo *in situ* gelation under physiological conditions. Once formed, the gel not only retains the microspheres but also shields them from immediate clearance by interstitial fluids, thereby preventing drug washout. Moreover, by adjusting the polymer composition such as using thermosensitive polymers (e.g., Pluronic F127), natural biopolymers (e.g., chitosan, alginate, or gelatin), or synthetic biodegradable materials (e.g., PEG–PLGA blends) the release rate and mechanical strength of the system can be finely tuned to match therapeutic requirements (Xu et al., 2023).

Microspheres in nanofibers

Incorporating drug-loaded microspheres within electrospun nanofibers provides a dual advantage of localized targeting and controlled drug release. Similar to SiO_2/PVDF microspheres enhancing structural and functional properties, drug-encapsulated microspheres embedded in the nanofibrous matrix act as sustained reservoirs. The nanofiber network confines and protects the microspheres, allowing gradual diffusion of the drug while maintaining mechanical flexibility and stability. This hybrid system ensures prolonged therapeutic effect, reduced burst release, and precise site-specific drug delivery (Gao et al., 2018). Additionally, the integration of microspheres within nanofibers forms a hierarchical structure that mimics the extracellular matrix, promoting better cell adhesion and proliferation in tissue regeneration applications. The synergistic combination of nanofiber porosity and microsphere encapsulation enables the fine-tuning of drug release kinetics through the modulation of polymer composition and morphology. Such composite systems not only enhance the physicochemical stability of encapsulated therapeutics but also provide a versatile platform for multidrug delivery, wound healing, and localized treatment of chronic diseases (Ionescu et al., 2010).

Based on the principle of fibre coalescence, the incorporation of drug-loaded nanofiber microspheres into electrospun matrices represents a favourable advancement in both controlled and localised drug delivery systems. The morphology, size, and internal structure of these microspheres can be modified by optimising electrospinning and thermal crosslinking conditions. The resulting interconnected nanofibrous network stabilises the microspheres and regulates diffusion behaviour, enabling sustained and site-specific release. This hybrid system further enhances physicochemical stability, mechanical integrity, and biocompatibility, offering significant potential for advanced biomedical and pharmaceutical applications (Zhang et al., 2025).

Theranostic microspheres

Microspheres, which are visible in CT and MRI, are developed with the loading of chemotherapeutic agents and contrast agents, both of which are explored for their theranostic uses. (both diagnostic and therapeutic). Radioactive labelled resin, polymeric, and glass microspheres are widely applied as theranostics in the localised treatment of various solid organ tumors like liver, lung, pancreatic, and ovarian cancer. This locoregional approach of delivering radiation only to the targeted site helps minimize adverse effects on healthy tissue. Microspheres must be able to carry radionuclides, most commonly yttrium-90 and holmium-166, without leaching or leaking to avoid off-target radiation exposure. The biodegradable gel microspheres can also be utilized to perform transarterial radioembolization along with lung shunt fraction evaluation in patients with hepatocellular carcinoma (Jiang et al., 2025; Dong et al., 2024). Positron emitters like fluorine-18, gallium-68, and zirconium-89 are labelled in microspheres and have been developed recently to increase the resolution and quality of the image after PET scanning, which determines the *in vivo* biodistribution of the radiolabelled microspheres. Poly (L-lactic acid), Poly (lactic-co-glycolic acid), gelatin, alginates, chitosan, etc., are the polymers used to develop biodegradable polymeric microspheres used as theranostics (Gupta et al., 2024).

Microspheres equipped microneedles

Transdermal delivery of the chemotherapeutic agents can be successfully achieved using microneedles, which serve to improve the therapeutic availability of the drugs in the target site. Drugs are loaded into the microparticles to overcome their physicochemical barriers, which limit their absorption via skin into systemic circulation, such as being hydrophilic in nature. When such anticancer drugs are encapsulated inside a biodegradable polymer and equipped with microneedles, efficient transdermal delivery is possible due to the combination of sustained release by microspheres and good penetrability by microneedles. Anticancer agents loaded PLGA microparticles are explored for the controlled delivery, which, when integrated with dissolving microneedle patches, provide a minimally invasive approach to deliver them to the tumor site, avoid first pass metabolism caused by oral administration, and enhance patient compliance when compared to parenteral delivery of drugs (Nguyen et al., 2025).

Future perspectives

The upcoming years are expected to bring remarkable progress in the development of microparticles for targeted cancer treatment. Researchers are increasingly focusing on creating intelligent delivery systems that can respond to the unique conditions of the tumor environment, such as changes in pH, temperature, or enzyme levels. These smart microparticles are being designed to release drugs only when and where they are needed, which greatly minimizes harm to healthy tissues and enhances the effectiveness of therapy. The use of biodegradable and biocompatible materials, along with hybrid structures that combine polymers, lipids, and metals, is making these systems more efficient and safer for longterm use. Modern fabrication techniques like 3D printing and microfluidics are allowing precise control over particle size, shape, and internal structure, leading to better drug loading and sustained release profiles. In addition, surface modification with targeting molecules such as antibodies or peptides is improving the ability of these microparticles to recognize and bind to specific cancer cells. Looking ahead, artificial intelligence and computational modeling are expected to play a vital role in predicting drug release patterns and optimizing formulations for personalized cancer therapy. Combining microparticlebased systems with advanced treatments like immunotherapy and gene therapy could further enhance therapeutic success. Overall, these advancements point toward a future where microparticle based drug delivery systems become highly precise, adaptive, and capable of providing safer and more effective cancer treatments tailored to each patient's needs (Lengyel et al., 2019).

Conclusion

Microparticles are a groundbreaking advancement in delivering cancer drugs. They offer controlled release of medication, precise targeting of cancer cells, and the ability to use multiple treatment approaches at once, which helps overcome many issues with traditional chemotherapy. Progress in materials science, how drugs are made into particles, and personalized medicine are expanding what microparticles can do. As more studies are done and real-world results are gathered, microparticles are expected to play a key role in the future of cancer treatment, offering more effective, tailored, and safer options for patients (Lengyel et al., 2019).

References

Abdel-Hafez, S.M., Gallei, M., Wagner, S., Schneider, M., 2024. Inhalable nano-structured microparticles for extracellular matrix modulation as a potential delivery system for lung cancer. Eur. J. Pharm. Biopharm. 204. https://doi.org/10.1016/j.ejpb.2024.114512.

Alvarez, I., Gutiérrez, C., Gracia, I., Rodríguez, J.F., García, M.T., 2025. Synthesis of gemcitabine-loaded PLGA microparticles with green solvents. ACS Omega 10 (30), 33946–33958. https://doi.org/10.1021/acsomega.5c06385.

An, L., Jia, Y., Li, J., Xiao, C., 2023. Reduction-responsive dextran-based Pt (IV) nano-prodrug showed a synergistic effect with doxorubicin for effective melanoma treatment. Int. J. Biol. Macromol. 233.

Arabia, M., Maretti, E., Sedighidarijani, A., Rustichelli, C., Leo, E., 2025. Optimizing formulation conditions of PLGA microparticles to enhance indomethacin encapsulation. Part. Part. Syst. Char. 42 (2). https://doi.org/10.1002/ppsc.202400135.

Baek, J.S., Choo, C.C., Tan, N.S., Loo, S.C.J., 2017. Sustained-releasing hollow microparticles with dual-anticancer drugs elicit greater shrinkage of tumor spheroids. Oncotarget 8 (46), 80841–80852. https://doi.org/10.18632/oncotarget.20591.

Bakhtiary, Z., Barar, J., Aghanejad, A., Ata Saei, A., Nemati, E., Ezzati Nazhad Dolatabadi, J., Omidi, Y., 2017. Microparticles containing erlotinib-loaded solid lipid nanoparticles for treatment of non-small cell lung cancer. Drug Dev. Ind. Pharm. 43 (8), 1244–1253. https://doi.org/10.1080/03639045.2017.1310223.

Bhatt, Y., Shah, D., 2012. Influence of additives on fabrication and release from protein loaded PLGA microparticles. J. Chem. Pharmaceut. Res. 4 (3), 1708–1715.

Campos, F.L., de Alcântara Lemos, J., Oda, C.M.R., de Oliveira Silva, J., Fernandes, R.S., Miranda, S.E.M., Cavalcante, C.H., Cassali, G.D., Townsend, D.M., Leite, E.A., de Barros, A.L.B., 2022. Irinotecan-loaded polymeric micelles as a promising alternative to enhance antitumor efficacy in colorectal cancer therapy. Polymers 14 (22). https://doi.org/10.3390/polym14224905.

Chutoprapat, R., Witarat, J., Jongpanyangarm, P., Sung Thluai, L.M., Khankaew, P., Lai, W.C., 2024. Development of solid lipid microparticles (SLMs) containing asiatic acid for topical treatment of acne: Characterization, stability, in vitro and in vivo anti-acne assessment. Int. J. Pharm. 654. https://doi.org/10.1016/j.ijpharm.2024.123980.

Dong, Y., Yin, L., Huang, J., Hu, Di, Sun, J., Zhang, Z., Li, Z., Zhong, B.-Y., Zhu, R., Wang, G., 2024. 99mTc/90Y radiolabeled biodegradable gel microspheres for lung shutting fraction assessment and radioembolization in hepatocellular carcinoma theranostics. Mater. Today Bio 29. https://doi.org/10.1016/j.mtbio.2024.101367.

Esthar, S., Rajesh, J., Prakash, N., Ayyanaar, S., Bhaskar, R., Thanigaivel, S., Webster, T.J., Rajagopal, G., 2023. An effective biodegradable curcumin loaded magnetic microsphere: Applications for drug delivery and cancer treatment. Pharmacol. Res. Mod. Chin. Med. 6. https://doi.org/10.1016/j.prmcm.2023.100219.

Fahira, A.I., Amalia, R., Barliana, M.I., Gatera, V.A., Abdulah, R., 2022. Polyethyleneimine (PEI) as a polymer-based co-delivery system for breast cancer therapy. Breast Cancer 14, 71–83. https://doi.org/10.2147/bctt.s350403.

Gao, J., Li, B., Wang, L., Huang, X., Xue, H., 2018. Flexible membranes with a hierarchical nanofiber/microsphere structure for oil adsorption and oil/water separation. J. Ind. Eng. Chem. 68, 416–424. https://doi.org/10.1016/j.jiec.2018.09.001.

Gupta, A., Park, J.Y., Choi, H., Choi, T.H., Chung, Y., Kim, D.H., Lee, Y.S., 2024. Development of alginate-based biodegradable radioactive microspheres labeled with positron emitter through click chemistry reaction: Stability and PET imaging study. Mol. Pharm. 21 (10), 5005–5014. https://doi.org/10.1021/acs.molpharmaceut.4c00412.

Ionescu, L.C., Lee, G.C., Sennett, B.J., Burdick, J.A., Mauck, R.L., 2010. An anisotropic nanofiber/microsphere composite with controlled release of biomolecules for fibrous tissue engineering. Biomaterials 31 (14), 4113–4120. https://doi.org/10.1016/j.biomaterials.2010.01.098.

Jelvehgari, M., Hassanzadeh, D., Kiafar, F., Loveymi, B.D., Amiri, S., 2011. Preparation and determination of drug-polymer interaction and in-vitro release of mefenamic acid microspheres made of cellulose acetate phthalate and/or ethylcellulose polymers. Iran. J. Pharm. Res. 10 (3), 457–467.

Jiang, X., Chen, L., Xu, X., 2025. Advancements in the investigation of radioactive microspheres for brachytherapy. Front. Bioeng. Biotechnol. 13. https://doi.org/10.3389/fbioe.2025.1621418.

Jusu, S.M., Obayemi, J.D., Salifu, A.A., Clare Nwazojie, C., Obiageli Uzonwanne, V., Odusanya, O.S., Oluwole Soboyejo, W., 2021. PLGA-CS-PEG microparticles for controlled drug delivery in the treatment of triple negative breast cancer cells. Appl. Sci. 11 (15), 7112. https://doi.org/10.3390/app11157112.

Kállai-Szabó, N., Farkas, D., Lengyel, M., Basa, B., Fleck, C., Antal, I., 2024. Microparticles and multi-unit systems for advanced drug delivery. Eur. J. Pharmaceut. Sci. 194, 106704. https://doi.org/10.1016/j.ejps.2024.106704.

Kumar, V., Kumar, N., Mehra, A., Shrivastava, P., Maurya, P.K., 2021. Microparticles for Cancer Therapy Advanced Drug Delivery Systems in the Management of Cancer. Elsevier, India, pp. 359–371. https://doi.org/10.1016/B978-0-323-85503-7.00019-5.

Lengyel, M., Kállai-Szabó, N., Antal, V., Laki, A.J., Antal, I., 2019. Microparticles, microspheres, and microcapsules for advanced drug delivery. Sci. Pharm. 87 (3), 20. https://doi.org/10.3390/scipharm87030020.

Li, C., Gao, L., Zhang, Y., Simpson, B.K., 2019. Preparation of quercetin loaded microparticles and their antitumor activity against human lung cancer cells (A549) in vitro. Curr. Pharm. Biotechnol. 20 (11), 945–954. https://doi.org/10.2174/1573407215666190628145902.

Li, W., Chen, J., Zhao, S., Huang, T., Ying, H., Trujillo, C., Molinaro, G., Zhou, Z., Jiang, T., Liu, W., Li, L., Bai, Y., Quan, P., Ding, Y., Hirvonen, J., Yin, G., Santos, H.A., Fan, J., Liu, D., 2022. High drug-loaded microspheres enabled by controlled in-droplet precipitation promote functional recovery after spinal cord injury. Nat. Commun. 13 (1). https://doi.org/10.1038/s41467-022-28787-7.

López-Iglesias, C., López, E.R., Fernández, J., Mariana, L., García-González, C.A., 2020. Modeling of the production of lipid microparticles using PGSS® technique. Molecules 25 (21). https://doi.org/10.3390/molecules25214927.

Lu, X., Miao, L., Gao, W., Chen, Z., McHugh, K.J., Sun, Y., Tochka, Z., Tomasic, S., Sadtler, K., Hyacinthe, A., Huang, Y., Graf, T., Hu, Q., Sarmadi, M., Langer, R., Anderson, D.G., Jaklenec, A., 2020. Engineered PLGA microparticles for long-term, pulsatile release of STING agonist for cancer immunotherapy. Sci. Transl. Med. 12 (556). https://doi.org/10.1126/SCITRANSLMED.AAZ6606.

Lukova, P., Katsarov, P., Pilicheva, B., 2023. Application of starch, cellulose, and their derivatives in the development of microparticle drug-delivery systems. Polymers 15 (17). https://doi.org/10.3390/polym15173615.

Luna Lazo, R.E., de Paula Oliveira, B., Cobre, A.d.F., Mota Ferreira, L., Bettega Felipe, K., de Oliveira, P.R., Seigi Murakami, F., 2023. Engineering porous PLGA microparticles for pulmonary delivery of sildenafil citrate. Powder Technol. 430. https://doi.org/10.1016/j.powtec.2023.118999.

Medipelli, A., Chinthala, P., 2025. Study on effect of formulation variables on drug release of bosentan microspheres. Biosci. Biotechnol. Res. Asia 22 (1), 255–266. https://doi.org/10.13005/bbra/3358.

Miles, C.E., Bernstein, A.D., Osborn Popp, T.M., Murthy, N.S., Nieuwkoop, A.J., Gormley, A.J., 2021. Control of drug release from microparticles by tuning their crystalline textures: A structure-activity study. ACS Appl. Polym. Mater. 3 (12), 6548–6561. https://doi.org/10.1021/acsapm.1c01254.

Motiei, M., Mišík, O., Truong, T.H., Lizal, F., Humpolíček, P., Sedlařík, V., Sáha, P., 2023. Engineering of inhalable nano-in-microparticles for co-delivery of small molecules and miRNAs. Discov. Nano 18 (1). https://doi.org/10.1186/s11671-023-03781-0.

Nguyen, H.X., Kipping, T., Banga, A.K., 2025. Enhancement of transdermal drug delivery: Integrating microneedles with biodegradable microparticles. Mol. Pharm. 22 (2), 984–1009. https://doi.org/10.1021/acs.molpharmaceut.4c01202.

Park, K., Otte, A., Sharifi, F., Garner, J., Skidmore, S., Park, H., Jhon, Y.K., Qin, B., Wang, Y., 2021. Formulation composition, manufacturing process, and characterization of poly (lactide-co-glycolide) microparticles. J. Contr. Release 329, 1150–1161. https://doi.org/10.1016/j.jconrel.2020.10.044.

Pooresmaeil, M., Namazi, H., 2020. pH-sensitive ternary Fe3O4/GQDs@G hybrid microspheres; synthesis, characterization and drug delivery application. J. Alloys Compd. 846. https://doi.org/10.1016/j.jallcom.2020.156419.

Sood, A., Dev, A., Das, S.S., Kim, H.J., Kumar, A., Thakur, V.K., Han, S.S., 2023. Curcumin-loaded alginate hydrogels for cancer therapy and wound healing applications: A review. Int. J. Biol. Macromol. 232. https://doi.org/10.1016/j.ijbiomac.2023.123283.

Verma, D., Dua, K., Kapoor, D.N., Bhatia, A., Chopra, S., Prasher, P., Gupta, G., Tambuwala, M.M., Chellappan, D. K., Aljabali, A.A.A., Sharma, M., 2021. Advancements on Microparticles-Based Drug Delivery Systems for Cancer Therapy Advanced Drug Delivery Systems in the Management of Cancer. Elsevier, India, pp. 351–358. https://doi.org/10.1016/B978-0-323-85503-7.00003-1.

Vieira, W.S., Pinto, J.C., Lopes, R.T., de Souza, M.N., 2020. Development of hybrid microspheres for assessment of multiphase processes. Appl. Radiat. Isot. 158, 109035. https://doi.org/10.1016/j.apradiso.2020.109035.

Vlachopoulos, A., Karlioti, G., Balla, E., Daniilidis, V., Kalamas, T., Stefanidou, M., Bikiaris, N.D., Christodoulou, E., Koumentakou, I., Karavas, E., Bikiaris, D.N., 2022. Poly (Lactic acid)-based microparticles for drug delivery applications: An overview of recent advances. Pharmaceutics 14 (2), 359. https://doi.org/10.3390/pharmaceutics14020359.

Wan, B., Andhariya, J.V., Bao, Q., Wang, Y., Zou, Y., Burgess, D.J., 2021. Effect of polymer source on in vitro drug release from PLGA microspheres. Int. J. Pharm. 607. https://doi.org/10.1016/j.ijpharm.2021.120907.

Wang, J., Heshmati Aghda, N., Jiang, J., Habib, A.M., Ouyang, D., Maniruzzaman, M., 2022. 3D bioprinted microparticles: Optimizing loading efficiency using advanced DoE technique and machine learning modeling. Int. J. Pharm 628. https://doi.org/10.1016/j.ijpharm.2022.122302.

Xu, Y., Wang, F., Zhang, P., Lu, C., Liu, W., Guo, Y., Ni, Z., Wang, J., Lu, B., Lou, Q., Liang, X., Liu, J., 2024. High-precision 3D printing by deploying expandable microspheres. Cell Rep. Phys. Sci. 5 (8). https://doi.org/10.1016/j.xcrp.2024.102113.

Xu, Z., Zhang, Q., Fan, C., Xiao, M., Yang, R., Yao, Y., Wu, Y., Nie, X., Wang, H., Liu, W., 2023. A gel microparticle-based self-thickening strategy for 3D printing high-modulus hydrogels skeleton cushioned with PNAGA hydrogel mimicking anisotropic mechanics of meniscus. Bioact. Mater. 26, 64–76. https://doi.org/10.1016/j.bioactmat.2023.02.020.

Yadav, K.S., Raut, H.C., Nijhawan, H.P., 2023. Inhalable spray-dried polycaprolactone-based microparticles of sorafenib tosylate with promising efficacy on A549 cells. Pharmaceut. Dev. Technol. 28 (8), 755–767. https://doi.org/10.1080/10837450.2023.2251148.

Yan, Y., Zhang, J., Ren, L., Tang, C., 2016. Metal-containing and related polymers for biomedical applications. Chem. Soc. Rev 45 (19), 5232–5263. https://doi.org/10.1039/c6cs00026f.

Zhao, J., et al., 2022. Injectable, anti-cancer drug-eluted chitosan microspheres against osteosarcoma. J. Funct. Biomater. 13.

Zhang, L., Lu, Z., Ma, L., Liu, N., Bai, Z., 2025. Preparation of nanofiber microspheres and investigation of coalescence performance enhanced by the coupled swirling flow field. Chem. Eng. Sci. 316, 121854. https://doi.org/10.1016/j.ces.2025.121854.

CHAPTER

26

Microneedles for anticancer drug delivery

Vikas, Justin Jablonski, Maddelyn Hoehn, Nurhaliza Syukur and Jason R. McCarthy

Department of Biomedical Research and Translational Medicine, Masonic Medical Research Institute, Utica, NY, United States

Introduction

Cancer is a growing disease, with prevalence increasing worldwide. In 2022, 20 million new cases and 9.7 million cancer-associated mortalities were diagnosed globally (Bray et al., 2024). Typical cancer treatments include surgical resection, radiation therapies, and chemotherapies, with the former two typically localized to cancerous areas and the latter a systemic approach (Abbas and Rehman, 2018). Although the strategies are effective at killing cancer cells, they also pose undesirable side effects. Surgery and radiotherapy can remove healthy tissues, leaving scarring, and are linked to cancer relapse, while chemotherapy leads to hair loss, chronic nausea and fatigue, immunocompromise, and organ toxicity (Abbas and Rehman, 2018). Studies are ongoing on the use of biological controls for cancer, such as stem cell-based immunomodulation, antiangiogenic factors, antibodies, and hormone therapies, as well as investigating novel methods and devices for diagnosing cancers and delivering the therapeutics (Abbas and Rehman, 2018). FDA-approved cancer drug delivery systems, such as liposomal formulations, nanoparticle-bound drugs, implantable wafers, and antibody-drug conjugates, have significantly improved cancer treatment by improving drug targeting while reducing systemic toxicity. However, these systems face numerous challenges, including insufficient penetration into tumor tissues, off-target effects on other body regions, elicitation of immune responses, high production costs, and the need for frequent administration in clinical settings (Oostra and Macrae, 2014; Iuchi et al., 2022; Barenholz, 2012; Ghahremanloo et al., 2025; Miele et al., 2009; Shi et al., 2017; Tong et al., 2024; Metselaar and Lammers, 2020).

Advanced Cancer Therapeutics
https://doi.org/10.1016/B978-0-443-44185-1.00004-5

Microneedle-based drug delivery systems offer an effective strategy for addressing several challenges associated with conventional formulations, including the need for intravenous administration, systemic toxicity, and limited patient compliance. Through minimally invasive, localized delivery, microneedles have the potential to enhance safety, improve user experience, and enable at-home administration. Microneedle arrays are small patches containing numerous tiny "needles", which are small and short enough to avoid pain and discomfort in patients. Depending on the design of these needles, various drugs and diagnostic agents can be delivered, and fluid samples can be taken, facilitating the detection and treatment of tumors and diffuse cancers. The use of microneedles to treat cancers allows for improved patient comfort, ease-of-use, and localization of treatment, allowing for the use of potent chemotherapeutics and novel drugs while reducing many of the off-target effects. Despite the lack of FDA approval for cancer treatment, microneedles are being investigated for their ability to deliver chemotherapeutic agents, immunotherapies, and cancer vaccines in preclinical models. Potential benefits include reduced systemic toxicity, controlled or extended drug release, and the ability to administer multiple therapeutic agents at the same time. Following promising results in preclinical studies, microneedle-based therapies, are currently undergoing early phase clinical trials (A Trial to Evaluate Placebo Microneedle Arrays in Healthy Human Volunteers, 2021). Challenges remain, including the limited number of drugs that can be administered, penetration depth, scalability of production, and the need for comprehensive clinical data. Addressing these challenges could position microneedles as a significant advancement in cancer treatment administration (Hema et al., 2025). This chapter investigated the potential of microneedle-based delivery of drugs as an alternative treatment for cancer. Microneedles provide a minimally invasive platform with considerable potential for translation into clinical applications and improved patient compliance. Additionally, the components and characterization methods of microneedles were discussed, various preclinical studies focused on cancer treatment and diagnosis were reviewed, and the challenges encountered in this field were addressed.

Essential components of microneedles

The array

Microneedle arrays are a three-dimensional geometric grid of small "microneedle" structures arranged on a supporting base. These microneedles, which may or may not resemble actual needles depending on the type of array, allow transdermal delivery of a drug to enhance the absorption of pharmaceuticals, avoiding large systemic doses. The most important aspects of microneedle arrays are the needles that can be tuned as per the requirement. Shape, size, material, fabrication method, and type of needle are all interlinked, which determine the drug release from the array (AL-Japairai et al., 2020; Aldawood et al., 2021). The base of the array may be manufactured as a single piece with the microneedles, or may be made separately as a simple or layered structure, depending on flexibility requirements, method of manufacture, and other specific needs (AL-Japairai et al., 2020; Aldawood et al., 2021; Xue et al., 2025; Xiang et al., 2024). Reservoirs can be incorporated into the base of the needle to increase drug loading capacities (Shao et al., 2024). The base of the array can be functionalized to further improve the efficacy of the microneedle delivery system, with different technologies used to enhance drug delivery. Xue et al. (2025) utilized a microneedle array with a composite circuit in the base to apply ultrasound to the skin beneath the array, which worked with nanoparticles injected by the needles to improve the generation of reactive oxygen species (ROS) for cancer therapy (Xue et al., 2025). Oungeun et al. (2024) developed a patch that used light-emitting diodes to activate photo-sensitizers for ROS therapy (Oungeun et al., 2024). Shao et al. (2024) used a multilayered base with a powdered iron layer for a self-heating oxidation reaction that thermally enhanced the release of the drug from the microneedle array (Shao et al., 2024). Functionalization of the microneedle base is uncommon due to the higher costs and complexities of manufacturing, but it allows new approaches and improvements in microneedles for various cancer therapies.

Needle geometries

Microneedles are patient-friendly with zero pain and discomfort, and allow sustained drug delivery for longer action (AL-Japairai et al., 2020). Microneedles are typically approximately 1 mm in length or smaller. This allows the needles to penetrate the stratum corneum and the upper epidermal layers effectively, creating perforations in the hydrophobic skin barrier through which the drug can then enter easily (Wang et al., 2025; Zhu et al., 2025). The microneedle length plays a crucial role, as shorter lengths are less likely to penetrate sufficiently, while longer lengths are more likely to cause pain and discomfort in patients (Wang et al., 2025). The other aspects of microneedle geometries are their shape. Needle shapes are often conical or pyramidal, giving a strong support base with a narrow tip for more effective skin penetration (AL-Japairai et al., 2020; Wang et al., 2025; Zhu et al., 2025). Needles may also have hexagonal or octagonal bases, increasing the edges of the needles to enhance swelling capabilities (Zhu et al., 2025). Cylindrical needles may also be used, due to easier manufacturability and increased internal volume for drug loading (Wang et al., 2025). Variations in thickness and geometries are often chosen to influence drug release kinetics and delivery to the target site.

Materials

Numerous materials can be used to construct microneedle arrays based on their design and manufacturing method. In cases where higher rigidity is prioritized, microneedles are often made of inorganic materials such as silicon, alloys, ceramics, and rigid polymers (AL-Japairai et al., 2020; Aldawood et al., 2021; Zhu et al., 2025; Cammarano et al., 2024). These materials have high structural integrity, enhancing microneedle penetration to the skin. However, these materials have lower biocompatibility and pose a risk of fracture and residues. Additionally, manufacturing limitations and costs make these materials less commonly used in microneedle arrays. For anticancer drug-loaded microneedles design, natural and biocompatible polymers are preferred. These consist of carbohydrates (alginate, trehalose, chitin, and hyaluronan), proteins (silk, collagen), polyvinyl pyrrolidone (PVP), methylacrolyl (MA) polymers, and polyvinyl alcohol (PVA), and other synthetic polymers (AL-Japairai et al., 2020; Xiang et al., 2024; Cammarano et al., 2024). Though these microneedles tend to have lower penetration strength, there is less concern over breakage since many of these polymers are biodegradable and will not require removal. Additionally, these polymers may form hydrogels upon contact with fluid (AL-Japairai et al., 2020; Zhu et al., 2025). This allows more flexible methods of drug loading and delivery (Chen et al., 2017; Ingrole and Gill, 2019; Lan et al., 2018).

Classification of needles

Microneedle arrays are typically classified based on the method of drug delivery, as different types of microneedles have distinct drug release profiles. There are commonly six types of microneedles: solid, coated, porous, hollow, dissolvable, and swellable (Tang et al., 2024). Fig. 26.1 shows the drug delivery mechanism of different types of microneedles, as reproduced from Zhu et al. (2025) (Zhu et al., 2025).

Solid microneedles

Unlike other microneedle types, solid microneedles do not contain a drug within the needles or the patches that support the needle array. Instead, these microneedles work through perforation of the stratum corneum and upper epidermis, creating small breaks in the barrier of the skin to allow drugs to diffuse into the lower epidermis and underlying dermis easily (AL-Japairai et al., 2020; Aldawood et al., 2021; Wang et al., 2025; Sadeqi et al., 2022). A drug-containing patch or cream is then applied over the perforated area, allowing enhanced transdermal absorption of the drug, as compared to intact skin. This method of drug delivery may be referred to as the "poke-and-patch" method, with the microneedles "poking" the skin before the "patch" of drug is delivered, although in some cases the medication may be applied first before the microneedle array helps drive the medication deeper (AL-Japairai et al., 2020; Wang et al., 2025). The purpose of these needles is mechanical strength and durability. Solid microneedles are usually made of strong, rigid materials, such as metals, alloys, ceramics, and nondegradable polymers (AL-Japairai et al., 2020; Aldawood et al., 2021; Zhu et al., 2025). Due to their solid design and the higher strength of these materials, solid microneedles tend to be more durable and are cheaper and easier to manufacture (Aldawood et al., 2021; Wang et al., 2025). Additionally, these needles are reusable. However, the nonbiodegradable nature of solid microneedle materials raises concerns of enhanced inflammation and residues left in the skin (Aldawood et al., 2021; Zhu et al., 2025; Sadeqi et al., 2022).

Coated microneedles

Coated microneedles are solid microneedles that have been coated with a pharmaceutical agent. These are manufactured as solid microneedle arrays, but a drug coating is applied to the needles before use via dipping or spraying (Wang et al., 2025; Ingrole and Gill, 2019). The drug-coated needles are applied to the skin to perforate the stratum corneum as before, allowing the drug from the coating layer to reach the deep epidermal layers for absorption

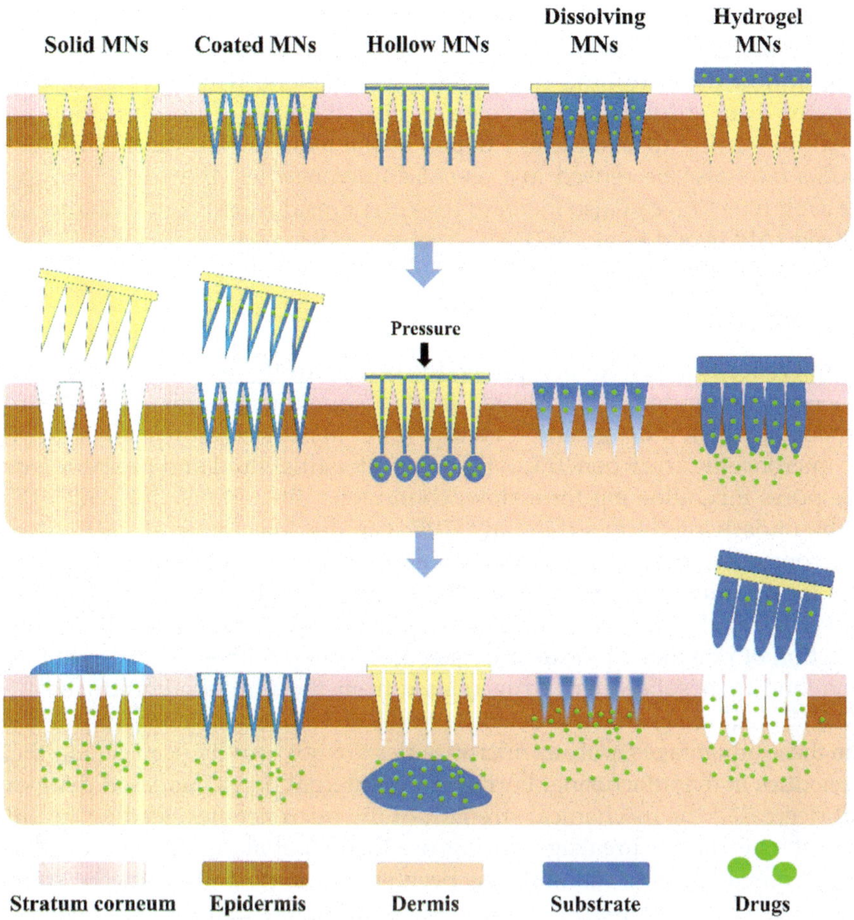

FIGURE 26.1 **Drug delivery mechanism of different types of microneedles.** Solid microneedles create microchannels for passive drug diffusion. Coated microneedles release surface-coated drug upon insertion. Hollow microneedles deliver liquid formulations under pressure. Dissolving microneedles dissolve within the skin to release encapsulated drugs. Hydrogel microneedles absorb interstitial fluid and enable sustained drug release through swelling *Reproduced from Zhu , Lanqi, Qiao, Guanlin, Gao, Huiyang, Jiang, Aowei, Zhang, Linan & Wang, Xiaobing. (2025). Enhancing melanoma therapy with hydrogel microneedles. Front. Oncol., 15. https://doi.org/10.3389/fonc.2025.1590534, licensed under CC BY (https://creativecommons.org/licenses/by/4.0/).*

(AL-Japairai et al., 2020; Aldawood et al., 2021; Zhu et al., 2025). The dissolution of the coated layer allows quick delivery of a set amount of drug; however, the release is poorly controlled due to the limited swelling time of the microneedle arrays and the thinness of the drug coating layer (Aldawood et al., 2021; Zhu et al., 2025). Compared to solid microneedles, material choice and surface functionalization of coated microneedles are more important to ensure retention of the coated drug layer. Polymeric coatings may be used to enhance drug loading, especially if both hydrophobic and hydrophilic drugs are utilized (Wang et al., 2025). However, a limited amount of drug can be coated onto the microneedles, where the surface-coated nature restricts the amount of drug that can be delivered (Aldawood et al., 2021; Wang et al., 2025; Zhu et al., 2025). Additionally, the uniformity and location of the coating are critical in controlling drug release parameters, with uneven coatings leading to inconsistent drug absorption, and coatings near the base of needles often failing to be properly absorbed due to insufficient depth in the skin (Ingrole and Gill, 2019). Coated microneedles may also be reused just as solid microneedles, the surface properties optimized for drug retention can also increase the risk of residue and contamination if not properly sterilized (Aldawood et al., 2021).

Porous microneedles

Porous microneedles seek to incorporate the drug directly into solid microneedles. These needles incorporate randomly distributed pores throughout the microneedle, providing an interior space in which a drug can be loaded (Li et al., 2017; van der Maaden et al., 2015). When the microneedle array penetrates the skin, interstitial fluid and preloaded drug within the needle pores mix, allowing for a slow, continuous diffusion of drug out of the needles and into the underlying dermis (Li et al., 2017; van der Maaden et al., 2015). Compared to coated microneedles, porous microneedles are capable of delivering larger amounts of drug over longer time periods, making them more suitable for controlled or sustained drug releases (Li et al., 2017; van der Maaden et al., 2015). Fig. 26.2 illustrates the diagrammatic depiction of polymeric porous microneedles loaded with solid drugs before and after application, and their subsequent drug release from the skin, as reproduced from Sadeqi et al. (2022) (Sadeqi et al., 2022).

Despite these advantages, porous microneedles are not heavily used due to their delicacy and complexities in manufacturing. Formation of internal pores increased drug carrying capacity but decreased the mechanical strength of the microneedles, leading to difficulties in insertion of the needles or breakage during use (Sadeqi et al., 2022; van der Maaden et al., 2015). Use of metals such as titanium has been shown to help alleviate the strength issues and has been used to form porous microneedles strong enough for skin penetration; however, the use and manufacture of these materials is costly (Li et al., 2017). Needle strength can also be increased by using a solid-cored needle with a porous external coating; however, these coatings still have low mechanical properties and risk of breakage in the skin (van der Maaden et al., 2015). Additionally, as the solid core is increased and the porous coating is thinned, the volume and controlled-release nature of the pores are lost, and the microneedle becomes functionally similar to the coated microneedles.

Hollow microneedles

Unlike porous microneedles, hollow microneedles function similarly to a typical injection. These microneedles contain fully open internal reservoirs and an open tip, allowing for even larger volumes of drug to be loaded inside the needle (Aldawood et al., 2021; Wang et al., 2025; Zhu et al., 2025). When this microneedle array is then placed on the skin, the hollow needles allow the drug to flow out the tip and into the epidermis, like a shallower version of a subcutaneous injection. Due to the small size and large number of needles, manual

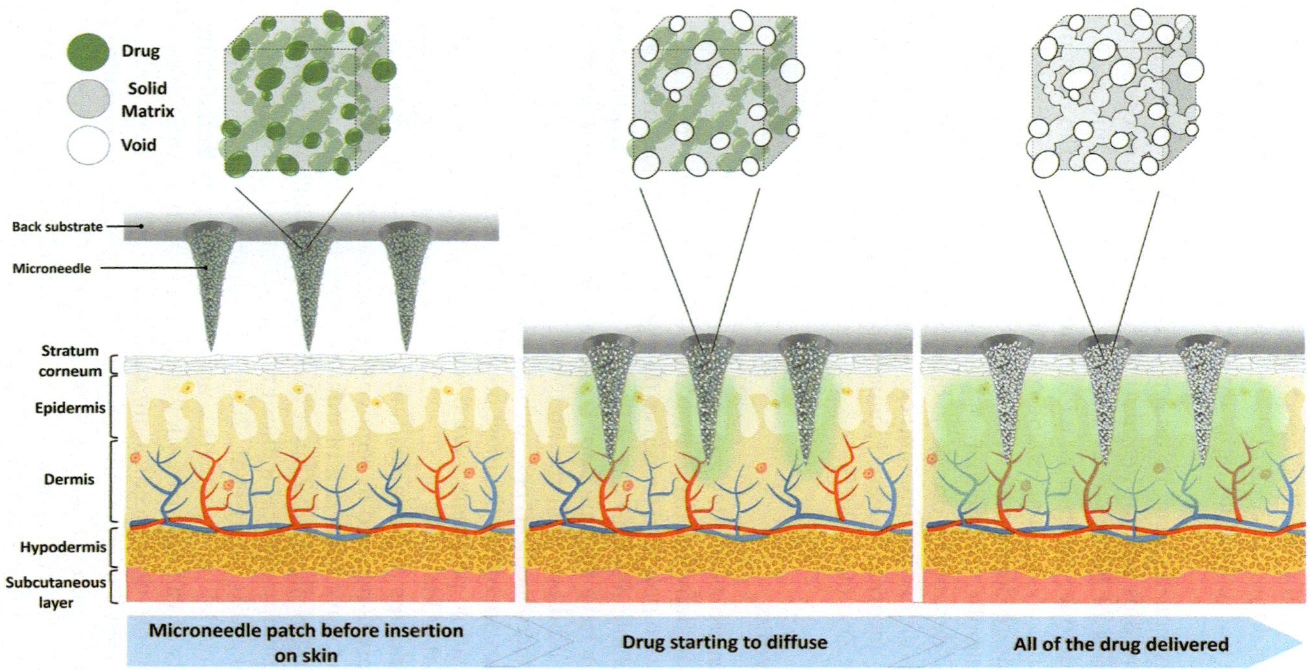

FIGURE 26.2 The diagrammatic depiction of polymeric porous microneedles loaded with solid drugs before and post application, and after drug release from the skin. Upon insertion, interstitial fluid dissolves the drug, enabling diffusion while leaving behind voids. The rigid resin preserves microneedle integrity during penetration. *Reproduced from Sadeqi , Aydin, Kiaee, Gita, Zeng, Wenxin, Rezaei Nejad, Hojatollah & Sonkusale, Sameer. (2022). Hard polymeric porous microneedles on stretchable substrate for transdermal drug delivery. Sci. Rep., 12(1). https://doi.org/10.1038/s41598-022-05912-6, licensed under CC BY 4.0 (http://creativecommons.org/licenses/by/4.0/).*

pressure is not often used to inject the drug, with delivery of the pharmaceutical instead often relying on diffusion out of the needle reservoir (AL-Japairai et al., 2020; Aldawood et al., 2021). Geometries of the needles, aperture sizes at the tip, and formulation of the loaded drug can all be modified to control the release profile of the drug, allowing for hollow microneedles to be useful for both rapid dosing and time-release therapies (Aldawood et al., 2021).

Although hollow microneedles can be adapted to a wide range of dosage amounts and regimens, these microneedles are not heavily utilized due to their cost and delicacy. The complex open geometries of hollow microneedles make manufacture more difficult and expensive than other microneedle options, with greater care needed in designing these needles (Aldawood et al., 2021; Wang et al., 2025). Additionally, storage and application of these microneedle arrays is more delicate as well, since the needles can be more easily bent or broken due to their thin-walled hollow nature (Aldawood et al., 2021). Finally, as controlled drug release is heavily dependent on the geometry and size of the apertures of hollow microneedles, blockages of the apertures and clogging of the needle risks impairing drug delivery and may lead to incorrect release kinetics or incomplete dosages (Aldawood et al., 2021; Wang et al., 2025; Zhu et al., 2025).

Dissolvable microneedles

The three previous microneedle designs rely on rigid, nondegradable materials that are used to break the skin to deliver a drug, then are removed. While these designs allow for stronger microneedles with potential for reuse, they pose risks for inflammation, needle fracture, and nonbiodegradable residues left at the site of application (Aldawood et al., 2021). Biodegradable polymers have become popular materials for microneedle manufacture due to their inherent compatibilities with the body (AL-Japairai et al., 2020), allowing for the development of new microneedle types such as dissolvable and swellable microneedles. Dissolvable microneedles are one of the most popular designs for microneedle arrays. These needles utilize biocompatible polymers loaded with a drug to provide for controlled release (AL-Japairai et al., 2020; Aldawood et al., 2021; Wang et al., 2025). As the needles are implanted, the polymeric tips degrade, leading to drug release into the epidermis and underlying dermis. As there is no need to remove the microneedles, these microneedle arrays can be easier to use and have little risk of inflammatory residues that other microneedles may leave behind (Wang et al., 2025; Zhu et al., 2025). Additionally, the ability to preload the microneedles with pharmaceutical without risk of leakage improves their ease of application (AL-Japairai et al., 2020; Xiang et al., 2024). Dissolvable microneedles have been used for drug delivery, vaccine delivery, cosmetics, and cell delivery, with the ability to encapsulate various components of various sizes allowing for flexibility in their applications (Xiang et al., 2024). As dissolvable microneedles are made of biodegradable polymers, they are often more delicate than solid microneedles and require more care in handling and insertion to prevent unintended fracture of the needles. Additionally, manufacture of dissolvable microneedles can be complex and typically requires careful casting and demolding to preserve the geometry of the microneedles (Aldawood et al., 2021; Wang et al., 2025).

Swellable microneedles

Swellable microneedles are formed from biocompatible hydrogels, which swell upon exposure to the water present in interstitial fluids. Once such microneedles are embedded into the skin, they absorb water and grow in size, forming pores and channels that allow the drug to diffuse out of the needles and enter the surrounding tissue (Wang et al., 2025; Zhu et al., 2025). Depending on the composition of these microneedles, they may be left in the tissue to biodegrade or may be removed from the tissue after drug release. The swelling property and channel formation of these microneedles can also be used outside of drug delivery, with some studies utilizing the swelling of these hydrogels to collect interstitial fluid for diagnosis (Jung et al., 2025; Huang et al., 2023). Swellable microneedles share many of the same challenges as dissolvable microneedles, with lower mechanical strength leading to difficulties in sufficient needle penetration and complex manufacturing (Wang et al., 2025; Zhu et al., 2025). Additionally, the rate of swelling of the polymer dictates the release profile of the incorporated drug, often driving slower sustained release rates over the course of hours to days (AL-Japairai et al., 2020).

Microneedle fabrication techniques

There are numerous ways to manufacture microneedles. Manufacturing options may be chosen based on microneedle design, material selection, and facility capabilities, with different methods having tradeoffs between precision, reproducibility, drug encapsulation capabilities, and cost.

Laser etching/laser ablation

For many inorganic materials or unloaded polymers, laser etching or laser ablation is often used. This technique utilizes a focused beam of light to precisely evaporate small amounts of material, burning away undesired sections with limited heat transfer to nearby areas (Aldawood et al., 2021; Ravi-Kumar et al., 2019). As excess material is removed, the shape of the microneedle array becomes apparent. Laser ablation allows for rapid production and high precision in manufacturing microneedle arrays, however the high costs associated with the devices and the loss of material during the ablation process limit the usefulness of this technique (Aldawood et al., 2021).

Lithography

Lithography techniques are another method of manufacturing microneedles and can be adapted to a wide range of materials. Lithography relies on the use of a "mask", or pattern, to dictate the shape of the resultant product, with photosensitive materials and the shadow pattern cast by the mask transferring the 2D design to the 3D product (Aldawood et al., 2021; Lee and Jung, 2012). Lithography techniques may be subtractive and use the mask to select material to remove from the microneedle array, or may be additive and may use the mask to dictate where material is added to the array (Lee and Jung, 2012). For example, Dardano et al. (2021) utilized photolithography with a UV-curable polymer system to manufacture hollow microneedles. The lithography mask was used to control UV exposure to the underlying UV-curable polymer, allowing only specific areas to cure to form the microneedle array and simplifying the manufacture of the complex hollow needle structure (Dardano et al., 2021). While lithography techniques are common and have both material adaptability and high precision, they require extended production times, high cleanliness, and careful mask alignment during the production of the microneedle array to ensure accurate needle formation (Aldawood et al., 2021; Dardano et al., 2021).

Micro-molding

Micromolding may also be used to produce microneedle arrays. Micromolding requires a master mold to be made, from which negative molds can be cast to form an individual microneedle array. This technique allows for the production of multiple identical arrays, making it efficient and popular in mass-production manufacturing (Aldawood et al., 2021). Additionally, the preset volume of micromolds allows for minimal loss of material during manufacturing, making this technique amenable to preloaded polymers such as those used in dissolvable microneedles. However, concerns must be taken with the specific materials used, as molding requires the material to be in a liquid form, and some polymers may exceed temperatures that will degrade the target pharmaceuticals (AL-Japairai et al., 2020).

It should also be noted that while popular, micromolding is not a stand-alone method for producing microneedle arrays. Another technique must be used to first create the master mold, with lithography or 3D printing often used (Aldawood et al., 2021). While this provides for another, often complex step in the manufacture of micromolded microneedles, the single mold produced allows for production of tens to hundreds of molded arrays, offsetting the additional costs and providing for enhanced reproducibility in microneedle production (Aldawood et al., 2021).

With micromolding, the small size of the molds and properties of the chosen materials may lead to trapped air or difficulties in properly filling the mold. As such, many micromolding techniques utilize methods to ensure proper filling of the mold, such as the application of heat or pressure to the mold (Aldawood et al., 2021). For example, Li et al. (2017) utilized injection molding to manufacture titanium microneedle arrays, which applies a vacuum to remove excess air and ensure successful filling of the mold (Li et al., 2017). Chen et al. (2017) utilized a hot-pressed method for similar purposes during the production of coated PLA microneedles, heating the polymer before applying direct pressure to ensure the PLA filled the mold entirely (Chen et al., 2017). These methods help to enhance the reproducibility and quality of the final microneedle arrays produced, but can increase the processing costs and time, and may require specialized equipment (Aldawood et al., 2021).

3D printing

3D printing is a newer but popular method for manufacturing microneedle arrays. 3D printing relies on the serial addition of material to the array, working layer-by-layer to build the microneedles (Zhu et al., 2025). Various types of 3D printing may be used. Fused Deposition Modeling (FDM), where materials are extruded and fused together to build the layers of a structure, is a common and cheaper method for printing structures but is limited by the resolution of the nozzle, curing speed of the deposited materials, and the complexity of the printed design (Olowe et al., 2022). Photopolymerization-based methods of 3D printing, such as Digital Light Processing, Stereolithography, Two-Photon Polymerization, and Selective Laser Sintering, allow for higher resolution and faster production times of microneedle arrays (Zhu et al., 2025; Olowe et al., 2022). These methods utilize lasers to cure successive layers of a structure, which may be either fully submersed in the liquid form of the printing material or may be held against a liquid or powder interface as material is sequentially added (Olowe et al., 2022). Depending on the method used, these forms of 3D printing require more delicate and expensive equipment than the more widely-available FDM printers.

Due to the nature of 3D printing technologies, it is often amenable to drug encapsulation within the microneedles, with biocompatible polymers preloaded with drug used to print dissolving or swellable hydrogel microneedles. The use of extrusion or laser-based curing is often mild enough to avoid damage to the pharmaceutical agents, making 3D printing popular for preloaded microneedle designs (Zhu et al., 2025).

Methods of drug loading

Loading of pharmaceutical agents into microneedles may occur during the manufacturing process or may be a subsequent step in the preparation of microneedles. For all types except solid microneedles, the drug must first be loaded before skin application, to allow the array to deliver the drug transdermally. For dissolvable microneedles and some swellable microneedles, encapsulation of the drug occurs during manufacture. The target drug is mixed in with the polymer that composes the microneedle array, and a gentler manufacturing process, such as micromolding or 3D printing, is used to form the microneedles (Aldawood et al., 2021; Lan et al., 2020; Luo et al., 2025; Kim et al., 2019; Cheng et al., 2023). This method is rather popular as it allows for easier and faster manufacturing of the final loaded array, but limits the manufacturing methods to those that will be safe for the encapsulated drug and will not cause degradation or denaturing of the pharmaceutical agent.

For other microneedles, such as coated, porous, hollow, and some swellable designs, drug encapsulation follows manufacture. Coated microneedles require that the drug be applied to the surface and often utilize coating solutions of the target drug dissolved in natural or biocompatible polymers such as sucrose or Polyvinyl alcohol (PVA) (AL-Japairai et al., 2020; Ingrole and Gill, 2019). The array may then be dipped or immersed in the coating, or the coating may instead be applied to the array via spray or inkjet printing to cover the microneedles with the drug (Chen et al., 2017; Ingrole and Gill, 2019). Porous and swellable microneedles may be loaded via submersion of the array into solutions containing the drug, allowing for diffusion of the drug into the microneedles to load the needles for future use (van der Maaden et al., 2015). Hollow microneedles may be loaded similarly, but many designs include an attached reservoir in the base of the array that can be preloaded with a drug before assembly or loaded after the array is complete for higher dosages (Aldawood et al., 2021; Dardano et al., 2021).

Characterization parameters

After the manufacture and loading of microneedle arrays, they must be characterized before use to ensure the successful delivery of the target pharmaceutical. When characterizing manufactured microneedles, the two key components that need to be considered are the mechanical properties of the array and the drug release properties of the system, unless it is a solid, uncoated array, which will have no drug to release.

Mechanical characterization

Mechanical characterization of microneedles is important to ensure that the needle array is able to successfully penetrate the skin without breakage, as failure to penetrate will prevent drug delivery, and breakage during penetration will also leave residue and increase inflammation. As such, testing both the axial and transverse failure strengths of microneedles is key to determining the likelihood of breakage (Aldawood et al., 2021). Any testing machines designed for mechanical stress tests can be used, and needles can either be tested to the point of failure or failure may be extrapolated from test data (Aldawood et al., 2021). Microscopy imaging is often used as well, both to characterize the geometries of the needles and to evaluate deformation or breakage sustained from mechanical testing (AL-Japairai et al., 2020; Aldawood et al., 2021). Characterization of the mechanical properties of microneedles allows for predictions of bending behavior and fracture risk in in vivo systems. It is also important to verify these findings with testing on actual skin sections. While mechanical testing allows for the prediction of the properties of the microneedle array during use, the irregular nature of skin (especially if tumors are present) may lead to inconsistent needle penetration. As such, skin insertion tests are often used to verify the success of the array in actual use (AL-Japairai et al., 2020; Aldawood et al., 2021). Skin samples of the target species should be used, although porcine skin is often utilized as a substitute for human skin samples. Additionally, live animal models may be used for penetration testing, allowing for better evaluation of inflammation and tissue responses to the array (AL-Japairai et al., 2020). The penetration success rate of the array (the number of needles that successfully pierce the skin to a depth sufficient for drug delivery) can be determined from these tests, with histology of the skin sections or 3D imaging techniques such as Optical Computed Tomography used to analyze the depth of penetration and geometry of pores formed by the microneedles (AL-Japairai et al., 2020; Aldawood et al., 2021).

Drug release characterization

Testing on simulated or actual skin can also assist with the characterization of the drug release profile of the microneedle system. A drug-loaded microneedle array can be applied to the test skin, with fluid samples taken from the other side of the skin at set times to measure the quantity of drug delivered through the skin over time (AL-Japairai et al., 2020). Similar testing may be completed in vivo on animals as well, often including fluorescent markers to help visualize drug release (van der Maaden et al., 2015; Luo et al., 2025; Fu et al., 2020), or may be completed in buffer solutions without the use of skin to characterize drug release rates into the surrounding fluid (AL-Japairai et al., 2020). Drug release characterization typically involves analytical techniques such as high-performance liquid chromatography (HPLC), UV–Vis spectroscopy, fluorescence imaging, and histological analysis. Key parameters assessed include release kinetics, diffusion depth, residual drug content, and skin retention time. These factors are essential for evaluating the release efficiency and therapeutic potential of microneedle formulations.

Fig. 26.3 Reproduced from Fu et al. (2020), illustrates a representative example of drug release behavior from microneedles fabricated using poly (vinylpyrrolidone–vinyl acetate) (PVPVA) as the base polymer, coloaded with cisplatin (CDDP) and IR820 (New Indocyanine Green). PVPVA was selected for its favorable water solubility, mechanical strength, and suitability for mold casting. Upon application to murine skin, the microneedles dissolve rapidly, releasing the loaded drugs. The figure presents bright-field and fluorescence microscopy images taken between 0 and 10 min after application, alongside UV–Vis absorption spectra, calibration curves, and residual drug quantification for both agents. These findings indicate successful microneedle insertion, rapid dissolution, and efficient drug release, underscoring the effectiveness of microneedles for localized combination drug delivery (Fu et al., 2020). Drug release profiles can also be simulated using various simulations and mathematical models (Yadav et al., 2020; Yang et al., 2025). As the materials and geometries of microneedles heavily influence drug release kinetics, modeling different designs can allow for characterization of drug release even before needles are manufactured (Yadav et al., 2020). Simulations are important in selecting needle types and designs to ensure the physical microneedle array has a high chance of working as desired, but these are typically supported by physical testing to ensure that the array behaves as expected (AL-Japairai et al., 2020; Yadav et al., 2020; Yang et al., 2025).

Microneedles: Emerging cancer drug delivery systems

Various drug delivery strategies have been explored to enhance the benefit-to-risk ratio by targeting medications directly to tumor sites (Imtiaz et al., 2025). Pegylated liposomal formulations of doxorubicin (DOX) have been used clinically to treat a wide range of cancers (Ghahremanloo et al., 2025). More recently, receptor-mediated targeted nanomedicines have gained attention for their promising results in preclinical models (Fan et al., 2023). Despite these advancements, many of these approaches require close medical supervision and may not be convenient for all patients. In settings where continuous medical oversight is not

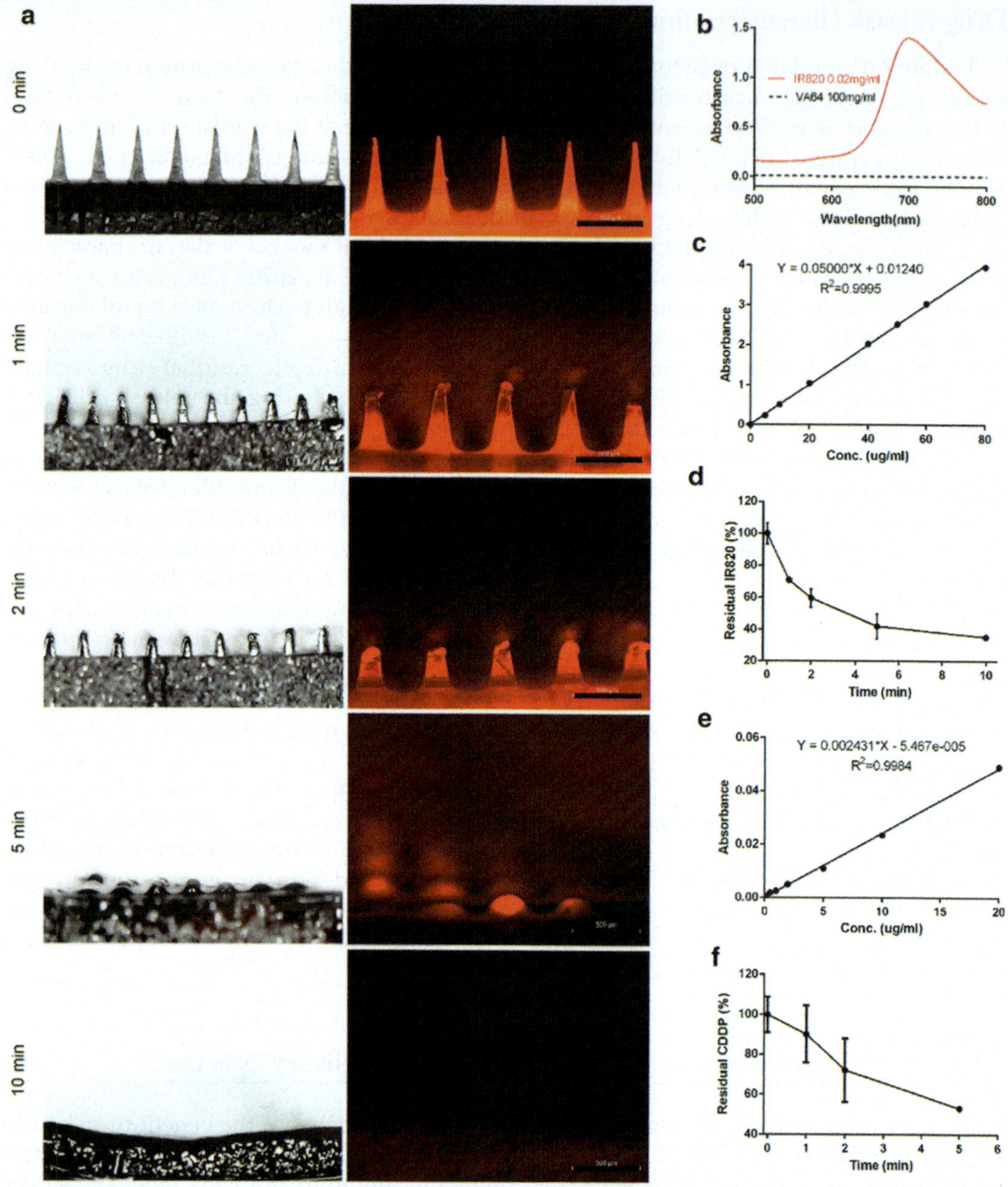

FIGURE 26.3 **Drug release profile from vinylpyrrolidone—vinyl acetate based microneedles.** a. Bright field and fluorescence microscope images of microneedles loaded with cisplatin and IR820, collected 0–10 min post in vivo application on mouse skin, with a scale bar of 500 μm. b. Visible absorption spectrum of PVPVA and IR820. c. Calibration curve for IR820. d. Residual percentage of IR820 in the microneedle. e. Calibration curve for CDDP. f. The remaining percentage of CDDP in the microneedle *Reproduced from Fu, J.j., Li, C.w., Liu, Y., Chen, M.y., Zhang, Q., Yu, X.y., Wu, B., Li, J.x., Du, L.r., Dang, Y.y., Wu, D., Wei, M.y., Lin, Z.q. and Lei, X.p. (2020). The microneedles carrying cisplatin and IR820 to perform synergistic chemo-photodynamic therapy against breast cancer. J. Nanobiotechnol., 18 (1). https://doi.org/10.1186/s12951-020-00697-0, licensed under CC BY 4.0 (https://creativecommons.org/licenses/by/4.0/).*

necessary, microneedle-based drug delivery systems offer a promising alternative due to their minimally invasive nature and potential for self-administration.

Microneedle for cancer treatment

The primary goal of drug delivery systems in cancer therapy is to deliver medication directly to the tumor site in sufficient concentration and duration. A wide range of cancer medications is currently being used (Li et al., 2025). Microneedle-based drug delivery systems provide more targeting options, not only for superficial or topical delivery, but also for malignant tumors that are accessible through or near the skin, depending on the cancer type and stage (Singh and Shukla, 2025).

While nanomedicine-based drug delivery systems have been extensively researched and shown promise in preclinical studies, there are still numerous challenges in translating these technologies into clinical and commercial applications (Patra et al., 2018; Metselaar and Lammers, 2020). Microneedle-based drug delivery systems provide numerous benefits, including improved patient compliance, minimally invasive administration, and the possibility of self-use (Waghule et al., 2019). Table 26.1 provides a comprehensive overview of recent advancements, including different microneedle designs, therapeutic agents, and targeted cancer treatment strategies assessed in preclinical investigations. Despite the challenges, their compelling pathway to commercialization makes them promising candidates for cancer treatment, especially in settings where close medical supervision is not required (Cammarano et al., 2024; Baker-Sediako et al., 2023).

Applications of microneedles in cancer therapy

Diagnosis

Interstitial fluid (ISF) is the extracellular fluid that envelops cells in the skin and various tissues, and it is significant in disease diagnosis. ISF encompasses a diverse array of biomarkers, including proteins, metabolites, nucleic acids, and exogenous compounds, which closely mirror those present in blood (Oharazawa et al., 2024; Kim and Prausnitz, 2021). The capability to extract interstitial fluid, especially through sophisticated microneedle technologies, represents a significant advancement as it facilitates a less invasive diagnostic method. ISF is an exceptional option for continuous monitoring and point-of-care applications, with the capacity to transform health assessment and disease management positively. Samant et al. (2020) utilized microneedle patches alongside mild suction to extract ISF from human dermis. This innovative method was favorably received by participants and enabled the collection of clinically significant volumes of ISF. The mass spectrometry analysis of samples from 21 human volunteers revealed multiple biomarkers commonly employed in research and clinical diagnostics in ISF and plasma (Samant et al., 2020).

Huang et al. (2023) developed a gelatin methacrylate acrylic acid based hydrogel microneedle patch, designed to extract samples from ISF with minimal invasiveness. Following insertion, hydrogel microneedles penetrate the stratum corneum and absorb ISF, which contains cancer-related biomarkers such as glycoantigen CA15-3 and carcinoembryonic antigen (CEA). The microneedle patch is prepared through ultraviolet crosslinking, forming a

TABLE 26.1 Recent advances in microneedle-based drug delivery for cancer treatment.

S. No.	Microneedle type	Basic components	Drug loaded	In vitro study	In vivo model	Outcomes	References
1.	Vinylpyrrolidone-vinyl acetate copolymer	• Vinylpyrrolidone-vinyl acetate copolymer (PVPVA) • Photosensitizer IR820 • Cisplatin (CDDP)	• Photosensitizer IR820 • Cisplatin (CDDP)	• MTT assay • Live/dead cell assay (calcein AM and PI) • Intracellular ROS detection (DCFH-DA and DHE probes) • Capase-3 activation assay	• Breast Cancer model using female Balb/c mice (6–8 weeks) • Subcutaneously injected with 4T1 breast cancer cells to establish tumors	• Significant tumor inhibition; enhanced cell apoptosis and reduced cell proliferation • Synergistic anticancer effect • Tumor inhibition ratios (TIR) were over 50% (90% for CDDP-IR820) (treatment reduced tumor size significantly compared to control group(s); high tumor suppression)	Fu et al. (2020)
	Wearable flexible ultrasound microneedle patch wf-UMP	• Hyaluronic acid (HA) • Piezocatalytic nanoparticles	• Modified KNN piezoelectric nanoparticles (mKNN PNPs)	• ROS measurement (using DCFH-DA fluorescence staining) • Flow cytometry analysis • Apoptosis assay (using FITC-Annexin V/PI staining) • Transwell assay • Cytotoxicity measurement (CCK8 assay)	• Subcutaneous tumor model of 4T1 breast cancer mice; female Balb/c mice (6–8 weeks old)	• Synergistic immunotherapy improved anticancer immunity (inhibiting distant tumor growth and tumor recurrence)	Xue et al. (2025)
	Polymeric porous microneedle (made from biocompatible and photo-curable resin)	• photo-curable resin • solid drug powder (lidocaine hydrochloride monohydrate and Ibuprofen sodium salt) • Polydimethylsiloxane (PDMS) and acrylic sheets	• Lidocaine and Ibuprofen (Anesthetic and nonsteroidal antiinflammatory drugs)	• Dye-loaded microneedle patch (ground sulforhodamine B dye, inserted microneedle patch into gelatin-based tissue model) • Drug release profile of Lidocaine and Ibuprofen (microneedle patches	• Ex vivo porcine skin model (isolated from a four-month-old male Yorkshire pig)	• Successful fabrication of porous microneedles • Effective drug loading and release • Reliable skin penetration • Strong mechanical properties • Versatility and conformability	Sadeqi et al. (2022)

			immersed in Dulbecco's phosphate buffered saline (DPBS) and drug concentration was measured using UV-Vis spectroscopy) • FTIR spectroscopy (confirm drug molecular structure remained intact)			
Supramolecular dissolving microneedle (DMN) patches	• Cyclodextrin (CD) derivatives	• Ability to load hydrophilic (RhB) and hydrophobic (ibuprofen) drugs	• Microneedles were tested on ex vivo skin models. • Mechanical strength, dissolution rate, drug loading and release were tested.	• Xylene-induced acute inflammation mouse model	• Fast dissolution (less than 30 s) • Rapid drug delivery and onset of therapeutic action • Successfully able to load both hydrophilic and hydrophobic drugs	Wang et al. (2022)
Coated polymer microneedle	• Polylactic acid (PLA)	• Sulforhodamine B	• Drug loading and delivery efficiency were measured using a microplate reader • Skin penetration test using porcine skin • Mechanical properties testing using a dynamometer	• Balb/c mouse model (8–10 weeks old female mice)	• Successful fabrication • Controlled drug loading and release • Effective skin penetration allowed for drug delivery to the subcutaneous tissue • 90% efficiency in skin penetration and drug release • In vivo mouse model displayed no skin injuries and allowed for natural skin recovery	Chen et al. (2017)
Gelatin methacryloyl (GelMA)	• Gelatin • Methacrylic anhydride (MA)	• Oncolytic Newcastle	• NDV release and expression detection using	• Mouse model (7-week-old female mice)	• Biocompatible and biodegradable with	Zhang et al. (2024)

(Continued)

TABLE 26.1 Recent advances in microneedle-based drug delivery for cancer treatment.—cont'd

S. No.	Microneedle type	Basic components	Drug loaded	In vitro study	In vivo model	Outcomes	References
	hydrogel microneedles	• 2-hydroxy-4'-(2-hydroxyethoxy)-2-methylphenylacetone	Disease Virus (NDV)	immunofluorescence and hemagglutination assays • Penetration tests (5% agarose gel and mouse model) • Swelling and degradation tests (GelMA blocks immersed in PBS and PBS with collagenase)		complete degradation within 24 h • Responsive to tumor-associated enzymes like collagenase were successful in vitro assay • Capable of penetrating skin • GelMA hydrogel successfully encapsulate and stabilize NDV • NDV release by delivery system was not detected; further experiments would need to be conducted	
	Photothermal therapy based Dissolving microneedle	• Semiconductor polymer nanoparticles (SPNs) • Hyaluronidase (hyalase) • Polyinosinic-polycytidylic acid (PIC) • Polyvinylpyrrolidone (PVP)	• Hyaluronidase-modififed semiconductor polymer nanoparticles (HSPN) • Polyinosinic-polycytidylic acid (PIC)	• Matrix degradation assay (tested hyaluronidase-modified nanoparticles to determine their ability to degrade extracellular matrix, specifically hyaluronic acid (major component of tumor stromal barrier) • Cell penetration and uptake (cancer cells were incubated with nanoparticles using 3D multicellular tumor spheroid (MCTS) model) • Cytotoxicity assay (CCK-8)	• C57BL/6 female mice (6-week-old that were injected subcutaneously with B16–F10 melanoma cells)	• Enhanced tumor penetration • Synergistic therapeutic effect (photothermal therapy with immune activation led to improved tumor suppression compared to treatment alone) • Enhanced immune response to tumor cells • Suppressed primary tumor growth and reduced likelihood of metastasis • Exhibited good photothermal performance and biocompatibility	He et al. (2021)

mechanically stable and highly swellable microneedle. The extent of cancer-specific biomarker levels was quantified from ISF for microneedles compared to traditional blood tests, and microCT and ultrasound imaging on a murine orthotopic 4T1 breast cancer model. Notably, there were higher levels of both the biomarkers in ISF through microneedle patch than in serum, indicating the potential of ISF biomarker-based diagnosis at earlier stages. In parallel, a genetically engineered MMTV-PyMT transgenic mouse model was used to investigate longitudinal biomarker expression during spontaneous tumor development. The results showed enhanced biomarker levels in ISF through microneedle, preceding serum changes. The findings suggest that microneedle-enabled ISF collection offers a rapid, local, and minimally invasive platform for early cancer diagnosis, highlighting its value for point-of-care screening and patient-friendly diagnostics (Huang et al., 2023).

Park et al. (2023) developed a hydrogel-based microneedle patch for the early detection of colorectal cancer in a separate study. The detection relies on identifying GPC-1 expression on exosomes originating from tumor cells. The microneedles comprise polycaprolactone (PCL) as the backing material, hydrogel tips formulated from alginic acid crosslinked with calcium chloride, and sucrose utilized as a swelling agent. Additionally, the hydrogel tips were enhanced with GPC1 (glypican-1) antibodies, which selectively bind to tumor-derived exosomes that overexpress GPC1, thereby increasing the specificity of cancer biomarker capture from ISF. The diagnosis strategy was validated using murine models for skin and colon cancer. The colon cancer model employed tumorigenesis by administering azoxymethane (AOM) and dextran sulfate sodium (DSS). The microneedles coated with 200 μL of alginate hydrogel extracted a higher volume of ISF and captured a significantly greater number of exosomes in cancer-bearing mice compared to healthy controls. Mice with colorectal cancer exhibited significantly elevated levels of GPC-1-positive exosomes in their ISF relative to healthy mice. The increase was detected using ELISA, demonstrating that the microneedles can differentiate between normal and cancerous states based on biomarker concentration. Nevertheless, in the context of a skin cancer model, the microneedles effectively extracted exosomes from ISF; however, GPC-1 did not demonstrate notable overexpression. The data indicate that, while exosome levels increase over time, skin tumors in this model do not exhibit the GPC-1 biomarker pattern observed in colorectal cancer. The findings highlight the specificity of GPC-1 as a biomarker for specific cancers, including colorectal cancer, and demonstrate the potential of microneedle-based ISF sampling for differential cancer diagnosis (Park et al., 2023).

Jung et al. (2025) developed hydrogel microneedles integrated with droplet digital PCR (ddPCR) for the efficient and minimally invasive lung cancer diagnosis. The microneedle patches of methacrylate hyaluronic acid are engineered to enhance mechanical strength and swellability, effectively extracting ISF. The optimized microneedle patches maintained their mechanical integrity while effectively extracting ISF from an agarose gel skin model within 10 min. Moreover, this study also demonstrated that RT-qPCR has a detection limit of approximately 1 pg/μL for identifying low-concentration miRNA biomarkers in ISF. On the other hand, the integrated droplet digital PCR (ddPCR) system increased sensitivity by 114-fold, resulting in a detection limit of 8.8 fg/μL. This innovative method enhances molecular diagnostics and patient outcomes by facilitating more accurate and accessible early cancer diagnosis (Jung et al., 2025). The amalgamation of sensitive detection methodologies, such as ddPCR, with microneedle-assisted ISF sampling created a solid foundation for accurate and minimally invasive cancer diagnostics. These methods can improve early disease detection through specific biomarker analysis, enhance patient comfort via minimally invasive techniques, and optimize sampling procedures.

Targeted chemotherapy

Microneedles may further be used for targeted delivery of chemotherapeutics to tumors or localized cancers, allowing for high local dosage at the targeted site with reduced systemic dosage for reduced side effects (Singh and Shukla, 2025). For example, Lan et al. (2018) developed a dissolving microneedle platform for head and neck squamous cell carcinoma, utilizing lipid nanoparticles carrying Cisplatin (Lan et al., 2018). Cisplatin precursor was encapsulated in lipid nanoparticles to overcome the poor solubility of cisplatin, and these nanoparticles were subsequently incorporated into a dissolving cellulose microneedle array manufactured by molding. In vitro studies demonstrated enhanced cellular uptake of the cisplatin and efficacy of the drug-loaded nanoparticles against squamous cell carcinoma cell lines, and in vivo studies against a xenograft model showed significant reductions in tumor volume and weight in treated groups compared to controls. Additionally, histological examination of organs found a lack of cisplatin-associated toxicity in the mice treated with the microneedle-nanoparticle therapy, whereas mice treated systemically showed notable cisplatin-associated organ toxicity (Lan et al., 2018). Use of microneedles to deliver localized doses of the chemotherapeutic agent successfully reduced systemic effects while providing efficacy against the targeted tumors.

Microneedle patches may also be functionalized to enhance the efficacy of chemotherapeutics delivered. Zhang et al. (2025) developed a microneedle system for the treatment of melanoma, using combined photothermal-chemotherapy with polypyrrole nanoparticles carrying DOX. Hydrogel microneedle arrays made of chitosan and polyvinyl alcohol were designed to deliver nanoparticles to the site of the tumor, where exposure to near-infrared light (NIR) was used to excite the polypyrrole particles and cause localized heating to potentiate DOX cytotoxicity (Zhang et al., 2025). The dual-modal therapy was confirmed by in vitro (B16 melanoma cells) and in vivo (A375 melanoma-bearing mice) studies. In vitro, microneedle mono-therapy reduced cancer cell viability to 60%. When supplemented with either DOX or phototherapy, the viability of the cells was further reduced to ~40%. The combined microneedle including DOX and NIR treatment resulted in maximal effects, giving ~20% cell viability and signifying a clear synergy among the therapeutic approach (Zhang et al., 2025). For in vivo studies, tumor-bearing mice were treated for 14 days, during which the control group did not receive any treatment. NIR treatment exhibited minimal effects, but microneedle treatment resulted in a 50% decrease in tumor volume. Microneedles loaded with DOX and or with NIR also moderately inhibited the growth of the tumor. The combined loading of DOX and NIR into the microneedle system led to the most significant antitumor effect, causing a much larger decrease in the volume of the tumor as compared to single treatment approaches (Zhang et al., 2025). This combination of localized drug delivery, bioactive nanoparticles, and phototherapy overcomes the major limitations of traditional chemotherapy and provides a more effective and patient-oriented treatment model, showing a promising approach for melanoma treatment.

In a similar vein, Oungeun et al. (2024) designed a dissolving DOX-loaded microneedle array that worked with LEDs for photo-driven cancer therapy, but they utilized a photosensitizer system instead of a photothermal system to enhance drug activity (Oungeun et al. 2024). Their microneedle array was made of the sugar alcohol sorbitol, preloaded with DOX and the photosensitizer chlorin-e6, and manufactured via micromolding. In-vitro and in-vivo studies on colorectal tumors also showed the efficacy of their microneedle-phototherapy system, with their chemotherapeutic and photosensitizer delivered by their microneedles working synergistically to increase apoptosis of cancerous cells to provide effective anticancer therapy (Oungeun et al. 2024). Fu et al. (2020) utilized the chemotherapeutic agent cisplatin with the photosensitizer IR820 in a dissolving microneedle array against breast cancer cells, and similarly found that the combination of photosensitizer and chemotherapeutic delivered the most effective cancer inhibition with no systemic toxicity (Fu et al., 2020). Shao et al. (2024) delivered thermally enhanced chemotherapy through the design of a multilevel self-heating microneedle array, which utilized iron oxidation to generate heat and improve the release of thymoquinone and 5-fluorouracil into the site of the cancer (Shao et al., 2024). Combined use of both drugs with the self-heating patch design was most effective at suppressing tumor growth in in-vivo studies without causing toxicity or systemic symptoms, further showing the flexibility of microneedle patches in developing effective combination therapies to enhance chemotherapeutic treatments of cancer with minimal side effects (Shao et al., 2024).

Immunotherapy

Immunotherapy employs the body's own immune system to treat cancer, helping the body to detect and eliminate cancer cells it otherwise fails to target properly. These therapies often work to enhance T-cell efficacy in clearing cancer cells, with antibodies targeting immune checkpoints often used to prevent tumor-initiated suppression of the immune system and thus to improve immune response against cancerous cells (Luo et al., 2025; Wang et al., 2016).

To enhance the efficacy of immunotherapy against tumors, Wang et al. (2016) designed a degradable microneedle patch to achieve localized and sustained delivery of antiPD1 (aPD1), a factor used to enhance T-cell activity in clearing tumors (Wang et al., 2016). This patch consisted of hyaluronic acid microneedles. The dissolving microneedles were loaded with dextran nanoparticles that encapsulated aPD-1 along with glucose oxidase (GOx). GOx catalyzes the oxidation of glucose to gluconic acid and hydrogen peroxide, generating a local acidic environment to enhance dissociation of the nanoparticles and thus release of the antibody. The localized enzymatic reaction ultimately promotes the degradation of the nanoparticles at a predictable rate to provide sustained release of aPD1 for about 72 h. This mechanism proves to be beneficial in promoting immune activation right at the tumor site and minimizing systemic release. In vivo studies with B16F10 melanoma-bearing mice showed that application of the microneedle patch achieved higher immune response over direct injections of aPD1 or patches without the GOx degradation trigger, demonstrating the efficacy of the microneedle-nanoparticle system in stimulating immunotherapies (Wang et al., 2016). Kim et al. (2019) used a similar modality for immunotherapy, developing a dissolving hyaluronic acid microneedle array to deliver a cytotoxic T-cell epitope peptide to stimulate the immune system response (Kim et al., 2019). The peptide was conjugated with low molecular weight hyaluronic acid to enhance immunogenicity, and the conjugates were incorporated into the dissolving needles during vacuum molding. In vivo testing in a murine melanoma model showed that mice immunized by the microneedle array had increased T-cell infiltration into cancer and reduced tumor growth, supporting the prophylactic role of the microneedle patch in enhancing immune response against cancer (Kim et al., 2019).

Just as with chemotherapeutics, combination therapies can enhance the efficacy of immunotherapy approaches as well. Xue et al. (2025) designed a dissolvable microneedle patch for aPD1 immunotherapy that included an integrated circuit and piezoelectric nanoparticles to provide ultrasound therapy to the region of microneedle application (Xue et al., 2025). The hyaluronic microneedle patch was preloaded with the antibody and the nanoparticles, which, upon delivery, were excited by the ultrasound transducer to induce ROS formation at the site of application. In-vitro and in-vivo analysis demonstrated enhanced immune response with the inclusion of the nanoparticles, providing another example of effective combination anticancer therapies being facilitated by the flexibility of microneedle design and application (Xue et al., 2025).

Metastasis and recurrence are the top contributors to cancer fatalities (Duong et al., 2023). Existing treatments lack the ability to sufficiently provide prolonged protection to patients, and as such, there is an urgent demand for novel long-lasting preventative measures. Use of immunotherapies against cancer can be expanded to vaccines against cancer, utilizing immune memory to provide long-term protection against cancer recurrence. Duong et al. (2023) developed a biodegradable two-layer microneedle patch to provide sustained release of a cancer DNA vaccine complex (Duong et al., 2023). The top layer contained a polyethylene glycol (PEG)-modified poly(sulfamethazine ester urethane) (PSMEU) polymer that degrades gradually over the course of 2 weeks, whereas the bottom layer consists of a polyvinylpyrrolidone/polyvinyl alcohol (PVP/PVA) combination that serves as the base for the array. Microneedles were loaded with an ovalbumen (OVA)-expressing DNA vaccine and the adjuvant polyinosinic-polycytidylic acid. Due to instability and inability to penetrate cell membranes, these compounds were encapsulated with deoxycholic acid-conjugated low-molecular-weight polyethyleneimine, which protects the compounds and promotes cell penetration. The resulting complexes were incorporated in the microneedle layer for prolonged intradermal delivery, enabling gradual uptake by antigen-presenting cells and eliciting a persistent tumor-specific immune response. This approach demonstrated vaccine release over the course of 10 days and marked lung metastasis inhibition in tumor models, providing a prospective clinical strategy for preventing recurrence (Duong et al., 2023).

Luo et al. (2025) designed a dissolving microneedle patch of modified hyaluronic acid for postsurgical inhibition, utilizing immune activators such as cGAMP and IL-2 and an antiCTLA-4 antibody to enhance immune function (Luo et al., 2025). This patch showed suppression of tumor recurrence in an incomplete tumor resection model, inhibiting tumor growth, prolonging mouse survival, and increasing T-cell infiltration into solid tumors. Additionally, the microneedle vaccine was compared to chemotherapy and radiotherapy, the current standards for preventing tumor recurrence, and serum and histology tests showed an absence of pathological changes in microneedle-treated mice, whereas both radiotherapy and chemotherapy were associated with organ-specific toxicities (Luo et al., 2025). Boone et al. (2020) utilized a polyvinylpyrrolidine dissolving microneedle array to deliver the plant-targeting cowpea mosaic virus (CMPV) to tumors to stimulate immune response, forming an "in-situ" vaccine relying on the tumor's own antigens (Boone et al., 2020). The application of a foreign virus, CPMV, into the tumor as an adjuvant functions to generate an acute immune response that induces antitumor immunity. CMPV was formulated into nanoparticles, which were loaded into the microneedle array during molding. Magnesium (Mg) was also loaded into the tips of the microneedle array. Upon application, dissolution of the Mg tips led to gas evolution and faster release of the CPMV into the tumor microenvironment, increasing the strength of the subsequent immune response in the area. In vivo studies of the microneedle patches showed enhanced mouse survival and tumor suppression over injections of CMPV, suggesting the use of the microneedle array in approving the strength of in situ vaccination strategies against cancer (Boone et al., 2020).

In a recent preclinical study, Xue et al. (2025) developed a wearable flexible ultrasound microneedle patch (wf-UMP) incorporating piezoelectric nanoparticles (mKNN PNPs) for cancer immunotherapy. This patch demonstrated both mechanical adaptability and electromechanical responsiveness, allowing for efficient application on curved and dynamic tissue surfaces. Upon ultrasound activation, the embedded nanoparticles generated ROS, inducing oxidative stress and immunogenic cell death in tumor cells. These effects collectively enhanced dendritic cell maturation and promoted macrophage polarization toward the M1 phenotype, effectively stimulating antitumor immunity. The ROS production in 4T1 tumor cells was visualized using DCFH-DA fluorescence staining, while JC-1 and flow cytometry assays confirmed apoptosis. The Transwell assay revealed significant inhibition of tumor cell invasiveness. In vivo, the wf-UMP treatment group showed marked tumor growth suppression, reduced tumor weights, and prolonged survival in murine models. Histological analysis demonstrated decreased proliferation (Ki-67), increased apoptosis (TUNEL), and reduced angiogenesis (CD31) in tumors following treatment. Furthermore, when combined with antiPD-1 checkpoint blockade, wf-UMP treatment significantly improved immune responses, effectively targeting both primary and distal tumors in dual tumor models and reducing recurrence by enhancing immune memory. These findings highlight the potential of microneedle-based platforms in delivering combination immunotherapies for effective and localized cancer treatment (Xue et al., 2025).

Theranostic

Microneedle drug delivery research is poised to significantly advance theranostics in the realm of cancer treatment. These innovative, minimally invasive devices seamlessly blend form and function, offering a compelling dual approach that empowers both precise diagnostic sampling and effective therapeutic delivery. The efficacy of drugs is improved by polymeric microneedles through the targeted delivery of anticancer agents and the acquisition of skin-derived biomarkers. This approach facilitates the immediate evaluation of therapeutic outcomes and encourages the development of personalized treatment strategies. Microneedle technologies have the potential to revolutionize minimally invasive approaches for cancer diagnosis and treatment, significantly improving patient outcomes and enhancing quality of life. Table 26.2 summarizes recent microneedle-based ISF sampling techniques developed for cancer diagnostics.

Dosta et al. (2023) developed a novel microneedle platform based on hyaluronic acid for the efficient delivery of nanoparticles containing cytosine-phosphate-guanine (CpG) oligonucleotides. The innovative microneedle system tracks therapeutic responses and facilitates

TABLE 26.2 Overview of microneedle platforms for ISF sampling in preclinical cancer models.

Microneedle tyle/material	Cancer type	Duration of application	Biomarker(s) detected	Analysis method	Outcomes	References
Hydrogel-coated microneedle: • Base material: polycaprolactone • Coating material: alginate hydrogel, sucrose, calcium chloride, poly-l-lysine • Drug delivery component: glypican-1 antibodies (GCP-1)	Colorectal	20 min	• Glypican-1 (GCP-1)	• ELISA assay • Fluorescence microscopy • Confocal laser scanning microscopy	• Successful interstitial fluid extraction • Tumor specific exosome detection • Enhanced diagnostic sensitivity	Park et al. (2023)
Hydrogel-based microneedle: • Microneedle matrix: hyaluronic acid, 8-arm PEG-NHS • Back layer: PGLA • Drug delivery component: CpG Oligodeoxynucleotides (cpG-ODNs), Poly(β-amino ester)s) (PBAEs))	Melanoma Colorectal	24 h	• Macrophages (CD11b+, F4/80) • Dendritic cells ($CD11c^+$, $MHCII^+$, $CD80^+$, $CD80^{hi}$, $CD45^+$) • Natural killer cells ($CD45^+NK^+$) • T cells ($CD4^+$ helper T cells, $CD8^+$ effector T cells, $CD8^+$/$CD4^+$ ratio)	• Flow cytometry • ELISA • Confocal microscopy • Histology • Dynamic light scattering	• Successful interstitial skin fluid extraction • Biomarker correlation (correlated with tumor) • Longitudinal monitoring (enabled serial tracking)	Dosta et al. (2023)
• Gelatin methacrylate (GelMA-AA)	Breast	1 min	• CA15-3 • Carcinoembryonic antigen (CEA)	• ELISA • Imaging-based: CT (Micro-CT) and ultrasound • Blood testing	• Successful interstitial skin fluid extraction • Improved interstitial fluid extraction efficiency in a shortened period of time	Huang et al. (2023)
Hydrogel based microneedle patches: • Methacrylate hyaluronic acid (HA-MeHA)	Lung	10 min	• miR-21 • miR-155 • miR-210	• Droplet digital PCR (ddPCR)	• Successful interstitial skin fluid extraction • High biomarker recovery efficiency • Precise differentiation of miRNA profiles • Superior sensitivity of ddPCR and maintained sensitivity during multiplex detection	Jung et al. (2025)
Dissolving microneedles: • Hyaluronic acid (HA) • Dextran, • Polyvinylpyrrolidone (PVP)	Melanoma	5 min	• Primary biomarker: STAT3 (signal transducer and activator transcription 3) • Secondary biomarkers: Bcl-xl, Bcl-2, Mcl-1, Survivin (antiapoptotic genes upregulated by STAT3) • Cyclin D1, c-Myc (cell cycle regulators influenced by STAT3) • MMP-2 (promotes tumor invasion and metastasis) • VEGF (stimulates angiogenesis)	• RT-PCR (measured mRNA expression levels in vitro and in vivo) • MTT antiproliferation assay (for cell viability and proliferation) • Histology (H and E staining)	• Efficiently delivered siRNA to melanoma cells • Achieved targeted gene silencing of STAT3 • Suppressed tumor growth in a dose-dependent manner • Safe and minimally invasive procedure	Pan et al. (2018)

transdermal drug delivery by analyzing immune cells collected within the microneedles following patch retrieval and digestion. The transdermal delivery of microneedles containing CpG-NPs in mice with orthotopic melanoma demonstrates a significant reduction in tumor growth and an enhancement in survival rates. The CpG-nanoparticle-loaded microneedles significantly decrease tumor size by actively stimulating innate immune cells. Intravital microscopy demonstrates the transport efficiency of CpG-NPs to the tumor microenvironment, highlighting their spatiotemporal accumulation. The analysis of ISF obtained through microneedles reveals immunological features similar to those present in bulk tumor homogenate, particularly an elevation in macrophages and effector T cells following treatment. Fig. 26.4 illustrates the application of a hyaluronic acid-based microneedle patch designed for the codelivery of CpG oligonucleotides and poly (β-amino ester) nanoparticles, alongside the sampling of interstitial fluid (ISF) for immune cell analysis. Panel A shows the schematic representation of the microneedle patch design, highlighting its capability to deliver immunomodulatory agents and simultaneously collect ISF for immune cell profiling. Panel B presents dynamic light scattering characterization of the CpG-containing nanoparticles, ensuring proper size and stability. Panel C demonstrates the efficient uptake of CpG-NPs by TLR9-expressing HEK 293 cells, confirming the functionality of the system. Panel D illustrates NF-κB activation in TLR9-expressing cells, confirming immune activation. Panel E shows the successful application of the microneedle patch on mouse skin. Finally, Panel G presents the in vitro release profile of CpG-NPs from the microneedles, showcasing sustained release, which further supports the potential of this platform for cancer immunotherapy (Dosta et al., 2023).

Advantages of microneedle drug delivery

Microneedle drug delivery systems offer several significant advantages, particularly in the context of cancer treatment. One key benefit is that microneedles can serve as an alternative drug delivery system for established therapeutics and diagnostic agents, allowing for the direct delivery of drugs through the skin and bypassing the limitations of traditional oral and intravenous routes (Waghule et al., 2019). This system can improve bioavailability and offer a more targeted approach to therapy, reducing systemic side effects. Another important advantage is the minimally invasive nature of microneedles, which eliminates the need for injections or infusions (Zhou et al., 2023). This makes treatment more comfortable and convenient for patients. Moreover, the potential for self-administration enables patients to manage their treatment. When recommended by a medical team and supported by proper training and resources, this approach can improve treatment adherence, reduce the burden on healthcare systems, and lower overall costs (Liu et al. 2023). Microneedles also enable theranostic applications, where both therapeutic and diagnostic agents can be delivered simultaneously (Alshammari et al., 2023). This dual functionality allows for real-time monitoring of the treatment's effectiveness and disease progression, facilitating personalized therapy. The ability to adjust treatment based on immediate feedback could significantly improve patient outcomes. In terms of biocompatibility, microneedles are typically made from materials that are well-tolerated by the body, reducing the risk of adverse immune responses. This is especially crucial for cancer patients who may already have weakened

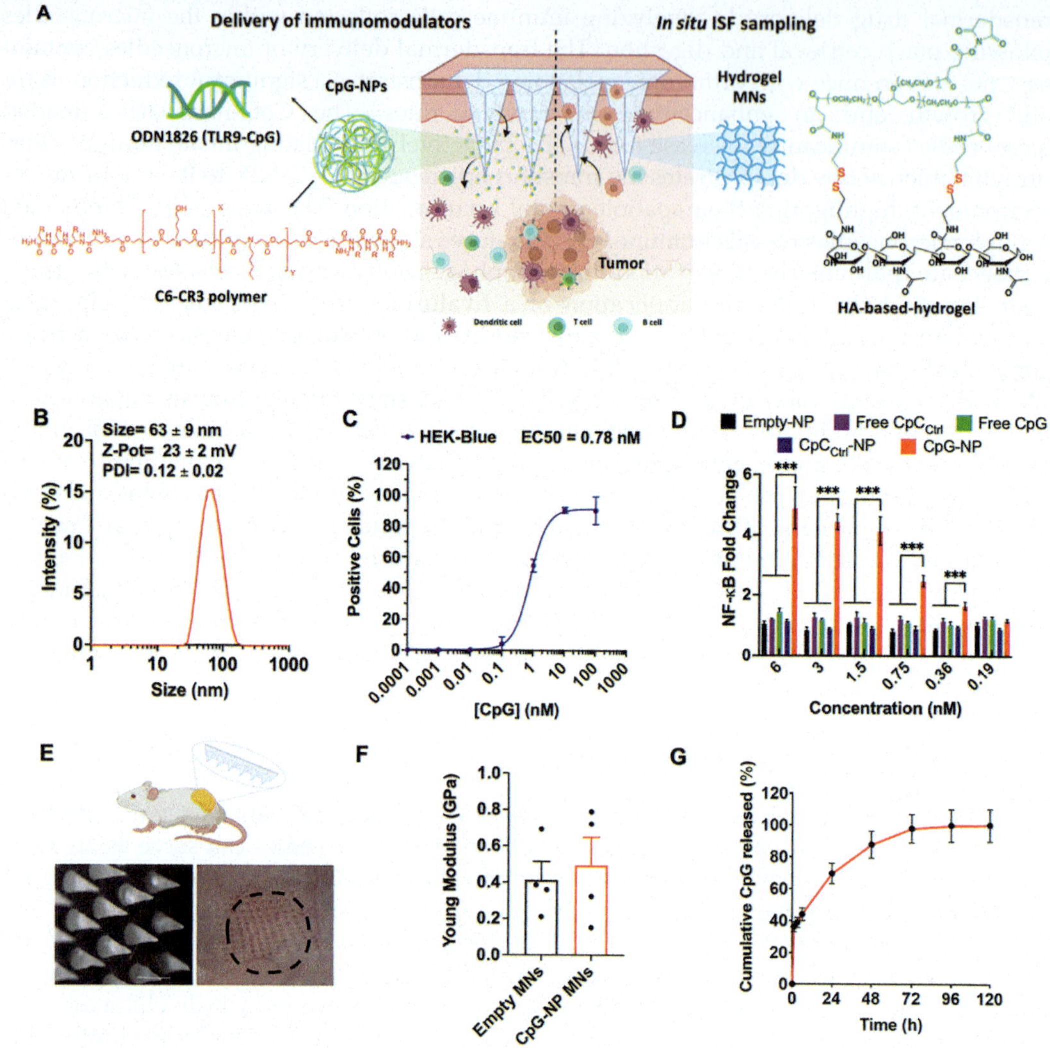

FIGURE 26.4 **Theranostic application of microneedle platforms for skin cancer.** (A) Schematic of hyaluronic acid based microneedle patch for co-delivery of CpG oligonucleotides complexed with poly (β-amino ester) s and simultaneous sampling of ISF for immune cell analysis. (B) Dynamic light scattering characterization of CpG-containing nanoparticles (NPs). (C) Quantification of CpG-NP uptake by TLR9-expressing HEK 293 cells via flow cytometry. (D) In vitro NF-κB activation in HEK293 TLR9 reporter cells treated with various formulations: Free CpG, CpCCtrl, CpG-NPs, CpCCtrl-NPs, and empty NPs. (E) microscopy image of HA-based microneedles (scale bar = 500 μm) and representative image of microneedle administration in mouse skin (dotted line marks tumour region). (F) Compression testing comparing the mechanical strength of empty microneedles (MNs) and CpG-NP-loaded microneedles. (G) In vitro release profile of fluorescently labelled CpG-NPs from microneedles at pH 7.4, 37°C. *Reproduced from Dosta, Pere, Puigmal, Núria, Cryer, Alexander M., Rodríguez, Alma L., Scott, Ella, Weissleder, Ralph, Miller, Miles A. and Artzi, Natalie. (2023). Polymeric microneedles enable simultaneous delivery of cancer immunomodulatory drugs and detection of skin biomarkers. Theranostics, 13(1), 1–15. https://doi.org/10.7150/thno.73966, licensed under CC BY 4.0 (https://creativecommons.org/licenses/by/4.0/).*

immune systems due to their condition or treatment (Maia et al., 2025). Another distinctive advantage is that microneedles can bypass the limitations of oral drug delivery, where first-pass metabolism often reduces drug efficacy (Wang et al., 2025).

Finally, the cost-effectiveness of microneedle systems is an important consideration. As microneedles can be used for self-administration, they can reduce the need for frequent healthcare visits, cutting down on overall treatment costs for both patients and healthcare systems (Richter-Johnson et al., 2018). Additionally, the adaptability of microneedles makes them more easily integrated across research, industry, and clinical settings compared to some other drug delivery technologies. Their scalability and ease of use in mass production make them particularly industry-friendly, allowing for smooth transitions from laboratory research to clinical application (Baker-Sediako et al., 2023). This level of adaptability is more challenging with other forms of drug delivery, which may face barriers in terms of scalability, regulatory hurdles, or patient compliance. Microneedles can be loaded with anti-cancer nanoparticles, resulting in an advanced drug delivery system with modified drug delivery for effective cancer therapy while minimizing drug-related systemic toxicity (Jha et al., 2024).

Limitations and challenges

Despite the promising advantages of microneedle-based drug delivery systems for cancer treatment, several limitations and challenges need to be addressed before they can achieve widespread clinical application. First, microneedles have a limited dosing capacity, which makes them less suitable for high-dose chemotherapy regimens typically required in cancer treatment. While effective for delivering small, localized doses or adjuvant therapies, microneedles may not be able to accommodate the higher doses needed for aggressive cancer treatments. To overcome this challenge, the development of high-dose microneedles or combining them with other drug delivery systems may be necessary (Jung and Jin, 2021; Li et al., 2021). Another limitation is the application area. Microneedles are designed primarily for skin-based delivery, restricting their use to accessible areas of the body. This makes them unsuitable for cancers located in internal organs, such as the brain, lungs, or liver, where access to skin surfaces is not feasible. Consequently, while microneedles are effective for localized cancers or skin treatments, their use in systemic cancer therapy remains limited (Zhu et al., 2024; Rad et al. 2021). Expanding their application through nanoparticle formulations or alternative delivery methods could help address this issue. One significant challenge with microneedles is the risk of infection at the site of skin puncture. Although microneedles create only shallow holes, they disrupt the skin's natural barrier, potentially allowing pathogen entry. This risk is heightened in cancer patients with compromised immune systems due to treatments like chemotherapy or radiation. To mitigate infection risks, strict sterility protocols and proper postapplication care are essential (Wu et al., 2024). Future research focused on innovative delivery systems that combine microneedles with other technologies may offer solutions for overcoming this challenge. In addition, clinical outcomes with microneedles can be variable, possibly due to variations in drug formulations, microneedle designs, or individual patient skin characteristics. More research is needed to optimize microneedle designs, formulations, and treatment regimens to improve clinical consistency (Ryan, 2018).

Conclusions

Microneedle-based drug delivery systems offer a minimally invasive, biocompatible, and self-administered alternative to traditional methods, addressing major limitations like bioavailability and patient compliance. They are particularly promising in oncology, enabling targeted chemotherapy, immunotherapy, and theranostic applications, combining treatment and diagnostic capabilities in one platform. However, challenges remain, including limited dosing capacity, skin accessibility, and risk of infection, all of which can impact clinical outcomes. Variations in microneedle design, drug formulation, and skin characteristics contribute to these inconsistencies. To realize their full potential, interdisciplinary research is necessary to refine designs, optimize clinical protocols, and ensure the safe and effective application of these technologies. Microneedles hold great promise for cost-effective, precise, and patient-friendly cancer therapies, but their success depends on continued innovation and standardization across scientific and clinical fields.

References

A Trial to Evaluate Placebo Microneedle Arrays in Healthy Human Volunteers (Part I), Followed by Proof of Concept Testing of Efficacy and Safety of Doxorubicin Microneedle Arrays in Subjects with Basal Cell Cancer (Part II). (2021).

Abbas, Z., Rehman, S., 2018. An Overview of Cancer Treatment Modalities. IntechOpen. https://doi.org/10.5772/intechopen.76558.

Alshammari, M.K., Albutayh, B.N.A., Alhabib, B., Alharbi, A.S., Almutairi, Y.S., Kamal, M., Aloraini, M.S., Alotaibi, M.M., Alhusayni, S.J., Al-Ahmad, I.F., Ali Alghamdi, N., Almutiri, B.B., Arshad, M.F., Imran, M., 2023. Cancer theranostics employing microneedles: Experimental and patented strategies. J. Drug Deliv. Sci. Technol. 83, 104402. https://doi.org/10.1016/j.jddst.2023.104402.

AL-Japairai, K.A.S., Mahmood, S., Almurisi, S.H., Reddy Venugopal, J., Rebhi Hilles, A., Azmana, M., Raman, S., 2020. Current trends in polymer microneedle for transdermal drug delivery. Int. J. Pharm. 587, 119673. https://doi.org/10.1016/j.ijpharm.2020.119673.

Aldawood, F.K., Andar, A., Desai, S., 2021. A comprehensive review of microneedles: Types, materials, processes, characterizations and applications. Polymers 13 (16). https://doi.org/10.3390/polym13162815.

Baker-Sediako, R.D., Richter, B., Blaicher, M., Thiel, M., Hermatschweiler, M., 2023. Industrial perspectives for personalized microneedles. Beilstein J. Nanotechnol. 14, 857–864. https://doi.org/10.3762/BJNANO.14.70.

Barenholz, Y.(C.), 2012. Doxil — The first FDA-approved nano-drug: Lessons learned. J. Contr. Release 160 (2), 117–134. https://doi.org/10.1016/j.jconrel.2012.03.020.

Boone, C.E., Wang, C., Lopez-Ramirez, M.A., Beiss, V., Shukla, S., Chariou, P.L., Kupor, D., Rueda, R., Wang, J., Steinmetz, N.F., 2020. Active microneedle administration of plant virus nanoparticles for cancer in situ vaccination improves immunotherapeutic efficacy. ACS Appl. Nano Mater. 3 (8), 8037–8051. https://doi.org/10.1021/acsanm.0c01506.

Bray, F., Laversanne, M., Sung, H., Ferlay, J., Siegel, R.L., Soerjomataram, I., Jemal, A., 2024. Global cancer statistics 2022: GLOBOCAN estimates of incidence and mortality worldwide for 36 cancers in 185 countries. CA Cancer J. Clin. 74 (3), 229–263. https://doi.org/10.3322/caac.21834.

Cammarano, A., Dello Iacono, S., Battisti, M., De Stefano, L., Meglio, C., Nicolais, L., 2024. A systematic review of microneedles technology in drug delivery through a bibliometric and patent overview. Heliyon 10 (23), e40658. https://doi.org/10.1016/j.heliyon.2024.e40658.

Chen, Y., Chen, B.Z., Wang, Q.L., Jin, X., Guo, X.D., 2017. Fabrication of coated polymer microneedles for transdermal drug delivery. J. Contr. Release 265, 14–21. https://doi.org/10.1016/j.jconrel.2017.03.383.

Cheng, X., Hu, S., Cheng, K., 2023. Microneedle patch delivery of PROTACs for anti-cancer therapy. ACS Nano 17 (12), 11855–11868. https://doi.org/10.1021/acsnano.3c03166.

Dardano, P., De Martino, S., Battisti, M., Miranda, B., Rea, I., De Stefano, L., 2021. One-shot fabrication of polymeric hollow microneedles by standard photolithography. Polymers 13 (4), 520. https://doi.org/10.3390/polym13040520.

Dosta, P., Puigmal, N., Cryer, A.M., Rodríguez, A.L., Scott, E., Weissleder, R., Miller, M.A., Artzi, N., 2023. Polymeric microneedles enable simultaneous delivery of cancer immunomodulatory drugs and detection of skin biomarkers. Theranostics 13 (1), 1–15. https://doi.org/10.7150/thno.73966.

Duong, H.T.T., Yin, Y., Le, T.M.D., Jeong, J.H., Lee, D.S., 2023. Highly prolonged release of the cancer vaccine and immunomodulator via a two-layer biodegradable microneedle for prophylactic treatment of metastatic cancer. Biomacromolecules 24 (3), 1209–1219. https://doi.org/10.1021/acs.biomac.2c01270.

Fan, D., Cao, Y., Cao, M., Wang, Y., Cao, Y., Gong, T., 2023. Nanomedicine in cancer therapy. Signal Transduct. Targeted Ther. 8 (1). https://doi.org/10.1038/s41392-023-01536-y.

Fu, J.j., Li, C.w., Liu, Y., Chen, M.y., Zhang, Q., Yu, X.y., Wu, B., Li, J.x., Du, L.r., Dang, Y.y., Wu, D., Wei, M.y., Lin, Z.q., Lei, X.p., 2020. The microneedles carrying cisplatin and IR820 to perform synergistic chemo-photodynamic therapy against breast cancer. J. Nanobiotechnol. 18 (1). https://doi.org/10.1186/s12951-020-00697-0.

Ghahremanloo, A., Erfani, B., Asgharzadeh, F., Mansoori, S., Gheybi, F., Isaac Hashemy, S., 2025. Reducing toxicity and enhancing efficacy of doxorubicin by liposomal doxorubicin and aprepitant in breast cancer. Sci. Rep. 15 (1). https://doi.org/10.1038/s41598-025-94291-9.

He, T., Luo, Y., Zhang, Q., Men, Z., Su, T., Fan, L., Chen, H., Shen, T., 2021. Hyalase-mediated cascade degradation of a matrix barrier and immune cell penetration by a photothermal microneedle for efficient anticancer therapy. ACS Appl. Mater. Interfaces 13 (23), 26790–26799. https://doi.org/10.1021/acsami.1c06725.

Hema, A.J., Bala, R., singh, A., 2025. A review on recent advances and challenges of microneedle technology for enhanced topical treatment of skin disorders. Arch. Dermatol. Res. 317 (1). https://doi.org/10.1007/s00403-025-04239-2.

Huang, H., Qu, M., Zhou, Y., Cao, W., Huang, X., Sun, J., Sun, W., Zhou, X., Xu, M., Jiang, X., 2023. A microneedle patch for breast cancer screening via minimally invasive interstitial fluid sampling. Chem. Eng. J. 472, 145036. https://doi.org/10.1016/j.cej.2023.145036.

Imtiaz, S., Tamanna Ferdous, U., Nizela, A., Hasan, A., Shakoor, A., Zia, A.W., Uddin, S., 2025. Mechanistic study of cancer drug delivery: Current techniques, limitations, and future prospects. Eur. J. Med. Chem. 290, 117535. https://doi.org/10.1016/j.ejmech.2025.117535.

Ingrole, R.S.J., Gill, H.S., 2019. Microneedle coating methods: A review with a perspective. J. Pharmacol. Exp. Therapeut. 370 (3), 555–569. https://doi.org/10.1124/jpet.119.258707.

Iuchi, T., Inoue, A., Hirose, Y., Morioka, M., Horiguchi, K., Natsume, A., Arakawa, Y., Iwasaki, K., Fujiki, M., Kumabe, T., Sakata, Y., 2022. Long-term effectiveness of Gliadel implant for malignant glioma and prognostic factors for survival: 3-year results of a postmarketing surveillance in Japan. Neurooncol. Adv. 4 (1). https://doi.org/10.1093/noajnl/vdab189.

Jha, A., Kumar, M., Goswami, P., Manjit, M., Bharti, K., Koch, B., Mishra, B., 2024. Hyaluronic acid-oleylamine and chitosan-oleic acid conjugate-based hybrid nanoparticle delivery via. dissolving microneedles for enhanced treatment efficacy in localized breast cancer. Biomater. Adv. 160. https://doi.org/10.1016/j.bioadv.2024.213865.

Jung, D., Kim, W., Song, Y., Yu, S.-bin, Rho, D., Nam, H.B., Kim, Y.T., Lee, K.G., Jung, J.H., 2025. Ultrasensitive and non-invasive multiplex miRNA detection for lung cancer diagnostics using hydrogel microneedles-integrated droplet digital PCR. Chem. Eng. J. 516, 164001. https://doi.org/10.1016/j.cej.2025.164001.

Jung, J.H., Jin, S.G., 2021. Microneedle for transdermal drug delivery: Current trends and fabrication. J. Pharm. Investig. 51 (5), 503–517. https://doi.org/10.1007/s40005-021-00512-4.

Kim, H., Seong, K.-Y., Jung, H.L., Park, W., Yang, S.Y., Hahn, S.K., 2019. Biodegradable microneedle patch delivering antigenic peptide–hyaluronate conjugate for cancer immunotherapy. ACS Biomater. Sci. Eng. 5 (10), 5150–5158. https://doi.org/10.1021/acsbiomaterials.9b00961.

Kim, Y., Prausnitz, M.R., 2021. Sensitive sensing of biomarkers in interstitial fluid. Nat. Biomed. Eng. 5 (1), 3–5. https://doi.org/10.1038/s41551-020-00679-5.

Lan, X., She, J., Lin, D.-an, Xu, Y., Li, X., Yang, W.-fa, Lui, V.W.Y., Jin, L., Xie, X., Su, Y.-xiong, 2018. Microneedle-mediated delivery of lipid-coated cisplatin nanoparticles for efficient and safe cancer therapy. ACS Appl. Mater. Interfaces 10 (39), 33060–33069. https://doi.org/10.1021/acsami.8b12926.

Lan, X., Zhu, W., Huang, X., Yu, Y., Xiao, H., Jin, L., Pu, J.J., Xie, X., She, J., Lui, V.W.Y., Chen, H.-J., Su, Y.-xiong, 2020. Microneedles loaded with anti-PD-1–cisplatin nanoparticles for synergistic cancer immuno-chemotherapy. Nanoscale 12 (36), 18885–18898. https://doi.org/10.1039/d0nr04213g.

Lee, K., Jung, H., 2012. Drawing lithography for microneedles: A review of fundamentals and biomedical applications. Biomaterials 33 (30), 7309–7326. https://doi.org/10.1016/j.biomaterials.2012.06.065.

Li, J., Liu, B., Zhou, Y., Chen, Z., Jiang, L., Yuan, W., Liang, L., Santos, H.A., 2017. Fabrication of a Ti porous microneedle array by metal injection molding for transdermal drug delivery. PLoS One 12 (2), e0172043. https://doi.org/10.1371/journal.pone.0172043.

Li, K., Guo, B., Gu, J., Na, T., Gu, J., Yu, H., Sun, M., Han, T., 2025. Emerging advances in drug delivery systems (DDSs) for optimizing cancer complications. Mater. Today Bio 30, 101375. https://doi.org/10.1016/j.mtbio.2024.101375.

Li, W., Song, L., Fan, X., Prausnitz, M.R., 2021. Microneedle patch designs to increase dose administered to human subjects. J. Contr. Release 339, 350–360. https://doi.org/10.1016/j.jconrel.2021.09.036.

Liu, F., Cheng, Z., Yi, H., 2023. NIR light-activatable dissolving microneedle system for melanoma ablation enabled by a combination of ROS-responsive chemotherapy and phototherapy. J. Nanobiotechnol. 21 (1). https://doi.org/10.1186/s12951-023-01815-4.

Luo, Z., Li, X., Zhu, D., Fu, W., Liu, Y., Zheng, L., Chen, P., Gong, C., Liu, X., 2025. Implantable immunostimulant microneedle patch for post-surgical prevention of cancer recurrence and distant tumor inhibition. ACS Appl. Mater. Interfaces 17 (15), 22362–22374. https://doi.org/10.1021/acsami.5c01155.

Maia, R.F., Machado, P., Rodrigues, R.O., Faustino, V., Schütte, H., Gassmann, S., Lima, R.A., Minas, G., 2025. Recent advances and perspectives of MicroNeedles for biomedical applications. Biophys. Rev. 17 (3), 909–928. https://doi.org/10.1007/s12551-025-01317-7.

Metselaar, J.M., Lammers, T., 2020. Challenges in nanomedicine clinical translation. Drug Deliv. Transl. Res. 10 (3), 721–725. https://doi.org/10.1007/s13346-020-00740-5.

Miele, E., Spinelli, G.P., Miele, E., Tomao, F., Tomao, S., 2009. Albumin-bound formulation of paclitaxel (Abraxane ABI-007) in the treatment of breast cancer. Int. J. Nanomed. 4 (1), 99–105.

Oharazawa, A., Maimaituxun, G., Watanabe, K., Nishiyasu, T., Fujii, N., 2024. Metabolome analyses of skin dialysate: Insights into skin interstitial fluid biomarkers. J. Dermatol. Sci. 114 (3), 141–147. https://doi.org/10.1016/j.jdermsci.2024.04.001.

Olowe, M., Parupelli, S.K., Desai, S., 2022. A review of 3D-printing of microneedles. Pharmaceutics 14 (12). https://doi.org/10.3390/pharmaceutics14122693.

Oostra, D.R., Macrae, E.R., 2014. Role of trastuzumab emtansine in the treatment of HER2-positive breast cancer. Breast Cancer 6, 103–113. https://doi.org/10.2147/BCTT.S67297.

Oungeun, M., Wanichwecharungruang, S., Miyako, E., 2024. Wireless light-emitting diode-driven functional microneedle devices for skin cancer therapy. Adv. Therapeut. 7 (11). https://doi.org/10.1002/adtp.202400233.

Pan, J., Ruan, W., Qin, M., Long, Y., Wan, T., Yu, K., Zhai, Y., Wu, C., Xu, Y., 2018. Intradermal delivery of STAT3 siRNA to treat melanoma via dissolving microneedles. Sci. Rep. 8 (1). https://doi.org/10.1038/s41598-018-19463-2.

Park, W., Maeng, S.-W., Won Mok, J., Choi, M., Cha, H.J., Joo, C.-K., Hahn, S.K., 2023. Hydrogel microneedles extracting exosomes for early detection of colorectal cancer. Biomacromolecules 24 (3), 1445–1452. https://doi.org/10.1021/acs.biomac.2c01449.

Patra, J.K., Das, G., Fraceto, L.F., Campos, E.V.R., Rodriguez-Torres, M.D.P., Acosta-Torres, L.S., Diaz-Torres, L.A., Grillo, R., Swamy, M.K., Sharma, S., Habtemariam, S., Shin, H.S., 2018. Nano based drug delivery systems: Recent developments and future prospects. J. Nanobiotechnol. 16 (1). https://doi.org/10.1186/s12951-018-0392-8.

Ravi-Kumar, S., Lies, B., Zhang, X., Lyu, H., Qin, H., 2019. Laser ablation of polymers: A review. Polym. Int. 68 (8), 1391–1401. https://doi.org/10.1002/pi.5834.

Rad, Z.F., Prewett, P.D., Davies, G.J., 2021. An overview of microneedle applications, materials, and fabrication methods. Beilstein J. Nanotechnol. 12, 1034–1046. https://doi.org/10.3762/BJNANO.12.77.

Richter-Johnson, J., Kumar, P., Choonara, Y.E., du Toit, L.C., Pillay, V., 2018. Therapeutic applications and pharmacoeconomics of microneedle technology. Expert Rev. Pharmacoecon. Outcomes Res. 18 (4), 359–369. https://doi.org/10.1080/14737167.2018.1485100.

Ryan, F.D., 2018. Clinical Translation and Industrial Development of Microneedle-based Products Microneedles for Drug and Vaccine Delivery and Patient Monitoring. Wiley, pp. 307–322. https://doi.org/10.1002/9781119305101.ch11.

Sadeqi, A., Kiaee, G., Zeng, W., Rezaei Nejad, H., Sonkusale, S., 2022. Hard polymeric porous microneedles on stretchable substrate for transdermal drug delivery. Sci. Rep. 12 (1). https://doi.org/10.1038/s41598-022-05912-6.

Samant, P.P., Niedzwiecki, M.M., Raviele, N., Tran, V., Mena-Lapaix, J., Walker, D.I., Felner, E.I., Jones, D.P., Miller, G.W., Prausnitz, M.R., 2020. Sampling interstitial fluid from human skin using a microneedle patch. Sci. Transl. Med. 12 (571). https://doi.org/10.1126/SCITRANSLMED.AAW0285.

Shao, J., Li, X., Li, Y., Lin, J., Huang, P., 2024. Self-heating multistage microneedle patch for topical therapy of skin cancer. Adv. Mater. 36 (15). https://doi.org/10.1002/adma.202308217.

Shi, J., Kantoff, P.W., Wooster, R., Farokhzad, O.C., 2017. Cancer nanomedicine: Progress, challenges and opportunities. Nat. Rev. Cancer 17 (1), 20–37. https://doi.org/10.1038/nrc.2016.108.

Singh, M., Shukla, R., 2025. Leveraging nanoengineered microneedle-augmented drug delivery in oncological intervention. Part. Part. Syst. Char. 42 (4). https://doi.org/10.1002/ppsc.202400181.

Tang, H., Cheng, X., Liang, L., Chen, B.Z., Liu, C., Wang, Y., 2024. A stimulus responsive microneedle-based drug delivery system for cancer therapy. Biomater. Sci. 12 (24), 6274–6283. https://doi.org/10.1039/d4bm00741g.

Tong, F., Wang, Y., Gao, H., 2024. Progress and challenges in the translation of cancer nanomedicines. Curr. Opin. Biotechnol. 85, 103045. https://doi.org/10.1016/j.copbio.2023.103045.

van der Maaden, K., Luttge, R., Jan Vos, P., Bouwstra, J., Kersten, G., Ploemen, I., 2015. Microneedle-based drug and vaccine delivery via nanoporous microneedle arrays. Drug Deliv. Transl. Res. 5 (4), 397–406. https://doi.org/10.1007/s13346-015-0238-y.

Waghule, T., Singhvi, G., Kumar Dubey, S., Pandey, M.M., Gupta, G., Singh, M., Kamal, D., 2019. Microneedles: A smart approach and increasing potential for transdermal drug delivery system. Biomed. Pharmacother. 109, 1249–1258. https://doi.org/10.1016/j.biopha.2018.10.078.

Wang, C., Ye, Y., Hochu, G.M., Sadeghifar, H., Gu, Z., 2016. Enhanced cancer immunotherapy by microneedle patch-assisted delivery of anti-PD1 antibody. Nano Lett. 16 (4), 2334–2340. https://doi.org/10.1021/acs.nanolett.5b05030.

Wang, H., Fu, Y., Mao, J., Jiang, H., Du, S., Liu, P., Tao, J., Zhang, L., Zhu, J., 2022. Strong and tough supramolecular microneedle patches with ultrafast dissolution and rapid-onset capabilities. Adv. Mater. 34 (51). https://doi.org/10.1002/adma.202207832.

Wang, T., Liu, H., Li, M., Ji, Z., Zhang, X., Wang, N., Chen, Y., Sun, J., Liu, F., 2025. Microneedle-based nanodrugs for tumor immunotherapy. J. Contr. Release 380, 539–562. https://doi.org/10.1016/j.jconrel.2025.02.003.

Wu, C., Yu, Q., Huang, C., Li, F., Zhang, L., Zhu, D., 2024. Microneedles as transdermal drug delivery system for enhancing skin disease treatment. Acta Pharm. Sin. B 14 (12), 5161–5180. https://doi.org/10.1016/j.apsb.2024.08.013.

Xiang, M., Yang, C., Zhang, L., Wang, S., Ren, Y., Gou, M., 2024. Dissolving microneedles for transdermal drug delivery in cancer immunotherapy. J. Mater. Chem. B 12 (24), 5812–5822. https://doi.org/10.1039/d4tb00659c.

Xue, H., Jin, J., Huang, X., Tan, Z., Zeng, Y., Lu, G., Hu, X., Chen, K., Su, Y., Hu, X., Peng, X., Jiang, L., Wu, J., 2025. Wearable flexible ultrasound microneedle patch for cancer immunotherapy. Nat. Commun. 16 (1). https://doi.org/10.1038/s41467-025-58075-z.

Yadav, P.R., Han, T., Olatunji, O., Pattanayek, S.K., Das, D.B., Modelling, M., 2020. Simulation and optimisation of microneedles for transdermal drug delivery: Trends and progress. Pharmaceutics 12 (8), 693. https://doi.org/10.3390/pharmaceutics12080693.

Yang, P., Song, Q., Zhang, L., Liu, Z., Ma, H., 2025. Numerical modeling and simulation for microneedles drug delivery: A novel comprehensive swelling-obstruction-mechanics model. Eur. J. Pharm. Biopharm. 206, 114583. https://doi.org/10.1016/j.ejpb.2024.114583.

Zhang, Q., Na, J., Liu, X., He, J., 2024. Exploration of the delivery of oncolytic newcastle disease virus by gelatin methacryloyl microneedles. Int. J. Mol. Sci. 25 (4), 2353. https://doi.org/10.3390/ijms25042353.

Zhang, Y., Liu, C., Li, Z., Liu, Y., Zheng, H., Lin, Q., Yu, L., Boo, Y.J., Chan, B.Q.Y., Loh, X.J., Wu, Y.-L., Song, Q., Li, P., Chan, S.Y., 2025. Microneedle-mediated synergistic photothermal and chemotherapy for targeted melanoma treatment. ACS Appl. Mater. Interfaces 17 (10), 14952–14967. https://doi.org/10.1021/acsami.4c20844.

Zhou, Q., Li, H., Liao, Z., Gao, B., He, B., 2023. Bridging the gap between invasive and noninvasive medical care: Emerging microneedle approaches. Anal. Chem. 95 (1), 515–534. https://doi.org/10.1021/acs.analchem.2c01895.

Zhu, L., Qiao, G., Gao, H., Jiang, A., Zhang, L., Wang, X., 2025. Enhancing melanoma therapy with hydrogel microneedles. Front. Oncol. 15. https://doi.org/10.3389/fonc.2025.1590534.

Zhu, W., Wei, T., Xu, Y., Jin, Q., Chao, Y., Lu, J., Xu, J., Zhu, J., Yan, X., Chen, M., Chen, Q., Liu, Z., 2024. Non-invasive transdermal delivery of biomacromolecules with fluorocarbon-modified chitosan for melanoma immunotherapy and viral vaccines. Nat. Commun. 15 (1). https://doi.org/10.1038/s41467-024-45158-6.

CHAPTER

27

Implants for anticancer drug delivery

Manish Kumar[1, 2], *Viresh Kumar*[1], *Shruti Srivastava*[3] and *Abhishek Sharma*[4]

[1]ISF College of Pharmacy, Moga, Punjab, India; [2]KIET School of Pharmacy, Krishna Institute of Engineering & Technology (KIET), Pharmaceutics, Ghaziabad, Uttar Pradesh, India; [3]Directorate of Research, Innovation & Consultancy, Chandigarh University, Unnao, Uttar Pradesh, India; [4]Department of Pharmaceutical Engineering and Technology, Indian Institute of Technology (BHU), Varanasi, Uttar Pradesh, India

Introduction

The development of anticancer drugs began in the 1940s, with nitrogen mustards that created a new foundation for cancer treatment. For a long time, the common practice was to administer cytotoxic drugs systemically to ensure their circulation throughout the body and target rapidly dividing cells. However, this technique is inevitably constrained due to a narrow therapeutic window and nonselective distribution to all main organs (Basak et al., 2022). These medications also affect normal fast-dividing cells, such as bone marrow and the endothelium lining (Schirrmacher, 2019). In the clinical setting, a lack of selectivity frequently causes significant and dose-limiting toxicities that affect numerous organ systems. Acute chemotherapy-related toxicities are expected to occur in 20%–80% of individuals. Certain pharmacological classes are well-known for having distinct side effects; for example, anthracyclines are notorious for cardiotoxicity, and platinum-based drugs are frequently associated with nephrotoxicity (Livshits et al., 2014). This is due to off-target distribution in normal organs, which results in low cellular bioavailability in cancer cells. To be therapeutically effective, a drug administered systemically must have a high plasma concentration that delivers an adequate amount to the tumor site or in cancer cells. As a result, a high dose is required for maintaining the drug's pharmacokinetics; however drug level in healthy tissues and the bloodstream rises while the amount that reaches the tumor may remain insufficient. Therefore, clinicians had to balance the therapeutic dose of antitumor drugs with the risk of significant systemic side effects (Li et al., 2023). To circumvent this and reduce anticancer drugs-associated adverse effects, targeted administration via

Advanced Cancer Therapeutics
https://doi.org/10.1016/B978-0-443-44185-1.00017-3

Implantable drug delivery systems (IDDS) is used. IDDS prevents anticancer drugs from entering the systemic circulation and allows for continuous site-specific delivery of drugs directly to the tumor mass or surgical margins (Rajgor et al., 2011). IDDS effectively reforms the therapeutic window by limiting the therapeutic agent's distribution to the target tissue. They offer high drug levels at the tumor site while minimizing drug levels at the systemic site. This technique stands out for the local efficacy from systemic side effects, allowing for more effective therapies (Wolinsky et al., 2012). IDDS are especially beneficial in situations where: (a) the side effects of systemic treatment are too severe for the patient to tolerate; (b) the local disease cannot be operated on or managed using standard methods; or targeted tumor control is needed to provide palliative relief or to facilitate a less invasive surgical procedure (Huanbutta et al., 2024).

IDDS emerged in the 1960s, with early experiments using materials such as silicone rubber as vehicles for long-term, controlled delivery of drugs. The first notable clinical and commercial achievements of IDDS occurred in other domains, specifically the approval by the U.S. FDA of a subcutaneous testosterone pellet product, Testopel, in 1972, and a contraceptive implanted device, Norplant, in 1990. These pioneering techniques demonstrated that implanted polymers can function as drug depots (Kleiner et al., 2014). IDDS emerged in the 1960s, with early experiments using materials such as silicone rubber as vehicles for long-term, regulated drug administration. The first major clinical and commercial triumphs of IDDS occurred in other areas, including the approval by the United States Food and Drug Administration of a subcutaneous testosterone pellet product, Testopel, in 1972 and the introduction of a contraceptive implanted system, Norplant, in 1990. These pioneering techniques demonstrated that implanted polymers might function well as drug depots (Kleiner et al., 2014). The subsequent development of IDDS for cancer treatment has been influenced by a continual technological push for greater control and independence. This advancement can be divided into several distinct stages of innovation. Passive reservoirs, like Norplant, are nondegradable and rely on passive diffusion to release drugs. However, they provide limited control (Huanbutta et al., 2024). Second, biodegradable implants were a significant breakthrough since they eliminated the need for surgical removal and minimized associated patient complications (Huanbutta et al., 2024). The third category is smart and controlled systems, which include reducing implant sizes, enabling remote-control functions, and developing systems that track a patient's status and alter drug doses instantly (Quarterman et al., 2021). This historical evolution indicates a clear shift in the perspective, from static and passive depots to dynamic, interactive, and programmable therapeutic platforms.

Principles and rationale of implantable drug delivery systems

The main goal of IDDS is to improve the pharmacokinetics (PK) and pharmacodynamic (PD) responses. The goal is to maximize the drug's C_{max} (peak concentration) and AUC (overall exposure) in the tumor and minimize the systemic levels of the drug to minimize the risk of toxicity at the bedside (Magill et al., 2023). In vivo experiments are giving unequivocal and quantifiable evidence of this reversal of pharmacokinetics. A study of biodegradable implants using doxorubicin (DOX) for intratumoral chemotherapy in an osteosarcoma model was a clear example of this concept (Glassman and Muzykantov, 2019). Twelve hours after implantation, the DOX concentration in tumor tissue reached its peak of 1266.96 ng/g. In great contrast, the concentration in plasma was only 2.83 ng/mL. In the control group, where an equivalent systemic (intraperitoneal) dosage was given, there was a reversal of the pharmacokinetic profile. Tumor concentration only reached 178.91 ng/g (about seven times less than the implant), while plasma concentration only reached 268.1 ng/mL (about 94 times more than the implant) (He et al., 2022). This large change in the pharmacokinetic profile of the drug has unique pharmacodynamic advantages. Initially, the enhanced and prolonged concentration of the drug at the site of action enhances antitumor activity, an important factor for preoperative adjuvant treatment and prevention of tumor recurrence. Moreover, the precipitous decrease of systemic drug concentrations brings about a commensurate decrease of adverse effects. Within the osteosarcoma study, drug levels in key organs of the body, such as the heart, liver, spleen, lungs, and kidneys, were measured and showed concentrations 20 to 58 times higher in animals that were given systemic injections than those that received the implant. These observations highlight a significant reduction in systemic exposure and risk of off-target toxicities, particularly doxorubicin-related cardiotoxicity (He et al., 2022; Sun et al., 2024). Achieving the desired PK/PD profile requires carefully designing an implantable system through the fine-tuning of several engineering parameters that often conflict with one another. Precise regulation of these factors is essential for maximizing therapeutic effectiveness and maintaining patient safety (Trucillo, 2024). The most critical design considerations include biocompatibility, drug encapsulation, release kinetics, morphology, mechanical properties and stability.

Biocompatibility

Materials used in the fabrication of implants should be biodegradable, free of toxic components, and should not trigger immune responses like chronic inflammation. The biocompatibility of such materials is often determined using in vitro assays (MTT and cytoskeletal staining), as well as in vivo implantation studies (Omidian and Wilson, 2025). In this context, a recent approach integrates electrospun polysulfone (PSu) nanofibers with bioactive ceramics to develop implantable systems for localized delivery of anticancer drugs. Owing to its strong chemical resistance and biocompatibility, especially under the acidic tumor conditions (pH 3–5). PSu has been utilized as a carrier for 5-fluorouracil (5-FU), while its apatite-forming ability further enhances its suitability for implant applications (Saravanabhavan and Dharmalingam, 2013).

Drug-loading

The implanted system should be fabricated to accommodate high drug loading and, more crucially, consistent and well-controlled release kinetics. A major issue with polymer-based delivery methods is initial burst release, in which a considerable part of the drug is released quickly, promptly following implantation. This sudden release may generate toxicity in surrounding tissues and prematurely deplete the drug reservoir, disrupting the implant's anticipated long-term release pattern (Liu et al., 2023). In one approach, nanotubular implant surfaces were repeatedly exposed to DOX or Apo2L/TRAIL solutions under vacuum, enabling the drug molecules to become securely trapped within the polymer-supported nanotube structures. After removing surface residues, the loaded drug content was quantified, demonstrating the material's high loading capacity. Subsequent release studies in PBS at physiological conditions showed a controlled, gradual drug release profile, measured via fluorescence and BCA assays. Such efficient loading and sustained release behavior highlight the importance of choosing implant polymers and surfaces that support stable drug incorporation and long-term therapeutic delivery (Maher et al., 2017). Thus, the selection of polymers should be done carefully for the design of an implant with the desired release kinetics.

Morphology

Research on the marketed leuprolide acetate product (Eligard) has shown the effect of implant morphology, like shape, size, as well as their surface-to-volume ratio, on the drug release profile (Yu et al., 2023). Morphology of anticancer implants, including shape, size, porosity, and surface-to-volume ratio, plays a crucial role in governing hydration, erosion, and drug diffusion pathways. Studies on marketed leuprolide acetate implants such as Eligard demonstrate that smaller, thinner rods or implants with higher surface-to-volume ratios hydrate and erode faster, leading to an increased initial release and shorter duration of therapy, whereas bulkier geometries promote more prolonged release. Surface morphology, including micro and nanopores or roughness introduced during fabrication, further modulates interstitial fluid penetration and polymer degradation, thereby fine-tuning the balance between burst and sustained release. Consequently, rational design of implant morphology is a key formulation lever to achieve predictable, long-acting local chemotherapy or hormone therapy with minimized systemic exposure (Benhabbour et al., 2019; Zare et al., 2008).

Mechanical properties

The implant must have sufficient mechanical strength, including compressive strength, to resist physiological forces used for implantation (Yu et al., 2023). Mechanical properties of anticancer implants are tailored to provide sufficient strength, flexibility, and structural integrity while withstanding physiological loads and tissue movements. Recent PLGA/PDMS in situ forming implants show injectable Newtonian flow with viscosity optimized for easy administration, yet they rapidly solidify into robust matrices that resist fragmentation and maintain depot integrity at the tumor site. Key mechanical parameters such as tensile strength, elastic modulus, and hardness are engineered to match surrounding tissue, minimizing stress shielding and implant failure over time (Maged et al., 2024). Additionally, careful control of polymer composition and crosslinking ensures that mechanical stability is retained throughout the degradation period, supporting consistent local drug release in vivo (Moghadasi et al., 2022).

Stability

The implant carrier must be stable throughout its shelf life, maintaining its physicochemical properties like appearance, porosity, pH, and mechanical strength. It should maintain the stability of the payload, avoiding drug degradation during fabrication, sterilization, storage, or administration (Imtiaz et al., 2025). Recent work on chitosan–poloxamer in situ implants for doxorubicin in breast cancer shows stable gel formation, predictable rheology, and sustained release without significant drug degradation over extended in vitro testing (Sahoo et al., 2024). Similarly, long-acting PLGA-based in situ forming implants have demonstrated minimal drug loss and preserved activity for several months under accelerated and real-time storage, indicating robust physicochemical stability of the payload as well as formulation (Pouso et al., 2025). Biodegradable polymeric systems further emphasize that optimizing polymer composition (e.g., PLGA, PCL, PLA), crystallinity, and hydrophilicity is critical to prevent burst release and ensure stable long-term local chemotherapy from injectable or implantable depots (Kim et al., 2025).

Classification of anticancer implants

Anticancer implants can be classified into various categories as follows.

Based on material fate

This classification system distinguishes implants based on whether they are intended to remain permanently in the body or degrade over time. Nonbiodegradable implants are made of strong, durable polymers such as silicone, poly(ethylene-co-vinyl acetate) PEVA, or polyurethanes, which are all stable, biostable polymers. Their design is generally straightforward and, in large part, dependent on passive diffusion. A major benefit of these systems is the availability of a constant and very predictable release profile. Nonetheless, a major drawback exists in the need for an additional surgical intervention to remove the implant after the drug reservoir is exhausted, an intervention that could result in infection, tissue damage, and patient discomfort (Stewart et al., 2018; Xu et al., 2024). Biodegradable implants consist of polymers that decompose within the human body to harmless substances, which are further absorbed or eliminated. Commonly used materials are poly(lactic-co-glycolic acid) (PLGA), poly(caprolactone) (PCL), and polyanhydrides. One of the main advantages is that the surgical removal is not required. However, this can add another complexity as the drug release may depend upon the rate at which the polymer degrades, a process which can vary significantly from patient to patient (Stewart et al., 2018).

Based on the mechanism of action

Passive implants are the most widely used category and include straightforward devices that contain no moving components. These systems depend on natural, physical, or chemical mechanisms to release the drug, mainly through passive diffusion from the material or through the gradual erosion or breakdown of the polymer matrix. Their drug-release pattern is typically governed by diffusion (first-order kinetics), which leads to a decreasing release rate as time progresses (Stewart et al., 2018). Active implants rely on a driving force or energy-dependent mechanism to provide a more controlled drug release. Although many such systems use electromechanical components, a well-known polymer-based example is the osmotic pump. In this type of implant, the drug reservoir is enclosed by a semipermeable membrane. The difference in osmotic pressure between the implant and bodily fluids causes a constant flow of water into the system. This incoming water increases internal pressure, which then pushes the drug out through a precisely created opening. The major benefit of this approach is its ability to deliver the drug at a constant rate (zero-order release), which is ideal for keeping drug levels consistently within the therapeutic range (Stewart et al., 2018; Kumar and Pillai, 2018).

Based on form and structure

The physical form-factor of an implant dictates its method of administration and its suitability for specific anatomical locations. Common forms include polymeric wafers, hydrogels, scaffolds, and in-situ film-forming gel. Polymeric Wafers are solid, preshaped discs, with the Gliadel wafer being the most well-known example. They are intended to be placed inside a surgical resection cavitysuch as after removing a brain tumor, to provide high, localized doses of chemotherapy directly to the surrounding surgical area (Xing et al., 2015). Hydrogels are water-swollen, three-dimensional cross-linked polymer networks that can be preformed or, more commonly, used as in situ forming systems. Nanofibrous Scaffolds are made using electrospun or self-assembled polymer fibers, forming a scaffold with a large surface area that can be infused with therapeutic agents. They are commonly explored for their combined use in drug delivery and tissue regeneration (Merati et al., 2019). In situ forming implants (ISFIs) are an important innovation in minimally invasive drug delivery. They are administered as a liquid formulation that usually contains a biodegradable polymer such as PLGA dissolved in a biocompatible solvent like N-methyl pyrrolidone. After the solution is injected into subcutaneous or intramuscular tissue, the solvent gradually diffuses out, and water enters the system. This triggers the polymer to solidify at the injection site, creating a depot that enables controlled and prolonged drug release (Woodring et al., 2023).

Biomaterials in focus: The building blocks of anticancer implants

Natural and semi-synthetic polymers

Natural polymers, in contrast to synthetic polymers, are renowned for their biological activity, the intrinsic biocompatibility, low toxicity, and ease of biodegradation. In the case of drugs for oncology, the most used natural polymers are polysaccharides such as alginate, chitosan, and hyaluronic acid. Chitosan, derived from crustacean shells, is a cationic polysaccharide well known for its mucoadhesive properties and its ability to increase drug uptake. Alginate, derived from seaweed, is an anionic polymer that forms hydrogels under gentle, physiological conditions in contact with divalent cations. Among the natural polymers that are exploited in the field of oncology, hyaluronic acid (HA) has a prominent place. Its functionality goes far beyond that of a mere carrier, being a versatile, intelligent biomaterial (Wong et al., 2020). Hyaluronic acid (HA) offers targeting due to its high binding affinity with the CD44 receptor. The receptor is often overexpressed on the surface of many cells in the body and is linked to cancer progression, making HA-modified nanoparticles a promising platform for active and selective drug delivery. The tumor microenvironment (TME) typically contains high levels of hyaluronidases, which are the mediators of the hydrolysis of hyaluronic acid (HA). This characteristic can be exploited in designing TME-responsive implants for controlled drug release at the tumor site (Wong et al., 2020).

Synthetic biodegradable polymers

Synthetic aliphatic polyesters are the workhorse materials for modern, resorbable implants, largely due to their FDA-approved status and, most importantly, their tunable properties. Poly(lactic-co-glycolic acid) (PLGA) is one of the most widely used polymers in controlled drug delivery owing to its biocompatibility, biodegradability, and tunable properties. Since it is a copolymer based on lactic acid (LA) and glycolic acid (GA), its properties can be individually tailored by varying the share of LA to GA. Increasing the glycolide (GA) content increases the hydrophilic nature of the polymer, thus degrading faster and releasing the drug at a higher rate. In contrast, increasing the amount of lactide (LA) makes it more hydrophobic, slowing the breakdown of the polymer. This flexibility allows the deliberate design of implants that can deliver drugs for a period of time from several weeks up to several months (Rajgor et al., 2011; Kumari et al., 2010). Polycaprolactone (PCL) is a semi-crystalline polyester with a high degree of flexibility, low glass transition temperature, and an extremely slow rate of degradation. Owing to its high crystallinity and hydrophobicity, the penetration of water is limited to a certain extent, making it suitable for long-term sustained release systems, which can last for several months or years (Sun et al., 2006). Poly-lactic Acid (PLA) is a relatively brittle polymer with high tensile strength. Its degradation occurs more slowly than that of PLGA but faster than PCL, providing a drug-release duration that ranges from a few days to several months (Stewart et al., 2018). The selection of a synthetic polymer is thus an engineering decision based on the clinical need. The key properties of these materials are summarized in Table 27.1.

Nondegradable materials

Nondegradable materials are used for permanent implants, often in applications where long-term structural integrity is required. The innovation in this field lies in repurposing these established, structurally inert materials into active therapeutic devices. Titanium (Ti) and its Alloys are the material of choice for orthopedics and dental implants because of their superior mechanical strength, corrosion resistance, and excellent biocompatibility. Recently, Ti-based biomaterials have been functionalized for antitumor use. By modifying the surface, for example, by the creation of titanium nanotubes (TNTs) or by the application of drug-loaded polymeric bilayer films, an inert Ti implant can be converted into a local drug delivery (LDD) system with the capacity for sustained, targeted release of chemotherapeutics

TABLE 27.1 Comparative properties of synthetic biodegradable polymers.

Property	Polycaprolactone (PCL)	Polylactic acid (PLA)	Poly(lactic-co-glycolic acid) (PLGA)
Glass transition (T_g)	Approx.-60°C	Approx. 60°C	40°C–60°C
Melting point (T_m)	58°C–61°C	150°C–160°C	Amorphous (variable)
Crystallinity	High (semi-crystalline)	Variable (amorphous to crystalline)	Amorphous
Degradation rate	Very slow (months-years)	Slow (days-months)	Tunable (fast, weeks-months)
Key feature	Flexibility; long-term release	High tensile strength	Tunable degradation via LA: GA ratio

(Yan et al., 2025). Poly(methyl methacrylate) (PMMA) is an acrylic polymer widely used as an acrylic bone cement in orthopedic oncology to stabilize pathological fractures or to fill voids after tumor resection. Traditionally regarded as a simple grout material, it is now being used as a dual-function device. When impregnated with antineoplastic agents, PMMA is no longer just a structural support, but a drug-eluting implant, therefore can provide mechanical stabilization and localized chemotherapy (Madadi and Sohn, 2024).

Clinical applications and landmark case studies

Central nervous system tumors: Implant for overcoming the blood-brain barrier

The blood-brain barrier makes most systemic chemotherapeutic agents ineffective in the treatment of primary tumors of the brain. The Gliadel wafer (carmustine implant) is a landmark example of an intratumoral drug delivery designed to overcome this barrier. The wafer is made of a biodegradable polyanhydride copolymer that carries a chemotherapeutic agent, carmustine (BCNU). It is designed to be implanted directly into the surgical resection cavity after the neurosurgeon has resected a high-grade glioma (HGG). The wafer breaks down over several weeks and releases high concentrations of BCNU directly into the surrounding brain tissue, and will obtain local exposures that are impossible to get through systemic administration. The clinical performance of the Gliadel wafer, however, highlights the complex realities of implant-based therapy. A systematic review and meta-analysis of its application in newly diagnosed HGG patients showed a nuanced and rather ambiguous record of success (Wolinsky et al., 2012). Efficacy on Survival: Meta-analysis showed statistically significant improvement of overall survival (OS) of patients treated with the wafer with a mean difference of 2.64 months compared to untreated patients. Efficacy on Recurrence. On the other hand, in the meta-analysis, the researchers found no statistically significant difference in progression-free survival (PFS) ($P = 0.55$), which means that although the implant extended the patient's life, it did not clearly delay tumor recurrence. The wafer is linked to a relatively higher rate of complications, such as infection, poor wound healing, and increased cerebral edema; however, the meta-analysis did not find a statistically significant difference ($P = 0.53$). The controversial profile of the Gliadel wafer (which has a small, but significant, OS benefit, no PFS benefit, and a perceived risk of complications) has limited its widespread adoption, but it remains an important case study to understand in the translation of localized therapy (Ricciardi et al., 2022).

Breast cancer: Implant for localized therapy post-lumpectomy

The current standard of care for early stage breast cancer often includes breast-conserving surgery (lumpectomy) and radiotherapy. A major reason for the failure of therapy is local recurrence, which is caused by the deposition of malignant cells remaining in the affected area. This clinical problem represents an optimal target as an implantable drug delivery system (IDDS). A new generation of biodegradable implants, such as biopolymeric scaffolds and nanocomposite materials, is currently being developed for placement directly into the lumpectomy cavity at the time of the surgical procedure. This strategy creates a synergistic model where the surgeon removes the main tumor mass, and the implant acts as an adjuvant in the treatment, delivering a large, localized dose of chemotherapy to the surgical margins to kill residual microscopic disease. By taking advantage of the pharmacokinetic advantages of the implant, this strategy is intended to prevent local recurrence, which is the major cause of treatment failure (Pial et al., 2022).

Prostate cancer: Hormonal and brachytherapy implants

The treatment of prostate cancer is one of the most successful and prevalent uses of implantable technology, and this helps to further define drugs to include radiation. Brachytherapy (BT) is one of the main treatment methods for localized prostate cancer that involves the placement of sealed radioactive sources directly into the prostate gland. This is a quintessential example of localized therapy. The objective is to deliver a curative dose of radiation to the tumor, but the rapid dose fall-off of the radioactive seeds spares adjacent healthy organs, such as the bladder and the rectum. This principle is similar to that of chemical IDDS, high local dose with low systemic or adjacent dose, but is carried out by nuclear physics rather than pharmacology (Zaorsky et al., 2017). Two primary techniques used are Low-Dose-Rate (LDR) Brachytherapy and High-Dose-Rate (HDR) Brachytherapy. LDR Brachytherapy involves the permanent implantation of small radioactive seeds (e.g., Iodine-125 or Palladium-103). HDR Brachytherapy involves the temporary placement of catheters into the prostate, through which a single, high-activity source (e.g., Iridium-192) is remotely advanced to deliver the dose in a highly controlled, computer-optimized manner (Koukourakis et al., 2009). In the context of a disease with a higher risk of recurrence, brachytherapy is often used in conjunction with adjunctive treatment, such as external beam radiation therapy (EBRT) or hormone therapy (HT). Research shows that brachytherapy combined with hormone therapy improves 5-year and 10-year biochemical progression-free survival (bPFS) rates, but this practice has not been shown to improve overall survival compared with brachytherapy alone (Zaorsky et al., 2017; Koukourakis et al., 2009).

Pancreatic and liver cancer: Implant for targeting non-resectable tumors

For highly aggressive and often nonresectable malignancies like pancreatic carcinoma, implants can have a pivotal dual function: prolongation of life and palliation. Patients suffering from pancreatic carcinoma with hepatic metastases, for example, have a historically unfavorable prognosis, with half of all patients dying after three to 6 months. Radioactive 125I seed implantation (brachytherapy) has been used as a treatment method for such unresectable tumors. A retrospective cohort study of patients with pancreatic carcinoma and unexpected hepatic metastases showed that 125I seed implantation coupled with postoperative chemotherapy had a mean overall survival of 16.3 months compared with 10 months for patients who received seed implantation without chemotherapy. More significantly, the implants provided a significant palliative effect with 84.6% of patients experiencing postoperative pain relief. This case study describes the ability of IDDS to improve the quantity and quality of life in the more demanding oncological scenarios (Li et al., 2020, 2021).

Ocular oncology: Implants for retinoblastoma and uveal melanoma

In ocular oncology, the major goal of treatment is two-fold: to save the patient's life and to protect the ocular organ, and if possible, to conserve the patient's visual acuity. Historically, malignant tumors such as retinoblastoma in children and uveal melanoma in adults were treated by the removal of the eye by surgery (enucleation). The discipline has undergone a paradigm shift toward minimally invasive, organ-sparing, and targeted interventions, including different modalities of brachytherapy. By implanting a radioactive plaque or using other methods of localized radiation delivery, oncologists can deliver a high therapeutic dose to the intraocular tumor while exposing the rest of the globe to a minimal dose of radiation, thereby providing the best chance to preserve vision (Vasalaki et al., 2017; Phull et al., 2021).

Bone sarcomas and metastases: Drug-eluting bone cement implants

Metastatic bone lesions and primary sarcomas are frequently associated with surgical intervention with reconstruction, posing a high risk of tumor recurrence or reconstruction failure. This has resulted in the development of dual-function implants that deliver both structural support and local chemotherapy. Poly(methyl methacrylate) (PMMA) and calcium phosphate cements (CPCs) are usually used to achieve mechanical stabilization. By embedding active ingredients, such as antineoplastic drugs, Doxorubicin (DOX), directly into the cement, these types of passive structural materials can be converted into active, drug-eluting devices (Pountos and Giannoudis, 2018). Nevertheless, this application highlights an important engineering challenge, that localization alone is not sufficient; control of release is still paramount. The formulation problem: The simple incorporation of DOX into PMMA gives a poor formulation. The drug gets trapped, and only about 6% is released in 100 days. Advanced composites, for example, PMMA supplemented with a gamma cyclodextrin (g-CD), are required to achieve a controlled, therapeutically relevant release of close to 100% over a period of 100 days. The Local Toxicity Problem. The whole point of IDDS, in getting high local levels of drugs, can become a liability. A review of studies on chemo bone cements found that all six studies that assessed local toxic effects found negative effects on healthy bone structure. This goes to show that a "high local concentration" is a double-edged sword. The local toxicity is not a failure of the concept of localization, but a failure of formulation and release control. This provides evidence for the need for "smart" systems that could be used to better modulate drug release (Cyphert et al., 2022).

The next frontier: Smart and stimuli-responsive implants

The limitations of passive implants, such as burst release, potential for local toxicity, and release kinetics that are not adaptable to patient needs, have driven the development of smart or stimuli-responsive systems. These devices are engineered to release their therapeutic payload in a controlled, on-demand fashion by sensing and reacting to specific triggers.

On-demand drug release

This class of implants is designed to be autonomous and respond to internal stimuli that are unique to the tumor microenvironment (TME). The TME is an abnormally chaotic and aggressive environment, with aberrant physiological and chemical properties that can be used as triggers. Common internal stimuli are low pH, enzymes, ROS, or redox potential. Low pH (Acidosis) in many solid tumors is due to the Warburg effect. Polymers and linkers can be made to be stable at physiological pH (7.4) but dissolve or cleave in an acidic environment. The TME has a much greater concentration of reducing agents (especially glutathione, GSH) than is found in the extracellular space. This gradient may be exploited to initiate the release from implants that are built with disulfide connections, which are sensitive to redox. Enzymes: Certain enzymes (e.g., matrix metalloproteinases, MMPs) are often upregulated in tumors and play a key role in the invasion and metastasis of tumors. Implants can be made with enzyme-cleavable linkers, which serve as a sensor that delivers its payload only when tumor-specific enzymatic action is present (Thomas et al., 2020; Taghizadeh et al., 2015). For example, a pH-responsive titanium implant coated with polydopamine has been shown to release doxorubicin more rapidly in the acidic tumor microenvironment than at physiological pH, achieving strong antiosteosarcoma activity while sparing healthy bone cells (Xiao et al., 2024). In another study, an injectable nanocomposite hydrogel incorporating gold nanorods provided dual NIR/pH-responsive release of doxorubicin, allowing clinicians to pulse drug output noninvasively using near-infrared light for spatiotemporally controlled chemophotothermal therapy (Xu et al., 2017). These autonomous systems represent a significant leap in selectivity, as the drug is released only when and where the chemical signature of a tumor is detected.

Externally triggered systems

If systems of internal stimuli are autonomous, systems of external stimuli are physician-controlled. These implants are engineered to be inert until a noninvasive, external energy

TABLE 27.2 Mechanisms of externally-triggered drug release.

Stimulus	Mechanism	Description of action	References
Light (NIR)	Photothermal effect (PTE)	Light-absorbing agents (e.g., gold nanorods) convert light to heat, causing a phase change or degradation of the carrier (e.g., liposome, gel) to release the drug.	Fomina et al. (2012)
	Photodynamic effect (PDE)	Light activates a sensitizer to produce reactive oxygen species (ROSs), which then cleave ROS-sensitive bonds within the carrier to release the drug.	Saravanakumar et al. (2017)
Ultrasound (US)	US thermal effect	Focused ultrasound generates localized heat, inducing a phase transition in thermosensitive carriers (e.g., liposomes).	Grüll and Langereis (2012)
	Sonodynamic effect (SDE)	Ultrasound activates an acoustic sensitizer to generate ROS, which disrupts ROS-sensitive components of the carrier, facilitating drug release.	Wang et al. (2025)

source is applied from outside the body, providing the clinician with the ability to control dosing on demand. This approach brings a new paradigm to the science of personalized medicine, allowing precise control over the timing, dosage, and duration of the release of the drug. Common external triggers include light and ultrasound (Table 27.2). Near-infrared (NIR) light is often used because of its tissue-penetrating capability. Light may trigger the release of drugs by two main mechanisms. First, the photothermal effect (PTE) occurs as light-absorbing nanoparticles, such as gold nanorods, within the implant convert the light into heat. This localized heating causes a phase change or degradation of the carrier—be it thermosensitive liposome or hydrogel leading to the release of drugs. Second, the photodynamic effect (PDE) consists of light activation of a photosensitizer, which produces reactive oxygen species (ROS). These ROS then reverse the ROS-sensitive bonds in the carrier matrix. The ultrasound (US) offers another noninvasive trigger that can be focused deeply within the body. It is responsible for triggering the release of the drug through two mechanisms: the ultrasound thermal effect (USTE), where the conversion of acoustic energy into thermal energy, by melting, is used to release the thermosensitive carrier; and the sonodynamic effect (SDE), where the acoustic activation of an acoustic sensitizer generates ROS that in turn breaks the drug carrier (Hu et al., 2024; Pham et al., 2020). Magnetic Fields can cause localized heating in magnetic nanoparticles (magnetic hyperthermia) or physically disrupt a magnetic-responsive carrier, triggering drug release (Pham et al., 2020).

Microchip: Programmable and multi-drug dosing

At the technological end of the controlled-release systems are microchip-based microelectromechanical systems (MEMS). These high-tech devices represent the culmination of all the trends described above, and they provide an ultimate platform for programmable, personalized therapy. The microchips have a series of discrete reservoirs, each of which can be individually addressed and opened. The advantages of this architecture are profound; programmable release offers precise, digital control over the rate as well as timing of release. Multi-drug therapy, made possible by loading the different reservoirs with different drugs, allows complex, sequential, or combination chemotherapy regimens to be carried out from a single implant. Pulsatile dosing, which opens and closes reservoirs at command, allows pulsatile release, which may be more physiologic or effective than continuous release (Saha et al., 2025; Eltorai et al., 2016). Drug Protection, the reservoirs can be hermetically sealed, protecting unstable biologic drugs (e.g., proteins, antibodies) from degradation in vivo (Eltorai et al., 2016). Various research is focused on developing these devices to be refillable, which would create a permanent, implantable, and programmable portal for chronic disease management, including cancer therapy.

Manufacturing, regulatory, and translational challenges

From bench to bedside: Navigating the translational gap

The translation of a novel implant is posing a challenge on two fronts that require innovation in engineering and regulatory strategy. A real-life story of the translation of an implantable microdevice (IMD) for oncology presents the situation perfectly. The engineering-clinical hurdle was that the laboratory device needed to be completely redesigned to fit in with the existing clinical workflows. This redesign incorporated adaptations for percutaneous implantation using a standard interventional needle and, most importantly, the development of a retrieval method that left the surrounding tissue intact for later analysis. A device that requires a complicated, novel surgical method is not likely to be accepted. The reason for the regulatory hurdle was that, as a first-in-class device, there was no existing regulatory pathway. The translational team led the way in a novel approach that successfully adapted existing FDA microdosing regulations originally designed for pharmacokinetic (PK) studies and applied them to their device, which measures pharmacodynamic (PD) response. This effort involved defining their drug-polymer matrix as a new chemical entity so that they would have the opportunity to move forward with the agency. This case study shows that the key to translational success will often be less about the novelty of the bench science and more about the disciplined interdisciplinary effort to solve these real-world integration challenges (Dominas et al., 2022).

Manufacturing and sterilization

On an industrial scale, drug-eluting implants present formidable manufacturing challenges. As combination products, their manufacture must comply with Current Good Manufacturing Practice (cGMP) regulations for both the device component (under 21 CFR 820) and the drug component (under 21 CFR 211) (Sheehy et al., 2016). Sterilization is a crucial, yet often overlooked, bottleneck. The final, packaged implant should be sterile. Nevertheless, conventional terminal sterilization methods (gamma irradiation, electron-beam (e-beam), or heat sterilization by autoclaving) can be harmful for the product. Radiation or heat may degrade the active pharmaceutical ingredient, thereby reducing its potency.

Moreover, the sterilization process can affect the properties of the polymer, for example, by cleavage of polymer chains, thereby impacting the degradation profile and therefore the carefully designed drug release kinetics. On the other hand, the drug itself can alter the mechanical properties of the device. This sterilization Catch-22 requires that manufacturers often turn to more complex and expensive aseptic manufacturing processes. Inside this workflow, both drug and device components are sterilized separately before assembly in an entirely sterile environment, hence significantly increasing the cost and complexity of production (Somayaji, 2016).

The regulatory pathway: FDA and EMA perspectives on combination products

Drug-eluting implants are regulated as combination products by such regulatory bodies as the US Food and Drug Administration (FDA) and the European Medicines Agency (EMA). Navigating this pathway is complicated because the product does not fit neatly into one of the categories of drug or device. In the United States, the regulatory pathway is based on one very important classification: the Primary Mode of Action (PMOA). The PMOA is defined as the single mode of action—drug, device, or biologic—that makes the greatest contribution to the overall intended therapeutic effects of the product. The FDA's Office of Combination Products (OCP) assigns the product to a lead center, either the Center for Drug Evaluation and Research (CDER) or the Center for Devices and Radiological Health (CDRH) based on this PMOA determination. This assignment determines the entire regulatory and clinical trial pathway (Singh et al., 2024). A drug-led combination product (like Gliadel wafer, where the effect of the drug is primary) will usually go through the New Drug Application (NDA) process, which requires extensive Phase I–III clinical trials. A device-led combination product (e.g., of a drug-eluting stent, where the primary action of the stent is mechanical) will follow the Premarket Approval (PMA) path. This PMA determination is arguably the singular most important strategic decision in the development of an implant, in terms of determining both the timeline (in years) and cost (in hundreds of millions of dollars) that will be needed to get the implant on the market (Reis et al., 2022).

Conclusion

Implantable drug delivery devices represent a paradigm shift in anticancer therapy, moving away from the nonselective, high-toxicity systemic administration model to a targeted, localized strategy. The primary advantage of implantable chemotherapy is its capacity to totally alter the pharmacokinetic profile of traditional chemotherapy, resulting in exceptionally high, sustained drug concentrations at the tumor site while avoiding systemic exposure and accompanying side effects. This chapter has followed the evolution of this sector, from simple, passive reservoirs to sophisticated, programmable systems in the future. This evolution is defined by a multi-decade pursuit of control: Spatial Control (Achieved by local implantation), Temporal Control (Engineered through the selection of biomaterials with tunable degradation rates, such as the PCL and PLGA polymer library), Kinetic Control

(Advanced from simple passive diffusion to active, zero-order release via osmotic pumps), Autonomous Control (Realized in smart systems that sense and respond to the internal tumor microenvironment) and Programmable Control (The technological apex, seen in multi-reservoir microchips capable of executing complex, on-demand, multi-drug regimens). Clinical case studies, ranging from the equivocal effectiveness of the Gliadel wafer to the confirmed efficacy of brachytherapy, show that when this control is accomplished, implants can increase survival, provide palliative care, and save organs. However, case studies in bone oncology highlight a fundamental point: localization without precise release control can merely transfer toxicity from a systemic to a local issue. This difficulty is currently the core focus of formulation science, and its solution is inseparable from the manufacturing and regulatory difficulties that represent the ultimate barrier to clinical translation.

References

Basak, D., Arrighi, S., Darwiche, Y., Deb, S., 2022. Comparison of anticancer drug toxicities: paradigm shift in adverse effect profile. Life 12 (1), 48. https://doi.org/10.3390/life12010048.

Benhabbour, S.R., Kovarova, M., Jones, C., Copeland, D.J., Shrivastava, R., Swanson, M.D., Sykes, C., Ho, P.T., Cottrell, M.L., Sridharan, A., Fix, S.M., Thayer, O., Long, J.M., Hazuda, D.J., Dayton, P.A., Mumper, R.J., Kashuba, A.D.M., Victor Garcia, J., 2019. Ultra-long-acting tunable biodegradable and removable controlled release implants for drug delivery. Nat. Commun. 10 (1). https://doi.org/10.1038/s41467-019-12141-5. Available from: http://www.nature.com/ncomms/index.html.

Cyphert, E.L., Kanagasegar, N., Zhang, N., Learn, G.D., von Recum, H.A., 2022. PMMA bone cement composite functions as an adjuvant chemotherapeutic platform for localized and multi-window release during bone reconstruction. Macromol. Biosci. 22 (5). https://doi.org/10.1002/mabi.202100415.

Dominas, C., Bhagavatula, S., Stover, E., Deans, K., Larocca, C., Colson, Y., Peruzzi, P., Kibel, A., Hata, N., Tsai, L., Hung, Y., Packard, R., Oliver, J., 2022. The translational and regulatory development of an implantable microdevice for multiple drug sensitivity measurements in cancer patients. IEEE (Inst. Electr. Electron. Eng.) Trans. Biomed. Eng. 69 (1), 412–421. https://doi.org/10.1109/tbme.2021.3096126.

Eltorai, A.E.M., Fox, H., McGurrin, E., Guang, S., 2016. Microchips in medicine: current and future applications. BioMed Res. Int. 2016, 1–7. https://doi.org/10.1155/2016/1743472.

Fomina, N., Sankaranarayanan, J., Almutairi, A., 2012. Photochemical mechanisms of light-triggered release from nanocarriers. Adv. Drug Deliv. Rev. 64 (11), 1005–1020. https://doi.org/10.1016/j.addr.2012.02.006.

Glassman, P.M., Muzykantov, V.R., 2019. Pharmacokinetic and pharmacodynamic properties of drug delivery systems. J. Pharmacol. Experim. Therap. 370 (3), 570–580. https://doi.org/10.1124/jpet.119.257113.

Grüll, H., Langereis, S., 2012. Hyperthermia-triggered drug delivery from temperature-sensitive liposomes using MRI-guided high intensity focused ultrasound. J. Contr. Release 161 (2), 317–327. https://doi.org/10.1016/j.jconrel.2012.04.041.

He, P., Xu, S., Guo, Z., Yuan, P., Liu, Y., Chen, Y., Zhang, T., Que, Y., Hu, Y., 2022. Pharmacodynamics and pharmacokinetics of PLGA-based doxorubicin-loaded implants for tumor therapy. Drug Deliv. 29 (1), 478–488. https://doi.org/10.1080/10717544.2022.2032878.

Hu, H., Busa, P., Zhao, Y., Zhao, C., 2024. Externally triggered drug delivery systems. Smart Mater. Med. 5 (3), 386–408. https://doi.org/10.1016/j.smaim.2024.08.004.

Huanbutta, K., Puri, V., Sharma, A., Singh, I., Sriamornsak, P., Sangnim, T., 2024. Rise of implantable drugs: a chronicle of breakthroughs in drug delivery systems. Saudi Pharm. J. 32 (12), 102193. https://doi.org/10.1016/j.jsps.2024.102193.

Imtiaz, S., Tamanna Ferdous, U., Nizela, A., Hasan, A., Shakoor, A., Zia, A.W., Uddin, S., 2025. Mechanistic study of cancer drug delivery: current techniques, limitations, and future prospects. Eur. J. Med. Chem. 290, 117535. https://doi.org/10.1016/j.ejmech.2025.117535.

Kim, Y., Kwak, J., Lim, M., Lim, S.Y., Chae, S., Ha, S.J., Won, Y.W., Kim, H.O., Lim, K.S., 2025. Advances in PCL, PLA, and PLGA-based technologies for anticancer drug delivery. Pharmaceutics 17 (10). https://doi.org/10.3390/pharmaceutics17101354.

Kleiner, L.W., Wright, J.C., Wang, Y., 2014. Evolution of implantable and insertable drug delivery systems. J. Contr. Release 181 (1), 1–10. https://doi.org/10.1016/j.jconrel.2014.02.006.

Koukourakis, G., Kelekis, N., Armonis, V., Kouloulias, V., 2009. Brachytherapy for prostate cancer: a systematic review. Adv. Urol. 2009, 1–11. https://doi.org/10.1155/2009/327945.

Kumar, A., Pillai, J., 2018. Implantable drug delivery systems: an overview. In: Nanostructures for the Engineering of Cells, Tissues and Organs, pp. 473–511.

Kumari, A., Yadav, S.K., Yadav, S.C., 2010. Biodegradable polymeric nanoparticles based drug delivery systems. Colloids Surf. B Biointerfaces 75 (1), 1–18. https://doi.org/10.1016/j.colsurfb.2009.09.001.

Li, C.G., Zhou, Z.P., Jia, Y.Z., Tan, X.L., Song, Y.Y., 2020. Radioactive 125I seed implantation for locally advanced pancreatic cancer: a retrospective analysis of 50 cases. World J. Clin. Cases 8 (17), 3743–3750. https://doi.org/10.12998/wjcc.v8.i17.3743.

Li, C.G., Zhou, Z.P., Jia, Y.Z., Tan, X.L., Song, Y.Y., 2021. Radioactive 125I seed implantation for pancreatic cancer with unexpected liver metastasis: a preliminary experience with 26 patients. World J. Clin. Cases 9 (4), 792–800. https://doi.org/10.12998/wjcc.v9.i4.792.

Li, J., Wang, Q., Xia, G., Adilijiang, N., Li, Y., Hou, Z., Fan, Z., Li, J., 2023. Recent advances in targeted drug delivery strategy for enhancing oncotherapy. Pharmaceutics 15 (9), 2233. https://doi.org/10.3390/pharmaceutics15092233.

Liu, L., Tang, H., Wang, Y., 2023. Polymeric biomaterials: advanced drug delivery systems in osteoarthritis treatment. Heliyon 9 (11), e21544. https://doi.org/10.1016/j.heliyon.2023.e21544.

Livshits, Z., Rao, R.B., Smith, S.W., 2014. An approach to chemotherapy-associated toxicity. Emerg. Med. Clin. 32 (1), 167–203. https://doi.org/10.1016/j.emc.2013.09.002.

Madadi, A.K., Sohn, M.J., 2024. Pharmacokinetic interpretation of applying local drug delivery system for the treatment of deep surgical site infection in the spine. Pharmaceutics 16 (1). https://doi.org/10.3390/pharmaceutics16010094. Available from: http://www.mdpi.com/journal/pharmaceutics.

Maged, A., Mabrouk, M., Nour El-Din, H.T., Osama, L., Badr-Eldin, S.M., Mahmoud, A.A., 2024. PLGA and PDMS-based in situ forming implants loaded with rosuvastatin and copper-selenium nanoparticles: a promising dual-effect formulation with augmented antimicrobial and cytotoxic activity in breast cancer cells. Front. Pharmacol. 15. https://doi.org/10.3389/fphar.2024.1397639.

Magill, E., Demartis, S., Gavini, E., Permana, A.D., Thakur, R.R.S., Adrianto, M.F., Waite, D., Glover, K., Picco, C.J., Korelidou, A., Detamornrat, U., Vora, L.K., Li, L., Anjani, Q.K., Donnelly, R.F., Domínguez-Robles, J., Larrañeta, E., 2023. Solid implantable devices for sustained drug delivery. Adv. Drug Deliv. Rev. 199, 114950. https://doi.org/10.1016/j.addr.2023.114950.

Maher, S., Kaur, G., Lima-Marques, L., Evdokiou, A., Losic, D., 2017. Engineering of micro- to nanostructured 3D-printed drug-releasing titanium implants for enhanced osseointegration and localized delivery of anticancer drugs. ACS Appl. Mater. Interfaces 9 (35), 29562–29570. https://doi.org/10.1021/acsami.7b09916.

Merati, A.A., Hemmatinejad, N., Shakeri, M., Bashari, A., 2019. Preparation, Classification, and Applications of Smart Hydrogels Advanced Functional Textiles and Polymers: Fabrication, Processing and Applications. wiley, Iran, pp. 337–364. https://doi.org/10.1002/9781119605843.ch12. Available from: http://onlinelibrary.wiley.com/book/10.1002/9781119605843.

Moghadasi, K., Mohd Isa, M.S., Ariffin, M.A., Mohd jamil, M.Z., Raja, S., Wu, B., Yamani, M., Bin Muhamad, M.R., Yusof, F., Jamaludin, M.F., Ab Karim, M.S.b., Abdul Razak, B.b., Yusoff, N.b., 2022. A review on biomedical implant materials and the effect of friction stir based techniques on their mechanical and tribological properties. J. Mater. Res. Technol. 17, 1054–1121. https://doi.org/10.1016/j.jmrt.2022.01.050.

Omidian, H., Wilson, R.L., 2025. PLGA implants for controlled drug delivery and regenerative medicine: advances, challenges, and clinical potential. Pharmaceuticals 18 (5). https://doi.org/10.3390/ph18050631. Available from: https://www.mdpi.com/journal/pharmaceuticals.

Pham, S.H., Choi, Y., Choi, J., 2020. Stimuli-responsive nanomaterials for application in antitumor therapy and drug delivery. Pharmaceutics 12 (7), 1–19. https://doi.org/10.3390/pharmaceutics12070630.

Phull, S.S., Rahimnejad Yazdi, A., Ghert, M., Towler, M.R., 2021. Bone cement as a local chemotherapeutic drug delivery carrier in orthopedic oncology: a review. J. Bone Oncol. 26, 100345. https://doi.org/10.1016/j.jbo.2020.100345.

Pial, M.M.H., Tomitaka, A., Pala, N., Roy, U., 2022. Implantable devices for the treatment of breast cancer. J. Nanother. 3 (1), 19–38. https://doi.org/10.3390/jnt3010003.

Pountos, I., Giannoudis, P.V., 2018. Drug-eluting implants for the suppression of metastatic bone disease: current insights. Expert Rev. Med. Dev. 15 (4), 301–311. https://doi.org/10.1080/17434440.2018.1456336.

Pouso, M.R., Melo, B.L., Gonçalves, J.J., Louro, R.O., Mendonça, A.G., Correia, I.J., de Melo-Diogo, D., 2025. Injectable and implantable hydrogels for localized delivery of drugs and nanomaterials for cancer chemotherapy: a review. Int. J. Pharm. 677. https://doi.org/10.1016/j.ijpharm.2025.125640. Available from: https://www.sciencedirect.com/science/journal/03785173.

Quarterman, J.C., Geary, S.M., Salem, A.K., 2021. Evolution of drug-eluting biomedical implants for sustained drug delivery. Eur. J. Pharm. Biopharm. 159, 21–35. https://doi.org/10.1016/j.ejpb.2020.12.005.

Rajgor, N., Bhaskar, V.H., Patel, M., 2011. Implantable drug delivery systems: an overview. Sys. Rev. Pharm. 2 (2), 91. https://doi.org/10.4103/0975-8453.86297.

Reis, M.E., Bettencourt, A., Ribeiro, H.M., 2022. The regulatory challenges of innovative customized combination products. Front. Med. 9. https://doi.org/10.3389/fmed.2022.821094.

Ricciardi, L., Manini, I., Cesselli, D., Trungu, S., Piazza, A., Mangraviti, A., Miscusi, M., Raco, A., Ius, T., 2022. Carmustine wafers implantation in patients with newly diagnosed high grade glioma: is it still an option? Front. Neurol. 13. https://doi.org/10.3389/fneur.2022.884158.

Saha, A., Khanna, A., Nair, A., Singh Butola, B., Sharma, N., Sharma, N., 2025. Precision beyond pills: the era of implantable microchips in controlled drug delivery. J. Biomed. Mater. Res. B Appl. Biomater. 113 (9). https://doi.org/10.1002/jbm.b.35645.

Sahoo, G.P., Rai, V.K., Pradhan, D., Halder, J., Rajwar, T.K., Mahanty, R., Saha, I., Mishra, A., Dash, P., Dash, C., Al-Tamimi, J., Manoharadas, S., Kar, B., Ghosh, G., Rath, G., 2024. A doxorubicin loaded chitosan-poloxamer in situ implant for the treatment of breast cancer. RSC Adv. 14 (46), 33952–33967. https://doi.org/10.1039/d4ra06253a.

Saravanabhavan, S.S., Dharmalingam, S., 2013. Fabrication of polysulphone/hydroxyapatite nanofiber composite implant and evaluation of their in vitro bioactivity and biocompatibility towards the post-surgical therapy of gastric cancer. Chem. Eng. J. 234, 380–388. https://doi.org/10.1016/j.cej.2013.08.076.

Saravanakumar, G., Kim, J., Kim, W.J., 2017. Reactive-oxygen-species-responsive drug delivery systems: promises and challenges. Adv. Sci. 4 (1). https://doi.org/10.1002/advs.201600124. Available from: http://onlinelibrary.wiley.com/journal/10.1002/(ISSN)2198-3844.

Schirrmacher, V., 2019. From chemotherapy to biological therapy: a review of novel concepts to reduce the side effects of systemic cancer treatment (Review). Int. J. Oncol. 54 (2), 407–419. https://doi.org/10.3892/ijo.2018.4661.

Sheehy, A., Lambert, B., Rapoza, R., 2016. Business Perspective: Case Study: Commercialized Cell-Free Cardiovascular Implant In Situ Tissue Regeneration: Host Cell Recruitment and Biomaterial Design. Elsevier Inc., United States, pp. 405–419. https://doi.org/10.1016/B978-0-12-802225-2.00021-0. Available from: http://www.sciencedirect.com/science/book/9780128022252.

Singh, S., Malik, A., Prakash Rawat, A., Tevetia, N., Aggarwal, R., Goswami, S., Sharma, K., Raghavendra Rao, N. G., Pathak, A., 2024. Regulatory considerations of material used for medical devices and combination products in different countries: a review. Mater. Today Proc. 103, 527–533. https://doi.org/10.1016/j.matpr.2023.10.045.

Somayaji, M.R., 2016. Perspectives on development and regulation of therapeutic products for CED-based therapy of neurodegenerative diseases. Curr. Pharm. Biotechnol. 17 (6), 495–512. https://doi.org/10.2174/1389201017666151030105055.

Stewart, S.A., Domínguez-Robles, J., Donnelly, R.F., Larrañeta, E., 2018. Implantable polymeric drug delivery devices: classification, manufacture, materials, and clinical applications. Polymers 10 (12). https://doi.org/10.3390/polym10121379. Available from: https://www.mdpi.com/2073-4360/10/12/1379/pdf.

Sun, H., Mei, L., Song, C., Cui, X., Wang, P., 2006. The in vivo degradation, absorption and excretion of PCL-based implant. Biomaterials 27 (9), 1735–1740. https://doi.org/10.1016/j.biomaterials.2005.09.019.

Sun, R., Chen, Y., Pei, Y., Wang, W., Zhu, Z., Zheng, Z., Yang, L., Sun, L., 2024. The drug release of PLGA-based nanoparticles and their application in treatment of gastrointestinal cancers. Heliyon 10 (18), e38165. https://doi.org/10.1016/j.heliyon.2024.e38165.

Taghizadeh, B., Taranejoo, S., Monemian, S.A., Moghaddam, Z.S., Daliri, K., Derakhshankhah, H., Derakhshani, Z., 2015. Classification of stimuli-responsive polymers as anticancer drug delivery systems. Drug Deliv. 22 (2), 145–155. https://doi.org/10.3109/10717544.2014.887157.

Thomas, R.G., Surendran, S.P., Jeong, Y.Y., 2020. Tumor microenvironment-stimuli responsive nanoparticles for anticancer therapy. Front. Mol. Biosci. 7. https://doi.org/10.3389/fmolb.2020.610533.

Trucillo, P., 2024. Biomaterials for drug delivery and human applications. Materials 17 (2), 456. https://doi.org/10.3390/ma17020456.

Vasalaki, M., Fabian, I.D., Ashwin Reddy, M., Cohen, V.M.L., Sagoo, M.S., 2017. Ocular oncology: advances in retinoblastoma, uveal melanoma and conjunctival melanoma. Br. Med. Bull. 121 (1), 107–119. https://doi.org/10.1093/bmb/ldw053.

Wang, H., Liu, Y., Li, Y., Zhao, Y., Li, X., 2025. Ultrasound-responsive drug delivery system for cancer therapy. Macromol. Biosci. 25 (11). https://doi.org/10.1002/mabi.202500082.

Wolinsky, J.B., Colson, Y.L., Grinstaff, M.W., 2012. Local drug delivery strategies for cancer treatment: gels, nanoparticles, polymeric films, rods, and wafers. J. Contr. Release 159 (1), 14–26. https://doi.org/10.1016/j.jconrel.2011.11.031.

Wong, K.H., Lu, A., Chen, X., Yang, Z., 2020. Natural ingredient-based polymeric nanoparticles for cancer treatment. Molecules 25 (16). https://doi.org/10.3390/molecules25163620. Available from: https://www.mdpi.com/1420-3049/25/16/3620.

Woodring, R.N., Gurysh, E.G., Bachelder, E.M., Ainslie, K.M., 2023. Drug delivery systems for localized cancer combination therapy. ACS Appl. Bio Mater. 6 (3), 934–950. https://doi.org/10.1021/acsabm.2c00973.

Xiao, Q., Wan, C., Zhang, Z., Liu, H., Liu, P., Huang, Q., Zhao, D., 2024. A pH-responsive Ti-based local drug delivery system for osteosarcoma therapy. J. Funct. Biomater. 15 (10), 312. https://doi.org/10.3390/jfb15100312.

Xing, W.K., Shao, C., Qi, Z.Y., Yang, C., Wang, Z., 2015. The role of Gliadel wafers in the treatment of newly diagnosed GBM: a meta-analysis. Drug Des. Dev. Ther. 9, 3341–3348. https://doi.org/10.2147/DDDT.S85943.

Xu, L., Wei, C., Deng, L., Wang, P., Zhong, W., Huang, W., 2024. A review of non-biodegradable alloys implantation induced inflammatory and immune cell responses. J. Alloys Compd. 977, 173086. https://doi.org/10.1016/j.jallcom.2023.173086.

Xu, X., Huang, Z., Huang, Z., Zhang, X., He, S., Sun, X., Shen, Y., Yan, M., Zhao, C., 2017. Injectable, NIR/pH-Responsive nanocomposite hydrogel as long-acting implant for chemophotothermal synergistic cancer therapy. ACS Appl. Mater. Interfaces 9 (24), 20361–20375. https://doi.org/10.1021/acsami.7b02307.

Yan, X., Liu, H., Zhang, Z., Xiang, D., Lin, M., Cai, Z., Tang, D., Wang, H., Wen, L., Zhao, D., 2025. Ti-based metallic biomaterials for antitumor applications. Materials 18 (10), 2262. https://doi.org/10.3390/ma18102262.

Yu, H., Liu, H., Shen, Y., 2023. Qiang Ao, Synthetic biodegradable polymer materials in the repair of tumor-associated bone defects. Front. Bioeng. Biotechnol. 11. https://doi.org/10.3389/fbioe.2023.1096525.

Zaorsky, N.G., Davis, B.J., Nguyen, P.L., Showalter, T.N., Hoskin, P.J., Yoshioka, Y., Morton, G.C., Horwitz, E.M., 2017. The evolution of brachytherapy for prostate cancer. Nat. Rev. Urol. 14 (7), 415–439. https://doi.org/10.1038/nrurol.2017.76.

Zare, M., Mobedi, H., Barzin, J., Mivehchi, H., Jamshidi, A., Mashayekhi, R., 2008. Effect of additives on release profile of leuprolide acetate in an in Situ forming controlled-release system: in Vitro study. J. Appl. Polym. Sci. 107 (6), 3781–3787. https://doi.org/10.1002/app.27520.

CHAPTER

28

Phytomedicine for cancer therapy

Hemangini Meher[1], *Alakh N. Sahu*[2] *and Debadatta Mohapatra*[2, 3]

[1]Department of Pharmacology, Guru Ghasidas Vishwavidyalaya, Bilaspur, Chhattisgarh, India; [2]Phytomedicine Research Laboratory, Department of Pharmaceutical Engineering & Technology, Indian Institute of Technology (BHU), Varanasi, Uttar Pradesh, India; [3]Leslie Dan Faculty of Pharmacy, University of Toronto, Toronto, ON, Canada

Introduction

Plant-based medications for disease prophylaxis and therapy have been a cornerstone of healthcare since ancient times. Plant-based treatments in Ayurveda have significantly shaped the foundations of current pharmacology and healthcare (Izah et al., 2024). Traditional herbal treatments remain prevalent, supported by cultural heritage, accessible, affordable, and perceived as safe (Yebirzaf et al., 2019). Phytomedicine, or herbal drugs or botanicals, are roots, stems, leaves, bark, fruit, seeds, or flowers with medicinal properties. It includes using whole or part of medicinal plants or their secretions, excretions, and exudations as whole extracts, purified extracts, enriched fractions, or formulations. The World Health Organization (WHO) defined phytomedicine or herbal drugs as herbs, herbal preparations, or herbal products that contain one or more active ingredients as parts of plants, plant materials, or their combinations. Phytochemically, herbal drugs are multicomponent mixtures. They can be prepared as single herb preparations or polyherbal formulations. Phytomedicine offers cancer therapy as a multifunctional approach by modulating various molecular mechanisms contributing to cancer progression. Plant-derived bioactive compounds can exhibit potent bioactivity, including anticancer, antioxidant, antiinflammatory, and immune-enhancing activities, and thus can be used for treating and mitigating cancer (Garcia-Oliveira et al., 2021). Numerous studies have reported the anticancer potential of phytomedicine over synthetic drugs, with minimal side effects. Moreover, many phytochemicals in a herbal extract simultaneously act on multiple molecular targets (e.g., modulating kinases, transcription factors, and epigenetic enzymes), which can overcome the single-target limitations of synthetic drugs. Phytomedicines exert anticancer action by induction of apoptosis, arresting cell cycle phases, dysregulating mitochondrial function,

Advanced Cancer Therapeutics
https://doi.org/10.1016/B978-0-443-44185-1.00009-4

blocking tumor angiogenesis, inhibiting proinflammatory markers, regulating gene expression, modulating immune responses, altering reactive oxygen species (ROS) production, and preventing cancer metastasis (Asma et al., 2022). However, due to larger molecular weight and chemical complexity, many phytoconstituents have poor pharmacokinetic properties (poor solubility, permeability, low absorption, and bioavailability). Such challenges can be addressed by developing novel drug delivery systems, such as nanoformulations. This chapter discusses the potential of phytomedicine as an anticancer therapeutic. The focus was on therapeutic targets, anticancer mechanism of phytomedicine, advanced phytoformulations, challenges and opportunities for formulation development, preclinical and clinical evidence, safety, toxicity, and pharmacokinetics aspects, and future perspectives.

Therapeutic targets and plant-derived compounds for cancer therapy

The conventional methods for cancer treatment are surgery, chemotherapy, radiation therapy, immunotherapy, hormone therapy, and stem cell transplantation. The treatment strategy aims to achieve complete eradication of cancer cells, but is associated with adverse effects, organ toxicity, resistance, and cancer relapse. This necessitated the search for novel therapeutics for improved cancer therapy. Hallmarks of cancer include (i) resistance to cell death, (ii) sustained proliferative signaling, (iii) evasion of growth suppressors, (iv) activation of invasion and metastasis, (v) replicative immortality, and (vi) angiogenesis (Hanahan and Weinberg, 2011). The therapeutics should participate in growth suppression (cyclin-dependent kinase inhibitors), immune inactivation (immunocheckpoints inhibitors), replicative immortality (telomerase inhibitors), inflammation (antiinflammatory drugs), invasion and metastasis (hepatocyte growth factor/mesenchymal-epithelial transition factor (HGF/c-Met) inhibitors), angiogenesis (vascular endothelial growth factor/VEGF inhibitors), genome instability and mutation (poly ADP-ribose polymerase/PARP inhibitors), cell proliferation (apoptotic drugs), altered cellular energetics (aerobic glycolysis inhibitors), and proliferative signaling (Epidermal Growth Factor Receptor/EGFR inhibitors) for effective cancer therapy (Hanahan and Weinberg, 2011). At the molecular level, cancer usually develops due to genetic mutations, epigenetic alterations, and disruptions in key regulatory pathways governing cell growth, differentiation, and death. Elucidating the molecular mechanisms in cancer is essential for identifying therapeutic targets. Molecular mechanisms of cancer include oncogene activation, tumor suppressor inactivation, cell cycle dysregulation, apoptosis evasion, angiogenesis, genomic instability, epigenetic alterations, immune evasion, and interactions with the tumor microenvironment (Hanahan and Weinberg, 2011). The molecular basis of cancer, key genes or proteins, and their implications in cancer are shown in Table 28.1, which can be targeted with traditional plants and phytomedicine for cancer therapy.

The use of medicinal plants in the treatment of human diseases, including cancer, has a well-documented history across various ancient medical systems, such as the Ayurvedic system of medicine, Siddha system of medicine, Unani system of medicine, Traditional Chinese Medicine (TCM), and ancestral healing practices in Africa and the Americas (Sharma et al., 2024; Izah et al., 2024). These ancient systems often recognized cancer-like conditions, described as abnormal. These traditional remedies used multiherbal mixtures as a holistic

TABLE 28.1 Molecular basis of cancer.

Molecular mechanism	Causes	Key genes/Proteins involved	Implications in cancer
Oncogene activation	Constitutive activation of growth and survival signaling	RAS, MYC, BRAF, EGFR, HER2	Promotes uncontrolled proliferation and resistance to apoptosis
Tumor suppressor inactivation	Suppression of intrinsic and extrinsic cell death pathways	TP53, RB1, PTEN, CDKN2A	Enables survival of genetically unstable cells
Cell cycle dysregulation	Overactivation of CDKs, checkpoint bypass	Cyclin D1, CDK4/6	Leads to rapid and unchecked cell division
Apoptosis evasion	Loss of cell cycle control, apoptosis inhibition	BCL-2, BCL-XL, BAX, caspases	Allows survival of damaged or mutated cells
Angiogenesis	Formation of new blood vessels	VEGF, VEGFR, HIF-1α, MMPs	Sustains tumor growth and metastasis
Genomic instability	Promotes inflammation, epithelial-mesenchymal transition, and invasion	BRCA1/2, ATM, MLH1, MSH2	Accelerates mutation accumulation and tumor heterogeneity
Epigenetic alterations	Aberrant gene silencing or activation	DNA methyltransferases, HDACs, miRNAs	Inactivates tumor suppressor genes or activates oncogenes
Immune evasion	Escape recognition and destruction by the host immune system	PD-1, PD-L1, TGF-β, IL-10	Allows tumor escape from host immune responses
Tumor microenvironment	Impaired DNA damage response and repair	CAFs, TAMs, ECM proteins, cytokines	Enhances tumor progression and metastasis

ATM, ataxia-telangiectasia; *BAX*, BCL2-associated X protein; *BCL-2*, B-cell lymphoma 2; *BCL-XL*, B-cell lymphoma-extra large; *BRCA1/2*, Breast Cancer gene 1 and 2; BRAF -Raf proto-oncogene, serine/threonine kinase; *CAFs*, Cancer-Associated Fibroblasts; *CDKN2A*, Cyclin-dependent kinase inhibitor 2A; *CDK4/6*, Cyclin-Dependent Kinase 4 and 6; *ECM*, Extracellular Matrix; *EGFR*, Epidermal Growth Factor Receptor; *HDACs*, Histone Deacetylases; *HER2*, Human Epidermal growth factor Receptor 2; *HIF-1α*, Hypoxia-Inducible Factor 1-alpha; *IL-10*, Interleukin-10; *MLH1*, MutL homolog 1; *MMPs*, Matrix Metalloproteinases; *MSH2*, MutS homolog 2; *MYC*, MYC Proto-Oncogene; *PTEN*, Phosphatase and TENsin homolog deleted on chromosome 10; *PD-1*, Programmed Cell Death Protein 1; *PD-L1*, Programmed Death-Ligand 1; *RAS*, Rat sarcoma; *RB1*, Retinoblastoma 1 gene; *TAMs*, Tumor-Associated Macrophages; *TGF-β*, Transforming Growth Factor beta; *TP53*, Tumor protein p53; *VEGF*, Vascular Endothelial Growth Factor; *VEGFR*, Vascular Endothelial Growth Factor Receptor.

approach for targeting the disease as well as overall health and immunity (Smith and Mallath, 2019). Traditional knowledge has directly contributed to current drug discovery, as demonstrated by *Catharanthus roseus*'s vincristine and vinblastine for leukemias and lymphomas, and *Taxus brevifolia*'s paclitaxel for lung, ovarian, and breast cancers. Clinical evidence on traditional medicinal plants, such as *Withania somnifera* (Ashwagandha), *Curcuma longa* (Turmeric/Curcumin), *Ocimum sanctum* (Tulsi), *Tinospora cordifolia* (Guduchi), *Moringa oleifera* (Drumstick), *Azadirachta indica* (Neem), *Phyllanthus Emblica*.L (Amla), *Piper nigrum* (Black Pepper), and *Allium sativum* (Garlic) revealed their anticancer against various cancers, including breast, oral, colorectal, head and neck, and liver (Reyaz et al., 2025). The isolates, exudates, and extractions of such plants known as phytocompounds can be used for effective management of cancer. Phytocompounds are natural, renewable, and economical with long histories of medicinal use. Due to their diverse chemical structures and bioactivity, natural products have always been a vital source of inspiration for drug discovery, especially for cancer therapy (Dehelean et al., 2021; Jenča et al., 2024). These sources are abundant, safe, and easily accessible (Reyaz et al., 2025). About 40% of FDA-approved drugs are natural or nature-inspired, and of these, nearly 74% are used in cancer therapy (Seca and Pinto, 2018). FDA-approved plant-derived anticancer drugs, such as paclitaxel (from *Taxus brevifolia* Nutt.), homoharringtonine (*Cephalotaxus harringtonii*), camptothecin (*Camptotheca acuminata*), vincristine and vinblastine (*Catharanthus roseus*), teniposide, and etoposide (*Podophyllum peltatum*) represented promising chemotherapeutics for the treatment of various cancers (Oyenihi et al., 2021). Over 60% of clinically used anticancer agents are derived from plants, microbes, or marine sources (Talib et al., 2020; Situmorang et al., 2024). Market-approved plant-derived anticancer drugs, such as atropine, bromelain, colchicine, doxorubicin, etoposide, morphine, paclitaxel, podophyllotoxin, quinine, topotecan, vincristine, and vinblastine, represent their anticancer and commercial potential (Reyaz et al., 2025). Phytomedicine simultaneously acts on multiple molecular targets (e.g., modulating kinases, transcription factors, and epigenetic enzymes), overcoming the single-target limitations of synthetic drugs (Mohapatra et al., 2023b; Talib et al., 2020). Furthermore, anticancer phytomolecules are structurally diverse, biocompatible, biodegradable, and less cytotoxic to healthy tissues than chemotherapeutics, suggesting plant-derived phytochemicals as key leads for anticancer drug discovery.

Integration of phytomedicine with conventional oncology

Integrative oncology combines evidence-based complementary therapies with conventional cancer treatments (chemotherapy, radiotherapy, immunotherapy, gene therapy, hormonal therapy, surgery) to reduce side effects, overcome multidrug resistance, manage symptoms, improve quality of life, boost immunity, and enhance therapeutic outcome (Alfonzetti et al., 2021; Ayaz et al., 2022; Puranik, 2024). Phytochemicals, such as quercetin with docetaxel (breast cancer), berberine with cisplatin (ovarian cancer), ellagic acid with doxorubicin (hepatocellular carcinoma), fisetin with paclitaxel (lung cancer), curcumin with 5-fluorouracil (colorectal cancer), resveratrol with 5-fluorouracil (melanoma), triptolide with oxaliplatin (colon cancer), emodin with tamoxifen (breast cancer), kaempferol with sorafenib (liver cancer) demonstrated improved anticancer activity through multiple mechanisms (Puranik, 2024; Lin et al., 2020). Codelivery of phytomolecules with other anticancer agents (chemotherapeutics, hormonal therapy, gene therapy, immunotherapy) through novel drug delivery systems (nanoparticle, micelle, liposomes, nanoemulsion) showed improved pharmacokinetics, enhanced therapeutic efficacy, reduced toxicity, and minimal adverse effects (Anwar et al., 2021). Many patients use medicinal plants to boost immunity and ease chemotherapy toxicity, though most view them as supportive rather than alternative options. Clinicians acknowledge the benefits of herbal drugs, but concerns remain about herb-drug interactions (Lin et al., 2020). Despite regional regulatory challenges, integrative medicine is increasingly incorporated into oncology centers, supported by professional guidelines, with emphasis on safety, evidence-based use, and open patient-clinician communication. Phytomedicines and their role in cancer supportive therapy are demonstrated in Table 28.2 (Puranik, 2024).

TABLE 28.2 Phytomedicines and their role in cancer supportive therapy.

Herbal medicine	Botanical name	Active phytochemicals	Pharmacological actions	Oncology applications
Turmeric	*Curcuma longa*	Curcumin	Antiinflammatory, antioxidant, anticancer	Adjunct for inflammation, tumor suppression
Ginger	*Zingiber officinale*	Gingerols, shogaols	Antinausea, antiinflammatory	Reduces chemotherapy-induced nausea and vomiting
Milk thistle	*Silybum marianum*	Silymarin	Hepatoprotective, antioxidant	Protects liver during chemotherapy
Ashwagandha	*Withania somnifera*	Withanolides	Adaptogenic, stress-relief, immunomodulatory	Enhances quality of life, reduces fatigue
Astragalus	*Astragalus membranaceus*	Polysaccharides, saponins	Immune support, enhances chemotherapy tolerance	Immune restoration postchemotherapy
Ginseng	*Panax ginseng*	Ginsenosides	Antifatigue, cognitive support, immune modulating	Reduces treatment-related fatigue
Holy basil	*Ocimum sanctum (Tulsi)*	Eugenol, ursolic acid	Antioxidant, antiinflammatory, adaptogenic	Reduces oxidative stress
Licorice	*Glycyrrhiza glabra*	Glycyrrhizin	Antiulcer, antiinflammatory	Protects GI mucosa during treatment
Cannabis	*Cannabis sativa*	Tetrahydrocannabinol, cannabidiol	Pain relief, antiemetic, appetite stimulation	Palliative care, improves appetite and sleep

Anticancer mechanism of phytomedicine

Phytomedicine can exert anticancer activity through various mechanisms, including apoptosis (e.g., curcumin, resveratrol, quercetin, artesunate, genistein, Epigallocatechin-3-gallate or EGCG), inhibiting cell proliferation and cell cycle progression (e.g., ellagic acid, quercetin), interfering with microtubule formation (e.g., taxanes, vinca alkaloids), acting on topoisomerase targets and preventing DNA replication (e.g., camptothecin, thymoquinone, berberine, curcumin, coptisine, myricetin, fisetin), inhibiting angiogenesis (e.g., curcumin, EGCG, genistein), modulating key signaling pathways (e.g., curcumin, resveratrol, EGCG), modulating tumor microenvironment (e.g., curcumin, resveratrol, silibinin), reversing multidrug resistance (e.g., flavonoids, alkaloids, terpenoids, polyphenols, coumarins), and activating immune cells and regulating immune function (polyphenols, terpenoids, polysaccharides) (Jenča et al., 2024; Talib et al., 2020). Fig. 28.1 demonstrates various mechanisms of action followed by phytomedicine for exhibiting anticancer activity.

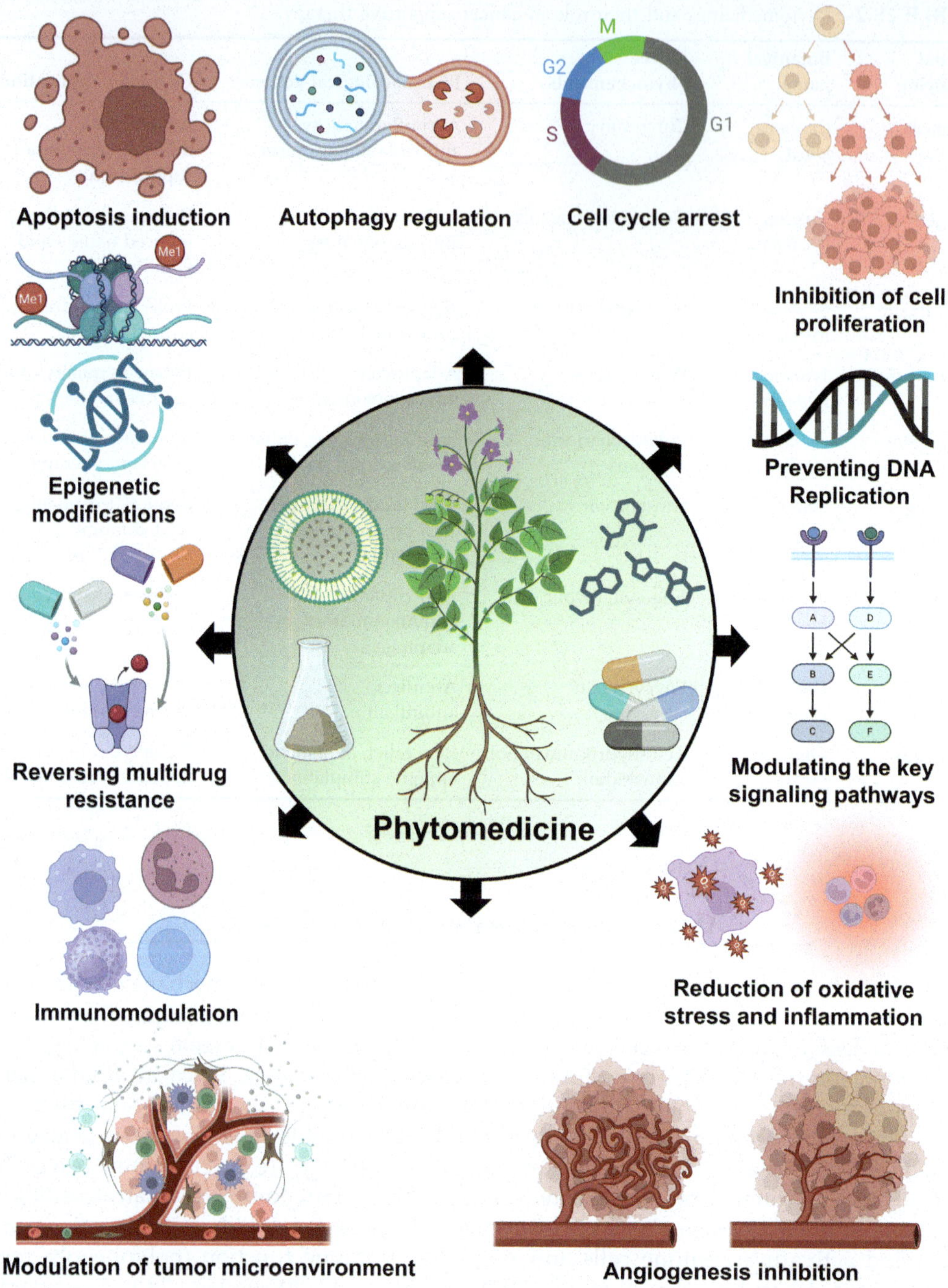

FIGURE 28.1 Anticancer mechanism of phytomedicine.

Apoptosis induction

Phytoconstituents can exert anticancer effects by inducing apoptosis through the regulation of apoptotic proteins and signaling pathways. Phytomedicine activates both the extrinsic (death receptor) and intrinsic (mitochondrial) apoptotic pathways in cancer cells (Puranik, 2024). For example, curcumin modulates Bcl-2 proteins, activates caspases, and regulates NF-κB, PI3K/Akt, and MAPK pathways to exert anticancer action against breast, colon, prostate, lung, and glioblastoma. It also enhances the chemotherapeutic efficacy of anticancer drugs such as paclitaxel. Similarly, resveratrol induces apoptosis in breast, prostate, and leukemia cells by regulating Bcl-2 proteins, activating caspases, and impairing mitochondrial function, while sensitizing tumors to chemotherapy. Beyond apoptosis, phytoconstituents can trigger autophagy and pyroptosis to suppress tumor growth. EGCG induces apoptosis by improving proapoptotic Bak and Bax levels and decreasing antiapoptotic genes Bcl-2 and Bcl-xL (Jenča et al., 2024).

Autophagy regulation

Autophagy is a cellular process that degrades and recycles damaged cellular organelles, misfolded proteins, and other debris through lysosomal pathways, maintaining cellular homeostasis (Ali et al., 2023). It plays a dual role in cancer development, acting as both a tumor promoter and suppressor. In the early stage of the tumor, autophagy maintains cellular homeostasis by eliminating damaged organelles, reactive oxygen species (ROS), and misfolded proteins, thereby averting genomic instability and malignant transformation. However, after tumor establishment, cancer cells utilize autophagy to survive under hypoxia, metabolic stress, and nutrient deprivation within the tumor microenvironment. Phytomolecules have been reported to exert anticancer effects through the regulation of autophagy (Puranik, 2024). Curcumin, berberine, emodin, silibinin, and resveratrol were reported to promote and regulate autophagy in various cancers, including breast, bladder, liver, melanoma, colon, ovarian cancer, etc. (Cui et al., 2025).

Cell cycle arrest and inhibition of cell proliferation

Phytoconstituents exert anticancer effects largely by blocking tumor growth through cell-cycle arrest (Puranik, 2024). They regulate cyclins, cyclin-dependent kinase (CDKs), and CDK inhibitors, often halting progression at G1/S or G2/M checkpoints. Phytoconstituents act by disrupting the delicate balance of cell cycle kinetics and influencing key signaling pathways that drive cancer progression. Ellagic acid has been reported to inhibit cell proliferation and induce cell cycle arrest at the G0/G1 and G2/M phases by targeting cyclin B1 and cdc2 kinase. Quercetin is reported for G2/M phase arrest by modulating the expression of cyclin B1, cdc2, and other pivotal mitotic regulators. Quercetin affects several signaling pathways related to cell cycle regulation, such as the PI3K/Akt, MAPK, and NF-κB pathways, resulting in the inhibition of cell proliferation and the induction of cell cycle arrest (Jenča et al., 2024).

Preventing DNA replication

Topoisomerases are crucial enzymes involved in DNA replication and repair. Targeting this enzyme represents a significant approach in cancer therapy. Phytomolecules and their derivatives inhibit these enzymes and prevent DNA replication in tumor cells, thereby disrupting the survival and growth of cancerous cells. Camptothecin and its derivatives, such as topotecan and irinotecan, inhibit topoisomerase I. Berberine, an alkaloid, is reported to inhibit topoisomerase II activity and increase DNA cleavage in various cancers (Jenča et al., 2024).

Angiogenesis inhibition

Inhibiting angiogenesis, the process of new blood vessel formation that supports tumors, represents a critical strategy in cancer therapy. Natural products, comprising diverse compounds and nutrients, can influence signaling pathways and transcription factors associated with angiogenesis, thereby limiting tumor growth and metastasis (Ali et al., 2023). Alkaloids, such as camptothecin and berberine, were reported to inhibit angiogenesis by inducing apoptosis of endothelial cells and decreasing the expression of angiogenic factors. Polyphenols, such as quercetin, ellagic acid, catechin, and baicalin have been reported to inhibit angiogenesis by targeting important signaling pathways and transcription factors involved in the process, such as vascular endothelial growth factor (VEGF) and its receptor, extracellular signal-regulated kinase (ERK), mitogen-activated protein kinase (MAPK), and hypoxia-inducible factor 1-alpha (HIF-1α) (Jenča et al., 2024).

Modulating key signaling pathways

Phytomolecules such as curcumin, EGCG, and resveratrol have been reported to influence key signaling pathways, thereby inducing apoptosis, inhibiting cell proliferation, and suppressing metastasis (Puranik, 2024; Talib et al., 2020). They were reported to modulate (Situmorang et al., 2024) nuclear factor kappa-B cells (NF-κB), MAPK, Phosphoinositide 3-kinase/protein kinase B (PI3K/Akt), and Janus kinase/signal transducer and activator of transcription (JAK-STAT) pathway with downregulation of various genes involved in cell proliferation, Hedgehog pathway, notch signaling pathway, wingless/integrated-beta-catenin (Wnt/β-catenin), apoptosis inhibition, and metastasis (Reyaz et al., 2025; Gupta et al., 2021; Jenča et al., 2024). Phytomolecules, such as EGCG, resveratrol, curcumin, genistein, quercetin, and luteolin, are reported to exert their anticancer activity through modulation of various molecular signaling pathways (Akt/PI3K, NF-κB, AMP-activated protein kinase/mechanistic/mammalian target of rapamycin (AMPK/mTOR), JAK/STAT3, Wnt/β-catenin) (Jia et al., 2023). Astaxanthin, baicalein, curcumin, paclitaxel, quercetin, and resveratrol are reported to act through the MAPK/ERK pathway. Apigenin, catechin, gallic (Situmorang et al., 2024) acid, hesperidin, and luteolin are reported to act through the TNF signaling pathway (Situmorang et al., 2024). Allicin, baicalein, curcumin, EGCG (Situmorang et al., 2024), and kaempferol act on death receptor pathways. Apigenin, garcinol, resveratrol, and silibinin are reported to act on the p53 pathway, whereas astaxanthin, baicalein, honokiol, resveratrol, and vitisin A act on the p38 pathway (Situmorang et al., 2024). Compounds such as fisetin, curcumin, migrastatin, and quercetin act through actin dynamics pathways, and phytomolecules, such as berberine, baicalein, EGCG, kaempferol, myricetin, withanolides, and silymarin, are reported to act on autophagy pathways in cancer.

Modulation of tumor microenvironment

The tumor microenvironment (TME) includes cancer cells and a complex network of surrounding immune cells, including cancer-associated fibroblasts (CAFs), endothelial cells, components of the extracellular matrix, tumor-associated macrophages (TAMs), regulatory T cells (Tregs), and myeloid-derived suppressor cells (MDSCs), which together influence tumor growth and metastasis, and therapeutic resistance. Phytomedicines have the ability to modify the tumor microenvironment, thereby offering anticancer effects. By targeting molecules and specific cells within the TME, these phytomolecules inhibit cancer cell invasion, adhesion, and metastasis. Silibinin, a polyphenolic flavonoid, was reported to inhibit the invasion and metastasis of prostate cancer cells by modulating CAFs. Curcumin was reported to transform immune-suppressive Treg cells into antitumor T helper 1 (Th1) cells. Berberine was reported to suppress Treg activation, reduce MDSCs, and boost tumor-infiltrating T cell immunity (Jenča et al., 2024).

Reversing multidrug resistance

Multidrug resistance (MDR) is a major obstacle in cancer therapy, as it enables tumor cells to evade multiple chemotherapeutic agents. Natural products show promise in overcoming MDR by inhibiting drug efflux pumps (e.g., P-glycoprotein (P-gp), Multidrug Resistance-associated Protein 1 (MRP1)), inducing DNA damage and cell cycle arrest, modulating apoptosis, and regulating resistance-related signaling pathways. Flavonoids such as baicalein, quercetin, and chrysin are reported to improve chemosensitivity of chemotherapeutics by induction of apoptosis, suppression of efflux proteins, and cell cycle control. Similarly, alkaloids such as berberine, matrine, and evodiamine are reported to reverse MDR by inhibiting P-gp and modulating apoptotic pathways, highlighting their potential as adjuvants in cancer therapy (Jenča et al., 2024).

Immune cell activation and immune function regulation

Activating immune cells and regulating immune function is a key strategy in cancer therapy. Natural products can enhance anticancer activity by modulating T cells, mast cells, macrophages, cytokines, and other components of TME. For example, resveratrol boosts Th1 responses and cytotoxic T lymphocytes ($CD8^{+}T$) activity by reducing immune checkpoint receptor/programmed cell death protein 1 (PD-1) expression, while curcumin is reported to lower programmed death-ligand 1 (PD-L1) expression, increase $CD8^+$ T cells, and decrease Tregs and myeloid-derived suppressor cells (MDSCs) in cancers (Jenča et al., 2024). Apigenin showed potent immunomodulatory activity across various cancer types through interactions with dendritic cells (DCs), tumor-associated macrophages (TAMs), natural killer (NK) cells, T lymphocytes, and MDSCs (Cui et al., 2025).

Antioxidants and antiinflammatory activities

Chronic inflammation and oxidative stress promote cancer, and many phytoconstituents counter both (Crawford, 2014). Polyphenols and flavonoids, with multiple hydroxyls and conjugated rings, scavenge reactive oxygen species (ROS), reactive nitrogen species (RNS), and activate endogenous antioxidants (Rudzińska et al., 2023). They also inhibit inflammatory signaling, including NF-κB, MAP Kinase, STAT3, and inflammasomes, reducing proinflammatory cytokines and COX-2 expression. This dual antioxidant and antiinflammatory action contributes to cancer prevention and therapy (Rudzińska et al., 2023). Curcumin, EGCG, ginsenosides, resveratrol, and ursolic acid are reported to show anticancer activities through antioxidant activity and other anticancer mechanisms (Cui et al., 2025). Ginsenosides, berberine, curcumin, emodin, and EGCG are reported to exert antiinflammatory and anticancer activities (Cui et al., 2025).

Epigenetic modification

Epigenetic modifications are heritable biochemical changes to DNA or histones. Key mechanisms include DNA methylation and posttranslational histone modifications. Aberrant hypermethylation or deacetylation can silence tumor suppressor genes in cancer (Puranik, 2024). Many Phytoconstituents act as epigenetic modulators. For instance, EGCG (green–tea catechin) inhibits DNA methyltransferases (DNMTs) and histone deacetylases (HDACs), reactivating silenced genes such as p16INK4a and hMLH1. Similarly, genistein reduces DNMT1/3 levels, alters histone modifications, and reactivates tumor suppressor genes such as RARβ, p16INK4a, and MGMT. Other dietary compounds, including curcumin, resveratrol, and sulforaphane, also modulate histone acetylation and methylation in cancer cells (Puranik, 2024). These Phytoconstituents can reverse oncogenic epigenetic changes, restore normal gene expression, and inhibit tumor-promoting pathways, highlighting their potential as epigenetic therapies in cancer.

Natural phytoconstituents targeting cancer

Medicinal plants are rich in bioactive phytomolecules with diverse pharmacological effects, including anticancer activities. These compounds are categorized into flavonoids (e.g., epigallocatechin, quercetin), alkaloids (e.g., berberine, vinblastine, vincristine, camptothecins), terpenoids (e.g., paclitaxel, camptothecin), polyphenols (e.g., curcumin, quercetin, resveratrol, EGCG, luteolin, and gossypol), stilbenoid (e.g., resveratrol), and saponins and glycosides (e.g., digoxin, ouabain, and bufalin). Ongoing research continues to reveal the therapeutic potential of these bioactives, paving the way for the discovery of new and effective therapeutic agents (Choudhari et al., 2020; Jenča et al., 2024).

Flavonoids

Flavonoids are polyphenolic compounds consisting of two aromatic rings connected by a three-carbon bridge and are subdivided into flavonols, flavones, flavanones, isoflavones, and anthocyanidins. Flavonoids demonstrate anticancer effects through several mechanisms, including inhibiting cell proliferation, suppressing angiogenesis, inducing apoptosis, and modulating signaling pathways associated with cancer progression. Quercetin has been reported to induce apoptosis and inhibit cancer cell growth (Jenča et al., 2024).

Alkaloids

Alkaloids are nitrogenous phytocconstituents with heterocyclic structures. Many alkaloids demonstrate anticancer potential by inducing apoptosis, inhibiting topoisomerases, and interfering with microtubule function (Puranik, 2024). For instance, vinca alkaloids disrupt cell division by binding β-tubulin, blocking microtubule polymerization, and arresting cells in metaphase. Similarly, camptothecins, a topoisomerase I inhibitor, stabilize DNA-enzyme complexes, leading to replication stress and apoptosis. Other alkaloids, such as colchicine, also hinder mitosis or damage DNA. Collectively, plant-derived alkaloids exert anticancer effects by blocking cell cycle progression and activating caspase pathways, with vinca alkaloids serving as a prime example (Jenča et al., 2024).

Terpenoids

Terpenoids, also known as isoprenoids, represent a diverse class of natural compounds composed of repeating five-carbon isoprene units. This class includes monoterpenes, sesquiterpenes, and diterpenes, many of which demonstrate anticancer properties. These agents primarily function by inhibiting cell proliferation, inducing apoptosis, suppressing angiogenesis, and modulating signaling pathways. For instance, paclitaxel, a diterpenoid, is an anticancer drug that disrupts microtubule dynamics, leading to cell cycle arrest and apoptosis (Jenča et al., 2024; Puranik, 2024).

Polyphenols

Polyphenols are a diverse group of phytocompounds represented by the presence of multiple phenolic rings. They are classified into stilbenes, phenolic acids, and lignans. These compounds have represented excellent anticancer activities through apoptosis induction, antioxidant activity, modulation of signaling pathways, and inhibition of angiogenesis. For example, resveratrol, a stilbene, has been reported to inhibit cell proliferation and induce apoptosis in several cancer cell lines (Jenča et al., 2024). Polyphenolic compounds, such as curcumin, quercetin, resveratrol, EGCG, luteolin, and gossypol, were reported to possess anticancer activity through various molecular mechanisms, including molecular pathway inhibition, apoptosis induction, and metastasis inhibition (Jia et al., 2023).

Saponins and glycosides

Saponins are glycosides represented by their soap-forming ability and belong to the steroidal or triterpenoid class. Plant saponins and glycosides exert anticancer effects through several mechanisms, including disruption of cancer cell membranes, induction of apoptosis or necrosis, inhibition of proliferation, angiogenesis, reversing MDR, and stimulation of immune responses (Puranik, 2024). Their amphiphilic structures allow interaction with lipid bilayers, creating pores and altering membrane potential. Diosgenin, a steroidal saponin from fenugreek and yams, inhibits prosurvival pathways such as TNF-α–activated NF-κB and IL-6-activated STAT3, thereby reducing proliferation and promoting apoptosis. It also enhances caspase-3 activity and regulates p53 and Bcl-2 expression (Sethi et al., 2018). In animal models, diosgenin suppresses tumor growth and improves the efficacy of chemotherapeutic drugs. Cardiac glycosides such as digoxin, ouabain, and bufalin act by inhibiting Na^+/K^+-ATPase, leading to calcium imbalance and elevated ROS, which trigger apoptosis. They further downregulate HIF-1α and NF-κB, causing cell cycle arrest and promoting immunogenic cell death (Schneider et al., 2017).

Phytoformulations for cancer therapy

Herbal formulations are earlier classified into traditional and conventional herbal formulations (Fig. 28.2). The traditional formulation approach was strictly based on the procedures given in traditional books. Conventional herbal formulations are similar to allopathic formulations; however the active pharmaceutical ingredient is replaced by a multicomponent plant extract or enriched fraction (Sahu, 2021). Recently, modern/novel herbal formulations emerged that offer improved solubility, permeability, absorption, stability, and tissue distribution along with dose reduction, side effect minimization, control over the release of incorporated medicament, and improved therapeutic activity over conventional herbal formulations (Fig. 28.3). Modern herbal formulations have integrated nanotechnology into traditional formulations, resulting in a system with enhanced cancer treatment potential (Jha et al., 2024). This provides for the selective accumulation of phytoconstituents in cancer cells, thereby minimizing anticancer drug-linked damage to normal cells, reducing the likelihood of drug resistance, and enhancing therapeutic effectiveness (Talib et al., 2020). Modern herbal formulation included nanoformulations (Fig. 28.3), such as liposomes, solid lipid nanoparticles, micelles, dendrimers, and quantum dots (Chavda et al., 2022; Puranik,

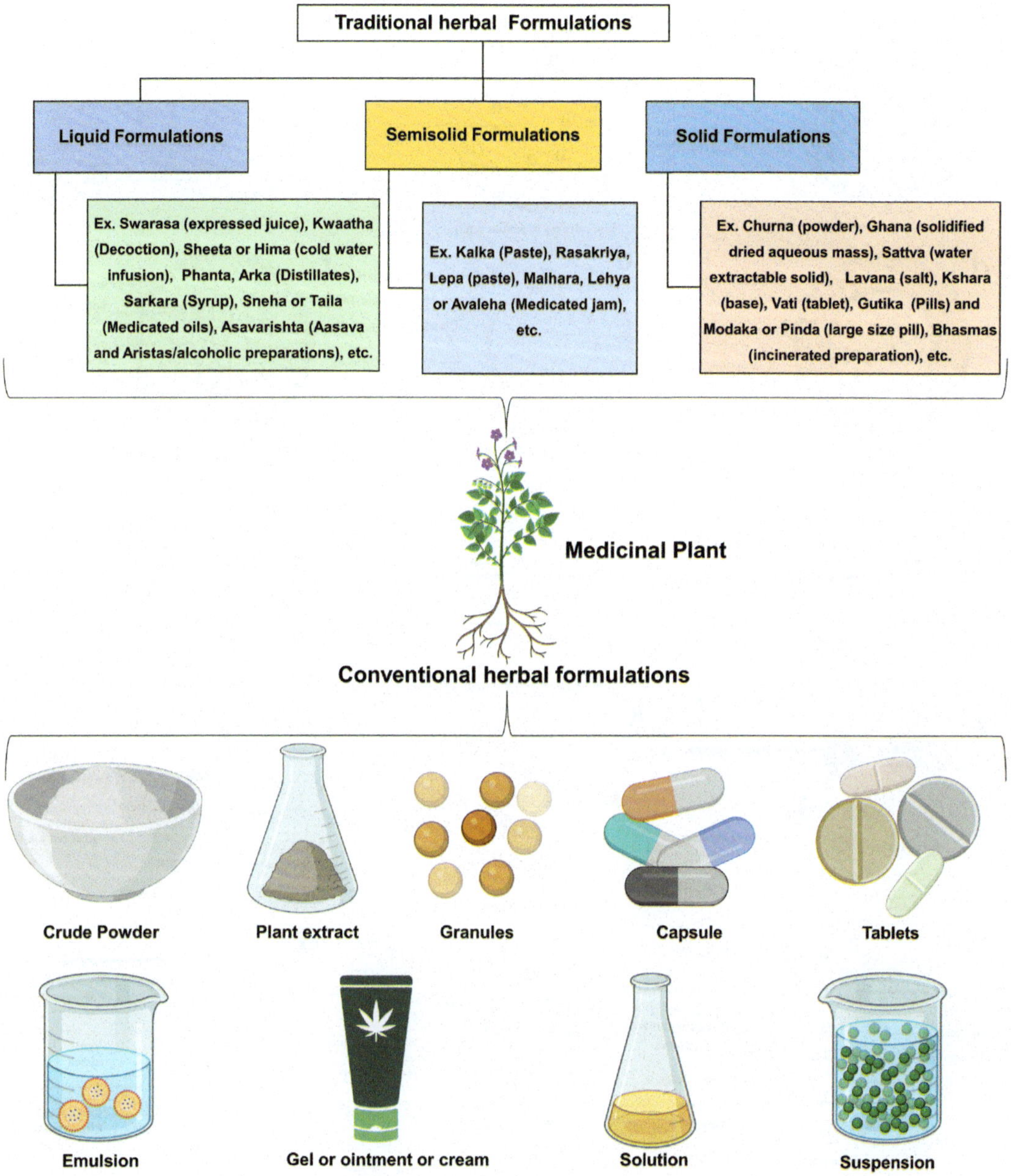

FIGURE 28.2 Traditional and conventional herbal formulations.

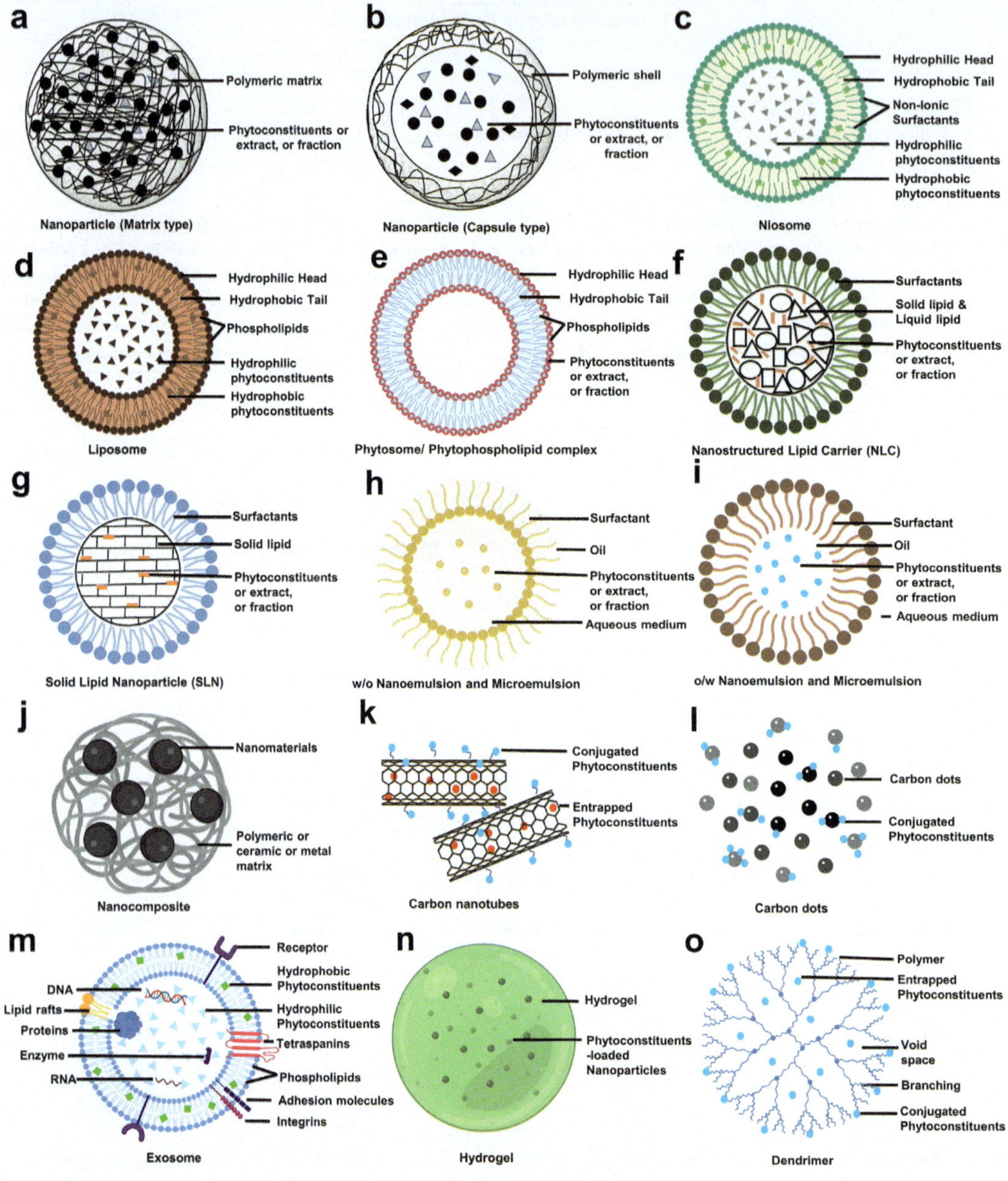

FIGURE 28.3 Schematic representation of novel drug delivery systems of herbal drug for cancer therapy (a and b) nanoparticle, (c) noisome, (d) liposome, (e) phytosome, (f) nanostructured lipid carrier, (g) solid lipid nanoparticle, (h and i) nanoemulsion and microemulsion, (j) nanocomposite, (k) carbon nanotube, (l) carbon dots, (m) exosome, (n) hydrogel, and (o) dendrimer.

2024). Commercially approved novel drug delivery systems of anticancer phytomolecules, such as Lipusu (paclitaxel-loaded liposome), Abraxane (paclitaxel-loaded albumin-bound Nanoparticle), Opaxio (paclitaxel-loaded polymeric nanoformulation), Marqibo (Vincristine-loaded liposome), Theracurmin (curcumin-loaded colloidal dispersion), and Meriva (curcumin-loaded phytosome), represent their significance for effective cancer therapy. Some of the nanoformulations of phytomolecules and herbal extracts are shown in Table 28.3.

Challenges in developing phytoformulations for cancer therapy

Herbal formulations face several challenges, including plant related challenges (chemical complexity, standardization, variability in the nature and proportion of chemical constituents, improper authentication, lack of quality due to adulteration or substitution) and pharmaceutical challenges (difficulty of preformulation study, difficulty in formulation and development, limited aqueous, lipid solubility, and poor bioavailability, instability, altered pharmacokinetics, and difficulty of shelf-life assessment) (Sahu, 2021). Regulatory and safety challenges further reduced the progress, with only a few nanophytoformulations receiving FDA approval due to variability in encapsulation and pharmacokinetics, stability issues, and high production costs (Puranik, 2024).

Preclinical and clinical evidence in cancer therapy

In vitro and in vivo studies

Preclinical studies demonstrated the anticancer activity of plant-derived compounds and extracts by multiple mechanisms (Puranik, 2024). In vitro assays showed that numerous phytoconstituents such as curcumin, resveratrol, EGCG, quercetin, rutin, Chrysis, lupeol, artemisinin, Withaferin A, D, andrographolide, betulinic acid, herbal extracts (*Panax ginseng, Aristolochia fontanesii, Artemisia annua, Andrographis paniculata, Allium sativum, Camelia sinensis, Centella asiatica, Cannabis sativa, Colchicum autumnale, Ginkgo biloba, Gossypium hirsutum, Linum usitatissimum, Moringa oleifera, Momordica charantia, Podophyllum peltatum, Silybum marianum*) can trigger apoptosis, inhibit proliferation, inhibition of angiogenesis, cell cycle arrest, cell invasion, ROS production, decrease mitochondrial membrane potential, alteration of molecular pathways and even reverse drug resistance in breast cancer, osteosarcoma, cervical cancer, colorectal cancer, melanoma, lung cancer, pancreatic cancer, and ovarian cancer (Dehelean et al., 2021; Sharma et al., 2024). In vivo models demonstrate tumor suppression and regression by numerous phytoconstituents, herbal extracts, and novel formulations in various animal models. Phytomedicines, such as resveratrol, curcumin, EGCG, quercetin, rutin, artemisinin, betulinic acid, ginseng extract are reported for anticancer activity in mice models through decreased tumor volume, growth rate, weight, and metastasis for treating breast cancer, cervical cancer, colorectal cancer, lung cancer, pancreatic cancer, and ovarian cancer (Dehelean et al., 2021). The delivery of phytomedicines through advanced phytoformulations, such as liposomes, gold nanoparticles, cyclodextrins, micelles,

TABLE 28.3 Phytomedicine loaded novel drug delivery systems for cancer therapy.

Type of novel herbal formulation	Phytomolecule/ Extract/fraction	Disease model	Overall outcome	Cancer	References
Nanoparticle	Hibiscus and curcumin extracts	In-vitro cytotoxicity against colorectal carcinoma cells (HCT-116) and breast cancer cells (MCF-7) cells	• Gold nanoparticles showed significant decrease in number of cells compared with control cells • Gold nanoparticle of hibiscus specimen showed a better inhibiting property than curcumin nanoparticles	Colon cancer and breast cancer	Akhtar et al. (2022)
	Boswellic acid	In-vitro cytotoxicity against human lung cancer (A-549) cell lines	• The nanoparticle showed significantly improved cytotoxicity compared with pure drug	Lungs cancer	Solanki et al. (2025)
Niosome	*Hedera Helix* extract (HHE) *Glycyrrhiza glabra* extract (GGE)	Cytotoxicity and cellular uptake using MCF-7 and BT-474 breast cancer cell lines Gene expression analysis and western blot	• Improved cellular uptake and anticancer property compared with extract • Niosomal HHE showed significant antitumor effects on breast cancer cells than niosomal GGE	Breast cancer	Akhlaghi et al. (2022)
	Hippadine	Cytotoxicity against two human ovarian carcinoma (A2780) and human skin cancer cells (A375)	• Niosomes demonstrated significantly improved cytotoxic activity compared with free hippadine	Ovarian cancer and skin cancer	Obeid et al. (2023)
Liposome	Orthosiphon aristatus var. aristatus extract	Antiproliferative activity against human lung adenocarcinoma (A549)	• Liposome showed improved anticancer activity	Lung cancer	Baharetha et al. (2025)
	Parthenolide	In-vitro cytotoxicity against human gastric adenocarcinoma cell line (AGS)	• Phytosome showed selective cytotoxicity to cancer cells than normal cells by activation of intrinsic apoptosis pathway.	Gastric adenocarcinoma	Ensaf et al. (2024)

Phytosome	*Barleria lupulina* Lindl. extract (BLSP)	In-vitro cytotoxicity against MCF-7 breast and HeLa cervical cancers	• Phytosome showed its potential for delivery of BLSP to treat breast and cervical cancer	Breast and cervical cancer	Banerjee et al. (2025)
	Hinokitiol	In-vitro cytotoxicity against breast cancer cell lines (MCF-7 and MDA-MB-231) Cell apoptosis study Cell cycle analysis (Yari et al., 2024)	• Hinokitiol-loaded phytosomes showed improved cytotoxicity, compared to pure hinokitiol with induction of apoptosis and cell cycle arrest at the G2/M and S phases	Breast cancer	Ahmed et al. (2024)
Nanostructured lipid carrier (NLC)	*Rosa damascena* essential oils (RDEOs)	In-vitro cytotoxicity against human breast cancer cell line (MDA-MB-231) Cell apoptosis study	• NLC showed its ability to stimulate apoptosis in the human breast cancer cell line • NLC showed improved cytotoxicity compared to RDEOs	Breast cancer	Yari et al. (2024)
	Carvacrol	In-vitro cytotoxicity against MCF-7 breast adenocarcinoma cell	• NLC showed 12-fold increase in cytotoxic effect of carvacrol	Breast cancer	Uchôa et al. (2025)
Solid lipid nanoparticle (SLN)	*Morus alba* extract	In-vitro cytotoxicity against MDA-MB231 cell line	• SLN showed significantly higher cytotoxic effects than extract • SLN demonstrated increased apoptosis compared with extract	Breast cancer	Palei et al. (2025)
	Curcumin	In-vitro cytotoxicity against triple-negative breast cancer cells (MDA-MB-231) Hemolysis and biocompatibility analysis In-vitro antioxidant activity Colony forming assay Wound healing assay/scratch assay Cellular uptake study Apoptosis assay by fluorescence-activated cell sorting In-vivo biodistribution assay in BALB/c mice	• SLN showed potent anticancer activity with induction of in MDA-MB-231 • SLN showed excellent hemocompatibility and antioxidant activity • Colony forming assay showed stronger antiproliferative capability of SLN compared with curcumin alone • SLN showed significant inhibition of cell migration • SLN-treated cells showed more early apoptotic • Cells (22.6%) than late apoptotic (10%) and necrotic cells (0.2%) • Demonstrated prolonged drug release profiles, elevated cellular uptake, and in vivo distribution	Breast cancer	Sarkar et al. (2025)

(*Continued*)

TABLE 28.3 Phytomedicine loaded novel drug delivery systems for cancer therapy.—cont'd

Type of novel herbal formulation	Phytomolecule/ Extract/fraction	Disease model	Overall outcome	Cancer	References
Nanoemulsion	*Cinnamomum Cassia* L. Essential oil	In-vitro cytotoxicity against lung adenocarcinoma cell line (A549)	• Improved cytotoxicity compared to essential oil	Lungs cancer	Alam et al. (2023)
	Celastrol	In-vitro cytotoxicity in non-small-cell lung cancer (A549) cell line Wound healing assay Clonogenic assay Spheroid assay Live-dead assay	• Nanoemulsion showed significant reduction of cell viability compared with neat phytomolecule with six-fold decrease in IC_{50} value • Nanoemulsion showed significant inhibition of cell migration compared with free phytomolecule • Coloni forming assay selected superior inhibitory effect of nanoemulsion over plain phytomolecule • Significant reduction in spheroid volumes was observed for nanoemulsion compared to the free drug • Nanoemulsion showed intensified red fluorescence with little to no green fluorescence, suggesting the presence of majorly dead cells.	Lungs cancer	Quadros et al. (2025)
Microemulsion and microemulge;	*Hygrophila auriculata* extract	In-vitro cytotoxicity against Human epidermoid carcinoma (A431) cells	• Microemulgel showed dose-dependent cytotoxicity	Skin cancer	Shaikh et al. (2024)
	Norcantharidin	Human colon cancer cell lines (HCT116 and HT29) In-vivo anticancer activity using BALB/c mice	• Microemulsion showed inhibition of tumor growth, migration and invasion in mice • Microemulsion increase the tumor-infiltrating T lymphocytes in mice with colon cancer	Colon cancer	Liu et al. (2025)

Nanocomposite	*Crocus sativus* extract	Cytotoxic activity against the HeLa cervical cancer cell line. Reactive oxygen species (ROSs) assay, matrix metalloprotease (MMP) levels Western blot analysis	• Bimetallic Ag@ZnO nanocomposite showed significant antitumor activity through the development of oxidative stress, inhibition of proliferation, and cell cycle arrest.	Cervical cancer	Yin et al. (2024)
	β–Sitosterol	In-vitro cytotoxicity against MCF-7 cells Free radical scavenging activity Pharmacokinetic studies in albino rats	• Alginate/Chitosan nanocomposite showed improved cytotoxicity and bioavailability compared with plain β–Sitosterol • Significantly higher antioxidant activity of nanocomposite compared with plain drug.	Breast cancer	Afzal et al. (2022)
Carbon dots	*Piper longum* leaves extract	In-vitro cytotoxicity against MDA-MB-231 (human breast cancer), SiHa (human cervical carcinoma), and B16F10 (murine melanoma) cell lines In-vitro antioxidant activity	• The carbon dots showed significantly improved cytotoxicity compared with neat extract • The DPPH and ABTS assay represented improved antioxidant activity of carbon dots compared to extract	Breast cancer Cervical cancer Melanoma	Mohapatra, Pratap, et al. (2023a)
	Quercetin	In-vitro cytotoxicity against Leukemia cancer cells (K-562). In-vitro antioxidant activity	• The developed carbon dots showed enhanced cytotoxic effect on leukemia cancer cells without affecting normal kidney cells • The carbon dots showed dose-dependent free radical scavenging activity	Leukemia	Naik et al. (2023)
Carbon nanotubes (CNTs)	*Olea europaea* L. extract	In-vitro cytotoxicity against Human breast adenocarcinoma (MCF7), human hepatocellular carcinoma (HepG2), and human colorectal cancer (SW620).	• The CNT resulted in the most significant inhibition cancer cell viability	Breast cancer Liver cancer Colon cancer	Alhajri et al. (2022)
	Ferulic acid and Diosgenin	In-vitro cytotoxicity against MCF-7 breast carcinoma cells, HepG2 hepatocellular carcinoma cells, and A549 non-small-cell lung cancer cells	• The CNT showed a promising drug delivery platform for improving the anticancer activity of phytomolecules	Breast cancer Liver cancer Lungs cancer	AbouAitah et al. (2024)
Exosome	*Oxalis corniculate* L.	In-vitro cytotoxicity against hepatocellular carcinoma (HuH7 cell) Apoptosis assay	• Exosomes improved the delivery and cytotoxic efficacy of the polyphenols	Liver cancer	Begum et al. (2025)

(*Continued*)

TABLE 28.3 Phytomedicine loaded novel drug delivery systems for cancer therapy.—cont'd

Type of novel herbal formulation	Phytomolecule/ Extract/fraction	Disease model	Overall outcome	Cancer	References
	Cannabidiol	Cell culture assays (MTT, colony forming) against drug-sensitive and resistant lung cancer cells Orthotopic lung tumor xenograft mouse-model	• Exosome showed antiproliferative and antiinflammatory activities against both lung cancer cells and reduce the colony forming ability. • Orally administered exosome showed superior tumor growth inhibition as compared with free cannabidiol	Lungs cancer	Moholkar et al. (2025)
Hydrogel (nano-loaded hydrogel)	*Piper longum* extract	In-vitro cytotoxicity against melanoma (B16F10) cells Ex-vivo skin permeability assay by Franz diffusion study and confocal laser scanning microscopy In-vivo anticancer activity in syngeneic transplantable tumor model using C57BL/6 mice.	• Transferosome showed improved cytotoxicity compared with neat extract • The transgelosome showed improved skin permeability compared with extract loaded plain gel. • Transgelosome showed significantly improved in-vivo tumor regression outcomes compared with extract loaded plain gel.	Melanoma	Mohapatra, Kumar, Shreya, Panigrahi, et al. (2023c)
	Berberine	In-vitro cytotoxicity against A431 carcinoma cell lines Depth of permeation by confocal laser scanning microscopy Dermatokinetic study	• The formulation showed significantly improved cytotoxicity compared to plain berberine • Nanoemulgel showed improved drug availability in skin	Skin cancer	Awasthi et al. (2024)
Dendrimer	*Peganum harmala* alkaloids and tannic acid	Cytotoxic activities against breast adenocarcinoma (MCF-7) cells	• The dendrimers showed significant increases in late apoptosis in MCF-7 cells relative to their respective free forms.	Breast cancer	Azzazy et al. (2022)
	Curcumin Methotrexate	In-vitro cell viability study using HeLa cancer cell lines Apoptosis assay Reactive oxygen species (ROSs) assessment	• Dendrimer exhibited significantly higher cytotoxicity than free drugs. • The codelivery of drugs synergistically improved the cytotoxicity. • Significant rising in ROS level was observed in dendrimer treated cells	Cervical cancer	Aghanejad et al. (2025)

solid dispersion, microcapsules, polymeric nanoparticles, and proniosomal gel, demonstrated significantly improved therapeutic activity compared with phytomolecule or extract in in vitro and in vivo cancer models (Dehelean et al., 2021; Puranik, 2024; Talib et al., 2020).

Clinical trials

Current and emerging clinical trials highlight the increasing role of herbal drugs in cancer therapy, both as first line anticancer agents and as adjuvants to conventional therapies. Despite challenges in quality control, standardization, bioavailability, formulation, and regulatory acceptance, the steady growth of well-designed trials reflects a global trend toward integrating phytomedicines into current oncology, aiming to improve efficacy, reduce toxicity, improve patient compliance, and therapeutic outcomes. Some of the ongoing clinical trials on herbal drugs for cancer therapy are listed in Table 28.4 (Clinicaltrials.gov, 2025).

Safety and toxicity considerations

Safety and toxicity considerations are required for using phytomedicine for cancer therapy. In general, herbal drugs are well-tolerated, but higher concentrations, often required for therapeutic efficacy, can pose safety and toxicity issues (Sharma et al., 2024). However, the bioavailability of many phytoconstituents is low, requiring high doses that might develop toxicity (Puranik, 2024). The regulation and approval of herbal medicines remain difficult because of poor standardization, leading to variability in quality, safety, and therapeutic outcomes. The diverse chemical composition, chemical complexity, formulation challenges, and analytical challenges in phytotherapy complicate the validation of phytomedicines for cancer therapy. Variability in plant constituents and external factors such as harvesting, storage, and environment further affect quality. Thus, reliable standardization and quality control remain critical but challenging when active compounds are not fully identified. Rigorous clinical trials and pharmacokinetic studies are required to establish the safety, toxicity, and pharmacokinetic profile of phytomedicines (Puranik, 2024).

Risk and benefits analysis for phytomedicine for cancer therapy

Multiconstituent-based complex herbal drugs offer multiple advantages over conventional single-drug therapy due to synergism among phytoconstituents. Despite the promising anticancer potential of herbal drugs, several challenges need to be addressed to fully incorporate them into mainstream cancer therapy (Jenča et al., 2024).

Benefits

- **Multitargeted mechanisms of action:** Many Phytoconstituents act on multiple signaling pathways simultaneously, targeting proliferation, apoptosis, angiogenesis,

TABLE 28.4 Ongoing clinical trials with herbal drugs for cancer therapy.

Clinical trial no.	Study title	Interventions	Phase of clinical trial	Type of cancer
NCT05152498	Fu Zheng Jie Du Hua Yu principle for treatment of severe HBV related hepatocellular carcinoma (FZJDHYPFTOSHBVHCC)	Drug: Fu Zheng Jie Du Hua Yu therapy	Early phase 1	Hepatocellular carcinoma
NCT03384667	Maekmoondong-tang on postoperative cough in patients with lung cancer	Drug: Maekmoondong-tang and placebo	Phase 3	Postoperative cough, lung cancer
NCT02510118	Synergistic antitumor effect of ChangTai Keli for colon cancer patients	Drug: mFOLFOX6, XELOX, placebo ChangTai Keli, ChangTai Keli	Phase 3	Colon cancer
NCT01975454	Study of TLBZT-based herbal therapy plus chemotherapy for metastatic colorectal cancer	Drug: Chemotherapy, herbal therapy	Phase 2	Metastatic colorectal cancer
NCT01142479	Compound herbal formula (TPE-1) for leukopenia and cancer-related fatigue in breast cancer patients with radiotherapy	Drug: Chinese herbal medicine decoction	Phase 3	Breast cancer
NCT00669656	Herbal therapy for treatment of recurrent prostate cancer	Drug: Prostate health cocktail	Phase 2	Prostate cancer
NCT00243022	Dietary, herbal and alternative medicine in glioblastoma multiforme	Drug: *Boswellia serrata* extract dietary supplement: Cyanocobalamin	Phase 2	Glioblastoma
NCT00079794	Iscar for supplemental care in stage IV lung cancer	Drug: Iscar, mistletoe	Phase 2	Lung cancer
NCT00064857	Pycnogenol for the treatment of lymphedema of the arm in breast cancer survivors	Drug: Pycnogenol	Phase 2	Lymphedema and breast cancer
NCT00028964	Combination chemotherapy after surgery with or without Chinese herbal therapy to treat symptoms in women with breast cancer	Dietary supplement: Chinese herbs Drug: Cyclophosphamide, doxorubicin hydrochloride	Phase 2	Breast cancer
NCT00028977	Herbal therapy in treating women with metastatic breast cancer	Drug: Herba scutellaria Barbatae (HSB)	Phase 2	Breast cancer

and metastasis. This pleiotropic activity is advantageous in addressing tumor heterogeneity (Cui et al., 2025).

- **Synergistic effects with standard therapies:** Phytoconstituents such as curcumin, resveratrol, and EGCG have shown synergistic effects with chemotherapy and radiotherapy, enhancing efficacy and reducing required drug doses (Lin et al., 2020).
- **Pharmacokinetic/Bioavailability enhancement:** Certain anticancer phytomolecules (piperine, quercetin, naringin) act as bioenhancers by inhibiting efflux pumps, drug metabolizing enzymes, and absorption. They improve the bioavailability of conventional synthetic chemotherapeutics (Gidwani et al., 2025; Kulkarni et al., 2022).
- **Chemopreventive potential:** Many plant-derived compounds can reduce cancer risk through antioxidant, antiinflammatory, and immunomodulatory effects, thereby playing a preventive role in high-risk populations (Dehelean et al., 2021; Lin et al., 2020).
- **Cost-effectiveness and accessibility:** In low and middle-income countries, phytomedicine may serve as a more affordable and locally available alternative or adjunct to expensive conventional drugs.
- **Selective toxicity and decreased side effects:** Herbal drugs are reported to alleviate the side effects of conventional anticancer drugs, improving treatment tolerance and allowing the continuation of treatment.
- **Sensitizer in drug resistance:** Herbal drugs are reported for potentiation of the tumoricidal effect of chemotherapeutic drugs by avoiding drug resistance by multiple mechanisms (inhibition of P-gp efflux, MRP, inducing DNA damage and cell cycle arrest, modulating apoptosis, and regulating resistance-related signaling pathways) (Dehelean et al., 2021).

Risks

- **Variability in composition and potency:** The phytochemical content of plant materials can vary depending on species, geographic origin, harvesting conditions, and processing methods, leading to inconsistent therapeutic outcomes (Puranik, 2024).
- **Poor bioavailability:** Many Phytoconstituents (e.g., curcumin, quercetin) experience limited absorption, fast metabolism, and low bioavailability, limiting their clinical efficacy unless advanced delivery systems are used (Puranik, 2024).
- **Potential herb-drug interactions and adverse effects:** Phytomedicines sometimes interact with synthetic chemotherapeutics, and may not provide therapeutic benefits (Allegra et al., 2023; Lin et al., 2020). Certain phytomedicines can interfere with drug-metabolizing enzymes, and membrane transporters, altering the pharmacokinetics of conventional anticancer agents.
- **Insufficient clinical evidence:** While numerous preclinical studies show promising anticancer activity, robust clinical trials are lacking for many phytomedicines, making regulatory approval challenging.
- **Risk of self-medication and misuse:** Patients may replace evidence-based cancer treatments with unproven herbal remedies, leading to disease progression or delayed access to appropriate care.

- **Regulatory barriers:** The use of herbal drugs as the main chemotherapy and their integration with standard herbal anticancer agents into clinical practice face regulatory and acceptance barriers due to a lack of scientific evidence, clinical trials, and chemical complexity. Further, improper product categorization, variation in regulation regarding premarket and postmarket control, also pose challenges for herbal drug use as the main anticancer therapy.
- **Other challenges:** In addition to above challenges, medicinal plant related challenges (chemical complexity, difficulty in following standardization protocol, lack of quality due to adulteration or substitution, lack of good agricultural and collection practices (GACP) and good manufacturing practices (GMP), presence of contaminants), and pharmaceutical challenges (difficulty of preformulation study, difficulty in formulation and development, instability, altered pharmacokinetics) need to be addressed (Sahu, 2021).

Future scopes for drug delivery systems and innovation

Integrating phytomedicines into modern cancer care holds promise for developing effective yet less toxic therapies. Progress will depend on well-structured clinical trials to evaluate phytoconstituents and strict adherence to GACP and GMP, supported by phytochemical databases and reference standards. Advanced tools such as genomics, metabolomics, pharmacogenomics, and artificial intelligence can enhance understanding, drug discovery, and personalized treatment design. Ethnopharmacological studies may reveal new bioactive compounds. Successful integration will further require updated regulations, professional training in phytotherapy, and dedicated oncology facilities, ultimately bridging traditional knowledge with modern biotechnology for sustainable, and personalized cancer treatment.

Conclusion

Cancer remains a major global health burden, and conventional therapies often suffer from high costs, limited efficacy, and severe side effects. Natural plant-derived compounds and complex herbal extracts have demonstrated promising potential for cancer prevention and treatment. Since cancer is multifactorial, it's wise to use multiconstituent-based standardized herbal drugs (extract/fraction) compared with single therapeutics, which may act in a multitargeting way simultaneously. Integrating phytomedicines into synthetic chemotherapeutics can improve outcomes, reduce side effects, and enhance patient quality of life. Delivery of phytomedicine through novel drug delivery systems will improve its targetability, stability, pharmacokinetic profile, and therapeutic efficacy with negligible toxicity. However, challenges such as variability in plant composition and limited clinical validation remain. Advancing phytotherapy requires collaborative research, optimized formulations, supportive regulatory frameworks, and integration into personalized care. Overall, medicinal plants hold promise as complementary tools in modern cancer treatment.

References

AbouAitah, K., Abdelaziz, A.M., Higazy, I.M., Swiderska-Sroda, A., Hassan, A.M.E., Shaker, O.G., Szałaj, U., Stobinski, L., Malolepszy, A., Lojkowski, W., 2024. Functionalized carbon nanotubes for delivery of ferulic acid and diosgenin anticancer natural agents. ACS Appl. Bio Mater. 7 (2), 791–811. https://doi.org/10.1021/acsabm.3c00700.

Afzal, O., Akhter, M.H., Ahmad, I., Muzammil, K., Dawria, A., Zeyaullah, M., Altamimi, A.S.A., Khalilullah, H., Mir Najib Ullah, S.N., Rahman, M.A., Ali, A., Shahzad, N., Jaremko, M., Emwas, A.H., Abdel Aziz Ibrahim, I., 2022. A β-sitosterol encapsulated biocompatible alginate/chitosan polymer nanocomposite for the treatment of breast cancer. Pharmaceutics 14 (8). https://doi.org/10.3390/pharmaceutics14081711. Available from: http://www.mdpi.com/journal/pharmaceutics.

Aghanejad, A., Kheiriabad, S., Ghaffari, M., Namvar Aghdash, S., Ghafouri, N., Ezzati Nazhad Dolatabadi, J., Andishmand, H., Hamblin, M.R., 2025. Targeted co-delivery nanosystem based on methotrexate, curcumin, and PAMAM dendrimer for improvement of the therapeutic efficacy in cervical cancer. Scient. Rep. 15 (1). https://doi.org/10.1038/s41598-024-82074-7. Available from: https://www.nature.com/srep/.

Ahmed, T.A., Milibary, G.A., Almehmady, A.M., Alahmadi, A.A., Ali, E.M.M., El-Say, K.M., 2024. Improving the cytotoxic activity of hinokitiol from drug-loaded phytosomal formulation against breast cancer cell lines. Int. J. Nanomed. 19, 10321–10339. https://doi.org/10.2147/IJN.S476667.

Akhlaghi, M., Taebpour, M., Lotfabadi, N.N., Naghib, S.M., Jalili, N., Farahmand, L., Haghiralsadat, B.F., Rahmanian, M., Tofighi, D., 2022. Synthesis and characterization of smart stimuli-responsive herbal drug-encapsulated nanoniosome particles for efficient treatment of breast cancer. Nanotechnol. Rev. 11 (1), 1364–1385. https://doi.org/10.1515/ntrev-2022-0080.

Akhtar, S., Asiri, S.M., Khan, F.A., Gunday, S.T., Iqbal, A., Alrushaid, N., Labib, O.A., Deen, G.R., Henari, F.Z., 2022. Formulation of gold nanoparticles with hibiscus and curcumin extracts induced anti-cancer activity. Arab. J. Chem. 15 (2). https://doi.org/10.1016/j.arabjc.2021.103594. Available from: http://colleges.ksu.edu.sa/Arabic%20Colleges/CollegeOfScience/ChemicalDept/AJC/default.aspx http://www.sciencedirect.com/science/journal/18785352.

Alam, A., Ansari, M.J., Alqarni, M.H., Salkini, M.A., Raish, M., 2023. Antioxidant, antibacterial, and anticancer activity of ultrasonic nanoemulsion of cinnamomum Cassia L. Essential oil. Plants 12 (4). https://doi.org/10.3390/plants12040834. Available from: www.mdpi.com/journal/plants.

Alfonzetti, T., Yasmin-Karim, S., Ngwa, W., Avery, S., 2021. Phytoradiotherapy: an integrative approach to cancer treatment by combining radiotherapy with phytomedicines. Front. Oncol. 10. https://doi.org/10.3389/fonc.2020.624663. Available from: http://www.frontiersin.org/Oncology/about.

Alhajri, H.M., Aloqaili, S.S., Alterary, S.S., Alqathama, A., Abdalla, A.N., Alzhrani, R.M., Alotaibi, B.S., Alsaab, H. O., 2022. Olive leaf extracts for a green synthesis of silver-functionalized multi-walled carbon nanotubes. J. Funct. Biomater. 13 (4). https://doi.org/10.3390/jfb13040224. Available from: http://www.mdpi.com/journal/jfb.

Ali, M., Wani, S.U.D., Salahuddin, M., Manjula, S.N., Dey, T., Zargar, M.I., Singh, J., 2023. Recent advance of herbal medicines in cancer- a molecular approach. Heliyon 9 (2). https://doi.org/10.1016/j.heliyon.2023.e13684. Available from: http://www.journals.elsevier.com/heliyon/.

Allegra, S., De Francia, S., Turco, F., Bertaggia, I., Chiara, F., Armando, T., Storto, S., Mussa, M.V., 2023. Phytotherapy and drugs: can their interactions increase side effects in cancer patients? J. Xenob. 13 (1), 75–89. https://doi.org/10.3390/jox13010007.

Anwar, D.M., El-Sayed, M., Reda, A., Fang, J.Y., Khattab, S.N., Elzoghby, A.O., 2021. Recent advances in herbal combination nanomedicine for cancer: delivery technology and therapeutic outcomes. Expert Opinion Drug Deliv. 18 (11), 1609–1625. https://doi.org/10.1080/17425247.2021.1955853.

Asma, S.T., Acaroz, U., Imre, K., Morar, A., Shah, S.R.A., Hussain, S.Z., Arslan-Acaroz, D., Demirbas, H., Hajrulai-Musliu, Z., Istanbullugil, F.R., Soleimanzadeh, A., Morozov, D., Zhu, K., Herman, V., Ayad, A., Athanassiou, C., Ince, S., 2022. Natural products/bioactive compounds as a source of anticancer drugs. Cancers 14 (24). https://doi.org/10.3390/cancers14246203. Available from: http://www.mdpi.com/journal/cancers/.

Awasthi, S., Hasan, N., Nadeem, M., Rizvi, M.A., Alam, K., Kesharwani, P., Ahmad, F.J., 2024. Optimized formulation of berberine hydrochloride loaded nanoemulgel for management of skin cancer. Colloids Surfaces A Physicochem. Eng. Aspects 687. https://doi.org/10.1016/j.colsurfa.2024.133406. Available from: https://www.sciencedirect.com/science/journal/09277757.

Ayaz, M., Nawaz, A., Ahmad, S., Mosa, O.F., Eisa Hamdoon, A.A., Khalifa, M.A., Sadiq, A., Ullah, F., Wadood, A., Kabra, A., Ananda Murthy, H.C., 2022. Underlying anticancer mechanisms and synergistic combinations of phytochemicals with cancer chemotherapeutics: potential benefits and risks. J. Food Qual. 2022. https://doi.org/10.1155/2022/1189034. Available from: https://www.hindawi.com/journals/jfq/.

Azzazy, H.M.E.S., Sawy, A.M., Abdelnaser, A., Meselhy, M.R., Shoeib, T., Fahmy, S.A., 2022. Peganum harmala alkaloids and tannic acid encapsulated in PAMAM dendrimers: improved anticancer activities as compared to doxorubicin. ACS Appl. Polymer Mater. 4 (10), 7228–7239. https://doi.org/10.1021/acsapm.2c01093.

Baharetha, H.M., Abdul Majid, A.M.S., Nazari, M.V., Samad, N.A., Al-Mansoub, M.A., Taleb Agha, M., Dahham, S. S., 2025. Optimised formulation and characterisation of liposomes for enhanced stability and antiproliferative efficacy of Orthosiphon aristatus var. aristatus extract in lung cancer treatment. Nat. Prod. Res. https://doi.org/10.1080/14786419.2025.2494638. Available from: https://www.tandfonline.com/action/journalInformation?journalCode=gnpl20.

Banerjee, S., Mukhopadhyay, S., Das, A., Banerjee, S., Bose, S., Banerjee, S., Casarcia, N., Bishayee, A., 2025. Preparation, characterisation, anticancer potential and safety evaluation of a soy lecithin phytosome delivery system loaded with constituents from Barleria lupulina. J. Microencap. 42 (3), 209–229. https://doi.org/10.1080/02652048.2025.2467046.

Begum, S., Mazumder, P.B., Das Talukdar, A., 2025. In vitro evaluation of anticancer activity of Oxalis corniculata L., by harnessing exosome for effective drug delivery against hepatocellular carcinoma. Pharmacol. Res. Nat. Prod. 8. https://doi.org/10.1016/j.prenap.2025.100298. Available from: https://www.sciencedirect.com/journal/pharmacological-research-natural-products.

Chavda, V.P., Patel, A.B., Mistry, K.J., Suthar, S.F., Wu, Z.X., Chen, Z.S., Hou, K., 2022. Nano-drug delivery systems entrapping natural bioactive compounds for cancer: recent progress and future challenges. Front. Oncol. 12. https://doi.org/10.3389/fonc.2022.867655. Available from: http://www.frontiersin.org/Oncology/about.

Choudhari, A.S., Mandave, P.C., Deshpande, M., Ranjekar, P., Prakash, O., 2020. Phytochemicals in cancer treatment: from preclinical studies to clinical practice. Front. Pharmacol. 10. https://doi.org/10.3389/fphar.2019.01614. Available from: http://www.frontiersin.org/Pharmacology.

Clinicaltrials.gov, 2025. Available from: https://clinicaltrials.gov/search?cond=Cancer&term=Herbal%20Medicine&intr=Herbal%20therapy&aggFilters=phase:0%201%202&sort=StudyFirstPostDate.

Crawford, S., 2014. Anti-inflammatory/antioxidant use in long-term maintenance cancer therapy: a new therapeutic approach to disease progression and recurrence. Ther. Adv. Med. Oncol. 6 (2), 52–68. https://doi.org/10.1177/1758834014521111.

Cui, D., Zhang, C., Zhang, L., Zheng, J., Wang, J., He, L., Jin, H., Kang, Q., Zhang, Y., Li, N., Sun, Z., Zheng, W., Wei, J., Zhang, S., Feng, Y., Wen, T., Zhong, Z., 2025. Natural anti-cancer products: insights from herbal medicine. Chin. Med. 20 (1). https://doi.org/10.1186/s13020-025-01124-y.

Dehelean, C.A., Marcovici, I., Soica, C., Mioc, M., Coricovac, D., Iurciuc, S., Cretu, O.M., Pinzaru, I., 2021. Plant-derived anticancer compounds as new perspectives in drug discovery and alternative therapy. Molecules 26 (4). https://doi.org/10.3390/molecules26041109. Available from: https://www.mdpi.com/1420-3049/26/4/1109/pdf.

Ensaf, P.K., Goodarzi, M.T., Tabrizi, M.H., Neamati, A., Hosseinyzadeh, S.S., 2024. Novel formulation of parthenolide-loaded liposome coated with chitosan and evaluation of its potential anticancer effects in vitro. Mol. Biol. Rep. 51 (1). https://doi.org/10.1007/s11033-024-09325-8. Available from: https://www.springer.com/journal/11033.

Garcia-Oliveira, P., Otero, P., Pereira, A.G., Chamorro, F., Carpena, M., Echave, J., Fraga-Corral, M., Simal-Gandara, J., Prieto, M.A., 2021. Status and challenges of plant-anticancer compounds in cancer treatment. Pharmaceuticals 14 (2), 1–28. https://doi.org/10.3390/ph14020157.

Gidwani, B., Bhairam, M., Shukla, S.S., Verma, H., Kumar Pandey, R., 2025. Herbal bioenhancers in pharmaceutical drug delivery: mechanisms, challenges, and future innovations. Chem. Biodivers. https://doi.org/10.1002/cbdv.202500760.

Gupta, P.K., Saraff, M., Gahtori, R., Negi, N., Tripathi, S.K., Kumar, J., Kumar, S., Aldhayan, S.H., Dhanasekaran, S., Abomughaid, M.M., Dua, K., Gundamaraju, R., Ojha, S., Ruokolainen, J., Jha, N.K., Kesari, K.K., 2021. Phytomedicines targeting cancer stem cells: therapeutic opportunities and prospects for pharmaceutical development. Pharmaceuticals 14 (7). https://doi.org/10.3390/ph14070676. Available from: https://www.mdpi.com/1424-8247/14/7/676/pdf.

Hanahan, D., Weinberg, R.A., 2011. Hallmarks of cancer: the next generation. Cell 144 (5), 646–674. https://doi.org/10.1016/j.cell.2011.02.013.

Izah, S.C., Ogidi, O.I., Ogwu, M.C., Salimon, S.S., Yusuf, Z.M., Akram, M., Raimi, M.O., Iyingiala, A.A., 2024. Historical perspectives and overview of the value of herbal medicine. Refer. Series Phytochem. 3164, 3–35. https://doi.org/10.1007/978-3-031-43199-9_1.

Jenča, A., Mills, D., Ghasemi, H., Saberian, E., Jenča, A., Forood, A.M.K., Petrášová, A., Jenčová, J., Velisdeh, Z.J., Zare-Zardini, H., Ebrahimifar, M., 2024. Herbal therapies for cancer treatment: a review of phytotherapeutic efficacy. Biol. Targets & Ther. 18, 229–255. https://doi.org/10.2147/btt.s484068.

Jha, A., Kumar, M., Bharti, K., Manjit, M., Mishra, B., 2024. Biopolymer-based tumor microenvironment-responsive nanomedicine for targeted cancer therapy. Nanomedicine 19 (7), 633–651. https://doi.org/10.2217/nnm-2023-0302.

Jia, W., Zhou, L., Li, L., Zhou, P., Shen, Z., 2023. Nano-based drug delivery of polyphenolic compounds for cancer treatment: progress, opportunities, and challenges. Pharmaceuticals 16 (1). https://doi.org/10.3390/ph16010101. Available from: https://www.mdpi.com/journal/pharmaceuticals.

Kulkarni, M., Bhat, R., Ingale, S., Date, A., 2022. Herbal Bioenhancers in Cancer Drug Delivery Drug Delivery Technology: Herbal Bioenhancers in Pharmaceuticals. De Gruyter, India, pp. 103–148. https://doi.org/10.1515/9783110746808-005.

Lin, S.R., Chang, C.H., Hsu, C.F., Tsai, M.J., Cheng, H., Leong, M.K., Sung, P.J., Chen, J.C., Weng, C.F., 2020. Natural compounds as potential adjuvants to cancer therapy: preclinical evidence. British J. Pharmacol. 177 (6), 1409–1423. https://doi.org/10.1111/bph.14816. Available from: http://onlinelibrary.wiley.com/journal/10.1111/(ISSN)1476-5381.

Liu, X., Fang, W., Lu, W., Xu, M., Wu, Z., Su, D., Ding, L., Zhang, Q., Ouyang, J., Wang, T., Sun, L., Gao, S., Cheng, H., Hu, R., 2025. Oral pH-sensitive solid self-microemulsion of norcantharidin wrapped in colon-coated capsule for selective therapy of colorectal carcinoma. AAPS PharmSciTech 26 (3). https://doi.org/10.1208/s12249-025-03056-0. Available from: https://www.springer.com/journal/12249.

Mohapatra, D., Pratap, R., Pandey, V., Shreya, S., Naik, G.G., Mandal, S.C., Otimenyin, S.O., Dubey, P.K., Parmar, A.S., Sahu, A.N., 2023a. Bioengineered dual fluorescent carbon nano dots from Indian long pepper leaves for multifaceted environmental and health utilities. Environm. Sci. Pollution Res. 30 (18), 52182–52208. https://doi.org/10.1007/s11356-023-25887-9.

Mohapatra, D., Kumar, D.N., Shreya, S., Pandey, V., Dubey, P.K., Agrawal, A.K., Sahu, A.N., 2023b. Quality by design–based development and optimization of fourth-generation ternary solid dispersion of standardized Piper longum extract for melanoma therapy. Drug Deliv. Trans. Res. 13 (12), 3094–3131. https://doi.org/10.1007/s13346-023-01375-y.

Mohapatra, D., Kumar, D.N., Shreya, S., Panigrahi, D., Agrawal, A.K., Sahu, A.N., 2023c. Quality-by-design-based development of ultradeformable nanovesicular transgelosome of standardized Piper longum extract for melanoma. Nanomedicine 18 (14), 963–985. https://doi.org/10.2217/nnm-2023-0069.

Moholkar, D.N., Kandimalla, R., Jeyabalan, J., Yan, J., Song, Z.H., Aqil, F., Gupta, R.C., 2025. Targeted oral delivery of exosomal formulation of cannabidiol against lung cancer. Adv. Therap. 8 (7). https://doi.org/10.1002/adtp.202400362. Available from: http://onlinelibrary.wiley.com/journal/10.1002/(ISSN)2366-3987.

Naik, G.G., Pratap, R., Mohapatra, D., Shreya, S., Sharma, D.K., Parmar, A.S., Patra, A., Sahu, A.N., 2023. From phytomedicine to photomedicine: quercetin-derived carbon nanodots—synthesis, characterization and healthcare applications. J. Mater. Sci. 58 (34), 13744–13761. https://doi.org/10.1007/s10853-023-08880-y.

Obeid, M.A., Ogah, C.A., Ogah, C.O., Ajala, O.S., Aldea, M.R., Gray, A.I., Igoli, J.I., Ferro, V.A., 2023. Formulation and evaluation of nanosized hippadine-loaded niosome: extraction and isolation, physicochemical properties, and in vitro cytotoxicity against human ovarian and skin cancer cell lines. J. Drug Deliv. Sci. Technol. 87. https://doi.org/10.1016/j.jddst.2023.104766. Available from: http://www.editionsdesante.fr/category.php?id_category=48.

Oyenihi, O.R., Oyenihi, A.B., Erhabor, J.O., Matsabisa, M.G., Oguntibeju, O.O., 2021. Unravelling the anticancer mechanisms of traditional herbal medicines with metabolomics. Molecules 26 (21). https://doi.org/10.3390/molecules26216541. Available from: https://www.mdpi.com/1420-3049/26/21/6541/pdf.

Palei, N.N., Sabapati, M., Samajdar, S., Dhar, A.K., 2025. Formulation of Morus alba extract loaded solid lipid nanoparticles: in silico, characterizations, and in vitro cytotoxicity study. Drug Develop. Indust. Pharm. 51 (1), 14–28. https://doi.org/10.1080/03639045.2024.2439930.

Puranik, N., 2024. Nano-formulation of Dietary Phytochemicals for Cancer Management. Springer Nature, Singapore. https://doi.org/10.1007/978-981-97-8005-1.

Quadros, M., Goyal, M., Chauhan, G., Gadhave, D., Gupta, V., 2025. An inhaled nanoemulsion encapsulating a herbal drug for non-small cell lung cancer (NSCLC) treatment. Pharmaceutics 17 (5), 540.

Reyaz, A., Qadri, S.S., Javaid, D., Ganie, S.Y., Reshi, M.S., 2025. Exploring the role of traditional medicinal plants in cancer therapy: present efficacy and future directions. Phytomed. Plus 5 (3). https://doi.org/10.1016/j.phyplu.2025.100845. Available from: https://www.sciencedirect.com/science/journal/26670313.

Rudzińska, A., Juchaniuk, P., Oberda, J., Wiśniewska, J., Wojdan, W., Szklener, K., Mańdziuk, S., 2023. Phytochemicals in cancer treatment and cancer prevention—review on epidemiological data and clinical trials. Nutrients 15 (8). https://doi.org/10.3390/nu15081896. Available from: http://www.mdpi.com/journal/nutrients/.

Sahu, A.N., 2021. Herbal Drug Formulation and Standardization.

Sarkar, T., Sarkar, T., Banerjee, S., Goswami, M., Das, P., Bhakat, A., Sarkar, K., 2025. Formulation of curcumin loaded solid lipid nano particles following response surface methodology to improve the anti-cancer activity in triple-negative breast cancer cells. Mater. Today Commun. 45. https://doi.org/10.1016/j.mtcomm.2025.112220. Available from: https://www.sciencedirect.com/science/journal/23524928.

Schneider, N.F.Z., Cerella, C., Simões, C.M.O., Diederich, M., 2017. Anticancer and immunogenic properties of cardiac glycosides. Molecules 22 (11). https://doi.org/10.3390/molecules22111932. Available from: http://www.mdpi.com/1420-3049/22/11/1932/pdf.

Seca, A., Pinto, D., 2018. Plant secondary metabolites as anticancer agents: successes in clinical trials and therapeutic application. Int. J. Mol. Sci. 19 (1), 263. https://doi.org/10.3390/ijms19010263.

Sethi, G., Shanmugam, M.K., Warrier, S., Merarchi, M., Arfuso, F., Kumar, A.P., Bishayee, A., 2018. Pro-apoptotic and anti-cancer properties of diosgenin: a comprehensive and critical review. Nutrients 10 (5). https://doi.org/10.3390/nu10050645. Available from: http://www.mdpi.com/2072-6643/10/5/645/pdf.

Shaikh, Z., Aher, S., Shah, S., Lale, S., Shaikh Mohammad, R., 2024. Hygrophilla auriculata extract loaded microemulsion gel for treatment of skin cancer. Int. J. Res. Pharm. Sci. 15 (3), 39–46. https://doi.org/10.26452/ijrps.v15i3.4685.

Sharma, A.N., Kumar Dewangan, H., Upadhyay, P.K., 2024. Comprehensive review on herbal medicine: emphasis on current therapy and role of phytoconstituents for cancer treatment. Chem. Biodivers. 21 (3). https://doi.org/10.1002/cbdv.202301468.

Situmorang, P.C., Ilyas, S., Nugraha, S.E., Syahputra, R.A., Nik Abd Rahman, N.M.A., 2024. Prospects of compounds of herbal plants as anticancer agents: a comprehensive review from molecular pathways. Front. Pharmacol. 15. https://doi.org/10.3389/fphar.2024.1387866. Available from: http://www.frontiersin.org/Pharmacology.

Smith, R.D., Mallath, M.K., 2019. History of the growing burden of cancer in India: from antiquity to the 21st century. J. Global Oncol. 2019 (5). https://doi.org/10.1200/JGO.19.00048. Available from: https://ascopubs.org/doi/pdf/10.1200/JGO.19.00048.

Solanki, N., Saini, S., Singh, S.K., Paudel, K.R., Goh, B.H., Dua, K., Dureja, H., 2025. Central composite designed boswellic acids loaded nanoparticles for enhanced cellular uptake in human lung cancer cell line A549. J. Drug Deliv. Sci. Technol. 105. https://doi.org/10.1016/j.jddst.2024.106591. Available from: https://www.sciencedirect.com/science/journal/17732247.

Talib, W.H., Alsalahat, I., Daoud, S., Abutayeh, R.F., Mahmod, A.I., 2020. Plant-derived natural products in cancer research: extraction, mechanism of action, and drug formulation. Molecules 25 (22). https://doi.org/10.3390/MOLECULES25225319. Available from: https://www.mdpi.com/1420-3049/25/22/5319/pdf.

Uchôa, A.F.C., Formiga, A.L.D., Cardoso, A.L.M.R., Pereira, G.M.A., Carvalho, L.M.M., Souza, P.H.O., Silva, A.L., Souza, R.R.M., Sobral, M.V., Silva, M.S., Barbosa-Filho, J.M., Xavier-Júnior, F.H., 2025. Optimized and functionalized carvacrol-loaded nanostructured lipid carriers for enhanced cytotoxicity in breast cancer cells. Pharmaceutics 17 (3). https://doi.org/10.3390/pharmaceutics17030363. Available from: http://www.mdpi.com/journal/pharmaceutics.

Yari, E., Sari, S., Kelidari, H., Asare-Addo, K., Nokhodchi, A., 2024. Effect of rosa damascena essential oil loaded in nanostructured lipid carriers on the proliferation of human breast cancer cell line MDA-MB-231 in comparison with cisplatin. J. Pharma. Innov. 19 (1). https://doi.org/10.1007/s12247-024-09809-x. Available from: https://www.springer.com/journal/12247.

Yebirzaf, Y., Esubalew, T., Workinesh, T., 2019. The dynamics of medicinal plants utilization practice nexus its health and economic role in Ethiopia: a review paper. Int. J. Biodivers. Conserv. 11 (1), 31–47. https://doi.org/10.5897/ijbc2018.1201.

Yin, Q., Zhou, Q., Hu, J., Weng, J., Liu, S., Yin, L., Long, L., Tong, Y., Tang, K., Ou, L., 2024. Fabrication of bimetallic Ag@ ZnO nanocomposite and its anti-cancer activity on cervical cancer via impeding PI3K/AKT/mTOR pathway. J. Trace Elem. Med. Biol. 84, 127437.

CHAPTER

29

Small molecules as delivery tools for enzymes employed in enzyme-prodrug therapy

Louay Abo Qoura[1, 2] *and Vadim S. Pokrovsky*[1, 2]

[1]Research Institute of Molecular and Cellular Medicine, People's Friendship University of Russia (RUDN University), Moscow, Russia; [2]Blokhin National Medical Research Center of Oncology, Ministry of Health of the Russian Federation, Moscow, Russia

Introduction

Enzyme prodrug therapy (EPT) is a promising cancer treatment strategy designed to overcome the limitations of conventional chemotherapy, including nonspecific toxicity and poor tumor selectivity. EPT uses the catalytic activity of enzymes, either naturally overexpressed within tumor tissues (endogenous enzymes) (Ma et al., 2023) (Fu et al., 2023), or introduced specifically into the tumor microenvironment (exogenous enzymes) (de la Fuente et al., 2021), to convert systemically administered inert prodrugs into cytotoxic agents in situ. EPT approaches can be broadly divided into two strategies: (1) direct enzyme delivery, referred to as antibody-directed enzyme prodrug therapy (ADEPT), where the active enzyme is conjugated to tumor-targeting moieties such as monoclonal antibodies (Bagshawe, 1987); and (2) indirect strategies, referred to as gene-directed enzyme prodrug therapy (GDEPT) (Friedmann and Roblin, 1972), where the gene encoding the prodrug-activating enzyme is delivered through viral or bacterial vectors, consequently enabling in situ enzyme synthesis directly within cancer cells.

The integration of nanotechnology has significantly improved enzyme delivery in EPT by using nanocarriers such as nanoparticles, PICsomes, extracellular vesicles, nanobubbles, and carbon nanotubes (Abo Qoura et al., 2024a). The incorporation of these nanocarriers significantly enhances enzyme stability, prolongs systemic circulation half-life, and promotes more efficient tumor tissue penetration. Furthermore, they can be functionalized with

Advanced Cancer Therapeutics
https://doi.org/10.1016/B978-0-443-44185-1.00014-8

targeting ligands to enable receptor-mediated cellular uptake and engineered for stimuli-responsive drug release, triggered by exogenous stimuli such as ultrasound or light, as well as by endogenous tumor microenvironmental factors, including pH and redox potential (Abo Qoura et al., 2024a). Additionally, recent advances in EPT have expanded the technological and biological aspects that have enhanced tumor selectivity and anticancer effects by using small, single-domain antibody fragments, known as nanobodies (Cortez-Retamozo et al., 2004), which have superior tumor penetration capabilities and reduced immunogenicity, making them a promising carrier for direct enzyme targeting to cancer cells. This chapter explores the growing use of exogenous enzymes from microbial sources for EPT, focusing on nanocarrier technologies and recent innovations in small molecules as delivery tools. A key highlight of this chapter is the discussion of a proprietary EPT system developed by our group, which targets hormone receptor-positive cancers by selectively engaging G-protein-coupled estrogen receptor 1 (GPER1) by using C115H methionine γ-lyase-daidzein and sulfoxide-based prodrugs, demonstrating the potential for highly selective and effective cancer therapy.

Current approaches for EPT in cancer therapy

EPT is a cancer treatment method that addresses the limitations of traditional chemotherapy, such as poor tumor specificity and significant systemic toxicity. This approach employs a two-step treatment strategy involving: (1) delivering and expressing a gene for a foreign enzyme or targeting an antibody-enzyme conjugate to the cancer cells; and (2) administering a nontoxic prodrug as a substrate for the expressed enzyme, which converts the prodrug into a cytotoxic drug, resulting in targeted cancer cell killing. Several strategies, including antibody-directed enzyme prodrug therapy (ADEPT) and gene-directed enzyme prodrug therapy (GDEPT), have been developed to enhance therapeutic precision, efficacy, and safety.

Antibody-directed enzyme prodrug therapy (ADEPT)

ADEPT is a cancer treatment strategy that uses full-length monoclonal antibodies conjugated to nonhuman enzymes to target cancer cells, allowing localized conversion of an inactive prodrug into its active cytotoxic form (Fig. 29.1) (Bagshawe, 1987). However, traditional ADEPT has significant limitations, including limited penetration into solid tumors due to the large size of enzyme-antibody complexes and rapid clearance from the body, that reduced the effectiveness of therapy (Stribbling et al., 1997). To overcome these challenges, current research on ADEPT has shifted towards next-generation targeting and conjugation strategies using small carriers such as nanobodies (Cortez-Retamozo et al., 2004), $F(ab')_2$ fragments (Yu et al., 2025), single-chain variable fragments (scFv) (Monnier et al., 2013), and complementation-dependent ADEPT (CoDEPT) systems (Nervig et al., 2022). These carriers enhance penetration into tumor tissue and facilitate homogeneous intratumoral distribution.

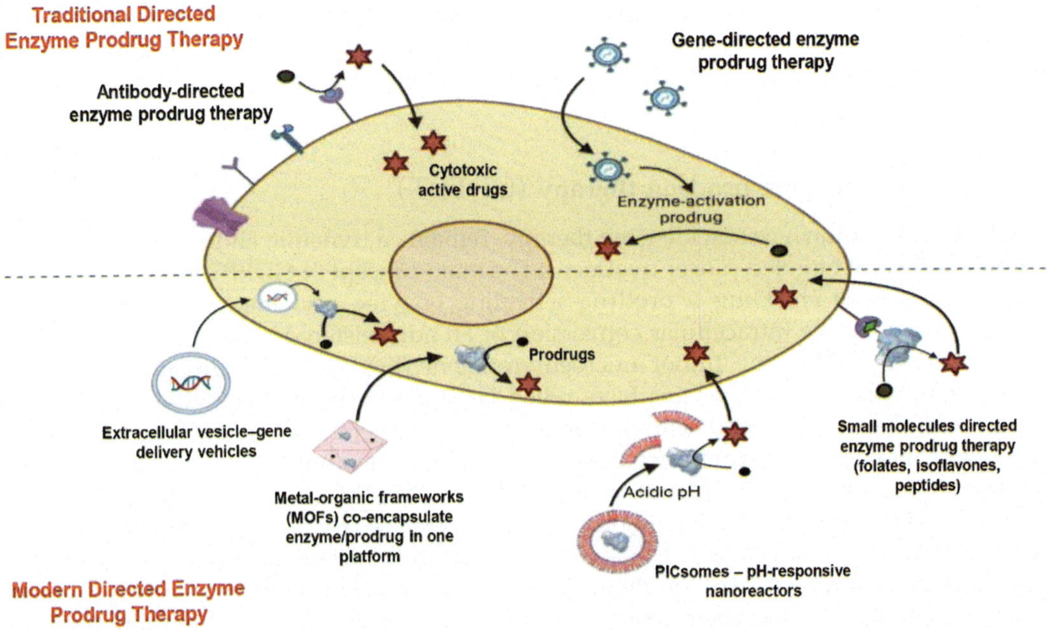

FIGURE 29.1 Traditional and modern strategies used in directed enzyme prodrug therapy.

Nanobodies (Nb), single-domain derived from heavy-chain antibodies in camelids and cartilaginous fish (Schiffelers et al., 2024), offer unique benefits due to their small size and structural stability. Their small size, generally between 12 and 15 kDa (Alexander and Leong, 2024), allows them to penetrate tumor tissues more deeply than monoclonal antibodies, improving targeting precision, minimizing off-target exposure, and reducing systemic toxicity (Fig. 29.1) (Wu, 2025). Nanobody-based ADEPT, such as Nb-HER2–2-cytosine deaminase (CD), is a fusion protein that combines a single anti-HER2 nanobody with two CD units. It converts the nontoxic prodrug 5-fluorocytosine (5-FC) into the active chemotherapy drug 5-fluorouracil (5FU), resulting in an eightfold increase in catalytic activity and fivefold increase in cytotoxicity in 3D spheroid cell cultures (Metcalf et al., 2021). Another fusion protein, β-lactamase cAntibody-carcinoembryonic antigen 5 (CEA5):βL, activates the release of the toxic phenylenediamine mustard from its cephalosporin nitrogen mustard prodrug on the surface of CEA-positive LS174T cancer cells, resulting in an excellent biodistribution profile and significant tumor growth inhibition in mouse models (Cortez-Retamozo et al., 2004). Similarly, $F(ab')_2$ fragments, generated by cleaving whole IgG, conjugated to carboxypeptidase G2 (CPG2), have improved tumor specificity in carcinoembryonic antigen (CEA)-positive tumors. Fusion proteins optimize tumor retention and pharmacokinetic profiles (Yu et al., 2025). In parallel, peptides targeting integrin receptors, such as RGD motifs, offer selective enzyme delivery by exploiting overexpressed vascular markers in tumors (Yu et al., 2025). The downsizing of antibody carriers in ADEPT has resolved constraints related to tumor penetration, intratumoral distribution homogeneity, immunogenicity, and off-target toxicity. Nanobodies, $F(ab')_2$ fragments, and single-chain variable fragments increase localized enzyme delivery, catalytic performance, and therapeutic selectivity, enhancing ADEPT's therapeutic index and potential for targeted cancer treatment.

Gene-directed enzyme prodrug therapy (GDEPT)

GDEPT, also known as suicide gene therapy, remains a dynamic and evolving approach within the field of targeted cancer treatment. The main concept of GDEPT involves the introduction of a gene encoding a prodrug-activating enzyme into malignant cells, thereby enabling the selective intracellular conversion of an administered nontoxic prodrug into a cytotoxic agent within the tumor microenvironment (Fig. 29.1) (Friedmann and Roblin, 1972). Traditional GDEPT systems have relied largely on viral and nonviral vectors, such as adenoviral, retroviral, and lentiviral systems, or synthetic carriers such as dendrimers and lipid nanoparticles, to transport and deliver enzyme-encoding DNA or mRNA to cancer (Friedmann and Roblin, 1972) (Hattori and Maitani, 2005; Poletti and Mavilio, 2021).

A new GDEPT approach by using extracellular vesicles (EVs) as gene delivery vehicles (Fig. 29.1) has been developed. EVs, which are naturally occurring lipid-bilayer vesicles, have unique advantages over synthetic carriers and viruses due to their ability to cross-biological barriers, protect their genetic cargo from degradation, and exhibit low immunogenicity (Abo Qoura et al., 2025). EVs carrying mRNA for bacterial enzyme HChrR6 and targeted with anti-HER2 scFv have shown effective delivery to HER2-positive breast cancer models, resulting in near-complete tumor growth arrest without significant off-target toxicity (Wang et al., 2018). Mesenchymal stem cell-derived EVs transporting yeast cytosine deaminase: uracilphosphoribosyl transferase (yCD:UPRT) have shown potent inhibition of glioblastoma progression in vitro and in vivo, leading to tumor regression and durable tumor resistance in treated rodents (Altaner and Altanerova). Recent advances have extended this approach to uveal melanoma (UM), wherein EVs secreted by UM cells genetically engineered to express the yCD:UPRT suicide gene release small vesicles encapsulating suicide gene mRNA, thereby effectively inhibiting the proliferation of both UM and cutaneous melanoma cells in vitro (Jakubechova et al., 2023). EV-mediated GDEPT, with its proven success across multiple tumor models, has the potential to overcome translational barriers and advance suicide gene therapy clinical application in oncology.

Microbial enzymes used in EPT

Cytosine deaminase/5-fluorocytosine (CD/5-FC)

The cytosine deaminase (EC 3.5.4.5; CD) and 5-fluorocytosine (5-FC) system represents one of the most extensively investigated and well-characterized EPT (Kilstrup et al., 1989). CD, found in fungi and bacteria, converts cytosine into uracil and ammonia and efficiently transforms the nontoxic prodrug 5-FC into the chemotherapeutic agent 5-fluorouracil (5-FU). This enzymatic conversion underpins a targeted GDEPT approach that selectively activates chemotherapy within tumors, minimizing systemic toxicity (El-Sayed et al., 2022). The active metabolite 5-FU inhibits thymidylate synthase, disrupting DNA synthesis and inducing cancer cell death, making this system effective against several cancers, including head and neck, gastrointestinal, and cervical cancers (Ghafouri-Fard et al., 2021). However, the main limitations that restrict clinical use of 5-FU are the short $t_{1/2}$, the drug resistance, and the relatively poor selectivity. Additionally, the unintended conversion of the prodrug 5-FC into 5-FU by commensal microbial flora can result in off-target exposure, contributing to adverse effects such as mucositis, dermatitis, and myelosuppression (Zhang et al., 2008). These challenges have driven the development of CD/5-FC suicide gene therapy, which aims to confine 5-FU generation specifically to the tumor microenvironment, thereby enhancing efficacy while minimizing systemic adverse effects. CD/5-FC strategy exhibits a pronounced bystander effect, wherein 5-FU produced within CD-expressing tumor cells diffuses into neighboring nontransduced cancer cells. This phenomenon substantially enhances the overall therapeutic efficacy, compensating for suboptimal gene transfer efficiencies. Preclinical studies have demonstrated that achieving CD expression in as few as 20% of tumor cells can lead to complete tumor regression, underscoring the potent amplification effect of this system (Lawrence et al., 1998).

The advancement of a translational platform for bCD has driven the engineering of enzyme variants to enhance substrate specificity and catalytic efficiency for clinical applications. Initial investigations revealed that the wild-type CD exhibited suboptimal activity in converting the 5-FC, prompting the development of mutants such as D314A and I525 variants with improved enzymatic properties (Fuchita et al., 2009). Additionally, the F186W mutant has demonstrated the ability to induce cell cycle arrest at lower 5-FC concentrations, suggesting a potential to mitigate systemic toxicity while maintaining therapeutic efficacy (Raza et al., 2015). Yeast-derived CD (yCD) is a superior option due to its higher substrate affinity and stability, resulting in greater therapeutic efficacy in mammalian systems. When coupled with *E. coli* uracil phosphoribosyltransferase (UPRT), a fusion protein can convert 5-FU to its active metabolites, resulting in a 100-fold increase in 5-FU generation (Kievit et al., 1999). In 2012, Li et al. successfully transfected MCF-7 cells with the recombinant plasmid pEGFP-KDRP/CD-TK using ultrasound targeted microbubble destruction (UTMD). The CD-TK fusion gene was expressed in MCF7 (KDR^+) cells compared with LS174T (KDR^-) cells, indicating that the KDR promoter can selectively regulate the expression of the suicide gene. The CD-TK fusion gene exhibits good synergy, with a higher rate of inhibition of MCF-7 growth with the administration of both 5-FC and GCV. The CD-TK double suicide gene was conjugated to anti-$\alpha V\beta 3$ integrin monoclonal antibodies to target the hepatocellular carcinoma cell line (HepG2) using cationic microbubbles (CMBs). The combination of the CD-TK suicide gene delivery system with CMBs targeting $\alpha v\beta 3$ or UTMD targeting KDRP has shown promising results in preclinical studies against different solid malignant tumors. A molecular-targeted US method was developed against bladder tumor cells (T-24) using thin-film hydration sonication, carbodiimide chemistry approaches, and electrostatic adsorption methods. The tumor growth was significantly slower when the mice were treated with US + CD-TK double suicide gene nanobubbles in the presence of 5-FC or GCV, with the slowest growth observed when both prodrugs were combined (Hu et al., 2020; Li et al., 2016).

Recent advancements in gene delivery strategies have led to MSCs as promising gene carriers due to their tumor-homing ability and immune tolerance (Ding et al., 2020). These cells can be genetically modified to express CD, enabling selective and sustained prodrug activation within the tumor environment. These cellular vehicles have shown improved targeting, increased local drug concentration, and reduced systemic side effects compared with traditional vector-based delivery. Innovative viral vectors, such as replication-competent adenoviruses and vaccinia strains expressing CD variants, have also improved transgene delivery efficiency and therapeutic enzyme persistence within tumor tissue (Ding et al., 2020). Combinatorial regimens, such as 5-FU with bevacizumab, enhance anticancer efficacy. The fusion of multiple enzymes, such as human beta-glucuronidase and a bCD: UPRT fusion protein, has synergistic antitumor effects, with studies showing that even 20% expression can lead to complete tumor regression in immunocompetent mice (Ochiai et al., 2012). Polyion complex vesicles (PICsomes) have been used to encapsulate CD (CD-PICsomes), enhancing the properties of the CD/5-FC. This encapsulation improves tumor accumulation and blood circulation of the enzyme, showing high antitumor activity in a subcutaneous model of C26 murine colon adenocarcinoma. However, the administration schedule for both CD-PICsomes and 5-FC still requires optimization. Encapsulation of exogenous enzymes within PICsomes could expand EPT treatment for various cancer types and facilitate coloading of multiple enzymes for prodrug-combination therapy (Goto et al., 2023). CD/5-FC has been undergoing multiple clinical trials, with several Phase I, Phase I/II, and Phase II/III trials completed or terminated (NCT02015819, NCT01562626, NCT01172964, NCT04657315, NCT04327011, NCT02576665, NCT01470794, NCT01985256, and NCT02414165). These trials are investigating CD/5-FC for recurrent high-grade gliomas, solid cancers, and malignant gliomas. A Phase I/II trial using mesenchymal stem cells for recurrent glioblastoma has also completed. These clinical trials highlight the significant clinical investment and ongoing efforts to translate the CD/5-FC system into a widely applicable cancer therapeutic.

Purine nucleoside phosphorylase/6-methylpurine deoxyriboside (PNP/MEP)

Purine nucleoside phosphorylase (EC 2.4.2.1; PNP) is a glycosyltransferase found in all eukaryotes, protozoa, and prokaryotes. Human PNP (hPNP) is crucial in the purine salvage pathway, and deficiency can affect T-cell activity without affecting B-cell function (Canduri et al., 2004). *E. coli* PNP (mPNP) has more hydrophobic purine-/ribose-binding sites, making it suitable for EPT (Russell and Khatri, 2006). Unlike hPNP, mPNP catalyzes 6-methylpurine, 2-deoxyriboside, and fludarabine into an active form, which undergoes intracellular phosphorylation by host adenine phosphoribosyltransferase (APRT) to generate cytotoxic nucleotides, disrupting cellular processes and causing cell cycle arrest in tumor cells (Parker et al., 1998). Three prodrugs, MeP-dR, F-dAdo, and F-araAMP, are studied, which are substrates of mPNP and cannot be detected by hPNP. F-araAMP has shown promising results in treating various types of cancer in vivo (Sorscher et al., 2012). Despite preclinical efficacy, clinical translation of EPT, such as PNP/MeP-dR has faced challenges in efficient delivery to tumor microenvironments. However, recent advancements in mechanistic understanding and innovative engineering have improved system efficacy and addressed delivery hurdles. Efforts are being made to modify hPNP forms to overcome immunogenicity, allowing them to use deoxyadenosine-based prodrugs as substrates. A double mutant of hPNP (Glu201Gln or Asn243Asp) efficiently cleaves adenosine-based prodrugs, catalyzing the phosphorolysis of F-dAdo to F-Ade (Afshar et al., 2009a). Additionally, hPNP has been fused to anti-HER2/neu single-chain Fv by using the ADEPT system, demonstrating cytotoxic effects against $HER2^+$ MCF7 cells with low immunogenicity (Afshar et al., 2009b).

Nanocarriers such as ultrasonic nanobubbles are being used to enhance the delivery of a PNP/fludarabine suicide gene system for treating hepatocellular carcinoma cell lines. Studies show that nanobubble/liposome-mediated plasmids have greater effects than plasmids alone, and ultrasound irradiation increases transfection efficiency (Zhang et al., 2018). Synergistic use of microbubbles, ultrasound, and nanoparticles enhances anticancer efficacy. The PNP/MEP treatment has completed a Phase I clinical trial in 12 head and neck cancer patients (NCT01310179), showing dose-dependent tumor responses and anticancer efficacy confined to tumors receiving intratumoral injections. Patient serum analysis confirmed the absence of systemic exposure to 2-fluoro-2′-deoxyadenosine (2-FA), minimizing systemic toxicity. Further clinical trials by using an ovine atadenovirus for prostate cancer (NCT00625430) and a replication-defective adenoviral vector for head and neck cancer (NCT03754933); however, the current status of these clinical trials remains unclear. The PNP/MeP-dR is a promising area of research in enzyme-prodrug therapy due to its tumor selectivity, potent bystander effect, and expanding range of active prodrugs. Advancements in enzyme engineering, nanocarriers, and gene therapy approaches are accelerating its potential for clinical translation, overcoming historical limitations and realizing the full therapeutic promise of this sophisticated enzyme/prodrug pair in targeted cancer therapeutics.

Carboxypeptidase G2/Nitrogen mustard (CPG2/CMDA)

Carboxypeptidase G2 (EC 3.4.17.11; CPG2), a zinc-containing metalloendopeptidase produced by *Variovorax paradoxus*, hydrolyzes urethanic, amidic, or orureidic bonds between L-glutamic acid and benzene rings. CPG2 cleaves the glutamic acid moiety from the prodrug 4-[(2-chloroethyl) (2-mesyloxyethyl) amino] benzoyl-L-glutamic acid (CMDA), generating the DNA-crosslinking mustard drug. CPG2 can be used in cancer therapy as a rescue agent in chemotherapy to convert methotrexate into a less toxic compound (Voraxaze) and a targeted treatment to activate prodrugs CMDA (Springer et al., 1990; Al-Qahtani et al., 2019). Unlike other combinations, CPG2 releases a toxic drug directly from CMDA without requiring modification by cellular enzymes, thereby reducing drug resistance. Additionally, the toxic drug activated by CPG2 can freely diffuse and impact neighboring cells, which can kill both proliferating and nonproliferating cancer cells without the need for a cosubstrate (Davies et al., 2005). This combination has demonstrated promising results in vivo in models of melanoma, breast, and colon cancer (Frei et al., 1988). CPG2/CMDA has been enhanced through various strategies, including the development of three-prodrugs for use with a mutant of CPG2 tethered to the outer tumor cell surface (stCPG2(Q)3) (Friedlos et al., 2002), a new CPG2 type from *Xenophilus azovorans* SN213, fusion proteins between vascular endothelial growth factor (VEGF) and CPG2 (Michael et al., 1996), CNGRC-CPG2 fusion proteins (Al-mansoori et al., 2021), and CPG2/ZD2767P (Yu and Li, 2023). These prodrugs have shown more effective therapeutic effects against various cancer cell lines, and their PEGylated form showed lower immunogenicity but higher efficacy against colon cancer HT1080. Recently, CPG2/ZD2767P has been used with ultrasound to modulate CPG2 activity, resulting in apoptosis and ferroptosis in cisplatin-resistant sublines, SKOV3/DDP and A549/DDP (Yu and Li, 2023). CPG2 has been enhanced through various strategies, including developing three-prodrugs with a mutant of CPG2 tethered to the tumor cell surface, a novel CPG2 type isolated from *Xenophilus azovorans SN213*, and fusion proteins. These proteins activate CMDA directly on the surface of cells expressing VEGFR2, and when combined with the prodrug ZD2767P, they show high cytotoxic effects against aminopeptidase N-expressing cancer cells (Friedlos et al., 2002). Current research is focused on screening CPG2 enzymes with epitopes engineered to evade immune system detection, employing immunosuppressive agents, utilizing protective polymer coatings, and optimizing intracellular delivery of the enzyme-drug conjugate. The development of nontoxic and stable nonviral vectors represents a promising approach to advancing GDEPT in clinical applications. Notably, the recently developed SEAKER cell platform, comprising engineered synthetic enzyme-armed killer cells that express CPG2, shows significant potential for repurposing glucarpidase as both a cytotoxic agent and a targeted delivery vector, particularly in tumors exhibiting antigenic heterogeneity.

Nitroreductase/CB1954 (NTR/CB1954)

Nitroreductase (NTR) is a flavin-containing oxidoreductase enzyme that reduces nitrogen-containing compounds, such as nitro groups on aromatic rings. NTR enzymes are classified into two types: oxygen-insensitive (type I) and oxygen-sensitive (type II). The type I enzyme from *E. coli* is particularly suitable for EPT because it can activate nitro-containing prodrugs under both oxygen-rich and hypoxic tumor conditions (Lehouritis et al., 2013). NTR is known to activate four classes of prodrugs: nitroindolines, dinitroaziridinyl benzamides, mustard dinitrobenzamides, and 4-nitrobenzyl carbamates. In the presence of NAD(P)H, NTR converts CB1954 (5-(aziridin-1-yl)-2,4-dinitrobenzamide) into a mixture of 2- and 4-hydroxylamine metabolites, which induce apoptosis in both proliferating and nonproliferating cancer cells (Knox et al., 1988). The NTR/CB1954 system helps overcome resistance to chemotherapeutic agents such as cisplatin and exhibits a strong bystander effect, enhancing the elimination of tumor cells beyond those directly expressing the enzyme (Green et al., 2003). NTR/CB1954, originally developed for ADEPT, encountered difficulties due to the need for administering its exogenous cofactor NAD(P)H or its analogs, which hindered its progression to clinical trials. Nevertheless, it has been successfully applied in GDEPT, where bacterial or viral vectors are used, and has advanced to clinical trials for the treatment of prostate and colon cancers (Patel et al., 2009; Palmer et al., 2004; Chung-Faye et al., 2001). The NTR/CB1954 system in GDEPT has several limitations due to liver enzymes activating the prodrug CB1954, which can lead to hepatic toxicity. The low Michaelis constant of the NTR for the CB1954 substrate also limits its efficiency. Researchers have explored alternative NTR variations from different sources, such as *E. coli* YieF and Allivibriofischeri flavin reductase (Frase I) (Swe et al., 2012), which have shown the ability to kill human colon carcinoma cells at lower concentrations. Advanced prodrugs such as 3,5-dinitrobenzamide-2-bromomustard SN 27,686, PR-104, and evofosfamide have also been investigated. The combination of NTR-armed oncolytic adenovirus ONYX-411 (ONYX-411-NTR) with PR-104 has shown efficacy against HCT116 xenografts (Singleton et al., 2007, 2022). New delivery systems for NTR, such as immobilizing modified NTRs onto gold-coated magnetic nanoparticles, have shown high anticancer activity against breast cancer cell line SKOV3 when combined with new dinitrobenzamide mustard prodrugs PR-104A and SN27686, aiming to improve targeted delivery and reduce systemic toxicity (Searle et al., 2004). The NTR/CB1954 system is a targeted therapeutic approach that uses hypoxic conditions in tumors. Current research focuses on improving enzyme efficiency, developing prodrugs, and refining delivery mechanisms, including nanoparticle-based strategies, to enhance its clinical utility.

Small molecules as delivery tools for enzymes in EPT

Small molecule-based approaches represent a refined strategy in EPT by facilitating targeted delivery of enzymes to cancer sites through conjugation with ligands possessing high affinity for tumor-associated receptors. This precise targeting enables selective enzyme localization within the tumor microenvironment, thereby minimizing systemic toxicity and reducing off-target effects. Moreover, the inherently small size of these ligands enhances tissue penetration and promotes rapid diffusion, effectively overcoming conventional biological barriers to improve therapeutic efficacy.

Ligand-directed enzyme prodrug therapy (LDEPT)

LDEPT strategy utilizes ligand-enzyme conjugates that selectively bind to cancer-specific receptors, facilitating localized enzymatic activation of prodrugs into their cytotoxic forms within the tumor microenvironment (Fig. 29.1). By confining drug activation to malignant cells, LDEPT enhances treatment precision, mitigates systemic toxicity, and significantly improves the therapeutic index relative to traditional chemotherapeutic strategies (Al-Jaber et al., 2025). CPG2, for instance, has been genetically fused to CNGRC (cyclic peptide Cys–Asn–Gly–Arg–Cys), which selectively binds to aminopeptidase N (APN), a tumor-associated antigen overexpressed in solid tumors (Al-mansoori et al., 2021; Yu and Li, 2023). Two distinct constructs were developed, one featuring a single CNGRC motif and another displaying CNGRC peptides at both N- and C-termini, facilitating targeted binding to APN-expressing cancer cells. The double-fused protein (X-CPG2-X) showed better binding affinity and catalytic efficiency compared with the mono-fused variant, likely due to dual ligand attachment (Al-mansoori et al., 2020; Al-mansoori et al., 2020). Both constructs effectively activated ZD2767P, selectively inducing apoptosis in APN-overexpressing cells. Importantly, immunogenicity assessments revealed reduced T-cell activation in response to the fusion constructs, and enzymatic activity was sustained for over two weeks in serum conditions, highlighting their stability and clinical applicability. Collectively, these findings represent a successful preclinical demonstration of LDEPT that integrates precise ligand–enzyme targeting with efficient prodrug activation, offering a compelling platform for tumor-selective chemotherapy with improved safety and efficacy.

Nanoparticle and biomaterial-based strategies

Nanoparticle and biomaterial-based delivery systems have significantly transformed EPT by overcoming many limitations associated with traditional strategies. Nanoscale carriers, typically ranging from 10 to 100 nm, enhance drug solubility, extend systemic circulation, and facilitate selective accumulation of therapeutic agents within tumors through the enhanced permeability and retention (EPR) effect (Manzari-Tavakoli et al., 2024). Recent developments encompass diverse platforms such as lipid-based nanocarriers (Cheng et al., 2024), polymeric nanoparticles (Begines et al., 2020), and inorganic materials (Tsuchida and Murakami, 2008), which provide the capacity to codeliver enzymes and prodrugs within a single system or transport nucleic acids encoding prodrug-activating enzymes. The benfits of using these platforms are (1) nano/microbubbles (NBs/MBs) enable ultrasound-guided, noninvasive gene delivery with transient expression and minimal side effects, demonstrating promising antitumor efficacy in preclinical models (Wu and Li, 2017); (2) Mesoscopic polyion complex vesicles (PICsomes) function as pH-responsive nanoreactors that selectively release enzymes in acidic tumor microenvironments (Fig. 29.1), thereby prolonging enzyme half-life and allowing repeated prodrug activation with reduced systemic toxicity (Goto et al., 2023); (3) Nanoparticles enhance enzyme stability, cellular uptake, and controlled release, while modifications such as near-infrared (NIR) activation and magnetic targeting increase tumor specificity and therapeutic efficiency (Tian et al., 2022); and (4) Magnetic nanoparticles, in particular, permit remote control of enzymatic activity under external magnetic fields, amplifying cytotoxic effects and limiting off-target toxicity (Torres-Herrero et al., 2023). The comparative overview of enzyme delivery methods and their preclinical efficacies is summarized in Table 29.1.

Beyond traditional nanoparticles, metal–organic frameworks (MOFs) have emerged as an innovative class of crystalline, porous materials composed of metal ions and organic linkers. Their high surface area, tunable pore size, and chemical versatility facilitate spatial separation and protection of enzymes and prodrugs within one platform (Fig. 29.1), minimizing premature activation and preserving enzymatic activity until release in the acidic or reductive tumor lysosomal environment. MOFs loaded with horseradish peroxidase (EC 1.11.1.7; HRP) and indole-3-acetic acid (IAA) preserve enzyme activity after delivery and efficiently trigger prodrug conversion within cancer cells. The encapsulated HRP and IAA demonstrate sustained and synchronized release, with the MOF nanocarriers enhancing enzyme delivery into cellular lysosomes, enabling endosomal escape, and effectively releasing both enzyme and prodrug inside cells within 48 h—outperforming the delivery capability of native HRP alone (Wang et al., 2020). Similarly, codelivery systems combining glucose oxidase with hypoxia-activated prodrugs exploit tumor microenvironmental features for selective activation and enhanced therapeutic synergy. Surface modification or biomimetic coating of MOFs further improves tumor targeting, circulation time, and biocompatibility (Li et al., 2023). While nanoparticles and MOF-based delivery

TABLE 29.1 Overview of nanocarrier-based enzyme for enzyme-prodrug therapy.

Nanocarrier system	Enzyme/ conjugated system	Targeting strategy	Targeted cancer cell lines/ Models	Administration mode	Key findings/Comments	References
Nano/ Microbubbles	HSV-*TK*	MB/US	A549 HT29 C26 EMT6	In vivo	Gene expression was detectable through 24h after transfection and significantly reduced after 48h. 4-fold decreased in tumor volume.	Aoi et al. (2008)
	pEGFP-KDRP/*CD-TK*	UTMD	MCF7 LS174T	In vitro	Good synergy effect of *CD-TK* to with high anticancer effect against MCF7. No effect against LS174T due to absence of receptor KDR on the surface of cells.	Li et al. (2012)
	anti-αVβ3/ *CD-TK*	CMBs/US	$HepG_2$	In vitro	High inhibition rate in compared with control or against normal L-02 cells.	Li et al. (2016)
	anti-VEGFR2/ *CD-TK*	CMBs/US	T-24	In vivo	Significantly slower in tumor growth in compared with control or one of the prodrugs.	Hu et al. (2020)
	pcDNA3.1-*PNP*	MB/US	$HepG_2$ SMMC7721	In vivo	The level of GFP showed high expression of the gene PNP in $HepG_2$.	Zhang et al. (2018)
	NP-DNA/ *TK-NTR*	MB/US	TNBC	In vivo	The successful transport of the *TK-NTR* gene was confirmed by converting nonfluorescent CytoCy5S into a highly fluorescent metabolite. Decrease in tumor volume by 2.3-fold in compared with control.	Devulapally et al. (2018)
	HSV-*TK*	HIFU/CMBs	Liver cells	In vivo	The combination therapy of HIFU + CMBs + GCV can target and kill liver cells, demonstrating that these targeted microbubbles, enhanced by HIFU treatment.	Liu et al. (2024)

(Continued)

TABLE 29.1 Overview of nanocarrier-based enzyme for enzyme-prodrug therapy.—cont'd

Nanocarrier system	Enzyme/ conjugated system	Targeting strategy	Targeted cancer cell lines/ Models	Administration mode	Key findings/Comments	References
PICsomes	*β*-gal	Encapsulated in PICsome	C26	In vivo	Encapsulated β-gal in PICsome can protect it from biodegradation, extending its half-life.	Anraku et al. (2016)
		Encapsulated in PICsome	4T1	In vivo	Tumor pH-responsive swelling increased from ~100 to ~200 nm. Prolonge nanofactories intratumoral retention for up to 1 week. Increased membrane permeability.	Japir et al. (2021)
		CAPsomes	HeLa	In vivo	CAPsomes protect enzymes from degradation. Reaction rate decreases with increased vesicular membrane thickness. CAPsomes overcome limitations in other nanoreactor systems through easy fabrication, efficient enzyme encapsulation, permeability, and accumulation at target areas.	Nishimura et al. (2017)
	C115H MGL	Encapsulated in PICsome	-	In vivo	Prolonged $T_{1/2}$ of the enzyme up to 42 h. After 24 h, over 50% of the enzymes still had their encapsulation in PICsomes 70 and 120.	(Morozova et al., 2019; Koval et al., 2022)
	CD	Encapsulated in PICsome	C26	In vivo	Increased antitumor activity.	Goto et al. (2023)
Nanoparticles	HRP	Chitosan (CSNP)	Bcap37	In vitro	Over 80% cell death when treated with HRP-CSN/IAA.	Cao et al. (2015)
		Hollow gold nanoparticles (HGNP)	-	In vivo	Increase survival of mice.	Gupta et al. (2023)
		Acetalated dextran	-	In vivo	Increased expression of gene in the targeted cells. Increased survival rates of mice.	Konhäuser et al. (2023)
	CD	Upconverting nanoparticles + NIR	CaCo-2	In vitro/in vivo	Targeting overexpression cells with EGFR. 2-Fold decrease in the growth of tumor.	Roy et al. (2022)
	MYP	Honeycomb-gold nanoparticles	4T1	In vivo	NIR used to release MYP near tumor cells. Increasing anticancer activity by ~43-fold.	Cheng et al. (2019)

Magnetic nanoparticles	HRP	MNPs + AMF	MIA-PaCa2	In vivo	10-Fold decrease in the growth of tumor compared with control. 3-Fold decrease in the growth of tumor compared with treatment without AMFs.	Torres-Herrero et al. (2023)
	HRP	MNPs	HCT116	In vivo	Increase $T_{1/2}$ of the enzyme by 280 times. Effectively targeting HRP to cancer cells.	Correa et al. (2019)
	NTR (NfnB-cys and YfkO-cys)	Gold-coated magnetic nanoparticles	SKOV3	In vivo	Increase in anticancer effect.	(Ball et al., 2021; Patel et al., 2009)
Extracellular vesicles	*CD: UPRT*	Gene *mRNA*	Schwan-nomas cell line	In vivo	Increase expression of the dual gene in the targeted cells.	Mizrak et al. (2013)
	TK-NTR	Minicircle	4T1, MDA-MB-231, MCF7, BT474	In vivo	Increase expression of the dual gene in the targeted cells.	Kanada et al. (2019)
	yCD:UPRT	MSCs	C6	In vivo	Increased survival of rats. Increased expression of the dual gene in the targeted cells.	(Tibensky et al., 2022; Altaner et al., 2014; Altanerova et al., 2012)
	pCMV-CD	Nanovesicles	C6	In vivo	Significantly increased cytotoxic effect.	Wang et al. (2014)

platforms demonstrate remarkable versatility and capability for enzyme-prodrug delivery, challenges persist concerning scalable manufacturing, uniform tumor penetration, long-term biosafety, and consistent in vivo behavior. Continued investigations aim to refine physicochemical properties and to clarify interactions within complex biological systems to enhance clinical translation.

Receptor-targeted small molecule–enzyme conjugates

Folate-directed enzyme prodrug therapy (FDEPT)

Folate receptors (FRs) are membrane proteins that facilitate the uptake of folic acid (FA), a crucial B9 vitamin for nucleotide biosynthesis and methylation reactions in cells. Cancer cells often upregulate high-affinity FRs to meet their increased demand for FA. Mammalian cells internalize folate through reduced folate carrier (RFC), proton-coupled folate transporter (PCFT), and FR-mediated endocytosis, which is predominantly expressed on cancers, activated macrophages, and kidney proximal tubule cells. There are four FR isoforms, with FRα being the most widely studied and frequently overexpressed in various epithelial tumors (Nkepang et al., 2014). Overexpression of FRs in cancer cells increases folate uptake, leading to tumor progression and drug resistance. FR has shown promising efficacy in vitro and in vivo (Nkepang et al., 2014). Lu et al. utilized an FA-penicillin-V amidase conjugate to specifically target cancer cells that overexpress folate receptors. In combination with the prodrug doxorubicin-N-p-hydroxyphenoxyacetamide (DPO), this strategy enabled the selective release of active doxorubicin within tumors, achieving an IC_{50} of approximately 0.6 μM (Lu et al., 1999). Additionally, folate-penicillin-G amidase (FA-PGA) conjugates have been synthesized and shown to efficiently hydrolyze the prodrug N-(phenylacetyl) doxorubicin. In vitro studies demonstrated specific enzyme delivery to folate receptor-positive HeLa and SKOV3 cells, resulting in a 3.1- and 3.3-fold reduction in IC_{50} values compared with free doxorubicin, respectively. These targeted approaches produced significant antitumor effects while reducing systemic toxicity compared with free drug administration (Zhang et al., 2006). The enzyme targeting was confirmed by competitive inhibition with free folic acid, and pharmacokinetic and biodistribution analyses showed rapid clearance of FA-PGA within 24 h and greater tumor accumulation compared with unconjugated penicillin-G amidase (Zhang et al., 2006). Recent advancements in folic acid conjugates have expanded their targeting capabilities beyond cell surface receptors to intracellular pathways, improving prodrug activation in tumor microenvironments. This development is crucial in cancer therapeutics, offering selective approaches to optimize efficacy and minimize systemic adverse effects.

Isoflavones

Isoflavones, such as daidzein and genistein, are small molecules derived from natural sources that have gained considerable attention as targeted ligands for enzyme delivery in cancer therapy (Fig. 29.1). Daidzein, firstly used by Israeli scientists, was conjugated with daunomycin to achieve specific binding to estrogen receptor-positive (ER^+) ovarian tumors. The resulting conjugates demonstrated direct tumor targeting while retaining cytotoxicity, and substantially reduced cardiotoxicity, thus highlighting the clinical potential of isoflavone-mediated delivery systems (Somjen et al., 2008). Further study demonstrated that daidzein conjugation to alliinase enables accumulation on the surface of ER^+ human ovarian adenocarcinoma cells, facilitating local generation of cytotoxic allicin in the presence of the substrate alliin (Appel et al., 2011). This strategy overcomes the instability and systemic toxicity associated with direct administration of thiosulfinates, allowing in situ production of the active anticancer agent (Appel et al., 2011). Similarly, genistein exhibits high binding affinity to estrogen receptors and has been employed both as a carrier molecule for therapeutic macromolecules and as a radiosensitizer in cancer models. Advances in linker chemistry have improved the stability and specificity of genistein-enzyme conjugates, while their antioxidant properties provide additional cellular protection. In parallel, daidzein-enzyme conjugates continue to show higher affinity to cancer cells that overexpress ER^+ and enable localized activity of both chemotherapeutics and catalytic proteins, reducing off-target effects and improving therapeutic indices (Falcão et al., 2018). Isoflavone-based targeting leverages receptor-mediated endocytosis to achieve enhanced tumor specificity, promoting sustained enzyme retention within tumor tissues and facilitating controlled release of cytotoxic metabolites. Current investigations into synthetic isoflavone derivatives, improved conjugation methodologies, and combinatorial dual-targeting approaches are broadening the clinical applicability of natural isoflavones as precise delivery vectors in enzyme-prodrug therapy.

C115H Methionine Gamma-Lyase-Daidzein/Propiin

Cancer cells display distinct metabolic vulnerabilities, notably an increased reliance on glucose—a phenomenon originally identified by Otto Warburg (1956)—as well as on essential amino acids such as methionine (L-Met), arginine, and asparagine (Pokrovsky et al., 2022; Gao et al., 2019; Cheng et al., 2007; Rytting, 2010), which are critical for sustaining their rapid proliferation. Among these metabolic dependencies, methionine addiction, also known as the Hoffman effect, represents a fundamental hallmark of numerous cancers (Pokrovsky et al., 2023; Abo Qoura et al., 2024b). This addiction is characterized by accelerated cancer cell growth and proliferation relative to normal cells and is associated with dysregulated transmethylation metabolism. Consequently, dietary restriction of L-Met is gaining attention as a viable adjunctive therapeutic approach, showing potential to inhibit tumor progression and enhance the efficacy of chemo- and radiotherapy. However, dietary or systemic reduction of L-Met levels alone may be inadequate to substantially decrease its bioavailability in the body to a degree sufficient for cancer regression or eradication (Epner et al., 2002; Pokrovsky et al., 2023). An alternative and potentially more effective approach involves the utilization of methioninase (METase; methionine γ-lyase, EC 4.4.1.11), an enzyme capable of enzymatically degrading circulating L-Met, thereby lowering its concentration in the bloodstream and inhibiting tumor growth. Despite demonstrating promising anticancer efficacy, the clinical translation of MGL has historically faced significant challenges, such as pronounced immunogenicity, cofactor instability, and enzyme degradation. Recent progress in enzyme engineering and the development of effective oral delivery systems are reinvigorating interest in MGL as a widely applicable therapeutic strategy in oncology (Abo Qoura et al., 2024b). To address these challenges, a genetically engineered

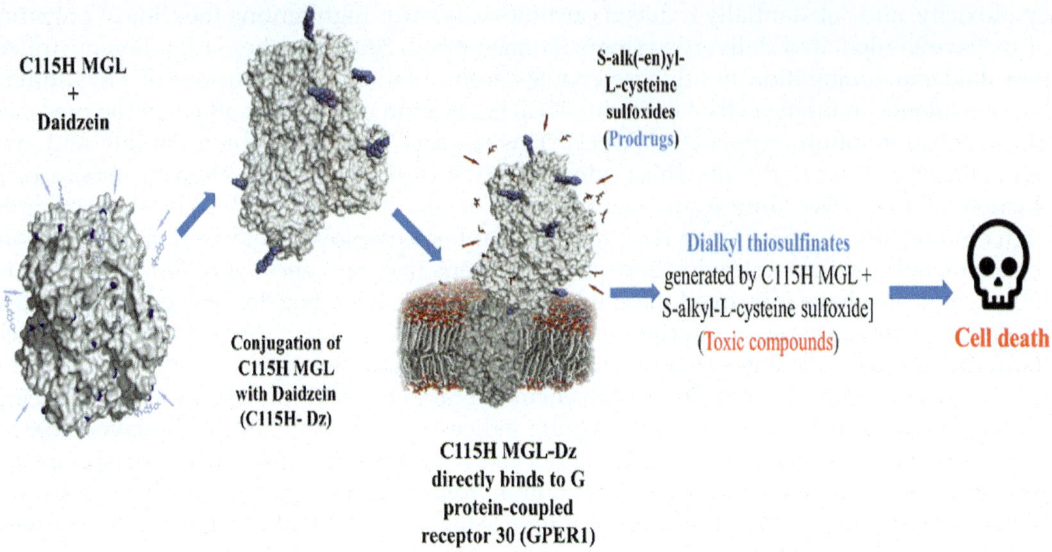

FIGURE 29.2 **Mechanism of action of C115H MGL-Dz in the presence of propiin.** The mutant C115H methionine γ-lyase conjugated with daidzein (C115H MGL-Dz) catalyzes the β-elimination of S-propyl-L-cysteine sulfoxide (propiin), resulting in the local production of cytotoxic dipropyl thiosulfinate at the surface of targeted cancer cells.

mutant of MGL derived from *Clostridium novyi*—in which cysteine at position 115 is substituted by histidine (C115H MGL)—has been developed in collaboration with Prof. Tatiana Demidkina's group from Engelhardt Institute of Molecular Biology, Moscow, Russia. This variant demonstrates significantly improved catalytic efficiency in activating the prodrug S-propyl-L-cysteine sulfoxide (propiin) (Fig. 29.2) (Morozova et al., 2022).

A significant advancement in targeted enzyme delivery is the chemical conjugation of the C115H MGL mutant to the natural isoflavone daidzein (C115H MGL-Dz). Daidzein selectively binds to estrogen receptors, including the G protein-coupled estrogen receptor (GPER1) (Ariyani et al., 2020), which are frequently overexpressed in breast, prostate, pancreatic, and colon cancers (see Section Isoflavones). This conjugation strategy preserves the enzymatic activity of C115H MGL ($k_{cat} = 16.9\ s^{-1}$, $K_m = 1.0$ mM) while incorporating approximately three daidzein moieties per enzyme subunit (Morozova et al., 2022). This modification enhances receptor affinity without compromising the enzyme's active site. Pharmacokinetic evaluation of the C115H MGL-Dz conjugate demonstrated an extended plasma half-life, increasing from 4.4 to 7.2 h, thereby improving its therapeutic potential (Morozova et al., 2022). In vitro investigations revealed pronounced cytotoxic effects of the conjugate against GPER1-positive cancer cell lines, including breast cancers MCF7 ($IC_{50} = 0.53$ μM) and SKBR3 ($IC_{50} = 1.15$ μM), as well as colon (HT29, $IC_{50} = 6.9$ μM), pancreatic (Panc1, $IC_{50} = 3.8$ μM), and prostate (22Rv1, $IC_{50} = 5.4$ μM) cancer models. The specificity of the targeting mechanism was corroborated by a substantially diminished cytotoxic response in receptor-negative cells, exemplified by SW620 colon cancer cells exhibiting an IC_{50} of 19.2 μM, thereby underscoring the crucial role of receptor-mediated uptake in the observed therapeutic activity (Abo Qoura et al., 2022).

The anticancer efficacy of the conjugate C115H MGL-Dz in combination with the prodrug propiin was evaluated in vivo across multiple xenograft tumor models. The therapeutic regimen achieved significant tumor growth inhibition (TGI%), ranging from 51% in HT29 colon xenografts to 85% in GPER1-positive breast cancer xenografts (SKBR3), with all outcomes reaching statistical significance ($P < .05$). The C115H MGL-Dz treatment did not result in a statistically significant reduction in tumor volume compared with the control group in SW620 xenografts, attributable to the low expression of daidzein-binding receptors on these cells. In contrast, control treatments involving either the unconjugated enzyme plus prodrug or the conjugate administered in the absence of propiin demonstrated negligible tumor suppression, highlighting the critical requirement for both targeted enzyme delivery and prodrug activation for optimal antitumor effect (Abo Qoura et al., 2022). The conjugate C115H MGL-Dz exhibits enhanced catalytic efficiency, selective receptor-mediated targeting, and improved pharmacokinetics, resulting in significant antitumor activity in GPER1-positive cancer models when combined with propiin. These findings underscore the necessity of both targeted enzyme delivery and prodrug activation for effective cancer therapy.

Conclusion

Since their emergence in the 1980s, ADEPT approaches have encountered challenges largely due to enzyme immunogenicity and prodrug activation specificity, limiting clinical translation compared with antibody–drug conjugates. Despite FDA approvals and clinical success, ADEPT research has progressed slowly, with only a few enzymes reaching clinical trials and limited recent activity. Small molecule–enzyme conjugates and LDEPT have demonstrated potential to overcome some key limitations by utilizing receptor- or metabolite-targeted small molecules, to achieve selective enzyme localization within tumors. Recent innovations, including the use of small molecule conjugates combined with enzymatic prodrug activation, and the engineering of enzyme variants with improved catalytic efficiency and reduced immunogenicity, offer promising avenues. These advances, integrated with complementary delivery platforms and ligand-mediated targeting, suggest a future where small molecule-assisted enzyme prodrug therapies can achieve improved specificity, deeper tumor penetration, and enhanced safety profiles. Overall, the convergence of antibody-based targeting with small-molecule delivery systems highlights a multifaceted evolution of enzyme prodrug therapies, pointing toward more precise, personalized, and effective cancer treatment modalities. Continued interdisciplinary research is critical to refining these approaches and translating them into clinically viable therapeutics.

Author contributions

Louay Abo Qoura: Writing - Original Draft; Vadim S. Pokrovsky: Writing - Review and Editing.

Funding

This study was supported by the Ministry of Health project of N.N. Blokhin Cancer Research Center, NUYO-2026-0043.

Conflict of interest

The authors declare no conflict of interest, financial or otherwise.

References

Abo Qoura, L., Babayeva, G., Kolpaksidi, A.P., Pokrovsky, V.S., 2025. l-lysine α-oxidase encapsulation in red blood cells - derived extracellular vesicles as biocompatible nanoplatform for cancer therapy. Biochem. Biophys. Res. Commun. 775, 152130. https://doi.org/10.1016/j.bbrc.2025.152130.

Abo Qoura, L., Morozova, E., Kulikova, V., Karshieva, S., Sokolova, D., Koval, V., Revtovich, S., Demidkina, T., Pokrovsky, V.S., 2022. Methionine γ-lyase-daidzein in combination with S-Propyl-L-cysteine sulfoxide as a targeted prodrug enzyme system for malignant solid tumor xenografts. Int. J. Mol. Sci. 23 (19), 12048. https://doi.org/10.3390/ijms231912048.

Abo Qoura, L., Morozova, E., Ramaa, C.S., Pokrovsky, V.S., 2024a. Smart nanocarriers for enzyme-activated prodrug therapy. J. Drug Target. 32 (9), 1029–1051. https://doi.org/10.1080/1061186x.2024.2383688.

Abo Qoura, L., Balakin, K.V., Hoffman, R.M., Pokrovsky, V.S., 2024b. The potential of methioninase for cancer treatment. Biochim. Biophys. Acta Rev. Canc 1879 (4), 189122. https://doi.org/10.1016/j.bbcan.2024.189122.

Afshar, S., Olafsen, T., Wu, A.M., Morrison, S.L., 2009a. Characterization of an engineered human purine nucleoside phosphorylase fused to an anti-her2/neu single chain Fv for use in ADEPT. J. Exp. Clin. Cancer Res. 28 (1). https://doi.org/10.1186/1756-9966-28-147.

Afshar, S., Sawaya, M.R., Morrison, S.L., 2009b. Structure of a mutant human purine nucleoside phosphorylase with the prodrug, 2-fluoro-2′-deoxyadenosine and the cytotoxic drug, 2-fluoroadenine. Protein Sci. 18 (5), 1107–1114. https://doi.org/10.1002/pro.91.

Alexander, E., Leong, K.W., 2024. Discovery of nanobodies: A comprehensive review of their applications and potential over the past five years. J. Nanobiotechnol. 22 (1). https://doi.org/10.1186/s12951-024-02900-y.

Al-Jaber, H., Biswas, K.H., Al-Mansoori, L., 2025. Advancing targeted therapy for colorectal cancer: Harnessing ligand-directed enzyme prodrug therapy for highly specific interventions. Front. Oncol. 15. https://doi.org/10.3389/fonc.2025.1570712.

Al-mansoori, L., Al Qahtani, A.D., Elsinga, P., Goda, S.K., 2021. Production of long-acting CNGRC–CPG2 fusion proteins: New derivatives to overcome drug immunogenicity of ligand-directed enzyme prodrug therapy for targeted cancer treatment. Technol. Cancer Res. Treat. 20. https://doi.org/10.1177/15330338211057371.

Al-mansoori, L., Bashraheel, S.S., Al Qahtani, A.D., O'Connor, C.D., Elsinga, P., Goda, S.K., 2020. In vitro studies on CNGRC-CPG2 fusion proteins for ligand-directed enzyme prodrug therapy for targeted cancer therapy. Oncotarget 11 (6), 619–633. https://doi.org/10.18632/oncotarget.27478.

Al-Qahtani, A.D., Bashraheel, S.S., Rashidi, F.B., O'Connor, C.D., Romero, A.R., Domling, A., Goda, S.K., 2019. Production of "biobetter" variants of glucarpidase with enhanced enzyme activity. Biomed. Pharmacother. 112. https://doi.org/10.1016/j.biopha.2019.108725.

Altaner, C., Altanerova, V., Cihova, M., Ondicova, K., Rychly, B., Baciak, L., Mravec, B., 2014. Complete regression of glioblastoma by mesenchymal stem cells mediated prodrug gene therapy simulating clinical therapeutic scenario. Int. J. Cancer 134 (6), 1458–1465. https://doi.org/10.1002/ijc.28455.

Altanerova, V., Cihova, M., Babic, M., Rychly, B., Ondicova, K., Mravec, B., Altaner, C., 2012. Human adipose tissue-derived mesenchymal stem cells expressing yeast cytosinedeaminase: Uracil phosphoribosyltransferase inhibit intracerebral rat glioblastoma. Int. J. Cancer 130 (10), 2455–2463. https://doi.org/10.1002/ijc.26278.

Altaner C, Altanerova U. Mesenchymal stem cell exosome-mediated prodrug gene therapy for cancer. In: Düzgüneş N (ed) Suicide Gene Therapy. New York, NY: Springer New York, pp. 75–85.

Anraku, Y., Kishimura, A., Kamiya, M., Tanaka, S., Nomoto, T., Toh, K., Matsumoto, Y., Fukushima, S., Sueyoshi, D., Kano, M.R., Urano, Y., Nishiyama, N., 2016. Kazunori Kataoka, systemically injectable enzyme-loaded polyion complex vesicles as in vivo nanoreactors functioning in tumors. Angew. Chem. Int. Ed. 55 (2), 560–565. https://doi.org/10.1002/anie.201508339.

Aoi, A., Watanabe, Y., Mori, S., Takahashi, M., Vassaux, G., Kodama, T., 2008. Herpes sSimplex virus thymidine kinase-mediated suicide gene therapy using nano/microbubbles and ultrasound. Ultrasound Med. Biol. 34 (3), 425–434. https://doi.org/10.1016/j.ultrasmedbio.2007.09.004.

Appel, E., Rabinkov, A., Neeman, M., Kohen, F., Mirelman, D., 2011. Conjugates of daidzein-alliinase as a targeted pro-drug enzyme system against ovarian carcinoma. J. Drug Target. 19 (5), 326–335. https://doi.org/10.3109/1061186X.2010.504265.

Ariyani, W., Miyazaki, W., Amano, I., Hanamura, K., Shirao, T., Koibuchi, N., 2020. Soy isoflavones accelerate glial cell migration via GPER-mediated signal transduction pathway. Front. Endocrinol. 11. https://doi.org/10.3389/fendo.2020.554941.

Bagshawe, K.D., 1987. Antibody directed enzymes revive anti-cancer prodrugs concept. Br. J. Cancer 56 (5), 531–532. https://doi.org/10.1038/bjc.1987.237.

Ball, P., Hobbs, R., Anderson, S., Thompson, E., Gwenin, V., Von Ruhland, C., Gwenin, C., 2021. The YfkO nitroreductase from Bacillus licheniformis on gold-coated superparamagnetic nanoparticles: Towards a novel directed enzyme prodrug therapy approach. Pharmaceutics 13 (4), 517. https://doi.org/10.3390/pharmaceutics13040517.

Begines, B., Ortiz, T., Pérez-Aranda, M., Martínez, G., Merinero, M., Argüelles-Arias, F., Alcudia, A., 2020. Polymeric nanoparticles for drug delivery: recent developments and future prospects. Nanomaterials 10 (7), 1403. https://doi.org/10.3390/nano10071403.

Canduri, F., Dos Santos, D.M., Silva, R.G., Mendes, M.A., Basso, L.A., Palma, M.S., De Azevedo, W.F., Santos, D.S., 2004. Structures of human purine nucleoside phosphorylase complexed with inosine and ddI. Biochem. Biophys. Res. Commun. 313 (4), 907–914. https://doi.org/10.1016/j.bbrc.2003.11.179.

Cao, X., Chen, C., Yu, H., Wang, P., 2015. Horseradish peroxidase-encapsulated chitosan nanoparticles for enzyme-prodrug cancer therapy. Biotechnol. Lett. 37 (1), 81–88. https://doi.org/10.1007/s10529-014-1664-5.

Cheng, L., Zhang, F., Wang, S., Pan, X., Han, S., Liu, S., Ma, J., Wang, H., Shen, H., Liu, H., Yuan, Q., 2019. Activation of prodrugs by NIR-triggered release of exogenous enzymes for locoregional chemo-photothermal therapy. Angew. Chem. Int. Ed. 58 (23), 7728–7732. https://doi.org/10.1002/anie.201902476.

Cheng, P.N.M., Lam, T.L., Lam, W.M., Tsui, S.M., Cheng, A.W.M., Lo, W.H., Leung, Y.C., 2007. Pegylated recombinant human arginase (rhArg-peg5,000mw) inhibits the in vitro and in vivo proliferation of human hepatocellular carcinoma through arginine depletion. Cancer Res. 67 (1), 309–317. https://doi.org/10.1158/0008-5472.CAN-06-1945.

Cheng, Z., Fobian, S.F., Gurrieri, E., Amin, M., D'Agostino, V.G., Falahati, M., Zalba, S., Debets, R., Garrido, M.J., Saeed, M., Seynhaeve, A.L.B., Balcioglu, H.E., ten Hagen, T.L.M., 2024. Lipid-based nanosystems: The next generation of cancer immune therapy. J. Hematol. Oncol. 17 (1). https://doi.org/10.1186/s13045-024-01574-1.

Chung-Faye, G., Palmer, D., Anderson, D., Clark, J., Dowries, M., Baddeley, J., Hussain, S., Murray, P.I., Searle, P., Seymour, L., Ferry, D., Kerr, D.J., Harris, P.A., 2001. Virus-directed, enzyme prodrug therapy with nitroimidazole reductase: A phase I and pharmacokinetic study of its prodrug, CB1954. Clin. Cancer Res. 7 (9), 2662–2668.

Correa, S., Puertas, S., Gutiérrez, L., Asín, L., de la Fuente, J.M., Grazú, V., Betancor, L., Marr, A.C., 2019. Design of stable magnetic hybrid nanoparticles of Si-entrapped HRP. PLoS One 14 (4), e0214004. https://doi.org/10.1371/journal.pone.0214004.

Cortez-Retamozo, V., Backmann, N., Senter, P.D., Wernery, U., De Baetselier, P., Muyldermans, S., Revets, H., 2004. Efficient cancer therapy with a nanobody-based conjugate. Cancer Res. 64 (8), 2853–2857. https://doi.org/10.1158/0008-5472.CAN-03-3935.

Davies, L.C., Friedlos, F., Hedley, D., Martin, J., Ogilvie, L.M., Scanlon, I.J., Springer, C.J., 2005. Novel fluorinated prodrugs for activation by carboxypeptidase G2 showing good in vivo antitumor activity in gene-directed enzyme prodrug therapy. J. Med. Chem. 48 (16), 5321–5328. https://doi.org/10.1021/jm0502182.

de la Fuente, M., Lombardero, L., Gómez-González, A., Solari, C., Angulo-Barturen, I., Acera, A., Vecino, E., Astigarraga, E., Barreda-Gómez, G., Therapy, E., 2021. Current challenges and future perspectives. Int. J. Mol. Sci. 22 (17), 9181. https://doi.org/10.3390/ijms22179181.

Devulapally, R., Lee, T., Barghava-Shah, A., Sekar, T.V., Foygel, K., Bachawal, S.V., Willmann, J.K., Paulmurugan, R., 2018. Ultrasound-guided delivery of thymidine kinase–nitroreductase dual therapeutic genes by PEGylated-PLGA/PEI nanoparticles for enhanced triple negative breast cancer therapy. Nanomedicine 13 (9), 1051–1066. https://doi.org/10.2217/nnm-2017-0328.

Ding, Y., Fan, J., Deng, L., Huang, B., Zhou, B., 2020. Antitumor efficacy of cytosine deaminase-armed vaccinia virus plus 5-fluorocytosine in colorectal cancers. Cancer Cell Int. 20 (1). https://doi.org/10.1186/s12935-020-01340-6.

El-Sayed, A.S.A., Mohamed, N.Z., Yassin, M.A., Amer, M.M., El-Sharkawy, R., El-Sayed, N., Ali, M.G., 2022. Microbial cytosine deaminase is a programmable anticancer prodrug mediating enzyme: Antibody, and gene directed enzyme prodrug therapy. Heliyon 8 (9). https://doi.org/10.1016/j.heliyon.2022.e10660.

Epner, D.E., Morrow, S., Wilcox, M., Houghton, J.L., 2002. Nutrient intake and nutritional indexes in adults with metastatic cancer on a phase I clinical trial of dietary methionine restriction. Nutr. Cancer 42 (2), 158–166. https://doi.org/10.1207/S15327914NC422_2.

Falcão, H.G., Handa, C.L., Silva, M.B.R., de Camargo, A.C., Shahidi, F., Kurozawa, L.E., Ida, E.I., 2018. Soybean ultrasound pre-treatment prior to soaking affects β-glucosidase activity, isoflavone profile and soaking time. Food Chem. 269, 404–412. https://doi.org/10.1016/j.foodchem.2018.07.028.

Frei, E., Teicher, B.A., Holden, S.A., Cathcart, K.N.S., Wang, Y., 1988. Preclinical studies and clinical correlation of the effect of alkylating dose. Cancer Res. 48 (22), 6417–6423.

Friedlos, F., Davies, L., Scanlon, I., Ogilvie, L.M., Martin, J., Stribbling, S.M., Spooner, R.A., Niculescu-Duvaz, I., Marais, R., Springer, C.J., 2002. Three new prodrugs for suicide gene therapy using carboxypeptidase G2 elicit bystander efficacy in two xenograft models. Cancer Res. 62 (6), 1724–1729.

Friedmann, T., Roblin, R., 1972. Gene Therapy for Human Genetic Disease? Proposals for genetic manipulation in humans raise difficult scientific and ethical problems. Science 175, 949–955.

Fu, Q., Shen, S., Sun, P., Gu, Z., Bai, Y., Wang, X., Liu, Z., 2023. Bioorthogonal chemistry for prodrug activation in vivo. Chem. Soc. Rev. 52 (22), 7737–7772. https://doi.org/10.1039/d2cs00889k.

Fuchita, M., Ardiani, A., Zhao, L., Serve, K., Stoddard, B.L., Black, M.E., 2009. Bacterial cytosine deaminase mutants created by molecular engineering show improved 5-fluorocytosine–mediated cell killing in vitro and in vivo. Cancer Res. 69 (11), 4791–4799. https://doi.org/10.1158/0008-5472.can-09-0615.

Gao, X., Sanderson, S.M., Dai, Z., Reid, M.A., Cooper, D.E., Lu, M., Richie, J.P., Ciccarella, A., Calcagnotto, A., Mikhael, P.G., Mentch, S.J., Liu, J., Ables, G., Kirsch, D.G., Hsu, D.S., Nichenametla, S.N., Locasale, J.W., 2019. Dietary methionine influences therapy in mouse cancer models and alters human metabolism. Nature 572 (7769), 397–401. https://doi.org/10.1038/s41586-019-1437-3.

Ghafouri-Fard, S., Abak, A., Tondro Anamag, F., Shoorei, H., Fattahi, F., Alireza Javadinia, S., Basiri, A., Taheri, M., 2021. 5-Fluorouracil: A narrative review on the role of regulatory mechanisms in driving resistance to this chemotherapeutic agent. Front. Oncol. 11. https://doi.org/10.3389/fonc.2021.658636.

Goto, A., Anraku, Y., Fukushima, S., Kishimura, A., 2023. Increased enzyme loading in PICsomes via controlling membrane permeability improves enzyme prodrug cancer therapy outcome. Polymers 15 (6), 1368. https://doi.org/10.3390/polym15061368.

Green, N.K., McNeish, I.A., Doshi, R., Searle, P.F., Kerr, D.J., Young, L.S., 2003. Immune enhancement of nitroreductase-induced cytotoxicity: Studies using a bicistronic adenovirus vector. Int. J. Cancer 104 (1), 104–112. https://doi.org/10.1002/ijc.10916.

Gupta, N., Sharma, R.K., Maitra, A., Shrivastava, A., 2023. In-vitro and in-vivo efficacy of hollow gold nanoparticles encapsulating horseradish peroxidase: Oxidative stress-mediated tumor cell killing. J. Drug Deliv. Sci. Technol. 79, 103979. https://doi.org/10.1016/j.jddst.2022.103979.

Hattori, Y., Maitani, Y., 2005. Folate-linked lipid-based nanoparticle for targeted gene delivery. Curr. Drug Deliv. 2 (3), 243–252. https://doi.org/10.2174/1567201054368002.

Hu, C., Jiang, D., Wu, M., Wang, J., Zhang, R., 2020. Ultrasound-mediated nanobubble destruction (UMND) facilitates the delivery of VEGFR2-targeted CD-TK-loaded cationic nanobubbles in the treatment of bladder cancer. J. Cancer Res. Clin. Oncol. 146 (6), 1415–1426. https://doi.org/10.1007/s00432-020-03160-7.

Jakubechova, J., Smolkova, B., Furdova, A., Demkova, L., Altanerova, U., Nicodemou, A., Zeleznikova, T., Klimova, D., Altaner, C., 2023. Suicide-gene-modified extracellular vesicles of human primary uveal melanoma in future therapies. Int. J. Mol. Sci. 24 (16), 12957. https://doi.org/10.3390/ijms241612957.

Japir, A.A.W.M.M., Ke, W., Li, J., Mukerabigwi, J.F., Ibrahim, A., Wang, Y., Li, X., Zhou, Q., Mohammed, F., Ge, Z., 2021. Tumor-dilated polymersome nanofactories for enhanced enzyme prodrug chemo-immunotherapy. J. Contr. Release 339, 418–429. https://doi.org/10.1016/j.jconrel.2021.10.015.

Kanada, M., Kim, B.D., Hardy, J.W., Ronald, J.A., Bachmann, M.H., Bernard, M.P., Perez, G.I., Zarea, A.A., Ge, T.J., Withrow, A., Ibrahim, S.A., Toomajian, V., Gambhir, S.S., Paulmurugan, R., Contag, C.H., 2019. Microvesiclemediated delivery of minicircle DNA results in effective gene-directed enzyme prodrug cancer therapy. Mol. Cancer Therapeut. 18 (12), 2331–2342. https://doi.org/10.1158/1535-7163.MCT-19-0299.

Kievit, E., Bershad, E., Ng, E., Sethna, P., Dev, I., Lawrence, T.S., Rehemtulla, A., 1999. Superiority of yeast over bacterial cytosine deaminase for enzyme/prodrug gene therapy in colon cancer xenografts. Cancer Res. 59 (7), 1417–1421. Available from: http://cancerres.aacrjournals.org/.

Kilstrup, M., Meng, L.M., Neuhard, J., Nygaard, P., 1989. Genetic evidence for a repressor of synthesis of cytosine deaminase and purine biosynthesis enzymes in Escherichia coli. J. Bacteriol. 171 (4), 2124–2127. https://doi.org/10.1128/jb.171.4.2124-2127.1989.

Knox, R.J., Friedlos, F., Jarman, M., Roberts, J.J., 1988. A new cytotoxic, DNA interstrand crosslinking agent, 5-(aziridin-1-yl)-4-hydroxylamino-2-nitrobenzamide, is formed from 5-(aziridin-1-yl)-2,4-dinitrobenzamide (CB 1954) by a nitroreductase enzyme in walker carcinoma cells. Biochem. Pharmacol. 37 (24), 4661–4669. https://doi.org/10.1016/0006-2952(88)90335-8.

Konhäuser, M., Kannaujiya, V.K., Kaltbeitzel, J., Winterwerber, P., Böhm, E., Breitenbach, B., Wich, P.R., 2023. Dual-responsive enzyme-polysaccharide conjugate as a nanocarrier system for enzyme prodrug therapy. Biomacromolecules 24 (5), 2138–2148. https://doi.org/10.1021/acs.biomac.3c00031.

Koval, V., Morozova, E., Revtovich, S., Lyfenko, A., Chobanian, A., Timofeeva, V., Solovieva, A., Anufrieva, N., Kulikova, V., Demidkina, T., 2022. Characteristics and stability assessment of therapeutic methionine γ-lyase-Loaded polyionic vesicles. ACS Omega 7 (1), 959–967. https://doi.org/10.1021/acsomega.1c05558.

Lawrence, T.S., Rehemtulla, A., Ng, E.Y., Wilson, M., Trosko, J.E., Stetson, P.L., 1998. Preferential cytotoxicity of cells transduced with cytosine deaminase compared to bystander cells after treatment with 5-flucytosine. Cancer Res. 58 (12), 2588–2593.

Lehouritis, P., Springer, C., Tangney, M., 2013. Bacterial-directed enzyme prodrug therapy. J. Control. Release 170, 120–131.

Li, J., Zhou, P., Li, L., Zhang, Y., Shao, Y., Tang, L., Tian, S., Pintus, G., 2016. Effects of cationic microbubble carrying CD/TK double suicide gene and αVβ3 integrin antibody in human hepatocellular carcinoma HepG2 cells. PLoS One 11 (7), e0158592. https://doi.org/10.1371/journal.pone.0158592.

Li, S., Wang, Q., Jia, Z., Da, M., Zhao, J., Yang, R., Chen, D., 2023. Recent advances in glucose oxidase-based nanocarriers for tumor targeting therapy. Heliyon 9 (10), e20407. https://doi.org/10.1016/j.heliyon.2023.e20407.

Li, X.-hua, Zhou, P., Wang, L.-hua, Tian, S.-ming, Qian, Y., Chen, L.-rong, Zhang, P., 2012. The targeted gene (KDRP-CD/TK) therapy of breast cancer mediated by SonoVue and ultrasound irradiation in vitro. Ultrasonics 52 (1), 186–191. https://doi.org/10.1016/j.ultras.2011.08.002.

Liu, Y., Zhang, Y., Du, Di, Gu, X., Zhang, X., Hong, G., Xing, L., 2024. Nanotargeted cationic lipid microbubbles carrying HSV-TK gene inhibit the development of subcutaneous liver tumor model after HIFU ablation. J. Ultrasound Med. 43 (1), 95–107. https://doi.org/10.1002/jum.16342.

Lu, J.Y., Lowe, D.A., Kennedy, M.D., Low, P.S., 1999. Folate-targeted enzyme prodrug cancer therapy utilizing penicillin-V amidase and a doxorubicin prodrug. J. Drug Target. 7 (1), 43–53. https://doi.org/10.3109/10611869909085491.

Ma, Q., Jiang, H., Ma, L., Zhao, G., Xu, Q., Guo, D., He, N., Liu, H., Meng, Z., Liu, J., Zhu, L., Lin, Q., Wu, X., Li, M., Luo, S., Fang, J., Lu, Z., 2023. The moonlighting function of glycolytic enzyme enolase-1 promotes choline phospholipid metabolism and tumor cell proliferation. Proc. Natl. Acad. Sci. 120 (15). https://doi.org/10.1073/pnas.2209435120.

Manzari-Tavakoli, A., Babajani, A., Tavakoli, M.M., Safaeinejad, F., Jafari, A., 2024. Integrating natural compounds and nanoparticle-based drug delivery systems: A novel strategy for enhanced efficacy and selectivity in cancer therapy. Cancer Med. 13 (5). https://doi.org/10.1002/cam4.7010.

Metcalf, K.J., Kimmel, B.R., Sykora, D.J., Modica, J.A., Parker, K.A., Berens, E., Dai, R., Dravid, V.P., Werb, Z., Mrksich, M., 2021. Synthetic tuning of domain stoichiometry in nanobody-enzyme megamolecules. Bioconjug. Chem. 32 (1), 143–152. https://doi.org/10.1021/acs.bioconjchem.0c00578.

Michael, N.P., Chester, K.A., Melton, R.G., Robson, L., Nicholas, W., Boden, J.A., Pedley, R.B., Begent, R.H.J., Sherwood, R.F., Minton, N.P., 1996. In vitro and in vivo characterisation of a recombinant carboxypeptidase G2: Anti-CEA scFv fusion protein. Immunotechnology 2 (1), 47–57. https://doi.org/10.1016/1380-2933(96)00033-4.

Mizrak, A., Bolukbasi, M.F., Ozdener, G.B., Brenner, G.J., Madlener, S., Erkan, E.P., Ströbel, T., Breakefield, X.O., Saydam, O., 2013. Genetically engineered microvesicles carrying suicide mRNA/protein inhibit schwannoma tumor growth. Mol. Ther. 21 (1), 101–108. https://doi.org/10.1038/mt.2012.161.

Monnier, P., Vigouroux, R., Tassew, N., 2013. In vivo applications of single chain Fv (variable domain) (scFv) fragments. Antibodies 2 (2), 193–208. https://doi.org/10.3390/antib2020193.

Morozova, E., Abo Qoura, L., Anufrieva, N., Koval, V., Lesnova, E., Kushch, A., Kulikova, V., Revtovich, S., Pokrovsky, V.S., Demidkina, T., 2022. Daidzein-directed methionine γ-lyase in enzyme prodrug therapy against breast cancer. Biochimie 201, 177–183. https://doi.org/10.1016/j.biochi.2022.05.007.

Morozova, E.A., Kulikova, V.V., Anufrieva, N.V., Minakov, A.N., Chernov, A.S., Telegin, G.B., Revtovich, S.V., Koval, V.S., Demidkina, T.V., 2019. Methionine γ-lyase in enzyme prodrug therapy: An improvement of pharmacokinetic parameters of the enzyme. Int. J. Biol. Macromol. 140, 1277–1283. https://doi.org/10.1016/j.ijbiomac.2019.08.224.

Nervig, C.S., Hatch, S.T., Owen, S.C., 2022. Complementation dependent enzyme prodrug therapy enables targeted activation of prodrug on HER2-positive cancer cells. ACS Med. Chem. Lett. 13 (11), 1769–1775. https://doi.org/10.1021/acsmedchemlett.2c00394.

Nishimura, T., Sasaki, Y., Akiyoshi, K., 2017. Biotransporting self-assembled nanofactories using polymer vesicles with molecular permeability for enzyme prodrug cancer therapy. Adv. Mater 29 (36). https://doi.org/10.1002/adma.201702406.

Nkepang, G., Bio, M., Rajaputra, P., Awuah, S.G., You, Y., 2014. Folate receptor-mediated enhanced and specific delivery of far-red light-activatable prodrugs of combretastatin A-4 to FR-positive tumor. Bioconjug. Chem. 25 (12), 2175–2188. https://doi.org/10.1021/bc500376j.

Ochiai, T., Masuda, T., Yagi, M., Kasai, R., Furuyama, T., Tsukamoto, K., Ito, H., Igari, K., Aihara, A., Kumagai, Y., Iida, M., Odajima, H., Tanaka, S., Arii, S., Yamazaki, S., 2012. Successful combination therapy of radical liver resection with 5-Fluorouracil/leucovorin, oxaliplatin, plus bevacizumab for ascending colon cancer with pulmonary and 43 liver metastases: Report of a case. Int. Surg. 97 (1), 6–13. https://doi.org/10.9738/cc88.1.

Palmer, D.H., Mautner, V., Mirza, D., Oliff, S., Gerritsen, W., Van der Sijp, J.R.M., Hubscher, S., Reynolds, G., Bonney, S., Rajaratnam, R., Hull, D., Horne, M., Ellis, J., Mountain, A., Hill, S., Harris, P.A., Searle, P.F., Young, L.S., James, N.D., Kerr, D.J., 2004. Virus-directed enzyme prodrug therapy: Intratumoral administration of a replication-deficient adenovirus encoding nitroreductase to patients with resectable liver cancer. J. Clin. Oncol. 22 (9), 1546–1552. https://doi.org/10.1200/JCO.2004.10.005.

Parker, W.B., Allan, P.W., Shaddix, S.C., Rose, L.M., Speegle, H.F., Gillespie, G.Y., Bennett, L.L., 1998. Metabolism and metabolic actions of 6-methylpurine and 2-fluoroadenine in human cells. Biochem. Pharmacol. 55 (10), 1673–1681. https://doi.org/10.1016/S0006-2952(98)00034-3.

Patel, P., Young, J.G., Mautner, V., Ashdown, D., Bonney, S., Pineda, R.G., Collins, S.I., Searle, P.F., Hull, D., Peers, E., Chester, J., Wallace, D.M., Doherty, A., Leung, H., Young, L.S., James, N.D., 2009. A phase I/II clinical trial in localized prostate cancer of an adenovirus expressing nitroreductase with CB1984. Mol. Ther. 17 (7), 1292–1299. https://doi.org/10.1038/mt.2009.80.

Pokrovsky, V.S., Abo Qoura, L., Morozova, E., Bunik, V.I., 2022. Predictive markers for efficiency of the amino-acid deprivation therapies in cancer. Front. Med. 9. https://doi.org/10.3389/fmed.2022.1035356.

Pokrovsky, V.S., Abo Qoura, L., Demidova, E.A., Han, Q., Hoffman, R.M., 2023. Targeting methionine addiction of cancer cells with methioninase. Biochemistry (Mosc.) 88 (7), 944–952. https://doi.org/10.1134/S0006297923070076.

Poletti, V., Mavilio, F., 2021. Designing lentiviral vectors for gene therapy of genetic diseases. Viruses 13 (8), 1526. https://doi.org/10.3390/v13081526.

Raza, A., Kohila, V., Ghosh, S.S., 2015. Redesigned Escherichia coli cytosine deaminase: A new facet of suicide gene therapy: Cytosine deaminase mutant in suicide gene therapy. J. Gene Med. 17, 132–139.

Roy, S., Curry, S.D., Corbella Bagot, C., Mueller, E.N., Mansouri, A.M., Park, W., Cha, J.N., Goodwin, A.P., 2022. Enzyme prodrug therapy with photo-cross-linkable anti-EGFR affibodies conjugated to upconverting nanoparticles. ACS Nano 16 (10), 15873–15883. https://doi.org/10.1021/acsnano.2c02558.

Russell, P.J., Khatri, A., 2006. Novel gene-directed enzyme prodrug therapies against prostate cancer. Expert Opin. Invest. Drugs 15 (8), 947–961. https://doi.org/10.1517/13543784.15.8.947.

Rytting, M., 2010. Peg-asparaginase for acute lymphoblastic leukemia. Expert Opin. Biol. Ther. 10 (5), 833–839. https://doi.org/10.1517/14712591003769808.

Schiffelers, L.D.J., Tesfamariam, Y.M., Jenster, L.M., Diehl, S., Binder, S.C., Normann, S., Mayr, J., Pritzl, S., Hagelauer, E., Kopp, A., Alon, A., Geyer, M., Ploegh, H.L., Schmidt, F.I., 2024. Antagonistic nanobodies implicate mechanism of GSDMD pore formation and potential therapeutic application. Nat. Commun. 15 (1). https://doi.org/10.1038/s41467-024-52110-1.

Searle, P.F., Chen, M.J., Hu, L., Race, P.R., Lovering, A.L., Grove, J.I., Guise, C., Jaberipour, M., James, N.D., Mautner, V., Young, L.S., Kerr, D.J., Mountain, A., White, S.A., Hyde, E.I., 2004. Nitroreductase: A prodrug-activating enzyme for cancer gene therapy. Clin. Exp. Pharmacol. Physiol. 31. https://doi.org/10.1111/j.1440-1681.2004.04085.x.

Singleton, D.C., Mowday, A.M., Guise, C.P., Syddall, S.P., Bai, S.Y., Li, D., Ashoorzadeh, A., Smaill, J.B., Wilson, W. R., Patterson, A.V., 2022. Bioreductive prodrug PR-104 improves the tumour distribution and titre of the nitroreductase-armed oncolytic adenovirus ONYX-411NTR leading to therapeutic benefit. Cancer Gene Ther. 29 (7), 1021–1032. https://doi.org/10.1038/s41417-021-00409-2.

Singleton, D.C., Li, D., Bai, S.Y., Syddall, S.P., Smaill, J.B., Shen, Y., Denny, W.A., Wilson, W.R., Patterson, A.V., 2007. The nitroreductase prodrug SN 28343 enhances the potency of systemically administered armed oncolytic adenovirus ONYX-411NTR. Cancer Gene Ther. 14 (12), 953–967. https://doi.org/10.1038/sj.cgt.7701088.

Somjen, D., Katzburg, S., Nevo, N., Gayer, B., Hodge, R.P., Renevey, M.D., Kalchenko, V., Meshorer, A., Stern, N., Kohen, F., 2008. A daidzein–daunomycin conjugate improves the therapeutic response in an animal model of ovarian carcinoma. J. Steroid Biochem. Mol. Biol. 110 (1–2), 144–149. https://doi.org/10.1016/j.jsbmb.2008.03.033.

Sorscher, E.J., Hong, J.S., Allan, P.W., Waud, W.R., Parker, W.B., 2012. In vivo antitumor activity of intratumoral fludarabine phosphate in refractory tumors expressing E. coli purine nucleoside phosphorylase. Cancer Chemother. Pharmacol. 70 (2), 321–329. https://doi.org/10.1007/s00280-012-1908-9.

Springer, C.J., Antoniw, P., Bagshawe, K.D., Searle, F., Bisset, G.M.F., Jarman, M., 1990. Novel prodrugs which are activated to cytotoxic alkylating agents by carboxypeptidase G2. J. Med. Chem. 33 (2), 677–681. https://doi.org/10.1021/jm00164a034.

Stribbling, S.M., Martin, J., Pedley, R.B., Boden, J.A., Sharma, S.K., Springer, C.J., 1997. Biodistribution of an antibody-enzyme conjugate for antibody-directed enzyme prodrug therapy in nude mice bearing a human colon adenocarcinoma xenograft. Cancer Chemother. Pharmacol. 40 (4), 277–284. https://doi.org/10.1007/s002800050659.

Swe, P.M., Copp, J.N., Green, L.K., Guise, C.P., Mowday, A.M., Smaill, J.B., Patterson, A.V., Ackerley, D.F., 2012. Targeted mutagenesis of the Vibrio fischeri flavin reductase FRase I to improve activation of the anticancer prodrug CB1954. Biochem. Pharmacol. 84 (6), 775–783. https://doi.org/10.1016/j.bcp.2012.07.002.

Tian, H., Zhang, T., Qin, S., Huang, Z., Zhou, L., Shi, J., Nice, E.C., Xie, N., Huang, C., Shen, Z., 2022. Enhancing the therapeutic efficacy of nanoparticles for cancer treatment using versatile targeted strategies. J. Hematol. Oncol. 15 (1). https://doi.org/10.1186/s13045-022-01320-5.

Tibensky, M., Jakubechova, J., Altanerova, U., Pastorakova, A., Rychly, B., Baciak, L., Mravec, B., Altaner, C., 2022. Gene-directed enzyme/prodrug therapy of rat brain tumor mediated by human mesenchymal stem cell suicide gene extracellular vesicles in vitro and in vivo. Cancers 14 (3), 735. https://doi.org/10.3390/cancers14030735.

Torres-Herrero, B., Armenia, I., Alleva, M., Asín, L., Correa, S., Ortiz, C., Fernández-Afonso, Y., Gutiérrez, L., de la Fuente, J.M., Betancor, L., Grazú, V., 2023. Remote activation of enzyme nanohybrids for cancer prodrug therapy controlled by magnetic heating. ACS Nano 17 (13), 12358–12373. https://doi.org/10.1021/acsnano.3c01599.

Tsuchida, K., Murakami, T., 2008. Recent advances in inorganic nanoparticle-based drug delivery systems. Mini Rev. Med. Chem. 8 (2), 175–183. https://doi.org/10.2174/138955708783498078.

Wang, F., Yang, J., Li, Y., Zhuang, Q., Gu, J., 2020. Efficient enzyme-activated therapy based on the different locations of protein and prodrug in nanoMOFs. J. Mater. Chem. B 8 (28), 6139–6147. https://doi.org/10.1039/d0tb01004a.

Wang, J.H., Forterre, A.V., Zhao, J., Frimannsson, D.O., Delcayre, A., Antes, T.J., Efron, B., Jeffrey, S.S., Pegram, M. D., Matin, A.C., 2018. Anti-her2 scfv-directed extracellular vesicle-mediated mRNA-based gene delivery inhibits growth of her2-positive human breast tumor xenografts by prodrug activation. Mol. Cancer Therapeut. 17 (5), 1133–1142. https://doi.org/10.1158/1535-7163.MCT-17-0827.

Wang, L., Yuan, Y., Lin, S., Cheng, Du, Wang, X., Jiang, Q., Shuai, X., 2014. Co-delivery of 5-fluorocytosine and cytosine deaminase into glioma cells mediated by an intracellular environment-responsive nanovesicle. Polym. Chem. 5 (15), 4542–4552. https://doi.org/10.1039/c4py00291a.

Warburg, O., 1956. On the origin of cancer cells. Science 123 (3191), 309–314. https://doi.org/10.1126/science.123.3191.309.

Wu, J., Li, R.K., 2017. Ultrasound-targeted microbubble destruction in gene therapy: A new tool to cure human diseases. Genes Dis. 4 (2), 64–74. https://doi.org/10.1016/j.gendis.2016.08.001.

Wu, Y., 2025. Trends in nanobody technology in industrialization. Discover Nano 20 (1). https://doi.org/10.1186/s11671-025-04200-2.

Yu, T., Li, X., 2023. Development of ZD2767P–carboxypeptidase G2–ultrasound therapy against cisplatin-resistant cancer. Front. Oncol. 13. https://doi.org/10.3389/fonc.2023.1151613.

Yu, T., Yu, T., Li, X., 2025. Prodrug–carboxypeptidase G2 therapy: Certain concerns on carboxypeptidase G2. Front. Pharmacol. 16. https://doi.org/10.3389/fphar.2025.1560834.

Zhang, B., Chen, M., Zhang, Y., Chen, W., Zhang, L., Chen, L., Sethi, G., 2018. An ultrasonic nanobubble-mediated PNP/fludarabine suicide gene system: A new approach for the treatment of hepatocellular carcinoma. PLoS One 13 (5), e0196686. https://doi.org/10.1371/journal.pone.0196686.

Zhang, N., Yin, Y., Xu, S.J., Chen, W.S., 2008. 5-Fluorouracil: Mechanisms of resistance and reversal strategies. Molecules 13 (8), 1551–1569. https://doi.org/10.3390/molecules13081551China.

Zhang, Q.i., Xiang, G., Zhang, Y., Yang, K., Fan, W.o., Lin, J., Zeng, F., Wu, J., 2006. Increase of doxorubicin sensitivity for folate receptor positive cells when given as the prodrug N-(phenylacetyl) doxorubicin in combination with folate-conjugated PGA. J. Pharmaceut. Sci. 95 (10), 2266–2275. https://doi.org/10.1002/jps.20714.

CHAPTER III

Clinical status, challenges, and future prospectives

An important step in improving cancer treatment outcomes is the successful translation of revolutionary anticancer drug delivery systems from lab research to clinical use. Although many approaches such as targeted drug conjugates and nanoparticle-based systems have shown promising results in preclinical studies, only a few have reached the stage of clinical application. This illuminates the importance of assessing safety, scalability, reproducibility, and patient compatibility along with therapeutic efficacy. Understanding the current clinical status of these systems also allows us to get valuable insight into the real-world performance and the steps needed for broader adoption of these studies. The advancement of anticancer drug delivery systems in a clinical setting, which also incorporates authorized formulations and those being studied in clinical trials, is highlighted in the Unit Clinical Status, Challenges, and Future Prospectives. It also discusses major barriers to clinical translation, including high development costs and challenges in large-scale manufacturing, along with issues related to stability, pharmacokinetics, and targeted delivery. Regulatory considerations play an important role in the development and approval of these systems. Strict requirements for quality, safety, efficacy, and risk management must be met before clinical use. The regulatory framework needs to be continuously updated in order to keep up with the developing technology, mainly in the field of nanomedicine and tailored therapeutics. Overall, future opportunities lie in overcoming the present constraints through transdisciplinary methods, enhanced design tactics, and more flexible regulatory pathways. Precision medicine and scalable manufacturing are given more importance, which helps to speed up clinical translation of novel drug delivery systems, which ultimately leads to closing the gap between clinical practice and research, which helps to develop cancer treatments that are safer, more efficient, and patient-centered.

CHAPTER

30

Clinical status of anticancer drug delivery systems

Dilip Panwar[1,2], *Madhu Sharma*[1], *Neha Agarwal*[1,3], *Avijit Kumar Bakshi*[1,2], *Pratiksha Tiwari*[1,2], *Prabhat Kumar Mishra*[1,3], *Sweety Das*[1,3] *and Prabhat Ranjan Mishra*[1,3]

[1]Division of Pharmaceutics and Pharmacokinetics, CSIR-Central Drug Research Institute, Lucknow, Uttar Pradesh, India; [2]Jawaharlal Nehru University, Delhi, New Delhi, India; [3]Academy of Scientific and Innovation Research (AcSIR), Ghaziabad, Uttar Pradesh, India

Introduction

Conventional cancer drug delivery systems, including oral tablets or intravenous injections, frequently have significant drawbacks of lower therapeutic efficacy as well as high adverse effects in vital organs. The complex biology of cancer, the systemic characteristics of conventional treatments, and the nonspecific distribution of anticancer drugs within the body are major concerns (Ezike et al., 2023). Conventional chemotherapy lacks precise delivery to the target site or selectivity towards anticancer cells, limiting pharmacological and therapeutic outcomes. This often leads to undesirable effects, such as hair loss, digestive disturbances, reduced bone marrow function, and a weakened immune system. Additionally, most anticancer drugs have poor physicochemical and pharmaceutical properties, resulting in low systemic absorption and minimal therapeutic exposure of the drug at the intended site of action. Additionally, tumor cells frequently develop multidrug resistance (MDR) due to overexpression of efflux pump transporters, such as P-glycoprotein, or alteration/dysregulation in key proteins of various cellular pathways, thereby gradually decreasing treatment efficacy and exacerbating the situation (Dong and Mumper, 2010). Conventional delivery systems have short plasma half-lives due to rapid clearance of the drug by hepatic metabolism and renal excretion, necessitating frequent or high-dose

Advanced Cancer Therapeutics
https://doi.org/10.1016/B978-0-443-44185-1.00032-X

administrations that further lead to increased systemic exposure of toxic anticancer drugs. Tumor microenvironment, such as dense extracellular matrix, high interstitial fluid pressure, and irregular vasculature, are other barriers that restricts drug penetration and uniform distribution within solid tumors (Campbell, 2006). All these factors together reduce treatment efficacy, increase organ toxicity (especially in the liver, kidney, heart, and bone marrow), and reduce patient compliance, which compromises treatment results and survival benefits. Modern cancer treatment has started the use of nanocarrier-based delivery systems for improved drug delivery and enhanced anticancer action. These carriers have reduced the unwanted side effects, addressed multidrug resistance, and improved drug pharmaceutical properties, such as solubility, permeability, and stability. It also improved accurate dosing and patient compliance to therapy (Wicki et al., 2015; Sharma et al., 2023). This chapter examines the application of nanotherapeutic approaches in cancer treatment, highlighting both their successful clinical applications and the challenges that limit their broader adoption in clinical practice.

Overview of anticancer drug delivery systems

Anticancer drug delivery systems (DDS) are carriers used to transport a drug to a specific site of the body by regulating the biodistribution and drug release. Nanomedicine for anticancer drug delivery utilizes passive delivery or active delivery through the use of targeting ligands or stimuli-responsive moiety for precise drug delivery. For instance, the release of doxorubicin from a pH-sensitive nanoparticle in response to the acidic pH of the tumor for selective delivery and higher tumor localization (Du et al., 2011; Panwar et al., 2023). It can improve the physicochemical properties of a drug such as solubility, permeability, and chemical stability, biodistribution, and cellular bioavailability, reducing off-target accumulation, systemic exposure, and thus organ toxicity, a crucial factor in the clinical management of cancer (Williams et al., 2013). It reduces overall dose and dosing frequency and simplifies dosing due to regulated drug release, responsible for improved patient adherence to the treatment. It can optimize the therapeutic potential of drugs under realistic and practical conditions, thereby improving their clinical performance.

Various nanocarriers utilized for the delivery of chemotherapeutic drugs consist of protein, lipid, or polymer substrates. Liposomes, consisting mainly of lipids, are spherical vesicles measuring 100–400 nm in diameter for hydrophilic as well as hydrophobic anticancer drugs. Polymer-based nanosystems are more diversified and generally consist of smaller structures ($\leq$100 nm in size) (Tiwari et al., 2024a). Besides, albumin-bound nanoparticles, antibody-drug conjugates (ADCs), and implants or localized DDS are other nanomedicines gaining popularity. Fig. 30.1 describes a range of nanomedicine platforms, such as drug conjugates, liposomes, polymeric carriers, inorganic nanoparticles, and virus-like nanoparticles that are being utilized in clinical cancer treatment. Tables 30.1 and 30.2 provide a comprehensive list of nanotherapeutics and antibody drug conjugates that are currently approved for clinical use. Table 30.3 enlists nanomedicine products that are in clinical studies.

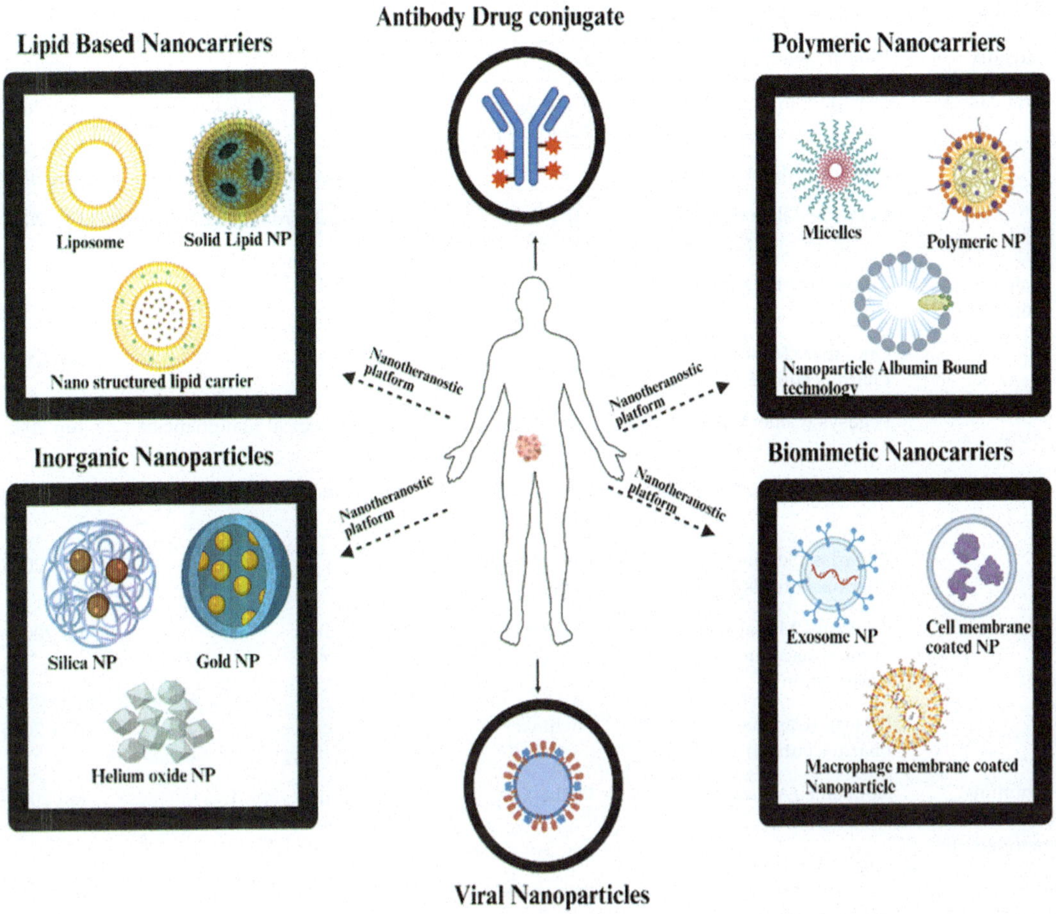

FIGURE 30.1 A range of nanomedicine platforms—Such as drug conjugates, liposomes, polymeric carriers, inorganic nanoparticles, and virus-like nanoparticles—Are being utilized in clinical cancer treatment.

Viral nanoparticles for anticancer drug delivery and clinical status

Viral nanoparticles (VNPs) are gaining attention in cancer treatment due to their ability to deliver genetic material, therapeutic proteins, or cytotoxic agents with high precision. One emerging strategy focuses on exploring tumor-seeking viruses by modulating them to produce or release therapeutic agents directly within the cancer site. Poxviruses such as myxoma and vaccinia preferentially replicate in malignant cells, aided by features such as impaired apoptosis, deregulated proliferation, and immune evasion mechanisms (Kirn and Thorne, 2009; Tiwari et al., 2024b). JX-594 (pexastimogene devacirepvec) is a genetically modified vaccinia virus that selectively replicates in tumor cells through activation of the EGFR–Ras–MAPK pathway and is engineered to express granulocyte colony-stimulating factor (G-CSF) to boost antitumor immunity. In an early intratumoral trial involving patients with primary or metastatic liver cancer, JX-594 led to partial remission in three patients and

TABLE 30.1 Clinically approved nanotherapeutics.

Category	Product [company]	Drug	Indications	Approval
Viral vaccine	Imlygic (BioVex Inc.)	Talimogene laherparepvec	Melanoma	Oct 2015
	Gardasil (Merck and Co.)		HPV-associated cancers	Jun 2006
	Cervarix (GlaxoSmithKline)	HPV16 and HPV18 L1 VLPs	VLPs made from the L1 proteins	Oct 2009
Protein-conjugates	Zinostatin stimalamer (Astellas Pharma Inc.)	Neocarzinostatin	Hepatocellular carcinoma	1994
	Oncaspar (Servier Pharmaceuticals)	L-asparaginase	ALL	Jul 2006
	Pegasys (Genentech)	Peginterferon alfa-2a	Haematological malignancies	Jun 2002
	PegIntron (Merck and Co.)	Peginterferon alfa-2b	Haematological malignancies	Mar 2011
	Asparlas (Servier Pharmaceuticals LLC)	Calaspargase pegol	ALL	Dec 2018
Micelles	Genexol-PM (Samyang Biopharmaceuticals Corporation)	Paclitaxel	Breast cancer	Jul 2006
	Paclical (Oasmia Pharmaceutical)	Paclitaxel	Ovarian cancer	Apr 2015
Albumin-bound nanoparticles	Abraxane (Abraxis BioScience)	Paclitaxel	Breast cancer, NSCLC, Pancreatic cancer	Jan 2005
Inorganic nanoparticles	Ferumoxytol (Feraheme injection, AMAG Pharmaceuticals)	Iron oxide		Jun 2009
	Hensify (Nanobiotix)	Hafnium oxide	Soft tissue sarcoma	Apr 2019
Liposomes	Doxil (Johnson and Johnson)	Doxorubicin	Karposi's sarcoma, Multiple myeloma, and Ovarian cancer	Nov 1995
	Caelyx (Baxter Corporation)	Doxorubicin	Karposi's sarcoma, multiple myeloma, breast and ovarian cancer	Jun 1996
	Lipo-Dox (Taiwan Liposome)	Doxorubicin	Karposi's sarcoma, ovarian and breast cancer	1998
	Myocet (Cheplapharm)	Doxorubicin	Breast cancer	Jul 2000
	Lipodox (Sun Pharmaceuticals)	Doxorubicin	Ovarian, colon, and stomach cancers	Feb 2013

TABLE 30.1 Clinically approved nanotherapeutics.—cont'd

Category	Product [company]	Drug	Indications	Approval
	DaunoXome (Gilead Sciences)	Daunorubicin	Karposi's sarcoma	Aug 1996
	DepoCyt (Pacira)	Cytarabine	Lymphomatous meningitis	Apr 1999
	Mepact (Takeda)	Mifamurtide	Osteosarcoma	Mar 2009
	Vyxeos (Jazz Pharmaceuticals)	Cytarabine and daunorubicin	AML	Aug 2017
	Onivyde (Ipsen Biopharmaceuticals)	Irinotecan	Metastatic pancreatic cancer	Oct 2015
	Onpattro (Alnylam Pharmaceuticals)]	Patisiran	Hereditary transthyretin-mediated amyloidosis	Aug 2018
	Taxol (Bristol-Myers Squibb (BMS))	Paclitaxel	Ovarian and breast cancer	Dec 1992
	Lipusu (Luye Pharmaceutical Co. Ltd.)	Paclitaxel	Ovarian, breast, and non-small-cell lung cancer	2003

disease stabilization in 6, with flu-like symptoms and elevated bilirubin being the main side effects (Park et al., 2008). In a phase I study in 23 patients, intravenous administration of JX-594 in patients with advanced solid tumors demonstrated successful tumor targeting within 24h of exposure, showed dose-related viral replication in 7 of 10 samples, and measurable antitumor activity, while healthy tissues just adjacent to the tumor showed uptake, but no viral replication (Breitbach et al., 2011). This trial provided the first clinical evidence of systemic delivery of an oncolytic virus leading to tumor response.

Viral nanoparticle-based therapeutics have made significant progress in clinical oncology. Oncorine (H101), an adenovirus-based therapy, became the first approved oncolytic virus in China in 2005 for the treatment of head and neck squamous cell carcinoma. It works by selectively replicating in tumor cells with defective p53 pathways, leading to cell lysis (Liang, 2018). The FDA (2015) and EMA approved Talimogene laherparepvec (T-VEC, Imlygic) for unresectable metastatic melanoma, marking another significant milestone. T-VEC is a genetically engineered herpes simplex virus type-1 that not only targets tumor cells but also produces GM-CSF, which stimulates systemic antitumor immunity. Patients were randomly distributed to receive either subcutaneous GM-CSF alone or several intralesional injections of T-VEC, a modified herpes simplex virus type 1 engineered to express GM-CSF, into nonvisceral melanoma lesions. The primary outcome measured was a durable response, defined as either partial or complete tumor regression lasting at least 6 months. In total, 16.3% of patients who received T-VEC achieved a sustained response, compared with only 2.1% in the GM-CSF group (Andtbacka et al., 2019). Furthermore, Bavarian Nordic's Modified Vaccinia Ankara (MVA)-based vectors are currently in Phase II/III trials for prostate cancer and other solid tumors, demonstrating the rising potential of viral platforms in these trials for prostate cancer and other solid tumors, which in turn highlights the increasing potential of viral platforms (Orlova et al., 2022). Additionally, vaccines based

TABLE 30.2 Approved ADCs formulations for clinical use.

ADCs drug	Brand name (company)	Payload	Target	Antibody	Linker	Tumor types	Approval date
Gemtuzumab ozogamicin	Mylotarg (Pfizer)	Calicheamicin	CD33	Gemtuzumab	Hydrazone	Acute myeloid lymphoma	May 2000 Sep 2017
Brentuximab vedotin	Adcetris (Seagen Takeda)	MMAE	CD30	Brentuximab	mc-VC-PABC	Hodgkin Lymphoma	Aug 2011
Trastuzumab emtansine	Kadcyla (Genentech)	DM1	HER2	Trastuzumab	SMCC	Breast cancer	Feb 2013
Inotuzumab ozogamicin	Besponsa (Pfizer)	Calicheamicin	CD22	Inotuzumab	Hydrazone	Acute lymphoblastic leukemia	Jun 2017 (EMA) Aug 2017 (FDA)
Moxetumomab pasudotox	Lumoxiti (AstraZeneca)	PE38	CD22	Moxetumomab	mc–VC–PABC	Hairy Cell Leukemia	Sep 2018
Polatuzumab vedotin	Polivy (Genentech)	MMAE	CD79b	Polatuzumab	mc–VC–PABC	Diffuse Large B-Cell Lymphoma	Jun 2019
Trastuzumab deruxtecan	Enhertu (AstraZeneca, Daiichi Sankyo)	DXD	HER2	Trastuzumab	tetrapeptide	Breast cancer	Dec 2019
Enfortumab vedotin	Padcev (Astellas, Seagen)	MMAE	Nectin-4	Enfortumab	mc–VC–PABC	Urothelial Cancer	Dec 2019
Sacituzumab govitecan	Trodelvy (Gilead Sciences)	SN-38	TROP2	Sacituzumab	CL2A	Breast cancer, Urothelial Cancer	Apr 2020
Disitamab vedotin	Aidixi (RemeGen)	MMAE	HER2	Disitamab	mc–VC–PABC	Gastric cancer UC	Jun 2021 (NMPA)
Loncastuximab tesirine	Zynlonta (ADCs Therapeutics)	PBD SG3199	CD19	Loncastuximab	mc–VC–PABC	Diffuse Large B-Cell Lymphoma	Apr 2021
Tisotumab vedotin	Tivdak (Seagen)	MMAE	TF	Tisotumab	mc–VC–PABC	Cervical cancer	Sep 2021
Mirvetuximab soravtansine	Elahere (ImmunoGen)	DM4	FRα	Mirvetuximab	Sulfo-SPDB	Ovarian cancer	Nov 2022

TABLE 30.3 Investigational nanomedicines in clinical development.

Formulation	NCT no.	Drug	Indication	Phase	Study type	References
Liposomes	NCT01158079	ALN-VSP02	Solid Tumor	Phase I	-	Tabernero et al. (2013)
	NCT01262235	TKM-080301	Solid Tumor or lymphoma	Phase II	Non-Randomized	A Dose Finding Study of TKM-080301 Infusion in Neuroendocrine Tumors (NET) and Adrenocortical Carcinoma (ACC) Patients (2019)
	NCT00938574	Atu027 (siRNA)	Solid Tumor	Phase I	Dose finding	Schultheis et al. (2014)
	NCT00024492	Mitoxantrone	Solid Tumor	Phase I	Randomized	Study of Liposome Encapsulated Mitoxantrone (LEM) in Patients With Advanced Cancer (2011)
	NCT01151384	Docetaxel	Solid Tumor	Phase I	Non-Randomized	Deeken et al. (2013)
	NCT06632574	Paclitaxel	Solid Tumor	Phase I	-	A Clinical Study of Paclitaxel Cationic Liposomes for the Treatment of Patients With Advanced Solid Tumors (2024)
	NCT00703170	Temsirolimus and Doxorubicin	Resistant Solid Malignancies	Phase I	-	Phase I Study of DOXIL and Temsirolimus in Resistant Solid Malignancies (2013)
	NCT03088813	Irinotecan	Small Cell Lung Cancer	Phase III	Randomized	Spigel et al. (2024)
	NCT04258631	Bupivacaine with or without Hydromorphone	Gynaecological Malignancies	Phase IV	Randomized	Liposomal Bupivacaine With or Without Hydromorphone for the Improvement of Pain Control After Laparotomy in Patients With Gynecological Malignancies (2024)
	NCT05429008	HMPL-A83	Advanced Malignant Neoplasm	Phase I	-	A Phase I Clinical Study of HMPL-A83 in Patients With Advanced Malignant Neoplasm (2025)
	NCT00024232	huJ591	Progressive Androgen-Independent Prostate Cancer	Phase II	-	Monoclonal Antibody Therapy in Treating Patients With Prostate Cancer (2013)

(*Continued*)

TABLE 30.3 Investigational nanomedicines in clinical development.—cont'd

Formulation	NCT no.	Drug	Indication	Phase	Study type	References
	NCT04895137	mFOLFOX6+ Bevacizumab + PD-1	Colorectal Cancer	Phase II		Das et al. (2015)
	NCT00051597	SGN-30	Hematologic Malignancies	Phase II	Non-Randomized	Bartlett et al. (2008)
	NCT00014495	Cytarabine and Bismuth-213-Labeled HuM195	Myeloid Malignancies	Phase II	-	Rosenblat et al. (2010)
Polymeric micelles	NCT01644890	NK 105 (Paclitaxel)	Metastatic Pancreatic Cancer	Phase III	-	Fujiwara et al. (2019)
	NCT01770795	Gemcitabine	Non-small-cell Lung Cancer	Phase II	-	Saif et al. (2010)
	NCT01426126	Gemcitabine and Platinum	Urothelial Cancer	Phase II	Non-Randomized	Lee et al. (2012)
Albumin-bound nanoparticle (nab)	NCT02646319	Rapamycin	Advanced cancer with mTOR mutations	Phase I	-	Nanoparticle Albumin-Bound Rapamycin in Treating Patients With Advanced Cancer With mTOR Mutations (2019)
	NCT03304210	Paclitaxel (PIPAC Nab-pac)	Stomach, Pancreas, Breast, Ovarian Cancer	Phase II	Randomized	Ceelen et al. (2022)
	NCT02392637	Gemcitabine, Cisplatin, Paclitaxel	Metastatic Biliary Cancer	Phase II	-	Shroff et al. (2019)
	NCT00629499	Paclitaxel Cyclophosphamide	Early-Stage Breast Cancer	Phase II	Non-Randomized	Yardley et al. (2010)
	NCT00662129	Paclitaxel Gemcitabine Bevacizumab	Metastatic Breast Cancer	Phase II		Northfelt et al. (2011)

Cancer vaccines	NCT00110695	Paclitaxel 5-Fluorouracil Epirubicin	Breast Cancer	Phase II	-	Robidoux et al. (2010)
	NCT00625456	JX-594 (pexastimogene devacirepvec)	Solid Tumor	Phase I	Dose escalation	Park et al. (2008)
	NCT00643097	Cyclophosphamide Temozolomide Sargramostim	Glioblastoma Multiforme	Phase II	Non-Randomized	Vaccine Therapy in Treating Patients With Newly Diagnosed Glioblastoma Multiforme (ACTIVATe) (2017)
	NCT03359239	Atezolizumab	Urothelial Cancer	Phase I	-	Saxena et al. (2025)
	NCT03639714	Nivolumab Ipilimumab	Non-small-cell lung, colorectal, urothelial, gastresophageal cancer		-	Palmer et al. (2022)
Cyclodextrins	NCT02055716	Sulforadex Alpha-cyclodextrin	Prostate Cancer	Phase I	-	Sulforadex in Healthy Human Males MAD (2015)
	NCT02769962	Camptothecin Olaparib	Small Cell Lung Cancer	Phase I and Phase II	Non-Randomized	Schmidt et al. (2020)
	NCT03138967	Rocuronium Sugammadex Neostigmine Glycopyrrolate	Bladder Cancer	Phase IV	Non-Randomized	*Investigation of Sugammadex in Outpatient Urological Procedures* (2020)
	NCT03039543	Rocuronium Sugammadex	Malignant Neoplasm of Urinary Tract	Phase IV	Non-Randomized	Koo et al. (2016)

on virus-like particles (VLPs), such as Cervarix and Gardasil, have received widespread approval to prevent cervical and other HPV-associated malignancies. These vaccinations demonstrate the safety and clinical utility of VNP-based approaches in oncology, primarily as preventive measures (de Sanjosé et al., 2007). VNP-based therapies hold great promise as direct oncolytic drug delivery and cancer immunotherapy delivery systems. The T-VEC, Oncorine, and HPV vaccines' clinical success to date offers strong support for the creation of more sophisticated viral nanoparticle delivery systems in the future for targeted anticancer treatment.

Synthetic polymer-based therapeutics and clinical status

Synthetic polymers have emerged as effective tools in cancer therapy, offering superior pharmacokinetics, specific tumor targeting, and lower systemic toxicity than conventional medicines. They can function as carriers, conjugates, or micelle-forming systems, enabling the regulated and site-specific administration of anticancer drugs. Ruth Duncan defined "polymer therapeutics" as polymeric pharmaceuticals with intrinsic activity, polymer-drug and polymer-protein conjugates, polymeric micelles with covalently linked medications, and polyplexes designed as nonviral gene delivery vectors (Duncan et al., 2006). These systems are often composed of hydrophilic polymers, which can be chemically modified into complex or well-defined structures to enhance drug delivery. One of the first methods was PEGylation, which involves attaching polyethylene glycol (PEG) to proteins or drugs to reduce immunogenicity and increase circulation time. This method, which was initially applied to proteins, was later adapted for small compounds such as irinotecan, paclitaxel, docetaxel, and camptothecin. Furthermore, synthetic polymers such as N-(2-hydroxypropyl) methacrylamide (HPMA) attracted attention due to their small nanoscale size (5–100 nm), which allows for rapid clearance through renal or hepatobiliary pathways (Duncan, 2003). Ideally, nanoscale conjugates accumulate in tumors due to enhanced permeability and retention (EPR) effects. Once internalized by endocytosis, the linker is broken down by the lysosomal enzymes and releases the therapeutic drug within the cell. The increase in applications is evident, as demonstrated by the development of biodegradable and nonbiodegradable copolymers in pharmaceutical pipelines. CRLX101 (camptothecin, Cerulean Pharma Inc.) is one of the most clinically advanced examples of a polymer–drug conjugate. A cyclodextrin-based polymer-drug conjugate formulation of camptothecin (topoisomerase I inhibitor) is currently in a late-stage of clinical trial. In addition to recurrent ovarian and advanced rectal cancers, it has been studied for several cancers, including advanced or metastatic gastric, gastro-oesophageal, and esophageal cancers. Cyclodextrin-based nanoparticles were used to deliver camptothecin to patients with advanced solid tumors in a phase 2 clinical study (CRLX-101). The formulation achieved a 64% overall response rate and showed a lower incidence of side effects when compared with free camptothecin. By reducing systemic toxicity and increasing camptothecin's therapeutic efficacy, the polymer–drug conjugate design makes CRLX101 a viable option for polymer-based anticancer treatment (Sanoff et al., 2019).

Polymer–protein conjugates operate in the same way based on the principle of polymer–drug conjugates, but the therapeutic component is a protein rather than a small molecule drug. A notable early successful example is Zinostatin stimalamer (SMANCS, Yamanouchi), which uses a poly (styrene-co-maleic acid) polymer as a carrier for neocarzinostatin, a DNA-damaging protein. Approved in Japan for hepatocellular carcinoma, SMANCS demonstrated improved plasma half-life, reduced bone marrow toxicity, and greater tumor accumulation compared with the free protein drug (Maeda, 2001). Another widely used example is Oncaspar (pegaspargase, Enzon/Sigma-Tau), a PEGylated form of E. coli L-asparaginase, indicated for acute lymphoblastic leukemia (ALL). PEGylation enhanced the clinical utility of L-asparaginase by reducing its hypersensitivity risks and lowering the dosing frequency from multiple times per week to once every 2 weeks (Graham, 2003). PEGylated Interferon-α, marketed as Pegasys and PegIntron, employs polyethylene glycol (PEG) as the polymer component. While these formulations were originally approved for the treatment of viral infections such as hepatitis B and C, they have also been explored in the context of hematological malignancies (Hehlmann et al., 2003). The attachment of PEG increases the stability and circulation time of interferon-α, allowing for less frequent dosing compared with the native protein. This outcome demonstrates the broader utility of PEGylation in enhancing the pharmacokinetics of anticancer drugs, reducing their immunogenicity, and promoting better patient compliance. A further advancement in polymer-protein conjugates is Calaspargase pegol (SC-PEG), which utilizes a succinimidyl carbonate linker instead of the traditional succinate for attaching the protein to PEG. This structural modification yields a more stable formulation, providing extended enzymatic activity and prolonged asparagine release in pediatric ALL patients, while maintaining comparable pharmacokinetic, pharmacodynamic, and toxicity profiles to the Oncaspar (Angiolillo et al., 2014).

Amphiphilic polymers can spontaneously form micelles in aqueous environments, consisting of a hydrophobic core surrounded by a hydrophilic shell. Depending on solubility and affinity, a drug can be positioned in different regions of the micelle. However, most poorly soluble drugs are encapsulated within the hydrophobic core, while hydrophilic drugs are typically encapsulated within the hydrophilic shell. Commonly used hydrophobic polymers include polyesters, polyethers, and poly (β-amino esters), while PEG is widely used for the hydrophilic shell (Sutton et al., 2007). A well-known example is Pluronic, a triblock copolymer composed of PEG and poly (propylene oxide) in a PEG-PPO-PEG arrangement (Kabanov et al., 2002). Polymeric micelles are attractive drug carriers because of their small size (5–100 nm), ability to encapsulate large amounts of hydrophobic drugs, and extended circulation half-life compared with free drugs. For instance, Genexol-PM (IG-100; Samyang Biopharm), a paclitaxel formulation free of Cremophor EL, reduces severe side effects such as hypersensitivity, hyperlipidemia, and peripheral neuropathy. It is approved in South Korea for metastatic breast cancer (MBC) and is under phase II trials for advanced NSCLC (Ahn et al., 2014). Several other polymeric micelle-based formulations are progressing through clinical development. Paclical (Oasmia Pharmaceutical), a paclitaxel micelle formulation, has received orphan drug designation for ovarian cancer by the US FDA. Similarly, Livatag [Doxorubicin Transdrug (BioAlliance Pharma)], based on biodegradable polyalkylcyanoacrylate nanospheres, was granted orphan status for hepatocellular carcinoma by the EU and later by the FDA. Both Paclical and Doxorubicin Transdrug are currently being evaluated in phase III clinical trials (Barraud et al., 2005). NK105 is a polymeric micelle formulation of paclitaxel, constructed using a poly (ethylene glycol)-poly (aspartate) block copolymer. It has progressed to phase III clinical trials for the treatment of gastric and breast cancers. By encapsulating paclitaxel within micelles, NK105 improves its solubility and changes its pharmacokinetic profile, which causes more efficient tumor delivery (Fujiwara et al., 2019). Additionally, this formulation helps reduce hypersensitivity reactions commonly associated with conventional paclitaxel formulations that require Cremophor EL as a solvent. Thus, NK105 represents a significant advancement in polymer-based nanotherapeutics, offering enhanced therapeutic efficacy while reducing systemic toxicity.

Natural protein and peptide nanocarriers and clinical status

Human serum albumin (HSA) has become an important DDS for clinical application due to its natural abundance, biocompatibility, and unique multiple binding sites for both endogenous and exogenous compounds, as well as the ability to associate with metal ions and form complexes. HSA serves as a versatile platform for therapeutic delivery. One of the earliest applications was the development of 99mTc-labeled albumin, used as a γ-emitting imaging agent for the detection of primary tumors and metastases in nuclear medicine (Elsadek and Kratz, 2012). Albumin-based drug conjugates exploit the natural transport pathways of albumin, which facilitate preferential tumor accumulation. Through binding to the gp60 receptor on endothelial cells, albumin undergoes transcytosis across the tumor vasculature. Once in the tumor microenvironment, albumin–drug complexes are retained by SPARC (Secreted Protein Acidic and Rich in Cysteine), resulting in enhanced drug deposition within the extracellular tumor space. In oncology, albumin-bound nanoparticles (nabs) were introduced to overcome the toxicities of solvent-based drug formulations. The most notable example is nab-paclitaxel (Abraxane, ABI-007; Abraxis/Celgene), approved by the FDA in 2005 for metastatic breast cancer (MBC) and subsequently in many countries. By avoiding Cremophor EL, nab-paclitaxel reduces hypersensitivity reactions and demonstrates improved tolerability, though neuropathy remains a concern in some patients. Clinical trials have also shown superior efficacy compared with solvent-based formulations, such as Taxotere (Yamamoto et al., 2011). Its indications have since expanded to non-small-cell lung cancer (NSCLC), pancreatic cancer, melanoma, and head and neck cancers. Beyond paclitaxel, other albumin-based formulations are under active development. Nab-docetaxel is in clinical evaluation for gastroesophageal junction adenocarcinoma, aiming to replicate the safety and delivery benefits of nab-paclitaxel (Wang et al., 2024). Additionally, several albumin–drug conjugates are advancing through early-phase trials, including rapamycin (mTOR inhibitor), 17-AAG (HSP90 inhibitor), and INNO-206 (a doxorubicin prodrug). These studies highlight the versatility of albumin as a drug carrier, reinforcing its role as a clinically validated and promising strategy for cancer therapy (Elsadek and Kratz, 2012).

Inorganic nanoparticles and clinical status

Inorganic nanoparticles have emerged as a valuable tool in cancer treatment due to their distinct physical and chemical properties, including large surface areas, structural stability, and the capacity to support multiple functions, such as in vivo imaging, targeted drug delivery, and heat- or radiation-based therapy (Kim et al., 2018). Gold, silica, iron oxide, and calcium phosphate nanoparticles are among the most widely studied nanoparticles for both diagnostic and therapeutic applications. Their natural tendency to accumulate within tumor tissue through the EPR effect, together with the flexibility to modify their surfaces with various ligands, positions them as promising platforms for advancing cancer therapeutics (Song et al., 2022). Ferumoxytol (Feraheme) is regarded as one of the most successful inorganic nanoparticle formulations in clinical use. It is an FDA-approved iron oxide nanoparticle originally developed for managing iron-deficiency anaemia. Although it does not carry formal approval for anticancer therapy, ferumoxytol has been investigated in several clinical studies as a tumor-imaging agent and as an immunomodulatory platform, which indicates that it may promote macrophage-driven antitumor activity (Toth et al., 2017). Another exciting example is AuroLase, a gold-silica nanoshell inorganic nanoparticle consisting of a silica core and a gold shell coated with PEG, developed for photothermal therapy. In this approach, nanoparticles are administered intravenously, and when they accumulate in tumors, near-infrared (NIR) light is used to activate them, generating heat and leading to localized tumor destruction (Riley and Day, 2017). AuroLase has progressed through the early stages of clinical evaluation in patients with head and neck cancers, where it has shown both a favorable safety profile and practical feasibility. Hafnium oxide nanoparticles (NBTXR3, Nanobiotix) represent another milestone in this field. NBTXR3 is designed as a radioenhancer, accumulating in tumor tissues and amplifying the effects of radiotherapy. Phase 2-3 randomized trial involving 176 patients compared NBTXR3 plus radiotherapy with radiotherapy alone. The primary endpoint was pathological complete response. The NBTXR3 group showed a significantly higher rate of complete response (16% vs. 8% in the radiotherapy-alone group) (Bagley et al., 2022). It received European approval in 2019 under the name Hensify for the treatment of locally advanced soft tissue sarcoma, making it one of the first inorganic nanoparticle-based systems approved specifically for cancer therapy. Clinical studies are also ongoing in other indications, including head and neck squamous cell carcinoma and hepatocellular carcinoma (Bonvalot et al., 2019). Other inorganic nanocarriers, such as mesoporous silica nanoparticles, calcium phosphate-based systems, and quantum dots, are currently under preclinical and clinical evaluation for use in drug delivery and imaging applications. These platforms are being explored for loading chemotherapeutics, siRNA, or targeted ligands to achieve precise delivery and minimize systemic toxicity (Pugazhendhi et al., 2018).

Liposomal drug delivery systems and clinical status

Liposomes are composed of an aqueous core enclosed by one or more phospholipid bilayers. They are both biocompatible and biodegradable, capable of encapsulating water-soluble drugs within their inner cavity, while incorporating water-insoluble drugs into the lipid layers. Depending on the size and number of bilayers, liposomes can exist as small unilamellar vesicles, large unilamellar vesicles, or multilamellar vesicles (Bozzuto and Molinari, 2015). First introduced in the late 1960s, liposomes have undergone continuous development to improve the delivery of poorly soluble small molecules while minimizing their toxicity (Allen and Cullis, 2013). Advancements in technology allow efficient drug loading into liposomes and precise control over their drug release rate. The rapid clearance issues of conventional liposomes, which are mainly caused by the immune system, have been significantly reduced through PEGylation of their surface (Allen and Cullis, 2013; Kumar et al., 2023). The main advantage of PEGylation is that it prolongs the circulation time of liposomes in the blood by preventing opsonization and degradation by reticuloendothelial system (RES) components, such as hepatocytes and Kupffer cells. Compared with conventional liposomes, PEGylated versions exhibit a longer half-life, reduced plasma clearance, smaller distribution volume, and improved tumor accumulation (as discussed by Milla et al.) (Milla et al., 2012). Despite the growing number of liposomal anticancer formulations being developed, only a limited few have received approval for use in cancer therapy. Although the potential of liposome technology has been significantly enhanced, further combining it with advancements such as gene editing and biosensing is expected to lead to significant developments in fields such as immunotherapy and vaccines (Kulkarni et al., 2018). The COVID-19 mRNA vaccine is a well-known example, in which liposomes serve as vital mRNA carriers (Hou et al., 2022). In the future, liposomes are expected to play a more significant role in cutting-edge medical applications, such as gene therapy, immune regulation, and personalized therapies. The EPR effect in tumors is generally created from their abnormal blood vessels, which have larger gaps between the endothelial cells than normal tissues, allowing nanoparticles under 200 nm to cross the endothelium more easily. Combined with poor lymphatic drainage, this leads to prolonged retention of macromolecules at tumor sites. First described by Maeda in 1986, the EPR effect plays a key role in concentrating nanoparticle-based therapies, such as liposomal paclitaxel or camptothecin, within tumors, thereby improving treatment effectiveness (Maeda, 1989).

Liposomal doxorubicin is one of the most well-known and widely used examples in clinical practice, particularly valued for its ability to reduce cardiotoxicity. The PEGylated form [PLD; marketed as Caelyx, Doxil (Johnson and Johnson), and Lipo-Dox (Taiwan Liposome)] has received approval in Europe for treating Kaposi's sarcoma, ovarian cancer, multiple myeloma, and metastatic breast cancer (MBC) (Duggan et al., 2011). The non-PEGylated formulation [Myocet (Cephalon)] is approved in the EU and Canada for MBC in combination with cyclophosphamide (Leonard et al., 2009). These liposomal formulations are engineered to raise drug levels within tumor tissue by exploiting the enhanced permeability of tumor blood vessels, while remaining largely restricted in healthy organs such as the heart, where the vascular barrier is intact. Both PEGylated and non-PEGylated liposomal doxorubicin exhibit slower blood clearance than standard doxorubicin; however, the non-PEGylated versions are more readily taken up by cells of the mononuclear phagocyte system. Clinically, PLD offers comparable efficacy to other monotherapies but with reduced cardiac and hematologic toxicity, though skin reactions may occur due to drug build-up in the skin. In contrast, Myocet is associated with fewer skin side effects but can cause significant hematologic toxicity, often linked to higher administered doses than those typically used in routine practice (Leonard et al., 2009). In addition to liposomal doxorubicin, several other liposomal formulations of anticancer and therapeutic agents have been approved for more specific indications. These include daunorubicin [DaunoXome (Galen)] for Kaposi's sarcoma (Petre and Dittmer, 2007), cytarabine [DepoCyt (Pacira)] for lymphomatous meningitis (Chhikara and Parang, 2010), and the immunomodulator mifamurtide [Mepact (Takeda)] for pediatric osteosarcoma (Frampton et al., 2010). Other approvals comprise doxorubicin [Lipodox (Sun Pharmaceuticals)] for ovarian, colon, and stomach cancers (Smith et al., 2016); a combination of cytarabine and daunorubicin [Vyxeos (Jazz

Pharmaceuticals)] for certain types of acute myeloid leukemia (Tzogani et al., 2020); irinotecan [Onivyde (Ipsen Biopharmaceuticals)] for metastatic pancreatic cancer (Passero et al., 2016); and patisiran [Onpattro (Alnylam Pharmaceuticals)] for hereditary transthyretin-mediated amyloidosis (Akinc et al., 2019) many anticancer agents embedded in liposomes have been subjected to clinical trials.

Most liposomal formulations generally exhibit improved tolerability compared with their free-drug counterparts; however, their therapeutic performance has often fallen short of expectations. A possible explanation for this reduced efficacy is the limited release of the encapsulated drug at or near its target site within cells. One potential strategy to enhance tumor drug delivery involves using cationic liposomes, which can interact with the negatively charged endothelial cells of tumor-associated neovasculature, thereby promoting cellular uptake (Awada et al., 2014). Various approaches have been investigated to increase the internalization of DDS, including the use of fusogenic lipids or any other membrane components that facilitate the fusion of liposomal membranes with the cell's plasma membrane, thereby improving the cellular penetration (Allen and Cullis, 2013). Another promising method is the use of receptor-mediated endocytosis, which offers greater selectivity, enhanced drug uptake, and the potential to bypass drug resistance. Significant progress has been made in developing ligand-targeted liposomes, starting with immunoliposomes that incorporate monoclonal antibodies or their fragments on the liposome surface. However, the clinical use of immunoliposomes remains limited, with most evidence coming from early-phase studies—for instance, phase I trials of anti-EGFR doxorubicin immunoliposomes employing cetuximab antigen-binding fragments as targeting ligands (Penel et al., 2012).

The first reported clinical trial of targeted liposomes tested GAH-coated, doxorubicin-loaded immunoliposomes (MCC-465) in individuals with metastatic gastric cancer. GAH, a human monoclonal antibody, binds to over 90% of gastric cancer cases (Hamaguchi et al., 2004). Treatment was administered at 3-week intervals for up to six cycles, with myelosuppression identified as the primary dose-limiting side effect. Among 18 patients assessable for response, 10 achieved disease stabilization, though no complete or partial remissions were recorded. Lipid-based nanocarriers are being actively explored for the systemic delivery of nucleic acids and other molecules with inherently short plasma half-lives (Li and Rana, 2014). While no such formulation has yet received clinical approval, early human trials have demonstrated the practicality and therapeutic potential of delivering siRNA (RNA interference) using lipid nanocarriers (Coelho et al., 2013). Several clinical studies in solid tumors have been completed, including NCT01158079 (Phase I) targeting kinesin spindle protein (KSP) and vascular endothelial growth factor (VEGF), NCT01262235 (Phase II) targeting polo-like kinase 1 (PLK1), and NCT00938574 (Phase I) targeting PKN3, a protein kinase C–related molecule in vascular endothelium. To date, several liposome-based nanocarrier platforms have entered clinical evaluation for delivering regulatory nucleic acids, aiming either to silence oncogenes such as Myc, c-Raf, and Bcl-2, or to restore tumor suppressors such as p53 and Fus1. One example, EphA2-siRNA-DOPC—a neutral lipid nanoliposome encapsulating siRNA against EphA2—is currently undergoing a Phase I trial in patients with ovarian cancer and other solid tumors (Wagner et al., 2017). A promising lipid-based strategy under preclinical investigation is squalenoylation technique, in which anticancer agents such as doxorubicin are covalently linked to the natural lipid squalene

(Maksimenko et al., 2014). This modification enables the conjugates to self-assemble in aqueous environments into nanoassemblies with distinctive features, including a high drug-loading capacity and extended circulation time in the body. In a mouse model of pancreatic cancer, squalene–doxorubicin nanoassemblies were able to reduce the tumor size by approximately 95%, compared with only 29% with free doxorubicin.

Antibody-drug conjugate and clinical status

Conventional cancer therapy, including chemotherapy and radiotherapy, is often limited because of significant side effects and suboptimal activity. To overcome these limitations, researchers have developed a new class of DDS known as antibody-drug conjugates (ADCs), which combine improved safety profiles and greater targeting precision (Li et al., 2021). The U.S. Food and Drug Administration (FDA) approved the first ADCs-based cancer therapy in 2000 with the introduction of Mylotarg, designed for acute myeloid leukemia (AML) patients who have to meet specific criteria—first relapse, age over 60, CD33-positive status, and unsuitability for standard cytotoxic chemotherapy (Norsworthy et al., 2018). Since then, the number of approved ADCs has grown to 13, as shown in- Table 30.2 below, with more than 100 candidates currently in different phases of clinical development (Fu et al., 2022).

An antibody-drug conjugates (ADCs) consists of three main components: a human-derived monoclonal antibody, a chemical linker, and a highly potent cytotoxic payload. The antibody recognizes and attaches to specific antigens present on the surface of target cells, leading to internalization through endocytosis. After internalization, the ADCs moves from early endosomes to lysosomes, where the acidic environment and lysosomal enzymes break down the ADCs (Fig. 30.2). This breakdown releases the active cytotoxic payload into

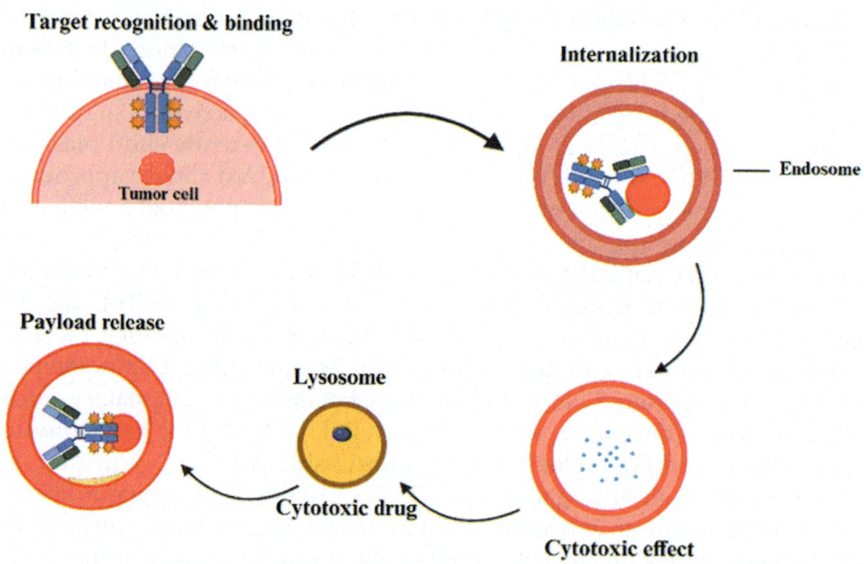

FIGURE 30.2 Intracellular metabolism of ADCs: A schematic diagram.

the cytoplasm, allowing it to act on intracellular targets such as DNA or microtubules. This causes disruption of essential cellular processes, leads to cell-cycle arrest, and ultimately induces programmed cell death (Tsuchikama and An, 2018). In ADCs, the drug-to-antibody ratio (DAR) is a key quality parameter for antibody–drug conjugates, reflecting the average number of cytotoxic payload molecules attached to each antibody. Increasing the DAR can enhance the cytotoxic potential of an ADCs; however, excessively high loading often increases hydrophobicity, promoting aggregation and accelerating clearance from the circulation, which can reduce its treatment efficacy. For this reason, establishing an appropriate DAR is essential to balance efficacy and safety. In practice, many clinically successful ADCs exhibit an average DAR between 2 and 4 (*Antibody-Drug Conjugates (ADCs) and Drug–Antibody Ratio (DAR)*, 2024).

The approval of Orthoclone (OKT3) in 1992 marked a major milestone in the treatment of haematological cancers and opened the door to the development of effective antibody-based therapies. In 2000, the FDA authorized gemtuzumab ozogamicin (GO) [Mylotarg (Pfizer/Wyeth)], an anti-CD33 monoclonal antibody coupled to a calicheamicin derivative, for patients with CD33-positive acute myeloid leukemia (AML). About a decade later, GO was withdrawn from the U.S. market after clinical data showed limited benefit. Later studies demonstrated that using a fractionated dosing schedule improves treatment outcomes and reduces toxicity, allowing higher cumulative doses to be given safely (Castaigne et al., 2012). Clinical studies such as MyloFrance-1 and AML-19 further assessed gemtuzumab ozogamicin in patients with CD33-positive AML. MyloFrance-1 reported some significant toxicities but also demonstrated therapeutic benefit when using a 3 mg/m^2 dosing schedule on days 1, 4, and 7. In contrast, AML-19 showed that treatment with GO improved overall survival in older patients unsuitable for intensive chemotherapy, with side effects that remained within a manageable range (Norsworthy et al., 2018; Amadori et al., 2016). These findings led the FDA to reapprove the GO in 2017 (Appelbaum and Bernstein, 2017). In paediatric AML patients, the AAML0531 trial also showed improved efficacy with GO treatment (Lamba et al., 2017). Moreover, further evidence indicates that GO enhances outcomes in newly diagnosed CD33-positive AML, particularly in intermediate-risk cases (Awada et al., 2023). When used alongside standard chemotherapy, it improves event-free survival in younger patients and enhances overall survival in individuals with NPM1 or FLT3 mutations, reinforcing its safety and therapeutic benefit at the time of initial AML diagnosis. Brentuximab vedotin (BV), developed by Seagen (formerly Seattle Genetics) in collaboration with Takeda, was the second antibody–drug conjugate to receive regulatory approval. It consists of a chimeric IgG1 monoclonal antibody that binds to the CD30 antigen, linked through a cleavable mc–VC–PABC dipeptide linker to the cytotoxic agent monomethyl auristatin E (MMAE), a potent microtubule inhibitor. BV is designed to specifically target CD30-expressing cancers, such as Hodgkin lymphoma and anaplastic large cell lymphoma (ALCL) (Nikolaenko and Nademanee, 2020).

Clinical studies have shown that brentuximab vedotin (BV) improves outcomes in cutaneous T-cell lymphomas, reducing symptoms without affecting quality of life (Horwitz et al., 2021). In 2018, the FDA approved BV with CHP for untreated systemic ALCL and other CD30-positive peripheral T-cell lymphomas (PTCLs) (Richardson et al., 2019). Real-world data (2020–22) reported a 64.5% response rate, with 12-month PFS (Progression-Free Survival) and OS (overall survival) at 77.2% and 79.9%, respectively, and neutropenia as the most common side effect (Zhang et al., 2023). In HIV-related HL, BV combined with chemotherapy achieved 100% complete remission, with 2-year PFS of 87% and OS of 92% (Rubinstein et al., 2023). Trastuzumab–emtansine (T-DM1), marketed as Kadcyla, is an FDA-approved antibody–drug conjugate for HER2-positive metastatic breast cancer. It combines trastuzumab with the microtubule inhibitor DM1, enabling targeted HER2 therapy while inducing apoptosis through microtubule disruption (Ballantyne and Dhillon, 2013). Approved in 2013, T-DM1 continues to be evaluated in phase II/III trials for early-stage HER2-positive breast and gastric cancers, showing strong antitumor activity, especially in patients with high HER2 expression (Miller et al., 2014). Inotuzumab ozogamicin (InO) is an ADCs targeting CD22 on B cells, where it delivers the cytotoxic agent calicheamicin to induce DNA damage and apoptosis. When compared with conventional chemotherapy, phase III trials have demonstrated greater recovery rates, longer cure periods, and improved quality of life in patients with relapsed or refractory acute lymphoblastic leukemia (ALL) (*Profile of inotuzumab ozogamicin and its potential in the treatment of acute lymphoblastic leukemia*, 2014). Moxetumomab pasudotox (MP), FDA-approved in 2018, is a CD22-targeting recombinant immunotoxin for the treatment of relapsed or refractory hairy cell leukemia patients with multiple prior therapies. In a Phase III trial, it produced long-lasting results with controllable safety, achieving a 75% overall response and a 41% total remission. It marked the first new HCL therapy in over 20 years (Kreitman et al., 2021).

Polatuzumab vedotin (PV), an ADCs targeting CD79b with MMAE (Monomethyl auristatin E) as a cytotoxic agent, is approved for relapsed/refractory DLBCL (Diffuse Large B-Cell Lymphoma) along with other therapies such as bendamustine and rituximab after multiple therapies. Clinical studies showed ~59% ORR (objective response rate), 46% CR (Complete Response), and improved survival, with neutropenia and fatigue as key side effects, supporting its role as an effective option for patients who are not eligible for transplants (Budde et al., 2024). Enfortumab vedotin (EV), an ADCs targeting Nectin-4, delivers MMAE to urothelial carcinoma cells, causing microtubule disruption and apoptosis. The FDA approved EV plus pembrolizumab (P) as first-line therapy for cisplatin-ineligible advanced cases. Trials showed strong tumor shrinkage, pain reduction, and preserved quality of life, with both EV + P and EV alone proving effective options (Milowsky et al., 2024). Trastuzumab deruxtecan (T-DXd) is an ADCs combining trastuzumab with a topoisomerase I inhibitor, offering a stronger bystander effect than T-DM1(Ogitani et al., 2016). The FDA approved it for HER2-positive metastatic breast cancer after prior anti-HER2 therapies and later for HER2-low breast cancer. DESTINY trials showed significant survival benefits over standard treatments, with manageable safety despite more grade $\geq$3 adverse events (André et al., 2023). Sacituzumab govitecan (SG) is a Trop-2–targeting ADCs carrying SN-38 through a CL2A (PEG8-and triazole-containing PABC-peptide-mc) linker with a high drug-to-antibody ratio, designed to limit off-target toxicity (Zaman et al., 2019). The FDA granted it accelerated approval in April 2020 for adults with metastatic triple-negative breast cancer (TNBC) after at least two prior therapies (Syed, 2020). Disitamab vedotin (RC48) is a HER2-targeted ADCs linking a humanized HER2 antibody to MMAE through a cleavable linker (Jiang et al., 2020). In June 2021, it became the first ADCs approved in China, authorized for HER2-positive locally advanced or metastatic gastric cancer (including gastroesophageal junction adenocarcinoma) after at least two prior treatments (Deeks, 2021). Loncastuximab tesirine (LT) is a CD19-targeted ADCs carrying a pyrrolobenzodiazepine toxin through a cleavable linker. It is approved for relapsed or refractory large B-cell lymphoma (LBCL), including DLBCL and high-grade subtypes, after two or more prior therapies (Lee, 2021). Tisotumab vedotin (TV) is a tissue factor (TF)-targeting ADCs linked to MMAE, approved for recurrent or metastatic cervical cancer after chemotherapy (Markham, 2021). TF overexpression in multiple solid tumors makes TV a promising targeted therapy option. Mirvetuximab soravtansine (MIRV) is a folate receptor α (FRα)-targeting ADCs linked to a microtubule-disrupting agent, approved for FRα-positive, platinum-resistant ovarian, fallopian tube, and primary peritoneal cancers after one to three prior therapies (Heo, 2023). ADCs have advanced from first-generation models such as Mylotarg, which used unstable linkers and showed high toxicity, to second-generation drugs such as BV and T-DM1, with improved antibodies and linkers but persistent off-target effects. Third-generation ADCs now feature fully humanized antibodies, site-specific conjugation, and potent payloads, offering better efficacy though toxicity from highly cytotoxic agents remains a concern (*Antibody-drug conjugates come of age in oncology, 2023*) (Dumontet et al., 2023).

Current challenges and barriers

Nanotherapeutics are the most advanced and promising techniques for cancer treatment. Thousands of reports and significant preclinical research have demonstrated its therapeutic potential in both in vitro and in vivo conditions. Despite promising findings, only a small percentage of nanocarriers have made it to clinical trials. The distinction emphasizes the enormous hurdles in the design and development of clinically feasible, optimized nanotherapeutic devices that must be overcome (Gaspar and Duncan, 2009).

Manufacturing complexity and scale-up issues

The large-scale production of nanotherapeutics faces considerable technical and regulatory hurdles, particularly in meeting the GMP requirements, due to their inherent polydispersity and complex physicochemical properties. As a result, stringent quality-control guidelines and more sophisticated CMC processes are essential to maintain uniformity and ensure product reliability (Zamboni et al., 2012). The Doxil shortage (2011–14) is a notable example due to issues with manufacturing and sterility, resulting in a hindered supply chain that led to treatment delays, increased expenses, and the need for alternative production methods (McBride et al., 2013). Bioconjugation processes require precise pH control, particularly in the case of pH-sensitive nanomedicines, while in a multistep synthesis process, the use of expensive raw materials increases costs. As shown by Abraxane and Doxil, nanoformulations are significantly more expensive than their free-drug counterparts, implying that their clinical benefits must be substantial to justify the higher production costs and market prices (Resnik and Tinkle, 2007). Therefore, proper characterization and uniformity are crucial for the production of nanoparticles that comply with GMP.

Regulatory hurdles and approval pathways

The FDA and EMA have approved a number of cancer nanomedicine formulations that satisfy current safety requirements. However, there is no dedicated regulatory framework for nanomaterial-based pharmaceuticals. In a 2014 advisory, the FDA described nanoparticles as materials with at least one dimension of 1–100 nm, or up to 1 μm if they exhibit nanoscale characteristics (Hamburg, 2012). In 2015, the EMA issued its own definition, highlighting ongoing efforts to standardize global standards for nanotechnology-based medicines. Because there are no standardized regulatory procedures, nanomedicine approvals are frequently granted on a case-by-case basis, which assures safety but can create market entrance delays. To increase oversight, authorities rely on specialized knowledge, such as the FDA's work with the Nanotechnology Characterization Laboratory (NCL) and Europe's EU-NCL under Horizon 2020, to provide standardized testing and regulatory support for nanomedicine products (European nanomedicine characterisation laboratory launches, 2020). Nanomedicine regulatory problems extend beyond approval and necessitate the use of advanced product characterization and quality control techniques. The FDA's 2013 approval of Lipodox, the first generic liposomal therapy, demonstrates the importance of establishing precise frameworks for the "nano-similars" (Tinkle et al., 2014). With the emergence of next-generation nanocarriers, approval processes will grow more complex, necessitating the refinement and harmonization of standards to assure the quality and timely access to new therapeutics.

Physicochemical characterization of nanotherapeutics

Size, shape, composition, surface chemistry, porosity, charge, and tendency to aggregate all have a substantial impact on large-scale manufacturing and pharmacodynamic performance. Because of their high variability, nanomedicine products must be characterized during manufacturing, storage, and application. Quantitative analytical processes must be capable of detecting all quality characteristics of nano-sized substances. Polydispersity (PD), which represents the degree of particle heterogeneity, is particularly essential among these factors. Even slight differences might alter biocompatibility, toxicity, pharmacokinetic behavior, and overall therapeutic effectiveness (Aillon et al., 2009). As a result, batch-to-batch testing employing complementary approaches is critical to assuring the dependability of nanomedicine development. The bulk of nanomedicine formulations are generated in aqueous buffers, but once delivered, they interact with biomolecules and serum proteins, causing aggregation and altering their physicochemical properties. Such interactions have the potential to alter therapeutic performance. This makes it critical to assess nanoparticle characteristics in clinically relevant settings. Furthermore, biodegradable polymer-based systems may suffer degradation in vivo, affecting particle diameters, drug encapsulation levels, and release kinetics (Vasir and Labhasetwar, 2007). There is an urgent need to improve the quality assessment of nanomaterials by defining clear and reproducible standards. Furthermore, in vitro and in vivo models that accurately mimic clinical conditions must be developed.

Safety concerns

Concerns regarding nanoparticles' toxicity to the environment and human health must be addressed due to their extensive usage. Similar to intracellular organelles or biomolecules involved in cell signaling, nanomedicine products have nanoscale dimensions. Nanoparticles may also have detrimental biological interactions, as per a number of studies. As a result, nanotoxicology has emerged as a separate field of study. An increasing amount of data regarding the toxicity of nanoparticles is growing. The need for better and more specialized testing methods is highlighted by the fact that the current toxicity studies available for conventional medications do not sufficiently address the distinct behaviors of nanoscale materials (Stone et al., 2009). The toxicity of nanomaterials is influenced by numerous factors. The interaction of nanomedicine with the biological interface is influenced by size, shape, charge, surface area, surface functional group, and hydrophobicity. The huge number of variables involved hampers a thorough toxicological investigation of nanomedicine products. Nanomedicine compounds can produce acute toxicity, including complement activation, hemolysis, inflammation, oxidative stress, and altered mitochondrial function. Chronic toxicity research is more difficult due to a scarcity of available data (Mayer et al., 2009). Risks in clinical testing can be reduced by combining more advanced or more accurate diagnostic techniques with creative targeting strategies, thereby identifying "safe-responders" and achieving tailored cancer therapy. Theranostic techniques present a tremendous opportunity in this direction. At the same time, the increasing usage of nanoparticles in industry raises concern about their environmental impact and potential health dangers to workers, necessitating ongoing monitoring and comprehensive risk evaluations.

Future perspectives and emerging trends

Modern anticancer DDS are progressively being designed with biocompatible, accurate, and patient-focused approaches. Researchers are investigating a variety of novel carriers, such as biodegradable polymers, lipid-based nanoparticles, extracellular vesicles such as exosomes, and biomimetic platforms that resemble the body's own cells, in order to increase therapeutic accuracy while reducing detrimental side effects. The application of stimulus-responsive nanocarriers is another expanding field of study. These intelligent systems are designed to only release the drug payload in response to particular stimuli of tumor environments, such as localized temperature changes, increased enzyme activity, or changed pH. The carriers ensure precise delivery to the target site by reacting to distinct biological cues of the tumor, lowering systemic toxicity and enhancing overall therapeutic outcome. Furthermore, by integrating genetic profiling, molecular biomarkers, AI-driven diagnostic and therapeutic approaches, personalized medicine is anticipated to revolutionize cancer treatment in the future. In addition to improving therapeutic results, administering the most effective dosage to the particular patient minimizes toxicity and undesired exposure. These combination techniques offer long-term survival, fewer instances of recurrence, and more sustained responses when compared with standard therapy. In general, the design of the upcoming generation of anticancer DDS is exceptionally patient-centered. Innovative materials, smart stimulus-responsive features, and strict GMP characterization standards are all combined in these new platforms. By providing safer, more flexible, and more effective therapies, the overall goal is not only to improve disease management but also to improve patients' quality of life. A summary of several nanomedicine formulations currently advancing through clinical development is already provided in- Table 30.3.

Conclusion

Although nanotechnology has previously investigated a number of ideas that could be applied in oncology, the field of nanomedicine is still in the beginning stages. The pharmaceutical industry faces difficulties in large-scale production as well as in designing and producing increasingly complicated nanosized medicinal formulations, despite the fact that research institutes contribute significantly to engineering. Production expenses and quality regulations probably hinder the clinical transfer of such sophisticated nanoparticles. The main problem for the environment and human health is the toxicity of the nanoparticles. In order to create better nanotherapeutics, future research will make use of previously published data and concentrate on investigations of acute and chronic toxicity. In summary, the development of nanotherapeutics in a variety of domains, including therapeutic and diagnostic applications in oncology, is aided by the substantial preclinical research.

Abbreviation

ADCs Antibody-Drug conjugates
ALCL Anaplastic Large Cell Lymphoma
ALL Acute lymphoblastic leukemia
AML Acute Myeloid Leukemia
CD Cluster of differentiation
CL2A PEG8-and triazole-containing PABC-peptide-mc linker
CMC Critical Micellar concentration
CR Complete Response
DDS Drug delivery system
DLBCL Diffuse Large B-Cell Lymphoma
DM1 Mertansine
DM4 Ravtansine
DOPC 1,2-dioleoyl-sn-glycero-3-phosphocholine
DXD deruxtecan
EGFR-RAS-MAPK Epidermal Growth Factor Receptor- Rat sarcoma- Mitogen-Activated Protein Kinase
EMA European Medicines Agency
EphA2 Ephrin type-A receptor two
EPR Enhanced permeability and retention
EU European Union
EU-NCL European Union-Nanotechnology Characterization Laboratory
FDA Food and Drug Administration
FRα Folate receptor alpha
G-CSF Granulocyte Colony-Stimulating Factor

GC Gastric cancer
GMP Good manufacturing practice
HCL Hairy Cell Leukemia
HER Human epidermal growth factor receptor
HL Hodgkin Lymphoma
HPMA N-(2-hydroxypropyl) methacrylamide
HPV Human papillomavirus infection
HSA Human serum albumin
KSP Kinesin spindle protein
MBC Metastatic breast cancer
mc-VC-PABC Maleimidocaproyl-Valine-Citrulline-p-Aminobenzoyloxycarbonyl
MDR Multidrug resistance
MMAE Monomethyl auristatin E
mTOR Mechanistic target of rapamycin
MVA Modified Vaccinia Ankara
NIR Near infrared
NSCLC Non-small-cell lung cancer
PD Polydispersity
PE38 modified Pseudomonas exotoxin A
PEG Polyethylene glycol
PEG-PPO-PEG poly (ethylene glycol)-poly (propylene oxide)
PKN3 Protein Kinase N3
PLD PEGylated Liposome delivery
PLK1 Polo-like kinase 1
RES Reticuloendothelial system
SC-PEG Calaspargase pegol
SMCC Succinimidyl 4-(N-maleimidomethyl) cyclohexane-1-carboxylate
SN-38 7-ethyl-10-hydroxycamptothecin
SPARC Secreted Protein Acidic and Rich in Cysteine
Sulfo- SPDB N-((4-(2-pyridyldithio) butanoate) oxy) carbonyl)-4-(2-sulfo) pyridyl)-2-pyridyldithio)-2-sulfo butanoate
TF Tissue factor
TNBC Triple negative breast cancer
Trop2 Tumor-associated calcium signal transducer two
UC Urothelial Cancer
VLPs Virus-like nanoparticles
VNPs Viral nanoparticles

Acknowledgments

The authors gratefully acknowledge the support and facilities provided by the Central Drug Research Institute (CSIR-CDRI), Lucknow, for extending resources during the preparation of this manuscript. The CDRI Communication number for this manuscript is 11181.

References

A Clinical Study of Paclitaxel Cationic Liposomes for the Treatment of Patients with Advanced Solid Tumors, 2024. https://www.clinicaltrials.gov/study/NCT06632574.

A Dose Finding Study of TKM-080301 Infusion in Neuroendocrine Tumors (NET) and Adrenocortical Carcinoma (ACC) Patients, 2019. https://clinicaltrials.gov/study/NCT01262235.

A Phase I Clinical Study of HMPL-A83 in Patients with Advanced Malignant Neoplasm, 2025. https://clinicaltrials.gov/study/NCT05429008?term=NCT05429008&rank=1.

Ahn, H.K., Jung, M., Sym, S.J., Shin, D.B., Kang, S.M., Kyung, S.Y., Park, J.W., Jeong, S.H., Cho, E.K., 2014. A phase II trial of cremorphor EL-free paclitaxel (Genexol-PM) and gemcitabine in patients with advanced non-small cell lung cancer. Cancer Chemother. Pharmacol. 74 (2), 277–282. https://doi.org/10.1007/s00280-014-2498-5.

Aillon, K.L., Xie, Y., El-Gendy, N., Berkland, C.J., Forrest, M.L., 2009. Effects of nanomaterial physicochemical properties on in vivo toxicity. Adv. Drug Deliv. Rev. 61 (6), 457–466. https://doi.org/10.1016/j.addr.2009.03.010.

Akinc, A., Maier, M.A., Manoharan, M., Fitzgerald, K., Jayaraman, M., Barros, S., Ansell, S., Du, X., Hope, M.J., Madden, T.D., Mui, B.L., Semple, S.C., Tam, Y.K., Ciufolini, M., Witzigmann, D., Kulkarni, J.A., van der Meel, R., Cullis, P.R., 2019. The onpattro story and the clinical translation of nanomedicines containing nucleic acid-based drugs. Nat. Nanotechnol. 14 (12), 1084–1087. https://doi.org/10.1038/s41565-019-0591-y.

Allen, T.M., Cullis, P.R., 2013. Liposomal drug delivery systems: From concept to clinical applications. Adv. Drug Deliv. Rev. 65 (1), 36–48. https://doi.org/10.1016/j.addr.2012.09.037.

Amadori, S., Venditti, A., Voso, M.T., Annino, L., De Fabritiis, P., Alimena, G., Mancini, M., Paoloni, F., Vignetti, M., Fazi, P., Aversa, F., Gaidano, G., Musso, M., Mazzone, C., Magro, D., Ramadan, S.M., Suciu, S., Meert, L., Selleslag, D., Hagemeijer, A., Baron, F., Muus, P., Dewitte, T., Willemze, R., 2016. Gemtuzumab ozogamicin versus best supportive care in older patients with newly diagnosed acute myeloid leukemia unsuitable for intensive chemotherapy: Results of the randomized phase III EORTC-GIMEMA AML-19 Trial. J. Clin. Oncol. 34 (9), 972–979. https://doi.org/10.1200/JCO.2015.64.0060.

André, F., Hee Park, Y., Kim, S.B., Takano, T., Im, S.A., Borges, G., Lima, J.P., Aksoy, S., Gavila Gregori, J., De Laurentiis, M., Bianchini, G., Roylance, R., Miyoshi, Y., Armstrong, A., Sinha, R., Ruiz Borrego, M., Lim, E., Ettl, J., Yerushalmi, R., Zagouri, F., Duhoux, F.P., Fehm, T., Gambhire, D., Cathcart, J., Wu, C., Chu, C., Egorov, A., Krop, I., 2023. Trastuzumab deruxtecan versus treatment of physician's choice in patients with HER2-positive metastatic breast cancer (DESTINY-Breast02): A randomised, open-label, multicentre, phase 3 trial. Lancet 401 (10390), 1773–1785. https://doi.org/10.1016/S0140-6736(23)00725-0.

Andtbacka, R.H.I., Collichio, F., Harrington, K.J., Middleton, M.R., Downey, G., Öhrling, K., Kaufman, H.L., 2019. Final analyses of OPTiM: A randomized phase III trial of talimogene laherparepvec versus granulocyte-macrophage colony-stimulating factor in unresectable stage III-IV melanoma. J. Immunother. Cancer 7 (1). https://doi.org/10.1186/s40425-019-0623-z.

Angiolillo, A.L., Schore, R.J., Devidas, M., Borowitz, M.J., Carroll, A.J., Gastier-Foster, J.M., Heerema, N.A., Keilani, T., Lane, A.R., Loh, M.L., Reaman, G.H., Adamson, P.C., Wood, B., Wood, C., Zheng, H.W., Raetz, E. A., Winick, N.J., Carroll, W.L., Hunger, S.P., 2014. Pharmacokinetic and pharmacodynamic properties of calaspargase pegol Escherichia coli L-asparaginase in the treatment of patients with acute lymphoblastic leukemia: Results from children's oncology group study AALL07P4. J. Clin. Oncol. 32 (34), 3874–3882. https://doi.org/10.1200/JCO.2014.55.5763.

Antibody-Drug Conjugates (ADCs) and Drug–Antibody Ratio (DAR), 2024. https://www.biointron.com/blog/adcs-and-drug-antibody-ratio-dar.html.

Antibody-drug Conjugates Come of Age in Oncology, 2023. https://pubmed.ncbi.nlm.nih.gov/37308581/.

Appelbaum, F.R., Bernstein, I.D., 2017. Gemtuzumab ozogamicin for acute myeloid leukemia. Blood 130 (22), 2373–2376. https://doi.org/10.1182/blood-2017-09-797712.

Awada, A., Bondarenko, I.N., Bonneterre, J., Nowara, E., Ferrero, J.M., Bakshi, A.V., Wilke, C., Piccart, M., 2014. A randomized controlled phase II trial of a novel composition of paclitaxel embedded into neutral and cationic lipids targeting tumor endothelial cells in advanced triple-negative breast cancer (TNBC). Ann. Oncol. 25 (4), 824–831. https://doi.org/10.1093/annonc/mdu025.

Awada, H., Abdelmalek, M., Cronin, T., Baron, J., Kashour, Z., Azad, F., Faisal, M.S., Faber, M., Gravina, M., Sung, P.J., Green, S.D., Przespolewski, A., Thompson, J.E., Griffiths, E.A., Wang, E.S., 2023. Gemtuzumab ozogamicin plus standard induction hemotherapy improves outcomes of newly diagnosed intermediate cytogenetic risk acute myeloid leukemia. Blood Cancer J. 13 (1). https://doi.org/10.1038/s41408-023-00910-x.

Bagley, A.F., Ludmir, E.B., Maitra, A., Minsky, B.D., Li Smith, G., Das, P., Koong, A.C., Holliday, E.B., Taniguchi, C. M., Katz, M.H.G., Tamm, E.P., Wolff, R.A., Overman, M.J., Patel, S., Kim, M.P., Tzeng, C.W.D., Ikoma, N., Bhutani, M.S., Koay, E.J., 2022. NBTXR3, a first-in-class radioenhancer for pancreatic ductal adenocarcinoma: Report of first patient experience. Clin. Transl. Radiat. Oncol. 33, 66–69. https://doi.org/10.1016/j.ctro.2021.12.012.

Ballantyne, A., Dhillon, S., 2013. Trastuzumab emtansine: First global approval. Drugs 73 (7), 755–765. https://doi.org/10.1007/s40265-013-0050-2.

Barraud, L., Merle, P., Soma, E., Lefrançois, L., Guerret, S., Chevallier, M., Dubernet, C., Couvreur, P., Trépo, C., Vitvitski, L., 2005. Increase of doxorubicin sensitivity by doxorubicin-loading into nanoparticles for hepatocellular carcinoma cells in vitro and in vivo. J. Hepatol. 42 (5), 736–743. https://doi.org/10.1016/j.jhep.2004.12.035.

Bartlett, N.L., Younes, A., Carabasi, M.H., Forero, A., Rosenblatt, J.D., Leonard, J.P., Bernstein, S.H., Bociek, R.G., Lorenz, J.M., Hart, B.W., Barton, J., 2008. A phase 1 multidose study of SGN-30 immunotherapy in patients with refractory or recurrent CD30+ hematologic malignancies. Blood 111 (4), 1848–1854. https://doi.org/10.1182/blood-2007-07-099317.

Bonvalot, S., Rutkowski, P.L., Thariat, J., Carrère, S., Ducassou, A., Sunyach, M.P., Agoston, P., Hong, A., Mervoyer, A., Rastrelli, M., Moreno, V., Li, R.K., Tiangco, B., Herraez, A.C., Gronchi, A., Mangel, L., Sy-Ortin, T., Hohenberger, P., de Baère, T., Le Cesne, A., Helfre, S., Saada-Bouzid, E., Borkowska, A., Anghel, R., Co, A., Gebhart, M., Kantor, G., Montero, A., Loong, H.H., Vergés, R., Lapeire, L., Dema, S., Kacso, G., Austen, L., Moureau-Zabotto, L., Servois, V., Wardelmann, E., Terrier, P., Lazar, A.J., Bovée, J.V.M. G., Le Péchoux, C., Papai, Z., 2019. NBTXR3, a first-in-class radioenhancer hafnium oxide nanoparticle, plus radiotherapy versus radiotherapy alone in patients with locally advanced soft-tissue sarcoma (Act.In.Sarc): Amulticentre, phase 2–3, randomised, controlled trial. Lancet Oncol. 20 (8), 1148–1159. https://doi.org/10.1016/S1470-2045(19)30326-2.

Bozzuto, G., Molinari, A., 2015. Liposomes as nanomedical devices. Int. J. Nanomed. 10, 975–999. https://doi.org/10.2147/IJN.S68861.

Breitbach, C.J., Burke, J., Jonker, D., Stephenson, J., Haas, A.R., Chow, L.Q.M., Nieva, J., Hwang, T.-H., Moon, A., Patt, R., Pelusio, A., Le Boeuf, F., Burns, J., Evgin, L., De Silva, N., Cvancic, S., Robertson, T., Je, J.-E., Lee, Y.-S., Parato, K., Diallo, J.-S., Fenster, A., Daneshmand, M., Bell, J.C., Kirn, D.H., 2011. Intravenous delivery of a multi-mechanistic cancer-targeted oncolytic poxvirus in humans. Nature 477 (7362), 99–102. https://doi.org/10.1038/nature10358.

Budde, L.E., Olszewski, A.J., Assouline, S., Lossos, I.S., Diefenbach, C., Kamdar, M., Ghosh, N., Modi, D., Sabry, W., Naik, S., Mehta, A., Nakhoda, S.K., Smith, S.D., Dorritie, K., Jia, T., Pham, S., Huw, L.Y., Jing, J., Wu, H., Ead, W. S., To, I., Batlevi, C.L., Wei, M.C., Chavez, J.C., 2024. Mosunetuzumab with polatuzumab vedotin in relapsed or refractory aggressive large B cell lymphoma: A phase 1b/2 trial. Nat. Med. 30 (1), 229–239. https://doi.org/10.1038/s41591-023-02726-5.

Campbell, R.B., 2006. Tumor physiology and delivery of nanopharmaceuticals. Anti Cancer Agents Med. Chem. 6 (6), 503–512. https://doi.org/10.2174/187152006778699077.

Castaigne, S., Pautas, C., Terré, C., Raffoux, E., Bordessoule, D., Bastie, J.N., Legrand, O., Thomas, X., Turlure, P., Reman, O., De Revel, T., Gastaud, L., De Gunzburg, N., Contentin, N., Henry, E., Marolleau, J.P., Aljijakli, A., Rousselot, P., Fenaux, P., Preudhomme, C., Chevret, S., Dombret, H., 2012. Effect of gemtuzumab ozogamicin on survival of adult patients with de-novo acute myeloid leukaemia (ALFA-0701): A randomised, open-label, phase 3 study. Lancet 379 (9825), 1508–1516. https://doi.org/10.1016/S0140-6736(12)60485-1.

Ceelen, W., Sandra, L., de Sande, L.V., Graversen, M., Mortensen, M.B., Vermeulen, A., Gasthuys, E., Reynders, D., Cosyns, S., Hoorens, A., Willaert, W., 2022. Phase I study of intraperitoneal aerosolized nanoparticle albumin based paclitaxel (NAB-PTX) for unresectable peritoneal metastases. EBioMedicine 82. https://doi.org/10.1016/j.ebiom.2022.104151.

Chhikara, B.S., Parang, K., 2010. Development of cytarabine prodrugs and delivery systems for leukemia treatment. Expert Opin. Drug Deliv. 7 (12), 1399–1414. https://doi.org/10.1517/17425247.2010.527330.

Coelho, T., Adams, D., Silva, A., Lozeron, P., Hawkins, P.N., Mant, T., Perez, J., Chiesa, J., Warrington, S., Tranter, E., Munisamy, M., Falzone, R., Harrop, J., Cehelsky, J., Bettencourt, B.R., Geissler, M., Butler, J.S., Sehgal, A., Meyers, R.E., Chen, Q., Todd, B., Hutabarat, R.M., Clausen, V.A., Alvarez, R., Fitzgerald, K., Gamba-Vitalo, C., Nochur, S.V., Vaishnaw, A.K., Sah, D.W.Y., Gollob, J.A., Suhr, O.B., 2013. Safety and efficacy of RNAi therapy for transthyretin amyloidosis. N. Engl. J. Med. 369 (9), 819–829. https://doi.org/10.1056/NEJMoa1208760.

Das, R., Verma, R., Sznol, M., Boddupalli, C.S., Gettinger, S.N., Kluger, H., Callahan, M., Wolchok, J.D., Halaban, R., Dhodapkar, M.V., Dhodapkar, K.M., 2015. Combination therapy with anti-CTLA-4 and anti-PD-1 leads to distinct immunologic changes in vivo. J. Immunol. 194 (3), 950–959. https://doi.org/10.4049/jimmunol.1401686.

Deeken, J.F., Slack, R., Weiss, G.J., Ramanathan, R.K., Pishvaian, M.J., Hwang, J., Lewandowski, K., Subramaniam, D., He, A.R., Cotarla, I., Rahman, A., Marshall, J.L., 2013. A phase i study of liposomal-encapsulated docetaxel (LE-DT) in patients with advanced solid tumor malignancies. Cancer Chemother. Pharmacol. 71 (3), 627–633. https://doi.org/10.1007/s00280-012-2048-y.

Deeks, E.D., 2021. Disitamab vedotin: First approval. Drugs 81 (16), 1929–1935. https://doi.org/10.1007/s40265-021-01614-x.

Dong, X., Mumper, R.J., 2010. Nanomedicinal strategies to treat multidrug-resistant tumors: Current progress. Nanomedicine 5 (4), 597–615. https://doi.org/10.2217/nnm.10.35.

Du, J.Z., Du, X.J., Mao, C.Q., Wang, J., 2011. Tailor-Made dual pH-sensitive polymer-doxorubicin nanoparticles for efficient anticancer drug delivery. J. Am. Chem. Soc. 133 (44), 17560–17563. https://doi.org/10.1021/ja207150n.

Duggan, S.T., Keating, G.M., Ferrandina, G., Kesterson, J.P., Lorusso, D., Muggia, F., 2011. Pegylated liposomal doxorubicin: A review of its use in metastatic breast cancer, ovarian cancer, multiple myeloma and AIDS-related Kaposis sarcoma. Drugs 71 (18), 2531–2558. https://doi.org/10.2165/11207510-000000000-00000.

Duncan, R., Ringsdorf, H., Satchi-Fainaro, R., 2006. Polymer therapeutics - polymers as drugs, drug and protein conjugates and gene delivery systems: Past, present and future opportunities. J. Drug Target. 14 (6), 337–341. https://doi.org/10.1080/10611860600833856.

Dumontet, C., Reichert, J.M., Senter, P.D., Lambert, J.M., Beck, A., 2023. Antibody–drug conjugates come of age in oncology. Nat. Rev. Drug Discov. 22 (8), 641–661. https://doi.org/10.1038/s41573-023-00709-2.

Duncan, R., 2003. The dawning era of polymer therapeutics. Nat. Rev. Drug Discov. 2 (5), 347–360. https://doi.org/10.1038/nrd1088.

Elsadek, B., Kratz, F., 2012. Impact of albumin on drug delivery - new applications on the horizon. J. Contr. Release 157 (1), 4–28. https://doi.org/10.1016/j.jconrel.2011.09.069.

European Nanomedicine Characterisation Laboratory Launches, 2020. https://www.drugtargetreview.com/news/5048/first-european-nanomedicine-characterisation-laboratory-launches/.

Ezike, T.C., Okpala, U.S., Onoja, U.L., Nwike, C.P., Ezeako, E.C., Okpara, O.J., Okoroafor, C.C., Eze, S.C., Kalu, O.L., Odoh, E.C., Nwadike, U.G., Ogbodo, J.O., Umeh, B.U., Ossai, E.C., Nwanguma, B.C., 2023. Advances in drug delivery systems, challenges and future directions. Heliyon 9 (6). https://doi.org/10.1016/j.heliyon.2023.e17488.

Frampton, J.E., Anderson, P.M., Chou, A.J., Federman, N.C., Ferrari, S., Kim, H.J., Loeb, D.M., Mori, K., 2010. Mifamurtide: A review of its use in the treatment of osteosarcoma. Pediatr. Drugs 12 (3), 141–153. https://doi.org/10.2165/11204910-000000000-00000.

Fu, L., Han, S., Zhang, 2022. Antibody drug conjugate: The "biological missile" for targeted cancer therapy. Signal Transduct. Targeted Ther. 7. https://doi.org/10.1038/s41392-022-00947-7.

Fujiwara, Y., Mukai, H., Saeki, T., Ro, J., Lin, Y.C., Nagai, S.E., Lee, K.S., Watanabe, J., Ohtani, S., Kim, S.B., Kuroi, K., Tsugawa, K., Tokuda, Y., Iwata, H., Park, Y.H., Yang, Y., Nambu, Y., 2019. A multi-national, randomised, open-label, parallel, phase III non-inferiority study comparing NK105 and paclitaxel in metastatic or recurrent breast cancer patients. Br. J. Cancer 120 (5), 475–480. https://doi.org/10.1038/s41416-019-0391-z.

Gaspar, R., Duncan, R., 2009. Polymeric carriers: Preclinical safety and the regulatory implications for design and development of polymer therapeutics. Adv. Drug Deliv. Rev. 61 (13), 1220–1231. https://doi.org/10.1016/j.addr.2009.06.003.

Graham, M.L., 2003. Pegaspargase: A review of clinical studies. Adv. Drug Deliv. Rev. 55 (10), 1293–1302. https://doi.org/10.1016/S0169-409X(03)00110-8.

Hamaguchi, T., Matsumura, Y., Nakanishi, Y., Muro, K., Yamada, Y., Shimada, Y., Shirao, K., Niki, H., Hosokawa, S., Tagawa, T., Kakizoe, T., 2004. Antitumor effect of MCC-465, pegylated liposomal doxorubicin tagged with newly developed monoclonal antibody GAH, in colorectal cancer xenografts. Cancer Sci. 95 (7), 608–613. https://doi.org/10.1111/j.1349-7006.2004.tb02495.x.

Hamburg, M.A., 2012. FDA's approach to regulation of products of nanotechnology. Science 336 (6079), 299–300. https://doi.org/10.1126/science.1205441.

Hehlmann, R., Berger, U., Pfirrmann, M., Hochhaus, A., Metzgeroth, G., Maywald, O., Hasford, J., Reiter, A., Hossfeld, D.K., Kolb, H.J., Löffler, H., Pralle, H., Queißer, W., Griesshammer, M., Nerl, C., Kuse, R., Tobler, A., Eimermacher, H., Tichelli, A., Aul, C., Wilhelm, M., Fischer, J.T., Perker, M., Scheid, C., Schenk, M., Weiß, J., Meier, C.R., Kremers, S., Labedzki, L., Schmeiser, T., Lohrmann, H.P., Heimpel, H., 2003. Randomized comparison of interferon α and hydroxyurea with hydroxyurea monotherapy in chronic myeloid leukemia (CML-study II): Prolongation of survival by the combination of interferon α and hydroxyurea. Leukemia 17 (8), 1529–1537. https://doi.org/10.1038/sj.leu.2403006.

Heo, Y.A., 2023. Mirvetuximab soravtansine: First approval. Drugs 83 (3), 265–273. https://doi.org/10.1007/s40265-023-01834-3.

Horwitz, S.M., Scarisbrick, J.J., Dummer, R., Whittaker, S., Duvic, M., Kim, Y.H., Quaglino, P., Zinzani, P.L., Bechter, O., Eradat, H., Pinter-Brown, L., Akilov, O.E., Geskin, L., Sanches, J.A., Ortiz-Romero, P.L., Weichenthal, M., Fisher, D.C., Walewski, J., Trotman, J., Taylor, K., Dalle, S., Stadler, R., Lisano, J., Bunn, V., Little, M., Miles Prince, H., 2021. Randomized phase 3 ALCANZA study of brentuximab vedotin vs physician's choice in cutaneous T-cell lymphoma: Final data. Blood Adv. 5, 5098–5106. https://doi.org/10.1182/bloodadvances.2021004710.

Hou, X., Tal, Z., Langer, R., Dong, Y., 2022. Author correction: Lipid nanoparticles for mRNA delivery (Nature reviews materials, (2021), 6, 12, (1078-1094), 10.1038/s41578-021-00358-0). Nat. Rev. Mater. 7 (1). https://doi.org/10.1038/s41578-021-00400-1.

Investigation of Sugammadex in Outpatient Urological Procedures, 2020. https://clinicaltrials.gov/study/NCT03138967?term=NCT03138967&rank=1.

Jiang, J., Li, S., Shan, X., Wang, L., Ma, J., Huang, M., Dong, L., Chen, F., 2020. Preclinical safety profile of disitamab vedotin:A novel anti-HER2 antibody conjugated with MMAE. Toxicol. Lett. 324, 30–37. https://doi.org/10.1016/j.toxlet.2019.12.027.

Kabanov, A.V., Batrakova, E.V., Alakhov, V.Y., 2002. Pluronic block copolymers as novel polymer therapeutics for drug and gene delivery. J. Contr. Release 82 (2–3), 189–212. https://doi.org/10.1016/S0168-3659(02)00009-3.

Kim, D., Kim, J., Park, Y.I., Lee, N., Hyeon, T., 2018. Recent development of inorganic nanoparticles for biomedical imaging. ACS Cent. Sci. 4 (3), 324–336. https://doi.org/10.1021/acscentsci.7b00574.

Kirn, D.H., Thorne, S.H., 2009. Targeted and armed oncolytic poxviruses: A novel multi-mechanistic therapeutic class for cancer. Nat. Rev. Cancer 9 (1), 64–71. https://doi.org/10.1038/nrc2545.

Koo, B.W., Oh, A.Y., Seo, K.S., Han, J.W., Han, H.S., Yoon, Y.S., 2016. Randomized clinical trial of moderate versus deep neuromuscular block for low-pressure pneumoperitoneum during laparoscopic cholecystectomy. World J. Surg. 40 (12), 2898–2903. https://doi.org/10.1007/s00268-016-3633-8.

Kreitman, R.J., Dearden, C., Zinzani, P.L., Delgado, J., Robak, T., le Coutre, P.D., Gjertsen, B.T., Troussard, X., Roboz, G.J., Karlin, L., Gladstone, D.E., Kuptsova-Clarkson, N., Liu, S., Patel, P., Rotolo, F., Mitry, E., Pastan, I., Giles, F., 2021. Moxetumomab pasudotox in heavily pre-treated patients with relapsed/refractory hairy cell leukemia (HCL): Long-term follow-up from the pivotal trial. J. Hematol. Oncol. 14 (1). https://doi.org/10.1186/s13045-020-01004-y.

Kumar, A., Panwar, D., Bhavana, V., Thakor, P., Singh, P.K., Mehra, N.K., 2023. Lipid-based Nanomaterials: A Brief Note on Composition, Development, and Drug Delivery Applications Nanomaterial-Based Drug Delivery Systems: Therapeutic and Theranostic Applications. Springer International Publishing, India, pp. 65–98. https://doi.org/10.1007/978-3-031-30529-0_3.

Kulkarni, J.A., Cullis, P.R., Van Der Meel, R., 2018. Lipid nanoparticles enabling gene therapies: From concepts to clinical utility. Nucleic Acid Therapeut. 28 (3), 146–157. https://doi.org/10.1089/nat.2018.0721.

Lamba, J.K., Chauhan, L., Shin, M., Loken, M.R., Pollard, J.A., Wang, Y.C., Ries, R.E., Aplenc, R., Hirsch, B.A., Raimondi, S.C., Walter, R.B., Bernstein, I.D., Gamis, A.S., Alonzo, T.A., Meshinchi, S., 2017. CD33 splicing polymorphism determines gemtuzumab ozogamicin response in de novo acute myeloid leukemia: Report from randomized phase III children's oncology group trial AAML0531. J. Clin. Oncol. 35 (23), 674–2682. https://doi.org/10.1200/JCO.2016.71.2513.

Lee, A., 2021. Loncastuximab tesirine: First approval. Drugs 81 (10), 1229–1233. https://doi.org/10.1007/s40265-021-01550-w.

Lee, J.L., Ahn, J.H., Park, S.H., Lim, H.Y., Kwon, J.H., Ahn, S., Song, C., Hong, J.H., Kim, C.S., Ahn, H., 2012. Phase II study of a cremophor-free, polymeric micelle formulation of paclitaxel for patients with advanced urothelial cancer previously treated with gemcitabine and platinum. Invest. N. Drugs 30 (5), 1984–1990. https://doi.org/10.1007/s10637-011-9757-7.

Leonard, R.C.F., Williams, S., Tulpule, A., Levine, A.M., Oliveros, S., 2009. Improving the therapeutic index of anthracycline chemotherapy: Focus on liposomal doxorubicin (Myocet). Breast 18 (4), 218–224. https://doi.org/10.1016/j.breast.2009.05.004.

Li, W.Q., Guo, H.F., Li, L.Y., Zhang, Y.F., Cui, J.W., 2021. The promising role of antibody drug conjugate in cancer therapy: Combining targeting ability with cytotoxicity effectively. Cancer Med. 10 (14), 4677–4696. https://doi.org/10.1002/cam4.4052.

Li, Z., Rana, T.M., 2014. Therapeutic targeting of microRNAs: Current status and future challenges. Nat. Rev. Drug Discov. 13 (8), 622–638. https://doi.org/10.1038/nrd4359.

Liang, M., 2018. Oncorine, the world first oncolytic virus medicine and its update in China. Curr. Cancer Drug Targets 18 (2), 171–176. https://doi.org/10.2174/1568009618666171129221503.

Liposomal Bupivacaine with or without Hydromorphone for the Improvement of Pain Control After Laparotomy in Patients with Gynecological Malignancies, 2024. https://clinicaltrials.gov/study/NCT04258631?a=14.

Maeda, H., 1989. Principle and therapeutic effect of lipophilic anticancer agent [smancs/lipiodol]: selective targeting with oily contrast medium. Jpn. J. Cancer Chemother. 16 (10), 3323–3331.

Maeda, H., 2001. SMANCS and polymer-conjugated macromolecular drugs: Advantages in cancer chemotherapy. Adv. Drug Deliv. Rev. 46 (1–3), 169–185. https://doi.org/10.1016/S0169-409X(00)00134-4.

Maksimenko, A., Dosio, F., Mougin, J., Ferrero, A., Wack, S., Reddy, L.H., Weyn, A.A., Lepeltier, E., Bourgaux, C., Stella, B., Cattel, L., Couvreur, P., 2014. A unique squalenoylated and nonpegylateddoxorubicin nanomedicine with systemiclong-circulating properties and anticancer activity. Proc. Natl. Acad. of Sci. U S A 111 (2), E217. https://doi.org/10.1073/pnas.1313459110.

Markham, A., 2021. Tisotumab vedotin: First approval. Drugs 81 (18), 2141–2147. https://doi.org/10.1007/s40265-021-01633-8.

Mayer, A., Vadon, M., Rinner, B., Novak, A., Wintersteiger, R., Fröhlich, E., 2009. The role of nanoparticle size in hemocompatibility. Toxicology 258 (2–3), 139–147. https://doi.org/10.1016/j.tox.2009.01.015.

McBride, A., Holle, L.M., Westendorf, C., Sidebottom, M., Griffith, N., Muller, R.J., Hoffman, J.M., 2013. National survey on the effect of oncology drug shortages on cancer care. Am. J. Health Syst. Pharm. 70 (7), 609–617. https://doi.org/10.2146/ajhp120563.

Miller, K.D., Diéras, V., Harbeck, N., Andre, F., Mahtani, R.L., Gianni, L., Albain, K.S., Crivellari, D., Fang, L., Michelson, G., De Haas, S.L., Burris, H.A., 2014. Phase IIa trial of trastuzumab emtansine with pertuzumab for patients with human epidermal growth factor receptor 2-positive, locally advanced, or metastatic breast cancer. J. Clin. Oncol. 32 (14), 1437–1444. https://doi.org/10.1200/JCO.2013.52.6590.

Milowsky, M.I., O'Donnell, P.H., Hoimes, C.J., Petrylak, D.P., Flaig, T.W., Moon, H.H., Friedlander, T.W., Mar, N., McKay, R.R., Srinivas, S., Gravis, G., Ramamurthy, C., Bupathi, M., Bracarda, S., Wright, P., Hepp, Z., Carret, A.-S., Yu, Y., Dillon, R., Kataria, R., Beaumont, J.L., Purnajo, I., Rosenberg, J.E., 2024. Patient-reported outcomes in patients with advanced urothelial cancer who are ineligible for cisplatin and treated with first-line enfortumab vedotin alone or with pembrolizumab. J. Clin. Oncol. 42 (12), 1403–1414. https://doi.org/10.1200/JCO.23.01547.

Milla, P., Dosio, F., Cattel, L., 2012. PEGylation of proteins and liposomes: A powerful and flexible strategy to improve the drug delivery. Curr. Drug Metabol. 13 (1), 105–119. https://doi.org/10.2174/138920012798356934.

Monoclonal Antibody Therapy in Treating Patients with Prostate Cancer, 2013. https://clinicaltrials.gov/study/NCT00024232?term=NCT00024232&rank=1.

Nanoparticle Albumin-Bound Rapamycin in Treating Patients with Advanced Cancer with mTOR Mutations, 2019. https://clinicaltrials.gov/study/NCT02646319?term=NCT02646319&rank=1.

Nikolaenko, L., Nademanee, A., 2020. Brentuximab vedotin and its use in the treatment of advanced Hodgkin's lymphoma. Future Oncol. 16 (29), 2273–2282. https://doi.org/10.2217/fon-2020-0026.

Norsworthy, K.J., Ko, C.W., Lee, J.E., Liu, J., John, C.S., Przepiorka, D., Farrell, A.T., Pazdur, R., 2018. FDA approval summary: Mylotarg for treatment of patients with relapsed or refractory CD33-positive acute myeloid leukemia. Oncologist 23 (9), 1103–1108. https://doi.org/10.1634/theoncologist.2017-0604.

Northfelt, D.W., Dueck, A.C., Flynn, T.P., Zander, P.J., Stella, P.J., Melnik, M., Pavey, E.S., Perez, E.A., 2011. Phase II trial combining nab-paclitaxel (NP), gemcitabine (G), and bevacizumab (B) in patients (pts) with metastatic breast cancer (MBC): NCCTG N0735. J. Clin. Oncol. 29 (15_Suppl. l), 1126. https://doi.org/10.1200/jco.2011.29.15_suppl.1126.

Ogitani, Y., Aida, T., Hagihara, K., Yamaguchi, J., Ishii, C., Harada, N., Soma, M., Okamoto, H., Oitate, M., Arakawa, S., Hirai, T., Atsumi, R., Nakada, T., Hayakawa, I., Abe, Y., Agatsuma, T., 2016. DS-8201a, a novel HER2-targeting ADC with a novel DNA topoisomerase I inhibitor, demonstrates a promising antitumor efficacy with differentiation from T-DM1. Clin. Cancer Res. 22 (20), 5097–5108. https://doi.org/10.1158/1078-0432.CCR-15-2822.

Orlova, O.V., Glazkova, D.V., Bogoslovskaya, E.V., Shipulin, G.A., Yudin, S.M., 2022. Development of modified vaccinia virus ankara-based vaccines: Advantages and applications. Vaccines (Basel) 10 (9). https://doi.org/10.3390/vaccines10091516.

Palmer, C.D., Rappaport, A.R., Davis, M.J., Hart, M.G., Scallan, C.D., Hong, S.J., Gitlin, L., Kraemer, L.D., Kounlavouth, S., Yang, A., Smith, L., Schenk, D., Skoberne, M., Taquechel, K., Marrali, M., Jaroslavsky, J.R., Nganje, C.N., Maloney, E., Zhou, R., Navarro-Gomez, D., Greene, A.C., Grotenbreg, G., Greer, R., Blair, W., Cao, M.D., Chan, S., Bae, K., Spira, A.I., Roychowdhury, S., Carbone, D.P., Henick, B.S., Drake, C.G., Solomon, B.J., Ahn, D.H., Mahipal, A., Maron, S.B., Johnson, B., Rousseau, R., Yelensky, R., Liao, C.Y., Catenacci, D.V.T., Allen, A., Ferguson, A.R., Jooss, K., 2022. Individualized, heterologous chimpanzee adenovirus and self-amplifying mRNA neoantigen vaccine for advanced metastatic solid tumors: Phase 1 trial interim results. Nat. Med. 28 (8), 1619–1629. https://doi.org/10.1038/s41591-022-01937-6.

Panwar, D., Thakor, P., Sharma, M., Bakshi, A.K., Bhavana, V., Srivastava, V., Mishra, P.R., Singh, S.B., Mehra, N.K., 2023. Hyaluronic acid-engineered Bcl-2 inhibitor nanocrystals for site-specific delivery to breast tumor cells. Nanomedicine 18 (15), 1005–1023. https://doi.org/10.2217/nnm-2023-0132.

Park, B.H., Hwang, T., Liu, T.C., Sze, D.Y., Kim, J.S., Kwon, H.C., Oh, S.Y., Han, S.Y., Yoon, J.H., Hong, S.H., Moon, A., Speth, K., Park, C., Ahn, Y.J., Daneshmand, M., Rhee, B.G., Pinedo, H.M., Bell, J.C., Kirn, D.H., 2008. Use of a targeted oncolytic poxvirus, JX-594, in patients with refractory primary or metastatic liver cancer: A phase I trial. Lancet Oncol. 9 (6), 533–542. https://doi.org/10.1016/S1470-2045(08)70107-4.

Passero, F.C., Grapsa, D., Syrigos, K.N., Saif, M.W., 2016. The safety and efficacy of Onivyde (irinotecan liposome injection) for the treatment of metastatic pancreatic cancer following gemcitabine-based therapy. Expert Rev. Anticancer Ther. 16 (7), 697–703. https://doi.org/10.1080/14737140.2016.1192471.

Petre, C.E., Dittmer, D.P., 2007. Liposomal daunorubicin as treatment for Kaposi's sarcoma. Int. j. nanomed. 2 (3), 277–288.

Penel, N., Adenis, A., Bonneterre, J., 2012. Role of the investigator in phase 1 trials of anticancer drugs. Lancet Oncol. 13 (12), 1177–1179. https://doi.org/10.1016/S1470-2045(12)70502-8.

Phase I Study of DOXIL and Temsirolimus in Resistant Solid Malignancies, 2013. https://clinicaltrials.gov/study/NCT00703170.

Profile of Inotuzumab Ozogamicin and its Potential in the Treatment of Acute Lymphoblastic Leukemia, 2014. https://www.dovepress.com/profile-of-inotuzumab-ozogamicin-and-its-potential-in-the-treatment-of-peer-reviewed-fulltext-article-BLCTT.

Pugazhendhi, A., Edison, T.N.J.I., Karuppusamy, I., Kathirvel, B., 2018. Inorganic nanoparticles: A potential cancer therapy for human welfare. Int. J. Pharm. 539 (1–2), 104–111. https://doi.org/10.1016/j.ijpharm.2018.01.034.

Resnik, D.B., Tinkle, S.S., 2007. Ethics in nanomedicine. Nanomedicine 2 (3), 345–350. https://doi.org/10.2217/17435889.2.3.345.

Richardson, N.C., Kasamon, Y.L., Chen, H., de Claro, R.A., Ye, J., Blumenthal, G.M., Farrell, A.T., Pazdur, R., 2019. FDA approval summary: Brentuximab vedotin in first-line treatment of peripheral T-cell lymphoma. Oncologist 24 (5), e180. https://doi.org/10.1634/theoncologist.2019-0098.

Riley, R.S., Day, E.S., 2017. Gold nanoparticle-mediated photothermal therapy: Applications and opportunities for multimodal cancer treatment. Wiley Interdiscip. Rev. Nanomed. Nanobiotechnol. 9 (4). https://doi.org/10.1002/wnan.1449.

Robidoux, A., Buzdar, A., Quinaux, E., Jacobs, S., Rastogi, P., Fourchotte, V., Younan, R.J., Pajon, E.R., Shalaby, I. A., Desai, A.M., Fehrenbacher, L., Geyer, C.E., Mamounas, E.P., Wolmark, N., 2010. A phase II neoadjuvant trial of sequential nanoparticle albumin-bound paclitaxel followed by 5-fluorouracil/epirubicin/cyclophosphamide in locally advanced breast cancer. Clin. Breast Cancer 10 (1), 81–86. https://doi.org/10.3816/CBC.2010.n.011.

Rosenblat, T.L., McDevitt, M.R., Mulford, D.A., Pandit-Taskar, N., Divgi, C.R., Panageas, K.S., Heaney, M.L., Chanel, S., Morgenstern, A., Sgouros, G., Larson, S.M., Scheinberg, D.A., Jurcic, J.G., 2010. Sequential cytarabine and α-particle immunotherapy with bismuth-213-lintuzumab (HuM195) for acute myeloid leukemia. Clin. Cancer Res. 16 (21), 5303–5311. https://doi.org/10.1158/1078-0432.CCR-10-0382.

Rubinstein, P.G., Moore, P.C., Bimali, M., Lee, J.Y., Rudek, M.A., Chadburn, A., Ratner, L., Henry, D.H., Cesarman, E., DeMarco, C.E., Costagliola, D., Taoufik, Y., Ramos, J.C., Sharon, E., Reid, E.G., Ambinder, R.F., Mitsuyasu, R., Mounier, N., Besson, C., Noy, A., Barta, S.K., Hamdan, A., Boué, F., Delobel, P., Galicier, L., Coppo, P., Ghesquières, H., 2023. Brentuximab vedotin with AVD for stage II–IV HIV-related Hodgkin lymphoma (AMC 085): Phase 2 results from an open-label, single arm, multicentre phase 1/2 trial. Lancet Haematol. 10 (8), e624. https://doi.org/10.1016/S2352-3026(23)00157-6.

Saif, M.W., Podoltsev, N.A., Rubin, M.S., Figueroa, J.A., Lee, M.Y., Kwon, J., Rowen, E., Yu, J., Kerr, R.O., 2010. Phase II clinical trial of paclitaxel loaded polymeric micelle in patients with advanced pancreatic cancer. Cancer Invest. 28 (2), 186–194. https://doi.org/10.3109/07357900903179591.

de Sanjosé, S., Diaz, M., Castellsagué, X., Clifford, G., Bruni, L., Muñoz, N., Bosch, F.X., 2007. Worldwide prevalence and genotype distribution of cervical human papillomavirus DNA in women with normal cytology: a meta-analysis. Lancet Infect. Dis. 7 (7), 453–459. https://doi.org/10.1016/S1473-3099(07)70158-5.

Sanoff, H.K., Moon, D.H., Moore, D.T., Boles, J., Bui, C., Blackstock, W., O'Neil, B.H., Subramaniam, S., McRee, A.J., Carlson, C., Lee, M.S., Tepper, J.E., Wang, A.Z., 2019. Phase I/II trial of nano-camptothecin CRLX101 with capecitabine and radiotherapy as neoadjuvant treatment for locally advanced rectal cancer. Nanomed. Nanotechnol. Biol. Med. 18, 189–195. https://doi.org/10.1016/j.nano.2019.02.021.

Saxena, M., Anker, J.F., Kodysh, J., O'Donnell, T., Kaminska, A.M., Meseck, M., Hapanowicz, O., Niglio, S.A., Salazar, A.M., Shah, H.R., Kinoshita, Y., Brody, R., Rubinsteyn, A., Sebra, R.P., Bhardwaj, N., Galsky, M.D., 2025. Atezolizumab plus personalized neoantigen vaccination in urothelial cancer: A phase 1 trial. Nat. Cancer 6 (6), 988–999. https://doi.org/10.1038/s43018-025-00966-7.

Schmidt, K.T., Huitema, A.D.R., Dorlo, T.P.C., Peer, C.J., Cordes, L.M., Sciuto, L., Wroblewski, S., Pommier, Y., Madan, R.A., Thomas, A., Figg, W.D., 2020. Population pharmacokinetic analysis of nanoparticle-bound and free camptothecin after administration of NLG207 in adults with advanced solid tumors. Cancer Chemother. Pharmacol. 86 (4), 475–486. https://doi.org/10.1007/s00280-020-04134-9.

Schultheis, B., Strumberg, D., Santel, A., Vank, C., Gebhardt, F., Keil, O., Lange, C., Giese, K., Kaufmann, J., Khan, M., Drevs, J., 2014. First-in-human phase I study of the liposomal RNA interference therapeutic Atu027 in patients with advanced solid tumors. J. Clin. Oncol. 32 (36), 4141–4148. https://doi.org/10.1200/JCO.2013.55.0376.

Sharma, M., Panwar, D., Tiwari, P., Kumar, A., Gautam, S., Marwaha, D., Rai, N., Singh, N., Kumar Bakshi, A., Agarwal, N., Singh, N.K.C., Mitra, K., Prajapati, V.M., Mishra, P.R., 2023. Immobilized doxorubicin and ribociclib carbamate linkers encaged in surface modified cubosomes spatially target tumor reductive environment to enhance antitumor efficacy. Biomater. Adv. 155, 213672. https://doi.org/10.1016/j.bioadv.2023.213672.

Shroff, R.T., Javle, M.M., Xiao, L., Kaseb, A.O., Varadhachary, G.R., Wolff, R.A., Raghav, K.P.S., Iwasaki, M., Masci, P., Ramanathan, R.K., Ahn, D.H., Bekaii-Saab, T.S., Borad, M.J., 2019. Gemcitabine, cisplatin, and nab-paclitaxel for the treatment of advanced biliary tract cancers: A phase 2 clinical trial. JAMA Oncol. 5 (6), 824–830. https://doi.org/10.1001/jamaoncol.2019.0270.

Smith, J.A., Costales, A.B., Jaffari, M., Urbauer, D.L., Frumovitz, M., Kutac, C.K., Tran, H., Coleman, R.L., 2016. Is it equivalent? evaluation of the clinical activity of single agent lipodox compared to single agent doxil in ovarian cancer treatment. J. Oncol. Pharm. Pract. 22 (4), 599–604. https://doi.org/10.1177/1078155215594415.

Stone, V., Johnston, H., Schins, R.P.F., 2009. Development of in vitro systems for nanotoxicology: Methodological considerations in vitro methods for nanotoxicology Vicki Stone et al. Crit. Rev. Toxicol. 39 (7), 613–626. https://doi.org/10.1080/10408440903120975.

Song, W., Jia, P., Zhang, T., Dou, K., Liu, L., Ren, Y., Liu, F., Xue, J., Hasanin, M.S., Qi, H., Zhou, Q., 2022. Cell membrane-camouflaged inorganic nanoparticles for cancer therapy. J. Nanobiotechnol. 20 (1). https://doi.org/10.1186/s12951-022-01475-w.

Spigel, D.R., Dowlati, A., Chen, Y., Navarro, A., Yang, J.C.H., Stojanovic, G., Jove, M., Rich, P., Andric, Z.G., Wu, Y. L., Rudin, C.M., Chen, H., Zhang, L., Yeung, S., Benzaghou, F., Paz-Ares, L., Bunn, P.A., Clingan, P., Hayes, T., Underhill, C., Demey, W., Forget, F., Lambrechts, M., Nackaerts, K., André Franke, F., Azambuja, A.A., Guimaraes, R., Mourao Dias, J., Santos, V., Cezar Uchoa Junior, B., Alves, G.V., De Melo Sette, C.V., Bi, M., Cui, J., Fang, J., Shi, J., Wang, K., Wang, Z., Yu, X., Dayen, C., Greillier, L., Quere, G., Baraniskin, A., Bischoff, H., Griesinger, F., Waller, C., Csoszi, T., Galffy, G., Laczo, I., Losonczy, G., Tehenes, S., Delmonte, A., Follador, A., Batura-Gabryel, H., Centkowski, P., Danielewicz, I., Kazarnowicz, A., Ramlau, R., Muntean, A.S., Oprean, C.M., Schenker, M., Tiut, C., Adrian Udrea, A., Ungureanu, A., Karaseva, N., Kislov, N., Poddubskaya, E., Rozhkova, I., Solovyeva, E., Zimina, A., Andric, Z., Kovcin, V., Petrovic, M., Radojevic, Z., Stojanovic, G., Hong, S., Kim, S.W., Lee, K.H., Shim, B.Y., Alonso Garcia, M., Calles Blanco, A., Calderon, V.G., Juan Vidal, O.J., Massuti Sureda, B., Navarro Mendivil, A., Palmero Sanchez, R., Ho, C.L., Lin, S.H., Liu, C.Y., Yang, C.H., Cicin, I., Gumus, M., Harputluoglu, H., Ozguroglu, M., Selcuk Seber, E., Sezer, A., Adamchuk, H., Bondarenko, I., Hotko, Y., Kobziev, O., Koshelenko, O., Kurochkin, A., Semegen, Y., Sinielnikov, I., Tarasenko, T., Trukhin, D., Carlisle, J., Carr, L., Chaudhry, A., Chen, H.,

Chen, Y., Dowlati, A., Duvivier, H., Edenfield, W., Hussein, M., Jotte, R., Jujjavarapu, S., Lingerfelt, B., McCune, S., Nagajothi, N., Rubin, P., Scilla, K., Spigel, D., Srkalovic, G., Weise, A., Zuniga, R., 2024. RESILIENT Part 2: A randomized, open-label phase III study of liposomal irinotecan versus topotecan in adults with relapsed small cell lung cancer. J. Clin. Oncol. 42 (19), 2317–2326. https://doi.org/10.1200/JCO.23.02110.

Study of Liposome Encapsulated Mitoxantrone (LEM) in Patients with Advanced Cancer, 2011. https://clinicaltrials.gov/study/NCT00024492.

Sulforadex in Healthy Human Males MAD, 2015. https://clinicaltrials.gov/study/NCT02055716?term=NCT02055716&rank=1.

Sutton, D., Nasongkla, N., Blanco, E., Gao, J., 2007. Functionalized micellar systems for cancer targeted drug delivery. Pharm. Res. 24 (6), 1029–1046. https://doi.org/10.1007/s11095-006-9223-y.

Syed, Y.Y., 2020. Sacituzumab govitecan: First approval. Drugs 80 (10), 1019–1025. https://doi.org/10.1007/s40265-020-01337-5.

Tabernero, J., Shapiro, G.I., LoRusso, P.M., Cervantes, A., Schwartz, G.K., Weiss, G.J., Paz-Ares, L., Cho, D.C., Infante, J.R., Alsina, M., Gounder, M.M., Falzone, R., Harrop, J., White, A.C.S., Toudjarska, I., Bumcrot, D., Meyers, R.E., Hinkle, G., Svrzikapa, N., Hutabarat, R.M., Clausen, V.A., Cehelsky, J., Nochur, S.V., Gamba-Vitalo, C., Vaishnaw, A.K., Sah, D.W.Y., Gollob, J.A., Burris III, H.A., 2013. First-in-humans trial of an RNA interference therapeutic targeting VEGF and KSP in cancer patients with liver involvement. Cancer Discov. 3 (4), 406–417. https://doi.org/10.1158/2159-8290.CD-12-0429.

Tinkle, S., Mcneil, S.E., Mühlebach, S., Bawa, R., Borchard, G., Chezy Barenholz, Y., Tamarkin, L., Desai, N., 2014. Nanomedicines: Addressing the scientific and regulatory gap. Ann. N. Y. Acad. Sci. 1313 (1), 35–56. https://doi.org/10.1111/nyas.12403.

Tiwari, P., Shukla, R.P., Yadav, K., Panwar, D., Agarwal, N., Kumar, A., Singh, N., Kumar Bakshi, A., Marwaha, D., Gautam, S., Rai, N., Mishra, P.R., 2024a. Exploring nanocarriers as innovative materials for advanced drug delivery strategies in onco-immunotherapies. J. Mol. Graph. Model. 128, 108702. https://doi.org/10.1016/j.jmgm.2024.108702.

Tiwari, P., Yadav, K., Shukla, R.P., Kumar Bakshi, A., Panwar, D., Das, S., Mishra, P.R., 2024b. Extracellular vesicles-powered immunotherapy: Unleashing the potential for safer and more effective cancer treatment. Arch. Biochem. Biophys. 756, 110022. https://doi.org/10.1016/j.abb.2024.110022.

Toth, G.B., Varallyay, C.G., Horvath, A., Bashir, M.R., Choyke, P.L., Daldrup-Link, H.E., Dosa, E., Finn, J.P., Gahramanov, S., Harisinghani, M., Macdougall, I., Neuwelt, A., Vasanawala, S.S., Ambady, P., Barajas, R., Cetas, J.S., Ciporen, J., DeLoughery, T.J., Doolittle, N.D., Fu, R., Grinstead, J., Guimaraes, A.R., Hamilton, B. E., Li, X., McConnell, H.L., Muldoon, L.L., Nesbit, G., Netto, J.P., Petterson, D., Rooney, W.D., Schwartz, D., Szidonya, L., Neuwelt, E.A., 2017. Current and potential imaging applications of ferumoxytol for magnetic resonance imaging. Kidney Int. 92 (1), 47–66. https://doi.org/10.1016/j.kint.2016.12.037.

Tsuchikama, K., An, Z., 2018. Antibody-drug conjugates: Recent advances in conjugation and linker chemistries. Protein Cell 9 (1), 33–46. https://doi.org/10.1007/s13238-016-0323-0.

Tzogani, K., Penttilä, K., Lapveteläinen, T., Hemmings, R., Koenig, J., Freire, J., Márcia, S., Cole, S., Coppola, P., Flores, B., Barbachano, Y., Roige, S.D., Pignatti, F., 2020. EMA review of daunorubicin and cytarabine encapsulated in liposomes (Vyxeos, CPX-351) for the treatment of adults with newly diagnosed, therapy-related acute myeloid leukemia or acute myeloid leukemia with myelodysplasia-related changes. Oncologist 25 (9), e1414. https://doi.org/10.1634/theoncologist.2019-0785.

Vaccine Therapy in Treating Patients with Newly Diagnosed Glioblastoma Multiforme (ACTIVATe), 2017. https://clinicaltrials.gov/study/NCT00643097?term=NCT00643097&rank=1.

Vasir, J.K., Labhasetwar, V., 2007. Biodegradable nanoparticles for cytosolic delivery of therapeutics. Adv. Drug Deliv. Rev. 59 (8), 718–728. https://doi.org/10.1016/j.addr.2007.06.003.

Wagner, M., Mitra, R., Mcarthur, M.J., Wallace, B., Barnhart, K., Wu, S.Y., Rodriguez-Aguayo, C., Zhang, X., Coleman, R.L., Lopez-Berestein, G., Sood, A.K., 2017. Preclinical mammalian safety studies of EPHARNA (DOPC Nanoliposomal EphA2-Targeted siRNA). Mol. Cancer Therapeut. 16 (6), 1114–1123. https://doi.org/10.1158/1535-7163.MCT-16-0541.

Wang, Z., Chen, D., Li, H., Yang, M., Lin, R., Cheng, Y., Li, Z., Huang, X., Wang, W., Li, H., Liu, H., Dai, Y., Wang, J., Zhao, X., Yang, Y., Qu, X., Zhao, J., Zhang, Z., Zeng, Y., Xu, R.-H., 2024. Phase II randomized clinical trial comparing albumin-bound docetaxel vs. docetaxel in patients with previously treated advanced gastric or gastroesophageal junction adenocarcinoma. J. Clin. Oncol. 42 (16_Suppl. l), e16018. https://doi.org/10.1200/jco.2024.42.16_suppl.e16018.

Wicki, A., Witzigmann, D., Balasubramanian, V., Huwyler, J., 2015. Nanomedicine in cancer therapy: Challenges, opportunities, and clinical applications. J. Contr. Release 200, 138–157. https://doi.org/10.1016/j.jconrel.2014.12.030.

Williams, H.D., Trevaskis, N.L., Charman, S.A., Shanker, R.M., Charman, W.N., Pouton, C.W., Porter, C.J.H., 2013. Strategies to address low drug solubility in discovery and development. Pharmacol. Rev. 65 (1), 315–499. https://doi.org/10.1124/pr.112.005660.

Yardley, D., Burris, H., Peacock, N., Raefsky, E., Melnik, M., Inhorn, R., Shipley, D., Hainsworth, J., 2010. A pilot study of adjuvant nanoparticle albumin-bound (nab) paclitaxel and cyclophosphamide, with trastuzumab in HER2-positive patients, in the treatment of early-stage breast cancer. Breast Cancer Res. Treat. 123 (2), 471–475. https://doi.org/10.1007/s10549-010-1047-0.

Yamamoto, Y., Kawano, I., Iwase, H., 2011. Nab-paclitaxel for the treatment of breast cancer: Efficacy, safety, and approval. OncoTargets Ther. 4, 123–136. https://doi.org/10.2147/OTT.S13836Japan.

Zaman, S., Jadid, H., Denson, A.C., Gray, J.E., 2019. Targeting trop-2 in solid tumors: Future prospects. OncoTargets Ther. 12, 1781–1790. https://doi.org/10.2147/OTT.S162447.

Zamboni, W.C., Torchilin, V., Patri, A.K., Hrkach, J., Stern, S., Lee, R., Nel, A., Panaro, N.J., Grodzinski, P., 2012. Best practices in cancer nanotechnology: Perspective from NCI nanotechnology alliance. Clin. Cancer Res. 18 (12), 3229–3241. https://doi.org/10.1158/1078-0432.CCR-11-2938.

Zhang, X., Qiao, H., Chai, X., Gao, X., Ma, R., Li, Y., Zhu, Z., Zhang, M., 2023. Brentuximab vedotin in treating Chinese patients with lymphoma: A multicenter, real-world study. Cancer Med. 12 (24), 21725–21734. https://doi.org/10.1002/cam4.6733.

CHAPTER

31

Challenges and future prospectives in anticancer drug delivery

Abhishek Sharma[1], *Shreya Singh*[2], *Shilpi Arora*[3] *and Sundeep Chaurasia*[4]

[1]School of Pharmaceutical Sciences, SDGI Global University, Ghaziabad, Uttar Pradesh, India; [2]Pharmacology Department, Bharat Institutions - Pharmacy, Mangalpally, Ibrahimpatnam, Telangana, India; [3]Himachal Institute of Pharmacy, Paonta Sahib, Himachal Pradesh, India; [4]Department of Pharmaceutics, National Institute of Pharmaceutical Education and Research (NIPER), Mohali, Punjab, India

Introduction

Cancer is one of the leading causes of death around the globe in subjects under 85 years of age (Siegel et al., 2024). Cancer is a multifaceted cluster illness where a few body cells propagate violently, leading to the bizarre growth of specific tissues, along with the propagation of this uncontrolled expansion to different parts of the body. Characteristics of cancer associate nonstop growth signaling and the suppression of growth suppressors, leading to violent cell proliferation and cell division. Declining cellular apoptosis, augmentation of angiogenesis for malignant tissues, attacking systemic circulation along with distant body organs, prompting genetic alterations, and ceasing immune responses contrary to cancerous tissues are also found associated as distinctive traits of cancer (Fouad and Aanei, 2017). Plentiful grounds, including lifestyle adoptions (alcohol consumption, smoking, diet, etc.), radiation contact, anxiety or stress, viral and bacterial infections, and exposure to chemicals, are various factors for these characteristics and the incidence of cancer (Wu et al., 2024). Fig. 31.1 portrays the vital characteristics of cancer cells, displaying important pathological phenomena imperative to the development and progression of cancer. Cancer is accountable for nearly 10 million deaths per annum globally, and is considered to be the second deadliest disease after cardiovascular ailments, as per the World Health Organization (WHO) (WHO Cancer Factsheet, 2025). Cancer burden is nonuniformly spread around the globe, and remarkable variances in burden occur among regions and countries. These variances

Advanced Cancer Therapeutics
https://doi.org/10.1016/B978-0-443-44185-1.00006-9

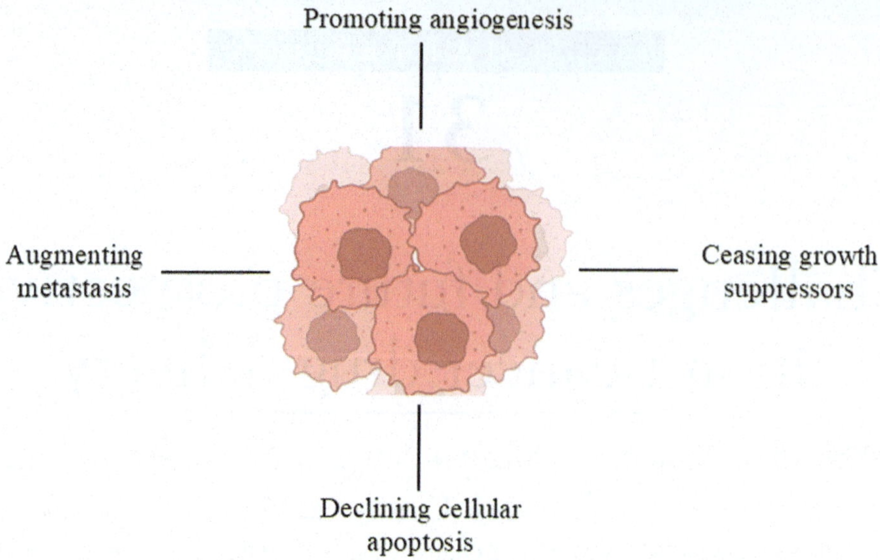

FIGURE 31.1 Distinctive characteristics of cancer cells.

are ascertained through a multifaceted exchange of determinants such as lifestyle, environmental factors, socioeconomic factors, and access to healthcare services. The incidence and mortality of several cancers also differ geographically. The incidence and prevalence patterns are imperative while intending targeted prevention and control policies according to the specific requisites of different populations. Additionally, patterns of cancer occurrence and mortality over a larger time frame should be monitored to recognize the impact of current interventions and to identify challenges in anticancer drug delivery (Bray et al., 2024).

Chemotherapy is the first-line treatment option utilized in cancer therapy for complete cancer eradication and to avoid cancer relapse post surgery or radiation therapy. The FDA (Food and Drug Administration) has approved over 300 chemotherapeutic medicines with various modes of action to treat cancer. Despite their potent anticancer potential, therapeutic results could alter, probably due to drug-associated challenges, complex tumor heterogeneity, and varying cellular responses and patient physiology, resulting in varying and subtherapeutic effects. Their effectiveness against cancer could also be constrained by drug efflux, the multidrug resistance phenomenon, and patient health. Anticancer drugs are usually given through intravenous administration or as oral tablets. This results in nonselective distribution to all major organs of the body and is thus associated with toxicity issues. A list of chemotherapeutic drugs with their mechanism of action and key adverse effects has been shown in Table 31.1. The subtherapeutic effect of anticancer drugs could be due to various reasons, including tumor biology, drug physicochemical properties and pharmacokinetics, drug resistance or genetic mutations, interpatient variability, and formulation-related issues. These challenges are discussed below to understand and overcome them with advanced cancer therapy strategies.

TABLE 31.1 Chemotherapeutical agents and their mode of action along with key adverse effects.

Drug Category	Subcategory	Name of drugs	Key adverse effects
Alkylating drug	Nitrogen mustard	Cyclophosphamide	Alopecia, myelosuppression, gonadal damage, and hemorrhagic cystitis
	Platinum agents	Carboplatin, cisplatin, oxaplatin	Neurotoxicity, nephrotoxicity, ototoxicity, and myelosuppression
Antimetabolite drugs	Pyrimidine derivatives	Gemcitabine, 5-fluorouracil, floxuridine, capecitabine	Pulmonary embolism, leukopenia, pyrexia, neutropenia, thrombocytopenia, and diarrhoea
	Antifolates	Methotrexate	Hepatotoxicity, nausea, vomiting, mucosal disorders, and loss of appetite
Antimitotic drugs	Taxanes	Cabazitaxel, docetaxel, paclitaxel	Infusion reactions, febrile neutropenia, fluid retention, and fatigue
	Vinca alkaloids	Vinblastine, vincristine	Chest pain, acute pulmonary effects, neurotoxicity, acute cardiac ischemia, hand-foot syndrome, hepatic and pulmonary toxicity
Topoisomerase inhibitor drugs	Topoisomerase-I inhibitors	Irinotecan, topotecan	Myelosuppression GI toxicity, alopecia, cardiotoxicity, and secondary leukaemia
	Topoisomerase-II inhibitors	Etoposide	
Antitumor-antibiotic drugs	Anthracyclines	Daunorubicin, doxorubicin, epirubicin, idarubicin, valrubicin	Cardiotoxicity, tissue necrosis, and alopecia
	Others	Mitoxantrone, bleomycin	Alopecia, febrile neutropenia, bone marrow suppression, and cardiotoxicity
Hormonal drugs	Selective estrogen receptor modifier	Raloxifen, tamoxifen,	Vaginal dryness, hot flashes, weight gain, depression, and sleep disturbances

Reprinted with permission from G. Kumar, T. Virmani, A. Sharma, K. Pathak, Codelivery of phytochemicals with conventional anticancer drugs in form of nanocarriers Pharmaceutics. 15 (3) (2023). doi: 10.3390/pharmaceutics15030889.

Challenges in anticancer drug delivery

Tumor biology and microenvironment

Tumor heterogeneity

One of the biggest obstacles to efficient oncology medication delivery is tumor heterogeneity. Even within the same tumor mass, neoplastic masses show significant genetic, epigenetic, and phenotypic diversity across cancer cells (Yang et al., 2015). Drug absorption, distribution, metabolism, and treatment response are all impacted by this variability (Zhu et al., 2021). Differential drug sensitivity may result from subpopulations that change cell surface receptors or overexpress efflux transporters (Zhang et al., 2020). As a result, it becomes extremely difficult to achieve consistent drug distribution and efficacy within the tumor, which recurrently leads to partial responses or recurrence (Zhu et al., 2021; El-Sayes et al., 2021).

Hypoxia and acidic microenvironment

Solid tumors, owing to their aberrant and disorganized vasculature, frequently have hypoxic areas (Li and Sun, 2018). Hypoxia-inducible factors (HIFs), which stimulate angiogenesis, glycolysis, and drug resistance, are overexpressed when there is hypoxia (Zhou et al., 2020). Moreover, tumor cells depend on anaerobic glycolysis, which causes lactic acid to build up, lowering the pH outside of cells (Dharmaratne et al., 2021). Therapeutic results may be lowered by this acidic environment's capacity to deactivate weakly basic chemotherapeutic medications, decrease membrane permeability, and impair drug release kinetics and nanoparticle stability (Li and Sun, 2018; Mo and Gu, 2016).

Dense extracellular matrix and poor vascularization

Collagen, fibronectin, and hyaluronan make up the extracellular matrix (ECM), which becomes overly dense in many solid tumors (He et al., 2020). This creates a physical barrier that restricts the diffusion and penetration of therapeutic molecules and nanoparticles (He et al., 2020; Gouarderes et al., 2020). Tumor vasculature is also often uneven, leaky, and poorly perfused, which results in heterogeneous blood flow and poor drug delivery to tumor cores that are hypo-perfused (Ghosh Dastidar et al., 2020). Intratumoral medication accumulation and therapeutic efficacy are greatly decreased when inadequate vascularization and high interstitial fluid pressure coexist (Gouarderes et al., 2020; Paresishvili and Kakabadze, 2023).

Pharmacokinetic and pharmacodynamic barriers

Poor solubility and stability

Even though many of the approved medications still have high systemic toxicity, primarily because of their lack of tumor selectivity and current pharmacokinetic problems, such as low water solubility, which impair the drug's circulation time and bioavailability, anticancer research has produced impressive results in recent decades (Ioele et al., 2022). The stability experiments have shown how sensitive anticancer medications are to a wide range of factors, whether they were conducted in benign settings during development or under stressful exposure to high temperatures, hydrolytic media, or light sources (Ioele et al., 2022; Lorscheider et al., 2021).

Degradation products are therefore assessed in pharmaceutical formulations as well as in the safety and toxicity parameters during stability assessments. Too far, many formulations have been produced to improve medication stability, reduce harmful side effects, and achieve tissue-specific drug targeting (Lorscheider et al., 2021). An implied approach to targeted cancer therapy is the creation of prodrugs, which increase the stability, efficacy, and selectivity of active ingredients. According to recent research, anticancer medications can be made more stable, soluble, and with enhanced pharmacokinetics by incorporating them into vesicular systems such as polymeric micelles or cyclodextrins, or by employing nanocarriers that contain chemotherapeutics that conjugate to monoclonal antibodies (Lorscheider et al., 2021; Alqosaibi, 2022).

Many anticancer drugs have low aqueous solubility and chemical instability, especially new molecular and lipophilic chemicals (Viswanathan et al., 2017). These traits make systemic delivery difficult, which leads to erratic pharmacokinetics and limited bioavailability. Toxic solubilizers are frequently required due to formulation issues, which can make clinical applications even more difficult in cancer drug delivery. Improving oral bioavailability may lessen the medication load and related side effects. Self-emulsifying drug delivery systems (SEDDS) can limit efflux transport, circumvent hepatic metabolism by lymphatic absorption, and improve in-vivo solubility and drug absorption from the gastrointestinal tract (Viswanathan et al., 2017; Pandya et al., 2022).

Rapid clearance and nontarget effects

The quick systemic clearance of anticancer medications, which hinders sufficient exposure of tumor tissues to therapeutic concentrations, is one of the main pharmacokinetic challenges in cancer treatment (Chidambaram et al., 2011). Plentiful long-established chemotherapy drugs, including paclitaxel, cisplatin, and doxorubicin, have molecular weights on the lower side and a hydrophilic character, which makes them vulnerable to hepatic biotransformation and urinary filtration (Senapati et al., 2018). A substantial quantity of the medications is promptly removed through the kidneys or metabolized by hepatic cytochrome P450 enzymes after systemic transfer, before they approach the tumor location. Systemic toxicity is aggravated by the short plasma half-life of conventional chemotherapeutic agents, which brutally ruins absorption of these medications, and therefore, high dosages or recurrent dosages are required to accomplish therapeutic effectiveness (Kawish et al., 2024).

The nontarget effects and rapid clearance of these conventional chemotherapeutic medications highlight the need for site-specific drug delivery methods that may accomplish controlled release, prolonged circulation, and selective cancer tissue targeting. Stimuli-responsive release mechanisms (pH, redox, enzyme, or temperature sensitive), surface modification with targeting ligands (antibodies, peptides, or aptamers), and nanocarriers designed to capitalize on the enhanced permeability and retention (EPR) effect are some of the emerging strategies to overcome these challenges (Senapati et al., 2018; Allahou et al, 2021; Li et al., 2025). By reducing systemic disruption of drugs and augmenting tumor-specific delivery, these technologies aim to enhance treatment efficacy while reducing the debilitating, unwanted side effects that have traditionally constrained chemotherapy.

Blood and organ-specific barriers

Blood-brain-barrier (BBB) signifies one of the most considerable physiological barriers in rendering anticancer doses, especially for brain tissue neoplasms and metastatic lesions. The structural veracity of the Blood-Brain-Barrier is upheld by pericytes, endothelial tight junctions, and astrocytes, which altogether form a highly selective permeability barrier (Alyautdin et al., 2014). Furthermore, metabolic enzymes such as cytochrome P450s and active efflux transporters such as P-glycoprotein (P-gp) and breast cancer resistance protein (BCRP) further limit the entry and retention of chemotherapeutic medications (Moorthy et al., 2025). Consequently, only a minor fraction of chemotherapeutic drugs, even after being administered systemically, inhibits attainment of therapeutic levels of drugs within the central nervous system (CNS), resulting in a lack of therapeutic efficacy for glioblastomas and metastatic brain tumors (Moorthy et al., 2025).

Beyond BBB, organ-specific blockades present additional drug-delivery challenges in cancer therapeutics. Specified tissues, which are resistant to numerous conventional cancer treatments, are found to get protection by the blood and testis barrier, placental barrier, and ocular barrier, which all tightly control molecular transport of chemotherapeutic agents (Moorthy et al., 2025; Zahednezhad et al., 2024). Additionally, mechanical resistance and hiked interstitial pressure through substantial stromal encapsulation and desmoplasia in pancreatic and hepatic malignancies hinder medication transport and vascular perfusion. In addition to limiting drug penetration, this microenvironmental stiffness produces an immunosuppressive and hypoxic environment that increases tumor survival (Grippo et al., 2012; Shihadeh et al., 2025).

Drug resistance mechanisms

Efflux pumps and multi-drug resistance (MDR)

Chemotherapeutic agents have been reported to actively efflux from cancer cells once ATP-binding cassette (ABC) transporters, including P-glycoprotein (P-gp), multidrug resistance-associated proteins (MRPs), and breast cancer resistance protein (BCRP), are highly overexpressed (Wang et al., 2022). This efflux and subsequent multi-drug resistance (MDR) abridge cytotoxic efficiency and intracellular chemotherapeutic drug accumulation, which is one of the foremost grounds of therapy failure that relapse and spread in various types of malignancies (Robey et al., 2018).

Genetic mutations and signaling pathway adaptations

Mutations in cancer genes and tumor expression suppressor genes (e.g., TP53, KRAS, EGFR) can amend drug targets and downstream signaling, making targeted therapies less efficacious (Bhat et al., 2024; Sheeba et al., 2014). Tumor cells can rewire signaling networks or activate compensatory endurance pathways such as PI3K/AKT or MAPK cascades. Epigenetic modifications and cancer stem cell populations further contribute to adaptive resistance, necessitating combinatorial or sequential therapeutic strategies as essential and posing challenges towards currently available drug delivery in cancer therapeutics (Bhat et al., 2024; Sheeba et al., 2014; Cheng et al., 2020).

Patient-specific and clinical challenges

Variability in drug metabolism and genetics

Interpatient variance in drug ADME (absorption, distribution, metabolism, and excretion) of antineoplastic agents is influenced by genetic polymorphisms in metabolizing enzymes (e.g., CYP450 isoforms), transporters, and various receptors (Narendra et al., 2022). This pharmacogenetic variability affects both efficacy and toxicity profiles of anticancer agents, obscuring dose optimization and therapeutic monitoring. Tailored individual dosing strategies are frequently required to balance therapeutic benefits with safety in such cases for the delivery of cancer therapeutics (Narendra et al., 2022; Bertholee et al., 2017).

Adverse effects and considerations for quality of life

Adverse effects are being considered as a substantial disapproval for the cancer treatments available in the current era, even with progressions in targeted treatment (Nurgali et al., 2018). Impairment to normal tissues, immune suppression, and systemic toxicity combined abridge patient compliance and poor life quality for cancer victims are key issues. Common side effects include chronic tiredness, myelosuppression, mucositis, and nausea (Rock et al., 2007). To overcome these obstacles and clinical issues with existing drug therapy in cancer treatment, drug delivery strategies that ensure tumor selectivity, minimize systemic exposure, and maintain patient well-being over long-term treatment are obligatory in modern cancer therapy modules. Phyto-cannabinoids have been in the limelight for screening for a long time to overcome the above-mentioned adverse effects for modern-day cancer treatment and management of other life-threatening ailments (Nurgali et al., 2018; Abalo et al., 2017; Sharma et al., 2025).

Formulation related challenges

Drug-related challenges

Anticancer agents often display native physical and chemical limitations that hamper the development of their effective formulation and thus clinical application. Several chemotherapeutic and targeted anticancer agents hold poor hydrophilicity, resulting in erratic dissolution, unpredictable pharmacokinetics, and low bioavailability (Alqosaibi, 2022). Adding to this, exalted hydrophobicity often demands the use of abrasive solvents or surfactants that can cause tissue-related toxicities (Gyanani et al., 2021). Molecular instability, such as predisposition to enzymatic breakdown, hydrolysis, or oxidation, supplement formulation design, chiefly for emerging treatment modalities such as RNA-based and peptide-based drugs. Antineoplastic drugs may also present a narrow therapeutic index, signifying that even the slightest disparities in dosing regimen can lead to severe toxicity (Gyanani et al., 2021; Torres et al., 2020). One more major challenge arises from the large molecular weight antineoplastic agents, which limit their tissue permeability and intracellular uptake (Torres et al., 2020). Furthermore, anticancer agents targeting intracellular pathways must possess the potential to traverse multiple biological barriers such as cell and nuclear membranes and endosomal compartments, ensuring their effective delivery. These drug-linked challenges collectively impede consistent therapeutic exposure and present rising exigency for innovative carrier systems and formulation strategies (Alqosaibi, 2022; Gyanani et al., 2021; Torres et al., 2020).

Excipients-related challenges

Excipient assortment for anticancer active drug delivery is restrained by compatibility issues, safety profiles, and geographic regulatory obligations (Jog and Burgess, 2018). Since cancer patients are frequently reported to carry compromised immune responses, any excipient-prompted sensitivity or inflammation may intensify the clinical risk of unmanageable oncological reactions (Lorscheider et al., 2021; Gyanani et al., 2021). Various practical excipients employed in advanced cancer therapeutics, including surfactants, polymers, cationic-lipids, and targeting ligands, may display dose-dependent toxicity, organ accumulation, specifically in the liver and spleen, and hemolysis. Furthermore, interactions amongst active pharmaceutical ingredients and excipients may lead to drug precipitation, its degradation, and transformed release kinetics, or disturbed bioactivity. The condition is more multifaceted for nanocarriers, where excipients impact surface chemistry, particle charge, particle size, and stability; minor variations can lead to extremely altered bio-distribution and therapeutic results (Alqosaibi, 2022; Azman and Wong, 2025). Real-world examples of excipients in nano-therapeutic cancer drug delivery employ lipids such as oleic acid, polysaccharides such as alginate, chitosan, and pectin, which are used to develop nanocarriers such as micelles, liposomes, and solid lipid nanoparticles. Other instances are biopolymers such as gelatin and heterocycles such as porphyrins, which form nanocarriers with specific required characteristics (Azman and Wong, 2025). Furthermore, different regulatory bodies of different regions necessitate a wide-ranging characterization of residual solvents, purity, and leachables within the excipients, presenting noteworthy challenges throughout nano-therapy development for cancer. Rising need for specific excipients that are both safe and functional in oncotherapy underscores the importance of designing next-generation biomaterials with enhanced degradability, biocompatibility, and aligned physicochemical characteristics (Jirvankar et al., 2025).

Scaling-up challenges

Translation of lab-scale drug-delivery systems for clinically feasible, scientifically, and industrially scalable drug delivery products relies on one of the major bottleneck challenges in oncology drug delivery [80]. Polymeric nanotherapeutics employing dendrimers and micelles denote a substantial number of formulation approaches established over the past decades. Though when equated with lipid-based nanotherapeutics and liposomes, polymeric nanotherapeutics have abridged clinical translation from laboratory scale. Chief shortcomings of polymeric nanotherapeutic formulations for low clinical translation have been the futile reproducibility in formulating steady and homogeneous large-scale industrial batches (Paresishvili and Kakabadze, 2023; Mahmud et al., 2024; Herdiana et al., 2022). Issues such as particle size nonuniformity, encapsulation efficiency loss, batch-to-batch variability, aggregation, and poor reproducibility often arise through scaling-up procedures. Moreover, dedicated equipment modules, such as high-pressure homogenizers and microfluidic mixers, may not be extensively accessible or economically viable for large-scale production of these types of drug delivery for cancer (Mahmud et al., 2024; Muthu and Wilson, 2012; Rosenblum et al., 2018). Maintaining sterile conditions and good manufacturing practices (GMP) compliance is found to be challenging, especially for biologically derived materials. Furthermore, complex formulations may need several labor-intensive and yield-loss-prone purifying procedures. Global regulatory standards also need thorough characterization, reliable quality control measures, and validated analytical techniques, all of which increase complexity. The rising necessity for scalable drug-delivering technologies in cancer highlights the fact that these scale-up difficulties recurrently cause major delays in their clinical translation and commercialization (Mahmud et al., 2024; Herdiana et al., 2022; Rosenblum et al., 2018).

Stability-related challenges

For anticancer medication formulations to remain effective and safe during production, storage, transit, and clinical use, stability is the most essential parameter (Sarvepalli et al., 2025). Chemical instability makes many chemotherapeutic drugs vulnerable to hydrolysis, oxidation, photodegradation, or thermal breakdown, all of which can produce hazardous degradation products. Due to their propensity for aggregation, fusion, leakage, or structural disintegration over time, nanocarriers, dendrimers, liposomes, micelles, and biological formulations (such as chitosan, mRNA, siRNA, proteins, or CRISPR-Cas components) pose such additional difficulties in nano drug delivery for cancer (Sarvepalli et al., 2025; Rahman and Mondal, 2024). Temperature fluctuations, pH variations, and mechanical strain, while handling these drug delivery systems, can cause destabilization of carrier-drug complexes. Lyophilization is frequently exercised to augment stability, but studies demonstrated that it could alter particle morphology or reduce bioactivity if not optimized accordingly (Sarvepalli et al., 2025; Ioele et al., 2022).

Future prospectives in cancer therapeutics

Computational modeling and AI in drug delivery for cancer

Artificial intelligence (AI) and computational modeling are transforming drug delivery optimization and discovery (Harkos et al., 2025; Rana et al., 2025). To improve delivery effectiveness, machine learning algorithms can emulate tumor and medication interfaces, optimize nanoparticle size and surface features, and predict pharmacokinetic modeling for the chemotherapeutic compound. By making it simpler to identify novel ligands and biomaterials for targeted distribution, AI-driven in-silico screening enhances the evidence-based theories for laborious experimental preclinical in-vitro examinations (Moradi Kashkooli et al., 2021b). Drug diffusion, release kinetics, and intracellular trafficking inside intricate tumor architectures are being modeled increasingly by employing computational fluid dynamics (CFD) and molecular dynamics (MD) simulations (Moradi Kashkooli et al., 2021a). When combined, these data-driven technologies have enormous potential to speed up the development of intelligent drug delivery systems, increase predictability, and absolute implementation of vast research on nano-formulations for cancer, and can reduce the time it takes to move ideas from the labs to the clinic and finally to the patients (Kamal et al., 2025).

Theranostics-amalgamation of therapies and diagnostics

A striking pattern shift in cancer management has been brought about by the expansion of theranostic nanoplatforms, which combine therapeutic and diagnostic capabilities into a single system (Kumar and Antal, 2025). This fusion of methods enables physicians to see drug accumulation and therapeutic efficacy at the same time by combining drug administration with real-time radiological studies and imaging, biodistribution stalking, and response monitoring. For illustration, iron oxide nano-carriers, and gold have been developed to enable MRI, CT, or fluorescence imaging while delivering genetic or chemotherapeutic payloads as medicine. By abridging the uncertainty and empowering early diagnosis of resistance or recurrence, this convergence of therapy and diagnostics simultaneously promotes image-guided and adaptive treatment regimens (Kumar and Antal, 2025; Anitha et al., 2024). Future advancements in multifunctional theranostic systems should make it possible for dynamic, feedback-controlled cancer therapy, in which the course of treatment is continuously adjusted in response to biological reactions in real time (Rajora et al., 2024).

Merging therapies with multifunctional carriers

Multimodal and synergistic therapy approaches are frequently necessary to overcome the complexity of cancer (Conte and Cauda, 2022). Codelivering chemotherapeutic drugs, gene modulators, and immunostimulatory molecules within a single multifunctional carrier is the goal of the upcoming generation of anticancer drug delivery systems. By targeting several cancer hallmarks at once, including angiogenesis, immune evasion, metastasis, and proliferation, such combination therapies lower the chance of treatment resistance, such as multimodal approaches in pancreatic ductal adenocarcinoma have been widely assessed (Conte and Cauda, 2022; Fan et al., 2017). Reactive linkers that release medicine as payloads sequentially or in response to certain stimuli such as pH, enzyme activity, or redox gradients are being employed in the design of polymeric micelles, liposomes, dendrimers, and exosome-based carriers (Fan et al., 2017).

Furthermore, rigorous preclinical studies have further demonstrated encouraging outcomes for clubbed immunotherapy with chemotherapy or gene therapy through combined delivery methods for cancer drug delivery (Hopkins et al., 2022). A new era of combinatorial therapy designed for continuing and restorative cancer treatment outcomes has been placed in demand by this confluence of precision technology and a multichannel treatment model in drug delivery for cancer (Hopkins et al., 2022; Luo et al., 2019).

Conclusion

From realistic chemotherapy and radiotherapy regimens to logically designed, targeted, and stimulus-responsive platforms such as precision medicine and cancer vaccines, the field of anticancer medication delivery has undergone an extraordinary revolution. Tumor heterogeneity, biological barriers, nontargeted and undesired effects, variance in genetic makeup and drug metabolism, and adaptive resistance are only a few of the major translational and clinical impediments that persist despite mammoth scientific advancements in drug delivery for cancer. Accordingly, the next-gen cancer therapies must merge scientific advancements with patient and system-level intelligence to address patient-specific factors, clinical practicalities, and molecular and cellular complexities.

Anticancer drug delivery paradigms are evolving towards more integrated, sophisticated, and customized solutions. Traditional cancer treatments are being replaced or enhanced by smart nanocarriers, multimodal synergistic therapies, theranostics, codelivery, and hybrid systems with controlled drug release. When combined with advancements in imaging, molecular diagnostics, and analytics, these delivery systems have the potential to change cancer treatment from reactive to predictive and adaptive management. Therapeutic interventions can be specifically adjusted to each patient's tumor microenvironment features, pharmacogenomic family history, and response towards treatment employing personalized nanomedicine, which is steered by genomic and proteomic analysis.

References

Abalo, R., Uranga, J.A., Pérez-García, I., de Andrés, R., Girón, R., Vera, G., López-Pérez, A.E., Martín-Fontelles, M.I., 2017. May cannabinoids prevent the development of chemotherapy-induced diarrhea and intestinal mucositis? experimental study in the rat. Neuro Gastroenterol. Motil. 29 (3). https://doi.org/10.1111/nmo.12952.

Allahou, L.W., Madani, S.Y., Seifalian, A., 2021. Investigating the application of liposomes as drug delivery systems for the diagnosis and treatment of cancer. Int. J. Biomater. 2021. https://doi.org/10.1155/2021/3041969.

Alqosaibi, A.I., 2022. Nanocarriers for anticancer drugs: Challenges and perspectives. Saudi J. Biol. Sci. 29 (6). https://doi.org/10.1016/j.sjbs.2022.103298.

Alyautdin, R., Khalin, I., Nafeeza, M.I., Haron, M.H., Kuznetsov, D., 2014. Nanoscale drug delivery systems and the blood-brain barrier. Int. J. Nanomed. 9 (1), 795–811. https://doi.org/10.2147/IJN.S52236Malaysia.

Anitha, K., Chenchula, S., Surendran, V., Shvetank, B., Ravula, P., Milan, R., Chikatipalli, R., Ra, P., 2024. Advancing cancer theranostics through biomimetics: A comprehensive review. Heliyon 10 (6). https://doi.org/10.1016/j.heliyon.2024.e27692.

Azman, B., Wong, T.W., 2025. Excipient nanoparticles as cancer therapeutics: Mechanistic actions, delivery and manufacturing perspectives. Int. J. Pharm. 681. https://doi.org/10.1016/j.ijpharm.2025.125866.

Bertholee, D., Maring, J.G., van Kuilenburg, A.B.P., 2017. Genotypes affecting the pharmacokinetics of anticancer drugs. Clin. Pharmacokinet. 56 (4), 317–337. https://doi.org/10.1007/s40262-016-0450-z.

Bhat, G.R., Sethi, I., Sadida, H.Q., Rah, B., Mir, R., Algehainy, N., Albalawi, I.A., Masoodi, T., Subbaraj, G.K., Jamal, F., Singh, M., Kumar, R., Macha, M.A., Uddin, S., Akil, A.S.A.S., Haris, M., Bhat, A.A., 2024. Cancer cell plasticity: from cellular, molecular, and genetic mechanisms to tumor heterogeneity and drug resistance. Cancer Metastasis Rev. 43 (1), 197–228. https://doi.org/10.1007/s10555-024-10172-z.

Bray, F., Laversanne, M., Sung, H., Ferlay, J., Siegel, R.L., Soerjomataram, I., Jemal, A., 2024. Global cancer statistics 2022: GLOBOCAN estimates of incidence and mortality worldwide for 36 cancers in 185 countries. CA Cancer J. Clin. 74 (3), 229–263. https://doi.org/10.3322/caac.21834.

Cheng, D.-B., Qiao, Z.-Y., Xuan, L., Wang, H., 2020. Recent advances of morphology adaptive nanomaterials for anti-cancer drug delivery. Prog. Nat. Sci. Mater. Int. 30 (5), 555–566. https://doi.org/10.1016/j.pnsc.2020.09.002.

Chidambaram, M., Manavalan, R., Kathiresan, K., 2011. Nanotherapeutics to overcome conventional cancer chemotherapy limitations. J. Pharm. Pharmaceut. Sci. 14 (1), 67. https://doi.org/10.18433/j30c7d.

Conte, M., Cauda, V., 2022. Multimodal therapies against pancreatic ductal adenocarcinoma: A review on synergistic approaches toward ultimate nanomedicine treatments. Adv. Therapeut. 5 (11). https://doi.org/10.1002/adtp.202200079.

Dharmaratne, N.U., Kaplan, A.R., Glazer, P.M., 2021. Targeting the hypoxic and acidic tumor microenvironment with ph-sensitive peptides. Cells 10 (3), 1–14. https://doi.org/10.3390/cells10030541.

El-Sayes, N., Vito, A., Mossman, K., 2021. Tumor heterogeneity: A great barrier in the age of cancer immunotherapy. Cancers 13 (4), 806. https://doi.org/10.3390/cancers13040806.

Fan, W., Yung, B., Huang, P., Chen, X., 2017. Nanotechnology for multimodal synergistic cancer therapy. Chem. Rev. 117 (22), 13566–13638. https://doi.org/10.1021/acs.chemrev.7b00258.

Fouad, Y.A., Aanei, C., 2017. Revisiting the hallmarks of cancer. J. Cancer Res. 7 (5), 1016–1036.

Ghosh Dastidar, D., Ghosh, D., Chakrabarti, G., 2020. Tumor vasculature targeted anti-cancer therapy. Vessel Plus 4. https://doi.org/10.20517/2574-1209.2019.36.

Grippo P.J, Munshi. Hidayatullah G, Pancreatic Cancer and Tumor Microenvironment. In: Grippo Paul J, Munshi Hidayatullah G, Transworld Research Network, Transworld Research Network, 2012.

Gouarderes, S., Mingotaud, A.F., Vicendo, P., Gibot, L., 2020. Vascular and extracellular matrix remodeling by physical approaches to improve drug delivery at the tumor site. Expert Opin. Drug Deliv. 17 (12), 1703–1726. https://doi.org/10.1080/17425247.2020.1814735.

Gyanani, V., Haley, J.C., Goswami, R., 2021. Challenges of current anticancer treatment approaches with focus on liposomal drug delivery systems. Pharmaceuticals 14 (9). https://doi.org/10.3390/ph14090835.

Harkos, C., Hadjigeorgiou, A.G., Voutouri, C., Kumar, A.S., Stylianopoulos, T., Jain, R.K., 2025. Using mathematical modelling and AI to improve delivery and efficacy of therapies in cancer. Nat. Rev. Cancer 25 (5), 324–340. https://doi.org/10.1038/s41568-025-00796-w.

He, X., Yang, Y., Li, L., Zhang, P., Guo, H., Liu, N., Yang, X., Xu, F., 2020. Engineering extracellular matrix to improve drug delivery for cancer therapy. Drug Discov. Today 25 (9), 1727–1734. https://doi.org/10.1016/j.drudis.2020.06.029.

Herdiana, Y., Wathoni, N., Shamsuddin, S., Muchtaridi, M., 2022. Scale-up polymeric-based nanoparticles drug delivery systems: Development and challenges. OpenNano 7. https://doi.org/10.1016/j.onano.2022.100048.

Hopkins, C., Javius-Jones, K., Wang, Y., Hong, H., Hu, Q., Hong, S., 2022. Combinations of chemo-, immuno-, and gene therapies using nanocarriers as a multifunctional drug platform. Expert Opin. Drug Deliv. 19 (10), 1337–1349. https://doi.org/10.1080/17425247.2022.2112569.

Ioele, G., Chieffallo, M., Occhiuzzi, M.A., De Luca, M., Garofalo, A., Ragno, G., Grande, F., 2022. Anticancer drugs: Recent strategies to improve stability profile, pharmacokinetic and pharmacodynamic properties. Molecules 27 (17), 5436. https://doi.org/10.3390/molecules27175436.

Jirvankar, P., Agrawal, S., Shaikh, F., Borse, K., 2025. Natural excipients: Role in nano drug delivery system. Current Nanomater. 10 (3), 246–255. https://doi.org/10.2174/0124054615248522231211105002.

Jog, R., Burgess, D.J., 2018. Excipients Used in Oral Nanocarrier-Based Formulations Fundamentals of Nanoparticles: Classifications, Synthesis Methods, Properties and Characterization. Elsevier, United States, pp. 279–342. https://doi.org/10.1016/B978-0-323-51255-8.00010-0.

Kamal, I.R., El-atty, S.M.A., El-Zoghdy, S.F., Soliman, R.F., 2025. Intelligent deep learning model for targeted cancer drug delivery. Sci. Rep. 15 (1). https://doi.org/10.1038/s41598-025-96149-6.

Kawish, S.M., Sharma, S., Gupta, P., Ahmad, F.J., Iqbal, M., Alshabrmi, F.M., Anwer, M.K., Fathi-karkan, S., Rahdar, A., Aboudzadeh, M.A., 2024. Nanoparticle-based drug delivery platform for simultaneous administration of phytochemicals and chemotherapeutics: emerging trends in cancer management. Part. Part. Syst. Char. 41 (12). https://doi.org/10.1002/ppsc.202400049.

Kumar, R.R., Antal, S., 2025. Advances in theranostic nanomedicine: Integrating diagnosis and therapy for precision cancer treatment. Curr. Stem Cell Res. Ther. https://doi.org/10.2174/011574888X362719250603073728.

Kumar, G., Virmani, T., Sharma, A., Pathak, K., 2023. Codelivery of phytochemicals with conventional anticancer drugs in form of nanocarriers. Pharmaceutics 15 (3). https://doi.org/10.3390/pharmaceutics15030889.

Li, J., Wang, J., Chen, Z., 2025. Emerging role of exosomes in cancer therapy: Progress and challenges. Mol. Cancer 24 (1). https://doi.org/10.1186/s12943-024-02215-4.

Li, W., Sun, X., 2018. Recent advances in developing novel anti-cancer drugs targeting tumor hypoxic and acidic microenvironments. Recent Pat. Anticancer Drug Discov. 13 (4), 455–468. https://doi.org/10.2174/1574892813666180831102519.

Lorscheider, M., Gaudin, A., Nakhle, J., Veiman, K.L., Richard, J., Chassaing, C., 2021. Challenges and opportunities in the delivery of cancer therapeutics: Update on recent progress. Ther. Deliv. 12 (1), 55–76. https://doi.org/10.4155/tde-2020-0079.

Luo, Q., Zhang, L., Luo, C., Jiang, M., 2019. Emerging strategies in cancer therapy combining chemotherapy with immunotherapy. Cancer Lett. 454, 191–203. https://doi.org/10.1016/j.canlet.2019.04.017.

Mahmud, M.M., Pandey, N., Winkles, J.A., Woodworth, G.F., Kim, A.J., 2024. Toward the scale-up production of polymeric nanotherapeutics for cancer clinical trials. Nano Today 56. https://doi.org/10.1016/j.nantod.2024.102314.

Mo, R., Gu, Z., 2016. Tumor microenvironment and intracellular signal-activated nanomaterials for anticancer drug delivery. Mater. Today 19 (5), 274–283. https://doi.org/10.1016/j.mattod.2015.11.025.

Moorthy, T., Yalamandala, B.N., Huynh, T.M.H., Lien, H.W., Pan, W.C., Iao, H.M., Chang, Y.H., Hu, S.H., 2025. Beyond borders: engineering organ-targeted immunotherapies to overcome site-specific barriers in cancer. Drug Deliv. Transl. Res. 15 (11), 4217–4259. https://doi.org/10.1007/s13346-025-01935-4.

Moradi Kashkooli, F., Soltani, M., Momeni, M.M., Rahmim, A., 2021a. Enhanced drug delivery to solid tumors via drug-loaded nanocarriers: An image-based computational framework. Front. Oncol. 11. https://doi.org/10.3389/fonc.2021.655781.

Moradi Kashkooli, F., Soltani, M., Momeni, M.M., 2021b. Computational modeling of drug delivery to solid tumors: A pilot study based on a real image. J. Drug Deliv. Sci. Technol. 62. https://doi.org/10.1016/j.jddst.2021.102347.

Muthu, M.S., Wilson, B., 2012. Challenges posed by the scale-up of nanomedicines. Nanomedicine 7 (3), 307–309. https://doi.org/10.2217/nnm.12.3.

Narendra, G., Choudhary, S., Raju, B., Verma, H., Silakari, O., 2022. Role of genetic polymorphisms in drug-metabolizing enzyme-mediated toxicity and pharmacokinetic resistance to anti-cancer agents: A review on the pharmacogenomics aspect. Clin. Pharmacokinet. 61 (11), 1495–1517. https://doi.org/10.1007/s40262-022-01174-7.

Nurgali, K., Jagoe, R.T., Abalo, R., 2018. Editorial: adverse effects of cancer chemotherapy: Anything new to improve tolerance and reduce sequelae? Front. Pharmacol. 9. https://doi.org/10.3389/fphar.2018.00245.

Pandya, M., Chatterjee, B., Ganti, S., 2022. Self-emulsifying drug delivery system for oral anticancer therapy: constraints and recent development. Curr. Pharm. Des. 28 (31), 2538–2553. https://doi.org/10.2174/0366622060614344З.

Paresishvili, T., Kakabadze, Z., 2023. Challenges and opportunities associated with drug delivery for the treatment of solid tumors. Oncol. Rev. 17. https://doi.org/10.3389/or.2023.10577.

Rahman, M.H., Mondal, M.I.H., 2024. Stability, challenges, and prospects of chitosan for the delivery of anticancer drugs and tissue regenerative growth factors. Heliyon 10 (21). https://doi.org/10.1016/j.heliyon.2024.e39879.

Rana, N., Sharma, K., Sharma, A., 2025. In Deep Learning and Computer Vision: Models and Biomedical ApplicationsDiagnostic Strategies Using AI and ML in Cardiovascular Diseases: Challenges and Future Perspectives. https://doi.org/10.1007/978-981-96-1285-7_72025.

Rajora, A., Rajora, S., Bhattacharya, Z., 2024. Emergence and impact of theranostic-nanoformulation of triple therapeutics for combination cancer therapy. Smart Med. 3. https://doi.org/10.1002/SMMD.20230035.

Robey, R.W., Pluchino, K.M., Hall, M.D., Fojo, A.T., Bates, S.E., Gottesman, M.M., 2018. Revisiting the role of ABC transporters in multidrug-resistant cancer. Nat. Rev. Cancer 18 (7), 452–464. https://doi.org/10.1038/s41568-018-0005-8.

Rock, E.P., Scott, J.A., Kennedy, D.L., Sridhara, R., Pazdur, R., Burke, L.B., 2007. Challenges to use of health-related quality of life for food and drug administration approval of anticancer products. J. Natl. Cancer Inst. Monogr. 37, 27–30. https://doi.org/10.1093/jncimonographs/lgm006.

Rosenblum, D., Joshi, N., Tao, W., Karp, J.M., Peer, D., 2018. Progress and challenges towards targeted delivery of cancer therapeutics. Nat. Commun. 9 (1). https://doi.org/10.1038/s41467-018-03705-y.

Sarvepalli, S., Pasika, S.R., Verma, V., Thumma, A., Bolla, S., Nukala, P.K., Butreddy, A., Bolla, P.K., 2025. A review on the stability challenges of advanced biologic therapeutics. Pharmaceutics 17 (5). https://doi.org/10.3390/pharmaceutics17050550.

Senapati, S., Mahanta, A.K., Kumar, S., Maiti, P., 2018. Controlled drug delivery vehicles for cancer treatment and their performance. Signal Transduct. Targeted Ther. 3 (1). https://doi.org/10.1038/s41392-017-0004-3.

Sharma, A., Singh, R., Virmani, T., Chouhan, N.K., Kapoor, G., Kumar, G., Bhutani, R., Rana, N., Sharma, S., 2025. Cannabichromene, a key non-psychotropic phytocannabinoid in treatment of major depressive disorder: In silico and in vivo explorations. N. Schmied. Arch. Pharmacol. 398 (11), 15611–15630. https://doi.org/10.1007/s00210-025-04236-2.

Sheeba, C.J., Marslin, G., Revina, A.M., Franklin, G., 2014. Signaling pathways influencing tumor microenvironment and their exploitation for targeted drug delivery. Nanotechnol. Rev. 3 (2). https://doi.org/10.1515/ntrev-2013-0032.

Shihadeh, H., Yousef, A., Al-Leimon, A., Abu-Rumman, H., Kreshan, L., 2025. Targeting stromal components in pancreatic ductal adenocarcinoma: A review. Ecancer med. sci. 19. https://doi.org/10.3332/ecancer.2025.1996.

Siegel, R.L., Giaquinto, A.N., Jemal, A., 2024. Cancer statistics, 2024. CA Cancer J. Clin. 74 (1), 12–49. https://doi.org/10.3322/caac.21820.

Torres, J., Dhas, N., Longhi, M., García, M.C., 2020. Overcoming biological barriers with block copolymers-based self-assembled nanocarriers. Recent advances in delivery of anticancer therapeutics. Front. Pharmacol. 11. https://doi.org/10.3389/fphar.2020.593197.

Viswanathan, P., Muralidaran, Y., Ragavan, G., 2017. Challenges in oral drug delivery: A nano-based strategy to overcome. Nanostructures for Oral Med. 173–201. https://doi.org/10.1016/B978-0-323-47720-8.00008-0.

Wang, C., Li, F., Zhang, T., Yu, M., Sun, Y., 2022. Recent advances in anti-multidrug resistance for nano-drug delivery system. Drug Deliv. 29 (1), 1684–1697. https://doi.org/10.1080/10717544.2022.2079771.

2025 10 5 2025 2 3 WHO Cancer Factsheet https://www.who.int/news-room/fact-sheets/detail/cancer.

Wu, Z., Xia, F., Lin, R., 2024. Global burden of cancer and associated risk factors in 204 countries and territories, 1980–2021: a systematic analysis for the GBD 2021. J. Hematol. Oncol. 17 (1). https://doi.org/10.1186/s13045-024-01640-8.

Yang, Q., Parker, C.L., McCallen, J.D., Lai, S.K., 2015. Addressing challenges of heterogeneous tumor treatment through bispecific protein-mediated pretargeted drug delivery. J. Contr. Release 220, 715–726. https://doi.org/10.1016/j.jconrel.2015.09.040.

Zahednezhad, F., Allahyari, S., Sarfraz, M., Zakeri-Milani, P., Feyzizadeh, M., Valizadeh, H., 2024. Liposomal drug delivery systems for organ-specific cancer targeting: Early promises, subsequent problems, and recent breakthroughs. Expert Opin. Drug Deliv. 21 (9), 1363–1384. https://doi.org/10.1080/17425247.2024.2394611.

Zhang, J., Du, Q., Song, X., Gao, S., Pang, X., Li, Y., Zhang, R., Abliz, Z., He, J., 2020. Evaluation of the tumor-targeting efficiency and intratumor heterogeneity of anticancer drugs using quantitative mass spectrometry imaging. Theranostics 10 (6), 2621–2630. https://doi.org/10.7150/thno.41763.

Zhou, Y., Chen, X., Cao, J., Gao, H., 2020. Overcoming the biological barriers in the tumor microenvironment for improving drug delivery and efficacy. J. Mater. Chem. B 8 (31), 6765–6781. https://doi.org/10.1039/d0tb00649a.

Zhu, L., Jiang, M., Wang, H., Sun, H., Zhu, J., Zhao, W., Fang, Q., Jia, Y., Chen, P., Wu, S., Zheng, Z., He, Y., 2021. A narrative review of tumor heterogeneity and challenges to tumor drug therapy. Ann. Transl. Med. 9 (16). https://doi.org/10.21037/atm-21-1948.

CHAPTER

32

Regulatory considerations for anticancer drug delivery systems

Kanchan Bharti, Deepika Deepika and Vikas Kumar

Institut de Recerca Biomèdica Catalunya Sud (IRBCatSud), Department of Chemical Engineering, Universitat Rovira I Virgili (URV), Tarragona, Spain

Introduction

Incurable malignancies are being treated aggressively as they pose a serious threat to life. Toxic chemicals or biological products intended to destroy tumor tissue or inhibit cell division are commonly used in antineoplastic therapies. Even though many anticancer drugs are highly toxic, careful dosing, clinical monitoring, and toxicity management make the side effects less hazardous than the disease. To achieve dosage optimization, an appropriate drug delivery system and drug targeting are required. The United States Food and Drug Administration's (US FDA) Division of Oncology Drug Products at the Center for Drug Evaluation and Research (CDER) recognizes the importance of developing new anticancer therapies and the need for promising compounds to enter clinical trials as soon as possible. As a result, the US FDA issued a number of guidelines for industry to follow, assisting sponsors in developing effective anticancer medicines. This chapter provides a regulatory viewpoint on the preclinical development of novel anticancer therapies with the aim of elucidating the distinctions from the preclinical testing of nanoncology therapies and outlining the evidence necessary for human testing and marketing (DeGeorge et al., 1997).

The process of developing a novel drug delivery system for targeted therapy is intricate and multifaceted, which calls for specific knowledge in the fields of materials science, chemistry, biology, and regulatory affairs. Reaching such important benchmarks is crucial for developing a safe and efficient drug delivery system that enhances cancer treatment. Though many treatment modalities have been approved, there is a notorious requirement for refining the regulatory landscape so that more effective and safe treatment options reach the patient's bedside. Regulatory obstacles, safety and efficacy issues, manufacturing scalability, cost-effectiveness, and intellectual property rights are a few of the concerns. Regulatory approval procedures are frequently drawn out and differ by nation,

Advanced Cancer Therapeutics
https://doi.org/10.1016/B978-0-443-44185-1.00002-1

necessitating early agency interaction to ensure alignment. Thorough preclinical research assessing toxicity and pharmacological characteristics is necessary to guarantee patient safety. Similarly, well-designed animal studies are necessary to evaluate therapy outcomes to demonstrate efficacy. Clinical translation requires scalable and repeatable manufacturing, while cost constraints require the utilization of effective, inexpensive materials and techniques. Finally, managing licensing and intellectual property rights can be difficult, which emphasizes the importance of working with legal and business partners (Bartkowski et al., 2025).

Development of nanoparticle-based drug delivery systems, whose properties can be predicted from existing data, would significantly facilitate the creation of product-specific regulatory guidelines. To enable this, a well-designed, up-to-date nanomaterial database is needed to curate relevant data and assign nanostructure-based annotations. This knowledge can aid in the production of nanoparticles with decisive or almost expected properties, under biological conditions. With this goal in mind, the United States, the European Union, and a few other nations launched the Nanoinformatics Roadmap 2030 (Nanoinformatics Roadmap, 2030; Yan et al., 2020). By storing and exchanging data, the project aimed to integrate all the information about nanomaterials and create a shared understanding among academics, industry, and regulators about nanoparticles and any health hazards (Junnuthula et al., 2022). By using this approach, all the most recent data about nanoparticles will be accessible on a single platform, supporting the expansion of research and the creation of stringent regulations for nanomaterials, as well as their clinical translation. This chapter attempts to highlight important aspects related to clinical, nonclinical, and advanced methodologies such as PBPK modeling, which contribute to the development of effective anticancer drug delivery systems.

Designing the nonclinical studies

The ICH S9 guideline outlines a flexible, streamlined approach to nonclinical testing of anticancer pharmaceuticals in patients with advanced malignancies. As cancer patients face life-threatening diseases and can tolerate greater risk, the guideline permits modifications in study design and timing compared with conventional drug development (EMA/CHMP/ICH/646107/2008, 2010). Key recommendations of the guideline include incorporating safety-pharmacology endpoints (cardiovascular, respiratory and central nervous system function) into general toxicology studies, so stand-alone safety pharmacology studies are only needed if specific concerns arise, and allowing the more detailed absorption, distribution, metabolism and excretion (ADME) characterization to be generated later, in parallel with ongoing clinical trials rather than being fully completed beforehand. In early phase trials in advanced cancer, first-in-human studies can proceed with minimal animal data, where no fixed no-observed-adverse-effect level (NOAEL) is required. In such cases, toxicology studies should approximate the intended clinical dosing schedule rather than following standard study durations. If patients respond and continue treatment beyond the tested duration, no new animal studies are mandated solely due to extended dosing. Recovery cohorts to assess reversibility of toxicity are omitted by default; a nondosing recovery period is included only if severe toxic effects at clinically relevant exposures make reversibility uncertain, and even then, complete recovery need not be demonstrated (Hansen et al., 2015).

In line with 3Rs (Reduction, Refinement, Replacement) principles, the ICH S9 guideline allows fewer animal species to be used in nonclinical studies when justified. For example, a single relevant rodent species may suffice for repeat-dose toxicity if the drug is a genotoxic agent targeting rapidly dividing cells. Reproductive toxicology studies are not required in the initial stage. Embryo-fetal development studies must be completed by the marketing stage, but are not required before trials in advanced cancer patients, and they may be waived entirely if the therapy's class or mechanism is already known to cause developmental toxicity. Fertility and pre/postnatal development studies are generally not warranted at all for advanced cancer indications; any potential effects on fertility can be inferred from the histopathology of reproductive organs in the general toxicity studies (*Oncology Pharmaceuticals: Reproductive Toxicity Testing and Labeling Recommendations Guidance for Industry*, 2019). Genotoxicity testing is not considered essential before first-in-human studies in this setting, although a standard battery should be completed by the time of marketing. Notably, if in vitro genotoxicity assays are positive, ICH S9 guidelines do not call for the usual in vivo follow-up assay in animals, given the expectation that many anticancer agents are genotoxic by design. Long-term carcinogenicity studies in rodents are not required to support marketing approval for drugs treating advanced cancer, reflecting the patients' limited lifespan and the acceptance of potential secondary malignancy risks (*Oncology Pharmaceuticals: Reproductive Toxicity Testing and Labeling Recommendations Guidance for Industry*, 2019). Immunotoxicity assessment is normally built into routine toxicology evaluations, without separate immune function studies, unless the drug has a specific immunomodulatory action, in which case endpoints such as immune cell phenotyping can be incorporated into the toxicity study design. Photosafety testing is handled pragmatically; an initial phototoxicity risk assessment is done in pre-Phase I, and if a potential risk is identified, patients in early trials should use protective measures. A definitive photosafety study is only conducted by the marketing stage if the risk is characterized inadequately (*PHOTOSAFETY EVALUATION OF PHARMACEUTICALS S10*, 2013).

Nonclinical evidence to inform clinical trial design and marketing authorization

This guideline explicitly links nonclinical study duration to clinical development phases: short-term toxicity studies in appropriate species generally suffice to support first-in-human and Phase II trials, and repeat-dose studies of up to 3 months are considered adequate to support marketing authorization for most advanced-cancer therapies. However, the combined nonclinical package supporting Phase I, together with the emerging human safety data from Phase I, is usually sufficient to proceed to Phase II and even first-or second-line therapy trials in the target cancer population. Unlike traditional limits, ICH S9 guidelines also allow clinical dose escalation beyond the highest dose tested in animals, provided that careful monitoring and smaller dose increments are used if animal data show a steep toxicity dose-response without clear warning markers. For combination therapies, no dedicated animal toxicity study is generally needed as long as each component drug's toxicity profile is known; if one component is novel or uncharacterized in humans, a limited nonclinical study (typically a pharmacodynamic/pharmacology study that also observes basic safety endpoints such as mortality, body weight, clinical signs) should demonstrate added therapeutic benefit without synergistic toxicity before proceeding in patients. Trials in pediatric cancer populations are usually initiated only after adult Phase I data establishing a reasonably safe dose. Notably, these guidelines do not require juvenile animal studies to include pediatric patients, unless existing adult data are insufficient to evaluate specific pediatric safety concerns. The guideline draws special attention to drug delivery platforms and conjugated systems, acknowledging that novel formulations require tailored evaluations. For antibody–drug conjugates (ADCs) or other conjugated products (drugs covalently attached to carriers such as proteins, polymers, or lipids), the safety of the whole conjugate is the primary concern and is thoroughly characterized, whereas the unconjugated (released) drug and linker are examined in a more limited fashion. This includes demonstrating the conjugate's stability in circulation (in both animal models and human plasma) and performing toxicokinetic analyses to measure both the conjugated form and the free payload after administration. Similarly, for liposomal formulations and analogs such as nanoparticle or carrier-based delivery systems, a full repetition of all toxicology on the free drug is not warranted if that active ingredient is already well-characterized. Instead, the emphasis is on evaluating the liposome-encapsulated product's safety profile, with only a targeted assessment of the free drug and the liposomal excipient/carrier as needed. The same principle applies to other novel carriers. The nonclinical studies should address the unique attributes of the delivery system, such as altered biodistribution or sustained release, without duplicating known information on the active moiety (EMA/CHMP/ICH/646107/2008, 2010).

Other considerations for nonclinical evaluation of anticancer pharmaceuticals

Toxicokinetic measurements are recommended to quantify both the encapsulated and free drug in vivo, whenever feasible, to inform exposure–toxicity relationships for each component. ICH S9 guidelines also provide pragmatic guidance on ancillary chemistry-related safety issues, for example, human metabolites detected during development that were not present in animal studies do not automatically require separate toxicity qualification for an advanced cancer indication. In addition, acceptable impurity limits may be relaxed beyond the usual ICH Q3A/Q3B thresholds for oncologic products, recognizing that the negligible-risk standards for chronic use may be inappropriate in the setting of life-threatening cancer. Sponsors can justify higher impurity levels in the marketing application by considering factors such as the serious nature of the disease, the patient population and life expectancy, the pharmacologic/toxicologic profile of the drug, the limited treatment duration, and the feasibility of further impurity reduction in manufacturing. In particular, the guideline notes that the conventional lifetime cancer risk limits for genotoxic impurities are not pertinent for advanced cancer patients; higher impurity thresholds can be set with scientific justification using the above risk-benefit considerations (EMA/CHMP/ICH/646,107/2008, 2010). Overall, ICH S9 reflects a science-driven, risk-balanced paradigm that streamlines nonclinical requirements for anticancer drug development. It focuses on essential safety information to protect patients without unnecessary studies, enabling more efficient development of promising cancer therapies for those with urgent medical needs.

Regulatory considerations for clinical studies of anticancer drug delivery systems

Recent regulatory guidance on clinical evaluation of anticancer therapies increasingly recognizes the diversity of drug-delivery modalities and includes delivery-specific expectations in trial design. The 2023 EMA CHMP (*Concept paper on the revision of the guideline on the 4 evaluation of anticancer medicinal products and 5 appendices, 2025*) guideline on the clinical evaluation of anticancer medicinal products provides overarching requirements for all stages of development but distinguishes between cytotoxic agents, noncytotoxic targeted therapies, monoclonal antibodies, immune-modulating agents, including tumor vaccine,s and chemoprotective or radio/chemosensitising agents, with separate sections for each modality. It emphasizes comprehensive characterization of pharmacokinetics to support selection of dose, dosing schedule, and route of administration, including mass-balance studies, assessment of food effects for orally administered products, and organ-impairment studies where distribution or elimination may be altered, as well as population pharmacokinetic analyses to quantify variability in systemic exposure across patient subgroups. The guideline further highlights that biologics such as therapeutic proteins and monoclonal antibodies (MABs) require reference to specific clinical pharmacology guidance, reflecting their long half-lives, immunogenic potential, and often parenteral delivery, and that combination regimens and radio/chemosensitizers demand careful evaluation of administration sequence and schedule to optimize tumor exposure while limiting normal-tissue toxicity. Complementing this, the 2021 Japanese Ministry of Health guideline defines the scope of anticancer drugs for clinical evaluation to include small-molecule compounds, antibody drugs, cell therapies, and vaccines, but explicitly excludes cell- and gene-therapy products such as CAR-T cells because their manufacturing, biodistribution, and risk profile require distinct regulatory treatment (Minami, 2022). Nevertheless, the document stresses that the general principles of stepwise development, early studies to establish ADME, pharmacokinetics, and recommended dosage, followed by exploratory and confirmatory trials, apply across these delivery platforms, and that ethnic differences in pharmacokinetics and pharmacodynamics must be considered when extrapolating doses and exposure from global programs to Japanese patients. A related 2021 commentary on the revised Japanese guidelines (Minami et al., 2021) further underlines how delivery modality shapes regulatory expectations by focusing on immune-checkpoint inhibitors, noting that their parenteral administration, prolonged receptor occupancy and durable immune activation lead to delayed antitumor effects and late-onset immune-related toxicities, so clinical studies must incorporate extended follow-up and may rely on surrogate endpoints and conditional approval pathways, particularly in rare molecular subtypes, while still monitoring for interethnic differences in exposure and safety.

The safety, efficacy, and tolerability conundrum

In cancer therapy, the antitumor efficacy of the drug remains paramount. However, in incurable malignancies, rigorous evaluation of dose-related toxicity becomes essential, because they have a significant impact on quality of life and they possess the potential to elevate noncancer mortality. Randomized controlled trials (RCTs) are considered to be the most standard to assess the benefit-to-risk ratio, yet their safety data are frequently inadequate and potentially misleading. Most RCTs underestimate the toxicity endpoints, limiting detection of clinically meaningful between-arm differences, and rare but severe adverse events often escape identification within typical trial sample sizes and durations. When examining the links between drug exposure and outcomes for particular patients, it is crucial to take into account the temporal relationships of events to drug exposure as well as experience with drug challenge and rechallenge (if safe to do) (Thynne and Gabb, 2023).

Regulatory guidance for dose optimization of drugs and biological products

The US FDA, in its guidelines to industry made a paradigm shift from the administration of the traditional maximum tolerated dose (MTD) approach, which often yielded high, poorly tolerated doses, to an exposure–response-driven strategy for dose selection. Developed under the influence of Project Optimus, which is the FDA Oncology Center of Excellence initiative to reform oncology dose selection by maximizing efficacy and safety, this guidance urges sponsors to initiate dose optimization early in clinical development and to engage proactively with the FDA (e.g., through formal meetings or the Model-Informed Drug Development (MIDD) paired meeting program) to discuss dose-finding plans (Fourie Zirkelbach et al., 2022). Rigorous model-informed approaches, such as the collection of comprehensive pharmacokinetic or pharmacodynamic data to enable population pharmacokinetic modeling and exposure–response analyses for both safety and efficacy, are supported by sponsors guided by the FDA's related guidance on Population Pharmacokinetics and Exposure–Response relationships (Fig. 32.1). FDA encourages sponsors to collect robust PK/PD data early so they can build population pharmacokinetic models. These models support exposure–response analyses to guide dose selection and evaluate both safety and efficacy, in line with FDA guidance on population pharmacokinetic and exposure–response relationships. The guidance further advises to evaluate relevant intrinsic and extrinsic factors, such as patient pharmacogenomics, organ dysfunction, or food–drug interactions, early in development to refine dose selection. For oral therapies, the effect of food on drug pharmacokinetics and safety characterization in early trials is advised (Miao et al., 2023). To identify an optimal dose, sponsors are expected to compare multiple dose levels in trials, often through randomized, well-controlled dose-ranging studies with stratification or blinding to dose whenever feasible. Innovative trial design elements, including adaptive or crossover designs and even intrapatient dose titration schemes, may be employed with appropriate prespecified analysis plans to characterize dose exposure response relationships robustly. Key dose optimization endpoints extend beyond tumor efficacy to include detailed safety and tolerability metrics, such as the proportion of patients able to complete therapy without dose reduction and the rates of dose interruptions,

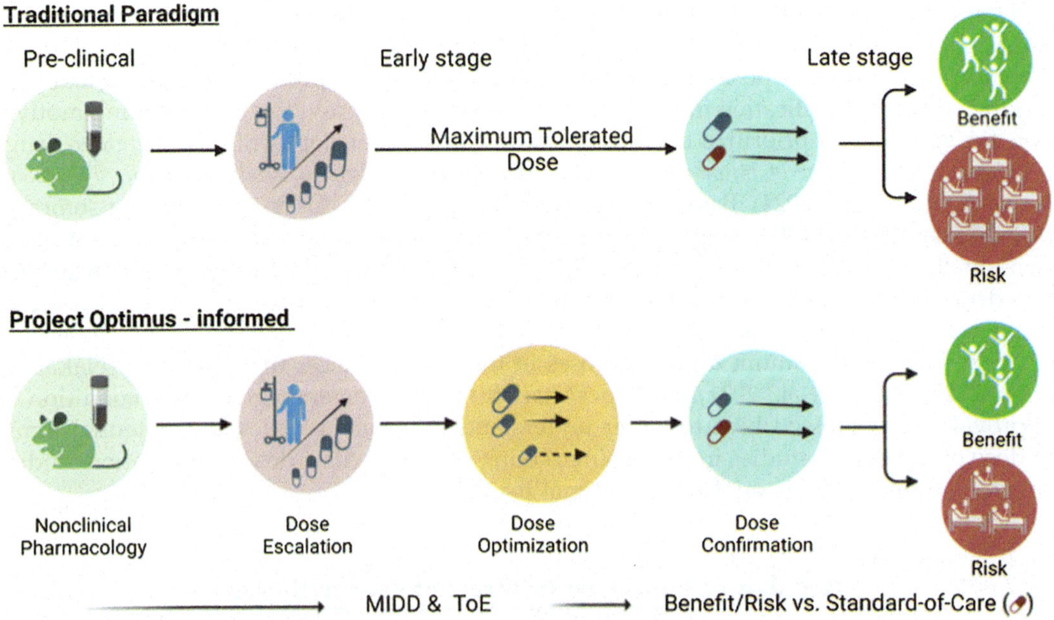

FIGURE 32.1 **Comparison of the traditional oncology development paradigm, which escalates to a single maximum tolerated dose in early phases before late-stage benefit–risk evaluation, with the project optimus–informed framework that integrates nonclinical pharmacology, dose escalation, formal dose optimization, and dose confirmation. The latter relies on model-informed drug development (MIDD) and a totality-of-evidence (ToE) approach to define regimens that maximize clinical benefit and minimize risk relative to the standard-of-care control arm.** *The image is adapted from W. Gao, J. Liu, B. Shtylla, K. Venkatakrishnan, D. Yin, M. Shah, T. Nicholas, Y. Cao, Realizing the promise of Project Optimus: Challenges and emerging opportunities for dose optimization in oncology drug development. CPT Pharmacometrics Syst. Pharmacol. 2163-8306. 13 (5) (2024), 691–709, https://doi.org/10.1002/psp4.13079. under the license, which permits use and distribution in any medium. The original work is an open-access article under the terms of http://thecreativecommons.org/licenses/by-nc-nd/4.0/.*

reductions, or discontinuations at each dose level (Gao et al., 2024). The inclusion of patient-reported outcome measures is also recommended to quantitatively capture symptomatic side effects and their impact on patients' quality of life and functional status. The guidance addresses practical formulation considerations for oral drugs. Dosage optimization must account for formulation factors such as pill burden and palatability, and multiple dose strengths should be developed. In such cases, manufacturing challenges are not an acceptable excuse for avoiding multiarm dose studies (*Optimizing the Dosage of Human Prescription Drugs and Biological Products for the Treatment of Oncologic Diseases*, 2024). Additionally, oral dosing strategies should consider food effects and dosing convenience. For parenteral drugs, the feasible concentration, injection volume, and dosing schedule at different dose levels should be considered when selecting the final dose and formulation. Overall, the FDA's dose-optimization guidance makes clear that oncology drugs (small molecules or biologics) should enter pivotal trials at a clinically optimized dose. This is enforced after the considerations of the results obtained after pharmacologic modeling, empirical dose–response data, and patient-centric tolerability assessments. These principles apply even to combination regimens or novel delivery modalities, which may require case-by-case consultation with them. The FDA emphasizes its position by warning that a crucial trial protocol suggesting a dosage lacking sufficient justification might be put on clinical hold, providing a compelling motivation for sponsors to prioritize dose optimization in the development of anticancer drugs (*Optimizing the Dosage of Human Prescription Drugs and Biological Products for the Treatment of Oncologic Diseases*, 2024). Based on this guideline, there is a classic case study of sotorasib (Lumakras) developed by Amgen, approved by the USFDA for the indication of metastatic non–small-cell lung cancers (NSCLCs). A dose comparison study had to be conducted for this drug postmarketing due to the pharmacokinetic profile and the overall response rate of the cohort of patients taking a lower dose (Shah et al., 2021). This challenges the notion of approving the maximum tolerated doses in the case of cancer drug delivery (Nakajima et al., 2022; Ratain et al., 2021). Such postmarketing requirements, given as a condition of approval, are addressed here to better understand the characteristics and potential limits of dose optimization studies in the postmarketing scenario. Also, dose optimization studies ensure optimum patient safety and minimal toxicity.

Regulatory landscape of targeted cancer therapy

Cancer immunotherapy is a relatively recent approach that selectively inhibits key immune checkpoints involved in tumor development. Monoclonal antibodies (MABs) have the ability to initiate tumor-antigen-specific immune responses (Weiner et al., 2009; "Monoclonal Antibodies for the Treatment of Cancer," 2017). In past years, out of 160 MABs that were approved by the US FDA, 42% were approved for the treatment or diagnosis of cancer (Shapiro, 2024). This section specifically navigates through regulatory acceptances of MABs as an effective cancer treatment modality.

The first therapeutic MAB, muromonab, was approved in 1986 for treating acute allograft rejection in renal transplant recipients, but the broader clinical potential of MABs was not fully recognized until the late 1990s. In the decade following muromonab's approval, 12 additional MABs were licensed: 7 as therapeutics, including 2 for oncology and 5 as imaging agents, 4 of which were indicated for tumor imaging to define tumor location and extent. The first MAB approved specifically for an oncology indication was rituximab in 1997, for patients with relapsed or refractory low-grade or follicular B-cell non-Hodgkin's lymphoma. This was followed by trastuzumab in 1998 for metastatic breast cancer in patients with overexpressed Human Epidermal Growth Factor Receptor 2 (HER2) tumors and had received at least one prior chemotherapy regimen for metastatic disease. Since their initial approvals, both rituximab and trastuzumab have been approved for other indications such as autoimmune diseases.

The limited success of many early MABs was attributed to incomplete characterization of antigen specificity and function or intended mechanism of action, suboptimal preclinical development, inadequately designed clinical trials, and inappropriate target selection (Glennie and van de Winkel, 2003; Stein, 1997). Most approved MABs are of the IgG isotype, though several marketed products consist solely of variable-region–derived fragments, single-chain variable fragments, or single-domain antibodies. Over time, nonhuman variable region engineering has evolved beyond immunogenicity reduction to address affinity optimization, developability and manufacturability (Bailly et al., 2020; Negron et al., 2022; Xu et al., 2019), as well as improved half-life (Igawa et al., 2010). Early development studies are used to identify problematic amino acid motifs that may confer unfavorable quality attributes, such as aggregation-prone sequences, potential immunogenic epitopes, or residues susceptible to posttranslational modifications, including nonhuman variable region glycosylation (Xu et al., 2019).

Although some earlier products have been withdrawn, by the end of 2023, more than 160 novel and biosimilar MABs had been approved by the FDA (Fig. 32.2). Approximately 42% of these approvals are for oncology indications, including 4 imaging agents, 12 antibody–drug conjugates (ADCs, one incorporating a bacterial toxin), 9 bispecific antibodies, a coformulated MAB combination, and 13 biosimilar MABs. Several of these products incorporate Fc-engineered sequences or are produced in glycoengineered cell lines. While most oncology MABs are still administered as intravenous infusions, some have been reformulated with recombinant human hyaluronidase for subcutaneous delivery, enabling substantially shorter administration times compared with standard intravenous infusions (Frost, 2007). Collectively, these developments highlight the need for modality-specific regulatory frameworks that rigorously address MAB quality, safety, and delivery route when used as anticancer drug delivery systems.

Route of administration changes

Switching an anticancer drug from intravenous (IV) to oral or otherwise changing the route, is usually aimed at improving the efficacy of the formulation. Before proposing an oral phase I trial for a drug, which was previously studied on the IV route, additional nonclinical work should be examined to check whether oral dosing increases liver injury, causes direct GI toxicity, or alters metabolism through gut microbiota, intestinal enzymes/transporters, or hepatic first-pass. These concerns can be addressed with oral animal toxicity studies that include bioavailability readouts, or oral efficacy studies that explicitly assess GI and hepatic safety, using a dosing schedule that is similar to the planned human phase I regimen. If metabolites are supposed to impact the efficacy or toxicity, then characterization of the circulating molecular species is suggested. Prior human pharmacokinetic profile from the IV form helps inform the initial oral dose, though it is not strictly required.

When there is a shift from prior oral clinical experience to IV administration for a drug, the primary risk that is more likely to be encountered is increased systemic exposure (e.g., higher C_{max} and AUC) and consequent toxicity. Before initiating an IV phase I trial, there should be supporting data coming from either an IV nonclinical toxicity study conducted on the intended clinical schedule or from human pharmacokinetic data with the oral product demonstrating that estimated IV exposures will remain within an acceptable safety margin.

Similarly, formulation changes for orally administered anticancer drugs must address the potential for increased systemic exposure. The extent of additional work depends on the human bioavailability of the original formulation and the likelihood that the new formulation

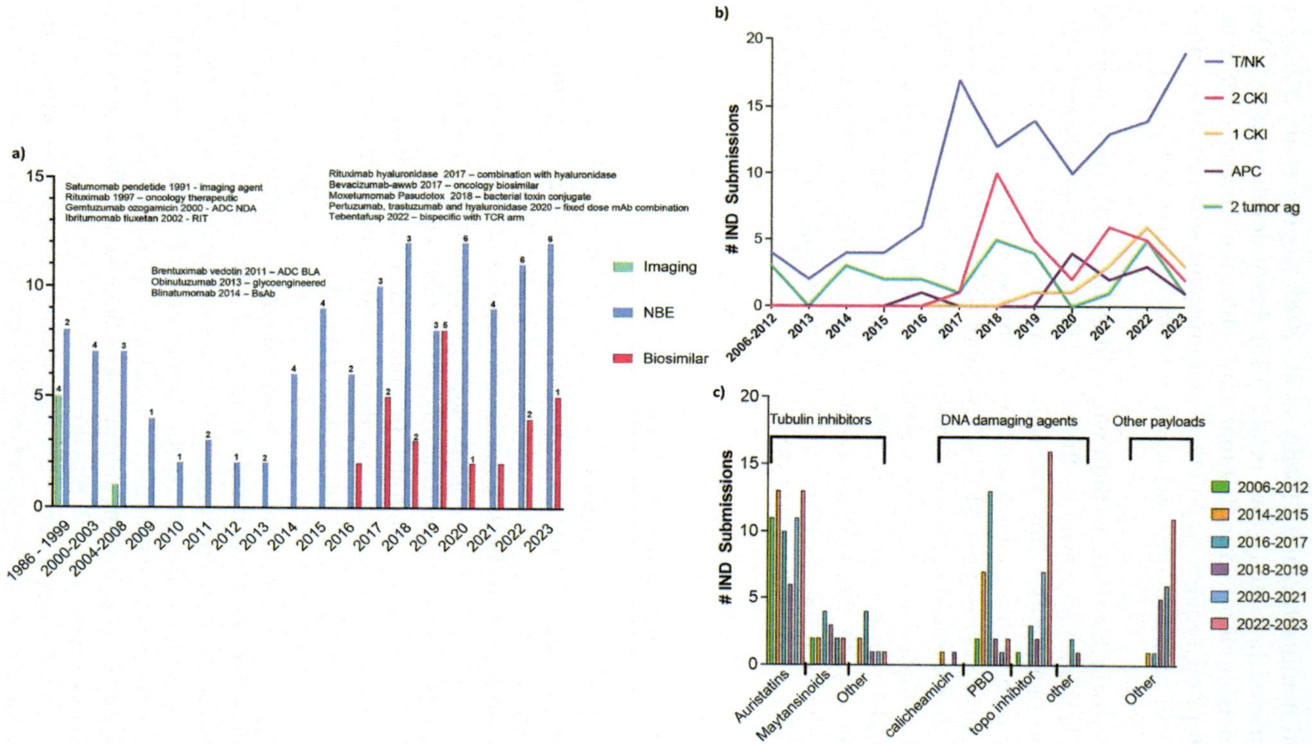

FIGURE 32.2 Regulatory and development trends in monoclonal antibody–based oncology products. (a) FDA approvals of monoclonal antibodies from 1986 to 2023, stratified as imaging agents (green), novel biologic entities (NBE; blue), and biosimilars (magenta). Labels denote "first-in-class" oncology products (e.g., first imaging agent, first ADC, first glyco-engineered mAb, first bispecific, first mAb–hyaluronidase combination). Numbers above bars indicate the number of oncology approvals in that year (b) Trends in bispecific antibody IND submissions for oncology indications between 2006 and October 2023, categorized by target configuration (c) Antibody–drug conjugate (ADC) IND submissions over time (2012–October 2023), grouped by payload class, illustrating diversification of cytotoxic warheads and sustained growth of ADC development for oncology. *The image is adapted from M.A. Shapiro, Regulatory considerations in the design, development and quality of monoclonal antibodies and related products for the diagnosis and treatment of cancer. Front. Oncol. 2234-943X. 14 (2024), https://doi.org/10.3389/fonc.2024.1379738. under the license, which permits use and distribution in any medium. The original work is an open-access article under the terms of the Creative Commons Attribution License (CC BY).*

could meaningfully enhance the bioavailability. If the original oral formulation exhibits ~100% bioavailability, the risk of exposure-driven toxicity is minimal, and additional studies might not be required. Conversely, with low original bioavailability, a comparative bioavailability study in a suitable animal species should be considered to estimate the exposure shift with the new formulation. These data can inform an appropriate starting dose for the initial phase I study of the revised product. In a few cases, it may be acceptable to proceed directly to a reduced first-in-human dose of the new formulation without new animal studies, provided the dose reduction adequately accounts for potential increases in bioavailability.

Considerations for different drug delivery systems

Administration of anticancer agents as depots, carrier-bound species, or specialized encapsulated formulations can substantially enhance therapeutic performance. Potential advantages of these delivery approaches include: (a) preferential targeting of the drug to the tumor tissue, (b) reduction of off-target toxicity, (c) maintenance of therapeutic concentrations over prolonged periods, (d) improved intracellular delivery of hydrophilic agents, and (e) more practical administration of highly lipophilic compounds. Representative platforms comprise copolymer implants, human albumin microspheres, monoclonal antibody--drug conjugates, and liposomal products. Such carrier or depot-based systems generally require additional nonclinical evaluation beyond that conducted for conventional cytotoxics. For antibody drug conjugates, key safety concerns are (i) toxicity from abrupt payload release and (ii) unanticipated, target-mediated toxicity of the conjugate in normal human tissues. In vitro stability studies in human plasma, conducted under conditions relevant to the proposed release mechanism, help determine the need for further toxicology. Where warranted, toxicology studies using the released drug species can reveal clinically important toxicities. A broad tissue cross-reactivity panel using human tissues from at least three donors is recommended, and if the antigen is absent in standard animal models, a tolerance study in Pongidae apes at ≥2-fold the planned human starting dose should be considered. The tissue reactivity screen and ape tolerance study can identify potential organ-specific toxicities, whereas standard repeat-dose toxicology primarily defines nonspecific effects. Additional in vitro specificity studies comparing binding or cytotoxicity in cell lines with and without target expression further assess the difference between on-target and off-target toxicity. When feasible, pharmacokinetic investigations that separately quantify intact conjugate, free antibody, and free drug are highly informative for the interpretation of toxicology findings and interspecies comparisons. Clinical starting dose selection should integrate conjugate toxicology, conjugate stability, and the intrinsic toxicity of the released drug.

For liposomal agents, standard nonclinical toxicology of the delivery system, the free drug, and the final liposomal formulation is critical to characterize safety. Because liposomes typically prolong systemic exposure, preclinical studies should mimic the intended clinical repeat-dose schedule to capture potential toxicities related to accumulation. When the delivery system is designed to modify absorption, distribution, biotransformation, excretion, or target organ distribution, even minor formulation changes can markedly alter overall toxicity; therefore, conducting toxicology with the final clinical formulation is preferred. Comparative pharmacokinetic studies of the liposomal product versus the free drug help inform dosing regimens and interpretation of any shifts in toxicity profile. In some cases, evaluating blank liposomes coadministered with free drug can clarify efficacy changes associated with the liposomal product, as blank vesicles alone may alter the pharmacokinetics of the free agent sufficiently to yield therapeutic benefit (Kim et al., 1987). Preclinical development of depot formulations generally parallels that of liposomal products, with the added requirement for a local toxicity study at the intended site or compartment of administration, including histopathological assessment of surrounding tissues. If the depot formulation does not substantially alter the toxicity profile, initial clinical doses comparable with the total dose previously administered in human studies with the nondepot formulation may be used.

Key considerations for polymeric therapeutics

In oncology, the urgent need for safer and more effective therapies has driven the development of advanced anticancer drug delivery systems, including polymer therapeutics, PEGylated conjugates, nanoparticles, and other nanomedicines. These next-generation systems are expected to further improve cancer care, but their progression from laboratory research to first-in-human trials must be strictly controlled through a rigorous benefit: risk framework. This transition, and subsequent progression to marketing authorization, is continuously overseen by regulatory bodies (e.g., FDA, MHRA, EMA, or other European agencies), whose review in practice runs in parallel with the entire research, development, and clinical program rather than occurring only at the end. No anticancer product or delivery procedure is entirely risk-free. The role of these authorities is to ensure that novel drug delivery systems actually confer clinically meaningful benefit and that their risks remain acceptable relative to expected gains in survival and quality of life. To achieve an objective judgment, regulators integrate evidence on quality, safety, and efficacy, and they continue to monitor these aspects postapproval through stringent pharmacovigilance. This is particularly important for nanoparticle-based drug delivery systems that, once in routine use, may be administered across heterogeneous global patient populations differing in age, ethnicity, genetics, and environmental exposures. Contrary to the perception that regulatory processes hinder innovation, these agencies are intended to enable the timely introduction of truly innovative, safe anticancer delivery technologies that provide tangible public health benefits, while ensuring that they are also cost-effective, practical to use, and ideally globally accessible. Indeed, PEG-protein, PEG-peptide, and PEG-aptamer conjugates already established in clinical practice (Veronese and Mero, 2008) have undergone formal pharmacoeconomic assessment, demonstrating that such conjugates can be cost-effective and even cost-saving in cancer care.

Within this broader context, nanotechnology-enabled anticancer delivery systems raise specific regulatory questions. Nanomedicines, which include liposomes, polymer–drug conjugates, and nanoparticles, offer clear clinical and societal advantages but also introduce potential risks related to both intentional patient exposure and unintentional environmental or occupational exposure (Maynard et al., 2006). Governmental and expert bodies worldwide are therefore examining nanomaterial exposure, their increasing use in healthcare, and the ethical and societal implications of these technologies (Helmus, 2007). Public discourse around "nano" has tended to oscillate between enthusiastic overstatement of the future promise of nanopharmaceuticals and alarm over hypothetical hazards, often neglecting the fact that first-generation nanomedicines, such as liposomal formulations (Torchilin, 2005), colloidal nanoparticles (Couvreur and Vauthier, 2006), and polymer therapeutics (Veronese and Mero, 2008), have been in routine oncology practice for almost two decades. The historical development of these systems reflects early recognition by pharmaceutical scientists that successful anticancer nanomedicines require a sound biological rationale combined with robust, reproducible manufacturing and characterization. All first-generation oncology nanomedicines were evaluated under the regulatory standards in place at the time of approval and met those requirements. Since then, the regulatory framework has evolved but continues to apply a case-by-case assessment, which has proven sufficiently flexible and robust to allow safe translation of these nanopharmaceuticals to the market, benefitting thousands of cancer patients. Going forward, new-generation anticancer nanomedicines and polymer-based delivery systems will be expected to build explicitly on the prior experiences, integrating early regulatory dialogue, rigorous characterization of nano-specific risks, and clear demonstration that the added complexity of the delivery system is justified by meaningful improvements in clinical outcomes and overall benefit: risk.

How PBPK can contribute to regulatory acceptance

Physiologically based pharmacokinetic (PBPK) models are extensively applied across academia and industry to characterize internal dosimetry underlying observed adverse effects in humans and other species. Their use has expanded markedly in recent decades, particularly alongside alternative, nonanimal testing approaches such as in vitro assays and in silico quantitative structure–activity relationship (QSAR) predictions. Data generated from these new approach methodologies (NAMs) can be incorporated as model inputs, increasing confidence in PBPK simulations for substances lacking in vivo datasets for calibration. Nevertheless, despite substantial progress in good modeling practice (GMP) for PBPK model development and evaluation, regulatory authorities remain cautious about their routine use in chemical risk assessment.

Another interesting aspect of utilizing PBPK modeling for dosing characterization is the rising attention towards the development of PBPK ontology (Kumar et al., 2024). The PBPK ontology provides a standardized way to describe physiological, physicochemical, and biochemical parameters used in various models across different software platforms, hence facilitating data harmonization. Apart from this, the PBPK ontology also enables the automation of model building and annotations, thereby decreasing the manual errors and enhancing the efficiency. This will ultimately enhance the regulatory acceptance by helping the researchers and agencies consistently evaluate the models by providing a clear, transparent framework for assumptions and data sources.

To increase the regulatory acceptance of outcomes from PBPK studies, it becomes important to understand how PBPK models are actually being used in practice and what specific barriers are limiting their regulatory uptake. A study done by Paini et al., (2017) reports the outcomes of a survey circulated within the modeling community to characterize how frequently PBPK models are used, for which applications, and in what regulatory contexts. The survey also aimed to establish a network of PBPK practitioners with GMP expertise who can serve as peer reviewers to strengthen the credibility and regulatory acceptability of PBPK models (Paini et al., 2017).

Role of pharmacokinetic modeling and simulation in precision dosing of anticancer drugs

Precision dosing is particularly important in oncology because many anticancer agents have a narrow therapeutic index, large interindividual variability in exposure, and are used in vulnerable populations with multiple comorbidities and comedications. Conventional body-surface-area–based dosing only weakly correlates with clearance and volume of distribution, leading to highly variable systemic exposure and inconsistent benefit: risk profiles across patients. PBPK modeling and model-informed precision dosing provide a quantitative framework to characterize interindividual variability, link exposure to covariates and clinical outcomes, and support individualized dose selection, especially where traditional clinical trials in special populations or complex drug–drug interaction (DDI) settings are difficult to conduct. The PBPK and DDI models can be developed to provide a basis for rational, evidence-based use of this drug in normal and special population (Jing et al., 2022; Liu et al., 2025).

PBPK modeling approaches relevant for precision dosing

Precision dosing aims to individualize therapy by accounting for patient-specific factors that influence drug exposure and response. In this context, Darwich et al., (2017) distinguish three complementary modeling paradigms: (i) population PK/PD based on nonlinear mixed-effects modeling, which quantifies variability in PK parameters and identifies influential covariates; (ii) PBPK modeling, which represents organs and tissues as mechanistic compartments parameterized by blood flows, tissue volumes, and enzyme/transporter expression; and (iii) "middle-out" approaches that combine population-PK and PBPK, fitting mechanistic PBPK structures to clinical data to refine physiological parameters. Population PK/PD is dominant in the literature (≈75% of studies), while PBPK modeling accounts for a smaller but growing fraction (~8%), especially for predicting metabolic DDIs, biopharmaceutic effects, and extrapolation to special populations (Darwich et al., 2017).

Quantifying variability and covariate effects

Covariate analysis within population PBPK models is central to precision dosing. Demographic factors (body weight, body surface area, sex, age), organ function (renal and hepatic impairment), genotype/phenotype, and disease-related pathophysiology are included as dichotomous or continuous effects on clearance and distribution parameters, allowing prediction of individual exposure from patient characteristics before dosing and refinement using a small number of blood samples or routine therapeutic drug monitoring. Across 393 oncology modeling publications, body weight and other demographic covariates were the most frequently retained, with additional work on special populations such as pediatrics, organ impairment, and elderly patients (Darwich et al., 2017; Joerger, 2012).

Applications across the anticancer drug life-cycle

PBPK modeling is used throughout drug discovery and development. In early phases, population-PK/PD and PBPK models support candidate selection, translation of preclinical exposure–response, and ADME characterization. In clinical development, these models guide first-in-human dose selection, dose escalation, schedule optimization, and dose bridging between populations (e.g., adult-to-pediatric extrapolation for docetaxel). PBPK models that incorporate oncology-specific physiological changes such as altered plasma proteins, inflammatory status, or hematocrit value have been used to better reproduce the exposure of drugs such as midazolam, saquinavir, docetaxel, and irinotecan in cancer patients compared with healthy-volunteer physiology, thereby informing dose adjustment in the real-world oncology population.

Model-informed precision dosing in clinical practice

There are three types of clinical implementation of model-informed precision dosing (MIPD): (i) real-time implementation in healthcare systems, where Bayesian forecasting tools are integrated with electronic health records to combine prior population models with patient-specific TDM data for example dashboards used to optimize high-dose methotrexate therapy and timing of rescue treatment; (ii) mechanistic modeling and extrapolation, where PBPK models predict exposure under DDIs or in special populations to inform dose recommendations when dedicated trials are not feasible; and (iii) model-derived dose banding, where PBPK models are used to define practical dosing strata based on covariates such as body weight or renal function, as illustrated by model-based dose banding for pembrolizumab that reduced drug wastage without materially changing exposure. Classical examples such as renal-function guided carboplatin dosing and PBPK-guided 5-fluorouracil dosing demonstrate that model-informed approaches can improve target-exposure attainment, enhance response, and reduce toxicity compared with body-surface-area-based dosing (Darwich et al., 2017; Tsamandouras et al., 2015; Wong et al., 2016).

Challenges and future directions

Despite substantial progress in regulatory science for anticancer drug delivery systems, several cross-cutting challenges continue to limit the efficient translation of innovative platforms from bench to bedside. At the nonclinical stage, ICH S9 has successfully streamlined requirements for advanced cancer indications, but its deliberately lean framework can be difficult to reconcile with the growing complexity of modalities such as antibody–drug conjugates, liposomes, polymer therapeutics, and other nanosystems. Such modalities often require additional data on carrier behavior, payload release, long-term biodistribution, immunotoxicity, and impurities, studies on which can be difficult to conduct with constraints such as timelines and reduced animal use. Similar concerns arise when there are modifications in formulation and route-of-administration that can alter the toxicity profile. In such cases, any prior knowledge about the drug moiety can help warrant the safety of the drug product with nonclinical studies. On the clinical side, regulators are moving from empirical maximum tolerated dose strategies toward exposure–response–driven dose optimization, but implementation is not yet uniform. Project Optimus and EMA/Japanese guidelines expect multiarm, model-informed dose-finding, careful assessment of intrinsic and extrinsic factors, and incorporation of tolerability and patient-reported outcomes.

The efficacy of targeted therapies such as monoclonal antibodies, antibody drug conjugates, and polymeric or nanoparticle-based systems is highly dependent on the biology of the target, carrier engineering, and route of administration of the drug product. This increases the complexity of trial design, deciding the appropriate specifications with the potential to be applied across the global regulatory authorities. At the same time, long-acting immune checkpoint inhibitors and other immunotherapies pose challenges related to delayed onset of action, late-onset toxicities, and the need for prolonged follow-up, which existing frameworks do not address completely. In line with the advanced drug delivery systems, extensive methodological development, and numerous case studies, the routine implementation of PBPK-based precision dosing in cancer research also remains limited. Key barriers include the absence of robust exposure–response or exposure–toxicity relationships for many newer targeted agents and monoclonal antibodies, limited evidence on patient-level clinical and economic benefit of MIPD strategies, and practical constraints such as the availability of multiple dose strengths or flexible formulations required to operationalize individualized regimens.

Future regulatory thinking will likely place more emphasis on patient-centric outcomes and implementation feasibility. For drug delivery systems, this means not only demonstrating superior exposure or tumor targeting, but also showing tangible advantages in terms of tolerability, quality of life, treatment convenience, healthcare resource use, and global accessibility. As health-technology assessment bodies and sponsors increasingly scrutinize the cost-effectiveness of complex delivery platforms, regulators, developers, and clinicians will need to work together to ensure that added technological sophistication translates into meaningful clinical benefit at a sustainable cost. If these scientific, regulatory, and economic challenges can be addressed in a coordinated way, the next generation of anticancer drug delivery systems supported by streamlined nonclinical strategies, rational dose optimization, and robust model-informed frameworks has the potential to deliver personalized, safer, and more effective cancer therapy.

References

Andres, H., Frederick, K., 2018. EU US Roadmap Nanoinformatics 2030. German Federal Institute of Risk Assessment (BfR). Department of Chemical and Product Safety. Germany. Pennsylvania Bio Nano Systems, LLC, USA. https://doi.org/10.5281/zenodo.1486012.

Bailly, M., Mieczkowski, C., Juan, V., Metwally, E., Tomazela, D., Baker, J., Uchida, M., Kofman, E., Raoufi, F., Motlagh, S., Yu, Y., Park, J., Raghava, S., Welsh, J., Rauscher, M., Raghunathan, G., Hsieh, M., Chen, Y.-L., Nguyen, H.T., Nguyen, N., Cipriano, D., Fayadat-Dilman, L., 2020. Predicting antibody developability profiles through early stage discovery screening. mAbs 12 (1). https://doi.org/10.1080/19420862.2020.1743053.

Bartkowski, M., Calzaferri, F., Giordani, S., 2025. Toward clinical translation of carbon nanomaterials in anticancer drug delivery: The need for standardisation. Beilstein J. Nanotechnol. 16, 2092–2104. https://doi.org/10.3762/bjnano.16.144.

Concept Paper on the Revision of the Guideline on the 4 Evaluation of Anticancer Medicinal Products and 5 Appendices, 2025. https://www.ema.europa.eu/en/evaluation-anticancer-medicinal-products-scientific-guideline.

Couvreur, P., Vauthier, C., 2006. Nanotechnology: Intelligent design to treat complex disease. Pharm. Res. 23 (7), 1417–1450. https://doi.org/10.1007/s11095-006-0284-8.

Darwich, A.S., Ogungbenr, K., Hatley, O.J., 2017. Amin Rostami-Hodjegan, Role of pharmacokinetic modeling and simulation in precision dosing of anticancer drugs. Transl. Cancer Res. 6 (S10), S1512. https://doi.org/10.21037/tcr.2017.09.14.

DeGeorge, J.J., Ahn, C.-H., Andrews, P.A., Brower, M.E., Giorgio, D.W., Anwar Goheer, M., Lee-Ham, D.Y., David McGuinn, W., Schmidt, W., Joseph Sun, C., Tripathi, S.C., 1997. Regulatory considerations for preclinical development of anticancer drugs. Cancer Chemother. Pharmacol. 41 (3), 173–185. https://doi.org/10.1007/s002800050726.

EMA/CHMP/ICH/646107/2008 EMA 2010. European Medicine Agency "Guidance for Industry S9 Nonclinical Evaluation for Anticancer Pharmaceuticals." https://www.fda.gov/regulatory-information/search-fda-guidance-documents/s9-nonclinical-evaluation-anticancer-pharmaceuticals.

Fourie Zirkelbach, J., Shah, M., Vallejo, J., Cheng, J., Ayyoub, A., Jiang, L., Hudson, R., Sridhara, R., Ison, G., Amiri-Kordestani, L., Tang, S., Gwise, T., Rahman, A., Pazdur, R., Theoret, M.R., 2022. Improving dose-optimization processes used in oncology drug development to minimize toxicity and maximize benefit to patients. J. Clin. Oncol. 40 (30), 3489–3500. https://doi.org/10.1200/jco.22.00371.

Frost, G.I., 2007. Recombinant human hyaluronidase (rHuPH20): An enabling platform for subcutaneous drug and fluid administration. Expert Opin. Drug Deliv. 4 (4), 427–440. https://doi.org/10.1517/17425247.4.4.427.

Gao, W., Liu, J., Shtylla, B., Venkatakrishnan, K., Yin, D., Shah, M., Nicholas, T., Cao, Y., 2024. Realizing the promise of Project Optimus: Challenges and emerging opportunities for dose optimization in oncology drug development. CPT Pharmacometrics Syst. Pharmacol. 13 (5), 691–709. https://doi.org/10.1002/psp4.13079.

Glennie, M.J., van de Winkel, J.G.J., 2003. Renaissance of cancer therapeutic antibodies. Drug Discov. Today 8 (11), 503–510. https://doi.org/10.1016/s1359-6446(03)02714-4.

Hansen, A.R., Cook, N., Stacey Ricci, M., Razak, A., Le Tourneau, C., McKeever, K., Roskos, L., Dixit, R., Siu, L.L., Hinrichs, M.J., 2015. Choice of starting dose for biopharmaceuticals in first-in-human phase I cancer clinical trials. Oncologist 20 (6), 653–659. https://doi.org/10.1634/theoncologist.2015-0008.

Helmus, M.N., 2007. The need for rules and regulations. Nat. Nanotechnol. 2 (6), 333–334. https://doi.org/10.1038/nnano.2007.165.

Igawa, T., Tsunoda, H., Tachibana, T., Maeda, A., Mimoto, F., Moriyama, C., Nanami, M., Sekimori, Y., Nabuchi, Y., Aso, Y., Hattori, K., 2010. Reduced elimination of IgG antibodies by engineering the variable region. Protein Eng. Des. Sel. 23 (5), 385–392. https://doi.org/10.1093/protein/gzq009.

Jing, J., Chen, Y., Musib, L., Jin, J.Y., Cheung, K.W.K., Yoshida, K., Sane, R., 2022. Assessment of cytochrome P450 3A4-mediated drug–drug interactions for ipatasertib using a fit-for-purpose physiologically based pharmacokinetic model. Cancer Chemother. Pharmacol. 89 (5), 707–720. https://doi.org/10.1007/s00280-022-04434-2.

Joerger, M., 2012. Covariate pharmacokinetic model building in oncology and its potential clinical relevance. AAPS J. 14 (1), 119–132. https://doi.org/10.1208/s12248-012-9320-2.

Junnuthula, V., Kolimi, P., Nyavanandi, D., Sampathi, S., Vora, L.K., Dyawanapelly, S., 2022. Polymeric micelles for breast cancer therapy: Recent updates, clinical translation and regulatory considerations. Pharmaceutics 14 (9), 1860. https://doi.org/10.3390/pharmaceutics14091860.

Kim, S., Kim, D.J., Howell, S.B., 1987. Modulation of the peritoneal clearance of liposomal cytosine arabinoside by blank liposomes. Cancer Chemother. Pharmacol. 19 (4). https://doi.org/10.1007/bf00261478.

Kumar, V., Deepika, D., Kumar, S., Sharma, S., 2024. P05-47 an ontology of Physiologically Based Pharmacokinetic Model (PBPK) for harmonization and automation of modeling framework (PBPKO). Toxicol. Lett. 399, S150. https://doi.org/10.1016/j.toxlet.2024.07.382.

Liu, S.-T., Ke, C.-J., Su, J., Qian, Y.-D., Wu, W.-H., Lin, X., Lin, W.-W., 2025. Precision dosing of perampanel in pediatric patients receiving oxcarbazepine combination therapy: Physiologically based pharmacokinetic modeling and simulation. Expert Rev. Clin. Pharmacol. 18 (6), 425–436. https://doi.org/10.1080/17512433.2025.2527079.

Maynard, A.D., Aitken, R.J., Butz, T., Colvin, V., Donaldson, K., Oberdörster, G., Philbert, M.A., Ryan, J., Seaton, A., Stone, V., Tinkle, S.S., Tran, L., Walker, N.J., Warheit, D.B., 2006. Safe handling of nanotechnology. Nature 444 (7117), 267–269. https://doi.org/10.1038/444267a.

Miao, X., Wu, L.S., Lin, S.X.W., Xu, Y., Chen, Y., Iwaki, Y., Kobos, R., Stephenson, T., Kemmerer, K., Uhlar, C.M., Banerjee, A., Goldberg, J.D., Trancucci, D., Apte, A., Verona, R., Pei, L., Desai, R., Hickey, K., Su, Y., Ouellet, D., Samtani, M.N., Guo, Y., Garfall, A.L., Krishnan, A., Usmani, S.Z., Zhou, H., Girgis, S., 2023. Population pharmacokinetics and exposure–response with teclistamab in patients with relapsed/refractory multiple myeloma: Results from MajesTEC-1. Targeted Oncol. 18 (5), 667–684. https://doi.org/10.1007/s11523-023-00989-z.

Minami, H., Kiyota, N., Kimbara, S., Ando, Y., Shimokata, T., Ohtsu, A., Fuse, N., Kuboki, Y., Shimizu, T., Yamamoto, N., Nishio, K., Kawakami, Y., Nihira, S.-ichi, Sase, K., Nonaka, T., Takahashi, H., Komori, Y., Kiyohara, K., 2021. Guidelines for clinical evaluation of anti-cancer drugs. Cancer Sci. 112 (7), 2563–2577. https://doi.org/10.1111/cas.14967.

Minami, H., 2022. SY07-1 New guidelines for clinical evaluation of anti-cancer drugs in Japan. Ann. Oncol. 33, S430. https://doi.org/10.1016/j.annonc.2022.05.443.

Monoclonal antibodies for the treatment of cancer. Anticancer Res. 37 (11), 2017. https://doi.org/10.21873/anticanres.12040.

Nakajima, E.C., Drezner, N., Li, X., Mishra-Kalyani, P.S., Liu, Y., Zhao, H., Bi, Y., Liu, J., Rahman, A., Wearne, E., Ojofeitimi, I., Hotaki, L.T., Spillman, D., Pazdur, R., Beaver, J.A., Singh, H., 2022. FDA approval summary: Sotorasib for KRAS G12C -mutated metastatic NSCLC. Clin. Cancer Res. 28 (8), 1482–1486. https://doi.org/10.1158/1078-0432.ccr-21-3074.

Negron, C., Joyce, F., McPherson, M.J., Blaine Stine, W., McCluskey, A.J., 2022. Separating clinical antibodies from repertoire antibodies, a path to in silico developability assessment. mAbs 14 (1). https://doi.org/10.1080/19420862.2022.2080628.

Oncology Pharmaceuticals: Reproductive Toxicity Testing and Labeling Recommendations Guidance for Industry, 2019. https://www.fda.gov/regulatory-information/search-fda-guidance-documents/oncology-pharmaceuticals-reproductive-toxicity-testing-and-labeling-recommendations-guidance.

Optimizing the Dosage of Human Prescription Drugs and Biological Products for the Treatment of Oncologic Diseases, 2024. https://www.fda.gov/regulatory-information/search-fda-guidance-documents/optimizing-dosage-human-prescription-drugs-and-biological-products-treatment-oncologic-diseases.

Paini, A., Leonard, J.A., Kliment, T., Tan, Y.-M., Worth, A., 2017. Investigating the state of physiologically based kinetic modelling practices and challenges associated with gaining regulatory acceptance of model applications. Regul. Toxicol. Pharmacol. 90, 104–115. https://doi.org/10.1016/j.yrtph.2017.08.019.

Photosafety Evaluation of Pharmaceuticals S10, 2013. https://database.ich.org/sites/default/files/S10_Guideline.pdf.

Ratain, M.J., Tannock, I.F., Lichter, A.S., 2021. Dose optimization of sotorasib: Is the US food and drug administration sending a message? J. Clin. Oncol. 39 (31), 3423–3426. https://doi.org/10.1200/jco.21.01371.

Shah, M., Rahman, A., Theoret, M.R., Pazdur, R., 2021. The drug-dosing conundrum in oncology — when less is more. N. Engl. J. Med. 385 (16), 1445–1447. https://doi.org/10.1056/nejmp2109826.

Shapiro, M.A., 2024. Regulatory considerations in the design, development and quality of monoclonal antibodies and related products for the diagnosis and treatment of cancer. Front. Oncol. 14. https://doi.org/10.3389/fonc.2024.1379738.

Stein, K.E., 1997. Overcoming obstacles to monoclonal antibody product development and approval. Trends Biotechnol. 15 (3), 88–90. https://doi.org/10.1016/s0167-7799(96)10075-5.

Thynne, T.R.J., Gabb, G.M., 2023. Editorial: Limitations of randomised controlled trials as evidence of drug safety. Aust. Prescr. 46 (2), 22–23. https://doi.org/10.18773/austprescr.2023.005.

Torchilin, V.P., 2005. Recent advances with liposomes as pharmaceutical carriers. Nat. Rev. Drug Discov. 4 (2), 145–160. https://doi.org/10.1038/nrd1632.

Tsamandouras, N., Rostami-Hodjegan, A., Aarons, L., 2015. Combining the 'bottom up' and 'top down' approaches in pharmacokinetic modelling: Fitting PBPK models to observed clinical data. Br. J. Clin. Pharmacol. 79 (1), 48–55. https://doi.org/10.1111/bcp.12234.

Veronese, F.M., Mero, A., 2008. The impact of PEGylation on biological therapies. BioDrugs 22 (5), 315–329. https://doi.org/10.2165/00063030-200822050-00004.

Weiner, L.M., Dhodapkar, M.V., Ferrone, S., 2009. Monoclonal antibodies for cancer immunotherapy. Lancet 373 (9668), 1033–1040. https://doi.org/10.1016/s0140-6736(09)60251-8.

Wong, K.M., Capasso, A., Gail Eckhardt, S., 2016. The changing landscape of phase I trials in oncology. Nat. Rev. Clin. Oncol. 13 (2), 106–117. https://doi.org/10.1038/nrclinonc.2015.194.

Xu, Y., Wang, D., Mason, B., Rossomando, T., Li, N., Liu, D., Cheung, J.K., Xu, W., Raghava, S., Katiyar, A., Nowak, C., Xiang, T., Dong, D.D., Sun, J., Beck, A., Liu, H., 2019. Structure, heterogeneity and developability assessment of therapeutic antibodies. mAbs 11 (2), 239–264. https://doi.org/10.1080/19420862.2018.1553476.

Yan, X., Sedykh, A., Wang, W., Yan, B., Zhu, H., 2020. Construction of a web-based nanomaterial database by big data curation and modeling friendly nanostructure annotations. Nat. Commun. 11 (1). https://doi.org/10.1038/s41467-020-16413-3.

Index

Note: 'Page numbers followed by *f* indicate figures, *t* indicate tables.'

D

F

G

H

N

O

P

U